Timothy Kidd
Honorable Cadet
VT 2007

WEST POINT

THE BICENTENNIAL BOOK

WEST POINT

THE BICENTENNIAL BOOK

Agostino von Hassell
and Herm Dillon

HOWELL PRESS
Charlottesville, Virginia

Designed by Lisa Wayand
Edited by Meghan M. Mitchell and James R. Knowles

Library of Congress Cataloging-in-Publication Data

Von Hassell, Agostino.
    West Point: the bicentennial book / Agostino von Hassell with Herm Dillon.
        p. cm.
    Includes bibliographical references.
    ISBN 1-57427-120-2 (hardcover)
    1. United States Military Academy--History. I. Dillon, Herm, 1947- II. Title.

    U410.L1 V65 2002
    355'.0071'173--dc21

                                                    2002039715

    ISBN 1-57427-120-2

    10 09 08 07 06 05 04 03 02 01
    10 9 8 7 6 5 4 3 2 1

Printed in China

Published by Howell Press
1713-2D Allied Lane
Charlottesville, VA 22903
(434) 977-4006
www.howellpress.com

TABLE OF CONTENTS

ACKNOWLEDGMENTS

Anyone who has ever worked with the administration at West Point knows that there is the Army way of doing things and there is the West Point way of doing things. The West Point way is similar to the Army way only it is a bit more complicated. This is not a criticism, simply an observation. In writing this book we were quite fortunate to have had the opportunity to work with Mr. Michael D'Aquino, a specialist in the West Point Public Affairs Office (PAO). There are actually many people in the PAO to whom we are indebted for helping us schedule visits, interviews and photo shoots during the research and production of this book. We were transported on everything from golf carts and six-bys to boats, jeeps, and humvees. Mike arranged for all of this, as well as introductions to Cadets who took us under their wing and showed us around the Academy with the Cadet's point of view. To Mike and other staff at the PAO we are extremely grateful for their help and cooperation. Another individual to whom we are greatly indebted is Dr. Stephen Grove, US Military Academy Historian, for his conscientious review of information presented in this book.

We also owe many thanks to Cadet Meghan Wilmore, who invited us as her guests to Christmas Dinner and allowed us to report on an event that few outside of West Point have ever experienced. She also did double duty in helping us recruit Cadets for the uniform photos and helped us out at football games. Speaking of Christmas Dinner at Washington Hall, we were very fortunate to meet Keith Thomaier, who runs the mess hall at West Point and does an incredible job. Keith—like John Leggio, the tailor whom we write about—is a perfect example of the enthusiasm and dedication that civilian staff bring to the Academy and contribute to its high standards of excellence.

Two individuals made major contributions. Leslie Jean-Bart is a photographer in New York City who assisted with some of the key shots in this book, in particular the portraits. The photos that Leslie produced were choreographed and set up by Keith Crossly. Keith, now a story board artist and film producer in New York, was a combat artist for the United States Marine Corps in Vietnam. Many thanks to both.

We also need to thank Christian Ulrich von Hassell, who patiently helped with the editing of many thousands of slides. And deep thanks to our publisher, Ross Howell, and our editors, Meghan Mitchell and James Knowles.

Many others contributed to this book and it is impossible to name them all. We, as authors, are extremely appreciative and consider ourselves very fortunate to have had the opportunity to work with them. We also are grateful to the US Marine Corps, which taught us to understand and view the military. In consideration of this we donate a portion of the proceeds of this book to the Marine Corps Law Enforcement Foundation.

AGOSTINO VON HASSELL
HERM DILLON

INTRODUCTION

West Point was once just a bend in a river, then a fort, and then a school founded on the idea that leaders could be trained for military service. Today the words "West Point" are neither a place nor a school, but rather a meaning, a reputation, a description earned by a long line of proven leaders dedicated to high ideals and public service.

The concept of leadership training requires a learning experience that I believe is in constant evolution in order to help young, motivated participants develop five essential elements of leadership: integrity, competence, confidence, compassion, and awe.

The bedrock lifestyle commitment of West Point is integrity. The United States Military Academy's Honor System has through the decades differentiated a West Point graduate from graduates of other universities, schools, and training programs. The Honor System, which is of the Corps, by the Corps, and for the Corps, instills within each Cadet the recognition that integrity is the foundation upon which trust is built. And without trust, there can be no leadership.

A diverse and constantly evolving academic and training curriculum imparts the knowledge and skills required to be a competent military leader. In the beginning, the West Point experience included the basic drill, equestrian, engineering and social skills—all considered essential to military leadership. Through the years, as the art of war has evolved, so too has the curriculum and training at the United States Military Academy. The goal has never been to follow change, but rather to lead the development of new and improved methods of waging war with the conviction that by ensuring victory against any would-be foe, war can be deterred. Where skill with the sword and horse once were critical, today skill with computers and analysis are essential.

The challenge of developing diverse personalities with different physical and intellectual skills into men and women with a well grounded, unwavering sense of confidence has been the genesis of many of the proudest and perhaps most notorious West Point traditions. From mandatory boxing to daily oral recitations to leadership positions within the Corps that are affirmed upon graduation—each graduate eventually realizes that fear, hesitancy, and uncertainty can be overcome.

The close, family-like relationship developed within the Corps, which often lasts a lifetime, builds within each graduate the ability to look beyond the uniform and rank to the person within. Compassion becomes the tie that binds one Cadet to another. Whether it is helping a tired classmate during a long forced march, tutoring a struggling student, or cheering a Cadets' Corps Squad or intramural team, Cadets understand the need for personal reinforcement and understanding. Working together in mandatory training, athletics, and studies designed for a total experience rather than the particular strengths of an individual, Cadets learn to work together, building upon each other's strengths and compensating for their weaknesses.

Lastly, the focus of all training and work is toward the objective of military service. Each Cadet realizes that one day all training, studies, preparation, and tests will end, and they will become responsible for the lives and well-being of other human beings assigned to their command. The business of their unit and their profession is war. War, which Napoleon described as "the business of barbarians" and what others have called "man's greatest inhumanity to man," is the eventuality for which the West Point leader is prepared. The uniquely American perspective that wars are fought not to enrich or to enlarge, but rather to protect, makes the likelihood of war more real. No other job, position, or career has the awesome responsibility of leading young men and women into the face of death. No other leader has the privilege and burden of knowing that the lives of others hang in the balance of his competence and skill.

West Point, once a place and then a school, is today a presumption of integrity, competence, confidence, compassion and awe in the person of a military leader. A graduate of the United States Military Academy, a West Pointer, is a leader to whom we as a nation can entrust our most treasured resources—our sons, daughters, fathers, mothers, sisters, and brothers—and know with certainty that their lives will be cherished and their full potential realized. If the West Point tradition has been pre-served, West Point leaders will, time and time again, inspire those around them to reach within themselves for that hidden potential to challenge fate and change the world for the betterment of mankind.

As one West Point graduate, I have been blessed with the opportunity to pass among those who went before and those who are coming after. For that I am grateful. May this book be a reminder to all of us of what has been, what is, and what can be.

PAUL BUCHA
WEST POINT CLASS OF 1965
MEDAL OF HONOR, 1968

West Point

WEST POINT
HEROES

"WHEN I ATTENDED WEST POINT, ON R-DAY ALL NEW CADETS WERE REQUIRED TO STRIP DOWN AND POSE FOR POSTURE PHOTOS. AT THAT MOMENT I REALIZED THAT ALL OF US WERE EQUAL. NOTHING WE BROUGHT WITH US—MATERIAL POSSESSIONS, HONOR, RANK, OR ANCESTRY—MATTERED. WE WERE ALL THE SAME ON THE OUTSIDE. THE DIFFERENCE, AS WE WOULD COME TO LEARN, WAS WHAT WAS ON THE INSIDE. I BEGAN TO REALIZE THEN THAT WHAT YOU HAVE, YOU HAVE WITHIN YOU."

—CAPT. PAUL BUCHA, CLASS OF 1965, 1968 MEDAL OF HONOR RECIPIENT

It was March 1968, just over a month after the Tet offensive. There was an unprecedented amount of NVA activity throughout the country as North Vietnam reveled in its numerous victories, accomplished through a series of surprise attacks on villages, cities, and jungle real estate that was believed to have been firmly under South Vietnamese and US control. The situation was no different near Phuoc Vinh in Binh Duong Province. Company D of the Third Battalion, 187th Infantry, Third Brigade, 101st Airborne Division was dropped by helicopter on a search-and-destroy mission into an area known to have a high concentration of enemy forces.

What the men of D Company encountered at Phuoc Vinh was far beyond their worst nightmares. Two days into the mission, they encountered heavy small weapons fire, supported by machine gun fire, rockets, mortars, and grenades. Claymores were everywhere; it was as if they had been expected. What soon became obvious was that D Company was up against an enemy force estimated to be battalion size.

Pinned down by machine gun fire, the company commander, Capt. Paul Bucha, crawled to a concealed bunker and single-handedly destroyed it with hand grenades. Throughout a fearful night filled with small arms fire, the captain, wounded from shrapnel, moved among his troops, distributing ammo, encouragement, and leadership of the kind seldom seen. Guiding his company in repelling the human wave assaults, Bucha directed artillery fire and air support on the enemy strongholds, marking their positions

OPPOSITE: *The American Soldiers Statue depicting three World War II infantrymen was the first monument at the academy to honor the nation's enlisted personnel. The bronze sculpture by Felix de Weldon was presented to the Academy and the Corps of Cadets by the classes of 1935 and 1936.*

with smoke grenades. At one point during the encounter, as an element rescuing casualties was cut off from the perimeter, he advised his soldiers to pretend they were dead and called in artillery fire around them.

Exposing himself to enemy sniper fire, Bucha used a flashlight to direct medical evacuations of seriously wounded men and the helicopter re-supply of his unit. At dawn, he personally led a rescue party to recover the dead and wounded members of his unit. "On a night like that all you truly have to rely on is your men and what you have within you," Bucha says.

Never having dreamed that he would be placed in a situation in which his entire outfit's well-being depended on his decisions and his actions, Paul Bucha may have been a reluctant hero. His actions at Phuoc Vinh that night represent the most profound and most important kind of heroism and placed him among America's most elite group of heroes—soldiers who have been awarded the Congressional Medal of Honor.

Before he saved innumerable lives in Vietnam, Paul Bucha was a competitive swimmer, good enough to be named all-American for three consecutive years. His swimming skill earned him a scholarship to Yale University. Yale, however, was not in the cards; after his entrance interview there, his father suggested he consider the United States Military Academy.

On a visit to West Point, Bucha liked what he saw. He came from a closely knit immigrant family, and in the Academy he saw the opportunity to belong to something that would support and develop the values and mores that had already made an indelible mark on his character. He was intrigued by the concept of honor at West Point, and he believed that he could more easily realize his true potential there than at Yale.

Bucha graduated from West Point in 1965. He left the US Army soon after being awarded the Medal of Honor for his valor in Vietnam. Today, he is chairman of Wheeling-Pittsburgh Steel Corporation in Wheeling, West Virginia. But the titles of Medal of Honor recipient and senior corporate executive don't begin to describe the depth of his character.

He has, through his experiences at West Point and in Vietnam, developed a unique perspective on heroism. Humility is no small part of it. "You only need valor when you've made a mistake," he says. "If all goes smoothly, then there's no need for it." He laments ten names on "the Wall," the names of men who were killed that night in Vietnam.

Paul Bucha is just one of many exceptional Americans whose path included West Point. Since 1802 Academy graduates have stood up to the supreme examination—battle. In two hundred years West Point has produced seventy-four Medal of Honor recipients. American fighting troops in all conflicts dating back to the Civil War have been led with inspiration, dedication, honor, and commitment by West Point graduates. John J. Pershing, Class of 1886, led America's army in Europe during World War I. Dwight D. Eisenhower, Class of 1915, held that post in World War II. Douglas MacArthur, Class of 1903, who served as superintendent of West Point from 1919 to 1922, went on to lead US forces in Korea. William C. Westmoreland, Class of 1936 and superintendent from 1960 to 1963, commanded US troops in Vietnam. H. Norman Schwarzkopf, Class of 1956, led American troops to decisive victory in the Persian Gulf. Wesley Clark, Class of 1966, led US troops in Kosovo.

West Pointers dominated both Confederate and Federal ranks in America's Civil War.

Ulysses S. Grant, Class of 1843, and Robert E. Lee, Class of 1829, led the two opposing armies. Pierre G. T. Beauregard, Class of 1838, became Academy superintendent in early 1861 but was recalled after just five days due to his home state's threat of secession. One month later, on February 20, he resigned his US commission and accepted a senior command as brigadier general in the Confederate army, a position from which he would lead the defenses at Charleston, South Carolina. Other West Point graduates taking prominent roles in the Civil War were Jubal A. Early, George E. Pickett, Stonewall Jackson, George B. Meade, William Tecumseh Sherman, Philip Sheridan, and Braxton Bragg.

More recently, Omar Bradley, George S. Patton, and Matt Ridgeway distinguished themselves and the Academy.

In the first forty-five years, from 1802 to 1847, 1,365 young men graduated from West Point. By 1847, sixty-eight of these graduates had been killed in battle, and eighty-one had received brevet promotions "for gallantry." By 1860, more than seventy-five percent of the officers in the regular Army had graduated from the Point.

In the words of General Pershing, "Though relatively small in number, men of West Point have always been the leaven and have ever given the guiding impulse that has carried our armies to victory. No other institution has furnished to the country as great a proportion of distinguished citizens as West Point." When he said this, in June 1920, thirty-four of thirty-eight senior officers in his American Expeditionary Force in France were West Point graduates. Some years later, during World War II, the class of 1915 earned the nickname "the class the stars fell on." Of 164 graduates, fifty-nine reached at least the rank of brigadier general.

As the new millennium began, the West Point tradition of excellence was firmly in place. By the year 2001 a solid thirty percent of all generals in the US Army had attended the School on the Hudson, and one West Point graduate had just relieved another as Army chief of staff. Cadet Alison M. Jones, meanwhile, had joined the list of honored Cadets with a decoration of her own.

Jones, Class of 1999, was serving a summer internship at the United States Embassy in Nairobi, Kenya, on August 7, 1998, when a terrorist bomb left the building a rubble of burning fuel tanks, live electrical wires, and toxic gases. One of the first to arrive on the scene after the explosion, Jones immediately helped secure the building. She then led a search for survivors, administered first aid, and helped recover the dead. In May 1999 she received the Soldier's Medal, the highest honor awarded for selfless and heroic action in peacetime.

★　★　★

The West Point legacy does not begin and end with military duty. In the 1960s, the Academy was one of the first places NASA looked for candidates for its astronaut program. Six of the country's first thirty astronauts were Academy graduates, including Buzz Aldrin and Mike Collins, who flew the first manned mission to the moon. Aldrin became the second man to walk on the moon. Frank Borman was a space commander aboard the American craft that accomplished the first rendezvous in space, and West Point graduate Ed White died in a launch fire aboard Apollo 1 at Cape Kennedy.

What enables West Point to consistently turn out such leaders? What is the special magic of this school on the Hudson? What is the secret to taking a young person from the plains of Kansas, such as Gen. Eisenhower, or from the Mississippi Valley, such as Gen. Roscoe Robinson, Jr., the first African-American to achieve the rank of four-star general in the Army, and creating a leader? "West Point takes the richest and the poorest, the farmer's son and the factory worker's boy," said Gen. Omar Bradley, Class of 1915, in 1952.

West Point's mission is simply stated: "To educate, train and inspire the Corps of Cadets so that each graduate is a commissioned leader of character committed to the values of Duty, Honor, Country; professional growth throughout a career as an officer in the United States Army; and a lifetime of selfless service to the Nation." This mission has been largely the same since 1802, when a reluctant Congress finally authorized the establishment of the school. The record shows that West Point has been successful in producing exemplary officers and talented engineers for two hundred years. The Academy has been equally successful at preparing young professionals for success in the civilian world.

West Point begins with some of the nation's most talented young people and gives them a solid, diversified education in the sciences. It then adds the potent combination of duty, honor, and country. And it has shown an extraordinary ability to adapt to changing times, though it means hard work. Integrity, competence, confidence, compassion, and awe have been added to the mix as a great school enters its third century of shaping America's leaders.

RIGHT: *Alison M. Jones, Class of 1999, receiving the Soldier's Medal.*

OPPOSITE PAGE: *Sylvanus Thayer, known as the "father of the US Military Academy," served as its superintendent from 1817 to 1833, the longest tenure in Academy history. The Thayer monument was sculpted by Carl Conrad and erected in 1883.*

COLONEL THAYER,
FATHER
OF THE
MILITARY ACADEMY

ABOVE: *A cairn of remembrance is displayed atop the grave of Lieutenant Colonel Edward H. White, II, Class of 1952, the first American to walk in space. White was killed in the tragic fire at Cape Kennedy in Apollo 1. White's parents are buried just to the left of his grave. His father was an Academy graduate, Class of 1924. There is also a stone for White's brother, James B. White, a Vietnam MIA.*

LEFT: *General Dwight D. Eisenhower keeps watch over the Plain. Ike's nine-foot tall bronze statue was sculpted by Robert L. Dean, Jr., Class of 1953, and erected in May 1983. Eisenhower was a 1915 graduate of the Academy.*

TWO

THE FOUNDING OF
WEST POINT

"FOURTHLY. ACADEMIES, ONE OR MORE FOR THE INSTRUCTION OF THE ART MILITARY; PARTICULARLY THOSE BRANCHES OF IT WHICH RESPECT ENGINEERING AND ARTILLERY, WHICH ARE HIGHLY ESSENTIAL, AND THE KNOWLEDGE OF WHICH, IS MOST DIFFICULT TO OBTAIN. ALSO MANUFACTORIES OF SOME KINDS OF MILITARY STORES."
—GEORGE WASHINGTON, SENTIMENTS ON A PEACE ESTABLISHMENT, 1783

West Point had its beginning as a key defense site during the American Revolution. The view of the Hudson and the sharp S-curves in the river just north of West Point provided an excellent location from which to attack and halt British ships attempting to make their way to the northern colonies.

Only fifty miles north of New York City, this point of land juts into the Hudson River from the west and commands a view of breathtakingly beautiful, glacier-carved canyons, ancient mountains, and sheer cliffs. The view was so solemn and beautiful that it gave rise to the first internationally recognized Hudson River School, the first American school of landscape painting, active from 1825 to1870. It seems fitting that on this dominant position, a fledgling country born and made of war should found this institution of learning.

In 1776, however, all of this was well in the future. In one of its first acts, on May 25, 1775, the Continental Congress passed a resolution providing for the establishment of posts to command the Hudson. Three years later, further recognizing the strategic importance of West Point's location, a heavy iron chain was stretched across the river to Constitution Island, serving as a blockade to any insurgents from the north or south. As the topography is too mountainous for an army to cross, West Point was thus protected from a redcoat attack by land or by sea.

At the outbreak of the Revolutionary War, both the colonists and the British realized the importance

OPPOSITE: *A boat ride up the Hudson reveals a river that narrows tightly to its shores and turns sharply with sheer rock cliffs on either side. "It always scares me a bit," said the skipper of a modern-day Army boat while navigating up the Hudson past West Point. It was undoubtedly a formidable barrier to eighteenth-century captains.*

of gaining possession of the Hudson River valley, and West Point became of strategic value to the defense of the colonies. Gen. George Washington established his headquarters there in 1779, and in 1780 Maj. Gen. Benedict Arnold was given command of the post. Arnold, embittered by Congressional slights and newly married into a loyalist family, attempted to betray the post to the British. He failed and fled.

In February 1776, George Washington, in a letter to his military secretary Joseph Reed, complained about a lack of leadership among his soldiers and the need for training in officership. Over the next quarter century the shape and training of the new country's armed defenses would be the subject of considerable national debate.

Most politicians, and even many military men, believed that the best way to defend the colonies was with a standing militia. State militias had repeatedly demonstrated that they could stand up to Indian attacks, and they represented themselves well even against Great Britain. Political leaders of the new nation feared that a standing professional army, and even more so a military academy, would result in an elite force of fighting men that would justify its existence through the instigation of war, whether warranted or not. There were also concerns that academy-trained soldiers would revolt against the US government.

In 1783, Washington asked Gen. Ebenezer Huntington for his views on a military academy. Huntington, an experienced infantry officer, recommended West Point as a location, suggesting that the fortifications there be maintained and held in a constant state of readiness. "With a small additional expense," noted Huntington, "an academy might be here instituted for instruction in all branches of the military art." Washington incorporated Huntington's recommendations into "Sentiments Upon a Peace Establishment," his argument for a military academy, which he sent to Alexander Hamilton in 1783 and which stated that provisions should be made "for instructing a certain number of young gentlemen in the theory of the art of war." Ten years later, over the objections of Thomas Jefferson, President Washington repeated those convictions in a 1793 message to the US Congress. But tight budgets, coupled with military ignorance and an economic focus, doomed Washington's recommendations to slow-acting committees that were unable to come to any consensus.

Meanwhile, West Point was already being used in a limited fashion as an educational institution. The Corps of Invalids had been sent to West Point in 1781 to advise in the organization of artillery garrisons and fortifications that would be used to thwart enemy traffic on the Hudson River. The corps had been established in 1777 and was charged with employing disabled soldiers and propagating military knowledge and discipline. Invalids had been used in rear positions and for teaching young soldiers since the very early days of warfare. The year after Washington's address to Congress in 1794, a Corps of Artillerists and Engineers was authorized by the legislature. It was located at West Point and authorized to consist of four battalions, each with eight Cadets plus officers and enlisted men. The secretary of war was ordered to obtain books, instruments, and teaching aids for the corps, which would bring young men into service as Cadets and train them in military leadership.

A few years later the concept was revisited, this time by Hamilton himself, who in November 1799 placed before Secretary of War James McHenry a plan for a military academy that would instruct all military services, navy included, in the fundamentals of war. A copy of Hamilton's plan was sent to George Washington at Mount Vernon, Virginia. In his last letter relating to public business, Washington responded, "the establishment of such an institution as you describe has ever been considered by me as an object of primary importance to this country." Washington died two days later, but he had given Hamilton the confidence he needed to push the concept forward and through the Congress. The proposal was incorporated into the secretary of war's annual report to Congress on January 13, 1800. Congress proceeded to debate it for well over a year.

Acting on his own while Congress deliberated, Thomas Jefferson—now president, clearly influenced by the threat of war with France and willing to abandon his earlier opposition to an academy—ordered the establishment of a military school at West Point, naming Maj. Jonathan Williams the first superintendent. Williams was the great-nephew of Benjamin Franklin and had served as a colonial government representative in France during the American Revolution. Afterward, he had collaborated with his great-uncle on scientific experiments, and in 1800 he translated de Scheel's *A Treatise of Artillery* from the original French.

A year later, on March 16, 1802, Congress finally passed an act establishing a "Corps of Engineers" that would consist of ten Cadets at West Point. Section 27 of the act states:

"And be it further enacted, That the said corps, when so organized shall be stationed at West Point, in the state of New York, and shall constitute a military academy. . . ."

This date, March 16, 1802, is generally recognized as the founding date of the US Military Academy.

TOP: Artillery Drill, *c. 1827. Painting by George Catlin. (Courtesy of West Point Museum, USMA)*

BOTTOM: View of West Point from Bull Hill, *c. 1840. Painting by Victor DeGrailly. (Courtesy of West Point Museum, USMA)*

Although West Point had been occupied continuously by troops since 1778, it did not become government property until 1790, when Congress appropriated the money for its purchase. Since then there have been numerous acquisitions, and today the reservation occupies approximately sixteen thousand acres.

Drill! Drill! Drill! Cadets love close order drill or "Reviews," as they are referred to at West Point. The Academy uses virtually any excuse to have a "Review."

The architectural style at West Point has been described as "Military Gothic." The hand-cut gray granite lends an air of strength and fortitude to the Academy and blends into the steel gray of the mountainside and the banks of fog from the Hudson River that frequently shroud West Point.

ABOVE AND LEFT: *The USMA Silent Drill Team performs at parades and other special affairs, exhibiting precision drill exercises including a unique rifle inspection involving elaborate spins and tosses of the ten and one-half pound M-1 rifle.*

OVERLEAF: *Cadets stand in formation on the Plain. In the background left is the superintendent's quarters. Cadet parades on the Plain are almost weekly events during football season, and of course, to commemorate important events.*

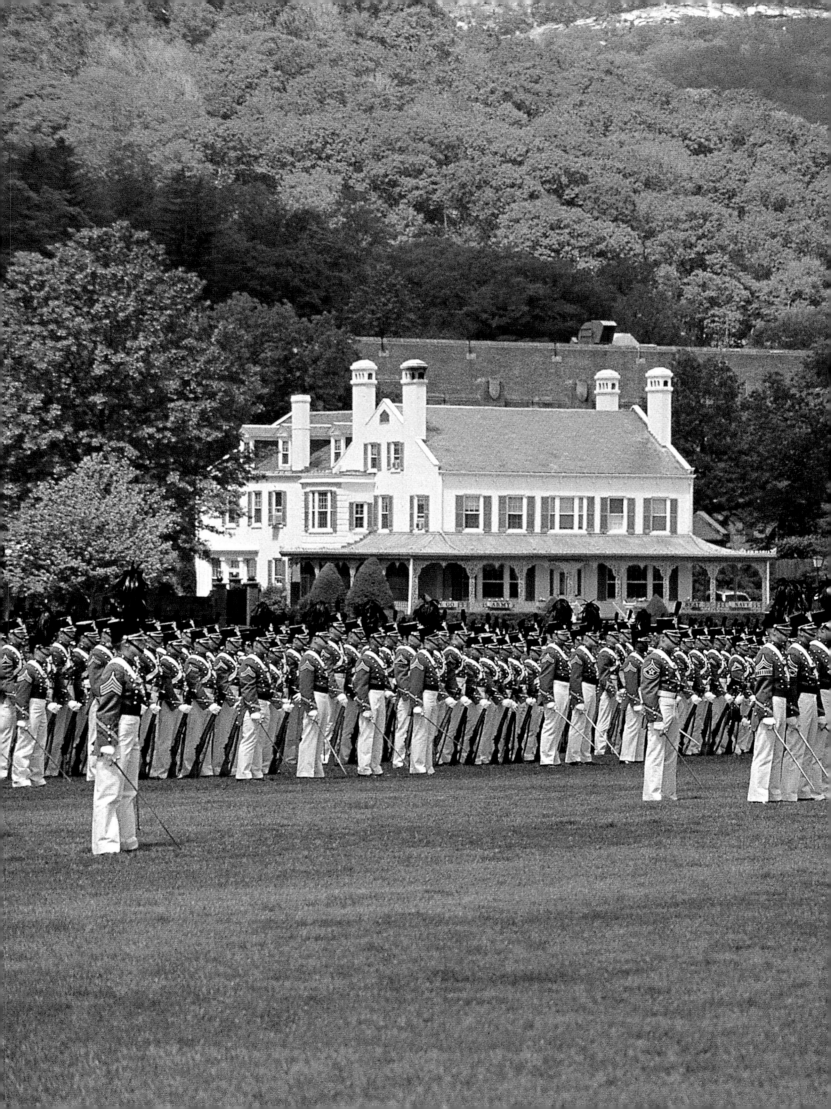

INNOVATION FROM THE VERY BEGINNING

"EVERY ONE OF MY AMERICAN ASSOCIATES . . . WHETHER OR NOT A FORMER CADET, AGREES THAT WEST POINT SYMBOLIZES THE THINGS THAT SHOULD GUIDE US. HER MOTTO EMBRACES THEM ALL. THE ONE-HUNDRED-FIFTY-YEAR RECORD OF HER GRADUATES REMINDS US THAT WEST POINT IS A NATIONAL ASSET BEYOND ALL PRICE."
—DWIGHT D. EISENHOWER, CLASS OF 1915, APRIL 1951

The US Military Academy set the standard for military instruction and education from the start. Few of the European academies already in place at the turn of the eighteenth century sought to train young men to be officers in an organized program. Although West Point's founders almost certainly were influenced by the French schools l'École Spéciale Militaire (1802) and École Polytechnique (1794), both of which had been visited by the Academy's first superintendent, Jonathan Williams, the result was distinctly modern.

Indeed, the military academy at West Point was established at a time of profound change in the way wars were fought and men prepared to fight them. Until about 1800, the profession of arms was essentially a gentleman's endeavor. Officers were the sons of nobility, trained from youth in riding, fencing, hunting, trapping, and other such arts believed essential to the leading of armies. The knowledge needed for senior leadership and generalship was learned on the job—"at the cannon's mouth." As late as 1764, "cadet" was defined as "a young gentleman who chooses to carry arms in a marching regiment, as a private man. His views are to acquire some knowledge in the art of war, and to obtain a commission in the army." A formal education was utterly dispensable.

So dispensable, in fact, that in many European countries, particularly in Great Britain, it was completely acceptable to purchase commissions. Famous generals such as Wellington purchased their first commissions. Even the rank of colonel could be acquired regardless of the buyer's qualifications.

But two major developments in warfare occurred at the end of the eighteenth century—the evolution

OPPOSITE: *This Cadet carries the USMA colors in a commemorative parade.*

West Point's oldest books, many of which were collected in France, are famed texts on fortifications, such as those written by Vaubaun, and complex studies of logarithms needed to properly lay a gun. Assembling a superb collection of books was one of the earliest missions of the Academy, and two officers, Col. William McRee and Maj. Sylvanus Thayer (pictured here), were abroad from 1815 to 1817 acquiring the foundation of the library. Upon his return, Thayer was appointed superintendent of the Academy.

The library has been amply fed by West Point graduates, who have shown themselves to be prolific writers. The report on the 1902 Centennial Celebration lists 15,708 articles and books authored by West Point graduates in the first one hundred years. (Photo: Leslie Jean-Bart)

of more complex fortifications and major advances in artillery. To understand the elements of either requires both skill and "book knowledge"; the effective soldier now had to have a solid understanding of engineering, mathematics, and geometry, topics not easily mastered on the job. These new skills were not part of the usual repertoire of a "young gentleman." In Prussia and Austria-Hungary, regiments of artillery and combat engineers quickly made commissions available to non-nobles.

The need for such technical proficiency is in large part the reason why West Point was established. It took the scientific training of Cadets one step further than its European counterparts, placing such a heavy emphasis on civil engineering that the Army Corps of Engineers, rather than the regular Army, was in direct control of West Point until 1866. The early emphasis on science and engineering influences the Academy's curriculum to this day.

Fears that a military academy would breed a nation of warmongers were also behind the up-to-date curriculum. West Point was charged not only with training skilled military officers, but also with educating young engineers who could build roads, bridges, canals, and other infrastructure critical to the nascent country.

Many West Point graduates have gone on to serve as noted engineers throughout America's history. The famous Intracoastal Waterway, one of the East Coast's major transportation arteries, was designed by West Point graduates serving in the Army Corps of Engineers. George Washington Goethals, Class of 1880, was the chief engineer of the Panama Canal. Robert E. Lee (pictured at left), Class of 1829 , became a surveyor upon graduation and is credited with mapping much of the South prior to and during the Civil War.

West Point today is steeped in tradition. But the Academy has changed with the times, offering this nation new visions, new ideas, and new horizons. It has consistently been first in line when society demanded change. The Point was among the first service academies to open its doors to women. Today women make up about fifteen percent of the Corps of Cadets, and ethnic and racial minorities account for twenty percent.

Leading other educational and military training institutions through social change, academic change, and even changes in leadership training has been hard on the Academy and often difficult for the Cadets. But long before the nation overall had the heart and mind to acknowledge many of the important changes that have occurred in society, education, technology, and leadership training, West Point consistently showed the way.

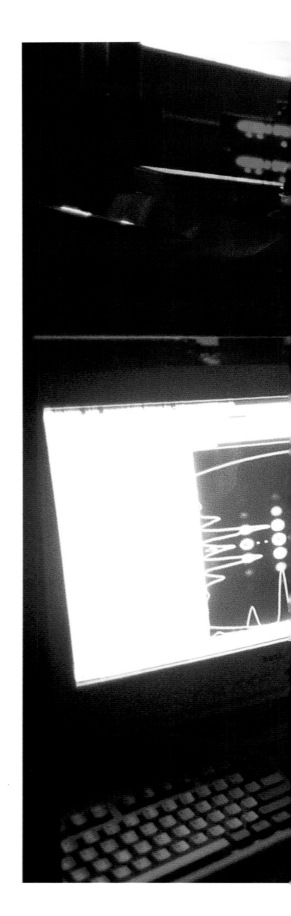

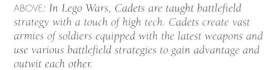

ABOVE: *In Lego Wars, Cadets are taught battlefield strategy with a touch of high tech. Cadets create vast armies of soldiers equipped with the latest weapons and use various battlefield strategies to gain advantage and outwit each other.*

RIGHT: *The Laser Laboratory teaches Cadets some of the fundamentals of light and how lasers and photonics technology are applied in the areas of photoacoustic spectroscopy, laser-induced carbonization of polymers, photorefractive devices, ultrafast optoelectronics and switching, optical information processing, and simulated rotational Raman scattering.*

FOUR

ACADEMICS

"[THE MILITARY ACADEMY] COULD NOT STAND ON MORE APPROPRIATE GROUND, AND ANY
GROUND MORE BEAUTIFUL CAN HARDLY BE. THE COURSE OF EDUCATION IS SEVERE, BUT WELL
DEVISED AND MANLY."
—CHARLES DICKENS, AMERICAN NOTES, 1841

An inversion covers most of the surrounding mountains. Patches of green forest emerge slowly, painting
the mountainside in its spring greenery. A faint, momentary rainbow appears over the Hudson as slivers
of sunlight begin to cut their way through a fog that moves slowly, eerily, down the river.

A whippoorwill ending its night-long vigil cuts the silence. A lonely dove coos sweetly to its mate.
Distant voices echo gently from the mountains, from the water, from buildings that have carved their way
into history for over two hundred years.

The mellow sound of a bagpipe beckons the morning, playing its lonely tune over the graves of those
who have served. Their memories are alive here. They are called upon day after day to reinforce a tradition that is known nowhere else on this earth. They are beckoned, again and again, to teach, coach, and
counsel those who aspire to serve the Long Gray Line.

Statues and cannons line the pathways, commemorating those who taught, who fought, who fell. As
the fog lifts, perspective emerges—perspective on what has transpired here for two centuries. One may
begin to understand the depth of sacrifice of the officers who fought here, the soldiers who died here, and
the patriots who have trodden this hallowed ground in their bold, unselfish effort to make and keep a
nation free. It is solemn. It is sobering.

A trumpet sounds. The reveille cannon fires. A flag marked with fifty brilliant stars rises to its pinnacle, almost lost in the still rising fog. Another day begins for the young leaders at the School on the Hudson.

OPPOSITE: *After a morning of classes, hungry Cadets crowd into the mess hall for lunch.*

★ ★ ★

West Point isn't just a hill above the river, or mammoth granite buildings, or eloquent statues. West Point is people. Young men and women. Experienced military leaders. Trained teachers and professors. Priests, ministers, and rabbis. All of whom stand on the shoulders of those who came before—the men and women who have helped build America into its greatness. Not just generals and heroes who made their mark in battle, but explorers who helped settle the West, engineers who dug canals and built the bridges across them, government and civic leaders, inventors, and even scientists.

The nation's most qualified students provide the raw material for these exceptional Americans. The US Military Academy typically receives more than eleven thousand applications for admission. After careful screening, roughly ten percent of the applicants are admitted. Physical and dental exams are reviewed as closely as SAT (Scholastic Achievement Test) scores. Today, the average combined SAT score of a West Point Cadet is 1,268, well above the national average of 1,013. Some fifty-seven percent of students accepted to West Point are members of the National Honor Society, and eighty-eight percent wear varsity letters for excellence in high school sports. About eighteen percent have been active in student government.

Once at West Point, these accomplished students continue to excel. Since 1923 the Academy has ranked fourth among US universities producing Rhodes Scholars. Seventeen West Point Cadets have received Marshall Scholarships since 1983, nearly twice as many as the Naval Academy and four times more than the Air Force Academy. The school on the Hudson ranks third behind MIT and Stanford University in the number of Hertz Scholarships awarded since 1969.

Not surprisingly, West Point has gained a reputation as one of the nation's finest engineering schools. But it is much more than an institution of advanced learning for America's youth. The Academy teaches a broad curriculum in engineering while it molds young men and women into military leaders.

It was founded in 1802 to do just that. The United States Military Academy at West Point has embodied a rigid program of leadership development from its inception, and it is leadership development that pervades every aspect of Cadet life.

Contrary to the beliefs of many denied applicants, the stringent physical requirements for admission to West Point are not a recent addition. In 1943, Army regulations specified that "No candidate will be accepted unless he has a minimum of six serviceable vital masticating teeth." In a reference perhaps to the rocky hills that surround West Point, the regulations further stated that "Candidates should walk as well as run over the hilliest countryside available to them" in preparation for matriculation.

Whether plebe (freshman) or firstie (senior), life for a West Point Cadet is rigorous, challenging, and rewarding. Cadets learn quickly to take pride in their accomplishments and their unique status as a member of the corps. An astronomical number of activities fill each Cadet's day, most of them centered around leadership skills, ethics, physical training, and education.

Most weekdays begin at 0520. After the completion of various duties and responsibilities, there is a reveille formation at 0655. The Cadets then proceed to breakfast at 0700. Classes begin at 0735 and run until lunch formation at 1205. There is a half-hour for lunch. Following additional Cadet duties, classes resume for the afternoon at 1350. Following afternoon classes, Cadets either participate in some type of sport (intercollegiate or intramural) or participate in drill and ceremonies. Dinner is at 1745. Cadets spend most of the evening addressing the considerable amount of homework they accumulated until taps sounds at 2330.

A Cadet's first two years of coursework at the Academy focus heavily on military science, ethics, and leadership. Because they affect the military, current events, both national and international, are a frequent topic of study. Cadets learn about military unit organization, particularly in terms of battlefield situations and tactical planning. In these early years they begin to think about fields of specialization and the location of their first duty station.

This is also the part of the West Point curriculum that has undergone the most revolutionary change. More and more, Cadets are taught to be diplomats as well as warriors. In response to the US Army's anticipation that it will take on larger roles in peacekeeping, dealing with terrorism, and disaster relief, Cadets no longer just learn borders on a map; they are taught about cultures in countries throughout the world. There is increased emphasis on what West Point calls the "principles of officership":

Duty . . . always first, subordinating personal interests
Honor . . . physical and moral courage, integrity, doing the right thing, always
Loyalty . . . upward to Commander in Chief, down to all subordinates
Service to Country . . . the officer's motivation . . . and legacy
Competence . . . as a moral imperative
Teamwork . . . modeling civility and respect, placing the group and mission over self
Subordination . . . to civilian control while exercising rights of citizenship
Leadership . . . always by example.

This framework, these virtues, are what make Cadet life and a career as an Army officer rewarding and attractive to young people.

OPPOSITE: *Cadets stand at attention during lunch formation.*

ABOVE: *Learning to tie knots at West Point goes way beyond what most of us learned in Boy Scouts or Girl Scouts.*

LEFT: *"Well this is how I got my answer, sir." Engineering courses that emphasize math and physics are basic to every Cadet's academic instruction at West Point. (Photo: Leslie Jean-Bart)*

R-DAY

BUILDING LEADERS THE
WEST POINT WAY

"MAKE US CHOOSE THE HARDER RIGHT INSTEAD OF THE EASIER WRONG..."
—FROM THE CADET PRAYER

R-Day (Reception Day) is the day future Cadets report to the Academy to begin their military training. It's a masterpiece of planning and logistics. Everything is organized and orchestrated. For the new Cadets, it's a day characterized by anxiety, confusion, perplexity, humility, and pride.

Cadets report to the Academy, typically with their families, early on a late June day. The Cadet's trek toward membership in the Long Gray Line begins in a queue outside Michie Stadium, to which "new Cadets" and their family members are admitted some fifty at a time. After a briefing on what each—Cadet and parent—can expect during R-Day, the new Cadets are given a short time to say their good-byes.

With hugs and handshakes in memory, the new Cadets line up to make their second important march of the day. While it may be one of the shortest marches they'll make over the next four years, it is a most significant one. Bolstered by the applause and proud shouts of family, the new Cadets make their way across the football field. They all carry documents received in the mail weeks before Cadet training begins. They also carry luggage. Some have brought a simple overnight bag. Others drag suitcases on wheels. One carries a portable TV cloaked in a nylon bag. It's getting heavy already.

The walk across Michie Stadium is a long, lonely one. All know that they are walking away from one life and entering a new one, but at this point none can imagine what the new life will be, what rewards it can bring, or what price they will pay to attain them. Most likely, none of the new Cadets knows anyone else. No one knows precisely what will happen next—not in the next few minutes, not in the summer of rigorous training before them, not in the next four years.

OPPOSITE: *Now it begins. The first stop for Cadets reporting for Cadet Basic Training on R-Day is Arvin Gymnasium, where they will be issued part of their new wardrobe and begin the mustering-in process at West Point.*

What's ahead is one of the most intense physical and mental training programs of any institution in the world, a program that has been developed over the course of two hundred years with one goal in mind: to develop the finest men and women to lead the nation's army in peace and in war. Over the next four years, these Cadets will be changed into a corps of officers prepared to lead.

Waiting for them in the bowels of the stadium is a cadre of Army officers, NCOs, and upper-class Cadets who will launch these young civilians into the Corps of Cadets. As they emerge from the opposite side of the stadium into which they only moments ago marched, the faces of the new Cadets are instantly transformed. They are solemn. The smiles are gone. Their eyes are focused straight ahead. Muscles are tensed. The new Cadets board a bus and travel to Arvin Gymnasium, where they will spend the next few hours being outfitted with military clothing and gear before taking an oath to serve the United States of America.

The oath is a crossroads for many. Cadets are required to read it carefully before reciting it, swearing to God to obey it, and signing it. With about two hours of Army life behind them, an occasional few decide this life is not for them, and they are mustered out as quickly as they were mustered in.

For those who stay, the next few hours are dedicated to equipping the soldier. Underwear, T-shirts, uniforms, web belts, canteens, shots, shoes, socks, hats and boots, rucksacks and e-tools—all are poured into a blue nylon bag that by the end of the day weighs in at about eighty pounds.

On R-Day, new Cadets are organized into squads of ten, four of which make up a platoon, four of which make up a company, eight of which make up the regiment. They're assigned to rooms and roommates. They learn to salute, to stand at attention, and to stand at parade rest. *Right face*, *left face*, and *about face* become part of their repertoire, as does the proper way to address a senior officer. New Cadets don't have many options when addressing superiors: "Yes, sir," "No, sir," "No excuse, ma'am," and "Ma'am, I do not understand." Upper-class Cadets are involved in every step of the process, which is a critical part of their own leadership training.

Not a minute is lost. Though the new Cadets don't know it, by the end of this first day they will march respectably—though perhaps not with true West Point precision—in front of their parents as West Point Cadets.

Having said their good-byes to their families, new Cadets march across the field at Michie Stadium and board a bus that will take them to Arvin Gymnasium for processing.

ABOVE: *Proud mother of a new Cadet.*

OPPOSITE: *Cadets learn immediately
where their eyes belong—straight ahead.*

CADET
ISSUE/SIZING IN

Name PARIKH SAMAR H (MI)
(First)

Co. 33   PLEASE PRINT

                                SLEEVE
HEIGHT 7 1/2   DRESS
                        SHOES
CHEST 40   COMBAT
                        BOOTS
WAIST 31

SEAT

IN-SEAM

1. Carry this tag with you to all issue points for the
   next three days

2. Tie the string tag to your barracks bag for
   identification.   (Edition of May 98 is obsolete)

USMA FORM 6-11
May 99

PARIKH SAMAR HEM
029629501
CO: D

R-DAY Processing
for Cadet Ba

ID Photo
Barber Shop
Issue Point 2
Issue Point 3
Orientation Detail
Administration Det
Supply Detail
Plebe Bag Checked by
Squad Leader / New
R-Day Drill # 1 (over)
Lunch Meal
R-Day Drill # 2 (over)
Trousers Issued

USMA FORM 2-176
(Rev Feb 85)

ARMY

ABOVE: *New Cadets leave behind fashions by brand-name designers for new designs by ARMY. Throughout R-Day, each Cadet will have virtually every part of his physique measured for the uniforms that will be tailored for him at the Uniform Factory.*

LEFT: *Each new Cadet is tagged, bagged, and hustled from one clothing station to another throughout the day. This Cadet has just learned how to stand at parade rest, a marching order he will be required to know for the R-Day parade held later that evening.*

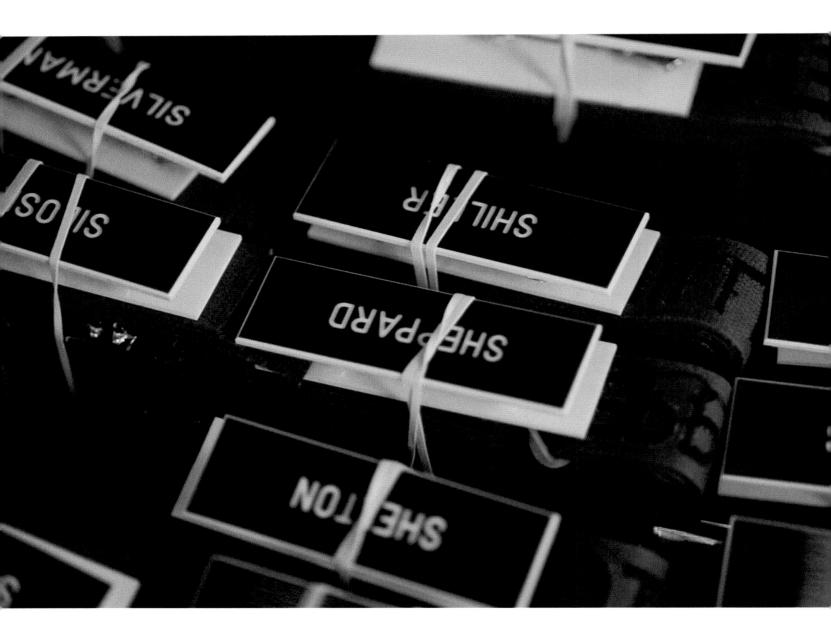

A testament to West Point's organization is the fact that all 1,000 incoming Cadets are fully equipped with uniform items already marked with their names.

Shirts, shorts, and other gymnastic and underclothing are fitted and
stuffed into bags for each new Cadet.

ABOVE: *Shoes and socks are available in black, black, or black.*

OPPOSITE TOP: *R-Day is the first time Cadets take an oath to serve the United States of America. This oath is reaffirmed each year while at West Point and taken again as part of graduation day ceremonies.*

ABOVE: *This Cadet is learning the basic vocabulary that he will use for the first few days at West Point. "Yes ma'am," "No ma'am," "No excuse, ma'am," and "Ma'am, I do not understand."*

BEAST
THE FOUNDATION

"THE DISCIPLINE WHICH MAKES THE SOLDIERS OF A FREE COUNTRY RELIABLE IN BATTLE IS NOT TO BE GAINED BY HARSH OR TYRANNICAL TREATMENT. ON THE CONTRARY, SUCH TREATMENT IS FAR MORE LIKELY TO DESTROY THAN TO MAKE AN ARMY. HE WHO FEELS THE RESPECT WHICH IS DUE TO OTHERS CANNOT FAIL TO INSPIRE IN THEM REGARD FOR HIMSELF, WHILE HE WHO FEELS, AND HENCE MANIFESTS, DISRESPECT TOWARDS OTHERS, ESPECIALLY HIS SUBORDINATES, CANNOT FAIL TO INSPIRE HATRED AGAINST HIMSELF."

—MAJ. GEN. JOHN M. SCHOFIELD, ADDRESS TO THE CORPS OF CADETS, AUGUST 11, 1879

Its formal name is Cadet Basic Training (CBT), but it is much better known as Beast Barracks. No one is sure of the nickname's origin, but it is the first test of a new Cadet's mettle. Only after these six weeks of rigorous training are new Cadets recognized as members of the Corps of Cadets, at which point they get to drop the "new."

Beast Barracks begins on R-Day and has a variety of goals, not the least of which is to turn a young civilian into a West Point Cadet. Training is vigorous, intense, and usually carried out during hot summer days and nights.

Cadets change physically during Beast; some lose weight, while others build muscle and gain weight. All add stamina. They learn military customs and courtesies, and they begin the four-year-long training in leadership and West Point's revered honor code. They learn to march and to dismantle and clean their weapons, and they become familiar with Army jargon and songs.

The method is simple: Cadets are taught, given the opportunity to practice, and then tested. For instance, Cadets spend one full day learning how to treat battlefield wounds. The training occurs in the field, where lifelike dummies with open wounds and very real-looking simulated blood are dressed and treated. At the end of the day of intensive training, the unsuspecting Cadets are divided into patrols and sent on a march through the woods. Smoke grenades have been placed at key points on the trail. Also

OPPOSITE: *New Cadets compete to see which team can get all of its members over the wall first.*

along the trail are dummies with simulated injuries. As the Cadets march through the forest, an M-60 (shooting blanks) opens up, and grenades begin to detonate. It is the first time these Cadets have been fired upon, and for most, the first time they have experienced the rapid fire of a machine gun. They are expected to provide protective fire, find and treat the wounded dummies, and then carry them off the battlefield.

The Academy has taken a unique approach to CBT, one that permeates its academic program as well. In typical military training environments, those who bring up the rear in an exercise are chastised for their inability to keep up. At West Point, the opposite occurs. Cadets, the thinking goes, should not fail—neither at scaling a wall nor at nuclear physics. After all, these young men and women come from America's brightest and most athletic stock. New Cadets who have difficulty completing a physical task are encouraged by the cadre. Their comrades will run, crawl, climb walls, and swim across lakes to encourage floundering new Cadets not to quit, not to give in to the pain and fatigue, and to push on.

While new Cadets are acquiring basic skills, cows (juniors) and firsties (seniors) are learning advanced leadership skills. Most of CBT is organized and operated by upper-class Cadets, who operate a regimental headquarters and assume such key roles as regimental commander, executive officers, battalion commanders, and supply officers. They also fill senior NCO ranks, such as regimental sergeant major. Throughout CBT, upper-class Cadets teach by example. They are strict, tough, and demanding. They also make it clear to their trainees that plebes, or fourth-class Cadets, are lower than every other class.

Just two weeks after R-Day, change is noticeable in the new Cadets. During the first few days, many of them stood in formation looking visibly nervous. They were extremely cautious. They couldn't march with any precision, and watching a company dressed in full field gear march was comical. New Cadets maintain no interval, and some lag behind and have to run every once in a while to catch up to the hapless formation. Confidence is nowhere to be found.

Throughout CBT, *tactical officers work to instill the seven Army values of loyalty, duty, respect, honor, integrity, selfless service, and personal courage into the new Cadets. They talk about these values one-on-one, in informal group sessions, and in formal speeches. As Dr. Ray O. Wood, a member of the Department of Physical Education, explained, "At most universities around the world, they teach profit and loss. A failure in their program and someone loses money. Here at West Point we teach life and death. If there's a failure in our program, people die."*

But with every step these new Cadets take, they come closer to the life of a professional Army officer. After just two weeks, they are highly motivated, and there is strong evidence of team-building. They appear more comfortable with their environment, although some of the confidence they will need over the next four years is still lacking. They have already been introduced to the Academy's three bedrock principles—duty, honor, country—and they've begun to understand the moral and ethical responsibilities of an officer in the US Army. Inside each is a growing awareness of the unique individual he or she is becoming.

The culmination of Beast occurs at Lake Frederick, a former resort area for officers located near Camp Buckner. Here the Cadets bivouac for a week, sleeping in pup tents and getting a real taste of Army life in the field. It's an exciting time. After six weeks of hard marching, physical training, and learning about military life, they are counting down the days. But they have made friends, and they are feeling just a bit more comfortable about their decision to enter West Point. The transition from civilian to Cadet is almost complete.

During the week at Lake Frederick, Cadets and their units compete in a wide variety of activities designed to test what they've learned over the past six weeks. There are competitions in military protocol, rifle sharpshooting, hand-to-hand combat, tactical operations, first aid, and command and leadership. Individual achievement is important, but on the final day only outstanding units will be recognized.

More important than the testing and evaluation, however, is the confidence that the week-long exercise is designed to provide. Capt. Gillian Boice, Class of 1989 and the executive officer for CBT 1999, remembers her week at Camp Frederick as a Cadet. "All of the Cadets at West Point come from leadership positions in civilian life. Some were president of their high school class or held leadership positions in boy scouts or church or community organizations. This confidence is eroded on R-Day, when new Cadets become part of a large group of equals. They are not allowed to lead, only to follow. In the weeks that follow, as the new Cadets are given one challenge after another during Beast, they begin to regain their confidence bit by bit. By the time we come to Lake Frederick it all gels, and they look at each other and say, 'Wow, I did it.'"

While it might be the last day of Beast, the events of the day represent a lot of firsts for the new Cadets. In fact, they will lose their titles as "new Cadets" and now become plebes, as each is assigned to his or her academic unit. On the last day of Beast, an early afternoon formation is interrupted by a group of Cadets wearing full face paint and combat gear and emerging from the lake. With them they carry a sign bearing the slogan the class has selected for its crest. Evidently someone stole the sign in the middle of the night, and now concerned upperclassmen have been kind enough to rescue it from the depths of Lake Frederick.

The return of the slogan is cause for celebration, and for the first time, the new Cadets begin to dance and party. It's a raucous celebration, with loud music coming from loudspeakers the size of refrigerators in front of the lakeside formation. The new Cadets sing, dance, and cheer, saying good-bye to Beast Barracks.

Following an awards presentation and a spirit rally, the brigade tactical officer climbs aboard a picnic bench, otherwise known as a field podium, and addresses the soon-to-be plebes. One such recent address, given by Col. Joseph Adamczyk, Class of 1972, is an excellent summary of what Beast Barracks—and indeed, the entire West Point experience—is about.

"As the brigade tactical officer, I want to tell you what I'm about. I'm about taking care of soldiers. I'm about getting missions accomplished. I'm about telling it like it is.

Soldiers expect their leaders to care for them. They expect their leaders to enforce, respect, and adhere to established standards. And that's exactly what the Class of 2003 has done this summer. They set the standard. Huah?

Soldiering is meeting tough standards. Soldiering is accomplishing the mission. Soldiering is about taking care of soldiers. And I congratulate you on that. . . . Now we're getting ready to go into the academic year. And that's part of your mission too. Academics is a mission. Academics is a duty. And you have to approach it like that. And if you approach it like that, you're going to be successful in academics also.

You may wonder why you have been successful thus far. I'm going to tell you why. Look around you. I want you to give a round of applause to your great cadre.

You got that way because that cadre cared about you. Because that cadre trained before they trained you, because they understood what the standards were, because they set the standards, because they invoked the standards, because they adhered to the standards. Cadre, good job!

Now, what can you expect in the academic year? You can expect the same thing from your cadre. . . . You can expect disciplined training. You can expect to be held to those standards, and they should lead you by positive inspirational leadership and by example. They should set a standard for you that you want to achieve. You should be saying, 'I want to be like them.' And if not, then you make them set that standard for you. I'm going to challenge you to that. I'm going to challenge you, Class of 2003, the class of the twenty-first century, to set that standard, to continue to make West Point what makes West Point special.

Now I want to talk to you about the bedrock of the Army, and I want to talk to you about the bedrock of the Military Academy. The bedrock of the Army is the seven Army values, and you know them. I would dare to say that you are truly the first class that has focused on those seven Army values from the day you entered the Academy here at West Point. You know about loyalty, you know what duty is, what respect is, selfless service, honor, integrity and personal service, you know what moral and physical courage are. Don't let yourself down. Continue to hold those values as you measure yourself in accomplishing all your missions this year. Academics, military, physical, moral, ethical—these are the guideposts.

Now there are a couple of bedrocks at West Point: honor and respect. Honor is what makes every graduate of this institution special. Everyone understands the honor code at West Point. . . . The bedrocks of our Army are built upon trust. Soldiers must have trust in each other. Soldiers have to know that there is a mutual respect, whether on the battlefield, in the classroom, in the barracks or off duty. They have got to know that their friend, their fellow soldiers are going to take care of them. They've got to know that they respect them regardless of their gender, they respect them regardless of their ethnicity, they respect them regardless of their race, religion, creed, whatever. They respect them because we are all soldiers. And soldiers take care of each other. And it is that mutual trust that allows soldiers to deploy, to fight, to win, to accomplish the mission on the battlefield and return home to their loved ones.

So you must expect that mutual respect; you are to expect to be treated with dignity. And if you are not, then you should never, ever tolerate it. . . . That is not what our Army is about. That's the bottom line, the true bedrock. No doubt about it. No, no doubt about it."

★　　★　　★

Beast is almost over, and the Cadets are anxious to get back to West Point and begin the academic year. There remain, however, fifteen miles between them and the school on the Hudson. They begin the traditional "March Back" at 0245 the day after the celebration at Lake Frederick. The longest trek the new Cadets have endured thus far is made in the dark over rugged terrain.

About midway through the march, as the Cadets approach a difficult uphill portion, an unseen bagpipe plays the marching tune and stirs the adrenaline needed to crest the top of the mountain.

At mid-morning the Cadets assemble and begin their final cadence as new Cadets, marching down Washington Road to Jefferson Road and passing in review in front of Quarters 100. In a few short days, they will be inducted into the Corps of Cadets and march proudly in the Acceptance Day Parade as full-fledged West Point Cadets.

ABOVE: *Colonel Joseph Adamczyk, Class of 1972, and Brigade Tactical Officer, knows what West Point is all about and he shares that knowledge daily with Cadets.*

OPPOSITE: *Watersports is an important part of Cadet Basic Training, including "walking the plank." Here Cadets are required to walk across a narrow beam, step up two steps and then jump down. The consequence if you miss? First a series of push-ups and then the opportunity to try again.*

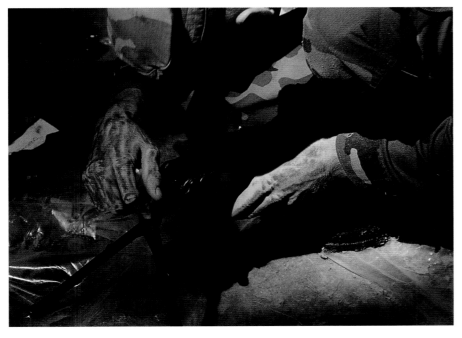

ABOVE: *Most of CBT occurs at nearby Camp Buckner. Cadets train not far from the ruins of artillery redoubts built during the Revolutionary War. Here, Cadets receive small boat training on one of the many lakes.*

OPPOSITE: *The "slide for life" is one of the highlights of CBT. While the maneuver is designed to get soldiers from one side of a river to the other without getting wet, new Cadets are forced to drop at the end of the slide and get soaked.*

LEFT: *Learning to assemble, disassemble and maintain weapons is an important part of Cadet Basic Training.*

RIGHT: *Prior to attending the Academy, this Cadet applied cosmetic makeup to her face. Now it's camo, applied in the same meticulous fashion as rouge.*

OPPOSITE: *In CBT, Cadets climb a lot of hills and learn how to rappel back down them.*

BELOW AND OVERLEAF: *Sit-ups and push-ups the West Point way.*

Cadets learn emergency first aid under simulated battlefield conditions.

CBT provides each Cadet with basic soldiering skills, a familiarity with basic Army values and traditions, and experience at succeeding in a difficult environment.

OPPOSITE: During Beast, Cadets learn to apply camouflage and how to wear and use a variety of field gear, ranging from the M-16 rifle to rappelling equipment.

Cadets learn to assemble a pontoon bridge under battlefield conditions.

Beast is almost over and these Cadets reflect on how they have
changed over the last six weeks. Tomorrow is the March Back from
Lake Frederick and preparation for the academic year.

The March Back from Lake Frederick—a fifteen-mile forced march wearing full military gear—marks the end of Beast.

UPPER-CLASS
LIFE ON CAMPUS

"I HAD THE LAYMAN'S NOTION THAT THIS WAS A STIFF, REGIMENTED PLACE WHERE ROBOTS MOVE
TO NUMBERS. I HAVE FOUND IT'S A LITTLE DIFFERENT . . . IN PRINCETON AND VIRGINIA THERE IS
SOMETHING A LITTLE SLOPPY WHICH IS NOT HERE . . . I'M INCLINED TO THINK THAT A MILITARY
BACKGROUND WOULDN'T HURT ANYBODY."
—WILLIAM FAULKNER, APRIL 1962, VISITING WEST POINT

While working hard academically, upper-class Cadets enjoy a rich social life, most of it styled and coor-
dinated in Army fashion. The last two years of a West Point education also include many milestones that
are celebrated with pomp and circumstance.

West Point may be the last place in the world where Cadets still attend formal dances called hops. The
dances are used to teach Army etiquette and protocol, and Cadets attend several during their four years
at the Point. Yearling Winter Weekend, which highlights West Point's winter sports, is accompanied by a
banquet and a hop for yearlings (sophomores) and their guests.

Another important hop is held on 500th Night, which marks five hundred days until graduation for
cows, who are second-class, or third-year, Cadets. A similar celebration is held on 100th Night, which
marks one hundred days until graduation for firsties, or first-class Cadets in their final year at the
Academy. The 100th Night Show, a musical written, directed, and performed by members of the graduating class, is based upon events and activities unique to that class's West Point experience.

But before 100th Night comes Ring Weekend, a rite of passage that reflects another age-old West Point
tradition. In August, just prior to the start of their fourth academic year, Firsties march down the Plain to
the band shell at Trophy Point, where they receive their class rings. They then assemble in the Cadet Area,
where plebes carry out a tradition called Ring Poop: they recite rhymes while begging for permission to
touch "the bold mold of rolled gold."

OPPOSITE: *100th Night—a Cadet greets his classmate's date for the hop.*

The very tradition of wearing class rings, now practiced at educational institutions throughout the US, started at West Point in 1835. West Point rings are further distinguished by the fact that each class's ring design is unique. Molded into each ring is the class crest, which is designed by new Cadets during their first summer and revealed to the entire class at the culmination of Beast Barracks. The class crest carries with it memories of the friendships and camaraderie formed in the first months of Cadet life, and it becomes a rallying point. Opposite the class crest is the crest of the US Military Academy.

Between Ring Weekend and graduation, first-class Cadets wear their rings with the class crest facing inward, to symbolize the leadership responsibilities the class has within the Corps of Cadets. Upon graduation, the newly commissioned officers wear the ring with the class crest facing outward and the Academy crest facing inward—symbolizing leadership responsibilities to the United States.

The Class of 1958 recently added to the mystique of West Point class rings, establishing a Class Ring Memorial Program whereby graduates (or graduates' descendants) may bequeath West Point class rings for the specific purpose of incorporating the gold into the class rings of future graduates. The program was instituted with the class rings of the Bicentennial Class of 2002. A total of twenty-nine rings and portions of two others were given and used for the inaugural "meltdown," including a ring that had been taken into space by astronaut Col. Bill McArthur, Class of 1973. A small portion of melted gold was drawn from the kiln and reserved to be incorporated into the rings of the next class, thereby extending the gold in the Long Gray Line.

Graduation, the culmination of four years of hard work and dedication, is a week-long series of events that culminates in a parade, a formal banquet, the last hop—held on the Friday evening before graduation— and the graduation ceremony on Saturday.

Graduation day begins as a solemn occasion. Cadets acknowledge their TACs, professors, coaches, and administrators. It ends, however, in a raucous free-for-all that begins when the newly commissioned officers throw their caps into the air. Young children, who have been waiting behind the graduating class in Michie Stadium, charge into the area and collect the discarded caps; they are rewarded by change or a message in the name pocket inside.

Another highlight of graduation week is the naming of the class goat, the Cadet ranked last in the class academically. Along with a degree, the class goat is typically presented with a gag gift from the graduating class, such as a crumpled up paper bag containing a dollar bill donated by each class member.

The notoriety surrounding class goats, not to mention the monetary rewards, created a bit of a problem for the Academy years ago. As senior class members learned their class rank prior to taking their finals, those vying for class goat walked a fine line on their last exams between finishing last and actually failing.

OPPOSITE: *First-class Cadets share a dance at the 100th Night hop.*

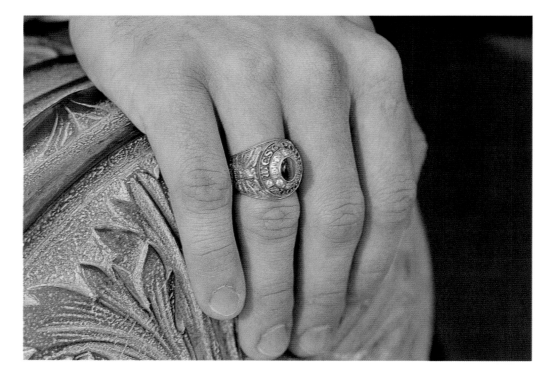

ABOVE: *Class rings have been a tradition at West Point since 1835.*

OPPOSITE: *A major part of barracks life for a Cadet is keeping every-thing neat and orderly, including his or her closet, where uniforms are hung in regulation fashion.*

OPPOSITE, AND FOLLOWING: *Graduation Day. As Cadets sit solemnly in Michie Stadium, each graduating Cadet is called to the podium to receive his or her diploma. While returning to their seats, Cadets often make rounds in the audience to thank their TACs, professors, and other significant staff members to whom they are especially grateful.*

After each Cadet receives his or her degree, there is a final oath to serve the country, and the newly commissioned second lieutenants fling their caps high into the air. Behind them, waiting anxiously, is a large group of young children who scramble to get one of the white caps, many of which contain money or mementos inside the hat band.

Graduating last from an elite institution does not mean failure
in life, and there have been many famous goats. Col. George A. Custer, Class of
1861, was a class goat, as was Gen. George E. Pickett, Class of 1846. Gen.
Gene E. Russy, Class of 1812, is the only goat to have served as superintendent
of West Point (1833–38). There were only eighteen Cadets in his class.

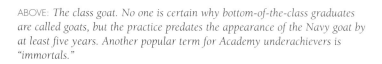

ABOVE: *The class goat. No one is certain why bottom-of-the-class graduates
are called goats, but the practice predates the appearance of the Navy goat by
at least five years. Another popular term for Academy underachievers is
"immortals."*

HONOR

A CADET WILL NOT LIE, CHEAT, STEAL, NOR TOLERATE THOSE WHO DO
THE HONOR CODE

"TO BE GOOD OFFICERS YOU MUST BE GOOD MEN—TRUE, FAITHFUL, HONEST, HONORABLE, SOBER, INDUSTRIOUS. AND ABOVE ALL, LOVE YOUR COUNTRY, AND YOUR PROFESSION, WITH AN ARDOR IN COMPARISON WITH WHICH EVERY OTHER FEELING WILL PALE AS THE RUSH-LIGHT IN THE SUN."
—GEN. WILLIAM TECUMSEH SHERMAN, COMMENCEMENT ADDRESS, 1869

Perhaps the most renowned and yet least understood element of West Point is its concept of an honor code, which dates to the Academy's founding. Jonathan Williams, West Point's first superintendent, realized from the start that honor among the corps was of paramount importance, but his reasoning was more practical than lofty. At the time, officers in the corps were given considerable responsibility for reports, muster rolls, supply inventories, and even pay records. They also handled the large sums of money that funded new fortifications and structures at West Point. Williams knew that trust had to exist among these officers, and he lectured Cadets often on the importance of an officer's word. The Army also required that all reports signed by the officer in charge be accompanied by the written statement, "I certify on my honor that the above is a faithful statement."

An officer's "word of honor" was and still is a hallmark of the profession of arms. Based upon the code of conduct of medieval knights, honor and its defense have been central to officers' lives for at least a thousand years. "Loyalty to truth and to the pledged word" was defined by French scholar Léon Gautier as one of the key commandments of chivalry. Many were the duels fought over honor. Because of the code, an officer's word sufficed for centuries.

The concept of honor among the Corps of Cadets was emphasized and further developed by the Academy's fourth superintendent, Sylvanus Thayer, who stressed that a Cadet's statement must be accepted as truth and that a man's word is his bond. Lying and stealing were not tolerated by Thayer, and Cadets

OPPOSITE: *The practice of placing stones or a cairn atop a grave marker is believed to have had its origin in Gaelic clan custom. As each warrior is summoned to battle by the chief he brings with him a stone, which he leaves at the meeting place. When the warriors return from battle, each collects his stone. Each stone remaining represents a fallen warrior.*

proven to have done so were court-martialed. But then, as now, there were very fine lines to draw in enforcing the honor code, and the severity of the violation, the circumstances, and allowances for youthful indiscretion often temper punishments.

Many years passed before the honor code expanded beyond lying. Despite Thayer's efforts, cheating was condoned until well into the twentieth century. In 1905, the Academy's adjutant stated that Cadets caught cheating would be severely punished but not dismissed, but very soon thereafter, Superintendent Hugh L. Scott issued a directive that included cheating in the honor code. It wasn't until 1926, however, that West Point's academic board developed regulations elucidating how honor would apply to the classroom. Even so, honor violations in the classroom continued to be ignored, and most Cadets caught cheating were given a second chance.

Stealing became a part of the honor code in the 1920s. Prior to that time, it was an offense worthy of court-martial; if the Cadet was found guilty, he was generally separated from the Academy with no further punishment, unless the offense was flagrant.

Gen. Douglas MacArthur, during his tenure as superintendent in the 1920s, is credited with having made the most significant changes to the honor system. MacArthur started by instituting a Cadet honor committee and formalizing the system. He then emphasized what has become the fourth tenet of the honor code, the concept of non-toleration of violations. Referred to unflatteringly as "squealing," this requirement that Cadets police their own ranks had been espoused as early as 1908, when a student journalist wrote in *Bugle Notes*, the annual publication of the Corps of Cadets, "The high standards of integrity for which the institution is famous cannot be maintained if toleration for such is known. A thief, a liar and a coward cannot be extenuated in the eyes of the Corps." By the time non-toleration was formally added to the honor code in 1970, Cadets who tolerated honor code violations in their midst had long met with dismissal.

Non-toleration remains the most difficult of the four honor code tenets for Cadets, but it continues to be critical to the Academy's mission. A white paper published by the Center for the Professional Military Ethic at West Point (CPME), dated February 10, 2000, notes that "Exceptional provisions like the Non-toleration Clause, which hold the Cadet to standards of behavior above and beyond societal norms, provide concrete and constant, if not always gentle, reminders of the extraordinary nature of their moral duty to the people they have freely chosen to serve."

In 1998, the honor code was changed from "A Cadet will not lie, cheat, steal or tolerate those who do" to "A Cadet will not lie, cheat, steal, **nor** tolerate those who do." According to the Cadets who initiated and supported the change, the old wording could have been interpreted to mean that intolerance was an optional element of the code.

Today, Cadets have a strong role in the honor system at West Point. An ongoing "honor action plan" promotes discussion and review of the system, which at its best maintains a critical balance between time-honored principles and modern needs. The honor committee itself is made up of seventy-six Cadets charged with educating the corps and enforcing the code. The committee's chairperson, executive officer, vice chair for investigations, vice chair for education, and numerous other officers ensure balanced representation for the entire corps.

Gen. Daniel W. Christman, Academy superintendent at the turn of the twenty-first century, made honor code education a priority. He assigned a more prominent role in the honor system to the commandant, and both are now responsible for imposing sanctions on Cadets found to be in violation of the code. Before deciding on the disposition of an honor violation, the superintendent or the commandant reviews the entire case file and recommendations from the chair of the honor committee, the Cadet's company commander, tactical officers, and the chain of command, as well as a special assistant to the commandant for honor matters.

The standard sanction for all honor code violations remains separation, or discharge, from the Academy. The superintendent has discretion if the investigation indicates that it is warranted—when the violation proves to be an isolated mistake, for example, and doesn't represent a Cadet's true character. The Cadet is expected to accept full responsibility for the violation and demonstrate that he or she can live up to the code in the future. Typically, if leniency is shown to a Cadet who violates the code, the Cadet will enter a "sus-

While it may sound like a simple concept in Army terms—*"The way to be is to do, and unless the Cadet can do, and ultimately be, all that is required morally, he or she will not have attained the moral-ethical standards required of a professional officer in our Army"*—*the requirement that Cadets report honor code violations is a difficult one.*

pended separation" process, which means entering a six-month-long mentoring program that requires a full self-evaluation, maintenance of a diary, and a written review of the violation. The Cadet continues to attend classes and training exercises but becomes an active duty enlisted soldier in the Army. Upon completion of the program, which is overseen by a commissioned or noncommissioned officer, the Cadet can graduate if he or she does not have any subsequent violations of the honor code.

In 1998, West Point created the Center for the Professional Military Ethic to develop, coordinate, and execute character development programs that contribute to the moral and ethical development of the Corps of Cadets. During four years at West Point, each Cadet receives over sixty hours of "values education training." Each Cadet also receives some twenty hours of instruction related to the honor code itself over the first three years, most of it under the guidance and monitoring of CPME.

CPME's mission goes beyond West Point and the Army, extending into the halls of civilian educational institutions and even into the boardrooms of leading American corporations. The National Conference on Ethics, held at West Point each fall, brings undergraduate students from colleges and universities all over the United States to a three-day conference on ethical issues on campus and in career fields. Using mentors from the ranks of college professors and administrators, lawyers, and Army officers, the conference leads students in discussions that center on contemporary ethical challenges, including the efficacy of ethical codes and character education. On CEO Day, business leaders from the corporate community lead discussions involving ethical dilemmas in management.

TOP: *Advised by one regular Army JAG, Cadets review cases of honor code violations in a real trial setting.*

BOTTOM: *Folding the flag.*

NINE

EVERY CADET AN ATHLETE EVERY ATHLETE CHALLENGED

"UPON THE FIELDS OF FRIENDLY STRIFE ARE SOWN THE SEEDS THAT UPON OTHER FIELDS, ON OTHER DAYS, WILL BEAR THE FRUITS OF VICTORY."
—GENERAL DOUGLAS MACARTHUR

Physical education is one of the three core platforms underlying the West Point experience. Each Cadet takes classes in boxing (or self-defense, the equivalent for women), gymnastics, aquatics, close-quarters combat, grappling, personal fitness, and lifetime fitness. Additionally, each Cadet is expected to compete in two or three intramural or varsity sports per year. It's hard to think of a sport that is not played at the Academy, and the Army has even invented some games of its own.

The highlight of the athletic year is the Army-Navy football game. Celebrated nationwide, the rivalry brings out as much adrenaline in the stands as it does on the field. Superintendent Christman refers to it as the "Army-Navy mystique," adding, "You feel it in your heart. It's one of the most emotional times in any school year." A week of spirit rallies, parades, parties, and prayers precedes the game. Alumni travel thousands of miles—their Army sweaters, insignia, and flags clearly visible on I-95—to tailgate with class-mates and cheer their alma mater on to victory. As General Christman says, "[The game is] a tremendous bonding force for our alumni. They come together in hundreds of places across the globe around the TV set or radio." The Army points to this dedication as evidence of the strongest bond—the one with the "twelfth man," the US Corps of Cadets.

The first Army-Navy game was played in 1890, but the rivalry so quickly got out of hand that the annual meetings were discontinued after only a few years. After a cooling-off period, the contests resumed, and in 1999 the Army-Navy football game was played for the one hundredth time. *Gray Matter*,

OPPOSITE: *The importance of West Point football was epitomized by Gen. George C. Marshall, who as Army chief of staff during World War II needed an officer to train and lead a ranger-type battalion for a secret mission. Marshall said, "I want an officer for a secret and dangerous mission. I want a West Point football player."*

published by the Association of Graduates, described the atmosphere in the barracks in the weeks leading up to the big game. "What is it like to be vastly outnumbered and surrounded by the enemy? Just ask a couple of Navy Midshipmen who are exchange Cadets at West Point this semester. They are feeling the force of West Point's spirit as the furor mounts before the Army-Navy football game Saturday.

"Midshipmen Eliza Colquitt, from Norfolk, Virginia, and Tim Strabbing, from Hudsonville, Michigan, have been the target of some plebe spirit missions. Colquitt has had most of her clothes taken from her room and was caught in the middle of a pillow fight. Strabbing has had all of his clothes, books, computer, and bed taken and hidden away. Strabbing retaliated against the plebes in his company by taking every computer mouse ball while the plebes were gone, and Colquitt has plans to tie all the plebe doors shut after taps."

Midshipmen, meanwhile, broke into the mess hall and labeled all the condiments on the 440 tables with large blue Ns. Someone painted "Go Navy Beat Army" on the sidewalk in front of Thayer Hall and Bartlett Hall, the library. The *coup de grâce* for the middies was a "Go Navy" banner hung inside Taylor Hall, the building that houses the superintendent's and the dean's offices.

Army lost to Navy in the historic hundredth outing, but Army has racked up more wins overall, with a 48-45-7 record. The rivalry continues into the twenty-first century.

★   ★   ★

At one of the first Army-Navy games, held in Philadelphia in 1895, the Midshipmen arrived from Annapolis with a goat. The Corps of Cadets reacted by hastily selecting a mule as the official mascot for the Point, and a tradition was born.

In the years since, the Academy has embraced its curious mascot. The image of the Army mule is almost everywhere—on book covers and posters, on the bright yellow USMA windbreakers worn by proud parents, on the exercise uniforms of Cadets. A small bronze statue of a mule decorates the house of the superintendent.

The real-life mules—Raider, Traveller (named after Gen. Robert E. Lee's famous battle charger), and Trooper—live and work at West Point. Outfitted with standard US Cavalry tack, these mules, a gift from generous alumni, accompany the football team and delight children and adults alike at community functions. All are over ten years old and exceptionally well trained; during football games, they charge up and down the field carrying Cadets with sabers drawn, ignoring the cannon fire that celebrates touchdowns. A select group of Cadets cares for and trains the adored mascots.

When their service is up, the mules likely will be retired to farms throughout the United States. They may even be buried at West Point, as have past mascots.

The Army mule and the Army horse, which have long carried heavy loads and dragged artillery pieces into inaccessible mountain passes, get their due in a large plaque mounted inside Thayer Hall.

OPPOSITE: *Monument to West Point athletics. The words of the inscription are from Gen. Douglas MacArthur.*

OVERLEAF: *Army spirit.*

UPON THE FIELDS OF FRIENDLY STRIFE,
ARE SOWN THE SEEDS THAT, UPON
OTHER FIELDS, ON OTHER DAYS,
WILL BEAR THE FRUITS OF VICTORY.
DOUGLAS MACARTHUR · USMA CLASS OF 1903

Army football games at West Point are sold-out events with alumni traveling thousands of miles to see their alma mater play. Homecoming Weekend is the most popular weekend for class reunions and other alumni activities.

ABOVE: *While baseball doesn't enjoy the popularity of football at the Point, the Army baseball team placed four of its members on the Patriot League conference's two all-star teams.*

OPPOSITE: *The Army women's basketball team competes in the Patriot League against teams like Notre Dame, Colgate, American University, and yes, they have their own version of the Army-Navy game.*

Character is important to victory in any sport,
but it is especially important in fencing, a
club-level sport in which West Point teams
excel.

Crew is one of the fastest-growing collegiate sports. The Hudson River provides an excellent opportunity for West Point teams to practice and compete.

The Army mule, West Point's mascot, attends all West Point football games and wears a familiar mark.

THE RESIDENCE
OF THE SUPERINTENDENT

"WE HAVE A FINE GARDEN WITH A POND IN IT AND SEVERAL MEADOWS. THERE IS QUITE A NICE GREENHOUSE WITH A SPLENDID LEMON TREE IN IT."
—FROM THE 1853 DIARY OF AGNES LEE, DAUGHTER OF ROBERT E. LEE

Quarters 100, right on the edge of the Plain and across from Washington Hall, has been the residence of every superintendent since Sylvanus Thayer first lived there in 1820. Once a simple wooden structure, the residence has been expanded many times but retains much of its original character. It is still easy to envision superintendents in the 1850s sitting on the southern-style porch and observing parade practice while sipping juleps (likely, considering how many of the superintendents were Southerners).

The supe's quarters are believed to be the second-oldest structure still standing at the Point. Quarters 101, the residence of the commandant next door, is a few months older.

Adjacent to Quarters 100 sits a magnificent formal garden, an excellent setting for receptions, promotion ceremonies, and even the occasional wedding. The pond mentioned by Agnes Lee is long gone, but forty-five of the fifty states are represented by state trees and flowers, such as the Alabama azaleas, the blue phlox from Louisiana, the bleeding heart of Nebraska, and the Alaska potentilla.

Inside the house there is—apart from ghosts mentioned by staffers—a magnificent collection of antiques that trace West Point's heritage. Included are several Hudson River School paintings, along with grand portraits of Robert E. Lee, Sylvanus Thayer, and Joseph Swift, the Academy's very first graduate. The furniture includes a writing desk used by every superintendent since Robert E. Lee donated it to West Point.

Above a table capable of seating more than twenty dinner guests hangs a particularly meaningful crystal chandelier. The chandelier was bequeathed to West Point by the daughter of William C. Muschenheim, a partner in and proprietor of the former Astor Hotel in New York City's Times Square. Muschenheim was born and grew up in Germany, where at an early age he decided to become a professional chef. In 1880, soon after emigrating to America at the age of seventeen, Muschenheim learned that the food being served

OPPOSITE: *Quarters 100 as seen from across the Plain.*

in the officers' mess at the US Military Academy was in dire need of improvement. Young Muschenheim secured a position there, and in a short time was reported to have made remarkable improvements in the quality of the cuisine. Eventually, he turned the officers' mess into a first-class restaurant.

Muschenheim became a part owner of the Astor Hotel after a series of other ventures, but he never forgot where he got his start, and the hotel became a haven for Cadets and officers, who enjoyed "favorable rates." Some time after his death, while the hotel was being demolished, his daughter Emma Radley Koehler rescued the chandelier, under which many West Point Cadets had been entertained, and gave it to the Academy. Muschenheim's obituary in the *New York Times* on October 26, 1918, stated, "It was once said of the almost affectionate relations existing between the proprietor of the Hotel Astor and the Army officers that 'Muschenheim belongs to the Army and the Army belongs to Muschenheim.'"

The crystal chandelier, now over 150 years old, has lit many a ceremonial meal at Quarters 100. Beyond serving as quarters for the superintendent and his family, the residence is used for social events and formal dinners. US presidents, foreign heads of state, and senior officers have occupied the comfortable, period-decorated guest rooms. The house staff boasts that they have the busiest social schedule of any post in the Army.

Emma Radley married Herman John Koehler, who was in charge of physical education at West Point and earned the nickname "Father of Army Physical Education." In 1885, Koehler became the first to earn the title Master of the Sword. More than a century later, his influence is still felt by the US Army. In December 2000, a new United States Army Physical Fitness School Headquarters at Fort Benning, Georgia, was dedicated in his name.

OPPOSITE: *General Daniel W. Christman, superintendent (1996-2001) and graduate of the Class of 1965, stands before the portrait of Robert E. Lee in the supe's quarters. (Photo: Leslie Jean-Bart)*

ABOVE: *The formal garden adjacent to the superintendent's quarters is the perfect setting for receptions, promotion ceremonies, and even the occasional wedding.*

OPPOSITE: *Robert E. Lee's writing desk (top), and a place setting in the formal dining room at Quarters 100.*

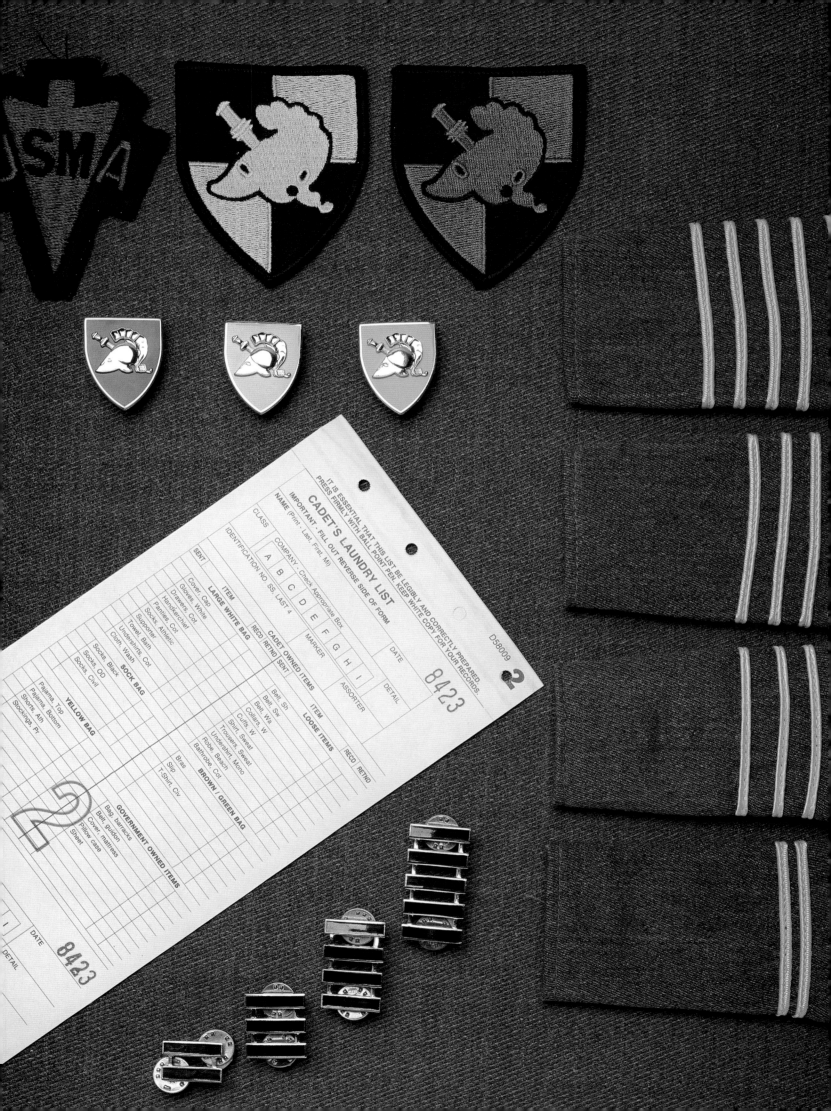

ELEVEN

THE CADET
UNIFORM FACTORY

"Q. WHAT IS THE ORIGIN OF CADET GRAY?

A. THIS COLOR WAS INTRODUCED BY SUPERINTENDENT PARTRIDGE IN THE FALL OF 1815. DUE TO THE INABILITY OF THE GOVERNMENT TO FURNISH THE TROOPS WITH BLUE UNIFORMS AT THAT PARTICULAR TIME, GENERAL BROWN'S REGULAR TROOPS WERE CLOTHED IN GRAY. THE BRITISH INITIALLY THOUGHT THEY WERE UP AGAINST GRAY-CLAD MILITIA TROOPS, WHICH THEY HAD EARLIER DEFEATED. GENERAL WINFIELD SCOTT WAS ONE OF BROWN'S BRIGADE COMMANDERS AT THIS BATTLE."
—BUGLE NOTES '98

As you enter the Cadet Uniform Factory at West Point, a sign reminds you that the same pride that goes into molding Cadets goes into the design, tailoring, and production of their uniforms. Each uniform is tailored to fit one Cadet.

The factory uses approximately thirty thousand yards of Cadet Gray cloth each year. This cloth, woven strictly to proprietary USMA specifications, is cut into patterns designed at the factory and sewn into uniforms with special thread and sewing techniques. More than one hundred thousand buttons are added to these uniforms annually.

On R-Day, one of the first stops a Cadet makes is the fitting room, where uniform factory fitters measure and fit each Cadet for his or her uniforms. It takes about eight hours to make one complete uniform, but by four o'clock on the afternoon of R-Day, each new Cadet has a tailored pair of trousers to wear in their first parade later that evening. Cadets return to the uniform factory during their summer training for further fittings, and by September, most have their dress grays. They receive their dress coats shortly thereafter. The long overcoats are completed last and distributed to Cadets in November, just in time for the upcoming Army-Navy game, for which they have become trademark attire.

Sixteen uniforms are issued to and paid for by each Cadet. With the exception of athletic gear, each is tailor-made. As Cadets gain or lose weight through active physical training, their uniforms are refitted, always by staff at the Cadet Uniform Factory.

OPPOSITE: *Stripes, badges, insignia, medals . . . there is a virtual laundry list of them at West Point—a list that every Cadet must know and understand.*

Born deaf in Ragusa, Italy, on November 10, 1940, John A. Leggio began an apprenticeship in tailoring in Palermo. He went on to study fashion design in Rome, and became a master tailor in 1962.

Six years later, Leggio moved to New York and began work for Brooks Brothers, one of the world's most famous clothiers. But when he learned of a job opening at the United States Military Academy, he moved sixty miles up the Hudson and began a thirty-year career as the Master Tailor of Cadet Gray.

During his time at West Point, Leggio oversaw numerous design changes to Cadet attire, and he worked on all of the uniforms produced by the Cadet Uniform Factory. The factory became so well known that other military organizations came to have uniforms designed and produced by Leggio and his team. He is credited with designing not only the USMA full dress coat but also the uniform of the Old Guard, the US Army's oldest active duty infantry unit and escort to the president of the United States.

John Leggio retired on March 3, 2000, exactly thirty years to the day after his arrival at West Point. He now lives in Florida with his wife.

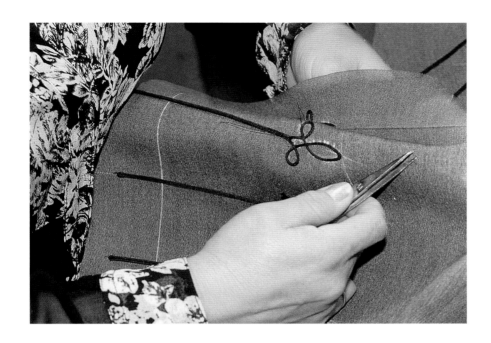

LEFT AND BELOW: *The skilled men and women of the Cadet Uniform Factory still do much of their work the old-fashioned way—by hand.*

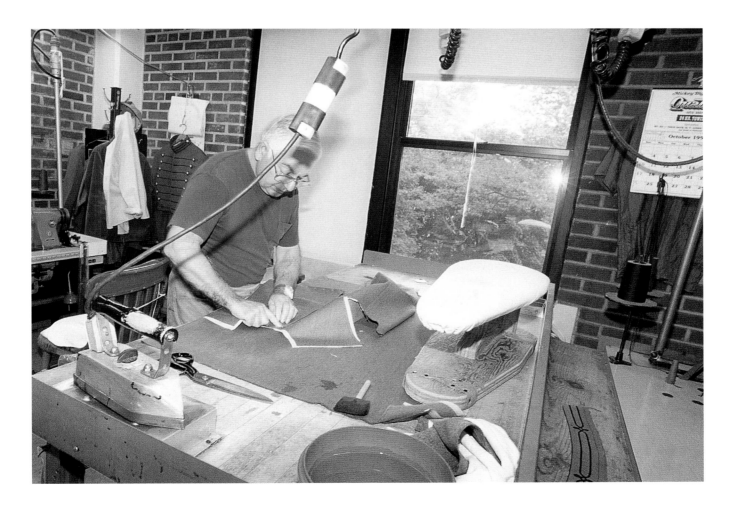

Perhaps the most recognizable attire at West Point is the Dress Gray uniform, adopted as the formal uniform for hops, parades, and formal dinners in the mid-1880s and worn here by Cadets Susan Woo, Class of 2001, and Duane S. Enger, Class of 2000. In the summer, this uniform is worn with white trousers or a white skirt. (Photo: Leslie Jean-Bart)

The original West Point Cadet uniform was blue, the same color worn by the regular Army of the day. However, because of a wartime shortage of blue wool, the uniform was changed to gray in 1814. At that time the Cadet jacket was redesigned to include brass buttons, over which a white leather cross belt was worn in a manner very similar to today's Full Dress Under Arms (left), worn here by Cadet David J. Martin, Class of 2002. Underclassmen always wear this uniform with a bayoneted M-14 rifle, which requires the white cloth cross belt and tar bucket carried at the rear waist. Only first-class Cadets may wear the saber (right), which is accompanied by a single white shoulder belt and a red sash, demonstrated here by Cadets David A. Mattox, Class of 2000, and Greg Barber, Class of 2002.

The black cock feather plume was adopted at West Point around 1820, and Cadets were required to wear it at all times, even while studying in the barracks. Cadets complained that the five-pound leather cap, or shako, was too heavy to wear constantly, and the regulation was rescinded by Superintendent Delafield in 1839. Today, the shako is worn only for parades. (Photos: Leslie Jean-Bart)

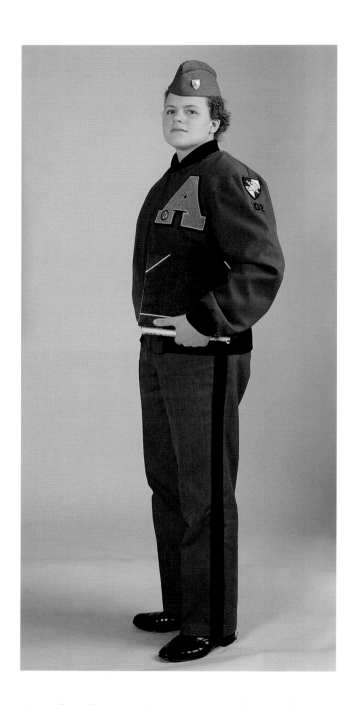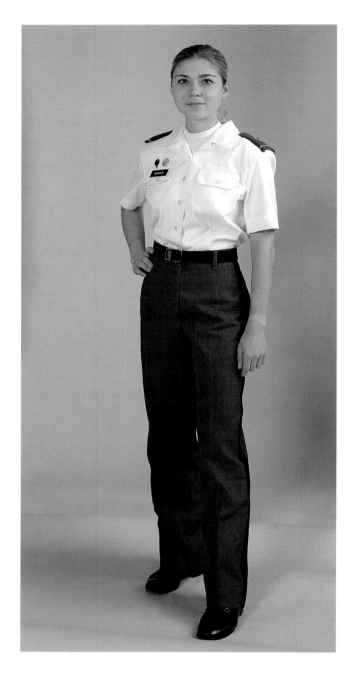

During the academic year, the most common uniform is As for Class. When it is worn with the gray jacket in winter (left), as demonstrated here by Cadet Erin Springsteen, Class of 2002, it is called As for Class under Gray. Cadet Agatha M. Glowacki (right), Class of 2000, wears White over Gray, a summer duty uniform. (Photos: Leslie Jean-Bart)

ABOVE LEFT: *The uniform Cadets have the opportunity to wear the least is India Whites. Shown here on Cadets Meghan B. Wilmore and Christian Catron, Class of 2001, India Whites are worn only twice by most Cadets during their four-year stay at West Point: during the Camp Illumination dance, which follows summer training in a Cadet's second year, and during Ring Weekend, the first weekend of the senior academic year.*

ABOVE RIGHT: *Like India Whites, the Long Overcoat sees very limited use. It was designed to give Cadets a dramatic and uniform look at the Army-Navy football game. It is traditionally worn with the top two buttons showing and the long flaps turned up, as shown here on Cadet Robert K. Beale, Class of 2002, but it can also be worn with the flaps down and buttoned in front, which gives the appearance of a cape. (Photos: Leslie Jean-Bart)*

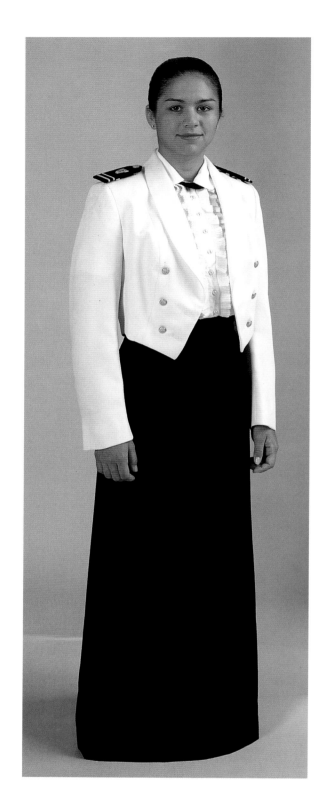

ABOVE LEFT: *Cadet Jana K. Smith, Class of 2001, wears the Dress Mess, a relatively new uniform at West Point that is worn for such special occasions as Thanksgiving and Christmas dinner. There is no male equivalent to this uniform.*

ABOVE RIGHT: *The only uniform issued to Cadets that is virtually identical to a regular Army uniform is the Battle Dress Uniform, or BDU. Consisting of a cap, blouse, and trousers and worn here by Cadet Charles Schwab, Class of 2002, this utility uniform is worn on field exercises, marches, and work details. BDUs are always worn with a brown or green crew neck T-shirt under the blouse, the sleeves of which may be rolled up or buttoned down as the weather dictates or as specified. When rolled up, the sleeves should be within one inch of the forearms when the arm is bent at a ninety-degree angle. A green tape bearing the Cadet's name is sewn onto the blouse above the right breast pocket, and the trouser legs are bloused with straps just above the boot. (Photos: Leslie Jean-Bart)*

Gym A is a physical training uniform for playing intramural sports and working out in the gym. It is also a favorite of Cadets just hanging out in the barracks. Cadet William R. Duncan, Class of 2002, wears the shorts and T-shirt (right), and Cadet Stacy L. Gervelis, Class of 2002, wears Gym A with the optional Running Suit (left), which is the newest uniform at West Point. The gray jacket of the Running Suit, designed for the protection of Cadets running in the dark, has a reflective surface which turns white in bright light. (Photos: Leslie Jean-Bart)

THE MESS HALL
PRECISION PERSONIFIED

"THE COMMISSION INSPECTED THE MESS HALL OR COMMONS OF THE CADETS REPEATEDLY AT DIN-
NER TIME. THEY REGRET TO SAY THAT THEY FOUND IT IN A STATE FAR FROM SATISFACTORY, AND THE
COMPLAINTS OF THE CADETS, LOUD AND CONCURRENT, WERE QUITE JUSTIFIED BY THE FOOD UPON
THE TABLES. IT WAS NEITHER NUTRITIOUS NOR WHOLESOME, NEITHER SUFFICIENT NOR NICELY
DRESSED."—REPORT OF A CONGRESSIONAL COMMISSION INVESTIGATING WEST POINT IN 1860

If there is one thing that most all West Point Cadets have in common, it's a voracious appetite. In the field, Cadets have food stuck in every nook and cranny of their rucksacks, in every pocket of their fatigues, and in first aid and ammo pouches worn on their cartridge belts. Give a Cadet a five-minute break, and he or she nearly always turns to an MRE (Meal Ready-to-Eat).

When they are not in the field, Cadets eat in a mess hall that constitutes the largest building on campus, employs the largest number of civilian employees, and utilizes the greatest amount of electricity of any unit at West Point.

The Cadet Mess Hall occupies more than 260,000 square feet—nearly six acres. Its first section, known as Washington Hall, was built in 1929. Two additions have been made since. The original entrance to Washington Hall remains in the center of the now six wings that extend from the door like spokes on a wheel.

Inside, the kitchen is enormous, designed for maximum efficiency and equipped with huge kettles and ovens. It's quite a sight to see ten thousand hot dogs being boiled simultaneously. A bakeshop equipped with complicated rotating ovens is capable of baking five hundred pies at a time.

Completely renovated in 1998 at a cost of over thirty million dollars, the kitchen is highly automated, impeccably clean, and extremely organized. Three times a day, 4,450 meals are prepared, distributed onto a conveyor belt, and transferred to hot carts that are wheeled out into the dining area. Everyone is served within six minutes.

The timing of the meals, from preparing the food through serving it, is an exercise in superior planning and execution. Every one of the 280 employees, who collectively work around the clock, must be counted upon to do his job. Except for the Naval and Air Force academies, whose mess halls function in a similar fashion, no other institution in the United States can serve a hot meal to as many people.

OPPOSITE: *USMA standard-issue milk cartons stashed on a Cadet's barracks windowsill.*

★ ★ ★

The Cadet Mess Hall isn't just about feeding Cadets. It brings the corps together at least twice a day, reinforcing the sense of community. And it's an extension of the lessons in leadership, precision, and even etiquette that pervade the West Point experience.

Except on Sundays, when there is a morning brunch and evening dinner, the Cadet mess offers three meals a day. Of the dinners, only Thursday night is obligatory. Lunch, which is obligatory daily, is preceded by a noon formation outside Washington Hall. Thursday formations double as haircut inspections.

Once the entire regiment is seated, forty waiters serve the meal. Usually, the entrée is on dinner plates, and vegetables and desserts are passed family style. Cadets sit ten to a table, with the table commandant seated at one end and a plebe at the other. The plebe, who is the last to sit, stands at parade rest in front of his chair until the Corps is assembled and ordered to "take seats." It is his or her responsibility to announce the menu and to know and serve each person's preferred beverage. When dessert is cake or pie, the plebe cuts it into perfectly equal portions based on the number of diners who wish to have dessert—once again, without asking. At the end of the meal, the plebe reports to the senior Cadet at the table how much of each dish is left in the serving containers.

In the minutes preceding each meal, you can watch plebes carefully checking their respective tables and place settings. They take care to straighten the condiments properly: ketchup, peanut butter, and milk containers must all be positioned with the West Point logo facing the diners. On special occasions the milk cartons even carry slogans, such as "Beat Navy."

Mounted on the exterior walls of the Poop Deck are sets of four lights visible to all the Cadets. When "Attention to Orders" is read, about halfway through the meal, the first light in each set is lit, and firsties are allowed to depart the Mess Hall. When the second light is lit, cows may disperse, and yearlings are dismissed with the third light. Plebes wait for the fourth light, which comes on only when the order is given for the brigade to rise.

Once the Cadets have departed, the job of cleaning 445 tables, straightening 4,450 chairs, and washing thousands of dishes (of which there is only one set) begins. The linen on each table needs to be changed, the six acres of slate floor cleaned, condiments replenished, and each table reset—all in a few hours' time.

Although Cadets still spurn baked fish in favor of pizza pockets and pasta, the fare is much improved since 1860, when Cadet Lieutenant Adelbert Ames, Class of May 1861, said: "The fish, in odor and taste, is sometimes disgusting. . . . Bugs will be found in the sugar, and cockroaches in the soup." That same year Joseph C. Ives, Class of 1852, then a first lieutenant, wrote, "The fare is very bad. I have lived on bread for days, rather than eat the other food provided."

For a good part of the nineteenth century, the West Point menu included boiled beef or boiled salt pork, stewed rhubarb, and molasses with nearly every single meal. Fresh vegetables were a novelty and lard a staple: in 1860, Academy Cadets consumed more than four thousand pounds of lard.

This recipe from the West Point mess, which yields food for five thousand people, illustrates the enormous quantities of ingredients that go into a single meal.

TURKEY POT PIE WITH FLAKY CRUST

1,250 pounds turkey breast, cooked
200 pounds frozen peas
200 pounds frozen carrots, sliced
75 10-lb. cans whole white potatoes
25 10-lb. cans large pearl onions
450 pounds fresh celery

140 pounds margarine
150 pounds flour
5 jars wine sherry
5 1-lb. jars chicken base
20 ounces poultry seasoning

Cut potatoes and celery. Cut turkey into pieces ¾" square. Divide turkey into pot(s), cover with stock, and heat through. Drain stock and reserve for gravy. Cook vegetables separately. Drain pearl onions. Add potatoes and vegetables to turkey, divide sauce, heat, and season. Top with flaky crust.

Like most everything at West Point, the Cadet mess reflects the history and traditions of the Academy. The walls of the wings are hung with pre–Revolutionary War flags, portraits of former superintendents, and the flags of the fifty states. Today the portraits are covered with Plexiglas, the consequence of a food fight that erupted at a "spirit night" dinner prior to the 1984 Army-Navy game. The entire corps was called back to clean up.

A conspicuous and very unusual work of art adorns the entire back wall of the C Wing. The 2,450-square-foot mural, painted in 1936 by T. Loftin Johnson, captivates onlookers. It took Johnson one year to paint the mural, which consists primarily of battle scenes, some going back thousands of years. But no one knows why the work depicts King Richard the Lion Hearted with two right hands or why a man, seemingly bowing to Queen Elizabeth, has no face. There are other anomalies—a horn from an old car, a sparkplug, a gas mask, and other incongruous objects appear here and there, though few people have been able to find the bottle of Coca-Cola or the pack of cigarettes rumored to be present.

In the center of the Cadet mess, above the original Washington Hall doorway, is a room used by the Academy superintendent for formal dining. The Poop Deck, as it is called, is capable of seating twelve people and looks out over the six wings of Washington Hall (see overleaf).

LEFT: *Meals in the Cadet Mess Hall are orchestrated events. Three times a day, more than 4,000 Cadets, officers, and guests are served in less than six minutes.*

ABOVE: *Try buying this ketchup in your commissary. Several makers of condiments and beverages have agreed to supply their products with the West Point name.*

T. Loftin Johnson's 1936 mural adorns the entire back wall of the mess hall's C Wing.

Christmas

On holidays and special occasions, the Cadet mess treats Cadets to more than the usual pomp and circumstance. The Graduation Banquet, 100th Night, 500th Night, Yearling Banquet, Plebe/Parent Banquet, Thanksgiving dinner, speeches by notables, and the annual presentation of the Thayer Award are among the causes for extra fanfare. Cadets look forward especially to the Christmas meal.

The Christmas season at West Point officially begins with a tree-lighting ceremony held during the first week of December, just after the legendary Army-Navy football game. With the game out of the way—won or lost—Cadets begin to focus on three things: the end of the first academic term, final exams, and the Christmas holidays, when many will make their first visits home in six months. The Corps Christmas Dinner commemorates this trilogy—the game, finals, and the holidays. It takes place at the semester's end, before the arduous week of final exams, and like most everything else at West Point, it is steeped in tradition. Cadets wear their full dress uniforms and are served an elaborate turkey dinner.

And yet the evening has its lighthearted and even raucous side. Cadets entering the mess hall are greeted by Christmas carols being played and sung by the West Point Jazz Band. The air is electric. Some Cadets exchange gifts and begin their good-byes, snapping photographs to take home to their families. Uniforms are decorated with bows, bells, and other festive symbols. A few Cadets are dressed as Santa.

The 445 tables, meanwhile, are unlike anything a civilian has ever seen. It's the duty of the plebes to decorate them, and no rules apply. Some tables are shrouded in pup tents; others are wrapped as Christmas gifts. Quite a few bear Christmas lights, some are circled by model railroads, and still more sprout trees ranging in height from one to six feet. Prizes are awarded, including one for best military design, best Christmas theme, and best decoration overall.

The first order of business for the dinner is a noble one. All of the chefs, cooks, waiters, and mess hall personnel who serve the corps faithfully and efficiently every day assemble on the Poop Deck and receive a clamorous round of applause for their dedication. Properly saluted, the staff goes to work serving the formal Christmas dinner.

After the meal, the corps rises and sings "The Twelve Days of Christmas." They wish each other happy holidays and then place one chair in the center of their respective tables, now littered with decorations, empty plates, and dirty utensils. Plebes clamber aboard the chairs and stand at attention while their tablemates lift the tables into the air and over their heads. Each piece of solid wood furniture weighs well in excess of three hundred pounds. More ambitious groups create pyramids of chairs or lift two plebes, one piggybacking the other. The tables go up and down haphazardly, creating a sea of rolling waves. There are some spectacular accidents.

Chimes sound. The boom of a gavel reverberates through the Black and Gold Room at Washington Hall. A senior officer gives the order to post the colors. A bugle sounds the call to attention; a drum rolls. Those in the room are standing.

There is a brief invocation, followed by toasts to the visiting dignitaries. "To His Majesty, the king of the Belgians." "To His Majesty." "To the president of the United States." "To the president."

And so it goes. This is a mock exercise, as much a part of Cadet education at West Point as battlefield training, and the US Army protocol of Dining In is instilled with all the finesse and panache of the real event.

Each Cadet's education in this venerated military tradition consists of hosting such a formal affair for family or a small group of classmates. The Black and Gold Room, equipped with silverware, china, crystal, serving dishes, and other accoutrements designed specifically for the US Military Academy, is the training ground. The young host is responsible for scheduling the affair, creating the guest list, choosing and issuing invitations, planning the menu, arranging the tables and seating, and selecting the toasts, wines, and even cigars.

Seven courses, each accompanied by a complementary wine or champagne in an appropriate goblet, are not unusual. A typical menu might look like this:

COURSE	SERVING	WINE
1	shrimp cocktail, oysters, clams on the half shell	Chablis
2	soup (usually clear)	sherry
3	fish (hot or cold)	Rhine
4	main course (beef or game) and vegetable	claret or Burgundy
5	salad	claret or Burgundy
6	dessert (ice cream or sherbet)	Champagne
7	fruit (pears, grapes, etc.)	Champagne

After-dinner coffee is always served, frequently with cigars and Port. In much the same way that blanks are used as ammunition for battlefield training, Cadets are served sparkling cider and other nonalcoholic beverages throughout the evening.

A presentation or address often follows the meal, after which the presiding officer announces, "Retire the Colors." The sound of the gavel reverberates again, this time twice, and the chimes follow. The Dining In is complete.

As the festivities end, thousands of Cadets retire into the cold night and gather in front of Washington's monument, where they light the cigars that were included in their place settings. Smoking, of course, is prohibited at West Point—with this single exception. As almost everyone lights up, the smoke perfumes the night, providing a memorable end to a memorable evening.

THIRTEEN

THE CHAPELS

"HELP US MAINTAIN THE HONOR OF THE CORPS UNTARNISHED AND UNSULLIED AND TO SHOW
FORTH IN OUR LIVES THE IDEALS OF WEST POINT IN DOING OUR DUTY TO THEE AND TO OUR
COUNTRY."
—FROM THE CADET PRAYER

The main chapel dominates the West Point skyline, prominent not only in the hearts and minds of Cadets but in location as well. Dedicated in 1910 and erected as part of the West Point expansion that coincided with America's emergence as a world power, the building was designed by Bertram G. Goodhue, and it fits perfectly into its surroundings. It looks more like a castle than a house of worship, and its design appears to have been taken from a handbook on medieval battlements.

Known to some as the Cadet Chapel and to others as the Cathedral of the US Army, the main chapel is dominated by two large stained-glass windows—gifts from graduating classes—located on either side of the nave. They are an eloquent testimony to the generosity of West Point alumni, who contribute millions of dollars to the Academy each year.

The north window is dedicated to West Point graduates who died in World War I, and a series of stained-glass windows nearby depicts the triumph of Christ over sin and death. The glorious sanctuary window uses Old and New Testament heroes to represent the "Genius and Spirit of West Point." Cut glass depicts the "then and now," framed at the bottom with the words, "To the glory of the God of battles and in faithful memory of the departed graduates of the United States Military Academy erected by living alumni MCMX." The sanctuary window also depicts the crucifixion of Christ, soldiers of the Roman Guard, the coats of arms of the United States and the Academy, and Moses receiving the Ten Commandments.

Other chapels add to the beauty of West Point. Built in 1836 adjacent to the Plain, the Old Cadet Chapel was the primary house of worship until 1910, when the new Cadet Chapel was dedicated. Generous alumni interceded with plans to demolish the older building, and the chapel was carefully dis-

OPPOSITE: *Stained glass of the Cadet Chapel's sanctuary window.*

mantled, stone by stone, and reconstructed in 1911 right inside the gates of the West Point Cemetery. Its soaring columns and nearly all-white interior make an exemplary setting for protestant services, wedding ceremonies, and funerals.

The Synagogue, a dramatic structure befitting an institution whose very first graduate was Jewish, was completed in May 1984. The Catholic Chapel was begun in 1899 and dedicated in 1900. And the Post Chapel, dedicated June 4, 1944, is noteworthy for its single stained-glass window. It is dedicated to four Army chaplains who, on February 3, 1944, were serving aboard the transport ship *Dorchester* when it was torpedoed by the Germans off Greenland. When the chaplains realized there was a shortage of life jackets, they handed theirs to fellow soldiers and went down with the ship, in prayer.

The Cadet Chapel is a steady reminder that weddings can take place just after graduation, though not before. In an average year, fifteen to twenty Cadet weddings—elaborate events conducted with complete Army protocol—take place at West Point's various chapels within twelve days of graduation.

As many as twenty percent of female graduates go on to marry members of their graduating class, creating thoroughly West Point families.

Cadets ring the chapel bells from high inside the belfry. Getting there,
up numerous flights of a narrow stairwell, requires stamina.

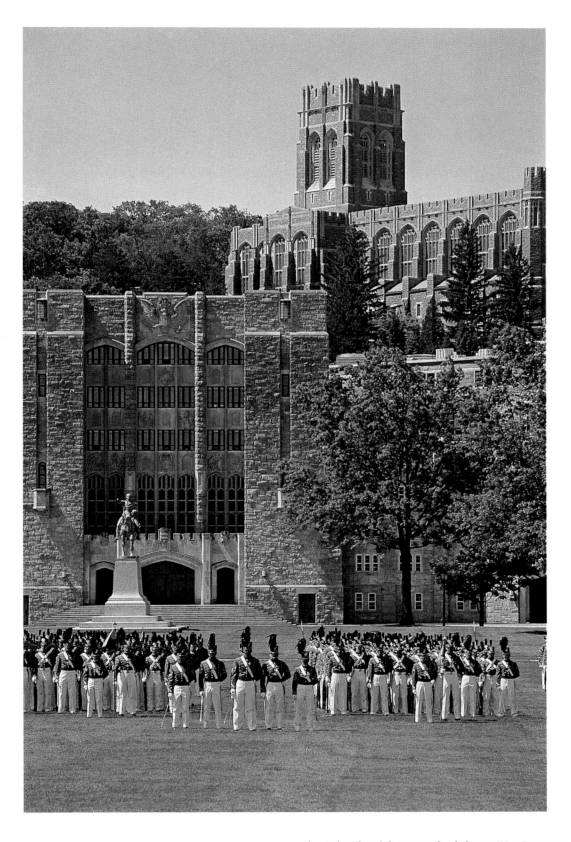

The Cadet Chapel dominates the skyline at West Point, its tall bell tower visible from nearly everywhere on campus.

147

Cadets are encouraged to practice their own religion at West Point.
Hymns sung in the chapel come from the Book of Worship for US
Forces.

SO VERY LITTLE RANCOR
WEST POINT'S LEADING
ROLE IN THE CIVIL WAR

"IT IS PROPER FOR WEST POINT TO TAKE PRIDE, NOT OF NECESSITY IN THE RIGHTNESS OF ITS CONFEDERATE GRADUATES BUT IN THEIR UPRIGHTNESS."
—GENERAL MAXWELL D. TAYLOR, JANUARY 19, 1952

Ask a Southerner just what he thinks of the Confederate cannons, mortars, and other captured booty assembled at West Point's Trophy Point, and he'll likely tell you that the Academy ought to return them to their rightful owners. But West Point and its graduates have played an enormous role in healing the wounds of that terrible conflict, and a strong case could be made for absolution.

During the War between the States, the Academy, like the nation, was divided in two. When fighting broke out, more than three hundred of West Point's alumni, or about half of those living, joined the Confederacy, and a good number of Cadets went south to join their brethren prior to graduation. In the end, leaders on both the Northern and the Southern sides had been educated on the Hudson. Of the Class of 1846's fifty-nine members, for instance, ten men—Darius Nash Couch, John Gray Foster, John Gibbon (who entered West Point with the class of 1846 but graduated in 1847), George Henry Gordon, George Brinton McClellan (who graduated second in the class, after Charles Seaforth Stewart, who advanced only to the rank of colonel), James Oakes, Jesse Lee Reno, Truman Seymour, George Stoneman, and Samuel Davis Sturgis—served as Union generals. Ten more became generals in the Confederate army—John Adams, Birkett Davenport Fry (who attended West Point but was dismissed prior to graduation), William Montgomery Gardner, Ambrose Powell "A. P." Hill, Thomas Jonathan "Stonewall" Jackson, David Rumph Jones, Dabney Herndon Maury, Samuel Bell Maxey, George Edward Pickett, and Cadmus Marcellus Wilcox. Still other members of the class advanced to flag rank after the war.

The dual role of West Point graduates during the Civil War created a firestorm of criticism in the press and in Congress. In one particularly vicious attack, Senator Zachariah Chandler of Michigan said that West Point "has produced more traitors within the last fifty years than all the institutions of learning and education that have existed since Judas Iscariot's time." But the criticism eventually died down, and in many cases the bonds formed in the classroom tempered deep divisions among politicians and families at critical times. Many historians believe that the shared lessons of West Point helped Grant and Lee fashion a surrender that gave Southerners a sense of pride and honor despite their loss.

OPPOSITE: *Bronze relief depicting the death of an officer in the Civil War.*

In the years after the war, West Point contributed to the nation's recovery by making a point of celebrating heroes both Northern and Southern. Hence Grant Hall next to Lee Hall; hence plaques and monuments to graduates who fought on both sides. Cadets from Southern states whose parents had served the Confederacy came to West Point and were fully accepted by the Corps of Cadets.

Equal treatment, always. And no rancor. In later years, when class notes included the obituaries of Civil War veterans, their careers in either the South or the North were treated respectfully. And during celebrations of West Point's 150th birthday in 1952, a portrait of Robert E. Lee in his Confederate uniform was unveiled "to symbolize the end of sectional differences in our country." Keynote speaker Gen. Maxwell D. Taylor said, "To most of us it appears high time to lay aside such historical blinders in viewing our graduates, and to acclaim with pride the fact which every schoolboy knows—that Robert E. Lee was not only a distinguished graduate of West Point, a superintendent who contributed notably to the development of the Academy, a brilliant officer of the United States Army worthy to be offered the supreme command but also the immortal battle leader of the Confederacy, whose deeds will stir men's souls as long as future generations find time to read the history of this country." The portrait, now in the main room of the library, hangs next to an 1866 painting of Ulysses S. Grant.

As tensions mounted between North and South, the Academy hurried to educate young officers. Two classes were graduated in 1861, one in May and one in June, the latter after abbreviated schooling. Alumni of these small classes (with forty-five and thirty-four graduates, respectively), went on to varying degrees of success and infamy. Henry Algernon du Pont, who graduated first in the Class of May 1861, received the Medal of Honor in the battle of Cedar Creek. After the war he was a principal in his family's chemical business, the Dupont Company, served as US Senator from Delaware, and was instrumental in procuring restitution for the Virginia Military Institute, which was burned down by Union troops. The goat of the June class, now buried in the West Point Cemetery, was George Armstrong Custer.

Cadet Jefferson Davis
Class of 1828

LEFT: *In the early days of the Academy, drawing was considered an important prerequisite for Cadets to learn mapmaking and other field communications skills. This drawing, typical of early Cadet assignments, is by Cadet Jefferson Davis, Class of 1828. (Courtesy of West Point Museum, USMA)*

BELOW: *1841 painting by Cadet Ulysses S. Grant, afterwards General of the Army and president of the United States. (Courtesy of West Point Museum, USMA)*

It is estimated that three hundred ninety cannons used in the American Civil War still exist today, most as monuments to the nation's bloodiest conflict. Some were made at the West Point foundry at Cold Spring, New York, and many are still displayed at the Academy. This one, at Trophy Point, pays homage to those who lost their lives in the Battle of Gettysburg.

MEMORIES
OF VALOR

"THEY ARE HERE IN GHOSTLY ASSEMBLAGE,

THE MEN OF THE CORPS LONG DEAD,

AND OUR HEARTS ARE STANDING AT ATTENTION,

WHILE WE WAIT FOR THEIR PASSING TREAD."

—"THE CORPS," ANTHEM OF THE CORPS OF CADETS

Aside from Arlington National Cemetery, no place in our country better represents courage, duty, honor, and the commitment to freedom than the West Point Cemetery. It is a registry of the inhabitants of the Home of the Brave, and its polished granite stones and solemn monuments pay homage to the people who have made and kept the United States of America free. It is difficult to walk through these fourteen acres of hallowed ground, with its more than seven thousand graves, without coming face to face with the gravity of West Point's refrain: duty, honor, country.

The cemetery, which overlooks the Hudson River, served as a burial ground for area residents and Revolutionary War soldiers even before 1817, when it officially became a military cemetery. The oldest grave commemorates an ensign in the Ninth Connecticut Infantry, a native of Cork, Ireland, named Dominick Trant. His burial here is a reminder of the early days of the Revolutionary War, when a handful of Connecticut infantrymen were first to occupy the Point. Across the cemetery lie the graves of Susan Warner and Anna B. Warner, who lived on Constitution Island, which they willed to the Academy. The sisters are credited with writing many songs and books, including the children's melody "Jesus Loves Me."

Since those early days, America's toil for freedom has laid many exceptional men and women to rest in this great place. Guarding the wrought-iron gates at the entrance to the cemetery is the Old Cadet Chapel, whose whitewashed walls are heavily decorated with dark marble plaques commemorating those who fought in such conflicts as the Revolutionary War, the War of 1812, and the Mexican wars. History and

OPPOSITE: *One of the largest monuments in the Cadet Cemetery is the columned memorial for Major General Daniel Butterfield, who composed the bugle call "Taps."*

Joseph G. Swift, the Academy's first graduate, came very close to losing that distinction. When he reported to West Point for duty in October 1801, before it became the US Military Academy, he was invited by some other officers to dine in the artillery mess. This demonstration of favoritism did not sit well with Professor Baron, a recently hired teacher of arts and sciences. Baron sent a servant to inform Swift that he would have to dine with other Cadets, but Swift ignored the order. When called to account, Swift told Baron that he refused to honor an oral order from a servant. Baron called him a mutinous young rascal, at which point Swift jumped from his chair and lunged at the professor. Baron ran to his quarters and locked the door.

Charges were lodged against both: Baron for conduct unbecoming an officer, and Swift for showing disrespect to a superior. Both were found guilty, but only Baron was discharged. After the Academy was formally established the following year, Swift went on to become its first graduate. From 1812 to 1814, he served as superintendent of West Point.

stories are everywhere. One curious marble plaque lists only a birth date, 1740, and the rank of major general; the place where a name should be is blank. This is the memorial that was earmarked for Benedict Arnold before discontent led him to treason. Another plaque commemorates the first Cadet to graduate from West Point, Joseph G. Swift.

Gen. Winfield Scott's pew is marked with a small silver plaque much like those in today's Cadet Chapel commemorating Academy superintendents. Though Scott never served as superintendent, he spent a great deal of time at West Point and lobbied its cause in Washington. His own military career had begun with a brief stint as a corporal in the Virginia militia. Later, when President Jefferson asked Congress to authorize an additional six thousand men to complement eight new regiments for the Army, Scott used political favors to get an audience with the president and a promise that, if Congress approved his request, Scott would be granted a commission as a captain. On April 8, 1808, Congress voted to triple the size of the Army, and Winfield Scott's career as one of this country's greatest military leaders began. In 1841, he was named a major general and commander in chief of the Army. He retired during the Civil War, after laying down the strategy for the Union army's victory.

The cemetery's monument to another luminary, George Custer, is itself an interesting story. On a knoll across from Washington Hall, a granite gravestone topped by an obelisk reads, "George A. Custer, Lt. Colonel 7th Cavalry, Killed with his entire command at the Battle of Little Big Horn on June 25, 1876." But this is not what was originally erected to commemorate the aggressive Indian fighter. Two years after Custer's death, Congress allocated bronze from twenty cannons to a larger-than-life-size statue of the general. Sculptor Wilson MacDonald designed the monument, which depicted Custer in full dress uniform, long hair waving in the breeze, wearing jackboots and holding a saber in one hand and a pistol in the other.

Custer's widow, Libby, who had not been consulted, objected to everything about the statue. She didn't think MacDonald sufficiently accomplished as an artist to warrant the commission. Nor did she favor the manner in which her husband was depicted—as a desperado, she felt, copiously armed and dressed in an improper uniform. In 1884, after Mrs. Custer had spent years lobbying for the statue's removal in Washington, DC, all but the base of it was removed. In 1905, at Mrs. Custer's behest, the granite obelisk was added. What happened to the statue remains a mystery to this day.

Not far from Custer's diminished tombstone, on the far southeastern corner of the burial ground, is the Cadet Memorial. Erected in 1818, this beacon overlooking the Hudson may be the most moving of the cemetery's shrines. Shaped like a huge lighthouse and adorned with gargoyles at its pinnacle, its bricks are engraved with the names of Cadets who have died while at the Academy. Most were not yet twenty-one.

The West Point Cemetery is a place that makes one proud to be an American. It's a place to give thanks for freedom. The tribute on Gen. Winfield Scott's marker brings home the level of heroism and gratitude that gives visitors an almost eerie sensation: "Winfield Scott, born Dinwiddie County, Virginia on June 13, 1786. Died at West Point on May 29, 1866. History records his eminent services as a warrior, pacificator, and General in Chief of the Armies of the United States. Medals and an equestrian statue ordered by Congress in the Capital of his country are his public monuments. This stone is a mark of the love and veneration of his daughters. Requiescat in pace."

Winfield Scott was a brilliant leader, but his name is not widely known in American history, and he was a controversial figure to those who knew him. Robert E. Lee wrote of Scott, "The General, of course, stands out prominently, but he appears the bold, sagacious, truthful man he really is." Ulysses S. Grant remarked on his tendency to write in the third person, which allowed him to "bestow praise on the person he was talk-

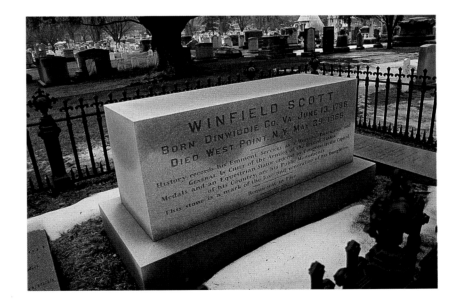

ing about without the least bit of embarrassment." Scott was egotistical, aggressive, and independent, and he served with great passion. That combination led to at least one duel, several courts-martial, and, perhaps, his obscurity. His grave in the West Point Cemetery is a suitable monument to the hero he was and his place as a knight of the American legend.

The West Point Cemetery sits on a promontory once known as "German Flats," behind the old Cadet Chapel and over-looking the Hudson River and Constitution Island. There are more than six thousand men and women buried there, including soldiers who died in nearly every armed conflict in which the United States has taken part.

OPPOSITE: *Erected in 1818, the Cadet Memorial is one of the most hallowed monuments at the Academy. It was originally built in honor of Cadet Vincent M. Lowe, who was killed by a premature discharge of a cannon the year before. Today, the sides of the monument are inscribed with the names of Cadets and faculty members who died on duty at West Point.*

ABOVE: *Battle Monument at Trophy Point. The base of the monument is inscribed with 2,230 names, representing only a small portion of the regular Army soldiers who died in the Civil War.*

ABOVE: *Monument to George Armstrong Custer.*

CONTEMPLATING A
NEW BEGINNING

"THE LONG GRAY LINE HAS NEVER FAILED US. WERE YOU TO DO SO, A MILLION GHOSTS IN OLIVE

DRAB, IN BROWN KHAKI, IN BLUE AND GRAY, WOULD RISE FROM THE WHITE CROSSES THUNDERING

THOSE MAGIC WORDS: DUTY, HONOR, COUNTRY."

—GENERAL DOUGLAS MACARTHUR, 1962

What is it that draws young people to serve their nation? What values or interests underlie first the curiosity and then the drive to join America's military elite? There is no single answer to these questions, and today, the answers have become very complex.

National pride is a good beginning. Most Americans will agree that the foundation upon which America has been built is worth protecting. But patriotism alone is not enough. The Academy seeks to train a new kind of leader, one who performs not only in war but also in peace. This is part of the new vision at West Point. This is a new kind of soldier, one West Point has never trained before. Twenty-first century leaders must be capable of dealing with changing geographical and political boundaries, new threats, new weapons, and new adversaries. The Academy has never faced such profound changes.

★ ★ ★

Class of 1965

To place the Academy's present and future challenges into context, it is instructive to examine the achievements of one remarkable class from West Point's recent past. Most of the Cadets who reported for R-Day in June 1961 didn't know what a cold war was. The Bay of Pigs invasion had just occurred but meant little to high school seniors. They had no idea where Vietnam—then spelled Viet Nam—was located or what was happening there. Little could they imagine what their fate would be over the next ten years.

What they witnessed, what they experienced and lived during that decade and the next, was fundamental change in the social, political, and military structure of their country and the world. They saw social and political havoc and the rise of rogue nations; they experienced victory and defeat in battle; they witnessed the near-catastrophic moments of the cold war and then watched it end, suddenly, with the destruction of the Berlin Wall.

OPPOSITE: *An equestrian statue of General George Washington keeps watch over the Plain.*

About halfway through the Class of 1965's training at West Point came the infamous shot heard around the world. The president of the country, whose constitution they had sworn to protect, had been assassinated. The United States had just upped the ante with a quarantine on Cuba that prevented Russian ships from placing nuclear weapons just off America's shores. As they studied at West Point, the Soviet Union was building a wall in Germany that would separate much more than just ideologies, and Vietnam's first democratic president was overthrown and assassinated. By Graduation Day 1965, there would be more than 175,000 US troops in Vietnam, in a war that was escalating daily. Twenty-four of the 595 class members who served in southeast Asia gave their lives there. And yet, despite the turmoil, this class has worn its historical hash marks proudly.

Vietnam veterans dealt with the stigma of returning from an unpopular war in many ways. Many vets were never able to heal the invisible wounds, but members of West Point's Class of '65 knew that no matter what, they had each other. That enabled healing to take place.

"Most [members of the class] will tell you that it was their training as Cadets at West Point that allowed them to face the disappointment of Vietnam, to watch the deterioration of leadership in America, and to find the confidence to forge onward with their own lives and their own careers," says Lt. Gen. Joseph DeFrancisco (Ret.).

"When you go to school here, and you walk around these monuments, and you study military history, you come to the realization that there will be no end to war. When I went to Vietnam the first time, I had the feeling that it was my turn to pay back; this was my turn to do something for my country, and I was getting the opportunity to do it rather quickly."

Members of the Class of '65 have served in Vietnam, Panama, Granada, Desert Storm, and Bosnia. Of the 595 graduates, 417, or seventy percent, have been decorated. Ninety-four class members have been awarded the Silver Star; 173, the Bronze Star with Valor; 473, the Bronze Star; 56, the Commendation Medal with Valor; 472, the Army Commendation Medal; 818, the Air Medal; and 59, the Air Medal with Valor. Fifty-three members of the class have received the Distinguished Flying Cross, and seventeen wear the Distinguished Service Medal. The Legion of Merit has been awarded to members of this class 194 times; the Meritorious Service Medal, 405 times. One member wears the Navy Commendation Medal, one wears the National Defense Service Medal, and one was awarded the Prisoner of War Medal. The Purple Heart has been pinned on the chests of 133 class members. In total, 3,128 medals have been awarded to members of the Class of '65.

Because of the social, cultural, and political change that has occurred since the mid-sixties, the Class of 1965 also offers a good benchmark to measure the Academy's own change. Gen. Daniel W. Christman, himself a member of the Class of '65, became superintendent of West Point in 1996. "When I graduated in '65, we were commissioned into a service that was caught in the middle of the cold war. We knew who the enemy was; the enemy was the Warsaw Pact, the enemy was aggressive communism in southeast Asia. We knew where we were going to end up . . . Vietnam. But that was part of a larger US tapestry of opposition to aggressive policies throughout the world. That all changed one fall night in October, eleven years ago, when the Berlin Wall came down. As an institution, we are still wrestling with what that means. The Army itself is going through an incredible transformation.

"What we are producing right now are junior leaders who, compared to graduates thirty-five years ago, are much more mentally and strategically agile, capable of negotiation with a Serbian chief, capable of fighting the Republican Guards in Basra, capable of feeding the homeless in Hungary and Rwanda or repairing utility lines in Dade County, Florida. We are preparing graduates to respond to a much broader and more diverse mission of international tasks than was ever the case here at West Point."

Along with the Classes of 1966, 1967, and 1968, West Point's Class of 1965 bore the brunt of the Vietnam experience, and it has traversed some difficult social and political terrain. But its members have much in common with graduates of the Class of 2001 and even the Class of 1865. Their training and service have been rooted in the same principles. A long gray thread joins them—and drives them to be the world's greatest leaders, in war and in peace.

★   ★   ★

The Future of West Point

While Cadets still wear uniforms that have remained virtually unchanged for over 150 years, and the parade drills still resemble those executed by Cadet Douglas MacArthur in 1903, a sea change is occurring at the Academy in response to the demands and threats of a rapidly changing world. The end of the cold war, the new arms race among rogue nations striving to acquire nuclear arsenals, and the changing geophysical and political landscape all require massive adaptation by the country's military forces. The entire defensive fabric of the United States, from the Army chief of staff to the Department of Defense, the Department of State, and Congress, is calling for the country's military establishment to evolve accordingly.

That evolution begins and ends with the training of soldiers and officers. Cadets who graduate in the twenty-first century face challenges American soldiers have not faced before. They will confront new threats, and they will use new weapons. They will find themselves on the defensive against new weapons in the heat of battle in environments that are almost impossible to envision, much less define.

"In the face of the most incredible change any of us have seen in the Army's operating environment, West Point has to keep asking, are we getting this right? Are we preparing our Cadets for officership in ways that are relevant for what they are, and will be asked to do?" —Gen. Daniel W. Christman, Superintendent, 1996–2001

Technological advances are resulting in a revamping of the soldier. Gone is the old Army warrior—a king of the battlefield backed by a fearsome arsenal of small arms, heavy artillery, tanks, ships, and air support. The new soldier is envisioned as a peacekeeper and diplomat first and a one-man terminator second. Researchers are developing a concept called Future Warrior 2025, a single soldier as lethal as an M1 Abrams tank. A key proponent of the concept is Army Chief of Staff Gen. Eric Shinseki, Class of 1965, who spearheaded the organization of new rapidly deployable brigades, which can engage in battle effectively without the heavy artillery and tanks that slow down invasion forces.

Instilling the leadership skills required of the new peacekeeping soldier equipped to wreak havoc if necessary is a formidable and novel challenge for the Academy. Change is already visible on R-Day and at Beast Barracks, where the focus is on training young officers to deal with the new threats. The concept of honor is presented more often and earlier. Because today's military officer is an interface between the United States and the international communities in which US troops are stationed, there is greater emphasis on human interaction, diplomacy, cultural differences, and geography. New science courses teach the principles and technology of future weapons and communications systems. Independence is also critical to the development of the leadership skills necessary in this particular age, and Cadets have more of it than they once did.

Since 1969, West Point has graduated 199 *international Cadets, and is authorized to enroll as many as forty at a time. These alumni go back to their own countries with a strong understanding of American values and traditions. Examples include Fidel Ramos, president of the Philippines; Pichitra Kullavanijaya, deputy supreme commander of the Thai army, and Jose Maria Figuerres, president of Costa Rica. They follow in the footsteps of the Point's first foreign graduate, Guatemala's Antonio Barrios, Class of 1889.*

As the United States and the rest of the world continue to change, both geopolitically and socioeconomically, West Point will be forced to evolve as well—not haphazardly, not quickly, but deliberately and without sacrifice of its basic tenets. In the most important sense, today's military officers are challenged no differently than nineteenth century West Point Cadets learning how to strike an azimuth for an artillery shell.

★   ★   ★

Epilogue: 9 ★ 11

"These acts of mass murder were intended to frighten our nation into chaos and retreat, but they have failed. . . .Those who make war against the United States have chosen their own destruction. We will smoke them out of their holes. We'll get them running and we'll bring them to justice."
—*President George W. Bush, September 11, 2001*

On September 11, 2001, the President of the United States declared war on terrorism in response to a vicious terrorist attack on American icons of peace, economic prosperity, and freedom. It was a new war, not one against a specific country or culture, not to be fought within any geographical confines, not even a war against a specific nationality. It was a war against a difficult-to-define enemy that uses all forms of terror to kill and win psychological and territorial victories.

For years, teachers at the US Military Academy had approached the subject of terrorism in mostly theoretical terms, although in many respects Cadets were already learning the important lessons necessary to lead and respond to this newest form of warfare. What happened on September 11, 2001, just sixty miles downriver from the Academy, gave these lessons a new reality that no teacher or Cadet will ever forget.

The first reactions at West Point were almost routine. The Academy was immediately secured with extra guards performing careful searches of anyone entering or exiting its two main gates. The campus was closed to the public and only service providers and visitors with an appointment were allowed entrance. Military police were added to Cadet barracks, training areas and classrooms. All liberty and off-post visits by Cadets were canceled.

OPPOSITE: *The Cadet Color Guard is one of only three permanent color guards in the Army.*

Cadets, of course, were appalled at the actions of this new enemy willing and capable to ambush civilians and non-military installations. But the mettle of the Point, its administration and teachers, and its young Cadets, showed through. Brigadier General Daniel J. Kaufman, Dean of the Academic Board at the Academy, is noted for his knowledge and experience in national security and international relations. At West Point his presence has a calming effect on Cadets, particularly when he talks about where we are today.

He notes that the Cadets who graduate in 2002, West Point's bicentennial year, were nine years old when the Berlin Wall came down. "They lived in a world of unprecedented economic growth, when things were always getting better. They experienced unprecedented advances in medicine and science and watched a world globalize and grow, always getting better for everybody. Now with the events of September 11, one of the deadliest days in American history, that has all changed. We now have to face the fact that life in America may have to be a lot different." West Point graduates will come to learn this better than most Americans.

Some have referred to the young people in America's colleges today as the Millennium generation or the generation of "innocents." They have not seen any major wars or conflicts. In many ways, however, they are no more "innocent" than many other past graduates of the Academy. Early graduates of the Academy were trained to fight against well-drilled infantry moving in long lines against each other. These graduates were not prepared to face the more sophisticated guns and artillery they faced in 1812. The Class of 1902, many of whom went on to fight in World Wars I and II, had no concept of how airplanes, high-level bombing, tanks, and submarines would change the way wars were fought. Most Army officers, including West Pointers, have never been trained specifically to fight terrorists. They have, however, been trained as leaders, and as thinkers; this background equips them to defeat any enemy.

Looking retrospectively at its training and curriculum after September 11, West Point officials say they may see a need to beef up instruction in information technology, and a second course has already been added on that subject; but courses and training in light operations, interim brigade combat teams, and international cultures have been in place for some time and provide the necessary basis for Army officers to lead in the war now facing America.

General Kaufman says that September 11 was a day of reckoning for this generation of Cadets: learning that the stock market is not always going to go up, the quality of life for all Americans may not continue to get better and better, and in fact, we may be involved in a campaign of some length and at some cost. He reminds Cadets of what he calls "First Principles"; that is, "the fundamental strength of this nation and that which unites us is much stronger than that which divides us."

The honor, duty, and resolve of the Long Gray Line remain not only intact, but strengthened by the events of September 11. As the Academy approaches its 200th year, the insights of George Washington, Thomas Jefferson, Sylvanus Thayer and others who saw a need for a military academy have been affirmed one more time as the Unites States embarks on a new kind of war in confronting terrorism. Never has the need for well-trained men and women to lead the country into battle been more critical to our nation's future.

BIBLIOGRAPHY

The following is an annotated selection of books and articles consulted by the authors in the preparation of this work. It is by no means a complete list of available sources.

Atkinson, Rick. *The Long Gray Line: The American Journey of West Point's Class of 1966.* Boston: Houghton Mifflin Company, 1989. A detailed and highly readable review of the Vietnam experiences of the Class of 1966.

Ashley, Robert and Fant, Joseph L. *Faulkner at West Point.* New York: Random House, 1964. Report on William Faulkner's celebrated visit to West Point in April 1962.

Barkalow, Carol. *In the Men's House: An Inside Account of Life in the Army by One of West Point's First Female Graduates.* New York: Poseidon Press, 1990. A gripping account on what it was like to be one of the very first female Cadets at West Point in 1976.

Baumer, William. *Not All Warriors: Portraits of 19th Century West Pointers who Gained Fame in Other than Military Fields.* Freeport, New York: Books for Libraries Press, 1971. Reports on seven nineteenth-century West Pointers who gained fame: Benjamin Louis Eulalie de Bonneville, Jefferson Davis, Leonidas Polk, Edgar Allan Poe, Henry du Pont, James McNeill Whistler, Horace Porter.

Carhart, Tom. *The Offering: A Generation Offered their Lives to America in Vietnam—One Soldier's Story.* New York: William Morrow and Company, Inc., 1987. Written by a graduate of the Class of 1966 and airborne troop commander in Vietnam, this book tells of the agony of West Pointers going to Vietnam and returning so very much unappreciated. It is an excellent description of the shock a young officer experiences in going from the Academy to active combat within a few months of graduation. It is also an example of how values taught at the Point sustain young officers in the field.

Chandler, David and Ward, Patrick. *Sandhurst: The Royal Military Academy.* London: Harmony House, 1991. An absolutely superb photographic record of this crown jewel of military education, but sadly with only limited text.

Dupuy, R. Ernest. *Men of West Point: The Story of the First One Hundred and Fifty Years of the United States Military Academy.* New York: William Sloane Associates, 1951. A book packed with facts and details.

Efaw, Amy. *Battle Dress: Never Surrender.* New York: Harper Collins, 2000. Aimed at teenagers, this book describes the experiences of a young girl at West Point. Written by a 1989 graduate.

Endler, James R. *Other Leaders, Other Heroes: West Point's Legacy to America Beyond the Field of Battle.* Westport, Connecticut: Praeger, 1998. An essential book, contributing significantly to the general study of how West Point graduates have helped build America.

Galloway, Joseph L. and Pasternak, Douglas. "The Warrior Class." *U.S. News & World Report,* July 5, 1999. Article on the Class of 1939, which would bear much of the burden of World War II.

Galloway, K. Bruce and Johnson, Robert Bowie Jr. *West Point: America's Power Fraternity.* New York: Simon and Schuster, 1973. Written by former Army officers who saw action in Vietnam and one graduate (Johnson, Class of 1965), this is a polemical, highly negative view of the Academy. Written clearly under the impact of the Vietnam War, this is probably the single most anti-West Point book we encountered.

Hancock, H. Irving. *Dick Prescott's First (Second, Third & Fourth) Year at West Point.* Philadelphia: Henry Altemus Company, 1911. A four-volume novel written for young men and teenagers about West Point. As with so many West Point novels, the honor code takes center place.

Hughes, Libby. *West Point.* New York: Dillon Press, 1993. A quick tour of the Academy.

Kauffman, Bill. "The West Point Story." *American Enterprise*, July/August 1999. A somewhat critical look at West Point. This issue also has other articles on the US Naval Academy and related matters.

Kirshner, Ralph. *The Class of 1861: Custer, Ames, and Their Classmates after West Point.* Carbondale and Edwardsville: Southern Illinois University Press, 1999. A detailed analysis of young officers serving in the Civil War.

Krist, Bob. *West Point.* Prospect, Ky.: Harmony House Publishers, 1987. A photographic portrait.

Lipsky, David. "War and Peace: A Year in the Life of the New West Point." *Rolling Stone*, November 25, 1999 (part one) and December 16, 1999 (part two). Photographs by Mark Seliger. A detailed, honest look at West Point illustrated with magnificent photographs. Probably one of the most important articles on the Academy in the past decade. Writer Lipsky is currently researching a more detailed report on West Point for a new book.

Maihafer, Harry J. *Oblivion: The Mystery of West Point Cadet Richard Cox.* Washington and London: Brassey's, Inc., 1996. This book tells the disappearance of a Cadet in 1950 with possible intelligence implications. Good descriptions of life at the Point in the early 1950s.

Morrison, James L., Jr. *The Best School: West Point, 1833-1866.* Kent, Ohio & London: The Kent State University Press, 1986. Another detailed examination of how the Civil War became a contest between classmates from West Point.

O'Neil, Thomas E. *Home at Rest: The Story of the West Point Cemetery.* Brooklyn, New York: Arrow and Trooper Publishing, 1991. A very useful guide to the cemetery.

Pahl, David. *West Point.* New York: Exeter Books, 1987. A general report on West Point with some decent photographs.

Ploetz, Ludwig von. *Kein Raum: Eine Kadettengeschichte.* Berlin: F. Fontane & Co., 1897. Titled "No Space," this simple novel describes better than any West Point novel the pain felt by a young cadet caught up in military life but somewhat unsuited for it.

Puryear, Edgar F., Jr. *American Generalship—Character is Everything: The Art of Command.* Novato, CA: Presidio Press, 2000. An excellent study on what has formed senior military leaders in America's history. Many of them are West Point Graduates and the impact of that school on their leadership style is examined in often minute detail.

Rapp, Kenneth W. *West Point: Whistler in Cadet Gray, and other Stories about the United States Military Academy.* North River Press, 1978. Nice collection of anecdotes and small stories about West Point.

Ruggero, Ed. *The Academy: A Novel of West Point.* New York: Simon & Schuster, 1997. One of the many novels of West Point, written by a graduate as well as former instructor at the Academy. Good examination of the honor code.

Simpson, Jeffrey. *Officers and Gentleman: Historic West Point in Photographs.* Tarrytown, NY: Sleepy Hollow Press, 1982. An indispensable resource of historical photographs.

Truscott, Lucian K., IV. *Dress Gray.* New York: Doubleday & Company, 1978. Written by a West Point graduate, this classic novel examines all aspects of the honor code. The author comes from a family of West Point graduates.

Truscott, Lucian K., IV. *Full Dress Gray.* New York: William Morrow and Company,

1998. Follow-up to *Dress Gray* and a superb look at a changed West Point with women and "modern" problems yet with the same powerful honor code.

Van Creveld, Martin. *The Training of Officers: From Military Professionalism to Irrelevance.* New York: The Free Press, 1990. An insightful discussion of how training of military officers evolved.

Waugh, John G. *The Class of 1846—From West Point to Appomattox: Stonewall Jackson, George McClellan and Their Brothers.* New York: Warner Books. A superb study of how this famous class served a divided nation with skill and honor. Elaborates on the often wrenching emotional turmoil created by the Civil War's divisions between close classmates and friends.

Wildenbruch, Ernst von, and King, Charles. *Noble Blood and a West Point Parallel.* New York: F. Tennyson Neely, 1896. This book, aimed at teenagers, combines two novels: *Noble Blood: A Prussian Cadet Story*, written by a Prussian officer, and *A West Point Parallel: An American Cadet Story* written by a US Army captain. Both stories are virtually identical, examining how young Cadets deal with issues of honor and commitment. It is an excellent example of just how very similar major cadet schools were in the closing days of the 19th Century.

Government & West Point Publications

The Association of the Graduates of the United States Military Academy, Annual Reunion, June 12th, 1908, and *June 10th, 1909.* West Point: USMA, 1908 and 1909. Excellent examples of how both Union and Confederate West Point graduates are treated with equal respect in the obituaries.

Bradley, John H. *West Point and the Hudson Highlands in the American Revolution.* West Point: USMA, 1976.

Bugle Notes '98. West Point: US Corps of Cadets, 1998. A hardbound version of the Cadet handbook, with pictures and some limited advertising.

The Centennial of the United States Military Academy at West Point, New York. 1802-1902, Volume II, Statistics and Bibliographies. Washington: Government Printing Office, 1904. A somewhat dry resource of data and names.

The Chapels. Charlotte, NC: C. Harrison Conroy Co. A short guide to all West Point chapels.

Foreman, Sidney. *The Beginning of the West Point Library.* West Point: USMA, 1959.

Information Relative to the Appointment and Admission of Cadets to the United States Military Academy, West Point, New York. Edition 1944. Washington, D.C.: United States Government Printing Office, 1943. A fascinating look at the admission requirements as well as the curriculum during World War II.

New Cadet Handbook CBT '99, Class of 2003 "Beast Barracks." West Point: US Corps of Cadets, 1999. An annual publication issued to new Cadets and full of basic knowledge about all aspects of the Academy. New Cadets routinely get drilled on this "knowledge" by senior Cadets.

Official Register of the Officers and Cadets: United States Military Academy, 5 June 1956. West Point: USMA, 1956. This is but one example of such listings, great in detail on all academic and military class rankings, details on the curriculum and even the deficiencies recorded.

Report of the Commission to Examine into the Organization, System of Discipline, and Course of Instruction of the United States Military Academy at West Point. Washington, D.C.: Government Printing Office, 1881. This report, first published on December 13,

1860, was the result of a major congressional investigation of West Point. The Commission was led by West Point graduate and then Senator Jefferson Davis who would, within months, become the president of the Confederacy. This report is a fascinating accounting of West Point around 1860, within weeks of the outbreak of the Civil War.

The Sesquicentennial of the United States Military Academy: An Account of the Observance January–June, 1952. West Point, New York, 1952. A rather dry report on the celebration of the first 150 years of the Academy.

Important Web Sites

www.aog.usma.edu. The Association of Graduates website. Contains a wealth of information on current alumni activities as well as past classes.

www.usma.edu. The Official West Point web site.

Films

Assault at West Point, the history of a black West Point Cadet in 1880.

The Long Gray Line, directed by John Ford. A classic.

THE LONG GRAY LINE
CADET ROSTER 1802-2001

1802 Joseph Gardner Swift 1 Simon Magruder Levy 2 **1803** Walker K. Armistead 3 Henry Burbeck Jackson 4 John Livingston 5 **1804** Samuel Gates 6 Hannibal Montesque Allen 7 **1805** George Bomford 8 William McRee 9 Joseph Gilbert Totten 10 **1806** William Gates 11 Julius Frederick Heileman 12 Pascal Vincent Bouis 13 Auguste Pierre Chouteau 14 Alden Partridge 15 Charles Gratiot 16 Eleazer Derby Wood 17 William Partridge 18 Prentiss Willard 19 Joseph Proveau Proveaux 20 Thomas Bennett 21 Ethan Augustus Allen 22 Robert Lucas 23 John Duncan Wyndham 24 Louis Loramier 25 **1807** Justus Post 26 Saterlee Clark 27 John Anderson 28 Samuel Champlin 29 Samuel Noah 30 **1808** Daniel Ashley Buck 31 Samuel Babcock 32 Sylvanus Thayer 33 Samuel B. Rathbone 348 Louis Valle 35 Heman Allen Fay 36 Oliver George Burton 37 Minor Huntington 38 Milo Mason 39 George P. Peters 40 James Gibson 41 Samuel Newman 42 Alpheus Roberts 43 Luther Leonard 44 Samuel H. Holley 45 **1809** Christopher Van De Venter 46 Solomon G. Conkling 47 Augustus William Magee 48 Milton Haxton 49 Anson Hall 50 Abraham L. Sands 51 Theodore Randell 52 **1811** Alexander John Williams 53 Marie V. Boisaubin 54 Adam Larrabee 55 Henry A. Hobart 56 Thomas Ketchum 57 James D. Cobb 58 Armstrong Irvine 59 Thomas Jones Beall 60 James Dalliba 61 Gustavus Loomis 62 Ezra Smith 63 Richard H. Ashley 64 Hippolite Henry Villard 65 John Bliss 66 Henry A. Burchstead 67 Ormond Marsh 68 George Ronan 69 Benjamin Field 70 John James Abert 71 **1812** Joseph M. Wilcox 72 Augustus Conant 73 Londus L. Buck 74 Alexander Ramsey Thompson 75 John R. Bell 76 Francis Benoni Murdock 77 George Templeman 78 Thomas Beverly Randolph 79 William F. Hobart 80 William Sumter 81 George W. Hight 82 John S. Brush 83 Nathaniel W. Osgood 84 George Morley 85 Alexander C. W. Fanning 86 William Cutbush 87 William Wallace Smith 88 Rene Edward De Russy 89 **1813** George Trescot 90 **1814** George W. Gardiner 91 Charles S. Merchant 92 Nathaniel G. Dana 93 John Monroe 94 John Sylvanus Allanson 95 Lewis Gustavus De Russy 96 Thomas Childs 97 Stephen Birdsall 98 John Wright 99 Edmund Brooke 100 John Armstrong 101 James Wolfe Ripley 102 Daniel Turner 103 Isaac E. Craig 104 Charles Mynn Thruston 105 Henry William Fitzhugh 106 Jackman J. Davis 107 Thomas T. Stephenson 108 Evans Humphrey 109 Samuel Waldo Wetmore 110 William Wells 111 William Lee Booth 112 Thomas J. Baird 113 Jabez Parkhurst 114 Robert L. Armstrong 115 James P. Badollet 116 George Washington Gardner 117 Bradley S. A. Lowe 118 Thomas Randolph Broom 119 Hilary Brunot 120 **1815** Henry Middleton 121 William F. Rigal 122 James Simonson 123 John Hills 124 Simon Willard 125 John Symington 126 William Washington Gordon 127 Henry Roger Dulaney 128 John Roe Sloo 129 Henry William Griswold 130 James Monroe 131 Robert Carroll Brent 132 Abraham Wendell 133 George Augustin Washington 134 Robert J. Scott 135 Alonzo Brewer 136 Francis Nathaniel Berier 137 George Cooper 138 Henry Smith 139 Alexander Fulton Cochrane 140 Michael F. Van de Venter 141 Milo Johnson 142 Aaron G. Gano 143 Robert M. Forsyth 144 Thomas W. Lendrum 145 George Blaney 146 Thomas Jefferson Leslie 147 William Sanford Eveleth 148 Robert W. Pooler 149 William Henry Chase 150 Wolvert Ecker Williams 151 William B. Davidson 152 John Alexander Webber 153 Thomas Jefferson Gardner 154 Benjamin L. E. Bonneville 155 Samuel Cooper 156 Charles Davies 157 James R. Stubbs 158 Peter Embury 159 Richard Mansfield White 160 **1817** Augustus Louis Roumfort 161 James M. Spencer 162 Isaac Austin Adams 163 William Montrose Graham 164 James Duncan Graham 165 Charles Despinville 166 John C. Kirk 167 John Rogers Vinton 168 Richard Bland Lee 169 Frederick L. Griffith 170 Edward John Lambert 171 William Gibbs McNeill 172 Angus W. McDonald 173 Henry Berryman 174 Constant Mathieu Eakin 175 John D. Orr 176 Ethan Allen Hitchcock 177 John Macrae Washington 178 Ambrose Madison 179 **1818** Richard Delafield 180 Andrew Talcott 181 Samuel Stanhope Smith 182 Horace Webster 183 Samuel Ringgold 184 Harvey Brown 185 Joseph N. Chambers 186 Samuel Mackenzie 187 Giles Porter 188 George Washington Corprew 189 John Jay Jackson 190 Edward Harding 191 Benjamin Chew Vining 192 Henry H. Loring 193 Joseph F. Daingerfield 194 Joseph Strong 195 John B. F. Russell 196 George Webb 197 Hartman Bache 198 William S. Newton 199 Leonard O. Brooke 200 Henry Giles 201 John Taylor Pratt 202 **1819** William Alexander Eliason 203 Frederick Augustus Underhill 204 Cornelius Austin Ogden 205 Edward Deering Mansfield 206 Henry Brewerton 207 John Randolph Bowes 208 Henry A. Thompson 209 Zebina J. D. Kinsley 210 William Turnbull 211 Joshua Baker 212 Justin Dimick 213 George Washington Whistler 214 Benjamin Walker 215 Daniel Tyler 216 John Francis Hamtramck 217 Ethan C. Sickles 218 James S. Hepburne 219 John L'Engle 220 John E. Edwards 221 Austin Brockenborough 222 William Malcolm 223 John Mackenzie 224 Joseph D. Rupp 225 Jacob Adrian Dumeste 226 James Riddle Blaney 227 Roswell Conant 228 Jasper Strong 229 Henry Gilbert 230 William Henry Swift 231 **1820** Stephen Tuttle 232 Andrew Jackson Donelson 233 Thomas Emery Sudler 234 William Haywood Bell 235 William Chetwood De Hart 236 Francis Noel Barbarin 237 Robert S. Brooke 238 James A. Chambers 239 Edward Geo. Washington Butler 240 Daniel D. Tompkins 241 John Henry Winder 242 William Pinckney Buchanan 243 Samuel B. Dusenberry 244 Henry James Feltus 245 Nicholas Cruger 246 Rawlins Lowndes 247 Lewis Nelson Morris 248 Joshua Barney 249 George F. Lindsay 250 John Mills Tufts 251 Benjamin Gorham 252 Samuel McRee 253 Thomas Noel 254 Thomas McArthur 255 Charles Guerrant 256 George Douglas Ramsay 257 Edgar Samuel Hawkins 258 William Seton Maitland 259 Aaron Burr Skinner 260 William Walton Morris 261 **1821** Edward Henry Courtenay 262 Clark Burdine 263 Jonathan Prescott 264 William Wayne Wells 265 Charles Dimmock 266 John C. Holland 267 Edward C. Ross 268 Washington Wheelwright 269 David Wallace 270 Robert Francis Withers Allston 271 John Fell Scott 272 James Grier 273 John Benjamin Scott 274 Joseph Pentland 275 Alexander Hamilton Morton 276 William Warren Gaillard 277 Seth Makepeace Capron 278 Jefferson Vail 279 James Henshaw 280 Otis Wheeler 281 Henry Bainbridge 282 Jason Rogers 283 David Montgomery Porter 284 Julius Adolphus d'Lagnel 285 **1822** George Dutton 286 Joseph K. Fenno Mansfield 287 Charles Goodrich Smith 288 Thomas R. Ingalls 289 Horace Bliss 290 William Cook 291 William Rose 292 Walter Gwynn 293 Campbell Graham 294 Thompson B. Wheelock 295 James H. Cooke 296 William Clark Young 297 Augustus Canfield 298 David Hammond Vinton 299 John Jacob Schuler 300 John Pickell 301 Isaac Ridgeway Trimble 302 Henry H. Gird 303 Benjamin Hall Wright 304 William M. Boyce 305 St. Clair Denny 306 Westwood Lacey 307 Eustace Trenor 308 George Wright 309 David Hunter 310 George Archibald McCall 311 Albert Lincoln 312 Francis Lee 313 James R. Stephenson 314 John D. Hopson 315 Thompson Morris 316 John R. Wilcox 317 Thomas Johnston 318 George Washington Folger 319 Thomas McNamara 320 Gary Merick Wright 321 John Joseph Abercrombie 322 Samuel Wragg 323 David Moniac 324 Henry Clark 325 **1823** Alfred Mordecai 326 George Sears Greene 327 George C. Richards 328 Reuben Holmes 329 Samuel Mercer Southerland 330 Lucien Bonaparte Webster 331 Frederick L. Guion 332 George Nauman 333 Alfred Beckley 334 Frederick Searle 335 Richard De Treville 336 Andrew Kinnard 337 George Washington Waters 338 John Farley 339 Levi M. Nute 340 Mark W. Batman 341 Lorenzo Thomas 342 Julius Jesse Backus Kingsbury 343 George Andrews 344 Richard D'Cantillon Collins 345 William Reynolds 346 Joseph Rowe Smith 347 Hannibal Day 348 Henry R. Stewart 349 Elias Phillips 350 Joseph Augustus Phillips 351 Asa Richardson 352 John E. Newell 353 John Nicholls 354 George Hampton Crosman 355 Charles Holt 356 John Winslow Cotton 357 Edmund Brooke Alexander 358 Albert S. Miller 359 Egbert B. Birdsall 360 **1824** Dennis Hart Mahan 361 John W. A. Smith 362 Robert Parker Parrott 363 R. Edward Hazzard 364 John King Findlay 365 Napoleon Bonaparte Bennett 366 John N. Dillahunty 367 Francis L. Jones 368 George Washington Long 369 John Milton Fessenden 370 William Phillips Bainbridge 371 John M. W. Picton 372 Horatio A. Wilson 373 Nicholas Tilllinghast 374 William George Williams 375 Anthony Drane 376 Louis Thornton Jamison 377 William Bickley 378 Ephraim W. Low 379 Joseph Cadle 380 Alexander Johnston 381 William L. Harris 382 William Bloodgood 383 William Washington Eaton 384 Timothy Paige 385 Francis Day Newcomb 386 Dixon Stansbury Miles 387 Electus Backus 388 Julius Catlin 389 Joseph Van Swearingen 390 William Beverhout Thompson 391 **1825** Alexander Dallas Bache 392 Peter McMartin 393 Alexander Hamilton Bowman 394 Thompson Skinner Brown 395 Daniel S. Donelson 396 Stephen Van Rensseler Ryan 397 Raphael Cummings Smead 398 Benjamin Huger 399 Francis Taylor 400 Abbott Hall Brisbane 401 William Fenn Hopkins 402 William Anderson Thornton 403 Joseph Whipple Harris 404 Matthew Jouett Williams 405 Robert Anderson 406 Alexander D. Mackay 407 James Ramsay Irwin 408 Horace Smith 409 Charles Ferguson Smith 410 Washington Seawell 411 Lawrence F. Carter 412 Frederick Norcom 413 Nathaniel Heath Street 414 Joseph Swazey Worth 415 Nathaniel Sayre Harris 416 Osborne Cross 417 Joseph Bonnell 418 William Reading Montgomery 419 Henry St. James Linden 420 James J. Anderson 421 James Duff Burnham 422 Gustavus Dorr 423 Frederick Thomas 424 George Washington Garey 425 James Engle 426 Joseph Clay 427 Samuel Rogers Allston 428 **1826** William H. C. Bartlett 429 Thomas S. Twiss 430 William Bryant 431 Thomas Jefferson Cram 432 Charles G. Ridgely 433 John McClellan 434 Bennett H. Henderson 435 Albert Sidney Johnston 436 Edward Brickell White 437 Francis Littleberry Dancy 438 Joseph Donaldson Searight 439 Joel C. Townsend 440 Daniel S. Herring 441 George Woodbridge 442 Michael Marye Clark 443 Maskell C. Ewing 444 Samuel Peter Heintzelman 445 Theophilus B. Brown 446 Danforth H. Tufts 447 Augustus James Pleasanton 448 Martin Philips Parks 449 John Breckinridge Grayson 450 John Williamson 451 Henry J. Griffin 452 John Archer 453 Samuel Hollongs Ridgely 454 John McPherson Berrien 455 Edwin Burr Babbitt 456 Richard Woodward Colcock 457 Charles L. C. Minor 458 William H. Sims 459 Francis J. Brooke 460 Nathaniel Chapman Macrae 461 James George Allen 462 Alexander G. Baldwin 463 Amos Beebe Eaton 464 Moses Emery Merrill 465 Charles Colerick 466 Silas Casey 467 Thomas Harris Pearce 468 Ephraim Kirby Smith 469 **1827** Ebenezer Sproat Sibley 470 John Childe 471 William Maynadier 472 James Andrew Jackson Bradford 473 Lucien Irainba Bibb 474 Napoleon Bonaparte Buford 475 Edwin Schenck 476 Leonidas Polk 477 Essex Sterrett 478 George Fetterman 479 William E. Aisquith 480 Thomas Worthington 481 Gabriel James Rains 482 John Gano Furman 483 William Braxton Magruder 484 Thomas Baylies Stockton 485 Alexander Seymour Hooe 486 William W. Flanigan 487 George Houghton Prentiss 488 David Perkins 489 Samuel Hitchcock 490 Alexander Jenkins Center 491 Philip St. George Cooke 492 Thomas Sterne Trask 493 Abner Riviere Hetzel 494 Joseph Hatch La Motte 495 Edgar Martin Lacey 496 Levin Gale 497 Isaac Pierce Simonton 498 Jefferson Van Horne 499 Washington Hood 500 Isaac Lynde 501 Nathaniel Jackson Eaton 502 Stephen M. Westmore 503 Jonathan Kimball Greenough 504 William Shaler Stilwell 505 Abraham Van Buren 506 Nelson N. Clark 507 **1828** Albert E. Church 508 Richard Cooke Tilghman 509 Hugh Weedon Mercer 510 Robert Emmet Temple 511 Charles O. Collins 512 Ivers James Austin 513 Edmund French 514 Joseph Lorenzo Locke 515 George Edward Chase 516 John F. Lane 517 William Palmer 518 Thomas Boylston Adams 519 Robert Emmet Clary 520 Robert Sevier 521 William Williams Mather 522 Enos Gardwood Mitchell 523 James Farley Izard 524 Thomas Cutts 525 William Henry Baker 526 James L. Thompson 527 Gustave Sebastian Rousseau 528 Benjamin Willis Kinsman 529 Jefferson Davis 530 William L. E. Morrison 531 Samuel Kelly Cobb 532 Samuel Torrence 533 Amos Foster 534 Thomas Fenwick Drayton 535 Thomas Clark Brockway 536 John Randolph Barent Gardenier 537 Crafts James Wright 538 James Wilkinson Penrose 539 Philip R. Van Wyck 540 **1829** Charles Mason 541 Robert Edward Lee 542 William Henry Harford 543 Joseph Allen Smith Izard 544 James Barnes 545 Catharinus Putnam Buckingham 546 Joseph Smith Bryce 547 John Mackay 548 Charles William Hackley 549 Miner Knowlton 550 John Charles Casey 551 William Robertson McKee 552 Joseph Eggleston Johnston 553 John Francis Kennedy 554 Ormsby McKnight Mitchel 555 Gustavus Brown 556 Sidney Burbank 557 William Hoffman 558 Charles Petigru 559 Franklin Eyre Hunt 560 Lancaster P. Lupton 561 Seth Eastman 562 Thomas Swords 563 Albemarie Cady 564 Thomas Alfred Davies 565 Albert Gallatin Blanchard 566 Chileab Smith Howe 567 Caleb Chase Sibley 568 James Hampton Wright 569 George Augustine Sterling 570 Joseph Hiester Pawling 571 Antes Snyder 572 William Henry Warfield 573 James Clark 574 James Allen 575 Jonathan Freeman 576 John P. Davis 577 George Russel James Bowdoin 578 Edwin Ramsay Long 579 Benjamin William Brice 580 Robert Wallace Burnet 581 James Seaborn Moore 582 Charles O. May 583 Theophilus Hunter Holmes 584 Edward R. Williams 585 Richard R. Screven 586 **1830** Alexander Joseph Swift 587 William Elon Basinger 588 Walter Scott Chandler 589 Francis Vinton 590 William Nelson Pendleton 591 George Washington Lawson 592 Thomas Jefferson Lee 593 John Waller Barry 594 Thomas Beasly Linnard 595 Benjamin Poole 596 Simon Henry Drum 597 James Henry Prentiss 598 Robert H. Kirkwood Whitely 599 Edwin Rose 600 John Bankhead Magruder 601 Albert Taylor Bledsoe 602 John S. Stoddard 603 John Wilkins Murray 604 James West 605 James Madison Hill 606 Samuel Kinney 607 Jesse Henry Leavenworth 608 Meriwether Lewis Clark 609 John T. Collinsworth 610 Lloyd James Beall 611 William Cruger Heyward 612 Joseph Ritner 613 John Henry K. Burgwin 614 Thomas Ludwell Alexander 615 James H. Taylor 616 Robert Christie Buchanan 617 Camilus C. Daviess 618 John Suthpen Vanderveer 619 Thomas Jefferson Royster 620 George Wilson 621 George Waynefleet Patten 622 Willliam Eustis 623 David A. Manning 624 George Washington McClure 625 Richard H. Ross 626 John Miller Clendenin 627 Stephen Bruce Legate 628 **1831** Roswell Park 629 Henry Clay 630 James Allen 631 Henry Epaminondas Prentiss 632 Albert Miller Lea 633 Richard H. Peyton 634 William Augustus Norton 635 George W. Turner 636 Samuel Chase Ridgely 637 Samuel H. Miller 638 George Henry Talcott 639 Jacob Ammen 640 Andrew Atkinson Humphreys 641 William Hemsley Emory 642 William Chapman 643 Charles H. Larnard 644 Elbridge Gerry Eastman 645 Moses Scott 646 Thomas Jefferson McKean 647 Henry Van Rensselaer 648 Edmund Augustus Ogden 649 Lucius Ballinger Northrop 650 Erasmus F. Covington 651 Horatio Philips Van Cleve 652 Bradford Ripley Alden 653 Thomas Stockton 654 Samuel Ryan Curtis 655 James Seymour Williams 656 Ingham Wood 657 Frederick Wilkinson 658 John Gailard Harvey 659 Charles Whittlesey 660 John Conrad 661 **1832** George Washington Ward 662 Robert Percy Smith 663 Benjamin Stoddert Ewell 664 George Washington Cass 665 Jacob Whitman Bailey 666 Philip St. George Cocke 667 Henry G. Sill 668 Joseph C. Vance 669 George Watson 670 Erasmus Darwin Keyes 671 Franklin McDuffee 672 Lewis Howell 673 William Wall 674 John Navarre Macomb 675 Edward Deas 676 John Ely Brackett 677 Ward Benjamin Burnett 678 James Hervey Simpson 679 Alfred Brush 680 Richard Gammon Fain 681 Henderson K. Yoakum 682 Tench Tilghman 683 William Henry Pettes 684 Theophilus F. J. Wilkinson 685 Lorenzo Sitgreaves 686 George Bibb Crittenden 687 Jacob Brown 688 Daniel Powers Whiting 689 Randolph Barnes Marcy 690 James P. Hardin 691 Thomas McCobb Hill 692 Roger Sherman Dix 693 Robert Harris Archer 694 James Voty Bomford 695 Richard Caswell Gatlin 696 William H. Storer 697 George Hancock Griffin 698 John Beach 699 William Overton Kello 700 Henry Swartwout 701 Gaines Pease Kingsbury 702 Humphrey Marshall 703 James Monroe Bowman 704 Asbury Ury 705 Albert Gallatin Edwards 706 **1833** Frederick

Augustus Smith 707 John Gross Barnard 708 George Washington Cullum 709 Rufus King 710 Francis Henney Smith 711 William Henry Sidell 712 David Bullock Harris 713 Roswell Walter Lee 714 William Wallace Smith Bliss 715
Erastus A. Capron 716 Isaiah Garrett 717 John Henry Miller 718 David Emerson Hale 719 Robert Richard Mudge 720 John Addison Thomas 721 James Lucius Davis 722 Edmund Schriver 723 Henry Walter 724 John Howard Allen
725 Alexander Eakin Shiras 726 Henry Du Pont 727 Benjamin Alvord 728 George D. Dimon 729 Isaac R. D. Brunett 730 Jacob Edmund Blake 731 John Locke Hooper 732 Joel Riggs 733 John W. McCrabb 734 Henry Walton
Wessells 735 John P. Center 736 George Herbert Pegram 737 Abraham Charles Myers 738 George Hay Ringgold 739 Daniel Ruggles 740 James Willoughby Anderson 741 James McClure 742 John Chester Reid 743 Thomas
Johns 744 Benjamin E. Du Bose 745 Joseph P. Harrison 746 Henry Lee Scott 747 Augustine Fenton Seaton 748 Nathaniel Wyche Hunter 749 **1834** William Davidson Fraser 750 John Sanders 751 Harrison Loughborough 752
Thomas Armstrong Morris 753 Robert T. P. Allen 754 James Duncan 755 Epaphras Kibby 756 William Telfair Stockton 757 John Fitzgerald Lee 758 Charles Alexander Fuller 759 Curran Pope 760 Charles Bainbridge Chalmers 761
John Eaton Henderson 762 Morris Smith Miller 763 William Grigsby Freeman 764 Louis A. du Barth Walbach 765 James Fairlie Cooper 766 Gabriel Rene Paul 767 George P. Field 768 Cary Harrison Fry 769 Henry Smith Turner
770 Seneca Galusha Simmons 771 Thomas Osborne Barnwell 772 Henry McKavett 773 Goode Brown 774 Joseph Leander Coburn 775 James G. Reed 776 Phillip Nordbourne Barbour 777 Arnold Harris 778 Richard Somers
Smith 779 Eustace Robinson 780 William Scott Ketchum 781 Forbes Britton 782 John Graham 783 William Harrison Price 784 Alexander Montgomery 785 **1835** George Webb Morell 786 Charles Henry Bigelow 787 John Henry
Martindale 788 Charles Jarvis Whiting 789 George Mackey Legate 790 Alfred Herbert 791 Arnoldus Vanderhorst Brumby 792 Joseph Roberts 793 Horace Brooks 794 James McCready Morgan 795 Robert M. Renick 796 Richard
Henderson 797 James N. Ellis 798 John Low Keais 799 William Spencer Brown 800 Henry Lane Kendrick 801 James Hughs Stokes 802 Montgomery Blair 803 George Gordon Meade 804 William H. Betts 805 George G.
Waggaman 806 Weightman Key Hanson 807 Henry Morris Naglee 808 Archibald Campbell 809 Alexander Saranac Macomb 810 John H. Hanley 811 William Henry Griffin 812 Abraham Robinson Johnston 813 Peter Cheves
Gaillard 814 Henry Prince 815 Herman Haupt 816 Samuel Moses Plummer 817 Alexander M. Mitchell 818 Alexander Harper Tappan 819 William Henry De Forest 820 Philip Roots Thompson 821 William M. D. McKissack 822
Stephen Theodore Tibbatts 823 James Mayo Wells 824 William Seaton Henry 825 John M. Scott 826 George Washington Shaw 827 Joseph Horace Eaton 828 Jones Mitchell Withers 829 Isaac Van Duzer Reeve 830 John Wood
Scott 831 Larkin Smith 832 Marsena Rudolph Patrick 833 Thomas Boyal Arden 834 Joseph H. Whipple 835 Lucius Bradbury 836 Robert Auchmuty Wainwright 837 Benjamin Stone Roberts 838 William Nicholson Grier 839 Thomas
Lee Brent 840 Hugh McLeod 841 **1836** George Lewis Welcker 842 James Louis Mason 843 Danville Leadbetter 844 Joseph Reid Anderson 845 Montgomery Cunningham Meigs 846 Daniel Phineas Woodbury 847 Fisher Ames
Lewis 848 Samuel J. Bransford 849 Augustus Porter Allen 850 William Horace Warner 851 Barnabas Conkling 852 William Bradford Wallace 853 Marlborough Churchill 854 David Porter De Witt 855 James Lowry Donaldson 856
John Paul Jones O'Brien 857 Roland Augustus Luther 858 Thomas West Sherman 859 John Frederick Roland 860 Charles Bostwick Sing 861 Alexander Parker Crittenden 862 Henry Hayes Lockwood 863 Christopher Albert Greene
864 John Wolcott Phelps 865 Peter Valentine Hagner 866 Muscoe Livingston Shackleford 867 Christopher Quarles Tompkins 868 Martin John Burke 869 John W. Judson 870 Israel Carle Woodruff 871 William Brickett Arvin 872
John Samuel Hatheway 873 Robert Allen 874 William Frazer 875 George Cummins Thomas 876 Arthur Breese Lansing 877 Charles Belding Daniels 878 William Mock 879 Robert Fulton Baker 880 Charles Hoskins 881 Samuel
Whitehorn 882 Collinson Reed Gates 883 Marcus Claudius M. Hammond 884 Richard G. Stockton 885 Thomas Philoteus Chiffelle 886 Lloyd Tilghman 887 Thomas McCrate 888 Henry Clay Moorhead 889 Charles Henry Edward
Spoor 890 **1837** Henry Washington Benham 891 John Williams Gunnison 892 Edwin Wright Morgan 893 John Bratt 894 Braxton Bragg 895 Alexander Byrdie Dyer 896 William Warren Chapman 897 William Whann Mackall
898 Eliakim Parker Scammon 899 Lewis Golding Arnold 900 Israel Vogdes 901 Thomas Williams 902 Robert Tignall Jones 903 Francis Woodbridge 904 Asa Park Gregory 905 Edward Davis Townsend 906 William Thomas Martin
907 Jubal Anderson Early 908 Edmund Bradford 909 Henry Clay Pratt 910 Bennett Hoskin Hill 911 William Henry French 912 George Taylor 913 John Sedgwick 914 Joshua Hall Bates 915 George Clayton Rodney 916 John
Clifford Pemberton 917 William Armstrong 918 Joseph Hooker 919 John Marshall Harvie 920 Charles F. Wooster 921 Arthur Middleton Rutledge 922 Arnold Elzey 923 Edward Jenner Steptoe 924 William Henry Fowler 925 Samuel
Woods 926 Robert Milligan McLane 927 Walter Sherwood 928 John Blair Smith Todd 929 James Russell Soley 930 Samuel D. J. Moore 931 Randolph Ridgely 932 Francis Octavus Wyse 933 William Gain Grandin 934 Nevil
Hopson 935 William Henry Talbot Walker 936 Levi Platt Davidson 937 Robert Hall Chilton 938 William Hardia 939 Franklin Saunders 940 **1838** William Henry Wright 941 Pierre Gustuve T. Beauregard 942 James Heyward
Trapier 943 Stephen Henderson Campbell 944 Jeremiah Mason Scarritt 945 Alexander Hamilton Dearborn 946 John Thomas Metcalfe 947 Thomas Casey 948 Isaac Stockton Keith Reeves 949 Buckner Board 950 William B. Blair
951 Thomas Lee Ringgold 952 James M. Ketchum 953 Henry Constantine Wayne 954 Lucius Pitkin 955 William H. Shover 956 William Farquhar Barry 957 Milton A. Haynes 958 William Augustus Nichols 959 John Calvin Fletcher
960 Leslie Chase 961 Langdon Cheves Easton 962 Irvin McDowell 963 Rowley S. Jennings 964 William Austine 965 William Joseph Hardee 966 Hamilton Wilcox Merrill 967 Robert Seaman Granger 968 Owen P. Ransom 969
John H. Mathews 970 Henry Hopkins Sibley 971 Edward Johnson 972 Ripley Allen Arnold 973 Constant Freeman 974 Alexander Welch Reynolds 975 Andrew Jackson Smith 976 Charles John Hughes 977 William Hulbert 978
Robert M. Cochran 979 Justus McKinstry 980 Ferdinand Suydam Mumford 981 Carter Littlepage Stevenson 982 Richard Hill Graham 983 Charles Frederick Ruff 984 Zebulon Montgomery Pike Inge 985 **1839** Isaac Ingalls Stevens
986 Robert Quarles Butler 987 Henry Wager Halleck 988 Jeremy Francis Gilmer 989 Henry Lyon Smith 990 Michael Simpson Culbertson 991 George Thom 992 Franklin Dyer Callender 993 Henry Stanton Burton 994 Joseph Abel
Haskin 995 Henry Dearborn Grafton 996 James Lee Rankin 997 Alexander Robert Lawton 998 Henry Bethel Judd 999 Lucius Hamilton Allen 1000 James Brewerton Ricketts 1001 Edward Otto Cresap Ord 1002 Joseph B. Boyd 1003
Henry Jackson Hunt 1004 William Irvin 1005 William Sooy Smith 1006 Samuel Kennedy Dawson 1007 Augustus Abel Gibson 1008 Eleazer A. Paine 1009 Garrett Barry 1010 Charles Wickliffe 1011 Thomas Hunton 1012 Edgar
Basil Gaither 1013 William Henry Korn 1014 Edward Richard Sprigg Canby 1015 John Howard Hill 1016 **1840** Paul Octave Hebert 1017 Charles Peoble Kingsbury 1018 John McNutt 1019 William Page Jones 1020 William
Gilham 1021 William Tecumseh Sherman 1022 Job Roberts Hamilton Lancaster 1023 William Hunter Churchill 1024 Stewart Van Vliet 1025 John Porter McCown 1026 Francis Newman Clarke 1027 George Henry Thomas 1028
Richard Stoddert Ewell 1029 James Green Martin 1030 George Washington Getty 1031 Horace B. Field 1032 Henry Whiting 1033 William Hays 1034 Fowler Hamilton 1035 Bryant Parrott Tilden 1036 Thaddeus Higgins 1037
Oscar Fingal Winship 1038 Bushrod Rust Johnson 1039 Charles Henry Humber 1040 James Nelson Caldwell 1041 John William Tudor Gardiner 1042 Reuben Philander Campbell 1043 Pinckney Lugenbeel 1044 Henry Wardwell
1045 William Robertson 1046 William Steele 1047 Robert Plunket Maclay 1048 Oliver Lathrop Shepherd 1049 Henry Davies Wallen 1050 Stephen Decatur Captenter 1051 Joseph Libbey Folsom 1052 William Gould Torrey 1053
Daniel G. Rogers 1054 William Brooke Johns 1055 Douglass Simms Irwin 1056 Thomas Jordan 1057 John Danforth Bacon 1058 **1841** Zealous Bates Tower 1059 Horatio Governour Wright 1060 Masillon Harrison 1061 Smith
Standsbury 1062 Amiel Weeks Whipple 1063 Josiah Gorgas 1064 Thomas Jackson Rodman 1065 Albion Parris Howe 1066 Philip W. MacDonald 1067 George Washington Ayers 1068 Nathaniel Lyon 1069 Joseph Fenley Irons
1070 Leonidas Jenkins 1071 John Love 1072 Harvey Abner Allen 1073 Julius Peter Garesche 1074 Sewall L. Fremont 1075 Samuel Smith Anderson 1076 Samuel Jones 1077 Simon Snyder Fahnestock 1078 Richard Pincell Hammond
1079 Joseph Bennett Plummer 1080 John Milton Brannan 1081 Schuyler Hamilton 1082 James Totten 1083 John Fulton Reynolds 1084 Robert Selden Garnett 1085 Robert Bogardus Parker 1086 Richard Brooke Garnett 1087 Richard
Huston Bacot 1088 Claudius Wistar Sears 1089 Don Carlos Buell 1090 John Green Burbank 1091 Alfred Sully 1092 Franklin Foster Flint 1093 John Beardsley 1094 Patrick Calhoun 1095 Israel Bush Richardson 1096 John Marshall
Jones 1097 Andrew W. Bowman 1098 Edward Murray 1099 Francis Nelson Page 1100 Anderson D. Nelson 1101 Benjamin A. Berry 1102 Alexander Contee Darne 1103 William Thomas Harbaugh Brooks 1104 Elias Kent Kane
1105 Levi Gantt 1106 Mortimer Rosecrants 1107 Rudolph F. Ernst 1108 Abraham Buford 1109 Charles Frederick Morris 1110 **1842** Henry Lawrence Eustis 1111 John Newton 1112 George Washington Rains 1113 John Daniel
Kurtz 1114 William Stark Rosecrans 1115 Theo. Thadeus Sobieski Laidley 1116 Barton Stone Alexander 1117 Gustavus Woodson Smith 1118 Mansfield Lovell 1119 Calvin Benjamin 1120 James Gilchrist Benton 1121 Alexander
Peter Stewart 1122 Edward Griffin Beckwith 1123 Henry Macomb Whiting 1124 Isaac Bowen 1125 Martin Luther Smith 1126 John Pope 1127 Joseph Stewart 1128 Richard William Johnston 1129 John Hillhouse 1130 David
Gibson 1131 Charles Lawrence Kilburn 1132 Seth Williams 1133 Abner Doubleday 1134 Hachaliah Brown 1135 Lucien Loeser 1136 Frederick John Denman 1137 Daniel Harvey Hill 1138 Napoleon Tecumseh Dana 1139 Allen
Higbee Norton 1140 Armistead T. Mason Rust 1141 John Swayze McCalmont 1142 Patrick Noble 1143 Henry Clament Story 1144 Jenks Beaman 1145 John Donnell Clark 1146 Ralph Wilson Kirkham 1147 Cyrus Hall 1148
George Sykes 1149 Richard Herron Anderson 1150 George William Lay 1151 James Wall Schureman 1152 George Thompson Mason 1153 Charles Downs Jordan 1154 Henry Whiting Stanton 1155 Andrew Jackson Williamson
1156 Eugene Eckel McLean 1157 Lafayette McLaws 1158 Thomas C. Hammond 1159 Charles Tainter Baker 1160 Samuel Brinckle Hayman 1161 Earl Van Dorn 1162 Christopher Raymond Perry 1163 James Longstreet 1164
James William Abert 1165 James Overing Handy 1166 **1843** William Buel Franklin 1167 George De Shon 1168 Thomas Jefferson Brereton 1169 John Henry Greeland 1170 William Franklin Raynolds 1171 Isaac Ferdinand Quinby
1172 Roswell Sabin Ripley 1173 John James Peck 1174 John Preston Johnstone 1175 Joseph Jones Reynolds 1176 James Allen Hardie 1177 Henry Francis Clarke 1178 Jacob John Booker 1179 Samuel Gibbs French 1180 Theodore
Lincoln Chadbourne 1181 Christopher Columbus Augur 1182 Franklin Gardner 1183 George Stevens 1184 Edmunds Balard Holloway 1185 Lewis Neill 1186 Ulysses Simpson Grant 1187 Joseph Haydin Potter 1188 Robert Hazlitt
1189 Edwin Howe 1190 Lafayette Bowyer Wood 1191 Charles Smith Hamilton 1192 William Kumble Van Bokkelen 1193 Alfred St. Amand Crozet 1194 Charles Edward Jarvis 1195 Frederick Steele 1196 Henry Raymond Selden
1197 Rufus Ingalls 1198 Frederick Tracy Dent 1199 John Courts McFerran 1200 Henry Moses Judah 1201 Norman Elting 1202 Cave Johnson Couts 1203 Charles George Merchant 1204 George C. McClelland 1205 **1844**
William Guy Peck 1206 Joseph Hotchkiss Whittlesey 1207 Samuel Gill 1208 Daniel Marsh Frost 1209 Asher Robbins Eddy 1210 Francis John Thomas 1211 Alfred Pleasonton 1212 Thomas Jefferson Curd 1213 Augustus Cook
1214 John Young Bickness 1215 Simon Bolivar Buckner 1216 John Trevitt 1217 Rankin Dilworth 1218 Erastus Burton Strong 1219 William Turnbull Burwell 1220 William Read 1221 James Sterrett Woods 1222 Winfield Hancock
1223 James M. Lake Henry 1224 Alexander Hays 1225 George Wainwright 1226 Henry B. Schroeder 1227 Joseph Poinsett Smith 1228 John Jordan Crittenden Bibb 1229 George Washington Hawkins 1230 **1845** William Henry
Chase Whiting 1231 Edward Bissell Hunt 1232 Louis Hebert 1233 William Farrar Smith 1234 Thomas John Wood 1235 Thomas Grimke Rhett 1236 Charles Pomroy Stone 1237 Fitz-John Porter 1238 Josiah Howard Carlisle 1239
George Edwards 1240 Henry Coppee 1241 Francis Collins 1242 Joseph Francis Farry 1243 Louis Dwight Welch 1244 George Pearce Andrews 1245 Thomas Bradford J. Weld 1246 John Porter Hatch 1247 John Alexander Richey
1248 Henry Merrill 1249 Patrick Alden Farrelly 1250 Abram B. Lincoln 1251 Bezaleel Wells Armstrong 1252 William Thomas Allen 1253 James G. Soulard Snelling 1254 Edmund Kirby Smith 1255 Thomas Jefferson Montgomery
1256 John Wynn Davidson 1257 James Noble Ward 1258 James Morrison Hawes 1259 Newton Curd Givens 1260 Richard Carlton Walker Radford 1261 Delos B. Sacket 1262 Bernard Elliott Bee 1263 William Rhea 1264
Gordon Granger 1265 Henry Boynton Clitz 1266 William Henry Wood 1267 David Allen Russell 1268 Joseph McElvain 1269 Thomas Gamble Pitcher 1270 William Logan Crittenden 1271 **1846** Charles Seaforth Stewart 1272
George Brinton McClellan 1273 Charles Edward Blunt 1274 John Gray Foster 1275 Edmund Lafayette Hardcastle 1276 Francis Theodore Bryan 1277 George Horatio Derby 1278 Jesse Lee Reno 1279 Clarendon J. L. Wilson 1280
Thomas M. Whedbee 1281 Edmund Hayes 1282 Edward Carlisle Boynton 1283 Darius Nash Couch 1284 Henry B. Sears 1285 William Dutton 1286 John A. Brown 1287 Thomas Jonathan Jackson 1288 Albert Lewis Magilton
1289 Truman Seymour 1290 Colville Jackson Minor 1291 Charles Champion Gilbert 1292 Marcus de Lafayette Simpson 1293 Rufus J. Bacon 1294 Hamilton Leroy Shields 1295 John Adams 1296 Richard Henry Rush 1297 Henry
Astor Ehninger 1298 Thomas Foster Castor 1299 Orren Chapman 1300 Alexander Perry Rodgers 1301 Oliver Hazzard Perry Taylor 1302 Samuel Davis Sturgis 1303 George Stoneman 1304 James Oakes 1305 William Duncan
Smith 1306 George F. Evans 1307 Dabney Herndon Maury 1308 Innis Newton Palmer 1309 James Stuart 1310 Parmenas Taylor Turnley 1311 David Rumph Jones 1312 Alfred Gibbs 1313 George Henry Gordon 1314 Frederick
Myers 1315 DeLancey Floyd-Jones 1316 John Dariah Wilkins 1317 Joseph Nelson Garland Whistler 1318 Thomas Easley 1319 Nelson Henry Davis 1320 Thomas Rush McConnell 1321 Matthew Rider Stevenson 1322 George S.
Humphreys 1323 William Henry Tyler 1324 Cadmus Marcellus Wilcox 1325 William Montgomery Gardner 1326 Edmund Russell 1327 Archibald Blair Botts 1328 Samuel Bell Maxey 1329 George Edward Pickett 1330 **1847**
John Cleves Symmes 1331 John Hamilton 1332 Joseph Jackson Woods 1333 Julian McAllister 1334 George Washington Hazzard 1335 Daniel Tompkins Van Buren 1336 Samuel Fletcher Chalfin 1337 Orlando Bolivar Willcox 1338
John Sanford Mason 1339 George Patten 1340 John H. Dickerson 1341 Daniel M. Beltzhoover 1342 Otis Hammond Tillinghast 1343 James Barnett Fry 1344 Ambrose Powell Hill 1345 Anson Jones Cook 1346 Horatio Gates
Gibson 1347 Ambrose Everett Burnside 1348 Richard Henry Long 1349 John Gibbon 1350 Clermont Livingston Best 1351 Romeyn Beck Ayres 1352 Charles Griffin 1353 Henry More Black 1354 Henry Bascom Hendershott 1355
Tredwell Moore 1356 Thomas Hewson Neill 1357 William Wallace Burns 1358 Edward Fifield Abbott 1359 Egbert Ludovicus Viele 1360 Washington Posey Street 1361 Montgomery Pike Harrison 1362 Lewis Cass Hunt 1363
Augustus Henry Seward 1364 Peter W. L. Plympton 1365 John De Russy 1366 Edward DeVeux Blake 1367 Henry Heth 1368 **1848** William Petit Trowbridge 1369 Andrew Jackson Donelson 1370 James Chatham Duane 1371
Walter Husted Stevens 1372 Robert Stockton Williamson 1373 Rufus A. Roys 1374 Nathaniel Michler 1375 James Milton Haynes 1376 Joseph Claypole Clark 1377 William Edmonson Jones 1378 John Caldwell Tidball 1379
William G. Gill 1380 Benjamin Davis Forsythe 1381 Thomas Smith Rhett 1382 James Holmes 1383 John Buford 1384 Truman K. Walbridge 1385 Edward Benjamin Bryan 1386 Richard Irving Dodge 1387 Grier Tallmadge 1388
William Alloway Slaughter 1389 Robert Milton Russell 1390 Charles Humphrey Tyler 1391 John C. Booth 1392 Thomas Klugh Jackson 1393 George H. Paige 1394 Nathaniel Henry McLean 1395 Andrew Galbraith Miller 1396
Charles Henry Ogle 1397 William N. R. Beall 1398 Ferdinand Paine 1399 Thomas Denton Johns 1400 William Thompson Mechling 1401 George Clinton Barber 1402 Daniel Huston 1403 Nathan George Evans 1404 George
Hume Steuart 1405 George Washington Howland 1406 **1849** Quincy Adams Gillmore 1407 John Grubb Parke 1408 Stephen Vincent Benet 1409 Thomas Jefferson Haines 1410 Johnson Kelly Duncan 1411 William Silvey 1412
Beekman DuBarry 1413 Delavan Duane Perkins 1414 Absalom Baird 1415 William A. Nimmo 1416 Milton Cogswell 1417 Edward Dorsey Stockton 1418 Edward Russell Platt 1419 Chauncey McKeever 1420 William Henry Lewis
1421 John Kellogg 1422 John Creed Moore 1423 Rufus Saxton 1424 Thomas Wright 1425 Horace F. DeLano 1426 Daniel W. McClure 1427 Edward McKenney Hudson 1428 John Withers 1429 Washington Carroll Tevis 1430
Beverly Holcombe Robertson 1431 Joseph Lorenzo Tidball 1432 Charles William Field 1433 Seth Maxwell Barton 1434 Duff C. Green 1435 Richard W. Johnson 1436 Samuel Beckley Holabird 1437 Thomas Greenhow Williams
1438 Thornton Augustin Washington 1439 John W. Frazer 1440 Alfred Cumming 1441 Thomas Cooper English 1442 Joseph Hunter McArthur 1443 James Philip Roy 1444 Charles Benjamin Alvord 1445 Davius D. Clark 1446
Louis Henry Marshall 1447 Samuel H. Reynolds 1448 James McQueen McIntosh 1449 **1850** Frederick Edward Prime 1450 Governeur Kemble Warren 1451 Silas Crispin 1452 Cuvier Grover 1453 Powell T. Wyman 1454 Joseph
Henry Wheelock 1455 Jacob Culbertson 1456 Oscar Addison Mack 1457 Hugh E. Dungan 1458 Achilles Bowen 1459 William Thomas Magruder 1460 Adam Jacoby Slemmer 1461 Richard Arnold 1462 James Persons Flewellen
1463 Lucius March Walker 1464 John A. Mebane 1465 Armistead Lindsay Long 1466 Robert Ransom 1467 Eugene Asa Carr 1468 William Passmore Carlin 1469 Amos Beckwith 1470 Charles Sidney Winder 1471 Francis
Henry Bates 1472 Jonas P. Holliday 1473 Elisha Gaylord Marshall 1474 Nicholas Bartlett Pearce 1475 William Ransom Calhoun 1476 Robert Johnston 1477 Thomas Bingham 1478 Austin Nelson Colcord 1479 Robert Macfeely
1480 John W. Alley 1481 William Lewis Cabell 1482 James Hamilton Wilson 1483 Henry Cary Bankhead 1484 Alden Sargent 1485 Robert Granderson Cole 1486 John James A. A. Mouton 1487 Joseph Tristam Haile 1488
James Lawrence Corley 1489 Zetus Stilwell Searle 1490 Joseph Edward Maxwell 1491 Frederick M. Follett 1492 Donald Chester Stith 1493 **1851** George Leonard Andrews 1494 James St. Clair Morton 1495 George Thatcher
Balch 1496 William Thomas Welcker 1497 Alexander Piper 1498 James Thompson 1499 Caleb Huse 1500 Kenner Garrard 1501 Ben Hardin Helm 1502 Edward Henry Day 1503 Alvan Cullem Gillem 1504 DeWitt Noyes Root
1505 Alexander James Perry 1506 Isaiah N. Moore 1507 John Edwards 1508 Albert J. Stiffan Molinard 1509 Henry Eveleth Maynadier 1510 David Bell 1511 Robert Williams 1512 John Mendenhall 1513 Martin Philip Parks
1514 Hyatt Clark Ransom 1515 Alexander McRae 1516 Charles E. Norris 1517 Gurden Chapin 1518 John Cunningham Kelton 1519 William Hopkins Morris 1520 James Curtiss 1521 Robert Emmett Patterson 1522 Thomas
Jonathan Coffin Amory 1523 William Dennison Whipple 1524 Henry Clay Hodges 1525 Junius Daniel 1526 Roger Jones 1527 Adolphus Freeman Bond 1528 Melancthon Smith 1529 Edward Augustus Palfrey 1530 John Thomas

Shaaff 1531 Henry F. Witter 1532 Joseph Green Tilford 1533 James B. Greene 1534 Lawrence Simmons Baker 1535 **1852** Thomas Lincoln Casey 1536 Newton F. Alexander 1537 George Henry Mendell 1538 George Wilson Rose 1539 Joseph Christmas Ives 1540 John W. Todd 1541 Henry Warner Slocum 1542 James Van Voast 1543 David Sloan Stanley 1544 George Burgwin Anderson 1545 Jerome Napoleon Bonaparte 1546 Henry De Veuve 1547 James Watts Robinson 1548 Milo Smith Hascall 1549 John Mullan 1550 Sylvester Mowry 1551 George Blake Cosby 1552 Robert Brenham Thomas 1553 George Lucas Hartsuff 1554 Charles Robert Woods 1555 Matthew L. Davis 1556 John Horace Forney 1557 Marshall Tate Polk 1558 Peter Tyler Swaine 1559 Charles Henry Rundell 1560 Andrew Wallace Evans 1561 John Dawes O'Connell 1562 John Nugen 1563 Hugh Brady Fleming 1564 Alexander McDowell McCook 1565 Henry Douglass 1566 William Myers 1567 Philip Stockton 1568 George Augustus Williams 1569 August Valentine Kautz 1570 Lawrence Albert Williams 1571 Lyman Mack Kellogg 1572 George Crook 1573 Arthur Pendleton Bagby 1574 John Parker Hawkins 1575 Edwin D. Phillips 1576 Richard Vanderhorst Bonneau 1577 Hezekiah H. Garber 1578 **1853** James Birdseye McPherson 1579 William Price Craighill 1580 Joshua Woodrow Sill 1581 William Robertson Boggs 1582 Francis John Shunk 1583 William Sooy Smith 1584 John McAllister Schofield 1585 Matthew Marsh Blunt 1586 Thomas Hight 1587 George Russell Bissell 1588 Thomas McCurdy Vincent 1589 Henry Clay Symonds 1590 John S. Bowen 1591 George Bell 1592 James Dodley Burns 1593 William Rufus Terrill 1594 Louis Henry Pelouze 1595 Owen Fort Solomon 1596 La Rhett Loralzo Livingston 1597 Richard Cornell Duryea 1598 John Gorham Chandler 1599 Robert Ogden Tyler 1600 Walworth Jenkins 1601 Nelson Bowman Sweitzer 1602 James Lyon White 1603 Benjamin Allston 1604 Benjamin Franklin Chamberlain 1605 John Henry Edson 1606 Thomas Wilson 1607 William Warren Lowe 1608 John Randolph Chambliss 1609 William McEntire Dye 1610 Henry B. Davidson 1611 Philip Henry Sheridan 1612 William Appleton Webb 1613 John Lawrence Grattan 1614 Elmer Otis 1615 Alfred Eugene Latimer 1616 Benjamin Franklin Smith 1617 Silas Parsons Higgins 1618 Henry Harrison Walker 1619 Edmund Charles Jones 1620 Alexander Chambers 1621 John Bell Hood 1622 James Argyle Smith 1623 Robert Finley Hunter 1624 Thomas Marshall Jones 1625 Augustus H. Plummer 1626 James B. McIntyre 1627 Lucius Loomis Rich 1628 Reuben Reddick Ross 1629 William Craig 1630 **1854** George Washington Custis Lee 1631 Henry Larcom Abbot 1632 Thomas Howard Ruger 1633 Oliver Otis Howard 1634 Thomas James Treadwell 1635 Charles Nesbit Turnbull 1636 James Deshler 1637 Henry Whitney Closson 1638 Judson David Bingham 1639 John Pegram 1640 Charles Geddings Rogers 1641 Thomas Jefferson Wright 1642 James Ewell Brown Stuart 1643 Archibald Gracie 1644 John Radcliff Smead 1645 Michael Ryan Morgan 1646 Stephen Dill Lee 1647 Milton T. Carr 1648 William Dorsey Pender 1649 Loomis Lyman Langdon 1650 John Trout Greble 1651 John Brodenave Villepique 1652 Henry Adams Smalley 1653 Samuel Kinsey 1654 Abner Smead 1655 Oliver Duff Greene 1656 Stephen H. Weed 1657 Edwin Franklin Townsend 1658 Alfred B. Chapman 1659 George Alexander Gordon 1660 John Osmond Long 1661 Benjamin Franklin Davis 1662 James Wright 1663 Waterman Palmer 1664 David Porter Hancock 1665 Samuel Turner Shepperd 1666 William M. Davant 1667 Charles Greene Sawtelle 1668 Levi L. Wade 1669 John T. Mercer 1670 Zenas Randall Bliss 1671 Edgar O'Connor 1672 John Mulins 1673 David Hammett Brotherton 1674 Horace Randal 1675 John McCleary 1676 **1855** Cyrus Ballou Comstock 1677 Godfrey Weitzel 1678 Cornelius Van Camp 1679 George Henry Elliot 1680 Junius Brutus Wheeler 1681 Ebenezer Gay 1682 Samuel Breck 1683 David McMurtie Gregg 1684 Frederick Lynn Childs 1685 Dubois John Van Deusen 1686 Michael Peter Small 1687 Francis Reddin T. Nicholls 1688 Alexander Stewart Webb 1689 John Wesley Turner 1690 Francis Asbury Shoup 1691 John Reuben Church 1692 Albert V. Colburn 1693 James Wheeler 1694 George David Ruggles 1695 Lewis Merrill 1696 Alfred Thomas A. Torbert 1697 Charles William Thomas 1698 James Hoffman Hill 1699 Edward L. Hartz 1700 Clarence Edmund Bennett 1701 William Woods Averell 1702 Timothy Matlack Bryan 1703 William Babcock Hazen 1704 Henry Williams Freedley 1705 Henry Martyn Lazelle 1706 William Russell Pease 1707 Jesse K. Allen 1708 Robert Clinton Hill 1709 George McGunnegle Dick 1710 **1856** George W. Snyder 1711 David Crawford Houston 1712 Miles Daniel McAlester 1713 Charles Cochrane Lee 1714 Henry V. De Hart 1715 Orlando Metcalfe Poe 1716 John Tipton 1717 Herbert Austin Hascall 1718 Andrew Parker Porter 1719 Francis Laurens Vinton 1720 George Dashiell Bayard 1721 Thomas Crook Sullivan 1722 John Walker Barriger 1723 Lorenzo Lorain 1724 John Bennett 1725 Wesley Owens 1726 Guilford Dudley Bailey 1727 John Brognard Shinn 1728 Hylan Benton Lyon 1729 Edmund Cooper Bainbridge 1730 Lunsford Lindsay Lomax 1731 Richard Lodor 1732 James Patrick Major 1733 Jeremiah Howard Gilman 1734 Thomas Edwin Miller 1735 Charles Bryant Stivers 1736 William Gaston 1737 James William Forsyth 1738 Thomas Woodruff Walker 1739 George Jackson 1740 Joseph Hancock Taylor 1741 John Francis Ritter 1742 John Kemp Mizner 1743 Frank Stanley Armistead 1744 Herman Biggs 1745 William Thomas Gentry 1746 James Barton Stone Alexander 1747 William Hicks Jackson 1748 Owen Kenan McLemore 1749 Richard S. C. Lord 1750 William Price Sanders 1751 James McMillan 1752 William Burton Hughes 1753 Samuel Sprigg Carroll 1754 Fitzhugh Lee 1755 John McLean Hildt 1756 Brayton C. Ives 1757 Herbert Merton Enos 1758 Arthur Sinclair Cunningham 1759 **1857** John Carver Palfrey 1760 Richard Kidder Meade 1761 Edward Porter Alexander 1762 Henry Martyn Robert 1763 George Crockett Strong 1764 Joseph Lee Kirby Smith 1765 Thomas Gregory Baylor 1766 Haldimand Sumner Putnam 1767 William Proctor Smith 1768 George Amos Kensel 1769 Thomas J. Berry 1770 Charles Hale Morgan 1771 Oliver Hazzard Fish 1772 Abram Calvin Wildrick 1773 Charles Jones Walker 1774 Francis Beach 1775 William Sinclair 1776 Augustus Gilman Robinson 1777 Samuel Wragg Ferguson 1778 Marcus Albert Reno 1779 Edward Raynsford Warner 1780 Manning Marius Kimmel 1781 George Henry Weeks 1782 John T. Magruder 1783 George Alfred Cunningham 1784 Henry C. McNeill 1785 Ira Wallace Claflin 1786 Aurelius Franklin Cone 1787 Paul Jones Quattlebaum 1788 John Sappington Marmaduke 1789 George Waller Holt 1790 Joseph Speed Conrad 1791 Edward J. Conner 1792 George Ryan 1793 Robert Houstoun Anderson 1794 Charles E. Farrand 1795 Thomas Jefferson Lee 1796 Lafayette Peck 1797 **1858** William Cushing Paine 1798 Moses James White 1799 Joseph Dixon 1800 William Holding Echols 1801 John Seldon Saunders 1802 James Henry Hallonquist 1803 Thomas Redding Tannatt 1804 Marcus Peter Miller 1805 Charles H. Ingraham 1806 Leroy Napier 1807 Solomon Williams 1808 Richard Henry Brewer 1809 Samuel McKee 1810 James Judson Van Horn 1811 Andrew Jackson 1812 Charles Garrison Harker 1813 Sardine P. Reed 1814 Royal Thaxter Frank 1815 Edward Potter Cressey 1816 Asa Bacon Carey 1817 William Hemphill Bell 1818 Bryan Morel Thomas 1819 William Joseph Leonard Nicodemus 1820 Oliver Paul Gooding 1821 William George Robinson 1822 George Nicholas Bascom 1823 Charles Edward Jesup 1824 **1859** William Emery Merril 1825 Samuel Henry Lockett 1826 Charles Read Collins 1827 Chauncey B. Reese 1828 Orlando G. Wagner 1829 Robert Franklin Beckham 1830 Moses Hanibal Wright 1831 Edward Geer Bush 1832 Francis Luther Guenther 1833 Elias Brown Carling 1834 Martin D. Hardin 1835 Eugene Mortimer Baker 1836 Norman J. Hall 1837 Roderic Stone 1838 Francis James Crilly 1839 Allen Latham Anderson 1840 Edwin Henry Stoughton 1841 Caleb Henry Carlton 1842 Joseph Wheeler 1843 John Jacques Upham 1844 Abraham Kerns Arnold 1845 Henry Augustus F. Worth 1846 **1860** Walter McFarland 1847 John Alphonse Tardy 1848 Horace Porter 1849 Nicholas Bowen 1850 Theodore Edson 1851 James Harrison Wilson 1852 Benjamin F. Sloan 1853 James M. Whittemore 1854 Alanson Merwin Randol 1855 Cornelius Hook 1856 William Westwood McCreery 1857 John Moulder Wilson 1858 Josiah Holcomb Kellogg 1859 Stephen Dodson Ramseur 1860 Edward R. Hopkins 1861 Daniel Darius Lynn 1862 Samuel A. Foster 1863 Alexander C. McWhorter Pennington 1864 John Marshall Kerr 1865 Albert Micajah Powell 1866 Alfred Theophilus Smith 1867 Wesley Merritt 1868 James Porter Martin 1869 John R. B. Burtwell 1870 William Graham Jones 1871 Martin Van Buren Lewis 1872 Salem Sumner Marsh 1873 Wade Hampton Gibbes 1874 Charles Stuart Bowman 1875 Samuel Tobey Cushing 1876 Frank Huger 1877 Robert Henry Hall 1878 John Newman Andrews 1879 Edward Bishop Dudley Riley 1880 William Henry Jordan 1881 John Jay Sweet 1882 Lyman Mishler 1883 George S. Hollister 1884 George Washington Vanderbilt 1885 James Meech Warner 1886 Harold Borland 1887 **1861** Henry Algernon Du Pont 1888 Charles E. Cross 1889 Orville Elias Babcock 1890 Henry Walter Kingsbury 1891 Adelbert Ames 1892 Llewellyn Griffith Hoxton 1893 Adelbert Rinaldo Buffington 1894 Emory Upton 1895 Nathaniel Rives Chambliss 1896 Edmund Kirby 1897 John Isaac Rodger 1898 Samuel Nicoll Benjamin 1899 John Adair 1900 John Whitney Barlow 1901 Charles Edward Hazlett 1902 Charles E. Patterson 1903 Judson Kilpatrick 1904 Franklin Harwood 1905 George Warren Dresser 1906 Charles McKnight Loeser 1907 Henry Cornelius Hasbrouck 1908 William Anthony Elderkin 1909 Francis Asbury Davies 1910 Charles Carroll Campbell 1911 Malbone Francis Watson 1912 John Benson Williams 1913 Guy Vernor Henry 1914 Jacob Henry Smyser 1915 Jacob Beekman Rawles 1916 Erskin Gittings 1917 Jacob Ford Kent 1918 Eugene Beauharnais Beaumont 1919 Leonard Martin 1920 John Scroggs Poland 1921 Robert Langdon Eastman 1922 Henry Beach Noble 1923 Leroy Lansing Janes 1924 Campbell Dallas Emory 1925 James F. McQueston 1926 George Oscar Sokalski 1927 Olin F. Rice 1928 Wright Rives 1929 Charles Henry Gibson 1930 Mathias Winston Henry 1931 Sheldon Sturgeon 1932 Patrick Henry O'Rorke 1933 Francis Ulric Farguhar 1934 Arthur Henry Dutton 1935 Clarence Derrick 1936 Daniel Webster Flagler 1937 Thomas Carr Bradford 1938 Richard Mason Hill 1939 William Hamilton Harris 1940 Alfred Mordecai 1941 David Hillhouse Buel 1942 Stephen Carr Lyford 1943 Alonzo Hersford Cushing 1944 Charles Caroll Parsons 1945 John Rufus Edie 1946 Lawrence Sprague Babbitt 1947 George Augustus Woodruff 1948 Joseph Crain Audenried 1949 Julius Walker Adams 1950 Peter Conover Hains 1951 Francis Henry Parker 1952 Joseph Pearson Farley 1953 Joseph Boyd Campbell 1954 Henry Erastus Noyes 1955 Philip Halsey Remington 1956 William Duncan Fuller 1957 Justin E. Dimick 1958 James Pierre Drouillard 1959 Leroy S. Elbert 1960 Charles Henry Brightly 1961 Eugene Carter 1962 Samuel Peter Ferris 1963 George Owen Watts 1964 Frank A. Reynolds 1965 George Armstrong Custer 1966 **1862** Ranald Slidell Mackenzie 1967 George Lewis Gillespie 1968 George Burroughs 1969 Charles Russell Suter 1970 Jared Augustine Smith 1971 Samuel Mather Mansfield 1972 Henry Clifton Wharton 1973 Clemens Clifford Chaffee 1974 Morris Schaff 1975 Jasper Myers 1976 William Augustus Marye 1977 Frank Brown Hamilton 1978 Isaac Arnold 1979 Tully McCrea 1980 James Madison Lancaster 1981 John Egan 1982 Asa Bolles 1983 James A. Sanderson 1984 Clifton Comly 1985 William Chambers Bartlett 1986 James Eveleth Wilson 1987 John Haskell Calef 1988 Samuel Bates McIntire 1989 Albert M. Murray 1990 James Hickman Rollins 1991 James Henry Lord 1992 Frederick Joseph James 1993 Charles Nelson Warner 1994 **1863** John Rogers Meigs 1995 Peter Smith Michie 1996 James David Rabb 1997 William Joseph Twining 1998 William Rice King 1999 William Henry Harrison Benyaurd 2000 Charles Wagoner Howell 2001 Asa Hopkins Holgate 2002 John Randolph McGinness 2003 George Wilson McKee 2004 Frank Huntington Phipps 2005 James William Reilly 2006 Josiah Horace Vincent Field 2007 Charles Farnam Rockwell 2008 William Sully Beebe 2009 Thomas Ward 2010 Jacob Henry Counselman 2011 George Douglass Ramsay 2012 Henry C. Dodge 2013 John Gazzam Butler 2014 Robert Catlin 2015 Charles Harris Lester 2016 Kenelm Robbins 2017 James Madison Johnson Sanno 2018 James Riley Reid 2019 **1864** Garrett J. Lydecker 2020 Arthur Hubert Burnham 2021 Amos Stickney 2022 James Wayne Cuyler 2023 Alexander Mackenzie 2024 Oswald Herbert Ernst 2025 David Porter Heap 2026 William Ludlow 2027 Charles Blanchard Phillips 2028 William Albert Jones 2029 John T. Cantwell 2030 Andrew Neaf Damrell 2031 Charles Douglas Waterman 2032 Vanderbilt Allen 2033 Charles Julius Allen 2034 Cullen Bryant 2035 Martin Luther Poland 2036 Alexander Sanford Clarke 2037 Elias Van Arsdale Andruss 2038 William Ennis 2039 John Elliott 2040 Melville Richard Loucks 2041 Isaac Walker Maclay 2042 Rezin Gist Howell 2043 William Preston Vose 2044 Edward D. Wheeler 2045 Samuel Hall Kinney 2046 **1865** Charles Walker Raymond 2047 Lewis Cooper Overman 2048 Alexander Macomb Miller 2049 Micah Ryder Brown 2050 Milton Butler Adams 2051 William Roscoe Livermore 2052 David Wells Payne 2053 William Henry Heuer 2054 William Sanford Stanton 2055 William Howard Chase 2056 Thomas Henry Handbury 2057 Reuben Winslow Petrikin 2058 James Clarence Post 2059 John Kinsman Hezlep 2060 Alex Nisbet Lee 2061 James Fingal Gregory 2062 Alfred Elliott Bates 2063 Henry Brockholst Ledyard 2064 Thomas Murray Tolman 2065 John Patten Story 2066 Ormsby McKnight Mitchel 2067 David Rittenhouse Porter 2068 James Harrison Hall 2069 Appleton Downer Palmer 2070 James Larned Sherman 2071 William Augustus Rafferty 2072 Cyrus M. Allen 2073 Albert Gallatin Forse 2074 William Henry McLaughlin 2075 Clinton Jacob Powers 2076 Seneca Hughes Norton 2077 Charles M. Reid 2078 Edward Harris Totten 2079 George Hall Burton 2080 George T. Olmsted 2081 Edwin Mauck 2082 Frederick W. Bailey 2083 Thomas Lee Brent 2084 Charles Henry Breckinridge 2085 James M. Marshall 2086 William Sylvanus Starring 2087 William Krause 2088 Charles Phillips Smith 2089 Jared Lawrence Rathbone 2090 Thomas Jefferson Lloyd 2091 Francis H. Ross 2092 Edward Hunter 2093 William Augustus Garland 2094 Alexander William Hoffman 2095 Edgar Campbell Bowen 2096 Charles Keller 2097 Benjamin Dwight Critchlow 2098 Malcolm McArthur 2099 John Edward Hosmer 2100 Samuel Meyers Mills 2101 William David O'Toole 2102 Charles Erastus Moore 2103 Joseph Keyes Hyer 2104 George Gordon Greenough 2105 James Duncan Graham 2106 Warren Carpenter Beach 2107 Charles Morris 2108 Satterlee Clark Plummer 2109 Archibald Henry Goodloe 2110 Cass Durham 2111 Robert Buchanan Wade 2112 Peter Elmendorf Sloan 2113 Charles Adam Dempsey 2114 **1866** Henry Martyn Adams 2115 James Mercur 2116 Charles Edward Law Baldwin Davis 2117 Benjamin Dwight Greene 2118 John Hull Weeden 2119 George Montague Wheeler 2120 Eugene Augustus Woodruff 2121 James Baird Quinn 2122 Daniel Wright Lockwood 2123 William Patterson Butler 2124 Frank Soule 2125 Edward Maxwell Wright 2126 Richard Cuyler Churchill 2127 Charles Sidney Smith 2128 Hiero Benjamin Herr 2129 James O'Hara 2130 Charles Evans Kilbourne 2131 Abner Hopkins Merrill 2132 Henry Harrison Chase Dunwoody 2133 Robert Craig 2134 William Preston Dixon 2135 Charles King 2136 James Edwin Eastman 2137 Isaac Talman Webster 2138 William Henry Upham 2139 Solon Orr 2140 Elbridge Romeyn Hills 2141 Joseph Gardner Swift 2142 Francis Lowell Hills 2143 George Ogilvie Webster 2144 Rufus Porter Brown 2145 John Scott Payne 2146 John Perry Walker 2147 Quintin Campbell 2148 John Franklin Stretch 2149 Albert John Neff 2150 William Wirt Fleming 2151 Charles Louis Umbstaetter 2152 Will Jenkins Moberley 2153 John Charles Thompson 2154 James Blakeslee Cole 2155 **1867** Ernest Howard Ruffner 2156 John Conrad Mallery 2157 Clinton Brooks Sears 2158 Thomas Turtle 2159 Joseph Evan Griffith 2160 William Evans Rogers 2161 Lewis Muhlenberg Haupt 2162 John Edwin Greer 2163 Edward Maguire 2164 John Pitman 2165 Frederick August Mahan 2166 Charles Francis Powell 2167 Frederick Augustus Hinman 2168 William Floyd Reynolds 2169 Charles Shaler 2170 Charles Stuart Heintzelman 2171 John Moore Kelso Davis 2172 Crosby Parke Miller 2173 Charles George Eckhart 2174 Luigi Lomia 2175 James Edward Bell 2176 Robert Morris Rogers 2177 Thomas Henry Barber 2178 John Mitchell Johnson 2179 John McClellan 2180 Thomas Tipton Thornburgh 2181 Eugene Peter Murphy 2182 Samuel Roberts Jones 2183 Ephraim Thos Carroll Richmond 2184 Henry Brown Osgood 2185 James Bassel 2186 Sedgwick Pratt 2187 Allyn Capron 2188 Henry Davies Wallen 2189 Arthur Cranston 2190 Alexander DeBois Schenck 2191 Oliver Ellsworth Wood 2192 Edward Munro Merriman 2193 Edwin Styles Curtis 2194 George Armstrong Garretson 2195 Jacob Almy 2196 William Judson Sartle 2197 Leander Townsend Howes 2198 Henry Clay Danes 2199 Walter Howe 2200 Barnet Wager 2201 Medorem Crawford 2202 Edward Davis 2203 Arthur Tracy Lee 2204 Henry Nixon Moss 2205 Stanislaus Remak 2206 Horatio Morgan Jones 2207 Edward Settle Godfrey 2208 William James Roe 2209 Christopher Columbus Wolcott 2210 John Augustus Campbell 2211 Gilbert Palmer Cotton 2212 Eliphalet Nott Chester 2213 George William Cradlebaugh 2214 William Bascom McCallum 2215 Orsemus Bronson Boyd 2216 Thomas Randolph Adams 2217 John Henry Gifford 2218 **1868** Albert Henry Payson 2219 John George David Knight 2220 Richard Leveridge Hoxie 2221 Edgar Wales Bass 2222 James Bond Mackall 2223 Richard Henry Savage 2224 William Louis Marshall 2225 Joseph Henry Willard 2226 Henry Metcalf 2227 Frank Heath 2228 William John Hamilton 2229 Robert Fletcher 2230 John Joseph Casey 2231 Clarence Orville Howard 2232 David Dick Johnson 2233 James Campbell Morrison 2234 Charles Ridgly Barnett 2235 Eugene Oscar Fechet 2236 William Everett 2237 Paul Dahlgren 2238 Charles William Whipple 2239 George Wagener Deshler 2240 David Stewart Denison 2241 Alexander Logan Morton 2242 Christopher Tomkins Hall 2243 William Philo Clark 2244 Samuel Miller Swigert 2245 William Preble Hall 2246 Joshua Lounsbury Fowler 2247 John Pope 2248 William Jefferson Volkmar 2249 James Henry Jones 2250 Richard Edward Thompson 2251 John Black Rodman 2252 Patrick Thomas Brodrick 2253 William Curtis Forbush 2254 John Deane Charles Hoskins 2255 Frank L. Shoemaker 2256 James Worden Pope 2257 Chancellor Martin 2258 William Thomas Ditch 2259 George Washington Pyle 2260 James Edwin Batchelder 2261 Frank Webster Russell 2262 George Montgomery Harris 2263 Thomas Jefferson March 2264 Harrison Samuel Weeks 2265 Loyall Farragut 2266 Thomas Moseley Willey 2267 Charles Francis Roe 2268 Delancey Astor Kane 2269 Sumner Homer Bodfish 2270 Patrick Fitzpatrick 2271 William Henry Coombs 2272 **1869** Eric Bergland 2273 Leonard Gansevoort Hun 2274 Samuel Escue Tillman 2275 Phillip M. Price 2276 Daniel Morgan Taylor 2277 William Crittenden Fitzsimmons 2278 William Penn Duvall 2279 Jacob Arnold Augur 2280 Henry Leavenworth Harris 2281 Arthur Sherburne Hardy 2282 John Gregory Bourke 2283 David Alexander Lyle 2284 Worth Osgood 2285 Remembrance Hughes Lindsey 2286 Charles Henry Rea 2287 James Ezekiel Porter 2288 Frank Edward Nye 2289 William Thomas Craycroft 2290 Charles Braden 2291 John Aspinwall 2292 John Wesley Pullman 2293 Franklin Yeaton 2294 Earl Dennison Thomas 2295 William Isaac Reese 2296 Charles Morton 2297 Charles Henry Rockwell 2298 Wells Wilner Leggett 2299 Jenifer Hanson Smallwood 2300 William Frederick Smith 2301 George Robert Bacon 2302 Henry Pratt Perrine 2303 William Wallace Robinson 2304 Wentz Curtis Miller 2305 William Rawson 2306 Edward Wright Brady 2307 Henry Warner Sprole 2308 Martin Briggs Hughes 2309 William Gerhard 2310 Mason Marion Maxon 2311 **1870** Francis Vinton Greene 2312 Winfield Scott Chaplin 2313 Edward Singleton Holden 2314 Carl Follen Palfrey 2315 James Rockewell 2316 Edward Edgar Wood 2317 William Bayard Weir 2318 William Russell Quinlan 2319 Edward Silas Chapin 2320 Henry Albert Reed 2321 William Bradford Homer 2322 Rollin Augustus Ives 2323 James Alfred Dennison 2324 Edward Godfrey Stevens 2325 Edgar Swartwout Dudley 2326 Clarence Ashley Postley 2327 Charles William Burrows 2328 Ira MacNutt

2329 William Edward Birkhimer 2330 Walter Scribner Schuyler 2331 Benjamin Harrison Randolph 2332 Charles Adam H. McCauley 2333 Richard Algernon Williams 2334 Edward Coke Edgerton 2335 Daniel Crosby Pearson 2336 Clinton Hale Tebbetts 2337 Alexander Oswald Brodie 2338 Charles William Larned 2339 Edmund Monroe Cobb 2340 Austin Lamartine Peirce 2341 Edward Allison Godwin 2342 Samuel Warren Fountain 2343 Frederick King Ward 2344 Robert Edward Coxe 2345 Peter Sporr Bomus 2346 Edward John McClernand 2347 Frederick Elisha Phelps 2348 Robert Goldthwaite Carter 2349 Dexter Wright Parker 2350 Charles Brewster Schofield 2351 Frederick William Kingsbury 2352 John Gowdy Kyle 2353 Jerauld Aubray Olmsted 2354 Frank Michler 2355 Benjamin Hubert Hodgson 2356 Edwin Henry Shelton 2357 Otto Louis Hein 2358 Sebree Smith 2359 Orlando Luther Wieting 2360 Winfield Scott Edgerly 2361 John Brown Kerr 2362 Clarence Augustus Stedman 2363 Isaiah Heylin McDonald 2364 John Conline 2365 Robert Newton Price 2366 Daniel Hezekiah Floyd 2367 Lovell Hall Jerome 2368 Levi Pettibone Hunt 2369 **1871** James Robert Wasson 2370 Edgar Zell Steever 2371 James Cooper Ayres 2372 Andrew Howland Russell 2373 George Smith Anderson 2374 Vinton Augustus Goddard 2375 Frank Heartt Edmunds 2376 Reid T. Stewart 2377 Charles Clifford Morrison 2378 George Breckenridge Davis 2379 Charles Albert Woodruff 2380 Walter Scott Wyatt 2381 Wallace Mott 2382 George E. Bacon 2383 Thomas Mayhew Woodruff 2384 Leverett Hull Walker 2385 Richard Henry Poillon 2386 Henry Peoble Kingsbury 2387 Andrew Humes Nave 2388 Frederick Schwatka 2389 John Augustine McKinney 2390 James Nicholls Allison 2391 James Burke Hickey 2392 Charles Henry Ribbel 2393 George Francis Chase 2394 Ulysses Simpson Grant White 2395 Thomas Taylor Knox 2396 Francis Worthington Mansfield 2397 James Fornance 2398 Henry Eleazer Robinson 2399 William Baker Wheeler 2400 Daniel Harmon Brush 2401 John McAdams Webster 2402 Charles Richard Ward 2403 Alexander McCook Guard 2404 Thomas Staniford Mumford 2405 Frederick Dent Grant 2406 Thomas Gerry Townsend 2407 William Reddy Hoag 2408 Fayette Washington Roe 2409 Julius Hayden Pardee 2410 **1872** Rogers Birnie 2411 Overton Carr 2412 Stanhope English Blunt 2413 Marcus Ward Lyon 2414 Frank Baker 2415 Frank Obadiah Briggs 2416 Emerson Griffith 2417 William Abbot 2418 George Daniel Wallace 2419 Harry Dewitt Moore 2420 Henry Rowan Lemly 2421 Charles Dyer Parkhurst 2422 Benjamin Hidden Gilman 2423 Abram Epperson Wood 2424 John Timothy VanOrsdale 2425 George Ruhlen 2426 Charles Albert Varnum 2427 Frank West 2428 Henry Moore Harrington 2429 Richard Thompson Yeatman 2430 Jacob Rhoads Riblett 2431 George Enoch Pond 2432 Mitchell Ford Jamar 2433 Addis Morgan Henry 2434 George Brinton Walker 2435 Thomas Childs Woodbury 2436 Charles Albert Phelps Hatfield 2437 James Allen 2438 Charles Austin Booth 2439 John William Wilkinson 2440 Ralph Wilson Hoyt 2441 Charles Henry Watts 2442 Leven Cooper Allen 2443 Austin Henely 2444 William Campbell McFarland 2445 William Foster Norris 2446 George Thomas Tillman Patterson 2447 William Boerum Wetmore 2448 Charles Anthony Worden 2449 William Haven Miller 2450 Thomas Brainard Nichols 2451 John Jefferson Dougherty 2452 Alfred Hibbard Rogers 2453 Thaddeus Winfield Jones 2454 Alexander Ogle 2455 Robert Hanna 2456 Joseph Hall 2457 George LeRoy Brown 2458 George Howard Evans 2459 Herbert Everett Tutherly 2460 William Hale Low 2461 Henry Wygant 2462 William Henry Williams James 2463 Henry Hutton Landon 2464 Thomas Corbin Davenport 2465 Frank Patrick Reap 2466 Millard Fillmore Goodwin 2467 **1873** William Herbert Bixby 2468 Henry Sheldon Taber 2469 William Trent Rossell 2470 Thomas Norton Bailey 2471 John August Lundeen 2472 Charles Adiel Lewis Totten 2473 Jacob Emanuel Bloom 2474 William Harrison Coffin 2475 Joseph Haddock Dorst 2476 Albert Simpson Cummins 2477 Joseph Garrard 2478 Ezra Bond Fuller 2479 Alexander Brydie Dyer 2480 Joshua Legrand Knapp 2481 George Summers Hoyle 2482 Edward Thomas Brown 2483 George Hussey Paddock 2484 Robert London 2485 Bainbridge Reynolds 2486 George Francis Edward Harrison 2487 John Edward Myers 2488 Frederick Appleton Smith 2489 George Anthony Cornish 2490 Edwin Thomas Howard 2491 Calvin Duvall Cowles 2492 George Oscar Eaton 2493 Daniel Cornman 2494 Henry Clayton LaPoint 2495 Dillard Hazelrigg Clark 2496 Hoel Smith Bishop 2497 Augustus Cleveland Tyler 2498 Charles Mallon O'Connor 2499 Samuel Nelson Holmes 2500 Edward Wanton Casey 2501 William Harding Carter 2502 Hugh T. Reed 2503 Cornelius Gardner 2504 Louis Philip Brant 2505 Edgar Swazie Beacom 2506 Quincy O'Maher Gilmore 2507 Joseph Francis Huston 2508 **1874** Thomas William Symons 2509 Arthur Murray 2510 Henry Merritt Andrews 2511 Montogomery Meigs Macomb 2512 James Lewis Wilson 2513 Frank Sabinus Rice 2514 John Thomas Honeycutt 2515 George Lucius Anderson 2516 John Philip Wisser 2517 Joseph Shillington Oyster 2518 Orin Burlingame Mitcham 2519 Albert Hastings Mellen 2520 Clarence Deems 2521 Wright Prescott Edgerton 2522 Edgar Brooks Robertson 2523 Edmund Kirby Webster 2524 Russell Thayer 2525 George Russell Cecil 2526 Harrison Gail Otis 2527 Charles Henry Cabaniss 2528 Charles Water Rowell 2529 Frederick William Sibley 2530 Charles Carroll Norton 2531 Charles Erskine Scott Wood 2532 Luther Rector Hare 2533 Willis Wittich 2534 George Lemuel Turner 2535 Alfred Reynolds 2536 William Logan Geary 2537 William Staring Davies 2538 Christian Cyrus Hewitt 2539 Henry Perrine Walker 2540 Louis Aleck Craig 2541 Edward Ervin Hardin 2542 Charles Richard Tyler 2543 Charles Andrew Williams 2544 Marion Perry Maus 2545 Charles Frederick Lloyd 2546 Theodore Henry Eckerson 2547 William Henry Wheeler 2548 James Hansell French 2549 **1875** Smith Stallard Leach 2550 Dan Christie Kingman 2551 Eugene Griffin 2552 Willard Young 2553 Lotus Niles 2554 William Augustus Simpson 2555 Charles Albert Tingle 2556 Tasker Howard Bliss 2557 Charles Hobart Clark 2558 John Percival Jefferson 2559 Victor Horace Bridgman 2560 John Mary Baldwin 2561 Elbert Wheeler 2562 Erasmus Morgan Weaver 2563 Myron Winslow Howe 2564 James Richard McAuliffe 2565 James Mills Jones 2566 Eli DuBose Hoyle 2567 James Clark Bush 2568 Edwin Proctor Andrus 2569 William Nelson Dykman 2570 George Benjamin Backus 2571 Stanton Augustus Mason 2572 Robert P. Page Wainwright 2573 William Abram Mann 2574 Henry Dustan Huntington 2575 Timothy Arthur Touey 2576 William Baird 2577 James Garland Sturgis 2578 Alexander Rodgers 2579 George Rodney Smith 2580 Joseph Henry Gustin 2581 George Lawson Scott 2582 Francis Eugene Eltonhead 2583 Samuel Austin Cherry 2584 Thomas Francis Davies 2585 James Buick Goe 2586 John Green Ballance 2587 Edwin Bradford Bolton 2588 Arthur Lockwood Wagner 2589 Thomas Sydney McCaleb 2590 Robert Kennon Evans 2591 Charles Wilson Williams 2592 **1876** John R. Williams 2593 Herman Dowd 2594 Lawrence Laurenson Bruff 2595 Alexander Samuel Bacon 2596 William Crozier 2597 Henry Hunt Ludlow 2598 John Theodore French 2599 William Morgan Medcalfe 2600 Charles Booth Satterlee 2601 Leonard Austin Lovering 2602 William Thomas Howard 2603 Samuel Richard Douglas 2604 Edward Edgerly Gayle 2605 William Reeve Hamilton 2606 Henry Dana Borup 2607 Eugene Albion Ellis 2608 Granger Adams 2609 Sevier McClellan Rains 2610 Edward Everett Dravo 2611 Charles William Foster 2612 Herbert Sidney Foster 2613 Oscar Fitzalan Long 2614 Charles Hartwell Bonesteel 2615 Carver Howland 2616 Edward Samuel Farrow 2617 William Cathcart Buttler 2618 Frederic Edward Greydene-Smith 2619 Charles Scott Hall 2620 Eben Swift 2621 Ernest Albert Garlington 2622 James Parker 2623 George Allen Dodd 2624 Harry Lee Bailey 2625 John Chowning Gresham 2626 George Andrews 2627 Hugh Lenox Scott 2628 Horatio Gates Sickel 2629 Loyd Stone McCormick 2630 Charles Elias Garst 2631 Charles Lyman Hammond 2632 Albert Judson Russell 2633 John Pitcher 2634 Samuel Speece Pague 2635 James Alexander Hutton 2636 George Palmer 2637 Joseph Franklin Cummings 2638 Alfred Mason Fuller 2639 Hamilton Rowan 2640 **1877** William Murray Black 2641 Walter Leslie Fisk 2642 Solomon William Roessler 2643 Thomas Calvin Patterson 2644 Albert Todd 2645 William Brandon Gordon 2646 Howard Abraham Springett 2647 William Watts Galbraith 2648 Solon Frederick Massey 2649 John January Haden 2650 Charles Gwinn Woodward 2651 Adam Slaker 2652 John Vasser White 2653 Frederick Marsh 2654 David Price 2655 Francis Preston Blair 2656 James Clayton Shofner 2657 Fred Waldron Foster 2658 Theophilus Parker 2659 Edward Hinkley Plummer 2660 Medad Chapman Martin 2661 Augustus Perry Blocksom 2662 Charles Bare Gatewood 2663 Jacob Garretson Galbraith 2664 Cunliffe Hall Murray 2665 Richard Hulbert Wilson 2666 Calvin Esterly 2667 Edward Chynoweth 2668 Francis Jarvis Patten 2669 John Herbert Philbrick 2670 Henry Joseph Goldman 2671 Wilber Elliott Wilder 2672 Monroe Parker Thorington 2673 James V. Seaman Paddock 2674 Curtis Bushrod Hoppin 2675 James Defrees Mann 2676 Robert Ratcliff Stevens 2677 Henry Kirby 2678 Thomas Henry Barry 2679 John Francis Guilfoyle 2680 William Carey Brown 2681 William Thomas Wood 2682 Robert Eliel Safford 2683 Charles Judson Crane 2684 Harry Truett Hammond 2685 John Bigelow 2686 Ammon Arthur Augur 2687 George White Baxter 2688 Charles Allen Bradley 2689 Henry Ossian Flipper 2690 John James Brereton 2691 Oscar James Brown 2692 Robert Temple Emmet 2693 Ben Israel Butler 2694 John McMartin 2695 Robert Doddridge Read 2696 Samuel Pierce Wayman 2697 Edwin Forbes Glenn 2698 Stephen Crosby Mills 2699 George Nathan Chase 2700 Millard Fillmore Eggleston 2701 William Herbert Baldwin 2702 John Elston Baxter 2703 Heber Mansfield Creel 2704 James Berryman Jackson 2705 Alexander McCarrell Patch 2706 George King Hunter 2707 Daniel Alfred Frederick 2708 Wallis Olwin Clark 2709 Matthias Walter Day 2710 Samuel Howard Loder 2711 David Newton McDonald 2712 James Alison Maney 2713 John Frederick Charles Hegewald 2714 Ariosto McCrimmon 2715 Frederic Halverson French 2716 **1878** George McClellan Derby 2717 James Loring Lusk 2718 Frank Emery Hobbs 2719 Edwin McNeill 2720 George Percival Scriven 2721 James Sumner Pettit 2722 Douglas Alexander Howard 2723 Frederick Wooley 2724 John Reynolds Totten 2725 William Pierce Evans 2726 Edgar Wellington Howe 2727 Solomon Eaton Sparrow 2728 Lewis Douglass Greene 2729 John Thomas Barnett 2730 Edward Bernard Ives 2731 Albert Sidney Bailey 2732 William Langdon Buck 2733 Charles Melanckton Schaeffer 2734 Abner Pickering 2735 John Charles Fremont Tillson 2736 John Fulton Reynolds Landis 2737 Frank deLaunay Carrington 2738 John Nelson Glass 2739 Donald Winston 2740 Frank Porter Avery 2741 Charles Grenville Starr 2742 Millard Fillmore Waltz 2743 Baldwin Day Spilman 2744 Henry Olcot Sheldon Heinstand 2745 James Russell Richards 2746 John Leatherman Cox 2747 Charles Marim Carrow 2748 Elijah Heading Merrill 2749 Robert Nelson Getty 2750 Nat Poyntz Phister 2751 Fred Wheeler 2752 William John Elliott 2753 James Franklin Bell 2754 Elon Farnsworth Willcox 2755 Abiel Leonard Smith 2756 Silas Augustus Wolf 2757 Henry Fletcher Kendall 2758 Ormentiz John C. Hock 2759 **1879** Frederic Vaughn Abbot 2760 Thomas Lincoln Casey 2761 Theodore Alfred Bingham 2762 Curtis McDonald Townsend 2763 Gustav Joseph Fiebeger 2764 William Wesley Gibson 2765 Walter Stone Alexander 2766 Frank Stowell Harlow 2767 James Edward Runcie 2768 George Henry Goodwin Gale 2769 William Alexander Shunk 2770 Francis Henry French 2771 John Martin Porter 2772 Edmund Dickinson Smith 2773 Frederick Steinman Foltz 2774 Luther Scott Welborn 2775 Lorenzo Las Casas Brooks 2776 Henry Alexander Greene 2777 James Ormond Mackay 2778 Frank Loring Dodds 2779 Guy Evans Huse 2780 Edwin Palmer Pendleton 2781 John Alexander Johnston 2782 William Dorrance Beach 2783 Archie Gibson 2784 Thomas Cruse 2785 Alfred McCartney Ogle 2786 Charles Rutherford Noyes 2787 Allen Robertson Jordan 2788 Alonzo Lee O'Brien 2789 Micah John Jenkins 2790 James Alexander Leyden 2791 Charles Henry Grierson 2792 Lloyd Milton Brett 2793 Charles Marcellus Truitt 2794 Samuel Churchill Robertson 2795 Albert Leopold Mills 2796 Augustine Francis Hewit 2797 James Lockett 2798 Charles Paul Stivers 2799 Hunter Liggett 2800 John Spry Parke 2801 Thomas Jefferson Lewis 2802 Henry DeHart Waite 2803 Walter Lowrie Finley 2804 William Butler Reynolds 2805 Robert Wingmund Dowdy 2806 Christopher Comstock Miner 2807 James Anderson Irons 2808 Frank French Eastman 2809 Charles McClure 2810 Charles Lee Steele 2811 Daniel Lane Howell 2812 Edward Harrison Browne 2813 Benjamin Ward Leavell 2814 John Skinner Mallory 2815 Willis Thompson May 2816 Samuel Warren Miller 2817 Frank Beall Jones 2818 Charles William Taylor 2819 Marion Boling Saffold 2820 Percy Parker 2821 Arthur Charles Ducat 2822 William Ellery Almy 2823 Nathaniel Johnson Whitehead 2824 Walter Alonzo Thurston 2825 Guy Roosevelt Beardslee 2826 **1880** Oberlin Matthies Carter 2827 George Washington Goethals 2828 Sidney Edwin Stuart 2829 William Carroll Rafferty 2830 John Loomis Chamberlain 2831 Charles Sumner Burt 2832 Henry Albert Schroeder 2833 Charles Justin Bailey 2834 Frank Harrison Peck 2835 Edward Harwood Catlin 2836 Frederick Smith Strong 2837 Wilbur Loveridge 2838 David Jacob Rumbough 2839 Millard Fillmore Harmon 2840 Charles Hodge Hunter 2841 George William Van Deusen 2842 Edgar Hubert 2843 James Buchanan Aleshire 2844 Samuel Wadsworth Dunning 2845 Edward Spaw Avis 2846 Warren Hayden Cowles 2847 James Brailsford Erwin 2848 Charles Edward Hewitt 2849 Hugh Jocelyn McGrath 2850 Elias Chandler 2851 William Sherley Scott 2852 Walter Mason Dickinson 2853 George Leroy Converse 2854 Frederick Duane Holton 2855 Daniel Lisle Tate 2856 Pierce Mason Butler Travis 2857 George Horace Morgan 2858 Albert Blackstone Scott 2859 James Walker Benet 2860 Benjamin Samuel Wever 2861 James Seymour Rogers 2862 Henry Buckman Moon 2863 Harris Lee Roberts 2864 James Rolla Chapman 2865 John Y. Fillmore Blake 2866 James Hendricks Gains Wilcox 2867 Francis Joseph Andrew Darr 2868 George Bell 2869 Charles Berard Vogdes 2870 George Henry Sands 2871 Henry Granville Sharpe 2872 George William Goode 2873 Zerah Watkins Torrey 2874 Charles Stewart 2875 George Ritter Burnett 2876 James Waterman Watson 2877 Percy Edwards Trippe 2878 **1881** John Millis 2879 John Biddle 2880 Edward Othniel Brown 2881 Harry Foote Hodges 2882 James Goold Warren 2883 Edwin St. John Greble 2884 Williston Fish 2885 Samuel Edward Allen 2886 Daniel Hall Boughton 2887 George True Bartlett 2888 Melzar Clinton Richards 2889 Charles Asa Bennett 2890 Charles Leonard Phillips 2891 Clarence Page Townsley 2892 Albert Church Blunt 2893 Joseph Alfred Gaston 2894 Guy Carleton 2895 Francis Joseph Kernan 2896 Reuben Banker Turner 2897 John Lewis Barbour 2898 Albert Scott McNutt 2899 Rowland Gardner Hill 2900 Henry Clay Hodges 2901 Franklin Oliver Johnson 2902 Benjamin Franklin Handforth 2903 John Frank Morrison 2904 Joseph Theodore Dickman 2905 James Taggart Kerr 2906 James Henry Waters 2907 Daniel Edward McCarthy 2908 Enoch Herbert Crowder 2909 Charles Henry Barth 2910 Albert James Griffiths 2911 Andrew Goodrich Hammond 2912 Frederick Grady Hodgson 2913 Virgil Jefferson Brumback 2914 Lester Warren Cornish 2915 John Charles Waterman 2916 Lyman Hall 2917 Jonas Aden Emery 2918 John Miller Stotsenburg 2919 Andrew Summers Rowan 2920 Parker Whitney West 2921 Britton Davis 2922 Frank Burton Andrus 2923 Harry Alex Lee 2924 Walter Riggs Stoll 2925 John Howard Wills 2926 John Harry Gardner 2927 Lyman Walter Vere Kennon 2928 Simeon Moses Dinkins 2929 John Bacon McDonald 2930 Frederick Thrall Van Liew 2931 **1882** Edward Burr 2932 Oscar Terry Crosby 2933 Lansing Hoskins Beach 2934 Graham Denby Fitch 2935 Eugene Jaccard Spencer 2936 Warren Putnum Newcomb 2937 Harry Coupland Benson 2938 Ormund Mitchell Lissak 2939 George Franklin Barney 2940 Adelbert Cronkhite 2941 John Taliaferro Thompson 2942 Harvey Clarence Carbaugh 2943 Charles Gould Treat 2944 Edward Alexander Millar 2945 Richard Whitehead Young 2946 Samuel Rodman 2947 Benjamin Alvord 2948 Victor Emanuel Stottler 2949 George Willcox McIver 2950 Henry Tureman Allen 2951 William Hampden Sage 2952 William Woods Forsyth 2953 George Hermann Patten 2954 Magnus Olin Hollis 2955 Barrington King West 2956 John Henry Beacom 2957 Francis Gibson Irwin 2958 Charles Pinckney Elliott 2959 Charles Josiah Stevens 2960 Blanton Charles Welsh 2961 Thomas Buchanan Dugan 2962 James Albert Goodin 2963 William Herbert Allaire 2964 Woodbridge Geary 2965 James Oscar Green 2966 Charles Lee Collins 2967 George Patrick Ahern 2968 **1883** George Arthur Zinn 2969 William Campbell Langfitt 2970 Henry Ely Waterman 2971 William Frederick Hancock 2972 Henry Clarence Davis 2973 Beverly Wyly Dunn 2974 Samuel Diggs Freeman 2975 William Francis Flynn 2976 Robert John Duff 2977 Thomas Ridgway 2978 John Wilson Ruckman 2979 Alfred Baury Jackson 2980 William Porter Stone 2981 William Ewen Shipp 2982 Ira Allen Haynes 2983 Willoughby Walke 2984 Edwin Conover Bullock 2985 Chase Wilmot Kennedy 2986 Louis Ostheim 2987 Charles Gould Morton 2988 Samuel Effinger Adair 2989 Godfrey Harry Macdonald 2990 Herbert Howland Sargent 2991 Matthew Forney Steele 2992 Edwin Alvin Root 2993 John Mitchell Neall 2994 William Harvey Smith 2995 Isaac William Littell 2996 George Hamilton Cameron 2997 Walter King Wright 2998 Tyree Rodes Rivers 2999 Roger Bates Bryan 3000 John Wilkinson Heard 3001 John Henry Shollenberger 3002 Charles Henry Osgood 3003 Harry Clay Hale 3004 Robert Douglas Walsh 3005 Charles Herschell Cochran 3006 Elmore Findlay Taggart 3007 George Windle Read 3008 Samson Lane Faison 3009 Alfred Hasbrouck 3010 Jacob Fordney Kreps 3011 Henry Coalter Cabell 3012 Charles Case Teare 3013 Edgar Smith Walker 3014 Charles McQuiston 3015 Thomas Wilson Griffith 3016 Frederick Perkins 3017 Omar Bundy 3018 Lawrence Davis Tyson 3019 Clarence Ransom Edwards 3020 **1884** Irving Hale 3021 James Clark Sanford 3022 Hiram Martin Chittenden 3023 Cassius Erie Gillette 3024 David DuBose Gaillard 3025 Harry Taylor 3026 William Luther Sibert 3027 John Conklin 3028 Charles Loring Corthell 3029 Stephen Miller Foote 3030 Isaac Newton Lewis 3031 Eugene Frederick Ladd 3032 Samuel Davis Sturgis 3033 Wendell Lee Simpson 3034 Everard Enos Hatch 3035 Frederick Langworthy Palmer 3036 James Alfred Cole 3037 DeRosey Carroll Cabell 3038 Edwin Burr Babbitt 3039 Elisha Spencer Benton 3040 Farrand Sayre 3041 Wilds Preston Richardson 3042 Hugh John Gallagher 3043 Clarence Eugene Dentler 3044 Grote Hutcheson 3045 James Kaster Thompson 3046 George Oscar Cress 3047 Ernest Smith Robins 3048 Henry Delp Styer 3049 John Bellinger Bellinger 3050 Waldo Emerson Ayer 3051 Robert Houston Noble 3052 David Cary Shanks 3053 Benjamin Clark Morse 3054 John Thornton Knight 3055 James Bryan Hughes 3056 Powhatan Henry Clarke 3057 **1885** Joseph Ernst Kuhn 3058 William Edward Craighill 3059 Michael James O'Brien 3060 Cornelis deWitt Willcox 3061 Haydn Samuel Cole 3062 Arthur Franklin Curtis 3063 John Crafts Wright Brooks 3064 Charles Henry Muir 3065 John Davenport Barrette 3066 Charles Foster Parker 3067 Robert Alexander Brown 3068 Lorenzo Paul Davison 3069 Elmer Wilcox Hubbard 3070 John Miller Carson 3071 Austin Hastings Brown 3072 Almon Lee Parmerter 3073 Willard Ames Holbrook 3074 Frank DeWitt Ramsey 3075 John Kirby Cree 3076 Henry Pinckney McCain 3077 Frank Atwood Cook 3078 William Shepard Biddle 3079 John Little 3080 Lewis M. Koehler 3081 George Smith Cartwright 3082 Robert Edward Lee Michie 3083 Robert Lee Bullard 3084 Samuel Ewing Smiley 3085 Daniel Bradford Devore 3086 Beaumont Bonaparte Buck 3087 Philip Augustus Bettens 3088 George Logan Byram 3089 George Israel Putnam 3090 Edward Robinson Gilman 3091 Charles Dennis Towsley 3092 James Watson Benton 3093 William Franklin Martin 3094 Herbert Sydney Whipple 3095 Edward Percival Lawton 3096 **1886** Henry Clay Newcomer 3097 Mason Mathews Patrick 3098 Charles Swift Riche 3099 Thomas Henry Rees 3100 Charles Lewis Potter 3101 John Alexander Towers 3102 Arthur Thayer 3103 Robert Lincoln Hirst 3104 Lucien Grant Berry 3105 Frank McIntyre 3106 John Eugene McMahon 3107 Walter Nicholas Paine Darrow 3108

John Taylor Haines 3109 Avery DeLano Andrews 3110 Cecil Stewart 3111 Charles Thomas Menoher 3112 Samuel Reber 3113 Floyd Walter Harris 3114 William Homer Camp 3115 John Torrence Nance 3116 Harry Freeland 3117 Robert Grider Procter 3118 George Durfee DeShon 3119 Colville Mott Pettit 3120 Albert Decatur Kniskern 3121 Frank Green Kalk 3122 Charles Carroll Walcutt 3123 William Heebner Bean 3124 David Jewett Baker 3125 John Joseph Pershing 3126 Peter Edward Traub 3127 Thomas Bentley Mott 3128 Benjamin Andrew Poore 3129 Edward William McCaskey 3130 Gustave Woodson Smith Stevens 3131 Joseph Charles Byron 3132 Jesse McIlvaine Carter 3133 Frank Benton Fowler 3134 Harry George Trout 3135 Edwards Cranston Brooks 3136 Chauncey Brooke Baker 3137 Malvern Hill Barnum 3138 Letcher Hardeman 3139 Edmund Sehon Wright 3140 Bertram Tracy Clayton 3141 William Henry Hay 3142 James Eugene Nolan 3143 James Henry McRae 3144 Stephen Habersham Elliott 3145 Amos Blanchard Shattuck 3146 William Maclay Swaine 3147 Walter Henry Gordon 3148 James Lewis Druien 3149 Armand Isidore Lasseigne 3150 James Henly Frier 3151 George John Godfrey 3152 Henry Clay Keene 3153 George Burwell Davis 3154 Frederick Clark Kimball 3155 Charles George Lyman 3156 Arthur Johnson 3157 Frank Long Winn 3158 Charles Clarenden Ballou 3159 Erneste Virgil Smith 3160 George Brand Duncan 3161 Robert Clarence Williams 3162 Lucius Loyd Durfee 3163 Charles Grattan Dwyer 3164 Julius Augustus Penn 3165 Edward Mann Lewis 3166 Richard Clayborne Croxton 3167 Edward Nathaniel Jones 3168 Seward Mott 3169 Dwight Ely Holley 3170 William George Elliot 3171 Marcus Maxwell 3172 David William Fulton 3173 **1887** Francis Rawn Shunk 3174 James Joseph Meyler 3175 Eugene Willett Van Court Lucas 3176 Charles Brewster Wheeler 3177 Edward Clinton Young 3178 Richmond Pearson Davis 3179 George Owen Squier 3180 Ernest Hinds 3181 Wirt Robinson 3182 John Murray Jenkins 3183 Edgar Russel 3184 George Foreman Landers 3185 George Washington Gatchell 3186 Harry Eugene Wilkins 3187 Oscar Itin Straub 3188 Alfred Milton Hunter 3189 Fremont Pearsons Peck 3190 Edson Arthur Lewis 3191 Charles Henry Martin 3192 John David Miley 3193 P. D. Lochridge 3194 Thomas Horace Slavens 3195 Nathaniel Fish McClure 3196 William Cannon Rivers 3197 Herman C. Schumm 3198 James Calvin Bourke 3199 William Weigel 3200 Frederick Amasa Tripp 3201 Ellwood Waller Evans 3202 Robert Glasgow Paxton 3203 John Caldwell Gregg 3204 John Hanks Alexander 3205 John Alexander Harman 3206 Thomas Quinton Donaldson 3207 George McKnight Williamson 3208 Thomas Grafton Hanson 3209 Francis Henry Beach 3210 Thomas Winthrop Hall 3211 Ambrose Irving Moriarty 3212 Alonzo Gray 3213 William Estcourt Bruce 3214 Herman Hall 3215 Pierrepont Isham 3216 Arthur Blossom Foster 3217 Marcus Daniel Cronin 3218 Alexander Lucien Dade 3219 Charles Stewart Farnsworth 3220 Charles Gerhardt 3221 Samuel Seay 3222 William Pitt Baker 3223 Eugene Lincoln Loveridge 3224 James Theodore Dean 3225 Ulysses Grant McAlexander 3226 William Kinley Jones 3227 Edmund Wittenmyer 3228 Frederic Dahl Evans 3229 Michael Joseph Lenihan 3230 William Hudspeth Wassell 3231 Mark Leslie Hersey 3232 Walter Lucian Taylor 3233 Bard Pendleton Schenck 3234 Henry Ranney Adams 3235 Samuel Aaron Smoke 3236 Frank Herman Albright 3237 **1888** Henry Jervey 3238 Charles Hedges McKinstry 3239 William Voorhees Judson 3240 George Washington Burr 3241 Charles Corser Gallup 3242 John Louis Hayden 3243 Charles Day Palmer 3244 William Sullivan Peirce 3245 John Sheridan Winn 3246 Peyton Conway March 3247 Eugene Trimble Wilson 3248 James William McAndrew 3249 Solomon Pervis Vestal 3250 Charles Aloysius Hedekin 3251 Francis John Koester 3252 John Simon Grisard 3253 Charles Perren Russ 3254 Claiborne Lee Foster 3255 Charles Wendell Fenton 3256 John Daniel Leinbach Hartman 3257 Clough Overton 3258 William Jefferson Davis Horne 3259 Robert Lee Howze 3260 Edward Roberts Chrisman 3261 Guy Henry Preston 3262 Edwin Moore Suplee 3263 Andrew Gregg Curtin Quay 3264 John Paul Ryan 3265 William Roderick Sample 3266 Edward Anderson 3267 Peter Charles Harris 3268 Munroe McFarland 3269 William Horace Hart 3270 William Tolivar Wilder 3271 William Herman Wilhelm 3272 Charles Victor Donaldson 3273 George Edward Stockle 3274 William Robert Dashiell 3275 Eli Alva Helmick 3276 Alexander Wallace Perry 3277 William Thomas Littebrant 3278 Charles Grant French 3279 Capers Daniel Vance 3280 Matthew Calbraith Butler 3281 **1889** Eben Eveleth Winslow 3282 Albert Miligan D'Armit 3283 Clement A. Finley Flagler 3284 Chester Harding 3285 William Wright Harts 3286 Robert McGregor 3287 Edmund Molyneux Blake 3288 John Thomas Martin 3289 Francis Wallace Willcox 3290 Wilmot Edward Ellis 3291 William Lacy Kenly 3292 William George Haan 3293 Sidney Sauzade Jordan 3294 Walter Augustus Bethel 3295 Alvin Humphrey Sydenham 3296 Ben Johnson 3297 Morris Keene Barroll 3298 Ralph Harrison 3299 Delamere Skerrett 3300 Edward Fenton McGlachlin 3301 Archibald Campbell 3302 John Power Hains 3303 William Lassiter 3304 George LeRoy Irwin 3305 Charles Baldwin Hagadorn 3306 Charles Dudley Rhodes 3307 Harry Raymond Lee 3308 Edwin Victor Bookmiller 3309 Alexander Ross Piper 3310 Edward Thomas Winston 3311 Winthrop Samuel Wood 3312 George Tayloe Langhorne 3313 Ulysses Grant Kemp 3314 Matt Ransom Peterson 3315 Edwin Tuttle Cole 3316 William Allen Phillips 3317 John Rodgers Meigs Taylor 3318 George William Kirkman 3319 Francis Edmond Lacey 3320 Sydney Amos Cloman 3321 Charles Crawford 3322 William Sidney Graves 3323 Frank Daniel Webster 3324 Joseph Dugald Leitch 3325 Samuel Burkhardt 3326 James Edward Normoyle 3327 Edward Villeroy Stockham 3328 Antonio Barrios 3329 Charles Young 3330 **1890** Edgar Jadwin 3331 Charles Keller 3332 Herbert Deakyne 3333 Charles Summers Bromwell 3334 Colden l'Hommedieu Ruggles 3335 William Orlando Johnson 3336 Henry Davis Todd 3337 John Clifford Rennard 3338 James Hamilton 3339 Thomas Winfield Winston 3340 Alfred Charles Merillat 3341 Maurice Gaston Krayenbuhl 3342 George Montgomery 3343 Clint Calvin Hearn 3344 William Church Davis 3345 James Robert Lindsay 3346 Hiram McLemore Powell 3347 Robert Bruce Wallace 3348 Francis Cutler Marshall 3349 Frank Gratin Mauldin 3350 Daniel Warren Ketcham 3351 Milton Fennimore Davis 3352 William Sharp McNair 3353 William Josiah Snow 3354 George Grant Gatley 3355 Thomas Briggs Lamoreux 3356 Fred Winchester Sladen 3357 James Augustine Ryan 3358 Harry Hill Bandholtz 3359 Henry Thornburg Ferguson 3360 Frank Merrill Caldwell 3361 Henry Grant Learnard 3362 James Joseph Hornbrook 3363 William Franklin Clark 3364 Samuel Goode Jones 3365 John Henry Wholey 3366 Melvin Weston Rowell 3367 George Marion Brown 3368 James Madison Andrews 3369 Peter Murray 3370 Paul Alexander Wolf 3371 Henry Gideon Lyon 3372 George Davis Moore 3373 Willis Uline 3374 Lawrence Julian Fleming 3375 Hugh Swain 3376 Charles Jacobs Symmonds 3377 Ernest Bertrand Gose 3378 Charles Carr Clark 3379 Joseph Cincinnatus Fox 3380 Oren Browning Meyer 3381 Frank Browne Keech 3382 Edmund Luther Butts 3383 Vernon Avondale Caldwell 3384 **1891** Spencer Cosby 3385 John Stephen Sewell 3386 Charles Patton Echols 3387 James Francis McIndoe 3388 Jay Johnson Morrow 3389 Odus Creamer Horney 3390 Leroy Springs Lyon 3391 Andrew Hero 3392 Tiemann Newell Horn 3393 Edward D. Anderson 3394 Truman Oscar Murphy 3395 George Philip White 3396 Lawson Mayo Fuller 3397 Louis Charles Scherer 3398 John William Furlong 3399 Richard Larremore Livermore 3400 Thomas Michael Corcoran 3401 Robert John Fleming 3402 Edwin Baruch Winans 3403 William Thomas Johnston 3404 William Headley Osborne 3405 Francis Henry Schoeffel 3406 Harold Palmer Howard 3407 William Harry Bertsch 3408 Ross Leonard Bush 3409 Joseph Laviallle Donovan 3410 Elmer Lindsley 3411 John Bradbury Bennet 3412 Joseph Thadeus Crabbs 3413 William Jefferson Glasgow 3414 Frank Spear Armstrong 3415 Melville Shinn Jarvis 3416 John William Heavey 3417 Harry Jean Hirsch 3418 Charles DeLano Hine 3419 Joseph Frazier 3420 Robert Lee Hamilton 3421 LaRoy Sunderland Upton 3422 Harry Alexander Smith 3423 Hollis Chenery Clark 3424 George Coolidge Saffarrans 3425 Palmer Eddy Pierce 3426 Lutz Wahl 3427 William Payne Jackson 3428 Albert Bernard Donworth 3429 Charles Cornell Ogden 3430 Gordon Voorhies 3431 John Leonard Hines 3432 Guy Howard Berard Smith 3433 Walter Monteith Whitman 3434 Matthias Crowley 3435 Jacques deLivandais Lafitte 3436 John Jewsbury Bradley 3437 Douglas Settle 3438 John Singleton Switzer 3439 Herbert Owen Williams 3440 George Dickinson Guyer 3441 William Frederick Grote 3442 William Henry Henley Chapman 3443 Herbert Nathan Royden 3444 Isaac Colburn Jenks 3445 Alfred Wettermak Drew 3446 Hanson Edward Ely 3447 Lewis Stone Sorley 3448 David Price Cordray 3449 **1892** James Bates Cavanaugh 3450 James Postell Jervey 3451 Frank Ephraim Harris 3452 George Blakely 3453 Jay Edgar Hoffer 3454 Tracy Campbell Dickson 3455 Arthur Wallace Chase 3456 Frank Winston Coe 3457 Kenneth Morton 3458 William Ruthven Smith 3459 Henry Howard Whitney 3460 Samuel Alexander Kephart 3461 Louis Ray Burgess 3462 Charles Clark Jamieson 3463 James Ancil Shipton 3464 Sawyer Blanchard 3465 George Columbus Barnhardt 3466 William Chamberlaine 3467 John McAuley Palmer 3468 Charles Pelot Summerall 3469 William Gerald Fitzgerald 3470 James Haynes Reeves 3471 Kirby Walker 3472 John Kramer Miller 3473 Claude Bernard Sweezey 3474 Jacob H. G. Lazelle 3475 Henry Alexander Pipes 3476 Sterling Price Adams 3477 Traber Norman 3478 Horace Maynard Reeve 3479 Alexander Macdonald Davis 3480 Julian Robert Lindsey 3481 Edmund Mortimer Leary 3482 Julius Theodore Conrad 3483 Howard Russell Hickok 3484 Samuel Benjamin Arnold 3485 Willard E. Gleason 3486 William Newman 3487 Frank Allen Wilcox 3488 John James O'Connell 3489 Henry Greene Cole 3490 George Sumner Harison 3491 Hansford Lee Threlkeld 3492 William Hart Anderson 3493 Peter Weimer Davison 3494 Leonard Morton Prince 3495 Marcus Butler Stokes 3496 Samuel McPherson Rutherford 3497 John Henry Parker 3498 George Williams Kirkpatrick 3499 John Edwin Woodward 3500 William Walter Haney 3501 Dennis Mahan Michie 3502 Frederic Thomas Stetson 3503 James Thaddeus Moore 3504 William David Davis 3505 George McDougall Weeks 3506 Isaac Erwin 3507 Samuel Vinton Ham 3508 George Hunter McMaster 3509 Robert Walter Mearns 3510 Horace George Hambright 3511 **1893** George Pierce Howell 3512 Charles Willauer Kutz 3513 Meriwether Lewis Walker 3514 Robert Pulliam Johnston 3515 Robert Rossiter Raymond 3516 William Mackey Cruikshank 3517 Gordon Graham Heiner 3518 John Hodgen Rice 3519 George Henry McManus 3520 Edward Julius Timberlake 3521 Henry Charles Le Comte 3522 David Matson King 3523 Lincoln Clark Andrews 3524 Samuel Chrisman Hazzard 3525 Samuel John Bayard Schindel 3526 William Renwick Smedberg 3527 Howard Louis Laubach 3528 Otho Willard Burnham Farr 3529 Robertson Honey 3530 Elmer Wright Clark 3531 John M. Morgan 3532 Louis Bowen Lawton 3533 Andrew Erwin Williams 3534 Amos H. Martin 3535 Walter Crosby Babcock 3536 William Yates 3537 Herbert Ball Crosby 3538 Buell Burdett Bassette 3539 Benjamin Bremner Hyer 3540 Mathew Charles Smith 3541 Edward Buchanan Cassatt 3542 Thomas Lee Smith 3543 Kenzie Wallace Walker 3544 Arthur Morris Edwards 3545 Harry Howard Pattison 3546 Edward Edgar Hartwick 3547 Charles Greene Sawtelle 3548 Howard Rand Perry 3549 George Edmund Houle 3550 Lincoln Fay Kilbourne 3551 Verling Kersey Hart 3552 Robert Edward Lee Spence 3553 William Cauldwell Rogers 3554 Frank Bornemann McKenna 3555 George Hairston Jamerson 3556 Edward Colby Carey 3557 Edward Taylor 3558 Hamilton Allen Smith 3559 Hunter Bithal Nelson 3560 Albert Laws 3561 Mathew Edward Saville 3562 **1894** William Baker Ladue 3563 William Jones Barden 3564 William Perry Pence 3565 Clarence Charles Williams 3566 James Marks Williams 3567 John Warren Joyes 3568 Edward Philip O'Hern 3569 Samuel Hof 3570 Clarence Edward Lang 3571 Charles William Castle 3572 Warren Halsey Mitchell 3573 Francis Le Jau Parker 3574 George French Hamilton 3575 Dwight Edward Aultman 3576 William Herman Paine 3577 Alston Hamilton 3578 Paul Bernard Malone 3579 John White Craig 3580 John Curtis Gilmore 3581 Rogers Finch Gardner 3582 John Fisher Preston 3583 Hugh Douglas Berkeley 3584 Albert Eugene Saxton 3585 Hamilton Smith Hawkins 3586 Butler Ames 3587 Frederick George Lawton 3588 Charles Frederic Crain 3589 Frank Sherwood Cocheu 3590 Ora Elmer Hunt 3591 Frank Parker 3592 John Campbell McArthur 3593 Thomas Gillespie Carson 3594 Frank David Ely 3595 William Alfred Sater 3596 Edwin Bell 3597 Otho Bane Rosenbaum 3598 George Henson Estes 3599 George Vidmer 3600 Dana Willis Kilburn 3601 Oliver Edwards 3602 Thomas Walter Connell 3603 John Somerville Battle 3604 Charles Lyman Bent 3605 William Ernest Welsh 3606 Frederick G. Stritzinger 3607 Charles Curtis Smith 3608 Frank Leslie Wells 3609 Briant Harris Wells 3610 John William Barker 3611 Ralph Reverdy Stogsdall 3612 James Paxton Harbeson 3613 Hugh Douglas Wise 3614 Pegram Whitworth 3615 James Alfred Moss 3616 **1895** Edward Hugh Schulz 3617 Harry Burgess 3618 John Asa Gurney 3619 Jens Bugge 3620 Casper Hauzer Conrad 3621 Harry Ernest Smith 3622 Harry Howard Stout 3623 Herbert Arthur White 3624 Joseph Lippincott Knowlton 3625 Charles Harman Paine 3626 Thales Lucius Ames 3627 Conway Hillyer Arnold 3628 Nathan King Averill 3629 Harry La Tourrette Cavenaugh 3630 Joseph Wheeler 3631 Adrian Sebastian Fleming 3632 Brooke Payne 3633 Mortimer Osborne Bigelow 3634 William Gray Sills 3635 August Carl Nissen 3636 Thomas Walter Darrah 3637 Americus Mitchell 3638 Perry Lester Miles 3639 Milton Loomis McGrew 3640 Clyde Emile Hawkins 3641 Lorrain Thompson Richardson 3642 James Southard Parker 3643 Charles Roscoe Howland 3644 Francis Pierpont Siviter 3645 Morton Fitz Smith 3646 Louis Meredith Nuttman 3647 Glenn Hedges Davis 3648 Franklin Swart Hutton 3649 Joseph Sutherland Herron 3650 Henry Benjamin Dixon 3651 Albert Sidney Brookes 3652 George Barnard Pritchard 3653 Thomas Francis Dwyer 3654 Fine Wilson Smith 3655 Walter Scott McBroom 3656 Louis Hoffman Lewis 3657 David Sheridan Stanley 3658 Benjamin Taylor Simmons 3659 Joseph Numa Augustin 3660 Samuel George Creden 3661 Girard Sturtevant 3662 Louis Hermann Bash 3663 Anton Springer 3664 Frank Bingley Watson 3665 Oscar Jerome Charles 3666 Thomas Absalom Pearce 3667 Daniel Duncan 3668 **1896** Edwin Roy Stuart 3669 George Matthias Hoffman 3670 Harry Frederick Jackson 3671 Robert Emmet Callan 3672 William Harvey Tschappat 3673 Samuel Victor McClure 3674 William Slann Guignard 3675 Eugene Postell Jervey 3676 Edwin Landon 3677 LeRoy Eltinge 3678 Clarence Henry McNeil 3679 Joseph Powell Tracy 3680 John Buffalo Christian 3681 Lloyd England 3682 Thomas Ferrers Howard 3683 James William Hinkley 3684 George Williams Moses 3685 Alga Prestina Berry 3686 Percy Myers Kessler 3687 Newton Davidson Kirkpatrick 3688 Lucian Stacy 3689 Charles Ezra Stodter 3690 Johnson Hagood 3691 Haydon Young Grubbs 3692 Alexander Macomb Miller 3693 Celwyn Emerson Hampton 3694 Paul Reisinger 3695 Charles Bryant Drake 3696 Charles McKinley Saltzman 3697 George Thomas Patterson 3698 John Morrison 3699 Frank Kerby Fergusson 3700 Harry Ormiston Willard 3701 Herschel Tupes 3702 Lucius Roy Holbrook 3703 George Henry Shelton 3704 John Parsons Wade 3705 Isaac Newell 3706 Robert Morris Brookfield 3707 Elvin Ragnvald Heiberg 3708 Stephen Morris Kochersperger 3709 Ola Walter Bell 3710 Abraham Grant Lott 3711 Frank Homer Whitman 3712 Francis Gurney Smith 3713 Clarence Newcomb Purdy 3714 Merch Bradt Stewart 3715 Frederick Worthington Lewis 3716 Edward Leonard King 3717 Charles Ernest Russell 3718 Dennis Edward Nolan 3719 James Newell Pickering 3720 William Arthur Burnside 3721 Duncan Norbert Hood 3722 Reynolds Johnston Burt 3723 Samuel Field Dallam 3724 William Kelly 3725 Russell Creamer Langdon 3726 George Thomas Summerlin 3727 Harry Herbert Tebbetts 3728 Charles Trumbull Boyd 3729 Thomas Aloysius Wansboro 3730 Houston Valle Evans 3731 Arthur Raphael Kerwin 3732 Henry Charles Whitehead 3733 George Swazey Goodale 3734 William Dixon Chitty 3735 Benj Minton Hartshorne 3736 Frank Crandall Bolles 3737 Alfred Eldrekin Kennington 3738 Lanning Parsons 3739 Edward Percy Orton 3740 Robert Boyd Powers 3741 **1897** William Durward Connor 3742 John Calvin Oakes 3743 Louis Casper Wolf 3744 Henry Sims Morgan 3745 Sherwood Alfred Cheney 3746 Frederick William Alstaetter 3747 Harley Bascom Ferguson 3748 Charles DuVal Roberts 3749 Robert Swepston Abernethy 3750 John Kirkpatrick Moore 3751 Francis Horton Pope 3752 Edwin Oliver Sarratt 3753 Albert Jesse Bowley 3754 Matthew Elting Hanna 3755 Bertram Charles Gilbert 3756 Lawrence Sprague Miller 3757 George Edward Mitchell 3758 Winfield Scott Overton 3759 Pierce Ambrose Murphy 3760 Mervyn Chandos Buckey 3761 Frederick Theodore Arnold 3762 Frederick Edgar Johnston 3763 Claude Hamilton Miller 3764 James Noble Munro 3765 Harold Benjamin Fiske 3766 Earle D'Arcy Pearce 3767 William Stanley Valentine 3768 Arthur Stewart Conklin 3769 Henry Carpenter Smither 3770 Roy Beveridge Harper 3771 John Hendricken Hughes 3772 Thomas Arnett Roberts 3773 Edgar Alexander Stirmyer 3774 Frank Ross McCoy 3775 George Willis Helms 3776 Chalmers Gaither Hall 3777 Rufus Estes Longan 3778 Frank Marion Savage 3779 Thomas Taylor Frissell 3780 Edward Anthony Roche 3781 William Mason Fassett 3782 Henry Magdeburg Dichmann 3783 Halstead Dorey 3784 Clarence Richmond Day 3785 George Franklin Baltzell 3786 Benjamin Martin Koehler 3787 Willard Herman McCornack 3788 James Francis Brady 3789 Hugh LaFayette Applewhite 3790 Seth Mellen Milliken 3791 Edgar Thomas Conley 3792 John Carrington Raymond 3793 Roderick Leland Carmichael 3794 Harry Gore Bishop 3795 Henry Abbot 3796 Andrew Moses 3797 Edgar Thomas Collins 3798 Fred Anderson Pearce 3799 Seaborn Green Chiles 3800 Lyman Mowry Welch 3801 Thomas Quinn Ashburn 3802 Sam Frank Bottoms 3803 Warren Sumner Barlow 3804 John Girardin Workizer 3805 Willard Douglas Newbill 3806 Charles Higbee Bridges 3807 Harold Edward Cloke 3808 **1898** Frank Cranstoun Boggs 3809 Clarke Stull Smith 3810 William Preston Wooten 3811 Lytle Brown 3812 Robert David Kerr 3813 Earl Ivan Brown 3814 Amos Alfred Fries 3815 Manus MacCloskey 3816 John Edmondson Stephens 3817 Thomas Emery Merrill 3818 Monroe Crawford Kerth 3819 Charles Harold Munton 3820 George Adolphus Nugent 3821 William West Hamilton 3822 Curtis William Otwell 3823 William Edward Cole 3824 Fox Conner 3825 Henry Wolf Butner 3826 Francis Key Meade 3827 Marcellus Garner Spinks 3828 Lambert Whitfield Jordan 3829 Jacob Calvin Johnson 3830 Henry Loew Newbold 3831 William Franklin Nesbitt 3832 James Bartholemew Gowen 3833 Harvey Wolfarth Miller 3834 Edwin Dyson Bricker 3835 Thomas Francis Maginnis 3836 William Watson Fiscus 3837 Ernest Darius Scott 3838 Daniel Greenwood Berry 3839 Edmund Nathaniel Benchley 3840 Malin Craig 3841 Harold Hammond 3842 Ralph Elliott Ingram 3843 Robert Courtney Davis 3844 Joseph Frank Janda 3845 Alvan Chambliss Read 3846 Ira Clinton Welborn 3847 Clarke Churchman 3848 David Edwin Wesley Lyle 3849 Alexander Elliott Williams 3850 Romulus Foster Walton 3851 Charles Wesley Exton 3852 Guy Vernor Henry 3853 Edward Hugh Martin 3854 Herbert Adams Lafferty 3855 David Porter Wheeler 3856 Conrad Stanton Babcock 3857 Edgar Ridenour 3858 Chauncey Benton Humphrey 3859 Berkeley Enochs 3860 William Louis Murphy 3861 Robert Jayne Maxey 3862 G. Maury Cralle 3863 Joseph Franklin Gohn 3864 James Heyward Bradford 3865 Wallace Bryan Scales 3866 David Lamme Stone 3867 **1899** James Albert Woodruff 3868 William Kelly 3869 Horton Whitefield Stickle 3870 Lewis Hathaway Rand 3871 Edward Murphy Markham 3872 Thomas Herbert Jackson 3873 LeVert Coleman 3874 Alfred Burpee Putnam 3875 George Woodbury Bunnell 3876 Hubert Llewellyn Wigmore 3877 Albert Edwin Waldron 3878 Jesse Crook Nicholls 3879 Frank Carson Jewell 3880 Fred Hayes Gallup 3881 Michael Joseph McDonough 3882 Patrick William Guiney 3883 Hugh Auchincloss Roberts 3884 Charles Brooks Clark 3885 Herman Walter Schull 3886

Henry Blow Farrar 3887 Clifton Carroll Carter 3888 Leon Benjamin Kromer 3889 Charles Annesley Romeyn 3890 Irvin Leland Hunt 3891 Henry Benjamin Clark 3892 George Sherwin Simonds 3893 Llewellyn Noel Bushfield 3894 James Buchanan Ray 3895 Francis Neal Cooke 3896 Stanley Dunbar Embick 3897 Samuel Tilden Ansell 3898 Ralph Stuart Granger 3899 Robert Halford Peck 3900 Evan Harris Humphrey 3901 Halsey Edward Yates 3902 Clement Augusta Trott 3903 George VanHorn Moseley 3904 Charles Cook Farmer 3905 Wilson Bryant Burtt 3906 Walter Stevens Brown 3907 Josiah Charles Minus 3908 Charles Michael Bundel 3909 Stuart Heintzelman 3910 Gwynn Richard Hancock 3911 Henry Leavenworth Harris 3912 Laurence Halstead 3913 Pierce Currier Foster 3914 Frederick William Van Duyne 3915 Charles Douglas Herron 3916 John Dudley Long 3917 Robert Bernard Calvert 3918 George Deveraux Jarrett 3919 Grayson Villard Heidt 3920 James Cooper Rhea 3921 James Hanson 3922 Fred Radford Brown 3923 William Topping Merry 3924 Frederick Blair Kerr 3925 Lawrence DuVal Cabell 3926 Clyffard Game 3927 George Washington Stuart 3928 Robert Cherry Foy 3929 Henry Newell Way 3930 William Taylor Patten 3931 Duncan Kennedy Major 3932 James Justice 3933 Llewellyn William Oliver 3934 Arthur Sidney Cowan 3935 Hector Arsene Robichon 3936 Reginald Edwards McNally 3937 Ephraim Geoffrey Peyton 3938 Albert N. McClure 3939 **1900** George Bigelow Pillsbury 3940 Edward Maguire Adams 3941 Gustave Rudolph Lukesh 3942 Edmund Moore Rhett 3943 John Rodolph Slattery 3944 Charles Robert Lawson 3945 Francis Amory Pope 3946 Gilbert Albin Youngberg 3947 Paul Stanley Bond 3948 Joseph Augustus Baer 3949 Frank Outhouse Whitlock 3950 Charles Fletcher Martin 3951 Robert Elkington Wood 3952 Willis Virlin Morris 3953 William Provines Stokey 3954 William Irving Westervelt 3955 Edwin Griffith Davis 3956 Walter Schuyler Grant 3957 Frederick Leroy Buck 3958 Jay Paul Hopkins 3959 Charles Macon Wesson 3960 Leroy Turner Hillman 3961 Upton Birnie 3962 Archibald Henry Sunderland 3963 Clarence Deems 3964 Raymond Hope Fenner 3965 Morton Claire Mumma 3966 Charles Lewis John Frohwitter 3967 Frank Porter Amos 3968 Edward Porter Nones 3969 Herman Glade 3970 Arthur Penrhyn Stanley Hyde 3971 Clifford Carleton Carson 3972 Harry Elwood Mitchell 3973 Julian Arnold Benjamin 3974 Ernest Edwin Allen 3975 John Watson 3976 Samuel Reid Gleaves 3977 Frank Sayles Bowen 3978 Fred Charles Doyle 3979 Lewis Sidney Morey 3980 James Parsons Robinson 3981 James Goethe 3982 Robert Fenwick Jackson 3983 Varien Delmar Dixon 3984 Verne LaSalle Rockwell 3985 Pressley Kennedy Brice 3986 George Thompson Perkins 3987 John William Wilen 3988 John McManus 3989 George Blanchard Comly 3990 Augustine McIntyre 3991 Charles Godfrey Harvey 3992 Richard Morgan Thomas 3993 **1901** Edward Neele Johnston 3994 Clarence Osborne Sherrill 3995 John Hudson Poole 3996 Ernest Dichmann Peek 3997 Walter Hatch Lee 3998 George Redfield Spalding 3999 Elliott Johnstone Dent 4000 William Goff Caples 4001 Henry Clay Jewett 4002 Arthur Williams 4003 Wildurr Willing 4004 William Leo Guthrie 4005 William Stacy Browning 4006 Clarence Hollister Knight 4007 Nathaniel Ephraim Bower 4008 Francis William Clark 4009 Joseph Fauntleroy Barnes 4010 Edward Canfield 4011 Walter Driscoll Smith 4012 William Peirce Ennis 4013 Harry Birdwhistell Jordan 4014 Arthur Henry Bryant 4015 Frank Purdy Lahm 4016 Willis Grandy Peace 4017 Orlando Collette Troxel 4018 William Poisson Platt 4019 Guy Elliott Carleton 4020 Eugne Ragland West 4021 Creed Fulton Cox 4022 Robert McCandlass Beck 4023 Dennis Hadley Currie 4024 Beverly Fielding Browne 4025 George Moor Russell 4026 Edward Marsh Shinkle 4027 Lewis Brown 4028 William Reese Bettison 4029 Raymond Silas Pratt 4030 Alfred Allen Maybach 4031 Jerome Gray Pillow 4032 Ralph Noble Hayden 4033 Alden Farley Brewster 4034 John Anderson Berry 4035 Leonard William Prunty 4036 Gordon Robinson 4037 Henry Michael Dougherty 4038 Louis Soleliac 4039 Edward Harrison DeArmond 4040 Edmund Kearsley Sterling 4041 Wiley Peters Mangum 4042 Charles Jacob Naylor 4043 Kerr Tunis Riggs 4044 Carl Henry Muller 4045 Allen Collins Keyes 4046 John Alonzo Pearson 4047 Prince Albert Oliver 4048 Charles Burnett 4049 Arthur James Lynch 4050 Claude Ernest Brigham 4051 Richard Furnival 4052 Daniel Dixon Gregory 4053 John Symington 4054 Walter Herbert Smith 4055 William Tidball 4056 George Hathaway Baird 4057 William Manley Cooley 4058 William Nafew Haskell 4059 James Prentice 4060 Henry Adolphus Meyer 4061 Frank Keller 4062 Fred Linden Deen 4063 Guy Kent 4064 Copley Enos 4065 Emory Jenison Pike 4066 Albert Hecker Mueller 4067 **1902** William Augustus Mitchell 4068 Warren Thomas Hannum 4069 Francis Fielding Longley 4070 Robert Ross Ralston 4071 Mark Brooke 4072 Laurence Verner Frazier 4073 J. Franklin Bell 4074 Gilbert Henry Stewart 4075 Wade Hampton Carpenter 4076 Frederic William Hinrichs 4077 Samuel Frankenberger 4078 Adam Floy Casad 4079 Charles Martin Allen 4080 John Epps Munroe 4081 John Maury Gibert 4082 Stephen Abbot 4083 John Cargill Pegram 4084 Charles Howard Jennings 4085 Harry Lumsden Hodges 4086 Edward Jay Moran 4087 William Francis Morrison 4088 William Howell Williams 4089 Rigby Dewoody Valliant 4090 Myron Sidney Crissy 4091 Victor Sidney Foster 4092 Ned Bernard Rehkopf 4093 Walter King Wilson 4094 John Preston Terrell 4095 Samuel Wilson Robertson 4096 Herbert Zettler Krumm 4097 Oscar Foley 4098 Frederick Dudley Griffith 4099 William L. Stevenson 4100 Albert Bowdre Dockery 4101 William Moragne Davis 4102 Henry Edmistoune Mitchell 4103 Edmund Loughborough Zane 4104 Nelson Allen Goodspeed 4105 Charles McHenry Eby 4106 William Henry Cowles 4107 John Richard McGinness 4108 Henry Meredith Nelly 4109 Frederick Frasier Black 4110 William Alexander McCain 4111 John Knowles Herr 4112 Philip Henry Sheridan 4113 Joseph Fulton Taulbee 4114 James Marcellus Hobson 4115 David Henry Bower 4116 Andrew William Smith 4117 Hiram Marshall Cooper 4118 Troup Miller 4119 Benjamin Franklin Miller 4120 William Waller Edwards 4121 **1903** Douglas MacArthur 4122 Charles Tileston Leeds 4123 Harold Chamberlayne Fiske 4124 Max Clayton Tyler 4125 Charles Telford 4126 Ulysses S. Grant 4127 Julian Larcombe Schley 4128 Levi Galloway Brown 4129 William Henry Rose 4130 Ferdinand Williams 4131 Owen Glenn Collins 4132 Richard Curtis Moore 4133 Scott Baker 4134 Lewis Milton Adams 4135 Frederic Harrison Smith 4136 William Morse Nichols 4137 Marion William Howze 4138 Olan Cecil Aleshire 4139 Emil Peter Laurson 4140 Frederick Ernest Shnyder 4141 George Arthur Lynch 4142 Grayson Mallet-Prevost Murphy 4143 George Wilbur Cocheu 4144 Charles Herman Patterson 4145 Lewis Turtle 4146 Henry Sayles Kilbourne 4147 Clifford Jones 4148 Wilford Judson Hawkins 4149 Louis Cass Brinton 4150 Thomas Fraley Van Natta 4151 Thomas Etholen Selfridge 4152 Henning Ferdinand Colley 4153 Paul Delmont Bunker 4154 James Andrew Mars 4155 George Lynn Morrison 4156 Orville Norris Tyler 4157 James Andrew Shannon 4158 Allan Melvill Pope 4159 Quinn Gray 4160 Reynolds James Powers 4161 Samuel Minter Parker 4162 Robert Morgan Lyon 4163 John Carter Montgomery 4164 James Sumner Jones 4165 Louis Robinson Dice 4166 William Mechling Colvin 4167 Edward Marie Zell 4168 Francis Hamilton Farnum 4169 Benjamin Edwards Grey 4170 Elvid Hunt 4171 Dorsey Read Rodney 4172 Alexander Mortimer Milton 4173 Hugh Samuel Johnston 4174 Francis Maurice Hinkle 4175 Benjamin Franklin McClellan 4176 Campbell Blackshear Hodges 4177 Jacob Winfield Scott Wuest 4178 Max Bruce Garber 4179 Leo Israel Samuelson 4180 Corbit Strickland Hoffman 4181 Carl Boyd 4182 Walter Vincent Gallagher 4183 Stephen Wilson Winfree 4184 Ephraim Foster Graham 4185 Clifton Morgan Butler 4186 Edmund Llewellyn Bull 4187 Truman William Carrithers 4188 George Francis Rozelle 4189 Arthur Emmett Ahrends 4190 Charles Franklin Severson 4191 Harry Surgisson Grier 4192 Reuben Chapman Taylor 4193 Charles Beatty Moore 4194 Clark Lynn 4195 Cornelius Stockmar Bendel 4196 Robert Emlen Boyers 4197 Burt Wellington Phillips 4198 Ben Frazer Ristine 4199 Albert Gilmor 4200 George Rendel Guild 4201 Stuart Ainslee Howard 4202 John Francis Franklin 4203 William Cissua Russell 4204 Roland Wallace Boughton 4205 John Southworth Upham 4206 Keith Sumner Gregory 4207 Irving Monroe Madison 4208 Ellery Farmer 4209 Everett Newton Bowman 4210 Homer Neill Preston 4211 Jesse Gaston 4212 Edward Aloysius Brown 4213 Charles Ferguson Smith 4214 **1904** Charles Roberts Pettis 4215 William Dandridge A. Anderson 4216 Ralph Talbot Ward 4217 John Jennings Kingman 4218 Robert Philip Howell 4219 Henry Harris Robert 4220 Joseph Haynsworth Earle 4221 Thomas Matthews Robins 4222 Roger Derby Black 4223 Theodore Harwood Dillon 4224 Lesley James McNair 4225 Charles Russell Alley 4226 James Garfield McIlroy 4227 Vaughn Washington Cooper 4228 Chauncey Lee Fenton 4229 Lucian Barclay Moody 4230 George R. Allin 4231 Pelham Davis Glassford 4232 William Bryden 4233 Donald Cowan McDonald 4234 Fulton Quintus C. Gardner 4235 Robert Charlwood Richardson 4236 Francis Webster Honeycutt 4237 Robert Madison Campbell 4238 John William McKie 4239 Jay Benedict 4240 Philip Henry Worcester 4241 George Veazey Strong 4242 Charles School Blakely 4243 Charles Thomas Smart 4244 George Bowditch Hunter 4245 Joseph Warren Stilwell 4246 Robert Melville Danford 4247 James Brownrigg Dillard 4248 Leo Paul Quinn 4249 Arthur Wood Copp 4250 Quincy Adams Gillmore 4251 James Kerr Crain 4252 Edmund Louis Gruber 4253 Carr Wilson Waller 4254 Richard James Herman 4255 David McCandless McKell 4256 Matthew Arthur Cross 4257 Edward Lorenzo Hooper 4258 Albert Howell Barkley 4259 Stanley Koch 4260 Irving Joseph Phillipson 4261 Carroll Wilder Neal 4262 Harry Smith Berry 4263 Edmund Bristol Gregory 4264 Wilbur Alexander Blain 4265 Walter Singles 4266 Stephen Clark Reynolds 4267 William Valux Carter 4268 Robert Burns Parker 4269 Gordon Rives Catts 4270 Henry Conger Pratt 4271 Donald Cameron Cubbison 4272 Christopher Jensvold 4273 Ursa Milner Diller 4274 Rollo Fred Anderson 4275 Edwin Butcher 4276 Russell Vernon Venable 4277 Arthur James Davis 4278 Roderick Dew 4279 Kinzie Bates-Edmunds 4280 Martin Christian Wise 4281 Andrew Jackson White 4282 Walter Scott Drysdale 4283 Edward Ellis Farnsworth 4284 Ralph Dickinson 4285 Riley Estel Scott 4286 Charles Andrew Meals 4287 Matthew Henry Thomlinson 4288 Charles Sherman Hoyt 4289 Horatio Balch Hackett 4290 Joseph Alexander Atkins 4291 Jacob Arthur Mack 4292 Charles Fullington Thompson 4293 Henry Joseph Reilly 4294 Augustus Bissell Van Wormer 4295 Thomas Leslie Crystal 4296 James Joseph O'Hara 4297 Albert Courtney Wimberly 4298 Wilton Stuart Dowd 4299 Arthur Dryhurst Budd 4300 Ralph Rigby Glass 4301 Erle Martin Wilson 4302 Merrill Ellicott Spalding 4303 Joseph James Grace 4304 Roy Weber Holderness 4305 John Donald Burnett 4306 Joseph Alexander McAndrew 4307 Robert Bailey Hewitt 4308 Henry Rodney Adair 4309 William Fitzhugh Lee Simpson 4310 Merrill Dole Wheeler 4311 Bernard Philip Oswalt 4312 Richard Rembert Pickering 4313 Lowe Abeel McClure 4314 James Scott Greene 4315 Gerald Clark Brant 4316 Charles Frederick Conry 4317 Clement Hale Wright 4318 William Ross Scott 4319 Winn Blair 4320 Eugene Victor Armstrong 4321 William Washington Harris 4322 Harry Lincoln Simpson 4323 Napoleon William Riley 4324 Otto Louis Brunzell 4325 George Carson Lawrason 4326 Robert Pattison Harbold 4327 James Barton Woolnough 4328 Innis Palmer Swift 4329 Joseph Dodge Park 4330 Arthur H. Wilson 4331 Walter Robson Fulton 4332 John Jay Moller 4333 Sherburne Whipple 4334 Harry Hawley 4335 Thomas Norton Gimperling 4336 Hugh Lawson Walthall 4337 John Buchanan Richardson 4338 **1905** DeWitt Clinton Jones 4339 Ernest Graves 4340 Francis Bowditch Wilby 4341 Clarence Self Ridley 4342 Alvin Barton Barber 4343 William Fitzhugh Endress 4344 Jarvis Johnson Bain 4345 Thomas Henry Emerson 4346 Robert Spencer Thomas 4347 Carlos John Stolbrand 4348 Douglas Imrie McKay 4349 Roger Garfield Powell 4350 John Neal Hodges 4351 Thomas Marshall Spaulding 4352 Arthur Rudolph Ehrnbeck 4353 Rolland Webster Case 4354 Thomas Bartwell Doe 4355 Charles Stuart Donavin 4356 Louis Herbert McKinlay 4357 Norman Foster Ramsey 4358 James Francis Curley 4359 Benj. Henderson Lorne Williams 4360 Thomas Dewey Osborne 4361 Otho Vaughan Kean 4362 Halsey Dunwoody 4363 David Curtis Seagrave 4364 William Henry Dodds 4365 John de Barth Walbach Gardiner 4366 LeRoy Bartlett 4367 John Lund 4368 Robert Collins Eddy 4369 George Dillman 4370 Patrick Henry Winston 4371 Julius Charles Peterson 4372 John Stevens Hammond 4373 DeWitt Clinton Tucker Grubbs 4374 Basil Gordon Moon 4375 James Frederick Walker 4376 Thomas West Hammond 4377 Charles Roemer 4378 Ellery Willis Niles 4379 Calvin Pearl Titus 4380 Philip John Radcliffe Kiehl 4381 Clarence Kumukoa Lyman 4382 Adelno Gibson 4383 Charles Dudley Daly 4384 Albert Terrell Bishop 4385 Haldan Urling Tompkins 4386 Charles Lewis Scott 4387 James Saye Dusenbury 4388 Lloyd Burns Magruder 4389 Robert Henry Lewis 4390 Francis Bowen Upham 4391 Arthur Hazelton Carter 4392 William Charles Miller 4393 Sidney Howland Guthrie 4394 William Adams Dallam 4395 James Hoop Dickey 4396 Ralph Talbot 4397 William Nicholas Hensley 4398 Charles Exton Bamford 4399 Frederick Willis Manley 4400 Arthur Willis Lane 4401 Walter Evans Prosser 4402 Henry Tacitus Burgin 4403 Louis Piaget Schoonmaker 4404 Carroll Henley Gardner 4405 Nathan Horowitz 4406 Bernard Lentz 4407 Karl Daenzer Klemm 4408 Edward Cornelius Hanford 4409 Clifford Lee Corbin 4410 Berkeley Thorne Merchant 4411 Frederic Coleman Test 4412 Arthur Charles Tipton 4413 Owen Stedman Albright 4414 Fred Hendrickson Baird 4415 Hugh Hunt Broadhurst 4416 Clifford Cabell Early 4417 Arthur William Holderness 4418 George Frank Waugh 4419 Louis Albert O'Donnell 4420 Allan Rutherford 4421 William Henry Hawes 4422 Joseph Ray Davis 4423 Oscar Arden Russell 4424 Sherman Miles 4425 William Seward Weeks 4426 Avery Duane Cummings 4427 Harry Telemach Herring 4428 Charles Smith Caffery 4429 Allen Wyant Gullion 4430 Louis Albert Kunzig 4431 John Pearson Bubb 4432 John George Hotz 4433 Clarence Andrew Mitchell 4434 John Roy Starkey 4435 Felix Waggoner Motlow 4436 Joseph Edward Barzynski 4437 Ralph Dwight Bates 4438 William Eaton Merritt 4439 Ben Waller Feild 4440 Robert Morrisson 4441 Bloxham Ward 4442 Paul Hedrick Clark 4443 Thomas Hixon Lowe 4444 Herndon Sharp 4445 Torrey Borden Maghee 4446 William Whitehead West 4447 George Washington Maddox 4448 Walter Eldridge Pridgen 4449 Jas. Wilson Hemphill Reisinger 4450 Rupert Algernon Dunford 4451 Charles Carr Bankhead 4452 **1906** Harold Storrs Hetrick 4453 William Albert Johnson 4454 James Josephus Loving 4455 Frederick Blundon Downing 4456 Edmund Leo Daley 4457 Henry Abercrombie Finch 4458 Edward Dahl Ardery 4459 Frederic Erastus Humphreys 4460 Charles Kellog Rockwell 4461 George Milburn Morrow 4462 Richard Coke Burleson 4463 James Wilson Riley 4464 Lloyd Patzlaff Horsfall 4465 Charles Gearhart Mettler 4466 Charles Baehr Gatewood 4467 Joseph Halley Pelot 4468 Morgan Lewis Brett 4469 Arthur Dean Minick 4470 Henry Walter Torney 4471 Forrest Estey Williford 4472 James Syer Bradshaw 4473 Earl McFarland 4474 Joseph Andres Green 4475 Alexander Garland Pendleton 4476 Jonathan Mayhew Wainwright 4477 Frederick Thibaut Dickman 4478 Walter Stephen Sturgill 4479 John Cleves Henderson 4480 Charles Alexander Lewis 4481 Harold Wood Huntley 4482 Adna Romanza Chaffee 4483 Roy F. Waring 4484 Walter Marantette Wilhelm 4485 Edward White Wildrick 4486 Walter Donahue Stuart 4487 Paul Revere Manchester 4488 Alexander Garfield Gillespie 4489 Dawson Olmstead 4490 Byard Sneed 4491 George Williamson DeArmond 4492 John George Quekemeyer 4493 Frank Maxwell Andrews 4494 Oscar Westover 4495 Harry Dale Ross Zimmerman 4496 Edwin DeLand Smith 4497 Cortlandt Parker 4498 John Sedgwick Pratt 4499 Joseph Choate King 4500 Hally Fox 4501 Martyn Hall Shute 4502 Matt Enright Madigan 4503 William Edward Lane 4504 Fred Alden Cook 4505 Ralph McTyeire Pennell 4506 George Gordon Bartlett 4507 Henry Black Clagett 4508 Clyde Rush Abraham 4509 Pierre Victor Kieffer 4510 George LeRoy Converse 4511 Harry Albert Schwabe 4512 John Conrad Maul 4513 George Harris Paine 4514 Donald Allister Robinson 4515 Rene Edward DeRussy Hoyle 4516 George Englemann Turner 4517 Philip Mathews 4518 Richard Herbert Jacob 4519 Ralph Allen Jones 4520 Calbert Lloyd Davenport 4521 Horace Fletcher Spurgin 4522 Robert Nelson Campbell 4523 Howard Kendall Loughry 4524 Hugo Daniel Selton 4525 Max Akin Elser 4526 George Rivers Byrd 4527 William Torbert MacMillan 4528 Marcellus Hagans Thompson 4529 William Watts Rose 4530 **1907** James Gordon Steese 4531 Roger Gordon Alexander 4532 John Augur Holabird 4533 James Alexander O'Connor 4534 Lewis Hayes Watkins 4535 Gilbert Edwin Humphrey 4536 Richard Park 4537 Richard Herbert Somers 4538 Daniel Isom Sultan 4539 Thomas Lee Coles 4540 John Boursiquot Rose 4541 Truman Darby Thorpe 4542 Nathaniel Pendleton Rogers 4543 Charles Tillman Harris 4544 Maxwell Murray 4545 Geoffrey Bartlett 4546 William Edgar Shedd 4547 Edwin Eastman Pritchett 4548 James Arthur Gallogly 4549 Hunter Ball Porter 4550 Royal Kemp Greene 4551 Robert Price Glassburn 4552 Harry Kenneth Rutherford 4553 Paul Jones Horton 4554 Roy Boggess Staver 4555 Fred Taylor Cruse 4556 James Preston Marley 4557 Robert Arthur 4558 John Patrick Keeler 4559 Lucian Dent Booth 4560 Henry Lee Watson 4561 Arthur Robert Calvo 4562 Waldo Charles Potter 4563 Henry Henderson Pfeil 4564 Thurman Harrison Bane 4565 Clyde Leslie Eastman 4566 Jesse Cyrus Drain 4567 Wiley Evans Dawson 4568 Alexander Wheeler Chilton 4569 Nathaniel Lamson Howard 4570 William Eric Morrison 4571 Donald James MacLachlan 4572 Charles Henry Rice 4573 Warren Lott 4574 Irving John Palmer 4575 Melvin Guy Farris 4576 Alexander William Maish 4577 William Jackson McCaughey 4578 Eugene Ross Householder 4579 James Gilbert Taylor 4580 Eugene Santschi 4581 William Addleman Ganoe 4582 Elmer Franklin Rice 4583 Edwin Colyer McNeil 4584 Augustine Warner Robins 4585 Benjamin Frederick Castle 4586 William Ducachet Geary 4587 Charles Lloyd Wyman 4588 Edward Hall Teall 4589 Hayden Waite Wagner 4590 Fred Hughes Coleman 4591 Emil Pehr Pierson 4592 Clark Porter Chandler 4593 John Walton Lang 4594 George Thomas Everett 4595 Henry Harley Arnold 4596 Walter Raymond Wheeler 4597 Arthur William Hanson 4598 George Frederick Ney Dailey 4599 Richard Huntington Kimball 4600 Abbott Boone 4601 Barton Kyle Yount 4602 Denham Bohart Crafton 4603 William Lewis Moose 4604 Charles Dunbar Rogers 4605 Ray Corson Hill 4606 Lewis Cassidy Rockwell 4607 Frederick Story Snyder 4608 William Eliot Selbie 4609 William Carroll Christy 4610 Sloan Doak 4611 Patrick Joseph Morrissey 4612 John Logan Jenkins 4613 Charles Henry White 4614 Alvin Gustav Gutensohn 4615 Stanley Livingston James 4616 Percy Alexander 4617 Robert Lee Lounsbury 4618 John Stephen Sullivan 4619 Ellwood Stokes Hand 4620 Leland Wadsworth 4621 David Grover Cleveland Garrison 4622 Seth William Scofield 4623 James Lawton Collins 4624 Herbert Bainbridge Hayden 4625 Lewis Vance Greet 4626 Bruce Bradford Buttler 4627 Evan Elias Lewis 4628 Paul Alexander Larned 4629 Harry Stevens Gillespie 4630 William Caldwell McChord 4631 William Rudicil Henry 4632 James Howard Laubach 4633 George Richard Harrison 4634 Ralph Wayne Dusenbury 4635 Thomas Charles Spencer 4636 George Francis Patten 4637 Throop Martin Wilder 4638 Robert Mercer Cheney 4639 William Logan Martin 4640 Fauntley Muse Miller 4641 **1908** Glen Edgar Edgerton 4642 Charles Lacey Hall 4643 Virgil Lee Peterson 4644 George Rodman Goethals 4645 John Wesley Niesz Schulz 4646 Clarence Lynn Sturdevant 4647 Earl James Atkisson 4648 Richard Tide Coiner 4649 Lawrence Wright McIntosh 4650 Robert Starrs Aloysius Dougherty 4651 William Eugene Dunn 4652 James Henry Burns 4653 Everett Strait Hughes 4654 Thomas Jefferson Smith 4655 Halvor Geigus Coulter 4656 Roger Sheffield Parrott 4657 West Chute Jacobs 4658 Oliver Andrews Dickinson 4659 Richard Edgar Cummins 4660 Telesphor George Gottschalk 4661 Harvey Douglas Higley 4662 James Wilbur Lyon 4663 Harold Geiger 4664 Rodney Hamilton Smith 4665 Alexander Long James 4666 Albert Lawrence Loustalot 4667 Richard Donovan 4668 Robert Clive

Rodgers 4669 Homer Havron Slaughter 4670 Sanderford Jarman 4671 Clair Warren Baird 4672 Edward Willis Putney 4673 Gilbert Marshall 4674 Henry Clinton Kress Muhlenberg 4675 Louis Lindsay Pendleton 4676 John Francis Curry 4677 James Eugene Chaney 4678 Thomas Alexander Terry 4679 Edward Nicoll Woodbury 4680 Philip Gordon 4681 William Jay Fitzmaurice 4682 Carl Cogswell Oakes 4683 John Thomas Kennedy 4684 Blaine Andrew Dixon 4685 Ray Longfellow Avery 4686 Horace Meek Hickam 4687 Owen Riggs Meredith 4688 James Clifford Williams 4689 Edward Alexander Stockton 4690 Homer McLaughlin Groninger 4691 Robert Emmett O'Brien 4692 James Hutchings Cunningham 4693 Charles Shattuck Jackson 4694 Youir Montefiore Marks 4695 Stewart Oscar Elting 4696 Edward Seery Hayes 4697 Francis Ludwig Sward 4698 Simon Bolivar Buckner 4699 John Kimball Brown 4700 George Washington Beavers 4701 Charles Hartwell Bonesteel 4702 Richard David Newman 4703 Elbert Lynn Grisell 4704 Thomas Jefferson Johnson 4705 Allison Barnes Deans 4706 Robert Howe Fletcher 4707 William Henry Garrison 4708 Frederick Ambrose Barker 4709 Agard Hyde Bailey 4710 Sumner McBee Williams 4711 Chester Amos Shephard 4712 George Cleveland Bowen 4713 Henry Wallace Hall 4714 John Hutchison Hester 4715 Franklin Langley Whitley 4716 Alfred Harold Hobley 4717 Edwin Vose Sumner 4718 H Fairfax Ayres 4719 Arthur James Hanlon 4720 Olin Oglesby Elis 4721 Gibbes Lykes 4722 Elmer Cuthbert Desobry 4723 Arthur Earl Wilbourn 4724 Emile Victor Cutrer 4725 Harry Bowers Crea 4726 Robert Christie Cotton 4727 George Barrett Glover 4728 Henry John Weeks 4729 Roy Alison Hill 4730 Arthur Edward Bouton 4731 Nathan Crary Shiverick 4732 Enoch Barton Garey 4733 Leonard H. Drennan 4734 Charles Kilbourne Nulsen 4735 Lawrence Campbell Ricker 4736 Leighton Wilson Hazlehurst 4737 John Harold Muncaster 4738 Theodore Kendall Spencer 4739 Ernest Grove Cullum 4740 Edwin Martin Watson 4741 William Walter Erwin 4742 Charles Dudley Hartman 4743 Edgar Simpson Miller 4744 Thomas Clement Lonergan 4745 Albert Lee Sneed 4746 Lester David Baker 4747 George Auguste Matile 4748 Walter Reed Weaver 4749 **1909** Stuart Chapin Godfrey 4750 Francis Clark Harrington 4751 Cleveland C. Gee 4752 John Marvin Wright 4753 John Roy Douglas Matheson 4754 William Hampden Sage 4755 Charles Joel Taylor 4756 Edwin Hall Marks 4757 Earl North 4758 Albert Hilands Archer 4759 Gilbert VanBuren Wilkes 4760 John Clifford Hodges Lee 4761 Frank Schaffer Besson 4762 Lindsay Coates Herkness 4763 Albert K. B. Lyman 4764 Charles Todd Richardson 4765 Clarence Edward Partridge 4766 Leo James Ahern 4767 Donald M. Beere 4768 Thomas H. McNabb 4769 Homer Ray Oldfield 4770 Herman Erlenkotter 4771 Claude B. Thummel 4772 Norton Meade Beardslee 4773 William C. Whitaker 4774 Harold Earl Miner 4775 James Alexander Brice 4776 N. Butler Briscoe 4777 James Leo Dunsworth 4778 Dana Harold Crissy 4779 Elbert Eli Farman 4780 Ronald DeVore Johnson 4781 George Lane VanDeusen 4782 Edward Aloysius Everts 4783 Thomas Benton Catron 4784 Robert Butcher Parker 4785 Edwin St. John Greble 4786 Francis Greason Delano 4787 Jacob Loucks Devers 4788 Philip Hayes 4789 Francis August Doniat 4790 Raphael Robert Nix 4791 James Lawrence Walsh 4792 Carl Adolph Baehr 4793 Elkin Leland Franklin 4794 George Smith Patton 4795 Henry Horace Malven 4796 Edward Luke Kelly 4797 Frederick Weeden Teague 4798 James Garesche Ord 4799 Thruston Hughes 4800 Robert Stanley Donaldson 4801 Wallace Copeland Philoon 4802 Charles Bartell Meyer 4803 Cuthbert Powell Stearns 4804 Herbert LeRoy Taylor 4805 James Rowland Hill 4806 Frederick Arthur Mountford 4807 Horace Hayes Fuller 4808 Fordyce LaDue Perego 4809 Delos Carleton Emmons 4810 Arnold Norman Krogstad 4811 Eley Parker Denson 4812 Thomas DeWitt Milling 4813 Roy Howard Coles 4814 Henry Dorsey F. Munnikhuysen 4815 Philip Stearns Gage 4816 Robert Lawrence Eichelberger 4817 Monte Jackson Hickok 4818 Stanley Maddox Rumbough 4819 Robert Charles Frederick Goetz 4820 Frederick Hanna 4821 Archibald Toombs Colley 4822 Edwin Forrest Harding 4823 Joseph Caldwell Morrow 4824 Hugh Henry McGee 4825 Theodore Mosher Chase 4826 Warder Higgins Roberts 4827 Raymond Durno Smith 4828 Carleton George Chapman 4829 Arthur Rutledge Underwood 4830 Ying Hsing Wen 4831 Robert Sears 4832 Thomas South Bowen 4833 William Allison Reed 4834 Joseph Plassmeyer 4835 Chester Paddock Mills 4836 William Harrison Anderson 4837 Lee Dunnington Davis 4838 Edwin Russell Van Deusen 4839 Frank Leroy Purdon 4840 Merle Paul Schillerstrom 4841 Carlin C. Stokely 4842 Louis Philip Ford 4843 John May McDowell 4844 Clifford Bluemel 4845 Wentworth Harris Moss 4846 Francis Robert Hunter 4847 Guy William McClelland 4848 Manton Campbell Mitchell 4849 William Hood Simpson 4850 Walker Evans Hobson 4851 Ting Chia Chen 4852 **1910** Frederick S. Strong 4853 Creswell Garlington 4854 William Carrington Sherman 4855 Daniel Dee Pullen 4856 Carey H. Brown 4857 Oscar Nathaniel Solbert 4858 Beverly Charles Dunn 4859 Donald Hilary Connolly 4860 Raymond Foster Fowler 4861 David McCoach 4862 James Gillespie Blaine Lampert 4863 Edgar Warren Taulbee 4864 Dwight Knowlton Shurtleff 4865 Francis Henry Miles 4866 Fred Clute Wallace 4867 Harry Torrey Pillans 4868 Burton Oliver Lewis 4869 Jose Martin Calvo 4870 Herbert Ray Odell 4871 Reginald Bifield Cocroft 4872 Legrand Beaumont Curtis 4873 Clyde Andrew Selleck 4874 Kenneth Bailey Harmon 4875 Ernest Joseph Dawley 4876 Elmore Beach Gray 4877 Herbert O'Leary 4878 Louis Arnold Beard 4879 Willard K. Richards 4880 Harry Dwight Chamberlin 4881 James Irvin Muir 4882 John Julius Waterman 4883 Ivens Jones 4884 Frank Drake 4885 Martin Hasset Ray 4886 Meade Wildrick 4887 Frederick Arthur Holmer 4888 Daniel Huston Torrey 4889 John Millikin 4890 Walter Browning Robb 4891 Fred Seydel 4892 Durward Saunders Wilson 4893 Parker Cromwell Kalloch 4894 Maurice Duncan Welty 4895 Charles Albert Chapman 4896 Harvey Morrison Hobbs 4897 Joseph Eugene Carberry 4898 Robert William Barr 4899 Frank Floyd Scowden 4900 Herbert Edgar Marshburn 4901 Charles Hines 4902 Jack Whitehead Heard 4903 Wm. Armistead Pendleton 4904 Walter Kilshaw Dunn 4905 Lawson Moore 4906 Charles Mann Haverkamp 4907 Thomas Sheldon Bridges 4908 Walter Hale Frank 4909 Walter Howard Williams 4910 Walter William Vautsmeier 4911 Guy W. Chipman 4912 Fred Barnes Carrithers 4913 Frederick Elwood Uhl 4914 Edgar Willis Burr 4915 Harvey Henry Fletcher 4916 John Erie Beller 4917 Jasper Alexander Davies 4918 John Frederick Landis 4919 Joseph Stephens Leonard 4920 John Arner Robenson 4921 Joseph P. Aleshire 4922 Walter Moore 4923 Oscar Woolverton Griswold 4924 Harding Polk 4925 Duncan Grant Richart 4926 Robert Horace Dunlop 4927 John Richard Walker 4928 Chester Piersol Barnett 4929 Allen Richland Edwards 4930 Emil Fred Reinhardt 4931 Calvin McClung Smith 4932 John Gray Thornell 4933 William Augustus Beach 4934 David Owen Byars 4935 **1911** Philip Bracken Fleming 4936 John Wesley Stewart 4937 Joseph Cowles Mehaffey 4938 Paul Sorg Reinecke 4939 Raymond Albert Wheeler 4940 William Benjamin Hardigg 4941 Curtis Hoppin Nance 4942 Harry Russell Kutz 4943 Charles Adam Schimelfenig 4944 Thompson Lawrence 4945 Freeman Wate Bowley 4946 Charles Reuben Baxter 4947 Gustav Henry Franke 4948 John Cabeen Beatty 4949 Hubert Gregory Stanton 4950 John Everard Hatch 4951 Charles Anderson Walker 4952 Bethel Wood Simpson 4953 Neil Graham Finch 4954 Harold F. Nichols 4955 Harry James Keeley 4956 Charles Philip Hall 4957 Alexander Day Surles 4958 William Edmund Larned 4959 Franklin Kemble 4960 Alfred John Betcher 4961 Charles L. Byrne 4962 Philip James Kieffer 4963 Karl Slaughter Bradford 4964 Herbert Arthur Dargue 4965 John Griffeth Booton 4966 Frederick Gilbreath 4967 George Richmond Hicks 4968 James Blanchard Crawford 4969 Haig Shekerjian 4970 Charles Sea Floyd 4971 Benjamin Curtis Lockwood 4972 Robert W. Clark 4973 Harrison Henry Cocke Richards 4974 Carroll Armstrong Bagby 4975 Arthur Bayard Conard 4976 Oliver S. McCleary 4977 Frederick Gilbert Dillman 4978 Gregory Hoisington 4979 Robert Lincoln Gray 4980 Ziba Lloyd Drollinger 4981 Frank Butner Clay 4982 Jesse Amos Ladd 4983 Paul William Baade 4984 Joseph Lamar Wier 4985 Frank Hall Hicks 4986 James Roy Newman Weaver 4987 James Daniel Burt 4988 Emanuel Villard Heidt 4989 John Porter Lucas 4990 William Henry Harrison Morris 4991 Herbert Sidney Foster 4992 Carl Fish McKinney 4993 Roscoe Conkling Batson 4994 Allen Russell Kimball 4995 Wilfrid Mason Blunt 4996 Ira Adelbert Rader 4997 Alvan Crosby Sandeford 4998 William Jay Calvert 4999 William Burrus McLaurin 5000 Kenneth Ebbecke Kern 5001 David Hamilton Cowles 5002 Ira Thomas Wyche 5003 James Craig Riddle Schwenck 5004 Arthur Clyde Evans 5005 William Patrick Joseph O'Neill 5006 John Lewis Homer 5007 Robert Clyde Gildart 5008 T. Jonathan Jackson Christian 5009 Frank Lazell Van Horn 5010 George Derby Holland 5011 Joseph William McNeal 5012 Howell Marion Estes 5013 John Furman Wall 5014 Max Stanley Murray 5015 Leo Gerald Heffernan 5016 Edwin Noel Hardy 5017 **1912** Howard Sharp Bennion 5018 Rudolph Charles Kuldell 5019 Roscoe Campbell Crawford 5020 Earl Grady Paules 5021 Bradford Grethen Chynoweth 5022 Milo Pitcher Fox 5023 Lee Otis Wright 5024 Lewis Andrews Nickerson 5025 Philip Ries Faymonville 5026 Russell Lamonte Maxwell 5027 William Coffin Harrison 5028 John Shirley Wood 5029 Charles Janvrin Browne 5030 Robert Henry Lee 5031 William Henry Walmsley Youngs 5032 David McLean Crawford 5033 Oscar James Gatchell 5034 John Nathaniel Hauser 5035 Karl C. Greenwald 5036 Thomas Jay Hayes 5037 Richard Emmanuel Anderson 5038 d'Alary Fechet 5039 Cris Miles Burlingame 5040 Raymond Vincent Cramer 5041 William Hale Wilbur 5042 Sidney Parker Spalding 5043 Byron Quinby Jones 5044 Leonard Lovering Barrett 5045 Stephen Harrison MacGregor 5046 James Albert Gillespie 5047 Wesley Moter Bailey 5048 Edgar Staley Gorrell 5049 Basil Duke Edwards 5050 Davenport Johnson 5051 James Kirk 5052 Robert McGowan Littlejohn 5053 Wade Hampton Haislip 5054 Robert Nall Bodine 5055 William Dean 5056 James Harve Johnson 5057 Harry Albert Flint 5058 Walter Melville Robertson 5059 John Henry Lindt 5060 Pearl Lee Thomas 5061 Sidney Vincent Bingham 5062 Otto Emile Schultz 5063 Bird S. DuBois 5064 Issac Spalding 5065 Cyril Augustine Phelan 5066 Harry James Malony 5067 John Hartwell Hinemon 5068 Henry Lytton Flynn 5069 Robert Lee Hyatt 5070 Harold Marvin Rayner 5071 Charles Nathaniel Sawyer 5072 Gilbert Richard Cook 5073 Max Weston Sullivan 5074 Stephen Marston Walmsley 5075 Franklin Cummings Sibert 5076 Archibald Vincent Arnold 5077 John Nicholas Smith 5078 William Gaulbert Weaver 5079 Stephen J. Chamberlin 5080 John Traylor McLane 5081 William Horace Hobson 5082 Walter Glenn Kilner 5083 George McClellan Chase 5084 Raymond Oscar Barton 5085 James Sylvester Mooney 5086 Houston Latimer Whiteside 5087 Henry William Harms 5088 John Earle Lewis 5089 Walton Harris Walker 5090 Millard Fillmore Harmon 5091 John Duncan Kelly 5092 Thorne Deuel 5093 Edward Chamberlin Rose 5094 Albert Eger Brown 5095 William Nalle 5096 Gustav Jacob Gonser 5097 Ralph Cadot Holliday 5098 Robert Emmet Patterson 5099 Adrian Weeks 5100 Carl Peterson Dick 5101 Charles Chisholm Drake 5102 George LeRoy Brown 5103 Earl Barlow Hochwalt 5104 William Joseph Morrissey 5105 Robert Theodore Snow 5106 Henry Charles McLean 5107 Joseph Edmund McDonald 5108 Frank Victor Schneider 5109 Frank Joseph Riley 5110 Benjamin Franklin Delamater 5111 Theodore Wilis Martin 5112 **1913** Francis Kosier Newcomer 5113 Charles Francis Williams 5114 Gordon Russell Young 5115 Richard Ulysses Nicholas 5116 Lewis King Underhill 5117 Myron Bertman 5118 Leo Jerome Dillow 5119 James Archer Dorst 5120 Rufus Willard Putnam 5121 Lunsford Errett Oliver 5122 Demetrio Castillo 5123 William Chalmers Young 5124 William Carey Crane 5125 William Bleecker Rosevear 5126 Carlos Brewer 5127 David Edward Cain 5128 John Eugene McMahon 5129 Francis Augustus Englehart 5130 Allen G. Thurman 5131 William Ashley Copthorne 5132 George Wessely Sliney 5133 Selby Harney Frank 5134 Eugene Tritle Spencer 5135 Willis Dale Crittenberger 5136 Robert Heber Van Volkenburgh 5137 Alfred Bainbridge Johnson 5138 Falkner Heard 5139 Roland Louis Gaugler 5140 Samuel John Heidner 5141 Junius Wallace Jones 5142 Stuart Warren Cramer 5143 Harold Smith Martin 5144 Thoburn Kaye Brown 5145 Manning Marius Kimmel 5146 John Huff Van Vliet 5147 Leland Swarts Devore 5148 Silas Miram Ratzkoff 5149 Geoffrey Keyes 5150 Frederick John Gerstner 5151 Charles Addison Ross 5152 Douglass Taft Greene 5153 Vern Scott Purnell 5154 Clarence Earl Bradburn 5155 Joseph Wadsworth Viner 5156 Robert Meredith Perkins 5157 Lawrence Babbitt Weeks 5158 Clarence Hagbart Danielson 5159 James Nixon Peale 5160 John Arthur Considine 5161 David Beauregard Falk 5162 William Cooper Foote 5163 Francis Reuel Fuller 5164 Clinton Warden Russell 5165 William Richard Schmidt 5166 Earl Lindsey Canady 5167 Louis Aleck Craig 5168 George Lester Hardin 5169 George Edward Lovell 5170 Otis Keilholtz Sadtler 5171 William Henry Jones 5172 John Erskine Ardrey 5173 Desmore Otts Nelson 5174 Carlyle Hilton Wash 5175 Henry Pratt Perrine 5176 Dennis Edward McCunniff 5177 Henry Balding Lewis 5178 Henry Barlow Cheadle 5179 Wyndham Meredith Manning 5180 Stewart Shepherd Giffin 5181 Samuel Alexander Gibson 5182 Paul Woolever Newgarden 5183 Harley Bowman Bullock 5184 Charles Andrew King 5185 Dana Palmer 5186 Alexander McCarrell Patch 5187 Charles Bishop Lyman 5188 Robert Lily Spragins 5189 George Washington Krapf 5190 Ward Elverson Duvall 5191 James Brown Gillespie 5192 Charles Harrison Corlett 5193 Charles Lawrence Kilburn 5194 Hans Robert Wheat Herwig 5195 Redondo Benjamin Sutton 5196 Howard Calhoun Davidson 5197 William Lynn Roberts 5198 William Alexander McCulloch 5199 Paul Duke Carlisle 5200 Bernard Peter Lamb 5201 William Augustus Rafferty 5202 Lathe B. Row 5203 John Flowers Crutcher 5204 Francis Joseph Toohey 5205 **1914** William Henry Holcombe 5206 James Bell Cress 5207 Charles Philip Gross 5208 Bernard August Miller 5209 Peter Cleary Bullard 5210 Brehon Burke Somervell 5211 Xenophon Herbert Price 5212 Robert Walter Crawford 5213 Frederick Snowden Skinner 5214 Dabney Otey Elliott 5215 Allen Parker Cowgill 5216 George Fenn Lewis 5217 Harrison Brand 5218 Frederick William Herman 5219 John Hill Carruth 5220 Philip Loomis Thurber 5221 William Chester Houghton 5222 John Churchill Wyeth 5223 Arthur Ringland Harris 5224 Lester Earl Moreton 5225 Roy Melvin Smyth 5226 La Rhett Livingston Stuart 5227 Alfred Earl Larabee 5228 John Adams Brooks 5229 Cleveland Hill Bandholtz 5230 John Green Burr 5231 Albion Ray Rockwood 5232 Frank Lawrence Hoskins 5233 Arthur Dow Newman 5234 John Hamilton Jouett 5235 John William Butts 5236 John Benjamin Anderson 5237 Cedric Watterson Lewis 5238 Fritz Philip Lindh 5239 Joseph De Moss McCain 5240 Harry Clyde Ingles 5241 James Lester Bradley 5242 Willis James Tack 5243 Edward Leuffer Nevin Glass 5244 Charles Watson Foster 5245 William Edward Burr 5246 Eugene Villaret 5247 Cuyler Llewellyn Clark 5248 Reiff Hesser Hannum 5249 Clarence Corinth Benson 5250 Thomas Henry Rees 5251 Floyd Randall Waltz 5252 John Henry Woodberry 5253 Carl Eugene Fosnes 5254 Harold Francis Loomis 5255 Leland Harold Stanford 5256 Walter Woolf Wynne 5257 James Cooper Waddell 5258 Weldon Williamson Doe 5259 William Abbot Robertson 5260 Richard Bolles Paddock 5261 Carl Spaatz 5262 Harold Roe Bull 5263 Charles Carleton Griffith 5264 James Byron Haskell 5265 Charles Morton Milliken 5266 James Fred Byrom 5267 Joseph Bradford Treat 5268 Woodfin Grady Jones 5269 Joseph Wilson Byron 5270 James Patrick Hogan 5271 Paul Clarence Paschal 5272 John Leo Parkinson 5273 Warren Philip Jernigan 5274 Rudolph Gwinn Whitten 5275 Louis Thomas Byrne 5276 Gooding Packard 5277 Glenn Preston Anderson 5278 Walter Cyrus Gullion 5279 Francis Rusher Kerr 5280 Francis Marion Brannan 5281 Vicente Lim 5282 Adam Empie Potts 5283 William Rutledge Orton 5284 Francis Henry Forbes 5285 Rufus Sumter Bratton 5286 Thomas George Lanphier 5287 Sylvester De Witt Downs 5288 Robert Dyer McDonald 5289 Jefferson Reese Davenport 5290 Orlando Ward 5291 John Prince Markoe 5292 Benjamin G. Weir 5293 Ralph Royce 5294 William Ord Ryan 5295 Harry Milford Brown 5296 Thomas H. Monroe 5297 Roger Burnett Harrison 5298 Joseph Webster Allison 5299 Benjamin F. Hoge 5300 Frederick Herr 5301 Clifford James Mathews 5302 Howard Prescott Milligan 5303 Frank William Milburn 5304 John Warren Weissheimer 5305 Isaac Gill 5306 John Kennard 5307 John Bellinger Thompson 5308 Hamner Huston 5309 Jens Anderson Doe 5310 Sheldon Harley Wheeler 5311 Lester Leland Lampert 5312 **1915** William Edward Raab Covell 5313 Edwin Richardson Kimble 5314 Joseph Dogan Arthur 5315 Ernest Frederick Miller 5316 John Stewart Bragdon 5317 George Jacob Richards 5318 Alexander Pennington Cronkhite 5319 John Scott Smylie 5320 Lehman Wellington Miller 5321 Douglas Lafayette Weart 5322 Earl Ewart Gesler 5323 Edwin Alexander Bethel 5324 John French Conklin 5325 Alfred Laing Ganahl 5326 John E. Harris 5327 William Frazer Tompkins 5328 Douglas Hamilton Gillette 5329 Paul Alfred Hodgson 5330 Donald Angus Davison 5331 Henry Spiese Aurand 5332 Thomas Bernard Larkin 5333 Edwin Coit Kelton 5334 James Allen Lester 5335 Mason James Young 5336 Layson Enslow Atkins 5337 Herman Beukema 5338 Herbert S. Struble 5339 Francis Joseph Dunigan 5340 Edwin A. Zundel 5341 Clinton Wilbur Howard 5342 Charles Manly Busbee 5343 Albert Whitney Waldron 5344 Parley Doney Parkinson 5345 John Hobert Wallace 5346 Raymond Marsh 5347 Harold Eugene Small 5348 Henry Benton Sayler 5349 Joseph May Swing 5350 Charles Wolcott Ryder 5351 Stafford Le Roy Irwin 5352 Joseph Taggart McNarney 5353 Pearson Menoher 5354 Albert Henry Warren 5355 Omar Nelson Bradley 5356 Paul John Mueller 5357 Leland Stanford Hobbs 5358 John Frederick Kahle 5359 Edwin Bowman Lyon 5360 Reinold Melberg 5361 Clarence Brewster Lindner 5362 John Henry Cochran 5363 Logan Wellington Series 5364 Carl Conrad Bank 5365 Charles Calvert Benedict 5366 Vernon Evans 5367 Roscoe Barnett Woodruff 5368 John Kimberly Meneely 5369 Joseph Jesse Teter 5370 John Storrie MacTaggart 5371 Lewis Clarke Davidson 5372 Dwight David Eisenhower 5373 Harold William James 5374 Hume Peabody 5375 Martin John O'Brien 5376 Joseph Cumming Haw 5377 James Basevi Ord 5378 John Ellis Rossell 5379 Earl Larue Naiden 5380 Henry McElderry Pendleton 5381 Whitten Jasper East 5382 Iverson Brooks Summers 5383 Edmund De Treville Ellis 5384 Robert William Strong 5385 Clifford Randall Jones 5386 John Beugnot Wogan 5387 Sidney Carroll Graves 5388 Clesen Henry Tenney 5389 Jo Hunt Reaney 5390 Clifford Barrington King 5391 Paul Russell Frank 5392 Frank Edwin Emery 5393 Edward Caswell Wallington 5394 Carl Ernest Hocker 5395 John William Leonard 5396 William Sumner Teall Halcomb 5397 Richmond Trumbull Gibson 5398 John Aloysius McDermott 5399 Edward Campbell McGuire 5400 Clyde Raymond Eisenschmidt 5401 Edward Bolton Hyde 5402 John McDonald Thompson 5403 James Alward Van Fleet 5404 Louis Alfred Merillat 5405 Edward Gill Sherburne 5406 Walter Wood Hess 5407 Michael Frank Davis 5408 Luis Raul Esteves 5409 Thomas Joseph Brady 5410 John Fuller Davis 5411 Stuart Clarence MacDonald 5412 Herbert Robison Corbin 5413 Metcalfe Reed 5414 Hubert Reilly Harmon 5415 Benjamin Greeley Ferris 5416 Charles Samuel Ritchel 5417 Thomas Guerdon Hearn 5418 Donald Henley 5419 Joseph Daly Coughlan 5420 Reese Maughan Howell 5421 Henry Jervis Friese Miller 5422 Harry Aloysius Harvey 5423 Alfred Schrieber Balsam 5424 Frank D. McGee 5425 Harry Benson Anderson 5426 Norman Jay Boots 5427 George Pulsifer 5428 Otto Al Busch Hooper 5429 Howard Donnelly 5430 Anastacio Quevedo Ver 5431 John Nicholas Robinson 5432 Hugh P. Avent 5433 Victor Vaughan Taylor 5434 Tom Fox 5435 Thomas James Hanley 5436 Jacob John Gerhardt 5437 Horace Stringfellow 5438 Stanley McNabb 5439 Leo Andrew Walton 5440 Ralph Pittman Cousins 5441 Charles Hosmer Chapin 5442 William Putnam Cherrington 5443 John Franklin Stevens 5444 Charles Robert Finley 5445 Vernon Edwin Prichard 5446 Blackburn Hall 5447 Robert Bishop Lorch 5448 Adlai Howard Gilkeson 5449 Gilbert Smith Brownell 5450 Richard Carlton Stickney 5451 Philip

Kitchings McNair 5452 Edward James Dwan 5453 Jesse Beeson Hunt 5454 John Benjamin Duckstad 5455 John Ross Mendenhall 5456 Norman Randolph 5457 Joseph Monroe Murphy 5458 George Edward Stratemeyer 5459 Eustis Lloyd Hubbard 5460 William Berkeley Peebles 5461 Frederic William Boye 5462 Leroy Hugh Watson 5463 Karl Hartman Gorman 5464 Henry Harold Dabney 5465 John Hamilton Chew Williams 5466 Melchior McEwen Eberts 5467 Oscar Andruss Straub 5468 Earl Marvin Price 5469 Arthur Arnim White 5470 John Keliher 5471 Benjamin Willis Mills 5472 Thomas Fenton Taylor 5473 Marshall Henry Quesenberry 5474 Robert Livingston Williams 5475 Charles Curtis Herrick 5476 **1916** John Howard Wills 5477 Raymond George Moses 5478 Wilhelm Delp Styer 5479 John Francis Woodman Fraser 5480 Charles Holmes Cunningham 5481 Dwight Frederick Johns 5482 William Arthur Snow 5483 Thomas Dewees Finley 5484 William Hamilton Britton 5485 Elroy Sandy Jackson Irvine 5486 Stanley Eric Reinhart 5487 Notley Young DuHamel 5488 William Henry Henderson 5489 Rovert George Guyer 5490 Dean Hudnutt 5491 Louis Emerson Hibbs 5492 Edward Clark Smith 5493 Jesse Frank Tarpley 5494 Robert Allen Sharrer 5495 Ludson Dixon Worsham 5496 Edward Goring Bliss 5497 Horace Logan McBride 5498 Ralph Gillett Barrows 5499 Holland Luley Robb 5500 Hamilton Ewing Maguire 5501 Ray Corrigan Rutherford 5502 Frederick Walter Bonfils 5503 Robert Reese Neyland 5504 William Morris Hoge 5505 William R. Woodward 5506 Stanley Lonzo Scott 5507 Tattnall D. Simkins 5508 Albert William Draves 5509 Alfred King King 5510 H. Crampton Jones 5511 Latham Loomis Brundred 5512 Leslie Thomas Saul 5513 Benjamin Sloan Beverly 5514 Frederick James Williams 5515 Carl Lee Marriot 5516 James Arthur Pickering 5517 James Knox Cockrell 5518 Charles Augustus Bayler 5519 Hugh Allen Ramsey 5520 William Spence 5521 John White Rafferty 5522 Willis McDonald Chapin 5523 Fred Beeler Inglis 5524 Robert Bruce McBride 5525 Paul Vincent Kane 5526 DeRosey Carroll Cabell 5527 Richard Parker Kuhn 5528 Ralph Irvine Sasse 5529 William Ewen Shipp 5530 Carl Smith Doney 5531 William Hieatt Cureton 5532 Fay Brink Prickett 5533 Calvin DeWitt 5534 James Mitchell Crane 5535 Lucien Samuel Spicer Berry 5536 John Alexander Street 5537 Victor William Beck Wales 5538 Sidney Herkness 5539 William Earl Chambers 5540 Joseph Merit Tully 5541 James deBarth Walbach 5542 Warner William Carr 5543 Pettus Harvey Hemphill 5544 High Mitchell 5545 Robert LeGrow Walsh 5546 Richard Mar Levy 5547 Thomas Lyle Martin 5548 Geoffrey Prescott Baldwin 5549 John Bennington Bennet 5550 Weir Riche 5551 Clarence Scott Maulsby 5552 Kenneth Macomb Halpine 5553 George Sidney Andrew 5554 Roland P. Shugg 5555 William Rosser Wilson 5556 Rafael Larrosa Garcia 5557 Ellicott Hewes Freeland 5558 Raymond Potter Campbell 5559 Spencer Albert Townsend 5560 Richard C. Birmingham 5561 Felix Rosseter McLean 5562 Craigie Krayenbuhl 5563 John Edward Martin 5564 Paul Barrows Parker 5565 Arthur Marion Jones 5566 William Edgerton Morehouse 5567 James Cornelius Ruddell 5568 Thomas Green Peyton 5569 Joseph Hamilton Grant 5570 Joseph James O'Hare 5571 Arthur Monroe Ellis 5572 Maurice Levi Miller 5573 Junius Henry Houghton 5574 Abram Vorhees Rinearson 5575 Benjamin Anthony Yancey 5576 William G. Patterson 5577 Douglas Jenkins Page 5578 James Nephew Caperton 5579 Charles Compton Smith 5580 Harrison Herman 5581 Frank Clark Scofield 5582 George Joseph Newgarden 5583 John David Miley 5584 William Edwin Coffin 5585 John Forest Goodman 5586 Ferdinand Francis Gallagher 5587 Barrington Lockart Flanigen 5588 Spencer Atkins Merrell 5589 William Worth Dempsey 5590 Robert Kenneth Whitson 5591 Otto Frederick Lange 5592 Harlan Leslie Mumma 5593 George Hollenbeck Blankenship 5594 Alexander Mathias Weyand 5595 Walter David Mangan 5596 Robert Rau Duncon McCullough 5597 Elon Albert Abernethy 5598 Nelson Bateman Russell 5599 Henry Parker Blanks 5600 Bartlett James 5601 **1917** Harris Jones 5602 Francis L. Palmer 5603 William F. Heavey 5604 Harold Roger Richards 5605 Robert Marks Bathurst 5606 John Jefferson Flowers Steiner 5607 Daniel Noce 5608 Willis Edward Teale 5609 William Harrison Saunders 5610 Clark Kittrell 5611 Samuel Rairigh Irwin 5612 Charles Everett Hurdis 5613 Henry Hutchings 5614 Henry John Schroeder 5615 James Kivas Tully 5616 John Matthew Devine 5617 Harold Albert Nisley 5618 Fenton Harrison McGlachlin 5619 Francis Eugene Dougherty 5620 James Louis Guion 5621 George Douglas Wahl 5622 Basil Harrison Perry 5623 Harold Rufus Jackson 5624 Lyman Lewis Parks 5625 Ray Hartwell Lewis 5626 Solomon Foote Clark 5627 Augustus Milton Gurney 5628 John Trott Murray 5629 Morris Keene Barroll 5630 Warfield Monroe Lewis 5631 Walter Wilton Warner 5632 Oliver Byron Cardwell 5633 William Osmond Butler 5634 Rex Webb Beasley 5635 J. Lawton Collins 5636 Walter Francis Vander Hyden 5637 James Oscar Green 5638 Daves Rossell 5639 Ira Adam Crump 5640 Elbert Louis Ford 5641 Samuel Jinkston Bradbury 5642 Ray Harrison 5643 William Foster Daugherty 5644 Harold McClave White 5645 James Lord Hayden 5646 Scott Brewer Ritchie 5647 John Tupper Cole 5648 George Sampson Beurket 5649 Stephen Huntting Sherrill 5650 Charles Hunter Gerhardt 5651 Lincoln F. Daniels 5652 Walter Herman Schulze 5653 Frederick Augustus Irving 5654 Burnett Ralph Olmsted 5655 Herbert Charles Holdridge 5656 Matthew Bunker Ridgway 5657 Albert Cowper Smith 5658 Nicholas Winn Lisle 5659 Richard Mars Wightman 5660 Percy Gamble Black 5661 Charles Walter Yuill 5662 William Willis Eagles 5663 Francis Anthony Markoe 5664 Louis Salvosa y Rada 5665 Joel Grant Holmes 5666 Albert Charles Stanford 5667 James Arthur Code 5668 John James McEwan 5669 Laurence Bascum Meacham 5670 William Sackville 5671 Louis Leroy Martin 5672 John Allen Stewart 5673 William Kelly Harrison 5674 Leroy Henry Lohmann 5675 Josiah Furman Morford 5676 Ernest Nason Harmon 5677 George Wilbur Sackett 5678 Francis Graves Bonham 5679 Norman Daniel Cota 5680 Christian Gingrich Foltz 5681 Joseph Scranton Tate 5682 Robert Bundy Ransom 5683 Arthur McKinley Harper 5684 Carleton Coulter 5685 Aaron Bradshaw 5686 James Henly Frier 5687 John Wesley Confer 5688 Herbert Norman Schwarzkopf 5689 Leo James Erler 5690 Robert Newton Kunz 5691 Robert Denis Newton 5692 Charles Solomon Kiburn 5693 Willis Richardson Slaughter 5694 George Hatton Weems 5695 Roy Lindsay Bowlin 5696 Charles Radcliffe Johnson 5697 William Claude McMahon 5698 William Warwick Cowgill 5699 Bertrand Morrow 5700 Bates Compton 5701 Harry Russell Pierce 5702 Francis Michael Brennan 5703 Lawrence Collamore Mitchell 5704 Milton B. Halsey 5705 Charles Love Mullins 5706 Thomas Simons Sinkler 5707 George Francis Wooley 5708 Sterling Alexander Wood 5709 William F. Redfield 5710 Mark Wayne Clark 5711 Stewart Whiting Hoover 5712 Alexander Hunkins Campbell 5713 David Sheridan Rumbough 5714 Francis John Heraty 5715 Marvil Groves Armstrong 5716 Donovan Swanton 5717 Francis Atherton Macon 5718 Laurence Bolton Keiser 5719 Homer Caffee Brown 5720 Clare Hibbs Armstrong 5721 Harris Marcy Melasky 5722 Sidney Hooper Young 5723 John Clement Whitcomb 5724 Wallace James Redner 5725 Charles David Lewis 5726 Edward William Leonard 5727 Paul Hancock Brown 5728 William Stuart Eley 5729 Paul Winters York 5730 Ferdinand Gustav Von Kummer 5731 Joseph Pescia Sullivan 5732 Henry Henley Chapman 5733 Asa Parmele Pope 5734 Edwin Howard Clark 5735 Lewis Perrine 5736 Clarke Kent Fales 5737 John Addison Weishampel 5738 Malcolm Boord Helm 5739 John Richard Nygaard 5740 Herman Henry Pohl 5741 Gerald Alford Counts 5742 Hiram B. Ely 5743 Kenneth Mason Moore 5744 Charles Dashiel Harris 5745 Edmond Harrison Leavey 5746 Thomas Dodson Stamps 5747 Bartley Marcus Harloe 5748 Thurston Elmer Wood 5749 Starr Clifton Wardrop 5750 Dean Ingersoll Piper 5751 Girard B. Troland 5752 Llewellyn B. Griffith 5753 John Michael Johnson 5754 Joseph Isadore Cohen 5755 William O. Reeder 5756 William Karl Kolb 5757 William R. Gerhardt 5758 Otto Max Jank 5759 Theodore Earl Buechler 5760 Herman Uth Wagner 5761 Frederick Edwin Tibbetts 5762 Samuel Durand Ringsdorf 5763 Redmond Francis Kernan 5764 Philip Stevens Day 5765 Theodore Leslie Futch 5766 Russell Luff Meredith 5767 William Innes Wilson 5768 Harold Allum Cooney 5769 John Thornton Knight 5770 Henry Anson Barber 5771 Miles Andrew Cowles 5772 Lawrence McCeney Jones 5773 Gordon Graham Heiner 5774 George Walter Hirsch 5775 Forrest Clifford Shaffer 5776 Edward Joseph Wolff 5777 William Riley Deeble 5778 Frank Fenton Reed 5779 John Will Coffey 5780 Frank Celestine Meade 5781 Lawrence Dwight 5782 Everett T. Brown 5783 Grayson Cooper Woodbury 5784 Robert Alston Willard 5785 Clyde Hobart Morgan 5786 Willard Merrill Hall 5787 Tracy Campbell Dickson 5788 Robert Wilson Hasbrouck 5789 Howard Patterson Faust 5790 John Taylor deCamp 5791 Wallace Duncan Collins 5792 Sargent Prentiss Huff 5793 William Henry Donaldson 5794 Duncan Gregor McGregor 5795 Thomas Jackson Heavey 5796 Henry Maris Black 5797 Wallace Francis Safford 5798 Willard David Murphy 5799 Council Bryan Palmer 5800 John Claron Hawkins 5801 Joshua Ashley Stansell 5802 John Marcus Erwin 5803 Fidel Ventura Segundo 5804 Raymond E. S. Williamson 5805 David Charles George Schlenker 5806 Harry Tremaine Wood 5807 Earl Frank Knoob 5808 Robert Earl Symmonds 5809 John Richard Wilmot Diehl 5810 Rudolph Daniel Delehanty 5811 William Beggs Carswell 5812 William Henry Whiting Reinburg 5813 Elmer Hugo Almquist 5814 Frank Leslie Carr 5815 Frank Edmund Bertholet 5816 Marion Carson 5817 Wilson Gunning Bingham 5818 Charles Cope Bartley 5819 Rossiter Hunt Garity 5820 Salvador Formoso Reyes 5821 Frank Charles Jedlicka 5822 Robert MacDonald Graham 5823 Leo Buffington Conner 5824 John Boersig Saunders 5825 Arthur Burnola Custis 5826 Rudolph Francis Whitelegg 5827 Loyd Van Horne Durfee 5828 John Henry Norton 5829 William Winchester Paca 5830 Desmond O'Keefe 5831 Hal Marney Rose 5832 Frederick John Durrschmidt 5833 John Ter Bush Bissell 5834 Milton Wickers Davis 5835 John Bellinger Bellinger 5836 Charles Aloysius Mahoney 5837 George Senseny Eyster 5838 Henry Richard Anderson 5839 William McCaskey Chapman 5840 Kenneth Paul Murray 5841 Roger Walton Stembridge 5842 Norman McNeill 5843 Glen Henry Anderson 5844 Bryant Edward Moore 5845 Leo Vincent Warner 5846 Alston Deas 5847 Henry William Bobrink 5848 Onslow Sherburne Rolfe 5849 Louis Armistead Freeman 5850 Henry Perkins Gantt 5851 Jesse Brooke Matlack 5852 Julius Earl Schaefer 5853 Theodore Desmond Schmidt 5854 Parry Weaver Lewis 5855 Edward Wrenne Timberlake 5856 Vincent Nicholas Taylor 5857 William Wallace Jenna 5858 William Richard Fleming 5859 Paul Wallace Cole 5860 Francis Porter Simpson 5861 Harry Cooper Barnes 5862 Robert John Hoffman 5863 Clare Wallace Woodward 5864 John Stevenson Mallory 5865 Frederick Dent Sharp 5866 William Sydney Barrett 5867 Paul Ryan Goode 5868 Harry Niles Rising 5869 Josephus Benjamin Wilson 5870 Henry C. Demuth 5871 Lowell Meeker Riley 5872 Edwin Clark Maling 5873 George Draper Watts 5874 Emil Krause 5875 Robert Lynn Bacon 5876 Walker Gibson White 5877 Earle Everett Sarcka 5878 Edwin Jacob House 5879 Arthur Charles Purvis 5880 James Jackson Hea 5881 Edgar Bruce Moomau 5882 Frank Sidney Long 5883 Carlisle Brittania Wilson 5884 William Edward Whittington 5885 Harold Lewis Milan 5886 Robert Amedee Bringham 5887 Horace Harding 5888 Earle Adams Billings 5889 Royal Harry Place 5890 John Thomas Bell 5891 **1918** John Paul Dean 5892 Patrick Henry Timothy 5893 Hugh John Casey 5894 Robert Earle Hamilton 5895 Patrick Henry Tansey 5896 Hans Kramer 5897 Albert Gordon Mathews 5898 Amos Blanchard Shattuck 5899 Leland Hazelton Hewitt 5900 Michael Charles Grenata 5901JUN Preston W. Smith 5902 Ken Wang 5903 Thomas Francis Kern 5904 Ralph Edward Cruse 5905 Lewis Tenney Ross 5906 Roland Stenzel 5907 Charles Francis Baish 5908 Clarence Lionel Adcock 5909 Keryn Ap Rice 5910 Charles Stuart Ward 5911 Henry Morehead Underwood 5912 James Bryan Newman 5913 James Marshall Young 5914 James Creel Marshall 5915 Walter Ernest Lorence 5916 Meyer Loshie Casman 5917 Lucius Du Bignon Clay 5918 Lloyd Ernst Mielenz 5919 Pierre Alexander Agnew 5920 Alexander Murray Neilson 5921 Hoel Smith Bishop 5922 Charles Emmett McKee 5923 Robert Habersham Elliott 5924 Samuel Davis Sturgis 5925 Thomas Hay Nixon 5926 Anderson Thomas William Moore 5927 Reginald Whitaker 5928 Eugene Mead Caffey 5929 Roland Mac Gray 5930 Julius Joseph Mussil 5931 Robert Johnson Horr 5932 Charles Ellicott Hoffman 5933 Henry Milton Alexander 5934 James Milligan Gillespie 5935 John Loughlin Grant 5936 Hugh Ambrose Murrill 5937 Milo Benson Barragan 5938 Oscar Alfred Axelson 5939 Paul Ludwig Deylitz 5940 Paul Bernard Malone 5941 Leo Myron Kreber 5942 Ernest William Gruhn 5943 Edwin Luther Sibert 5944 George Bicker Aigeltinger 5945 Edwin Hunter Crouch 5946 William Crosby Coogan 5947 Joseph S. Robinson 5948 James Faulkner Pichel 5949 O'Ferrall Knight 5950 Roy Douglas Paterson 5951 John Haleston 5952 Charles Clifton Blanchard 5953 Clyde Beauchamp Bell 5954 John Lawrence Hanley 5955 Paul Eleanor Hurt 5956 Henry Winston Holt 5957 John Magruder Bethel 5958 Clarence Page Townsley 5959 Robert Hilton Offley 5960 John Paul Zachman 5961 James Hubert Roemer 5962 John Mesick 5963 Albert Edwin Marks 5964 Elton Thomas Cobb 5965 Francis Parker Tompkins 5966 John Arthur Weeks 5967 Frederick William Gerhard 5968 Edward Alvin Grupe 5969 Cornelius Comegys Jadwin 5970 Donald Coray 5971 Jacob Gunn Sucher 5972 Howard Harvey Newman 5973 Francisco Cintron 5974 Richard Gray McKee 5975 William F. H. Godson 5976 Ernest Lenwood Stephens 5977 Nevins Dorsey Young 5978 William Lillard Barriger 5979 Julian Lamar 5980 Frederick Williams Fenn 5981 Elmer Quillen Oliphant 5982 Joseph Charles Kovarik 5983 Benjamin Franklin Manning 5984 Paul William George 5985 Jonathan Lane Holman 5986 Wynot Rush Irish 5987 Francis Earle Rundell 5988 Royal Adam Machle 5989 Leonard Randall Nachman 5990 Clark Hazen Mitchell 5991 William Maynadier Miley 5992 George Baird Hudson 5993 Duncan Hodges 5994 Edmund Bellinger Bellinger 5995 Wayne Wallace Wells 5996 Harry Clay Mewshaw 5997 Alfred Armstrong McNamee 5998 Joseph Perry Catte 5999 Francis Joseph Achatz 6000 Harold Strong Kelley 6001 Leon C. Boineau 6002 Harold Wilbert Gould 6003 Maxwell Michaux Corpening 6004 Howard Parrill Richardson 6005 George Bittman Barth 6006 Peter Lee Atherton Dye 6007 Harry Benham Sherman 6008 Frank Thorpe Turner 6009 Albert Francis Ward 6010 John Templeton Newland 6011 Carroll Tye 6012 Benjamin Ransom McBride 6013 Thomas Quinton Donaldson 6014 Philip Edward Gallagher 6015 Carroll Kimball Leeper 6016 Edward Nathaniel Jones 6017 Herbert Benjamin Williams 6018 Harold Berkeley Lewis 6019 Charlie Quillian Lifsey 6020 Hugh McCalla Wilson 6021 Dwight Terry Francis 6022 William Nimmons Davis 6023 Dorr Hazlehurst 6024 Robert Trueheart Foster 6025 Robert Edwin Bagby 6026 Edwin Davis Dando 6027 Frederick von Harten Kimble 6028 David Wood Griffiths 6029 Bernard Skinner Stearns 6030 Arthur William Pence 6031 Leslie Richard Groves 6032 Henry Gray Lodge 6033 Lemuel Pope 6034 James Logan Rhoads 6035 Frederic Bates Butler 6036 Leverett Griggs Yoder 6037 Harry Alexander Montgomery 6038 Wilson Gordon Saville 6039 Mark Mayo Boatner 6040 David Ayres Depue Ogden 6041 Fredrick Adolph Platte 6042 Karl Browne Schilling 6043 John Hawkins Elleman 6044 Elmer Ellsworth Barnes 6045 William Wesley Wanamaker 6046NOV Beverly Carradine Snow 6047 Richard Lee 6048 Howard Louis Peckham 6049 John Southworth Niles 6050 Charles Richard Bathurst 6051 Wendell Phillips Trower 6052 Robert Gilbert Lovett 6053 Cornman Louis Hahn 6054 Edwin Potter Lock 6055 George Brooke McReynolds 6056 Morris Williams Gilland 6057 David Terrill Johnson 6058 Edwin Gunsolus Shrader 6059 Randolph Piersol Williams 6060 Otto Praeger 6061 Allison Miller 6062 Newell Lyon Hemenway 6063 Archie Trescott Colwell 6064 Frederick Atherton Stevens 6065 Arthur Joseph Sheridan 6066 James George Christiansen 6067 Benjamin Franklin Chadwick 6068 Charles Dickson Jewell 6069 Heath Twichell 6070 Joseph Jones Twitty 6071 Harrison Shaler 6072 Edmund Wilson Searby 6073 Roger Mannng Wicks 6074 Benjamin Abbott Dickson 6075 Robert Everett York 6076 Chester Krum Harding 6077 William Victor Hesp 6078 Hugh Archer Palmer 6079 William Clarence Bennett 6080 Claude Henry Chorpening 6081 George Vernon Keyser 6082 Frank Otto Bowman 6083 James Postell Jervey 6084 Joseph Shirley Gorlinski 6085 George Sackett Witters 6086 Albert Riani 6087 Orville Ernest Walsh 6088 Drexler Dana 6089 Peter Paul Goerz 6090 Robert Blake Coolidge 6091 John Peter Dietrich 6092 William Aylett Callaway 6093 Howard Voorheis Canan 6094 Vere Alfred Beers 6095 Homer William Blair 6096 Doswell Gullatt 6097 John Bell Hughes 6098 Lawrence Bradford Bixby 6099 Eugene Luther Vidal 6100 Harry Crawford 6101 William Washington Webster 6102 John Hamilton Hinds 6103 John Marks Moore 6104 George Gage Eddy 6105 Charles Edward Morrison 6106 Eugene Germanus Miller 6107 William Powell Blair 6108 William James Epes 6109 John Hinton 6110 Joseph Coolidge Kilbourne 6111 Eric Spencer Molitor 6112 Brooks Scott 6113 Charles Mason Wells 6114 Richard August Ericson 6115 Richard Brobst Madigan 6116 James Vincent Carroll 6117 Arthur Emil Mickelsen 6118 Paul Boyle Kelly 6119 Leon Harold Dunn 6120 William Henry Barlow 6121 Ernest Calhoun Norman 6122 Christian Knudsen 6123 William Bobbs Miller 6124 Charles Rolland Gildart 6125 Richard Carrick Babbitt 6126 Francis Bassett Valentine 6127 Wade Rushton Cothran 6128 Percival Bolling Banister 6129 Gerald Alexander O'Rouark 6130 Claude Desha Anderson 6131 James Clyde Styron 6132 Charles Edward Hixon 6133 Hammond McDougal Monroe 6134 Bryan Evans 6135 Bonner Frank Fellers 6136 Richard Ravenel Spring 6137 John William Middleton 6138 Melton Adams Hatch 6139 Kenneth Seymour Stice 6140 Francis Andrew March 6141 George Maurice Badger 6142 John Sheridan Winn 6143 Marion Van Voorst 6144 Edwin Boyd Fitzpatrick 6145 Clarence Arthur Rosendahl 6146 Dean Richard Dickey 6147 Roger Williams Autry 6148 Frank Johnstone Cunningham 6149 Myrl Milton Miller 6150 William Amberson Sexton 6151 Thomas Tipton Thornburgh 6152 Hobart Reed Yeager 6153 Alfred Nathan Bergman 6154 William Covington Benton 6155 Stuart Millikin Bevans 6156 John Hiram Lewis 6157 Gervais William Trichel 6158 Vincent John Conrad 6159 Thomas William Munford 6160 James Longstreet Whelchel 6161 David Adams Taylor 6162 Edward Ward Smith 6163 Ronald Austin Hicks 6164 John Hadley Fonvielle 6165 John Bartlett Sherman 6166 Elmer Vaughan Stansbury 6167 Joe David Moss 6168 Edwin Leslie Hogan 6169 John Creel Hamilton 6170 John Joseph Breen 6171 Mark Rhoads 6172 Edward Arthur Dolph 6173 Joseph Kittredge Baker 6174 Felix Max Usis 6175 James Arthur Kehoe 6176 Charles William Leng 6177 Edward Ward Hendrick 6178 Frederick Pearson 6179 Charles Frederick Colson 6180 De Witt Hicks 6181 Albert Walker Johnson 6182 Donald Frederic Carroll 6183 Bernard Wellington Slifer 6184 Willard Ames Holbrook 6185 Austin Monroe Wilson 6186 Samuel Powell Walker 6187 Robert Alwin Schow 6188 John Harrison Stokes 6189 Jesse Ellis Graham 6190 Fred Glover Sherrill 6191 Soloman Mark Lipman 6192 Jerome David Cambre 6193 William Howell Cocke 6194 Eustaquio S. Baclig 6195 Burrowes Goldthwaite Stevens 6196 Alexander Thomas McCone 6197 Thomas Markham Brinkley 6198 John Kennedy Buchanan 6199 William Theodore Powers 6200 Ivans LaRue Browne 6201 Kenneth Willey Leslie 6202 Beverley Saint George Tucker 6203 John Trites Brown 6204 James Coachman Cullens 6205 Reginald Worth Hubbell 6206 Lee Earl Gray 6207 Donald William Sawtelle 6208 Wesley Collins Dever 6209 John May Tatum 6210 Gerald Burnett O'Grady 6211 Paul Wilkins Kendall 6212 John Franklin Farley 6213 Charles Henry Moore 6214 James Wentworth Freeman 6215 Linson Edward Dzau 6216 Alexander John Mackenzie 6217 Wiley Vinton Carter 6218 Ira Platt Swift 6219 Wilbur Eugene Dunkelberg 6220 James Hicks Carney Hill 6221 Victor Crippen Broome 6222 Thomas Reynolds Denny 6223 Frank Mathews Corzelius 6224 Julius Lynch Piland 6225 Arthur Pulsifer 6226 Farrin Allen Hillard 6227 William Jesserel Mason 6228 Elliott Watkins 6229 Francis James Gillespie 6230 Jesse Lewis

Gibney 6231 Robert Hale Vesey 6232 Clarence Miles Mendenhall 6233 Kester Lovejoy Hastings 6234 George McKnight Williamson 6235 Howard Waite Brimmer 6236 Charles Milner Smith 6237 Albert Brownfield Goodin 6238 Walter Joseph Muller 6239 Harry Lovejoy Rogers 6240 George Bryan Conrad 6241 William Stephen Murray 6242 Harry Krieger 6243 Raymond Wainwright Odor 6244 James Clyde Welch 6245 Miner Welsh Bonwell 6246 John Perry Pence 6247 John Leo Binder 6248 Joseph Magoffin Glasgow 6249 Elmer Mike Jenkins 6250 James Lawrence Keasler 6251 Rutherford Dent McGiffert 6252 Richard Bryan Wheeler 6253 Thomas Roswell Aaron 6254 Charles Llewellyn Gorman 6255 **1919** Louis George Horowitz 6256 David Albert Newcomer 6257 Boyd Wheeler Bartlett 6258 Alfred Maximilian Gruenther 6259 Laurence Van Doren Harris 6260 Herbert Bernard Loper 6261 Ivan Crawford Lawrence 6262 Benjamin Mace Hedrick 6263 Williston Birkhimer Palmer 6264 Robert Gibbins Gard 6265 Robert Ammons Hill 6266 David Hom Whittier 6267 Sydney Ward Gould 6268 Herbert Maury Jones 6269 Fred William Marlow 6270 Orville Wells Martin 6271 William Joseph Regan 6272 Roy Green 6273 Forrest Eugene Cookson 6274 John Paul Kennedy 6275 Alexander Sharp Bennet 6276 Horace Miller Buck 6277 George Sheldon Price 6278 Carl Spencer Molitor 6279 Philip Stueler Lauben 6280 Wybum Dwight Brown 6281 Robert Miller Montague 6282 Charles Pollard Jones 6283 Anthony Clement McAuliffe 6284 Robert Leonard Johnson 6285 Lester Francis Rhodes 6286 Albert Rhett Stuart Barden 6287 Romeo Francis Regnier 6288 Don Gilmore Shingler 6289 Harlan Nelson Hartness 6290 Louis Brainard Ely 6291 Julius Easton Slack 6292 Bertram Francis Hayford 6293 Ernest Aaron Bixby 6294 Robert Rossiter Raymond 6295 Harris Fulford Scherer 6296 Donald Miller Davidson 6297 Ernest John Riley 6298 Clarence Emil Burgher 6299 Thomas Benoit Hedekin 6300 Joseph Vincil Phelps 6301 Charles Norton McFarland 6302 Charles Alvin Pyle 6303 Alexander Griswold Kirby 6304 John R. Hardin 6305 Herbert Weldon Semmelmeyer 6306 William Wilkeson Barton 6307 Maurice Place Chadwick 6308 Walter Ernest Bullock 6309 Foster Joseph Tate 6310 Carl Robinson 6311 Richard Tobin Bennison 6312 Henry John D Meyer 6313 Elton F. Hammond 6314 Ernest Marion Brannon 6315 Francis George McGill 6316 Rollin Franklin Risen 6317 Luther L. Hill 6318 Oscar Alan Saunders 6319 John Wyville Sheehy 6320 James Battle Rivers 6321 John J. Burns 6322 Leslie Edgar Jacoby 6323 John R. Vance 6324 Clarence John Kanaga 6325 Richard P. Ovenshine 6326 Edwin Virgil Kerr 6327 Thomas McGregor 6328 Harrison How'l Dodge Heiberg 6329 William Irvin Allen 6330 Paul Andrew Donnally 6331 James Edmund Parker 6332 William Wesson Jervey 6333 George Raymond Burgess 6334 Edward Lynde Strohbehn 6335 Maurice Keyes Kurtz 6336 William Holmes Wenstrom 6337 Paul Lewis Harter 6338 Leo Clement Paquet 6339 Thomas Maurice Crawford 6340 Eugene McGinley 6341 Hugh Brownrigg Waddell 6342 Lester De Long Flory 6343 Paul Robert Menzies Miller 6344 Isaac Haiden Ritchie 6345 Augustine Francis Shea 6346 Carlisle Visscher Allan 6347 Marion Patton Echols 6348 Roy Anthony Moore 6349 John Edward McCarthy 6350 Francis Otis Wood 6351 Hobart Hewett 6352 Richard Thomas Rick 6353 Waldemar S. Broberg 6354 James H. Phillips 6355 John Edwin Leahy 6356 George Washington Lewis 6357 Frederick W. Drury 6358 Leander Dunbar Syme 6359 Ellis Vern Williamson 6360 LeRoy Clark Wilson 6361 Nathaniel Alanson Burnell 6362 William Goebel Stephens 6363 John B. Murphy 6364 James Lowe Harbaugh 6365 Virgil Farrar Shaw 6366 Paul Alpheus Noel 6367 Michael Gibson Smith 6368 Syril Emerson Faine 6369 Arthur Maxon Parsons 6370 Harry Welling Barrick 6371 William Travis Van de Graff 6372 John Wheelwright Brownell 6373 Howard Rand Perry 6374 Edward Hamilton Young 6375 Nathan Arthur Smith 6376 Gerald St. Claire Mickle 6377 Benjamin Randolph Farrar 6378 Henry Ellis Sanderson 6379 Hugh French Thomason Hoffman 6380 Davis Stanley Holbrook 6381 Walter Scott Winn 6382 Willard Gordon Wyman 6383 John Leonard Whitelaw 6384 Edward Henry Bowes 6385 Edwin Malcolm Sutherland 6386 Joseph Andrew Holly 6387 Henry Baldwin Nichols 6388 William Douglas McNair 6389 Charles Forrest Wilson 6390 Robert Francis Carter 6391 Hugh Garnett Elliott 6392 Nathan Farragut Twining 6393 William John Crowe 6394 George Whitfield MacMillan 6395 L. Hoyt Rockafellow 6396 Percy Emery Hunt 6397 Douglas Olcott 6398 Roland William McNamee 6399 John Carpenter Raaen 6400 Lenithon Wheeler 6401 Winfred George Skelton 6402 Lambert Benel Cain 6403 Edmund Bower Sebre 6404 Ignatius Lawrence Donnelly 6405 Merritt B. Booth 6406 Raymond Clay Barlow 6407 Frank Green Davis 6408 Emmett James Bean 6409 Donald Allen Fay 6410 Charles Henry Noble 6411 Walter Towle O'Reilly 6412 Kenneth Pierce 6413 Charles Henry Bryan 6414 John Endler 6415 John Howell Collier 6416 Dean Luce 6417 Vincent Coyle McAlevy 6418 George Gordon Elms 6419 John Dimmick Armstrong 6420 Ralph Francis Stearley 6421 Donald Handley Nelson 6422 Edward Ora Hopkins 6423 John Victor Dominey 6424 James Verne Cole 6425 Horace Parker Sampson 6426 Ralph Bernard Kindley 6427 John Adam Bruckner 6428 Clarence Archibald Frank 6429 Frederick Bradstreet Dodge 6430 Clarkson Deweese McNary 6431 Bernard Albert Byrne 6432 Charles Ream Jackson 6433 George Lincoln Dillaway 6434 Warren Wilson Christian 6435 Dale Wilford Maher 6436 Robert Barett Hutchins 6437 Joseph William Kullman 6438 George Dewey Rogers 6439 Harold Edward Marsden 6440 Robert Jones Merrick 6441 William Henry Dunham 6442 Landon Garland Daniel 6443 Raymond Francis Kilroy 6444 Irvin Alexander 6445 John Harvey Madison 6446 George Edward Bruner 6447 Thomas Llewellyn Waters 6448 Urban Niblo 6449 Thomas Houston Dameron 6450 Roger Sherman Evarts 6451 Charles L. Williams 6452 Harry M. Rex 6453 Kenneth Sharp Olson 6454 William Leighton McEnery 6455 Robert Montgomery Springer 6456 Russell John Nelson 6457 Charles Maine Wolff 6458 Simon Foss 6459 Davis Ward Hale 6460 Edward Melvin Starr 6461 Joseph Sladen Bradley 6462 Arthur Launcelot Moore 6463 Robert William Crichlow 6464 Martin Anthony Fennell 6465 Ralph Harris Bassett 6466 Harold Allen Brown 6467 Albert S. Johnston Stovall 6468 Donald Carson Hardin 6469 Wayne C. Zimmerman 6470 John Thomas Keeley 6471 Albert Smith Rice 6472 James Wellington Boyd 6473 Joseph Conrad Odell 6474 Vincent Harold Kelly 6475 Josiah Toney Dalbey 6476 Logan Osburn Shutt 6477 Stuart Little 6478 Hilton Edward Heineke 6479 Galen Magnus Taylor 6480 John Francis Lavagino 6481 Royal Wheeler Park 6482 Daniel Philip Buckland 6483 Philip McIlvaine Whitney 6484 John Morris Works 6485 Christian Hildebrand 6486 Joseph Holleman Warren 6487 Edgar Mortimer Gregory 6488 John David Frederick 6489 Richard Ray Coursey 6490 William Ramsey Bready 6491 Joseph Charles Panzarella 6492 Dwight Lyman Adams 6493 John Charles Hyland 6494 Thomas Gordon Cranford 6495 Lester George Degnan 6496 Henry Bennett Sheets 6497 Archie William Cooey 6498 Edwin Robert Samsey 6499 William Robert McMaster 6500 Paul Revere Carl 6501 Cornelius Emmett O'Connor 6502 Joseph Alfred Cranston 6503 Maurice Ladin Rosenthal 6504 Willard Leslie Isaacs 6505 Horace Speed 6506 Fred William Makinney 6507 William Benjamin Kean 6508 Harold Robert Emery 6509 David Sanderson Mc Lean 6510 William Joseph Moroney 6511 Russell Lowell Williamson 6512 Charles Leslie Keerans 6513 Howard Adams White 6514 Howard Dohla Johnston 6515 Albert Carroll Morgan 6516 Franklin LeRoy Rash 6517 Robert Watson Child 6518 Edgar Harvey Snodgrass 6519 Claude Birket Ferenbaugh 6520 Adna Chaffe Hamilton 6521 Harold Stuart Ruth 6522 Sterling Eugene Whitesides 6523 Lewis Stone Sorley 6524 Albert Coady Wedemeyer 6525 David Best Latimer 6526 Ralph J. Miller 6527 Isaac W. Finley 6528 John Leighton Denny 6529 Roswell Boyle Hart 6530 Halvor Hegland Myrah 6531 Herbert J. Riess 6532 Martin Loeb 6533 Henry Ignatius Szymanski 6534 Ulric Lee Fomby 6535 Frederick Brenton Porter 6536 Bryan Sewall Halter 6537 Gordon Leslie Chapline 6538 Hughes Steele 6539 **1920** James Barlow Cullum 6540 Francis Hudson Oxx 6541 Thomas Henry Stanley 6542 Donald Greeley White 6543 Henry George Lambert 6544 William Weston Bessell 6545 Charles G. Holle 6546 Charles Sheafe Joslyn 6547 Arthur Martin Andrews 6548 Edward Crosby Harwood 6549 John W. Moreland 6550 Wayne Stewart Moore 6551 Henry F. Hannis 6552 Arthur Lee McCullough 6553 Arthur Vinton Linwood James 6554 Edward A. Routheau 6555 Theodore Temple Knappen 6556 Godfrey Douglas Adamson 6557 Wilson Burnett Higgins 6558 Albert Newell Tanner 6559 William Alter Watson 6560 Frederick Lord Hayden 6561 Warren Cressman Rutter 6562 Harold Frank Handy 6563 Richard Clare Partridge 6564 Edward John McGaw 6565 Willis Willis McDonald 6566 Harold T. Miller 6567 John C. Felli 6568 Volney Archer Poulson 6569 Tyree Rivers Horn 6570 William C. Coe 6571 James W. Clark 6572 Robert Henry Vic'ery Stackhouse 6573 Joseph L. Langevin 6574 Willard Pierce Larner 6575 William H. Hill 6576 Louis Jacob Claterbos 6577 Herbert Ralph Pierce 6578 Carl Victor Erickson 6579 Auguste Rhu Taylor 6580 James K. Mitchell 6581 Frank Andrew Henning 6582 Ewart Gladstone Plank 6583 James Malcolm Lewis 6584 Donald Eddy Cummings 6585 Bernard L. Robinson 6586 John Robert Culleton 6587 James Goodrich Renno 6588 Charles Steinhart Whitmore 6589 James Hobson Stratton 6590 Loper Bailey Lowry 6591 Lee A. Denson 6592 Lawrence Granger Smith 6593 Edward Haviland Lastayo 6594 Alexander R. MacMillan 6595 Roy Winne Barhydt 6596 George DeGraaf 6597 James Vincent Walsh 6598 Lathrop Ray Bullene 6599 Bertram Wright Randles 6600 James Alexander Samouce 6601 William W. Ford 6602 George Dewey Vanture 6603 Charles Barney Harding 6604 Pastor Martelino 6605 Harry Earl Fisher 6606 Donald Sylvester Burns 6607 Donald James Leehey 6608 Carl Edwin Berg 6609 Joseph Eugene Harriman 6610 Coleman Romain 6611 George Joseph Loupret 6612 William Squier Wood 6613 Thomas Arnett Roberts 6614 Verne Donald Mudge 6615 Morrison Page Chitterling 6616 John L. Goff 6617 Francis Henry Morse 6618 Edward Macon Edmonson 6619 Robert Barrett Donnelly 6620 Ben Miller Campbell 6621 William Gordon Holder 6622 Halstead Clotworthy Fowler 6623 Joseph R. Stauffer 6624 Lyman L. Lemnitzer 6625 Leslie Burgess Downing 6626 William Ignatius Brady 6627 Eugene Martin Link 6628 John Simpson Hastings 6629 Charles Himmler 6630 John States Seybold 6631 Cornelius Garrison 6632 William Harry Bartlett 6633 Donald Breen Herron 6634 Edward C. Gillette 6635 Russell Owen Smith 6636 Freeman G. Cross 6637 Rex Van Den Corput 6638 Homer Watson Kiefer 6639 James Myron McMillin 6640 Joseph Harris 6641 John G. Howard 6642 Ford Trimble 6643 Robert H. Kreuter 6644 Laurence W. Bartlett 6645 Donald Frank Stace 6646 Earl Henry Blaik 6647 Reynolds Johnston Burt 6648 Edgar Allan Gilbert 6649 Leslie E. Mabus 6650 John D. Mitchell 6651 Clarence Henry Schabacker 6652 Ewart Jackson Strickland 6653 Fred Lebbeus Hamilton 6654 Robert S. Trimble 6655 John Francis Cassidy 6656 Gainer Brown Jones 6657 John Foxhall Sturman 6658 Joseph Jacob Billo 6659 Wilbert Engdahl Shallene 6660 George Leo Doolittle 6661 Robert F. Watt 6662 Clarence Clemens Clendenen 6663 William Carleton McFadden 6664 Eugene C. Johnston 6665 James Ludwell Lake 6666 Hugh Whitaker Winslow 6667 James Hess Walker 6668 Claude E. Haswell 6669 Russell V. Eastman 6670 Lyman Lincoln Judge 6671 Frank Needham Roberts 6672 Francis Henry Lanahan 6673 Lawrence Edward Schick 6674 Courtney Parker Young 6675 Henry C. Hine 6676 Charles Frederick Beattie 6677 John Donald Robertson 6678 Elias Sanford Gregory 6679 William Price Withers 6680 Frederick R. Pitts 6681 Sherman V. Hasbrouck 6682 Arthur Kenly Hammond 6683 Crump Garvin 6684 Martin Charles Casey 6685 Hamilton Peyton Ellis 6686 Thomas Dresser White 6687 Frederick Mixon Harris 6688 William Wallace McMillan 6689 Dwight Acker Rosenbaum 6690 Kenneth Gilpin Hoge 6691 James Frederick Wahl 6692 Donald Robert Van Sickler 6693 Richard C. Singer 6694 John Henry Hoffecker Hall 6695 Aladin J. Hart 6696 Powell Paxton Applewhite 6697 Robert Edwards 6698 Jefferson Denman Box 6699 William Richter Tomey 6700 Joseph Honore Rousseau 6701 Lawrence Joseph Carr 6702 Frederic S. Dixon 6703 Maurice W. Daniel 6704 Robert D. Durst 6705 Alexander Hamilton Perwein 6706 Clovis Ethelbert Byers 6707 Tracy Enfield Davis 6708 Oscar R. Johnston 6709 George Andrew Rehm 6710 Edward C. Engelhart 6711 Charles Whitney West 6712 Park Brown Herrick 6713 Herbert C. Reuter 6714 Helmer William Lystad 6715 Harold Edward Smyser 6716 Esher Claflin Burkart 6717 Thomas Eginton Whitehead 6718 Alexander George 6719 Charles Kenon Gailey 6720 Mortimer Frederick Wakefield 6721 Francis William Farrell 6722 Wilmer Brinton Merritt 6723 Harry C. Wisehart 6724 Harold Julius Chapman 6725 John Irvin Gregg 6726 John Russell 6727 Charles Merton Adams 6728 Frank Hoben Blodgett 6729 John Ferral McBlain 6730 Richard Meade Costigan 6731 Gustave H. Vogel 6732 Basil Girard Thayer 6733 Edward Joseph Sullivan 6734 James Perrine Barney 6735 Wilbur Sturtevant Nye 6736 Charles Harlan Swartz 6737 Leland Stuart Smith 6738 Wayne Latta Barker 6739 Francis Selwyn Gay 6740 Carl F. Duffner 6741 Wilburn Vastine Lunn 6742 Millard Pierson 6743 Francis Ward Walker 6744 Harold Oliver Sand 6745 Cyril Drew Pearson 6746 Raymond H. Reece 6747 Harlan Thurston McCormick 6748 Henry Peter Burgard 6749 Alexander Gilbert Sand 6750 Ray Olander Welch 6751 George William Richard Wilson 6752 John Lamont Davidson 6753 Julian Erskine Raymond 6754 Abraham Sheridan Abel 6755 George Honnen 6756 Charles Porter Amazeen 6757 Edward Thomas Williams 6758 Frank Thweatt Searcy 6759 George William Bailey 6760 Henry Kirk Williams 6761 Alan L. Fulton 6762 Terence John Tully 6763 William McKinley Laumeister 6764 Paul C. Kelly 6765 Sidney Ginsberg 6766 James Miller Rudolph 6767 William E. Crist 6768 William Roe Brewster 6769 Claude M. McQuarrie 6770 Charles W. Smith 6771 William Lemuel Mitchell 6772 Harrison Guinther Travis 6773 Escalus Emmert Elliott 6774 Milton Cogswell Shattuck 6775 Jos. Vincent de Paul Dillon 6776 Francis James Starr 6777 William Edward Ryan 6778 Hayden A. Sears 6779 Newton Nevada Jacobs 6780 John Thomas Lynch 6781 John B. Reybold 6782 John Raoul Guiteras 6783 William Dickey Long 6784 Henry Irving Hodes 6785 Clifford Augustine Taney 6786 Paul Earl Tombaugh 6787 Harvey Kenneth Greenlaw 6788 William Joel Tudor Yancey 6789 Leon E. Lichtenwalter 6790 Sidney R. Hinds 6791 John Aloysius McNulty 6792 Halley Grey Maddox 6793 Snowden Ager 6794 John English Nelson 6795 Randolph Burt Wilkinson 6796 Dean L. Sharrar 6797 John Talbot Curtis 6798 George Hasbrouck Krause 6799 Harold T. Turnbull 6800 Hugo Peoples Rush 6801 John William Wofford 6802 Wray Bertrand Avera 6803 Charles Fox Ivins 6804 Walter D. Buie 6805 John Taylor Ward 6806 John E. Reierson 6807 Edward Maurice Flexner 6808 Henry Jackson Hunt 6809 George Huston Bare 6810 **1921** Morris H. Marcus 6811 Frank Z. Pirkey 6812 Karl William Hisgen 6813 Joseph Patterson Wardlaw 6814 James H. Marsh 6815 Francis Warren Crary 6816 John Baylis Cooley 6817 John Elmer Freeman 6818 Selby Francis Little 6819 Milo G. Cary 6820 Harold J. Conway 6821 Gustin McCallister Nelson 6822 Frank Joseph Spettel 6823 Carroll Frederick Sullivan 6824 Rupert Harris Johnson 6825 Francis Joseph Magee 6826 Burwell Baylor Wilkes 6827 **1922** Charles Joseph Barrett 6828 George H. Olmsted 6829 Otto Spaulding Tinkel 6830 Maxwell D. Taylor 6831 Henry James Woodbury 6832 Louis Jacob Rumaggi 6833 Edmund Lynch 6834 Francis Jennings Wilson 6835 Alfred August Kessler 6836 Paschal N. Strong 6837 Cortlandt Van R. Schuyler 6838 Lawrence Coy Leonard 6839 Mervin Eugene Gross 6840 Arthur William Glass 6841 Harry B. Albert 6842 Robert Wayne Raynsford 6843 Harry Evans Bodine 6844 LeRoy Judson Stewart 6845 Edward S. Gibson 6846 John Francis Uncles 6847 Giles Richard Carpenter 6848 David James Crawford 6849 William Field Sadtler 6850 Du Pre Rainey Dance 6851 Earl Foster Thomson 6852 Charles Newsom Branham 6853 John Hughes Wallace 6854 Francis Borgia Kane 6855 Daniel Allen Terry 6856 William Stevens Lawton 6857 Richard Wilson Johnson 6858 William Augustine Burns 6859 Albert Svihra 6860 Theodore Fredrick Straub 6861 Arthur A. Klein 6862 Slator M. Miller 6863 Granger Anderson 6864 Alfred Eugene Kastner 6865 Edwin Paul Crandell 6866 Francis Martin Greene 6867 Mark McClure 6868 Benjamin Wiley Chidlaw 6869 Myron Leedy 6870 Alba Carelton Spalding 6871 James Kendrick Whetton 6872 Robert L. Taylor 6873 Edwin Norman Clark 6874 Stephen Cecil Lombard 6875 Howard Gillespie Davidson 6876 Fred James Woods 6877 Kenneth Francis Pughe 6878 Robert Smith McClenaghan 6879 Francis Xavier Mulvihill 6880 Charles Hancock Reed 6881 Toy Rhea Gregory 6882 Walter Russell Hensey 6883 Orval Raoy Cook 6884 Perry McCoy Smith 6885 James Wrathall Spry 6886 Gordon Sherman Armes 6887 Henry Edwin Tyler 6888 Frederick W. Hein 6889 Raymond Balliet Bosserman 6890 DeWitt Liggett McLallen 6891 Charles Rufus Smith 6892 Harold A. Meyer 6893 Jerre Land Dowling 6894 Robert Earle Blair 6895 Harold Thomas Molloy 6896 William Harvey Kyle 6897 James Dunne O'Connell 6898 Gilman Clifford Mudgett 6899 Leonard Edwin Stephens 6900 Numa Augustin Watson 6901 Wesley W. Yale 6902 Frederick Stevens Lee 6903 Harry Howard Stout 6904 Robert Wilkins Douglass 6905 Oscar Louis Beal 6906 Oliver W. Hughes 6907 Robert V. Murphy 6908 Aloysius Eugene O'Flaherty 6909 Melville Fuller Grant 6910 James Edward Rees 6911 James Robinson Pierce 6912 Lemuel Mathewson 6913 George Harold Carmouche 6914 Glenn Castle Wilhide 6915 Martin Augustine McDonough 6916 Thomas Varon Webb 6917 Harry Herman Haas 6918 George Edward Mitchell 6919 William Henry Schildroth 6920 Darius Donald Thorpe 6921 Clarence Dean 6922 Orlando Augustus Greening 6923 James Edward McDavid 6924 George Arthur Taylor 6925 Paul Sylvanus Graham 6926 Holmes Ficklen 6927 Alfred Lawrence Price 6928 Charles Holt Dobbs 6929 Frank L. Beadle 6930 Landon Carter Catlett 6931 Zeng T. Wong 6932 Gilbert Hayden 6933 Francis E. Cothran 6934 Thomas Herbert Maddocks 6935 Charles Perry Holweger 6936 David Marion Fowler 6937 Edward Arthur Kleinman 6938 Blackshear Morrison Bryan 6939 John Lawson Ballantyne 6940 Hilbert Milton Wittkop 6941 Donald Quitman Harris 6942 John Percy Kennedy 6943 Charles Mehegan 6944 Townsend Griffiss 6945 William Andrew Wedemeyer 6946 Edwin Carlo Greiner 6947 William B. Goddard 6948 Donald Harold Hayselden 6949 Philip Howard Raymond 6950 Oliver Perry Newman 6951 Ronald Gorrie MacDonald 6952 John H. Stodter 6953 Phillips Shirley Sears 6954 Thomas Edward Lewis 6955 Stewart Tiffany Vincent 6956 Paul Henry Mahoney 6957 James Clyde Fry 6958 Austin Folger Gilmartin 6959 **1923** Francis Rarick Johnson 6960 High Wagner Downing 6961 Glenn H. Palmer 6962 Royal Bertrand Lord 6963 Kenner Fisher Hertford 6964 Ray Carl Milton 6965 Steven L. Conner 6966 Miles Reber 6967 Charles West Stewart 6968 Wm. Francis Merwin Longwell 6969 John Rutherford Noyes 6970 Lyle Rosenberg 6971 William Randolph Winslow 6972 William Newton Leaf 6973 David M. Dunne 6974 Frank McAdams Albrecht 6975 Theodore M. Osborne 6976 Ralph Arnold Tudor 6977 Robert Farnsworth Hallock 6978 Kenyon Moore Hegardt 6979 Hebert Davidson 6980 Stuart Alfred Beckley 6981 Harold David Kehm 6982 John Wesley Warren 6983 James Warner Fletcher 6984 John Albert Chambers 6985 Isidore Sass 6986 Einar Bernard Gjelsteen 6987 William Elgie Carraway 6988 John Mark Pesek 6989 Thomas Magnor Conroy 6990 Mark Hampton Galusha 6991 Joseph Caldwell King 6992 Herbert B. Enderton 6993 John Battle Horton 6994 Woodson Lewis 6995 Alfred L. Johnson 6996 Lawrence Barroll 6997 Joseph Leander Hardin 6998 Carter B. Magruder 6999 William Joseph D'Espinosa 7000 Will Walter White 7001 William Jackson Morton 7002 Frank Edwin Wilder 7003 Wilbur R. Pierce 7004 Donald Henry Galloway 7005 Howard W. Serig 7006 Benjamin Franklin Caffey 7007 Daniel F. J. De Bardeleben 7008 Patrick Weston Timberlake 7009 Edgar Hoffman Price 7010 Clyde K. Rich 7011 Paul W. Wolf 7012 David Larr 7013 Laurence Carbee Craigie 7014 Philip R. Dwyer 7015 Sylvester John Keane 7016 Allen Lloyd Keyes 7017 Damon Mott Gunn 7018 Charles Metz Seebach 7019 Harry McKenzie Roper 7020 James H. Workman 7021 Charles Wesley Gettys 7022 Henry James Pitt Harding 7023 William

Shepard Biddle 7024 George Francis Heaney 7025 Wade Hampton Heavey 7026 Donald Alexander Beck 7027 John Humphrey Evans 7028 William Remsburgh Grove 7029 Wade L. Kerr 7030 Douglas Ewart Christie 7031 George Lewis Dewey 7032 Saverio Hardy Savini 7033 John Harvey Farrow 7034 James Frederick Torrence 7035 Douglass G. Pamplin 7036 Dan Chandler 7037 Charles White Lawrence 7038 George Edward Waldo 7039 Michael Buckley 7040 Benjamin Stern 7041 Wallace Evan Whitson 7042 Lloyd Shepard 7043 Rex Eugene Chandler 7044 Russell J. Minty 7045 Rowland Randolph Castle 7046 Sheffield Edwards 7047 John Roper Burnett 7048 Edgar Lee Love 7049 Raymond Stone 7050 John Joseph Binns 7051 Walter Burnside 7052 Birney Kellogg Morse 7053 Ben L. Wells 7054 Stewart Leon Thompson 7055 James Francis Joseph Early 7056 Howard John Vandersluis 7057 Ulysses John L. Peoples 7058 Wilfred Henry P. Weber 7059 Morris K. Voedisch 7060 Richard Briggs Evans 7061 Everett Clement Merrwether 7062 Alden Rudyard Crawford 7063 Winston Jennings Eaddy 7064 George Gareld Rusk 7065 Rochester Flower McEldowney 7066 Thomas Merritt Lowe 7067 Kevin O'Shea 7068 Carl Douglas Silverthorne 7069 Louis William Haskell 7070 David Myron Schlatter 7071 Charles Trovilla Myers 7072 Waldemar Fritz Breidster 7073 Eugene Ware Ridings 7074 Charles Woodford Cowles 7075 Kenneth Eugene Webber 7076 William Ernst Winter 7077 Alexander Davidson Reid 7078 Leslie Page Holcomb 7079 Charles A. Hennessey 7080 Raymond Chesley McCormick 7081 Frank Hinton Bunnell 7082 Charles Vinson Bromley 7083 John William Harmony 7084 Philip H. Enslow 7085 Ernest Byron Thompson 7086 Elwyn Donald Post 7087 Franklin K. Gurley 7088 Wilfrid Henry Hardy 7089 Louis Wagner Marshall 7090 James A. Evans 7091 Leslie Martin Grener 7092 Joseph Smith 7093 Henry Lee Shafer 7094 Kenneth Shearer Sweany 7095 Joseph H. Hicks 7096 Guy Haines Stubbs 7097 Ernest Herman Pfeiffer 7098 Ralph Christian Bing 7099 Clinton John Harrold 7100 Louis Henri Imhof 7101 Russell Emerson Bates 7102 Earl Shuman Gruver 7103 Warren Cole Stout 7104 David Barbour Barton 7105 Paul Russell Covey 7106 William Augustus Davis Thomas 7107 Dudley Carl Roth 7108 Eugene Lynch Harrison 7109 Bernard Aye Tormey 7110 Joseph Ingham Greene 7111 Abner Judson McGehee 7112 Valentine Roy Smith 7113 George William Hartnell 7114 Joseph Anthony Cella 7115 James Boyce Carroll 7116 John Ellsworth Adkins 7117 Cecil Ward Nist 7118 Robert Chaffee Oliver 7119 James Eugene B. McInerney 7120 Francis Arthur Garrecht 7121 Frank Dorn 7122 Allen Welty Smith 7123 Nathaniel Lancaster 7124 Charles Oscar Moody 7125 Noble Penfield Beasley 7126 Charles Edward Woodruff 7127 Donald McLean 7128 Hartwell Rodney Cragin 7129 Bruce R. King 7130 Paschal Hoover Ringsdorf 7131 Harry Tatum Rowland 7132 Stuart Cowles 7133 John Maurice Weikert 7134 George Pierce Howell 7135 Warren A. Robinson 7136 John Hensel Pitzer 7137 Herbert Robert Campbell 7138 William Lawrence Scott 7139 Dean Stanley Ellerthorpe 7140 Bernard H. Sullivan 7141 Guy Nathaniel Irish 7142 Roswell Hitchcock Harriman 7143 George Conrad Mergens 7144 Horton Vail White 7145 James Edward Bowen 7146 Austin Curtia Cunkle 7147 John Hamilton White 7148 Briscoe Allen Trousdale 7149 Francis Townsend Dodd 7150 Charles C. Cavender 7151 George Stanley Smith 7152 William C. Lucas 7153 Charles Heath Heyl 7154 Harvey K. Palmer 7155 Wendell G. Johnson 7156 Paul Downing Michelet 7157 Howard Edward C. Breitung 7158 Paul Kenneth Porch 7159 Edward Elford Lutwack 7160 James Sifly Jefferies 7161 John George Salsman 7162 John Guy Wilson 7163 Lyman O'Dell Williams 7164 Temple Graves Holland 7165 Lew Myers Morton 7166 Alejandro DeJose Garcia 7167 Paul Cyril Serff 7168 Lawrence Leroy Skinner 7169 Edward F. Adams 7170 Vincent Paul O'Reilly 7171 Thomas S. Timberman 7172 Cyril Quentin Marron 7173 George Franklin Williams 7174 John Delaney Sureau 7175 Robert Herman Krueger 7176 Louis John Storck 7177 Santiago Garcia Guevara 7178 Donald Cameron Tredennick 7179 Paul Philip Hanson 7180 John Adams Austin 7181 John Cyrus Graffin 7182 David Sherman Babcock 7183 James J. Carnes 7184 Joseph Winfield Boone 7185 Garrett Bartlett Drummond 7186 Walter Busill Tully 7187 Harry Lang Scheetz 7188 Hugh Chauncey Johnson 7189 James Michael Fitzmaurice 7190 Frederick Tuttle Manross 7191 Charles Calvin Higgins 7192 George Craig Stewart 7193 Louis Peter Leone 7194 Robert Leroy Dulaney 7195 James Clarke Carter 7196 Robert M. Smith 7197 Richard Edmondson Russell 7198 Hoyt Sanford Vandenberg 7199 Lawrence Varsi Castner 7200 Henry Granville Fisher 7201 Hal Clark Granberry 7202 Ralph M. Neal 7203 John Valentin Grombach 7204A Stewart Warren Towle 7204 Edwin B. Howard 7205 Frederick Edward Phillips 7206 John P. Evans 7207 William Harold Schaffer 7208 Sidney Lee Douthit 7209 Allen Dwight Raymond 7210 Oscar Carlton Stewart 7211 James Cyril Short 7212 Louis Carrier Barley 7213 David Franklin Stone 7214 Walter Cornelius White 7215 Lynn Edwin Brady 7216 Glen Clifford Jamison 7217 James Robert Lindsay 7218 Roy M. Foster 7219 Bordner Fred Ascher 7220 **1924** Wallace Howard Hastings 7221 Albert Fox Glenn 7222 Joseph Atticus Morris 7223 Emerson L. Cummings 7224 Robert V. Lee 7225 Earle Everard Partridge 7226 Fisher Shinolt Blinn 7227 Donald C. Hill 7228 Benjamin S. Mesick 7229 Adolph P. Rasmussen 7230 Reginald Langworthy Dean 7231 Merrow Egerton Sorley 7232 Philip Robison Garges 7233 John Ludden Mousseau des Islets 7234 Gerald Joseph Sullivan 7235 George Dakin Crosby 7236 Arthur G. Trudeau 7237 John Henry Brewer 7238 John Held Riepe 7239 Emerson C. Itschner 7240 Ernest Orrin Lee 7241 Howard Ker 7242 Charles D. Palmer 7243 Herbert D. Vogel 7244 Fremont Swift Tandy 7245 Allan Dawson 7246 Frank Lawrence Lazarus 7247 Emil J. Peterson 7248 Gordon Edmund Textor 7249 Everett C. Wallace 7250 Vernum Charles Stevens 7251 Otis McCormick 7252 Wendell Blanchard 7253 Thomas DuVal Roberts 7254 Clinton Frederick Robinson 7255 Frederic Allison Henney 7256 David Jerome Ellinger 7257 Francis J. Clark 7258 Leonard L. Bingham 7259 Floyd Allen Mitchell 7260 Samuel Vance Krauthoff 7261 Joseph P. Shumate 7262 Robert Lee Miller 7263 John I. Hincke 7264 George Arthur Duerr 7265 Fred Arley Ingalls 7266 Herbert Theodore Schaefer 7267 Raymond T. Beurket 7268 Heyward Bradford Roberts 7269 Charles G. Meehan 7270 Victor Allen Conrad 7271 Robin Bernard Pape 7272 John F. Williams 7273 Harry Jordan Theis 7274 Amel Thomas Leonard 7275 Clyde Massey 7276 Bruce Woodward Bidwell 7277 Elmer Ernest Count 7278 Robert Ward Berry 7279 Harry Van Wyk 7280 Glenn Bruce McConnell 7281 Harold P. Tasker 7282 William Howard Arnold 7283 Robert Lyle Brookings 7284 Claude Earl Moore 7285 Raymond H. Coombs 7286 Wellington A. Samouce 7287 Francis Elmer Kidwell 7288 William Hubbard Barksdale 7289 Eugene Barber Ely 7290 Grayson Schmidt 7291 Leslie Earl Simon 7292 Charles Trueman Lanham 7293 Richard Warburton Stephens 7294 John Henry Haile 7295 Robert Clement Lawes 7296 Richard Longworth Baughman 7297 Edwin Henry Harrison 7298 Cary Judson King 7299 Lawrence R. Dewey 7300 Ralph Irvin Glasgow 7301 Oren Wilcox Rynearson 7302 William Armstrong Bugher 7303 Wilbur Kincaid Noel 7304 Jesse Bernard Wells 7305 James Wm. Alexander McNary 7306 Cecil Ernest Henry 7307 George Anthony Bicher 7308 James Thomas Loome 7309 Harold P. Gard 7310 William Lloyd Richardson 7311 Andrew Allison Frierson 7312 Craig Alderman 7313 John Sewell Thompson 7314 Ovid Thomason Forman 7315 Leslie S. Fletcher 7316 Charles Raeburne Landon 7317 George W. Palmer 7318 Arthur R. Grimm 7319 Thomas E. Binford 7320 Clark Cornelius Witman 7321 Ernest A. Merkle 7322 Carl W. A. Raguse 7323 Leo Douglas Vichules 7324 Thomas Carey Ryan 7325 George Arthur Hadsell 7326 Earl Mattice 7327 Herbert T. Benz 7328 Uzal Girard Ent 7329 Henry Sterling Jernigan 7330 Worth Harper 7331 James Stewart Willis 7332 Karl Augustus Woltersdorf 7333 Frank Jay Thompson 7334 Augustine D. Dugan 7335 Donald Dean Rule 7336 Clarence Everett Rothgeb 7337 Marcus Butler Stokes 7338 Francis Marion Day 7339 Charles G. Stevenson 7340 William Herbert Schaefer 7341 Robert Hoffner Paton 7342 Clarence W. Bennett 7343 George B. Finnegan 7344 Gordon Byrom Rogers 7345 Bernard Francis Luebbermann 7346 Peter W. Shunk 7347 James Angus Watson 7348 George C. Claussen 7349 James Frederick Howell 7350 Russell Layton Mabie 7351 Ewing Hill France 7352 William J. Eyerly 7353 George Dunbar Pence 7354 Murray Bradshaw Crandall 7355 William J. Reardon 7356 Lester Joseph Tacy 7357 Emil Pasolli 7358 Charles Lanier Dasher 7359 Sanford Joseph Goodman 7360 Edward F. Booth 7361 Gerald Goodwin Gibbs 7362 William Hill Lamberton 7363 George William Busbey 7364 William Louis Howarth 7365 Hayden Lemaire Boatner 7366 Frank Stuart Lyndall 7367 David Marcus 7368 Cary Brown Hutchinson 7369 Clarence Keith Darling 7370 Joe L. Loutzenheiser 7371 Zachery W. Moores 7372 William Bellemere Wren 7373 Perry William Brown 7374 James E. Moore 7375 Silas W. Hosea 7376 Ellis Spurgeon Hopewell 7377 Harold James Keeley 7378 Stephen Stanley Koszewski 7379 Donald G. Storck 7380 John C. Smith 7381 Peter C. Hains 7382 Monro MacCloskey 7383 George Edmund Young 7384 Hardy Cross Dillard 7385 Ricardo Poblete 7386 Lindsay Patterson Caywood 7387 Czar James Dyer 7388 Richard Emmel Nugent 7389 Walter Allen Buck 7390 John Phillips Kirkendall 7391 Vonna F. Burger 7392 Charles D. Daniel 7393 Joseph Aloysius Kielty 7394 Albert Delmar Miller 7395 Cleland Charles Sibley 7396 James Edward McGraw 7397 Robert Roy Selway 7398 James A. Davidson 7399 John Gilbert Moore 7400 Edward Lynn Andrews 7401 James G. Anding 7402 Darwin Denison Martin 7403 George Avery Tucker 7404 Joseph Rogers Burrill 7405 Leslie Alfred Skinner 7406 Francis Anthony Kreidel 7407 Lawrence Wendall Adams 7408 Nathaniel Clay Cureton 7409 Harry Taylor Cavenaugh 7410 Clarence Sterling Raymond 7411 John Alfred McComsey 7412 George Morgan Kernan 7413 George Buford Leonard 7414 James Edwards Poore 7415 Maxwell Wood Tracy 7416 Howard Everett Kessinger 7417 Francis E. Gillette 7418 Walter A. Linn 7419 Albert Kellogg Stebbins 7420 Washington Mackey Ives 7421 William L. Johnson 7422 Richard Givens Prather 7423 Douglas B. Smith 7424 Robert Edward Cullen 7425 Randall Sollenberger 7426 John Jacob Williams 7427 Walton Gracy Procter 7428 Merton Goodfellow Wallington 7429 Eleazar Parmly 7430 Luther Stevens Smith 7431 Bernard Warren Justice 7432 Samuel Glenn Conley 7433 Stephen W. Ackerman 7434 Lewis Spencer Kirkpatrick 7435 Charles Hunter Coates 7436 Frank Glover Trew 7437 Edward Orlando McConahay 7438 Otto L. Nelson 7439 William Henry Kendall 7440 Warfield R. Wood 7441 John Curtis Lafayette Adams 7442 William Joseph Cleary 7443 Albert George Foote 7444 Robert Wells Harper 7445 Augustus Jerome Regnier 7446 Howard McMath Turner 7447 Walter Louis Weinaug 7448 Willard Koehler Liebel 7449 Oliver Malcolm Barton 7450 Bjarne Furuholmen 7451 Charles Pelot Summerall 7452 Thomas George McCulloch 7453 John Archer Stewart 7454 Leonard Henry Rodieck 7455 Robert Chester McCloud 7456 Frederick C. Pyne 7457 John Harry Stadler 7458 Louis Chadwick Friedersdorff 7459 David P. Page 7460 Walter D. Merrill 7461 Lewis Curtis Barkes 7462 Alexander George Greig 7463 John Lyman Hitchings 7464 Kenneth C. Strother 7465 William Ernest Slater 7466 George Alvin Millener 7467 Robert H. Thompson 7468 Daniel F. Healy 7469 George Hinkle Steel 7470 John P. Maher 7471 Russell Andrew Baker 7472 Frank Smith Kirkpatrick 7473 George W. Vaughn 7474 Paul Cooper 7475 Lee William Gilford 7476 Laurence Knight Ladue 7477 Leo Harold Towers 7478 Ralph Pulsifer 7479 Logan Carroll Berry 7480 Thomas J. Holmes 7481 Onto Price Bragan 7482 Gilbert F. Baillie 7483 Robert Joseph McBride 7484 Charles Ward Van Way 7485 Harry Dillon McHugh 7486 William Harry Bertsch 7487 William Reineman Forbes 7488 Gerald J. Reid 7489 Edward Higgins White 7490 James William Clyburn 7491 James Hewins 7492 Roy Deck Reynolds 7493 David S. Stanley 7494 David G. Erskine 7495 Armistead Davis Mead 7496 Albert Newton Stubblebine 7497 Charles Harold Royce 7498 Denis J. Mulligan 7499 Robert Charles Cameron 7500 Paul A. Pickhardt 7501 George Patrick O'Neill 7502 Oswaldo de la Rosa 7503 William Olmstead Eareckson 7504 William L. Coughlin 7505 William Thaddeus Sexton 7506 Henry Coates Burgess 7507 Francis Robert Stevens 7508 Robert Augustus Ellsworth 7509 George E. Wrockloff 7510 Campbell Weir 7511 James Edgar Macklin 7512 Richard Weigand Gibson 7513 Armand J. Salmon 7514 Carroll Riggs Griffin 7515 Frederick Raymond Keeler 7516 Charles E. Hart 7517 Kenneth Negley Decker 7518 George Almond Ford 7519 Edward A. Chazal 7520 Felix Marcinski 7521 Thomas Allen Jennings 7522 Rupert D. Graves 7523 Reed Graves 7524 Mark Edward Smith 7525 John Gillespie Hill 7526 Joseph Massaro 7527 Wolcott Kent Dudley 7528 James Barry Kraft 7529 Andrew Suter Gamble 7530 Howard Jehn John 7531 Charles Mansfield Reading 7532 John Reynolds Hawkins 7533 Earl Lynwood Scott 7534 Charles L. Booth 7535 Andrew Paul Foster 7536 John Jacob Outcalt 7537 Melvin Eugene Meister 7538 Emil Lenzner 7539 Hobart Amory Murphy 7540 William Henry Maglin 7541 Camille H. Du Val 7542 Ralph Emanuel Fisher 7543 William S. Triplet 7544 George Winfered Smythe 7545 John Harold Claybrook 7546 Jesse Thomas Traywick 7547 Leslie Ellis Griffith 7548 Philip McCaffrey Kernan 7549 Howard A. Malin 7550 James Earl Purcell 7551 John Archer Elmore 7552 John Wesley Ramsey 7553 Francis William Johnson 7554 Francis John Graling 7555 Nye K. Elward 7556 James Pierce Hulley 7557 Samuel Wayne Smithers 7558 Ralph A. Koch 7559 Kenneth Rector Bailey 7560 Lucien Francis Wells 7561 Richard T. Mitchell 7562 George Edward Lightcap 7563 Samuel H. Fisher 7564 Dennis Milton Moore 7565 Charles Rogers Bonnett 7566 Houston Val Evans 7567 Clark Norace Bailey 7568 George J. Smith 7569 Victor Emmanuel Phasey 7570 Clyde D. Eddleman 7571 Russell Leonard Moses 7572 John O'Day Murtaugh 7573 Sarratt Thaddeus Hames 7574 Peyton Fentrell McLamb 7575 James Barclay Dickerson 7576 Virgil Rasmuss Miller 7577 James Somers Stowell 7578 Arthur LeRoy Bump 7579 Bertel Eric Kuniholm 7580 William John Renn 7581 Michael Henry Cleary 7582 Briant H. Wells 7583 Robert C. Polsgrove 7584 George Edwin Penton 7585 William W. O'Connor 7586 Reeve Douglas Keiler 7587 George Emmert Elliott 7588 William Wallace Cornog 7589 Demas Thurlow Craw 7590 Henry Isaac Kiel 7591 Daniel H. Hundley 7592 William Walrath Lloyd 7593 Jacob Robert Moon 7594 Thomas Harrison Allen 7595 Raymond Rodney Robins 7596 Peter Sather 7597 Irving Ballard Greene 7598 Richard Garner Thomas 7599 Frank Faron Carpenter 7600 Ralph P. Eaton 7601 Harold Currie King 7602 Richard Gemant Herbine 7603 Henry Dahnke 7604 Clement H. Dabezies 7605 Ralph Houston Lawter 7606 George Harvey Doane 7607 Walter D. Gillespie 7608 Robert Carlyle Andrews 7609 Herbert Frank McG. Mathews 7610 Buford Alexander Lynch 7611 William J. Brunner 7612 Noah Mathew Brinson 7613 Albert John Dombrowsky 7614 Jean D. Scott 7615 Robert W. Stika 7616 Ovid Oscar Wilson 7617 Leighton Marion Clark 7618 Martin F. Hass 7619 Edward John Hirz 7620 Cornelius Walter Cousland 7621 Clarence William Hoeper 7622 Tao Hung Chang 7623 Edward Allen Robins 7624 Samuel Martin Strohecker 7625 **1925** Charles Henry Barth 7626 Standish Weston 7627 John William Bowman 7628 Charles Eskridge Saltzman 7629 Raymond Burkholder Oxrieder 7630 Gerald Edward Galloway 7631 Harrod George Miller 7632 Charles Hare Mason 7633 Louis Charles Scherer 7634 Harry Gordon Spillinger 7635 Carl Rueben Dutton 7636 George Kenyon Withers 7637 Arleigh Todd Bell 7638 Thomas Leonard Harrold 7639 Kenneth William Treacy 7640 Vincent Joseph Esposito 7641 Edgar William Garbisch 7642 Robert Lee Howze 7643 Leland Berrel Kuhre 7644 Colby Maxwell Myers 7645 Ralph Tibbs Garver 7646 William Ludlow Ritchie 7647 Amos Tappan Akeman 7648 Allen Annesley Cavenaugh 7649 Everett Sprague Emerson 7650 John Henry Farrell Haskell 7651 Raymond Wheeler Toms 7652 Philip Wing Nye 7653 Olive Cass Torbett 7654 James Albert Channon 7655 Rogers Alan Gardner 7656 Albert Harvey Burton 7657 Bruce Cooper Clarke 7658 William Adgate Lord 7659 John Henry Beatty 7660 Carl W. Meyer 7661 Albert Reno Dowling 7662 Richard Thomas Clark 7663 John Henry Dulligan 7664 David Henry Tulley 7665 Walter Grant Bryte 7666 Kryl L. F. deGravelines 7667 Warren Nourse Underwood 7668 Miles Merrill Dawson 7669 Charles P. Nicholas 7670 Russell Edward Randall 7671 Carl Warren Holcomb 7672 Armand Hopkins 7673 Timothy Lawrence Mulligan 7674 Finis Ewing Dunaway 7675 Charles Woodruff Scovel 7676 Benjamin Cobb Fowlkes 7677 John Wilson Huyssoon 7678 Wilfred Paul Champlain 7679 Wilmer Coalscott Gullette 7680 Frank Gilbert Fraser 7681 Stanley James Horn 7682 Frank Andrew Pettit 7683 William O'Connor Heacock 7684 Walter William Hodge 7685 William Henry Nutter 7686 Oscar Carl Maier 7687 Ralph Augustus Lincoln 7688 Gilbert Edward Linkswiler 7689 Aubrey Strode Newman 7690 Ernest Victor Holmes 7691 William Frank Steer 7692 Wiley Thomas Moore 7693 Ronald Montgomery Shaw 7694 C. Stanton Babcock 7695 Thomas Elton Smith 7696 John Ignatius Brosnan 7697 Alvin Truett Bowers 7698 Harold Shaffer Gould 7699 William Francis McLaughlin 7700 William Henry Bigelow 7701 Lewis Ackley Riggins 7702 Harold Foster Wiley 7703 William Gardner Plummer 7704 Willard Lamborn Wright 7705 John Frederick Gamber 7706 Ernest Andrew Barlow 7707 John Loomis Chamberlain 7708 Frank John Hierholzer 7709 Carl Frederick Tischbein 7710 John Salisbury Fisher 7711 Charles Pearre Cabell 7712 Alexander McNair Willing 7713 James Joseph Deery 7714 Allen Ward Dewees 7715 Archer Frank Freund 7716 Roland Ainslee Browne 7717 Milo Howard Matteson 7718 William John Carne 7719 John Stephen Henn 7720 Henry Randolph Westphalinger 7721 Raymond Cecil Conder 7722 Ralph Frederick Bartz 7723 James Wentworth Clinton 7724 Arthur Bliss 7725 William Holmes Wood 7726 John William Black 7727 Lucien Eugene Bolduc 7728 Alfred Boyce Devereaux 7729 Paul Maurice Seleen 7730 Henry Ewell Strickland 7731 Wilmer George Bennett 7732 Arthur Charles Boll 7733 Clifford Palmer Bradley 7734 Hubert Merrill Cole 7735 John Daniel 7736 Gustavus Wilcox West 7737 George Peter Berilla 7738 Daniel Hamilton Robertson 7739 Branner Pace Purdue 7740 George Joseph Deutermann 7741 Lebbeus Bigelow Woods 7742 George Arthur Grayeb 7743 Peter Paul Liwski 7744 Haydon Young Grubbs 7745 William Albert Fuller 7746 Ralph Edmund Tibbetts 7747 Stanley Meservey Plaister 7748 Edwin Lynds Johnson 7749 Clyde Eugene Steele 7750 Ernest Holmes Wilson 7751 Norman Holmes Smith 7752 John Wingo Dansby 7753 Robert Milchrist Cannon 7754 Arthur Anton Ruppert 7755 Charles Cavelli 7756 William Harrison Morford 7757 Thomas Byrd Whitted 7758 James Wilbur Mosteller 7759 Meredith Cornwall Noble 7760 George Henry McManus 7761 Leo Francis Kengla 7762 Robert Emmett Burns 7763 John Amos Hall 7764 Donald Janser Bailey 7765 Nicholas Joseph Robinson 7766 John Murphy Willems 7767 Joseph Cyril Augustin Denniston 7768 Gerard William Kelley 7769 John Franklin Bird 7770 George Frederic Bruner 7771 Henry Beane Margeson 7772 Nathaniel Claiborne Hale 7773 Donald Elwood Mitchell 7774 Claude Franklin Burbach 7775 Raymond M. Barton 7776 William Lloyd Burbank 7777 Donald Hudson Bratton 7778 Wallace Hallock Honnold 7779 John Frederick Powell 7780 Emmor Graham Martin 7781 Daniel Franklin Crosland 7782 Walter Scott Strange 7783 Graham Kirkpatrick 7784 Welborn Barton Griffith 7785 John H. McCormick 7786 William N. Gillmore 7787 Hubert Whitney Ketchum 7788 Marcel Gustave Crombez 7789 Milton Taylor Hankins 7790 Harry Oscar Ellinger 7791 John William Gaddis 7792 Raymond Kimball Quekemeyer 7793 William Everton Pheris 7794 Alexander Andrew Dobak 7795 John Howard Bennett 7796 Littleton Adams Roberts 7797 Harry Clifton Larter 7798 Wayne Carleton Smith 7799 Godwin Ordway 7800 Harry Jean Harper 7801 Solomon E. Senior 7802 Arnold S. Greensweight 7803 Robert Pepper Clay 7804 Edward Clement Mack 7805 William Leon Kost 7806 Ira Kenneth Evans 7807 Earl Walter Barnes 7808 John W. Bryan 7809 Porter Bush Fuqua 7810 Samuel Adrian Dickson 7811 Dwight Harvey 7812 William E. Long 7813 John Llewellyn Lewis 7814 John W. Davis 7815 Edwin Bascum Kearns 7816 Rinaldo Van Brunt 7817 George

P. Lynch 7818 John Francis Holland 7819 Robert Matheny Sampson 7820 John Porter Kidwell 7821 Clarence Harwood Smith 7822 Paul Leroy Weitfle 7823 Thaddeus Elmer Smyth 7824 Waldemar Noya Damas 7825 James Durward Barnett 7826 Claude A. Black 7827 Joe Oriel McMahon 7828 Russell T. Finn 7829 Harry Wells Crandall 7830 Joseph Pringle Cleland 7831 Enoch Joseph Scalan 7832 John Laing DePew 7833 John Robert McGinness 7834 Edward Daniel McLaughlin 7835 William Griffith Stephenson 7836 Thomas Quinn Ashburn 7837 George B. Peploe 7838 Samuel Selden Lamb 7839 Curtis D. Renfro 7840 William Delano Brackett 7841 Charles Henry Caldwell 7842 James Edward Boudreau 7843 Joseph Blair Daugherty 7844 Haskell Hadley Cleaves 7845 Albert Aaron Horner 7846 Louis Quarles McComas 7847 Mitchell Alonzo Giddens 7848 Leif Neprud 7849 Theodore Lamar Dunn 7850 Elliott Bickley Gose 7851 William Bruce LeFavour 7852 John Irene Soule 7853 Floyd Ellsworth Dunn 7854 George Wellington M. Dudley 7855 Michael John Geraghty 7856 Theodore Anderson Baldwin 7857 Donald Dunford 7858 Arthur Superior Peterson 7859 Ralph Randolph Sears 7860 Judson M. Smith 7861 Edgar Turner Noyes 7862 John M. Brabson 7863 David E. Bradford 7864 James K. DeArmond 7865 Ernest A. Suttles 7866 August William Farwick 7867 Samuel Mason Lansing 7868 Pierre B. Denson 7869 Jesus Airan 7870 **1926** William Clyde Baker 7871 William Livingston Bayer 7872 Herbert William Ehrgott 7873 Turner Ashby Sims 7874 Francis LeRoy Ankenbrandt 7875 William Hunt Mills 7876 Keith Richard Barney 7877 Elvin Ragnvald Heiberg 7878 Boone Gross 7879 Francis Xavier A. Purcell 7880 Harold Anthony Brusher 7881 Ray Coleman Maude 7882 Samuel Wallace VanMeter 7883 Richard Wyman Pearson 7884 Charles Edward Martin 7885 Irving Arthur Duffy 7886 William Preston Corderman 7887 C. Rodney Smith 7888 Fiorre John Stagliano 7889 Parker Montrose Reeve 7890 Harry Warren Johnson 7891 Rufus Leonidas Land 7892 James Norvell Krueger 7893 Robert Kinzie McDonough 7894 Donald Prentice Booth 7895 Arthur August Gerhart Kirchhoff 7896 William Murlin Creasy 7897 Alfred Henry Johnson 7898 Ralph Morris Osborne 7899 Norman Arthur Matthias 7900 Lincoln Jones 7901 Harlie Heston Parks 7902 Malcolm Raymond Kammerer 7903 Charles Daniel Sugrue 7904 Robert Eugene M. des Islets 7905 William Edward House 7906 James Roy Andersen 7907 Benjamin E. Thurston 7908 Harold McClure Forde 7909 William Alexander Walker 7910 John Colt Beaumont Elliott 7911 Hamilton Smith Hawkins 7912A Samuel Russ Harris 7912 Lewis Sherrill Griffing 7913 Waldo Eugene Laidlaw 7914 Thomas Francis Plummer 7915 Sidney Merrick Wheeler 7916 Horace Maynard Daniels 7917 Hamer Pace Ford 7918 Robert Clifford Broadhurst 7919 John Ensor Perman 7920 George William Hickman 7921 Earl Jerome Murphy 7922 Holger Nelson Toftoy 7923 Harold Doud 7924 Edward Davis Raney 7925 David Louis Van Syckle 7926 Wallace Hayden Barnes 7927 Shelton Ezra Prudhomme 7928 John Paul Doyle 7929 Leon William Johnson 7930 Richard Walden Mayo 7931 Earl Lewis Ringler 7932 George Voegele Ehrhardt 7933 Walter Clement Stanton 7934 Frank Sayles Bowen 7935 Malcolm Dudley Jones 7936 William Peirce Ennis 7937 Guy Beasley Henderson 7938 Edward Lowe Rhodes 7939 Richard Keith McMaster 7940 Francis Patrick Malloy 7941 Charles Dutton McNerney 7942 Clair McKinley Conzelman 7943 Henry Ross 7944 Samuel Pickens Collins 7945 John Cline Strickler 7946 Oscar James Levin 7947 Edwin Howard Feather 7948 Theodore Charles Wenzlaff 7949 William Jesse Deyo 7950 Benjamin Peter Heiser 7951 John Lawrence Ryan 7952 Egon Roland Tausch 7953 Alexander Randolph Sewall 7954 Prentice Edward Yeomans 7955 Paul Hamilton 7956 Charles Clifford Sloane 7957 Charles Winchell McGeehan 7958 James Russell Wheaton 7959 Basil Littleton Riggs 7960 Malcolm Hobson Harwell 7961 Henry Raymond Baxter 7962 Roy Kaylor 7963 Tyler Calhoun 7964 Richard Hanson Grinder 7965 Charles Augustus Meny 7966 Edwin James Van Horne 7967 Robert Charles Ross 7968 Harry Purnell Storke 7969 Thomas Edward Pickett Barbour 7970 Joseph Halversen 7971 Warren Milton Richardson 7972 Marvin Westlake Peck 7973 William Evans Dean 7974 George Albert Smith 7975 Eugene Charles Smallwood 7976 James Robert Davidson 7977 Frank Freeman Miter 7978 John Prichard Woodbridge 7979 Thomas Edward de Shazo 7980 Maurice Melville Condon 7981 Kenneth Frease March 7982 Frederick Francis Scheiffler 7983 Virgil Richard Pogue 7984 Robert Sylvester Nourse 7985 Richard Edward O'Connor 7986 John Sieba Roosma 7987 Gabe Edward Parker 7988 Paul Churchill Hutton 7989 John Anthony McFarland 7990 Morris Robert Nelson 7991 Kenneth Perry McNaughton 7992 John Harvey Kane 7993 Alvin Andrew Heidner 7994 Russell Potter Reeder 7995 Merson Leon Skinner 7996 Charles Draper William Canham 7997 Edward Harold McDaniel 7998 Thomas Benton Gailbreath 7999 Willet John Baird 8000 Paul John Black 8001 Clifton Coleman Carter 8002 Paul Leroy Carroll 8003 Edward Lyman Munson 8004 James Bell Burwell 8005 Frederick Prall Munson 8006 Thomas Howard James 8007 James Arthur Willis 8008 Wilson Turner Douglas 8009 John Robert Burns 8010 Marvin John McKinney 8011 Thomas Benjamin White 8012 William Benjamin Hawthorne 8013 Robert Alan Gaffney 8014 Walter Young 8015 Thomas Randall Horton 8016 Roy Jacob Herte 8017 Arthur Edwin Watson 8018 James Oka Wade 8019 Brookner West Brady 8020 Paul Avery Werner 8021 Harry McNeil Grizzard 8022 **1927** Hans William Holmer 8023 Harold Kurstedt 8024 Edward Grow Daly 8025 Donald Chamberlain Hawkins 8026 Theodore Addison Weyher 8027 Robert Hammiell Naylor 8028 Julian Montgomery West 8029 Paul Dunn Berrigan 8030 Henry Gordon Douglas 8031 Joseph Winston Cox 8032 George Townsend Derby 8033 Max Sherred Johnson 8034 Lee Bird Washbourne 8035 John Robert Crume 8036 George Woodburne McGregor 8037 John Leonard Hines 8038 Charles Albert Harrington 8039 Charles H. McNutt 8040 Herman Walter Schull 8041 E. Blair Garland 8042 Loren Davis Pegg 8043 Garrison Holt Davidson 8044 William Henderson Minter 8045 Woodbury Megrew Burgess 8046 Manuel Jose Asensio 8047 Cecil Winfield Land 8048 Frederick Everett Day 8049 Frederick Joseph Brown 8050 Edwin William Chamberlain 8051 Alvin Louis Pachynski 8052 Harry Oliver Paxson 8053 Henry Joseph Hoeffer 8054 Robert Kirby Perrine 8055 Maurice Francis Daly 8056 Fred Wallace Kunesh 8057 Alexander Macomb Miller 8058 Gerald Francis Lillard 8059 George Fenton Peirce 8060 William Hamilton Hunter 8061 Francis Cecil Foster 8062 James Wilson Green 8063 Parmer Wiley Edwards 8064 Francis Elliot Howard 8065 Laurence Sherman Kuter 8066 Fox Brandreth Conner 8067 William Perry Pence 8068 Thomas Morgan Watlington 8069 William Lewis McNamee 8070 Thomas John Hall Trapnell 8071 John Raymond Lovell 8072 Raymond Wiley Curtis 8073 Kenneth Earl Thiebaud 8074 Reynolds Condon 8075 Charles Brundy Brown 8076 Edward Gilbert Farrand 8077 Mason Fred Stober 8078 Willard Burton Carlock 8079 Benjamin Whitehouse 8080 James Wilson 8081 George McCoy 8082 George Lucien Richon 8083 Thomas Kessler McManus 8084 Charles Richard Hutchison 8085 Stanley Burton Bonner 8086 Edward Pont Mechling 8087 Julius Theodore Flock 8088 Robert Graham Lowe 8089 Charles Everett Dunham 8090 George Edward Martin 8091 John Milton Burdge 8092 Bertram Arthur Holtzworth 8093 Frederick Andrew Granholm 8094 Daniel Phipps Miller 8095 Samuel James Simonton 8096 Charles Pennoyer Bixel 8097 Robert Griffith Turner 8098 Alex N. Williams 8099 James Douglas Curtis 8100 Jeremiah Paul Holland 8101 Howard Auguste K. Perrilliat 8102 John Mills Sterling 8103 Edward James Francis Glavin 8104 Mark Kincaid Lewis 8105 Joseph Howard Gilbreth 8106 William Lewis Hoppes 8107 James Francis Collins 8108 Horace Alvord Quinn 8109 Lee Roy Williams 8110 Herbert Bryant Kirkpatrick 8111 Joseph Coleman Timberlake 8112 Thomas Frank Trapolino 8113 Edward Davis McLaughlin 8114 James Virgil Thompson 8115 Henri Anthony Luebberman 8116 Harold James Coyle 8117 Paul Edwin Meredith 8118 Olaf Helgesen Kyster 8119 Orin Leigh Grover 8120 Harry Forrest Townsend 8121 Francis Scoon Gardner 8122 Forester Hampton Sinclair 8123 Walter Morris Johnson 8124 Harold Stanley Isaacson 8125 Willis Webb Whelchel 8126 Albert Harvey Dickerson 8127 Leander LaChance Doan 8128 Arthur Edwin Solem 8129 Theodore Kalakuka 8130 Charlie Wesner 8131 Henry Magruder Zeller 8132 Orville Melvin Hewitt 8133 Arthur Layton Cobb 8134 Meredith Donald Masters 8135 John Anthony Schwab 8136 Lewis Hinchman Ham 8137 Virgil Miles Kimm 8138 Milton Merrill Towner 8139 Robert Curtis White 8140 William Jordan Verbeck 8141 Aloysius Joseph Lepping 8142 Joseph Ganahl 8143 Fay Roscoe Upthegrove 8144 John Marion Moore 8145 Stuart Wood 8146 Lawrence Edward Shaw 8147 Matthew Kemp Deichelmann 8148 Nathan Alton McLamb 8149 William Jefferson Glasgow 8150 Charles Bertody Stone 8151 Frank Thomas Ostenberg 8152 George Asnip 8153 Ruby Elderidge Hunter 8154 Ernest Godfrey Schmidt 8155 John Harold Kochevar 8156 Ernest Benjamin Gray 8157 Douglas Campbell 8158 William Joseph Phelan 8159 Joy Thomas Wrean 8160 John Joseph Holst 8161 Guy Ernest Thrams 8162 Arthur Roth 8163 Carl Sherman Graybeal 8164 David Morgan Hackman 8165 John Thomas Hopper 8166 Ralph Wise Zwicker 8167 Woodson Finch Hocker 8168 James Albemarle Harron 8169 William Edgar Thomas 8170 Cyril Edward Williams 8171 Arthur Milner Burghduff 8172 Joseph v Vincent 8173 Robert Martin Wohlforth 8174 Vachel Davis Whatley 8175 George Edward Levings 8176 Harry Ellery McKinney 8177 Carl Elliott Lundquist 8178 Antulio Segarra 8179 Bernard Cecil Rose 8180 Guy Stanley Meloy 8181 George Van Horn Moseley 8182 Roy William Axup 8183 John Walter Kirby 8184 Forrest Anthony Hornisher 8185 Raymond Earle Bell 8186 Dudley George Strickler 8187 Dana Powers McGown 8188 Charles Boal Ewing 8189 Felix Alex Todd 8190 Barney Avant Daughtry 8191 John Ogden Kilgore 8192 Philip DeWitt Ginder 8193 Ralph Edwin Doty 8194 Howell Hopson Jordan 8195 Robert Frederick Sink 8196 Elmer Matthew Webb 8197 John Prame Kaylor 8198 Christian Gotthard Nelson 8199 Martin Joseph Morin 8200 Gilbert McKee Allen 8201 Calvin Louis Whittle 8202 George Emericus Bender 8203 Jack Henry Griffith 8204 Robert Campbell Aloe 8205 Montgomery McKee 8206 David Stuart Loughborough 8207 Nelson Irving Fooks 8208 Malcolm Frederick Bauer 8209 Lawton Butler 8210 Marion Huggins 8211 Frederick Funston 8212 Martin Moses 8213 R. John West 8214 Edgar Daniel Stark 8215 David Drew Hedekin 8216 James William Smyly 8217 Raymond Gregory Stanton 8218 Neil Bosworth Harding 8219 Jesse Floyd Dressler 8220 Willis Small Matthews 8221 Robert Lewis Easton 8222 Henry Malone Bailey 8223 Fred LeRoy Thorpe 8224 William Rapier Francis Bleakney 8225 **1928** Luke William Finlay 8226 James L. Green 8227 Thomas Alphonsus Lane 8228 Theodore Scott Riggs 8229 Frederick Jensen Dau 8230 Albert Lea Alexander 8231 William T. Hefley 8232 Roland Clough Brown 8233 Samuel R. Browning 8234 Lyle E. Seeman 8235 John Craig Banta 8236 Raphael B. Ezekiel 8237 W. Dixon Smith 8238 Thomas F. Van Natta 8239 Robert S. Israel 8240 David Andrew Watt 8241 Donald Bertrand Smith 8242 Rudolph Ethelbert Smyser 8243 Charles Daniel Curran 8244 Francis Howard Falkner 8245 Alan J. McCutchen 8246 David William Heiman 8247 Robert John Fleming 8248 David Peter Laubach 8249 Benjamin S. Shute 8250 William E. Potter 8251 Edmund Koehler Daley 8252 William Joseph Matteson 8253 Webster Anderson 8254 Paul Lester Sanders 8255 James Elbert Briggs 8256 Richard M. Ludlow 8257 Harry C. Kirby 8258 John Stewart Mills 8259 George M. Cole 8260 Nelson Jacob DeLany 8261 Duncan Sloan Somerville 8262 David W. Traub 8263 Thomas J. Wells 8264 George W. Mundy 8265 Alfred R. Maxwell 8266 Paul Harold Johnston 8267 William Ross Currie 8268 Peter Duryea Calyer 8269 Edward Bernard Keller 8270 Walter Godley Donald 8271 Lyndon Gibson Pearl 8272 Roscoe C. Wilson 8273 Walter E. Todd 8274 William Henry Hennig 8275 Bryant L. Boatner 8276 Nathan Bedford Forrest 8277 Edward Murphy Markham 8278 Dwight Lewis Mulkey 8279 John J. Earle 8280 Robert F. Tate 8281 Church Myall Matthews 8282 Richard Jerome Handy 8283 Karl Gustaf Eric Grimmler 8284 Samuel Robert Brentnall 8285 Charles T. Leeds 8286 John Blanchard Grinstead 8287 John Paul Breden 8288 Howard H. Hasting 8289 Henry Francis IV Beaumont 8290 Mayer H. Halff 8291 Harvey Weston Wilkinson 8292 Clayton John Mansfield 8293 Paul Denver Peery 8294 Walter E. Johns 8295 Charles Franklin Born 8296 Daniel McCoy Wilson 8297 Frank Fort Everest 8298 Roy Henry Guertler 8299 Frank Q. Goodell 8300 Garrison B. Coverdale 8301 Leslie Haynes Wyman 8302 John J. Morrow 8303 Mercer Christie Walter 8304 Theodore J. Dayharsh 8305 Frank Jerdone Coleman 8306 Thomas Joseph Brennan 8307 Robert Loyal Easton 8308 Elmer B. Thayer 8309 James Stewart Neary 8310 John Benjamin Allen 8311 Norris B. Harbold 8312 John Cogswell Oakes 8313 Leslie George Ross 8314 George Raymond Bienfang 8315 Roger Woodhull Goldsmith 8316 Russell Alger Wilson 8317 David Raymond Gibbs 8318 Charles G. Goodrich 8319 Elmo S. Mathews 8320 Stephen Clark Reynolds 8321 Paul Amos Gavan 8322 Thomas Lynch Rich 8323 Leroy Cullom Davis 8324 Alvord V. P. Anderson 8325 Robert Jones Dwyer 8326 John H. Hinrichs 8327 Frederick Lewis Anderson 8328 Marion George Pohl 8329 John Archibald Sawyer 8330 John S. Upham 8331 Thayer S. Olds 8332 Samuel L. Myers 8333 Richard Perry O'Keefe 8334 Robert A. Howard 8335 Thomas Joseph Counihan 8336 Ephraim Hester McLemore 8337 James Easton Holley 8338 Frederick G. Stritzinger 8339 Robert Falligant Travis 8340 John Dabney Billingsley 8341 Lewis A. Vincent 8342 Thomas J. Cody 8343 Robert G. Butler 8344 Carl Herman Sturies 8345 Joseph Anthony Michela 8346 John Bourke Daly 8347 William Henry Tunner 8348 Robert Tryon Frederick 8349 Ralph E. Koon 8350 Verdi Beethoven Barnes 8351 Oren Ranald Meacham 8352 Howard G. Bunker 8353 Edward C. Reber 8354 Henry Leo Flood 8355 Gordon R. Williams 8356 Allison R. Hartman 8357 Stuart G. McLennan 8358 John Alexander Samford 8359 Douglas Glen Ludlam 8360 Legare Kilgore Tarrant 8361 Harry W. Halterman 8362 William Mattingly Breckinridge 8363 Arthur R. Thomas 8364 Paul Anthony Leahy 8365 Whitfield Jack 8366 Madison Clinton Schepps 8367 James L. Hathaway 8368 George Albert Brickman 8369 Douglas Crevier McNair 8370 Fred Obediah Tally 8371 Walter Emerson Finnegan 8372 Russell Blair 8373 Charles Ralph Pinkerton 8374 Edwin Augustus Cummings 8375 Powhatan Moncure Morton 8376 William Webb Browning 8377 Lionel C. McGarr 8378 Theodore D. Ellsworth 8379 James M. Lamont 8380 Montgomery B. Raymond 8381 Noble J. Wiley 8382 Wilhelm Paul Johnson 8383 Alfred Norman Webb 8384 Roger Maxwell Ramey 8385 Horace Lincoln Beall 8386 Harold Brown 8387 Carl Ferdinand Fritzsche 8388 John Peter Doidge 8389 Forrest G. Allen 8390 Thomas Oslin Huddleston 8391 Joseph Lovejoy 8392 Leigh Austin Fuller 8393 John Thomas Murtha 8394 George W. Baker 8395 Ralph J. Butchers 8396 John Severin Knudsen 8397 Samuel Egbert Anderson 8398 Everett D. Peddicord 8399 James G. Bain 8400 August William Schemacher 8401 Robert Franklin Tomlin 8402 Louis T. Vickers 8403 John Paul Boland 8404 Joseph A. Bulger 8405 Kilbourne Johnston 8406 Robert Bernard Beattie 8407 Ralph H. Sievers 8408 John Raymond Gilchrist 8409 Frank Rudolph Maerdian 8410 George Francis Will 8411 George F. Smith 8412 Allen W. Reed 8413 Desmond Henry O'Connell 8414 Arthur William Meehan 8415 Cyril Harvey McGuire 8416 Walter G. Staley 8417 Kent Ellsworth Nourse 8418 Frank Leonard Bock 8419 Thomas Joseph Moran 8420 James Elmer Totten 8421 Truman H. Landon 8422 Richard Ralph Middlebrooks 8423 Charles F. Howard 8424 Hampden Eugene Montgomery 8425 Elmer Wentworth Gude 8426 Maurice Clinton Bisson 8427 Harry E. Wilson 8428 Charles Bowler King 8429 Robert Williams Warren 8430 John F. Wadman 8431 Delmar Taft Spivey 8432 Maury Spotswood Cralle 8433 Ramon Antonio Nadal 8434 Carroll H. Prunty 8435 August W. Kissner 8436 Walter Simon 8437 Edgar E. Enger 8438 LaVerne George Saunders 8439 Tito George Moscatelli 8440 Louis Russell Delmonico 8441 George Henry Lawrence 8442 George C. Willette 8443 Frank Leroy Skeldon 8444 Francis Henry Boos 8445 Gaulden McIntosh Watkins 8446 Thomas L. Sherburne 8447 John F. Farra 8448 Stanhope B. Mason 8449 Eugene Thomas Lewis 8450 Allen Thayer 8451 Rex L. Smith 8452 Emmett O'Donnell 8453 John Oliver Williams 8454 Richard Wetherill 8455 Donald Winston Titus 8456 Emmett F. Yost 8457 Alfred H. Parham 8458 James W. Lockett 8459 Paul D. Adams 8460 Evan M. Houseman 8461 Ralph Thomas Nelson 8462 Robert Kinder Taylor 8463 James Morrow Ivy 8464 Gellert Arthur Douglas 8465 William G. Caldwell 8466 William T. Moore 8467 Paul Jones Mitchell 8468 Alfred B. Denniston 8469 James W. Brown 8470 William C. Sams 8471 Robert Harper Kelly 8472 Joseph F. Trent 8473 Edward Felix Shepherd 8474 Foster Richard Dickey 8475 Samuel H. Lane 8476 Francis W. Haskell 8477 Andrew T. McNamara 8478 Thomas Mason Tarpley 8479 James F. Olive 8480 Edgar A. Sirmyer 8481 Elmer E. Scudder 8482 Robert G. Wiesenauer 8483 Harold Francis Moran 8484 Thomas Webster Steed 8485 Paul Elliott MacLaughlin 8486 **1929** Horace Fennell Sykes 8487 Raymond Leslie Hill 8488 Frank Lee Blue 8489 George Arthur Lincoln 8490 Kenneth David Nichols 8491 Don Zabriskie Zimmerman 8492 Ernest Ward Carr 8493 James Adolph Ostrand 8494 Charles Theodore Tench 8495 Frank Hartman Forney 8496 Frederick Rodgers Dent 8497 Harold Huntley Bassett 8498 Paul Williams Thompson 8499 Howard Moore 8500 John Floyd McCartney 8501 Carl Roemer Jones 8502 James Lee Majors 8503 Alvin Galt Viney 8504 Walter King Wilson 8505 Bruce Douglas Rindlaub 8506 Herbert Milwit 8507 Ward Terry Abbott 8508 Benjamin Richard Wimer 8509 John Lloyd Person 8510 Harry Gage Montgomery 8511 Frank Eugene Fries 8512 Thomas Atkins Adcock 8513 Thomas John Sands 8514 John Stein Walker 8515 James Burt Evans 8516 Frederic Henry Chaffee 8517 Roger James Browne 8518 Joseph Jennings Ladd 8519 Richard David Wentworth 8520 Robert George Henry Meyer 8521 Warren Cecil McDermid 8522 William J. Thompson 8523 James Percy Hannigan 8524 John Gresham Minniece 8525 DeVere Parker Armstrong 8526 Merle Russell Thompson 8527 Douglas Golding Dwyre 8528 Clayton Earl Hughes 8529 Paul Singer Thompson 8530 Franklin Pierce Miller 8531 Dominick Joseph Calidonna 8532 John Martin McKeague 8533 David Ferdinand Brown 8534 Thomas Ludwell Bryan 8535 John Knox Poole 8536 Philip Henry Draper 8537 George Ross Sutherland 8538 Richard Lee Scott 8539 Paul Elias 8540 Paul William Shumate 8541 Harold Quiskey Huglin 8542 William Lewis Bell 8543 Andrew McKeefe 8544 James Theodore Barber 8545 Andrew Samuels 8546 Lawrence McIlroy Guyer 8547 Harold George Hayes 8548 Joseph Horridge 8549 Carl Henry Jark 8550 Donald Philip Graul 8551 Charles Blake McClelland 8552 Robert Emzy Chandler 8553 Edwin Hugh John Carns 8554 Charles Sommers 8555 Joseph Milton Colby 8556 Roy Eugene Hattan 8557 John James LaPage 8558 Wayland Henry Parr 8559 John Elliot Theimer 8560 William Price Connally 8561 John Coleman Horton 8562 George William Peake 8563 Dale Raymond French 8564 Walter Elmer Kraus 8565 Marshall Stanley Roth 8566 Stanley Henry Ayre 8567 David Mural Perkins 8568 Rudolph Fink 8569 Robert Maurice Kraft 8570 Oliver Hardin Gilbert 8571 Ralph Robert Mace 8572 Edwin George Griffith 8573 William Lewis McCulla 8574 Norman Edwin Poinier 8575 Roy Garfield Cuno 8576 Laurance Hilliard Brownlee 8577 John David Francis Phillips 8578 Bert Crawford Muse 8579 Sidney Andrew Ofsthun 8580 George Richard Carey 8581 William Evens Hall 8582 John Dennison Crary 8583 Frederic Harrison Smith 8584 William James Latimer 8585 Donald John Keirn 8586 Luster Azil Vickrey 8587 Philip Chauncey Bennett 8588 Donald Wilbur Armagost 8589 Airel Burr Cooper 8590 William Miller Vestal 8591 Myles Wilkenson Brewster 8592 Dwight Bahney Schannep 8593 George Waite Coolidge 8594 James Franklin Brooke 8595 Kenneth Johnson Woodbury 8596 Norman Alverton Congdon 8597 Robert Moffat Losey 8598 Daniel Norman Sundt 8599 James Lee Beynon 8600 William Tremlett Kirn 8601 William Hopkins Greear 8602 Harold Stevens Whiteley 8603 John J. O'Hara 8604 Charles Sherlock Vanderblue 8605 John Spencer Nesbitt 8606 Milton Andre Acklen 8607 James Gordon Harding 8608 Chandler Prather Robbins 8609 Emery Scott Wetzel 8610 Frank M.

Steadman 8611 William Lafayette Fagg 8612 Jacob George Reynolds 8613 William Darwin Hamlin 8614 Francis Emmons Fellows 8615 John Myron Underwood 8616 Thomas West Hammond 8617 Henry Ray McKenzie 8618 Edmund C.R. Lasher 8619 Paul Donal Harkins 8620 Thomas Fowler Taylor 8621 Mortimer Ernest Sprague 8622 Dexter M. Lowry 8623 Edward Jamet McNally 8624 Eric Hilmer Frithiof Svensson 8625 Donald Alexander Poorman 8626 William Milstead Talbot 8627 George Milton Beaver 8628 George Elial Bush 8629 William Carson Bullock 8630 Calvin Luther Partin 8631 Robert William Ward 8632 Frank Dow Merrill 8633 George Rodolphus Hays 8634 Louis M. de Lisle de Riemer 8635 George Eldridge Keeler 8636 Hugh Warner Stevenson 8637 Roy Vance Keyes 8638 Robert Loomis Anderson 8639 James Leitch Grier 8640 Harland Holmes DeKaye 8641 Joseph Reisner Ranck 8642 Joseph Marcellus Lovell 8643 Edward Blackburn Hempstead 8644 William Ernest Karnes 8645 George Rich Barnes 8646 Robert Gordon Crandall 8647 Theodore Rudolph Redlack 8648 Donald Manzanato Schorr 8649 Kai Eduard Rasmussen 8650 John Wesley Hammond 8651 Laurence Neville Buck 8652 Howard Earl Pearson 8653 Paul Wyatt Caraway 8654 Elmer Elsworth Kirkpatrick 8655 William Fulton McKee 8656 Wayne James Dunn 8657 William Gilmer Bowyer 8658 Eugene Louis Moseley 8659 Edgar Thomas Conley 8660 John Reynolds Callery 8661 Kenneth Milton Briggs 8662 Ezekiel Wimberly Napier 8663 Richard Claire Carpenter 8664 Paul William Steinbeck 8665 Charles Clarke White Allan 8666 Harlan Robinson Statham 8667 James Bernard Quill 8668 William Kerr Ghormley 8669 Robert Little Cook 8670 James Maurice Gavin 8671 Fred Winchester Sladen 8672 George Francis McAneny 8673 Ralph Nisley Woods 8674 Morris Goldberg 8675 Russell Lowell Vittrup 8676 Dale Joel Kinnee 8677 John Drury Cone 8678 Samuel Victor Stephenson 8679 Lester Skene Bork 8680 Ralph Bishop Strader 8681 Edward Auld Dodson 8682 Ernest Fred Heidland 8683 Ralph Van Strauss 8684 Charles Greene Calloway 8685 George Robert Evans 8686 John William Stribling 8687 William Hastings Francis 8688 Thomas Benton McDonald 8689 Charles Theodore Arnett 8690 Louis Anderson Hammack 8691 Daniel William Quinn 8692 John Russell Seward 8693 Melie John Coutlee 8694 Helm George Wilde 8695 Thomas Jefferson DuBose 8696 Daniel Campbell Doubleday 8697 Harlan Clyde Parks 8698 Paul Lamar Freeman 8699 James Joseph Mathews 8700 Marshall Stubbs 8701 Joseph Allen McNerney 8702 Clarence Renshaw 8703 Frederick Giddings 8704 Charles Newton Hunter 8705 Jerald Worden McCoy 8706 John Alfred Nichols 8707 Logan Clarke 8708 Randolph Bolling Hubard 8709 George Edward Lynch 8710 Hugh Mackintosh 8711 David Xavier Angluin 8712 William Erwin Maulsby 8713 Donald Archibald Stevning 8714 Carl Bascombe Herndon 8715 Charles Guthrie Rau 8716 Pearl Harvey Robey 8717 Charles Glendon Williamson 8718 James Julius Winn 8719 Wesley Carlton Wilson 8720 John Lyford Hornor 8721 Daniel Fulbright Walker 8722 John Kauffman Bryan 8723 George Putnam Moody 8724 Nelson Marquis Lynde 8725 Charles Dudley Wiegand 8726 Charles Howard Treat 8727 Thomas Bolyn Smothers 8728 John Francis Regis Seitz 8729 Bruce Easley 8730 Edgar Wright 8731 William Lester Nave 8732 Edward Edgecombe Cruise 8733 William Edward Murphy 8734 Brendan McKay Greeley 8735 Ralph Copeland Cooper 8736 John Ambrose Geary 8737 John Warren Joyes 8738 Everett Clifton Hayden 8739 William Henry Shimonek 8740 David Haytor Buchanan 8741 Stanley Walker Jones 8742 Francis Hobdy Lynch 8743 Roy Frederick Vincent 8744 Ronald John Pierce 8745 Keene Watkins 8746 James Joseph Fitzgibbons 8747 Robert Henry Chard 8748 Herbert John Vander Heide 8749 Luke Bruce Graham 8750 Rexford Wellington Andrews 8751 James Oliver Stephenson 8752 George Mulick Reilly 8753 Norris Slingluff Longaker 8754 Cornelius Zane Byrd 8755 George Franklin Baltzell 8756 Robert Fletcher Sadler 8757 Charles Randolph Kutz 8758 Normando Antonio Costello 8759 John Nicholas Stone 8760 Phineas Kimball Morrill 8761 Philip William Merrill 8762 Thomas Richard Lynch 8763 Allan Gullick Fadness 8764 Samuel Fayette Silver 8765 Charles Freeman Kearney 8766 Julian Broster Lindsey 8767 Charles Armstrong Lynch 8768 Robert Lawrence Love 8769 Thomas Norfleet Griffin 8770 Thomas Charles Dolan 8771 George Frederick Conner 8772 Henry Lloyd Knight 8773 Clebert Leon Hail 8774 Arthur Knight Noble 8775 William Franklin Stevenson 8776 Harding Palmer 8777 Samuel Edwin Mays 8778 Robert Campbell Johnson 8779 William Richard Parient 8780 Robert Van Meter Smith 8781 George Van Millett 8782 Lionel Theo. Roosevelt Trotter 8783 Edwin Michael Van Bibber 8784 Whitside Miller 8785 **1930** Paul Frailey Yount 8786 William Arnold Carter 8787 William Whipple 8788 Charles Keller 8789 Ralph Powell Swofford 8790 James Keller Herbert 8791 Frederick Walker Castle 8792 Paul Ernest Ruestow 8793 Philip Frederick Kromer 8794 Clement Van Beuren Sawin 8795 LeRoy Bartlett 8796 Robert Blake Lothrop 8797 Emil F. Klinke 8798 George Fletcher Schlatter 8799 Edward Fenlon Kumpe 8800 Robert Lynn Lancefield 8801 William Dewoody Dickinson 8802 Lawrence Arthur Bosworth 8803 Cyrus Lawrence Peterson 8804 Clarence Harvey Gunderson 8805 Donald Ralph Neil 8806 Elmer Landen Meguire 8807 Frederick Garside Terry 8808 Oscar Benjamin Beasley 8809 Irvin Rudolph Schimmelpfennig 8810 James Judson Heriot 8811 Robert William Porter 8812 John Henderson Dudley 8813 Andrew Mark Wright 8814 Lyman Huntley Shaffer 8815 Albert Eugene Dennis 8816 William Herschel Allen 8817 Howard Monroe McCoy 8818 Carl Henry Fernstrom 8819 Swasti Pradisdh 8820 Charles William Haas 8821 Darwin Worth Ferguson 8822 Hubert Du Bois Lewis 8823 Charles Lee Heitman 8824 Louis Theilmann Heath 8825 Albert Joseph Mandelbaum 8826 Andrew Pick O'Meara 8827 Clark Neil Piper 8828 Robert Jefferson Wood 8829 Aubrey Kenneth Dodson 8830 Mark Edward Bradley 8831 Philip Campbell Wehle 8832 Douglas Mitchell Kilpatrick 8833 Wiley Duncan Ganey 8834 George Clifford Duehring 8835 Francis Frederick Uhrhane 8836 Charles Granville Dodge 8837 Herbert Voivenelle Mitchell 8838 James Nugent Vaughn 8839 Thetus Cayce Odom 8840 Alexander Graham Stone 8841 Jacquard Hirshorn Rothschild 8842 Stuart Francis Crawford 8843 Truman William Carrithers 8844 Walter Campbell Sweeney 8845 Henry Bing Kunzig 8846 Keith Hartman Ewbank 8847 Thomas Irwin Edgar 8848 Herbert Charles Gibner 8849 Robert Foster Haggerty 8850 Frank Kowalski 8851 Albert Mark Smith 8852 Hamilton Hawkins Howze 8853 Harry Hollingsworth Geoffrey 8854 John Xavier Walsh 8855 Harry Brown Packard 8856 Robert James Watson 8857 Ralph Cooper Barrow 8858 Robert Highman Booth 8859 Arthur Leonard Fuller 8860 Mahlon Smith Davis 8861 Winfield Wilber Sisson 8862 Anthony Eugene Curcio 8863 Maximiano Saqui Janairo 8864 Morris John Lee 8865 John Joseph MacFarland 8866 Wendell Holmes Langdon 8867 Harry Raymond Boyd 8868 Ernest Emil Holtzen 8869 Samuel Lynn Morrow 8870 Albert Watson 8871 Marvin Lewis Harding 8872 Franklin Fearing Wing 8873 James Owen Curtis 8874 Birrell Walsh 8875 Henry Bittinger Croswell 8876 William Fletcher Grisham 8877 Phillips Waller Smith 8878 Alva Revista Fitch 8879 Dana Stuart Alexander 8880 James Quayle Brett 8881 Joseph Henry Twyman 8882 Percy Howard Brown 8883 Paul Clark 8884 Edward Sedgwick Berry 8885 David Hodge Baker 8886 Albert Everett Harris 8887 James Sylvester Sutton 8888 Richard Churchill Hutchinson 8889 James Theopold Darrah 8890 Roy Ernest Lindquist 8891 Sidney Clay Wooten 8892 Robert Edwin Cron 8893 Ross Thatcher Sampson 8894 William Henry Sterling Wright 8895 Archibald William Stuart 8896 Willis Almeron Perry 8897 Grant Eugene Hill 8898 John Frank Greco 8899 Alden Pugh Taber 8900 Charles Joseph Odenweller 8901 Edwin Sanders Perrin 8902 Neal Edwin Ausman 8903 George Goodrell Garton 8904 Robert Louis Brunzell 8905 Raymond Davis Millener 8906 Robert William Timothy 8907 Aubrey Dewitt Smith 8908 Barksdale Hamlett 8909 Brainard Spencer Cook 8910 Troup Miller 8911 William Ewing Grubbs 8912 William Dole Eckert 8913 Frederick Reginia Weber 8914 Charles Clinton Cloud 8915 O'Neill Keren Kane 8916 Arthur Carey Peterson 8917 Harold Eugene Brooks 8918 Paul Arthur Roy 8919 Bream Cooley Patrick 8920 William Henry Harris 8921 Tom Robert Stoughton 8922 Thomas Weldon Dunn 8923 Lauris Norstad 8924 Adam Andrew Koscielniak 8925 James Snow Lunn 8926 Marvin Chandler Johnson 8927 John Brazelton Fillmore Dice 8928 Millard Lewis 8929 Othel Rochelle Deering 8930 James Frederick Ammerman 8931 Leon Clarence Scott 8932 John Chesley Kilborn 8933 William Naille Taylor 8934 Frederick Dwight Atkinson 8935 William Warner Harris 8936 Carl Amandus Brandt 8937 Frederick Gardner Crabb 8938 Buford Russell Nyquist 8939 John Charles Hayden 8940 Robert Allen Ports 8941 Roderick Leland Carmichael 8942 Carl Irven Hutton 8943 George Wareham Gibbs 8944 Arthur Cleveland Goodwin 8945 Roy Whitman Muth 8946 Richard Shafle Freeman 8947 Walter William Thiede 8948 Harold L. Smith 8949 Jaromir Jan Pospisil 8950 Richards Montgomery Bristol 8951 Edward Irving Sachs 8952 Marshall Hill Hurt 8953 Samuel Philbrick Kelley 8954 George William Lermond 8955 Norman Ray Burnett 8956 Charles Lind Olin 8957 Samuel Roth 8958 Joe Clifton East 8959 Eugene Anthony Kenny 8960 John Livingood Pauley 8961 Frank Theodore Folk 8962 Robert Craig Sutherland 8963 Joseph Farrell Haskell 8964 Richard Joseph O'Keefe 8965 Carleton Merritt Clifford 8966 Noel Adrian Neal 8967 Howard Walter Quinn 8968 Raymond Charles Brisach 8969 Charley Paul Eastburn 8970 George William Perry 8971 Clifton Donald Blackford 8972 Ephraim M. Hampton 8973 Thomas Ferguson Wall 8974 Jack Griffin Pitcher 8975 James Sawyer Luckett 8976 Myron Albert Quinto 8977 Joseph Arthur Miller 8978 Ned Dalton Moore 8979 Christian Hudgins Clarke 8980 Claude Emerson Jurney 8981 John Herhold Murrell 8982 Thomas Mifflin 8983 Daniel Russell Taylor 8984 James Knox Wilson 8985 Francis Joseph Corr 8986 Camron Sudasna 8987 Kurt Martin Landon 8988 Alexander Richard Appelman 8989 Gerry Leonard Mason 8990 Hubern Paul Dellinger 8991 Winston Rose Maxwell 8992 Aubrey Ellis Strode 8993 Daniel Anderson Cooper 8994 Theodore Roberts Kimpton 8995 Earl Hugh Heimerdinger 8996 John Simpson Guthrie 8997 Allan Duard MacLean 8998 Richard Cloyd Parker 8999 Howard Russell Moore 9000 James Lowell Richardson 9001 Francis Hill Dohs 9002 Ludlow King 9003 Eli Stevens 9004 Jacob Samuel Sauer 9005 Joseph Eakens James 9006 Charles Edward Beauchamp 9007 Paul Aloysius Chalmers 9008 Thomas Kent 9009 Sory Smith 9010 Henry Estil Royall 9011 Paul William Blanchard 9012 Jasper Joseph Riley 9013 Theodore Francis Bogart 9014 Thad Adolphus Broom 9015 Guy Emery 9016 Harry Curns Anderson 9017 Walter Edwin Ahearn 9018 Herman William Ohme 9019 Henry Alan Winters 9020 Paul Russell Weyrauch 9021 William Holtz Diddlebock 9022 Orin Doughty Haugen 9023 Morton Elmer Townes 9024 Frederick James Simpson 9025 Charles Lewis 9026 **1931** Kenneth Adelbert McCrimmon 9027 Walter Henry Esdorn 9028 Chester William Ott 9029 Richard Lee Jewett 9030 Frederick Gilman Saint 9031 Frederick Hayes Warren 9032 Charles Hartwell Bonesteel 9033 Louis Russell Wirak 9034 Wilbur Stone Jones 9035 William White Ragland 9036 Marvin Lyle Thomas 9037 Edward John Cotter 9038 Gunnard William Carlson 9039 Stephen Read Hanmer 9040 Edward Minter Parker 9041 Rufo Calingat Romero 9042 Walter Krueger 9043 Jaime Velasquez 9044 Champlin Fletcher Buck 9045 Chester Lavaughn Landaker 9046 William Frederick Cassidy 9047 Edward Aloysius Brown 9048 Walker Wilson Milner 9049 George M. Wertz 9050 John Philips Daley 9051 Marshall Sylvester Carter 9052 Clarence Jonathan Hauck 9053 Angelo Ralph DelCampo 9054 Jergen Bernhart Olson 9055 John Barclay Sullivan 9056 Elwin Herklas Eddy 9057 Lawrence Herbert Rogers 9058 Glenn Frederick Rogers 9059 Clifton Lee MacLachlan 9060 Daniel Francis Callahan 9061 Theodore William Parker 9062 Roger Willard Moore 9063 Cornelius Ardalion Lichirie 9064 George Robert Huffman 9065 Marcellus Duffy 9066 Jesse Huckett Veal 9067 James Francis Stroker 9068 John William Hansborough 9069 Alfred Christian Gay 9070 Walter Ferris Ellis 9071 Robert Alan 9072 Robert Hackett 9073 James Donald Sams 9074 Grosvenor Francis Powell 9075 Charles Frederick McNair 9076 William White Dick 9077 Merwin Scott Dickson 9078 Donald Cubbison Little 9079 Howard William Hunter 9080 John William Cave 9081 Gordon Aylesworth Blake 9082 Joseph Francis Carroll 9083 William Charles Hall 9084 Donald Bowie Webber 9085 Sidney Glenn Brown 9086 Richard Hanna Lane 9087 Peter Schmick 9088 John Larimer Inskeep 9089 Milton Hughes Pressley 9090 Philip Bessom Stiness 9091 Anthony Sherwood Howe 9092 Alphonse Alfred Greene 9093 A. J. McVea 9094 Frank Pickering Corbin 9095 Charles Walker Raymond 9096 Michael Martin Irvine 9097 Gaspare Frank Blunda 9098 George Sebastian Speidel 9099 Julian Merritt Chappell 9100 Norman Ernest Tipton 9101 Richard Holmes Harrison 9102 James William Park 9103 Lucius Nash Cron 9104 Frederick Theodore Berg 9105 Arthur Deane Gough 9106 Gordon King Cusack 9107 William Frew Train 9108 Loren Fletcher Cole 9109 Tom Victor Stayton 9110 Warren Harlan Hoover 9111 Donald Norton Yates 9112 John Archibald Barclay 9113 Merillat Moses 9114 August Schomburg 9115 James Bertram Corbett 9116 Clyde Robinson McBride 9117 Elmo Clark Mitchell 9118 Hoyt Daniel Williams 9119 Miller Osborne Perry 9120 Scott Mock Sanford 9121 Herbert Walter Mansfield 9122 Fielder Price Greer 9123 William Eaton Chandler 9124 Frank Arthur Bogart 9125 Harold Lucas Bays 9126 C. Coburn Smith 9127 Charles Robert Bard 9128 Paul Gordon Miller 9129 Camden William McConnell 9130 Charles Breckinridge Duff 9131 Samuel Smellow 9132 Wilbur Manly Skidmore 9133 William John Bell 9134 James Chester Blanning 9135 Harry James Fleeger 9136 Milan George Weber 9137 Ernest Moore 9138 William Arthur Davis 9139 Royden Eugene Beebe 9140 Chester Joseph Diestel 9141 Philip Higley Bethune 9142 Earle Fremont Cook 9143 William Lamar Parham 9144 Johnson Hagood 9145 John Maurice Brown 9146 Earle William Hockenberry 9147 Frederick Richard Redden 9148 Albert Frederick Cassevant 9149 Richard Sylvester Spangler 9150 Percy Hotspur Lash 9151 John Edwin Barr 9152 Carl Edward Green 9153 Hamilton Murray Peyton 9154 Louis Augustine Guenther 9155 John Newlin Raker 9156 Augustus William Dannemiller 9157 Milton Wylie Arnold 9158 Forrest Caraway 9159 Paul Burns 9160 David Northup Motherwell 9161 Harry Bryant Cooper 9162 Jermain Ferdinand Rodenhauser 9163 Addison Vincent Dishman 9164 Millard Chester Young 9165 John Anderson Berry 9166 William Harris Isbell 9167 Philip Van Dick 9168 Norton Bailey Wilson 9169 Robert Perkins Holland 9170 Mervyn Mackay Magee 9171 Lawrence Turner Talcott 9172 Henry Keppler Mooney 9173 Eugene William Hiddleston 9174 John Knight Waters 9175 William Ayres Hampton 9176 Robert Merrill Lee 9177 Robert Freeman Fulton 9178 P. Francis Passarella 9179 Donald Donaldson 9180 Orlando Collette Troxel 9181 Francis Thomas Pachler 9182 Harold Ambrose Hughes 9183 Charles Roger Urban 9184 Donald Rosser Patterson 9185 Horace Wayne Taul 9186 John Thomas Westermeier 9187 Glenn Aloysius Farris 9188 Dean Coldwell Strother 9189 Clifford Christopher Wagner 9190 Richard Byington Carhart 9191 Robert Daniel Johnston 9192 Leonard Daniel Henry 9193 George Edwin Dietz 9194 George Frederick Hartman 9195 Louis Victor Hightower 9196 Edwin John Messinger 9197 Carl Wilbert Carlmark 9198 Robert Leander Cardell 9199 Charles North Howze 9200 Richard Hungerford Wise 9201 Charles Francis Densford 9202 John Robert Skeldon 9203 Leo Wilbur Cather 9204 Orville Zelotes Tyler 9205 Raymond Silas Pratt 9206 Walter Foster Gallup 9207 Maynard Norwood Levenick 9208 Gunnar Carl Carlson 9209 Jacob Edward Smart 9210 George Edward Fletcher 9211 Hugh Pate Harris 9212 Irving William Jackson 9213 Robert Quinney Brown 9214 Chas. Edward Nason Howard 9215 Gordon Singles 9216 John Robert Beishline 9217 Field Hunter Tapping 9218 Russell Bowman Semple 9219 Richard Hunter Lawson 9220 John William Mackay Read 9221 Lester Leroy Hilman Kunish 9222 Robert Edward Lee Eaton 9223 John Joseph Davis 9224 Carl Fillmore Damberg 9225 Wendell Washington Bowman 9226 Charles Pence Westpheling 9227 James Irvine King 9228 Thomas Joseph Marnane 9229 Joseph Buford Zimmerman 9230 Ernest Fred Easterbrook 9231 Curtis James Herrick 9232 Edward Kenly Purnell 9233 Howard Max Pahl 9234 Howard Harrison Dudley 9235 Richard Spencer Carter 9236 Hilbert Fred Muenter 9237 Elmer Lee Thompson 9238 Ashton Miller Haynes 9239 John Autrey Feagin 9240 Blair Arthur Ford 9241 Richard Klemm Boyd 9242 Charles Lowman Decker 9243 Merle Lucius Fisher 9244 Arthur Hamilton Hogan 9245 Edwin Anderson Walker 9246 Orrin Charles Krueger 9247 William Potter Turpin 9248 Raymond Taylor Lester 9249 Charles Edward Hoy 9250 Richard Francis Reidy 9251 William Leonard Hardick 9252 Harrison Schermerhorn Markham 9253 Richard Steinbach 9254 Loren Albert Ayers 9255 Harry Winston Candler 9256 Dean Ambrose Herman 9257 William David Davis 9258 William Taylor 9259 Arthur Raster Hercz 9260 Terrence Robert Joseph Hickey 9261 Earle Bradford Leeper 9262 Seiss Ertel Wagner 9263 Joseph Barlow Coolidge 9264 John Clarence Gordon 9265 John Hugh McAleer 9266 Arthur Raphael Kerwin 9267 Peter Otey Ward 9268 Carl William Kohls 9269 John Thomas Malloy 9270 Harold Robert Uhlman 9271 Donald Knox Armstrong 9272 Andrew Joseph Adams 9273 Victor James MacLaughlin 9274 Charles Bowman Dougher 9275 William Rogers Woodward 9276 James Willard Pumpelly 9277 Charles Ingram Humber 9278 David William Hutchison 9279 Irving Lehrfeld 9280 Paul Christian Heim Walz 9281 Phineas Harvey Adair 9282 Roy Luttrell Leinster 9283 Robert Everett Quackenbush 9284 Charles Elder Frederick 9285 Samuel Edward Jones 9286 Howard Hart Reed 9287 Gustave Marinius Heiss 9288 Joseph Kingsley Dickey 9289 John Frank Ruggles 9290 Harry George Roller 9291 Roy Kirschman Kauffman 9292 Donald Frank Buchwald 9293 John Hugh McGee 9294 Van Hugo Bond 9295 Marvin James Coyle 9296 Ernest Clyde Peters 9297 Gerald Evan Williams 9298 Clarence David McGowen 9299 Eugene Lewis Brown 9300 John Edward Leary 9301 Daniel Turner Workizer 9302 Alexander Johnston Sutherland 9303 James Edward Maloney 9304 Alfred Cookman Marshall 9305 James Thomas McClellan 9306 Robert Moorman Cheal 9307 Merrick Hector Truly 9308 Houston Parks Houser 9309 William James Mahoney 9310 Richard Robert Danek 9311 James Henry Carlisle 9312 Edward Julius Timberlake 9313 John Tazewell Helms 9314 Paul Arthur Mayo 9315 Theodore Beck Beck 9316 William Addison Magee Morin 9317 Charles Pugh Baldwin 9318 Augustus George Elegar 9319 John Hubert Matthews 9320 John Walter Brady 9321 Oral Grant Willis 9322 Russell Hunter Griffith 9323 **1932** Rush Blodget Lincoln 9324 Stanley Tanner Wray 9325 Ellsworth Ingalls Davis 9326 Andrew Hero 9327 George Kumpe 9328 William Ruthven Smith 9329 Frank Schaffer Besson 9330 Richard Roberts Arnold 9331 Herrol James Skidmore 9332 Francis Ray Hoehl 9333 Julian David Abell 9334 Chih Wang 9335 Frederick Raleigh Young 9336 John Chandler Steele 9337 Allen Fraser Clark 9338 Thore Fritjof Bengtson 9339 Christian Frederick Dreyer 9340 William Francis Powers 9341 James McCormack 9342 Russell Manly Nelson 9343 Stanley Ronald Stewart 9344 Arnold Sommer 9345 Charles Kissam Allen 9346 Sam Carroll Russell 9347 James Hutchings Cunningham 9348 John Henry Weber 9349 Roger Derby Black 9350 Archibald William Lyon 9351 Edward Ellis Farnsworth 9352 Daniel Stickley Spengler 9353 Joseph Percival Greenwood 9354 Norman Robert Ford 9355 John Campbell Street 9356 Milton Leonard Ogden 9357 Alexander Graham 9358 Ralph Hemmings Davey 9359 William Menoher 9360 George Wilson Power 9361 William Burns Fraser 9362 James Aloysius Cain 9363 Kenneth Frederick Zitzman 9364 John Earl Metzler 9365 George Robinson Mather 9366 Harrison Alan Gerhardt 9367 Stanley Sawicki 9368 Leo Peter Dahl 9369 Howard Raymond Martindell 9370 Edgar Northrop Chace 9371 Frank Lester Howard 9372 Frank Hamilton Britton 9373 Byron Leslie Paige 9374 Torgils Grimkel Wold 9375 John Bevier Ackerman 9376 Charles Ray Longanecker 9377 Irving Donald Roth 9378 James Karrick Woolnough 9379 Lauri Jacob Hillberg 9380 Samuel Watson Horner 9381 Philip Vibert Doyle 9382 Robert Augur Hewitt 9383 Benjamin Jepson Webster 9384 Earle Gilmore Wheeler 9385 Edwin Simpson Hartshorn 9386 James

Forsyth Thompson 9387 Charles Michael Baer 9388 William Alden Call 9389 Roger Barton Derby 9390 Roland Capel Bower 9391 Dwight Benjamin Johnson 9392 Joseph Edward Gill 9393 Everett Wayne Barlow 9394 Frederick William Ellery 9395 Loren Boyd Hillsinger 9396 Horace King Whalen 9397 John Paul McConnell 9398 Preston Steele 9399 Robert Douglass Glassburn 9400 Joe William Kelly 9401 Walter Allen Rude 9402 Walter Parks Goodwin 9403 Erven Charles Somerville 9404 John Abner Meeks 9405 Clifford McCoy Snyder 9406 Gilbert Nevius Adams 9407 Aaron Meyer Lazar 9408 John Clifford McCawley 9409 John Morgan Price 9410 Edward Gibbons Shinkle 9411 Robert Lockwood Williams 9412 John Joseph Hutchison 9413 Robert Earl Schukraft 9414 Carl Morton Sciple 9415 Harry Cecil Porter 9416 Dwight Edward Beach 9417 William Little 9418 William Massello 9419 Arthur Walter Blair 9420 Daniel Stone Campbell 9421 Richard Johnson Hunt 9422 Theodore George Burton 9423 Stephen Michael Mellnik 9424 Louis Watson Truman 9425 Dale Eugene Means 9426 Hugh Willard Riley 9427 William Sammis Coit 9428 Ray James Stecker 9429 Curtis Alan Schrader 9430 Charles Leonard Hassmann 9431 William Fletcher Spurgin 9432 Kenneth Burton Hobson 9433 John Reynolds Sutherland 9434 Donald Linwood Hardy 9435 Richard Tide Coiner 9436 Floyd Allan Hansen 9437 James Edward Godwin 9438 Harold Walmsley 9439 Gerald George Epley 9440 Bernard William McQuade 9441 John Brinton Heyburn 9442 Ashton Herbert Manhart 9443 Harald Simpson Sundt 9444 Horace Freeman Bigelow 9445 Charles Albert Clark 9446 James Bates Rankin 9448 David Emory Jones 9449 Harvey Porter Huglin 9450 Robert Folkes Moore 9451 Bernard Thielen 9452 George Dowery Campbell 9453 Karl Laurance Scherer 9454 Charles Hardin Anderson 9455 Dwight Drenth Edison 9456 Jefferson Davis Childs 9457 John Aloysius Gavin 9458 Todd Humbert Slade 9459 John Ramsey Pugh 9460 Joseph Edward Stearns 9461 Charles Ratcliffe Murray 9462 Wallace Hawn Brucker 9463 Francis Garrison Hall 9464 Charles Louis Williams 9465 William Barnes Moore 9466 William Russell Huber 9467 Bogardus Snowden Cairns 9468 Delbert Abraham Pryor 9469 Willard Sterling Garrison 9470 Charles Edward Wheatley 9471 Meyer Abraham Braude 9472 Chester Hammond 9473 John George Ondrick 9474 Byram Arnold Bunch 9475 I. Sewell Morris 9476 Gerard Charles Cowan 9477 Hunter Harris 9478 Gordon Whitney Seaward 9479 Henry Graham McFeely 9480 Walter Marquis Tisdale 9481 Ira Webster Porter 9482 Charles Albert Piddock 9483 Nelson Landon Head 9484 Walker Raitt Goodrich 9485 William Harvie Freeland 9486 Thomas Henry Harvey 9487 William Halford Maguire 9488 David Hamilton Kennedy 9489 Merle Robbins Williams 9490 William Whitfield Culp 9491 Kenneth Edward Tiffany 9492 Nicholas Earnest Powel 9493 Norman Herbert Lankenau 9494 Mom L. Chuan Chuen Kambhu 9495 William Bing Kunzig 9496 Robert Bruce McLane 9497 Andrew Meulenberg 9498 Charles Marvin Iseley 9499 Edwin Guldlin Simenson 9500 Sam Houston Wiseman 9501 William Gordon Beard 9502 Harvey Herman Fischer 9503 Robert Haynes Terrill 9504 Avery Madison Cochran 9505 Samuel Arthur Daniel 9506 Frank Vines Johnston 9507 Albert Edward Reiff Howarth 9508 James Lee Massey 9509 Albert Edward Stoltz 9510 Thomas Connell Darcy 9511 Edmond Michael Rowan 9512 Edward Green Winston 9513 Milton Skerrett Glatterer 9514 William Henry Mikkelsen 9515 Hugh Thomas Cary 9516 Sewell Marion Brumby 9517 Bun Mar Praband 9518 Clifford Harcourt Rees 9519 Arnold Leon Schroeder 9520 Graves Collins Teller 9521 Richard Henry Smith 9522 Roscoe Constantine Huggins 9523 Francis Deisher 9524 Eugene Porter Mussett 9525 Lon Harley Smith 9526 Edward Willis Suarez 9527 Paul Delmont Bunker 9528 Edward Joseph Burke 9529 Walden Bernald Coffey 9530 George Reynolds Grunert 9531 James Ellison Glattly 9532 David Peter Schorr 9533 William George Davidson 9534 John Clinton Welborn 9535 Edwin Charles Momm 9536 Herbert Bishop Thatcher 9537 Charles Salvatore D'Orsa 9538 Frederick Milton Hinshaw 9539 Robert Broussard Landry 9540 Luigi Giulio Guiducci 9541 William Hyatt Bache 9542 William Anderson McNulty 9543 Joe Edwin Golden 9544 Eldon Frederick Ziegler 9545 Frank Greenleaf Jamison 9546 James Winfield Coutts 9547 Dan Gilmer 9548 Wilfred Joseph Lavigne 9549 George Thigpen Duncan 9550 Harry Celistine Quartier 9551 Roy Edwin Moore 9552 Harley Niles Trice 9553 James Ernest Beery 9554 A. Ward Gillette 9555 Harold Edward Shaw 9556 Charles Gates Herman 9557 Charles Alexander Carrell 9558 Lawrence Bartlett Babcock 9559 William Roy Thomas 9560 Loris Ray Cochran 9561 Robert Lynn Carver 9562 Henry Chestnutt Britt 9563 Thomas Randall McDonald 9564 Orville Wright Mullikin 9565 Romulus Wright Puryear 9566 David Harrison Armstrong 9567 Earl Sipple Eckhart 9568 John William Keating 9569 John Garnett Coughlin 9570 Thomas Robertson Hannah 9571 William Madison Garland 9572 William Elwood Means 9573 George Louis Descheneaux 9574 Thomas Charles Morgan 9575 John William Bowen 9576 Frank Ward Ebey 9577 James Walter Gurr 9578 James Madison Churchill 9579 Robert Lee Scott 9580 Lewis Ray Briggs 9581 Harold Randall Everman 9582 Keith Allen Thompson 9583 Thomas Benjamin Spratt 9584 Erskine Clark 9585 **1933** Kenneth E. Fields 9586 George Wood Beeler 9587 John Joseph Danis 9588 Duncan Hallock 9589 Alfred Dodd Starbird 9590 John Douglas Matheson 9591 Richard Davis Meyer 9592 Alden Kingsland Sibley 9593 Paul R. Gowen 9594 Charles Wheeler Thayer 9595 Marshall Bonner 9596 Lawrence Joseph Lincoln 9597 Clayton Samuel Gates 9598 James Vance Hagan 9599 John Steven Conner 9600 Robert Campbell Tripp 9601 Edward George Herb 9602 William Jonas Ely 9603 John Thomas Honeycutt 9604 William Allen Harris 9605 Charles Russell Broshous 9606 Percival Ernest Gabel 9607 John Gardner Shinkle 9608 Bernard Card 9609 Rodney Cleveland Gott 9610 Hoy D. Davis 9611 Alvin Charles Welling 9612 William Harris Ball 9613 Douglas Charles Davis 9614 Ellsworth Barricklow Downing 9615 Robert Amrine Turner 9616 David Warren Gray 9617 Frank Sherman Henry 9618 William Orin Blandford 9619 Walter Adonis Downing 9620 Guy Cecil Lothrop 9621 Robert Crain Leslie 9622 John Edward Watters 9623 Francis Joseph McMorrow 9624 Charles Golding Dunn 9625 Thomas Allen Glass 9626 Thomas Samuel Moorman 9627 Harry Julian 9628 William Cunningham Reeves 9629 Dabney Ray Corum 9630 Lauren Whitford Merriam 9631 Herbert George Sparrow 9632 Howard Elwyn Webster 9633 Robert Wolcott Meals 9634 Walter August Jensen 9635 Winton Summers Graham 9636 Edward Bodeau 9637 William Livingston Travis 9638 Thomas Burns Hall 9639 Chalmer Kirk McClelland 9640 Ferdinand Marion Humphries 9641 David Nicholas Crickette 9642 John Denton Armitage 9643 Theodore John Conway 9644 Clayton Earl Mullins 9645 Paul Elton LaDue 9646 Edward Joseph Hale 9647 William J. Daniel 9648 Chester Arthur Dahlen 9649 John Joseph Lane 9650 Travis Monroe Hetherington 9651 Tayloe Stephen Pollock 9652 Edgar O. Taylor 9653 Ira Whitehead Cory 9654 William York Frentzel 9655 Thomas Kocher MacNair 9656 James Hilliard Polk 9657 John Glenn Armstrong 9658 Samuel Edward Otto 9659 Robert Richard Lutz 9660 Donald Gordon McGrew 9661 Harry Winfield Schenck 9662 Lamar Cecil Ratcliffe 9663 Gerald Chapman 9664 Robert John Lawlor 9665 Arthur Alfred McCrary 9666 Daniel Parker 9667 Edgar Haskell Kibler 9668 Harold Cooper Donnelly 9669 Morris Oswald Edwards 9670 William Oscar Senter 9671 Frank Joseph Zeller 9672 Richard Louis Matteson 9673 Sidney Francis Giffin 9674 Robert Beall Franklin 9675 William Gordon Bartlett 9676 Paul Nelson Gillon 9677 John Hardy Lewis 9678 Paul Rudolf Walters 9679 Vernon Cleveland Smith 9680 Edward Thorndike Ashworth 9681 William Bruce Logan 9682 Lafar Lipscomb 9683 Harry Stephen Bishop 9684 Harry Sheldon Tubbs 9685 Herman Henry Kaesser 9686 Francis Hill 9687 Herbert Charles Plapp 9688 Lassiter Albert Mason 9689 Joseph Henry O'Malley 9690 Frederic Henry Fairchild 9691 Emory Edwin Hackman 9692 George Hobart Chapman 9693 Francis Iden Pohl 9694 Patrick William Guiney 9695 J. Frederick Thorlin 9696 Frank Harris Shepardson 9697 William George Fritz 9698 H. Taylor Henry 9699 Jack Wellington Turner 9700 Robert Worman Hain 9701 Charles Goyer Patterson 9702 Clyde Lucken Jones 9703 Victor Edward Maston 9704 Ethan Allen Chapman 9705 Oren Eugene Hurlbut 9706 Harrison King 9707 George Warren White 9708 Richard Park 9709 Beverly Dewitt Jones 9710 William Hadley Richardson 9711 Frank Petterson Hunter 9712 Richard Channing Moore 9713 George Harold Crawford 9714 Harold Roth Maddux 9715 John Roosevelt Brindley 9716 Dwight Divine 9717 Samuel McF. McReynolds 9718 Marcus Tague 9719 Joseph Leonard Cowhey 9720 Edward Deane Marshall 9721 George Leon Van Way 9722 Newell Charles James 9723 Charles Henry Chase 9724 David Virgil Adamson 9725 John William Ferris 9726 Robert Penn Thompson 9727 Russell Roland Klanderman 9728 James Leo Dalton 9729 Neil Merton Wallace 9730 William Paul Whelihan 9731 Marshall Woodruff Frame 9732 Robin George Speiser 9733 William James Given 9734 Harry Nelson Burkhalter 9735 Avery John Cooper 9736 Laurence Browning Kelley 9737 Stephen Ogden Fuqua 9738 Hardin Leonard Olson 9739 Benedict Ray 9740 Cam Longley 9741 Carlyle Walton Phillips 9742 Robert Benton Neely 9743 Phillip Henshaw Pope 9744 William John Ledward 9745 Joseph Warren Stilwell 9746 Peter Paul Bernd 9747 Arthur Robert Cyr 9748 Arthur Wilson Tyson 9749 Joseph Menzie Pittman 9750 George Allen Carver 9751 Robert Allen Brunt 9752 Gordon Pendleton Larson 9753 Thomas Joseph O'Connor 9754 George Rushmore Gretser 9755 James Monroe Royal 9756 Robert Totten 9757 Douglas Moore Cairns 9758 Sherburne Whipple 9759 Edgar Collins Doleman 9760 Cyril Joseph Letzelter 9761 William Orlando Darby 9762 Daniel Light Hine 9763 Jack Wallace Rudolph 9764 John Abell Cleveland 9765 George Thomas Powers 9766 Frank James Carson 9767 Joshua Robert Messersmith 9768 Roy Tripp Evans 9769 Edwin Martin Cahill 9770 William Francis Ryan 9771 Raymond Emerson Kendall 9772 James Henry Skinner 9773 Anthony Frank Kleitz 9774 Paul Thomas Carroll 9775 Richard John Meyer 9776 Randolph Whiting Fletter 9777 Joseph Lockwood MacWilliam 9778 Horace Benjamin Thompson 9779 Charles Harlow Miles 9780 Humbert Joseph Versace 9781 Milton Frederick Summerfelt 9782 Franklin Guest Smith 9783 William Henry Baumer 9784 Gabriel Poillon Disosway 9785 James Pugh Pearson 9786 Earl Jacob Macherey 9787 Ralph Alspaugh 9788 Emile Jeantet Greco 9789 Gerald Lorenzo Roberson 9790 Joseph Edward Bastion 9791 Jewell Burch Shields 9792 Thomas Herbert Beck 9793 Maurice Evans Kaiser 9794 Benjamin Thomas Harris 9795 Gardner Wellington Porter 9796 Harry William Sweeting 9797 Franklin Stone Henley 9798 Cyrus Abda Dolph 9799 John Martin Breit 9800 Harold Lindsay Richey 9801 Charles Fauntleroy Harrison 9802 Thomas Bowes Evans 9803 Walter Andrews 9804 Franklin Gibney Rothwell 9805 Leo Harold Heintz 9806 William Howard Thompson 9807 William Fant Damon 9808 William Gray Sills 9809 Robert Evans Arnette 9810 F. Clay Bridgewater 9811 Luell Leyton Stube 9812 Ernest Mikell Clarke 9813 Victor H. King 9814 Daniel W. Smith 9815 Thomas Denyse Flynn 9816 Harold Keith Johnson 9817 James Orr Boswell 9818 David Parker Gibbs 9819 William Howard Garrett Fuller 9820 Gordon Milo Eyler 9821 Randall Elwood Cashman 9822 Cordes Frederich Tiemann 9823 Maddrey Allen Solomon 9824 Lyle William Bernard 9825 Shelby Francis Williams 9826 Richard Glatfelter 9827 Jean Evans Engler 9828 Corwin Paul Vansant 9829 Walter Abner Huntsberry 9830 Andrew Donald Stephenson 9831 Douglas Graver Gilbert 9832 Frank Laurence Elder 9833 Donald Cameron Cubbison 9834 Amaury Manuel Gandia 9835 Samuel Abner Mundell 9836 Robert Harrold Bayne 9837 Bruce Von Gerichten Scott 9838 Felix Louis Vidal 9839 Gwinn Ulm Porter 9840 Frederick Robert Zierath 9841 Robert Hulburt Douglas 9842 Carl Darnell 9843 Ira Bashein 9844 Joseph Brice Crawford 9845 Frederick William Coleman 9846 Raymond Wiltse Sellers 9847 Matthew William Kane 9848 Alton Alexander Denton 9849 Richard Ensign Myers 9850 Jules Verne Richardson 9851 Frederick William Gibb 9852 Norman Kemp Markle 9853 Charles Edmund Voorhees 9854 Jesse Martin Hawkins 9855 Ralph Talbot 9856 Charles Ellsworth Leydecker 9857 Austin Andrew Miller 9858 Henry Walter Herlong 9859 Morris King Henderson 9860 Earl Francis Signer 9861 Richard Thomas King 9862 John Daniel O'Reilly 9863 Roland Arthur Elliott 9864 Waldemar Justin Thinnes 9865 Lloyd Ralston Fredendall 9866 Edson Schull 9867 Joel Lyen Mathews 9868 Royal Reynolds 9869 George Hollie Bishop 9870 Stephen B. Mack 9871 Lawrence Kermit White 9872 Graydon Casper Essman 9873 Russell Franklin Akers 9874 Claude Leslie Bowen 9875 Duff Walker Sudduth 9876 Charles Vincent Wynne 9877 David Wagstaff 9878 Clyde Jarecki Hibler 9879 James Rhoden Pritchard 9880 James Dennis Underhill 9881 Robert Emmett Gallagher 9882 Samuel Edward Gee 9883 Alston Grimes 9884 Nelson Parkyn Jackson 9885 Frederick Otto Hartel 9886 Ivan Walter Parr 9887 William Roberts Calhoun 9888 Roy Dunscomb Gregory 9889 Karl Truesdell 9890 William Anderson Hunt 9891 Glenn Howbert Garrison 9892 Edson Duncan Raff 9893 Chester Braddock deGavre 9894 Erdmann Jellison Lowell 9895 William Agin Bailey 9896 Seymour Eldred Madison 9897 Robin Bruce Epler 9898 John Newman Scoville 9899 William Field Due 9900 Peter Demosthenes Clainos 9901 John Frederick Schmelzer 9902 Sydney Dwight Grubbs 9903 John Caldwell Price 9904 David Thomas Jellett 9905 Millard Loren Haskin 9906 Joseph Anthony Remus 9907 Ben Harrell 9908 Richard Churchfield Blatt 9909 Richard Allen Risden 9910 Joseph Ermine Williams 9911 Miller Payne Warren 9912 Stanley Nelson Lonning 9913 Robert Moore Blanchard 9914 William Wilson Quinn 9915 Charner Weaver Powell 9916 Charles Pearce Bellican 9917 Edward Spalding Ehlen 9918 Travis Albert Beck 9919 Thomas Tallant Kilday 9920 Richard Mattern Montgomery 9921 Arthur Adrian Holmes 9922 Charles Hoffman Pottenger 9923 John Roberts Kimmell 9924 William Vernard Thompson 9925 Paul Douglas Wood 9926 J.J. Jimenez Velazquez 9927 Gerald Carrington Simpson 9928 Robert Wilkinson Rayburn 9929 John Baird Shinberger 9930 Emmanuel Salvador Cepeda 9931 Adrian Leonard Hoebeke 9932 **1934** Charles Francis Tank 9933 Thomas DeForth Rogers 9934 John Burroughs Cary 9935 James Fuller Miller 9936 Robert Erlenkotter 9937 John Heughes Donoghue 9938 Staunton Lindsley Brown 9939 Richard Moser Sieg 9940 Joseph Lemual Johnson 9941 Ferdinand Julian Tate 9942 Burton Blodgett Bruce 9943 Robert George MacDonnell 9944 Paul Carter Ashworth 9945 Charles Leon Andrews 9946 Walter Jackson Renfroe 9947 William Joslin Himes 9948 Robert Beauchamp Miller 9949 Rudolph Green 9950 Charles Francis Fell 9951 Charles Rea Revie 9952 Joseph Ochsenschlager Killian 9953 Thomas Heber Lipscomb 9954 James Edward Walsh 9955 Austin Wortham Betts 9956 John Page Buehler 9957 Paul Henry Berkowitz 9958 Edward Walter Moore 9959 Seymour Irving Gilman 9960 Curtis Delano Sluman 9961 Byron Elias Brugge 9962 Robert Butler Warren 9963 Thompson Brooke Maury 9964 Wilford Edward Harry Voehl 9965 John Jay Stark 9966 William Sebastian Stone 9967 Jonathan Owen Seaman 9968 Kermit LeVelle Davis 9969 Ellis O. Davis 9970 William Loveland Rogers 9971 George Bernard Dany 9972 Harvey Julius Jablonsky 9973 Urquhart Pullen Williams 9974 Peter Samuel Peca 9975 Lawson S. Moseley 9976 Richard Ringo Moorman 9977 J. Paul Craig 9978 James Oscar Baker 9979 Lewis Kaspar Beazley 9980 John Hicks Anderson 9981 Severin R. Beyma 9982 Thomas Leslie Crystal 9983 Frederic Wood Barnes 9984 William Beehler Bunker 9985 Theodore Frelinghuysen Hoffman 9986 Miles Birkett Chatfield 9987 Howard Marshall Batson 9988 Karl William Bauer 9989 Charles Henry White 9990 Arthur B. Proctor 9991 William Jack Holzapfel 9992 Mathew Valois Pothier 9993 Joseph Sylvester Piram 9994 George Edward Adams 9995 Almon White Manlove 9996 John DuVal Stevens 9997 Yale Harold Wolfe 9998 John Farnsworth Smoller 9999 Craig Smyser 10000 Franklin Kemble 10001 Henry Richardson Hester 10002 Gersen Leo Kushner 10003 Richard Edward Weber 10004 Robert Waight Fuller 10005 James Alexander Costain 10006 Charles Warren Schnabel 10007 Harold Charles Davall 10008 Carl Delbert Womack 10009 Robert Gardner Baker 10010 Ronald LeVerne Martin 10011 George Julius Weitzel 10012 Charles Wadsworth Hill 10013 Gene Huggins Tibbets 10014 Donald Oliver Vars 10015 George Francis Wells 10016 Henry William Ebel 10017 Paul T. Hanley 10018 Jack Edward Shuck 10019 David Belmont Routh 10020 Lee Carl Miller 10021 Travis Ludwell Petty 10022 Peter James Kopcsak 10023 Robert Griffith Finkenaur 10024 William Scott Penn 10025 John de P. Townsend Hills 10026 Frank Willoughby Moorman 10027 Horace Lake Sanders 10028 Merlin Louis DeGuire 10029 Alexander James Stuart 10030 Harrison Francis Turner 10031 William Dowdell Denson 10032 Percy Thomas Hennigar 10033 William Monte Canterbury 10034 Kenneth Riffel Kenerick 10035 Richard Lee McKee 10036 Jerome Edward Blair 10037 Stacy William Gooch 10038 Clark Lynn 10039 Edward Flanick 10040 Leo William Henry Shaughnessey 10041 Harry Jenkins Hubbard 10042 Samuel Knox Yarbrough 10043 Joe Free Surratt 10044 Charles John Bondley 10045 William Milton Gross 10046 Claude Morris Howard 10047 Dale Orville Smith 10048 Gordon Graham Warner 10049 Hudson Hutton Upham 10050 Edward French Benson 10051 Albert Patterson Mossman 10052 Robert Carl Bahr 10053 Frank Carter Norvell 10054 Vincent Shaw Lamb 10055 John Walker Darrah 10056 Robert Hawkins Adams 10057 Donald Glover McLennan 10058 John Francis Franklin 10059 Theodore Gilmore Bilbo 10060 Perry Bruce Griffith 10061 Berton Everett Spivy 10062 Stilson Hilton Smith 10063 Kenneth Alonzo Cunin 10064 Lawrence Kent Meade 10065 Thomas Eugene Wood 10066 Fredric Carson Cook 10067 Lloyd Elmer Fellenz 10068 Joseph Michael Cummins 10069 Percival Stanley Brown 10070 Thomas Clary Foote 10071 John Huber Squier 10072 Charles Bernadou Elliott 10073 James Richard Winn 10074 Louis Lee Ingram 10075 Daniel Henry Heyne 10076 Harry Evans Lardin 10077 Paul Burlingame 10078 Wilson Hawkes Neal 10079 Elvin Seth Ligon 10080 Charles H. Wood 10081 Jack Jerome Neely 10082 John Wentworth Merrill 10083 Charles Burton Winkle 10084 Herbert Marvin Baker 10085 George Rolfe Walton 10086 Theodore Fiquet Hurt 10087 Thew Joseph Ice 10088 Dana Watterson Johnston 10089 Daniel Murray Cheston 10090 John Monroe Hutchison 10091 Edmund Waller Wilkes 10092 Daniel Edward Still 10093 Clifford Guldlin Simenson 10094 Richard Albert Smith 10095 Arno Herman Luehman 10096 Paul Lawrence Barton 10097 Frank Joseph Caufield 10098 James William Snee 10099 Ralph Emerson Bucknam 10100 Floyd Felice Forte 10101 James Dudley Wilmeth 10102 Joseph Aloysius Cleary 10103 Stanley Holmes 10104 William Starr Van Nostrand 10105 Raymond Judson Reeves 10106 Harry Lester Hillyard 10107 Robert Hugh Bennett 10108 William Hutcheson Craig 10109 William Harvey Wise 10110 Richard Andrew Legg 10111 Ralph Doak McKinney 10112 Gerald Joseph Higgins 10113 Tirso Gimenez Fajardo 10114 Harvey Thompson Alness 10115 Paul Earl Johnson 10116 John Thomas Hillis 10117 Charles Edward Johnson 10118 Robert Carson Kyser 10119 John Dixon Lawlor 10120 Russell William Volckmann 10121 Donald Linscott Durfee 10122 Victor Charles Huffsmith 10123 Sidney Thompson Telford 10124 Hallett Daniel Edson 10125 Edwin Rusteberg 10126 Albert Theodore Wilson 10127 Karl Trueheart Gould 10128 Harold Webb Browning 10129 Herbert Hadley Andrae 10130 William Frederick Northam 10131 George Lowe Eatman 10132 John Berchman Stanley 10133 John William White 10134 John Stotsenburg Kromer 10135 Charles Edward Brown 10136 Nathaniel Plummer Ward 10137 James Buchanan Wells 10138 Donald Adams McPheron 10139 Edmundo Valdez Valdez 10140 Thomas Hogan Hayes 10141 Robert Herbert Sanders 10142 Paul Lee Turner 10143 Arthur Lafayette Inman 10144 Stanley Joseph Donovan 10145 Henry Agnew Sebastian 10146 Harold Conly Brookhart 10147 Edward Messmore O'Connell 10148 Russell Walker Jenna 10149 Gerhard LeRoy Bolland 10150 William Bentley Kern 10151 Louis Alfred Walsh 10152 James Frederick Harris 10153 George Horner Gerhart 10154 Thomas Andrew McCrary 10155 John George Benner 10156 Eugene Harrington Cloud 10157 Dale Emerson Huber 10158 Travis Tabor Brown 10159 Edwin Gantt Hickman 10160 John

Elwood Mead 10161 Arthur Ferdinand Meier 10162 David Lyon Hollingsworth 10163 William Alex Cunningham 10164 Edward Ernest Bruno Weber 10165 John Edwards Diefendorf 10166 Meade Julian Dugas 10167 Thomas Almon O'Neil 10168 Emory Alexander Lewis 10169 Samuel Alfred Luttrell 10170 William Joseph Mullen 10171 William Hammond Waugh 10172 Henry Neilson 10173 Bey Mario Arosemena 10174 William Graham Barnwell 10175 Robert Hector McKinnon 10176 Oliver Prescott Robinson 10177 Dennis John McMahon 10178 James O'Hara 10179 Robert Nabors Tyson 10180 Joseph Edward Barton 10181 John Buchanan Richardson 10182 **1935** John Drake Bristor 10183 Donald Abeel Phelan 10184 Aaron Evan Harris 10185 David Hamilton Gregg 10186 Albert Joseph Shower 10187 David Campbell Wallace 10188 Arthur Houston Frye 10189 Herbert Caran Gee 10190 Jack Wallis Hickman 10191 Donald Allen Elliget 10192 Clyde Calhoun Zeigler 10193 Leighton Ira Davis 10194 Charles Bernard Rynearson 10195 Oliver Joseph Pickard 10196 John Blackwell Davenport 10197 Otto Jacob Rohde 10198 John Somers Buist Dick 10199 William Winston Lapsley 10200 James Devore Lang 10201 George Rosse Smith 10202 Charles Jephthiah Jeffus 10203 Henry Lewis Hille 10204 John Lathrop Throckmorton 10205 George Ruhlen 10206 Cornelis deWitt Wilcox Lang 10207 John Richards Parker 10208 Clarence Carl Haug 10209 John Sutton Growdon 10210 John Joseph Duffy 10211 Warren Sylvester Everett 10212 Carl Watkins Miller 10213 Salvatore Andrew Armogida 10214 William Paulding Grieves 10215 Stanley Tage Birger Johnson 10216 James Van Gorder Wilson 10217 Frank Alexander Osmanski 10218 Bernard Sanders Waterman 10219 Frederick Benjamin Hall 10220 Langfitt Bowditch Wilby 10221 John Dudley Cole 10222 George Raymond Wilkins 10223 Harry James Lewis 10224 Elmer John Koehler 10225 Charles Albert Symroski 10226 Henry Chaffee Thayer 10227 James Yeates Adams 10228 Harry Jacob Lemley 10229 Duncan Sinclair 10230 John Kimball Brown 10231 Geoffrey Dixon Ellerson 10232 Robert Morris Stillman 10233 Ray Allen Pillivant 10234 William Henry Brearley 10235 Ellery Willis Niles 10236 George Blackburne 10237 Robert Rigby Glass 10238 George Stafford Eckhardt 10239 Richard Elmer Ellsworth 10240 Clyde Benjamin Sims 10241 Alvin Dolliver Robbins 10242 Sidney George Spring 10243 Edward Stephen Bechtold 10244 Seth Lathrop Weld 10245 Harry John Harrison 10246 Ivan Clare Rumsey 10247 Raymond William Sumi 10248 Daniel John Murphy 10249 Clarence Bidgood 10250 Walter Albert Simpson 10251 Edward Gray 10252 Hugh McClellan Exton 10253 Durward Ellsworth Breakefield 10254 Robert Whitney Wood 10255 Sanford Welsh Horstman 10256 Kelso Gordon Clow 10257 David Gilbert Presnell 10258 Harry Herndon Critz 10259 Henry Porter Van Ormer 10260 Clifford Wellington Hildebrandt 10261 Edward Kraus 10262 Kenneth Irwin Curtis 10263 Joseph Charles Moore 10264 Earl Leo Barr 10265 John Alexis Gloriod 10266 Nathaniel Macon Martin 10267 Joseph G. Russell 10268 S. Fred Cummings 10269 James Martin Worthington 10270 James Michael Donohue 10271 Robert Clarence McDonald 10272 Joseph Waters Keating 10273 Halford Robert Greenlee 10274 Kenneth Paul Bergquist 10275 John Newton Wilson 10276 Richard Marvin Bauer 10277 Lawrence Robert St. John 10278 Gerald Frederick Brown 10279 Willard George Root 10280 Robert Van Roo 10281 Arthur Allison Fickel 10282 Charles MacLean Peeke 10283 Horace Wilson Hinkle 10284 Raymond Boyd Firehock 10285 Downs Eugene Ingram 10286 Milton Lawrence Rosen 10287 Edgar Allen Clarke 10288 James Mobley Kimbrough 10289 John Ralph Wright 10290 Harrison Barnwell Harden 10291 Edward Moseley Harris 10292 Carl Mosby Parks 10293 James Luke Frink 10294 Elmer John Gibson 10295 Julius Desmond Stanton 10296 James Howard Walsh 10297 Walter Joseph Bryde 10298 Thomas Washington Woodyard 10299 Stuart Gilbert Fries 10300 Harry Rich Hale 10301 Charles Frederick Leonard 10302 James Frank Skells 10303 Eugene Nall 10304 Willis Fred Chapman 10305 Seneca Wilbur Foote 10306 James Willoughby Totten 10307 William Henderson Baynes 10308 Eugene Henry Walter 10309 Norman Arthur Loeb 10310 Albert Curtis Wells 10311 Russell Melroy Miner 10312 John Nevin Howell 10313 John Mason Kemper 10314 Maynard Denzil Pederson 10315 Hamilton Austin Twitchell 10316 Russell Eugeune Nicholls 10317 Thomas Wildes 10318 Alfred Ashman 10319 Aaron Warner Tyer 10320 James Dyce Alger 10321 Ralph Edward Haines 10322 Franklin Bell Reybold 10323 Ewing Chase Johnson 10324 Robert Monroe Hardy 10325 Francis Johnstone Murdoch 10326 Pennock Hoyt Wollaston 10327 German Pierce Culver 10328 Carl Theodore Isham 10329 Francis Mark McGoldrick 10330 Wilhelm Cunliffe Freudenthal 10331 John Alfrey 10332 Joseph Rieber Russ 10333 John Henry Dilley 10334 Kermit Richard Schweidel 10335 Eugene Charles Orth 10336 Thomas Duncan Gillis 10337 Autrey Joseph Maroun 10338 Willard Leo Egy 10339 Milton Clay Taylor 10340 George Frederick Marshall 10341 Robert Morris 10342 Joseph Cobb Stancook 10343 John Brown Morgan 10344 William Robert Murrin 10345 Albert Frederick Johnson 10346 Joseph Henry Wiechmann 10347 Lea Campbell Roberts 10348 John Foster Rhoades 10349 Richard C. Boys 10350 George Robert Oglesby 10351 John Calvin Stapleton 10352 William Vincent Martz 10353 Kent Kane Parrot 10354 Robert Edward Frith 10355 Norman Arvid Skinrood 10356 Noel Maurice Cox 10357 Joseph Crook Anderson 10358 J. Hart Caughey 10359 Lawrence Edward Schlanser 10360 Edwin Major Smith 10361 Henry Thomas Cherry 10362 LeRoy William Austin 10363 Charles Jordan Daly 10364 Samuel Cummings Mitchell 10365 Edgar Joseph Treacy 10366 Paul Montgomery Jones 10367 Reuben Henry Tucker 10368 William Genier Proctor 10369 Lamont Saxton 10370 Caesar Frank Fiore 10371 Elmer Hardic Walker 10372 Clair Beverly Mitchell 10373 John Williamson 10374 John Pearson Sherden 10375 Jack Jones Richardson 10376 Charles Phelps Walker 10377 Louis Duzzette Farnsworth 10378 Charles Joseph Hoy 10379 Vernon Price Mock 10380 John Allen Beall 10381 Lamar Fenn Woodward 10382 Orin Houston Moore 10383 Charles Wythe Gleaves Rich 10384 Donald William Bernier 10385 Harvey Bower 10386 Allen Harvey Foreman 10387 Wilson Dudley Coleman 10388 Floyd Garfield Pratt 10389 Thomas Cebern Musgrave 10390 Glenn Cole 10391 Edward William Sawyer 10392 William Lee Herold 10393 William Bradford Means 10394 John Eidell Slaughter 10395 Robert Gibson Sherrard 10396 John Alfred Metcalfe 10397 Andrew Jackson Boyle 10398 Stephen Disbrow Cocheu 10399 John Neiger 10400 Thomas Joseph Gent 10401 Albert Ambrose Matyas 10402 Benjamin Walker Hawes 10403 Benjamin White Heckemeyer 10404 Nassieb George Bassitt 10405 Ducat McEntee 10406 William Robert Patterson 10407 Oscar Rawles Bowyer 10408 John James Davis 10409 Norman Basil Edwards 10410 Pelham Davis Glassford 10411 Robert Eugene Tucker 10412 Herbert Frank Batcheller 10413 Robert Hollis Strauss 10414 Maurice Monroe Simons 10415 Richard Cathcart Hopkins 10416 Alfred Kirk duMoulin 10417 Walter Edward Bare 10418 Ralph Shaffer Harper 10419 Charles Barry Borden 10420 Paul James Bryer 10421 Raymond Clarence Adkisson 10422 Emerson Oliver Liessman 10423 Burnis Mayo Kelly 10424 Lester Lewes Wheeler 10425 Carmon Ambrose Rogers 10426 Russell Batch Smith 10427 Marcus Samuel Griffin 10428 James George Balluff 10429 Richard Hayden Agnew 10430 Francis Regis Herald 10431 John LeRoy Thomas 10432 George Brendan O'Connor 10433 Russell Lynn Hawkins 10434 Eric Per Ramee 10435 Edwin Hood Ferris 10436 Jack Roberts 10437 Robert Middelton Booth 10438 George Madison Jones 10439 David Albaugh DeArmond 10440 Rives Owens Booth 10441 Wilson Larzerlere Burley 10442 James Louis McGehee 10443 Walter Albert Riemenschneider 10444 William Pierce O'Neal 10445 George Place Hill 10446 Melville Brown Coburn 10447 Alvin Louis Mente 10448 Harry Franklin Sellers 10449 David Bonesteel Stone 10450 Roland Joseph Rutte 10451 Glenn Curtis Thompson 10452 Samuel Barcus Knowles 10453 Jack Moore Buckler 10454 James Baird Buck 10455 Ralph O. Lashley 10456 Thomas Robert Clarkin 10457 John Pope Blackshear 10458 John Trueheart Mosby 10459 **1936** Oliver Garfield Haywood 10460 Herbert M. Cady 10461 Charles Henry Waters 10462 Ralph Dickson King 10463 Raymond John Harvey 10464 Bruce Palmer 10465 William Reeves Shuler 10466 Roy Dean McCarty 10467 John Herbert Kerkering 10468 Cecil Edward Combs 10469 Pierre Victor Kieffer 10470 Karl Theodore Klock 10471 Richard Rawlins Waugh 10472 Arthur Milton Jacoby 10473 Charles Barnard Stewart 10474 Dwight Oliver Monteith 10475 Robert Warren Davis 10476 Walter Alexander Faiks 10477 George Ervin White 10478 Carroll K. J. Bagby 10479 Gilbert M. Dorland 10480 Thomas Reuben Conner 10481 Thomas Jay Hayes 10482 Gordon Henry Holterman 10483 George Alexander Finley 10484 William Mellard Connor 10485 Henry Jacob Katz 10486 Wright Hiatt 10487 Arthur Kramer 10488 Howard Allen Morris 10489 Stephen Elliott Smith 10490 Edgar Hall Thompson 10491 William David Milne 10492 John Keeler Neff 10493 Benjamin Oliver Davis 10494 James Benjamin Lampert 10495 Gerald Herman Duin 10496 Reginald Joseph Beauregard Page 10497 Lawrence Edward Laurion 10498 Walter Bernard Bess 10499 Clarence Albert Cozart 10500 Andrew Davis Chaffin 10501 William Nott Beard 10502 John Lindsay Bower 10503 John Edward Kelly 10504 Stephen Walsh Holderness 10505 James Emmett Goodwin 10506 William Parrish Fickes 10507 Paul Francis Oswald 10508 Gordon Harrison Austin 10509 Cecil Eldon Spann 10510 Foster Leroy Furphy 10511 Jay Dean Rutledge 10512 Warren Smith Blair 10513 Robert Frederick Frost 10514 Howard Pinkney Persons 10515 Clement Wirt Crockett 10516 Adam Stephen Buynoski 10517 John Daniel McElheny 10518 Kenneth Einar Madsen 10519 Eugene Roberts Patterson 10520 Edwin Van V. Sutherland 10521 Thea Lewis Lipscomb 10522 Robert Dean Gapen 10523 Oren Swain 10524 David McCoach 10525 Robert Henry Kessler 10526 Harry Edgar Mikkelsen 10527 William Henry Kinard 10528 Eugene Everett Lockhart 10529 Maxwell Morrison Kallman 10530 Howell Marion Estes 10531 Ralph Richard Ganns 10532 Everett George Hahney 10533 Clifford Frederick Cordes 10534 Robert Matthew Burnett 10535 John Knox Arnold 10536 Clinton Dermott Vincent 10537 Richard Henry Mattern 10538 David Woodrow Hiester 10539 Charles Dudley Hartman 10540 John James Phelan 10541 Selwyn Dyson Smith 10542 Raymond Lemuel Cato 10543 Irwin Walton Rogers 10544 John Walter Romlein 10545 William Aldrich Davis 10546 William Charles Hay 10547 Edward Alexander Grove 10548 Joseph B. Yost 10549 Seward William Hulse 10550 Richard Henry Carmichael 10551 Robert Bruce Partridge 10552 Edward Worthington Williams 10553 Frank Walter Gillespie 10554 James Rutland Gunn 10555 Wilmer Charles Landry 10556 Hervey Bennett Whipple 10557 Nicholas Tate Perkins 10558 Eldred George Robbins 10559 Napoleon Robertson Duell 10560 Howard McCrum Snyder 10561 Carl Kenneth Bowen 10562 Orville Newton Stokes 10563 James Edward Landrum 10564 John Davis Torrey 10565 Albert Patton Clark 10566 William Raymond Prince 10567 Eugene Virgil Reece 10568 Donald Gilbert Grothaus 10569 Ned Taylor Norris 10570 William Childs Westmoreland 10571 John Earl Barlow 10572 John Richard Kelly 10573 Kenneth Francis Dawalt 10574 Harold William Wolf 10575 Norman Calvert Spencer 10576 Benjamin Merritt Warfield 10577 Frederick Reynolds Terrell 10578 Leonard Copeland Shea 10579 Charles Bernard Tyler 10580 Frederick Bell 10581 Harold Roy Low 10582 Frederick Charles Bothwell 10583 Philip Carey Whitehead 10584 Beverley Evans Powell 10585 Donald Read Bodine 10586 Charles Milton McCorkle 10587 Edward Lawrence Parsons Burke 10588 Earl Franklin Holton 10589 Leland Rodman Drake 10590 Ridgway Pancoast Smith 10591 Robert Hall Safford 10592 Edward Clare Dunn 10593 Chester Victor Clifton 10594 William Denton Cairnes 10595 John Godfrey Brimmer 10596 William Hamilton Jordan 10597 Wilbur Maben Griffith 10598 Langdon Andrew Jackson 10599 Wilfred Henry Tetley 10600 Joshua Asher Finkel 10601 James Walter Twaddell 10602 William Russell Grohs 10603 Henry David Lind 10604 Donald Paul Christensen 10605 Clarence Edward Gooding 10606 Carl Laverne Rickenbaugh 10607 William Swinton Steele 10608 John Milton Bartella 10609 Loyd Kenneth Pepple 10610 William Charles Haneke 10611 James Tillman Willis 10612 Karl William Schwering 10613 Claude Lee Crawford 10614 Robert George Fergusson 10615 Francis McDonald Oliver 10616 Robert Edward McCabe 10617 John Joseph Jakle 10618 Clinton Utterback True 10619 Turner Clifton Rogers 10620 Robert Walter Breaks 10621 William Loud Longley 10622 Louis Frederick deLesdernier 10623 Frederick Harold Gaston 10624 Roy Wheaton Cole 10625 James Rainier Weaver 10626 George Paul Champion 10627 Carl Baehr 10628 John Arnold Heintges 10629 Charles Chaney Segrist 10630 Harry Ripley Melton 10631 John Harold Daly 10632 Robert James Quinn 10633 Edward Daniel Mohlere 10634 William Francis Meany 10635 Peter Woods Garland 10636 Ned Butler Broyles 10637 Randolph Charles Dickens 10638 Elmer Willford Grubbs 10639 Lawrence Frederick Prichard 10640 Fred Livingood Walker 10641 George Weldon Childs 10642 John Henry Chiles 10643 Creighton Williams Abrams 10644 Edwin Gregory Beggs 10645 William Thomas Ryder 10646 William Edward Sievers 10647 Hilwert Schuyler Streeter 10648 William John Priestley 10649 Russell Victor Dolmar Janzan 10650 Alfred William Hess 10651 Karol Anthony Bauer 10652 William Jackson Hanlon 10653 James Latham Crandell 10654 Thomas Worthington Cooke 10655 William Garnett Lee 10656 McPherson LeMoyne 10657 Louis Stewart Chappelear 10658 Laurence John Ellert 10659 Richard Wilkins Ripple 10660 Robert Emmett O'Brien 10661 Philip Sheffield Greene 10662 Thurman Wesley Morris 10663 Albert Burnton Turner 10664 Clyde Lafayette Layne 10665 Jesse Cyrus Drain 10666 John Marvin Williams 10667 David Henry Brown 10668 Carl Theodor Goldenberg 10669 Jackson Holt Gray 10670 Warren Newcomb Wildrick 10671 Austin Glenwood Fisher 10672 Charles Lee Simpson 10673 Robert Thomas Crowder 10674 Allen Leeds Peck 10675 John Hersey Michaelis 10676 Franklin Rogers Sibert 10677 James Michael Illig 10678 Henry Kreitzer Benson 10679 Augustus Herbert Bode 10680 John Proctor Stone 10681 Duncan Buist Dowling 10682 Von Roy Shores 10683 William Ellerbe Covington 10684 Philip Stearns Gage 10685 Robert Francis Curran 10686 Thomas Edgar Clifford 10687 Charles B. Milliken 10688 Peter McGoldrick 10689 Allen Clinton Miller 10690 James Renwick Hughes 10691 Leonard Clement Godfray 10692 William Hartman Hendrickson 10693 Howard Franklin McManus 10694 Robert John Trout 10695 Raymond Horace Tiffany 10696 John Clarke Goldtrap 10697 John Ridgen Van Dickson 10698 John Roland Singletary 10699 William Barrett Sullivan 10700 Glenn Austin Sikes 10701 William Maurice McBee 10702 Godfrey Arthur Fowler 10703 Clark Lewis Hosmer 10704 Donald Wallace Noake 10705 William Wesley Jones 10706 David Lincoln Edwards 10707 Benjamin Otto Turnage 10708 Thomas James Lawlor 10709 William Pelham Yarborough 10710 Aloysius Elliott McCormick 10711 Joseph James Nazzaro 10712 Charles Morgan Prosser 10713 Frank Edward Shea 10714 Charles Billingslea 10715 Benjamin Franklin Evans 10716 Louis Shepard 10717 James Billy Leer 10718 Edmund Writner Miles 10719 William Levere Kimball 10720 Robert Sears Blodgett 10721 Leon Flores Punsalan 10722 Henry Andrews Mucci 10723 Thomas Walker Chandler 10724 Frederick Caesar Augustus Kellam 10725 John Matthew Lynch 10726 Charles Manly Pack 10727 Ernest Samuel Holmes 10728 Thomas Ryall Davis 10729 Wallace Conrad Barrett 10730 Theodore Janof 10731 Frank Pattillo Norman 10732 Conrad Francis Necrason 10733 Victor H. Wagner 10734 William Arthur Joyce 10735 **1937** Arthur William Oberbeck 10736 Campbell Hodges Snyder 10737 David Bennett Parker 10738 Frederick James Clarke 10739 Eugene Joseph Stann 10740 Jack Norman Donohew 10741 Fred Earl Ressegieu 10742 Augustine Patterson Little 10743 Charles Francis Mitchim 10744 Frederick Miller Thompson 10745 William Bayer Strandberg 10746 Charles Moses McAfee 10747 Charles Stanley Kuna 10748 Gerard Joseph Forney 10749 John Dudley Stevenson 10750 Julian Vincent Sollohub 10751 Charles Boes Hines 10752 Nils Olof Ohman 10753 George Lawrence Holcomb 10754 Edward Chandler Spaulding 10755 Peter Clarke Hyzer 10756 James Stephen Barko 10757 William Ray Clingerman 10758 Hamilton William Fish 10759 Ellis Edmund Wilhoyt 10760 Charles Lewis Register 10761 Leigh Cole Fairbank 10762 Asher Burtis Robbins 10763 John Manning Cromelin 10764 William Horace Lewis 10765 Frederick Otto Diercks 10766 David Tice Griffin 10767 William Edwin Wilson Farrell 10768 Walter Eckman 10769 Giles Lincoln Evans 10770 Jay Alan Abercrombie 10771 Douglass Phillip Quandt 10772 John B. Randolph Hines 10773 William Noel Snouffer 10774 Richard Phillip Klocko 10775 Robert Francis Seedlock 10776 John Gamble Schermerhorn 10777 Robert Stanley Palmer 10778 Houghton Ross Hallock 10779 Charles Aloysius Pfeffer 10780 Noel Houk Ellis 10781 Eric Dougan 10782 Jack West Chapman 10783 George Henry Walker 10784 Harold Bell Wright 10785 George Joseph Murray 10786 Carlin Hamlin Whitesell 10787 William Clements Chenoweth 10788 Alexander Day Surles 10789 Thomas Truxtun 10790 Henry Alfred Byroade 10791 Robert Carl Miller 10792 Walter Cinn DeBill 10793 John Francis Batjer 10794 Donald Wilt Shive 10795 Thomas Alexander Holdiman 10796 Perry Huston Eubank 10797 Kenneth Sayre Wade 10798 John Graham Zierdt 10799 Donald Bowen Brummel 10800 Raymond William Rumph 10801 John Gordon Eriksen 10802 William Lafayette Black 10803 Henry Mershon Spengler 10804 Elwyn Norman Kirsten 10805 Milton Harvey Clark 10806 Edgar John Ingmire 10807 Amzi Rudolph Quillian 10808 Robert William Griffin 10809 Harry Francis Van Leuven 10810 Gale Eugene Ellis 10811 Richard Risley Barden 10812 Edwin Allen Russell 10813 Alfred Eugene Diamond 10814 Victor Earl Mansfield 10815 Paul Bates Whittemore 10816 Charles Louis Robbins 10817 Horace Greeley Davisson 10818 Monte Jackson Hickok 10819 James Armitt Scott 10820 Wilbur Harvey Stratton 10821 John Franklin Foy 10822 Richard William Fellows 10823 William George Easton 10824 George Franklin Leist 10825 John Martin Cone 10826 Whiteford Carlisle Mauldin 10827 William Perry Baldwin 10828 Manob Suriya 10829 Edward Morris Lee 10830 Elmer Carl Blaha 10831 Manuel Quiaoit Salientes 10832 John Bowen Nance 10833 Bruce Keener Holloway 10834 James Haynes Reeves 10835 Roy Lee Mapes 10836 LeRoy Hubert Rook 10837 Alvord Rutherford 10838 John McMullan Gulick 10839 Carlos Antonio Nadal 10840 Godfrey Roland Ames 10841 Emmette Young Burton 10842 Maurice Arthur Preston 10843 Philip Gatch Lauman 10844 William James Dunmyer 10845 Robert Harley Fitzgerald 10846 Ivan Wilson McElroy 10847 William Kienle Horrigan 10848 George Vernon Underwood 10849 William Jack Worcester 10850 Chester Lee Johnson 10851 Charles Stuart O'Malley 10852 Alan Doane Clark 10853 James Nixon Peale 10854 Ben Wells Porterfield 10855 Robert Hensey Herman 10856 William Wise Bailey 10857 Edgar Major Teeter 10858 Daniel Allen Richards 10859 Edward C. David Scherrer 10860 Linscott Aldin Hall 10861 Thomas Charles Compton 10862 Arthur Harrison Wilson 10863 Oscar Baker Steely 10864 David B. Nye 10865 Thomas McGarey Metz 10866 Don Richard Ostrander 10867 Thomas Denman Neier 10868 Albert Ollie Connor 10869 Stanley John Cherubin 10870 Floyd Joaquin Pell 10871 Meyer Arendt Edwards 10872 Robert Clyde Gildart 10873 Fred Pierce Campbell 10874 Robert Fales Lesser 10875 James Early Norvell 10876 Robert Henry Stumpf 10877 Homer Harvey Uglow 10878 George Caldwell McDowell 10879 George Haines Minor 10880 Harry Leonard Stiegler 10881 James Young Parker 10882 Joseph Brady Mitchell 10883 Sam W. Agee 10884 Robert Taylor 10885 Wilbur Emmet Davis 10886 Lukas Ernest Hoska 10887 Edward Marion Postlethwait 10888 Battle Malone Barksdale 10889 Martin Levering Green 10890 Joseph Ludger Chabot 10891 John Thomas Shields 10892 Richard Ellis Nelson 10893 Luis F. Mercado 10894 Robert Maurice Stegmaier 10895 Charles Janvrin Browne 10896 Maurice Wuchter Musgrave 10897 Woodrow Wilson Stromberg 10898 Harold Everett Marr 10899 Dan Cashemere Russell 10900 Cecil Himes 10901 Curtis Raymond Low 10902 Joseph Harper

Hodges 10903 Ferdinand Thomas Unger 10904 Walter Clem Conway 10905 John Lawrence Powers 10906 Charles Grinnell Dannelly 10907 Coy Lyman Curtis 10908 Richard Hilton Hackford 10909 Charles Glen Young 10910 Max Shields George 10911 Stanley Lowell Smith 10912 Harry Edwin Hammond 10913 Posheng Yen 10914 Jack Edward Caldwell 10915 Edwin Borden Broadhurst 10916 Richard Frederick Hill 10917 Charles Bainbridge Westover 10918 James Stanfield Hatfield 10919 Carl Lawrence Lindquist 10920 Horace John Greeley 10921 Bernard Peter Major 10922 Richard Gates Williams 10923 Joseph Alfred Miller 10924 Samuel Charles Gurney 10925 John Hincks Montgomery 10926 Harvey Charles Dorney 10927 James Robert Johnson 10928 LeRoy Lutes 10929 Robert H. Van Volkenburgh 10930 George Maliszewski 10931 James Samuel Brierly 10932 Andrew Jackson Lynch 10933 Charles Robert Meyer 10934 Conrad Henry Diehl 10935 Paul William Scheidecker 10936 Oscar Gordon Kreiser 10937 Harry Walter Elkins 10938 John Whitelaw Browning 10939 James John Cosgrove 10940 Charles Andrews Sprague 10941 William Henry Traeger 10942 Robert Besson 10943 William Leslie Robinson 10944 Walter Gibson Gleye 10945 James Ferris Pearsall 10946 Stanley Warren Connelly 10947 Charles Junious Harrison 10948 Kelsie Loomis Reaves 10949 William Emmett McDonald 10950 B. Franklin Taylor 10951 Robert Sorrel Kennedy 10952 Ernest Hertel Laflamme 10953 Jasper Newton Durham 10954 John Russell Ulricson 10955 Alfred Allen Maybach 10956 Lawrence Augustus Spilman 10957 Kelton Seymour Davis 10958 William Grover Hipps 10959 John D. Haltom 10960 John Randal Weikel 10961 Hueston Richard Wynkoop 10962 Joseph George Focht 10963 Marshall Randolph Gray 10964 Wood Guice Joerg 10965 Parker Calvert 10966 Victor Edward Sinclair 10967 Augustin Mitchell Prentiss 10968 William Riddick Crawford 10969 Maxwell Awyn Tincher 10970 Charles Thomas Clagett 10971 John Houghton Hydle 10972 Bryan Coffield Arnold 10973 Robert Bronson Hubbard 10974 Carroll David Wood 10975 Philip Delano Brant 10976 Delk McCorkle Oden 10977 George Alexander McGee 10978 William Dawes McKinley 10979 Walter R. Lawson 10980 Winfield Lee Martin 10981 Charles Sherman Hoyt 10982 Colin Purdie Kelly 10983 Kenneth Witt Driskill 10984 Hugh Sawyer 10985 Woodrow William Dunlop 10986 William Allen Dodds 10987 Kelley Benjamin Lemmon 10988 Gilbert Fulghum Bell 10989 James Hunter Drum 10990 Kenneth Oliver Sanborn 10991 Elery Martin Zehner 10992 George Bidwell Sloan 10993 Arthur Kirkham Amos 10994 Edward Chynoweth Hobbs 10995 Carl Freeman Lyons 10996 Olen John Seaman 10997 John Jarvis Tolson 10998 Frederick John Dooley 10999 John Huff Van Vliet 11000 James Francis Faber 11001 Edwin Walter Richardson 11002 James Howard Skeldon 11003 Harold McDonald Brown 11004 William Joseph Cain 11005 James Wilson Duncan 11006 Noel Ambrose Menard 11007 Malcolm Green 11008 Thomas Everett Powell 11009 Ephraim Foster Graham 11010 Charles William Stark 11011 William Barrett Travis 11012 George Millard Simmons 11013 George Russell Cole 11014 Frank William Andrews 11015 John Oliver Frazier 11016 Raymond Clayton Cheal 11017 Gordon Custer Leland 11018 Morton David Magoffin 11019 Philip Columbus Sterling 11020 William Ragland Maxwell 11021 James Theo Posey 11022 Gordon Talmage Kimbrell 11023 Benjamin Turner Workizer 11024 Howard Norrington Smalley 11025 Wesley Skilton Calverley 11026 Eads Graham Hardaway 11027 William Brackett McClellan Chase 11028 Render Dowdell Denson 11029 Frank Ray Harrison 11030 John Fleming Polk 11031 John Powers Connor 11032 Charles William Blauvelt 11033 **1938** John Robert Jannarone 11034 Matthew John Altenhofen 11035 Robert Allen Breitweiser 11036 George Willard Bixby 11037 Desloge Brown 11038 James Burney Chubbuck 11039 Alexander John Frolich 11040 Paul Theodore Preuss 11041 John Eugene Kelsey 11042 Robert Worrell Love 11043 Morris Frederick Taber 11044 William Allen Orr 11045 Richard Giles Stilwell 11046 Irwin Miles Parry 11047 John William Thompson 11048 Harold Killian Kelley 11049 James Linn Lewis 11050 William Atha Gay 11051 Donald Glazier Williams 11052 Charles Howard Anderson 11053 Kenneth Gregory Wickham 11054 William Stoddard Crocker 11055 William Brett Kieffer 11056 Clarence Clinton Harvey 11057 Leo Vernon Harman 11058 William Ward Smith 11059 Clarence Alan Langford 11060 Andrew Carl Dapprich 11061 Benjamin Marcus Tarver 11062 Robert Marshall Batterson 11063 Edward Alfred Bailey 11064 Robert Joseph Kasper 11065 Milton Paul Barschdorf 11066 Vincent Martin Elmore 11067 Francis Woodworth Jenkins 11068 George Gray O'Connor 11069 Robert Claude McCabe 11070 Walter Edward Lotz 11071 William Kenneth Skaer 11072 Clair Edwood Hutchin 11073 Prescott Miner Spicer 11074 Samuel Mason Hogan 11075 Harold Nelson Moorman 11076 Rolf Olaf Wulfsberg 11077 Melvin Rhodes Russell 11078 Trevor Nevitt Dupuy 11079 Barry Duran Browne 11080 Henry Leland Crouch 11081 Laurence Edward Wernberg 11082 Glenn Preston Anderson 11083 Dallas Fernald Haynes 11084 Glenn Craddock Coleman 11085 Iver Arthur Peterson 11086 Fillmore Kennady Mearns 11087 William Welby Beverley 11088 Roland Bennett Anderson 11089 Alfred John D'Arezzo 11090 Frank Wade Norris 11091 John Fouche Brownlow 11092 Roy Cleveland Heflebower 11093 Burton Robert Brown 11094 George Arthur Bosch 11095 Sherwood Ernest Buckland 11096 Richard Gay Ivey 11097 Antonio Pabalan Chanco 11098 John Dale Ryan 11099 Frederick Charles Lough 11100 William Braden Latta 11101 William McGregor Lynn 11102 Joseph Conigliaro Conell 11103 Charles Joseph Blake 11104 Albert Peterson Sights 11105 George Kappes 11106 Omar Ellsworth Knox 11107 Frederick Adam Miller 11108 Walter Stephen Gray 11109 Alvar Bertil Sundin 11110 Gregory Hoisington 11111 Ole W. Danielson 11112 Howard Edward Michelet 11113 Samuel Knox Eaton 11114 Ted Irving Sawyer 11115 Milton Edward Lipps 11116 Jesse Fuller Thomas 11117 John Robert Bailey 11118 Tracy Bovard Harrington 11119 Martin Lockwood Webb 11120 Albert Joseph Weinnig 11121 Frank Pleasants Sturdivant 11122 Paul Canning Davis 11123 Philip Yeager Browning 11124 John Harland Swenson 11125 Norman Lester Tittle 11126 William Hollis Vail 11127 Lloyd Earl Johnson 11128 Francis Burnett Harrison 11129 Alvin Lee Burke 11130 Howard Doan Kenzie 11131 William Henry Corbett 11132 Edward Joseph York 11133 Bertram Cowgill Harrison 11134 Elliott Woodrow Amick 11135 William Thomas Weissinger 11136 Joseph Rhett Barker 11137 Paul Revere Cornwall 11138 William K. Kincaid 11139 Clifford Field Macomber 11140 Edgar Stanton Rosenstock 11141 Frederick John Gerlich 11142 Harvey Pettibone Barnard 11143 Arthur Wellesley Skerry 11144 Arthur Joseph Smith 11145 Douglas Clinton Polhamus 11146 William Anthony Sussmann 11147 Louis Edward Coira 11148 Arpad Arthur Kopcsak 11149 Robert Lee Snider 11150 Ashley Burdett Packard 11151 John Charles Nickerson 11152 Lawrence Chandler Baldwin 11153 Donald Ward Saunders 11154 Simon Rudel Sinnreich 11155 William Peek Brett 11156 Richard Joseph Long 11157 Robert Alan Zaiser 11158 Ferdinand Joseph Chesarek 11159 John Dean Moorman 11160 Gailon Myers McHaney 11161 Jack Lee Grubb 11162 Kenneth Glade 11163 Edgar Stanton McKee 11164 John Herbert Spangler 11165 James Taylor 11166 Ralph Burton Praeger 11167 Charles Winfield Sherburne 11168 Nicholas Horace Chavasse 11169 Henry Charles Huglin 11170 Alan Seff 11171 William Emmett Ekman 11172 Harry Cornelius Morrison 11173 John Barkley Pattison 11174 Jaroslav Thayer Folda 11175 Edwin Nevin Howell 11176 James Russell Holmes 11177 John C. Fremont Tillson 11178 John Burns Hamilton 11179 John Bennet Herboth 11180 Richard Franklin Bromiley 11181 Henry Brooks Wilson 11182 Maurice Raymond Lemon 11183 James Albert Bassett 11184 Lorenzo Dow Adams 11185 John Robert Hopson 11186 Virgil Lee Zoller 11187 Robert Carleton McBride 11188 Charles Loyd Jackson 11189 John Charles Damon 11190 Neil David Van Sickle 11191 John Cozart Pitchford 11192 Harlan Keith Holman 11193 Elmer Ellsworth Hallinger 11194 Donald Roy Matheson 11195 David Wallace Hayes 11196 Merton Singer 11197 Edwin Lee Clarke 11198 Jefferson Johnson Irvin 11199 Samuel Llewellyn Barbour 11200 George William Rhyne 11201 Philip Robert Hawes 11202 Robert Chilton Works 11203 Gordon Madison Clarkson 11204 William Hugh Blanchard 11205 Castex Paul Conner 11206 Edward Francis Gillivan 11207 Charles Little Haley 11208 Joseph Gray Duncan 11209 William Albert Johnson 11210 Wilbur Charles Strand 11211 Robert Carl Erlenbusch 11212 Hubert Emmet Strange 11213 Hugh Douglas Wallace 11214 Robert Davis Offer 11215 Earle Metzger Shiley 11216 Francis Henry Patrick 11217 William Adolph Sundlof 11218 James Henry Lynch 11219 Allen Douglas Hulse 11220 Clarence Earle Beck 11221 James Rhea Luper 11222 William Patrick Wansboro 11223 Carter Eugene Duncan 11224 Rudolph Laskowsky 11225 Rollin Benedict Durbin 11226 Fred Murray Dean 11227 Alexander Bruce Pendleton 11228 Joseph Benedict Missal 11229 James Terry Craig 11230 Arthur Fulbrook Gorham 11231 Warren Rand Williams 11232 George Henderson Lee Dillard 11233 John Milton Finn 11234 Harvey Lloyd Brown 11235 Eugene Joseph Sweeney 11236 Frank Elmer Glace 11237 Melvin Charles Brown 11238 Robert William Rulkoetter 11239 Thomas Lauten McCrary 11240 Robert Sherwood Demitz 11241 Arthur Sylvester Collins 11242 Willard Gregory Walsh 11243 William Henry Frederick 11244 Frank Milton Izenour 11245 Vincent Morgan Miles 11246 Donald Walker Thackeray 11247 Joseph Breece Wells 11248 Charles William Walson 11249 James Edward Mrazek 11250 Harris Edward Rogner 11251 Frank Dickson Miller 11252 William Henry Jaynes 11253 Richard Augustine Broberg 11254 David Owen Byars 11255 Leland Oscar Krug 11256 Robert Lee Wolverton 11257 Joseph Stephen Kujawski 11258 Thomas Nelson Sibley 11259 Roy Ray Brischetto 11260 Mark Francis Brennan 11261 Philip Charles Feffer 11262 Gibson Emerson Sisco 11263 Richard Elam Sims 11264 Vincent Keator 11265 Edwin Arthur Machen 11266 James Willis Rhymes 11267 Ben Sternberg 11268 Ralph Allen Jones 11269 Charles 11270 Richard Carl Thomas 11271 Louis Nathaniel Dosh 11272 Robert John Bruton 11273 Charles Mathes Young 11274 Charles Joseph Denholm 11275 Merrick Bayer 11276 John Joseph Carusone 11277 John Thomas English 11278 Arthur Anthony Maloney 11279 Robert Alois Barker 11280 John Alexander Norris 11281 Littleton James Pardue 11282 Franklin Henrie Hartline 11283 Edward George DeHart 11284 Arthur Maxwell Murray 11285 John Eliason Boyt 11286 Henry Sylvanus McDonald 11287 Vincent Wallace Siren 11288 Robert Belden Kuhn 11289 Robert Leaning Ashworth 11290 Walter Nicholas Guletsky 11291 Victor Charles Warren 11292 Myrl Fay Smith 11293 Wallace Stafford Ford 11294 Coral Max Talbott 11295 Edgar Hayden Dale 11296 Joseph Claude Reddoch 11297 Warren Thomas Hannum 11298 Robert Hodson Rhine 11299 Clifford Thomas Riordan 11300 John Winthrop White 11301 Shelby Young Palmer 11302 Gabrielle Caldwell Russell 11303 Edward Henry Lahti 11304 John Harlan Chambers 11305 Birdsey Lee Learman 11306 John Thomas Corley 11307 John Thomas Ewing 11308 James Eugene Henderson 11309 Frederick Starr Wright 11310 William Clark Jackson 11311 Edward Raymond Skinner 11312 William Conyers Fite 11313 Stephen Radford Batson 11314 Andy Archer Lipscomb 11315 Edward Walter Jacunski 11316 James Kent Schmidt 11317 Joe Reese Brabson 11318 George Cornell Abert 11319 Robert John Hill 11320 Ward Sanford Ryan 11321 Edward Stephenson 11322 Robert Howard York 11323 George Artman 11324 Ralph Brown Lister 11325 George Rapp Zohrlaut 11326 David Gibson Sherrard 11327 Frank Edward Hartman 11328 William Folwell Neff 11329 Samuel Salvatore Campanella 11330 Edward Gustave Aaron Chalgren 11331 James Horace Isbell 11332 Collin Baston Whitehurst 11333 John Boddie Coleman 11334 **1939** Stanley Walter Dziuban 11335 Andrew Jackson Goodpaster 11336 Delmer Joseph Rogers 11337 Louis Albert Kunzig 11338 John Spoor Samuel 11339 Richard D. Wolfe 11340 Wilmot Ruet McCutchen 11341 Edmund Kirby-Smith 11342 Charles Elting Coates 11343 Harvey Reed Fraser 11344 Albert Edgar McCollam 11345 Walter Woodrow Farmer 11346 Jay Phelps Dawley 11347 Montgomery Lee Webster 11348 Roscoe Campbell Crawford 11349 Charles Marsden Duke 11350 Harry Nathan Brandon 11351 Woodrow William Wilson 11352 John W. Medusky 11353 David Mason Matheson 11354 James Lewis Cantrell 11355 Norman Farrell 11356 Robert Riis Ploger 11357 James Donald Richardson 11358 James Lloyd McBride 11359 George Yount Jumper 11360 Walter Lloyd Winegar 11361 Nicholas Paraska 11362 Walter Johnson Wells 11363 Riel Stanton Crandall 11364 William Thomas Bradley 11365 Mahlon Wilkins Caffee 11366 Henry Crandall Newcomer 11367 Joseph George Perry 11368 Sidney Taylor Martin 11369 Robert Harriman Curtin 11370 John Henry Davis 11371 Edward John Gallagher 11372 Walter Evans Brinker 11373 John Ernest Linwood Huse 11374 Norman James McGowan 11375 Charles Edward White 11376 John Joseph Pavick 11377 Lawrence Leroy Beckedorff 11378 T. Jonathan Jackson Christian 11379 Robert Francis Cassidy 11380 John Alexander Chechila 11381 Josephus Alan Bowman 11382 Robert William Studer 11383 Robert Benjamin Miller 11384 James Lawton Collins 11385 Ladislaus Casimir Maslowski 11386 John Wilson Carpenter 11387 Julian Johnson Ewell 11388 Harmon Lampley 11389 Wayne Laverne O'Hern 11390 Wilbur Eugene Showalter 11391 Joseph Harold Frost 11392 Edward Boyd Leever 11393 Hugh Albert Griffith 11394 Robert Hyde Camp 11395 Daniel Joseph Minahan 11396 Chandler George Lewis 11397 Robert Mabry Williams 11398 James Irvin Muir 11399 Ralph Lemoine Lowther 11400 John Joseph Wald 11401 Milton Abraham Laitman 11402 George Edmund Howard 11403 Edward Harry Kurth 11404 Burrell Washington Helton 11405 Robert Penn Haffa 11406 Raymond Walter Allen 11407 Belmont Stuart Evans 11408 Walter MacRae Vann 11409 Walter Charles Dolle 11410 Philip Martin Royce 11411 Adam Kirk Breckenridge 11412 Roland Wallace Boughton 11413 John Arthur McDavid 11414 John R. Schrader 11415 George Peterson Winton 11416 Joseph Richardson Reeves 11417 John Ray 11418 Edward McCleave Dannemiller 11419 Albert F. Rollins 11420 Charles Crenshaw Pulliam 11421 John Godfrey Urban 11422 Rufus Hardy Holloway 11423 Allen Forrest Herzberg 11424 Thomas James Bartley Shanley 11425 Jasper Jackson Wilson 11426 Henry Riggs Sullivan 11427 Thomas James Webster 11428 Donald Roy Boss 11429 Joseph Lawrence Dickman 11430 Paul Joseph Long 11431 Harry McNeill Myers 11432 Carroll William Dietz 11433 John Dalton Byrne 11434 Charles Henry Hillhouse 11435 Henry Clay Walker 11436 Harold Mortimer Crawford 11437 Philip Henry Lehr 11438 Roger Edwards Phelan 11439 Robert Merwyn Wray 11440 William Albert Hinternhoff 11441 Andrew John Kinney 11442 Charles Russell Bowers 11443 Clarence Edward Seipel 11444 Kenneth Charles Griffiths 11445 Charles McNeal Mount 11446 Vernon Gustavus Gilbert 11447 John William Dobson 11448 Charles James Long 11449 Livingston Nelson Taylor 11450 Arthur Whitney Bollard 11451 Haskett Lynch Conner 11452 Eugene Allen Romig 11453 James Clarence Evans 11454 Leonard Kaplan 11455 Frederick Henry Foerster 11456 Paul Richard Okerbloom 11457 Orin Henry Rigley 11458 Richard DeForest Cleverly 11459 John Putnam Scroggs 11460 Kenneth Leon Yarnall 11461 Jack Kummer Norris 11462 David Young Nanney 11463 Joel Furman Thomason 11464 James McMenamin Shepherd 11465 Raymond Anthony Janowski 11466 David Kenneth White 11467 James Howard Keller 11468 Eloy Alfaro 11469 Elbert Owen Meals 11470 Sterling Russell Johnson 11471 Ulrich Georg Gibbons 11472 Edwin John Latoszewski 11473 Barton George Lane 11474 Hugh Wright Caldwell 11475 Arthur Wayne Reed 11476 Christopher C. Coyne 11477 Michael John Krisman 11478 Martin George Megica 11479 Charles David Thomas Lennhoff 11480 Theodore Norman Hunsbedt 11481 William Robards Buster 11482 Keith Maughan Hull 11483 Charles David Kepple 11484 Edward Millar Geary 11485 Richard Daniel Curtin 11486 Frank Wallace Iseman 11487 James Barclay Knapp 11488 Frederic William Boye 11489 Albert Leroy Robinette 11490 John Warren Frick 11491 Donald Chessman Beere 11492 Cecil Cerel McFarland 11493 Ralph John Hanchin 11494 Paul Vernon Tuttle 11495 John Campbell Bane 11496 Francis Kosier Newcomer 11497 Raymond Bradner Marlin 11498 Laird Woodruff Hendricks 11499 John Watt 11500 Benoid Earl Glawe 11501 William Herbert Price 11502 Joseph Irving Coffey 11503 Albert Ray Brownfield 11504 Robert Carver Sears 11505 Carl Herbert Wohlfeil 11506 Frank Thomas Holt 11507 Stanley Clippinger Scott 11508 Robert Evans Greer 11509 Ralph Edward Jordan 11510 Shepler Ward FitzGerald 11511 Joseph Seifres Lester 11512 William Clark George 11513 David Badger Goodwin 11514 John George Pickard 11515 Philip Randall Seaver 11516 Robert Roy Little 11517 Burnham Lucius Batson 11518 Hulen Dee Wendorf 11519 Clifford Betsworth Haughton 11520 James Frederick Roberts 11521 Richard Turner Bowie 11522 William Whitehead West 11523 Carl Davis McFerren 11524 Roger Merrill Lilly 11525 Albert Leslie Evans 11526 John Seymour Brearley 11527 Paul Barton Cozine 11528 William J. Henry 11529 John Gordon Johnson 11530 Edwin Lowrey Hoopes 11531 Claude Lee Shepard 11532 James Sykes Billups 11533 Robert John Hill 11534 Benton Raymond Duckworth 11535 John Edgar Beier 11536 Philip Melchus Breitenbucher 11537 William Secor Clark 11538 George Edward Pickett 11539 Marshall Ralston Hickok 11540 Warren Chester Chapman 11541 Galen Pickering Eaton 11542 Darwin Kingsley Oliver 11543 John Boiler Maxwell 11544 Edgar Jarvis Jordan 11545 William Dean Chadwick 11546 James Max Cochran 11547 Robert Cochrane Twyman 11548 Seth Foster Hudgins 11549 George Thaddeus Breitling 11550 Frank Joseph Kobes 11551 Clark Wilson Mayne 11552 Richard Steele Morrison 11553 Samuel Alton Madison 11554 William Joseph Boyle 11555 Charles James Hackett 11556 William Graham Dean 11557 Heinz Weisemann 11558 Warner Winston Croxton 11559 Thomas Bernard Whitehouse 11560 Daniel Farrington Tatum 11561 Elwood Paul Donohue 11562 Lincoln A. Simon 11563 Philip William Long 11564 Walter Thomas Kerwin 11565 James Richard Gifford 11566 Maurice Myron Miller 11567 Joseph Alexander McChristian 11568 Eugene Albert Trahan 11569 Richard Gordon Lycan 11570 Phillip Buford Davidson 11571 George Wallace Roger Zethren 11572 Donald Richard Snoke 11573 Ernest Beverly Maxwell 11574 Strother Banks Hardwick 11575 Vester Melvin Shultz 11576 Robert Charlwood Richardson 11577 John Brereton Bestic 11578 Marshall Wallach 11579 Charles Urban Brombach 11580 Casper Clough 11581 Welborn Griffin Dolvin 11582 John William Watt 11583 William Ames Garnett 11584 Thomas Mull Crawford 11585 Hall Cain 11586 Wiley Burge Wisdom 11587 Donald Max Simpson 11588 Walter Martin Higgins 11589 Daniel Andrew Nolan 11590 Elliott Vandevanter 11591 Harry William Osborn Kinnard 11592 Wilbur Winston Bailey 11593 Frank Thomas Mildren 11594 Carl Lentz 11595 Charles Henry Bowman 11596 James Louis LaPrade 11597 Edward Traywick McConnell 11598 William Milligan Herron 11599 Oliver Ellsworth Wood 11600 Arthur Dean Poinier 11601 Donald Burnell Newman 11602 Harry Thomas Smith 11603 Robert Henry Schellman 11604 George Mercer Higginson 11605 Jack Gordon Merrell 11606 Christopher Joseph Heffernan 11607 Stephen J. Mancuso 11608 Joel Terry Walker 11609 Robert Moorhouse Coleman 11610 Raymond Joseph Belardi 11611 Robert Watson Crandall 11612 John Willis Walker 11613 William Stein Boyd 11614 Victor Leroy Johnson 11615 William Thomas Smith 11616 Patrick David Mulcahy 11617 William Mulford Van Harlingen 11618 Howard B. St. Clair 11619 Donald Busby Miller 11620 Thomas Bennett Bartel 11621 Alfred Virgil Walton 11622 Harry de Metropolis 11623 Stephen Charles Farris 11624 Charles Langley Patrick Medinnis 11625 Percy De Witt McCarley 11626 John Keith Boles 11627 Tilden Perkins Wright 11628 Matt Combes Cavendish Bristol 11629 Robert George Cole 11630 William Lee McDowell 11631 Ray Joseph Will 11632 Rudyard Kipling Grimes 11633 Robert John Rogers 11634 Lyle Everett Peterson 11635 Arthur Wright Allen 11636 Howard Vincent Cooperider 11637 John Porter Tomhave 11638 William Charles Jones 11639 Matthew

Comerford Smith 11640 John Shotwell Wintermute 11641 Lionel Burke DeVille 11642 Robert Sewall Chester 11643 Estel Burkhead Culbreth 11644 Edwin Joseph Ostberg 11645 Perry Milo Hoisington 11646 Karl Frederick Ockershauser 11647 Oliver Burtis Taylor 11648 Walter Charles Wickboldt 11649 Lee Manning Kirby 11650 Geoffrey Lavell 11651 Leon Robert Vance 11652 Michael Shannon Davison 11653 William James McConnell 11654 Salvatore Edward Manzo 11655 William LeRoy Turner 11656 Leonard Neil Palmer 11657 Fidelis David Newcomb 11658 George N. Brown 11659 Melvin Verner Engstrom 11660 Thomas Walker Davis 11661 Clarence Riley Bess 11662 William Kemp Martin 11663 Robert David Hunter 11664 Jaime Eduardo Alfaro 11665 Edward Paul Smith 11666 Robert Royce Gideon 11667 William Joseph McCaffrey 11668 Carl Walter Hollstein 11669 Donald Franklin Hull 11670 John Olav Herstad 11671 James David Garcia 11672 John Neary Davis 11673 John Osburn Dickerson 11674 Samuel Goodhue Kail 11675 Ernest Patricio Lasche 11676 Benjamin Mart Bailey 11677 William Carter Stone 11678 James LeRoy Rogers 11679 Malcolm Frank Gilchrist 11680 John William Jaycox 11681 Walter James Alsop 11682 Robert Beirne Spragins 11683 Bernard George Teeters 11684 Robert Clarence Whipple 11685 DeWitt Nalley Hall 11686 Prentiss Davis Wynne 11687 William Henry Stubbs 11688 Herbert Raymond Odom 11689 Raymond Thompson Petersen 11690 Richard Arthur White 11691 Donald Kuldell Nickerson 11692 Ellsworth Reily Jacoby 11693 Edward MacDonald Serrem 11694 Robert Chapman Williams 11695 Charles George Fredericks 11696 Walter Herbert Grant 11697 Stanley Robert Larsen 11698 James Barclay Carvey 11699 Victor Frederick Crowell 11700 James Joseph Kelly 11701 William Calvin Banning 11702 William Montgomery Preston 11703 Lester Leland Lampert 11704 Frank Goodwin Forrest 11705 Matthew Whalen 11706 Shields Warren 11707 William Holloman Barnett 11708 John Bodine McConville 11709 James Thomas Lowe Schwenk 11710 Ned Woods Glenn 11711 Richard Van Wyck Negley 11712 Richard Moushegian 11713 William Henderson Patterson 11714 James Vincent Reardon 11715 Joseph Theodore Kingsley 11716 Charles Bradford Smith 11717 Matthew Leon Legler 11718 Jacob Kopf Rippert 11719 Edward Elliot Rager 11720 John Christian Habecker 11721 Herbert Henry Eichlin 11722 Charles Wesley Florance 11723 Robert William Page 11724 Kenneth Lansing Scott 11725 Frank Campbell Sellars 11726 Elmer Earl Rager 11727 Wiley Lee Dixon 11728 John Eric Olson 11729 John McMillan Banks 11730 William Walter Nichols 11731 Clyde Terry Sutton 11732 Charles Wilmarth Kouns 11733 Homer Griswold Barber 11734 John Carlos Edwards 11735 Robert Allen Matter 11736 Earle Livingstone Lerette 11737 Harold MacVane Brown 11738 Paul Tucker Clifford 11739 John Tyler Davis 11740 Robert Emmet McMahon 11741 James Anderson Roosa 11742 Robert Pennell 11743 Harry Lawrason Murray 11744 John Louis McCoy 11745 Willard Barber Atwell 11746 Loren Chester Grieves 11747 William Jackson Fling 11748 Charles Manly Walton 11749 Edward Randall Ford 11750 Ernest Frederick Brockman 11751 Allen Woodrow Ginder 11752 Clifford Lore Miller 11753 George Thomas Coleman 11754 Joseph Everett Reynolds 11755 George Richard Harrison 11756 Newton Elder James 11757 John Patrick Aidan Kelly 11758 Carl August Buechner 11759 Edwin Peter Schmid 11760 John Peter Mial 11761 James Law McCrorey 11762 James Elmer Mather 11763 Lewis Wilson Stocking 11764 Matthew James McKeever 11765 Vincent Laurence Boylan 11766 William Robinson Reilly 11767 Jack Reeson Looney 11768 Edward Smith Hamilton 11769 Edgar William Schroeder 11770 Benjamin Franklin Avery 11771 James Oren McCray 11772 Kenneth Wilson Collins 11773 Benjamin Charles Chapla 11774 Josiah Scott Kurtz 11775 Levin Lane Lee 11776 Harry Watson McClellan 11777 James Walter Wilson 11778 David Samuel Dillard 11779 Joseph Adams Hill 11780 V. Paul Yale 11781 Milton Bernard Adams 11782 John H. Meyer 11783 Constant August Troiano 11784 Lindsay Coates Herkness 11785 James Deimel Green 11786 Charles John Parsons 11787 William Herbert Hale 11788 John Joseph Kelly 11789 Arthur Tilman Williams 11790 **1940** Harold Clifton Brown 11791 Alan Edward Gee 11792 John Finzer Presnell 11793 John William Burfening 11794 John Anthony Graf 11795 Winston C. Fowler 11796 Robert Gibson Cooper 11797 Lawrence Cutwright Sheetz 11798 Charles Bellows Hazeltine 11799 Leo Erway Dunham 11800 Alton Parker Donnell 11801 George Francis Dixon 11802 Ashod Michael Ahmajan 11803 Lawrence Joseph Fuller 11804 Paul Francis O'Neil 11805 Lawrence Gordon Forbes 11806 Samuel Richard Peterson 11807 Eugene Joseph Carr 11808 Austin James Russell 11809 David Stuart Parker 11810 Harry Albright French 11811 Earl McFarland 11812 Joseph Vincent Iacobucci 11813 Raymond Harold Goodrich 11814 Edward Aiken Flanders 11815 Edward Thomas Podufaly 11816 Herbert Edward Pace 11817 Marvin Leroy Jacobs 11818 Clayton Allen Rust 11819 Howard Wilson Penney 11820 Robert Ila Wheat 11821 Thomas Duvall Quaid 11822 Raymond Maurice Clock 11823 Robert Carter Pfeil 11824 Louis Aloysius Thommen 11825 Francis Richard Sullivan 11826 James Arthur Plant 11827 Leonard Landon Haseman 11828 Richard Henry Free 11829 Edward Gaylord Cook 11830 Walter E. Gunster 11831 Vincent Ebol Gepte 11832 Milford Franklin Stablein 11833 Montgomery Cunningham Meigs 11834 Nathan Louis Krisberg 11835 Felicisimo Sulit Castillo 11836 Paul Hobart Krauss 11837 Robert Edward Applegate 11838 Thaddeus Michael Nosek 11839 Ivan Sattem 11840 Carey Law O'Bryan 11841 Laurence Joseph Legere 11842 Oval Hale Robinson 11843 Paul David Phillips 11844 Charles Harvey Banks 11845 William Harvey Roedy 11846 Charles Carmin Noble 11847 Ralph Morris Rogers 11848 John Bunyan Corbly 11849 Philip Lovell Elliott 11850 Luther Dixon Arnold 11851 Cuyler Llewellyn Clark 11852 Gerhard E. Brown 11853 John Edward Minahan 11854 William Regis Shanahan 11855 James Pershing Strauss 11856 Robert Irving Dice 11857 Charles Edmund Harrison 11858 Urey Woodson Alexander 11859 William Payne Francisco 11860 Jack Stewart DeWitt 11861 Delano Edgell 11862 Elbert Dotterer Hoffman 11863 Alan Greene Rorick 11864 Woodrow Maurice Smith 11865 David Roger Guy 11866 Robert Ray Williams 11867 James Montgomery Moore 11868 Wendell John Coats 11869 Edward Patrick Wynne 11870 Walter Ferrell Winton 11871 Bernard Ambrose Ferry 11872 Lawrence Ronald Klar 11873 Frederick Jacob Yeager 11874 George Mayo 11875 Raymond Renola 11876 Clarence William Clapsaddle 11877 Morris Loeb Shoss 11878 Cephas Bryan Sitterson 11879 Edward Verner 11880 Robert Moore Brewer 11881 Kenneth McRae Lemley 11882 John Thomas Harvey Spengler 11883 Raymond Leroy Shoemaker 11884 Nils Martin Bengtson 11885 Anthony Benvenuto 11886 Edward Hamilton Kyle 11887 Homer Barron Chandler 11888 Charles Richard Fairlamb 11889 Dean Titus Vanderhoef 11890 Stephen Silvasy 11891 Charles Webster Bagstad 11892 Donald Haldeman Baumer 11893 John Joseph Murphy 11894 Robert Hamilton Warren 11895 Manford Jay Wetzel 11896 Dean Marti Benson 11897 Edward Joseph Walker 11898 Henry Augustine Miley 11899 John Zachariah Endress 11900 James Robert Wendt 11901 Clarence Talmage Marsh 11902 Rolland Woodrow Hamelin 11903 Clarence Edward Gushurst 11904 Clyde Henry Webb 11905 Raymond Weir Millican 11906 Donald Vivian Bennett 11907 William Clark Craig 11908 Henry Allen Cunningham 11909 Woodrow Wilson Vaughan 11910 Richard Josiah Kent 11911 James Willard Walters 11912 George Daniel Carnahan 11913 Samuel Merrick Patten 11914 John Paul Gerald 11915 Robert John Fate 11916 James Kirkbride Taylor 11917 Edwin Fahey Black 11918 Willis Franklin Lewis 11919 Robinson R. Norris 11920 William Henry Harrison Mullin 11921 Burdett Eugene Haessly 11922 Thomas Huntington Monroe 11923 William Elliott Heinemann 11924 Hobart Burnside Pillsbury 11925 William Wilbur Wilcox 11926 Virgil Alvin Schwab 11927 Richard Sargent Abbey 11928 Theodore Louis Hoffmann 11929 Manley Calbraith Perry 11930 John Jacob Beiser 11931 William Henry Birrell 11932 Bradley Foote Prann 11933 Donald Boyle Stewart 11934 Charles Simonton Brice 11935 Thomas Henderson Scott 11936 Francis Joseph Crown 11937 Walter Wellman Lavell 11938 Everett DeWitt Light 11939 Francis Clare Gideon 11940 William Everett Marling 11941 Charles Alexander Shaunesey 11942 John Andrew O'Brien 11943 Victor Woodfin Hobson 11944 Joseph Richard Couch 11945 Joseph Michael Cole 11946 Jerry Spears Addington 11947 James Garland Dubuisson 11948 Sydney Gilbert Fisher 11949 Solomon Theodore Wills 11950 Joseph Patrick Donohue 11951 Leonard Milton Orman 11952 Otis Maxwell Ulm 11953 Edward Henry Hendrickson 11954 Dennis Ladislaus Barton 11955 Philip Courtney Loofburrow 11956 Alan Griffith Baker 11957 Orloff Lake Bowen 11958 Richard Levin Belt 11959 Harry Thompson Simpson 11960 Walter Joseph Fellenz 11961 Paul Schroeder Deems 11962 John MacNair Wright 11963 Robert Campbell Cassibry 11964 William Clay 11965 Michael Paulick 11966 James Lavern Smiley 11967 Arthur Austin McCartan 11968 Charles Gillies Esau 11969 Harry Lee Wilson 11970 Jerry Geza Toth 11971 Victor Stanisla Zienowicz 11972 Robert Jerome Delaney 11973 William Roscoe Kintner 11974 Wendell Burley Sell 11975 Robert Lamar Williams 11976 Davison Dalziel 11977 William Edward Buck 11978 Frank Armand deLatour 11979 James Ralph Taylor 11980 George Joseph LaBreche 11981 Thomas Bowman Hargis 11982 Charles Langworthy Beaudry 11983 Chester Kieser Britt 11984 James Elroy Tyler 11985 Richard Hobbs Fraser 11986 Edwin Carroll Haggard 11987 Melvin Herbert Rosen 11988 Donovan Paul Yeuell 11989 Stewart Lawrence McKenney 11990 Edison Albert Lynn 11991 Bertil Andrew Johnson 11992 Alan Philip Thayer 11993 Raymond Starrat Sleeper 11994 John Joseph Pidgeon 11995 Frederic Watson Oseth 11996 John Robert Wilbraham 11997 Jordan Joseph Wilderman 11998 Arthur Harold Nelson 11999 John Stevens Harnett 12000 Robert Leonard Colligan 12001 James Frederick Kreitzer 12002 John Edward Aber 12003 James Lawson Orr 12004 Alan Martin Strock 12005 James Harold Pitman 12006 William Beverly Campbell 12007 Gilbert Hume Woodward 12008 George Columbus Hines 12009 Robert Thorn Tuck 12010 Harry Frank Bunze 12011 Osmund Alfred Leahy 12012 James Butler Bonham 12013 Howard Thomas Wright 12014 James Anthony Lotozo 12015 George Alexander Aubrey 12016 Paul S. Cullen 12017 Thomas Frederick Gordon 12018 Joe W. Leedom 12019 John Joseph Kenney 12020 John Joseph Smith 12021 John Edmund Collins 12022 Michael Francis Bavaro 12023 William Frederick Horton 12024 Olin Lee Bell 12025 Herbert Mead Bowlby 12026 Scott Montgomery Case 12027 Francis Edward Kramer 12028 Rowland Herman Renwanz 12029 James W. Milner 12030 James Fant Berry 12031 Joseph Schuyler Hardin 12032 Jules David Yates 12033 Glenwood Gordon Stephenson 12034 Sanford Patrick England 12035 William Goodnow Stoddard 12036 Jack Pershing Thompson 12037 James Richard Maedler 12038 Dill Baynard Ellis 12039 Roy Hubert Kinsell 12040 Everett Houston Ware 12041 Philip John Moore 12042 Ronald Maurice Kolda 12043 James Scott Greene 12044 Hugh Jefferson Turner 12045 Salvo Rizza 12046 John Robert McLean 12047 John Deber Townsend 12048 John Harold Wohner 12049 Charles Henry Colwell 12050 Wing Fook Jung 12051 Thomas Corwin Chamberlain 12052 Cornelius Arthur Murphy 12053 Francis Michael Rooney 12054 James Thomas Hennessy 12055 Ralph Edward Zahrobsky 12056 Walter Israel Wald 12057 Robert Edwin Maxwell 12058 Robert Anthony O'Brien 12059 John Christie Emery 12060 Joseph William Ruebel 12061 Reginald James Clizbe 12062 Delbert Earle Munson 12063 Jas. Holland Stephen Rasmussen 12064 Roderick Wetherill 12065 Craig Lowe Moore 12066 Arthur Robert Barry 12067 Bryce Frederic Denno 12068 Augustus John Cullen 12069 Ernest Bryant Jones 12070 Robert Russell Dodderidge 12071 Thomas Franklin Mansfield 12072 Maurice Earle Parker 12073 Wallace Leo Clement 12074 William Benjamin Wright 12075 Dan Porter Briggs 12076 Ford Prioleau Fuller 12077 Robert Phineas Knapp 12078 James Francis Downing 12079 Arthur Dudley Maxwell 12080 Frank Colacicco 12081 Donald Lionel Bierman 12082 John Thomas O'Keefe 12083 Samuel McClure Goodwin 12084 Robert Carroll Cameron 12085 Wallace James Hackett 12086 Ralph Anderson Osborn 12087 David Barbour Byrne 12088 Lester Frank Schockner 12089 John Dibble 12090 Raymond Henry Bates 12091 Harry Ami Stella 12092 Joseph Lee McCroskey 12093 Harry Bert Lane 12094 William Eugene Farthing 12095 Martin Bell Chandler 12096 Henry Patrick Heid 12097 Rush Spencer Wells 12098 George John Bayerle 12099 Fred Hughes Coleman 12100 Albert Park Richards 12101 John Karl Roberts 12102 George Hans Mueller 12103 James McLaurin Ridgell 12104 Neri Philip Cangelosi 12105 Charles Edward Balthis 12106 Leland George Cagwin 12107 Thomas Henry Muller 12108 William Parham Kevan 12109 Silvio Emil Gasperini 12110 Harmon Porter Rimmer 12111 James David Loewus 12112 William Fielding Lewis 12113 David Rockwell Crocker 12114 Leonard Edward Symroski 12115 Andre Ringgold Brousseau 12116 William Kasper 12117 Frank Meszar 12118 John Ross East 12119 Richard Thomas Cassidy 12120 Lester Cecil Hess 12121 Robert William Strong 12122 Henry Hudson Norman 12123 Lee Watson Fritter 12124 Eugene Orville McDonald 12125 Franklin Stapf Shawn 12126 Morrill Elwood Marston 12127 Milton Carlton Barnard 12128 Sanford Harvey Webster 12129 John William Norvell 12130 James Frederick Williams 12131 Edward Deming Lucas 12132 George Washington England 12133 Allan Ashley Crockett 12134 Robert Francis O'Donnell 12135 Frederick Anthony Schmaltz 12136 Warren Curtis Stirling 12137 Gilford Dalton Green 12138 Mercer Patton Davis 12139 Raymond John Downey 12140 Frank C. Mandell 12141 Emory Sherwood Adams 12142 Archie Joyce Knight 12143 Arthur Gordon Malone 12144 Roy Willard Nelson 12145 Howard Lewis Peter 12146 Carter Burdeau Johnson 12147 Richard Ware Mabee 12148 Florian John Erspamer 12149 Andrew d'Elia 12150 Charles Eugene Oglesby 12151 Charles Theodore Biswagner 12152 Arthur Theodore Frontczak 12153 Ralph Adair Colby 12154 Bidwell Moore 12155 Thaddeus Philip Floryan 12156 Albert Dale Epley 12157 Lloyd Webster Hough 12158 Anthony Lewis Paul Wermuth 12159 Andrew Donald Budz 12160 Frank Talman Watrous 12161 Durward Henry Galbreath 12162 Jodie Gibson Stewart 12163 James Edward McGinity 12164 Eben French Swift 12165 Theodore Weisman Davis 12166 Robert Neville Mackin 12167 Richard Alexander Shagrin 12168 Louis Gonzaga Mendez 12169 James Byington McAfee 12170 William Joseph Gildart 12171 Joseph Jackson Eaton 12172 Stanton Thomas Smith 12173 Melville Offers 12174 Mark Ransom Hudson 12175 Sidney Vincent Bingham 12176 Stephen Bernard Morrissey 12177 Julius Boswell Summers 12178 Karl Tweeten Rauk 12179 Mark Clair Baugher Klunk 12180 Edward Franklin Hoover 12181 John Patrick Dwyer 12182 Victor George Conley 12183 Leon Luther Clarke 12184 Roland Merrill Gleszer 12185 Joseph Lee Mastran 12186 William Francis Coleman 12187 Walter Drummond Swank 12188 William Norman Holm 12189 Franklin Wolfram Horton 12190 Paul Sorg Reinecke 12191 Ralph Edward Miner 12192 Edward Aloysius Murphy 12193 Robert Charles Raleigh 12194 Edward Dunphy Fitzpatrick 12195 Burton Elmo McKenzie 12196 Julian Aaron Cook 12197 James Mason Shelley 12198 Irvine Harrison Shearer 12199 George Thomas Larkin 12200 Page Egerton Smith 12201 Henry Force Daniels 12202 William White Saunders 12203 Aquilla Ballard Hughes 12204 Frank Benjamin Wagner 12205 Henry Harley Arnold 12206 William Powell Litton 12207 Marvin Hatfield Merchant 12208 Alvan Cullom Gillem 12209 Chester Moffet Freudendorf 12210 Russell Joseph Manzolillo 12211 Benjamin Franklin Delamater 12212 Jack Borden 12213 Theodore Ross Milton 12214 Raymond John LaRose 12215 Philip Robert Cibotti 12216 Marshall Cloke 12217 Henry Randolph Brewerton 12218 Albert Eger Brown 12219 Harlan Benton Ferrill 12220 Francis Thomas Devlin 12221 Ralph Newlin Ross 12222 Frederick Leif Andrews 12223 Landon Albert Witt 12224 Kermit Robert Dyke 12225 John Bertram Coontz 12226 Evan Harris Humphrey 12227 Milton David Lederman 12228 John Richard Knight 12229 William Lyon Porte 12230 Graham Charles Sanford 12231 Albert Henry Bethune 12232 Percy Charles Stoddart 12233 Frederick Grinnell White 12234 Thomas Klauder Spencer 12235 Alfred Jennings Floyd 12236 Lyman Oscar Heidtke 12237 Michael Kuziv 12238 William John Bennett 12239 **1941** Alfred Judson Force Moody 12240 Elmer Parker Yates 12241 Wadsworth Paul Clapp 12242 John Clifford Hodges Lee 12243 Edwin Lloyd Powell 12244 John Roy Oswalt 12245 John Frederick Harris 12246 Allen Jensen 12247 Raymond Ira Schnittke 12248 Vincent Paul Carlson 12249 William Charles Gribble 12250 Curtis Wheaton Chapman 12251 Sears Yates Coker 12252 Howard Warren Clark 12253 Charles Leonard Peirce 12254 Richard Gentry Tindall 12255 Frank A. Gerig 12256 Cargill Massenburg Barnett 12257 Roy Skiles Kelley 12258 Paul Wyman Ramee 12259 Donald Haynes Heaton 12260 Jesse Paul Unger 12261 Charles Henry Schilling 12262 David Seavey Woods 12263 John Edward Schremp 12264 John Field Michel 12265 Richard Delaney 12266 William Thomas Seawell 12267 Howard Clarke Goodell 12268 Guy Harold Goddard 12269 Robert Mack Tarbox 12270 Kenneth Wade Kennedy 12271 Lynn Cyrus Lee 12272 Fred John Ascani 12273 James William Strain 12274 Robert Graham Waitt 12275 Herbert Campbell Clendening 12276 James Henry Carroll 12277 Harold Edward Nankivell 12278 Harry Van Horn Ellis 12279 Harry Charles Besancon 12280 Stanley Meriwether Ramey 12281 Joseph Jackson Thigpen 12282 William Miles Linton 12283 Robert Sealey Kramer 12284 Kenneth O'Reilly Dessert 12285 Harrington Willson Cochran 12286 Frederick John Baker 12287 Hume Peabody 12288 Joseph Ingram Gurfein 12289 Ben Isbel Mayo 12290 Paul Demetrius Duke 12291 Joseph Stanley Grygiel 12292 George Philip Seneff 12293 John Webb Van Hoy 12294 Emory Ashel Austin 12295 Mills Carson Hatfield 12296 Thomas L. Fisher 12297 Gordon Thomas Gould 12298 Edward Leon Rowny 12299 Robert Merrill Tuttle 12300 Ernest Durr 12301 John Langford Locke 12302 Herbert Richardson 12303 Walter E. Mather 12304 Robert Walter Samz 12305 Cecil Leo Smith 12306 Robert Patterson Pierpont 12307 Richard Magee Osgood 12308 Charles Dorsey Maynard 12309 Richard Bradford Polk 12310 Clarence John Lokker 12311 Joseph Meryl Silk 12312 John Holmes Camp 12313 Burnside Elijah Huffman 12314 Atanacio T. Chavez 12315 Denis Blundell Grace 12316 Alexander Ramsey Nininger 12317 James William Roy 12318 Norman Kitchner Coker 12319 John William Burtchaell 12320 Wayne Edgar Rhynard 12321 Ralph Edward Kuzell 12322 James William Stigers 12323 John F.T. Murray 12324 A. George Woodrow Johnson 12325 Richard John Rastetter 12326 Jack Curtright McClure 12327 Stephen Thaddeus Kosiorek 12328 George Lawrence Slocum 12329 Roy J. Clinton 12330 Lee Bradley Ledford 12331 John Rose Richards 12332 Henry Nathan Blanchard 12333 Charles Edwin Jones 12334 Straughan Downing Kelsey 12335 John Miles Henschke 12336 John Millikin 12337 LeMoyne Francis Michels 12338 Robert Vaughn Elsberry 12339 George Winfield Stalnaker 12340 John Jay Easton 12341 Joseph Andrew McCulloch 12342 Richard Pressly Scott 12343 Henry Richard Bodson 12344 David Gabriel Gauvreau 12345 Edward Harleston deSaussure 12346 Donald Leroy McMillan 12347 Glenn Alfred Lee 12348 Ernest Jeunet Whitaker 12349 Malcolm Corwin Johnson 12350 Walter James Woolwine 12351 Perry Thompson Jones 12352 Lloyd Robert Salisbury 12353 Leroy Hugh Watson 12354 John Nathaniel Hauser 12355 William M. Petre 12356 Frank Pleasants Stainback 12357 John Gabriel Redmon 12358 Edward Joseph Geldermann 12359 George Bissland Moore 12360 David Ernest Kunkel 12361 George Roopen Adjemian 12362 Mortimer Buell Birdseye 12363 Harry Kendall Bagshaw 12364 Max Woodrow Hall 12365 Max Campbell Tyler 12366 Wallace Michael Lauterbach 12367 Gregg LaRoix McKee 12368 Frederick Clinton Stanford 12369 Robert Stanley Reilly 12370 Clarence Lewis Elder 12371 Roger Stevens Neumeister 12372 James Gerard Healy 12373 Robert James Colleran 12374 Curtis Francis Betts 12375 Elkin Leland Franklin 12376 Floyd Sturdevan Cofer 12377 Willis Bruner Sawyer 12378 Paul George Skowronek

12379 Joseph Hester Ward 12380 Wilson Russell Reed 12381 Duward Lowery Crow 12382 Marshall Warren Carney 12383 Frank Ely Locke 12384 John Adams Brooks 12385 Alpheus Wray White 12386 Duval West 12387 Robert Edward Panke 12388 Robert Duncan Brown 12389 Jonathan Edwards Adams 12390 Clifford E. Cole 12391 Arnold Svere Torgerson 12392 Charles Arthur Cannon 12393 Isaac Owen Winfree 12394 Hugh Franklin Foster 12395 Eric Thomas de Jonckheere 12396 Charles William Fletcher 12397 William LeRoy Mitchell 12398 George William McIntyre 12399 Lanham Carmel Connally 12400 William Frank Starr 12401 Dan Holton Eaton 12402 Leon Herman Berger 12403 George Lawrence Theisen 12404 John Benjamin Manley 12405 Charles Knighton Harris 12406 George Hamilton Stillson 12407 James Oscar Green 12408 Edwin Watson Brown 12409 Thaddeus J. Shelton 12410 Roger Longstreet Lawson 12411 William Eugene Clifford 12412 Paul Rutherford Larson 12413 Richard Waggener Couch 12414 John Moore Christensen 12415 Walter Francis Molesky 12416 John Norton 12417 Richard Van Pelt Travis 12418 David Cooper 12419 R. Potter Campbell 12420 Malcolm Graham Troup 12421 Harold Wesley Norton 12422 Oscar Charles Tonetti 12423 Charles Joseph Canella 12424 Paul Chester Day 12425 Herbert Welcome Frawley 12426 Thomas Depher Collison 12427 Joseph Lippincott Knowlton 12428 Lyman Saunders Faulkner 12429 Arthur Lloyd Meyer 12430 Lawrence Vivans Greene 12431 Charles Gleeson Willes 12432 Samuel Bertron Magruder 12433 Matthew Clarence Harrison 12434 Paul von Santen Liles 12435 Miroslav Frank Moucha 12436 Albert Howell Snider 12437 Morton McDonald Jones 12438 Jack Leith Bentley 12439 Joseph Patrick Ahern 12440 Andrew Julius Evans 12441 Jacob Heffner Towers 12442 James Henry King 12443 Leo Charles Henzl 12444 Horace Maynard Brown 12445 Michael J. L. Greene 12446 John Charles Linderman 12447 Robert William Horn 12448 Walter Leon Moore 12449 Windsor Temple Anderson 12450 Robert Putnam Detwiler 12451 James Fuller McKinley 12452 William Morris Hoge 12453 Michael Frank Aliotta 12454 Robert Edward Lanigan 12455 Willard Russell Gilbert 12456 Ralph Robinet Hetherington 12457 Roy Leighton Atteberry 12458 William Hunter Woodward 12459 Harley Truman Marsh 12460 Donald Vincent Thompson 12461 James Philip Walker 12462 Thomas Winston Curley 12463 George William Cooper 12464 Richard William Kline 12465 Thomas Rodgers Lawson 12466 Auburon Paul Hauser 12467 William Graham Gillis 12468 Hill Blalock 12469 Robert Evarts Clark 12470 Benjamin McCaffery 12471 Henry Boswell 12472 Maurice Guthrie Miller 12473 Patrick Henry Tansey 12474 Clyde Arnold Thompson 12475 James Edward McElroy 12476 Harold Alexander Tidmarsh 12477 Robert John Coakley 12478 George Henry Pittman 12479 Robert Huff Edger 12480 Robert Channing Borman 12481 Heister Hower Drum 12482 Paul James O'Brien 12483 Thomas Rees Cramer 12484 Robert Paul Johnson 12485 Francis Cornelius Fitzpatrick 12486 Matthew Gordon Harper 12487 John Leonard Robinson 12488 Arnold Jacob Hoebeke 12489 Thomas Abbott Hume 12490 George Bibb Pickett 12491 Benjamin Berry Kercheval 12492 Merritt Lambert Hewitt 12493 Paul Gray 12494 Max Price 12495 John Calvin Clark 12496 Gibson Niles 12497 Moody Elmo Layfield 12498 Ralph Allen McCool 12499 Reynolds Robert Keleher 12500 James Raine Laney 12501 William Wallace Brier 12502 Dick Stanley von Schriltz 12503 Clinton Field Ball 12504 Howard Frank Adams 12505 Arnold Ray Thomas 12506 Gerard Anthony LaRocca 12507 Joseph Scott Peddie 12508 Charles Manly Busbee 12509 Rod Reed McNagny 12510 Jesse Duncan Thompson 12511 Wendell Pollitt Knowles 12512 Felix John Gerace 12513 Peter Kirkbride Dilts 12514 William Thomas Gleason 12515 Herbert Irving Stern 12516 Harry Howard Ellis 12517 Charles MacArthur Carman 12518 Frank Benton Howze 12519 William Faye Roton 12520 Fred Milas Hampton 12521 John Coles Barney 12522 Samuel Wilson Parks 12523 Ira Boswell Cheaney 12524 Edwin Boynton Buttery 12525 Leon Arthur Briggs 12526 Linton Sinclair Boatwright 12527 Joseph Tuck Brown 12528 Ben Marshall West 12529 Robert Willoughby Garrett 12530 George Lincoln Andrews 12531 William Augustus Purdy 12532 William Harold Gurnee 12533 Victor Woodrow Campana 12534 John Carl McIntyre 12535 Charles Robert Murrah 12536 William John Dooley Vaughan 12537 Paul Crawford Root 12538 Richard Mar Levy 12539 Thomas Wilson Sharkey 12540 James Isaac Cox 12541 Charles Love Mullins 12542 Edwin Charles Kisiel 12543 Irving Richard Perkin 12544 Alfred George Hayduk 12545 Walter Raleigh Mullane 12546 Thomas Ward Maxwell 12547 Ralph Earl Freese 12548 Paul Edgar Pique 12549 Maynard George Moyer 12550 Charles S. Seamans 12551 James Richardson 12552 Theodore Knox White 12553 Thomas Courtenay O'Connell 12554 Henry Durand Irwin 12555 Nelson Paul Monson 12556 Carroll Freemont Danforth 12557 Thomas J. Cleary 12558 James Henderson Dienelt 12559 Peer DeSilva 12560 Wharton Clayton Cochran 12561 Harry Niles Rising 12562 James Daniel Fowler 12563 William Annesley Kromer 12564 Walter Singles 12565 Charles Llewellyn Flanders 12566 William Kneedler Cummins 12567 Gwynne Sutherland Curtis 12568 John Raymond Sands 12569 Alexander Frank Muzyk 12570 John Ellis Rossell 12571 Daniel Salinas 12572 Thomas Edwin Reagan 12573 John Gavin Tyndall 12574 Horace Grattan Foster 12575 Hector John Polla 12576 John William Meador 12577 Donald Lyons Driscoll 12578 Paul Richard Kemp 12579 Ernest Franklin Poff 12580 George Scratchley Brown 12581 Robert Lloyd Cummings 12582 Benjamin Alvord Spiller 12583 Mercer Presley Longino 12584 Richards Abner Aldridge 12585 Riley Smith King 12586 Edward Joseph McGrane 12587 Harwell Leon Adams 12588 David Burch Taggart 12589 Justus MacMullen Home 12590 Leroy Pierce Collins 12591 Hamilton King Avery 12592 Angelo Augustine Laudani 12593 Joseph Scranton Tate 12594 Robert Toombs Dixon 12595 Albert Samuel Dalby 12596 Truman Eugene Deyo 12597 James Paul Forsyth 12598 Joseph John Weidner 12599 John B. Deane 12600 Howard Lawrence Felchin 12601 Stanton Claude Hutson 12602 Martin Andrew Shadday 12603 Earl Vincent Brown 12604 Leslie Wilmer Bailey 12605 James Rayford Sykes 12606 Thomas Martin Ward 12607 John Henry Zott 12608 Bradish J. Smith 12609 Harry Lee Jarvis 12610 William Gardner 12611 Bert Stanford Rosenbaum 12612 George Luther Hicks 12613 Stephen Kellogg Plume 12614 Sam H. Barrow 12615 Edison Kermit Walters 12616 Burton Curtis Andrus 12617 Maxwell Weston Sullivan 12618 Rudolph Adolph Matheisel 12619 Francis Joseph Troy 12620 Edgar Clayton Boggs 12621 Charles Fuller Matheson 12622 Bernard Schultz 12623 Ralph Reed Upton 12624 James Wetherby Graham 12625 Edgar Thronton Poole 12626 Theodore Bernarr Celmer 12627 Peter Schuyler Tanous 12628 Robert Hendrick Brinson 12629 William John Hershenow 12630 Robert Harold Rosen 12631 Junius Edward Dillard 12632 Robert Bernard Keagy 12633 Francis Joseph Myers 12634 Roscoe Barnett Woodruff 12635 Charles Herbert Humber 12636 Thomas Goldsborough Corbin 12637 Harry Canavan Harvey 12638 Alden George Thompson 12639 Clinton Earle Male 12640 William Doyle Pratt 12641 Earl K. Buchanan 12642 John Wilson Callaway 12643 Roderic Dhu O'Connor 12644 Harry White Trimble 12645 Edgar Mathews Sliney 12646 James Lawrence Kaiser 12647 George Hollenback Welles 12648 Robert Gilman Loring 12649 William Thomas McDaniel 12650 Frank Holroyd Linnell 12651 Bruce Wilds P. Edgerton 12652 Charles Edwin Thomas 12653 Lester Strode White 12654 Roy G. Hendrickson 12655 Edward Benedict Zarembo 12656 John Vincent D'Esposito 12657 John Earl Atkinson 12658 Edwin Forrest Harding 12659 Clare Hibbs Armstrong 12660 Kenneth Oswalt Due 12661 Bruce Campbell Cator 12662 Earle Wayne Brown 12663 **1942** James Hart Hottenroth 12664 James Henry Hayes 12665 Henry Preston Halsell 12666 Thomas Henry Lauer 12667 Elliott Carr Cutler 12668 Sam Ellsworth Cumpston 12669 George Edward Hesselbacher 12670 Robert Paul Young 12671 John Moore McMurray 12672 James Bryan Newman 12673 John Reiley Finney 12674 Hugh Pat Williams 12675 Richard Malcolm Horridge 12676 Irving Rock Obenchain 12677 John Earle Kennedy 12678 William Harold Morgan 12679 Lawrence Willard Vogel 12680 George Chambers Hozier 12681 Pedro Roxas FlorCruz 12682 John Winthrop Barnes 12683 William Ward Watkin 12684 Leon Joseph Hamerly 12685 Edward Ambrose Martell 12686 John Arnot Hewitt 12687 Yates Michel Hill 12688 Francis Paul Koisch 12689 Daniel Arthur Raymond 12690 Jerrold Duster Snow 12691 Joseph John Schmidt 12692 Eric Castlereigh Orme 12693 Paul Robert Cerar 12694 Robert Maurice Rawls 12695 Alvin Dumond Wilder 12696 Philip George Krueger 12697 William Tuttle Hamilton 12698 Miles Lowell Wachendorf 12699 Robert Peyton Tabb 12700 Frederick Charles Roecker 12701 Fred Edgar Rosell 12702 John Clement Mottina 12703 Frank Clyde Smiley 12704 Mahlon Eugene Gates 12705 John Pierce Beeson 12706 Robert Langdon Ferguson 12707 John Emory Gimperling 12708 Roger Lee Russell 12709 Richard Louis Hennessy 12710 Charles Emerson Ragland 12711 Thomas Adrian Norwood 12712 Edward McWayne Wright 12713 Roger Alley Barnes 12714 Seymour Rubenstein 12715 Theodore James Michel 12716 John Wallis Leonard 12717 Edmond Harrison Farrington 12718 Francis Eugene Voegeli 12719 Eugene Leland Weeks 12720 John Preston Sheffey 12721 Carter Williamson 12722 John Warmington Atwood 12723 John Baker 12724 Harold Archer Ogden 12725 Clyde Raymond Eisenschmidt 12726 Wayne Leonard Bart 12727 William Hampton Edwards 12728 Charles Marshall Fergusson 12729 Peter Richard Moody 12730 Horace Allan Lawler 12731 Thomas Francis Farrell 12732 Gerhardt Christopher Clementson 12733 Russell Peter Bonasso 12734 Thomas Matthew Rienzi 12735 Theodore James McAdam 12736 Louis Polcari 12737 Charles Fred Shutrump 12738 David Rowland 12739 Rollin Thomas Steinmetz 12740 Carl Helmstetter 12741 John William Harrell 12742 Alexander McCarrell Patch 12743 Edwin Felix Pezda 12744 Ben Franklin Hardaway 12745 William Russell Kraft 12746 Richard Eddy Gaspard 12747 Charles Malcom Mizell 12748 Raymond Patrick Murphy 12749 John Clinton Cockrill 12750 Arthur Lawrence Lambert 12751 Garrard Foster 12752 Kenneth Frederick Hanst 12753 Andrew Stevenson Low 12754 Garth Stevens 12755 Lawrence Lofton Cobb 12756 Wilbur Deane Snow 12757 Campbell Palfrey 12758 Robert Davis Terry 12759 Carl William Stapleton 12760 Carey Herbert Brown 12761 Robert Bryan Short 12762 El Roy Paul Master 12763 Robert Walter Fritz 12764 Stanton Wayne Josephson 12765 William Edward Corley 12766 Jack Lester Bogusch 12767 John Randle Watson 12768 Roy Orval Smith 12769 Jere Washington Maupin 12770 James Alfred Vivian 12771 Philip Edward Horan 12772 John Marion Baker 12773 Thurman McCord Brandon 12774 Philip Shaw Wood 12775 Philip Henry Riedel 12776 Lee Glasier Jones 12777 Marshall Waller 12778 Dale Eldon Buchanan 12779 George R. Allin 12780 Lawrence Lahm 12781 Paul Berkshire Woodward 12782 Fred Ernest Holdrege 12783 Selmer Gustaves 12784 Leonard John Pasciak 12785 James Francis Clark Hyde 12786 Joseph Richard Elliott 12787 Thomas Taylor Galloway 12788 Floyd Irvin Robinson 12789 Charles Curtis George 12790 John Paul Omans 12791 George Raybourn O'Neal 12792 John Douglas Reid 12793 Cyrus Edson Manierre 12794 Matthew John Redlinger 12795 Donald Eugene Simon 12796 Albert Oliver Witte 12797 Andrew Hudson Weigel 12798 Glen William Russell 12799 John Carter Ford 12800 John Munroe Anderson 12801 Charles Elbridge Howe 12802 Donald Hilary Connolly 12803 John Edward Craig 12804 William Burr Clark 12805 Richard Arthur House 12806 Robert Clark Kates 12807 Edward Allan Munns 12808 Walter Dean Short 12809 Joel John Dilworth 12810 Benjamin Ira Hill 12811 George Rogers Seip 12812 Lowell Stanley Nickodem 12813 Charles Howard Garvin 12814 Arvol Duane Allen 12815 Edgar Allan Rickman 12816 Samuel Hubbard Hays 12817 Roy William Ballard 12818 Richard Wood Maffry 12819 Harold Windsor Rice 12820 Sam Powell Wagner 12821 William Robert Hughes 12822 Robert Horatio Clagett 12823 Frank Clark Scofield 12824 James Knox Cockrell 12825 Henry Compton Benitez 12826 John Ashton Ely 12827 Wayne G. McCarthy 12828 Jesse Lee Lewis 12829 Thomas James Hanley 12830 Severino Martinez 12831 John Joseph Short 12832 Jay Jaynes 12833 James Madison Caviness 12834 Carl Comer Ulsaker 12835 Robert William Carpenter 12836 Cecil Kenneth Charbonneau 12837 John Dennis Sitterson 12838 James Edwin Wise 12839 Francis Joseph Roberts 12840 Chester Reed Ladd 12841 William Davis Tatsch 12842 Albert Nichols Thompson 12843 Samuel Alexander Gibson 12844 John Aloysius Ryan 12845 Mark Howard Terrel 12846 Harry Franklin Boone 12847 Frederic Homer Sargent Tate 12848 Carl Columbus Hinkle 12849 John Clarence Peck 12850 James Woodrow Bigbee 12851 Walter Walton Dillon 12852 Henry Premyslaus Kozlowski 12853 Leon Bilstin 12854 John Russell Deane 12855 Miles Alderman Gayle 12856 James Edmund Buckley 12857 John Lloyd McKee 12858 James Boone Bartholomees 12859 Jacob Baer Cooperhouse 12860 Karl Nelson Retzer 12861 Frank Dwight Waddell 12862 Henry Harmeling 12863 James Nicholas Studer 12864 Roy Stanley Geiger 12865 Richard Atlee Wise 12866 Byron Arthur Evans 12867 Thomas Peter Iuliucci 12868 Robert Henry Ivey 12869 Ira Welch Thompson 12870 Thomas Harvey Tarver 12871 William Charles Warren 12872 Edward Lawrence Corcoran 12873 Philip Alfred Wyman 12874 Allen Everett Frawley 12875 VanCleave Parrott Warren 12876 George Thad Buck 12877 George Denny Hughes 12878 William Franklin Smith 12879 Lawrence Francis McGuire 12880 Ollie William Reed 12881 Howard Lay Burris 12882 Leon Stann 12883 Galen Person Robbins 12884 Fred Cutting Tucker 12885 Charles Brooks Gracey 12886 Wyley Lovelace Baxter 12887 Archibald Donald Fisken 12888 John Ott Sanders Damron 12889 Donald Frank Blake 12890 Robert Hilton Offley 12891 Charles Marmaduke Grimshaw 12892 Samuel William Koster 12893 Walter Harlen Peirce 12894 Olmedo Alfaro 12895 Richard David Reinbold 12896 Thomas Patrick Furey 12897 Charles Eugene Robbs 12898 William Cloyd Plott 12899 Linwood Fogg Jordan 12900 William Henry Crosson 12901 James Norwood Wood 12902 U. Grant Jones 12903 Walter Franklin Griffin 12904 Claire Alfred Pelton Duffie 12905 Ralph James White 12906 Harvey Wirt Courtland Shelton 12907 Philip Marshall Costain 12908 Charles Berra 12909 Robert Henry Hinckley 12910 Robert Houston Townsend 12911 Pierce Anthony Doyle 12912 William Carroll Garland 12913 Willis Dale Crittenberger 12914 Donald George Jackson 12915 Alfred Francis Franklin Grieco 12916 Lawrence Haley Caruthers 12917 Joe Dean Hennessee 12918 Albert Edward Hunter 12919 Douglas Cunningham Murray 12920 Lawrence Augustus Adams 12921 Roy Walter Johnson 12922 Raymond Laurence Miller 12923 Richard Paul Yeilding 12924 Hal Creighton McMaster 12925 James Richard Pendergrast 12926 William Edgar Gernert 12927 Wayne Norbury Bolefahr 12928 Robert Ramsey Evans 12929 Lee Emir Cage 12930 Robert William Beers 12931 Frank Wharton Williams 12932 Robert Arnold Berman 12933 Joel Beck Stephens 12934 Edwin Griffin Clapp 12935 Arthur Robert King 12936 Robert Elmer Winkelmeyer 12937 Howard Martin Fender 12938 Radcliffe Spencer Simpson 12939 Thomas Hunter Crary 12940 August Dorsey Parker 12941 Forrest Stewart Gatchel 12942 Wallace Biddle Frank 12943 Frederick Weston Hyde 12944 John Clayton Adams 12945 Robert MacDougall Bringham 12946 Howard Wesley Slaton 12947 Mark John Burke 12948 John Richard Murphy 12949 Richard Robert Clark 12950 Joseph Morgan Cannon 12951 James Elwood Josendale 12952 Altus Grant Steadman 12953 Thomas Kennedy Trainer 12954 Robert Morris Blair 12955 Edwin Hall Marks 12956 Albert Charles Reinert 12957 Frank Butner Clay 12958 Leonard John Blissenbach 12959 Richard Cutler Miles 12960 Charles Russell Hill 12961 Claude Cleo Lumpkin 12962 Sidney Hooper Young 12963 Charles Kelly Bortell 12964 John Raymond Moran 12965 Walter Alfred Divers 12966 David Darwin May 12967 Peter Talbot Russell 12968 John Fuller Davis 12969 Jack Willard Pryor 12970 Gene Clifford Smith 12971 Charles Wolcott Ryder 12972 David Clark Clagett 12973 John Wilkinson Heard 12974 Vincent Lincoln Coates 12975 Robert Burnett Spilman 12976 John Hurst Westenhoff 12977 Daniel Edward Halpin 12978 James Stanley Woolfolk 12979 John William Guckeyson 12980 John Boursiquot Rose 12981 Ernest Johnson White 12982 Luis John Flanagan 12983 Clifford Cobb Sherman 12984 Richard Martin Scott 12985 William Francis Loughman 12986 Henry William Urrutia 12987 Charles Ray Rogers 12988 Edgar Bergman Colladay 12989 Keith Grayson Chatfield 12990 Donald Eugene Deffke 12991 William Edgar Shedd 12992 Charles Carroll Fishburne 12993 Richard Patrick Brice 12994 Joseph Bell 12995 Joe Virgil Morey 12996 George Lawrence Eckert 12997 Leonard Samuel Marshall 12998 Timothy Asbury Pedley 12999 Jesse Richard Miles 13000 George Rayens Grant 13001 Frederick Dana Standish 13002 Donnelly Paul Bolton 13003 James Savage Braden 13004 Allan Richard Scullen 13005 Charles Andrew Beaucond 13006 Lynn DeWitt Sifford 13007 Charlie Calhoun Coleman 13008 George Williams 13009 Samuel Withers Howell 13010 Allen Monroe Otis 13011 William Morris Zimmerman 13012 James Simmons Timothy 13013 Albert Edward Seifert 13014 George Robert Rew 13015 Jerome Pershing Ellis 13016 Thomas Seelye Arms 13017 Ellwood Tyler Claggett 13018 Boyd Freeze Walker 13019 Kenneth Earl Dyson 13020 Edward Joseph Aileo 13021 Lucius DuBignon Clay 13022 William Ross Scott 13023 Frederick Charles Uhler 13024 George Doan Rehkopf 13025 Wilfred Craig Ford 13026 Samuel Hampton Henton 13027 Thaddeus Francis Dziuban 13028 Albert McConnell Ward 13029 Robert George Brugh 13030 John Myrddin Davies 13031 Austin Patrick Byrne 13032 Richard Stockton Field 13033 Alden McLellan 13034 Charles Campbell Ettlesen 13035 Thomas Hasset Ray 13036 John Denis Crowley 13037 **1943 JAN** Dimitri Alexander Kellogg 13038 Richard Traber Batson 13039 Charles Calvert Benedict 13040 Edward Lee Sheley 13041 John Hugh Buckner 13042 John Jones Upchurch 13043 William Allen Knowlton 13044 Lawrence Harold Bixby 13045 DeWitt Clinton Armstrong 13046 Keith Gordon Lindell 13047 Robert Nelson Smith 13048 George Anthony Rebh 13049 Howard Deane Elliott 13050 Samuel N. Karrick 13051 Edward James Hardebeck 13052 Frank Ambler Camm 13053 Fred Brenning Waters 13054 Edmond Lawrence Faust 13055 Arthur Leslie Freer 13056 James Raymon Dempsey 13057 Douglas King Blue 13058 Howard Franklin Wehrle 13059 Paul Roscoe Ellis 13060 John McClure 13061 Louis Theodore Seith 13062 Robert Ralph Fishel 13063 James Oliver Frankosky 13064 Maxwell Adolph Neumann 13065 Thomas Daniel Harrison 13066 Edward Elmer Bennett 13067 Ernest Crews Lacy 13068 Edward Joseph Bielecki 13069 Walter Hugh Cook 13070 Robert Creel Marshall 13071 William Johnson Talbott 13072 Darrie Hewitt Richards 13073 Clarke Duncan Hain 13074 Albert Emmanuel Saari 13075 Milton Ernst Stevens 13076 Cecil George Young 13077 Keith Edward Canella 13078 Richard Lewis Evans 13079 William Love Starnes 13080 Vernon Keith Sanders 13081 Robert Guthrie Hillman 13082 Charles William Lenfest 13083 Clough Farrar Gee 13084 Thomas Quinton Donaldson 13085 Jack Jean Jones 13086 Mitchel Goldenthal 13087 Lowell Boyd Fisher 13088 Robert Belleau Burlin 13089 Woodrow Wilson Pratt 13090 John Carpenter Raaen 13091 George Kunkel Sykes 13092 Edward Michael Costello 13093 Emmett Robinson Reynolds 13094 Charles Glenn Glasgow 13095 James Randolph Richardson 13096 Franklin P. Shaw 13097 Herbert Gordon Kolb 13098 Francis Hamilton Bonham 13099 Ralph Mills Hofmann 13100 Charles Stuart MacVeigh 13101 Frederick Mark Smith 13102 Arthur B. Grace 13103 Charles Clifford Pinkerton 13104 Conrad Epping Koerper 13105 Alvin Mann Bachrach 13106 Frederick Sherwood Porter 13107 Edward Rice Ardery 13108 Edmund Cornish Suor 13109 Milton Albert Behn 13110 Robert Morse Wood 13111 John Franklin White 13112 Roger Alexander Bertram 13113 James Edward Brook 13114 Ralph Lincoln Cadwallader 13115 Thomas Henry Beeson 13116 Robert Emil Fiss 13117 Leslie Buckingham Harding 13118 William Robert Myers 13119 Rexford Herbert Dettre 13120 James Berhardt Cobb 13121 Joseph Louie Hamilton 13122 Harry Alfred Saunders 13123 Walter William Hogrefe 13124 Henry Frederick

Grimm 13125 Charles Asbury Holt 13126 Robert Seton Maloney 13127 John Leroy Weber 13128 Michel Andre George Robinson 13129 Francis Xavier Kane 13130 Stephen Otto Benner 13131 Berry B. Skaggs 13132 Quentin James Goss 13133 John George Moses 13134 Cleo Merton Bishop 13135 Thomas Hutson Martin 13136 William Earnest Hensel 13137 Earl L. Hehn 13138 Thomas Everett Griess 13139 Dan Morey Parker 13140 Wendell Lowell Bevan 13141 James Alfred McKinney 13142 Raymond C. Zettel 13143 John Frank Johnson 13144 John Foster Stephens 13145 Robert Francis McDermott 13146 Donald Henry Vlcek 13147 Vernon Edward Trinter 13148 Hiram Glenn Turner 13149 John Laurence Shortall 13150 Harold James Bestervelt 13151 Charles Edward Hardy 13152 Turner Mason Chambliss 13153 Frank Edward Boyd 13154 Joseph Harrison Dover 13155 John Jacob Shultz 13156 John Arthur Kerig 13157 James Dumont Wright 13158 John Robert Nickel 13159 James McClain Huddleston 13160 Edmund Barber Edwards 13161 John Miller Wilson 13162 Robert Muldrow 13163 Ralph Joseph Truex 13164 James Foster Reynolds 13165 Stewart Canfield Meyer 13166 Frederick Clayton Spann 13167 Thomas Isaac Cary 13168 Floyd Oralee Tobey 13169 Frederick Martin King 13170 Edmund James Carberry 13171 William Reed Hahn 13172 Ben Lee Baber 13173 Henry Anson Barber 13174 George Spoor Weart 13175 John Clair Stahle 13176 Paul Edward Andrepont 13177 Lawrence Philip Bischoff 13178 John Gray Wheelock 13179 Wendell Lapsley Clemenson 13180 Gregg Henry 13181 Frank Webb Griffen 13182 Lowell L. Wilkes 13183 Marion Hopkins May 13184 William Bernard Smith 13185 McGlachlin Hatch 13186 Vasco John Fenili 13187 Robert Tompkins Blake 13188 Malcolm Alexander Smith 13189 Rex David Minckler 13190 Francis Casimir Kajencki 13191 Adrian St. John 13192 John Joseph Courtney 13193 Leo Mose Blanchett 13194 Merle Landry Carey 13195 Alfred Lukacs Toth 13196 Kirby Alexander Gean 13197 Russell McKee Herrington 13198 Robert Guy Kurtz 13199 Walter Richard Taliaferro 13200 George William Porter 13201 Clifford James Moore 13202 Edwin James Willcox 13203 George Warner Dixon 13204 Richard Joseph Hynes 13205 John Jacob Luther 13206 William Frederick Pitts 13207 Arthur Anson Marston 13208 Richard Howell Broach 13209 Joseph William Benson 13210 John Erwin Kuffner 13211 Edward Potter Foote 13212 Clifton Lewis Butler 13213 Roderic Thomas Wriston 13214 Donald Eugene Wilbourn 13215 John Hixon Shaffer 13216 Dana Lee Stewart 13217 James R. Michael 13218 John Kenneth Hocker 13219 James Edward Kelleher 13220 Roy Alexander Sanders 13221 Moses Joseph Gatewood 13222 Hugh Mease 13223 John Jay Gorman 13224 Francis Anthony Thomas 13225 John Alden Hine 13226 Lester George Taylor 13227 Lee Boyer James 13228 William Hayes Fritz 13229 John Gregory Hoyt 13230 William Albert Kerr 13231 Louis Locke Wilson 13232 Douglas Blakeshaw Netherwood 13233 James Willis Ledbetter 13234 Burwell Baxter Bell 13235 Harold Kilburn Roach 13236 Henry John Ebrey 13237 Patrick Gerald Wardell 13238 James Justus Cobb 13239 Algin James Hughes 13240 Howard Louis Lambert 13241 Robert Ernest Lacy 13242 Younger Arnold Pitts 13243 Warren J. Lane 13244 Harold Stcats Walker 13245 William Edmund Larned 13246 Roy L. Bowlin 13247 Thomas Walsh Flatley 13248 Arvid Paul Croonquist 13249 Charles Francis Alfano 13250 George Mayer Eberle 13251 Robert Sprague Beightler 13252 James Emerson Bush 13253 Arthur Joseph Sebesta 13254 Joseph Bartholomew Conmy 13255 Donald Maurice Stangle 13256 Joseph Peeler Stabler 13257 Russel Price Harris 13258 Jessup David Lowe 13259 Raymond Cecil Brittingham 13260 Jesse Benjamin Hollis 13261 Oliver Williams DeGruchy 13262 Victor Vaughan Taylor 13263 Albert Earl Stoll 13264 John Shirley Wood 13265 Clarence Maude Davenport 13266 Roger Louis Fisher 13267 Victor Arnold Franklin 13268 William Lamar Hardy 13269 Russell Jackson Smith 13270 Robert LeVerne Davis 13271 Herschel Ashby Jarrell 13272 Virginio Lorenzo Antonioli 13273 Donald Hepburn Bruner 13274 John Riley Mitchell 13275 Arthur Pearson Wade 13276 James Leslie Doyle 13277 John Crocker Catlin 13278 Walter Edwin Nygard 13279 Thomas Bates Windsor 13280 Robert Eugene Baden 13281 George William Criss 13282 Donald Warren Thompson 13283 Hal Fitzgerald Crain 13284 Richard Turner Schlosberg 13285 Robert James Rader 13286 John Gilmore McNamara 13287 Arthur Vincent Jackson 13288 George Bradley Lundberg 13289 Howard Anthony Linn 13290 Robert E. Harrington 13291 Edward Alexander McGough 13292 Gerard Vincent Cosgrove 13293 John Willard Baer 13294 Sidney Zecher 13295 John Winthrop Armstrong 13296 Robert Logan Edwards 13297 John Roy Ross 13298 James Fisher Frakes 13299 Robert Morehead Cook 13300 John Henry Featherston 13301 John Keeler Eckert 13302 Willard Bruce Wilson 13303 William Diebold Brady 13304 Norman David Greenberg 13305 Norman Daniel Cota 13306 Frank Terry Ellis 13307 George Kameil Maertens 13308 Pete Daniel Pavick 13309 John Frederick Daye 13310 George Luck Danforth 13311 James Edwin Hickey Rumbough 13312 Henry Joseph Mazur 13313 Dick Elmo Hall 13314 Harry H. Pritchett 13315 James Wentworth Freeman 13316 James Alfred Rippin 13317 John Edgar Van Duyn 13318 Richard Baldwin Jones 13319 Edward Michael Flanagan 13320 Joseph A. Stuart 13321 John Edward Roberts 13322 John Jacob Norris 13323 Altus Emory Prince 13324 John Dennis Healy 13325 Thomas Edward Ramsey 13326 Daugherty Mason Smith 13327 Thomas Robert Watson 13328 William Edwin Waters 13329 John Francis Phelan 13330 John Thomas Russell 13331 Robert John Walling 13332 Cecil Wray Page 13333 Albert Lossen Lane 13334 Charles Alvin Wirt 13335 Benjamin Norris 13336 Richard Maddox Combs 13337 William Eugene Lewis 13338 Burton Francis Hood 13339 Edward Henry Murray 13340 John Everard Hatch 13341 James Marshall Little 13342 Myron Haines Dakin 13343 Herbert S. Lewis 13344 Henry Hodgen Kirby 13345 Kearie Lee Berry 13346 Joseph Anthony Riccio 13347 Malcolm Seth Wardrop 13348 Barton Kyle Yount 13349 George Harvey Watson 13350 William Robert Stewart 13351 Herbert Eugene Kemp 13352 Theodore Thomas Lutrey 13353 James Roland Anderson 13354 Hubert James Fiander 13355 Charles Lester Heltzel 13356 Robert Leonard Lawrence 13357 Darwin Jaques Mendoza 13358 Ernest Darius Scott 13359 Jacob Whitman Klerk 13360 Lester Meltzer 13361 William Harrell Scott 13362 William Johnston Hovde 13363 James Hamlin Schofield 13364 William Douaire Neale 13365 William Boyce Brice 13366 John Leopold Dworak 13367 Charles Herbert Burr 13368 John Daniel McGowan 13369 James Daniel Moore 13370 Robert Bernard Tresville 13371 Donald Franklin Powell 13372 Robert Victor Whitlow 13373 Barton James Mallory 13374 Norvin Leslie Davis 13375 Donald Ernest Griffin 13376 James Franklin Hackler 13377 John William Barnes 13378 Thomas Wilson Brown 13379 Charles Robert Finley 13380 Hugh Fagan Jordan 13381 Kenneth Ecklund Buell 13382 William Hiram Pietsch 13383 Robert Lee Bullard 13384 William Martin Thompson 13385 William Joseph Cook 13386 Britt Stanaland May 13387 Lyle Marvin Lappin 13388 George Romanta Kinney 13389 William D. Kyle 13390 Elvy B. Roberts 13391 Edward A. Doran 13392 Robert Hugh Fautt 13393 Chester John Butcher 13394 George Thomas Prior 13395 John Remington Northrop 13396 John Milton Cutler 13397 John Rossignol Lovett 13398 Boone Seegers 13399 Arthur Pershing Hurr 13400 Sidney Conrad Peterman 13401 Wesley James Curtis 13402 Ernest Charles Raulin 13403 David Harvey Barger 13404 William Hall Tallant 13405 Henry Benton Sayler 13406 Carlos Maurice Talbott 13407 Robert McNeely Peden 13408 Everett Edward Lowry 13409 Thomas Henderson Farnsworth 13410 John Joseph Nazzaro 13411 James C. Huntley 13412 Morton Campbell Carmack 13413 Joseph Edward Nett 13414 William F. Dolby 13415 Jack Francis Clark 13416 Elbert Pritchett Epperson 13417 Everard Kidder Meade 13418 Harry Richard Stroh 13419 Lucian Dalton Bogan 13420 Marvin Jay Berenzweig 13421 Jack Fontaine Dulaney 13422 Clyde Kelsey Sellers 13423 Raymond Francis Ruyffelaere 13424 Edward Hale Brooks 13425 Howard Everett Moore 13426 William Harold Dannacher 13427 Victor Anthony Cherbak 13428 James Stephen Changaris 13429 Jonathan Waverly Anderson 13430 William Haywood Hume 13431 Thomas A. Mesereau 13432 Melvin Sidney Thaler 13433 John Parsons Wheeler 13434 Patrick Wester Wheeler 13435 Daniel Dawson Waters 13436 Roy Robertson Wilson 13437 John Harvey Linton 13438 Eugene August Wink 13439 William Henry Tucker 13440 Frederick Seaton Kremer 13441 Robert Wood Dailey Guthrie 13442 Stanley Livingstson James 13443 Belmonte Pasquale Cucolo 13444 James Anthony Aleveras 13445 Benjamin Willis Mills 13446 **1943 JUN** Thomas Kilbury Oliver 13447 Lawrence Edwin Swank 13448 Coleman Cabell Richards 13449 Jesse LeRoy Fishback 13450 Richard Tilghman Hemsley 13451 Edward Stanley Ott 13452 Wallace Clifton Magathan 13453 John Francis Buyers 13454 Arthur William Holderness 13455 Walker Jamar 13456 Gabriel Alexander Ivan 13457 Richard Francis Shaefer 13458 Bernard William Rogers 13459 Alan Walter Jones 13460 John Joseph Kelly 13461 Harold Ferguson Knowles 13462 David Smith Chamberlain 13463 Richard Hemmig Meyer 13464 Richard Curry McAdam 13465 Stanley Carter Pace 13466 Richard Henry Reitmann 13467 Frank William Rhea 13468 Donald John Mehrtens 13469 Robert Edward Mathe 13470 J. Weller Smith 13471 Samuel W. Pinnell 13472 Robert Bernard Callan 13473 Robert William Newman 13474 Boyd Blaine Chambers 13475 Ralph Meloy Scott 13476 David Baldwin Conard 13477 Harry Jesse Kenyon 13478 Francis John Dirkes 13479 Frank Bertram Smith 13480 J. Duane Wethe 13481 Charles Myers Jones 13482 James Allen Betts 13483 James Franklin Deatherage 13484 William Daniel Falck 13485 Douglas Lipp Deal 13486 William Edward Cramsie 13487 Gordon Albert Schraeder 13488 John Jacob Neuer 13489 Donald DeForset McClure 13490 Roger Hilsman 13491 James Franklin Greene 13492 Roland Alfred Brandt 13493 Ranald Otis Whitaker 13494 Albert John Bowley 13495 Frank McCoy McMullen 13496 William M. Glasgow 13497 Ernest Arthur Buzalski 13498 Charles Allan Wilson 13499 Bobbie Allen Griffin 13500 James Vincent Christy 13501 John Seymoure Chandler 13502 Henry Romanek 13503 Norman Erland Pehrson 13504 Warren Rogers 13505 Harold Robert Parfitt 13506 Clare Francis Farley 13507 Walter James Hutchin 13508 Jonathan Sawyer Vordermark 13509 Robert Emmet Burrows 13510 William Wintle Martin 13511 Lowell B. Smith 13512 James Howard Watkins 13513 Richard Bocock Willis 13514 Clyde Tener Earnest 13515 Robert Ernest Plett 13516 Jack Henderson Whitson 13517 Eduardo Tolentino Suatengco 13518 Edward Francis McCabe 13519 Robert Maxwell Hancock 13520 Albert Raymond Shiely 13521 Rafael Manio Ileto 13522 William Hill McKenzie 13523 Lorres Charles Thomas 13524 Richard Concklin Snyder 13525 Robert John Barickman 13526 John Walter Myrtetus 13527 Frank James Harrold 13528 Arthur Thurston Surkamp 13529 Hiram Garrett Fuller 13530 John Calvin Bell 13531 Fred Ordway Wickham 13532 LeVerne Edwin Blount 13533 William Joseph Kilpatrick 13534 Howard Beverly Coffman 13535 Thomas Matkins Johnston 13536 Lloyd Zuppann 13537 Charles Sumner Reed 13538 Lawrence Middleton Watson 13539 Milton Ernst Steinbring 13540 Bruce Carlton Koch 13541 James Edward Browning 13542 John Price Mattfeldt 13543 Burrowes Goldthwaite Stevens 13544 Firman Edward Susank 13545 Richard Donald Sullivan 13546 Harvey Haroldson Latson 13547 George Howard Ingham 13548 Kenneth Bates Smith 13549 Edwin Milton Rhoads 13550 Kenneth Trevor Sawyer 13551 Charles William Carson 13552 Louis Charles Wieser 13553 Stanley Marcell Staszak 13554 James Cleveland Miller 13555 Richard Henry Parker 13556 Anthony Raymond Durante 13557 Reginald Bifield Cocroft 13558 Francis Earle Rundell 13559 Lucius Featherstone Wright 13560 John James Swisshelm 13561 James Cabell Reed 13562 Joseph Vincent Chaufty 13563 Franklin Woody Taylor 13564 Donald C. Pence 13565 Ralph Jamison Teetor 13566 Paul Gregory Atkinson 13567 Thomas William Essen 13568 Lansford Franklin Kengle 13569 William Edward Naylor 13570 James Robert Thomas 13571 John Blair Beach 13572 George Gordon Cantlay 13573 Robert Bruce McDowell 13574 Howard Grennlease Yeilding 13575 William Frederick Roos 13576 Edward Menefee Watkins 13577 Crawford Young 13578 Ronan C. Grady 13579 William Paul DeBrocke 13580 James H. Walker 13581 Christopher Henry Munch 13582 Donald Calhoun Spiece 13583 Fred Beaver Proctor 13584 Richard Ray Coursey 13585 John Woodland Morris 13586 Glenn Paul Ingwersen 13587 Jonas LeMoyne Blank 13588 Ullin Lee Hudson 13589 Fred Willard Herres 13590 James Alfred Bower 13591 William James Greenwalt 13592 Andrew Boreske 13593 Duane Paul Tenney 13594 Jack Willming Hammel 13595 James Moulton Keck 13596 Leslie Boone Hardy 13597 Milton Keith Pigg 13598 Ralph Joseph Renzulli 13599 Clare T. Ireland 13600 Leon Sembach 13601 Charles Skillman Waller 13602 Edward Burr 13603 Edward Mallory Almond 13604 Vincent Augustus Gaudiani 13605 Francis Harold Cloudman 13606 Richard Nichols Berry 13607 William Clarence Moore 13608 George Edward Newman 13609 Del Sullivan Perkins 13610 Arthur W. Van Schoick 13611 William David Lutz 13612 William Hunter Burns 13613 Eduardo Miguel Soler 13614 George Louis Alexander 13615 George Robert Moe 13616 Henry Merritt Fletcher 13617 Clarence Richard Westfall 13618 William Oliver Peak 13619 Robert William Hoffman 13620 Jammie Mendal Philpott 13621 Henry John Schroeder 13622 Gordon Lord Smith 13623 Clifford Charles Cornell 13624 Hubert Edward Tansey 13625 Robert W. Clark 13626 Charles Wendell Dickinson 13627 Joseph Wentworth Hartman 13628 Roger Ray 13629 David Emanuel Galas 13630 Clark Tileston Baldwin 13631 Kenneth Edgar Freed 13632 Richard Cameron Orphan 13633 John Taylor deCamp 13634 Robert John MacMullin 13635 Page Spencer Jackson 13636 LeRoy George Russell 13637 William Francis Malone 13638 Charles William Milmore 13639 Robin Olds 13640 Robert Louis McCanna 13641 Allen Mitchell Burdett 13642 Jack Coleman Winn 13643 Quellen Denis Boller 13644 Thomas McAdoo Love 13645 Robert D. Dwan 13646 Herman Turner Hunt 13647 Donald Alburtus Detwiler 13648 Hansford Nichols Lockwood 13649 Ned Schramm 13650 James Norris Lothrop 13651 Oliver Richard English 13652 Charles L. Crane 13653 Argonne Call Dixon 13654 Hal Thomas Rose 13655 George William Thompson 13656 Louis Konrad Nesselbush 13657 John Stanley Brady 13658 Warren T. Whittemore 13659 Alexander Russell Bolling 13660 Roger Leon Conarty 13661 Warren Leigh Taylor 13662 William Harold Brabson 13663 Felix Andrew Kalinski 13664 Gordon Winthrop Barrett 13665 Weston Fisher Maughan 13666 Benjamin Buckles Cassiday 13667 Robert Hansen Campbell 13668 Michael Zubon 13669 Harold Warren Gingrich 13670 John Buchanan Bond 13671 Walter George Mitchell 13672 John Walter Collins 13673 William Paul Brierty 13674 Robert Douglas Danforth 13675 Phillips Eastman 13676 Robert Hanna 13677 George Thomas Campbell 13678 Harry Ludwick Heintzelman 13679 Ernest Collier Price 13680 Lewis Frazer Webster 13681 Laurent Dupre Pavy 13682 Robert James Davenport 13683 Thomas McGahey Elgin 13684 Albert Caswell Metts 13685 William James Greene 13686 Richard Williams Stoddard 13687 Francis Wingate Saul 13688 Jeptha Charles Tanksley 13689 Oliver Boone Bucher 13690 Thomas James Laudani 13691 Richard Vincent Wheeler 13692 Joseph Hipolito Huau 13693 Richard David McCord 13694 James Alexander Brice 13695 Robert John Rooney 13696 Ivan Willard York 13697 Franklin Wood 13698 Stephen Oliver Brown 13699 Garland Cuzorte Black 13700 Earl Oren Olmstead 13701 Jack Talmadge Davis 13702 John McArthur Davis 13703 Robert Milton Holmes 13704 Daniel Francis Shea 13705 Roger Clawson Ball 13706 Vernon Richard Turner 13707 Cullen Albert Brannon 13708 John Henry Cochran 13709 Frank P. Breitenbach 13710 Richard Marshall Winfield 13711 Walter Neal Burnette 13712 Bernard Thomas Lewis 13713 William Michael Calnan 13714 Arthur Henry Rasper 13715 Leo Eugene Conway 13716 Ralph Kilbreth Jones 13717 Arnold Robert Tucker 13718 Stephen Ellison Gordy 13719 William Earl Evers 13720 Ralph Julian Hill 13721 Freeman Wate Bowley 13722 David Duncan Munro 13723 Marston Thorn Westbrook 13724 Norbert Joseph Oswald 13725 Teague Gray Harris 13726 John Mahlon Hommel 13727 Hamlet Robinson Carter 13728 William Jasper Brake 13729 James Dixon Fore 13730 Harry Mazur 13731 Jack Conrad Novak 13732 William Johnson Ray 13733 William Clyde Linton 13734 Robert Daniel Sonstelie 13735 James Richard Darden 13736 Henry Leon Hogan 13737 Ernest Thorpe Cragg 13738 Daniel Bernard Cullinane 13739 James Thomas Fitz-Gerald 13740 William Glenn Watson 13741 Richard Carlton Stickney 13742 Richard Frank Wilhelm 13743 Richard Victor Miracle 13744 Gayle Eugene Madison 13745 John Buchanan Stockton 13746 James Herschell Nash 13747 Robert Herman Clark 13748 Robert Lee Rooker 13749 Leo Cooper Brooks 13750 Lindsey M. Silvester 13751 Thomas Kelly Tannler 13752 John Porter Lucas 13753 Edward Hanson Connor 13754 Maurice Langhorne Martin 13755 Heber Cowan Brill 13756 Herbert Pierre Harper 13757 John Wyeth Earhart 13758 Alfred Dale Hagen 13759 Seth Roderick Frear 13760 Hubert Smith 13761 Stanley Livingston Wilson 13762 Alvin Ernest Orlian 13763 John Wills Moses 13764 Caleb Allen Cole 13765 James Rival Pugh 13766 Norman Lewis Williams 13767 Francis Veazy Walker 13768 George Gordon Bugg 13769 James Keith Glendening 13770 William Joseph Spahr 13771 Frank Williams Jones 13772 Mayo Jack Elliott 13773 Edward Joseph Rumpf 13774 Ernest Hinds 13775 Tonnis Boukamp 13776 Benedict Francis Hoffmann 13777 Walter Rea Beckett 13778 John Klotz Brier 13779 Raymond Carlton Blatt 13780 Archelaus Lewis Hamblen 13781 Mike Bedwell Davis 13782 Edward Joseph Walsh 13783 Alfred Ferdynand Tyrala 13784 Charles Donovan Warburton 13785 Alston Law Brown 13786 William Patrick Hunt 13787 Nicholson Parker 13788 John L. Butterfield 13789 Keith Albert Whitaker 13790 Frank Putnam Ball 13791 Arturo Rafael Espaillat 13792 Harold Halsey Dunwoody 13793 Clarence Walter Richmond 13794 Samuel Wright Jenkins 13795 Robert Sherman Culbertson 13796 Robert Dugald McClure 13797 Karl Everett Wolf 13798 Waldo Franklin Potter 13799 George Betts 13800 Peter John Ryan 13801 Harold William Woodson 13802 Harold Robert Aaron 13803 James Webster Cain 13804 Fearn Field 13805 Charles D. Puckett 13806 Earle Albie Johnson 13807 David Marston Chase 13808 Leo Victor Hayes 13809 Harry Langdon Reeder 13810 William Joseph Daner 13811 John Daniel Hughes 13812 Paul Leonard Steinle 13813 Lawrence Michel Fitzpatrick 13814 Ralph Junior Hallenbeck 13815 John Roger Kullman 13816 Eaton Arthur Gorelangton 13817 Paul Andre Hederstrom 13818 John William Rawlings 13819 John Patrick Schatz 13820 William Earnest Pulos 13821 Douglas Francis Parham 13822 James Donald Kidder 13823 William Joseph Whalen 13824 Edmond Harvey Curcuru 13825 Edward Jerome Hertel 13826 Thomas Terrell Jackson 13827 Frank Ernest Forrester 13828 John Hiley Cobb 13829 John Edward Abbott 13830 Jack Kenneth McGregor 13831 James Walter Phillips 13832 John Bell Hudson 13833 John Henry Norton 13834 Scott Brewer Ritchie 13835 Arthur Joseph Lacouture 13836 Ronald Dennis Cullen 13837 James Harvey Short 13838 Russell Lowell Maughan 13839 Thomas Lea Hutchings 13840 John Charles Piebes 13841 Thomas Archer Beckett 13842 Laurence Ronald MacDonnell 13843 Mark Mayo Boatner 13844 Randell Jacob Purcell 13845 David Lester Smith 13846 Phil Roy Phelps 13847 William Bradford Dudley 13848 Dale Fletcher McGee 13849 William Wayne Snavely 13850 John Robert McNiel 13851 Robert Wells Neilson 13852 Reading Wilkinson 13853 Robert Evans Orr 13854 Paul James Reinhalter 13855 Burton Clement Hanish 13856 Thomas Huntington Brown 13857 Preston Warham Easley 13858 Charles Edward Benson 13859 William Fontaine Scott 13860 Robert Joseph Gilles 13861 Edmund Augustus Wright 13862 Robert D. MacGregor Randall 13863 Owens Herbert Yeuell 13864 Wendell Grant VanAuken 13865 Albert Sidney J. Tucker 13866 Harold Alexander Neill 13867 Harold Sears Head 13868 Tom Bond Foulk 13869 Roule Cole Mozingo 13870 J. Craig Teller 13871 William Lawrence Bibby 13872 Austin James Canning 13873 Millard Othello Anderson 13874 Charles Arthur Gaignat 13875 Louis Sterling

Francisco 13876 Elwood Frank Smith 13877 Jack Patrick Loughman 13878 Edward Anthony Kreml 13879 Alan Francis Crump 13880 Frank David Derouin 13881 Robert Charles Foisey 13882 William W. Cover 13883 Martin Lee Harter 13884 Jarrett Mathew Huddleston 13885 Paul Joseph Hurley 13886 Harold Jacob Saine 13887 Warren Robert Hecker 13888 Albert Carl Hegenberger 13889 Joseph William Weyrick 13890 Edward Burke Burdett 13891 Edward Wellage Cutler 13892 Joseph Harry Eastmead 13893 John Russell Lloyd 13894 Dale Sidney Sweat 13895 Marvin E. Childs 13896 Fletcher Read Veach 13897 Edgar Jesse Fredericks 13898 Robert G. Gadd 13899 Edward Ryan Cleary 13900 Henry Grady Morgan 13901 Joseph Henry Rosness 13902 Luther Walker Hough 13903 John Bowler Hull 13904 Donald Joseph Jalbert 13905 William Cleveland Deekle 13906 John Metcalf Broderick 13907 Howard Tilghman Wickert 13908 David Gibbon Schwartz 13909 James Douglas Langstaff 13910 Thomas E. McCabe 13911 Robert Hamilton Mattox 13912 Quintus C. Atkinson 13913 Stephen Huntting Sherrill 13914 Heston Charles Cole 13915 Richard Edward Beck 13916 John Henry Nelson 13917 Max Verne Talbot 13918 Marion Scott Street 13919 Jack Mann McGregor 13920 Edgar Knowles Parks 13921 Russell Faux Scott 13922 Thorpe Coalson Grice 13923 Sidney Katz 13924 Edward Joseph Geaney 13925 Bethell Edrington 13926 Bernard Joseph Dyla 13927 Ralph Edgar Young 13928 Norman Jay Keefer 13929 William H. Tomlinson 13930 Charles Spieth 13931 Zaccheus Camp Richardson 13932 Norman Horace Frisbie 13933 Gordon Hall Steele 13934 Louis Blanton Umlauf 13935 William John Welsh 13936 Edmund Francis O'Connor 13937 Basil Dennis Spalding 13938 Stewart Shepherd Giffin 13939 Edward Fondren Shaifer 13940 Walter Leo Roe 13941 Alton Martin Shipstead 13942 Edward Julius Renth 13943 Joseph Francis Boyle 13944 James Kuykendall Wade 13945 Thomas S. Garrett 13946 Richard Hugh Houser 13947 Anthony Henry Richard 13948 Albert Murray Ellis 13949 Allen Wyant Gullion 13950 Jack Teague 13951 Ben Butler Barnes 13952 Donald Salmon Dargue 13953 Eber Eugene Simpson 13954 Charles Richard Abel 13955 William B. Arnold 13956 Lawton Davis 13957 Paul Joseph Curtin 13958 James Francis Keenan 13959 Robert Alvin Hersberger 13960 **1944** James Franklin Scoggin 13961 Ernest Graves 13962 Andrew King Keller 13963 Francis Joseph Hale 13964 Kenneth Banks Cooper 13965 Charles Coleman Martin 13966 Joseph R. Waterman 13967 John Henry Carlson 13968 John Franklin Kimbel 13969 Robert N. Ginsburgh 13970 George L. Ingersoll 13971 John Holloway Cushman 13972 Albert Lambert Bethel 13973 Donald Clarence Ingram 13974 Noel Degner Austin 13975 John W. Howell 13976 William Frederic Spalding 13977 Frank Cadle Mahin 13978 Robert Sherwood Day 13979 Charles J. Davis 13980 Owen Thornton Reeves 13981 John Pierre Bradley 13982 Frederick Adair Smith 13983 James Irvine 13984 Bernard Sohn 13985 Franklin Oliver Forthoffer 13986 Robert B. Codling 13987 Beverly C. Snow 13988 Robert C. Sellers 13989 Joseph Philip Barnes 13990 Robert Warren Conant 13991 Otto William Steinhardt 13992 Erwin Howard Kleist 13993 Donald Charles Vogler 13994 Geoffrey Cheadle 13995 Richard Erlenkotter 13996 William Milner Wallace 13997 William Byron Graham 13998 Edwin Radford Decker 13999 Franklin Boyd Moon 14000 Harlan Ware Holden 14001 Marshall E. Nolan 14002 Donald Foster Thompson 14003 John William Huling 14004 Albert Quincy Brooks 14005 William Earl Peugh 14006 William Elbert Steger 14007 Alan Evans Weston 14008 Jack Murph Pollin 14009 Howard C. Metzler 14010 David Ewing Ott 14011 Alexander M. Maish 14012 Pierre Anthony Tisdale 14013 Walter Allen Guild 14014 Henry Shaw Beukema 14015 Edwin Thomas O'Donnell 14016 Donald A. Gruenther 14017 Pierre Bontecou 14018 Kermit Orville Lindell 14019 Robert Boyd Robinson 14020 John Davis Calhoun 14021 Keith Edward Eiler 14022 Richard Llewellyn Dennen 14023 James Kenneth O'Brien 14024 Thomas Ben Ragland 14025 William Harry Goes 14026 Roger J. Hendrick 14027 Jean B. LaMarre 14028 Charles William Sampson 14029 James Todd White 14030 Albert G. Dancy 14031 Frank D. Henderson 14032 Alfred Mudge McCoy 14033 Arthur Derry Nelson 14034 Charles L. Steel 14035 Alvin Miles Wald 14036 Paul Bradshaw 14037 Thomas E. Mahoney 14038 Vicente Lim 14039 Dallas L. Knoll 14040 Donald Gribble MacWilliams 14041 Robert Clinton Dart 14042 William Justus Henderson 14043 Henry Spiese Aurand 14044 Martin Everett McCoy 14045 John Edward Glab 14046 Robert Henrik Brundin 14047 Jelks Henry Cabaniss 14048 John Goold Cleveland 14049 John Tardy Moore 14050 Robert Louis Algermissen 14051 Robert Charles Zott 14052 Robert Tharp Nixon 14053 Frank Errette Cash 14054 Winston Paine Anderson 14055 Louis A. Wilson 14056 Roald Max Andresen 14057 Louis George Gamble 14058 Richard Mansur Cowherd 14059 Theodore John Bartz 14060 John Wisdom Carley 14061 William John Nelson 14062 Jerry George Capka 14063 Glen Roger Hempleman 14064 William Charles Fullilove 14065 George R. Hayman 14066 Luther E. Armstrong 14067 Harry Lovejoy Rogers 14068 Bryan Henry Leeper 14069 Jack Brown Bruno 14070 James Richard Nelson 14071 William Randolph Sullivan 14072 George A. Tuttle 14073 Arthur Roy Marshall 14074 Walter Rawlins Harris 14075 John T. Coughlin 14076 Robert E. Morrison 14077 Arthur Peter Bick 14078 Robert M. Rodden 14079 John Stapleton Howland 14080 John James Tkacik 14081 Edward Charles Christl 14082 Luther Daniel Wallis 14083 Robert Odell Harper 14084 Douglas Warren Gallez 14085 Dixon Carle Rogers 14086 John Russell Geyer 14087 William Edward Burr 14088 James Thomas Blandford 14089 Hiram Baldwin Ely 14090 Frederick W. Gerhard 14091 Paul Jones 14092 William Henry Milnor 14093 Mason James Young 14094 George Van Swearingen 14095 Charles H. Czapar 14096 Alfred S. McCorkle 14097 John Shelden Doud Eisenhower 14098 Eugene Alexander Darrow 14099 Dennis P. McAuliffe 14100 Robert McClellan Mummey 14101 Paul Washington Phillips 14102 David Perry Wood 14103 Gerson K. Heiss 14104 James Wilkie Dunham 14105 Thomas E. Moore 14106 Patrick McAlester Neilond 14107 Harold G. De Arment 14108 John Nicholas Robinson 14109 William Henry Walters 14110 Robert William Faas 14111 Robert Evans Drake 14112 William Robert Hammond 14113 George Bellinger Brown 14114 Harold Blackwood Sloan 14115 James Shepard Douglas 14116 Robert Amos Mortland 14117 John Benedict Desmond 14118 Ralph Anthony Sciolla 14119 Howard Kaplan 14120 Robert Rogers Wessels 14121 Wilbur Leonard Kahn 14122 Stephen Harrison Smith 14123 John Case Trimmer 14124 James Bascom Giles 14125 William Madison Shirey 14126 Saul Aaron Jackson 14127 John Willson Donaldson 14128 James Cruden Gerhard 14129 Gregg F. Glick 14130 Alva Jeoffrey Forsythe 14131 Robert Taylor Martin 14132 Duncan Dixon Clore 14133 John G. Williams 14134 Robert Brown Callan 14135 Munson Hackett Pardee 14136 Thomas Francis Flynn 14137 Gerald Dean Hall 14138 Lloyd Barnett 14139 James Tuttle Bartley 14140 Robert Houstoun Murphy 14141 James R. Bandy 14142 William Best Murray 14143 Alan Clifford Edmunds 14144 Norman Courelius Shepard 14145 Joseph F. H. Cutrona 14146 Fielding Lewis Greaves 14147 Wendell Glen Allison 14148 Wilfred Lavern Dondanville 14149 James R. Cumberpatch 14150 Arthur Joseph McLean 14151 Roy Andrew Bahls 14152 Charles Roscoe Howland Bootz 14153 Wilson Clark Harper 14154 Edgar Willis Gregory 14155 John Clarence Stevens 14156 Francis Benedict Hennessy 14157 Ralph Leach Rhodes 14158 Edward W. Samuell 14159 Foster Lee Smith 14160 Raymond Janeczek 14161 Howard Hamlet Symons 14162 Henry Sweet Jones 14163 Eugene Quirn Steffes 14164 Charles Jay Keathley 14165 Dorsey Daniel Schaper 14166 Theodore Hess Geltz 14167 John Livermore Hazen 14168 Robert Warren Selton 14169 Robert Alexander Smith 14170 Leverett Norton Jenks 14171 Theodore John Altier 14172 William McGregor Stowell 14173 Harry Archer Buzzett 14174 Daniel Pryor Lee 14175 William Albert Baker 14176 Randolph Hutchinson Andrews 14177 Graham Castel Woodlaw 14178 Richard S. Ware 14179 Howard Wade Richards 14180 James Boniface Campbell 14181 Dale Denman 14182 Carl Leroy Peterson 14183 Robert Paul Reagan 14184 Robert White Parks 14185 Sam Dowty Hesse 14186 Andrew James DeGraff 14187 Winfield S. Scott 14188 Hugh Robert Burns 14189 John Christopher Pile 14190 James M. Connell 14191 John Oscar Lamp 14192 Warren Sanderson Conlon 14193 James Richard Lynch 14194 Leslie G. Callahan 14195 Gordon Emmons Burrell 14196 George Andrew Brown 14197 Robert Charles Daly 14198 Heath Bottomly 14199 Gerald St. Clair Mickle 14200 Stephen A. Farris 14201 Lewis Sheppard Norman 14202 Francis A. Cooch 14203 Nels A. Parson 14204 Henry Augustus Grace 14205 H. Minton Francis 14206 Richard Nalle 14207 Dee William Pettigrew 14208 Kern Phillips Pitts 14209 Rodney Walter Lindell 14210 William Clark Kennedy 14211 Robert McIntyre Pearce 14212 David Zillmer 14213 Robert Warren Samuel 14214 Steve Watson Mulkey 14215 Robert Chester Tompkins 14216 Roy Albert Hoffman 14217 Frederick Brenton Porter 14218 Willard Ainsworth Marks 14219 Drew Merritt Smith 14220 Robert L. Royem 14221 Charles Francis Frock 14222 Channing W. Gilson 14223 Thomas Joseph McGuire 14224 Henry P. Kutchinski 14225 Archer Lynn Lerch 14226 Douglas Douglas Kinnard 14227 George S. Blanchard 14228 Lorin Russell Klingle 14229 George Arthur Davis 14230 Robert Hawkins Armstrong 14231 Lawrence Frank Ciske 14232 John Francis Mangan 14233 James Thomas Milam 14234 Charles D. Daniel 14235 Carlyle Fairfax Whiting 14236 James Oliver Cowee 14237 Oliver Beirne Patton 14238 Lloyd R. Pugh 14239 Thomas Owen Mahon 14240 Carleton Paul Smith 14241 John W. Brown 14242 Walter Hugh Snelling 14243 Clarence W. Cyr 14244 Clifford Dixon Coble 14245 Harold I. Hayward 14246 Lester LeRoy Salzer 14247 Bruton Burke Schardt 14248 Thomas James Lynn 14249 Edgar Norman Millington 14250 Anthony Jack Vitullo 14251 John Peter Moore 14252 Noble Franklin Greenhill 14253 Douglas Lee Harris 14254 John Louis Grimmeison 14255 Andrew Joseph Cupper 14256 Elton Caron Parker 14257 Robert Graham Brotherton 14258 Maxwell Cole Murphy 14259 George Emmett Maxon 14260 Alan L. Partridge 14261 John Gordon Weir 14262 Ivan Windingland Nealon 14263 Bruce Keeley Deakin 14264 Arthur Siegmar Hyman 14265 William Lane Bingham 14266 Roy Aloysius Dunn 14267 Evarice C. Mire 14268 Harry Grandy Brickhouse 14269 Edward Conley Murphy 14270 Abraham Merton Glass 14271 Joseph R. Shelton 14272 John Leon Susott 14273 George Elmer Wear 14274 George Buford Norman 14275 Leo Hinkey 14276 Leonard H. Sims 14277 George S. Pappas 14278 Robert Milton Shoemaker 14279 Bernard E. McKeever 14280 Duncan Palmer 14281 Grady Olan White 14282 Cornelius J. Molloy 14283 John Joseph Hennessey 14284 John Bernard Brady 14285 David Blake 14286 Frederick Harry Black 14287 Raymond Adelbert Auringer 14288 John Martin Werner 14289 Philip Barrett Toon 14290 James Albert Downs 14291 John Creighton King 14292 Mark Joseph Klein 14293 Alexander C. Bridewell 14294 John Travis Lisenby 14295 Frank Edward Walton 14296 Donald E. Tripp 14297 David E. Fitton 14298 Robert Gist Pickens 14299 Dean Michael Bressler 14300 John Richard McPherson 14301 William C. McGlothlin 14302 Joseph W. Losch 14303 Joseph Carlton Petrone 14304 Malcolm Pitzer Mickelwait 14305 William Robert Buckley 14306 Michael E. Nicoletti 14307 Armond Di Silvio 14308 Thomas Byron Hoxie 14309 William Francis Enos 14310 James Joseph Patterson 14311 Henry Caleb Lindsey 14312 Chalmer Lee Deeter 14313 John William Gaffney 14314 William Edward Charlson 14315 Robin Schofield Kendall 14316 Richard Bernard Fowler 14317 Thomas McKee Tarpley 14318 George Edward Pickett 14319 Louis Verne Jones 14320 Corydon Fargo Schellenger 14321 Clarence E. Wolfinger 14322 John Mills Simmons 14323 Casimir Myslinski 14324 Harold Langford Wilhite 14325 Thomas Edward Lawrence 14326 Howard Nelson Tanner 14327 Philip Schuyler Grant 14328 Leslie H. Hendrickson 14329 Andrew Woloszyn 14330 Dean Garland Crowell 14331 Wallace Daniel Moore 14332 Gerard Francis Murphy 14333 Bruce Ingle Staser 14334 Paul James Hamm 14335 Richard Lawrence Creed 14336 James Gregory Monihan 14337 William N. Todd 14338 Simon Seelig Marks 14339 Leslie Harrison Halstead 14340 Lindley Corydon Ellis 14341 Robert Kelly Routh 14342 Peter Williams Almquist 14343 James Harvye Stewart 14344 Robert Homer Strecker 14345 John Peyton Kincaid 14346 Edward Heacock Hibbard 14347 Ralph Carl Hollstein 14348 George Harold Farne 14349 Lyall Davies de la Mater 14350 George Earl Hoffman 14351 Robert Francis Shannon 14352 William Johnston Humma 14353 Val Edward Prahl 14354 Wallace James Moulis 14355 Frederick Banks Gervais 14356 Frank E. Moore 14357 Charles Spurgeon Johnson 14358 Max Lawrence Marshall 14359 Robert Henry Hurst 14360 E. Paul Anderson 14361 Raymond Lee Gordon 14362 Vernon Everett Robbins 14363 Grey Fitzpatrick 14364 William Blackburn White 14365 Oliver George Becker 14366 Aloysius Arthur Norton 14367 Charles Harris Mullin 14368 William Taylor Courtney 14369 John O. McElvey 14370 James Wesley Weathers 14371 Eugene F. Callaghan 14372 John Robert Flynn 14373 William Thomas Miller 14374 Corbie Ralph Truman 14375 Arthur L. Handley 14376 Edward Schuyler Stahl 14377 Lawrence Locke Clayton 14378 Harold R. Emerson 14379 John N. Johnson 14380 Candler A. Wilkinson 14381 Edwin Moriel Aldrich 14382 Carl B. Anderson 14383 Thomas Oakley Phillips 14384 John Boning 14385 William Sidney Chandler 14386 William Edward Wightman 14387 John Tyler Elliott 14388 Buford Herman Melton 14389 Charles Byers Nye 14390 Odie David Minatra 14391 Nicholas Anthony Fuller 14392 Harold K. Boutwell 14393 John Thornton Peterson 14394 DeRosey Carroll Cabell 14395 Clarence A. Mitchell 14396 John S. Sullivan 14397 Randolph Jefferson Cary 14398 Henry Hastings Burnett 14399 Doniphan Carter 14400 Oscar E. Duttweiler 14401 Paul Casper Emley 14402 William Francis Bradley 14403 John Thomas Wells 14404 Hollis LeRoy Muller 14405 William Herman Fairbrother 14406 Leslie E. Babcock 14407 Alfe F. Erickson 14408 William Charles Jones 14409 John Francis Xavier McArdle 14410 Francis Ellis Merritt 14411 David Linton Silver 14412 Edward Basilio Di DiNapoli 14413 John Sanders 14414 Richard King Patch 14415 John Warren Hanley 14416 Louis William Howe 14417 Melville B. Withers 14418 James Harvey O'Connor 14419 Frederick John Keifer 14420 Robert Dorrance Ingalls 14421 Larkin Smith Tully 14422 Quitman Bellinger Jackson 14423 Robert P. Bright 14424 Robert M. Cowherd 14425 Wilson N. Boyles 14426 William Bell 14427 James Bradshaw Adamson 14428 Robert Stafford Rivers 14429 Edward J. Dravo 14430 Robert Nicholas Rudelic 14431 Robert Stephen Mills 14432 John William Combs 14433 William B. Tuttle 14434 **1945** Dwight Alban Riley 14435 Henry Perry Catts 14436 Ward Ellsworth Protsman 14437 Lochlin W. Caffey 14438 Warren Robert Stumpe 14439 Kenneth Lawrence Paape 14440 Robert R. Lochry 14441 Andrew G. Favret 14442 Leonard Joseph Gilbert 14443 Robert Francis Hegenberger 14444 Norman Douglas Mallory 14445 Cyril Joseph Brown 14446 Ernest Paul Braucher 14447 Paul Henry Ugis 14448 George Monroe Bush 14449 Fred Wharton Rankin 14450 Ira A. Hunt 14451 Garland S. Landrith 14452 Robert Wegley McBride 14453 William Brockenbrough Taylor 14454 Alfred Olivier Hero 14455 William Carl Trefz 14456 Dorsey Taylor Mahin 14457 Handford L. Cummings 14458 Colin McRae Carter 14459 William George Kratz 14460 William Garrett Stewart 14461 Joseph John Rochefort 14462 John Whelan Fehrs 14463 DeWitt Archibald Nunn 14464 Douglas Clark Atkins 14465 Robert Carl Erickson 14466 James Julius Heyman 14467 Richard Luther West 14468 Philip Jarvis Dolan 14469 Roscoe Allen Barber 14470 Wilbert Joe Kovar 14471 Amos Luther Wright 14472 Richard Atlee Chidlaw 14473 Hal Lloyd Fitzpatrick 14474 Glenn Samuel Brunson 14475 Wallace Gourley Hynds 14476 John Kilpatrick Boyce 14477 William Muir Nichols 14478 Ralph Severin Kristoferson 14479 George E. Wyatt 14480 Walter Raymond Hylander 14481 William Louis Barnes 14482 James Salter 14483 James R. Brownell 14484 Richard Edward McConnell 14485 George Frederick Bond 14486 Donald Robert Lunney 14487 William Alan Ekberg 14488 Roderick Harold Averill 14489 Paul Baker 14490 Charles F. Carter 14491 William Van Deusen Millman 14492 William Estes Farrar 14493 Delbert Marcom Fowler 14494 William Harvey McMurray 14495 John Lloyd Hadden 14496 Richard Raymond Moore 14497 John Henning Linden 14498 Gifford M. Holden 14499 James Mathew Mueller 14500 Frank Erhard Mehner 14501 John E. Reuler 14502 Robert Clough Nelson 14503 David Carleton Clymer 14504 Clark S. Campbell 14505 David James Crawford 14506 John Phillip Tyler 14507 Hugh Campbell Parker 14508 John Arthur Smart 14509 Harry James Shaw 14510 Walter Charles Gelini 14511 Harry Lane King 14512 James Arthur Summer 14513 Charles William Spann 14514 William Pringle Gardiner 14515 Henry Lee Warren 14516 Thomas J. Nichols 14517 Charles S. Adler 14518 Nile Warren Soik 14519 Richard Hulbert Groves 14520 George Albert Garman 14521 James Madison Garrett 14522 John Standish Stoer 14523 Carroll Edward Adams 14524 Ernest Edward Lane 14525 Howard James Dager 14526 Everett Eugene Love 14527 Albert Kellogg Stebbins 14528 John Henry Wirries 14529 Walter Jerome Slazak 14530 John E. Richards 14531 Arthur James Steele 14532 Ernest L. Hardin 14533 Maxwell Oscar Johnson 14534 Leon Arthur Cookman 14535 Marvin Louis Price 14536 E. Douglas Kenna 14537 Robert Carter McAlister 14538 John Kell Houssels 14539 Thomas E. Dowd 14540 James George Christiansen 14541 George E. Dexter 14542 Charles LeRoy Reynoldson 14543 John Washington Graham 14544 William Jackson Bowen 14545 Byron F. Knolle 14546 Kendall Russell 14547 Patrick O. Callahan 14548 Harvey Cooper Jones 14549 Oscar William Portman 14550 Raymond Iszard McFadden 14551 Ernest John Denz 14552 Thomas Russell Marks 14553 Vernon Wyatt Pinkey 14554 John Francis Lish 14555 Thomas Clinton Musgrave 14556 John James McCulloch 14557 John Taylor Rhett 14558 Richard Harold Johnson 14559 Richard Sides Hartline 14560 Houghton Lohn 14561 John Ross Karr 14562 Frank Alvin LaBoon 14563 Archibald V. Arnold 14564 Theodore Fadden Gerwin Adair 14565 Lawrence Wellburn Fagg 14566 Arthur Willis Walton 14567 Warren Marshall Briggs 14568 Lawrence John Klima 14569 Offa S. Nichols 14570 Richard Irving Kothrade 14571 Edward Michael Michalak 14572 William Tuinenburg Preston 14573 Philip Bertram Polak 14574 Arthur Pancratius Hanket 14575 James Arnold Reints 14576 William Mahl 14577 Arch Park Kimbrough 14578 John Ashley Noble 14579 Richard Walter Paul Boberg 14580 Roland Daniel Foley 14581 William Benson Wier 14582 Monor Collins Mabry 14583 Frank Freeman Marvin 14584 Donald J. Kohler 14585 Theodore Hays McLendon 14586 Harry Lee Maynard 14587 Francis Henry Klabouch 14588 Gabriel J. de La Guardia 14589 William R. Jarrell 14590 Reynold Martin Eckstrom 14591 Charles William Clark 14592 Bobby Lee Marlow 14593 James T. Neal 14594 Joseph P. Berg 14595 William D. McNaughton 14596 Leslie Sherman Ayers 14597 Vergil Calvin Givens 14598 Frederic William Hartwig 14599 Albion W. Knight 14600 Robert Eugene Duvall 14601 Martin Harvey Brewer 14602 James Frederick Holcomb 14603 Kelton Merrill Farris 14604 Daniel D. Whitcraft 14605 John W. Coffey 14606 John H. Holdridge 14607 James B. Townsend 14608 William James Love 14609 William D. Raymond 14610 Richard Joseph Hesse 14611 Douglas Albert Lott 14612 John Yates Bohn 14613 George O. Adkisson 14614 James Alva Munson 14615 Donal Joseph Wolf 14616 Fred Eugene Jones 14617 John Gibson Tomlinson 14618 Albert F. Muehlke 14619 Robert Leslie Marben 14620 James David Hume 14621 Cornelius W. Wakefield 14622 Donald Edward Fowler 14623 Horace Abbott Macintire 14624 Norwood Robinson 14625 Robert K. Reierson 14626 Bates Cavanaugh Burnell 14627 Abram Vorhees Rinearson 14628 Robert Harlie Bacon 14629 Marion Wiles Trotti 14630 Richard Clarkson Crane 14631 Roger Lundeen Johnson 14632 George F. Smith 14633 Robert Wallace Fye 14634 Ira B. Coldren 14635 John Baird MacWherter 14636 Keith C. Nusbaum 14637 Dale Earnest Lockard 14638 Geoffrey Brooks Keyes 14639 Nikitas Constantin Manitsas 14640

Palmer S. McGee 14641 Stanley Gunnison Calder 14642 Joseph P. O'Hanlon 14643 Dale Stanley Hall 14644 Albert Dermont Sheppard 14645 Robert Metcalf Hall 14646 Anthony Eugene Domey 14647 Frank Winthrop Draper 14648 John Charles Bennett 14649 Joseph George Hadzima 14650 Otis Collins Myers 14651 Malcolm N. Stewart 14652 Charles Richard Gorder 14653 William Atkinson Jones 14654 Alfred Gardner Thompson 14655 Jack Graham Crouch 14656 Richard P. Conniff 14657 Kenneth Mason Moore 14658 James Arthur Ruth 14659 William Robert Manlove 14660 George A. Williams 14661 Vernon Monroe Smith 14662 Kenneth Roland Ladensohn 14663 Albert R. Neville 14664 Robert L. Barr 14665 Ray Scott Basham 14666 Robert McChesney Smith 14667 Putnam Waldner Monroe 14668 William K. Moran 14669 David W. Crockett 14670 David Higgins 14671 Harold Dow Swain 14672 Chester A. Skelton 14673 John Edward Fox 14674 Earl W. Fuqua 14675 John P. Downing 14676 Henry E. Kelly 14677 Raymond Oscar Dietsche 14678 Donald H. Henderson 14679 Wallace Kieth Wittwer 14680 William Henry Norris 14681 William Vincent McGuinness 14682 John Lythgoe Black 14683 Philip Lewis Lansing 14684 Jeptha Hughes Evans 14685 Raymond Lavern Clark 14686 Edward Frederick McCarron 14687 Louis Renshaw Fortier 14688 Donald T. Nelson 14689 Bernard Moran James 14690 John Cutter Gage 14691 Charles Edward Barnett 14692 Franklin Case Davies 14693 Henry Hull Stick 14694 John Dorsey Nacy 14695 Mark E. Rivers 14696 Levin B. Broughton 14697 Robert Graham Valpey 14698 Carl Arnett Steinhagen 14699 Marshal Glenn Coulter 14700 Anthony Roberts Parrish 14701 Frank Sylvester Attinger 14702 Earl Milton Thompson 14703 John S. Holtze 14704 Fayette L. Worthington 14705 John Edward Ray 14706 Ward Winston Dworshak 14707 Dewey V. Cummings 14708 Richard Chapman Carnes 14709 Orlando Holway 14710 Robert Francis Mantey 14711 Clarence Richard Driscoll 14712 William Frank Gilbert 14713 Rabun Watson Griffith 14714 Herbert J. McChrystal 14715 Ralph J. Ford 14716 Howard Arthur Baldwin 14717 J. F. Allen 14718 Harry Thaddeus Stewart 14719 John Collingwood Hastie 14720 William Kimball Vaughan 14721 Charles L. Gandy 14722 Samuel Brown Adams 14723 Vernon Howard Harper Newman 14724 Wendell Jackson Long 14725 Arthur Lewis Wolfe 14726 John Bradley Chickering 14727 Robert George Lindsay 14728 Shelton Gillespie Spear 14729 Richard Byrd Minor 14730 Richard Louis Haley 14731 Bruce Olen McCracken 14732 Robert Muir Cunningham 14733 Robert M. Webster 14734 Patrick William Powers 14735 Robert Earl Hayes 14736 Thomas Everett Marriott 14737 Bernard James Wichlep 14738 David Erlenkotter 14739 James Richard Golden 14740 Harry Randolph Patrick 14741 John Broomhall Swartz 14742 Jack Chase Pettee 14743 Almon Richard Roth 14744 Joseph Russo 14745 James Lynn Henshaw 14746 Charles Jerome Avery 14747 Robert C. Lutz 14748 James Coleman Williams 14749 John William Storb 14750 Robert J. Mann 14751 George Anson Churchill 14752 Clifford Martin White 14753 Sylvan Edwin Salter 14754 Robert Ricketts Batson 14755 Harrison Larkin 14756 Joseph John Macur 14757 Robert Dias Hippert 14758 Kingdon Alva Davidson 14759 James H. O'Brien 14760 James Henry Elkey 14761 Harle Hoyt Damon 14762 Robert Goodman Lake 14763 Charles Francis Greer 14764 John Francis Suelzer 14765 George Fredendall Hoge 14766 George T. Forssell 14767 Edgar Marvin Munyon 14768 Edmund Gus Heilbronner 14769 John Thomas Fargason Milnor 14770 Robert Edward Dingeman 14771 Alfred William Klement 14772 Rupert W. Jernigan 14773 Paul B. Nelson 14774 Rupert Edward Hodges 14775 Billy Neel Hollis 14776 Cecil L. Rutledge 14777 William Sterling Wood 14778 Frederick Roy Einsidler 14779 Neil ImObersteg 14780 Glenwood William Flint 14781 Robert Paulle Eckert 14782 William Blount Craig 14783 Edmund Anthony Rafalko 14784 Edward A. Powers 14785 John G. Leghorn 14786 Richard Park Wallsten 14787 Alfred Jess Price 14788 Robert Clyde Loudermilch 14789 William Hopkins Stites 14790 Joseph Laird Woolley 14791 James Benjamin Tanner 14792 Basil A. Brockles 14793 Roy Leon Marston 14794 Theodore Franklin Wagner 14795 Edward Stanley Saxby 14796 Wilbur Henry Vinson 14797 William Robert Guthrie 14798 Alfred Henderson Jones 14799 Grant Harrison Fenn 14800 Samuel Kenric Lessey 14801 Earl Robert Velie 14802 Thomas Frederick Tuttle 14803 Lawrence M. Jones 14804 Luther Clyde Campbell 14805 Duncan Gault 14806 William Allen Walker 14807 George A. Daoust 14808 William T. Bess 14809 Harold Howard Buth 14810 James Arthur Herbert 14811 Charles Brown Rupert 14812 Randall Upson Pratt 14813 Henry M. M. Starkey 14814 Bernard E. Johnsrud 14815 John W. Pauly 14816 James Adolphus Giles 14817 John Orrien Truby 14818 Waldo Louis Carbonell 14819 David Murray Field 14820 Paul Allen Stough 14821 Clifford E. Myers 14822 Joseph C. Van Cleve 14823 Thomas Robert Gleason 14824 Claude Kitchin Josey 14825 Claude M. McQuarrie 14826 Michael Joseph Martin 14827 John M. Ferguson 14828 Warren W. Cobb 14829 Arthur Hadley Lozano 14830 Paul Clement Whelan 14831 George H. Troxell 14832 James B. Graham 14833 Camillus C. Sullivan 14834 Edgar Walker Nichols 14835 Calvert L. Estill 14836 Kenneth George Kochel 14837 Joe Ignacio Martinez 14838 Reamer Welker Argo 14839 William Doran Clark 14840 Wilson Patrick Hurley 14841 John William Campbell 14842 Henry Lee Cobb 14843 Perry Oldham Wilcox 14844 Thomas E. Fitzpatrick 14845 Laurence Louis Heimerl 14846 James B. Harrington 14847 Ernest James Davis 14848 Robert M. Herron 14849 John B. Bennet 14850 Jack Norman Hoffman 14851 Jesse B. Hearin 14852 Robert Joseph Parr 14853 Richard Charles Williams 14854 John Lewis Shadday 14855 Edward Francis Gudgel 14856 Joseph Denton Ledford 14857 John L. Kennedy 14858 Leonard Alfred Humphreys 14859 Robert Alfred Tolar 14860 Richard Frank DeKay 14861 William Edward McGlynn 14862 William Lee Clarkson 14863 Archie R. Patterson 14864 John Joseph Vallaster 14865 Karl Raymond Liewer 14866 James Lloyd Hayden 14867 John Robert Harman 14868 Joseph Lee Smith 14869 John Joseph Powers 14870 George Combs Berger 14871 Charles Frank Dubsky 14872 James Maxwell Shilstone 14873 Jack Harding Romney 14874 Jesse Cecil Gatlin 14875 James Wesley Gilland 14876 Benjamin Gunter Hussey 14877 Walter Harold Root 14878 Howard Johnston Hanson 14879 Edward Searles Eneboe 14880 Raymond Oscar Miller 14881 Richard Agnew Smith 14882 Arthur Raymond Morrison 14883 William A. Daugherty 14884 John Calvin Boleyn 14885 Fred Charles Parker 14886 Harry Oliver Amos 14887 Renato Vince Cervelli 14888 John Bernard Kusewitt 14889 Robert Francis Tansey 14890 Gordon Hughes Shumard 14891 Strathmore Keith McMurdo 14892 Robert Farrer Zeidner 14893 Russell Eugene Taliaferro 14894 Charles Howard King 14895 Charles Irvin Daubert 14896 John James Briscoe 14897 Harvey Stein Boyd 14898 Richard Wale Williver 14899 John Ewing Lawrence 14900 William Murray Ryan 14901 Ross Walton Campbell 14902 Alexander James Belmont 14903 John Duer Ludlow 14904 Claud Steward Hamilton 14905 John Malcolm Fitzpatrick 14906 Frederick Clifton Thayer 14907 William Roy Wolfe 14908 Harold Dale Wilson 14909 Donald Eugene Myers 14910 James Clark Wayne 14911 Walter Turbush Galligan 14912 Lucian King Truscott 14913 Theodore Harding Halligan 14914 John Joseph McGranery 14915 Arthur William Fridl 14916 Jesse Henry Johnson 14917 Lamar Weaver 14918 Woodbury Carter 14919 Edmund Randolph Preston 14920 James Lee Treester 14921 Robert Barton Waddington 14922 Donald Ray Bissell 14923 Joseph Tormin Adams 14924 John Thomas Burke 14925 Kincheon Hubert Bailey 14926 William Spearman Simpson 14927 Edward Francis Deacon 14928 Richard Allen Perez 14929 Taylor Kaye Castlen 14930 Rowland Charles W. Blessley 14931 Ralph Alan Ellis 14932 Edwin Harry Bailey 14933 James John Rouch 14934 John Francis Brown 14935 Clair Gene Whitney 14936 Kenneth Russell Scurr 14937 Roy William Farley 14938 Roland William McNamee 14939 Robert Grant Conrad 14940 Herbert Frank Haws 14941 William Kemper Cherry 14942 Harold Ballard Wohlford 14943 Kenneth Lee Jackson 14944 John Boone Martin 14945 Robert Clay Burgess 14946 Edward Jones Mason 14947 Harold Francis Hogan 14948 John Loren Goff 14949 Robert Victor Calvert 14950 George Magoun Wallace 14951 Robert Edward Pine 14952 Louis H. Boettcher 14953 John Wesley Sherwood 14954 Edward Leon Winthrop 14955 Charles William Cross 14956 James Morehead Alfonte 14957 R. Robert Siegel 14958 Charles Harry Curtis 14959 John Lawrence Wood 14960 Jared William Morrow 14961 James Robert Zeller 14962 Hugh Clifford Oppenheimer 14963 George S. Jones 14964 Joseph Edward McCarthy 14965 William F. Boiler 14966 Ray Stanley Jones 14967 Harry Richard Middleton 14968 Kenneth Homer Werner 14969 Robert Edward Stetekluh 14970 Augustus Raymond Cavanna 14971 Clark Woods Burton 14972 Robert Beeghly Tobias 14973 John Trompen Harmeling 14974 Stuart Lee Cowles 14975 William H. Holcombe 14976 Charles Sumner Pierce 14977 Earl Caldwell Hardy 14978 James Wingfield Morris 14979 Walter Albert Jagiello 14980 John Francis Myron 14981 Robert Finley Trimble 14982 Smith Barton Chamberlain 14983 Lincoln Landis 14984 David Fink 14985 Edwin Godwin Kellum 14986 John Jacob Knight 14987 Clarence Virgil Slack 14988 Richard Van Houten 14989 Ernest Scholten Ferguson 14990 Richard W. Davis 14991 Robert G. Breene 14992 Milton Henry De Vault 14993 Scott Anthony Kuntz 14994 Robert Lewis Babin 14995 Walter Gordon Allen 14996 Ralph Thomas Tierno 14997 Francis B. Kane 14998 Wilfred Lee Rogers 14999 James Franklin Holt 15000 Forrest Andrew Carhartt 15001 Charles Edward Moran 15002 Rayburn L. Smith 15003 Bert Frank Prentiss 15004 George William Casey 15005 David Harlan Thomas 15006 Fred Kochli 15007 James Asa Rasmussen 15008 John Wahl 15009 James Charles Bowman 15010 Dirck de Ryee Westervelt 15011 Bruce McCheane Barnard 15012 Robert R. Granik 15013 John Joseph McDonald 15014 Everett Orville Post 15015 Augustine Stephen Puchrik 15016 Frank Aloysius Lee 15017 John Adam Bruckner 15018 Harold Anton Van Hout 15019 Joseph E. Melanson 15020 James Gordon Mason 15021 Charles M. Seeger 15022 Robert Vincent Ridenour 15023 James Dudley Ingham 15024 Jack Winslow Spiller 15025 Clarence Leslie Linton 15026 Robert Simpson Bartron 15027 Glenn Chadwick Childs 15028 Yale Francis Trustin 15029 Edward Rexford McElroy 15030 Robert Charles Tongue 15031 Herman Smith Napier 15032 Robert Roff Horner 15033 Frederick Wadsworth Robinson 15034 Middleton McDonald 15035 F. C. Goeth 15036 Walter Davis Dabney 15037 Dale Eugene Mahan 15038 Robert Evans Woods 15039 James David Morrison Morris 15040 George Senseny Eyster 15041 R. Wheeler Ramey 15042 Chauncey Brooks Vandevanter 15043 Thomas Milton Dolan 15044 Jonas William Stuckey 15045 Robert R. Wallace 15046 Samuel Thomas Scarborough 15047 Homer S. Pitzer 15048 Chester Craig Sargent 15049 Winthrop William Wildman 15050 William Edward Glynn 15051 William B. Hankins 15052 Walter Branham Dillard 15053 Thomas Junior Godwin 15054 Robert Neale Mackinnon 15055 Daniel Jack Nelson 15056 Robert Barrett English 15057 Rolfe Louis Hillman 15058 Alfred Lewis Bailey 15059 Peter Van Matre 15060 Carl Bryant Nerdahl 15061 Lorrin Carlton Peterson 15062 Harris M. Findlay 15063 Charles William Cox 15064 George C. Lenfest 15065 Robert Gordon Krebs 15066 Ralph Moe Hinman 15067 George Baker Carrington 15068 Homer Robert Minckler 15069 James Albert Crowe 15070 James King Edwards 15071 James William Howe 15072 Walter Roberts Adkins 15073 James Thomas Farr 15074 William Lee Davis 15075 Harold G. Moore 15076 William James Reidy 15077 Norman Lawrence Lasker 15078 Arthur Bryan Greene 15079 George Craig Stewart 15080 Zean Goudy Gassmann 15081 Arthur L. Doyle 15082 David Uel Armstrong 15083 Joseph Rice Byron 15084 William Joseph Schibly 15085 John Ash Callahan 15086 Bickford E. Sawyer 15087 Theodore Mayer Fite 15088 Cole Dempster Bacon 15089 John Edward Coulahan 15090 Melvin Eugene Gustafson 15091 Nat D. King 15092 Donald Volney Rattan 15093 Walter Joseph Cain 15094 Neil J. O'Donnell 15095 George DuComb Kahlert 15096 Tom Lomax Schwinn 15097 Keith MacArthur Stewart 15098 Frank Armand Smith 15099 George Locke Robson 15100 Wade Harvey Shafer 15101 Robert Marshall Horan 15102 Earl Dudley Bruton 15103 Richard Warren Hurdis 15104 Ralph Francis Croal 15105 William Eugene Zook 15106 William Cannon Hanes 15107 Louis Lyon Martin 15108 Albert James Maris 15109 Charles Echols Spragins 15110 Alfred Henry Herman 15111 George L. Withey 15112 John Henry Johnson 15113 Ivan Leon Foster 15114 Claudius DaSilva Fingar 15115 Roger Eugene Miller 15116 George Benson Crowell 15117 Max Findell 15118 Robert Charles Waring 15119 John Colclough Geer 15120 Edmund d'Autremont Pickett 15121 John M. Gilligan 15122 Henry E. Hutcheson 15123 Lester Atchley Sprinkle 15124 Warren Wallace Drake 15125 Thomas D. Drake 15126 William Oliver Perry 15127 Jacques George Beezley 15128 Leon Alexander Dombrowski 15129 Thomas George McCunniff 15130 William Cary Sibert 15131 James T. Root 15132 James Kelley Patchell 15133 John W. Reynolds 15134 Fred John Archibald 15135 Russell Daniel McGovern 15136 John M. Forbes 15137 William Hayden Hughes 15138 Paul Robert Holland 15139 Charles William Pratt 15140 Earl William Bell 15141 Quentin Charles LaPrad 15142 Burton O. Lewis 15143 Leon Curtis Byrd 15144 Erskine Smith 15145 William Joseph Glunz 15146 Albert W. Childress 15147 Robert Inman Thompson 15148 Edwin John Gilmore 15149 John Wiley Warren 15150 John James Wuchter 15151 Earl Vane Wilkinson 15152 Randolph Carrington Heard 15153 Barney Groves Schneckloth 15154 Robert Allen Evans 15155 Donald Valen Crowe 15156 Arthur Theodore Flum 15157 Robert Edward Lee 15158 Robert Louis Woodward 15159 Marshall Pulliam 15160 John Pagenstecher Liebel 15161 William Collins 15162 Thomas Angelo Lombardo 15163 Harry Burt Hause 15164 Devol Brett 15165 Chester V. Braun 15166 Robert Price Smith 15167 Thomas B. Catron 15168 Robert Lee McDaniel 15169 Loxley Radford Scott 15170 Elmer Resides Haslett 15171 Norman Gardiner Sauer 15172 Marcello Joseph Del Vecchio 15173 Edmund David Poston 15174 Donald E. Huseby 15175 James Austin Stuart 15176 Walter A. Carter 15177 Robert Ingersoll Starr 15178 Morton Spiegel 15179 Harry Grady Walker 15180 Milton Dair Stone 15181 Joseph Schilling Senger 15182 Frederick Corbin Blesse 15183 James Calvin Hamilton 15184 Raymond James McCarrell 15185 Austin J. Yerks 15186 Alexander Otto Froede 15187 John DeSales Murphy 15188 John Henry Neff 15189 Frank N. Pavia 15190 Leonard William Lilley 15191 Daniel Crawford Perry 15192 George Crosland Fee 15193 Stewart Sylvester Stabley 15194 Edwin Bartlett Kerr 15195 Robert Northrup Ives 15196 Thomas Dick Longino 15197 Nathan Brown Chase 15198 Paul Ross Wheaton 15199 Joseph Francis McCaddon 15200 Eugene Joseph Gasior 15201 Harold Dale Wolaver 15202 Paul Kenneth Bullard 15203 Donald Edwin Gross 15204 Louis J. Schelter 15205 Donald Howard Rehm 15206 George Elden Shaffner 15207 Jose Luis Carrion 15208 Stephen Albion Day 15209 Harold Frederick Brenneman 15210 Frank Day McPeek 15211 John W. Fletcher 15212 Ernest Joseph Massari 15213 William Edward Whittington 15214 Robert Nelson Boehm 15215 William Philip Brown 15216 Charles Warren Partridge 15217 Alfred Dixon Blue 15218 Arthur Herbert Ringler 15219 George Daniel Jackson 15220 Bernard Clark Dailey 15221 Joseph Homer Hoffman 15222 Harry Drake 15223 Herbert Hamilton Price 15224 Stevan Meigs Olds 15225 Wilbur Raymond Pugh 15226 Robert Elias Spragins 15227 James Slade Nash 15228 Charles Edward Knudsen 15229 Harold Edwynne Curry 15230 Henry Joseph Hughes 15231 Robert Emmet Rochfort 15232 James Monroe Morris 15233 Arthur Henry Truxes 15234 Joseph Thomas O'Neal 15235 Arland Hertzog Wagonhurst 15236 Daniel C. Prescott 15237 Joseph Chamberlain Hill 15238 William Burton Crary 15239 Lyle Irving Edwards 15240 Walter Leslie Gerald 15241 John Victor McKerlie 15242 James Lockett Malony 15243 Robert Joseph St. Onge 15244 William Leonard Wood 15245 James Howard Dallman 15246 Thomas Brock Maertens 15247 Adolphus Worrell Roffe 15248 Richard Mark McBride 15249 John Harold Jones 15250 Paul Walker Field 15251 Lyman Screven Willcox 15252 John Terrell Carley 15253 George Charles Benson 15254 Thomas Hanley Curtis 15255 Donovan Low McCance 15256 Richard Orem Jett 15257 Thomas Humphreys McNiel 15258 William Van Dyke Ochs 15259 Stephen Pace 15260 Louis D. Gingras-O'Hara 15261 Lawrence J. Fox 15262 Thomas Henry Devlin 15263 William Clark Wood 15264 William Blum 15265 George Delano Nelson 15266 Joseph Corbett McDonough 15267 Hally D. Chesney 15268 Almon Leroy Shoaff 15269 William Robert Stickman 15270 Howard R. Bealmear 15271 Joseph John Stanowicz 15272 Jacksel M. Broughton 15273 Thomas Lewis Schroeder 15274 Daniel N. Silverman 15275 Carl H. Fischer 15276 Kyran M. Murphy 15277 Robert Milton Reese 15278 Charles Everett Limpus 15279 William H. Combs 15280 Daniel E. Farr 15281 Richard Burkhart Armstrong 15282 James Paul Donovan 15283 Kenneth Thompson Blood 15284 William Josiah Snow 15285 Andrew John Gatsis 15286 **1946** Wesley Wentz Posvar 15287 Milton Albert Strain 15288 Amos A. Jordan 15289 Andrew Burton Talbot 15290 William McCollam 15291 Edgar G. Braun 15292 George Gross Hagedon 15293 John McReynolds Wozencraft 15294 Earl Francis Poytress 15295 Robert G. Williamson 15296 Frederick C. Badger 15297 David Halstead Smith 15298 Edward A. Saunders 15299 Robert Hildebrand Ahlers 15300 Ferd E. Anderson 15301 James Carlisle Egan 15302 William George Simpson 15303 Evans Read Crowell 15304 Lawrence Lloyd Elder 15305 Max Marsh Ulrich 15306 Louis Gregory Creveling 15307 William Herbert McMaster 15308 Levi Aloysius Brown 15309 Jack G. Becker 15310 Dwight Comber Burnham 15311 William Alan Temple 15312 Robert Howell Bryan 15313 David Kirkwood Sheppard 15314 John Richard Hacke 15315 John Peter Daneman 15316 Leon B. Musser 15317 Charles T. Williams 15318 Charles R. H. Supplee 15319 Bernard Joseph Pankowski 15320 Arthur William Jank 15321 Ralph Hugh Pennington 15322 David Niesley Hutchison 15323 Bailey Toland Strain 15324 Frederic Alcott Frech 15325 John Perkins 15326 George T. Adams 15327 Jack Lawrence Schram 15328 Robert Benfred Stewart 15329 Rufus S. Garrett 15330 Louis Owen Elsaesser 15331 Joseph Tomlinson McKinney 15332 Alfred H. Victor 15333 Richard Glenn Patton 15334 Ray Moore Wagoner 15335 Francis George Gosling 15336 George Bernard Fink 15337 William Kappes Thomasset 15338 Brooke Albert 15339 Norman Theodore Stanfield 15340 Bernard Allen Petrie 15341 Gilbert Stewart Harper 15342 John Carl Ingram 15343 William Robert Wray 15344 David Thompson Bryant 15345 Arthur Andrew Murphy 15346 John Ember Sterling 15347 Roger Horace Lengnick 15348 Edmund G. Taylor 15349 Richard Cabell Tuck 15350 Allen Albert Wheat 15351 Charles M. Simpson 15352 Gordon Henry Oosting 15353 Bernard Earl Conor 15354 Joe H. Warren 15355 Wayne Allen Yeoman 15356 David Clayton Hinshaw 15357 Benjamin L. Landis 15358 Joseph Anthony Jansen 15359 Leonard Edelstein 15360 Benjamin Andrew Gay 15361 Robert Emmett Crowley 15362 Robert Fyfe Mein Duncan 15363 Laurence J. Cahill 15364 James Kerry Trimble 15365 Stanley Delbert Blum 15366 Rocco A. Petrone 15367 Saul Horowitz 15368 Robert Vernon Lee 15369 Wilton B. Persons 15370 John Russell Treadwell 15371 Peter Grosz 15372 Robert Joseph Malley 15373 William Powers Schneider 15374 Charles Edward Bonner 15375 Roy Pearl Beatty 15376 John C. Burney 15377 Robert Martin Rufsvold 15378 David T. Baker 15379 Billy Pat Pendergrass 15380 Robert Hamilton Berry 15381 Lewis William Rose 15382 Jack Keith Gilham 15383 Benjamin Neil Bellis 15384 Frank D. Conant 15385 Selwyn Phillips Rogers 15386 Daniel Marshall Leininger 15387 Stanford Alden Welch 15388 William Francis Studer 15389 Thomas David Blazina 15390 Albert L. Ramsey 15391 John G. Hill 15392 Jerome Frederick Naleid 15393 Wayne Stanley Nichols 15394 David Denison Bradburn 15395 Richard Gordon Beckner 15396 Ranald Trevor Adams 15397 Franklin Richard Day 15398 James McClure 15399 William W. Hall 15400 Kenneth Lee Tallman 15401 Murray Putzer 15402 W.

George Devens 15403 David Drummond Brown 15404 Roger Hurless Nye 15405 Leo John Miller 15406 Charles William Barker 15407 George Livingston Miller 15408 Herbert Ardis Schulke 15409 George S. Webb 15410 Frank Ellsworth Cole 15411 Richard Robert Sandoval 15412 Anderson Watkins Atkinson 15413 Richard Minter Wildrick 15414 Everett Eugene Christensen 15415 James Edward Coleman 15416 Wade Hampton Pitts 15417 William Charles Hall 15418 Mason P. Rumney 15419 Donald Gould Albright 15420 Ray Lawrence Burnell 15421 Frederick LeRoy Hafer 15422 Alexander Robert McBirney 15423 Lew Allen 15424 Oscar W. Traber 15425 Robert Lee Eyman 15426 Thornton Mitchell Milton 15427 Martin Grimes Colladay 15428 Lewis Benjamin Castle Logan 15429 Walter Alfred Lyman 15430 James Karnes Hoey 15431 Vernley Fred Thomas 15432 Paris Russell Burn 15433 Willis E. Schug 15434 Edward E. Fred Majeroni 15435 Russell Raymond Boyd 15436 William Jackson Whitener 15437 John Randolph Mathias 15438 David Seffers Lane 15439 Samuel Rucks Martin 15440 E. Lloyd Powers 15441 Harry Russell Knight 15442 Robert Johnson Hefferon 15443 Robert Kenneth Wright 15444 John Blackford Dayton 15445 Kenneth J. Steen 15446 John Linden Bennett 15447 Delbert Sylvester Barth 15448 Oliver D. Street 15449 Milton Sherman 15450 William Carl Fuller 15451 Ray Rodgers McCullen 15452 George Joseph MacDonald 15453 Kibbey Minton Horne 15454 Walter Francis Eanes 15455 Robert Lewis Frantz 15456 Richard Wendell Streiff 15457 Ralph Louis Ellis 15458 Norman Wahl 15459 James Edwin Hildebrandt 15460 Robert E. Bassler 15461 Alexander Earl Halls 15462 Robert Clarence Buckley 15463 Ernest Deloy Jernigan 15464 Matthew Reid Wallis 15465 Henry Kirk Williams 15466 William John Evans 15467 Calvin Lincoln Arnold 15468 Robert Carleton Key 15469 Jack Wilson Kopald 15470 Joseph Claypoole Clark 15471 Edward J. Roxbury 15472 Benjamin S. Hanson 15473 Paul Joseph Quinn 15474 Clarence Eugene Jordan 15475 Robert E. Knapp 15476 Donald Warner Stewart 15477 Lawrence Miller 15478 Robert Emil Lenzner 15479 Van Roy Baker 15480 Thomas Gibbs Gee 15481 William Ferdinand Scharre 15482 Lawson D. Bramblett 15483 Harold Clinton Friend 15484 Rutledge Parker Hazzard 15485 Charles Judd Hauenstein 15486 William W. Brothers 15487 Charles Robert Myer 15488 Harrison Lobdell 15489 Robert Thomas Gorman 15490 Jerry Dixmer Bowman 15491 Robert Hugh McDougal 15492 Benjamin Elliott Ivie 15493 James Clark Nelson 15494 Kenneth Wayne Anderson 15495 Robert Morin Shoemaker 15496 Howard R. Fuller 15497 Frederick Francis Hickey 15498 John George Kamaras 15499 Robert Langham March 15500 Wilbur Fields Joffrion 15501 James Edward Convey 15502 Kenneth Richard Chapman 15503 Gerald Samuel Epstein 15504 Edward Joseph Brechwald 15505 Harry Clayton Smythe 15506 John Charles Cassidy 15507 Harold Williams 15508 Herbert Z. Hopkins 15509 Robert Bradley Rheault 15510 William Fuller Pence 15511 Philip Henry Fryberger 15512 Ricardo Arturo Jimenez 15513 Stratis John Stratis 15514 Frank Gibson Lester 15515 Hal Edward Hallgren 15516 Everitt Fee Hardin 15517 Edward Francis McCue 15518 Alexander Gerardo 15519 George E. Sheffer 15520 Norman Emanuel Weiss 15521 Clyde B. MacKenzie 15522 Lloyd Charles Kurowski 15523 Harrison Howell D. Heiberg 15524 Carey Wayne Milligan 15525 Arthur Edward Hansen 15526 Stephen Orville Edwards 15527 Joe Fenton Lusk 15528 Robert Chase Toole 15529 James Thomas Dixon 15530 Norman Cooper Watkins 15531 Harold A. Terrell 15532 Charles James Simmons 15533 John Alan Barricklow 15534 Richard T. Blow 15535 John K. Paden 15536 Richard Boyer Diver 15537 Eugene P. Deatrick 15538 Oliver Moses 15539 William Croom Parker 15540 Hale Baugh 15541 Arthur James Lochrie 15542 W. Edward Chynoweth 15543 Richard Lloyd Dresser 15544 Richard Allan Johnson 15545 Amos Blanchard Shattuck 15546 Robert Bruce Bowen 15547 John C. McWhorter 15548 Marvin Stuart Weinstein 15549 Donald Ingram Hackney 15550 Theodore Robert Upland 15551 Thomas Jacob Agnor 15552 Harlan Winthrop Tucker 15553 John William Wiss 15554 Anthony Patrick Wesolowski 15555 Robert Overton Isbell 15556 Truman Kent Berge 15557 Benjamin Tullidge Hill 15558 Ralph Irving LaRock 15559 James Arthur Day 15560 William Theodore Lincoln 15561 Guy Kent Troy 15562 Salvador Enrique Felices 15563 George Frederick Otte 15564 Rex Webb Beasley 15565 Wayne Stetson Anderson 15566 Sam Hugh Smith 15567 Kenneth Cruikshank Van Auken 15568 Raoul Jean Quantz 15569 John Chambers Fischer 15570 Robert Franklin Morris 15571 John Stanley Baumgartner 15572 James Eugene Bruce 15573 Doyle Merritt 15574 Lloyd L. Dunlap 15575 Richard Leonard Stone 15576 Irving Granville Rouillard 15577 Edwin L. Weber 15578 George Walter Hirsch 15579 Robert N. Dosh 15580 Richard Benton Burgess 15581 Harold Joseph Stirling 15582 John Daniel Henry McDonough 15583 Walter J. DeLong 15584 James Joseph Dorney 15585 William Britton Teglund 15586 Duquesne Abraham Wolf 15587 Thomas H. McBryde 15588 Robert Trent Winfree 15589 Harris Harold Woods 15590 Alvan C. Hadley 15591 Philip Brian Brady 15592 Alexander Dominic Perwich 15593 Carcie C. Clifford 15594 Robert Hogan Stephenson 15595 John Eldredge Simpson 15596 Sam Sims Walker 15597 Maurice Serotta 15598 Robert Grewelle Cramer 15599 Stephen B. Elmer 15600 William Richard Stroud 15601 Vincent D. Gannon 15602 Charles M. Jaco 15603 Robert Francis Dickson 15604 Robert Carey Clemenson 15605 Ruel Fox Burns 15606 James Drummond Fitzgerald 15607 Guy Arnold Rogers 15608 Walter Fleming Hamilton 15609 Alford Edward Allen 15610 Samuel C. Skemp 15611 Robert Wallace Allen 15612 Daniel Orrin Graham 15613 Martin Bruce Feldman 15614 John Thomas Jones 15615 William Denton Baisley 15616 Keith Dennis Stidham 15617 Robert Fleming Carter 15618 Albert Marshall Leavitt 15619 Robert Irving Channon 15620 John R. Grace 15621 Jack Franklin Matteson 15622 Richard Harding Walker 15623 John Henry Grady 15624 Eugene Gibb Sharkoff 15625 John R. Thurman 15626 Robert R. Waggener 15627 Wilfred Everett Gassett 15628 Robert Reynolds Coller 15629 Donald A. Lundholm 15630 Richard George Walterhouse 15631 William Thomas Cound 15632 Robert T. Wagner 15633 Joseph Barnett Rogers 15634 Herbert Hesselton Flather 15635 Emory Robert Wells 15636 Faison Peirce Gibson 15637 James Richard Cavanaugh 15638 Lloyd Senter Adams 15639 Gunnar Einar Andersson 15640 Andrew W. LaMar 15641 John Eugene Molchan 15642 Felix Foster Cowey 15643 Richard Russell Galt 15644 Minter Lowther Wilson 15645 Milton Holmes Hamilton 15646 Roland Stephen Catarinella 15647 Patrick D. Doherty 15648 William H. Trotter 15649 Lawrence J. Luettgen 15650 Gilbert Chester Anthony 15651 George Robert Stallings 15652 John Griffin Parker 15653 Edward Joseph Collins 15654 John Robert Steele 15655 Bryce Poe 15656 Robert Carroll Hawley 15657 Jesse Simmons Harris 15658 Eugene Vincent Pfauth 15659 Edward John Morgan 15660 Charles Lafayette Robinson 15661 Charles D. Daniel 15662 Harrison Benson Kinney 15663 William H. Jenkins 15664 Reuben Pomerantz 15665 Earl S. Dye 15666 William Hayes Webb 15667 Hamilton Bruce Shawe 15668 Christopher Booth Sinclair 15669 Keith Burns Zimmermann 15670 James J. Gigante 15671 Elisha James Fuller 15672 Willis Dodge Cronkhite 15673 Malcolm Means MacWilliams 15674 Robert Earl Wayne 15675 Paul Shelby Ward 15676 Edwin D. Frazer 15677 Carshall Carter Carlisle 15678 Frank Stevens Hagan 15679 Raymond Edward Thayer 15680 Lewis Burton Tixier 15681 Robert Ernest Kren 15682 Walter Arthur Dumas 15683 Reginald Oras Shaw 15684 John William Vester 15685 Daniel Francis Mahony 15686 Francis Frazee Hamilton 15687 Alfred C. Haussmann 15688 Jean Krummel Joyce 15689 Thomas Jefferson Stapleton 15690 Calvert Potter Benedict 15691 John A. Riedel 15692 Paul M. Ireland 15693 John Morris Schuman 15694 John Prescott Doolittle 15695 Myron Jefferson Benefield 15696 William Randolph Bigler 15697 Walter Burnside 15698 Rodney Alger Blyth 15699 Daniel L. Levy 15700 John Frederick Green 15701 Josiah Ara Wallace 15702 Robert Webb Tribolet 15703 Harold G. de Moya 15704 Martin Al Kutler 15705 Percy Louis Wheeler 15706 Robert Francis Patterson 15707 Senour Hunt 15708 Edwin Sanders Van Deusen 15709 Farrel Elmore Dockstetter 15710 William Thaden Seeber 15711 Bernard Janis 15712 Edmund Keith Ball 15713 Robert Moody Williams 15714 John Emmett Pitts 15715 Robert Doyne Woodley White 15716 William Martin Harton 15717 Robert Earl Arnold 15718 Donald Wilson 15719 William Aiken Griffin 15720 Donald Scott Watson 15721 Robert Sidney Douthitt 15722 Howard Anthony Giebel 15723 Gerald Marshall Jones 15724 George Stanton Dorman 15725 Donald Warren Dreier 15726 William R. Kelty 15727 George Edward Hall 15728 James Patrick Hurley 15729 Clarence Wade Kingsbury 15730 Robert Milton Hamilton 15731 Marshall Sanger 15732 Gale Edward Stockdale 15733 William Martin Kiser 15734 David Arnold Newman 15735 Albert M. Nemetz 15736 Theodore G. Montague 15737 William Heaton Young 15738 John Max Minor 15739 John M. O'Connor 15740 Kent Keehn 15741 Harold Waldron Horne 15742 George Warren Griffith 15743 Elbert Satterlee Throckmorton 15744 Thomas Moore Huddleston 15745 John Merwin Shultz 15746 Richard Earl Lamp 15747 David Heber Plank 15748 Edwin Wallace Basham 15749 John Christopher Durr 15750 Thomas Gaetano Provenzano 15751 Francis Albert Richter 15752 William Arthur Humphreys 15753 Glennon Clyde Smith 15754 Robert S. Hughes 15755 Richard Taylor White 15756 Joseph O. Meerbott 15757 John Louis Umlauf 15758 Benjamin Wall Kernan 15759 Robert M. Lowry 15760 David E. Barnett 15761 Clifton Wellington Gray 15762 Roy Wilfred Gillig 15763 Joseph A. Giza 15764 James Morris Gridley 15765 Frank Beckwith Tucker 15766 James Wiley Johnson 15767 Theodore George Zeh 15768 Henry Hermann Bolz 15769 Jack Bain Hagel 15770 Frank Adair Doyle 15771 James C. Welch 15772 Robert Alexander Land 15773 John T. Price 15774 Elbert Madison Stringer 15775 Joe Bruton Flores 15776 Stephen Andrew Matejov 15777 Prentice Earle Whitlock 15778 Richard Sharon Pohl 15779 Roscoe Ellwood Patton 15780 Benjamin Ransom McBride 15781 Harley Eugene Venters 15782 Hunter Harry Faires 15783 Harry H. Roddenberry 15784 Warren Eastman Hearnes 15785 Philip Darlington Haisley 15786 William Craton Screven Simpson 15787 Jack Quentin Kimball 15788 James Robert Loome 15789 William Burns Castle 15790 James Ernest Paschall 15791 Tom Clifft Campbell 15792 Thomas L. McMinn 15793 Rolland Archibald Dessert 15794 Raymond Howard Glatthorn 15795 Joseph Fred Buzhardt 15796 Walter Leslie Frankland 15797 Harold F. Bentz 15798 Samuel P. Davis 15799 Jack T. Cairns 15800 Alan Homer Birdsall 15801 Robert Owen Bullock 15802 Arthur Emil Gay 15803 John Emil Vaci 15804 Marion Rich Richards 15805 Granville Watkins Hough 15806 Richard Allan Kellogg 15807 Guy E. Hairston 15808 Peter Gerald Arend 15809 Merl Galbreath Hutto 15810 John Alan Hoefling 15811 Edmond Charles Longarini 15812 James Madison McGarity 15813 Harold Thompson Dillon 15814 Philip Lee Clements 15815 Harry Griffith Cramer 15816 Clifford H. Parke 15817 Jere Otis Whittington 15818 Jack Lowman Bodie 15819 Alexander Papajohn 15820 Clyde Roscoe Denniston 15821 Everett Lipscomb Rea 15822 Lester Mykel Conger 15823 William Redfield Phillips 15824 Samuel Ewing Hill France 15825 James Burtram Hobson 15826 G. Hunter Bowers 15827 William Robert Parker 15828 Raymond E. Orth 15829 Eleazar Parmly 15830 Philip Riviere Safford 15831 Edwin R. Van Deusen 15832 Thomas Morton Constant 15833 Daniel W. Hickey 15834 Jesse Joseph Cohen 15835 William C. Bishop 15836 Robert Lee Steele 15837 Clair LaVern Book 15838 Richard Hugh Turner 15839 Steven L. Conner 15840 William W. Lewis 15841 Charles P. Baker 15842 Leslie E. Thompson 15843 Russell Edward Speake 15844 George Michael Sliney 15845 Kendrick B. Barlow 15846 Dudley S. Stark 15847 Arthur William Pence 15848 Bert Alison David 15849 John Edward Stannard 15850 Steven Edward Hill 15851 Gordon Ross Jacobsen 15852 Richard Arthur Patterson 15853 Stephen Garrett Henry 15854 Thomas Corbett Langstaff 15855 Thomas Harold Mahan 15856 Charles A. Waters 15857 Wayne Emerson Lawson 15858 William Price Withers 15859 William Howard Grisham 15860 William Welcome LaMar 15861 Joseph Roy Castelli 15862 Robert S. Daniel 15863 Charles Maurice Hall 15864 George C. Muir 15865 Frederick King Alderson 15866 David Lapham Colaw 15867 Kevin Albert Lynch 15868 William Gibson Richards 15869 James Edwin Thomas 15870 James T. Carbine 15871 Stephen Joseph Pagano 15872 James Von Kanel Ladd 15873 Johnny Rudd Castle 15874 Loren George DuBois 15875 Edward L. Flaherty 15876 Richard L. Conolly 15877 John Loveland Armstrong 15878 Arthur Johnston Bugh 15879 Joseph Peter Pepe 15880 Jesse Edwards Green 15881 James Montgomery Elder 15882 Harry John McPhee 15883 Donald R. Lynch 15884 Thomas Leigh Gatch 15885 DeBow Freed 15886 Frank M. Bowen 15887 Samuel Grier 15888 William Henry Bamber 15889 John C. Barrett 15890 Ralph Allen Starner 15891 Walter Donald Bauchman 15892 Corwin Boake 15893 Edward A. Lembeck 15894 Thomas Edward Gaines 15895 Arthur Burt Wilcox 15896 Martin Fish Zorn 15897 Robert O. Burke 15898 Earl Frederick Markle 15899 Don Walter Adair 15900 Beryl Leve 15901 Benjamin Clyde Brown 15902 Charles Gurley Williamson 15903 Richard J. Pitzer 15904 Robert Harry Case 15905 John Day Whitmore 15906 Billy McCall Prestidge 15907 Edward Joseph Cavanaugh 15908 William Preston Reed 15909 Benjamin Keller Chase 15910 Shirley S. Ashton 15911 Frank W. Porter 15912 Clarence E. McChristian 15913 Carroll R. O'Neill 15914 Byron D. Greene 15915 Samuel Hartman Title 15916 James Samuel Hutchins 15917 Patrick J. O'Connor 15918 Richard Glenn Carnright 15919 Harold Francis LaCouture 15920 Harry Alford Davis 15921 David Bartholomew Spellman 15922 Frederick Andrew Dodd 15923 Benjamin Bertram Williams 15924 Carl Paxton Schmidt 15925 Robert Lee Dobbs 15926 Alden Davis Korn 15927 Robert Seedorf Wilson 15928 Richard Edward Hale 15929 Louis Nelson Roberts 15930 Edwin Mortimer Joseph 15931 Fred W. Knight 15932 William S. Volmer 15933 Robert T. Richmond 15934 Robert Arthur Walsh 15935 John Donald McGregor 15936 Robert F. Hewett 15937 James Emmett Wirrick 15938 Robert M. White 15939 Ernest Anthony Pepin 15940 Thaddeus Stephen Skladzien 15941 Marvin O. Weber 15942 Albert Enzo Joy 15943 E. Scott Minnich 15944 Andrew Alexander McCoy 15945 William Marion Wright 15946 William L. Stone 15947 Alvin Ash 15948 William Thomas Reeder 15949 Calvin Ervin Glidewell 15950 Elisha M. Robinson 15951 John Charles Geary 15952 Francis Rene Baker 15953 Thomas Sawyer Owen 15954 Raymond Palmer Whitfield 15955 Glenn Willard Dettrey 15956 Elmer Raymond Ochs 15957 John Edward Barth 15958 Donald M. Messmore 15959 Lawrence Norman Gordon 15960 Stanley Dale Fair 15961 Meredith William Ghrist 15962 Raymond H. Gilbert 15963 John Edward Sauer 15964 E. Gene Sprague 15965 Robert Anderson Babcock 15966 Frederick B. Cordova 15967 James Luke Andrews 15968 Blucher S. Tharp 15969 Kyle Watson Bowie 15970 Roy G. Simkins 15971 James Donald Hughes 15972 William Robert Smith 15973 Herrold Emerson Brooks 15974 Cecil C. Larson 15975 George Lightfoot Dennett 15976 John J. Schmitt 15977 James Bjarne Furuholmen 15978 William Clinton Powers 15979 Benjamin C. Evans 15980 Corbin James Davis 15981 Theodore Julian Lepski 15982 Roy Ritter Hudspeth 15983 Harry Arthur Floyd 15984 Burton G. Cameron 15985 Charles Orion Wiedman 15986 Thomas Williams Pardue 15987 John W. Gillespie 15988 Edward Charles Drinkwater 15989 Pat W. Crizer 15990 John William Callaghan 15991 David Merritt Peters 15992 David Winthrop Brillhart 15993 George Silides 15994 Joseph George Rioux 15995 J. Edward Houseworth 15996 William Gilfillan Gavin 15997 John David Miley 15998 Arthur R. Moore 15999 William B. Yancey 16000 Roy Cuno Calogeras 16001 Frank C. Schoen 16002 William S. Culpepper 16003 Walter Stanley Mattox 16004 Charles Alexander FitzGerald 16005 William Joyce Kaliff 16006 James Robert Miller 16007 Robert T. Strudwick 16008 Joseph Dodge Park 16009 Max Milton Feibelman 16010 Joe Wesley Finley 16011 Fields Early Shelton 16012 George Jewel Porter 16013 John William Nance 16014 Robert John Eichenberg 16015 Waldron Berry 16016 Grover Woodrow Asmus 16017 Gilbert Everett Perry 16018 Daniel Reardon Moriarty 16019 Howard Ernst Pleuss 16020 Richard Martin Kinney 16021 Hobart Raymond Gay 16022 Robert Edward Kaplan 16023 Robert Vincent Kane 16024 John Neil Munkres 16025 Charles Edward Buckingham 16026 Richard Wanless Brunson 16027 James Malcolm Becker 16028 Richard Gordon Newell 16029 Elmo Eugene Cunningham 16030 Allan Curtis Torgerson 16031 John Francis Donahue 16032 Clarence F. Horton 16033 James Hubert McBride 16034 Alexander James Papatones 16035 Richard Henry Mealor 16036 Jack Harrison Montague 16037 Anastasio Somoza 16038 Horace Frederick Derrick 16039 Philip Anthony Farris 16040 Edward Francis Crowley 16041 Charles Ruggiero 16042 Robert Nathan Evans 16043 Edward Milton Carr 16044 William L. Clapp 16045 Joseph Easterbrook Collins 16046 Harold Paul Fox 16047 Thomas Edward Pfeifer 16048 Anthony A. Cucolo 16049 George Joseph Nelson 16050 William Joseph Kenney 16051 Cornelius McMillan 16052 James Sewell Elliott 16053 Stanley Jerome Love 16054 Rollin White Skilton 16055 Richard Anthony Bresnahan 16056 John Scholto Wieringa 16057 Needham Phillips Mewborn 16058 Jack Warren Morris 16059 Mose W. Gordon 16060 Charles William Brosius 16061 Henry L. Ingham 16062 Paul Miller Ellman 16063 Robert George Shackleton 16064 Raymond Turck Moore 16065 Albert Dunbar Wedemeyer 16066 Shepherd A. Booth 16067 Fred Brinson Roundtree 16068 Richard H. Bacon 16069 Marvin Chapman Reed 16070 Jerome Frederick Butler 16071 William Irving McKay 16072 Robert Irwin Rush 16073 Edward Joseph Conlin 16074 Warren Stanley Jungerheld 16075 Charles Gustavus Memminger 16076 William Franklin Ashby 16077 Philip John Frank 16078 Kenneth Wendell Hughes 16079 Robert J. Lamb 16080 Robert William Seaman 16081 Truman E. Boudinot 16082 Marshall McD. Williams 16083 Howard Byron Hirschfield 16084 Allen H. Wood 16085 Donald Sternoff Beyer 16086 Paul Ingram Barthol 16087 Albert R. Ives 16088 Eugene Emil Melo 16089 Thomas Vincent Hirschberg 16090 Robert Busill Tully 16091 Robert Clements Bradley 16092 Thomas Rodrick McCormick 16093 John Copeland Bartholf 16094 Norman Sturgis Wilcox 16095 James H. W. Inskeep 16096 Stephen Eugene Gray 16097 Francis Miller Palmatier 16098 George Smith Patton 16099 Alvyn Lofton Woods 16100 Roy Joseph Mossy 16101 Paul Aloysius Kelley 16102 John Marberger 16103 William Rogers Roney 16104 Edmond Alexander Kuna 16105 Philip Bird Hopkins 16106 Frank Earl Blazey 16107 Roland Arthur Kline 16108 Edgar S. Harris 16109 Richard Lincoln Ruble 16110 Ben Francis Boyd 16111 Robert Alexander Montgomery 16112 Leslie N. Shade 16113 Gene Kenyon Lawson 16114 John Alexander Martin 16115 Malcolm Eldridge MacDonald 16116 Ralph A. Meola 16117 William Henderson Mason 16118 Charles Leroy Wesolowsky 16119 Alexander Turner Cochran 16120 Morgan Joyce Murphy 16121 George Raney Bailey 16122 Robert Hazen Philips 16123 Robert Kniley Swab 16124 James Elbert Carter 16125 Richard L. Gruenther 16126 Sewall Harvey Emler Johnson 16127 Lynn W. Hoskins 16128 Robert Albert Chabot 16129 Charles Francis McCarty 16130 Peter Michael Jacula 16131 John Joseph Byrne 16132 Paul Maxfield Norris 16133 John Stuart Gayle 16134 Alvin Franklin Futrell 16135 Robert Batten Dunham 16136 Robert Lawrence Walker 16137 Ernest Willet Prevost 16138 Edward William Jones 16139 Harlan Gustave Koch 16140 John W. Dwyer 16141 Daniel Jarvis Finnegan 16142 Clarence M. Mendenhall 16143 Preston Heacock Hibbard 16144 Frank Salvatore Caruso 16145 Jesse A. Fields 16146 Del Rovis 16147 Hubert Sheldon Stees 16148 Robert X. Sheffield 16149 Robert Watt McCoy 16150 William Theodore Bowley 16151 Charles H. Parsons 16152 Jerome Vincent Halloran 16153 James David Lloyd Chatfield 16154 Earl R. Van Sickle 16155 John Wallace Jackson 16156 Robert Warren Storm 16157 John Ambler Sadler 16158 Ralph C. Davis 16159 Minor Lee Kelso 16160 Thomas Maldwyn Daye 16161 **1947** Robert Miller Montague 16162 Frank Coulter Boerger 16163

Melvin A. Rosen 16164 Junius Jay Bleiman 16165 John Wayne Mastin 16166 Roger R. Bate 16167 Merlin Willard Anderson 16168 John Joseph Lowry 16169 Howard L. Sargent 16170 John Edwin Mock 16171 James Russell Robinson 16172 James Franklin Fraser 16173 John Carter Faith 16174 Arthur Andrew Becker 16175 Peter Karter 16176 George Anthony Lynn 16177 Milum D. Perry 16178 James Betts Egger 16179 John Brooks Reese 16180 Jerome Boris Christine 16181 Shelton Brant Biles 16182 Donald Harry Steininger 16183 Norman Robert Rosen 16184 Sam David Starobin 16185 Bernard Michael Greenberg 16186 Richard Herman Allen 16187 Gonzalo Fernandez 16188 John James Murphy 16189 Donald Oren Robb 16190 James Byron Kennedy 16191 Jack Mathew Thompson 16192 Richard Freeman McAdoo 16193 Robert James Kennedy 16194 William Jackson Schuder 16195 Carroll C. Jacobson 16196 Edwin W. Robertson 16197 Burton Katz 16198 Robert Paul Babbitt 16199 Richard Joseph Steinborn 16200 Richard Lytle Yates 16201 Philip Thomas Boerger 16202 John Kenneth Lerohl 16203 John Elwood Hoover 16204 Hugh James Bartley 16205 Donovan Finley Burton 16206 Edwin Borchard Greene 16207 Richard Henry Sforzini 16208 Theodore Chester Biel 16209 Douglas Crowther Weaver 16210 John Joseph Sullivan 16211 James Smith Coolbaugh 16212 Paul J. Curry 16213 Frederick John Knauss 16214 Wallace Hull Griffith 16215 Forest Willard Crowe 16216 Marvin Henry Stock 16217 Robert Thornton Curtis 16218 Jack Vernon Pearce 16219 William Wright Gray 16220 Milton Leland Haskin 16221 James Allen Johnson 16222 Willard N. Munroe 16223 Kenneth Martin Hatch 16224 Raymond R. Hails 16225 John Franklin Piepenbrink 16226 George LeRoy Haugen 16227 Ralph C. Murrin 16228 Herbert C. Pinkerton 16229 John Jamison Anderson 16230 James David Heironimus 16231 John Love Gerrity 16232 Donald David Litt 16233 King D. Simon 16234 Robert Maurice Haas 16235 William Loyd Webb 16236 Richard A. Littlestone 16237 John Edward Culin 16238 Leslie Robert Stevens 16239 Cecil Edward Fox 16240 Einar Glenn Lundy 16241 Robert Blake Griffith 16242 Milton J. Chamberlain 16243 Robert Edward Keck 16244 Leonard Anthony Staszak 16245 Hal Clyde Richardson 16246 John Novomesky 16247 Brent Scowcroft 16248 Carlton J. Wellborn 16249 Louis Rachmeler 16250 Julius Fredrick Ickler 16251 Jack Van Dunham 16252 Kermit Clifton Kaericher 16253 Gerald Joseph Wojciehoski 16254 David Jarvis 16255 Harry Polk Ball 16256 Ralph Locker Bentley 16257 Albert Archer Van Petten 16258 Gordon Kendrick Dicker 16259 Warren Robert Gossett 16260 Harold Walter Grossman 16261 John Jay Kirby 16262 Bernard Jay Gardner 16263 William Jennings Sharpe 16264 John Guilford Paules 16265 Kermit Dean Reel 16266 Thomas Vincent Monahan 16267 Robert Jacob Baer 16268 Leland Dale Christensen 16269 Willis Howell Clark 16270 Hewitt Chemnitz Larsen 16271 Robert Wilson White 16272 George Levenback 16273 Melvin Vernon Leblanc 16274 Thomas E. Benson 16275 John More Miller 16276 Bennet Norman Hollander 16277 Edwin Connery Hightower 16278 Wallace Eugene Nickel 16279 Dandridge Featherston Hering 16280 James Lee Bushnell 16281 Donald Verner Schnepf 16282 George Fred Harrington 16283 David Anicker Odell 16284 Edson Leonard Garrabrants 16285 Frederick Gray Hudson 16286 George Martin Dell 16287 Joseph John Addison 16288 Robert Peter Lane 16289 John Delistraty 16290 Gerald Ross Toomer 16291 Marcos Emmet Kinevan 16292 John Edward Cottongim 16293 John Griffin Gaddie 16294 George Joseph Goldsborough 16295 Robert Miller Garvin 16296 James Philip Mattern 16297 Harold Jacob Eberle 16298 John Mackay Young 16299 William Douglas Grant 16300 William Smith 16301 Herschel Everett Fuson 16302 Richard Earl Dunlap 16303 William N. Nairn 16304 Clyde Calvin Reynolds 16305 Jean Prosper Burner 16306 Patrick J. O'Connell 16307 Donald Clement Helling 16308 Henry Cantzon Paul 16309 Robert Sattem 16310 John W. Lauterbach 16311 Alan David Sapowith 16312 Ralph Harold Beuhler 16313 Frank L. Taylor 16314 Lee Geoffrey Schlegel 16315 William Irvine West 16316 LeRoy Emil Majeske 16317 James Eugene Ecington 16318 William Thomas Kuykendall 16319 Bernard William Abrams 16320 William John Reckmeyer 16321 Rolland Valentine Heiser 16322 Robert Fletcher Halligan 16323 Robert DeWayne Peckham 16324 Robert Allan Beckelman 16325 Robert Haldane 16326 Winston Ousley Scoville 16327 Jack Francis Pierce 16328 Frank Joseph Lamattina 16329 Charles Carrington Stewart 16330 Angelo James Ellis 16331 James Walter Enos 16332 Joe Dean Johnston 16333 William Michael Sullivan 16334 Arnold William Mahlum 16335 David Newcomb 16336 William Fortune Coghill 16337 Alexander Lemberes 16338 Henry William Hill 16339 Robert James McNeil 16340 Robert Earl Hoffman 16341 Martin Michael Maloney 16342 Ira Warren Snyder 16343 James Edward Colburn 16344 Stuart Pounder MacLaren 16345 Calvin L. Bass 16346 Frank J. Kremser 16347 James Christopher Cosgrove 16348 Howard B. Arnold 16349 John Thompson Guice 16350 Herbert Owen Brennan 16351 Wells Brendel Lange 16352 Robert Lynn Ozier 16353 Stuart Gregory Force 16354 Homer P. Gainey 16355 Dean Stevens Gausche 16356 John L. Kennedy 16357 Kenneth Howe Farrier 16358 Theodore Solomon Spiker 16359 Richard Alexis McClure 16360 Earle LeRoy Bathurst 16361 Carl Kamp Russell 16362 Frederick Malcolm Wright 16363 Egbert H. Cofield 16364 Harold Stan Tavzel 16365 Tom Judson Perkins 16366 Stewart Meldred Vockel 16367 Otis E. Brannon 16368 Gordon James Duquemin 16369 Thomas Edmund Rogers 16370 Albert J. Geraci 16371 William Bernard Cronin 16372 Clifford G. Zimmer 16373 David Michael Dunham 16374 Alexander Meigs Haig 16375 Robert Burns Moore 16376 Alan Henry Gould 16377 James Crawford McKim 16378 Bernard Figueredo de Gil 16379 William S. Carpenter 16380 Robert Anthony Mahowald 16381 Robert Adair King 16382 James E. Smith 16383 William James Woldenberg 16384 Thomas Francis Hayes 16385 Walter Patrick Lukens 16386 Daniel L. Tate 16387 Norman Junior Salisbury 16388 Robert Ewing McCord 16389 Kenneth Moore Landis 16390 George Duane Heisser 16391 Young Arnold Tucker 16392 Peter Molnar 16393 Wayne Otis Hauck 16394 Henry Tomlinson MacGill 16395 Charles Hugh McKnight 16396 James Montgomery Breedlove 16397 Joseph John Williams 16398 Thomas Long Flattery 16399 Oliver Louis McDougell 16400 William Albert Carpenter 16401 William S. Henry 16402 Andrew Leon Hudgins 16403 Jesse James Gilliam 16404 Hubert Horace Lewis 16405 John D. Naill 16406 Charles Stuart Todd Mallett 16407 Wallace Francis Veaudry 16408 George Earl Bland 16409 Richard M. Hutchinson 16410 Park Brown Herrick 16411 Robert Bruce Fahs 16412 Arthur Emmett Coates 16413 John Richard Rantz 16414 Meade D. Wildrick 16415 William Donald Brown 16416 Willis Hickam Knipe 16417 David Welty Gibson 16418 James Edward Ryan 16419 William Donald Field 16420 Paul Charles Callan 16421 Donald M. Dexter 16422 Anthony Allan Alfano 16423 Gordon Malin Strong 16424 Albert W. Cretella 16425 Jack Harris Ray 16426 Harry Richard Kain 16427 Charles Edward Shields 16428 Charles A. Munford 16429 Harrison F. Meadows 16430 William Carl Ciamprone Baron 16431 Buford Bernell Biggs 16432 John Frost 16433 Frederick Walter Jacoby 16434 Allen Franklin Learmonth 16435 Stanley Warfield Crosby 16436 James Bernard Tatum 16437 Charles Kennicott Leech 16438 Walter Edward Johnson 16439 Edmund Mortimer Gregorie 16440 Milton Bellovin 16441 Jack M. Palmer 16442 Robert Bernard Coleman 16443 John Martin Coyne 16444 J. Robert Lilley 16445 William Gabriel McGee 16446 Robert Eugene Kettner 16447 John Patrick Tully 16448 Robert Francis Draper 16449 William E. Conger 16450 Graham Gunther Kent 16451 Selby Francis Little 16452 Leon Joseph Jacques 16453 George Aloysius Maloney 16454 Wilber Glenn Jones 16455 John S. Mallory 16456 Felix Anthony Blanchard 16457 William Lamble Cooper 16458 John W. McCullough 16459 Henry Everett Emerson 16460 Charles William Hill 16461 Conrad Normand Lajeunesse 16462 Robert W. Short 16463 Raul A. Roca 16464 Donald Warren Krause 16465 Glenn Woodward Davis 16466 Robert Joshua Koch 16467 Leland George Anderson 16468 Francis R. Perry 16469 William Dawes Williams 16470 Robert Maxwell Ehrlich 16471 **1948** Joseph Mortimer Kiernan 16472 Joel David Aron 16473 Joseph Key Bratton 16474 C. Arthur Borg 16475 Arnold Webb Braswell 16476 Gerald William Medsger 16477 Richard Dickson Cudahy 16478 Carl Andrew Anderson 16479 Robert Elwood Graf 16480 John Garnett Waggener 16481 Charles Anderson Wurster 16482 Walter Albert Della Chiesa 16483 James William Barnett 16484 John Charles Pickering 16485 William Mason Kaula 16486 Thomas Willard Bowen 16487 William Comstock Hayden 16488 William Curoe Burns 16489 Ennis C. Whitehead 16490 John J. Buckley 16491 Richard James Sequin 16492 Harrison Perry 16493 William Wallace Whitson 16494 Willard W. Scott 16495 Arthur Langley Whitley 16496 Louis LoConte 16497 Walker Syer Bradshaw 16498 Edward P. Sykes 16499 John Spier Egbert 16500 Wilho Richard Heikkinen 16501 Roger Frankland Conover 16502 Duane Lee Emerson 16503 Claron A. Robertson 16504 Otis Corcoran Moore 16505 Raymond Cameron Drury 16506 Edwin Dennis Patterson 16507 Thomas B. Tyree 16508 Charles N. French 16509 Thomas T. Jones 16510 Harvey R. Livesay 16511 Lee Thomas Doyle 16512 Stewart Young 16513 William Claude Burrows 16514 Norman Bertram Lovejoy 16515 Denman Murray Long 16516 Charles Harwood Shook 16517 William T. McGinness 16518 Charles Eads Coons 16519 William Loch Cook 16520 John W. Brennan 16521 Thomas Bledsoe Cormack 16522 James Gage Sandman 16523 Raymond Oscar Barton 16524 Benjamin Joseph Loret 16525 Reuben L. Anderson 16526 Harwell F. Smith 16527 John Arnold Edwards 16528 James Gates Tuthill 16529 Walter Frank Marciniec 16530 Benjamin Wynn Eakins 16531 Charles David Nash 16532 Jay Richard Brill 16533 John Bellinger Bellinger 16534 Alfred H. Kerth 16535 James F. Hooker 16536 Garland Ray McSpadden 16537 Paul Elwood Weaver 16538 George Warren Rutter 16539 George Adelbert LaPointe 16540 Jay Allan Hatch 16541 William G. Thomas 16542 William Henry Lynch 16543 Kenneth W. Olson 16544 Robert H. Cushing 16545 Thomas Ryan Clark 16546 Morton C. Mumma 16547 James Lloyd Jones 16548 Arthur deRohan Barondes 16549 Edward Ansel White 16550 Joseph Henry Meyer 16551 William Y. Smith 16552 Richmond J. Cooper 16553 Lowell B. Genebach 16554 Kenneth Irving Pressman 16555 Robert Marion Ward 16556 Thomas Albert Phillips 16557 John Bell Hughes 16558 Richard Lee Miner 16559 Donald Flint Packard 16560 James Allen Muehlenweg 16561 Frederick E. Tibbetts 16562 Stephen Murray Griffith 16563 Henry Barthold Stelling 16564 Edwin Blakely Nelson 16565 Jess B. Hendricks 16566 Alfred Arthur Pabst 16567 Andrew Benedict Witko 16568 Waldo Emmerson Bertoni 16569 Wallace Henley Hubbard 16570 Merle Gardner Sheffield 16571 Samuel White 16572 William Claiborne Buckner 16573 Patteson Gilliam 16574 James Cornelius Ruddell 16575 Lyle Edward Walter 16576 William Alvin Shuster 16577 Warren Reed Graves 16578 Donald Edward Deehan 16579 Walter William Plummer 16580 Richard Neil Stein 16581 John Winn McEnery 16582 John Joachim McCuen 16583 Harry Moody Bettis 16584 Louis Wellington Schalk 16585 Robert Couth Mathis 16586 Glenn C. Wilhide 16587 Saul Martin Resnick 16588 Fred Issac Chanatry 16589 Richard Glenn Weber 16590 William Reid Bandeen 16591 James Rodgers Allen 16592 Walter Burns Schlotterbeck 16593 Wallace Owens Enderle 16594 James Burnus Hall 16595 Alton Harold Quanbeck 16596 Andrew Broadus Anderson 16597 William Edmund Byers 16598 Joseph Eugene Gorrell 16599 Pierce H. Gaver 16600 Jay Silverman Josephs 16601 Rodman Saville 16602 Charles Samuel Horn 16603 Joseph Shindler Herbets 16604 Donald Charles McGraw 16605 David Wesley Armstrong 16606 Harry John Sternburg 16607 Norman Leander Robinson 16608 Edwin A. Rudd 16609 Elmer Cornelius Vreeland 16610 Robert Murray Pomeroy 16611 Louis Raymond Jones 16612 Edward F. Callanan 16613 Clarence Couch Elebash 16614 Joseph Pembroke Dorsey 16615 Lawrence V. Hoyt 16616 Thomas Allen Ware 16617 Kenneth E. Webber 16618 Mercer McConnico Doty 16619 Daniel DeFoe 16620 Francis Marion Williams 16621 James C. McManaway 16622 James E. Macklin 16623 J. Robert Taylor 16624 W. Grim Locke 16625 Benedict Ralph Jacobellis 16626 Ashby M. Foote 16627 Edward Leigh Scott 16628 L. Frank Robinson 16629 Ivan Morange Selig 16630 Sidney Bryan Berry 16631 Charles Frederick McGee 16632 Rees Jones 16633 Blaine R. Butler 16634 Christy Allen Murphy 16635 George M. Edwards 16636 William Meredith Lyon 16637 Kenneth Edward Ruddy 16638 Albert Feleciano Alfonso 16639 Carl Walter Schmidt 16640 Walter Edwin Meinzen 16641 Carey Bishop Barrineau 16642 Howard Edward Adams 16643 Evan William Rosencrans 16644 Vincent Paul Lewando 16645 Don Stuart McClelland 16646 Neil Rice Ayer 16647 Donn Albert Starry 16648 Eugene Priest Forrester 16649 Robert Francis Hallahan 16650 Robert L. Kirwan 16651 Fred E. Wagoner 16652 John H. Chitty 16653 Donal Denis Kavanagh 16654 Gaylord MacCartney 16655 David Saltonstall Mallett 16656 Nasor J. Mansour 16657 Hugh Thomason Hoffman 16658 James Webster Dingeman 16659 William Donald Mounger 16660 George Selby Thomas 16661 John Martin Nelson 16662 Rhonel Earl Morgan 16663 Donald Hood Reynolds 16664 Douglas Theodore Huie 16665 John Kesson Withers 16666 Donald Brunhoff Swenholt 16667 Charles L. Crouch 16668 Leslie Dillon Carter 16669 John Francis Creed 16670 James Arthur Blakeslee 16671 James W. Richardson 16672 Jesse Tompkins Kelsey 16673 Donald Charles Kipfer 16674 Irving Bernard Schoenberg 16675 James G. McCray 16676 William Francis Schless 16677 Samuel F. Hurt 16678 William B. Caldwell 16679 William A. Patch 16680 Floyd Allan Johnston 16681 Louis William Haskell 16682 Robert Wiley Marshall 16683 John Luke Osteen 16684 Hayden Julian Bayer 16685 Francis P. Cancelliere 16686 Hugh Wilson Perry 16687 Harry Thomas Adkins 16688 William Jepson Crosby 16689 George Newton Leitner 16690 William Harrison Travis 16691 Edward Anderton Kritzer 16692 William Charles Ocker 16693 Russell Conwell Ball 16694 Jack Rowland Miller 16695 John Baker Wadsworth 16696 Ralph Winston Pearson 16697 Harold Sherwood Gillogly 16698 James Frederick Walk 16699 Robert Armes Van Arsdall 16700 George W. Hartnell 16701 Richard Stanley Harsh 16702 Richard Ingram Skinner 16703 Louis Leland Anthis 16704 William Pinkerton Dougherty 16705 John W. Jones 16706 Keith Alden Boss 16707 Jacob Bernard Pompan 16708 Walworth Forman Williams 16709 Eugene Stanton Bierer 16710 Lake George Churchill 16711 Arnold M. Sargeant 16712 Carter W. Clarke 16713 Donald Albert Cerow 16714 Oscar F. Kochtitzky 16715 Robert A. Whitfield 16716 Philip McIlvanine Whitney 16717 Thomas W. Hazard 16718 Theodore Bruce Buechler 16719 George Alvis Swearengen 16720 Jack Lee Capps 16721 Edward T. Klett 16722 John Elliott Watkins 16723 Francis W. McInerney 16724 Rufus Johnston Hyman 16725 Edward Hiltner Bertram 16726 William Thomas O'Connell 16727 Robert Richard Finnegan 16728 Stanley Edward Thevenet 16729 John Kastris 16730 Robert Edwin Pater 16731 William J. Madden 16732 Robert James Petersen 16733 Harry Augustine Buckley 16734 Sam Cromwell Holliday 16735 Charles Henry Sunder 16736 Tenney Kutz Ross 16737 Lewis Chandler 16738 Samuel Grady Cockerham 16739 John McKenna Milton 16740 Joseph Philip Seymoe 16741 John Duncan Hamilton 16742 Richard P. Berry 16743 John Patrick Kean 16744 John Calvin Maple 16745 Walton Vernon Waller 16746 Michael J. Tashjian 16747 Philip S. Day 16748 Arthur Snyder 16749 Joseph William Huey 16750 Richard Lauren Warren 16751 Kenneth Hawthorne Barber 16752 Raymond Urban Bloom 16753 Jack Francis Peppers 16754 Charles P. Skouras 16755 Walter Beinke 16756 William Thomas Ryan 16757 Sims Gerald Dildy 16758 John Joseph Doody 16759 James C. Shively 16760 John Francis Dent 16761 David Draper Garrison 16762 David William McNeely 16763 James Alward Van Fleet 16764 Daniel Randall Beirne 16765 Odell W. Williamson 16766 Philip Steven Porter 16767 Frank L. McClaflin 16768 Robert Carroll Davis 16769 Houston Moore McMurray 16770 Eugene C. Fleming 16771 James Clyde Fry 16772 **1949** Richard Theron Carvolth 16773 Robert Clarence Stender 16774 Howard Lynn Strohecker 16775 Albert Hauck Goering 16776 Richard Grams Rumney 16777 Wade Dickinson 16778 Paul C. Dow 16779 Dan Lockwood McGurk 16780 Arthur Williams Banister 16781 Joseph H. Gilbreth 16782 Francis Anthony Wolak 16783 Kenneth Edwin McIntyre 16784 William Clay Robison 16785 William Edward Huber 16786 Russell Hinett Smith 16787 John William Armstrong 16788 Harry A. Griffith 16789 Abbott Congleton Greenleaf 16790 Hillman Dickinson 16791 Robert Charles Nelson 16792 Herman Theodore Boland 16793 Frederick Slocum Gallagher 16794 Edwin Stuart Townsley 16795 John P. Chandler 16796 William Frederick Luebbert 16797 Louis Pintard Bayard 16798 Richard Martin Connell 16799 William Addison Rank 16800 Dean Mount Teece 16801 James Marshall Neil 16802 Kenneth Hall Roper 16803 John Archer Poulson 16804 Patrick Joseph Donohoe 16805 Joseph Richard Stauffer 16806 Robert Stanley Slizeski 16807 Norman Dale Eaton 16808 Amos Clark Mathews 16809 James Richard McDaniel 16810 Patrick Kimball 16811 Howard Hollis Callaway 16812 Maurice K. Kurtz 16813 Raymond R. Battreall 16814 Marcus Bartlett Finnegan 16815 Richard Charles Henry 16816 Stephens Watson Nunnally 16817 Robert Harley Olson 16818 Chester Stuart Trubin 16819 James Alexander Willson 16820 John Joseph Costa 16821 William Charles Hiestand 16822 Wayne Aaron Norby 16823 Robert Frederick Swantz 16824 Donald Davis Klein 16825 Edward Roy Hindman 16826 Russell James Lamp 16827 George Howard Sylvester 16828 John Dickerson Mitchell 16829 John MacEwan Vander Vander Voort 16830 Charles Kenneth Heiden 16831 William Cavett Brown 16832 Thomas Ralph Mackenzie 16833 Frederick Robert Westfall 16834 William Thornton Moore 16835 Gerhard Wilhelm Schulz 16836 Richard Henry Wagner 16837 Norbert Otto Schmidt 16838 Avery Skinner Fullerton 16839 Marshall Edsel Neal 16840 William B. Terrell 16841 Richard Carl Bowman 16842 William Jackson Trautvetter 16843 Charles Gunter Olentine 16844 Charles Milton Adams 16845 Elsworth James Zimmerman 16846 Robert Murrell Rose 16847 Philip Cummings McMullen 16848 Charles Louis Spettel 16849 Schuyler Buell Brandt 16850 John Edward Ike 16851 Thomas Sheridan Pratt 16852 Wilbur John Mueller 16853 Meredith E. Hendricks 16854 Ralph Maurice Buffington 16855 William Howard Lake 16856 William Arthur Carroll 16857 William Battelle Liddicoet 16858 Richard H. Schoeneman 16859 Robert Edwin Pursley 16860 David F. Frech 16861 Hugh Wynne 16862 Anthony John Mione 16863 Fernando Francis Birch 16864 John Asa Hammack 16865 Bruce MacDonald Carswell 16866 Thomas Hutchins Williams 16867 Robert Adair Hansen 16868 Gilbert W. Kirby 16869 Charles Franklin Neef 16870 John Francis McArdle 16871 Robert Thomas O'Brien 16872 Donald Luther Gabel 16873 Edward Anthony Kostyniak 16874 William Henry Nordin 16875 Keith Eugene Sickafoose 16876 David Porter Barnes 16877 Edward Joseph Heesacker 16878 W. Hugh Jenkins 16879 George Stukhart 16880 Norman Fredrick Katz 16881 James Vincent Hartinger 16882 Louis H. Benzing 16883 Leslie Whittington Kirkpatrick 16884 Bernard Greenbaum 16885 James Henry Wroth 16886 William Walter Gustafson 16887 Charles Robert Kemble 16888 Kenneth Alden Main 16889 Edwin Arthur Nelson 16890 Robert Edward Leisy 16891 E. Hugh Kinney 16892 Frank Payne Clarke 16893 George Warner Tracy 16894 John Thomas Schall 16895 John Rodway Mackert 16896 John Howard Birrell 16897 Willis Homer Lowrey 16898 Hugh Mitchell 16899 Robert Benjamin Andreen 16900 William Eugene Dirkes 16901 Lee Eli Surut 16902 Robert A. Derrickson 16903 Joseph Jones Yeats 16904 Henry Turner Croonquist 16905 Joseph Lee Pospisil 16906 James Forrest Schmidt 16907 Everett Jacob Yacker 16908 Charles Gray Roebuck 16909 William Francis Gorog 16910 Lewis Maverick Jamison 16911 John Earl Sutton 16912 Stewart Martin Appelbaum 16913 Joseph Mario Pingitore 16914 William Thielman Paull 16915 Robert Thomas Marsh 16916 Dan A. Brooksher 16917 Homer S. Long 16918 Abner B. Martin 16919 Charles W. Anderson 16920 Edward R. Hilton 16921

William Roth Lambert 16922 Harold Carlton Fitz 16923 William Edward Mundt 16924 Lewis Franklin Moore 16925 Dean Berkeley Dickinson 16926 Raymond Joseph Rasmussen 16927 John L. Rust 16928 St. Clair Streett 16929 Jerry Bennett Lauer 16930 Robert Joseph Braun 16931 Frank Banker Bondurant 16932 Malcolm Joseph Agnew 16933 Robert Shebat 16934 Ralph Puckett 16935 Jack Dwight Finley 16936 Thomas Fuller Bamford 16937 Ray Francis Drummond 16938 Harry James Maihafer 16939 Mansfield Irving Smith 16940 Milton Arthur Kramer 16941 George A. Pollin 16942 James Blayney Rice 16943 Richard Nichols Bundy 16944 John George Albert 16945 Donald Raymond Keith 16946 William Carroll Ross 16947 Gerard Francis Helfrich 16948 Robert Cooke Barton 16949 Harvey Tipton Heckman 16950 Richard Eugene Gillespie 16951 Dan H. Williamson 16952 Harman Charles Agnew 16953 Robert Ernest Liichow 16954 Luther Henry Cassler 16955 Edward B. Wilford 16956 Robert Wilson Noce 16957 Carl F. Arantz 16958 Walter Reed Milliken 16959 David Hendrickson 16960 Stewart Van Vliet Spragins 16961 Ross Le Roy Johnson 16962 Arthur Herman Lindeman 16963 Tom Christian Oberst 16964 Ralph Christian Raabe 16965 Ranald David Council 16966 Albert Walker Singletary 16967 Martin Damon Howell 16968 Donald Rey Woods 16969 Albert Benjamin Suttle 16970 William Chapin Shiel 16971 Joseph Attwood Giddings 16972 Floyd Albert Stephenson 16973 Joseph Thomas Gibson 16974 James Harmon Holt 16975 Daniel Guyton 16976 Theron W. Knapp 16977 Davis Pendleton Parrish 16978 Robert Kent Estes 16979 Robert Paul Butler 16980 Robert Harley Gess 16981 Raymond James Klemmer 16982 Basil Pafe 16983 Miers C. Johnson 16984 James Walther Rawers 16985 John Edwin Miller 16986 John Richard Kiely 16987 Philip Robert Feir 16988 Lawrence P. Monahan 16989 Edwin George Triner 16990 Duane Howard Smith 16991 Leon Witcher McCrary 16992 William Alexander Cummings 16993 John W. Rasmussen 16994 John Thomas Wallace 16995 George Donald Summers 16996 John Powell Hawn 16997 Frank Gentry Barnes 16998 William Hayward Goodwin 16999 Robert Louis Erbe 17000 Murray Winn Williams 17001 Elmer Bruce Peters 17002 Thomas William Stockton 17003 Carl Raymond Crites 17004 George B. Chamberlin 17005 Milan Mosny 17006 Thomas Bernard Luzon 17007 John F. Magnotti 17008 Bartley E. Day 17009 John Charles Reed 17010 Arthur Joseph Kingdom 17011 Boyde Winston Allen 17012 Donald Eugene Whistler 17013 Harold Frederick Lombard 17014 John Louis Carr 17015 William McCoy Wadsworth 17016 Frederic Hine Maughmer 17017 Theodore Ernest Hervey 17018 Robert Michael Pfeiffer 17019 Anthony Cavalcante 17020 Timothy Cornelius Cronin 17021 John Arras Jenkins 17022 Virgil Millett 17023 Alexander Brown Culbertson 17024 Howard Francis Seney 17025 Joe B. Tye 17026 Henry Porterfield Taylor Corley 17027 Eugene Earle Hustad 17028 Albert M. Austin 17029 Frank Hawkins Brock 17030 William Leo Schlosser 17031 Robert M. Springer 17032 Robert Babcock Nelson 17033 John H. Madison 17034 Dolphin Dunnaha Overton 17035 Matthew David Lampell 17036 Robert Oliver Littell 17037 George Winfered Smythe 17038 Willum Harry Spillers 17039 Robert Lloyd Orem 17040 Arnold Winter 17041 John Henry Cronin 17042 William C. Workinger 17043 William Cremin Smith 17044 Cosby McBeath 17045 Charles Walz 17046 Alfred Bradford Hale 17047 Dean Jay McCarron 17048 Jesmond Dene Balmer 17049 Edgar Blair Ross 17050 Arthur James Mayer 17051 George C. Hoffmaster 17052 Edward Brinkley Howard 17053 Ward C. Goessling 17054 John Albert Maurer 17055 Donald Eugene Thompson 17056 Clyde B. Bell 17057 Arthur Roy Driscoll 17058 George D. Graham 17059 Ernst Edward Roberts 17060 Bernard S. Rosen 17061 Alan Joel Horton 17062 Charles William Kessler 17063 Francis Hinchion 17064 Jay Van Cleeff 17065 Louis Edward Abele 17066 Thomas Gray Hardaway 17067 Thomas Gifton Davis 17068 Earl Paul Ford 17069 Malcolm Kingsley Lewis 17070 William James Kennedy 17071 John J. Petranck 17072 M. J. Steger 17073 Charles Thomas Keffer 17074 Ogden S. Jones 17075 James Errington Milligan 17076 Charles Emmett Cheever 17077 John Vincent McDonald 17078 Ronald Emile Lemay 17079 Robert Thomas Fallon 17080 John Christopher Scholtz 17081 Joseph Robert Henry 17082 Orton Flournoy Spencer 17083 Charles R. Lehner 17084 Thomas M. Crawford 17085 Judson J. Conner 17086 Cleatus Jack Cox 17087 Jack Worrell Gillette 17088 Robert Louis Bradley 17089 Charles Thompson Baker 17090 Donald Norton Gower 17091 Clay Thompson Buckingham 17092 Michael Werner McNamee 17093 William F. Trieschmann 17094 William Kent Stemple 17095 Perry C. Hisken 17096 Joseph Daniel Toomey 17097 Wallace Addison Ford 17098 Cecil Earle Newman 17099 Morton Leo Marks 17100 Leo Kay Huber 17101 Donald Andrew McLean 17102 Paul Charles Fleri 17103 Joseph L. Schmalzel 17104 Marc Raphael Jartman 17105 Munro Magruder 17106 Jack Dawson Thomas 17107 Gerrit J. Van Westenbrugge 17108 Fred B. Deem 17109 Kirby Lamar 17110 Leon Luscher de Correvont 17111 Edward Joseph Campbell 17112 Don Reetz Swanke 17113 Alfred Erck Fagg 17114 Charles K. Nulsen 17115 Maurice Manuel Benitez 17116 John Taylor Hodes 17117 Marcellus William Bounds 17118 Roland Eustace Peixotto 17119 Louis Stanton Bush 17120 Joseph James Thompson 17121 Joseph Arthur May 17122 Ulmont R. Kendree 17123 John Howard Yepsen 17124 James Wesley Stansberry 17125 Henry Bennett Sheets 17126 John Franklin Forrest 17127 Richard Alexander Mackenzie 17128 William Wesley Bumpus 17129 George Anthony Nigro 17130 Paul Sherman Rufsvold 17131 Roy Cleveland Brunhart 17132 David Jarrett Chandler 17133 Lewis Carlton Lindsey Browne 17134 Douglas Spoor Weart 17135 Kelso Jones 17136 George Marvin Shepherd 17137 George Maurice Wentsch 17138 Robert Cannon Sanders 17139 Marion Collier Ross 17140 Chris A. Lay 17141 Carroll Stickney Meek 17142 Raymond Moss 17143 Theodore F. DeMuro 17144 Ralph E. Dougherty 17145 Irving Leonard Hammer 17146 Victor Reed Wakefield 17147 Roger Ray Kuhlman 17148 John Donald Woodson 17149 W. Griff Jenkins 17150 Frederick John Fritz 17151 Richard Joseph Tallman 17152 James Reddick Stillson 17153 Richard Arthur Fitzgerald 17154 William Harry Hoffmann 17155 James Delahunt Prescott 17156 Thomas Lyons Moses 17157 Robert Jack Stuart 17158 Harold Raymond Anderegg 17159 John B. Wogan 17160 William Oscar Ware 17161 Charles H. Brown 17162 Edward Weber Ivy 17163 John Norman McCarthy 17164 James Lampros 17165 James F. Marr 17166 John Pat Vollmer 17167 Mortimer B. Cameron 17168 Lewis Roy Baumann 17169 James Robert Hendricks 17170 John A. Walter 17171 Charles Goold Cleveland 17172 Emmet Tinley Everest 17173 Thomas Farris Bullock 17174 William V. Rice 17175 Charles Whitney Oliver 17176 Richard Earl Toth 17177 William Steven Vargovick 17178 William Lee Green 17179 Terence Andrew Powers 17180 Richard Arthur Eric White 17181 Louis Paul Murray 17182 Raymon C. Barlow 17183 Seth Sears Day 17184 Alfred Julius Anderson 17185 John Robert Boag 17186 Gilbert X. Cheves 17187 Robert McHugh Brown 17188 Winston Guerd Walker 17189 Charles Plumer Wason 17190 Robert James Howard 17191 Robert Russell Garrett 17192 Eugene Marder 17193 Herbert L. Hoot 17194 Albert Farrant Turner 17195 William Fletcher McMurry 17196 Robert Lucas Makinney 17197 Lucien Ell Messinger 17198 Philip R. O'Brien 17199 James E. Poore 17200 W. Clinton Norman 17201 Donald Richard Bonwell 17202 Clayton Louis Moran 17203 John Charles Burckart 17204 David Christian Krimendahl 17205 Earl Craig Betts 17206 S. V. Ellerthorpe 17207 Curtis L. Anders 17208 Robert Charles Miller 17209 Jay Allen Carey 17210 Robert Edwin Owen 17211 William Douglas Bush 17212 Emil Abraham Nakfoor 17213 Chester Charles Gilbert 17214 John Stebbins Andrus 17215 Charles Bopes Lee 17216 Bernard Charles Sabel 17217 David Endicott Bolte 17218 Robert Brower Ennis 17219 William Hale Wilbur 17220 Wayne Stewart Moore 17221 David Lee Arnold 17222 Edward Whitney Wagner 17223 Loren Scott Patterson 17224 Charles Artaud Byrne 17225 Robert Henry Schwarz 17226 Stanley Arthur Meyerhoff 17227 Leslie Earl Harris 17228 Nelson Trimble Levings 17229 Herbert Branch Turner 17230 Jefferson Allan Simpson 17231 Francis Leo Sarsfield 17232 Richard Lew Morton 17233 John Tilton Marley 17234 Robert William Howell 17235 Allan Jackson English 17236 John Arthur Bender 17237 Paul Allen Paulson 17238 I. Neal Judd 17239 John O. Vogel 17240 Trevor Washington Swett 17241 Frederick William Dederich 17242 Thomas Black Coughlin 17243 James Harris Steel 17244 Joseph P. St. Clair 17245 Allan Gregory Brown 17246 Billy Joe Rountree 17247 Goble Watson Bryant 17248 Richard Emmett Tobin 17249 John Irvin Saalfield 17250 William Alfred Gardner 17251 John Glennon Hayes 17252 Adrian Beecher Brian 17253 Mahlon Allison Smith 17254 Julian Perry Hunnicutt 17255 Joseph A. Guthrie 17256 J. Carver Wood 17257 Earl James Lochhead 17258 Robert Alexander Ronald 17259 Simeon M. Smith 17260 Robert Kirk Dalrymple 17261 J. Hayes Metzger 17262 David B. Rogers 17263 James J. Coghlan 17264 Harry Winfree Ware 17265 Arthur L. Gerometta 17266 John H. Saxon 17267 William Eugene Marfuggi 17268 Robert Orren Lynch 17269 Charles Nixon Bunn 17270 Charles Dana Palmer 17271 James H. Scholtz 17272 Robert Woolfolk Black 17273 Joseph Frank Sencay 17274 John Joseph Ragucci 17275 Andrew S. Dilts 17276 Tilton Lee Willcox 17277 Robert Johnson Gilroy 17278 Joseph Edward Muckerman 17279 Robert James Johnson 17280 Reed George Jensen 17281 Kenneth Ward Miller 17282 Richard David Rosenblatt 17283 Pennell Joseph Hickey 17284 Jack R. Hayne 17285 Jerome Jay Paden 17286 Edward Keller Yellman 17287 John Edward Ryan 17288 Lewis Lowenstein Zickel 17289 Joseph A. Eagers 17290 Stuart Fonda Martin 17291 Frederic Nathaniel Eaton 17292 Arthur R. Underwood 17293 James A. Whitmarsh 17294 Lawrence James Ogden 17295 Ernest William Denham 17296 Alexander Vincent Sarcione 17297 Samuel L. Barber 17298 William Stanley Kempen 17299 Donald Vincent Braun 17300 David James Colgan 17301 Paul David Terrien 17302 John Joseph Fatum 17303 John David Wightman 17304 Wayne Carleton Smith 17305 Charles Sidney Colson 17306 Courteny Chirm Davis 17307 Norman B. Hopkins 17308 Joseph Paul Kingston 17309 Douglas P. Stickley 17310 John Milton Sayler 17311 William Henry Marslender 17312 George William Tow 17313 George Soliday Orton 17314 Richard Tracy Dunphy 17315 David Gray Freeman 17316 Fenton McGlachlin Odell 17317 Stephen John White 17318 Edwin Saul Marks 17319 Dean Winston Meyerson 17320 Robert Bolenius Ritchie 17321 Charles Lee Smith 17322 Roger Joseph Kelly 17323 Richard Stirling Craig 17324 Willis Charles Newby 17325 William F. Earthman 17326 Joseph McLaughlin Turley 17327 Eugene Burlingame Mechling 17328 John Harwood Hastings 17329 Elwyn Phillips Rowan 17330 John Brandt Latimer 17331 James W. Spry 17332 Joseph B. Steffy 17333 Edmund Harwood Cave 17334 William Robert Penington 17335 Roger Lee Fife 17336 Herbert Edgar Marshburn 17337 Roy Thomas Byrd 17338 Thomas Hannah Burt 17339 Paul Ray Hinckley 17340 John Quirn Arnette 17341 Samuel Streit Coursen 17342 Frederick Augustus Johnson 17343 Barnard Cummings 17344 George Michael Crall 17345 Adrian Byron Arganbright 17346 **1950** William Bradford DeGraf 17347 Charles Ozro Eshelman 17348 James Mason Thompson 17349 Robert M. Wilson 17350 Monty Dale Coffin 17351 Stanley E. Reinhart 17352 Richard Brownson Keller 17353 Frank Borman 17354 John Richmond Brinkerhoff 17355 Paul J. Mueller 17356 Frank Norwood Watson 17357 James Laflin Kelly 17358 William F. Brandes 17359 Albert Leo Romaneski 17360 Leroy W. Henderson 17361 Henry Edward Tisdale 17362 Burke Whitehurst Lee 17363 Neal Bert Kindig 17364 Robert William Clement 17365 Albert B. Crawford 17366 Harvey W. Prosser 17367 David Herdman Cameron 17368 Richard Taylor Drury 17369 Richard Gurney Hoffman 17370 David Cullen Briggs 17371 Thomas Upton Greer 17372 Harold Aaron Gottesman 17373 Warde Franklin Wheaton 17374 Ira John Ward 17375 Thomas Francis Casserly 17376 Frederick J. Hamlin 17377 Rene Arthur Wolf 17378 Malcolm Dayton Johnson 17379 William Bonner Slade 17380 John Herbert Pigman 17381 Elmer Lawrence Birk 17382 Robert Burnett Hughes 17383 John Rutledge 17384 William Edgar Read 17385 Harry Michael Coyle 17386 John Emory Hurst 17387 Jay Bernard Durst 17388 Raymond Philip Singer 17389 Bennett Leonard Lewis 17390 Edmund J. Boyle 17391 Jared Bruce Schopper 17392 Russell B. Preuit 17393 Kenneth Lee Moll 17394 Charles Edgar Allbaugh 17395 John Raymond Hendry 17396 Jere Worth Sharp 17397 William Hayward Schwoob 17398 Albert Vernon Kinner 17399 Ray Samuel Hansen 17400 Tyler Winslow Tandler 17401 Myron Dow Snoke 17402 Herschel H. Liechty 17403 Walter M. Vannoy 17404 David Kay Carlisle 17405 James Raymond Hufnagel 17406 Carl A. Johnson 17407 John Aaron Fray 17408 Richard Maynard Strohm 17409 Fidel Valdez Ramos 17410 Paul Donald Triem 17411 Robert K. O'Connell 17412 Stephen Francis Cameron 17413 Robert Stanley Kubby 17414 William Smith Howe 17415 James Franklin Boylan 17416 George Rae Fullerton 17417 Robert Milton Hoover 17418 John Mansell Garrett 17419 Alan Clarke Fuller 17420 Jerome Noel Waldor 17421 Edward Peter Stefanik 17422 Manley Eaton Rogers 17423 George Sanders Oliver 17424 William H. Miehe 17425 Robert Rehm Werner 17426 John V. Parish 17427 Francis Rudolph Wondolowski 17428 Keith Wilson Loucks 17429 Richard C. Ewan 17430 Emmett Chambers Lee 17431 Lawrence Sherman Lodewick 17432 Cloyce Leland Mangas 17433 Nelson Loren Thompson 17434 Robert Francis Flinn 17435 Russell Eugene Leggett 17436 Arthur Hadfield Blair 17437 Maurice Denman Roush 17438 Edward C. West 17439 Lonnie H. Lumsden 17440 George Kenneth Patterson 17441 Karl Boromaeus Weber 17442 Patrick David Tisdale 17443 Malcolm E. Ryan 17444 Charles Passmore Graham 17445 George Everett Foster 17446 Robert G. Gard 17447 Harold W. Strickland 17448 Charles Junior Osterndorf 17449 Carl Berg Mitchell 17450 Lucien E. Bolduc 17451 Richard Lee Hunt 17452 John C. Maxwell 17453 Alfred Lee Griebling 17454 James Henderson Tormey 17455 I. Robert Ehrlich 17456 Earl Johnston 17457 Louis Gene Leiser 17458 John Arthur Magee 17459 William Ritter Henn 17460 Robert Bruce Ferguson 17461 James Edward Lynch 17462 Allen Burke Jennings 17463 Thomas M. Barry 17464 Ernest Collins Thomas 17465 George Bernard Shaffer 17466 Elbert Devore Holland Berry 17467 Paul Mason Ingram 17468 Edward Martin Pierce 17469 William George Aman 17470 Samuel Leroy Stapleton 17471 George Emory Lear 17472 Russell Alger Glenn 17473 George Harry Scithers 17474 Robert William Green 17475 John Paul Streit 17476 James F. Workman 17477 Pasquale Navarro 17478 Gerald Patrick Kelley 17479 Thomas Wesley Boydston 17480 Edward Barney Quinn 17481 Paul F. Gorman 17482 George Baylor Eichelberger 17483 Irwin I. Steinberg 17484 Donald Phillip Creuziger 17485 George Lynwood Price 17486 James L. Trayers 17487 Edward Paul Freedman 17488 John Horace Vanston 17489 Jack Robert Wheatley 17490 Thomas W. Fife 17491 John Harvey Smith 17492 Joe E. Anderson 17493 John Edward Wagner 17494 John Edmond Fox 17495 John Adams Wickham 17496 William Robert McDowell 17497 William Robert Miller 17498 Charles W. Hammond 17499 William Alexander Pogue 17500 Gerald Harry Monson 17501 Warren Carr Littlefield 17502 James Clayburn Donovan 17503 Thomas Cameron Loper 17504 Arthur Martens Apmann 17505 Philip Bruce Samsey 17506 Frederick Ramon Bonanno 17507 Charles William Newcomb 17508 Leonard W. Wegner 17509 Patrick Henry Zabel 17510 George Purefoy Tilson 17511 Joseph Fay Shankle 17512 Walter Clinton McSherry 17513 Robert Paul Leary 17514 Charles F. Baish 17515 John Marshall Cragin 17516 William M. Hinds 17517 Don Howard Payne 17518 Frank John Zagorski 17519 Leonard Joseph Garrett 17520 Philip Lawrence Bolte 17521 David Warren Mernan 17522 Robert Wayne Eastman 17523 Edward J. Gradoville 17524 Vaughn Lee Shahinian 17525 John Jacob Saalberg 17526 Lincoln David Faurer 17527 Blair Arthur Ross 17528 John Francis Roehm 17529 John Griffin Jones 17530 Richard Robert Wyrough 17531 Dale Jackson Crittenberger 17532 Robert Ambrose Shade 17533 William Arthur Rapp 17534 Howard Frank Reinsch 17535 Morris Joseph Herbert 17536 John E. O'Brien 17537 Melvin Henry Johnsrud 17538 Grady H. Banister 17539 Paul S. Ache 17540 Vance Saunders Brown 17541 Luther Bachman Aull 17542 Richard George Bastar 17543 John L. Fahs 17544 Donal Aloysius Fahey 17545 William K. Gearan 17546 Millard Henry Singleton 17547 Phillip Henry Donahue 17548 Emil Austin Pohli 17549 Thomas Prall Strider 17550 Reginald T. Lombard 17551 Robert Hays McCandlish 17552 Richard Stanley Fye 17553 William Frank Yeoman 17554 Kilbert Emile Lockwood 17555 Robert Andrew Hetz 17556 Abraham Noble Allan 17557 Francis Eugene Thompson 17558 Roy Elton Lounsbury 17559 Frank Peter Christensen 17560 Andy Joe Byers 17561 James C. Drewry 17562 Richard Neal Cody 17563 William E. Crist 17564 Robert Dale Willerford 17565 Robert Kirtland McCutchen 17566 Wilfred Donald Miller 17567 Archie Lee Wood 17568 David Davis Ray 17569 Linwood Bertram Mather 17570 Theodore Pyle Crichton 17571 William Francis Ward 17572 Robert Anthony Basil 17573 William E. Shambora 17574 Bobby Gene Vinson 17575 J. Coleman Bean 17576 Joe Flint Elliott 17577 Gerhard Leonard Jacobson 17578 Theodore Anderson Seely 17579 Daniel Lindsey Rogers 17580 William H. Tuttle 17581 George R. Middleton 17582 Fred Emmond Nickerson 17583 George C. Cannon 17584 John Richard Hall 17585 Willard Holbrook Coates 17586 Louis G. Hergert 17587 Carmelo Placido Milia 17588 Richard Louis Kramer 17589 Philo A. Hutcheson 17590 Glenn Warren Knauer 17591 Maurice Edward Melton 17592 Sidney R. Steele 17593 Wallace Hall Nutting 17594 Paul Blaine McDaniel 17595 Dan Robert McDaniel 17596 Walter Hope Baxter 17597 Carl Locklin Brunson 17598 John R. Gaffney 17599 Richard Whittier Nelson 17600 Herschel Eugene Chapman 17601 Douglas W. Poage 17602 Harold Louis Blank 17603 Louis Frederick Dixon 17604 Robert Joseph Lunn 17605 Raymond Richard Lunger 17606 David Page Pettit 17607 Cleyburn Lycurgus McCauley 17608 Roger Charles Lind 17609 Lloyd Eugene Darland 17610 James William Smyly 17611 Don Gerald Novak 17612 Martin Laverne Kammerer 17613 Alfred Lang Sanderson 17614 Lyman H. Hammond 17615 Henry Donald Spielman 17616 James R. Slay 17617 Donald Foster Dunbar 17618 James Cronin 17619 Stuart Wood 17620 Donald Richard Langren 17621 Lauris M. Eek 17622 Lucien Edward Rising 17623 James Wallace 17624 Roswell E. Round 17625 Joseph Bland Love 17626 Robert Frew Henry 17627 Richard Lee Johnson 17628 William W. Palmer 17629 Charles Alvin Gabriel 17630 George L. Ball 17631 Vernon Alfred Quarstein 17632 Walter F. Hester 17633 Philip Julian Pennington 17634 George Frederick Vlisides 17635 Clay D. Weight 17636 Albert McLees Paulger 17637 Norman Richard Smedes 17638 Marvin Wade Rees 17639 Charles Winthrop Hayward 17640 Florian Octave Cornay 17641 William Robert Stewart 17642 James A. Ross 17643 John Edward Kulpa 17644 William Irving MacLachlan 17645 Edward Painter Crockett 17646 O. Wolcott Parmly 17647 Grace G. Thomas 17648 Harry Eugene Rushing 17649 Clyde W. Spence 17650 Peter Howland Monfore 17651 John Henry Green 17652 Carl Evald Stone 17653 Robert Lee Miller 17654 Austin Kinsey Veatch 17655 Joseph R. Franklin 17656 Richard Y. Newton 17657 Robert W. Douglass 17658 Wendell Edward Phillips 17659 Kenneth Rohn Ebner 17660 Ralph Hadley Viskochil 17661 Peter Mallett 17662 Thomas E. McBride 17663 John E. McCleary 17664 Arthur C. Barker 17665 Herbert Patton Underwood 17666 Chester Morse Willingham 17667 Bert Benton Aton 17668 William Mastoris 17669 Hunter William Passmore 17670 Howard S. Mitchell 17671 John Samuel Hamel 17672 Joseph A. Gappa 17673 William Ridgely Lamdin 17674 Tarlton F. Parsons 17675 Clarence J. Matthiessen 17676 Warner Turner Bonfoey 17677 Arthur Francis Trompeter 17678 Lloyd Richardson Leavitt 17679 George Denys Klie 17680 Thomas Hogshead Tullidge 17681 Paul Costanzo Listro 17682 Walter Edwin Adams 17683 Thomas David Scofield 17684 George Ervine Hannan 17685 Graham Mcleod Sibbles 17686 Albert John Fern 17687 Claude H. Doughtie 17688 Edward Batchelor 17689

John Olin Bates 17690 Malcolm McMullen 17691 Richard Arthur Rein 17692 Frederick D. Hoham 17693 John Lonergan Weaver 17694 John Patrick Ahearn 17695 Matthew T. Henrikson 17696 Vernon R. Gatley 17697 Charles F. Kuyk 17698 John Fabian Wassenberg 17699 Lynn Holt Camp 17700 Francis King 17701 Mark Charles Rhoads 17702 George H. Hubbard 17703 Stanley David Osborne 17704 Allan Richard Packer 17705 Albert G. Breitwieser 17706 Howard E. Kessinger 17707 Duane Melvin Pederson 17708 Thomas A. Austin 17709 Peter Anthony Abbruzzese 17710 Clark Smith 17711 Boyd Truman Bashore 17712 Ralph W. Stephenson 17713 William G. O'Quinn 17714 Thomas C. Sharp 17715 Owen Smoot Nibley 17716 Michael Edward DeArmond 17717 Fredric William Haberman 17718 Kenton P. Cooley 17719 J. Clark Duncan 17720 Robert Charles Morrison 17721 Thurston Richard Baxter 17722 John Matheson McAlpine 17723 Thomas Patrick Greene 17724 Elliot Eclipse Heit 17725 Hugh Carter Holt 17726 Philip Elmer Nicolay 17727 William Lester Daugherty 17728 John Francis Loye 17729 Everett Lee True 17730 Wilbur Moore Warren 17731 Bruce Edward Petree 17732 William Franklin Whitfield 17733 John R. Shelley 17734 Robert Benjamin Peltz 17735 Joseph Nicholas Laccetti 17736 Grayson Dee Tate 17737 Clarence Murphy Watters 17738 Arthur Alten McGee 17739 August John Dielens 17740 Robert Marshall Grow 17741 Richard Greenleaf Trefry 17742 Lilbern Beryl Roberts 17743 Seymour Fishbein 17744 Philo B. Lange 17745 Eugene Charles Etz 17746 Charles Rufus Smith 17747 James Grant Howell 17748 Henry E. Strickland 17749 James Madison Lee 17750 Thomas O. Brandon 17751 Nathaniel Ambrose Gallagher 17752 Gerald Archie Rusch 17753 Robert Edward Whiting 17754 Thomas Watkins Ligon Hughes 17755 Peter Buck Farrell 17756 Mauro Elasio Maresca 17757 Ross F. Mayfield 17758 Frank A. Henning 17759 Allan S. Flynn 17760 Samuel W. Smithers 17761 Peter Blain Todsen 17762 William J. Baxley 17763 Charles Lewis Butler 17764 Samuel Newton Nicholson 17765 Robert Irven Weber 17766 Lewis A. Pick 17767 Ronald Robert Smith 17768 Lawrence Winfield Jackley 17769 Marshall Dillon Talbott 17770 Lloyd E. Mielenz 17771 David Sutton Meredith 17772 Richard Henry Lewandowski 17773 Robert Henry Hoisington 17774 Raymond Maladowitz 17775 Tyler Greene Goodman 17776 Mark McGuire 17777 Medon Armin Bitzer 17778 Winfred G. Skelton 17779 William Cooper Waddell 17780 John James Ross 17781 Martin White 17782 Louis Watkins Prentiss 17783 George Edward Morrissey 17784 Charles F. Dickerson 17785 John A. Barnet 17786 Charles Carroll Cunningham 17787 John S. Wagoner 17788 Wendell Gillham 17789 Lewis Anderson Page 17790 Patrick W. Wilson 17791 Winfield W. Scott 17792 William R. D. Jones 17793 Edwin Lyle Kennedy 17794 Robert Allen Williams 17795 John Ufner 17796 William Simmons Todd 17797 Carter Burdell Hagler 17798 Patrick Edmund McGill 17799 John E. DiGrazia 17800 Kelly Tresher Veley 17801 John Michael Murphy 17802 John Walton Best 17803 Robert Webb Robinson 17804 Edward Francis J. Mastaglio 17805 Andrew Madison Rutherford 17806 Gail Francis Wilson 17807 Paul A. Roach 17808 John Hunt Truesdale 17809 Howard N. Parks 17810 Robert Jordan Seitz 17811 Clifton A. Pritchett 17812 Donald Lee Bohn 17813 Ernest T. Hayes 17814 James Clarence Horsley 17815 Ralph D. Kaseman 17816 Howard O. Johns 17817 Ward Wertman Hemenway 17818 Ralph D. Pinto 17819 Bennie Luke Davis 17820 Reed E. Davis 17821 William Daniel Davis 17822 Robert Charles Edwards 17823 Malcolm W. Chandler 17824 John W. McCormick 17825 John Adams Dille 17826 Volney Frank Warner 17827 Donald Sprague Smith 17828 Raymond Ney Barry 17829 Samuel W. Lockerman 17830 Frank H. Duggins 17831 Merlin Ernest Pettigrew 17832 Robert Richard White 17833 William Leonard Knapp 17834 James A. Curtis 17835 Anderson Owen Hubbard 17836 Kenneth Arnold Tackus 17837 Jack Richard Hanson 17838 Harold Eugene McCoy 17839 David B. King 17840 Cyrus Phillip Barger 17841 Donald Earl Sampson 17842 Ernest Cook Dunning 17843 Howard J. Vandersluis 17844 Rudolph V. Cosentino 17845 James Miller Nold 17846 Allan Peter Scholl 17847 Karl Otto Kuckhahn 17848 Roy Woodson Easley 17849 Charles Franklin Means 17850 Elliott Reynolds Knott 17851 Harry Raymond Steffensen 17852 James Virgil Irons 17853 Harold Libert 17854 John D. Howard 17855 Courtenay Leonard Barrett 17856 Richard John Lorette 17857 Clarke Hickmott Allison 17858 Irvin Stafford Hirsch 17859 Paul Saxton Wood 17860 William Andrew Steinberg 17861 Lindsay Craig Rupple 17862 Henry Steele Sachers 17863 William D. Curry 17864 Gene Alton Dennis 17865 Charles Douglas Friedlander 17866 John D. Pennekamp 17867 George N. Earnhart 17868 Joseph Peter Buccolo 17869 Clyde Ross Cloar 17870 Robert P. Groseclose 17871 Dwight L. Adams 17872 Edmund Jones Lilly 17873 William Thrower Fitts 17874 William Lee Sweidel 17875 Michael Joseph Walsh 17876 Ray Michael Dowe 17877 James S. German 17878 Joseph M. McCrane 17879 Wiley M. Mangum 17880 John Tierney McKinney 17881 George Thomas Morris 17882 Francois X. Therrien 17883 Louis Bernard Hansotte 17884 Henry Alfred Gilbert 17885 Harry Eugene Dodge 17886 John David Scandling 17887 Robert Middleton Chambers 17888 John Charles Fogarty 17889 James Edward Higgins 17890 Ralph Hoyt Detherow 17891 Walter Edwin Price 17892 Clark Charles Martin 17893 William Goodjohn Fuller 17894 Paul L. Gurnee 17895 Ralph A. Ritteman 17896 George Wardman Bell 17897 George Cornelius Rees 17898 Joseph F. Green 17899 Victor N. Cuneo 17900 George Clark Fifield 17901 Edward Joseph Reidy 17902 Falkner Heard 17903 Dean Frederick Schnoor 17904 Edward Jay Fox 17905 David Anderson Campbell 17906 Garrett D. Buckner 17907 William Edwards Otis 17908 John Elbridge Miller 17909 Kenneth Walter Hall 17910 Jack Vincent Mackmull 17911 Louis A. Reinken 17912 Mark Ellis Jones 17913 Philip Dudley Fischer 17914 D. Duncan Joy 17915 John Jay Baughan 17916 Harold George Nabhan 17917 Robert Milton Abelman 17918 Thomas F. Dreisonstok 17919 James Frank Fooshe 17920 Malcolm Robert Cox 17921 Theodore Robert York 17922 Robert Thomas Luckese 17923 Robert Arnold Cheney 17924 Don Franklin Shreve 17925 Louis Vincent Genuario 17926 Frank Augustus Pierson 17927 Charles Hoey Bell 17928 Donald Anthony Coscarelli 17929 Ronald Rovenger 17930 Phillip George Bardos 17931 Briggs Howard Jones 17932 James C. Barnes 17933 James W. Stuff 17934 John Rex Jennings 17935 Salvatore Edward Fastuca 17936 James Robinson Pierce 17937 John Charles Trent 17938 Martin Joseph Small 17939 Stanley Paul Shankman 17940 John W. Allen 17941 Howard Gallaway Brown 17942 Ira L. Kimes 17943 Charles Kohl Farabaugh 17944 William N. Eichorn 17945 Joseph T. Griffin 17946 Richard George Steuart 17947 Norris E. Harrell 17948 Egbert L. Brady 17949 Charles E. Bell 17950 Arthur L. Shemwell 17951 David Maxwell Monihan 17952 John Walsh Goldsmith 17953 James Drexler Michel 17954 James Hoover Fette 17955 John W. Watson 17956 Bernard P. Matthey 17957 David Ralph Hughes 17958 Nelson Fred Ritter 17959 Stanley M. Prouty 17960 Philip Curtis Reybold 17961 Durward S. Wilson 17962 Pedro Ivan Schira 17963 James L. Guion 17964 Thomas Henry Ball 17965 James R. Mitcham 17966 Sidney Thomas Wright 17967 Milo David Rowell 17968 Paul Schuyler Vanture 17969 Charles William Elliot 17970 Aubrey Lee Benson 17971 Walter C. Stanton 17972 John Francis Irwin 17973 Arthur Gignilliat Porcher 17974 William Harold Kellum 17975 Robert Dana McBride 17976 Charles Frederick Tonningsen 17977 Walter Alexander Wood 17978 Arnold Anthony Galiffa 17979 Morton Ray 17980 Melville John Lougheed 17981 Will Hill Tankersley 17982 Clarence Q. Jones 17983 Francis E. Howard 17984 Thomas James Lobe 17985 Paul R. Zavitz 17986 James Rush Skove 17987 William Franklin Pierce 17988 Philip Harlan Harper 17989 Francis W. White 17990 John S. Matthews 17991 Frank E. Gaillard 17992 Edward J. Doyle 17993 John J. Koehler 17994 John William Fahy 17995 Kenneth Erwin Murphy 17996 William Edgar Slavins 17997 John Robert Shaffer 17998 John Sherman Harrold 17999 Leslie Page Holcomb 18000 Norman Failor Hubbard 18001 Mark James Hanna 18002 William H. Bloss 18003 Howard B. Blanchard 18004 Richard Lee Worley 18005 Robert Duncan Reed 18006 William Frederick Nelson 18007 Sidney R. Hinds 18008 Bruce Jean Leiser 18009 Francis Alois Sailer 18010 James Frank Dunn 18011 Warren Webster 18012 Frank Riley Loyd 18013 Andrew J. B. McFarland 18014 John Leo Begley 18015 James R. Wheaton 18016 **1951** Gordon Elmer Danforth 18017 Andrew Cunningham Remson 18018 Buzz Aldrin 18019 Richard Lee Harris 18020 William Lyman Lemnitzer 18021 William Edward Vandenberg 18022 Verle La Fayette Johnston 18023 Joseph Gordon Clemons 18024 Thomas B. Horgan 18025 Eben N. Handy 18026 Harold Dean Shultz 18027 Glenn Edward McChristian 18028 William Kenneth Stockdale 18029 Edward Rudolph Prince 18030 Richard Philip McLean 18031 Stanley Milward Umstead 18032 John Hartley Cousins 18033 John Eugene Schweizer 18034 Francis J. Waldman 18035 John R. Byers 18036 Joseph V. Fleming 18037 Lawrence Pope Crocker 18038 Thomas Roger Woodley 18039 John Richard Wasson 18040 Thomas Henry McMullen 18041 Alfred Dobson Norton 18042 Alan Arthur Frick 18043 Ronald Arthur Roberge 18044 Max Burton Scheider 18045 Thomas A. Stumm 18046 Robert Michael Isaac 18047 Charles B. Ewing 18048 Leo Fred Post 18049 Patrick Hugh Lynch 18050 Alan Arthur Lichtenberg 18051 Gorman Curtis Smith 18052 Bruce Harry Robertson 18053 Albert Crescenzo Costanzo 18054 Jack Wayne Martin 18055 Floy Lauren Ashley 18056 Kenneth Volkert Riley 18057 Donn Ferus Chandler 18058 Florencio Fernandez Magsino 18059 Edward Martin Willis 18060 Robert Elliot Fitch 18061 Larry James Larsen 18062 Guy E. Jester 18063 George Lawrence Harman 18064 Hugh Heflin Pattillo 18065 William W. Schooley 18066 Everette Sanford Parkins 18067 Frederick G. Rockwell 18068 Karl William Peltz 18069 Harley Earl Jeans 18070 Laurance Condon Dosh 18071 John Walter Granicher 18072 Ralph Cooper 18073 Marvin Joseph Krupinsky 18074 Walter J. Bacon 18075 Loyd M. Johnson 18076 George Peter Scheuerlein 18077 Louis John Storck 18078 William Gregory Moretti 18079 Anthony Joseph Delano 18080 George A. Bicher 18081 Edward P. Lukert 18082 Harry Warner Lombard 18083 Edward Compston Peter 18084 John David Daigh 18085 John Peter Hill 18086 Ernest Dishman Peixotto 18087 Charles Davis Phillips 18088 Otto C. Doerflinger 18089 Joseph St. Clair Smith 18090 John William Cunningham 18091 William Lloyd Richardson 18092 Walter Henry Johnson 18093 David Leroy Bills 18094 Samuel M. Guild 18095 William J. Veurink 18096 Robert Lerner 18097 Thomas Zadock James 18098 A.M. Robert Dean 18099 Richard Marshall Wells 18100 David Edward Leyshon 18101 John Broadus Lewis 18102 William Dwight Farrington 18103 Arnim L. Brantley 18104 James Gowen Boatner 18105 William F. Lackman 18106 Frank Edmund Hamilton 18107 David G. Carter 18108 Harold Edward Headlee 18109 William Sidney Monsos 18110 Frederick Lockwood Denman 18111 Donald David Zurawski 18112 William Anderson Allen 18113 Delmar L. Ring 18114 Derrick William Samuelson 18115 Robert De Witt Vincent 18116 Frank Ager Mullens 18117 George Davis Hardesty 18118 John Henry Strealdorf 18119 John Randolph Hook 18120 Joseph D. Lafleur 18121 Francis A. St. Mary 18122 Myles Standish Grant 18123 Roland Eugene Cooper 18124 John Charles Mousseau des Islets 18125 David Webster Huff 18126 Richard Alan Haggren 18127 Lee Edward Duke 18128 Donald J. Kasun 18129 Gerald Selah Reeve 18130 Thomas J. Wanko 18131 William Thomas Barnett 18132 Peter Anthony Beczkiewicz 18133 Robert William Snyder 18134 Daniel Spaulding Barnes 18135 John Little Moffat 18136 Harlan Warren Johnson 18137 Alan Clare Esser 18138 Joseph Paul Crocco 18139 Edward M. Markham 18140 David Alliene Carroll 18141 Richard Alfred Schwarz 18142 Charles Joseph Satuloff 18143 Leland Carl Pinkel 18144 Thomas G. Foster 18145 James Alden Check 18146 Roland Dean Tausch 18147 Dudley Thompson 18148 Robert Frank Niemann 18149 Frederic Allison Henney 18150 Robert Lloyd Johnson 18151 David M. Schlatter 18152 Francis Joseph Sheriff 18153 John Phillip Haumersen 18154 Frederick French Irving 18155 John Joseph Dorton 18156 Edward C. Meyer 18157 Norman James Brown 18158 Joseph H. Albenda 18159 Everette Taylor 18160 John Hinton 18161 Henry Charles Otten 18162 Samuel Thomas Dickens 18163 William J. Bradley 18164 Kennith Frank Hite 18165 Robert Parham Janssen 18166 John Ritchie 18167 Donald A. Van Matre 18168 Franklin Loeb Wilson 18169 George Henry Gardes 18170 Theodore John Charney 18171 Willet John Baird 18172 Gerald Keith Hendricks 18173 James Holden Phillips 18174 Ledyard Long 18175 Billy Joe Ellis 18176 William Rowland Richardson 18177 Lou Enlow Bretzke 18178 John Harrold Craigie 18179 Norman Eugene Dunlap 18180 George Gardner Ritter 18181 Frank Elliott Sisson 18182 Donald Dean Peifer 18183 Robert William Chapman 18184 Peter Rowland Kuhn 18185 Louis Brooks Martin 18186 John E. Shillingburg 18187 James William McDonald 18188 John Leslie Glossbrenner 18189 Herman Joseph Vetort 18190 Melvin C. Snyder 18191 Saul Antman Jacobs 18192 Seldon B. Graham 18193 Robert Orlikoff 18194 Michael Kovalsky 18195 Ralph L. Auer 18196 Richard Clay Breakiron 18197 Walter Brown Russell 18198 Duane Ray Tague 18199 Howard L. Peckham 18200 Barney M. Landry 18201 Jonathan L. Holman 18202 Julius R. Conti 18203 Stan Roger Sheridan 18204 Lawrence L. Eppley 18205 James S. Brett 18206 Paul R. Hilty 18207 Jack Lewis Price 18208 Charles D.W. Canham 18209 Charles Leland Knapp 18210 William E. Crouch 18211 James Roe Semmens 18212 Edward Allen Partain 18213 William Michael Quinn 18214 Wayne Dickson Miller 18215 Howard Olen Wiles 18216 Richard Crawford Allen 18217 Wallace C. Steiger 18218 James Addison Keeley 18219 Richard Gerry Dingman 18220 Francis Lally Winner 18221 Joseph W. Clarke 18222 William Joseph Ryan 18223 Edward P. Hartnett 18224 Newton Bedford Morgan 18225 Carleton Keith Sprague 18226 Harold Anthony Barton 18227 John W. Buckstead 18228 John Allen Hemphill 18229 Daniel James Myers 18230 Seth Ward Scruggs 18231 Joseph Lee Sites 18232 George M. Reid 18233 Donald L. Smith 18234 Irving Butler Reed 18235 Peter Louis Thorsen 18236 Thomas E. Aaron 18237 Francis Washington Craig 18238 Richard Joseph Buck 18239 Elmer Havens Birdseye 18240 David Eaithell Rogers 18241 Adam A. Gorski 18242 Robert Louis Jacobs 18243 Malcolm Brandt Tennant 18244 George Alden Sundlie 18245 John Garland Ballard 18246 John Robert Osborn 18247 James Richard Kintz 18248 Richard A. Perry 18249 Jose Andres Chacon 18250 James Myrick Lowerre 18251 Lewis Christian Buffington 18252 Donald Henry Roloff 18253 Thomas H. Williams 18254 David D. Detar 18255 Eric Ferdinand Antila 18256 Walter Richard Steidl 18257 Absalom Theodore Webber 18258 Charles Edwin Bryant 18259 John Cooper Powell 18260 Donald Albert McGann 18261 Paul Allin Coughlin 18262 Ransom Edward Barber 18263 Joseph W. Knittle 18264 William Neal Thomas 18265 Paul Dilwyn Summers 18266 Walter C. Phillips 18267 William C. Louisell 18268 James T. Barron 18269 Earl Loyd Keesling 18270 Rodney B. Gilbertson 18271 Gerald E. Dickson 18272 John Bernard Foster 18273 John F. Brown 18274 Edward John Mueller 18275 Walter B. Miller 18276 Joseph Francis Schuman 18277 Harold Gene Marsh 18278 John Vaughn Hemler 18279 Richard Carlyle McClure 18280 Frederick Jordan Hampton 18281 Philip Archinard Cuny 18282 Ronald Hugh Milam 18283 James R. Young 18284 Robert Earl Welch 18285 Aaron D. Bernstein 18286 Lawrence Lester Mintz 18287 Walter Albert Klein 18288 William Everitt Grugin 18289 Stephen Watsey 18290 John W. Croan 18291 John Colcock Hutson 18292 Bruce Allen Ackerson 18293 George Charles Filchak 18294 Redmond V. Forrester 18295 Loren Albin Anderson 18296 Bruno Antonio Giordano 18297 Richard Anthony Szymczyk 18298 J. Godfrey Crowe 18299 Frank George Penney 18300 Peter Matthews 18301 Daniel Hurlburt Wardrop 18302 William F. Magill 18303 Peter John Foss 18304 Patrick Matthew Brian 18305 Patrick Joseph Corrigan 18306 Kermit Douglas Johnson 18307 Bernard Zwerling 18308 Roscoe Robinson 18309 Garland Logan Owens 18310 Robert I. Simpson 18311 Russell Leroy Johnson 18312 George Shibata 18313 Don Charles Anker 18314 Edouard Albert Peloquin 18315 Frank Elliott Walker 18316 Edgar C. Thomas 18317 Hoyt Sanford Vandenberg 18318 Elmer D. Pendleton 18319 Daniel Gorman Sharp 18320 Allan Parker Hunt 18321 Donald James Norton 18322 John J. Bohan 18323 John Duke Ward 18324 Frank Paul Vellella 18325 Wayne Manford Dozier 18326 John Bennett Gordon 18327 William L. Givens 18328 Dean Duane Mulder 18329 Clyde Cocke 18330 William Hugh Cuthbertson 18331 Peyton Ellsworth Cook 18332 Clinton Edwon Granger 18333 Dain William Milliman 18334 Maynard Benjamin Johnson 18335 Guerdon Sterling Sines 18336 Charles R. Witmer 18337 John J. Stahl 18338 Diego Alonso Jimenez 18339 Edward Eli Matney 18340 Robert Michael Hechinger 18341 Raymond F. Sargent 18342 David A. Betts 18343 Robert Franklin McDonald 18344 Lew Sidney Robinson 18345 Edward Breed Atkeson 18346 Lynn Maynard McCrum 18347 Merton Juel Bangerter 18348 Robert Douglas Anderson 18349 Chandler Goodnow 18350 Desmond O'Keefe 18351 Richard Louis Ryan 18352 John Alexander Samotis 18353 William Andrew Malouche 18354 James S. Cox 18355 Charles Arthur Crowe 18356 Edwin T. Nance 18357 Robert H. McIlwain 18358 Samuel Ayer Lutterloh 18359 Juan Francisco Doval 18360 William Chauncey Barott 18361 Joseph Peter Rice 18362 Edwin Van Keuren 18363 Stanley Stuart Scott 18364 Richard Paul Guidroz 18365 Charles Rolland Gildart 18366 Thomas C. Odderstol 18367 Howard Cameron Williams 18368 George Allen Meighen 18369 Fred Gene Sartin 18370 Charles Crawford McIntosh 18371 Philip Neill Reed 18372 R. Joe Rogers 18373 Frank Reese Forrest 18374 Robert Earle Olson 18375 David Manker Abshire 18376 James Talbot Guyer 18377 John McGee Bohen 18378 Joseph W. Hutchinson 18379 Douglas Frederick Wainer 18380 Philip Sheridan 18381 Lincoln G. Jones 18382 Howard Wayne Snyder 18383 Richard Rougier McCullough 18384 Paul Richard Miller 18385 Alexander Mulqueen Weyand 18386 Herbert Roth 18387 William Carl Edler 18388 Joseph Albert Luger 18389 Fred Guillermo Reichard 18390 Franklin Herbert Hodgkins 18391 Michael J. Simpson 18392 Ernest Guy Rose 18393 Mathews McCleave Collins 18394 John P. Starrett 18395 Norman Dean Jorstad 18396 Frank R. Fischl 18397 Aaron Sherman 18398 Barry McKnight Harriss 18399 Robert Allan Prehn 18400 Charles Lynn Galloway 18401 Charles B. McLean 18402 John Hillman Gardiner 18403 Charles Nathan Wallens 18404 Louis G. Michael 18405 William G. Owens 18406 Philip Haines Gwynn 18407 Lewis Marquardt Casbon 18408 Richard Backer Dawson 18409 Fred Richard Miller 18410 Theodore W. Griesinger 18411 Lawrence Michael Kelly 18412 Joseph Lewis Fant 18413 Donald Thomas Sheridan 18414 Robert James Pazderka 18415 Leonard Paul Shapiro 18416 George Massle Gividen 18417 Robert Allen Rachek 18418 Carl Franklin Arnold 18419 Kenneth Guynn Herring 18420 Robert G. Yerks 18421 Philip Charles Barth 18422 John Ferguson Hook 18423 Raymond L. Toole 18424 John Daniel Foldberg 18425 Gerald Joseph Carlson 18426 Sanders A. Cortner 18427 Robert Edmond Bauers 18428 Robert Arthur Howes 18429 Hugh Stephen Galligan 18430 Norton Lacy Parks 18431 Serafino Arthur Scalise 18432 John B. Norvell 18433 John J. Moroney 18434 Cecil W. Nist 18435 William Brooks Woodson 18436 Gustave Villaret 18437 Donald Ray Schwartz 18438 Bruce Erland Elmblad 18439 Herbert Hugh Albritton 18440 John Lawton Ross 18441 James Mitchell Rockwell 18442 Robert William Flanagan 18443 Thomas B. De Ramus 18444 William Lawrence Depew 18445 Bruce Barton Bailey 18446 George Willis Stannard 18447 Donald J. Leehey 18448 John Thomas Derrick 18449 Charles Cowdry Pursley 18450 Howard M. Steele 18451 Henry C. Evans 18452 John Joseph Leffler 18453 Stuart L. Miller 18454 George Peter Psihas 18455 Christian F. Rupp 18456 Robert Allison Hyatt 18457 John M. Tatum 18458 Rex Douglas Michel 18459 George William Orton 18460 William Spence 18461 Floyd Gilbert Stephenson 18462 Robert L. Massenburg 18463 Charles Jenkins Walker 18464 Francis Edward Winfield 18465 Joseph Wyndham

Rawlings 18466 Edward Lauriston Zuver 18467 Frank Myer Bashore 18468 Thomas Ure Harrold 18469 Robert William Milburn 18470 Neil Oliver McCray 18471 Paul E. Niedringhaus 18472 James Richard Pitts 18473 Robert Eulass Macklin 18474 Robert B. Lins 18475 Roy J. Herte 18476 Russell Fleming Walthour 18477 Lowell Emmett Torseth 18478 Albert R. Knight 18479 Ryburn Glover Clay 18480 Robert Hartness Volk 18481 Albert Bayliss Akers 18482 Michael McQuatters Davis 18483 Kie O. Doty 18484 William F. Scheumann 18485 Dean de Laine Johnson 18486 James Donald Bick 18487 Thomas Hubert Hastings 18488 John A. Graham 18489 Teodoro Picado 18490 Jerry Shannon Ingram 18491 **1952** Harry L. Van Trees 18492 Harvey L. Arnold 18493 William L. Shields 18494 John Willard Shy 18495 Edgar Allan Gilbert 18496 George Richard Beiser 18497 Clyde A. Selleck 18498 William Francis Reilly 18499 Richard Davis Moore 18500 Charles Ross Wallis 18501 Edward Emil Wuthrich 18502 James Martin Gerhardt 18503 James H. Wallwork 18504 Thomas Watts Collier 18505 Thomas Walker Nelson 18506 James Bracken Lee 18507 James Watt Maloney 18508 John Douglas Butler 18509 Warren Joseph Hayford 18510 John Glenn Driskill 18511 Thomas Wilford Dowler 18512 Robert Lincoln Morgan 18513 Howell Linson Hodgskin 18514 Alfred F. Lawrence 18515 Thomas E. Courant 18516 Willard Lee McCullough 18517 John V. Foley 18518 Donald Edwin Hegberg 18519 John Lewis Cannon 18520 George M. Tronsrue 18521 Arthur C. Peters 18522 Ivan R. Mechtly 18523 Richard Straw Bullock 18524 David Kenneth Lyon 18525 David Frederick Piske 18526 George Robert Relyea 18527 Harry M. Roper 18528 Max L. Howard 18529 Donald Eugene Sells 18530 Reginald Hardy Mattox 18531 Thomas Frederick Cole 18532 Robert Joseph Haras 18533 John Royal Witherell 18534 Warren A. Spaulding 18535 Louis Vincent Tomasetti 18536 Clinton H. Winne 18537 Thomas Herbert Hobbs 18538 James Harold Sullivan 18539 Richard James Russomano 18540 Thomas Robert Hill 18541 John Edward Carlson 18542 Robert Samuel McGarry 18543 Herbert Deiss 18544 Robert Louis Rutte 18545 John F. Brewer 18546 James Laurence McAndie 18547 Thomas Frank Fiala 18548 Clarence Dunbar Gilkey 18549 Clarence Gerald Ruff 18550 Warren S. O'Sullivan 18551 John Raymond Aker 18552 John Theodore Olson 18553 Harry Stephen Wilson 18554 William L. Horn 18555 William Harold Geatches 18556 James H. Ivers 18557 Robert Earl Wright 18558 Henry Richard Meyer 18559 John William Sadler 18560 John Michael Misch 18561 Joseph A. Bulger 18562 Elmer Gordon Pahre 18563 Lewis Allen Williams 18564 William Paul Snyder 18565 John F. C. Kenney 18566 Joseph Anthony Hannan 18567 Edmund Randall Thompson 18568 Eugene J. Stokes 18569 Michael George Duerr 18570 Lawrence Duane Johnson 18571 Donald Richard Swygert 18572 Donald Gregory Weinert 18573 Lawrence Russell 18574 Thoralf M. Sundt 18575 William Harvey Dana 18576 Ralph Tibbs Garver 18577 Philip John Erdle 18578 Thomas Leese Kelsey 18579 Clyde T. Earnest 18580 Drake Wilson 18581 Daniel William Derbes 18582 Richard Joseph Miller 18583 James Benny Reaves 18584 Glenn H. Palmer 18585 Robert Fredrick Curry Winger 18586 John Christopher Knaggs 18587 Robert E. Day 18588 Robert Neill Kelley 18589 Edward Allen Brown 18590 Charles E. Sell 18591 Ashley Cobb Speir 18592 King James Coffman 18593 Herbert Yale Schandler 18594 Robert Ludwig Ackerson 18595 Leonard Andrew Sluga 18596 Herbert Charles Hollander 18597 Harry Victor Dutchyshyn 18598 Jay Earl Luther 18599 Robert Sylvester Holmes 18600 Paul W. Child 18601 Thomas Aquinas Kiernan 18602 Carl F. Dupke 18603 James Joseph Dietz 18604 Paul Jennings Brown 18605 Jack Richard Pilk 18606 John Edward Ralph 18607 Robert J. Craig 18608 Gilbert Leo Burns 18609 Robert Bruce Kendall 18610 John Dexter Smith 18611 Deane Elliott Welch 18612 Albert C. Lehman 18613 Robert Simpson Tickle 18614 Robert McCrindle 18615 James Eugene McInerney 18616 Frank T. Pimentel 18617 Robert Campbell Rounding 18618 Edward Higgins White 18619 Denis Francis Mullane 18620 Malcolm E. Craig 18621 Dayton Stanley Pickett 18622 Kent Goodwin Knutson 18623 Kenneth Adrian Simonet 18624 Charles William Yocum 18625 Corwin Anderson Mitchell 18626 Thomas Paul Casey 18627 William Alexander Walker 18628 Leon Eugene Lichtenwalter 18629 Birtrun S. Kidwell 18630 Paul B. Malone 18631 James M. Spell 18632 Graham Hildebrand 18633 Homer W. Kiefer 18634 William Russell Raiford 18635 Thomas D. Ayers 18636 John Robinson McLemore 18637 William Jesse Harrison 18638 James Everette Crow 18639 Thomas W. Moore 18640 Everett Dalton Richards 18641 James Edward Underwood 18642 James Arthur Michel 18643 Phillip Bruce Pickering 18644 Edward Eugene Lane 18645 James William Wensyel 18646 Gilbert Theodore Scott 18647 John William Feyrer 18648 Theodore Roosevelt Loeschner 18649 Jack Carl Kleberg 18650 Charles Edward Watkins 18651 John Joseph Halloran 18652 John Bernard Keeley 18653 Deryle Taylor Whipple 18654 Raymond Emmett Wallace 18655 Walter Gray Parks 18656 Kermit Dale Swanson 18657 James F. Lehan 18658 Roy Arthur Young 18659 Gerald Junior Naber 18660 Joseph L. Jordan 18661 Craig Alderman 18662 Donald Hilton Ross 18663 Harold Raymond Lamp 18664 Joseph Richard Paluh 18665 Charles A. Hoenstine 18666 Charles Evans Meikle 18667 Gordon David Carpenter 18668 Kenneth Harold Kronlund 18669 George William Miller 18670 Joseph John Urschel 18671 Cecil Ray Sykes 18672 Richard John Hall 18673 Arthur Rowland Stebbins 18674 Glennon M. Kingsley 18675 Michael Collins 18676 George Robert Dietz 18677 Terrell Butler Mallard 18678 Stephen Edward Nichols 18679 Joseph Clair Austin 18680 Ralph William Girdner 18681 Robert Silber McGowan 18682 Warren Alan Scaman 18683 Ronald Keith Dickinson 18684 William Thomas Leggett 18685 James Horace Reeves 18686 George Robert Underhill 18687 Albert N. Stubblebine 18688 Davis Charles Rohr 18689 Joseph A. De Angelis 18690 Russel Riegel Rentschler 18691 Don M. Bradley 18692 Carl De Leon Broadbent 18693 Clyde William Snodgrass 18694 Raymond Fred Koestner 18695 Robert Donald Woodward 18696 Clarence E. McKnight 18697 Arthur Le Roy Erickson 18698 Arthur P. Deverill 18699 John H. Tipton 18700 Donald Luther Richardson 18701 Preston Tyson Maddocks 18702 Stewart Paterson 18703 James Mitchell Peterson 18704 Ralph M. Cline 18705 Charles Jennings Luther 18706 David Christopher Ahearn 18707 William Guy Britton 18708 John Ross Morgan 18709 John David Bethea 18710 Edmund Albin Thompson 18711 Lewis Edward Beasley 18712 David Grayson Hansard 18713 Robert Nels Shelgren 18714 Robert James Cottey 18715 John Paul Rollston 18716 John Francis Robinson 18717 Robert Wesley Leach 18718 Henry Ingold Lowder 18719 William Charles Moore 18720 Lawrence Haynes Putnam 18721 Kenneth Newlon Good 18722 John Oliver Bovard 18723 John Raymond Espey 18724 John Edward Milner 18725 Larry Scott Mickel 18726 Edgar Byrd McClung 18727 Richard Ernest McCoy 18728 Walter Francis Ulmer 18729 Timothy Metz Seebach 18730 Glenn Alwin Cordell 18731 James Henry Rink 18732 John Landaker Baldner 18733 Edwin Joseph Upton 18734 Milton Dorhan Sullivan 18735 John Joseph Lentz 18736 Gordon Martin Hahn 18737 George Bennett Bartel 18738 Otis Augustus Moran 18739 Frank Barry Smith 18740 Albert J. Dombrowsky 18741 Peter Conower Hains 18742 Thomas Walsh Ashton 18743 Robert Lewis Russell 18744 James Northcutt Walter 18745 Leland Frederick Grossman 18746 Karl A. Woltersdorf 18747 Richard F. De Boalt 18748 John B. Garver 18749 Alvin Russel Gorby 18750 Robert Eugene Hubeli 18751 David Cornelius Bond 18752 Samuel John Hubbard 18753 Charles D. Youree 18754 James Walter Mueller 18755 Frank Eugene Robinson 18756 William L. Mitchell 18757 Richard J. Weyhrich 18758 Robert N. Wells 18759 Richard Xavier Larkin 18760 Karl George Koenig 18761 Frank Christopher Benedict 18762 Gerald Goodwin Gibbs 18763 Blair Buckley 18764 Stanley J. Kuick 18765 Henry Goldsborough Moseley 18766 Richard Neil Lang 18767 Thomas James McClung 18768 James Dickerson Hogan 18769 Theodore Osmer Gregory 18770 Thomas Arthur Rehm 18771 Louis Lawrence Churchill 18772 William J. Seaver 18773 Richard Thomas Shea 18774 Warren Howard Eisenhart 18775 Donald Rex Lasher 18776 William Lee Linkenhoger 18777 Emmett A. Niblack 18778 Robert Bennett King 18779 Arthur C. Elmore 18780 Richard Elmer Stanier 18781 Richard Joseph Rogers 18782 David Henry Martin 18783 John Adams Hettinger 18784 Jack Ward Burkheimer 18785 William DeWitt Gordon 18786 Robert Louis Craine 18787 Arthur E. Taylor 18788 Howard Hamilton Danford 18789 Charles Allen Edwards 18790 Benjamin M. Grafton 18791 Kenneth John Keating 18792 Frank A. Boyer 18793 Roy Nelson Berry 18794 Kennis Earl Lockard 18795 Leo Hugh Lennon 18796 Edmund Joseph Reinhalter 18797 Raymond F. Norton 18798 Robert Peter Pfeil 18799 Jeffrey Douglas Knight 18800 Gerald Alvin Kutz 18801 Francis Xavier Keilt 18802 Robert Lewis Wetzel 18803 Robert H. Dunn 18804 Harvey Herbert Perritt 18805 Reynold Thomas 18806 Vincent Patrick Bailey 18807 William Dearborn Landon 18808 Ronald Marvin Obach 18809 Donald Vance Pafford 18810 Henry Meadows West 18811 Peter Cotterill King 18812 Alfred Charles Griffin 18813 Alfred Lawrence Thieme 18814 Henry F. Carter 18815 Graham Wharton Rider 18816 Robert Preston Hand 18817 William Paul Bingham 18818 Elmer Mason Jenkins 18819 Arthur L. Webster 18820 James Richard Wiggins 18821 David Alfred Eachus 18822 Edward Norris Eckert 18823 Stephen W. Swatt 18824 Louis Francis Morin 18825 John Joseph Sullivan 18826 Freeman Luke Pendleton 18827 Robert Gene Kimmel 18828 Ralph Edmund Leonard 18829 Robert Angelo Carlone 18830 Laurean Thomas Esian 18831 Williams Ludwell Harrison 18832 James W. Woodward 18833 Hugh H. Broadhurst 18834 James Richard Erwine 18835 James Abel Rodrigues 18836 Robert Franklin Freeman 18837 Thomas Nelson Ellis 18838 John Craig Mauer 18839 Gerald J. Carey 18840 Carroll Valentine Jackson 18841 James E. Spence 18842 Raymond Joseph Tensfeldt 18843 Paul Allen Gray 18844 Douglas Alan Slingerland 18845 George W. Bowman 18846 Robert L. Sears 18847 Bruce Raymond Beard 18848 Ercell C. Hamilton 18849 Daniel Peter McMahon 18850 George L. Rule 18851 Michael Pettiss Juvenal 18852 Robert H. Truax 18853 Frederick A. Stevens 18854 Larry Boland Lucas 18855 James Stratton Pettit 18856 Joseph Edward Wasiak 18857 Philip D. Coleman 18858 Robert Joseph Wheeler 18859 Richard Carlton Coleman 18860 James Monroe Beasley 18861 Adalbert E. Toepel 18862 James Edward McDonnell 18863 Keith Lynn Comstock 18864 Louis McAlester Davis 18865 Wayne Neville White 18866 James H. Aldredge 18867 William Biffle Boyles 18868 Peter Craig Withers 18869 Gonzalo Maximo Casas 18870 Joseph N. Jaggers 18871 Raymond Owen Bergeson 18872 Robert Lansing Palmer 18873 James Lyons Tow 18874 Ernest Francis Condina 18875 Orville F. Ireland 18876 John Hiram Lewis 18877 Franklin Lawrence Reeder 18878 Thomas Daniel Pace 18879 Juan Guerrero Burciaga 18880 Raymond Carl Jess 18881 Herbert D. Vogel 18882 Donald Joe Gray 18883 Charles Norman Rainey 18884 Joseph F. Santilli 18885 Harold Kingston Peters 18886 Robert Everett Hatton 18887 Alfred McRae Bracy 18888 Donald Arthur Nixon 18889 Mahlon G. Weed 18890 William Albert Myers 18891 Edwin P. Horan 18892 Charles Sanford Steen 18893 John Vandever Gibney 18894 Donald William Barton 18895 Arthur B. De Wald 18896 George Franklin Barkley 18897 James E. Campbell 18898 James Harold Bremer 18899 Jerome Ira Brisman 18900 Robert Brooks Richardson 18901 Robert Louis Korchek 18902 James Edwin Armstrong 18903 Loyd P. Rhiddlehoover 18904 James Justice Turner 18905 Louis C. Bryan 18906 Robert Neal Hulley 18907 Leith J. Corbridge 18908 Edward Joseph Jelen 18909 Daniel Burnett Knight 18910 John Frederick Bart 18911 Thomas Theodore Brodin 18912 Richard Isaiah Wiles 18913 Thomas Selby Dunmire 18914 Winfield Andrew Holt 18915 Charles Vincent Harvey 18916 Philip W. Hamilton 18917 Robert Everett Durie 18918 Richard George Inman 18919 Owen C. Holleran 18920 John George Hill 18921 William A. Copthorne 18922 John W. Cooke 18923 Alfred Emanuel Smith Burkhard 18924 Richard Francis Lamb 18925 Ivan Ward King 18926 Thomas Edward Fitzpatrick 18927 Donald Nelson Williamson 18928 George L. MacGarrigle 18929 Wilbur Allen Ross 18930 Frank A. Allen 18931 William Howard Ritter 18932 MacPherson Conner 18933 William Herbert Duncan 18934 Arthur B. Custis 18935 Richard Briggs Haskell 18936 John R. Hermann 18937 Albert I. Lorenzen 18938 Robert Winfield Vining 18939 Joe Don Hendrickson 18940 Richard Byrd Ray 18941 Robert Turner Smyth 18942 Wesley Gale Jones 18943 Thomas John Murphy 18944 John Edward Panchisin 18945 Lope Baladad Rimando 18946 Joseph H. Devins 18947 Horace Whitley Brown 18948 Oscar Morales-Duvall 18949 Douglas G. Ludlam 18950 Thomas Edward Walls 18951 Wayne Houston Elliott 18952 Albert G. W. Biddle 18953 Harry H. Baird 18954 Sherman Lile Webster 18955 Daniel H. Hoge 18956 Richard Julian Baker 18957 Arthur Gerard Jackson 18958 William Bamford Holden 18959 Howard Charles Jelinek 18960 Kermit Wayne Bell 18961 Louis J. Rajchel 18962 Steven Zellem 18963 Bernard Morton Ashkenaze 18964 Richard F. Doody 18965 Vann A. Brewster 18966 Michael Alan Boos 18967 Manuel Jose Asensio 18968 William Thomas Waldrop 18969 Robert B. Tanguy 18970 William Gerard Finn 18971 Norbert Joseph Szymczyk 18972 John Macik 18973 Thompson Cummings 18974 Melvin Asher Young 18975 Joseph T. Clement 18976 Joseph Searle Simon 18977 James Patrick Paris 18978 Jorge Rene Pereyra 18979 William Patrick Gleason 18980 Wallace H. Hastings 18981 Marcus Ray Oliphant 18982 Raymond Ellwood Lash 18983 Neal Anthony Lespasio 18984 Lewis Joshua Henderson 18985 Graham Lacy Humble 18986 William H. Spencer 18987 Robert C. Turner 18988 John DeWitt Pelton 18989 William S. Schroeder 18990 William Norman Cowan 18991 John Thomas Quinn 18992 Harry Dwight Wagner 18993 Daniel Boone 18994 John Hanford Claybrook 18995 Loren Read Brooks 18996 David S. Smith 18997 Orin Robert Hilmo 18998 Raymond Charles Simmons 18999 James Wright Cain 19000 Scott H. Shipe 19001 Martin Joseph Celec 19002 Kelso A. Carroll 19003 Arthur Thomas Martin 19004 Robert Lawrence Burke 19005 Robert Shean Riley 19006 Carl Boyd Guess 19007 William James McClelland 19008 Marsden P. Earle 19009 Eugene Patrick Flanagan 19010 Alfred Emmanuel Crehan 19011 James Oliver Day 19012 James McGehee Lynch 19013 Stanley Lee Gregg 19014 Charles Van Der Veer Yarbrough 19015 George A. Grayeb 19016 Terry de la Mesa Allen 19017 Louis Celestino Scalzo 19018 **1953** Ed D. Davis 19019 Henry Augustus Flertzheim 19020 Raymond John Eineigl 19021 Edward Porcher Andrews 19022 Elvin R. Heiberg 19023 James Louis Lammie 19024 Thomas Daniel Mingledorff 19025 Allen Frederick Grum 19026 Arthur Johnson Cates 19027 Herman Louis Gilster 19028 James Lamar Appleton 19029 James Scarborough Sibley 19030 Robert Graham Bartlett 19031 Richard Edward Leonard 19032 Paul Eugene Suplizio 19033 Alvin Leo Hayes 19034 Glenn Edwin Schweitzer 19035 James R. Knox 19036 William Robert Bell 19037 Herbert Erb Friesen 19038 Michael Edward Kallman 19039 John Paul Angstadt 19040 Curtis Anderson Brewer 19041 Rodney Howe Smith 19042 Roy Leslie Sullivan 19043 Joe Harry Sheard 19044 Early Joseph Rush 19045 Charles James Fiala 19046 Jerald Lee Goetz 19047 Robert Eastman Ayers 19048 John Andrew Brinsko 19049 Roger Paddock Ellman 19050 Robert Erwin Barton 19051 Charles Maurice Lavender 19052 Craig West Gridley 19053 Harold Curtis Porter 19054 Sidney Wheeler Carter 19055 Edward Arthur Daggit 19056 Max Wilbur Noah 19057 Thorwald Roger Peterson 19058 O. Kirk Ehlers 19059 Kenneth Stanley Heitzke 19060 Laurence Walter Crevoiserat 19061 John Major Schuessler 19062 Donald Francis Davis 19063 Walter Henry Schmidt 19064 George Frye Garey 19065 John Beltz Hazlebeck 19066 Lawrence Byron Tatum 19067 Frederick Pratt Reynolds 19068 Bernard Charles Hughes 19069 Robert Lee Alexander 19070 Robert Norris White 19071 John Robert Eric Tumperi 19072 John Robert McDonald 19073 Glenn Kay Otis 19074 Donald Alexander Ramsay 19075 Leo Clare Morton 19076 Joseph Karl Brown 19077 G. Gerald Lohrli 19078 George Louis Egbert 19079 Maarten Vet 19080 Henry Lawrence Davisson 19081 James Francis McCluskey 19082 James Alfred Eubanks 19083 Fred L. Smith 19084 James Richard Effer 19085 Robert John Porter 19086 Ralph Longwell Sanders 19087 William Dudley Jones 19088 Robert Lee Crosby 19089 Alan Toops Horwedel 19090 William Russell Davis 19091 Richard Fleming Fischer 19092 William Arthur Burkhardt 19093 Howard Richards Matson 19094 Robert Clay Karns 19095 Robert William Hess 19096 Ollin Kemp Dozier 19097 John Smith Glenn 19098 Egerton King van den Berg 19099 Thomas H. Jones 19100 Andrew Michael Simko 19101 Albert Nelson Tardiff 19102 Anthony Peter Deluca 19103 Victor Luby 19104 William Jackson Jefferson 19105 Eugene Lee Fitzsimmons 19106 Milton Anthony Chojnowski 19107 Edgar Allen O'Hair 19108 Frederick George Gilmartin 19109 Donald Gary Fuqua 19110 Sam Ward Clay 19111 Frank Morehead Drew 19112 William Henry Stuart 19113 Walter F. Stepanek 19114 John William Seigle 19115 Hubert Wesley Lacquement 19116 Wayne Faessler Alch 19117 Morton Robert Saffer 19118 David Andrew Pistenmaa 19119 Hal Boyd Rhyne 19120 Charles Morgan Butler 19121 Joseph Clay Wilson 19122 G. Peter Bidstrup 19123 Guy Ernest Waller 19124 Arthur Leroy Spooner 19125 John Bullock Fitch 19126 Marion Alexander Todd 19127 Robert Lewis Kaplan 19128 George Allen Haas 19129 Richard Donald Boyle 19130 Harold Peyton Wheeler 19131 Greeley Horace Ellis 19132 Fred Kenneth Thompson 19133 Richard Thomas Remers 19134 Francis Vernon Gay 19135 Norman George Delbridge 19136 Edward Charles Metzcher 19137 John Powell Jones 19138 Montecue Judson Lowry 19139 David DuBois Horner 19140 Arthur A. Arduna 19141 Maxwell Rogers Murrell 19142 Arthur Raymond Phipps 19143 Randolph Vincent Araskog 19144 David Idris Lodwick 19145 Denell Delbert Zander 19146 John Baptist Oblinger 19147 Allen T. Lindholm 19148 Harold E. Gartrell 19149 Thomas Roger Canham 19150 John Toman 19151 William Dearl Horton 19152 Richard Day Lawrence 19153 Erhart Edward Demand 19154 Robert James Albert 19155 Bart Michael Filaseta 19156 Robert Daniel Rose 19157 Charles Joseph McGinn 19158 David A. Best 19159 James R. Stuart 19160 Raymond Ludwig Wm. Schroder 19161 Herbert Dean Peckham 19162 Stanley Valentine Wielga 19163 James Richard Endler 19164 James Paul Wade 19165 Ross Bruce Kenzie 19166 Robert Bruce Beveridge 19167 William Maddox Jewell 19168 John H.F. Haskell 19169 James Homer Elliott 19170 Gary Wayne Robbins 19171 Henry Earl Clements 19172 Lauren Steve Davis 19173 Dick Duane Neu 19174 John Charles Hall 19175 Neal Creighton 19176 Donald Joseph Hamilla 19177 Tom Harvey Brain 19178 Roy Fowler 19179 Mortimer Lenane O'Connor 19180 Dennis Dexter Whalen 19181 John Phillip Maher 19182 Burden Brentnall 19183 Robert Segal 19184 Ralph Arthur Koch 19185 John Francis Martin 19186 Louis Ernest Manfre 19187 Dyke McCarty 19188 William E. Rawlinson 19189 Jeremiah Joseph Brophy 19190 Robert Alexander Carter 19191 George Donald Waters 19192 John Richard Temp 19193 Bruce B. Hardy 19194 Donald Howard Becker 19195 Donald Lee Wilson 19196 Walter C. Cousland 19197 Robert LaFavor Smith 19198 Thomas Conant Davis 19199 Carl Lee Hammond 19200 Irvin Gray Kinnie 19201 Richard Raymond Davis 19202 Robert Eugene Butler 19203 John D. Meglen 19204 Donald Roger Martin 19205 Arthur Edmon Brown 19206 Charles Joseph Lowman 19207 Edwin Reed 19208 Robert F. Rogers 19209 Thomas Edward Nesbitt 19210 Donald Leslie Carter 19211 Ellietson David Rogers 19212 Joseph Richardson Walters 19213 Charles Mossi Borrell 19214 William August Miotke 19215 Adolph Ernest Mayer 19216 Gaillard Alvin Freimark 19217 Clarence Edgar Talley 19218 Allen Steventon Merritt 19219 Gerald Wilson Corprew 19220 Frank Joseph Marinaro 19221 Richard Gregg Vander Meer 19222 James Lawrence Jackson 19223 Jimmy Lee Pigg 19224 James Windle Hogg 19225 James Francis Miley 19226 William Wofford Hilley 19227 Thomas Edgar Williams 19228 Harold Elmer Bauer 19229 James Henry Harris 19230 Donald Wilbur Dunnuck 19231 Francis R. Hoyt 19232 Jack Odell Hayes 19233 John Coghill Phillips 19234 C. Clark

Neilson 19235 John Joseph Pimental 19236 Louis Chadwick Friedersdorff 19237 John R. Krobock 19238 Thomas Eugene Anderson 19239 Raymond Vincent Kotowski 19240 Robert Theodore Zargan 19241 James Robert Lindsay 19242 Drew Dowling 19243 Charles Joseph Tighe 19244 Charles E. Bishop 19245 David Lawrence Motycka 19246 John Worth Olsen 19247 Robert Joseph Thomas 19248 Daniel Paul Christman 19249 Louis Albert Kaufman 19250 William Walter Weihmiller 19251 William Louis Wubbena 19252 Donald Leonard Meyer 19253 Floyd Phillip Barrow 19254 John Hughes Young 19255 Gary Sherman Colonna 19256 Patton North Morrison 19257 William Franklin Sifford 19258 James Preston Selbe 19259 Joe John Volpe 19260 George John Dimtsios 19261 Gregorio Ramos Vigilar 19262 Benjamin Ray Battle 19263 Frank Anthony Iacobucci 19264 Harry Warren Halterman 19265 Joseph Paul Perlow 19266 James Gunder Hove 19267 Russell Glen Groshans 19268 John E. Johnson 19269 Robert Alan Boxell 19270 Donald Richard Schmidt 19271 Graham Wilson McIntyre 19272 Edgar Howard Smith 19273 Keith Leroy Born 19274 Robert Michael Joyce 19275 Arthur David Wells 19276 Allan Chester Biggerstaff 19277 Francis A. Nerone 19278 Robert Warren Blum 19279 Fred S. Taylor 19280 James Edgar Jones 19281 Robert Keith Potter 19282 Keith G. Kahl 19283 Graham Daniel Vernon 19284 Samuel Morgan Thomas 19285 Herbert Raymond Schmidt 19286 William Wilbur Yuengel 19287 Norman William Birchler 19288 Jack Allen Merrigan 19289 Otto Neal Riley 19290 Benjamin Eugene Tant 19291 Howard Barnett Thompson 19292 Dale Bernard Peloquin 19293 Douglas Richard Sliger 19294 Melburn Edward Laundry 19295 Stephen A. Belgau 19296 Max Earl Satchell 19297 James Andrew Currie 19298 Donald Earl Shaw 19299 Wallace William Noll 19300 Sam Burge Barrett 19301 Thomas John Victor Thorpe 19302 Gordon Allen Curran 19303 John William Parks 19304 James Frederick Bleecker 19305 Robert Lewis Schroeder 19306 Donald Lee McNutt 19307 Cary Brown Hutchinson 19308 Hiram Kellow Tompkins 19309 Roland Richard Sullivan 19310 William Alva Cole 19311 Harl Goronway Graham 19312 William Brooksbank Burdeshaw 19313 Rob Roy McGregor 19314 William Clyde Stinson 19315 John David Smythe 19316 Robert Francis Daly 19317 Jerry Wallace Nicks 19318 Robert Eugene Scofield 19319 Felix Lee Liveoak 19320 George Dudley Brosious 19321 Gilbert Andrew Volker 19322 Charles Emmett Harvey Edward 19323 William J. Campbell 19324 Alfred Mathiasen 19325 Montgomery Theodore Speir 19326 Robert Louis Rush 19327 Peter Smith Conzelman 19328 Donald Kunkel Sykes 19329 Richard Paul Geer 19330 Richard Alden Young 19331 Earl Ledlie Chambers 19332 Roger Littlefield Roderick 19333 Robert John Laflam 19334 Charles Willis Zipp 19335 Ramon Diaz Gonzalez-Artigas 19336 Frank Albert Mleko 19337 Thomas Oliver Pickett 19338 Ralph S. Greer 19339 Leon S. Zimmer 19340 Robert Laurence Mangels 19341 Frank Stanley Wilkerson 19342 Lewis Sutton Andrews 19343 Clay Bradford Jackson 19344 Douglas Gordon Waters 19345 James Edward Linka 19346 John Frederick Stoneburner 19347 James Wallace Leland 19348 James Joseph McGee 19349 Arthur Basil Shaw 19350 Henry Oswald Schneider 19351 James Gordon Donahue 19352 Harry Edwin Dunivant 19353 Edward A. Dinges 19354 Richard L. Durham 19355 William Raymond Colvin 19356 Leland C. Rew 19357 Russell Andrew Baker 19358 Theodore Darwin King 19359 Robert Olin Connor 19360 Guy S. Meloy 19361 John E. Wise 19362 Eugene R. Soja 19363 Richard W. Phillips 19364 David Kemper Rice 19365 Samuel H. Fisher 19366 Thomas Hoffman 19367 Donald Stewart Brown 19368 Halvor Hegland Myrah 19369 Richard Joseph Tchon 19370 Arthur Howard Ackerman 19371 David T. Wells 19372 Joseph Theodore Rears 19373 Alfred Esper Paulekas 19374 Eugene Randolph Currier 19375 John Derek Van Wyk 19376 H. Beecher Dierdorff 19377 Constantine James Blastos 19378 Kenneth E. Dawson 19379 James Leonard Dade 19380 Robert B. Maehr 19381 William James Sutton 19382 Clifford John Landry 19383 William Edward Walker 19384 Thomas Wesley Holcombe 19385 George Frederick Williams 19386 Thomas Daniel Brown 19387 John J. McFaull 19388 Lowell H. Skidmore 19389 Stuart Glover McLennan 19390 William A. Jolin 19391 Clifford Worthy 19392 John Brian Tanzer 19393 Robert Charles Breckenridge 19394 William Kunz Snead 19395 Donald A. Dennis 19396 Sarkis Semerjian 19397 Edward V. Coggins 19398 Frank C. Kincaid 19399 James Richard Bambery 19400 Elbert E. Fuller 19401 Daniel Edward Walker 19402 John Robert Englehart 19403 Craig Garrison Coverdale 19404 Kenneth John Sweeney 19405 Charles James Doryland 19406 James O. Dritt 19407 Stanley B. Sovern 19408 James Michael Burkland 19409 Rodney Miles French 19410 Lloyd Warren Boothby 19411 Monty William Walters 19412 Edward L. P. Bishop 19413 Edward Thomas Lynch 19414 Jerome F. O'Malley 19415 Herbert Sylvester Schaeffer 19416 Jack Walter Myers 19417 Daniel Sprague Rickard 19418 Jack Elvia Morton 19419 Ralph Edward Hickey 19420 Harold James Sarbacher 19421 William Heasley Harris 19422 Joseph Francis McGovern 19423 Louis C. Boone 19424 Paul Clinton Vose 19425 Charles William Prime 19426 David H. Rumbough 19427 Dale Ellwood Davis 19428 William F. Bauman 19429 Rocco F. Ventrella 19430 Ralph Carling Rich 19431 Worth L. Wardlaw 19432 Haydon Y. Grubbs 19433 William Donovan Renner 19434 Robert Nclasco Fernandez 19435 Martin Irwin Silberg 19436 Karl Richard Stewart 19437 Elden Q. Faust 19438 Robert H. Nutter 19439 James O. Sammons 19440 Thomas McGregor 19441 Frederic Gustave Agather 19442 James Alfred Loedding 19443 Sheldon Jerome Lustig 19444 Thomas Patrick McKenna 19445 John Lyman Balcom Bringham 19446 Gene Allen Seegmueller 19447 Frederick John Siebert 19448 Richard Allen Townsend 19449 LeRoy Perry Ades 19450 Donald Wayne Norris 19451 Richard Warren Flather 19452 John Calhoun Hammond 19453 Richard Wesley Cordill 19454 Robert George Day 19455 Walter Henderson 19456 Robert Evans Glasgow 19457 Robert Norman Martin 19458 Stephen J. Vogel 19459 Frederick French Van Deusen 19460 Arthur La Von Mavis 19461 Charles Oliver Neal 19462 Leonard James Greeley 19463 Charles E. Ramsgate 19464 William Talmadge Crim 19465 Francis Joseph Doyle 19466 Henry Purcell 19467 Jack Edwards Johns 19468 Lee Bond Gray 19469 Thomas George Sofis 19470 John J. P. Scoblick 19471 James R. Landreth 19472 William A. Fio Rito 19473 Miguel A. Bethencourt 19474 James Coleman Pfautz 19475 John Francis Jamieson 19476 Paul Edsel Floyd 19477 Raymond Cecil Conder 19478 Leland Patrick Luck 19479 Edward Kimmel Burdeau 19480 Francisco Roberto Prieto 19481 Chalmers Leslie Brewbaker 19482 Jack Adams Neuberger 19483 Charles J. Cheves 19484 Robert Tyler Beaucond 19485 Frederick William Glauner 19486 Edward L. Rhodes 19487 John Heughes Crerar 19488 Reubin Wallis Cochran 19489 John William Calvert 19490 James Tun Dare 19491 John W. Hughes 19492 Francis George LaBrash 19493 Richard Arthur Benz 19494 Gerald Eli Dresner 19495 John Anthony Nave 19496 John Walker Yale 19497 Howard Hazlett 19498 Thomas John Nugent 19499 John Robert Harmon 19500 William John Hosmer 19501 Conrad Mansur Osborn 19502 D. Clark Smith 19503 Rolfe Gunter Arnhym 19504 Bernard F. Hurless 19505 James E. Bowen 19506 Ennis A. Viereck 19507 Angel C. Ravelo 19508 John Philip Ceglowski 19509 Carson E. R. Holman 19510 Paul David Tomlingson 19511 Stanford M. Touchstone 19512 Walter Eugene Parker 19513 John Jay Burns 19514 Raymond Charles Rohlman 19515 Richard A. Miller 19516 Douglas S. Kimball 19517 Thomas Clifford Rote 19518 John Everett Hogan 19519 Adrian Pryor Reed 19520 Robert L. Dean 19521 Hugh J. Hall 19522 Joe Cecil Williams 19523 Jack Dale Wilson 19524 John Olin Cooper 19525 Francis Snyder 19526 Courtland C. Nordgren 19527 William Arthur Strickland 19528 John Howard Cooper 19529 Raymond John Lesinski 19530 **1954** Marion Frank Meador 19531 John Chapman Bard 19532 Richard Albert Farmer 19533 Donald Fred Newnham 19534 David Randolph Scott 19535 Walter John Martin 19536 Jackson Daniel Dennis 19537 Ames Scribner Albro 19538 Philip Lyman Brewster 19539 Gustav J. Freyer 19540 William L. Allan 19541 Paul Miller 19542 Harry E. B. Sullivan 19543 Lewis A. Mologne 19544 Marion Glenn Creath 19545 Paul Cyr Driscoll 19546 Richard Babcock Tyler 19547 Melvyn Douglas Remus 19548 William Locke Hauser 19549 Douglas Golding Dwyre 19550 Franklin Augustus Hart 19551 Richard Wright Hobbs 19552 Donald Palmer Shaw 19553 Robert Eldred Goodwin 19554 David L. Dimick 19555 Robert J. Morris 19556 Warren Alexander Samouce 19557 Dale Allen Vesser 19558 James Arthur Kriegh 19559 Richard Hunt Benfer 19560 William E. Albright 19561 William Lewis Wallace 19562 Teodorico Poblete Sanchez 19563 G. Wayne Cantrell 19564 James Henry Ahmann 19565 James J. Truscott 19566 Floyd Earl Siefferman 19567 William Henry Stroh 19568 William Young Epling 19569 Warren T. Palmer 19570 Andre George Broumas 19571 John A. Poteat 19572 Edwin Charles Keiser 19573 Richard Wells Diller 19574 Frederick Mertens Galloway 19575 Robert B. Sale 19576 Louis Gross 19577 Don McKnight Larson 19578 Charles Alan Debelius 19579 William Albert Orth 19580 Loren Mason Eberhart 19581 James Langton Carroll 19582 Earl D. Payne 19583 Alvin P. White 19584 Jack Richard Logan 19585 Robert Moffat Elton 19586 Bill Thomas Thompson 19587 Bradley John Honholt 19588 Louis Richard Mentillo 19589 Marvin Robert Kortum 19590 James Morrison Miller 19591 James Nick Halvatgis 19592 Henry Wallace Butler 19593 Kennon Bailey Stewart 19594 George Wayne Chancellor 19595 Maximiano R. Janairo 19596 James Myron Kirwin 19597 James William Daughtry 19598 Stanley Foster Choate 19599 Carl James Stark 19600 John Thomas Miller 19601 Darrell R. Anderson 19602 Joseph T. Palastra 19603 Rufus Daniel Hutcheson 19604 William Armstrong Boucher 19605 James J. Fraher 19606 John Richard Zartman 19607 Francis Carter Cobb 19608 Richard Harvey Sugg 19609 Frederick Byrd Bowling 19610 James Merton Lee Karns 19611 James Edward Thomas 19612 Mark Arthur McDermott 19613 Louis Carson Wagner 19614 Robert J. Harvey 19615 H. Everett Drugge 19616 Grayson C. Woodbury 19617 James Myron Zerkel 19618 James Robert Henry 19619 Charles David Richards 19620 Wilbur Craig Buckheit 19621 Richard Joseph Vossler 19622 Charles Robert Linton 19623 Sterling P. A. Darling 19624 Lloyd Jean Matthews 19625 Robert Malcolm McPherson 19626 Gerald Anthony Lodge 19627 George Theodore Neu 19628 George Stanley Kourakos 19629 Hugh Granville Robinson 19630 James Lee Scovel 19631 Robert Peter Kraujalis 19632 Eugene Francis Wirth 19633 William Pettit Boyd 19634 Sebastian Ambros Lasher 19635 Harold Frederick Barnes 19636 Leon Lester Kortz 19637 Clifford T. Flanigan 19638 Peter Walton Johnson 19639 John Lawson Ballantyne 19640 James Robert Randall 19641 Charles Donald Wood 19642 John Thomas Purdy 19643 Thomas Raymond Shukay 19644 John H. Farrar 19645 Richard Mack Renfro 19646 James Edward Dalton 19647 Thomas C. Young 19648 Gerald Herbert Parshall 19649 Charles E. Miller 19650 John Ernest Tilley 19651 Roger Russell Kolker 19652 Fletcher James Buckley 19653 Perry Louis Studt 19654 Joseph Ganahl 19655 Maurice Howard Leiser 19656 Richard Irwin Boe 19657 James Summers Knox 19658 James Edward Giles 19659 Milton L. Aitken 19660 Julius O. Thomas 19661 Richardson M. Bentley 19662 Raynor Garey 19663 Robert Merrill Gomez 19664 James Ellis Hays 19665 Robert James Ellis 19666 Virl Edward Haas 19667 Benjamin F. Breslauer 19668 Jack Donald Horner 19669 Leroy Thomas Lunn 19670 William Robert Baldwin 19671 Arnold Henry Winkelman 19672 Norman Hubert Bedell 19673 Richard E. Littlefield 19674 James Maclay Ingalls 19675 "Charles E., Jr. Storrs 19676" Robert Thomas Reed 19677 James H. Sloan 19678 James Frederick Ransone 19679 Gordon David Boose 19680 Robert Charles Riese 19681 Russell Wayne Parker 19682 John Herbert Klingberg 19683 John Henry Lohman 19684 Frederick Martin Anklam 19685 Alan Vinton Richard 19686 Robert Horace Muns 19687 Frederic Marvin Schweiger 19688 William McDonald Egan 19689 Thomas Holl Paprocki 19690 Clark Hamilton Benn 19691 Walter Clair Schrupp 19692 James Darwin Chandler 19693 George William Riess 19694 George Harrison Hilt 19695 John Alfred Wesner 19696 Arthur Frederick Lykke 19697 Samuel Lee Halliday 19698 George W. Kronsbein 19699 Daniel J. O'Mara 19700 Richard Dunphy Youngflesh 19701 James G. Plunkett 19702 Eldon T. Dahl 19703 Craig Eugene Mahaffy 19704 Robert Eugene Chapman 19705 Elliott Wesley Gritton 19706 John Kent Stephenson 19707 Alvin Sherman Milder 19708 David Peter Thoreson 19709 James Rufus Whitley 19710 John Severance Chesbro 19711 Duane Louis Hogan 19712 Joseph Rankin James 19713 Kenneth Edward Luckey 19714 Robert Ervin Ley 19715 Matthew P. Murphy 19716 Kerwood Wagner Barrand 19717 Prosper Newton Walker 19718 Jesse George Moore 19719 Luke L. Callaway 19720 Leland Roy Wood 19721 Edward Earl Roderick 19722 Robert Kenneth Garwood 19723 Robert Hugh Tawes 19724 Thomas D. Flaherty 19725 John Anthony Sulik 19726 Lewis H. Ham 19727 Lee Boardman Thackwray 19728 James Riley Stanley 19729 John George Pappageorge 19730 Leonard Hayes Fuller 19731 Robert J. Washer 19732 James E. Moore 19733 Leonard L. Griggs 19734 George William Milligan 19735 Gene Lynn Breeding 19736 Frederic John Delamain 19737 Robert Domenic Cicchinelli 19738 Edward O. Judd 19739 Frank Bentley Tiffany 19740 Edward W. McCloskey 19741 Francis Alphonse Ianni 19742 James Henry Slogar 19743 William Joseph Hilsman 19744 Allan C. Sterling 19745 Charles Duncan Beaumont 19746 Edward Merillat Moses 19747 William F. Acers 19748 Paul Gustav Erickson 19749 Jack Alton Lochner 19750 John Archie Koskella 19751 Orbun Fedrick Qualls 19752 Joseph James Heed 19753 James Warren Diebold 19754 James Francis Healy 19755 Craig Hamilton Spence 19756 Edward Perry Hart 19757 LuVern James Wooge 19758 Cornelius J. Sullivan 19759 Edward Albert Partridge 19760 Jerry James Curtis 19761 John R. LeMere 19762 John Elder Marcus 19763 Wilson C. Barnes 19764 Robert William Wells 19765 Ozro Richard Steigelman 19766 William R. Schulz 19767 Oliver B. Combs 19768 Lawrence Franklin Skibbie 19769 William Dean Liby 19770 Thomas Patrick Martin 19771 Kenneth Eugene Brant 19772 Edwin Eric Passmore 19773 Vincent Robert Suppicich 19774 John D'Aura 19775 Stanford Christian Pilet 19776 William D. Old 19777 Clarence William Hannon 19778 Andre Cavaro Lucas 19779 Ira Coron 19780 Richard Watts Griffin 19781 Norman A. Matthias 19782 Jerome Hartford Anderson 19783 Charles D. Ryan 19784 James Henry Brodt 19785 Louis Leon Bryant 19786 John Patrick Januleski 19787 Francis Lee Revere 19788 Duane Adams McMartin 19789 Henry James Mehserle 19790 Peter Charles Bunevich 19791 Duane Harold Erickson 19792 Francis J. Percy 19793 Joseph Aloysius Devlin 19794 Victor J. Hugo 19795 Edward Almon Saville 19796 Richard Bradshaw Moulton 19797 John Robert Borgatta 19798 Thomas Francis Healy 19799 Fred Holcomb Bartlit 19800 Joseph Masuck 19801 Thomas Alfred Stark 19802 Robert William Badger 19803 Daniel James Tobin 19804 William P. Emley 19805 Douglas J. O'Connor 19806 William Joseph Almon 19807 William Joseph Vipraio 19808 Manfred Allen Schalk 19809 Herbert Evans Williams 19810 Phillip Dean Vollmann 19811 Larimer Cushman McFarlane 19812 Owen E. Belville 19813 Robert Felts Anthis 19814 Hal William Howes 19815 Barron Fredricks 19816 Paul Hansen Reistrup 19817 Harlan Leslie Gurney 19818 Loren Verne Hart 19819 Newell E. Vinson 19820 Ronald Joseph Lemanski 19821 Kenneth Holmes Bell 19822 Paul Vincent Powers 19823 James Howard Kyker 19824 Jay Thomas Edwards 19825 Jerrold Martin North 19826 Robert Dill Resley 19827 Carl Richard Steimle 19828 Douglas Baird Stuart 19829 Benjamin Franklin Schemmer 19830 Robert James Blaisdell 19831 Robert Burnley Egelston 19832 Laurence Burton Bonner 19833 Fred Standwood Lindsey 19834 John M. Stark 19835 Alexander Patrick Dyer 19836 Donald Madison Rhea 19837 William Charles Royals 19838 John Nicholas Weiler 19839 Wilson Harry Nickerson 19840 Robert Earl Downen 19841 Gary Paul Thomas 19842 William Robert McKenney 19843 Louis J. Bahin 19844 Lawrence T. Drum 19845 John Rogers Galvin 19846 Peter Gaylord Jones 19847 James Weldon Surber 19848 Ralph E. Ennis 19849 Donald Clare Porter 19850 William Eldridge Odom 19851 William Jerome Weafer 19852 John Ismert Hincke 19853 Herbert Willoughby Booth 19854 Fred Kersh 19855 Kenneth Royale Sipes 19856 Donald Frederick Panzer 19857 Jack Maurice Beringer 19858 Allen L. Jennings 19859 Donald Gene Lewis 19860 Lee Edward Gilbreth 19861 Robert E. Fromm 19862 Lewis A. Walser 19863 Cyrus S. Avery 19864 Willis Garrett Bacon 19865 Ray Daniel Pace 19866 Jerome Henry Holmlund 19867 John Charles Eitel 19868 William A. Gager 19869 Robert L. Bullock 19870 Quinton Davis 19871 Robert Eugene Dorr 19872 Michael Drahushak Drake 19873 Paul Raymond Garneau 19874 John William Hudachek 19875 James Frederick Gibson 19876 John Robert Klein 19877 Henry S. Carroll 19878 William M. McVeigh 19879 Robert James Bullington 19880 Roman Joseph Peisinger 19881 Raymond F. Allen 19882 Ronald Frederick Gamble 19883 Warren James Alverson 19884 Thomas Wiley Moore 19885 Quay Carlton Snyder 19886 Charles McCabe Luce 19887 H. C. Tanner 19888 Andrew J. Maloney 19889 Chester Joseph Piolunek 19890 James Arthur Williams 19891 John Charles Shafer 19892 Rudolph Frank Wacker 19893 Glenn Kenge Matsumoto 19894 Robert Clark Forman 19895 Joseph Mason Massaro 19896 John Edward Arnet 19897 Richard Hanson Grinder 19898 Peter F. Witteried 19899 Howard William Hunter 19900 Edward Jan Paul Pawlowski 19901 Charles Wallace Carlson 19902 Robert Leigh Hunt 19903 George Baxter Calhoun 19904 John Ellsworth Lawson 19905 Arthur Kenneth Sirkis 19906 Robert Edward Keener 19907 William Vincent Paul 19908 William Nafew Haskell 19909 Arthur W. Wild 19910 John Anthony Wisniewski 19911 Charles Benjamin Hanson 19912 Frank Paul Colpini 19913 William Pace Purdue 19914 Ralph Emmett Porter 19915 Wilbur David Brickwell 19916 George Charles Soos 19917 Howard Markland Gabbert 19918 Leroy Clarence Turner 19919 Thomas John Wachowski 19920 Jack Edward Moore 19921 William E. McGuire 19922 Ronald Louis Salvador 19923 William Hemp Clarke 19924 William Lloyd Frier 19925 Shapleigh Morris Drisko 19926 Alan Leigh Devereaux 19927 Leonard F. B. Reed 19928 R. Jan LeCroy 19929 Robert H. Marcrum 19930 Joseph D. Lapchick 19931 Roger J. Browne 19932 Robert Leon Adams 19933 Sheldon John Burnett 19934 James C. Cooper 19935 Walton Joseph Christensen 19936 Samuel Hudson Wilson 19937 Brandt Fox Grubbs 19938 Louis H. Ginn 19939 Charles S. Stodter 19940 Robert Lee Lykens 19941 Charles Stuart Brown 19942 Clyde Winfred La Grone 19943 Edward Parry McNair 19944 Stanley Clifton Beck 19945 Jesse H. Martin 19946 John Vincent Craig 19947 Joseph Linden Yeager 19948 Paul Lansky 19949 Robert B. Short 19950 Earle Robert Evans 19951 James E. Briggs 19952 Roy William Muth 19953 Harry W. Emrick 19954 James R. L. Johnson 19955 Julian Burriss Edwards 19956 George W. McMillan 19957 Ronald Barry Lee 19958 Kenneth Rector Bailey 19959 Charles Robert Orr 19960 William Baynard Harper 19961 George Elmer Perrin 19962 Jesse R. Tippett 19963 Paul R. Jenkins 19964 William W. Welsh 19965 George Alexander Lacour 19966 Thomas F. Van Natta 19967 Edward V. Freeman 19968 Louis Charles Wagner 19969 Richard Alan Grifenhagen 19970 John Henry Wintrode 19971 John Wesley Gheen 19972 David Nord Holtam 19973 Wallace Kendall Haff 19974 John Alden Hall 19975 Marvin C. Jones 19976 Donald Shebat 19977 Lester Stanley Kirshner 19978 Jose LeRoy Chacon 19979 Richard Cassell Baughman 19980 Elmer Gene Allred 19981 John Joseph Morris 19982 Edward Martin Berko 19983 Judson Stillman Matthias 19984 William Miller Charles 19985 John Edward Krause 19986 Carl Bertil Lennart Johansson 19987 Fletcher K. Ware 19988 William Dickert Nelson 19989 Bruce Wesley Bidwell 19990 Elwin Rox Shain 19991 Derrol LeRoy Dennis 19992 James Francis Obendorfer 19993 Blackshear Morrison Bryan 19994 James Francis Bradel 19995 Gerald Socrates Vigee 19996 Robert Parker Morris 19997 Robert L. Gray 19998 Richard L. Weaver 19999 James L. Chapman 20000 John Louis Bonham 20001 Humbert Francis Sweeney 20002 Ernest A. Marvin 20003 David Thomas Teberg

20004 George C. Bennett 20005 Gerald Edward Van Valkenburg 20006 Samuel M. Mathews 20007 Alan Joseph Momberger 20008 Charles Ernest MacWilliam 20009 Eugene Joseph Alsperger 20010 Thomas E. DeSimone 20011 Joseph Edward Palumbo 20012 Charles R. Andreas 20013 William Wiley Phillips 20014 Robert Michael Mischak 20015 Kendell Olynn Iverson 20016 Joseph David Macklin 20017 Perin Mawhinney 20018 Wendell Frederick Grant 20019 Howard Prescott 20020 Jack Duncan Kincaid 20021 Dale Eugene Jenne 20022 Myron Warren Rose 20023 Jay William Gould 20024 James Phillips Jarrett 20025 William Joseph Ovberg 20026 Donald Keith Bradbury 20027 William Robert Thomas 20028 George H. Olmsted 20029 Don Joseph York 20030 Daryl Duane Jones 20031 Draper Bell Gregory 20032 George F. O'Brien 20033 George Hileman Storck 20034 John Hawkins Woodyard 20035 Edwin Mix Aguanno 20036 Robert Joseph Guidera 20037 Glen Wayne Stout 20038 Wendell Harrison Gilbert 20039 Robert Sutherland Clarke 20040 Samuel P. Walker 20041 Robert Allen Hamblin 20042 Ronald Lee Johnson 20043 Martin Paul Lachance 20044 Murray Burton Blume 20045 Carl Bobbitt Crews 20046 Eugene Stephen Procknal 20047 Norman Frank Stephen 20048 Jaime Ortiz-Lopez 20049 John G. Eckhardt 20050 Richard Paul Hoy 20051 Samuel Henry Fields 20052 Norwood William Potter 20053 Franklin Day Hicks 20054 James Paul Ryan 20055 Charles William Carroll 20056 Donald Thomas Geiger 20057 Mark Allen Ormsby 20058 James Helfrich Cronin 20059 Andrew Fillebrown Underwood 20060 Jackson Busic Carter 20061 Robert A. Ironside 20062 Joseph Allard Rude 20063 David Ford Harris 20064 Arthur McCarthy 20065 Robert Ernest Weeks 20066 William King Winston 20067 James Polk Spruill 20068 Ramon B. Aguilar Sanchez 20069 George Sterling Guy 20070 Robert Ernest Cottle 20071 Edward M. Knoff 20072 Emery Scott Wetzel 20073 Freddie A. D. Attaya 20074 James Kendall Allison 20075 James Gordon Higgs 20076 James Edward Moss 20077 Peter N. Leone 20078 Edward Cletus Bavaria 20079 Sayward Newton Hall 20080 Audrey John W. Short 20081 Lowell Edmund Toreson 20082 Joseph John Gerda 20083 Harry Franklin Ruhf 20084 William Thomas Sagmoen 20085 Richard George Ziegler 20086 Larry Elliott Willner 20087 Paul Schweikert 20088 Mercer Howell Patterson 20089 John R. Westervelt 20090 Yale Duane Weatherby 20091 Donald Ray Kirklighter 20092 Billy J. Cory 20093 William P. Grace 20094 Leo Peter Hobbs 20095 Ronald Kearney Knapp 20096 Emil Edward Levensky 20097 Robert Clark Preuitt 20098 Kevin Edward McKay 20099 Lowell Ellis Sisson 20100 William Taze Jessee 20101 Ronald Eugene Morris 20102 Charles Everett Wilson 20103 Kirk Fletcher Cockrell 20104 Herald F. Stout 20105 Leonard Victor Lundberg 20106 Kenneth Robert Kramer 20107 John W. Swaren 20108 Donald Joseph Alameda 20109 Robert Henry Gross 20110 William Thomas Archer 20111 John Edward Weaver 20112 Thomas Dabney Poor 20113 Jackson Lee Munsey 20114 Donald Edward Nowak 20115 Donald Eugene Gaston 20116 Peter C. Manus 20117 John William Gilboux 20118 Lindsey Beale Minturn 20119 Richard Harvell Bentz 20120 Thomas Cardwell Brown 20121 Dion Johnson 20122 William D. Kirby 20123 Robert Richard Stewart 20124 Robert Andrew Kaiser 20125 James Curtis Burris 20126 Lem Daavis Sugg 20127 Richard M. Boyle 20128 John Nicholas Koun 20129 Eugene Martin Donnelly 20130 Leland Ernest Bierlein 20131 Barnabe Ramirez Serrano 20132 Richard Wayne Townsley 20133 William E. Klein 20134 Willis Clifton Tomsen 20135 Neil Allen Chamberlin 20136 Cary Randolph Peyton 20137 Albert Carl Lieber 20138 Wade Hampton 20139 Thomas Sidwell Mayberry 20140 Robert Lee Geasland 20141 Norman Arthur Mattmuller 20142 Ralph Colby Ross 20143 Marvin Dale Danford 20144 John Crawford Bennett 20145 John Raymond Shelter 20146 Richard Douglas Kavanaugh 20147 Samuel Richard Harover 20148 John Grey Young 20149 William DeFord Bathurst 20150 Mark L. Reese 20151 George Nelson Stenehjem 20152 Edward Philip Cutolo 20153 John Martin Neas 20154 Joseph Thomas Gaffney 20155 Harold Roger Greer 20156 Ronald Earl Button 20157 John Grant Porter 20158 John W. Carnahan 20159 Thomas M. Watlington 20160 Thomas Jermone Abernathy 20161 John Carl Rogers 20162 George Stedman Petley 20163 **1955** Lee Donne Olvey 20164 John Thomas Hamilton 20165 William Bernard Streett 20166 Delbert Harold Jacobs 20167 Kaye Don Lathrop 20168 David Drew Gilpatrick 20169 George Arden Dulk 20170 Kenneth Edward Ginter 20171 Russell Levi Parsons 20172 John Edward Rudzki 20173 Martin Cyril McGuire 20174 Allen Dwight Raymond 20175 Harvey A. Garn 20176 Fred Bradford Phillips 20177 Thomas George Horst 20178 Francis James Adams 20179 David Eastwood Wheeler 20180 Raymond Alexander Karam 20181 Vane Quentin Bates 20182 Duane Wenzel Smetana 20183 William David Burroughs 20184 James R.C. Miller 20185 Philip Harrison Enslow 20186 Norman Wayne Sparks 20187 William Campbell Lucas 20188 Forrest Theodore Gay 20189 William Wiley Brown 20190 Paul Fetko 20191 Horace Schow 20192 Moody Echol Hayes 20193 Malcolm Vernon Meekison 20194 Charles R. Domeck 20195 Clifford Joseph Fralen 20196 Zach Hagedorn 20197 Robert Dollar Carpenter 20198 Robert C.H. Schmidt 20199 John Francis Sloan 20200 James Everman Drummond 20201 Reginald Roderick Davis 20202 Gordon Raynor Negaard 20203 Paul Bazilwich 20204 John Vincent Rock 20205 Carl John Bossert 20206 Joseph Powel Franklin 20207 Robert Wilson Hasbrouck 20208 John Thomas Gamble 20209 Alfred Merrill Worden 20210 Watha James Eddins 20211 George Robert Blitch 20212 Peter Nick Fikaris 20213 David Franklin Maurer 20214 James Evan Howard 20215 David W. Polly 20216 Alfred Joseph Spaulding 20217 Francis Martin Greene 20218 William Mervin Wix 20219 Lionel Robert Coyle 20220 Robert Oakley Wray 20221 Stanley Morgan Johnson 20222 Daniel Dean Ludwig 20223 Robert George Millard 20224 James Ralston Strickland 20225 Alexander Kratz Rupp 20226 Franz Peter Schauer 20227 Thomas Eugene Sims 20228 Charles Hiram Stevens 20229 Stanley Richard Sydenham 20230 Dennis James Cosca 20231 Raymond Edwin Dax 20232 William Frederick Sietman 20233 Thomas Tingey Craven 20234 George Alfred Straus 20235 Frederick Graham Johnson 20236 Lloyd Thomas Wolfe 20237 John Philip Lovell 20238 James Elliott Fleeger 20239 Robert Barrett Henry 20240 Norwood Wall Fleming 20241 Robert Lee LaFrenz 20242 John Stanton Lapham 20243 Edgar Ernest De Maris 20244 James Anthony Deveraux 20245 Carl Homer Cathey 20246 Richard Alfred Fontaine 20247 Karl Avrum Brunstein 20248 Alan Miller Edwards 20249 Robert Miller Sherman 20250 J. Gordon McCormack 20251 Richard Damon Johnson 20252 William Dale Norvell 20253 Jon Conrad Vanden Bosch 20254 Alfred Edwin Sheldon 20255 John Thomas Poirier 20256 Robert Dean McKelvey 20257 Ted Eugene Bishop 20258 Donald Herod Peterson 20259 Felix Dorough 20260 Robert Rugh McClelland 20261 Edward Richey Guthrie 20262 Jack Preston Campbell 20263 Jerome Douglas Hawkins 20264 Richard Sales Cheesborough 20265 Henry Albaum Klung 20266 George Wilson Page 20267 Russell Barry Hodges 20268 Kenneth Kiyoshi Ikeda 20269 David Dewees Finley 20270 James Fritz Heye 20271 Frank Lofton Donald 20272 Cecil Myron Minich 20273 Walter Earl Campbell 20274 John Scott Hardy 20275 John Rhodes Matteson 20276 Paul Richard Smor 20277 Richard Bradley Struss 20278 Peter Demetrios Booras 20279 Robert Bruce Chapman 20280 Rex Van Noy Perkins 20281 John Aubrey Feagin 20282 Ronald Eldredge Rule 20283 James Walter Staudaher 20284 Reed L. Stone 20285 James Edward Torrence 20286 Leon Ellington McKinney 20287 Ralph La Verne Henry 20288 Cyrus Curtis Cassells 20289 Philippe Ovide Bouchard 20290 William Andrews Axup 20291 Leo Vincent Warner 20292 James Elmer Fiscus 20293 Donald Arthur Andrews 20294 Richard Herbert Gray 20295 Henry Allen Hollensbe 20296 William Herbert Bottoms 20297 Leland Dwight Floyd 20298 Donald J. Sutton 20299 Donald Anthony Giza 20300 Eugene Richard Auer 20301 John Lawrence Schick 20302 Henry Watts Meetze 20303 Arthur Edward Muller 20304 Jack Durward Trawick 20305 Marshall William Dickson 20306 Norman Gene Blahuta 20307 Dean Albert Longbottom 20308 Macon Wesson Wells 20309 Robert Louis Soper 20310 James Albert McIntosh 20311 James Patrick Bergen 20312 Richard Hayes Prater 20313 Joseph Fraser Vincent 20314 William Daniel McWilliams 20315 Robert Joseph Cummins 20316 Walter Clifton McCrillis 20317 Robert Dudley Wiegand 20318 Henry Lee Sanderson 20319 Robert Louis Russell 20320 Paul Lawrence Martin 20321 Jose Dado 20322 Richard Neil Gottron 20323 Wilfred George Volkstadt 20324 Leo Anthony Hergenroeder 20325 Preston Brooks Mayson 20326 Gary William Munroe 20327 Bruce Abbott Wilburn 20328 Ronald William McNiven 20329 John Cruickshank Pearson 20330 Robert Anthony Meisenheimer 20331 James Frank Keegan 20332 James Francis Murphy 20333 John Jennings Beoddy 20334 Louis T. Tebodo 20335 Lewis Cortez Olive 20336 Billy Adair Arthur 20337 William Miles Carrington 20338 William Henry Edwards 20339 Robert Thornquist 20340 John Franklin Passafiume 20341 Richard Wayne Dinwiddie 20342 Brien Dale Ward 20343 Charles Richard Gersitz 20344 Robert Lee Shaffer 20345 John Leonard Pickitt 20346 Norb Ray Glidden 20347 Elisha Lloyd Gallup 20348 William James Goodwin 20349 Rawleigh Hazen Ralls 20350 Thomas Weller McCarthy 20351 Charles Fred Bliss 20352 James Edward Seay 20353 Richard Gustav Wargowsky 20354 Francis Edmund O'Brien 20355 Richard Vernon Secord 20356 Alexander Ronald Macdonald 20357 Herbert Selig Lichtenberg 20358 Daniel Boone Geran 20359 Lee Earl Erminger 20360 Cecil Donald Jellison 20361 Daniel Carlisle Dugan 20362 John Herbert Karnes 20363 Neil Louis Dorward 20364 Gerald Lewis 20365 Clarence Albert Delong 20366 Miguel Nieves 20367 Carl Herbert McNair 20368 Charles Horace Symonds 20369 James McKenney Cutchin 20370 Robert Winthrop Newton 20371 Herbert Charles Finger 20372 John Sheridan McDonald 20373 Robert Kirbo Strickland 20374 John William Crancer 20375 Robert Peter Johnson 20376 Clifford Jones 20377 Robert Bruce Brown 20378 Thomas James Phillips 20379 Charles Walton Roades 20380 John Garnett Senger 20381 William Carl Wildermuth 20382 John Ells Martling 20383 James Theopold Darrah 20384 Richard Adrian Regnier 20385 Marlin Richard Baker 20386 Robert Forrest Stanley 20387 John Farwell Hotchkiss 20388 Kenneth Anthony Dion 20389 Robert Elder Camp 20390 Lawrence Gilbert Michalove 20391 Harold Dean Frear 20392 Preston Standlee Harvill 20393 Don Philip Rundle 20394 Charles Augustus Steinman 20395 Robert Leroy Wallis 20396 Edwin McCoy Anderson 20397 Robert Arthur Jackson 20398 William Howard Wilcox 20399 Stephen Anthony Matuszak 20400 David August Hufnagel 20401 Ronald L. Cairns 20402 Gerald Duane Tebben 20403 Harold John Vandersea 20404 Richard Dean Shimunek 20405 Richard Morton Traut 20406 William Lee Anderson 20407 Paul Francis Parks 20408 Theodore Brooks Patterson 20409 Roy Thorvald Thorsen 20410 Loomis L. Crandall 20411 Richard Douglas Becker 20412 Rodney Lee Waterstrat 20413 Philip Taylor Blanton 20414 Donald Emerson Reid 20415 Fred Gerard Knieriem 20416 Robert Marble Hinrichs 20417 Edward Lee Trobaugh 20418 William Clifford Maus 20419 Martin Lewis McNamee 20420 William Perry Boyd 20421 Verne Golson Staffen 20422 Robert Emmett Joseph 20423 Peter Hampton Hornbarger 20424 George Lennox Monahan 20425 John Allen Myers 20426 John Cardinal McCloskey 20427 Theodore Eugene Vitori 20428 John Kanelos Leventis 20429 Royal Charles Bosshard 20430 John Bell Clayton 20431 Jerry Linwood Denman 20432 John Randolph Jeter 20433 Robert Charles Werner 20434 Donald Montgomery Buchwald 20435 Rudolph Sargus Malooley 20436 Daniel Karl Malone 20437 Billy Junior Chance 20438 Howard Francis Stone 20439 Gregory Inman Barras 20440 Alfred Anthony Cini 20441 Lawrence Chandler Herdman 20442 Sidney Echols Mason 20443 Graham Wayne Wood 20444 George Robert Kennebeck 20445 Frank George Walton 20446 John Meade Cohan 20447 Gerald John Samos 20448 William Edward Roth 20449 Albert Franklin Oppel 20450 William Whitmarsh Harris 20451 Joseph Henry Davis 20452 Michael Andrew Stevenson 20453 Charles Logan Flynn 20454 John Plympton Stuart Humphrey 20455 Harry Milton York 20456 Roland Leif Nordlie 20457 Leslie Delbert Pruitt 20458 Al Buie 20459 Kenneth Lee Donaldson 20460 James Benson Johnson 20461 David Lee Pemberton 20462 Alton Hugh Coleman 20463 Thomas Gerald Weaver 20464 Raymond Lowell Shideler 20465 David Crawford Young 20466 Edward Allen Mendell 20467 Dan Moses 20468 Charles Vincent Ewing 20469 John Edward Dryer 20470 William Grayson Peters 20471 Gerald George Chikalla 20472 Thomas John Brooks 20473 Todd Porter Graham 20474 Donald Keith Law 20475 Jack Goldstein 20476 Chester Hilton Pond 20477 Richard Dennis McCarthy 20478 Bud Thomas Hall 20479 Roy Saulsbury Dunaway 20480 Brewer Hamilton Young 20481 Paul Thomas Lenio 20482 Ronald Edwin Weissenborn 20483 Walter Joseph Ryan 20484 Roderic Bemis Vitty 20485 David Allen McNerney 20486 William Arthur Terrio 20487 John Colford Daly 20488 Thomas Patrick McGrevey 20489 Robert Frank Pheiff 20490 James Herbert Ryan 20491 William Stephen May 20492 John Sebree Farrington 20493 Judson Charles Faurer 20494 Kenneth Vincent Wilson 20495 Edward Wesley Nidever 20496 Thomas Crossley Wilkinson 20497 Alden Rudyard Crawford 20498 James Radcliffe Brokenshire 20499 Milton Joseph Herman 20500 William Edward Haas 20501 Francis Raymond Chura 20502 John Robert Sechrist 20503 William Joseph Hock 20504 Oscar Alberto Raynal 20505 James Irving Town 20506 John Walton Miller 20507 Edward John Zaborowski 20508 Jerry McClelland Gilpin 20509 James Edward Barker 20510 Robert Loyd Wheaton 20511 Leland Stanford Riggs 20512 William Ernest Lozier 20513 George Anthony Burkhart 20514 Thomas Lawrence Mullan 20515 James R. Miller 20516 John Alvin Viney 20517 Frederick Frank Woerner 20518 John Henry Pratt 20519 Gilbert John Weden 20520 Joseph John Skaff 20521 Clarence Lee Trentman 20522 Charles Gary Stoeckel 20523 J. Mitchell Brown 20524 Arthur Gordon Follett 20525 Lawrence Edward Stockett 20526 Frank Daniel Troyan 20527 Richard William Masson 20528 Bruce Stratton MacDonald 20529 John Charles Griggs 20530 Irvin George Katenbrink 20531 Thomas Allen Price 20532 Leo Robert St. Amour 20533 John Owen Funkhouser 20534 Walter Franklin Lecates 20535 Frederick Edward Pirkey 20536 Warren Alexander Jones 20537 Donald Carruthers Poorman 20538 Charles Allen Schuh 20539 Walter Howard Landers 20540 Billy Montgomery Tennant 20541 Ronald Stewart Murray 20542 Earl Vinton Singer 20543 Thomas Allan Turner 20544 Jack Wilson Frost 20545 Charles Homer Martin 20546 Francis Eugene Armour 20547 Carl Alan Rankin 20548 Raymond Eric Gunderson 20549 Thomas J. Auger 20550 James Hanlin Kinzer 20551 Robert Anthony Strati 20552 Albert Durfee McJoynt 20553 Edwin Francis Rumsey 20554 James William Grey 20555 Morris Thompson Warner 20556 Robert Everett Deardorff 20557 William Lewis McCulla 20558 Robert Ingomar Doerr 20559 Thomas James Bell 20560 Louis Vernon Pace 20561 Edmund Vulgas 20562 Edward Fox Grubbs 20563 Theodore Joseph Livesay 20564 Howard Clayton Whittaker 20565 Gerald Chadwick Brown 20566 Hugh Joseph Quinn 20567 Richard George Cardillo 20568 William McKell Hadly 20569 Harold Richard Hoeferkamp 20570 Haywood Shephard Hansell 20571 Norman Maynard Smith 20572 Richard Thomas Lilly 20573 Richard Anthony Stemle 20574 Roy Henry Lynn 20575 Madison Clinton Schepps 20576 Thomas Cato West 20577 John Gill Spellman 20578 Willard Ames Holbrook 20579 Paul James Sullivan 20580A Richard Lee Hargrove 20580 Frank Joseph Schlotter 20581 Dempsie Augustus Davis 20582 John Raymond Wing 20583 Wallace Greene Franklin 20584 William Hanion Chambers 20585 Benjamin Douglas Roberts 20586 David Wilson Patton 20587 Wilmer Lee McIlroy 20588 Charles Rodney Johnson 20589 Alva Barlett Bundren 20590 Samuel N. Lowry 20591 John Wiley Steakley 20592 Frank Upton Greer 20593 John Mark Hamilton 20594 Richard T. Hawkins 20595 Gilbert Rodney Batchman 20596 Thomas Wade Herren 20597 Paul James Jefferies 20598 Donald Eugene Smith 20599 Donald Haines Gransback 20600 Sterling Ramsdell Nichols 20601 James Allen Cooper 20602 William Totten Cummings 20603 Ira Woodruff Black 20604 William Trest Parks 20605 Jerome Francis Hagan 20606 Willard Luther Robinson 20607 Ted Eugene Thompson 20608 James Julian Pirtle 20609 John Howard Strom 20610 S. Jonathan Freed 20611 Joseph David Pettet 20612 Don Isbell 20613 Alton Brooks Parker 20614 Godwin Ordway 20615 Wynne Bennett Stern 20616 William Lloyd Welter 20617 Joseph Norman Thomer 20618 William Alexander Graham 20619 Daniel Wayne Dienst 20620 Richard James Bean 20621 Frank Jay Robertson 20622 Christopher Jesse Miller 20623 John Nicholas Calley 20624 Donald Constantine Hilbert 20625 Wayne Richard Smith 20626 Clyde Massey 20627 James Wyly Napier 20628 Robert Hugh Nourse 20629 John Harry James Giddings 20630 William Sylvester Burrus 20631 John Paul Doyle 20632 **1956** Robert Allan Stewart 20634 Frederick Stacer Holmes 20635 Gary Ray Phillips 20636 Lee Armistead Denson 20637 Marvin Francis Schwartz 20638 Don E. Ackerman 20639 George Kenyon Withers 20640 Frank Ligon Day 20641 Vincent Joseph Esposito 20642 James Kinard Strozier 20643 Larry Dean Fitzgerald 20644 Paul Michel Lion 20645 Elford Morgan Mayson 20646 B. Conn Anderson 20647 Robert Allison Ross 20648 Frederic Joseph Brown 20649 Richard Disbro Sylvester 20650 William Alfred White 20651 George Edmund Weeks Young 20652 Garrett Victor Sidler 20653 Thomas Charles Winter 20654 Heath Twichell 20655 William Hines Linder 20656 Bruce McClain Wallace 20657 Otis Peebles Studdard 20658 William R. Frederick 20659 George Erb Wien 20660 George Wayne Rostine 20661 John Milton Kamm 20662 John Carl Scholz 20663 Douglas Stoddard Johnson 20664 Alfred J. Hallisey 20665 James Anthony Harris 20666 Richard Joseph Daleski 20667 Robert Patrick St. Louis 20668 Silvio Pelosi 20669 Charles Richard Parker 20670 Dave Richard Palmer 20671 Joseph Patrick Waters 20672 William Charles Haponski 20673 Clayton Samuel Gates 20674 Thomas Edward Kirchgessner 20675 H. Norman Schwarzkopf 20676 Robert Chapman Beyer 20677 John Michael Kallfelz 20678 Marshall Delano Schoonmaker 20679 James Paradise 20680 Joseph Francis Stroface 20681 Warfield Monroe Lewis 20682 Howard Ray Cannon 20683 Robert Peter Judson 20684 George William Ward 20685 Harold Gordon Holmquist 20686 Richard Paul Thompson 20687 John Benton Tindall 20688 Roger Roy Redhair 20689 Roger Alan Root 20690 Christopher James Allaire 20691 Steven Loomis Canby 20692 Robert Everett Quackenbush 20693 Robert Gordon Farris 20694 James Hunter Sewell 20695 Richard Samuel Kem 20696 Robert Newton Richards 20697 William Robert Devoto 20698 Harold Philpott Southerland 20699 Robert Wetzel 20700 Mario Anthony Nicolais 20701 Gregory Welch Mitchell 20702 Zeb Boyce Bradford 20703 Charles William Robertson 20704 Roger Reckling Blunt 20705 Benjamin Gay Peterson 20706 James Lee Dozier 20707 Richard Patrick Dowell 20708 Perry McCoy Smith 20709 Thomas Eugene Ross 20710 Walter Lee McCahan 20711 Ernest Lewis Ruffner 20712 Robert Hunt Easton 20713 David Milton Corderman 20714 Richard Brayton Pierce 20715 Forrest James French 20716 Robert Douglas Krutz 20717 Irwin Benton Mayer 20718 Jerry Clark Frecka 20719 Lewis Stone Sorley 20720 Charles Blane Brinkley 20721 John William Woodmansee 20722 Marvin Marcy Williamson 20723 Jerome Glen Lake 20724 Samuel Anderson Alward 20725 Mark Edward Smith 20726 Arthur Eugene Dewey 20727 Edward Valence 20728 Eldon Doy Carr 20729 Philip Albert Stynes 20730 James Walsh McNulty 20731 Mark Joseph Sisinyak 20732 Thomas Edward Reinhardt 20733 Thomas LaRue Miller 20734 Donald Michael O'Shei 20735 David Carl Muntz 20736 Donald Ray Morelli 20737 Sidney Thomas Weinstein 20738 Charles Ellsworth Poole 20739 John Furman Wall 20740 Richard Lee Curl 20741 John Raymond Bray 20742 John Cline Snodgrass 20743 Wood Rene De Leuil 20744 Michael Grant Zeigler 20745 Richard Henning Hansen 20746 John Roger Conklin 20747 James Lewis Stroope 20748 Scott Beecher Smith 20749 Eugene Stanley Lynch 20750 George Ulrich Loffert 20751 Jerome Hirsch Werbel 20752 Robert Blair Tinsman 20753 William Mayo Hooker

20754 George Pearson Brandel 20755 James Neal Ellis 20756 William Robert Jarmon 20757 Gerald Ralph Aloysius Thompson 20758 George Weir Lee 20759 Charles Rowland Hamm 20760 Martin B. Zimmerman 20761 Joseph Mark Dougherty 20762 Herbert Henry Spaeni 20763 Donald Cubbison Little 20764 Michael Houston Alexander 20765 Harry Warren Johnson 20766 Stephen Richard Woods 20767 James Clarence Shirey 20768 Howard George Glock 20769 Robert Bruce Sheridan 20770 Romain Alton Young 20771 George Firmin Leonard 20772 Michael John Conrad 20773 Hugh Wilmot Munson 20774 Harlan Barry Bynell 20775 Hugh La Verne Filbey 20776 Charles Clayton Torrey 20777 Morrill Ross 20778 Gerald Zoel Demers 20779 John Martin Gromek 20780 Donald Adolph Fisch 20781 Matthew James Quinn 20782 Charles Wilson Bagnal 20783 Vernon Roy Van Vonderen 20784 Everette Gattis Caldwell 20785 Robert Dale Randall 20786 Edmund Leroy Van Dervort 20787 Richard Charles Malin 20788 Joven Gascon Villanos 20789 Edwin Woods Martin 20790 Herrol James Skidmore 20791 Ralph Mereline Griscom 20792 William Robert Johansen 20793 Aaron B. Loggins 20794 Anthony Joseph Ortner 20795 Frank Lee Smith 20796 Thomas Charles Harding 20797 James Paul Bolin 20798 Norman Clark Folden 20799 Edwin Till Holloway 20800 C. Theodore Ogren 20801 George Patrick Lynch 20802 James Walter Stanley 20803 Walter Charles Sager 20804 Jack Joseph Sharkey 20805 Robert David Cremer 20806 Bert Errol Tucker 20807 Joseph Jolly Haydon 20808 Charles John Garvey 20809 Lester Stearns McChristian 20810 Donald Cyril Lee 20811 Theodore Martin Faurer 20812 Patrick Norman Uebel 20813 Phillips Griffith Eliot 20814 Angelo Bortolutti 20815 Eugene Austin Fox 20816 William Franklin Crews 20817 Merrill Anson Green 20818 John William Foss 20819 Edmund Dederick Burhans 20820 Warren George Keinath 20821 Neale Malcolm Luft 20822 John Albert Shaud 20823 Ernest Edward Cross 20824 Griffith John McRee 20825 Richard Conant Chase 20826 James Harper Gordon 20827 Robert Kirk Nicholson 20828 Walter Bernard Liska 20829 H. Gregory Wold 20830 Thomas Martin Bowes 20831 Donald Clyde Graesser 20832 Jon Eugene Porter 20833 Robert Dale Hammond 20834 Rand Eliot Rensvold 20835 Robert Tyler Goodwyn 20836 William Carter Westcott 20837 Mervin Gilbert McConnel 20838 Walter Urbach 20839 Frank Albert Burd 20840 Robert English Grassberger 20841 Dennis Lee Butler 20842 Robert Charles Scully 20843 James Jolly Waldeck 20844 Robert Armstrong Flory 20845 John Blanchard Grinstead 20846 Lisle Greene Kendall 20847 Lowell Gene Smith 20848 G. Richard Schaumberg 20849 Ralph Joseph Chesnauskas 20850 Richard Lee Tripp 20851 Jerry Harold Huff 20852 Robert Kenneth Stein 20853 Frederick Rodgers Dent 20854 Gayle N. Linkenhoger 20855 Vernon Edward Ebert 20856 Paul Anthony Jakus 20857 William Leon Weihl 20858 William Louis Di Gennaro 20859 Samuel J. Roberts 20860 George John Stapleton 20861 John James Clark 20862 Nicholas Joseph Bruno 20863 John Hawley Oakes 20864 George Joseph Martin 20865 John Leroy Johnsen 20866 Alex Norwood Williams 20867 Edward Francis Neary 20868 John S. Sutherland 20869 Keith Andrew Barlow 20870 Richard Rinker 20871 Edward Harrison Redline 20872 Joe Edward Sanders 20873 Conrad Claude Ege 20874 John Alton Taylor 20875 Arvid Emerson West 20876 Donald August Hammel 20877 Richard Brent Washburn 20878 George David Kannapel 20879 Carl Louis Croft 20880 Everett Marion Yon 20881 David Finch Horton 20882 Stanley Elbert Wilker 20883 Julian Leo Abell 20884 Robert Patrick Sullivan 20885 Gerald Alan Richardson 20886 Richard Eugene Adams 20887 Jerry Joe Burcham 20888 Alan Leigh Thelin 20889 Everett Stanwood Diez 20890 William Taylor Wetzel 20891 Melvin Louis Wuest 20892 Samuel Murray Lansing 20893 William Ralph Crites 20894 James Ober Straub 20895 Richard Joseph Keating 20896 Ben Paul Saxton 20897 Steven Grosvenor Beebe 20898 John Carl Johnson 20899 Harry Kotellos 20900 Albert James Dye 20901 Richard Wetzel Lorey 20902 Reid Anderson Barrett 20903 Jan Edward Verfurth 20904 Thomas Joseph Cody 20905 Harry Allen Comeskey 20906 Steven Voorhees Boylan 20907 John Stephen Utz 20908 Edward Blaine Kime 20909 Charles Edward Trefzger 20910 Joel Stanley Hetland 20911 Joel Richard Campis 20912 Raymond Celeste 20913 Thomas Wesley Hanson 20914 James Arnold Cook 20915 John Patrick Haley 20916 Irving Alonzo Beauchamp 20917 Robert Augur Hewitt 20918 Donald Elmer Sheehan 20919 Stanley Herbert Meader 20920 Robert Lee Hull 20921 Farrell Gee Patrick 20922 Norman Levy 20923 John Lewis Liwski 20924 John William Nicholson 20925 Anthony Michael Jezior 20926 Charles Robert Kottich 20927 William Karl Schrage 20928 Walter Henry Knudsen 20929 John Albert Keutmann 20930 John Henry Higgins 20931 Edward Vallentiny 20932 William Philip Farmer 20933 Leslie Terence Prossner 20934 James Ambrose Linden 20935 Robert Arthur Goodman 20936 James Stephen McMahon 20937 Walter Douglas Williams 20938 Darold Wendle Clonts 20939 Edward Francis Daly 20940 James Lee Anderson 20941 Norris Brown Harbold 20942 John Randall Parker 20943 Harold Arthur Marvin 20944 William Cornelius Roll 20945 Paul Allen Lasley 20946 John Stanley Polickoski 20947 Stuart Waddington Bowen 20948 Anthony Andrew Benish 20949 Donald Lee Ernst 20950 Jarold Leroy Hutchison 20951 Carl Gerald Herrmann 20952 Alan Bishop Renshaw 20953 Ransom Jerome Amlong 20954 Frederic Lloyd Shean 20955 Gerald David Ankenbrandt 20956 Charles Richard Russell 20957 Bob Dennis Schuler 20958 John Hughes Stevenson 20959 David J. Scales 20960 Joseph Edward Gleason 20961 Paul Anthony Merola 20962 James Whitney Spires 20963 James Fulton Lane 20964 Darrell Leslie Anderson 20965 Donald Wade Satterfield 20966 Jerold Alan Morgan 20967 Jerald Henry Skatvold 20968 Dirk Henry Lueders 20969 William Penn Crum 20970 Carl Frank Hattler 20971 Roland Bertram Crase 20972 Kenneth Earl Lang 20973 Charles Benjamin Singletary 20974 Frank Owen Bonnarens 20975 Richard Reece Johnston 20976 Frank Emanuel Sharer 20977 Robert Ellsworth Brown 20978 Paul Hilger Greisen 20979 James Schmauch Bauchspies 20980 Mark Paul Binstein 20981 Gerald Daniel Goldberg 20982 William Christi Carey 20983 Robert Benton Danek 20984 Porter Nelson Medley 20985 Hiram Barricklow Turner 20986 Alfred Connor Bowman 20987 Kenneth James Knowles 20988 Robert Moulton Blocher 20989 Milton Cogswell Shattuck 20990 Luciano Cristoforo Salamone 20991 Paul Gustave Dougherty 20992 Ralph Hendrix Floyd 20993 Victor Thomas Bullock 20994 Henry Ronald Gaude 20995 Paul Wayne Rajala 20996 Thomas Norfleet Griffin 20997 John Dwight Schannep 20998 David Rea Larr 20999 Jack Thiel Munsey 21000 Michael Joseph McGrath 21001 Eugene Fox 21002 Harry Wilson Crandall 21003 Robert T. Barrett 21004 Robert LeRoy Pearson 21005 Nicholas Alexander Mavrotheris 21006 Gerard Michael Wynn 21007 Terry Wayne Creighton 21008 Winfield C. Frank 21009 Alfred Hoffman 21010 Walter Joseph Muller 21011 Joseph Edward Ragland 21012 Lawrence Alan Stebleton 21013 William Curtis McPeek 21014 Russell Aaron Mericle 21015 John Arthur Hampton 21016 Stainton Smith 21017 Robert Hunter Lindsey 21018 William Wallace McClung 21019 Gerald Lee Irwin 21020 Arthur Mowry Harris 21021 Gary Curtiss Hall 21022 Theodore Grant 21023 Lawrence Arthur Wange 21024 Theodore John Dayharsh 21025 Charles Cameron Snavely 21026 Harry George Christopher 21027 James Eugene Beal 21028 Donald Bertrand Smith 21029 Wallace Stanford Crain 21030 Robert Percy Caron 21031 William Francis Cody 21032 Rupert Charles Kinsloe 21033 Thomas Joseph McAniff 21034 Robert Coleman Bacon 21035 Charles Frederick Scott 21036 David Wardlaw Moore 21037 Peter Waller Lash 21038 John Charles Bahnsen 21039 Charles Francis Swezey 21040 Jack Adair Dunn 21041 Thorton Samuel Saferstein 21042 Michael Frederick Cavenaugh 21043 Robert Glen Andree 21044 Rudolph Booream DeFrance 21045 Jesse Eugene Blackwell 21046 Charles DeFitzer Sarkiss 21047 John Malcolm Kirk 21048 Harry James McGuire 21049 Ivar Walter Rundgren 21050 Thornton Akin Burns 21051 Everett Charles Updike 21052 Peter Joel Vann 21053 Thomas J. Masterson 21054 Jon Rutledge Matt 21055 Paul Hayne 21056 James Claud Blewster 21057 William Edward Narus 21058 Joseph Royall Carraway 21059 Randolph Adams McCreight 21060 David James Johnston 21061 Paul Patton Winkel 21062 Clifford Howard Baker 21063 Ward Morehouse LeHardy 21064 Theodore Clinton Jasper 21065 Edward Thomas Richards 21066 Robin George Speiser 21067 Carleton Coulter 21068 Gary Criswell Williams 21069 Charles Givens Prather 21070 Herbert Myers Wagenheim 21071 Michael Sanford Sirkis 21072 Rufus Renwick Hart 21073 Robert Malcolm Duncan 21074 Whit Lewis Coats 21075 William Purnell Baxter 21076 Donald Walter Holleder 21077 Charles Arvel Glenn 21078 Evangelos Dantos 21079 John Francis Wagner 21080 Frederick Ashby Rall 21081 Edward Francis Rhodes 21082 Leslie Hiram Weinstein 21083 Arthur Francis Boudreau 21084 Plato George Chambers 21085 Charles Campbell Gorlinski 21086 Wilbur Manly Skidmore 21087 Charles Eugene Eastburn 21088 Richard Edward Mackin 21089 Samuel Lindsay Lemmon 21090 Leroy Newton Suddath 21091 Cicero Council 21092 Jefferson Davis Childs 21093 David Tholin Berry 21094 George Joseph Woods 21095 Maury Spotswood Cralle 21096 Harry Jerrol Raymond 21097 Ernest Bayley Wilson 21098 Michael Joseph Pendino 21099 Henry Baldwin Miles 21100 Frederic John Fogh 21101 John Joseph McGinn 21102 William Edwin Lyon 21103 Francis Weems Matthews 21104 John William Keefe 21105 Dexter Harrison Shaler 21106 Donald Joseph Shannon 21107 Edgerton Thorne Crouter 21108 Roy Ernest Lindquist 21109 Bernard John O'Brien 21110 F. Javier Pozuelo 21111 Michael Francis West 21112 John Francis Sloan 21113 **1957** John Henry Vickers 21114 Wallen Michael Summers 21115 James Shepard Voorhees Edgar 21116 Herbert John Koops 21117 William Finch Carroll 21118 Charles Horne Cooper 21119 Archie Don Barrett 21120 Robert Alfred Langworthy 21121 Robert LaVern Wessel 21122 Edward Beeding Quill 21123 Richard Anthony Mollicone 21124 Maxim Icaak Kovel 21125 John Louis Wiegner 21126 Harper Brown Keeler 21127 John Robert Hocker 21128 Richard Michael Pastore 21129 William R. Ellis 21130 James Franklin Russell 21131 Donald Stanley Jenis 21132 Michael Scarth Higgins 21133 Carman Duane Negaard 21134 Robert Vernon Vermillion 21135 Frank Paul DeSimone 21136 Joseph William O'Neil 21137 Thomas Garth Adcock 21138 Edward Charles Olivares 21139 Charles E. Lea 21140 James Robert Murphy 21141 Samuel Morthland 21142 Robin John Roller 21143 Dana George Mead 21144 Donald Peyton Whalen 21145 Charles Matthew Radler 21146 James Arlen Chernault 21147 Gerald Edward Galloway 21148 Walter Joseph Rabe 21149 Leonard Plumer Wishart 21150 Joseph Anthony Beben 21151 Clifford Augustus Walton 21152 Harry Clifford Goodson 21153 Henry James Hatch 21154 Ronald Schuyler Gooding 21155 Richard Then White 21156 Donald Joseph Kutyna 21157 Martin Banks Carson 21158 Harry Edward Soyster 21159 Charles Custis Moses 21160 Jack Elwyn Hesse 21161 Edmund Anthony Wilhelm 21162 John Weber Purdy 21163 Robert Francis Comeau 21164 Stanley Theodore Johnson 21165 Paul Norman Chase 21166 Maurice Leonard Hazelrigs 21167 Douglas Patterson 21168 Frank Jackson Redd 21169 John Charles Burt 21170 Donald Raymond Pope 21171 Clyde Donald Sadler 21172 Kelly Mayo Harp 21173 William G. Liakos 21174 Joseph Adrian Bishop 21175 Nicholas Monaco 21176 John Joseph Ramsden 21177 Champlin Fletcher Buck 21178 Gerald Warren Chase 21179 Thomas Edward Olson 21180 James Robert Hamilton 21181 John Vernon Schafer 21182 Richard Van Arnam Huie 21183 E. Joe Shimek 21184 Richard Duane Kenyon 21185 Kenneth Anthony Parker 21186 George William Bruce Glen 21187 Leigh Madison Ogden 21188 William Henry Foster 21189 Marshall Lee Moore 21190 Donald Richard Stackhouse 21191 Ralph Wesley Stephenson 21192 William Francis Hurley Page 21193 Francis Robert Stevens 21194 Robert Edgar Bodenhamer 21195 Bruce Finley Stout 21196 William Echevarria 21197 Frederick Charles Freathy 21198 Charles Hunter Coates 21199 Louis Joseph Circeo 21200 Francis Whitney Hall 21201 Bernard William Basse 21202 Gordon Byrom Rogers 21203 Raymond Earle Bell 21204 Herman Eugene Day 21205 Gerald Thomas McCall 21206 James William Ray 21207 Francis Lawrence Hanigan 21208 Louis Stephen Quatannens 21209 Samuel James Newsom 21210 Charles Dewey Meng 21211 Leo Dennis McEvoy 21212 William Earl Yates 21213 John Robert De Sola 21214 Freeman Grant Cross 21215 Stanley Clarke Pore 21216 Robert Francis Martin 21217 Walter Leo Pritchard 21218 Benjamin Bowes Beasley 21219 James Arthur Pocock 21220 Gordon Ryon Moreland 21221 Elmer Russell Harris 21222 Richard Royer Manahan 21223 Robert Kinley Tener 21224 Homer Johnstone 21225 James Gerald Wood 21226 Arthur Berry Ellison 21227 Jerry Claude Scott 21228 Donald Eugene Seitz 21229 Ralph Edward Miles 21230 William Nathaniel Friend 21231 Jonathan David Nottingham 21232 Kermit Hoyt Gates 21233 David Pemberton Beurket 21234 Donald Richard Ley 21235 George Thomas Kilishek 21236 Gordon Edmund Williams 21237 John Nichols Politis 21238 Arthur Lawrence MacKusick 21239 John Burnham Dubbelde 21240 Edward LeRoy Gee 21241 Paul Jerome Schwehm 21242 Leslie John Prichard 21243 Theodore John Pearson 21244 Leon Delbert Bieri 21245 Gottfried Herman George Krafft 21246 William Kinley Wright 21247 W. Richard Magadieu 21248 Robert Lawrence McCoy 21249 Thomas Reichley Hicklin 21250 Charles Robert Sprague 21251 Morris Ralph McBride 21252 Edward Wendell Gale 21253 Stephen Barclay Place 21254 Kenneth Douglas Tobin 21255 Raymond Daryle Dixson 21256 Morton Franklyn Roth 21257 William Thomas Cudmore 21258 Thomas Wayne Roebuck 21259 John Dorsett Ellington 21260 Barnes Warland Rose 21261 Jack Burr Cooper 21262 Robert Calian Westerfeldt 21263 Hawkins Meador Conrad 21264 John Arthur Little 21265 William Thomas Carter 21266 Benjamin Edward Waller 21267 James Burr Kaiser 21268 William Lawrence Golden 21269 John James Patrick Meehan 21270 Julius Anthony Tieber 21271 Carl Henry Waldenmaier 21272 Gerald Thomas Dwyer 21273 Allan Arthur Bell 21274 Charles Howard Wheeler 21275 Donald Lee Winters 21276 Raymond Thomas Karsian 21277 Richard Graham Caldwell 21278 James Joseph Cortez 21279 Gene Edward Beimforde 21280 Donald Ray Schafer 21281 John Howard Peckham 21282 Lawrence Fallon McNeil 21283 Edward Ernest Hildreth 21284 John Harry Barbazette 21285 Anthony Maurice Solberg 21286 John Phillip Ritchey 21287 David Lawrence Smith 21288 Donald Leslie Miller 21289 Robert Henry Alsheimer 21290 William Risque Sowers 21291 Robert Frederick Markham 21292 John Curtis Wilkinson 21293 Alfred Harry Davidson 21294 John Taynton Murchison 21295 Warne David Mead 21296 Donald Dean Rowland 21297 Robert Parker Bateman 21298 Edward Lee Chase 21299 Richard Calvin Dean 21300 James Henrion Britton 21301 Johnny Coleman Ledbetter 21302 Anthony Francis Albright 21303 John Michael Witherow 21304 Robert Edward Winters 21305 Ronald Dean Kennedy 21306 Erman Milford Newman 21307 Charles Joseph Quinn 21308 Newton Bernard Penrose 21309 Thomas Philip Garigan 21310 Donald Campbell Bowman 21311 Jack Alfonso Apperson 21312 Albert Sidney Britt 21313 Donald Kieth Fitzpatrick 21314 H. Frederick Koehler 21315 Jefferson Zeno Amacker 21316 Mark Conover Heath 21317 Charles Bowler King 21318 William Louis Melton 21319 Peter Duryea Calyer 21320 Darrold John Erickson 21321 James Roy Jenkins 21322 Glaudis Pierre Gaspard 21323 Arcade George Boivin 21324 Ralph Allen Luther 21325 Jose Jesus Olvera 21326 Brian Franklin Head 21327 Richard Ballard Daluga 21328 Jesse Holland Ruder 21329 John Eugene Murphy 21330 Donald George Wells 21331 Byron Starr Fitzgerald 21332 Giles Dexter Harlow 21333 William Harvey Lowe Mullins 21334 Robert Edward Rawls 21335 John Martin McDonald 21336 Hardin Leonard Olson 21337 Joseph Bingham Mack 21338 Glen Lee Rhoades 21339 George Vaughn Rogers 21340 Norman Milton Vaughn 21341 David Paul Bernd 21342 William Myrlin Burke 21343 Tom Leo Lindholm 21344 Robert Purcell Christiansen 21345 Samuel Walter Focer 21346 Louis Barisano 21347 Veloy Jerald Varner 21348 John Algerton Witmer 21349 James Sutton Armstrong 21350 Richard Adrian Scholtes 21351 Bobby Gene Christy 21352 Frederic Harrison Smith 21353 Robert Leighton Merrick 21354 Donald Sanborn Tribe 21355 Owen O'Henley McIntyre 21356 Harold Blair Dyson 21357 J. David Preletz 21358 Henry Jerold Schumacher 21359 Michael Kay Stein 21360 William Royer Clark 21361 William Willson Campion 21362 John Lewis Hill 21363 Andrew Chase Johnson 21364 Howard Marcus Martinez 21365 Murray Glenn Swindler 21366 William Franklin Campbell 21367 Lofton Hugh White 21368 Glenn Miller Andrews 21369 Stanley Frederick Jensen 21370 Gene Ray Reget 21371 John Edmund Sobraske 21372 James Porter Woolnough 21373 William Thomas Huckabee 21374 Michael Roy Keating 21375 William Warren Gude 21376 Richard Iverson Edwards 21377 Dwight Carl Aller 21378 George Lee Richardson 21379 Edward Christian Kielkopf 21380 Albert Henry Krapf 21381 Robert Foster Gadd 21382 John Leonard Easterwood 21383 Theodore Dotzier Felber 21384 Robert Don Freeman 21385 James Fulton MacGill 21386 Stuart Ernest Wright 21387 Amherst Robert Lamb 21388 John Rusling Block 21389 Robert Newton Johns 21390 Cedric J. Zabriskie 21391 Houston Parks Houser 21392 Donald Herbert Cline 21393 William T. King 21394 Frank Wilson Willett 21395 John Michael McCarthy 21396 Carter Marion Kolb 21397 Craig Harrison Smyser 21398 Thomas Prentis Kehoe 21399 Richard Henry Morton 21400 John Eugene Setnicky 21401 James Foster Henthorne 21402 Timothy Gardner Lawton 21403 John Harrison Stokes 21404 Charles Bertody Stone 21405 Kendrick Harmon 21406 James Dorrance Powell 21407 Gerald Leon Jagrowski 21408 David Edward Schorr 21409 Rodney David McConnell 21410 Joseph Raymond Tedeschi 21411 Robert Emil Leard 21412 Howell Hopson Jordan 21413 Howard Francis Haupt 21414 Glenmore John Runnion 21415 Willis Edward Teale 21416 Richard Glenn Hurlburt 21417 Edwin Stanhope Olsmith 21418 George William McGovern 21419 Joe Bob Newman 21420 Luis Garcia San Andres 21421 Jay Charles Toole 21422 Lawrence Joseph Murphy 21423 John Thomas Gleason 21424 Jackson McDaniel 21425 Robert Wesley Faulkender 21426 Aubra Nelson Bone 21427 Richard Scott Hamner 21428 Charles Urban Hindman 21429 William Bentley Seely 21430 Neal Edwin Ausman 21431 Charles Leonard Raymond 21432 Earl Wendell Pettibone 21433 Herbert Charles Rice 21434 Benedict Emmanuel Glyphis 21435 Nicholas Brown Wilson 21436 John Leo Keefe 21437 James Donald Smith 21438 John Oren Hanford 21439 Clarence Earl Hall 21440 John Nathan Follansbee 21441 Edward Joseph Cutler 21442 Philip Allen Stein 21443 Robert Lynton Veal 21444 Bernard John Tullington 21445 Bruce Barry McDonough 21446 David Neal Thomas 21447 William Bryant Hall 21448 John Fletcher Elder 21449 Michael John Ilsemann 21450 Jerome Anthony Meyers 21451 Malcolm Matthew Duffek 21452 Thomas Vincent McMahon 21453 William Harrison Pope 21454 Robert Bruce Turnbull 21455 Jon Eckstorm Dunning 21456 Clarence Edward Wittman 21457 John Frederick Crater 21458 Douglas Wister Howell 21459 Guy Joseph Palmieri 21460 John Edward Schaefer 21461 Barry Perrin Fox 21462 James Donald Salzman 21463 Lester Edsel Bennett 21464 Jacob Erwin Lustig 21465 John William McClanahan 21466 Thomas Symington Bainbridge 21467 Albert Converse Kline 21468 Alex A. Vardamis 21469 John Charles Loberg 21470 James Louis Trainor 21471 Turner Maurice Gauntt 21472 Robert Paul McCoy 21473 William Patrick Hamm 21474 Bruno John Neukamm 21475 Theodore Bassett Voorhees 21476 Leon John Wilson 21477 Charles Kenneth Kyne 21478 John Edgar Blanck 21479 Allyn Bourke Ensign 21480 John Dean McSpadden 21481 Howard Elwyn Webster 21482 Christ John Poulos 21483 Jerry Kranz Patterson 21484 Donald Johnston Bowes 21485 Claude Greene Hammond 21486 Walter Camp Gordon 21487 John Lloyd Person 21488 Willis Morris Thomson 21489 Willard Merion Christenson 21490 Donald Alvin Buckner 21491 James Franklin Knight 21492 Andrew Michael Weber 21493 Phineas Kimball Morrill 21494 Leonard Sebastian Marrella 21495 Douglas Wilson Stockton 21496 Robert Alfred Dagle 21497 Harold Morris Carter 21498

Douglas Stuart Alexander 21499 Daniel Clancy 21500 Church Myall Matthews 21501 Gary Alan Stemley 21502 Kenneth Bryan 21503 William McKinley Bishop 21504 Richard Frederick Emery 21505 David Parker Gibbs 21506 Kenneth Richard Simila 21507 John Edmund Bloomfield 21508 Richard Charles Murtland 21509 Austin Eugene Miller 21510 Ricardo Delfino Tonda 21511 William Bryan Webb 21512 Cornell McCullom 21513 Nelson Marquis Lynde 21514 Jon Edward Bokovoy 21515 Theodore Manly Rosenberg 21516 Paul Osborne Olsen 21517 Robert Carothers Allen 21518 Nicholas John Robinson 21519 Arlyn Reese Madsen 21520 Thomas W. Keeley 21521 John Darwin Sankey 21522 Joseph Leonard Masterson 21523 George Dudley Iverson 21524 Robert Martin Reynolds 21525 Joseph Cygler 21526 David Preston Ray 21527 Edward I. Hickey 21528 Robert Charles Tilton 21529 Donald James Barlow 21530 Thomas Edmond Dayton 21531 Thomas Kilby Shuff 21532 Raymond Elliott B. Ketchum 21533 Eric Murray Christensen 21534 James Ward Dunn 21535 William Wendell Koch 21536 Thomas Steventon Gruhn 21537 Robin Mangum 21538 George Desire Landry 21539 William Douglass Deegan 21540 Frederick Leonard Wells 21541 Brian Thomas Kennedy 21542 Len Martin Hanawald 21543 Carl William Lohmann 21544 William Austin Duncan 21545 Gerald Samuel Hawley 21546 David Perry Perrine 21547 Michael James Petruno 21548 Duncan Padgett Smyly 21549 Robert Leonard Drudik 21550 William Allen Davies 21551 Carl Edward Vuono 21552 Craven Clark Rogers 21553 James Walter Mooring 21554 Wayne Brackett Nicoll 21555 Milton Donald Ewanus 21556 Robert Rodriguez 21557 John Harold Slaney 21558 Jesse Harion James 21559 Edward Szvetecz 21560 Richard William Pfeiffer 21561 Thomas Benton McDonald 21562 Martin Gilbert Bradley 21563 Jack Manuel Solomon 21564 Daniel J. Enxing 21565 William Ross Thompson 21566 Charles Don Erb 21567 Wesley Edward Kidd 21568 Russell Wilcox Ramsey 21569 William Harry Meyerholt 21570 Samuel L. Hylbert 21571 Robert Frederick Krueger 21572 Thomas Hugh Dougherty 21573 Thomas Earl Runyan 21574 L. Bradshaw Tate 21575 Donald Haydn Davis 21576 William Edward Murphy 21577 Anthony Richard Miklinski 21578 Jack Emerson Adams 21579 James Arnold Swenson 21580 William Lawrence Smith 21581 James Lawrence Siegel 21582 Fox McCarthy 21583 George William Bailey 21584 Justin Green La Porte 21585 Robert Adam Kyasky 21586 Thomas Allen Olsen 21587 John Dennis Shannon 21588 Robert Warren Arnold 21589 Guy Edward Wallace 21590 Stanley Dale Cass 21591 William Charles Ringler 21592 Robert Burrow Davis 21593 Jack Kyle Farris 21594 Richard William Christensen 21595 Thomas Anthony Rush 21596 Lee Burner 21597 Arthur Dale Johnson 21598 Julio Ernesto Heurtematte 21599 Joseph Wayne House 21600 Calvin De Witt 21601 Thomas George Thompson 21602 Dean Elwood Bates 21603 Durl Dale Zachgo 21604 George Michael Houser 21605 Franklyn Wayne Gross 21606 Peter Jay Chittick 21607 John Franklin Smith 21608 James Edward Maloney 21609 Andrew Robert Foster 21610 Bernard Loeffke 21611 John Leonard Waters 21612 Robert Warren Buckner 21613 Kenneth Edward Halloway 21614 Vincent Jerry Longo 21615 Barry Bruce Sturgis 21616 Richard Earl Stephenson 21617 Roger Melvin Currier 21618 John Paul Dodson 21619 Joseph Stephen Russo 21620 Thomas Dan McCrary 21621 Daniel Joseph De Lany 21622 John Cornelius Kilpatrick 21623 Walter Hoyt Kennett 21624 James Van Pelt Taylor 21625 Charles Marshall Hug 21626 Flay O. Goodwin 21627 Richard Anthony Fadel 21628 Stephen Arthur Glick 21629 James Robert O'Connor 21630 Peter Michael Leighton 21631 Robert Youngblood White 21632 Harlan Glenn Allen 21633 Franklin Delano Mastro 21634 George Losere O'Grady 21635 Charles Prentiss Scudder 21636 Robert Eugene Beckwith 21637 Carroll Wade Shaddock 21638 Marvin Howard Nilsen 21639 John Osborne McLaughlin 21640 Donald Emil Press 21641 Bernal Quiros 21642 Charles William Wheatley 21643 Cyril Louis Massar 21644 Gordon Michael O'Neal 21645 Richard Walter Seward 21646 Lawrence Henry Mulligan 21647 Charles Louis Williams 21648 Carl Ferdinand Burgdorf 21649 John Andrew Murphy 21650 Robert Leighton Jones 21651 Joseph Howard Spector 21652 Noel Ingebrigt Fedje 21653 Buel Trenton Rose 21654 Rudolph Nicholas Pataro 21655 Donald Blair Baughman 21656 James John Jameson 21657 Anthony Lawrence Bullotta 21658 Richard Horton Howes 21659 **1958** George William Patrick Walker 21660 Dan Allan Brookhart 21661 Anthony Allen Smith 21662 James Balmer Hall 21663 Richard Newland Groves 21664 Jack O'Brien Bradshaw 21665 James Stewart Willis 21666 Charles Hamilton Davis 21667 Francis Brian Crowley 21668 Robert Monroe Bunker 21669 James Edward Seltzer 21670 Peter Austin Penczer 21671 Charles Clark Hansult 21672 William Augustus Edwards 21673 Luis Manalang Mirasol 21674 Michael Stratton Jones 21675 Reginald Frederick Seiler 21676 John Oscar Bagot Sewall 21677 James Harrison Ramsden 21678 Alan Blanchard Salisbury 21679 Herbert Charles Puscheck 21680 Terence Jurdan Connell 21681 Duff Gerard Manges 21682 William L. Harry 21683 John Gaspard Schroeder 21684 Hugh P. Johnson 21685 Walter Mead Patterson 21686 Troy Dawson Chappell 21687 Robert Harry Julian 21688 Daniel Leon Johnson 21689 Jack Peter Bujalski 21690 LeRoy Robert Hayden 21691 James Joseph Kernan 21692 Paul Makowski 21693 James Patrick Mellin 21694 Joseph Anthony Lupi 21695 James Cameron Castle 21696 Josef Conrad Krankel 21697 William Troy Cooper 21698 Ronald Lawrence Bellows 21699 Terence Howard 21700 Robert William Giuliano 21701 Samuel Pickens Collins 21702 Richard Henry McManigell 21703 George Rogers Robertson 21704 George Warren Sibert 21705 William Robinson Parks 21706 Richard Dean Kittelson 21707 Larry Lee Shull 21708 Dick Shaw Oberg 21709 Bo Franklyn Craddock 21710 Donald Joseph Palladino 21711 Ashton Miller Haynes 21712 Cloin Gentry Robertson 21713 Richard Reese Price 21714 Sammy Howard Cardwell 21715 Lawrence Robert Tharp 21716 John Farmer Brinson 21717 John Bert Nun 21718 John Charles Buchanan 21719 Raymond Isaac Coffey 21720 William Preble Marshall 21721 Richard Stanley Kloskowski 21722 Wayne Arthur Weiss 21723 Samuel Leslie Myers 21724 Joseph August Shea 21725 Gerald LeRoy O'Barr 21726 Jerry Lee Burton 21727 Peter Jon Groh 21728 John Frederic Schaefer 21729 Hugh David Kevin 21730 Robert Ray Huskinson 21731 Robert Eugene Baker 21732 R.G. Ben Franklin 21733 James Wyatt Peck 21734 Edward Jackson Downing 21735 Robert Lawrence Grete 21736 Glenn Kennon Phillips 21737 Richard Walter Gell 21738 John Herbert Eliot 21739 John Lee Palmer 21740 George Morgan Hall 21741 Michael Joseph Dugan 21742 Curtis Rudolph Stender 21743 James Martin Sigler 21744 William Ray Miller 21745 Gordon Lee Goodman 21746 James William Chapman 21747 Thomas Francis Cameron 21748 John Joseph Madigan 21749 Robert Roy Foster 21750 Melvin Howard Farrar 21751 Alan Brian Claflin 21752 Roger Walter Waddell 21753 David William Livingston 21754 John Hilton Bradley 21755 Robert A. Dey 21756 Olen Aubry Brown 21757 Alexander Johnston 21758 William David Parsons 21759 Ronald Ernest Hudson 21760 Norbert Alfred Hulsman 21761 Victor John Gongola 21762 David Arthur Clarke 21763 Thomas Keith Smith 21764 Bill Cosmos Giallourakis 21765 Merwin Lamphrey Morrill 21766 Orland Kitchell Hill 21767 Donald Miles Forney 21768 Lon Arnold Spurlock 21769 Richard Francis Trabert 21770 John Paul Manos 21771 John Mark Dykes 21772 Robert Theodore Shellenberger 21773 James Clarence Bishop 21774 Leo Weber Smith 21775 John Michael Kubiak 21776 Harry Ray Kramp 21777 Dennis Augues Rupprecht 21778 Millard Leroy Pedersen 21779 Thomas Allen Sands 21780 James Richard Wade 21781 William Scott Stambaugh 21782 Larry Howard Hunt 21783 Nicholas Thomas Carlson 21784 Joseph Charles Luman 21785 Bruce Stevens Packard 21786 Richard Makoto Hirata 21787 Burton Tenney Miller 21788 Robert Francis Durkin 21789 William Joseph Wafer 21790 John Billy Abernathy 21791 Larry Kenneth Asbury 21792 David Frank Nidever 21793 Juan Edmundo Villanes 21794 Robert Ignatius McCann 21795 William Leo Parker 21796 Bruce McClung Hamilton 21797 James Harvey Hankee 21798 Arthur Wilbur Meyer 21799 George Bernard Mitchell 21800 Ernest Frederick Hasselbrink 21801 Louis Brand Rodenberg 21802 Anthony Paul West 21803 Joseph Albert Paes 21804 David Campbell Turner 21805 Jack Campbell May 21806 Daniel Edward Carter 21807 Charles Wesley Mitchell 21808 Donald Joseph Welch 21809 Thomas Hayden Davies 21810 Don Martin 21811 Robert Gardner Moscatelli 21812 John Henry Shimerda 21813 Charles Edwin Teeter 21814 Richard Brenard Webb 21815 Jerry Noel Hoblit 21816 Paul Martin Bons 21817 Thomas Montgomery Mason 21818 William Percy Gillette 21819 Robert Neil Mathis 21820 Robert Albert Bethmann 21821 Gerald Thomas Rudolph 21822 Robert Edward D'Amore 21823 Cline Gerald Cook 21824 Francis Aloysius Waskowicz 21825 Dwain Thate Moentmann 21826 Richard A. Simmers 21827 Gerald Clarence Mitchell 21828 Robert Phillip Gall 21829 Paul Gordon Ruud 21830 Charles Pearre Cabell 21831 William Ignatius Murphy 21832 Dale Eugene Hruby 21833 William P. Brower 21834 John Howard Lynne 21835 Glenn LaMar Bugay 21836 Wayne David Day 21837 John Harrison Roe 21838 James H. Weis 21839 Richard Sherwin Johnson 21840 Ronnie Dean Short 21841 Peter Burns Trainor 21842 Robert Walcott Meals 21843 Thomas Drexel Morgan 21844 John Carlson Burke 21845 Phillip Raign 21846 Leland Gilbert Fay 21847 John Michael Daley 21848 John Bernard Sampson 21849 Charles Williamson Glover 21850 Frederick Walter Kulik 21851 Jerry Wortham Betts 21852 Gerald Paul Schurtz 21853 Edwin Irwin Ofgant 21854 Robert Hassler Miller 21855 Harrell Glenn Hall 21856 Kenneth Stephen Herberger 21857 John Sylvester Rave 21858 Melville Anson Drisko 21859 Ernest Frank Geipel 21860 Charles August Normington 21861 George Clinton Huff 21862 John Burton Stone 21863 John Charles Galen 21864 Wayne Donald Hagberg 21865 Bruce Philip Mignano 21866 Thomas Edgar Carpenter 21867 Joseph Douglas Keyes 21868 William Alonzo Denson 21869 Ramon Antonio Nadal 21870 James Lawrence Rossetto 21871 Robert Earl Clark 21872 Ronald Kessinger Andreson 21873 Alexander Julius Pensiero 21874 Cecil L. Shrader 21875 Lawrence Francis Perreault 21876 John B. Cook 21877 Charles Elswood LeMere 21878 Joseph Conrad Tirre 21879 Crosbie Edgerton Saint 21880 John Wesley Loffert 21881 Olin Joel Moore 21882 Robert Maurice Clewell 21883 Davies Reed Powers 21884 Frederick Lewis Nuffer 21885 Kenneth Ervin Lager 21886 Richard Lee Smith 21887 Terry Dale Snyder 21888 Richard Duane Osborn 21889 Neil Seymour Williamson 21890 Roger Charles Gietzen 21891 Louis Joseph Prime 21892 Paul Thomas Schonberger 21893 William Wilkinson Foulkes 21894 Rupert Edwin Grimm 21895 Floyd Brown Spencer 21896 Karl E. Oelke 21897 Vernard McComb Stilson 21898 Kenneth Harold Montgomery 21899 Claude Belmont Donovan 21900 Hugh Homer Trumbull 21901 Frank Michael Harlem 21902 William Nourse Bicher 21903 Joseph Mitchell DeChant 21904 Harold Clifford Lyon 21905 Francis John Franks 21906 John Richard Larson 21907 Donald Ray Williams 21908 Will Garrison Merrill 21909 Peter James Young 21910 Edward Vincent DeBoeser 21911 Anthony George Bauer 21912 Garland Deloid O'Quinn 21913 James F.T. Corcoran 21914 John Wellington Devens 21915 Daniel Patterson Charlton 21916 Charles William Profilet 21917 Louis Basil Gennaro 21918 James Richard Wessel 21919 V. William Barta 21920 Milton Lee Miller 21921 Lloyd David Umbaugh 21922 William Farnham Brown 21923 John Rimmer Hill 21924 Leo Edward Sheehan 21925 George Newton Lancaster 21926 Richard Earle Thomas 21927 William G.T. Tuttle 21928 Otto Joseph Thamasett 21929 Robert Oliver Case 21930 Harold Jerry M. Williams 21931 Gary Lee Kosmider 21932 James Monteville Davis 21933 Philip William Ackerman 21934 Willis Clare Collett 21935 Paul Churchill Hutton 21936 Michael Paul Wagner 21937 Alan Carleton Chase 21938 James Howard Jones 21939 Edwin Nelson Dodd 21940 Edward Charles Weckel 21941 Richard John Buckalew 21942 Ronald Dean Turner 21943 John Allen Raymond 21944 Robert Lincoln Hultzen 21945 Harry Jenkins Hubbard 21946 Gary Gene Durkee 21947 Karl Frank Prunitsch 21948 John David Shetler 21949 George Sadtler Robertson 21950 Ernest Robert Lenart 21951 David Ernest Depew 21952 Carl White Sullinger 21953 John William Morrison 21954 George Gregory Wees 21955 J.H. Henry Curtis Ballard 21956 Paul Gordon Rice 21957 George Carr Lawton 21958 Robert Thomas Barker 21959 Glenn Allan Lane 21960 William John Shepard 21961 Dale Sherwood Cockle 21962 Roderic Edward Ordway 21963 John Francis Reilly 21964 Robert Gardner Rhodes 21965 Zane Kyle Rector 21966 William Walter Shely 21967 Clark Jonathan Bailey 21968 Thomas Arthur Francis Conti 21969 Loren Douglas Reid 21970 Richard Lamar Reynard 21971 Arvid Spencer Doucette 21972 Bradfield Fellowes Eliot 21973 Harry Lee Shedd 21974 Glenn Allison Brown 21975 Stanley Bacon 21976 Robert Degen 21977 Frederick John Schluter 21978 John David George 21979 Vichitra Sookmark 21980 Richard Keith Clements 21981 Clifford Bruce Trott 21982 Kenneth Woodyard Clark 21983 Thomas Joseph Kelly 21984 Garret Garrison Roosma 21985 Clarke McCurdy Brintnall 21986 Richard Gordon Graves 21987 Frank Mathias Smith 21988 Peter Darcey Hidalgo 21989 Donald Richard Garrett 21990 Stanley Edward Dus 21991 Dennis Paul Sharon 21992 Frank Sayles Bowen 21993 Thomas Peter Maliska 21994 Paul Frederic Ciasullo 21995 Kenneth Arthur Lohr 21996 William Christopher Melnik 21997 Hugh Whitford Morgan 21998 Branch Alvin Worsham 21999 John Francis Holecek 22000 Herbert Richard Johnson 22001 Frank Joseph Guenther 22002 Robert James Moore 22003 Robert William Puff 22004 Gary Perkins Graves 22005 Joseph Henry Schwar 22006 Charles Herbert Oxrieder 22007 David Schirmer Kyle 22008 Robert G. Finkenaur 22009 Daniel Joseph Yarr 22010 Jerome Dunn 22011 James Allen Godbey 22012 Clifford Daniel Victorine 22013 Roy Tripp Evans 22014 James Dunworth Stanton 22015 John Reynolds Sutherland 22016 Fred Wesley Hall 22017 Donald Eugene Wilson 22018 Donald A. DeJardin 22019 John Donald Crandall 22020 Robert Martin Higgins 22021 Leonard Joseph Kusek 22022 William Edward Serchak 22023 Henry Pratt Gardner 22024 Henry Edmund Bielinski 22025 Edward Joseph Burke 22026 Michael William York 22027 Richard Christopher Schonberger 22028 F. William Miles 22029 James M. Ryan 22030 William Arthur Shepherd 22031 Robert Edward Regut 22032 John Louis Isaacson 22033 Stanley Clarence Toney 22034 Robert Norton Tredway 22035 Robert Leroy Kirtley 22036 Benjamin John Pellegrini 22037 Jerome Francis Prochaska 22038 Michael David Mahler 22039 Donald Wright Johnson 22040 Douglass Alfred Sedgwick 22041 John William Peters 22042 David Warren Bourland 22043 Wallace William Ward 22044 Robert Thomas Donovan 22045 Richard Francis Reidy 22046 Barry Martin Zwick 22047 Harvey Raymond Jahn 22048 John Garrettson Evans 22049 John Albert Schaffer 22050 Milton Russell Wofford 22051 Charles Wilson Bond 22052 Philip Victor Di Mauro 22053 William Phillips Clary 22054 David Stuart Loughborough 22055 Lee Arthur Gaughan 22056 Lorin Ballantyne Farr 22057 Kelly Edward Robinson 22058 Lincoln Jones 22059 Joseph Kevin Brown 22060 Gerald Carl Capelle 22061 John Wilburn Schneider 22062 Clyde Orville Brown 22063 James Wayne McCauley 22064 Norman Herbert Monson 22065 Robert Waldemar Tallgren 22066 Robert Eugene Olson 22067 Ronald C. Olson 22068 Gerald Harwick Zimmer 22069 Thomas Hall Claffey 22070 Jude Joseph Theibert 22071 Donald R. Edwards 22072 William Miles Reynolds 22073 Jack Lloyd Halsey 22074 George Ellery Hussey 22075 Robert William Pointer 22076 Richard Swinney Beyea 22077 Heyward Groverman Hutson 22078 Mahlon Kirk 22079 George Edward Ellis 22080 Claude Emmanuel Fernandez 22081 Raymond Francis Hanson 22082 James Bruce Morgan 22083 Thomas Francis Cartwright 22084 James Noble Tilley 22085 R. Lewis Tony Munger 22086 Cary William Martin 22087 Theodore E. Childress 22088 Daniel Pleasant Brockwell 22089 William Saunders Graf 22090 Nelson Owen Conner 22091 Richard Daniel Garlick 22092 Roy Spencer Kirkpatrick 22093 Adam Benjamin 22094 Ola Robert Nelson 22095 Franklin Palmer Phillips 22096 Palmer McGrew 22097 Ronald Thomas Coleman 22098 James Albert Frick 22099 Peter Shunk 22100 Homer Bentley Jenkins 22101 Thomas Edward Stevens 22102 Stanley Arthur Maxson 22103 Eugene Gibson Wentworth 22104 Francis Milton Wright 22105 Robert Arthur Melott 22106 Bernard Michael Davall 22107 Julian John Levasseur 22108 Walter Andrew Hitchcock 22109 William Cibosky 22110 Eugene Allen Fisher 22111 John Ward Carson 22112 Douglass Stengrim Detlie 22113 Daryl George Jaschen 22114 Theodore Warren Hepner 22115 David Alan Hettinger 22116 James Edgerton Waller 22117 Kermit Mandes Henninger 22118 Walter James Barnes 22119 Walter Max Plaue 22120 Michael William Riordan 22121 Edward Whitehouse Matthews 22122 Thomas Linwood Orr 22123 Martin Larry Kirkegaard 22124 Frederick Flood Mayer 22125 Max Galen Pearsall 22126 Richard Thomas Lynch 22127 William Maxwell Young 22128 Frederick G. Stritzinger 22129 Robert Michael Hattler 22130 Paul Leonard Julius Klempnow 22131 David George Coury 22132 Joseph Daniel McElroy 22133 William Arnoux Roosma 22134 Leslie G. Gibbings 22135 John Daniel Herren 22136 Charles Francis Densford 22137 Thomas Arthur Forman 22138 John Hancock McKillop 22139 Henry John Gordon 22140 Charles Bernard Porciello 22141 J. Barrie Williams 22142 Paul Dudley Vanture 22143 Peter Frederic Bahnsen 22144 Alfred Rex Mason 22145 Hugh Albert Bauer 22146 Willis Aaron Smith 22147 Robert Edward Tierney 22148 Norman Lee Gustitis 22149 Joseph Mortimer Davis 22150 Dennis Russell Bruzina 22151 Thomas Anthony Forster 22152 Charles Sargent Moore 22153 William Harrison Dunning 22154 George William Yurick 22155 Peter Charles Byrne 22156 James Elmer Emmons 22157 Theodore Frank Smith 22158 Thomas Morris Thompson 22159 Edward John Lucci 22160 James Russell Wildey 22161 Nathan Harold Crow 22162 Ronald Shelton Brunner 22163 Pichitr Kullavanijaya 22164 William Timothy McLean 22165 Peter Edward Millspaugh 22166 Robert J. Matsumoto 22167 Townsend Allen Van Fleet 22168 Ben G. Crosby 22169 Gross Edwin Jenison 22170 Barry Phillip Eveleth 22171 Philip Alan Pryor 22172 Charles Anthony Miller 22173 Arthur Frederick Mace 22174 William James McCaffrey 22175 William Keppel Votruba 22176 Robert Edmund Lindquist 22177 Edward Joseph Jasaitis 22178 Joseph William Brandl 22179 Leonard Raymond McCormack 22180 Paul William Haushill 22181 Thomas Henry Harvey 22182 James Raymond Brooks 22183 Edward Gordon Hale 22184 Thomas Crawford Looney 22185 Larry Wendell Sutherland 22186 Bradley Jerome Johnson 22187 Brian Louis Koster 22188 Edward Julius Timberlake 22189 Frank McCarthy Brown 22190 Donald Joseph McCullough 22191 George Robert Michael 22192 Joseph Anthony Evans 22193 David Willits Swanson 22194 Joseph Martin DiTommaso 22195 Sterling Wayne Wyatt 22196 Warren Rubel 22197 Joseph Jacob Katz 22198 William Saunders Buchly 22199 George Octave Klotzbach 22200 John Anthony Nowak 22201 Zigmont Jody Le Towt 22202 Raymond Forrest R. Tomlinson 22203 William Guy Ganey 22204 Willie Jon Marshall 22205 Lawrence Lonero 22206 Fred Wesley Goodenough 22207 Harold Augustus Davenport 22208 Stanley Allen Slater 22209 Jerome Carter Lewis 22210 Richard Eugene Warner 22211 Richard Elmer Bauchspies 22212 Bernard Rogers Card 22213 Lawrence Michael Malone 22214 Raymond B. Riggan 22215 John Richard Deely 22216 Gennaro John Faiola 22217 Garth Hayden Payne 22218 Charles Nelson Toftoy 22219 Billy Frank Mathews 22220 Albert Douglas MacLeod 22221 Strube Jennings Jackson 22222 Donald James Roberts 22223 Eugene Johnson Scales 22224 Michael Frederick Easley 22225 W. John Soper 22226 Lawrence Hoover Bullis 22227 Turner D. Griffin 22228 William John Kelley 22229 Bruce Bradley Davenport 22230 John Francis Tierney 22231 Marius Stefan Sigurski 22232 **1959** James Leonard Abrahamson 22233 James Floyd Ray 22234 Stanley Martin Kanarowski 22235 C. Powell Hutton 22236 John Howard Veidt 22237 Albert Francis Dorris 22238 Jerome Bernard Hilmes 22239 James Joseph Satterwhite 22240 Donald Stuart Kendall 22241 Peter Miller Dawkins 22242 Freeman Irvin Howard 22243

Robert Walter Riordan 22244 John Southy Grinalds 22245 Jack Michael Warren 22246 Arthur Shiro Kubo 22247 Douglas Neil Campbell 22248 John Palmer Johnson 22249 Richard Delmas Welch 22250 Dwight Edward Beach 22251 Lewis Ray Martin 22252 John Benton Hyde 22253 Robert Archibald McDonald 22254 Michael James Gillette 22255 Leon Karol Moraski 22256 Raymond Thomas Beurket 22257 Joseph Herman Coreth 22258 Gerald Philip Stadler 22259 James Warren Van Loben Sels 22260 Andrew Karl Kuschner 22261 John Stephen Hurley 22262 Eugene Charles Mikelonis 22263 Edwin Matthews Moorman 22264 Donald Robert Reinhard 22265 Larry Michael Greene 22266 James Cameron Ferguson 22267 John Duncan Simpson 22268 Lawrence Calvin Ross 22269 George Roy Kleb 22270 David Henry Rogers 22271 Richard Albert Rothblum 22272 Mark Harge Magnussen 22273 Robert Alwyn Schow 22274 William Jackson Poole 22275 John Philip Huntingdon 22276 John Henry Moellering 22277 William Vance Murry 22278 F. David Ortman 22279 George Peter Johnson 22280 James Carter Rowe 22281 Bruce Campbell Johnson 22282 E. John Eberhard 22283 Robert Joseph Ranalli 22284 Willard McKenzie Burleson 22285 John Francis Corby 22286 William Wallace Breen 22287 David Lawrence McKinney 22288 James Wallace Taylor 22289 Lawrence Edgar Minnich 22290 Frederick John McConville 22291 Donald Bruce Williams 22292 Darel Stephen Johnson 22293 Richard Edwin Rogers 22294 Bruce Allan Porter 22295 Russell Alvoid Hewitt 22296 Anthony George Pokorny 22297 James Richard Turner 22298 J. Frank Campbell 22299 William Joseph Garcia 22300 Joseph Harrold Sullivan 22301 Thomas Button Russell 22302 Frederick Douglas Anderson 22303 Gerald Wayne Noga 22304 David Roger Carrier 22305 Harold Stephen Hughes 22306 Pedro Foronda Baraoidan 22307 Lee Roy Nunn 22308 William Daniel Isaac 22309 Richard C. Bennett 22310 Paul William Tomiczek 22311 Peter Leonard Stromberg 22312 Lawrence Athey Struble 22313 Orthus Knighton Lewis 22314 Donaldson Preston Tillar 22315 Donald James Fitchett 22316 James Andrew Gibbs 22317 Ronald William Brass 22318 Alan Wren Baldwin 22319 Thomas Koenig Seybold 22320 Arthur J. Siciliano 22321 Ronald Thomas Shelton 22322 Otis Pennell Tibbetts 22323 Clifford Wayne Mercer 22324 Carl Harry Groth 22325 Byron Drake Marsh 22326 Ronald Anthony Pistone 22327 Ronald Calvin Baldwin 22328 Joseph Enrico Todaro 22329 Frederick Melvin Franks 22330 Charles Edward Duke 22331 James Robert Krulcik 22332 Broder Lysholm Jervell 22333 Hubert Thomas Servis 22334 Paul Nelson Sper 22335 Richard Vincent Kocienda 22336 Gerald E. Weisenseel 22337 Dennis Ivyle Walter 22338 Benny Merle Carr 22339 Ronald Howard Templeton 22340 Don Markham 22341 William Stokes McDaniel 22342 Don Frederick Svendsen 22343 Samuel Donnell Gwin 22344 Gary Dean Beech 22345 Edward George Stauch 22346 Robert Hinkle Ryan 22347 Robert Grayson Crawford 22348 David Randolph Carroll 22349 Paul Edward Dearmin 22350 Robert Matthew Weekley 22351 Wayne Henry Bechthold 22352 Larry Norman Wiley 22353 Richard Owen Roberts 22354 William Thomas Zaldo 22355 David George Cotts 22356 Clayton Allen Fannin 22357 Haymon Harrellson Boggs 22358 Igor Dexter Gerhardt 22359 Donald Eugene Eckelbarger 22360 Joseph Wilson Hurst 22361 James W. Rosenoff Adams 22362 Charles Dale Darby 22363 William Earl Barry 22364 Robert Daniel Rizzi 22365 Donald Carlton Coen 22366 Nathan Irvin Broocke 22367 H. Charles Lymn 22368 George Donald Kissinger 22369 William Manford Toskey 22370 Patrick Francis Passarella 22371 Thomas Rodger Mooney 22372 Henry Emmett McCracken 22373 Richard George Toye 22374 Edward Nikolai Laughlin 22375 Stephen Klein 22376 Ashton Christal Lawrence 22377 Rush Spencer Yelverton 22378 Harold Lee Briggs 22379 Lewis Charles Ranch 22380 Richard Earl Forbes 22381 Alexander M. Grant 22382 John Adam Joh 22383 Wilbourne Anderson Kelley 22384 Bernard Emmett Watlington 22385 John Nourse Meloy 22386 Albert Augustine Breuel 22387 Roger Bruce Schlemmer 22388 Kevin John O'Neill 22389 Stanley John Delikat 22390 Alfred Boyce Devereaux 22391 Robert Huntley Burroughs 22392 Thomas Owen Young 22393 Bernard Joseph Battersby 22394 William Frew Train 22395 John Rhodes Harrell 22396 Nicholas Stephen H. Krawciw 22397 Richard Meyer Hotchkiss 22398 Sherwin Lewis Steinberg 22399 John Theodore Dannell 22400 Bruce Ray Bradley 22401 Kenneth George Norman 22402 Paul Joseph Elias 22403 Robert Dobson Evans 22404 Bruce E. Schmacker 22405 Donald Timothy Matthes 22406 John Cameron McNerney 22407 David Thomas Gray 22408 Louis John Schroeder 22409 Thomas William Gilligan 22410 Russell Keith Street 22411 Robert Joseph Croteau 22412 Claude Everett Lynch 22413 Christian Charles Thudium 22414 Jay Clifford Franz 22415 Geoffrey Curtis Davis 22416 Frederic Vincent Malek 22417 Cassius Joseph Mullen 22418 Thomas Francis McMorrow 22419 John Patrick Sheehan 22420 George Watson Williams 22421 Marvin L. Thomas 22422 Richard Paul Skowronek 22423 Alfred Whitby George 22424 Richard LeBrou Whitesides 22425 Erven Somerville Tyler 22426 William Lloyd Ramsay Stocker 22427 Milton Sims Newberry 22428 Reginald Walter Rhein 22429 John Paul Shock 22430 Dorsey Lynn Baker 22431 James Edward Chappell 22432 William Joseph Mullen 22433 Ronald Louis Ernharth 22434 David Comings Whitmore 22435 James Willard Madden 22436 Ronald Howard Salter 22437 Randall William Bell 22438 Martin Lloyd Plassmeyer 22439 Norman Harold Rosner 22440 James Lee Massey 22441 David Robert Wheeler 22442 James Clark Woods 22443 Charles Willard Hayes 22444 Jeryl Clyde Greenawalt 22445 Walter Tarleton Brown 22446 Riley Roy Moore 22447 Bernard Allen Knowles 22448 Benjamin Estes Dishman 22449 Dudley McBeth Moorhous 22450 Theodore William Simroe 22451 Francis Gary Gercz 22452 Joseph Albert Phillips 22453 Dick Tucker LeClere 22454 Alfred Edward Nordgren 22455 Richard Lee Clark 22456 Thomas Du Val Roberts 22457 Clayton John Mansfield 22458 Albert Virgil Goodpasture 22459 Frank Schaeffer Besson 22460 Ralph Robert Wensinger 22461 Dewitt Talmadge Monroe 22462 Henry Bernard Dorshow 22463 William Edward Temple 22464 Thomas Leib Moorhead 22465 Eugene Francis Madigan 22466 Robert West Beale 22467 Michael Morales 22468 Barrett Slocum Haight 22469 Robert Letchworth 22470 Godwin Patrick McLaughlin 22471 Jim Roddy Paschall 22472 Thomas Harrold White 22473 John Joseph Koisch 22474 Robert William Roth 22475 Brooks Hubbard Sisson 22476 Alfred Yim Kui Hew 22477 Louin Lester Beard 22478 Arleigh Todd Bell 22479 Donald Steadman Baker 22480 Edwin Hess Burba 22481 James Stanley Hahn 22482 David Alfred Lewis 22483 John Adikes McInerney 22484 William Anding Bush 22485 Thomas Gillis McInerney 22486 Charles Michael Lutz 22487 Thomas Clark Munz 22488 John Oman Neal 22489 Laurence Harrison Shuck 22490 Thomas Francis Plummer 22491 Richard Melvyn Cannon 22492 John Homer Ruth 22493 Raymond Chapman Baugh 22494 Albert Martin Lidy 22495 William Gailey 22496 Dennis Joseph Morrissey 22497 Frederick Lee Wilmoth 22498 Donald Clarence Gruschow 22499 James Montgomery Burwell 22500 Guy Hill Heath 22501 Michael Dominick Isacco 22502 Robert Bowman Howe 22503 Walter John Wosicki 22504 Joe Estill Williams 22505 Gilbert Eugene Roesler 22506 Charles Edward Johnson 22507 Robert Everett Holman 22508 Jimmie Dean Fielder 22509 Raymond Warren Fisher 22510 Ronald Richard Recher 22511 Charles Edward Tennant 22512 Donald William McClurg 22513 Warren Jay Warren 22514 Albert Stephen McSweeney 22515 Joseph Francis Enright 22516 Jimmy Calvin Hill 22517 Andrew P. O'Meara 22518 Russell Milroy Miner 22519 Wiley Valentine Harris 22520 Marvin Franklin Moss 22521 Thomas Henry Ballenger 22522 Phillip Galen Sheaffer 22523 James Edward Walsh 22524 LeRoy Vincent Greene 22525 Donald Lee Smart 22526 Roger Allan Quinn 22527 Jack Edward Bohman 22528 Ronald Leonard Schnick 22529 Robert George Shain 22530 John Junious Mayers 22531 John Franklin Orndorff 22532 Ollie Legree Langford 22533 Stanley James Zagalak 22534 John Frederick Carroll 22535 Julian Earl Weisler 22536 Michael Anthony Gabel 22537 Donald Doan Ingram 22538 Philip Lansdale Yeats 22539 Fitzhugh Horton Chandler 22540 Carl Everett Kinell 22541 Michael Molitoris 22542 David Eugene Fried 22543 Edward Bagdonas 22544 Eugene N. Smith 22545 James Holman Miller 22546 Jack Edward Ravan 22547 Carl Stephen Webster 22548 Roy Edgar Losey 22549 Thomas Henry Fletcher 22550 Jack Coldwell Smith 22551 David Paul Tulp 22552 Bertel Randolph Bertils 22553 Peter Haynes Foster 22554 Alvin Jackson Morefield 22555 George Charles Friedel 22556 William Henry Zierdt 22557 Donald Thomas Simpson 22558 Stuart Neil Bennett 22559 James A. Dorsey 22560 Herman V. Ivey 22561 Walter Busill Tully 22562 Peter Benjamin Schmidt 22563 Glenn Harold Dyer 22564 Conrad Lloyd Boyle 22565 Jon Alan Rindfleisch 22566 Hugh Henkel Renalds 22567 William Warren Wright 22568 William Gerald Rowe 22569 Henry Harris Covington 22570 John Wooten Gurr 22571 Thomas Vagn Borlund 22572 Larry Edward Burchell 22573 Ludvig Jarad Aamodt 22574 Wayne Winston Lambert 22575 Robert Howell Edwards 22576 William Atwood Fitzgerald 22577 Harry Clayton Abrams 22578 David Arnim Luedtke 22579 John Foster Harkins 22580 Charles Alan Millick 22581 Estan Francis Imler 22582 Arthur Henry Bair 22583 Andrew Michael Gasienica 22584 Richard Barton Johnson 22585 John Stewart Wilson 22586 William Cramer Pollock 22587 Douglas W. Sefton 22588 John R. Morrison 22589 Donald Richard Wands 22590 Hugh J. Socks 22591 Jerry Cleveland Mills 22592 Joel Kampf 22593 John Armand Cohan 22594 William Collins Buell 22595 Norvell Bonds DeAtkine 22596 Daniel Wallace Schrader 22597 William Kay Marshall 22598 James B. Patton 22599 Stephen Williams Fertig 22600 John Arthur O'Brien 22601 Richard Raymond Maglin 22602 Spencer Maddux 22603 William Arthur Luther 22604 John Albert Knebel 22605 John Edward Bryer 22606 Humbert Roque Versace 22607 Frank Merle Salvatore 22608 Frank Emilio Herrera 22609 James Thaddeus Freeland 22610 Warren Stanley Smith 22611 Paul Aloysius Chalmers 22612 Joseph Merton Shea 22613 Craig Randolph Bertolett 22614 Ralph Paul Weber 22615 Pierce Albert Rushton 22616 Howard James Stiles 22617 Carl Augusta Weaver 22618 Louis Caruso 22619 John Francis Milton 22620 William Lee Schwartz 22621 John Simpson Guthrie 22622 James Ervin Kennedy 22623 Richard Renner Peffenbach 22624 Harry Ned Walters 22625 Edward Charles Robinson 22626 Robert Warren DeMont 22627 Gregory David Page 22628 George Pierre Hannan 22629 Robert Allen Wheeler 22630 Richard Sheriden Sundt 22631 Robert Avera Turner 22632 Darwin Doris Boyd 22633 Eugene Leroy Oliver 22634 Larned Vesely Bearce 22635 Louis Victor Hightower 22636 Gary Simmons 22637 Richard Wells Harnly 22638 Roger Karl Paquette 22639 Stephen Kay Werbel 22640 Victor Michael Fernandez 22641 Richard Kenneth Jordan 22642 George Franklin Harrison 22643 Jean Helms Engler 22644 Thomas Boyd 22645 Edwin Arthur Netzloff 22646 John Michel Nash 22647 John Ferral McBlain 22648 Robert Michael Barry 22649 Kenneth Harold Joyce 22650 Russell Thomas Boyle 22651 John Bruce Medaris 22652 Edward Irwin Haskin 22653 Robert Martin Novogratz 22654 Henry Sofus Larsen 22655 Fred Vincent Manzo 22656 James Colton Corr 22657 Charles Edward Lytle 22658 Raymond Russell Ramsey 22659 William Alan Cohen 22660 Roger Blaine Ware 22661 William Joseph O'Meara 22662 Gregory John Kadlec 22663 Courtney Edward Prisk 22664 Jerald William McCoy 22665 William Edward Benagh 22666 John Herbert Farrell 22667 Nathaniel Fred Colby 22668 Arthur Ralph Griffin 22669 Hugh Thomas O'Connor 22670 George Ellis Day 22671 Arthur Robert Cyr 22672 Dan Moody Webster 22673 Theodore Danford Wells 22674 Laurence Sean O'Neill 22675 John Paul Porter 22676 Donald Richard Davis 22677 Tomas Rodolfo Letona Castaneda 22678 Marion Finney Graven 22679 Gerald Joseph Lhotak 22680 Thomas Walter Leo 22681 John Parko 22682 James Paul Walters 22683 Thomas Russell Soli 22684 Joseph Thomas Moriarty 22685 Richard Bruce McPeek 22686 Marlin Eugene McCahan 22687 William Ralph Weber 22688 Henry Kinmond Adamson 22689 Laurence James Palmer 22690 Gilbert Noyes Dorland 22691 Michael John Fletcher 22692 John Robert Cox 22693 John Forrester 22694 Peter Kenneth Keogh 22695 William Bradford Guild 22696 Donald Eugene Morgan 22697 Philip Edward Gibbs 22698 David Lee Roush 22699 Dwight Hunter Fuller 22700 James Stephens Dick 22701 James J. O'Brien 22702 William Richard Lehrfeld 22703 Allyn Clyde Houltry 22704 Thomas Gordon Bolick 22705 William Edward Clarke 22706 Sidney Hersh Yateman 22707 Louis Edward Sullenberger 22708 Charles Edward Getz 22709 Kirby Stanley Kapp 22710 William Stratton Callaghan 22711 Dennis Michael Duggan 22712 Ben Davis Faber 22713 Richard Torrence Harle 22714 Melecio Zamora Santos 22715 Frank Jay Redding 22716 Richard John Meyer 22717 Sean Howard Cummings 22718 Robert French Bowers 22719 Rody Mead Conway 22720 Robert Ivan Shapiro 22721 Donald Morgan Ludlam 22722 Leonard George Katsarsky 22723 Robert Stephen Frey 22724 Winston Moffatt Schepps 22725 Maurice Glen Hilliard 22726 Glen Edward Newman 22727 Roger Quinn Gaines 22728 George Whittington Parolini 22729 Joseph William Wheeler 22730 Alan Burgess Phillips 22731 **1960** Charles Paddock Otstott 22732 Robert Everard Montgomery 22733 James Jeremiah Stewart 22734 Wallace Hampton Duncan 22735 Edwin Augustus Deagle 22736 Thomas Henry Huber 22737 Ralph Fred Gerenz 22738 Vincent Robert Chitren 22739 Michael Denis Mierau 22740 Claude Leaman Clark 22741 Richard Stout Seaward 22742 Thomas Lee Bullock 22743 Edward Oliver Bierman 22744 Michael Stuart Lane 22745 Thomas Evangelista Valente 22746 Edward Allen Osborne 22747 William Joe Skinner 22748 John Anderson Berry 22749 Frederick Boyd Plummer 22750 Raymond Sherwood Andrews 22751 Paul Lindsay Miles 22752 Robert Nelson Bierly 22753 Leslie Gene Langseth 22754 Dean A. Herman 22755 Thomas Reed Bennett 22756 Eugene Price Reese 22757 Cyrus Clarke Wilson 22758 William Emer Yeager 22759 Larry Albert Bauermeister 22760 Edward Strasbourger 22761 Joel Elias Bernstein 22762 Charles R. Mandelbaum 22763 Grafton Jhung 22764 Richard James Hervert 22765 John Anthony Lopiano 22766 Eugene Munson Brisach 22767 Peter Frederick Lagasse 22768 Carl Dennis Miller 22769 Gordon Stuart Livingston 22770 Harold Newton Dreibelbis 22771 Milton Eustis Cooper 22772 Keith James Nance 22773 Theodore Russ Dunn 22774 Alfred Kenneth Richeson 22775 Lyle Thomas Jones 22776 Frank Almond Partlow 22777 Robert Harold Ammerman 22778 Ronald Frank Trauner 22779 Max Elden Rumbaugh 22780 Glenn Harris Lehrer 22781 Norman Julius Kuklinski 22782 Nathaniel Sill Fox 22783 Donald Joseph Stukel 22784 Berton Everett Spivy 22785 Donald James Usry 22786 Charles Maurice Dwyre 22787 Robert William Burnell 22788 Jonathan Walter Searles 22789 Raymond Reed Barrows 22790 William Andrew Rux 22791 John Hale Getgood 22792 Vincent Gregory Grande 22793 Charles Martin Titus 22794 Arthur Joe Dean 22795 Paul William Mandry 22796 John Roger Martz 22797 Ronald Alan Beltz 22798 John Scott Steele 22799 Henry Frederick Faery 22800 James R. Tichenor 22801 Lee Alexander Farmelo 22802 Richard Joseph Campbell 22803 Darryle Leslie Kouns 22804 Reynold Morin 22805 Joseph Michael Stehling 22806 Howard Theodore Harcke 22807 Davis Stevens Tarr 22808 Karl Trueheart Gould 22809 Kevin Emmett Carter 22810 John Allan Le Febvre 22811 Jerome Bailey York 22812 Henry Lee 22813 Joseph George Felber 22814 John Charles Depew 22815 Charlie Clarke Watkins 22816 Eugene Patrick Flannery 22817 Humphrey Francis Windsor 22818 Thomas Ellis Kopp 22819 Daniel Arthur Smith 22820 Terrence La Verne Rich 22821 Stillman Doane Covell 22822 Bertram Arnold Bunting 22823 Walter Rexford Good 22824 Thomas Bullene Throckmorton 22825 Robert Miller Myers 22826 Richard Webb Cato 22827 Stanford Wayne Hickman 22828 Edward James Brady 22829 John Kneeland Davidson 22830 Grant Arthur Schaefer 22831 Robert Donald Marcinkowski 22832 John Ulay Nix 22833 Harry Noel White 22834 Clayton Henry Carmean 22835 Richard Joseph Holleman 22836 John Jarrett Schneider 22837 Frank Louis Cloutier 22838 Jack Woodward Dice 22839 James Bryan Oerding 22840 Wayne Gordon Gillespie 22841 Kenneth Ray Hill 22842 Walker Hancock Flint 22843 Robert Ernest Klein 22844 Herman Thomas Eubanks 22845 Paul Anthony Roberts 22846 William Frederick Chamberlain 22847 Tom Adams Robinson 22848 Donald William Prosser 22849 David Howard Stem 22850 Frank Joseph Bochnowski 22851 John David Del Ponti 22852 Alonzo Coose 22853 Clarence Earl Endy 22854 John Kelly Keane 22855 Ross Andrew Gagliano 22856 Daniel Louis O'Leary 22857 Thomas Kelly O'Malley 22858 Frank Nevin Cremer 22859 Henry Charles Watson 22860 Russell Ashton Waters 22861 Edward Russell Baldwin 22862 William Ward Sartoris 22863 George Edmund Wrockloff 22864 Robert Charles Platt 22865 John Arthur Hixson 22866 William Warren Danforth 22867 Thomas Franklin Eynon 22868 Michael Thomas Ryan 22869 Eugene Donald Griffith 22870 Jerry Wayne Witherspoon 22871 John Randolph Berti 22872 William LeRoy Johnson 22873 Robert Gerald Totten 22874 William Smith Tozer 22875 Hartman Baxter Mowery 22876 William Orville Drollinger 22877 Robert Edward Burns 22878 Peter Brindley 22879 Gerald Chapman 22880 Joseph Grady Caldwell 22881 Richard Holt Gates 22882 John Evon Young 22883 William Montgomery Raymond 22884 Fletcher Hughes Griffis 22885 George Hornsby McManus 22886 Ned Natale Loscuito 22887 James Herbert Janszen 22888 Harry Charles Calvin 22889 Joal Le Roy Davis 22890 John Christian Birkholz 22891 Frederick Udo Schroeder 22892 Roger McKelvey Ryan 22893 Wilsie Horton Adams 22894 Jack Thomas Humes 22895 Anthony Harris Blackstone 22896 Glenn Edwin Dawson 22897 Kenneth Lloyd King 22898 Edward John Laurance 22899 Richard Hyde Gillespie 22900 William Henry Maloney 22901 John Howard Alban 22902 Bruce Stanley Nevins 22903 John Patrick Kane 22904 John Solomon Wilkes 22905 Robert J. Castleman 22906 Craig Goldsbrough Colter 22907 Larry William Pitts 22908 Phillip Lyle Blake 22909 Olin Rosco Thompson 22910 Robert Howard Mills 22911 Bobby Lee Owens 22912 Fred Nicholas Halley 22913 John William Hynd 22914 Robert Foye 22915 Leroy Allen Schmidt 22916 Johnny Ray Hubbard 22917 Daniel Wayne Shimek 22918 David J. MacAulay 22919 Alan Douglas Champ 22920 Warren Henry Glenn 22921 William Stanley Carpenter 22922 Richard Otto Sutton 22923 Robert Francis Clancy 22924 Larry Victor Kling 22925 James Berkley Fairchild 22926 William Geron Hanne 22927 Joseph Alexander Jascewsky 22928 Leslie Paul Mason 22929 Thomas Peter Van Riper 22930 Richard William Helbock 22931 Gregory Charles Clement 22932 Alfred Dunlop Bailey 22933 Homer William Jones 22934 Henry Allen Phillips 22935 Jay Hilyard Rodman 22936 Stephen Harlan Scott 22937 Wayne Clay 22938 Joe Middleton Cannon 22939 Henry Lewis Meloan 22940 Dan Harold Campbell 22941 Lee Allen 22942 Francis William Farrell 22943 Joseph Robert Cote 22944 Raymond Gordon Canant 22945 Terrance M. Gill 22946 Philip Augustus Walker 22947 Kenneth Reese Kirchner 22948 Richard W. Healy 22949 Michael Lambert Ferguson 22950 Robert Leland Leech 22951 Robert Lavern Keen 22952 Gerald Ramsey Jilbert 22953 Roland Dwight Fenton 22954 Philip Anthony Tripician 22955 John Paul Yeagley 22956 James Paul Fero 22957 John David Hogarth 22958 Martin William Cary 22959 Arthur Martin Giese 22960 Jimmy Donald Carver 22961 James Ellegood Humphreys 22962 Philip Vincent McGance 22963 Thomas Elbert Noel 22964 Robert John Schiemann 22965 George Alexander Finley 22966 Milledge E. Wade 22967 Arthur Thomas Carey 22968 Richard Allan Carnaghi 22969 William Thomas Veal 22970 Charles Richard Neely 22971 Thomas James Haycraft 22972 Phillip Edward Chappell 22973 Fenton Harris Griffith 22974 Michael Thomas Plummer 22975 Ercole Michael Barone 22976 James Joseph York 22977 Richard Nash McInerney 22978 Joseph Valentine Arnold 22979 Frederick James Lynn 22980 Paul George Cerjan 22981 Kenneth Richard Ludovici 22982 Dean Harvey Darling 22983 Joseph Carter Lucas 22984 E. Raymond Hapeman 22985 David Woodfin Bauer 22986 Craig Allan Hagan 22987 William Prado Manlongat 22988 Theodore Stephens Danielsen 22989 John Patrick

Kirby 22990 Charles Richard Nelson 22991 Charles Martin Valliant 22992 Denis Crowley Dice 22993 William Jan Hardenburg 22994 Richard Lafayette Cox 22995 Jack Phelan Hug 22996 James Timothy O'Connell 22997 Larry Morgan Williams 22998 O. George Everbach 22999 Anthony Benson Wood 23000 Harold Barroner Smith 23001 Patrick James O'Donnell 23002 John Roe Denton 23003 Daniel Hunter Wilson 23004 William Nathan Bailey 23005 George Keith Garner 23006 James George Garvey 23007 John Richard Burden 23008 James Houston Johnson 23009 Michael Joseph Hatcher 23010 Larry Duane Struck 23011 Darryl Snyder Krape 23012 Edward Reeves Garton 23013 Joseph Edward Naftzinger 23014 John Peter Fanning 23015 Jack Anthony Pellicci 23016 Robert Norman Johnson 23017 Irving Abram Lerch 23018 Robert Batson Davidson 23019 John Brad Seely 23020 Richard E. Walter 23021 Harold H. Lusky 23022 John Bolling Hubard 23023 William Ward Robocker 23024 John Francis Gulla 23025 Michael Ralph Eckmann 23026 John Franklin Geiger 23027 Edward Waldren Crum 23028 Joseph Daniels O'Keefe 23029 John Joseph McKinney 23030 Charles Roy Baker 23031 John Francis Hargrove 23032 David Francis Byrnes 23033 James Delano Ruppert 23034 Herbert William Barnett 23035 Walter Cornelius Tousey 23036 Don Allen Summers 23037 Jere King Forbus 23038 James William Klosek 23039 Alan T. Shost 23040 Williams Swift Martin 23041 Charles Rupert Schrankel 23042 Roy J. O'Connor 23043 James Richard Kane 23044 Merlin Duane Darling 23045 Jerome X. Lewis 23046 Frederic Benjamin Hall 23047 Donald Albert Hubbard 23048 Robert Campbell Johnson 23049 Edmond Howard Drake 23050 James Arthur Booker 23051 Joseph Patrick Wiley 23052 Hughes Lanier Ash 23053 Robert Douw Eckert 23054 Richard Tilford Schofield 23055 Edward John Handler 23056 William Neal McFaul 23057 Joseph William Squire 23058 Michael William Gilmartin 23059 William Fred Dawdy 23060 Michael Andrew Jezior 23061 John Lesesne DeWitt 23062 John Richard Blanton 23063 Randall A. Perkins 23064 James Rose Ramos 23065 Abraham Lincoln German 23066 Robert Anthony Trodella 23067 James Buchanan Lincoln 23068 Robert John Menzner 23069 Leslie Edward Beavers 23070 John Calvin Reid 23071 Bartley William Furey 23072 William Francis Murphy 23073 Arthur LeRoy Bloch 23074 George Michael Heckman 23075 John Clinton House 23076 Jay Scott Brown 23077 Thomas Allen Walker 23078 Victor T. Letonoff 23079 William Frederick Tamplin 23080 Francis Joseph Calverase 23081 Calvin Robert Johnson 23082 John Paul Misura 23083 Donald Frederick Straetz 23084 James Richard Smith 23085 Patrick Joseph Holland 23086 Edward Miller Crowley 23087 John Zollinger Miller 23088 David Loyal Hodge 23089 Joseph Edgar Fortier 23090 David Gordon Wilkie 23091 William Ray Harnagel 23092 Lyell Francis King 23093 Danford Milton Orr 23094 Ross H. Cullins 23095 Robert Neal Schannep 23096 George Frederick Kaiser 23097 Robert Hagerman Tripp 23098 Noble James Wiley 23099 Angel E. Olmeta 23100 Lawrence Raymond Coffey 23101 Julio Edgardo Perez 23102 Charles Stedman Nobles 23103 Henry Fredrick Drewfs 23104 John Lawrence Reber 23105 Joseph John Bobula 23106 Chris George Gigicos 23107 Robert Samuel Miser 23108 Donald Harvey Barrell 23109 Jennings Herbert Mease 23110 Thomas Alfred Koentop 23111 Daniel J. Donahue 23112 Richard Samuel Daum 23113 James Hildred Pearl 23114 Charles Gordon Luton 23115 Thomas Happer Taylor 23116 Richard Klemm Boyd 23117 Ernest Arthur Remus 23118 Ronald Frederick Desgroseilliers 23119 John Charles Fyfe 23120 George Peter Bare 23121 Donald Kenneth Allen 23122 Garrett Ross Sampson 23123 Ronald Wayne Halsall 23124 John Eugene Weiler 23125 Joseph Michael Robinson 23126 John Henry Willauer 23127 Joseph Warren Stilwell 23128 John Norman Taylor 23129 William Howard Willoughby 23130 George Joseph McElroy 23131 Frederick Colton Rice 23132 Frank Delaney Finn 23133 Jack Evans Elder 23134 Arthur Edward Judson 23135 James A. Hopper 23136 Robert Eugene Oswandel 23137 Brion Victor Chabot 23138 Herman Samuel Marmon 23139 William Joseph Hourihan 23140 James Maurice Crabbe 23141 James Nicholas Rowe 23142 Charles Ray Coon 23143 Thaddeus Joseph Bara 23144 Melvin Blair Hayes 23145 Fredrick Arthur Johnson 23146 Mark Perrin Lowrey 23147 Richard Kevin Queeney 23148 William Eugene Florence 23149 James Stewart Godwin 23150 Paul Stevens 23151 Kenneth Ellsworth Sindora 23152 Albert Clark Keating 23153 Ora Oscar Caldwell 23154 William Thomas Blitch 23155 William Thaddeus Sexton 23156 James Howard DeMent 23157 Elwyn Donald Post 23158 Charles Gene Belan 23159 Peter Maclachian 23160 Dyson Ramsey Conklin Miller 23161 Frederick Richard Trickett 23162 Harold Andrew Brownfield 23163 James Kenneth McCollum 23164 Robert Gene Drennan 23165 Philip Miles Croel 23166 Adolph Sutton 23167 James Anthony Dougalas 23168 Samuel Philbrick Kelley 23169 William Edwin Creighton 23170 Robert Scobie Fairweather 23171 John Guy Coombs 23172 Gerard Joseph Rivell 23173 Eugene Adair Howell 23174 William Martin Breit 23175 Harold Lee Ladehoff 23176 Charles Driscoll Collins 23177 Mark Lowry 23178 Charles T. Schmitt 23179 Paul Joseph Savio 23180 Michael Otto Preletz 23181 William A. Myers 23182 John Thomas Downey 23183 Darrell Gwynn Houston 23184 Gerald Francis Winters 23185 James Dane Starling 23186 William Peter Ruedel 23187 William Alexander Meder 23188 Harry Dillon Lambert 23189 Ira Dorsey 23190 Richard Phillip Shuey 23191 John Lloyd Casey 23192 Robert Francisco Estes 23193 John G. Hoaas 23194 Allyn Jay Barr 23195 Robert Kimball Mercado 23196 Joseph William Hutchison 23197 Floyd Donald Whitehead 23198 Edward Allen Bellis 23199 Frederick Garside Terry 23200 John Vincent Ello 23201 John Weller Wood 23202 William Irvine Scudder 23203 Walter Dinsmore Hastings 23204 Roger Graham Seymour 23205 James M. White 23206 Charles Benjamin Fegan 23207 Charles Decko 23208 Gene Raymond Wilson 23209 Thomas Pearson Maginnis 23210 Richard McDonald Greene 23211 Robert Gordon Morrison 23212 William N. Myers 23213 Ferdinand Clarence Bidgood 23214 Thomas Nelsen Whitmore 23215 Thomas J. Donahue 23216 William Ludlow Ritchie 23217 Edward John Walczak 23218 Joel Edward Sugdinis 23219 Judson Long Bireley 23220 Henry Bishop Fisher 23221 Thomas Francis Schatzman 23222 Julian Thomas Caraballo 23223 Charles Leonard Gallo 23224 Earl Whelbert Eubanks 23225 Clark Porter Chandler 23226 James Allan Powers 23227 Spencer Dee Marcy 23228 William Austin Vencill 23229 John Clayton Crump 23230 George Wayne Kramer 23231 Don Clark Chapman 23232 George Patrick McQuillen 23233 John Frederick Shelby 23234 Walter King Wilson 23235 Robert Sidney Rudesill 23236 David Brian Wentworth 23237 Rand Edelstein 23238 Ambrose William Brennan 23239 Larry Wilson Sapper 23240 Gerald George Epley 23241 Chandler Prather Robbins 23242 Eliot Vail Parker 23243 Richard Arthur Daniel 23244 Anthony David Baker 23245 Alan Edward Johnson 23246 Michael Finlay Field 23247 Paul Charles Swain 23248 James Frederick Schwoob 23249 John Pearson Sherden 23250 John Cecil Stanley 23251 George Nunzio Giacoppe 23252 Eugene Joseph McLaughlin 23253 William Clark Chase 23254 Michael Joseph Mooney 23255 Duncan Wilmore 23256 Robert Thomas Gerald Hackett 23257 Lawrence Nelson Geist 23258 George Robert Stanley 23259 Robert Paul Anderson 23260 Robert Philip Koontz 23261 Charles Ellis Sturgeon 23262 John Michael Lenti 23263 Hector Andres Carron 23264 Manuel Angel Hidalgo 23265 John Powell Hesford 23266 George Trent Crosby 23267 Albert John Dunlap 23268 Francis James Thompson 23269 Melvin W. Rollins 23270 Lyman Chandler Duryea 23271 William Peter Fay 23272 Berlis Fleming Ennis 23273 Richard Tyler Willson 23274 John Daniel Dobak 23275 Richard Alan Jaeckel 23276 William Tripp McNamara 23277 Stephen Preston Waldrop 23278 John Stephen Gibbs 23279 Benjamin Franklin Evans 23280 Charles H. Wood 23281 **1961** John Luther Kammerdiener 23282 Howard Dwayne Graves 23283 Larry Donald Budge 23284 John Merkel Dorr 23285 Russell Martin Cornelius 23286 Howard Harry Roberts 23287 Cyrus Newton Shearer 23288 James Edward Jenz 23289 Philip Gerald Dombrowski 23290 Theodore Vander Els 23291 David Lee Ackerman 23292 Richard Kent Jackson 23293 Henry Edward Lilienthal 23294 Darius William Gaskins 23295 Roy Lee Armstrong 23296 Peter David Heimdahl 23297 Richard George Knoblock 23298 James Burse Royce 23299 Douglas Frank Matthews 23300 Peter J. Offringa 23301 Frank Lawrence Heikkila 23302 Roger Lamon Cornelius 23303 James Franklin Oaks 23304 Brian Glen Schultz 23305 John Charles Sigg 23306 Bruce Peter Holmberg 23307 Bruce Mitchell Cowan 23308 William Lytle Heiberg 23309 Philip Halm Mallory 23310 Lawrence Abner Noble 23311 Daniel William Halpin 23312 John Clayton Jones 23313 William Richard Williamson 23314 Robert Harry Guerzenich 23315 William Terry Kirkpatrick 23316 Charles John Sollohub 23317 Benjaman Cyrus Glidden 23318 Arthur James Downey 23319 Walter Batchelor Ligon 23320 R. Michael Maus 23321 David Jens Teal 23322 Bruce Raul Abraham 23323 James John Harmon 23324 John Arthur Eielson 23325 James Milton Stokes 23326 William Eugene Seltz 23327 Morris Lee Marshall 23328 Ralph William Garens 23329 Roger W. Middlesteadt 23330 Douglas Alan Wold 23331 Willard Charles Conley 23332 Roy Frederick Busdiecker 23333 James Irving Crowther 23334 Harry George Rennagel 23335 Peter James Boylan 23336 Howard Ellwood McCreary 23337 Kim Edward Fox 23338 Robert Rigby Glass 23339 Thomas Harrison Rousseau 23340 Donald Lawrence McBee 23341 Franklin Thomas Tilton 23342 Warwick Paul Wadlington 23343 Rodney Allyn Bartholomew 23344 Pat C. Hoy 23345 Harold Michael Hannon 23346 Edward Aloysius Brown 23347 Bruce Brantley Halstead 23348 Edward Francis Bruner 23349 Philip Aiden Sykes 23350 Nicholas Stephen Plodinec 23351 Charles Howard Armstrong 23352 Daniel G. Barney 23353 Reginald Jude Brown 23354 John Michael Seidl 23355 Neil Sadler Grigg 23356 Charles Shaw Green 23357 William Henry Reno 23358 Howard Maxwell Potter 23359 George Sidney Smith 23360 John Bardonner Zimmerman 23361 Clinton Hays Coddington 23362 David Ainsworth Hastings 23363 Tarey Bessette Schell 23364 Thomas Francis Carroll 23365 Harvey Legrand Brown 23366 Charles Robert Hansell 23367 John Richard Nevins 23368 Carl Baird Sciple 23369 Bert Harris Custer 23370 Donald Arthur Dreesbach 23371 Robert Bogardus Cairns 23372 Charles Todd Westpheling 23373 Samuel Collins Nutt 23374 John Earle Skillman 23375 Basil Manly Parks 23376 Gary Robert Hyde 23377 John Frederick Votaw 23378 Howard William Randall 23379 Gary Reese Lord 23380 Lawrence Edward Welsh 23381 John Brennan Kampfer 23382 Thomas Robert Cuthbert 23383 Kenneth Eugene Siegenthaler 23384 Gerald Allen Vick 23385 Donald Allan Barbour 23386 Larry F. Smalley 23387 Robert Emmett McCarthy 23388 Robert Bernard Rosenkranz 23389 Martin Andrew Compton 23390 Richard John Davis 23391 J. Chism 23392 F. Walton Wanner 23393 James Pierson Cargile 23394 William Randolph Wright 23395 Gustav Henri Stiehl 23396 Frederick Donald Daniloff 23397 Frank Thomas Blanda 23398 Leroy Arthur Babbitt 23399 Thomas Richardson Stone 23400 James Dexter Jackson 23401 Robert Lynn Oliver 23402 Michael Gerard Breslin 23403 Heston W. Higginbotham 23404 Gordon Thomas Ericksen 23405 Robert James Steege 23406 Nicholas Charles Gilbert 23407 Julian Michael Olejniczak 23408 Holland Brewster Coulter 23409 Philip John Sands 23410 Marko Louis Popovich 23411 Gerard Henry Clements 23412 Roderick Anthony Cameron 23413 Steve Henry Denney 23414 Bruce Robert Seidel 23415 Dudley Cade Lancaster 23416 James Kuykendall Evetts 23417 Thomas Decker Matson 23418 Donn Gibson Miller 23419 Robert Reynolds Hardiman 23420 Roland Frederick Seylar 23421 Dallas Keith Gillespie 23422 Samuel David Wilder 23423 Charles Michael Swain 23424 Thomas Newton Sherburne 23425 Michael John Lombardo 23426 Robert Daw Hampton 23427 David Michael Brooks 23428 Thelmo Yilano Cunanan 23429 Gail Patrick Burchell 23430 James Bonade Taylor 23431 Bruce Gordon Heron 23432 Thomas Wilson Pusser 23433 Robert Frank Harris 23434 W. Scott Dillard 23435 Edwin Sterling Leland 23436 Stacy Carl Bragg 23437 John Knapp Solomon 23438 Joseph John McCann 23439 Lynn Alan Bender 23440 Charles Patrick Burns 23441 Gary W. Webster 23442 Walter Edward Stanley 23443 Donald Vincent Lockey 23444 Kenneth Homer Geiger 23445 William Dean Esselstein 23446 Herbert Theodore G. Benz 23447 John Francis McLaughlin 23448 Francis Joseph Fishburne 23449 Albert Vanderbush 23450 Bruce Jack Gronich 23451 John Brooks Oliver 23452 James Lee Tedrick 23453 Kenneth Wayne McCollister 23454 Lyman Gerard White 23455 James Calvin Connolly 23456 Robert James Kee 23457 Robert Reavis Protzman 23458 Grant Bruce Dalgleish 23459 William Ira Parks 23460 Barnwell Ingraham Legge 23461 David Shelby Price 23462 William Duncan Nesbeitt 23463 James Sinclair Mathison 23464 Robert Anthony Burns 23465 Dean Spalding Frazier 23466 Alan Henry Lubke 23467 Monroe Bailey Harden 23468 Robert Winfred Bunton 23469 James Bruce Raynis 23470 Henmar Ruskin Gabriel 23471 Hugh Harry Miller 23472 Michael Emmett Ekman 23473 Anderson Howel Walters 23474 Carl Joseph Wimmer 23475 Edward Todd Counts 23476 Joseph Glen Adams 23477 Michael Skotzko 23478 Donald Edward Landry 23479 Walter Gaines Robertson 23480 Thomas Michael Coyne 23481 Robert Hargreaves Kewley 23482 Dale Wendell Shipley 23483 Martin Walter Walsh 23484 Donald Michael Lionetti 23485 Benjamin Wilson Covington 23486 Darwin Lee Richards 23487 Martell De Vera Fritz 23488 Frank Collins Rauch 23489 Robert Francis Zielinski 23490 Carlton Elbridge Bacon 23491 Garry Michael Cook 23492 William Stuart Chandler 23493 John Winslow Lawrence 23494 William Johannes Theo. M. Born 23495 William Richard Griffiths 23496 Warren Leslie Miller 23497 Gilman John Hallenbeck 23498 Lucas Boeve 23499 Eugene Shirer Witherspoon 23500 Ephraim Whitworth Crews 23501 John Ernest Fischer 23502 William Arthur Jacob Mackie 23503 Robert Grantham Harrell 23504 Ray Lee Tilghman 23505 Regis John Reynolds 23506 William Michael Hale 23507 John Edward Jones 23508 George M. Hricz 23509 Hubert Byron Vaughn 23510 Richard Evan McNear 23511 Warren K. Watson 23512 Willard Samuel Belknap 23513 Andrew Franklin Bennett 23514 Harry E. Downing 23515 David Mackenzie Ritchie 23516 Gordon Spottswood Bounds 23517 Pringle Pat Hillier 23518 Warren Bellamy Shull 23519 Eugene Price Sanders 23520 Stanley Michael Conway-Clough 23521 William Townsley Deuel 23522 Richard A. Buckner 23523 Terry Lee Alexander 23524 Hans Otto Conrad Wagner 23525 Michael Leslie Underwood 23526 David Anthony Dluzyn 23527 David Harlan Mace 23528 James Armitt Scott 23529 George Alfred Joulwan 23530 Mark Norman Silverman 23531 Alan Parker Armstrong 23532 Ralph Bonner Garretson 23533 George Fox 23534 Robert Barry Hamilton 23535 James Dean Strachan 23536 Gunnar Carl Carlson 23537 James Francis Lynch 23538 William Austin Stricklen 23539 John Gordon Wildermuth 23540 Frank Walter Gillespie 23541 Ted Albert Showalter 23542 Joseph William Stewart 23543 Richard Frank Bitner 23544 Alvin Webster Kremer 23545 Howard Stuart De Witt 23546 William Ogden 23547 George Henderson 23548 Norman Northrop Cunningham 23549 Brendan McKay Greeley 23550 James Craig Manning 23551 Eugene Francis LaBorne 23552 John Rickert McCormick 23553 Richard Dale Sheeder 23554 John Alda Kemp 23555 Bruce Thomas Lammers 23556 Reid Reid Russell 23557 James Frederick Pryor 23558 Jay Cornell Cook 23559 David Leon Miller 23560 Richard Warren Van Riper 23561 Michael Edward O'Neill 23562 John William Goldtrap 23563 Richard August Behrenhausen 23564 Thomas Walter Paskewitz 23565 Charles Redfield Welsh 23566 Dale Gardner Campbell 23567 Patrick Michael Trinkle 23568 William Richards Ford 23569 Marshall Evan Harrington 23570 John Dean Veatch 23571 Robert Louis Janoska 23572 Nicolas Roskovanyi Vay 23573 William Ernest Hathaway 23574 Alexander James Stuart 23575 John O'Neill Turnage 23576 Laurence John Stoneham 23577 Raymond Elliott Starsman 23578 Robert P. Yavis 23579 Julius William Seibel 23580 Joseph Rudolph Tschamler 23581 Richard Curry Conant 23582 Francis Lee Gibson 23583 Thomas Henry Magness 23584 Wayne David Ploger 23585 Harmon Robert Parmele 23586 James William Tyler 23587 Richard Douglas Clarke 23588 James William Doherty 23589 William Bruce Bradford 23590 Robert Allan Liebman 23591 R. J. Wooten 23592 Jon Frank Nitkowski 23593 James Michael Coyle 23594 Donald Allen Walsh 23595 Robert Ames Montgomery 23596 W. Michael Younkin 23597 Ronald Dickerson Hines 23598 Michael Dent Eiland 23599 William Alan Weis 23600 Richard Hilmer Fanning 23601 Charles Bruce Hodell 23602 Joseph Anthony Czuberki 23603 Quinton Holton 23604 Gary Lee Flack 23605 Ronald R. Barrick 23606 Samuel Digges Freeman 23607 Richard Owen Cullum 23608 Jonathan Burrell Aaronsohn 23609 Richard Andrew Thompson 23610 Eugene Kenneth Goodell 23611 Jim Lee Madden 23612 George Dennis Lenhart 23613 Thomas John Minnehan 23614 Alexander Hamilton Evans 23615 Carl Thomas Hansen 23616 Robert Douglas Chelberg 23617 Francis Michael Williams 23618 Robert Lee Potts 23619 Russell Max Miller Phelps 23620 Steven Connor Walker 23621 Harry E. Woodward 23622 James Edward Struve 23623 Phillips Waller Smith 23624 Roger William Obermeier 23625 Henry Peter Van Gorder 23626 Robert Milnor Herrick 23627 Ronald Breen Neutzling 23628 Joseph Svensson Dahle 23629 James Michael Winters 23630 John Joseph Berinato 23631 Paul Carr Palmer 23632 Allan Raymond Wetzel 23633 Donald Charles Anselm 23634 Dominador Baldomero Bazan 23635 Robert Gerald Eveleth 23636 George Alexander Hartford 23637 Raymond R. Regan 23638 Thomas Richard Gordon 23639 Gilbert Richard Bilodeau 23640 James Patrick McGinnis 23641 Charles Norman Heiman 23642 Robert Maurice Dunning 23643 Byron Smith Baldwin 23644 Kenneth Lee Hruby 23645 Andrew Bateman Casani 23646 Thomas Truxton Moebs 23647 Morris Fredrick Hanson 23648 Harold Chester Gaither 23649 Joseph Frank Paone 23650 R. James Nicholson 23651 Clayton Imes Grant 23652 Henry James Kenny 23653 Steven Vass 23654 Frank Boyle Eyler 23655 Forrest Rodell Carlton 23656 James Leroy Livingston 23657 Lawrence Hurst Prather 23658 John L. Campbell 23659 Edward Patrick Barry 23660 Albert H. Hokins 23661 Arlen Clair Thomas Miller 23662 William Daniel Yost 23663 Robert Bruce McConnell 23664 Peter Dwight Burgess 23665 Howard Dale Himes 23666 Andrea Attilio Sarzanini 23667 Gene Arthur Adams 23668 Robert Andrew McCurdy 23669 William Lawrence Madsen 23670 Roger Cerasoli 23671 Nikolajs Robert Muiznieks 23672 John Joseph Java 23673 James Francis Xavier Looram 23674 David George Eaton 23675 Richard Walter Angstadt 23676 Donald Raymond Bonko 23677 Frank Joseph Habic 23678 George Larry Shamblee 23679 Paul Thomas DeVries 23680 George Philip Yancey 23681 Joseph Richard Maio 23682 Channing Miller Greene 23683 David William White 23684 Edward Burke Mucho 23685 Richard Gwyn Williams 23686 Robert Norris Gilliam 23687 Rodney Floyd Grannemann 23688 Joseph F. Pesek 23689 William Howard Sievers 23690 D. Peter Gleichenhaus 23691 Donald Wayne Watlington 23692 Walter William Hodge 23693 John Bruce Shroyer 23694 Rohlf Alexander Shaffer 23695 John Ronald MacLean 23696 Wayne Russell Williams 23697 John Owen Sommercamp 23698 Phillip Henry Ringdahl 23699 Joseph Gaius Brooks 23700 Emmanuel John Scivoletto 23701 Michael Coyne 23702 Beverley E. Powell 23703 Samuel Walter Enfield 23704 James Ross Corcoran 23705 Sanford Elihu Vedder 23706 William Edward Clancy 23707 Joseph Strong Stringham 23708 Roland Raymond Holz 23709 Howard Allan Bais 23710 Albert Lloyd Wells 23711 Joseph Francis Watt 23712 John Colby Cornelson 23713 James Steven Blesse 23714 Michael John Xenos 23715 Kenith Erwin Meissner 23716 Joseph Brian Amlong 23717 Richard C. Skaggs 23718 Travis Neal Dyer 23719 Henry Daniels Minor 23720 Francis G. Sisk 23721 James Leighton Stork 23722 Dan Alan Conner 23723 George Coleman Kopcsak 23724 William Galvin Tobin 23725 Gerald Armand Zingsheim 23726 Thomas John Lund 23727 Michael James Brady 23728 Larry Reynoldson Butterworth 23729 Monte Thomas Sloan 23730 Robert Scott Cain 23731 Robert Keith Bernard 23732

Glenn Miller Peters 23733 Lee Reuben Anderson 23734 James Arthur Goldstine 23735 George Murl Seckinger 23736 Michael Angelo Eggleston 23737 Glynn Clark Mallory 23738 John Parkinson Green 23739 Patrick James Murphy 23740 Michael Edmund Urette 23741 Ralph E. Pollard 23742 Thomas Kirn Mercer 23743 David Earl Biddinger 23744 Brendan J. Battle 23745 Harold Hampton Hodges 23746 George Martin Cherry 23747 James Edward Schall 23748 Barton Patrick Chambers 23749 Charles Nelson Haas 23750 Thomas Heritage Baird 23751 James Renfro Haise 23752 Gordon Kenneth Downey 23753 Bromley Newhall Cook 23754 John Dennis Guthrie 23755 Robert Hollis Strauss 23756 Ronald Lee Beckett 23757 Bruce Roger Kovac 23758 Conwell Barry Leinbach 23759 Lawrence Arthur Richards 23760 John T. Baker 23761 John Duncan Dewar 23762 Kenneth Lee Quinn 23763 John Joseph Neiger 23764 John Joseph Kilkenny 23765 Earl Wayne Gilmore 23766 James Emerson Altmeyer 23767 Benjamin Louis Willis 23768 James Anthony Cullen 23769 Thomas Eugene Leech 23770 Quinn Filmore Pearl 23771 Paul Franklin Vader 23772 Talbert Whiting Hughes 23773 Richard Carlton Boys 23774 Patrick Joseph Carroll 23775 Edgar D. Smith 23776 Harry Kyle Bayless 23777 Peter Louis Benzinger 23778 Donald Hugh Lewis 23779 Michael Maloney 23780 Charles Thomas Randolph 23781 Robert Scott Frix 23782 Dennis Michael Rooney 23783 Richard George Yule 23784 James Linden Chase 23785 Franklyn Arthur Erhardt 23786 Donald Andrew Couvillion 23787 John Louis Raible 23788 Paul Eugene Vallely 23789 Louis Charles Berra 23790 Donald William Sawtelle 23791 Walter E. Claassen 23792 Thomas Schiller Myerchin 23793 Earl Campbell Horan 23794 Lee Hugo Sager 23795 Robert Monte Gants 23796 Joseph Paul Russo 23797 John Jay Nichols 23798 Courtney Maxwell Rittgers 23799 James Wallace Connors 23800 Roland Marius Navarro 23801 John Rife Petty 23802 Sergei Vladimir Olive 23803 Martin Lewis Ganderson 23804 John Hassig Mack 23805 Robert Copelan Dickson 23806 David Woodrow Hiester 23807 Daniel Marshall DiCarlo 23808 Roger William Zailskas 23809 James John Roberts 23810 Jack McConnell Martin 23811 Francis Charles Egan 23812 Edwin Norman Olson 23813 Bruce Py Nichols 23814 Martin Joseph Zaldo 23815 **1962** John Herbert Fagan 23816 David Kerr Riggs 23817 Frank Barrett Horton 23818 Rudolf Ernest Penczer 23819 Richard Ernest Storat 23820 Ernest Gustave Zenker 23821 Walter Richard Menning 23822 Charles Rodney Chandler 23823 James Lee Kays 23824 Ed Walter Hendren 23825 Allan Dodge Robb 23826 Donald Richard Street 23827 Bernard Michael Martin 23828 James Raiford Ellis 23829 David A. Feldman 23830 Robert D. Zabik 23831 Will Myron Remington 23832 Philip J. Galanti 23833 Robert George Hufschmid 23834 Thomas Patrick Hueman 23835 John Ryan Landry 23836 Brian Vincent McKinley 23837 Charles G. Geiss 23838 Howard Taft Prince 23839 James Robert Martin 23840 Anthony Lynn Leatham 23841 Lawrence Thomas Sanders 23842 David John Phillips 23843 John Hobart Wagner 23844 Lawrence George Ailinger 23845 John Palmer Ferguson 23846 Arthur Stanley Brown 23847 Michael William Grebe 23848 Don Melville Snider 23849 Dan Leyland Denison 23850 Warner Deane Stanley 23851 Peter Siedzick 23852 James William Dunmyer 23853 Raoul Henri Alcala 23854 Jan Terry Molvar 23855 Robert J. Lilley 23856 Pierce Jude Hanley 23857 James Martin Worthington 23858 Frank Martin Cross 23859 Nicholas Richard Hurst 23860 Roy Shigeru Kobayashi 23861 Chalmers Hilliard Armstrong 23862 Christopher Hendrik Keuker 23863 Don Lee Lair 23864 Neil Kenneth Nydegger 23865 James John Heigl 23866 Bruce B. Parsons 23867 Craig Taylor 23868 Robert Edwin Douglas 23869 Richard Raymond Steinke 23870 William Crozier Meade 23871 David William Moore 23872 Donald Lee Williamson 23873 Walter Roger Shope 23874 Erik George Johnsson 23875 Frederick Erwin Sheaffer 23876 Michael Laurence Godshall 23877 Ronald Royce Henderson 23878 Frank Dickson Miller 23879 Richard Eli Helmuth 23880 Stephen Robert Schwam 23881 Donald Andrew Burns 23882 Robert G. Krause 23883 Allen Zehner Miller 23884 Edward Alfred Starbird 23885 Robert Leo Reid 23886 Thomas William McGarry 23887 Charles Russell Broshous 23888 Glen Alger Blumhardt 23889 George Wilhelm Kirschenbauer 23890 Paul Theodore Zmuida 23891 Charles Henry Ivy 23892 William G. Christopher 23893 Cal Duane Johnson 23894 Harry Meeth 23895 Donald Albert DeSapri 23896 John Edmund Easterbrook 23897 Lapsley Roger Caldwell 23898 Carl Rolland Morin 23899 Richard Edward Garvey 23900 Dwayne Donald Piepenburg 23901 Dennis William Gilstad 23902 William Charles Burns 23903 Jefferson Brian McCarthy 23904 Roy Vern Wallace 23905 John Henry Campbell 23906 Daniel Winston Wick 23907 George Thomas Mailey 23908 Kraig Ullman Hansen 23909 David Curtis Neumann 23910 George Richard Duncan 23911 Richard William Irwin 23912 Thomas Frank Ostenberg 23913 Paul Terry Murphy 23914 Joseph J. Wojcik 23915 Stephen Jay Kott 23916 Kenneth Dale Herring 23917 Joseph Edward Gross 23918 John Robert Meceda 23919 Wayne Donald Willis 23920 Jacob Roy Degenhardt 23921 Richard Joseph Randazzo 23922 Clifton R. Franks 23923 Clifford Moore McKeithan 23924 Ralph Lee Lurker 23925 Michael Moore 23926 Raymond Graham McDowall 23927 A. Thomas Fintel 23928 Richard Haven Gramzow 23929 David Andrew Armstrong 23930 Henry Domenick Urna 23931 Henry Wilson Worthington 23932 Dan Dale Buttolph 23933 Norman Donald Grahn 23934 Gary Lee Brown 23935 William George Kosco 23936 Philip Stuart Ball Fuller 23937 Donald Karrer 23938 Thomas Richard Middaugh 23939 Roger Wayne Franke 23940 David Paul Francis 23941 Roger A. Brown 23942 Eldon Lee Perdew 23943 Karl Martin Henn 23944 Benjamin Frederick Carter 23945 James Lau 23946 Richard William Fellows 23947 Joe W. Rigby 23948 Kenneth Robert Dolson 23949 Donald Johannes Voss 23950 Charles Elgin Dominy 23951 Arthur Frank Bondshu 23952 Harold Lewis Brown 23953 David Robert Spangler 23954 Michael Thomas O'Brien 23955 John Stevenson Habblett 23956 William Dooley Petty 23957 Alan McCauley Biddison 23958 Richard Irwin Carlson 23959 Donald William Hard 23960 Robert Charles Munsch 23961 Paul Wesley Burke 23962 George Burwell Sweet 23963 Ivan Leroy Waggoner 23964 Ronald Andrew Skarupa 23965 Dennis Joe Reimer 23966 John Franklin Meehan 23967 James Alexander Davidson 23968 Larry Dennis Smith 23969 James Henry Michael Malley 23970 Bertram Goldberg 23971 Douglas Willson Morgan 23972 Jeffrey Cornelius Alt 23973 Richard Glen Madden 23974 Robert Kenneth DeVries 23975 Samuel Kennett Wasaff 23976 Arthur N. Crowell 23977 David L. Mundt 23978 Arnold L. Larsen 23979 James S. Harrington 23980 Bertram Paul Finn 23981 David B. Garvin 23982 John J. Kelly 23983 Larry D. Bachelor 23984 Ronald Woodrum Witzel 23985 John B. Mumford 23986 Marshall B. Johnson 23987 John M. Vranish 23988 Bernard Skown 23989 Charles L. Fisher 23990 Kenneth V. Ishoy 23991 Ronald James Chisholm 23992 Ricardo E. D. Cesped 23993 Dan Talbott Stephenson 23994 James Francis McKay 23995 William Roberts Calhoun 23996 David Charles Minson 23997 Ervin Frank Kamm 23998 George Schein 23999 Jackson Custer Reavill 24000 Charles Lawrence Wuerpel 24001 Robert E. Holeman 24002 Dennis L. Benchoff 24003 Richard Rohrbacher 24004 Robert E. Rintz 24005 George Lawrence Gunderman 24006 Harry Raymond Boyd 24007 Roger Charles Andrews 24008 Russell O. Reich 24009 Todd L. Bergman 24010 Kenneth Michael Wallace 24011 William Joseph Dieal 24012 Ralph J. Finelli 24013 Joseph Anthony Petrolino 24014 William Thomas Reach 24015 Walter Ronald Brown 24016 Thomas Joseph Slaggie 24017 Ronald Anthony Borrello 24018 Morris Edgar Brown 24019 Stephen Horace Ellis 24020 John Frederick Nau 24021 Bill Pete Pfeifer 24022 Thomas Henry Merrell 24023 Ellis Miller Bailey 24024 Glenn Arthur Chadbourne 24025 William Arthur Hoos 24026 Robert Phillip Andrews 24027 Donald King Woodman 24028 Joseph Lawrence Guarino 24029 Samuel Sandeford Meyer 24030 Todd Darrah Stong 24031 Robert David Bauman 24032 Steventon Wagner 24033 Windsor Earl Ward 24034 Robert Dale Shuey 24035 Joseph George Porter 24036 Fred Augustus Gorden 24037 Dale H. Kuhns 24038 Charles D. Swick 24039 Richard Michael Gilligan 24040 John Philip Florence 24041 Richard Daniel Chegar 24042 Arthur Albert Lovgren 24043 Roger T. McNamara 24044 John Henry Dilley 24045 Elliott Guthrie Fishburne 24046 David O'Neal Treadwell 24047 Ronald Lewis Lane 24048 John Lee Novotny 24049 Clinton O'Neil Hyde 24050 Albert Richard Symes 24051 William Frank Daugherty 24052 Jay Herndon Witt 24053 John Norman Sloan 24054 Donald Allan Denton 24055 Herbert Charles Hertel 24056 Richard Evander Mayo 24057 Keith Edward Adams 24058 Lawrence Robert Crane 24059 Tyrus Raymond Cobb 24060 John Gregor Wilcox 24061 Richard William Wylie 24062 Robert Laird Ord 24063 Thomas Edward Murray 24064 Marshall N. Carter 24065 Francis Eugene Welper 24066 Jerry Dean Rose 24067 William Darrell Gertsch 24068 Kenneth O. Lutes 24069 Lawrence Craig Richardson 24070 Robert Joseph Weinfurter 24071 Robert L. Phillips 24072 Eldon H. Spradling 24073 Robert D. Greenwalt 24074 Charles William Tinnemeyer 24075 Edward J. Pabich 24076 Sylvain M. Loupe 24077 Kevin George Renaghan 24078 Terrance C. McCarthy 24079 Dale Franklin Smith 24080 Gary Lee Paxton 24081 William Lyle Miller 24082 Richard Collins Stephenson 24083 Joseph Alfred Simoneaux 24084 Peter Guild King 24085 James Randolph Furleigh 24086 Robert C. Carroll 24087 Wilton David McRae 24088 Rodney J. Schmidt 24089 David Merle Jones 24090 Lee Taylor 24091 Harold Dalton Baughman 24092 Gerald Albert Tysver 24093 Herbert Homer Hameister 24094 Stewart Sherard 24095 Wayne Allan Downing 24096 Charles Fredrick Bernitt 24097 Raife Edgar Snover 24098 Donald Neil Babb 24099 Stanley Edwin Whitmore 24100 John Edward Fee 24101 William Charles Whitehead 24102 Douglas Joyce Wauchope 24103 Robert Stafford Cooper 24104 Arthur Ray Miller 24105 Donald Allen Chafetz 24106 Wayne Brandt Parker 24107 Eugene Ramella 24108 William McCaw Hughes 24109 Frederick Eugene Comer 24110 James Gorman 24111 Arthur Milton Webb 24112 Frank Joseph Caufield 24113 David Loren Windom 24114 Leonard Anthony Butler 24115 John Edwin DeVore 24116 James M. Acklin 24117 Charles Edward Brown 24118 Steven L. Arnold 24119 Ernest LeRoy Webb 24120 John Robert Selby 24121 James D. Blundell 24122 Francis D. Westfall 24123 Charles Steuart Merriam 24124 John Leroy Franck 24125 Robert John Sikorski 24126 Theodore Glen Stroup 24127 John Wade Jones 24128 William Anderson Cauthen 24129 D. Edward Rowe 24130 William James Scott 24131 Jerry Joseph Seay 24132 George Walter Handy 24133 Stacy Edward Reeves 24134 Lawrence Richard Scheewe 24135 John James Hickey 24136 Jerry Vernon Lape 24137 Alfred Donovan Wilhelm 24138 John Henry King 24139 Stephen David Sperman 24140 Jack David Garrett 24141 Walter Joseph Bryde 24142 Ronald Lloyd Zinn 24143 Peter Joseph Oldfield 24144 Robert Barry Thomas 24145 Paul D. D. McNamara 24146 Gary Lee Seasholtz 24147 Russell DeVries 24148 William Leslie Ross 24149 Edward Albert Hamilton 24150 Billie Neal Thomas 24151 Paul Dale Schott 24152 Johann (Rudolph) Wilhelm Kohler 24153 Brian Raymond McEnany 24154 Harry Leon Fraser 24155 Rufus Claude Crow 24156 James M. Currin 24157 Donald E. Stewart 24158 James Lee Lindsey 24159 James F. McQuillen 24160 Larry Robert Needs 24161 Thomas Edward McMahan 24162 Willard Eugene Harrison 24163 Walter Alan Cooper 24164 Thomas John Kilmartin 24165 Charles O. Bennett 24166 Fred Rodney LaRoque 24167 Lewis Higinbotham 24168 Harry Wilber Nieuwboer 24169 William Allen Evans 24170 William H. Kinard 24171 David Alton Noake 24172 James Charles Ryan 24173 Roger Thomas Hilton 24174 Phillip Earl Nelson 24175 Raymond Joseph Lo Presto 24176 Robert Morgan Tarbet 24177 Michael George Schredl 24178 Robert Scott McGurk 24179 James A. Strohmeyer 24180 Jimmy Dale Mount 24181 Robert Walter Szymczak 24182 Phillip Atkinson Costain 24183 John Markle Grimshaw 24184 Frederick James Hillyard 24185 Joe Edward Pendergraft 24186 Joe Slade Johnson 24187 Michael Jeffrey Rosenberg 24188 Robert Yen Wong 24189 Anthony Borden Lawson 24190 Alfred Stephen Rushatz 24191 Paul James Kirkegaard 24192 James Gillis Andress 24193 John Charles Winkler 24194 Walter John Chrobak 24195 Grindley Cecil Curren 24196 Thomas Edward Faley 24197 Philip Yeager Browning 24198 Marlin Edward Schmidt 24199 Frederick Charles Bothwell 24200 Peter P. Horoschak 24201 Michael Allen Casp 24202 Howard Clifford Batt 24203 William Anthony Scherr 24204 William McEwan Cross 24205 Cornelius Cole Holcomb 24206 Francis Robert Scharpf 24207 Larry Lee Mengel 24208 Daniel David Clark 24209 Frederick Stanley Doten 24210 Robert Paul Garrett 24211 Edward Albaugh Gleichman 24212 Gene B. Tomlinson 24213 John David Finlayson 24214 Raymond Alden Pendleton 24215 James William Weiss 24216 Denne Aronson Sweeney 24217 Anthony Ronald De Amico 24218 Duane Lee Slater 24219 Christopher Wm Jerome Stanat 24220 Richard A. Lembo 24221 Richard Mark Chladek 24222 Thomas R. Kling 24223 Kenneth Lee Dean 24224 Harold Eugene Harris 24225 Ronny Joe Sayers 24226 Donald Norman Bergeron 24227 Gary Linn Sharp 24228 Dennis Don Flint 24229 Thomas Edward Walker 24230 William Francis Dworsak 24231 Richard Robert Sklar 24232 Paul Francis Wertz 24233 Roger Venton Havercroft 24234 Stanley Edward Thompson 24235 James Kennelly McCrorey 24236 Stephen Walsh Holderness 24237 David James Sholly 24238 David Vincent Harkins 24239 Ronald Adrian Tumelson 24240 Donald F. Pederson 24241 Richard Charles Cacioppe 24242 Harold Edwin Sprague 24243 Melvin Ernest Kriesel 24244 Alan Robert DeJardin 24245 Robert Harding Goode 24246 Thomas Emerson Buck 24247 John Turner Godwin 24248 John Joseph Kirby 24249 Thomas Charles Abbott 24250 James Michael Gleason 24251 Donald Fred Kauer 24252 Frederick Elmore Tilton 24253 George Joseph Telenko 24254 Thomas Leroy Mennie 24255 Paul Anthony Baltes 24256 Jerome Thomas Janicke 24257 William Phipps Cannon 24258 Charles Barry Butzer 24259 Kenneth R. Pakula 24260 Christopher Bennett Spivey 24261 Ronald Wayne Tumlin 24262 Matthew Bartholmew Whelton 24263 James L. Redmond 24264 Thurston Algee Griffith 24265 Dennis R. Bennett 24266 Thomas Dawson Pearson 24267 Vito Michael Caputo 24268 Thomas Arthur Herre 24269 Wilburn Layne Boozer 24270 Alan N. Scarsella 24271 Christopher Rutherford Robbins 24272 Francis Anthony Neil Fiore 24273 Wayne A. Snow 24274 Waide N. Rishel 24275 Gene Edward Baxter 24276 Jon Visart Lynn 24277 Robert Ferrell Wells 24278 Charles Calder Anderson 24279 Michael James Bartelme 24280 Patrick Oseth Kelly 24281 John Frederick Kendall 24282 Joseph Dale Nunnelee 24283 Phillip Ray Stewart 24284 Dean Lee Learish 24285 Ralph Marvin Fox 24286 Ardeen Richard Foss 24287 James Michael McDonough 24288 Paul Michael Jones 24289 Michael Anthony Guenther 24290 James Crawford Peterson 24291 David Roger McLaughlin 24292 John Leslie Taylor 24293 Thomas Anthony Simcox 24294 Ronald Paul Stock 24295 Thad Adolphus Broom 24296 Lawrence James Remener 24297 Evans Kellogg Whiting 24298 Edward James Dwyer 24299 Gerald George Garwick 24300 Joseph Duane Szwarckop 24301 Frank Stanley Reasoner 24302 Samuel Lindsey Steele 24303 Patrick Leo Canary 24304 William Floyd Smith 24305 John William O'Neal 24306 Ralph Regis Burr 24307 Roy Wheaton Cole 24308 Charles Leo Shaw 24309 Winston Blanton Clark 24310 Seth John Hudak 24311 Lawrence Roy Amon 24312 James Verlin Kimsey 24313 Marvin Peacock Norwood 24314 Thomas J. Teuten 24315 Laurence G. Mooring 24316 John Thaddeus Bode 24317 Livio Federico Pardi 24318 Steven George West 24319 Dan Graham Teed 24320 William Alfred Byrd 24321 Stanford Woodruff Shutes 24322 Thomas Richard Davis 24323 Robert Howard Fuellhart 24324 Sammie Tipton Carr 24325 Robert L. Ellis 24326 Paul James Dobbins 24327 James Joseph Spencer 24328 Thomas Richard Culver 24329 Alfred Frank Girardi 24330 William Walton Mogan 24331 Robert Charles Coyne 24332 John Winchester Byers 24333 Robert Edward Ricks 24334 James Edward Spurlock 24335 Alan Fleming McElhose 24336 Merle Robbins Williams 24337 John Baggett Walker 24338 Richard Allan James 24339 Michael Andrew Crabtree 24340 David William Logan 24341 Harry Edward Hagerty 24342 Trevor Nevitt Dupuy 24343 Robert Albert Redmond 24344 David Monroe Blynn 24345 Waldemar Philip Poulsen 24346 Charles L. Nahlen 24347 A. Richard Hartman 24348 David Edmund Symanski 24349 Alan Charles Tindale 24350 Richard Thomas Ryer 24351 James Edson Krause 24352 Michael R. N. McDonnell 24353 Joel Douglas Froeschle 24354 John Walter Dargle 24355 John Walker Darrah 24356 Thomas Frederick Eccleston 24357 James Randolph Tumpane 24358 Larry Wayne Parmenter 24359 Lawrence Elliot Waters 24360 Ralph Whittaker Pryor 24361 John Maxwell Ulmer 24362 Richard Albert Barry 24363 John Louis Schmidt 24364 Marcial David Samaniego 24365 Matthew Ronald Kambrod 24366 EdwardE. Eugene Krukowski 24367 James Francis Corr 24368 William H. Gavan 24369 Joseph Spangler Kieffer 24370 Charles Cavendish Darrell 24371 William Donald White 24372 Roger Conan Lee 24373 James Waldemer Dodd 24374 James Frederick Boyle 24375 Jerome Joseph Comello 24376 Donald Harold Woeber 24377 James Harper Cowles 24378 Robert Sewell Culp 24379 Anthony Arthur Pattarozzi 24380 Malcolm Jones Howard 24381 John Somers Regan 24382 Walter Dudley Taylor 24383 Jack L. Rucker 24384 Richard Steven Kent 24385 George Claude Sarran 24386 Geoffrey Dismukes Withers 24387 Robert Raymond Rumph 24388 John Gradwell Evans 24389 Michael Kenneth Gibson 24390 Robert Wray Jordan 24391 Francis Joseph Sazama 24392 Leonard Charles Henderson 24393 James Ronald Heldman 24394 Barry Lucius Gartrell 24395 Albert Francis Lynch 24396 John Dixon Porter 24397 Thomas Joseph Moore 24398 James Kooniger Schmidt 24399 Vincent Edward Murphy 24400 Philip Eugene Pons 24401 Thomas Clarence Brewer 24402 Donald Albert Price 24403 Charles Alex Murray 24404 Roger William Green 24405 Robert P. Brogi 24406 Robert Charles Dickinson 24407 Derek Gordon Sprouse 24408 George Perry Carnes 24409 Philip John Burns 24410 Rogelio Leon Luis 24411 Honald Noel Maidt 24412 Thomas Dale Culp 24413 Benjamin Russell Wilkerson 24414 Stephen Dwight Warner 24415 Martin Francis Bilafer 24416 **1963** Homer J. Holland 24417 Gary King Klauminzer 24418 George Thomas Hamilton 24419 Lionel Rowan Ingram 24420 Robert Edward Donovan 24421 Frank Cornelius Gibbs 24422 D. Clinton Seward 24423 Edward Morris Lee 24424 James Douglas Lang 24425 Clark Tilton Ballard 24426 Joseph William Lengyel 24427 James McDonald Ruth 24428 Galen Hideo Yanagihara 24429 Frank Cardile 24430 Pat M. Stevens 24431 Michael Joseph Bowers 24432 Douglas Merle Gladfelter 24433 Richard James Matteson 24434 Michael Oakley Moorman 24435 Edward George Tezak 24436 Glenn Nils Smith 24437 Ward Amory Lutz 24438 Jerry Calvin Harrison 24439 Lyndol Leon Cook 24440 Raymond Dennis Klopotek 24441 Donald Kenneth Griffin 24442 Norman Ellsworth Betaque 24443 Stephen Joseph Popielarski 24444 Martin Monroe Ischinger 24445 Paul Reginald Hable 24446 Francis Leo Lennon 24447 Christopher Patrick Tate 24448 Noel Andrew Brown 24449 David Keith Sallee 24450 Alexander Paul Shine 24451 James Donald Murff 24452 Richard Charles Gallagher 24453 Ralph Milton Drewfs 24454 Bruce Fessenden Miller 24455 Charles Edward Workman 24456 Terence Fairchild Sage 24457 Leonard Charles Gregor 24458 John Reed Robbins 24459 Donald Reid 24460 John Paul Bell 24461 Rodger Maurice Bivens 24462 Curtis Vinyard Esposito 24463 Gordon Converse Holterman 24464 Michael Edward Walsh 24465 Cary Andrew Fisher 24466 Allen Byron Clark 24467 Gordon Wade Arbogast 24468 Thomas Patrick Carney 24469 Robert A. Vogel 24470 William H. Alexander 24471 George Matthew Miller 24472 Michael Beggs Allen 24473 Philemon Andrews St. Amant 24474 Richard Allen Venes 24475 Robert John Boehlke 24476 James Cullin Nelander 24477 Stephen Joseph Best 24478 Peter Albert Kelly 24479 Luis Tomas Sanchez 24480 Richard Edward Weber 24481 Robert Hain O'Toole 24482 Thomas Marle Brendle 24483 Arthur Joseph Bianco 24484 Jorge Roberto Lambeth 24485 John William Wilson 24486 John Barneveld Wheeler 24487

Vesa Juhani Alakulppi 24488 William Homer George 24489 Leon Darius Rizio 24490 Clyde Woodrow Hotman 24491 Albert Joseph Genetti 24492 William Jerry Grabner 24493 Andrew Barre Seidel 24494 James Andrew Armogida 24495 Robert Herron Wood 24496 James Stuart Dickey 24497 Richard Allen Wilson 24498 Ray Jackson McQuary 24499 Douglas Kent Mosier 24500 Raymond Lee Jenison 24501 David Waldo Knowlton 24502 Harold Walter Nelson 24503 Phillip Harold Bosma 24504 Peter McIlvaine Hall 24505 Howard Daniel Embree 24506 Fred William Schaum 24507 Richard Anthony McKinnon 24508 Dean Edward Dowling 24509 Stephen Silvasy 24510 William Ottis Coomer 24511 Douglas Victor Myers 24512 William Craig Turpin 24513 Richard Daniel Scharf 24514 Robert Garman Vanneman 24515 Duane Hopper Myers 24516 Leon Garfield Thompson 24517 Ronald Duane Steinig 24518 George Alexander Orlicki 24519 Anthony Joseph Seiwert 24520 Fred Ernest Gantzler 24521 Michael Joseph Boyle 24522 Dennis Arthur DeSmet 24523 Didrik A. Voss 24524 George Compton DeGraff 24525 Olen Lee Earnest 24526 Jerome Roger Andersen 24527 Alan Haldane Scott 24528 Donald Louis Siebenaler 24529 Edward Feldin Hill 24530 Burton Kyle McCord 24531 George Webster Davenport 24532 Harold Ernest Caldwell 24533 John W. B. Shirley 24534 Charles Dudley Hartman 24535 Jay Joseph McClatchey 24536 Gilbert Charles Keteltas 24537 William Thomas Kelley 24538 Max Reeves Barron 24539 Donald Sinclair Dusenbury 24540 Alan Arthur LaVoy 24541 Louis Joseph Sturbois 24542 Lawrence Alan Britten 24543 Michael Holmes Summers 24544 James Raymond Hannigan 24545 Jack Steele Davis 24546 Robert Eugene Scheidig 24547 Chris Prince Wangsgard 24548 John Joseph Kauza 24549 John Patrick Riceman 24550 Paul Henry Henning 24551 Edward Martin Greybeck 24552 Gary James Marchand 24553 Armando Lujan 24554 Lewis Arnold Rice 24555 Alan Francis Jones 24556 Robert Oliver Odland 24557 Peter M. Kelly 24558 Victor Frank Bunze 24559 William Wayne Witt 24560 Michael Matthew Jenks 24561 Michael Joseph Vopatek 24562 Dennis James Prutow 24563 William Arthur Stacy 24564 John Carel Hamel 24565 Ronald George Barth 24566 Harvey Wendell Orndorf 24567 Edgar Banks 24568 Robert Bruce 24569 Richard Everett Eckert 24570 Timothy Richard Young 24571 Emmette Ward Smith 24572 Rudolph Harold Ehrenberg 24573 Donald Hector Coleman 24574 Joseph Alfred Almaguer 24575 Joseph Frederick Blackgrove 24576 Ramon Mario Ong 24577 William Robert Kuhns 24578 Alan Andrew Chapman 24579 Miles Murray Eberts 24580 Ralph James Rasmussen 24581 Jan Leo Senecal 24582 Paul August Reh 24583 James Edward DeWire 24584 Ivan Robert Farris 24585 Francis Garrison Hall 24586 Thomas Austin Wilson 24587 George Henry Lippemeier 24588 George Leon Moses 24589 Richard Benway Cole 24590 William Edward Hingston 24591 Jackie Orval Eitel 24592 William George Sipos 24593 Joseph Daughety Godsey 24594 Robert Malcolm Steele 24595 Stephen Charles Hustead 24596 William John Owen 24597 Michael John Cunningham 24598 Douglas Valentine Johnson 24599 Jon Frank VanZandt 24600 Karl Langford Beach 24601 Donald John Wolz 24602 Robert Kenneth Merrill 24603 Anthony Francis McGann 24604 Russell Vincent Hanson 24605 William Leslie McDonald 24606 William Jackson Silvey 24607 John Anthony Wyrwas 24608 David Ross Little 24609 Timothy James Grogan 24610 John Wade Hayes 24611 Joseph John Jaworowski 24612 Larry Reginold Capps 24613 George Marcellious Scherrer 24614 William Dixon Smith 24615 Michael Joseph Soth 24616 Kenneth Earl Wall 24617 Nicholas William Kuzemka 24618 J. William Stryker 24619 William George Lutz 24620 Peter Morgan Bentson 24621 Phillip Waldron Mock 24622 Luther Lee Woods 24623 Michael Stephen McCormack 24624 Gerald Nobuaki Nakashima 24625 John Claude Chalmere Roth 24626 Ronald Gary Chrisman 24627 Michael Andrew Clay 24628 Roger M. Smith 24629 Arthur Charles Meier 24630 C. Erik Chickedantz 24631 Richard Steven Kosevich 24632 R. Gordon Waugh 24633 John Howard Dorland 24634 James Vernon Dawson 24635 Bruce Herbert Ellis 24636 David Britton Almy 24637 Raymond Richard Moose 24638 Richard Grant Higgins 24639 Howard Helmut Guilhaus 24640 Frank John Karoly 24641 John Frederick Oliver 24642 Iain Reilly 24643 Arthur Chauncy Drewry 24644 Richard Robert Walsh 24645 Cliff Michael Natvig 24646 Peter Dow Adams 24647 Larry Ross Spear 24648 Laurence Richard Medlin 24649 William Alexander Robinson 24650 William John Cooke 24651 Jerome Alexander Pogorzelski 24652 William Northington Clark 24653 Clovis Olivier LaFond 24654 Durwood Ray Bagby 24655 Jack Edson Adams 24656 Frederick Howard Henderson 24657 Charles Overton Rolfe 24658 William Milton Boice 24659 Thomas Robert Brennan 24660 John Eldridge Counts 24661 Alden Michael Cunningham 24662 Kenny Dale Mitchell 24663 Wendell Roy Gideon 24664 Peter John Buckley 24665 Jonathan Wood Allen 24666 Robert Alan Zelley 24667 Edwin Hugh John Carns 24668 Lyle Gilchrest Robey 24669 Paul Turney Weyrauch 24670 Francis Thomas Mataranglo 24671 Garrett Smalley Hall 24672 William Marvin Sartor 24673 Richard George Young 24674 Roy Clinton 24675 Steven Paul Stahl 24676 Sam Ronald Davidson 24677 Allen Ryan Christensen 24678 George Harry Bentz 24679 Jon Earl Lundin 24680 Dale Findley Means 24681 Robert Theodore Coulson 24682 Arthur James Ryan 24683 John Milton Harrington 24684 William Lawrence Wilson 24685 Stephen Charles Goth 24686 Richard Howard Goldsmith 24687 Wayne E. Morehead 24688 Allan Kent Varnell 24689 William Joseph Grolemund 24690 John Alexander Dwyer 24691 Robert Jefferson Davis 24692 Glenn Robert Marrs 24693 James Stephen Hughes 24694 Eugene Dumar Cargile 24695 Thomas Keola Forsythe 24696 Richard Edward Entlich 24697 Gerald Francis Stonehouse 24698 David Samuel Jackson 24699 James Frederick Roberts 24700 Stephen Andrew Childers 24701 Michael Martin Quinlan 24702 S. Kent Wall 24703 Michael Lawrence Emerick 24704 John Nicholas McMullen 24705 Charles Christopher Curtis 24706 John Russell O'Donnell 24707 Emile Adrian Robert 24708 James Burrell Hewette 24709 Peter Livingston Sawin 24710 William Conrad Hawkins 24711 Richard Park Guthrie 24712 Kenneth Ray Silberstein 24713 Charles Lew Schmidt 24714 Terrence Francis Alger 24715 Robert Gary Sausser 24716 Henry Hensley Porper 24717 Arthur Camden Lewis 24718 Dennis Kay Taillie 24719 Roger Dean Manning 24720 James Leroy Cornfoot 24721 Andrew Francis Gothreau 24722 Richard Keeney Reinholtz 24723 Tom Jimison Vaughn 24724 Walter Daniel Downey 24725 James Edward Sorensen 24726 Robert Francis Winters 24727 David Lafayette Whidden 24728 David Lee Cole 24729 Steven Oliver Buchheim 24730 Ted Kazuo Yamashita 24731 Colin Purdie Kelly 24732 James Edward Daniels 24733 Frederick Butler Cummings 24734 Austin Courtnay Brightman 24735 Lloyd Thomas Asbury 24736 Lawrence Gilbert Dapra 24737 Walter David Nicholas 24738 John Curtis Ellerson 24739 Robert Cecil Palmer 24740 Edward White Wildrick 24741 Lynne Michael Patten 24742 Byron Eugene Bassett 24743 John Ryan Dwyer 24744 William James Whitehead 24745 Rocco Peter MacAllister 24746 Hiram Wilson Warder 24747 Thomas Eugene Casey 24748 Arthur William Hall 24749 Peter James McCullough 24750 Donald Gene Armstrong 24751 Michael William Keaveney 24752 Thomas W. Karr 24753 Michael Douglas White 24754 Paul Douglas Stanley 24755 Robert Lindley Sloane 24756 Paul Douglas Sutton 24757 Thomas Metz Solenberger 24758 Roy Lee Kingry 24759 Robert Louis McGarity 24760 John Edward Parker 24761 Raymond Howard Nickla 24762 Gary Franklyn Vote 24763 Donald Gill Byrne 24764 John Anthony Dunn 24765 Michael John Lawn 24766 Robert Charles Trucksa 24767 Robert Skeen Metzger 24768 William Michael Millerlile 24769 Will Ed DeMaret 24770 Tyron Spencer Tyler 24771 Arthur Hunter Swisher 24772 Robert James Stidham 24773 Robert Burita 24774 Malcolm Dean Otis 24775 Donald Henry Conrad 24776 Harry Ronald Dickson 24777 Robert Edward Brown 24778 James Arthur Jones 24779 Thomas Ray Griffith 24780 Arthur Roy Oxley 24781 Joe Franklin Galle 24782 Robert Wilder Drain 24783 Leigh Cole Fairbank 24784 John Raymond Ahern 24785 Daniel Demchuk 24786 Kenneth Norman Hollander 24787 Carl Wayne Mercer 24788 Stephen Andrew Lang 24789 Jack Spaulding Chase 24790 Alvin Joseph Marrow 24791 Warren Brooks Battis 24792 William Watson Little 24793 Kenneth Louis Loren 24794 Haldane Robert Mayer 24795 William Palma Merritt 24796 Dennis Anthony Leach 24797 Ronald Anthony Melanson 24798 Kenneth Romaine Graham 24799 Joseph David Halgus 24800 John Stein Walker 24801 Bruce Kennedy Heim 24802 John Thomas Goorley 24803 Benjamin Edward Benjamin 24804 William Henry Stennis 24805 Wolfgang A. Fletter 24806 Thomas Clare Mallison 24807 Paul Frederick Maxwell 24808 Charles Clifton Hogg 24809 James Thomas Nolan 24810 William Bronie Crumpler 24811 Stephen Hughes Chapman 24812 Russell Stephen Simonetta 24813 Leo Bernard Virant 24814 Ralph Molyneux Mitchell 24815 Michael John Barry 24816 Norman Edwin Beatty 24817 Michael David Miller 24818 Fred Robert Douglas 24819 Walter Lucius Goodnow 24820 Richard Hoover Roberts 24821 William Norman Baucum 24822 John Thomas Westermeier 24823 James Kent Creasy 24824 Lloyd Stanley Foight 24825 D. Brent Pope 24826 James Robert Herd 24827 Robert Forbes Lewsen 24828 John Clough Littlefield 24829 Geoffrey Dixon Ellerson 24830 Ralph P. Brown 24831 James R. Caywood 24832 Gary Quentin Coe 24833 Michael John McIntyre 24834 Robert Stephen Bowes 24835 Norton Bailey Wilson 24836 Karl Otto Schwartz 24837 William Lorence Ivy 24838 Robert Hayes McNeill 24839 Joe Berry Robertson 24840 Robert Clark Handcox 24841 Richard Edmond Dean 24842 James Hunter Shotwell 24843 John Francis Morgan 24844 Paul T. Brownback 24845 Robert Mitchell Clements 24846 Bradley Keith Jones 24847 Charles H. Kinsey 24848 Roland Banks Hudson 24849 James Lisman Blackwell 24850 Michael Vernon Gilbert 24851 Lawrence Stanley Janof 24852 Daniel Arthur Willson 24853 Thomas John Kelly 24854 Charles West Stewart 24855 John Thomas Shepard 24856 Michael Winston Kilroy 24857 Alexander James Thomson 24858 Gordon Andrew Dopslaff 24859 Roger Wilson Stribling 24860 Palmer Swift Haines 24861 Curry Ned Vaughan 24862 John Nils Ford 24863 Robert Lyons McCabe 24864 James Morris McCarver 24865 Arthur F. Conlon 24866 Kenneth Eugene O'Sullivan 24867 Rex Frank Pierson 24868 James W. Speed 24869 Douglas Thomas Williams 24870 Thomas Andrew Russell 24871 Frank John Kelly 24872 Henry Morris 24873 James Edward Sarn 24874 Heidi Baker Heiden 24875 Parker John Cowgill 24876 William Y. Robbins 24877 John Sherman Waller 24878 Thomas Archibald Dolighan 24879 Daniel Otterbein Struble 24880 Spencer A. Folsom 24881 Larry Lynn Spohn 24882 Reynold Antony Johnston 24883 Louis Francis Sill 24884 Jeffrey Lewis Dalia 24885 George Iver Perry Lodoen 24886 P. David Griffith 24887 Dale Martin Garvey 24888 John Wesley Byrns 24889 Eugene Bently Blackwell 24890 Thomas French Gallagher 24891 Charles Victor Nahlik 24892 Thomas Helmut Griffin 24893 James Michael O'Connor 24894 Lawrence Vincent Anderson 24895 John Malcolm Woods 24896 Michael David Simmons 24897 George Donald Fuller 24898 George Pappas 24899 Ralph Bamford Walker 24900 Edmond Michael Rowan 24901 Donald Job Smith 24902 Richard David James 24903 Alexander Kaleolani Olsen 24904 Dennis Charles Murphy 24905 James Edwin Doherty 24906 William Robert Brown 24907 George Everett Perry 24908 Louis Albert Mari 24909 Luis Allen Getella 24910 James Allen Green 24911 Wiley Wayne McCrary 24912 Robert Franklin Foley 24913 Tommy Robert Thompson 24914 Thomas Edward Harman 24915 David Mitchell Mabardy 24916 Joseph Albert Westbrook 24917 Charles Thomas White 24918 Alexander Wilson Whitaker 24919 Patrick R. Smith 24920 **1964** Jere Michael Richardson 24921 Don Lynn Renfro 24922 David Russell Perkins 24923 L. Patrick O'Connell 24924 Akos Dezso Szekely 24925 Raymond Edward Knell 24926 George Julian Domas 24927 John Barrett Kyle 24928 Jeffrey Victor Sutherland 24929 John Alexander Hottell 24930 Randolph Lee Price Harris 24931 Frank Ralph Giordano 24932 Ben Sternberg 24933 Michael Joseph Gray 24934 Dennis Reeves Gilson 24935 Dwayne Goldsmith Lee 24936 Dennis King Culp 24937 Kenneth Eugene Sprague 24938 Donald John Koterwas 24939 John Arthur Knutzen 24940 Arthur Lorenzo West 24941 Clair Hall Thurston 24942 William Vincent Cesarski 24943 Hugh French Boyd 24944 John Hester Ward 24945 John Lewis Richards 24946 Thomas Grover Faulds 24947 Michael Leonard 24948 Raymond William Anderson 24949 Stephen Elliot Draper 24950 William Charles Van Buskirk 24951 Carl Otto Percy Magnell 24952 Waldo Drake Freeman 24953 Robert Frank Serio 24954 John Richard Clark 24955 Anthony Elwood Hartle 24956 Mont Hubbard 24957 Robert Michael Amrine 24958 John Wallis Raymond 24959 Samuel Marion Burney 24960 Howard Eugene Boone 24961 Dennis L. Seiler 24962 Bernard Ambrose Ferry 24963 Daniel Howard Hornbarger 24964 Harold Raymond Winton 24965 Roy Stephen Finno 24966 Steven Perryman 24967 Richard George Williams 24968 Harold Milton Hatfield 24969 Kenneth Conrad Kvam 24970 John Kimble Winkler 24971 James David Brown 24972 Huba Wass de Czege 24973 Robert Joseph Almassy 24974 David Anthony Bramlett 24975 Karl Wilson Robinson 24976 Brink Prickett Miller 24977 James Raymond Harding 24978 Roger Francis Yankoupe 24979 Frederic Colbert Gray 24980 James Bunker McCutchan 24981 Gordon Paul Treweek 24982 Andrew Arthur Dykes 24983 Salvatore Joseph Culosi 24984 Robert James Walters 24985 James Henry Pedersen 24986 William Fordham Murdy 24987 Ted Miyoshi Kobayashi 24988 James Ford Harvey 24989 Howard Kane Schue 24990 Donald Martin Schwartz 24991 William James Mayhew 24992 John Harrison Darrow 24993 Owen Lee Spannaus 24994 Hugh Paul Morton 24995 Henry Coval Liverpool 24996 David Mansfield Latimer 24997 George Frank Hromyak 24998 Frederick Fenn Quist 24999 Sigmund Tatar Weiner 25000 William Francis Bailey 25001 Donald Albert Hall 25002 Warren Fletcher Miller 25003 Roy Charles Buckner 25004 Andrew Edward Andrews 25005 William Jerome Reynolds 25006 James Patrick Ryan 25007 Gerald Curtis Brown 25008 R. Bruce Foster 25009 Richard Vincent Oehrlein 25010 Kevin Charles Kelley 25011 Christian Muriel Shore 25012 Franklin Delano Knight 25013 John Austin Traylor 25014 Roger Clyde Higbee 25015 Maurice T. Lough 25016 John Howard Grubbs 25017 Clifford Newell Goff 25018 Morris Joseph Lent 25019 Robert Harold Carlson 25020 Leon Ryno Yourtee 25021 David Aral Corbett 25022 Robert David Hickson 25023 Mark Carl Galton 25024 William Ruble Vineyard 25025 Denis Wayne Galloway 25026 Wayne Richard Wheeler 25027 Terrance John Rusnak 25028 Lee Richard Grasfeder 25029 Robert Merchant Gregson 25030 David Alan White 25031 Arthur Robert Mack 25032 James Ernest Cornell 25033 Alan Mario Russo 25034 David Leonard Ugland 25035 Dirck Theodor Schou 25036 James Clifford McKittrick 25037 William Mellard Connor 25038 Daniel Harvey FitzGibbon 25039 Justice Wilson Neale 25040 Michel Robert Nawrosky 25041 John William Leyerzaph 25042 Arnold Houston Gaylor 25043 Philip Henry Shoemaker 25044 Fletcher McCarty Lamkin 25045 Max William Johnson 25046 Jay Fischer Bennett 25047 Pricha Claewplodtook 25048 Gary O'Neill Page 25049 Thomas Fred Reese 25050 George Alexander Fisher 25051 Robert Seney Ballagh 25052 James Melvin Daly 25053 Barry Richard McCaffrey 25054 Howard F. Bachman 25055 Gary Jack Walk 25056 Robert Rutherford Craighill 25057 Remo Melchiori 25058 Antonio Romualdez Janairo 25059 Robert Evans Monson 25060 Roger Lee Baldwin 25061 Stanley Aloysious McLaughlin 25062 Anthony Charles Trifiletti 25063 Barry James Roller 25064 James Peter Mozden 25065 Harold Paul Kindleberger 25066 Milivoj Tratensek 25067 Robert Albert Balderson 25068 Richard Carrol McAdams 25069 Martin Francis Ryan 25070 Joseph John Corey 25071 Gary Richard LaVoy 25072 Geoffrey Rickards Louis 25073 Peter Gerald Schmeelk 25074 LeRoy Harry Graw 25075 Joseph Robert Lake 25076 Harvey Reed Fraser 25077 Christopher Morrow Orndorff 25078 Donald Francis Ullmann 25079 William Jay Straub 25080 Steven Monroe Bettner 25081 Norman Lee Grunstad 25082 Carl Winter 25083 Joseph Coleman Arnold 25084 James Wilson Powers 25085 Robert Lee Johnson 25086 Herbert Dwight Raymond 25087 Joseph Charles Zengerle 25088 Ronald William Lind 25089 George Gregory Jacunski 25090 Ronald Howard Smith 25091 Joseph Gordon Seeber 25092 Michael Roderick Cook 25093 Thomas Neil Thomas 25094 Thomas William Chapman 25095 John Page Duffy 25096 Allyn Jon Palmer 25097 Mark Francis Brennan 25098 Leonard Dean Hardy 25099 Thomas Spencer Crain 25100 Stephen Lewis Weisel 25101 Donald Alexander Mac Isaac 25102 Richard Allen Chilcoat 25103 Christopher Oscar Bast 25104 Emil Theodore Lechner 25105 David Allan Bujalski 25106 Larry LaVern Bedell 25107 George Thomas Woolsey 25108 Frank Clarence Watson 25109 Michael John Raymond Moran 25110 Douglas Harmon Barr 25111 Joseph Bannan Missal 25112 Kent Lee Pietsch 25113 John Robert Cary 25114 James Robert McClure 25115 John Dalton Howard 25116 Michael Edward Harlan 25117 Charles Richard Macchiaroli 25118 James George Gantsoudes 25119 Martin John Michlik 25120 George Allen Carver 25121 Michael David Miller 25122 Daniel Marek Banovic 25123 Robert Lee Weathers 25124 Gary Monroe Boutz 25125 Peter Richard Danylchuk 25126 Michael Joseph Buckley 25127 Nicholas Boehm Kemp 25128 Robert Vaughn Moss 25129 David R. Holdsworth 25130 George Michael Hartley 25131 Jacob Carl Armstrong 25132 Michael Joseph Kowalchik 25133 Frank Carthorn Mashburn 25134 George Pierre Desjardins 25135 Robert Lawrence Blair 25136 Thomas Earl Bush 25137 Karl Robert Wilson 25138 Henry Larry Strickland 25139 Larry A. Bryan 25140 Michael Edwin Wikan 25141 John A. Farnsworth 25142 Eugene McKinnie McLemore 25143 Tyler Bennett Huneycutt 25144 Clifford Earl Williams 25145 Kent Richard Allen 25146 William Pressley Tanner 25147 James Thomas Pittman 25148 Albert Paul Fulco 25149 Norman Shiers Smith 25150 Gary Anthony Cecchine 25151 Gary Richard Johnson 25152 Lassiter Albert Mason 25153 Thurman McRoy Roberts 25154 Jack Harold Nunn 25155 Michael Benjamin Prothero 25156 James Herbert Macia 25157 Michael Shannon Davison 25158 Stephen Joseph Induni 25159 Michael Douglas Brooks 25160 Robert Kiyoshi Matsumoto 25161 Alan Nicholas Christensen 25162 William Hopping Seely 25163 Alfred Norman Webb 25164 Ronald von Freymann 25165 John Robert Rogers 25166 Wiley Ricks Smith 25167 Edwin George Winborn 25168 Samuel Palmer Lamback 25169 Jack Thomas Miller 25170 Thomas Craig Roberts 25171 Joseph Anthony Mastriani 25172 Bruce Lee Howard 25173 Eugene Raymond Sullivan 25174 James Richard Burnham 25175 Christopher Robert Kite-Powell 25176 Joseph James O'Brien 25177 Donald Douglas Dailey 25178 Henry Lucius Thomas 25179 A. Walter Temple 25180 David Michael Smith 25181 Jerome A. Chmielak 25182 Richard Allan Puckett 25183 Thomas Jacob Erdmann 25184 Arthur Edward Kierstead 25185 Robert Louis North 25186 Thomas Edwin Anthony 25187 James Francis McNulty 25188 Curtis Allen Davis 25189 James Franklin Schoonover 25190 William L. Jackman 25191 George Bruce Vondruska 25192 Jeffrey Lynn Merrill 25193 Daniel Edward Deter 25194 Robert Edward Wright 25195 John Walton Lang 25196 Carl T. Brown 25197 Norman William Gill 25198 George Francis Smith 25199 Charles Schreiner Miller 25200 David Earl Roesler 25201 Ian Buchanan Carter 25202 Michael Joseph Bowers 25203 Bob Fred McCoy 25204 Daniel Stewart Klunk 25205 Nicholas Michael Nahas 25206 Frederick Marvin Pope 25207 Kevin Robert Murphy 25208 Philip Jan Hughey 25209 Raymond Moylan Jones 25210 Ray Daniel Spinosa 25211 William James Miller 25212 Steven Paul Solomon 25213 James Irvin Muir 25214 Edward Paul Brinkman 25215 Michael Lee Horstman 25216 Terrell Gordon Covington 25217 Albert Cropper Williams 25218 Thomas William Butler 25219 Theodore Toshio Togashi 25220 Eddie Ray Sims 25221 Phillip Milton Sleet 25222 Peter Michael Elson 25223 Eugene Paul Markowski 25224 Robert Bruce Sinclair 25225 Per Ingvald Madsen 25226 Donald Benjamin Cotter 25227 Seavy Alexander Bain 25228 Gordon Thomas Rhoades 25229 Vichai Kongsuvan 25230 Jeffrey Alan Larson 25231 James Wayne Grisham

25232 Dennis James Gillem 25233 John Putnam Otjen 25234 Woods White Rogers 25235 David Gardner Binney 25236 Gerald Clifford Werner 25237 William Robert Beck 25238 John Frederick Roller 25239 J. B. Holeman 25240 Clifford Marcellus Beasley 25241 John Francis Murray 25242 Richard Warfield Davis 25243 John Stalker Price 25244 Louis Anthony Jerge 25245 Francis Lanier Fly 25246 Harold Dennis McCormack 25247 William Henry McMakin 25248 Stanley Sherwood Fracker 25249 David F. Stepek 25250 Richard Paul Dexter 25251 James Winghong Lew 25252 Crayon Cornelius Efird 25253 Clyde E. Woodle 25254 John Arthur Cope 25255 David George Kirkpatrick 25256 Robert Henry Orr 25257 John Donald Bergen 25258 Alvin David Treado 25259 Joseph William Simonis 25260 Everett Donald Grimes 25261 Harold Woodrow Smith 25262 John Henry Tate 25263 George Frederick Egner 25264 Dee Wayne Stone 25265 James Warren Normyle 25266 Michael Wayne Richard 25267 Thomas Lawrence Wright 25268 George McAulay Baseheart 25269 Lawrence Melvin Herdegen 25270 W. Arthur Russell 25271 Randy Kent Nanstad 25272 Michael Christopher Sanderson 25273 Charles Loyd Jackson 25274 Douglas Philip Bennett 25275 Patrick Howard Graves 25276 Stephen Miller Overton 25277 Thomas Lloyd Legan 25278 Gerard Vincent Palma 25279 David Michael Bergman 25280 Richard Gleason Knight 25281 Ronald Gordon Odom 25282 Gregory Michael Olson 25283 Raymond LeRoy Shoemaker 25284 Walter Ward Davis 25285 Edward John Lucyk 25286 Bruce Alden McKinley 25287 Jack William McWatters 25288 Clarence Barry Hartman 25289 James Richard Lindou 25290 Vukoslav Eneas Aguirre 25291 Arthur David Weiss 25292 Seth Foster Hudgins 25293 Tommy W. Harman 25294 James Stringfellow Cobbs 25295 Robert Joseph Klein 25296 George Ernest Lonsberry 25297 Robert Antoine Hillyer 25298 Arthur George Lozeau 25299 Robert John Michela 25300 Peter Joseph Meyer 25301 Peter Lloyd Drahn 25302 Larry James Bramlette 25303 Robert Ernest Wynn 25304 Charles Kirby Wilcox 25305 John Stephen Donovan 25306 James Leonard Koster 25307 Brendan Thomas Quann 25308 Joseph Edward Palko 25309 Calvin R. Kluess 25310 William McNair Annan 25311 Donald Wilt Shive 25312 Douglas Allen Alitz 25313 Melvin Elwood Case 25314 William Thomas Murphy 25315 John Paul Weber 25316 James Peter Downey 25317 Jose Angel Muratti 25318 William Earl Guthrie 25319 Martin Levering Green 25320 Thomas Edward Millacci 25321 Daniel Melvin Evans 25322 Edward Joseph Haydash 25323 William Albert Chescavage 25324 Milton J. Brokaw 25325 Thomas James Durfee 25326 John Clark Speedy 25327 Carl Edward Dye 25328 Arthur Michael Kelly 25329 Albert Arthur Caporaso 25330 James Bowdoin Stapleton 25331 George Oliver Hillard 25332 Geoffrey Hamilton Kleb 25333 Jon Thomas Little 25334 Roy Jones 25335 Roy John Faddis 25336 Peter Eaton Gleszer 25337 William Timothy DiNeno 25338 Ralph Jan Campbell 25339 Kearney Washington Crissman 25340 John Martin Harnisch 25341 Terry Don Manton 25342 Thomas Nelson Cunningham 25343 Henry Heil Zimmerman 25344 Benedict Trezza Marino 25345 James Lawrence Adams 25346 Peter Joseph McAteer 25347 Randall Phillips Kunkel 25348 David Johnny Baratto 25349 Richard LeRoy Carr 25350 James Edward O'Donnell 25351 Ronald Matthews Cross 25352 Watson Garrard Caudill 25353 Richard Harold Heydt 25354 Richard Stephen Schuley 25355 Neville Colburn 25356 Richard Anthony Piekarski 25357 Eric Lawrence Bischoff 25358 Roger Lewis Sornson 25359 Edward Ellsworth Mackey 25360 Dennis Frank O'Block 25361 Kenneth Roy Eklund 25362 Thomas Maxson Kullman 25363 Kenneth Edward Bloomfield 25364 Daniel Levin 25365 Robert Carl Moomaw 25366 Leo Vincent Spinelli 25367 Frederick Conant Taylor 25368 Kenneth Lansing Scott 25369 Francis Joel Stephenson 25370 Kenneth Kevin Ordway 25371 Stephen Bradley Pembrook 25372 Edmund C. Stone 25373 Francis Thomas Pachler 25374 Ronald Edwin Rezek 25375 James Raymond Jinks 25376 Richard Albert Nowak 25377 Michael J. Conway 25378 Chester Frank Kempinski 25379 John Quincy Mulvaney 25380 Richard Edward Plymale 25381 Edward Stanley Topor 25382 Paul Edward Cate 25383 Norman Lafayette Roberts 25384 Larry Keith Brewer 25385 Robert Joe Doolittle 25386 Donald Carl Reh 25387 James Wynn Hegglund 25388 James Anthony Kofalt 25389 Podge McCauley Reed 25390 William Joseph Luckie 25391 Robert Bruce Magruder 25392 Peter Michael Shaughnessey 25393 James Leonard Popp 25394 Robert Gerald Tetu 25395 David Bennett Dews 25396 Leroy Mills 25397 Justin Russell Hughes 25398 Charles Dudley Revie 25399 William Allen Ziegler 25400 Arthur Edward Parker 25401 Michael Joseph McKinley 25402 Edward Francis Roby 25403 Robert Arnold Ames 25404 Michael James Kiley 25405 Franklin Paul Lambert 25406 John Rodney Edward Sam 25407 Allen Falconer Jones 25408 Charles Thomas Hutchison 25409 Leo Desire Charron 25410 Robert Gwathmey Merritt 25411 William Harry Landgraf 25412 Jerrold Joseph Lynskey 25413 James E. Bigelow 25414 Richard Joseph Tiplady 25415 Michael Wade Griffith 25416 Geoffrey Smith Moakley 25417 Robert William Gesner 25418 Earl Robert Kelton 25419 Herbert Gwynn Vaughan 25420 Ted Gordon Morgan 25421 Russell Kryder Pells 25422 Dennis John O'Connor 25423 Thomas Ashby Badger 25424 David LeRoy Ramsay 25425 Robert Bruce Sandman 25426 William Arthur Henry 25427 James Conrad Powers 25428 Robert Francis Young 25429 Paul Thomas Rennie 25430 Willis H. Brucker 25431 David Riley Winters 25432 John Ward Arrington 25433 Charles Kimball Flint 25434 John Paul Scotnicki 25435 Helmuth Jan Heneman 25436 Gregory John Hayward 25437 Thomas Charles Kerns 25438 Glenn Richard Wilderman 25439 Ronald Frank Williamson 25440 Frederick Milton Hinshaw 25441 Samuel Anthony Biank 25442 Gary Peter Ponzoli 25443 Cornelius E. Mieras 25444 Jeffrey Knight Warner 25445 Ralph Corley 25446 Richard Edmund Peterson 25447 William Hall Adair 25448 Kenneth Moore Waldrop 25449 David Madsen Fishback 25450 Richard Laird Gray 25451 William Nesbitt Robertson 25452 Harold James Kaufman 25453 William Barrett Payne 25454 Frederick William Coleman 25455 Robert Martin Reich 25456 Kenneth Michael De Gon 25457 Ralph Peter Kufeke 25458 James Carl Kotrc 25459 Peter Louis D'Alessandro 25460 Leonard Anthony Kresefski 25461 Francis John Collins 25462 Paul Francis Bertelli 25463 William Ray Black 25464 William Ovid Hoover 25465 William Robert Bolen 25466 James Marsh Carson 25467 Howard Wayne Wilson 25468 Bruce Irwin Greiner 25469 Jerry Lee Shelton 25470 David Carlisle Wade 25471 George DuHadway Cromartie 25472 Robert Thomas Crowder 25473 John Meigs Graham 25474 Douglas Pierce O'Neal 25475 William Jewel Major 25476 Norman Leonard Anderson 25477 John Richard Stanko 25478 James Joseph Beierschmitt 25479 Edward Charles Schillo 25480 Thomas Michael Curran 25481 Harwood Sterling Nichols 25482 James Rudolph McCormack 25483 John Allen Nischwitz 25484 Thomas Francis Dooley 25485 **1965** Daniel William Christman 25486 James Ira Scheiner 25487 Thomas Charles Genoni 25488 James Reed Golden 25489 John Brundy Ritch 25490 Hubbert Lee Leverett 25491 David Vincent Mastran 25492 Thomas Duncan MacVicar 25493 John Irvin Alger 25494 James Henry McEliece 25495 James Marshall Paley 25496 Joseph Alexander McChristian 25497 David B. Kuhn 25498 Richard W. Chapman 25499 Edward Simpson 25500 Martin John Resick 25501 Gordon Alfred Long 25502 Paul William Bucha 25503 Frank Xavier Reller 25504 David Robert Brown 25505 Ken Yoshitani 25506 Emery John Chase 25507 Lloyd Clark Briggs 25508 Paul T. McDonald 25509 Grant Louis Fredricks 25510 Thomas Hawkins Johnson 25511 Walter Alfred Divers 25512 James Frederic Airy 25513 William Thomas Heller 25514 Ronald Bruce Bael Bailey 25515 William Edmund Byrne 25516 Omar Edwin Rood 25517 A. Edward Knauf 25518 John Michael Deems 25519 Harley Lester Moore 25520 Richard DeVere Mohlere 25521 Stanley George Genega 25522 Robert Michael Carini 25523 James Franklin Hennessee 25524 Howard Hammel Reed 25525 David Charles Bangert 25526 R. Chris Kinard 25527 Terrence Richard Tutchings 25528 Carl Robert Arvin 25529 Jack Miller Jannarone 25530 Robert Winston Baldinger 25531 Paul Fredrick Schultz 25532 Robert David Wolff 25533 Robert W. Huffhines 25534 Francis Real Skidmore 25535 Richard Magee Osgood 25536 Steven William Ellenbogen 25537 Camden White McConnell 25538 Charles Henry Moseley 25539 Dennis Andrew Shantz 25540 Charles Carroll McCloskey 25541 David Arthur Gabel 25542 John Bruce Gailey 25543 John Martin Wattendorf 25544 William Ralph Griffin 25545 Oleh B. Koropey 25546 Jerald Paul Eichelberger 25547 Henry William Sterbenz 25548 Frederick Joseph Charles 25549 Michael Lawrence Viani 25550 Michael Thomas Glynne 25551 Larry Louis Leskovjan 25552 Peter John Cahill 25553 William Earl Lyons 25554 Wayne John Scholl 25555 Alexander Jeremiah Clark 25556 Randolph Kent Guenther 25557 Richard Michael Hall 25558 Thomas Ray Satorie 25559 Richard Allan Sullivan 25560 Harry Nolan Joyner 25561 John Stephen Davis 25562 Jerry Ray Stockton 25563 Barry Warren Levine 25564 Leonard Douglas Davis 25565 John Richard Chaffer 25566 George Rex Brock 25567 Edgardo Querijero Abesamis 25568 Daniel Frederick Steinwald 25569 Robert Thomas Frank 25570 C. William Zadel 25571 Robert Bruce Cato 25572 Stephen Reagen Morrissey 25573 John Harold McCullough 25574 Richard Allen Knudson 25575 Lowry Arthur West 25576 Robert Maclay Frey 25577 Nicholas Harvey Merriam 25578 Paul John Singelyn 25579 John Anthony Madia 25580 Terrance Charles Ryan 25581 Glenn Roy Doughty 25582 Malcolm Stanton Gilchrist 25583 Lloyd Kent Brown 25584 Julian Emory Pylant 25585 Edward H. Zabka 25586 James Wilson Talbot 25587 Ronald Neil Williams 25588 Errol D. Alexander 25589 Lance Ray Stewart 25590 George Timothy Bell 25591 Clair Frederick Gill 25592 Fredric Lewis Laughlin 25593 David Pardee Gnau 25594 Frederick John Smith 25595 Beverly W. Motal 25596 Thomas Ross White 25597 Jon Richard Plaas 25598 John Daniel Knowles 25599 Glade McKay Bishop 25600 Douglas Lawrence Gibson 25601 Charles Spencer Nichols 25602 Arthur Cleveland Hester 25603 Henry Jackson Lowe 25604 Leslie Edwin Hagie 25605 Fred Martin Belanger 25606 Charles McKinley Cook 25607 Thomas Galloway Fergusson 25608 Kenneth Bruce Slutzky 25609 Richard Anderson Leary 25610 Eugene J. Parker 25611 Karl Julius Plotkin 25612 Steven Edward Philo 25613 Douglas John Richardson 25614 Bernard Lee Ziegler 25615 Royal Russel Garms 25616 Dennis Wayne Brewer 25617 Tadahiko Ono 25618 Lowell Baber Lawson 25619 Leighton Chapman Atteberry 25620 John Bertil Roseberg 25621 John M. Pickler 25622 Robert List Lee 25623 Claude M. Fligg 25624 Patrick D. Kenny 25625 David Leo Bodde 25626 Ralph Vito Locurcio 25627 Thomas H. Carll 25628 Paul F. Barber 25629 Robert A. Doughty 25630 Louis Stephan Csoka 25631 Robert D. Timbrook 25632 Ronald M. Wells 25633 Terry Axel Carlson 25634 Joe A. Weatherall 25635 Ray Garnie Woodruff 25636 Robert Anthony de Laar 25637 Bruce B.G. Clarke 25638 James S. Hume 25639 Lawrence George Bennett 25640 Donald Arthur Phillpotts 25641 Martin Wayne Andresen 25642 Neil Edward Brown 25643 Kenneth P. Moorefield 25644 John MacRae Vann 25645 Guenter Hennig 25646 Donald Stanley Rowe 25647 Thomas Clark Barron 25648 Michael Earl Hudson 25649 Michael Hollis Abbott 25650 Steven Clark Harman 25651 James Price Stephenson 25652 William Bryant Bachman 25653 Francis Joseph Probst 25654 David Evan Hurley 25655 Thomas Joseph Kovach 25656 James Rumsey Webb 25657 William John McKemey 25658 Robert Crawford White 25659 Anthony Horace Gamboa 25660 Ralph Alexander Hallenbeck 25661 Wayne Watson Marsh 25662 Robert John Molepske 25663 John Karl Swensson 25664 Martin LeRoy Johnson 25665 Edward James Sharkness 25666 Jim Wendell Holmes 25667 Richard Allen Boerckel 25668 Eric Thomas de Jonckheere 25669 Richard H. Sinnreich 25670 Michael Joe Huston 25671 Carmelito Arkangel 25672 Larry Harold Isakson 25673 Nicholas John Principe 25674 Frank John Prokop 25675 Thomas Anthony Cindric 25676 James Richard Harvey 25677 James L. Smith 25678 Peter M. Howard 25679 Robert Duncan Brown 25680 Joseph Kala Kukea 25681 Donald Clay Erbes 25682 James David Hopkins 25683 William August Beinlich 25684 Bernard John Mogan 25685 Robert Dennis Rood 25686 Charles Michael Aron 25687 Robert David Thompson 25688 Gordon A. Larson 25689 Bernard Francis Kistler 25690 James Martin Peters 25691 Joseph Anthony Zurlo 25692 Charles Ray Eckart 25693 George Edward Menninger 25694 Dennis James Sellers 25695 Michael J. O'Grady 25696 Raymond John Ludwig 25697 John Charles Thompson 25698 John Francis Concannon 25699 Leland Hazelton Hewitt 25700 Thomas Merritt Bumpass 25701 Richard Edward Pullen 25702 Jon Kay Thompson 25703 Walter Stanley Kulbacki 25704 Joseph Peter Koz 25705 James Alton Helberg 25706 Hugh Frederick Scruggs 25707 Walter Henry Oehrlein 25708 Gene Karl Manghi 25709 Benjamin Whitehouse 25710 Thomas William Van Dyk 25711 Robert Dean Stowell 25712 Donald C. Exelby 25713 Stephen David Clement 25714 John Edward McMillan 25715 Anthony Paul Pyrz 25716 Francis Paul Tantalo 25717 Paul Stephen Renschen 25718 George Henry Seaworth 25719 Eugene D. O'Neill 25720 Peter K. Becker 25721 Douglas Joel Sikorski 25722 Jerome P. Dufour 25723 Thomas Patrick Powers 25724 Calvin George Kahara 25725 Bedford Murray Pickup 25726 William Sherwood Birdseye 25727 Gilbert Warren Curl 25728 Norman Cale Boyter 25729 Charles Walter Boohar 25730 Hugh Allan Kelley 25731 Peter Bruere Lounsbury 25732 Thomas Robert Sheckells 25733 George W. Ruggles 25734 Gene Roger Farmelo 25735 Robert George Keats 25736 James Michael Kelly 25737 Kermit Donald Larson 25738 Grosvenor Wardwell Fish 25739 Thomas Joseph Matkov 25740 David Trevor Jones 25741 Charles Frank Shaw 25742 Karl Robert Savatiel 25743 Jerry Agnew Madden 25744 Ronald Lee Walter 25745 Michael Bernard Teeters 25746 John Thomas Anderson 25747 Daniel Edgar Speilman 25748 Nathan Kantor 25749 Donald James Parrish 25750 Robert John Hill 25751 Philip Robert Cooper 25752 Step Elmo Parlette Tyner 25753 Richard Arden Hennig 25754 Charles Raoul Heindrichs 25755 Merton Edward Munson 25756 Jay Eldon Vaughn 25757 Charles Henry Burgardt 25758 John Louis Salomone 25759 William Norman Ritch 25760 Richard LeRoy Endicott 25761 Lansing Tim Hewitt 25762 Philip Robert Olmsted 25763 Donald Gene Kurtz 25764 Jose Rafael Gonzalez Gonzalez 25765 Anthony Joseph Borrego 25766 Walter Lewis Saxon 25767 Gerald Anthony Buckosky 25768 Stephen James Kempf 25769 Robert Ronald Butterfield 25770 Terry Brunswick Grandstaff 25771 Lorin Craig Albright 25772 Stephen Clark Burrell 25773 John Wayne Cooley 25774 Michael J. Connor 25775 Stephen Carl Ganshert 25776 John Karl Lyons 25777 Jack Cocke Turner 25778 Robert William Mace 25779 Richard John Kuzman 25780 Charles Edward Brown 25781 Carl William Gentine 25782 Joseph Benjamin Anderson 25783 Barrie Emert Zais 25784 Jerome Michael Ledzinski 25785 Robert Henry Sterba 25786 Rance Hendrix Rountree 25787 Jerome Edmonds Kelly 25788 Ronald John Floto 25789 John Edward Longhouser 25790 Michael John Matteson 25791 Gordon Gregory Letterman 25792 Jon Douglas Scobie 25793 William Joseph Fields 25794 Thomas D. Thompson 25795 William C. Juchau 25796 Christopher Lowell Spire 25797 Nathan Hall Kniker 25798 Colin Oliver Halvorson 25799 Fred Whiting Timmerman 25800 John Berard Harrington 25801 Bruce Anthony Raybeck 25802 John Kendrick Hutton 25803 Leo Lawrence Konermann 25804 Paul Douglas Rau 25805 Dennis L. Chudoba 25806 Edwin Howard Klink 25807 Frank Marion Arnall 25808 Raymond John Schaltenbrand 25809 Douglas Kirby Gentzkow 25810 James Edward Ferguson 25811 William Brown Mitchell 25812 Warren M. Kennedy 25813 Edward Dewitt Winstead 25814 Burke Owen Buntz 25815 Jerry Dernar 25816 George Jerry Merges 25817 Eric Ken Shinseki 25818 Joseph Patrick O'Connor 25819 William Frederick Hecker 25820 Joseph Richard Barkley 25821 William Craig Bradley 25822 Roberto Rojas 25823 Joseph Emil DeFrancisco 25824 James Charles Hardin 25825 John Edward Connor 25826 James Michael Watson 25827 Robert Stephen Bradley 25828 James Lee Tillman 25829 Mitchell Ernest Bonnett 25830 John Eric Funk 25831 Harry Caum Haines 25832 James Thomas Seaburn 25833 James Ewell Echols 25834 Michael Momcilovich 25835 James Michael Coughlin 25836 Henry Martin Dermody 25837 Bruce Roland Marshall 25838 Charles Edgar Wuertenberger 25839 Richard Walter Tragemann 25840 Lyttle Preston Hughes 25841 Kim Harmon Olmstead 25842 C. Keyes Hudson 25843 Reginald W. Dryzga 25844 James Lee Dyer 25845 Roger William Wolf 25846 Carl August Peterson 25847 Timothy Shane O'Hara 25848 John Carl DeVitto 25849 Roger Alan Griffin 25850 Barre Stephen Bernier 25851 Thomas Joel Kelly 25852 Mark Elmer Sheridan 25853 Mark Richard Walsh 25854 Dennis Earle Hawker 25855 Thomas Francis Borkowski 25856 Orlin Lee Mullen 25857 John Hulsey Hays 25858 Richard Charles Williams 25859 Kendall McRae Lemley 25860 Earl Thomas Wiley 25861 John William Barwis 25862 Dennis R. Coll 25863 Stephen Louis Ammon 25864 Garrett Mark Davis 25865 Richard Larry Bryant 25866 Steven Michael Sperry 25867 Michael Patrick Shaver 25868 Christopher John Dorney 25869 Frank William Koleszar 25870 E. Graham Forrest 25871 Arpad Kovacsy 25872 Robert Francis Berdan 25873 Paul Richard Drass 25874 John Nolan Cullen 25875 Valentino Thomas Sammarco 25876 Gary Steven Kadetz 25877 Henry George Mickells 25878 Oscar Lee Atchley 25879 Ernest David Westpheling 25880 Francis William O'Brien 25881 David Michael Drinkwater 25882 Frederic Nelson Eichorn 25883 James Arthur Woodard 25884 Arthur Roth 25885 Donald Eugene Appler 25886 John Richard Smoak 25887 Peter James Long 25888 Walter J. Wells 25889 Grover Cleveland Starling 25890 Richard Earl Kramer 25891 Robert Louis Bedell 25892 Richard Eldridge Coleman 25893 Raymond George Pollard 25894 Robert Francis Fritz 25895 Robert Bowie Johnson 25896 Andrew Aloysius Zaleski 25897 Robert Arthur Guy 25898 Christopher James Needels 25899 Anthony George Livic 25900 Jerry Furman Clark 25901 Marvin Alvis Jeffcoat 25902 Richard James Donahuė 25903 Robert Jack Axley 25904 James Anthony Mirando 25905 Robert Campbell Jones 25906 James Vaughan Stewart 25907 James William Murphy 25908 Lee Edward Kleinmaier 25909 James Harry Hall 25910 John Warren Higley 25911 William Joseph Bradburn 25912 Kenneth Eugene Hjelm 25913 Michael Edward Berdy 25914 Richard Gordon Wirth 25915 Robert Emerson Gates 25916 Ballard Michael Barker 25917 John Michael Howell 25918 Robert Leslie Harter 25919 Leo Peter Allen 25920 Michael Robert Stanko 25921 James Ellis Lane 25922 Robert Leigh Clover 25923 Edwin Lee Armstrong 25924 Michael Thomas Shulick 25925 Dennis Blair Lewis 25926 John Austin Bell 25927 Hershall Don Hall 25928 Glennon Edward Nenninger 25929 Raymond James Hawkins 25930 Russell Lionel Dornier 25931 Harlan Frederick Fricke 25932 John Rahner Bohannon 25933 Robert Walter Higgins 25934 John Francis Keith 25935 Lawrence LeRoy Clewley 25936 William Russell Browder 25937 Thomas A. Ridenour 25938 William Hudson Tredennick 25939 William Albert Triick 25940 John Tilson Johnson 25941 Larry Thurston Neal 25942 Dean Richard Loftin 25943 Laban Phelps Jackson 25944 David Lee Benton 25945 Timothy James Simmons 25946 Walter Elliot Nelson 25947 Gerald Eugene Lipsit 25948 Milburn Kenneth Concannon 25949 James Robert Tomaswick 25950 Michael Peter Lapolla 25951 Gerald D. O'Leary 25952 Stephen Clark Darrah 25953 Dom Anthony DeSantis 25954 David Benton Vann 25955 Herbert J. Smith 25956 James Lawrence Berry 25957 Raymond Joseph Paske 25958 Paul Lewis Bergmann 25959 Curtis Dean Churchwell 25960 Americus Mack Gill 25961 James Peter Greene 25962 William Thomas McCreary 25963 Ralph Thomas Shaw 25964 Lewis Edward Green 25965 Marshall Wayne Schwartz 25966 Lawrence Michael Strassner 25967 John Richard Malpass 25968 Emanuel Paul Maimone 25969 Joseph David Hindsley 25970 James Edward Mims 25971 James Daniel Harmon 25972 Leo Raymond Kennedy 25973 Peter Christian Linn 25974 Charles Francis O'Donnell 25975 Jay Francis Stevison 25976 James Edward Bryan 25977 Frank Michael Applin 25978 Donald Edward Nowland 25979 Harold A. Jenkins 25980 Charles Lynn Hemmingway 25981 Frank Langdon Meier 25982 Thomas James Mushovic 25983 Louis

Lamborn Wheeler 25984 James Anthony Olivo 25985 John Kingsland Terry 25986 Kenneth Jefferson Cherry 25987 Julio Justin DeSantis 25988 Robert Maxwell Scott Anderson 25989 George Patrick O'Toole 25990 David Sargent deMoulpied 25991 Robert Emmett Scully 25992 James Tomotsu Miyashiro 25993 Robert Fielding Radcliffe 25994 Stephen Jack Spoerry 25995 Leroy Arthur Adam 25996 John Vincent Olson 25997 Ralph Wyatt Adams 25998 Roderick Wetherill 25999 William Edward Reisner 26000 Russell Alexander Campbell 26001 Zigmund James Roebuck 26002 Kevin Paul Toomey 26003 Thomas Lester Croak 26004 Frederick William Ammerman 26005 Jon Eliot King 26006 Ladd Hayden Metzner 26007 Jose Luis Sanchez 26008 Charles Clingman Dickey 26009 James Hayward Wood 26010 Chester Arthur Myers 26011 Edward A. Foehl 26012 John Hope Shuford 26013 Lewis Edward Maness 26014 Jack Lawrence Blau 26015 William James Lehman 26016 Kenneth Dickson McArthur 26017 Spotswood DeWitt 26018 Richard Glenn Horst 26019 Henry Louis Kelley 26020 Patrick Joseph Donovan 26021 C. Roland Stichweh 26022 Stephen Alan Olson 26023 Michael Leibowitz 26024 Ernest Jacob Knoche 26025 Richard Dexter Bunn 26026 Curtis Harper Adams 26027 Ronald James Riley 26028 William J. Connolly 26029 Arthur Bernard Mark 26030 John William Koletty 26031 John Timothy Thomasson 26032 Fred J. Shapiro 26033 Anthony Hugh Clay 26034 Bruce Daniel Hulin 26035 John Bartholomew Seymour 26036 Thomas R. Genetti 26037 Robert Omer Gagne 26038 Jesse Millard Whitten 26039 Richard Glen Collins 26040 Ronald Frederick Layer 26041 James Michael Hennen 26042 Ralph Eugene Asplund 26043 Preston Miller Motes 26044 Lawrence Parker Wiest 26045 Robert John Zonne 26046 Stephen Joseph Paek 26047 Michael H. Thompson 26048 William Walter Sherrell 26049 John Rocco McGurk 26050 Roger William Frydrychowski 26051 Lloyd Clinton Ray 26052 Charles Frank Pfeifer 26053 William Edward Brush 26054 Steven Ralph Leach 26055 Thomas Ryan Henneberry 26056 David Foster La Rochelle 26057 Jerry Reed McMillan 26058 Wesley Bayard Taylor 26059 Douglas Coleman Kline 26060 Francis Guy Riley 26061 Donald Craig Parcells 26062 Gregory Craig Steele 26063 Edward Roger Evans 26064 Harold Henri Klingler 26065 James Sylvester Conley 26066 George Silvy Gehringer 26067 Paul Jules Kantrowich 26068 A. Ross Wollen 26069 Frederick Ryan Grates 26070 Daniel Joseph Donaghy 26071 Carl Albert Letterie 26072 Terril Marquette Throckmorton 26073 Thomas Samuel Abraham 26074 Stephen Michael Bliss 26075 Robert Francis Selkis 26076 Bartholomew Dennis Barry 26077 Timothy James Vogel 26078 John Ware Thames 26079 Ronald Kenneth Kolzing 26080 Philip Vinson Harper 26081 **1966** Wesley Kanne Clark 26082 Paul Francis Mlakar 26083 Michael John Higgins 26084 William Wilson Kakel 26085 Jack Anathol LeCuyer 26086 Charles Loyd Moore 26087 David LeRoy Linder 26088 James Thomas Doyle 26089 Thomas Jay Hayes 26090 Samuel Frank Champi 26091 Richard Robert Sonstelie 26092 Richard Walter Thoden 26093 Arthur Crawford Mosley 26094 Jon Lee Steel 26095 John Howard Winger 26096 John Parsons Wheeler 26097 Richard Joseph Hlista 26098 David Clarence Pearce 26099 Theodore Preston Hill 26100 James Michael Cullem 26101 Michael Francis Grisafe 26102 Lanse Murray Leach 26103 James Richard Gardner 26104 Gilbert Charles Brunnhoeffer 26105 Terrall Martin de Jonckheere 26106 Frederick George Ernst 26107 Bernard Joseph Reilly 26108 James Seabury McCallum 26109 Michael Dunham Fry 26110 John Stuart Kelsey 26111 Steven Lewis Hanau 26112 Terrence Edward Durbin 26113 Edward Paul Kane 26114 James Kriebel 26115 John Hamilton Boyd 26116 Joseph Luke Welch 26117 Mark William Potter 26118 Robert Donald Bruegger 26119 John Martin Deponai 26120 Richard Allen Chatfield 26121 Frederick Robert Ulrich 26122 W. George Grandison 26123 William Gordon Gang 26124 Charles A. Walker Hines 26125 James Edmond Van Sickle 26126 Dale Roger Anderson 26127 John Charles Fremont Tillson 26128 Michael Wise Hustead 26129 John Joseph Petersberger 26130 James Hughland Lee 26131 Richard Vincent Gorski 26132 Paul Michael Root 26133 Frederick Edward Meurer 26134 Joseph Rodney Calek 26135 Alfred Arnold Lindseth 26136 Kurt Lee Rhymers 26137 C. Hilton Dunn 26138 Kenneth Graham Carlson 26139 Jon Wayne Loftheim 26140 Emery Folsom Hill 26141 Manuel E. Velazquez 26142 George Gose Peery 26143 Doctor Robert Crants 26144 William Karl Bergman 26145 Eugene Dale Atkinson 26146 Douglas S. Thornblom 26147 LeRoy Robert Fullerton 26148 Thomas Eugene Farewell 26149 Billy Dean Sims 26150 Richard Dean Woodward 26151 Eugene Joseph Driscoll 26152 William Thomas Harvey 26153 David Wessling Britain 26154 Richard Lowell Glassen 26155 Berry Ezell Morton 26156 Edward Norton Hathaway 26157 Gene Robert Canavan 26158 Larry Ronald Donnithorne 26159 Robert Edward Case 26160 Piers M. Wood 26161 Norman Elliott Fretwell 26162 William Wilton Hoyman 26163 Thomas William Eason 26164 Edgar Clifford Johnson 26165 Terrence Charles Salt 26166 Joseph August Bubriski 26167 Karl Stuart Snyder 26168 Robert David Lowry 26169 Raymond Frederick Rees 26170 William Edward Behan 26171 John Basil Kozak 26172 Rhesa Hawkins Barksdale 26173 Adrian Robert Wright 26174 Roger Arthur Grugle 26175 Richard John Wolak 26176 John Stephen McGuire 26177 Robert Allen Satter 26178 Charles Michael Baily 26179 James Ernest Jenkins 26180 Francis Richard Callahan 26181 Gerald Robert Lawrence 26182 Torrence Melvin Wilson 26183 James Michael Stepp 26184 Gordon Lowell Hall 26185 David Scott Berkman 26186 William Melton Kirtley 26187 Michael Thomas Campbell 26188 Gary Max Coggins 26189 Richard James Swift 26190 Theodore Vincent McCullough 26191 Kenneth Dale Buch 26192 Donald Leo Pelletier 26193 Jeremiah Christman Moll 26194 Dennis Dean Loftheim 26195 Michael Harry Brown 26196 Francis Leonard Swanson 26197 Charles Benjamin Chitty 26198 William John Newell 26199 Brian Wayne Ashbaugh 26200 Michael West Brennan 26201 William Edward Traubel 26202 Jack Kummer Norris 26203 John Kingston Ford 26204 Lawrence Donald Bryan 26205 Cooper Livingston Wright 26206 William Lawrence Helkie 26207 William Foster Hughes 26208 Franklin Young Hartline 26209 Robert Michael Meccia 26210 Daniel William Waldo 26211 Daniel Martin Smith 26212 William G. O'Connor 26213 Michael Karl Collmeyer 26214 David George Eichenberger 26215 Edmond Lawrence Faust 26216 Kenneth Paul Schroeder 26217 Thomas Edward Wagner 26218 David William Arthur 26219 Henry Stanley Langendorf 26220 Bryon Ernest Roshong 26221 William Douglas Booth 26222 William Einar Tews 26223 Samuel Anthony Rizzo 26224 Thomas Reed Miller 26225 Kenneth Anthony Foret 26226 William Francis Barry 26227 Robert Anthony Mentell 26228 Richard Dennis Doty 26229 Ronald Glenn Caldwell 26230 Arthur Andrew Schulcz 26231 Randall James Keener 26232 James William Suhay 26233 Robert Merritt Baker 26234 John Bernard Buczacki 26235 David James Kelley 26236 Henry Alan Nemec 26237 Kelso William Horst 26238 James Thomas Unger 26239 Stephen Charles Blackwell 26240 Gerald George Smith 26241 Thomas R. McLaughlin 26242 John Anthony Fera 26243 James Benjamin Peake 26244 Ted Raymond Lingle 26245 James Amis Dickens 26246 Lynn Jay Perey 26247 John Edward Burger 26248 Thomas Edward Swain 26249 Marc Lionel Tumas 26250 Richard Walter Darby 26251 Henry Ransaville Farrell 26252 Hermogenes D. Delarosa 26253 Randall Brannon Medlock 26254 Anthony Joseph Buetti 26255 Bruce Mackie Wilson 26256 John Wilson Marshall 26257 Richard Carl Larson 26258 Richard Lambert Jones 26259 Kenneth Russell Grice 26260 Leigh Franklin Wheeler 26261 Walter George Harper 26262 Boyce Clinton Morrow 26263 Gary Douglas Jackson 26264 Samuel Wilson Bartholomew 26265 John Martin Rice 26266 Jan Adams Van Prooyen 26267 Stephen Alan Williams 26268 Ronald L. Stenstrom 26269 Ronald Bert Carpenter 26270 Donald Reister Moore 26271 Deane C. Drury 26272 Michael Charles Higgins 26273 Matthew Francis DiFiore 26274 John Vernon Zehren 26275 Robert George Denney 26276 Richard T. Harper 26277 James Louis Morrison 26278 David Moore Anderson 26279 David Rockwell Crocker 26280 Fred Gordon Bertolino 26281 Reginald Lionel Audibert 26282 James Delmer Parker 26283 William Robert McKinney 26284 Michael Barnwell Silliman 26285 William Joseph Lewandowski 26286 Richard Nolan Clark 26287 Arthur Frederick Lincoln 26288 Eugene Welch Agnew 26289 Richard Vernon Howell 26290 John Thomas Hoskins 26291 William MacArthur Arrants 26292 Frank Anthony Rybicki 26293 Norman Richard Cooney 26294 Ronald Joseph Bartek 26295 Joseph Daniel Cavolick 26296 Stephen Charles Rinehart 26297 Floyd Cornelius Culhane 26298 Alfred John Sirutis 26299 George Norman Sandell 26300 Douglas James Behnke 26301 Vardell Edwards Nesmith 26302 Shird Bradford Hartley 26303 James Louis Selsor 26304 Larry Eugene Delp 26305 Terry Gaa Stull 26306 James Burton Ophus 26307 Richard Moody Swain 26308 Thom Patrick Garrett 26309 Richard Wayne Tarpley 26310 William Frederick Geiter Seith 26311 Jerome Goddard Edwards 26312 Michael Christopher Mewhinney 26313 Thomas Wade Ewart 26314 Thomas Joseph Kinane 26315 John Oi 26316 Robert Nicholson Seigle 26317 Earle Leroy Parker 26318 Robert Welles Catlin 26319 Charles Edward Figgins 26320 Paul Henry Roggenkamp 26321 William Edris Dock 26322 Raymond George Sepeta 26323 Frank Joseph Kobes 26324 Donald Lee Moffett 26325 Gary Lee Israelson 26326 Robert Eugene Huston 26327 Arthur George Mulligan 26328 Thomas Nahanee Almojuela 26329 Noble Eugene Hart 26330 Alan Douglas Gimian 26331 Gerald Arthur Sands 26332 David M. Schofield 26333 Stephen T. Ohotnicky 26334 Henry Francis Simon 26335 William Henry Correia 26336 Timothy Butler Jeffrey 26337 Richard William Thompson 26338 Bruce Daniel Andries 26339 Victor John Strokin 26340 Frederick Peter Fairchild 26341 Garry James Loysen 26342 Arthur Vernon Grant 26343 Francis Bernard Galligan 26344 James Creighton Gleason 26345 John Hamblen Eckert 26346 David Elmer Seibel 26347 Henry Sessam Foster 26348 Philip Dennis Riley 26349 Robert Mac Hammond 26350 John Cletus Eberle 26351 Robert Ruiz Hicks 26352 Frank Joseph Schap 26353 Patrick Haase Keating 26354 Jon Willard Blades 26355 Lawrence Michael Smith 26356 John Harvey Lester 26357 William Dewayne Basham 26358 Martin Keith Niskanen 26359 John Thomas Gatesy 26360 Kenneth Allen Woltz 26361 Arthur George Bonifas 26362 Willard Charles Guerrero 26363 John Redmond 26364 Wilson Val Kone 26365 David Reynolds Wilson 26366 Danny Lee Crawford 26367 Donald Hicks Scoggin 26368 Richard David Kline 26369 Chaunchy Francis McKearn 26370 Edward Paul Cattron 26371 Henry Eugene Dietz 26372 John Hughes Phillips 26373 Robert Blair Williams 26374 Ronald Dee Bowen 26375 James Winfred Cunningham 26376 Robert Charles Coats 26377 James David Ray 26378 Ralph Heller Cruikshank 26379 Gerald Ernest Dixon 26380 Phillip Allen Nelson 26381 William Marion Poole 26382 James Marshall Salander 26383 Glen McCord Harnden 26384 William Charles Rennagel 26385 William Reed Canning 26386 John Claypool Donovan 26387 Bryan Ray Cole 26388 Peyton F. Ligon 26389 Robert Hunter Turner 26390 John Wyman Detrick 26391 William McCarthy Stone 26392 James Wayne Turbish 26393 Jouni Keravuori 26394 Timothy Edward Daly 26395 George Mullin Alexander 26396 Wayne Lewis Poage 26397 James Churchill Glassford 26398 James McDonald Hayes 26399 Edward Gustav Anderson 26400 Ronald Edward Cox 26401 Charles Henry Blumenfeld 26402 Charles Brenne Hiller 26403 John Kenneth Kehres 26404 Hugh Robert McKibbin 26405 William Steven Pier 26406 Lawrence Ray Hinkle 26407 William Samuel Otto 26408 James Clark Britton 26409 Keith Lee Markey 26410 Douglas Kay Laipple 26411 George Edward Norton 26412 Robert Emery Seger 26413 Michael Nolan Penning 26414 Theodore Burns Borek 26415 Kevin Charles Gaynor 26416 Roger David Sherrard 26417 Joseph John Musiol 26418 Justin Kyle Pleasant 26419 David Carlton Brown 26420 Louis Salz 26421 Jan V. Pailes 26422 John Ralph Hayes 26423 James Wesley Gibson 26424 Billy Weldon Frazier 26425 Bruce Henry Schremp 26426 Marion Gibson Williams 26427 Daniel Richard Crooks 26428 Deme Michael Clainos 26429 Mark Butterworth Bailey 26430 Robert Martin Thompson 26431 Jeffrey Carl Shurtleff 26432 David Edward Youngquist 26433 Thomas Francis Hayes-Morrison 26434 George Thomas Cox 26435 Steven Daniel Berry 26436 Anthony Robert Mazzarella 26437 Douglas Arthur Sims 26438 Robert Llewellyn Gagnon 26439 Michael Patrick Fellenz 26440 Rex Arnold Nichols 26441 Shannon Curtis Cook 26442 Bryan Rowland Stevens 26443 Michael Walter Wynne 26444 Peter Michael Cecere 26445 Richard Elmo Hood 26446 Timothy George Fields 26447 James Theodore Ogle 26448 Jere Irving Huyck 26449 Freddy McFarren 26450 James Paul Connell 26451 James Kite Hackett 26452 David Lee Dickey 26453 Harry Edward Wise 26454 William Henry Stalker 26455 John Grant Christie 26456 Louis Robert Sustersic 26457 Chester Earl Keith 26458 Robert Jonathan Cresci 26459 Bohdan Andrij Sahan 26460 Richard Lawrence St. John 26461 Herbert William Fisher 26462 Marion Michael Hunter 26463 Edward Leo Andrews 26464 Jerry Glenn Fox 26465 Thomas Merritt Carhart 26466 Franklin Alford McGoogan 26467 William James Wight 26468 Gerald Thomas Cecil 26469 Theodore Tipton Sendak 26470 George Benjamin Utter 26471 Thomas Joseph Smith 26472 James Charles Nibbelink 26473 Bruce Philip Auer 26474 Edgar Wright 26475 Lynnford Samuel Wilson 26476 John William Smith 26477 Jeffrey Hartman Smith 26478 Richard White Manlove 26479 Robert Paul Fazen 26480 Russell Walker Jenna 26481 James Patrick Doogan 26482 Thomas James McNaughton 26483 Cameron Addison Ely 26484 John Julius LaRoche 26485 Joel Mark Gartenberg 26486 Arthur Middleton Parker 26487 Michael Hugh Kimel 26488 John Anthony Hanaberry 26489 Donald Jay Kievit 26490 John Joseph McDonnell 26491 William Carter Hunt 26492 George Hayden Groves 26493 Peter James Lantz 26494 William K. Sullivan 26495 William E. Ferguson 26496 Michael B. Fuller 26497 Peter M. Kronberg 26498 Steven Nicholas Brown 26499 Robert Michael Snell 26500 Allen Ross Culpepper 26501 Herbert Godley Miller 26502 Robert H. Scales 26503 Charles F. Hoffman 26504 John A. Ford 26505 Walter E. Brinker 26506 Walter Stanley Piskun 26507 Kenneth W. Fish 26508 John W. Wall 26509 John Graham Zierdt 26510 Thomas B. Davis 26511 William H. Wallace 26512 Matthew Clarence Harrison 26513 William Ashley Payne 26514 Arthur Ray Shepherd 26515 Gary Michael Stewart 26516 Timothy George Timm 26517 Russell Porter Grant 26518 Alvin Byron Dean 26519 Charles James Williams 26520 Douglas Brownlow Lawson 26521 Jan William Olkoski 26522 Emmitt Edison Gibson 26523 Boyd McCanna Harris 26524 Kenneth Richard Carlson 26525 Juel Gary Droubay 26526 Thomas Brew Dusel 26527 John Charles Carrow 26528 Alan Barry Nason 26529 James Davis Hallums 26530 John Wayne Bohuslar 26531 Robert Anthony Guerriero 26532 James Smiley Vivian 26533 Peter Francis Donnell 26534 Morris Robert Faber 26535 Charles Reynold Backlin 26536 Donald Thomas Murphy 26537 Lewis Houston James 26538 Paul Floyd Fantelli 26539 Paul Gene Gillenwater 26540 Warren Arthur Johnson 26541 Robert Nicholas Arnone 26542 Charles Frederick Coates 26543 Stanley Albert Brodka 26544 Paul Joseph Ekstrom 26545 Donald Jerome Prem 26546 John Glimis Pappas 26547 Kenneth Wenzel Kopecky 26548 Rogello Urbano Fernandez 26549 Michael Eugene Oshel 26550 Charles French Johnson 26551 James Robert Tarrant 26552 David Vance Crowell 26553 Dennis Leon Perkins 26554 Donald Joseph Fix 26555 Peter Erhardt Braun 26556 Melvin Oliver Liss 26557 Fred Warren Barnes 26558 James Hugh Proctor 26559 John Warren Geiger 26560 Nelson Hadley Newhouse 26561 Robert Hall Albright 26562 Samuel Hastings Wrightson 26563 Stephen Abraham J Eisenberg 26564 John Gregory Hoffman 26565 John Joseph Dobise 26566 Roger Gray Thompson 26567 Donald Edward Rose 26568 Robert Wayne Luecke 26569 Colin Edward Bludau 26570 Hugo Enrique Elvir 26571 Richard Narman Murray 26572 Curtiss Marion Lindler 26573 Robert Benjamin Ramsay 26574 Walter Michael Strickland 26575 William Edwin Pickens 26576 Robert Dennis Robbins 26577 Robert Carol Dunavan 26578 William Edward Thomas 26579 John Bowker Carber 26580 Morgan Garrott Roseborough 26581 Daniel Ayler Dodd 26582 Gordon Talmage Kimbrell 26583 Charles William Hargett 26584 Donald Richard Judd 26585 Daniel Victor James 26586 Donald Forrest Brown 26587 Carl E. Drewes 26588 Richard Philip Amatulli 26589 Niels Peter Biamon 26590 Philip Owen Benham 26591 Ronald Wayne Bashant 26592 Thomas Wilson Beasley 26593 Gill H. Ruderman 26594 Darryl Dean Magee 26595 John Austin Dubia 26596 Barry Myers DeBolt 26597 William Ernest Bishop 26598 Howard Clinton Kirk 26599 Ronald Eric Marvin 26600 Laurence Norman Hansen 26601 Dewey Jack Renneker 26602 Vincent Lawrence Casillo 26603 James Alfred Whicher 26604 John Thomas McKnight 26605 Kenneth Albert Waylonis 26606 Thomas Magann Donahey 26607 Charles Thomas Harris 26608 Courtenay Patrick O'Connell 26609 William Guernsey Haneke 26610 Ronald P. Meier 26611 Troy Calvin Scott 26612 Howard Samuel Pontuck 26613 Norman Earl Gunderson 26614 Thomas William Grabow 26615 Frank Marshall Hock 26616 Kermit Michael Morgan 26617 Frank Graham Pratt 26618 John McDowell Jenkins 26619 Lynn John Hunt 26620 Walter Edward Skowronski 26621 George Allen Crocker 26622 John James Strapac 26623 Michael Victor McKay 26624 Robert Edward Wysocki 26625 Frederick Charles Engelman 26626 Michael Joseph Brown 26627 Thomas Francis Zurla 26628 Thomas Martin Schroeder 26629 William F. Hixon 26630 Mark Alexander Scureman 26631 Stephen Lee Singer 26632 Billy Wayne Flynn 26633 David Irwin Haines 26634 John William Rantala 26635 Frank Meszar 26636 Warren Henry R. Albrecht 26637 Abney Alexander Smith 26638 Jack Donnelly Crabtree 26639 John Preston Isenhour 26640 William Paul Whelihan 26641 Robert H. Kesmodel 26642 John Roger Thomas 26643 David Fletcher Martin 26644 Frederick William Sparling 26645 Gordon James Wiser 26646 James Paul Backlin 26647 John Kushkowski 26648 Richard Albin Eklund 26649 Donald Campbell 26650 James Linden White 26651 Daniel Joseph Coonan 26652 Richard Ross Striegel 26653 Kevin Christopher Kelley 26654 Wright Edward Noble 26655 Charles Thomas Stowers 26656 John Robert Steenlage 26657 Frank Charles Cosentino 26658 Gaines Stockton Dyer 26659 Robert Frank Michener 26660 **1967** Ernest Clayton Heimberg 26661 Martin McCurdy Cassity 26662 Ronald Lee Weitz 26663 William Arthur Richards 26664 Robert James Carpenter 26665 Charles Philip Hernandez 26666 Wilbur Stone Jones 26667 Ernest R. Natalini 26668 Terry Davies Hand 26669 Roger Joseph Arango 26670 Roger James Purcell 26671 Norman Louis Nesterak 26672 Charles Jeffrey Mills 26673 Albert Jack Nahas 26674 Thomas Raymond Hankard 26675 Michael Bennis McBride 26676 Richard Ernest Radez 26677 William Douglas Brown 26678 Michael Alan Heyne 26679 John Daniel Montanaro 26680 Richard Arthur Jones 26681 Raymond John Winkel 26682 Lawrence Leonard Izzo 26683 Jim Neal Brantner 26684 Michael Frank Delleo 26685 Wallace Earl Walker 26686 Norbert Joseph Reder 26687 Charles Shrader Thomas 26688 George Beverly Winton 26689 Robert Howard Miller 26690 Peter Paul Summers 26691 Hobart Burnside Pillsbury 26692 William Walter Sharkness 26693 John Ruzick Hadorn 26694 Gerald Graham Threadgill 26695 Bruce Bagley Hedrick 26696 Vernon Parker Saxon 26697 Stephen Robert Sears 26698 John Stephen Garay 26699 Richard William Kline 26700 William Reed Morrell 26701 William Richard Lynn 26702 Mark Rowland Fischer 26703 Robert Allan Haeffner 26704 Harry Edward Rothmann 26705 Chad Whitney Keck 26706 Edward N. Tipton 26707 Jack Bruce Wood 26708 Daniel Roger Wells 26709 Karl Henry Jacobs 26710 John Edward Newton 26711 William Ray Pennington 26712 Bartholomew Bernard Bohn 26713 James Robert Sargeant 26714 William J. McDowell 26715 Brian Eugene Hayes 26716 Steven Peter Yambor 26717 Thomas Norman Swett 26718 Palmer John Penny 26719 Karl Donus Sakas 26720 John LeRoy Combs 26721 Christopher Scott Commons 26722 Robert Emmett Keenan 26723 Richard Hardwicke Rice 26724 William Wayne Obley 26725 Harry Alva Tucker 26726 John Edward Kelly 26727 Thomas Dale

Blaney 26728 Jon Stuart Behrens 26729 Brian James McCrodden 26730 David Lewis Powers 26731 James Thomas Reilly 26732 Gordon Mason Brown 26733 Robert Nelson Davie 26734 Thomas Paul Jacobus 26735 John Paul Kuspa 26736 Giuliano M. Toneatto 26737 Todd Lawren McConnell 26738 Jack Edward Obert 26739 Jeffrey Ross Madsen 26740 Monte Merryman Parrish 26741 Karl William Mills 26742 Charles William Streit 26743 Anthony Von Nida 26744 Richard Andrew Phalan 26745 Richard Henry LaBouliere 26746 Earl Richard Refsland 26747 Joseph Ernest Root 26748 Warren Michael Sands 26749 Edward John Dewey 26750 Nielsen Raymond Palmer 26751 Rufus Hale Shumate 26752 Stephen Allan May 26753 John Anthony Yankus 26754 Thomas Andrews Petrie 26755 John Elza Adamson 26756 David Carl Jones 26757 Thomas Marshal Curtis 26758 William Randolph Condos 26759 David Brice Bean 26760 Alexander R. Jansen 26761 Dennis Michael Mikale 26762 Edwin Paul Smith 26763 George Alphonse Schaefer 26764 James Byers Allen 26765 Richard Volney Gladstone 26766 Asa Alan Clark 26767 Richard Edward Foelsch 26768 David R.E. Hale 26769 David E. Peixotto 26770 Joseph Visconti 26771 Robert Leaming Portney 26772 Kent Edward Kraus 26773 James Kenneth Brierly 26774 William Edwin Cates 26775 John Richard James 26776 George Stephen Viney 26777 Ronald Edgar Dionne 26778 Hartmut Henning Lau 26779 James Byron Cowart 26780 Tidal Windham McCoy 26781 Calvin Bricker Delaplain 26782 William Langfitt Wilby 26783 Lawrence R. Smith 26784 Dennis Edward Coates 26785 William Henry Eggering 26786 Charles Costanza 26787 Walter Edward Mather 26788 Walter Lee Murfee 26789 Thomas R. Still 26790 Mark Wayne Miller 26791 Michael Minoru Kishiyama 26792 John Edward Goodnow 26793 Roger Thye Heimann 26794 Montgomery Cunningham Meigs 26795 Paul J. Kern 26796 Burk Everett Bishop 26797 Eddie L. Marion 26798 Robert Keith Williams 26799 Robert Peter Hagen 26800 Charles Harian Swanson 26801 Jerry Lee Hines 26802 Michael Joseph Aiello 26803 Alton Parker Donnell 26804 Christian Frank Vissers 26805 Steve Gradon Barbee 26806 James Harold Saine 26807 Charles Michael Rankin 26808 Richard Leslie Kiper 26809 Robert Arden Hixson 26810 Harvey Grant Taylor 26811 Richard Thomas Newell 26812 Richard Earl Waterman 26813 Frank Henry Kreger 26814 John Charles Gale 26815 Robert Neal Stromberg 26816 David Harold Kelley 26817 Reginald Graham Moore 26818 William Leonard Brigadier 26819 Thomas James Waraksa 26820 Richard Miller Hill 26821 Rand Karl Shotwell 26822 Edward Richard Hubshman 26823 Louis John Colella 26824 Tadashi Glenn Yuguchi 26825 Thomas Jackson Parr 26826 Paul Ballance Haseman 26827 Steven Thomas Kurtyka 26828 Gary Levone Hall 26829 Lawrence Hugh Marlin 26830 David Lee Tye 26831 Thomas Christopher Pettit 26832 Thomas Donald Thompson 26833 Frank Marchman Perry 26834 George Edward Dials 26835 J. Mare Ducharme 26836 David Joseph Bucchieri 26837 Carlton Gerald Savory 26838 Harry Oliver Taylor 26839 David Samuel Rowley 26840 Richard Michael Mullane 26841 Gary Lee Hyde 26842 Richard Adrian Ankener 26843 Dennis William Huyck 26844 James Edward Pryor 26845 Andrew William Maron 26846 John Harris Douglas 26847 Douglas James Pringle 26848 Donald William Dietz 26849 Thomas Bernard Dyer 26850 Gary Thomas Downs 26851 Jon Christopher Shuler 26852 Francis Lee Smith 26853 Joseph Garside Terry 26854 Richard Dabney Estes 26855 John Edward Cunningham 26856 Augusto Lim Palomar 26857 Charles Gordies Sutten 26858 William Alan Pittenger 26859 Robert Lewis Segal 26860 Donald Pedersen Albers 26861 James Robbins Balkcom 26862 Tom Emerson 26863 Roger Wayne Waltz 26864 John Edwin Severson 26865 Jan Phillip Askman 26866 James Anthony Tankovich 26867 Frederick Richard Schremp 26868 Max Powell Bailey 26869 James Daniel Fowler 26870 Michael Lewis Barney 26871 William Michael Langlois 26872 Robert Lee Harris 26873 Ronald James Naples 26874 William Frederick Hausman 26875 John B. Smith 26876 Robert Charles Keck 26877 John Spencer Caldwell 26878 Robert Springer Metzger 26879 Robert Kenaston Griffith 26880 Cole Wesley Minnick 26881 Richard Alan Grube 26882 Robert Felix LaRaia 26883 Daniel Patrick Ragsdale 26884 Kenneth Allen Rice 26885 Thomas Parnell McManus 26886 Robert Fields Shaw 26887 Frederick Howard Thomas 26888 Thomas Eugene White 26889 Marvin LaVerne Tieman 26890 Parker Tonjum Anderson 26891 Stephen L. Frankiewicz 26892 Charles M. Hickey 26893 Anson Slappey Ramsey 26894 Anthony Henry Cortese 26895 Robert Aldo Cenci 26896 David Mel Partridge 26897 Elmer Michael Casey 26898 David Robinson Ellis 26899 Malcolm Howard Philips 26900 Emmett Earl Hughes 26901 Richard H. Gooding 26902 Dean D. Hansen 26903 Frederick John Barofsky 26904 Michael Noboru Nii 26905 Richard T. Altieri 26906 James Judson Findley 26907 Michael W.L. Yap 26908 Benjamin Landis Weakley 26909 Gus Blakely Robinson 26910 Andrew Joseph Nusbaum 26911 Jerry Dale Walker 26912 Joseph Schuyler Hardin 26913 Robert Hughes Evans 26914 Peter Gustaf Hanelt 26915 Harry Douglas Hoskins 26916 Kenneth Roger Bush 26917 Michael R. Hardy 26918 Andrew Komblevitz 26919 Dean Masao Kunihiro 26920 John Albert Bornmann 26921 George Frederick Kolesar 26922 Mark Randall Hamilton 26923 Frank Allen Hill 26924 Arlin Cornelius Ruthven 26925 David Richard Mosser 26926 James Robert Baker 26927 Joe Melvin Dietzel 26928 Peter B. Krause 26929 David Merriam Snyder 26930 Ferdinand Loray Schwartz 26931 Richard Dale Releford 26932 Edward Van Schaick Moore 26933 Ralph G. Mohler 26934 George Atencio Rodriguez 26935 Charles Robert Meyer 26936 Michael William Shelton 26937 Lewis Prichard Kasper 26938 Colin Craig Smith 26939 Douglas Holland Starr 26940 Richard Angelo Comi 26941 Robert Irvin Curtis 26942 Gary Lee Moyer 26943 Robert John Love 26944 Henry Mathias Uberecken 26945 James Thomas Ralph Johnson 26946 Darrell LaVerne Mooney 26947 Robert Adam Wysocki 26948 William Joseph Donohue 26949 Daniel Patrick Schrage 26950 Robert Shiel McEldowney 26951 Gerald Joseph Molnar 26952 Richard Arthur Black 26953 John Thomas Boyt 26954 George Perry Hubert 26955 William Patrick Foley 26956 William Terence McMahan 26957 Randall William Moon 26958 John Joseph Boretti 26959 John Raymond Ouellette 26960 John Harry Jorgenson 26961 Michael Franklin Kush 26962 Gregory Arthur Rice 26963 Richard Curtis Adkins 26964 Daniel Leo Neuburger 26965 Jonathan Kent Burns 26966 Milford Berten Hutchinson 26967 Joseph Edmund DuBois 26968 George Paschal Lupton 26969 Robert Douglas Murrill 26970 Michael Francis Lascher 26971 Gary Michael Chambers 26972 Paul James Cmil 26973 Thomas Robert Guignon 26974 Joseph Porter Jackson 26975 William Gustav Held 26976 Mario Armando Loyola 26977 Bruce Shepley Richardson 26978 Randall Martin Pais 26979 David Richard McAdoo 26980 Robert Ralph Angeli 26981 Michael Edward Alverson 26982 John Patrick Brown 26983 Donald G. Helmstadter 26984 Ronald Lloyd Frazer 26985 Donald Homer Dwiggins 26986 George Harry Kellenbenz 26987 Henry Paul Timm 26988 Dana M. Groover 26989 Carl Allen Bowen 26990 Timothy Bruce Russell 26991 John Wilbert Thiltgen 26992 Thomas Lanyi 26993 Robert C. Doheny 26994 Paul Richard Kokonowski 26995 Leonard Lee Preston 26996 Steven A. Toelle 26997 James Michael Miley 26998 William A. MacDonald 26999 Virgil W. Stone 27000 Sealon R. Wentzel 27001 Michael T. Segraves 27002 William Carl Groman 27003 Barry E. Nickerson 27004 Richard S. Farr 27005 Garth L. Fowler 27006 Gary L. LaBelle 27007 Gordon L. Rankin 27008 Thomas H. Jackson 27009 William P. Moore 27010 Charles W. Trainor 27011 James Louis Walden 27012 Michael Norton 27013 David M. Hadly 27014 Michael Dirk Kelley 27015 Edward J. Beck 27016 James A. Alich 27017 Michael C. Winton 27018 George W. Watts 27019 Robert A. Frank 27020 Val D. Millard 27021 Glynn W. Hale 27022 Daniel Wayne Jinks 27023 Michael Montgomery Cain 27024 Jerry L. Nowels 27025 James Ray Horton 27026 Charles L. Baker 27027 Thomas Roy Hill 27028 Robert J. Mengert 27029 James F. Jackson 27030 Sherwood C. Spring 27031 Joel T. Matulys 27032 John R. Hall 27033 Gary A. Wikert 27034 Michael S. Lancaster 27035 Forrest D. Williams 27036 John Charles Mackerer 27037 Thomas A. Schwartz 27038 George Pejakovich 27039 Robin A. Walker 27040 James M. Weller 27041 William L. McMillan 27042 Jeffrey A. Stark 27043 Terry O. Atkinson 27044 Peter Economos 27045 James P. Jones 27046 Jack Arthur Windeler 27047 Philip A. Burkett 27048 Donald W. MacPherson 27049 John Thomas Corley 27050 James F. Ruhl 27051 Philip A. Hogue 27052 Richard B. Adams 27053 Richard Oliver Bickford 27054 Frank J. Fabish 27055 John E. Marshall 27056 John P. Canevet 27057 James P. DeSantis 27058 Bruce C. Baccei 27059 Richard L. Ehrenreich 27060 David Lynn Baggett 27061 Lloyd Philip Kinney 27062 W. Freed Lowrey 27063 Lodwick K. Alford 27064 Herbert Lewis Altshuler 27065 Clark A. Stave 27066 William Paulson Koch 27067 James E. Stewart 27068 Kenneth A. Harris 27069 Edward J. Locke 27070 Paul A. Bigelman 27071 Richard E. K. Brawn 27072 Paul E. Lima 27073 Gary Waldon Atkins 27074 John M. W. Graham 27075 William Lyman Haines 27076 Alan Eric Seyfer 27077 Carlan J. Kraft 27078 William Hoagland 27079 Donis R. Wolfe 27080 Claude P. Herman 27081 Thomas M. Murphy 27082 James F. Cali 27083 Norman B. Mekkelsen 27084 John E. Thomson 27085 Joseph C. Theis 27086 Thomas N. Thornton 27087 Gary William Carlson 27088 Randall Loftin Kinnard 27089 Frederick E. Hartman 27090 George R. Fischer 27091 Steven G. Honzo 27092 Douglas Taylor Gray 27093 James L. Milliken 27094 Phillip M. Fracker 27095 Michael Gramling Parr 27096 Thomas P. Condon 27097 Kenneth J. Leonardi 27098 Wayne A. Monroe 27099 Michael T. Spinello 27100 Dean P. Risseeuw 27101 Douglas E. Cole 27102 Myron S. Steere 27103 Alan D. Olson 27104 Loren H. Hohman 27105 Thomas J. Cullen 27106 Benjamin Rodriguez 27107 Everett Dennis Lucas 27108 David P. Rivers 27109 Gary L. Frazier 27110 Robert Lawson Sellars 27111 Michael Anthony Hood 27112 James Robert Adams 27113 Elwood M. Eme 27114 Emett R. White 27115 Richard W. Platt 27116 Terry L. Hegglin 27117 George E. Newman 27118 Raymond T. Roe 27119 Kenneth E. Williams 27120 Jack A. Ziemke 27121 John A. Frink 27122 Raymond Alonzo Heath 27123 James O. Vance 27124 Michael J. Cox 27125 Gerald S. Misurek 27126 Robert J. Nolan 27127 Joseph P. Stock 27128 Aaron E. Coe 27129 Robert F. Griffin 27130 James C. Crowley 27131 David Michael Bishop 27132 Jose Manuel Pena 27133 Gregory L. Crawford 27134 Louis Bailey Trevathan 27135 Dale J. Hikes 27136 Michael S. Lighthill 27137 John P. Charters 27138 Roger Alan Fulkerson 27139 John A. Rollow 27140 Gregory W. Smith 27141 David D. Horton 27142 Michael E. Dunn 27143 Edward A. Bryla 27144 Steven W. Kujawski 27145 William Francis Freccia 27146 Davis H. Loftin 27147 Derek L. Younkin 27148 William C. Gonser 27149 Hampton Allen Etheridge 27150 Thomas C. Rothrauff 27151 William Whitaker Horn 27152 John D. Hart 27153 William F. Cusack 27154 Kenneth D. Strong 27155 Donald J. Nelson 27156 F. Scott MacFarlane 27157 James E. Roberts 27158 James D. Osborne 27159 Craig Damien Butler 27160 John Joseph Avard 27161 George Ronald Sutton 27162 Robert James Lenz 27163 Michael C. Kempf 27164 Henry J. Berthelot 27165 Michael J. Neuman 27166 James R. Siket 27167 Sterling W. McColgin 27168 Gerry L. Fox 27169 Arnoldo A. Cano 27170 Robert D. Herb 27171 Ellis David Greene 27172 Michael G. Riess 27173 Charles M. Stancil 27174 Townsend Sutherland Clarke 27175 William J. Ervin 27176 Alfred E. Burer 27177 Christopher A. Biltoft 27178 Brian E. Mahoney 27179 Michael C. Wimert 27180 Robert E. Knapp 27181 Donald C. Hertzfeldt 27182 Paul M. Cline 27183 Robert C. Unterbrink 27184 Thomas Clifford Coker 27185 Edwin N. Jordan 27186 John Arthur Graziano 27187 Kerry Leigh O'Hara 27188 Lee Emir Cage 27189 Michael H. Warren 27190 Wesley J. Spincic 27191 Steven E. Doty 27192 Victor C. Pangle 27193 Robert J. Libutti 27194 Michael Leo Nathe 27195 Norman Ray Jones 27196 Robert M. Hartley 27197 William A. Pollitt 27198 Robert J. P. Begin 27199 Carrol Jaye Howard 27200 James M. Warner 27201 George L. Harmon 27202 John B. Landgraf 27203 Marshall Kirk Bolyard 27204 Gordon A. Socher 27205 Clarence E. Mahle 27206 John N. Stewart 27207 James O. Haas 27208 William A. Norton 27209 Thomas H. Sayes 27210 Mathew S. Mathews 27211 Terry Lee Ketter 27212 Raymond James Enners 27213 Robert McGarvey Colson 27214 Jimmy N. Bondurant 27215 William T. Platt 27216 William Frank Petruzel 27217 Hugh Bernard Brown 27218 Ward Dean 27219 John Hampden Murrell 27220 David K. Hewett 27221 Joseph C. Casey 27222 Michael Bland Ellzey 27223 Stephen K. Grove 27224 Timothy Paul Gilbert 27225 George Edward Perkins 27226 Richard T. Clapper 27227 Charles S. Horwath 27228 Robert A. Kunselman 27229 Manuel Alvarez 27230 Robert W. Rettig 27231 Howard M. Harmless 27232 Bobby G. Whaley 27233 Michael Allen Andrews 27234 Edward A. M. Sullivan 27235 John E. Mikula 27236 Charles T. Heisler 27237 Kenneth W. Smith 27238 Thomas R. Francisco 27239 Peter J. Gizzi 27240 David Gair Blanchard 27241 Wayne Keith Schaltenbrand 27242 Richard William Anastasi 27243 **1968** Lamar Cecil Ratcliffe 27244 Ray William MacDonald 27245 Michael Kell Sheaffer 27246 Edmund Rhodes Hobbs 27247 Andrew Lynne Dull 27248 Edward Dorsey Hammond 27249 Antone Charles Cerne 27250 John Robert Oneal 27251 Lawrence Anthony Rapisarda 27252 Daniel Dick Nettesheim 27253 Jerry Wayne Sorrow 27254 Robert Angelo Pinzuti 27255 Thomas Leggate McNaugher 27256 Richard Howard Witherspoon 27257 Howard W. Kympton 27258 Bruce Dixon Sweeny 27259 Franklin Pierce Robinson 27260 Eric Eugen Thomas 27261 Robert Dale Swedock 27262 Stephen Paul Donohue 27263 Gregory Bruce Johnson 27264 Barry George Hittner 27265 Thomas George Kurkjian 27266 Robert Arthur Firehock 27267 Robert Corby Kelly 27268 Jon Stockman Gardner 27269 Kenneth J. Moran 27270 Gordon Taylor Greeby 27271 Donald Robert Colglazier 27272 William Lafayette Nash 27273 Louis Paul Font 27274 John Lathrop Throckmorton 27275 John Thomas Martin 27276 Daniel Joseph Kaufman 27277 Daniel Eugene Adams 27278 James Arthur Tallman 27279 John William Morris 27280 Peter Perkins Wallace 27281 V. Paul Baerman 27282 George Van Devendorf Neill 27283 Michael Patrick Laing 27284 William Lewis Robinson 27285 John Anthony Dallen 27286 John William McDonald 27287 Robert Hewitt Fabrey 27288 Hugo William Croft 27289 Richard Phillip Gilliard 27290 Harold Langford Wilhite 27291 Joseph Vincent Creeden 27292 Nicholas Scott Dienes 27293 Mark Gordon Spelman 27294 Richard Ross Goodell 27295 Richard Frederick Keller 27296 Claude Daniel Lynes 27297 Wallace Clifton Magathan 27298 William Michael Brown 27299 Charles Percy Adkins 27300 Norman Eric Miller 27301 Bohdan Neswiacheny 27302 Victor Roma Farrugia 27303 Albert Sleder 27304 Roger Thomas Olson 27305 Frank Maxwell Puckett 27306 Frank Joseph Chapuran 27307 Michael Henrik Fellows 27308 Michael Edward Bruce 27309 Michael Lawrence Grygiel 27310 James Dean Kelly 27311 Gilbert James Reilly 27312 Michael Paul Peters 27313 Dan Popov 27314 Thomas Hellmuth Simmons 27315 William Taylor McCauley 27316 Jess Ralph Nickols 27317 Richard Robert Kent 27318 John Brian Copley 27319 Stephen Michael Herman 27320 Robert Hill Henderson 27321 Arnold Henry Soeder 27322 Norman Tyley O'Meara 27323 Richard Melvin Mason 27324 Craig Scott Carson 27325 Ronald Dennis Feher 27326 Thomas Nelson Burnette 27327 George Jacobs Prosnik 27328 Jack Edmund Gerke 27329 Steven George Lyons 27330 George Fredrick Adam 27331 Michael James Fisher 27332 George Kent Williams 27333 Mark Alan Edelman 27334 Martin Luther Bowling 27335 John Joseph Keane 27336 Michael Francis Palone 27337 Jesse Cecil Gatlin 27338 Richard Kenneth Wright 27339 Francis Allyn Cooch 27340 Albert James Madora 27341 Charles Robert James 27342 John Howard Cochran 27343 Russell L. Fuhrman 27344 Robert Charles Sweeney 27345 Timothy Wayne Brown 27346 Michael Lelon Patrow 27347 Charles Arthur Vehlow 27348 Arthur Coyne Sands 27349 Robert Allan Adams 27350 Werner John Stolp 27351 Harold Lee Timboe 27352 Frank Thompson Robinson 27353 John Joseph Gonzalez 27354 William Thomas Marriott 27355 Frederick Douglas Reynolds 27356 James David Craig 27357 George Bernard Shoener 27358 Mark F. Hansen 27359 Ronald Nochea Haruo Yasukawa 27360 Christopher Sal Iaconis 27361 Brian John McKenna 27362 John Reiley Finney 27363 Thomas Michael Moore 27364 Michael James O'Connell 27365 David Martin 27366 Terence Charles Holland 27367 Bogdan Michael Kulikowski 27368 Charles Richard Stroble 27369 Rand L. Allen 27370 Abe Lincoln Eustice 27371 Duncan F. Stewart 27372 Joseph Paul O'Connor 27373 Michael Martin Romash 27374 A. Patrick Jonas 27375 David Lee Alexander 27376 Carl Frederick Witschonke 27377 Robert Leonard Merritt 27378 Miguel Ontiveros Ruiz 27379 Larry James Petcu 27380 Harry S. Bennett 27381 Thomas Duane Onasch 27382 William J. Matlach 27383 Russell Peter Bonasso 27384 Maurice Dale Adams 27385 Edward Julius Lorentzen 27386 Dale Stanley Sharples 27387 Thomas Craig McConnell 27388 Joseph John Javorski 27389 David Warren Carraway 27390 Kendall Fielder Haven 27391 Richard Thomas Russell 27392 Earl William Flowers 27393 William Joseph Higgins 27394 Michael John Mann 27395 John Anthony Dodson 27396 Leo Edward Norton 27397 Theodore Joseph Trauner 27398 Peter Albert Lopes 27399 John Wesley Guinn 27400 William R. Clark 27401 Michael Joseph Cerrone 27402 R. Brickley Sweet 27403 Willard P. McCrone 27404 Richard Edward Fetterman 27405 Henry Mershon Spengler 27406 Larry Samuel Fulton 27407 Dennis Keith MacVittie 27408 David Allen Knecht 27409 Terrence J. Kennedy 27410 H. Michael Mears 27411 William Stanley Grabowski 27412 Thomas Keith Jewell 27413 Tay Yoshitani 27414 Lyle Eric Pirnie 27415 Dorsey David Hostler 27416 Louis W. Schlipper 27417 John Augustine Buckley 27418 Donald Joseph McLane 27419 David A. Schulte 27420 Frederic Leslie Tucker 27421 Don Wilson Jones 27422 Robert Spencer Lower 27423 Henry Frederick Gregor 27424 Neil A. McLean 27425 James Ken Worthen 27426 Daniel James Winter 27427 John Daniel Kruger 27428 James Reno Locher 27429 Maurice Edward Murphy 27430 Samuel Owen Lowry 27431 Gary Lee Schappaugh 27432 Joseph Creamer Fowler 27433 John Edward Heisel 27434 William Alan Bachman 27435 William James Peplinski 27436 Daniel Aloysius Ryan 27437 David Wolcott Olmsted 27438 Steven Rhodes Rader 27439 Robert Bruce Uhler 27440 James Ronald Swinney 27441 Charles Francis Besanceney 27442 Charles Wingard Jones 27443 Stephen Arthur Winsor 27444 Benjamin Franklin Heil 27445 Michael Carl Wells 27446 Kenneth Paul Knitt 27447 Toney Adams Mathews 27448 Jeffrey Louis House 27449 Charles Richard Miller 27450 Glen Martin Hewitt 27451 Richard Gordon Cliff 27452 Renata Frances Price 27453 Michael Elmore Havey 27454 Lee M. Schaeffer 27455 George Austin Gardes 27456 Charles Joseph Piraneo 27457 Donald Lewis Andrews 27458 Jay Douglas Johnson 27459 Hugh Andrew Shaffer 27460 Thomas Edmund Clare Margrave 27461 David Michael Hatcher 27462 John Hewett Munson 27463 John Joseph Bussa 27464 Michael L. Simonich 27465 Daniel Bruce Seebard 27466 John Donald Mayer 27467 Francis Stanley Delia 27468 Robert Harold Beahm 27469 Malcolm McLeod Murray 27470 Joel Edward Pigott 27471 Norman Donald Kulpa 27472 Robert L. Mills 27473 Victor F. Garcia 27474 Tyler Barnett Parsons 27475 Michael Douglas Selvitelle 27476 John Charles Cruden 27477 Michael Phillip Einbinder 27478 Howard Chowning McElroy 27479 Alvin Louis Mente 27480 Nelson Edward Laughton 27481 Joseph Daniel Durkan 27482 Karl Judd Leatham 27483 Anthony Ambrose 27484 Robert L. Sherman 27485 Louis Ellington Speer 27486 James Melvin Harter 27487 Karl Johan Gustafson 27488 Peter Michael Connor 27489 Edward Joe Heller 27490 Stephen Joe Frushour 27491 Ronald Marvin Warncke 27492 Gregory Michel Babitz 27493 Charles Douglas McKenna 27494 John Roger Williams 27495 Stephen Douglas Childers 27496 Dale Winslow Hansen 27497 Louis L. Pierce 27498 Peter Thomas Sowa 27499 C. Preston Miller 27500 James John Stettler 27501 John Francis Miller 27502 Roy Deen Miller 27503

Richard D. Shipley 27504 Richard John Scaglione 27505 John Brian Wing 27506 Charles Richard Myers 27507 Dean Brown Becker 27508 Larry Callan Baker 27509 William A. Kunzman 27510 Charles Robert Lieb 27511 William Dickson Shaffer 27512 David Harrison Clemm 27513 Leonard Arthur Wallin 27514 Paul Edward Ptasnik 27515 Edmund Alfred Thal 27516 Marvin Eugene Markley 27517 Michael Vance McClary 27518 Dennis Wayne Manske 27519 George William Schweitzer 27520 Bruce Edward Parry 27521 Thomas Lee Vollrath 27522 Michael Joseph Brennan 27523 James Dean Bodenhamer 27524 Edward Lee Milinski 27525 Lawrence George O'Toole 27526 Samuel Deering Wyman 27527 Timothy Alfred Fisher 27528 Fred Charles Parker 27529 Gregory Clark Camp 27530 Nicholas Nahorniak 27531 Marvin Sam Belasco 27532 Timothy Dean Balliett 27533 Andrew William Corcoran 27534 Henry W. Alward 27535 James Michael Tanski 27536 Jim Orvis Llewellyn 27537 Frederick Edward Burdette 27538 Steven John Coldwell 27539 Michael Thomas Toole 27540 John Anthony Calabro 27541 Robert Lee Keller 27542 Louis John Speidel 27543 Thomas Hugh Peirce 27544 Paul DeWitt Lovett 27545 Robert Douglas Hunt 27546 George Henry Fravel 27547 John Dewhurst Spengler 27548 Walton Wright Curl 27549 Michael Dean Vennum 27550 Gregory John Unangst 27551 Charles Richard Hill 27552 Paul Bradford Pedrotti 27553 Earl Eugene Newsome 27554 Dennis John Hergenrether 27555 James Lawrence Altemose 27556 Marvin Wooten 27557 William Francis Reichert 27558 Buren Riley Shields 27559 David Philip Ford 27560 Michael E. Benefield 27561 Alan Dean Catron 27562 John Christian Frinak 27563 Charles Lincoln Mackall 27564 Randall K. Witwer 27565 James Frederick Kelley 27566 Barton Jay McLellan 27567 George James Heckman 27568 Russell James Houck 27569 Robert Andrew Burns 27570 John Oscar Benson 27571 David Henry Ohle 27572 Stephen Jennings Marcuccilli 27573 Peter Byron Hanson 27574 William Roland Thygerson 27575 Neil Dwayne Hughes 27576 Francis Milton Creighton 27577 Denny Layton Johnson 27578 Richard Crowley Flanigan 27579 William George Easton 27580 Douglass Terrell Wheless 27581 Lee James O'Reilly 27582 Donald Arthur Johnson 27583 David Leslie Taylor 27584 Claude Alton Johnson 27585 Carl Frank Woessner 27586 Robert Christopher Galak 27587 Edward Martin Mendoza 27588 Jared Egerton Florance 27589 Harold Edward Yager 27590 Joseph F. Mance 27591 Ronnie Joe Lane 27592 Robert Michael Baker 27593 James Francis Lawton 27594 Walter Donald Gaddis 27595 William C. Jeffries 27596 Michael Robert Hart 27597 James Alexander Black 27598 James Porter Spencer 27599 Dale Rudolf Nelson 27600 Alan Brendan Aker 27601 Donald Francis Van Cook 27602 Steven Wayne Ader 27603 James Jude Jennings 27604 Robert Eugene Shimp 27605 Peter Alfred Swan 27606 Michael Leslie Trollinger 27607 Robert Adrian Brace 27608 G. Keith Quinney 27609 Joseph Shepard McCaffrey 27610 Robert C. Shaw 27611 Lawrence Thomas Hart 27612 David Thornton Maddux 27613 William M. Gardepe 27614 David Andra Smith 27615 Robert Michael Alexander 27616 John Michael Blevins 27617 William Morrow Reffett 27618 Dwight Earl Lee 27619 William Richard Kyzer 27620 Paul Alex DeCoursey 27621 George Rebovich 27622 James Michael Stefan 27623 Charles Fred Klein 27624 William Forssell Ericson 27625 Everett Theodore Wohlers 27626 Kenneth William Hauck 27627 F. Gordon Zophy 27628 James Lewis Greenberg 27629 Ralph D'Alessandro 27630 Edward Duane Larson 27631 John Francis Cullen 27632 William Michael Curran 27633 William Richard Schutsky 27634 Monte Royal Anderson 27635 John Duxbury Toraason 27636 Charles Thomas Olvis 27637 Mark Lee Barnett 27638 Donald Franklin Wantuck 27639 Ralph Reed Fraley 27640 George Louis Christensen 27641 William Ray Lynch 27642 Charles Robert Broderick 27643 Gordon Crupper 27644 Michael James Fay 27645 Frank Raymond Nader 27646 Robert Bryson Clarke 27647 Richard LeRoy Palke 27648 John H. Ludwikoski 27649 Robert Leon Hayes 27650 Ross Louis Nagy 27651 John Arndt Strand 27652 William Basil Raines 27653 Erin Francis Audrain 27654 William Lee Mulvey 27655 Robert Martin Brown 27656 Timothy Lee Carpenter 27657 Elwood Alexander Cobey 27658 Floyd T. Banks 27659 James Edward Garrison 27660 Gerald B. Weeks 27661 John Carl Crenshaw 27662 Clarence Austin Burrell 27663 Terence Keith Laughlin 27664 Michael Albert O'Neil 27665 Horst Gunter Rudolf Sperber 27666 William Joseph McAdams 27667 William Scott Miller 27668 Patrick Alan Toffler 27669 Douglas Maupin Cummings 27670 Howard Francis Harper 27671 Paul Thomas Krieger 27672 Robert Tudor Veidt 27673 Keith Fries Merritt 27674 James Gordon Decker 27675 Jerome Weber Holderness 27676 Larry Brian Main 27677 Terrence Kwock Hing Wong 27678 Richard John Wiedenbeck 27679 Jim Mann Bevans 27680 Charles R. Brooks 27681 Steven Alfred Shaw 27682 John Hayes Armstrong 27683 Gilbert Tijerina 27684 George Edward Germann 27685 Larry Reginald Jordan 27686 Warren Frank Bowland 27687 John Joseph Ryneska 27688 Victor Edward Hiatt 27689 Charles Dale Williams 27690 Richard Joseph Flynn 27691 John Clarence Johnston 27692 Robert John Balog 27693 James Ronald Adams 27694 Stephen Lee Bowman 27695 David A. Neyses 27696 George Robert Laswell 27697 William Nelson Campbell 27698 Daniel Russell Taylor 27699 Gordon E. Sayre 27700 Ronald Russell Kendall 27701 Arthur Cornwell Coogler 27702 Walter Denzin Meinshausen 27703 Dennis Max Burrell 27704 Richard Elliott McClelland 27705 John Edward Thomassy 27706 Frederic Holly Hoblit 27707 John Lewis Anderson 27708 Michael R. Soice 27709 Stephen James Harper 27710 Philip James Samuel 27711 Robert Alfred Stroud 27712 Robert Raymond Gora 27713 Charles Joseph Canella 27714 Joseph Cox Finley 27715 John T. Reed 27716 Alan George Vitters 27717 William Neil Lark 27718 Myles Joseph Crowe 27719 Christopher Robert Ohlinger 27720 Andrew Boyd Stratton 27721 Thomas Allan Barnes 27722 Arthur Weiman Ackerman 27723 James Miller Stanley 27724 Robert Bruce Messel 27725 Raymond Henry Puffer 27726 Douglas Edward MacFarlane 27727 Danny Ray Bunnell 27728 Richard Freeman Des Jardien 27729 Floyd Lee Perry 27730 Henry LeRoy Riser 27731 Michael August Noonan 27732 Ted Keith Broyhill 27733 Louis J. Hansen 27734 Bruce Michael Korda 27735 Alan Joseph Smith 27736 Gary Rikio Yoshizumi 27737 William Francis Little 27738 Jon B. Nolan 27739 Gilbert Arthur Jacobs 27740 Stewart David Beckley 27741 Michael William Potter 27742 Michael Fuchs Thuss 27743 Randolph Stephen Sprinkles 27744 Sam Brooks 27745 David Francis Cunningham 27746 James Paul Cima 27747 Allan Mac Crecelius 27748 David James Clappier 27749 William John Craven 27750 Hayden Clarence Poynter 27751 Andrew Ralston Anderson 27752 Robert Milton Echols 27753 Richard George Carlson 27754 Daniel Frederick Robinson 27755 Richard Denis Powell 27756 Jude Robert Rolfes 27757 William Edgar Dickerson 27758 Marvin Patrick Strong 27759 Patrick John Moe 27760 Gary William Halstead 27761 Gary Steven Williams 27762 Daniel Ernest Gooding 27763 James Richard Furr 27764 Robert Carl Lorbeer 27765 Stanley Alden Burwell 27766 Antonio William Medici 27767 Roy William Mase 27768 Michael Albert Dauth 27769 Jerald Melvin Cobb 27770 Richard Taylor Rhoades 27771 John Edward Darling 27772 George Edgar Fryer 27773 John Terence Wildrick 27774 Philip James Krueger 27775 Allen Stanley Parker 27776 Charles William Petruska 27777 Stephen James Rodgers 27778 Kenneth McAlpine Day 27779 John Joseph Clark 27780 Joseph Richard Henry 27781 Ronald Kemp Adams 27782 Gary Franklin Roberson 27783 Joaquin J. Perez 27784 Jerry Lee Buckley 27785 Charles Brian Utermahlen 27786 Daniel Ross Powell 27787 James Douglas Kohler 27788 Joseph Nicholas Mangino 27789 Louis Seaborn Davis 27790 Bruce Henry Brown 27791 David Ingham Drummond 27792 James William Carman 27793 William Edward Williams 27794 David Wallace Gerard 27795 John Stephen Westerlund 27796 Frank Joseph Lynch 27797 George John Ziots 27798 Michael Grant MacLaren 27799 Andrew Charles Silverthorn 27800 Gerald Ede Crawford 27801 Jeffrey C. Rogers 27802 Donald Lynn Roberts 27803 Charles S. Mahan 27804 J. Thomas Martin 27805 Barry Thomas Conway 27806 William Ross Irvin 27807 Gene Paul Austin 27808 Jonathan Boyd Dodson 27809 Charles Lowndes Steel 27810 Oliver R. Johnson 27811 James Foster Kimball 27812 Douglas Frank Stevenson 27813 Larry Lee Stevenson 27814 Thomas Eugene Pence 27815 Michael Edward Gorecki 27816 Arthur F. Torres 27817 Donald Craig Davis 27818 Robert George McDonald 27819 John Craig Allgood 27820 Jeffry Randal Riek 27821 Joseph Michael Cinquino 27822 George D. Nippell 27823 Charles Edward Beckwith 27824 Peter Grant Paulson 27825 Thomas Earl Stites 27826 Ernest Flowers 27827 David Lee Carl 27828 Joseph Gray Guignon 27829 Fred Joseph Shahid 27830 Thomas Michael Kecki 27831 Francis William Post 27832 Douglas Alan Cohn 27833 Gary Ernest Grant 27834 Craig E. O'Connor 27835 Orin Andrew Durham 27836 Michael Lee Billingsley 27837 Roland E. Olivier 27838 Donald Renay Workman 27839 John Pershing Bayer 27840 James John Thome 27841 James Thomas Baird 27842 Lewis Harold Robertson 27843 Karl William Volk 27844 Patrick Michael Curran 27845 James Henry Francis 27846 Robert McCall Hensler 27847 Wilson Lee Rorie 27848 Eric Richard Kunz 27849 Nicholas Michael Kurilko 27850 LeRoy Brookins Outlaw 27851 Stephen Jay Nyquist 27852 James Edwin Fourqurean 27853 Richard Warren Steiner 27854 John Patrick Walsh 27855 Thomas Albert Wantuck 27856 Fred Byron Johnson 27857 George Gordon Tillery 27858 Ralph Russell Tuccillo 27859 Kenneth John Kremenak 27860 John Curry Merriam 27861 Neil Foster Cowperthwaite 27862 Harry Ellis Hayes 27863 Michael Joseph Gilhuly 27864 Ardenne Stott Carleton 27865 Paul Fredrick Joseph 27866 John Charles Oventile 27867 Paul Howard Crist 27868 Richard Albert Brooke 27869 Edwin Harry Millson 27870 Jeffrey Duffin Wilcox 27871 Neil Michael Tangen 27872 John Nagle Williams 27873 Donald John Darmody 27874 John Charles Hedley 27875 Leslie Raymond Wright 27876 Daniel Bay Limbaugh 27877 Stephen Leslie Osborn 27878 James Francis Anderson 27879 Daniel Francis Carroll 27880 Charles Bernard Giasson 27881 Robert Theodore Jetland 27882 Stephen Lynn Murphy 27883 Jon Kelly Stallings 27884 Joseph Michael Dooley 27885 James T. Howard 27886 Bruce Francis Erion 27887 John Gilbert Hathaway 27888 Raymond Savage Vinton 27889 Russell Andrew Olsen 27890 Ralph Butler Tildon 27891 Jack James Reid 27892 James Alfred Gaiser 27893 William Earle Robinson 27894 Donald Gregory Hall 27895 John Trompen Harmeling 27896 Michael Anthony DiBenedetto 27897 Dennis LeRoy Rosenberry 27898 Larry Alan Manning 27899 Johnnie Miller 27900 Kenneth Thomas Cummings 27901 Kim Jury Henningsen 27902 Edward Bradford Cutting 27903 Virgil Foy Lambert 27904 Fred Ithel Rider 27905 James Ogden Younts 27906 James Franklin Walsh 27907 Richard Elton Bowers 27908 John A. Jones 27909 Benny LeRoy Robinson 27910 William Burg Dyer 27911 John Bruce Horn 27912 Charles F. Hawkins 27913 Manolo Natividad Diamante 27914 Kent Merrick Trexler 27915 John Carmine Peduto 27916 Lyle Raymond Rhodes 27917 Alvion Robert Kimball 27918 Leon Francis Morand 27919 David Stanley Jones 27920 Edward Lee Nelson 27921 Leslie Dale Krohnfeldt 27922 Henry Martin Toczylowski 27923 Larry Joe Van Horn 27924 Joseph Albert de Blaquiere 27925 Thomas Aquinas Beierschmitt 27926 Wilford Scott Vickers 27927 Surry Parker Everett 27928 Harrison Ulrich Jack 27929 James Edward McClain 27930 Michael Alexander Bressler 27931 Robert Edwin Szigethy 27932 Patrick James O'Keefe 27933 Russell Jacob Baker 27934 Wallace William Barton 27935 Leon Rudolph Griffin 27936 Jon Clifford Anderson 27937 John Holden Nerdahl 27938 Kenneth Robert Nicholson 27939 James Denton Horton 27940 James Arbon Orahood 27941 David Lee Sackett 27942 Robert Francis Casey 27943 James Von Hargis 27944 Daniel Joseph Donahue 27945 Jack Williams Swaney 27946 Andrew Bird Allen 27947 Keith Best Harrelson 27948 Richard Aspinall Hawley 27949 **1969** H. Jack Von Kaenel 27950 Wayne Kenneth Murphy 27951 Michael Diffley 27952 Bruce Hartig Laswell 27953 William Brockenbrough Taylor 27954 James Leonard Giacomini 27955 Frame John Bowers 27956 William John Gregor 27957 Robert Michael Kimmitt 27958 John Elson Furneaux 27959 Jack Burton Gafford 27960 Thomas W. McCaslin 27961 Kip Peter Nygren 27962 Dennis Robert Haydon 27963 Robert Henry Baldwin 27964 Kenneth Allan Eisenhardt 27965 Ralph Dozier Crosby 27966 Carl Dean Ozimek 27967 Jonathan Cameron Shine 27968 John Allen Guernsey 27969 Thomas Ray Wheelock 27970 Charles William Anderson 27971 Hugh James Donohue 27972 Forrest William Barnett 27973 William John Deller 27974 James Richard McDonough 27975 Ronald Lloyd Hunt 27976 John Frederick Brundage 27977 Scott Forrester Church 27978 William Hudson Thorne 27979 Ralph Reid White 27980 Kent Robert Gonser 27981 Luigi Bellotti Rose 27982 Salvatore Chris Malguarnera 27983 Brian David Owens 27984 Robert Carl Nechin 27985 James Andrew McCall 27986 Craig Roger Garrett 27987 Mark Lewis Frey 27988 Michael Egan McKay 27989 Matthew Jerome Zilinskas 27990 Peter Gerard Drower 27991 Larry Earl Anderson 27992 Edward William Mayer 27993 John James Woodrum 27994 Thomas Merrill Kiehne 27995 Jeffrey Blake Thompson 27996 Philip Vincent Coyle 27997 Harry Joseph Dolton 27998 Michael Francis Colacicco 27999 Arthur Lawrence Faris 28000 Mark Jay Kransdorf 28001 Lewis Dale Riggsby 28002 Terry Alan Bresnick 28003 Daniel Chambers Bird 28004 John Patrick Blumer 28005 Warren David Mueller 28006 William Anthony Aileo 28007 Howard Henry Hoege 28008 Robert Patrick Jones 28009 John William Bickel 28010 Douglas Semier Aykroyd 28011 Richard Magnus Frykman 28012 Michael P. Hagan 28013 Stephen Kale Rhyne 28014 Dennis Elvin Helsel 28015 Arthur Jeffery Hawking 28016 Philip Austin Clark 28017 Rickey Arthur Kolb 28018 Edward Louis Quinn 28019 Richard Chadwick Ashley 28020 Thomas William Fagan 28021 Claude Darius Alexander 28022 Arthur Roy Shean 28023 Paul Dallas Grant 28024 George Patrick Lasche 28025 Dennis William Tighe 28026 Adolf Carlson 28027 Joseph West Cornelison 28028 John Dashiell French 28029 Michael John Speltz 28030 Henry Paul Russell 28031 Jon Steven Davis 28032 David Warren Hill 28033 Ralph Artigliere 28034 James Robert Reinker 28035 Robin Reventar Cababa 28036 Donald Paul Wagner 28037 Terence G. Craig 28038 Robert Dewey Ramsay 28039 Frank Richard Savage 28040 Stephen M. Fall 28041 Terence Michael Freeman 28042 Robert Joseph Wilson 28043 Robert James McCloy 28044 Dale Layman Cross 28045 Milton D. Smith 28046 William Ross Taylor 28047 Earl Wayne Renner 28048 Carlos Enrique Araya Araya 28049 John Allen Lucas 28050 Joseph Lawier Olson 28051 James Leonard Narel 28052 John Frederick Suermann 28053 Roger Alan Vandenberg 28054 Charles William Leitzke 28055 Dale Evan Straw 28056 Robert Michael Tesdahl 28057 David Dent Harvey 28058 Gregory Christopher Binder 28059 Gerald William Ricker 28060 Robert Shelley Guest 28061 Terry Lee Rice 28062 Peter Heesch 28063 Robert Edgar Gregg 28064 Douglas Edward Taylor 28065 Douglas Cagney Fitzgerald 28066 Richard Gregor Whitney 28067 Stewart Herbert Bornhoft 28068 Francis Joseph Kopczynski 28069 Robert Allan Glacel 28070 John L. Davis 28071 William Garrard Foster 28072 John Ferguson Seck 28073 Emmett Eugene Stobbs 28074 Edward Stanley Babcock 28075 William Lloyd Jones 28076 Thomas Albert Dellwo 28077 Michael Joseph Nardotti 28078 Charles Ford Brower 28079 Larry Gene Kleinsteiber 28080 David Dale Kirby 28081 Lawrence James White 28082 Edward John Jahnke 28083 Glenn Richard Schiraldi 28084 Stephen Perry Traynor 28085 James Noble Carpenter 28086 Harrison Lobdell 28087 John Edward Oristian 28088 Thomas Francis Ramos 28089 William John Burke 28090 Patrick Joseph Spann 28091 William Earl Damon 28092 Roger Paul Balog 28093 Robert Donald Setzer 28094 Thomas Arthur Henderson 28095 Timothy James Slack 28096 Arthur S. Nabben 28097 Dana Charles Johnston 28098 Douglas Warren Marshall 28099 Charles J. Kibert 28100 Bruce Milton Eisentrout 28101 J. Ronald Hudnell 28102 William Emmert DuVall 28103 Douglas Hugh Madigan 28104 Michael A. Brennan 28105 Jerry Carl Mailey 28106 James Francis Reynolds 28107 Fredrick Lee Whitaker 28108 William Joseph Rice 28109 Benjamin G. Watts 28110 Robert Willis Wells 28111 James Craig Adamson 28112 William Herbert Selecman 28113 Douglas Willard Craft 28114 Joseph Anthony Silva 28115 Guy Estey Miller 28116 David Scott Barber 28117 Thomas Edward Kerestes 28118 Lloyd Elmer Fellenz 28119 Luis Bernardo Retana 28120 Daniel Joseph Cox 28121 Rene Goodloe Copeland 28122 Richard Roger Garay 28123 Thomas Timothy Brown 28124 Howard William Fleeger 28125 Clyde LeRoy Heffernan 28126 Randall You Choy Ho 28127 Jon Theriault Smrtic 28128 Robert Bruce McBane 28129 Russel Edward Milnes 28130 James Michael Johnson 28131 William Joseph Johnson 28132 Stephen Lloyd Herbert 28133 Daniel Francis Lennon 28134 Vernon Manuel Bettencourt 28135 Lewis Martin Killian 28136 Danwill Lee 28137 James Martin Bachta 28138 William Heavilin Leppig 28139 Richard Douglas West 28140 Michael William Maasberg 28141 David Gordon Hofstetter 28142 William Lee Johnsmeyer 28143 Jeffrey John Gilson 28144 Thomas Edward Karstens 28145 Brian Lee Raymond 28146 William Eugene Zook 28147 John Arthur Gloriod 28148 Stewart Oliver Olson 28149 Donald Wayne Tunstall 28150 Douglas Earl Johnson 28151 Gary Bill Bullock 28152 Richard Allen Carter 28153 Donald Ewan Stevenson 28154 William Francis Friese 28155 Douglas Arthur Freeley 28156 James Wallace Adams 28157 Douglas J. Jeffrey 28158 Laurence Ronald Sadoff 28159 Jeffrey George Klekner 28160 Ernest Eugene Bubb 28161 Carl Anthony Commons 28162 James Lee Ondo 28163 Daniel Clair Balough 28164 Michael Gene Snell 28165 Arnold J. Haake 28166 John Bruce Payne 28167 George Robert Steinbach 28168 William Michael Munson 28169 Kenneth A. Thomas 28170 Thomas Alfred Smith 28171 Joel Richard Alvarey 28172 James Patrick Russell 28173 Edwin Alexander Watson 28174 Nicholas Thomas Stafford 28175 Joseph Jay Wheeler 28176 Johnnie Woodrow Grant 28177 Howard LeRoy Hellerstedt 28178 Terrence Patrick O'Boyle 28179 Mark Ellsworth Dillon 28180 John Robert Vequist 28181 Kenneth Waldo Fleming 28182 Jay Bernard Haney 28183 Jose Arellano Syjuco 28184 Randall Haywood Bryant 28185 George Adams Woodbury 28186 Thomas Michael Hayes 28187 Alfred Louis Dibella 28188 John William May 28189 Francis Xavier McCullough 28190 William Henry Groening 28191 Roland Joseph LaVallee 28192 John J. Egan 28193 David Keith Wallestad 28194 John Louis LaBelle 28195 Thomas Dole Watson 28196 Thomas Floyd Hendrickson 28197 Vincent Charles Corica 28198 Andrew Joseph Bacevich 28199 Thomas Eugene Rogers 28200 John Anthony Champagne 28201 Charles John Pedersen 28202 James Andrew Ball 28203 Robert Allan Brigham 28204 William S. Wallace 28205 George Werner Albrecht 28206 Gregory Nosal 28207 Samuel Hopkins Bailey 28208 Billy Frank Brittenham 28209 Henry John Schroeder 28210 Joel Jenkins Snow 28211 Robert Neil Jannarone 28212 Michael Barszcz 28213 Joseph Charles Berenato 28214 Alan E. Edwards 28215 Bradley Earl Sparks 28216 James Joseph Rohacik 28217 Mark Louis Waple 28218 Thomas Marion Hall 28219 David Owen Byars 28220 Gilman Granville Hoskins 28221 George Pruitt Coan 28222 William F. Vanaskie 28223 Robert Alan Martray 28224 Leonard Roy Hawley 28225 Robert Andrews Bassett 28226 James Raymond Stelter 28227 Edward James Swenson 28228 Guy Virgile Nanney 28229 Thomas Pickett Byrd King 28230 Tinsley White Rucker 28231 Ronald Paul Hudak 28232 John Edward Hesson 28233 James Edward Walkenbach 28234 John Irvin McBeth 28235 John Robert Leone 28236 Andrew R. Wielkoszewski 28237 Fred Hayden Edwards 28238 Kenneth Andrew Nowak 28239 James William Kulbacki 28240 Donald Warren Nagel 28241 Brian Paul Murphy 28242 John Alfred Knabb 28243 Ernest Lewis Albanese 28244 Young Pinckney Oliver 28245 Edward Raymond Lachey 28246 William Baxter Rynearson 28247 Max Verl Terrien 28248 Richard Keith McCarty 28249 Charles Victor Anstrom 28250 Charles Frederick Thensted 28251 Bill Alphonse Schroeder 28252 David Hall Vaught 28253 George Anthony Lynn 28254 John Rasper Hamilton 28255 Robert Henry Nagle 28256

Daniel Hugh Sharphorn 28257 Dennis T. Nishida 28258 James Daniel Foss 28259 William Joseph Bahr 28260 Norman Michael Swaim 28261 Michael Edward Ludlow 28262 James Daniel Richards 28263 Carl Barry McGee 28264 Gerry Hubert Armstrong 28265 John William Harms 28266 Thomas William Garrett 28267 Steven Milan Korach 28268 Tony Clinton Singer 28269 Robert Eli Roseta 28270 Phillip Ray Smith 28271 David Keith Colbert 28272 Michael David Matthews 28273 Joseph E. Halloran 28274 James LeRoy Smith 28275 Allan Lee Erb 28276 Willis Bradley DeYoung 28277 Johnnie Douglas Shaw 28278 Brooks Aleshire Boye 28279 Fred Christian Sautter 28280 Douglas Glenn Farel 28281 Dennis Roy Hutchinson 28282 Walter Bernard Ballenberger 28283 Brent B. Barth 28284 David Scott Smith 28285 Anthony Lawrence Guerrerio 28286 John Woodrow Harre 28287 Michael H. Kelly 28288 Nicholas George Psaki 28289 Geoffrey H. Moran 28290 Robert Patrick Jordan 28291 Norviel Robert Eyrich 28292 Brian Boru O'Neill 28293 Russell Philip Roux 28294 Dennis Marshall Wance 28295 Howard Gray Curtis 28296 Tim Karle Beckworth 28297 Michael Kommers Lynett 28298 Ronald Dale McAdoo 28299 Charles Edward Stewart 28300 Dennis Charles McKelvey 28301 Mitchell McGeever Zais 28302 Paul J. Kedrow 28303 John Paul Abbott 28304 John Martinez Greathouse 28305 Terry Eugene Strickler 28306 James Murray Rowan 28307 Randall Franklin Jarmon 28308 Frank Robert Finch 28309 John Clarke Yeisley 28310 Kent Rex Crenshaw 28311 Bryan Heaton Schempf 28312 Dennis Ray Schonewetter 28313 Jeffrey Edward Furbank 28314 Donald Riley Crosby 28315 Albert Henry Schaaf 28316 Gary Harold Thorstens 28317 William B. Kerr 28318 Charles Eddington Adkins 28319 Michael Paul Hulten 28320 John Vernon Peters 28321 Anthony Kroll Curran 28322 Hurley Mitchell 28323 Paul Coburn Sawtelle 28324 Daniel Edwin Kersey 28325 Robert William Haines 28326 Ronald David Hilburn 28327 Michael Arden King 28328 John William Heath 28329 Paul Gregg Jones 28330 Paul Thomas Dimler 28331 David Wallace Hayes 28332 Herbert Maurice Kithcart 28333 John Michael Luchak 28334 Charles Arthur Hastings 28335 Joseph Leo McCarville 28336 Joseph Robert Megginson 28337 Kenneth C. Scull 28338 Frank Edwin Tabela 28339 Tom Andrew Hanna 28340 Thomas George Venard 28341 Robert V. Kennedy 28342 James Michael Wright 28343 Robert Weston Griffin 28344 David Lawrence Scibetta 28345 Charles Henry Tatum 28346 Leo Paul Carrigan 28347 Terris W. Mikelk 28348 Daniel Wesley Horne 28349 Charles Oren Bonebrake 28350 Alexander Mark Zupsich 28351 Robert B. Rowe 28352 Lester Martin Hunkele 28353 James Roger Nelson 28354 Sheldon Clark Wintermute 28355 Robert Joseph St. Onge 28356 Eric William Robyn 28357 Michael Allen Wright 28358 Roger Lee Caris 28359 Jerry Dean Morelock 28360 Donald Charles Randolph 28361 Michael Wayne Taylor 28362 John Joseph Black 28363 Michael C. Bible 28364 William Grady Beard 28365 Robert Daniel Merkle 28366 Daniel L. Kopp 28367 John Allan Dinger 28368 Henry R. Logan 28369 James William O'Toole 28370 David Kincaid Jamison 28371 John Elwin Rountree 28372 Philip Ward Holden 28373 Thomas E. Whitaker 28374 Keirn Clarke Brown 28375 Joseph Campbell Gelineau 28376 William Patrick Yonushonis 28377 Peter John Bazzel 28378 James Joseph Calandro 28379 William Thomas Slenker 28380 Stephen Frederick Davis 28381 Robert Philip Pratt 28382 George C. Hozier 28383 Danford Ryan Meischen 28384 Robert Lorne Leslie 28385 James Philo Isenhower 28386 Wallace Robins Lindsey 28387 Larry Michael Fettis 28388 David Alexander Himes 28389 Melvin Alton Tinker 28390 Patrick Lane Porter 28391 William Michael Casey 28392 Paul Sims Raglin 28393 Thomas Hart McCord 28394 Robert R. Harper 28395 Robert Rudolph Ivany 28396 Joseph Refugio Brillante 28397 Stephen Shane Overstreet 28398 H. Steven Hammond 28399 Richard Emanuel Cappiello 28400 Ronald Laurance Lucas 28401 Bruce DeLeon Schulz 28402 Roger Lyn Hoopengardner 28403 Roy Alexander Murray 28404 James Severance Gavitt 28405 Stephen Leighton Hunt 28406 Albert Francis Leister 28407 Robert Bronze Myers 28408 Eugene Thomas Murphy 28409 Frank B. Adams 28410 James Bryan Newman 28411 John Peter Staples 28412 Jimmy Morton Ford 28413 Michael Wade Jones 28414 David Michael Kaplan 28415 Paul Edward Murr 28416 William Ernest Pohlmann 28417 William A. Illingworth 28418 Robert Steven Hoffman 28419 David Francis Belden 28420 John Richard Wallace 28421 John Edward FitzGerald 28422 Glenn Alan Porter 28423 Lawrence Edward Swesey 28424 James Michael Allen 28425 Glenn Robert Ferraro 28426 Stephen Douglas Williams 28427 Stephen Ovid Allaire 28428 Fred Hamilton Van Atta 28429 Kip LeRoy Larson 28430 Reggie Leslie Pettitt 28431 Joseph Norwell Harper 28432 Charles Stephen White 28433 Charles F. Turk 28434 Patrick Foster Neeley 28435 Blaine Stephen Ball 28436 Kenneth Martin Bevis 28437 James Michael Potter 28438 Thomas Morriss Callaway 28439 George Cicero Fogle 28440 Richard Sinclair Jarman 28441 Emile Raymond Dupere 28442 G. Robert Brambila 28443 John Marshall Andrews 28444 Edwin Gilbert Northup 28445 Jerome Rodney Hackett 28446 Dennis Milton Moen 28447 Robert Warren Anderson 28448 Cornelius McNiel Cooper 28449 Albert Joseph Catani 28450 Frederick Franklin Lash 28451 James Harry Johnston 28452 George G. Cantlay 28453 Frederick Ernest Noll 28454 Brian Finley Wells 28455 Ronald Mervin Male 28456 Warren Scott Nix 28457 Wayne Edward McSwiggan 28458 Michael Anthoney Shafe 28459 James Thomas Fouche 28460 Randall Robert Peters 28461 Michael D. Modeen 28462 Linwood Earl Blackburn 28463 Edward Nye Rehkopf 28464 James Huntsman Johnson 28465 John Edward Hahn 28466 David James Kremenak 28467 Donald Blaine Smith 28468 Paul Scott Albright 28469 Sheridon Hale Groves 28470 Kenneth Wayne Hughes 28471 Onofre Torres 28472 James Byrnes 28473 Glen Toshio Hirabayashi 28474 Charles R. Funderburke 28475 James H. Hillebrand 28476 Thomas Theodore Reinhardt 28477 Gary R. Ferchek 28478 Orval Peter Schierholz 28479 Michael F. Fisher 28480 Michael V. Carr 28481 Robert Charles Foos 28482 Erwin D. Moulder 28483 G. Wilson Hester 28484 Jimmy R. Lucas 28485 Stephen J. Williams 28486 Thomas W. Mastaglio 28487 Henry J. Osterhoudt 28488 Stephen C. McGue 28489 John Charles Willut 28490 Jack W. Ellertson 28491 Dennis J. Frazier 28492 James D. Mullen 28493 Richard C. Anshus 28494 Terry R. Bacon 28495 Jeffrey Ladd Kimball 28496 Robert Allen Pitz 28497 Richard Gerald DiNicola 28498 Frank William Brittain 28499 James Michael Landrum 28500 Glen Floyd Weien 28501 Anton Charles Kaiser 28502 Paul Gregory Jones 28503 LeRoy Arnold Maxfield 28504 Arnold Robert Stankus 28505 James Albert Russell 28506 Louis Joseph Eyermann 28507 Steven Curt Anthony 28508 Mark Eldor Kannenberg 28509 Michael Edward Smith 28510 David Howard Krall 28511 Barry Charles Blay 28512 Robert C. Riddell 28513 George Demetriou 28514 Michael Deems Hanson 28515 Larry Jay Feigenbaum 28516 Gordon W. Urban 28517 Michael William Krzyzewski 28518 John Kenneth Christian 28519 Samuel Ray Granett 28520 William Chris Gagnaire 28521 Leroy R. Goff 28522 Rick Allen Wilber 28523 James Patrick Reams 28524 Thomas J. Brennan 28525 Michael Frank Ryan 28526 Henry Frederick Grimm 28527 Gary Eugene Dolan 28528 Harry Lindsay Thain 28529 Thomas Enrique Piazze 28530 Christopher Charles Cole 28531 Barry Jamesie Robella 28532 John F. Clapper 28533 Edward Bryson Poucher 28534 George William Morgan 28535 Joseph Chester Rose 28536 Donald Lee Navor 28537 Frank Borge Fell 28538 Richard S. Ploss 28539 Mark Bruce Hoffman 28540 Norman Alan Brown 28541 Kenneth Michael Wanless 28542 David Watson Dunaway 28543 Thomas Edison Bensberg 28544 Arthur Joseph Nigro 28545 M. Gregory Smith 28546 Douglas Charles Rogers 28547 Rodney Alan Taylor 28548 Donald E. Warner 28549 Phillip Arthur Weaver 28550 Richard Carl Taricska 28551 Arturo Francisco Guzman 28552 Gary Ross Calvert 28553 George Clinger Bass 28554 Ronald Walter Gray 28555 Gregory D. Foster 28556 Dwight Frederick Homann 28557 Geoffrey Gwynne Prosch 28558 John Thaddeus Jaccard 28559 Larry Alan Lemaster 28560 Edward Paul O'Connell 28561 William Anthony Pahissa 28562 John Tillman Bolger 28563 John Jester Russell 28564 Robert Charles Kuhn 28565 R. Daniel Gruenke 28566 Louis Joseph Curl 28567 Robert Tucker Lynch 28568 Bruce Ross Wheeler 28569 Paul Carter Campbell 28570 Thomas Joseph Spencer 28571 Frank Anthony LaPenta 28572 Bernard Francis King 28573 Francis Edward Schwabe 28574 Hugh Michael Stirts 28575 Paul Joseph Kessenich 28576 Larry Joe Wells 28577 Bruce Lester Helmich 28578 Lonnie Bothwell Adams 28579 Dana Christian Frandsen 28580 Gary Wallace Bogema 28581 Gerald Allan Burgess 28582 Richard Michael Seitz 28583 Randy Allen Wilson 28584 Peter Mirakian 28585 Charles William Karwan 28586 Gary Lynn Cantrell 28587 David William McDermott 28588 Roy Stewart Moore 28589 Johnnie L. Welsh 28590 Joseph D. Sebes 28591 Matthew Herbert Erickson 28592 James Stroh Kenady 28593 Ronald J. Hebert 28594 Charles Jackson Nesbitt 28595 John Lawrence Morris 28596 Gerald Robert Hayton 28597 Gary Martin Fahl 28598 Daniel Lee Tigges 28599 Gary Allan Bish 28600 John Thomas Sanders 28601 Terry Harold Young 28602 Gary Edward Marshall 28603 Robert Alexander King 28604 Victor George Smith 28605 James Fulford Love 28606 Lucian King Truscott 28607 Bidwell DeBost Moore 28608 Richard Lee Swick 28609 Robert William Molter 28610 Robert Theodore Schoville 28611 Peter Charles Miles 28612 Brian Eugene Morrill 28613 John Bacot 28614 Robert Joseph Hoffman 28615 Robert Sterling Noreen 28616 Robert John Jenkins 28617 Alan Mack Glazner 28618 John Thomas Daly Casey 28619 James Lawrence McCullough 28620 John Jacob Inselman 28621 George Marshal Olson 28622 James Frank Mesite 28623 R. James Moeller 28624 Frank George Oliver 28625 Steven Alan Bosshard 28626 Lemuel J. Cato 28627 Michael Elmer Rothermich 28628 Carl Leonard Remmel 28629 Arthur Paul Ireland 28630 George Michael Meier 28631 Matthew Shepard Beyeler 28632 James Merle Taylor 28633 David Michael Merhar 28634 William Alwin Mills 28635 Karl Ford Ivey 28636 Robert Ray Dickerson 28637 Carl Nelson Belack 28638 Glen Simmang Ivey 28639 Bill Gene Smith 28640 Robert Bruce Gallagher 28641 Lester Kenneth Johnson 28642 Helmut Herbert Haas 28643 Walter Michael Mischler 28644 Cornelius Jacob Westerhoff 28645 Daniel Anton Buechner 28646 Rodney Edgar Mosbacker 28647 Dennis Stephen Pogany 28648 Ronald George King 28649 Stanley Albert DeFilippi 28650 Jeffrey Michael Donaldson 28651 David Brian Dalum 28652 Stanley Cary Gaylord 28653 Tony Angelea Burgess 28654 Lenny Stanley Bay 28655 S. Stephen Vitucci 28656 James Gordon Cox 28657 Craig Stephen Schwender 28658 Robert Warren Yaap 28659 Michael Driscol Healy 28660 Peter James Skells 28661 James Hart Ruwet 28662 Eriberto Romeo Caranto 28663 Michael Maynard Williams 28664 T. James Blake 28665 Jonathan David Parobek 28666 Austin Joseph Yerks 28667 William Elmer Holbrook 28668 Allen Eugene Lavelle 28669 Charles William Whatton 28670 Richard Thomas Fowler 28671 Thomas C. Schafer 28672 Kenneth Henry Williams 28673 Joseph Louis Schatz 28674 John Stephen Yarnell 28675 Jodie Kenneth Glore 28676 Robert Stewart Tice 28677 Gary Allen Phelps 28678 Dennis Wayne Feuge 28679 John Arthur Ahlbrecht 28680 Clifford T. Rock 28681 Jon Harmon Anderson 28682 Kenneth Joseph Yonan 28683 Francis Darby Boyle 28684 Edward Dewey Simms 28685 Denis Eugene Gulakowski 28686 George Anthony Barstis 28687 Harold Lee Maxson 28688 Peter Anthony Dencker 28689 Michael Frederick McGovern 28690 Paul Stock Feyereisen 28691 Jack Ronald Schuyler 28692 Ronald Edward Williams 28693 Richard Lawrence Simmons 28694 Richard Walter Luecke 28695 Henry Bessemer Richmond 28696 Bernard John Tatro 28697 David Alan Metzler 28698 Preston Leach Forsythe 28699 Roger W. Loder 28700 Joseph Paul Sowa 28701 Thomas Guynne Lowry 28702 Edward J. Doyle 28703 Robert Jules DeClercq 28704 John Cranwell Fitz-Henry 28705 Joseph Casillo 28706 Ernest Carl Adams 28707 Walter Thomas Strother 28708 Robert Herman Behncke 28709 Henry Joseph Harmeling 28710 Donald Durell Parmeter 28711 Jay Carl Olner 28712 John Benton Legere 28713 James A. Minor 28714 William Clifford Crawford 28715 Peter Thomas Hyde 28716 James Richard Seiler 28717 William Harrison Ward 28718 Andrew Marshall Hatch 28719 Clemence Carl Oborski 28720 Richard Francis Duffy 28721 Paul Martin Salazar 28722 Paul David Silver 28723 Michael William Pettit 28724 William Kyle 28725 Charles Stuart Gwynne 28726 Edward John Tobin 28727 Hugh Garrette Fly 28728 Lewis Robert Levy 28729 Stephen Roger Metcalf 28730 Robert Duncan Allardice 28731 Charles Joseph Jarvis 28732 William Earl Knickerbocker 28733 David Lee Stoutner 28734 Gary Steven Eiber 28735 Dennis Wayne Hitzeman 28736 James Earl Nielson 28737 Terrance Wade Hoffman 28738 Laurence Leon Archer 28739 Wilson Lewis Maloz 28740 James Richard Wire 28741 Michael Francis Steele 28742 Michael Lee Thoreson 28743 Thomas Leonard McMinn 28744 Steven Warren Lindell 28745 Frederick Peter Mott 28746 Kip Clark Clapper 28747 Thomas Charles Domino 28748 Philip Delano Brant 28749 **1970** Jack Carl Zoeller 28750 Henry Alden Leonard 28751 Stephen Dahl Wesbrook 28752 Dean John Nickles 28753 James Alfred Kee 28754 David Earl Schroeder 28755 Stephen Henry Strom 28756 Michael Warren Bain 28757 William Wallace McBeth 28758 Charles Alan Lucente 28759 John Huff Van Vliet 28760 David Charles Valbracht 28761 Thomas Anthony Gerard 28762 James Boone Bartholomees 28763 James Charles Hunn 28764 Thomas David MacIver 28765 Gregory David Vuksich 28766 Robert Anthony Bauman 28767 Theodore Matthew Shadid 28768 Anthony Graham Barre 28769 James Edward Corfman 28770 Earle Howard Helgerson 28771 Steven James Pressler 28772 William Allen Knowlton 28773 Brian Campbell Davis 28774 John William Boslego 28775 Kenneth Howard Clow 28776 Thomas Rayburn Hall 28777 Gary Thomas 28778 Stephen Sayre Bagstad 28779 Richard Lee Goodyear 28780 Donald Ross Edmonston 28781 David Raymond Dinsmore 28782 Jeffrey Alan Schmidt 28783 Robert Louis Schaf 28784 Robert Nugent Brown 28785 Thomas Francis O'Meara 28786 George R. Allin 28787 Roger Ainsworth Rains 28788 David Lee Brown 28789 Thomas Anthony Lenox 28790 Thomas Harry Millar 28791 Harry Michael Ryan 28792 Cesare Francis Rosati 28793 Michael Warren Johnson 28794 Keith Brian Jarrett 28795 William Gerald Bishop 28796 Dale Edward Reagor 28797 Patrick James McGoldrick 28798 John Joseph Pavlick 28799 Charles Byron Hicks 28800 Russell Burton Jones 28801 Robert Francis Driscoll 28802 Michael Peter Murphy 28803 William Valere Adams 28804 L. Neal Ellis 28805 Steven S. Bailey 28806 William Cooper Taylor 28807 John Michael Greenwalt 28808 Steven Dale Wilson 28809 Peter Howze Jones 28810 William Myers Bowden 28811 Phillip John Linn 28812 Paul Alan Kowalczyk 28813 John Broderick Fishback 28814 Gregory Allan Holton 28815 Laurence Herman Foster 28816 George Michael Spinney 28817 Jon Gray Noll 28818 Joseph Eugene Henn 28819 Scott Preston Isaacson 28820 John Michael Boehm 28821 Clinton James Ancker 28822 William Allen Fogg 28823 Ronald James Baron 28824 Agapito de la Garza 28825 Richard H. Kelley 28826 Jonathan Edward Severson 28827 John Robert Lewis 28828 Kerry Mills Goodier 28829 Richard Henry St. Denis 28830 John David Huncharek 28831 Robert George Thomas 28832 Michael Samuel Meuleners 28833 Rolf William Knoll 28834 B. Joseph Alexander 28835 Howard Marshall Steinfeld 28836 Nelson Edward Kennedy 28837 William Cole Spracher 28838 Robert Ernest Hales 28839 Robert Sinclair Frank 28840 Edward George Beddow 28841 James Joseph Bellotty 28842 John H. Hanna 28843 Douglas James Drake 28844 Randall Arthur Sikes 28845 Edwin Kennedy Smith 28846 Glenn Windield Goodman 28847 Edwin Thomas Carlson 28848 Richard Albert Green 28849 Roger William Cross 28850 Robert Julius Cousar 28851 Thomas Upson Hannigan 28852 Joseph Wayne Patterson 28853 Mark Edward Meranda 28854 Ray C. Anderson 28855 Ira Kent Townsend 28856 Thomas Kevin Lawlor 28857 Dana Lafayette Newcomb 28858 Frederick Charles Lough 28859 Edward Martin De Castro 28860 Kenneth Lee Thomas 28861 Ronald Eugene Spears 28862 Richard Harvey Gasperini 28863 John Francis Joyce 28864 Herbert Ray Roberts 28865 Philip Charles Viehl 28866 Joseph Robert Faraguna 28867 Gary Lee Peckham 28868 Stephen Raymond Kupec 28869 Terrence Lee Nyhous 28870 James Gregory Mulligan 28871 Genous Sanders Hodges 28872 Gerry Stephen Gibson 28873 Michael John Zolidis 28874 Patrick Thomas Thornton 28875 Mark Quentin Barbour 28876 Earl Richard Albright 28877 Brian Dale Bryson 28878 James Edward Brink 28879 Donovan Frederick Jagger 28880 William Lanier Wallis 28881 Robert Tornow Babcock 28882 Robert David Conte 28883 Robert Price Thomson 28884 David Eugene Heineman 28885 James Patrick Hayes 28886 David Clinton Allbee 28887 David Dean Dawson 28888 William Leslie Campbell 28889 David Cressman Smith 28890 Thomas Michael Costello 28891 Frederick Zilian 28892 Stephen James Swain 28893 William A. Hedberg 28894 Julian Hall Burns 28895 Randall Arthur Carlson 28896 Robert N. Young 28897 Chris Gary Wittmayer 28898 Charles Wolcott Ryder 28899 David C. Rosenblum 28900 James Wilson Duncan 28901 Gregory Ronald Pohl 28902 Ray Thomas Williamson 28903 William Jonathan Hahney 28904 John Harry Shary 28905 John Joseph Dobiac 28906 Thomas C. Steidel 28907 Jeffrey Wayne Gault 28908 Russell Owen Morris 28909 Larry Keith Hartman 28910 Michael Neil Short 28911 Peter John Pella 28912 Robert Richard Heinen 28913 Kenneth Michael Mark 28914 Jonathan P. Deason 28915 Perry Franklin Baltimore 28916 Thomas Francis Page 28917 Terry John Treat 28918 Gary Vincent Wimberly 28919 Bruce Charles Michalowski 28920 Thomas Frank Armeli 28921 Johnny Mercer McClellan 28922 John M. Minor 28923 Robert Steven Young 28924 Charles Patrick Schafer 28925 William De Witt Lane 28926 Michael D. Haworth 28927 Terry J. Young 28928 Brooke Wain Jenkins 28929 Richard Edward Martin 28930 William Norman Vann 28931 Lynn Wendell Rolf 28932 Michael Richard Rundle 28933 Joseph Robert Stadelnikas 28934 John Norman Reese 28935 Paul Douglas Soucek 28936 Richard Pershing Moser 28937 William Ellis Beasley 28938 Larry Talmadge Brown 28939 Michael William Mahan 28940 William John Vogt 28941 John Chester Woloski 28942 Daniel Raymond Kibler 28943 Thomas G. Walker 28944 James William Henderson 28945 Gregory Hampton Knight 28946 Dennis Frederick Wehrle 28947 Jeffrey Richard Troxell 28948 Christopher Kuehne 28949 Arthur Roy Marshall 28950 Chester Allan Richardson 28951 David Allen Stainback 28952 Lewis Leonard Boyer 28953 Philip Walter Richard 28954 William Penn Watkinson 28955 John Curtis McDugald 28956 John William Ekegren 28957 Bruce Robert Galton 28958 William Carroll Geist 28959 Joseph Lanny White 28960 Richard Ogden Snider 28961 Larry Landis Henly 28962 David Walter Cortese 28963 Randall Craig Rutler 28964 Edward Patrick Ward 28965 Edward James Fletcher 28966 John Graham Senor 28967 Thomas Peter De Vito 28968 John Frederick Shull 28969 Paul John Dixon 28970 Geoffrey Bruce Charest 28971 David Wynne Wagner 28972 Thomas Lee Haller 28973 Terence Earl Keene 28974 Ronald Lee Rold 28975 Robert Arthur Meier 28976 Jimmie Stewart Avery 28977 David Wayne Trammel 28978 Randall Lee Cox 28979 James Francis Jeray 28980 Bristol W. Williams 28981 Gary Roy Swingle 28982 George Barnett Forsythe 28983 Lawrence J. Kimmel 28984 Robert John Kenevan 28985 Robert Townsend Richardson 28986 Richard Emery Thibodeau 28987 Gregory Emerson Smith 28988 Dennis Edward Williams 28989 Bruce Lee Schall 28990 Frank Eugene Seaman 28991 John Raymond Brown 28992 Don Beale Blakeslee 28993 John Thomas Connors 28994 John Valentine Cogbill 28995 John William Bickel 28996 David Michael Porreca 28997 Frederick E. White 28998 William Thomas Elliott 28999 Robert McClean Love 29000 Leonard Emil Weisman 29001 John Willis Adams 29002 Mitchell Kai Adams 29003 Donald Charles Frazer 29004 Lawrence Kermit White 29005 Charles Ray Miles 29006 Edwin David Selby 29007 Dennis Lee Fadden 29008 Steven A. Rank 29009 Thomas Willi Rabaut 29010 Charles Edward Davis 29011 William Joseph Wattendorf 29012

Stephen Wilfred Homoleski 29013 Robert Clayton Jarchow 29014 Dale Keith Marvin 29015 Thomas Joseph McNamara 29016 Thomas Lavell Secrest 29017 Warren Francis Geiger 29018 James A. Busack 29019 Lawrence Richard Clark 29020 Robert Ernest Pantier 29021 William Laurie Hagan 29022 Bruce Alexander Maki 29023 Lester Francis Sumner 29024 Thomas S. Lampley 29025 Steven Gage Starner 29026 Paul Anthony Mozoski 29027 Mathias Knorr 29028 William Albine Haislip 29029 Norman Wilson Etzler 29030 Carey Garland Thompson 29031 James Samson McHone 29032 John Bernard Ryan 29033 James Bolton Valliere 29034 Leslie Hinano Akoni Kahalekai 29035 Arthur Brent Alphin 29036 Lucas Harold Brennecke 29037 James Craig Cooper 29038 Wallace Bruce Olson 29039 Vincent Edward Reilly 29040 Robert Edward Laird 29041 Frank Joseph Gehrki 29042 James David Price 29043 Thomas Charles Bennett 29044 David Anthony Desannoy 29045 Robert Lee Heaton 29046 James B. Norwood 29047 William F. Pratt 29048 John Charles Abbott 29049 Charles Walter Ennis 29050 Carl A. Funke 29051 Dan Edward Schilling 29052 Stephen Dockstader Madley 29053 Donovan Mark Quimby 29054 Eric Benham 29055 Richard Steven Beahm 29056 William Francis Rose 29057 Philbert Cosman Doleac 29058 John James Marcello 29059 Edwin Thomas Bennett 29060 Christopher Michael Stall 29061 Thomas Pierce Gibbs Franklin 29062 Charles Lewis Gandy 29063 Rudolf Odd Siegesmund 29064 Michael Thurman Mitchell 29065 John Rhodes Gallogly 29066 Thomas Alex Brandtner 29067 William Charles Malkemes 29068 Ashby Allan McClanahan 29069 Russell Taylor Ray 29070 Robert Arthur Newman 29071 David Harlan Dvergsten 29072 Richard Harry Bronder 29073 Michael Allen Hawley 29074 John William Reitz 29075 Charles James Lauckhardt 29076 Scott Phillip Knight 29077 Lynn D. Moore 29078 Howard M. Lane 29079 Kerry Cornwall Lawrence 29080 Kim Richard Gibson 29081 Philip David Reifenberg 29082 Thomas William Weaver 29083 Anthony Verner James 29084 Robert E. Hilliard 29085 Mark Richard Olson 29086 Bernard Alan Zeper 29087 Thomas LeRoy Jatko 29088 Bradley Wayne Larsen 29089 John Marquis Biddle 29090 Thomas Edward Boytim 29091 Raymond P. Cossette 29092 Reginald Alexander Morrison 29093 Anthony William Sobul 29094 James Etchechury 29095 William Stephen Day 29096 Jon Peter Leckerling 29097 William Douglas Jackson 29098 Chester Nelson Ernst 29099 Kurt William Rorick 29100 Frank Sherman Montieth 29101 John Joseph Hennessey 29102 Daniel Lee Rhoads 29103 Gilbert Stewart Harper 29104 Robert Louis Sigmund 29105 Mark Guillen Goodell 29106 David Watson Phelan 29107 Scott Allen Patten 29108 Willard David Pease 29109 John David Brigadier 29110 James Robert Craig 29111 Eugene Amandus Studer 29112 Kurt Michael Markus 29113 William Stephen Hume 29114 John Landell McGill 29115 Robert Henry Millard 29116 Peter Byron Lilly 29117 William H. Squires 29118 John Patrick Cass 29119 Patrick Michael O'Hara 29120 Rodney James Backman 29121 William Neal Patterson 29122 Myhre Elroy Paulson 29123 Ralph George Rogers 29124 Michael Allen Boies 29125 Thomas Cyril Schmidt 29126 Peter Edward Billia 29127 Arthur John Alden 29128 Robert Lucien Beziat 29129 William Temple Cumiskey 29130 Bruce L. Spear 29131 Charles Francis McAteer 29132 Paul Vincent Passaro 29133 Francis John Monaco 29134 Ronald Marshall Riggs 29135 William A. Bruce 29136 George Edwin O'Malley 29137 Joseph Robert Reeder 29138 Rudolph Francis Basta 29139 Vernon Ray Stockwell 29140 Robert Alan Zollo 29141 John B. Becker 29142 Robert Stanley Wetherill 29143 Thomas Gilbert Dueker 29144 Phillip Gay Harris 29145 Giacomo Ramon Sabia 29146 Walton Eric Pedersen 29147 Kevin Collins Connolly 29148 Paul Ellsworth Selge 29149 Gilbert Pritchard 29150 Ross Claude Williams 29151 John Charles Brenner 29152 Phillip Lamar Curtis 29153 Paul D. Terry 29154 Wayne Marshall Barth 29155 Roger Lee McCormick 29156 Raymond Wood Gibbons 29157 James Judson Lovelace 29158 Timothy Charles Lavelle 29159 David Neal Muir 29160 Thomas Frank Kauza 29161 Roland Walter Carter 29162 Guillermo Daniel Chavez 29163 Paul Edward Cunningham 29164 William Charles Bennett 29165 Gary Alan Cornelison 29166 James Leonard Rushfeldt 29167 Robert Cabell Brand 29168 Loren Logan Todd 29169 Charles Parker Davidson 29170 Donald Fred Swanda 29171 Charles Ray Thompsen 29172 Joseph Peter O'Connell 29173 Michael Madigan Hoen 29174 Alan John Mellinger 29175 John P. Drinkwater 29176 B. Byron Price 29177 Steven Roberts 29178 Harold John Seifert 29179 Howard Lewis Guy 29180 Thomas Rickie Keller 29181 William Harris Green 29182 William Michael Naymick 29183 Clifford Jonas Gidlund 29184 Leonard Edwin Garrett 29185 Rolando Noca Floria 29186 Gerald Lee Wood 29187 William John Esmann 29188 Christopher Joseph Keegan 29189 Richard Dean Measner 29190 John Horn Colacicco 29191 Gary Gene Wilkins 29192 Michael Logan Grove 29193 William Paul Schmidt 29194 Nicholas Salvator Costantino 29195 Charles A. Morris 29196 Robert Francis Ryan 29197 Sean Egan Maxwell 29198 John Briane King 29199 David Dana White 29200 Thomas Gerard Mathews 29201 William Keith Fisher 29202 David Bruce Kent 29203 Louis Francis Sauter 29204 Danford Frederic Carroll 29205 Barry Valdean Pittman 29206 Eddie Mitchell 29207 Brian Marshall Smith 29208 Thomas Brock Maertens 29209 Daniel Wordsworth Reyen 29210 J. Patrick Moran 29211 Stephen Joseph Wood 29212 Sherman W. Crawford 29213 Michael Edward Schneider 29214 Henry Andrew Zimon 29215 Michael Dennis Anderson 29216 Michael David Snow 29217 Joseph Hugh Wehrle 29218 Richard Bruce Miller 29219 Dennis Wayne Lyons 29220 Victor Leonard Ross 29221 Lawrence Richard Verrochi 29222 Winston Edgar Diesto 29223 John Morris Forbes 29224 Brian Colin Campbell 29225 Maximiliano B. Kelly 29226 Richard Whitten Wise 29227 Charles Jerome Kerr 29228 Arthur Charles Lucia 29229 Howard Merle Parker 29230 Philip Eugene Terry 29231 Roger Clayton LeDoux 29232 Lowell Bernhard Ingwersen 29233 Brian Peter Locke 29234 Patrick Evans Sculley 29235 Marvin Scott Self 29236 Arthur Leslie Hudson 29237 Jak McGee Smith 29238 Joseph Edwin Aldrich 29239 Terry Alan Morford 29240 John Arthur Veenstra 29241 Jeff Woodward 29242 Richard Lee Rutledge 29243 James Ralph Snider 29244 Michael Alexander Kulungowski 29245 Barry Britton 29246 John Francis Lucas 29247 Tony Howard Brock 29248 Paul Joseph Bisulca 29249 Bruce Norman Peltier 29250 Joel David Smith 29251 Nicholas Harry Sebastian 29252 Mearl Edward Balmer 29253 Peter Bernhart McCall 29254 Ralph Charles Zychowicz 29255 Kim Burroughs Golden 29256 David Ralph Forinash 29257 John Joseph Mearsheimer 29258 Allan David Marple 29259 David Stevens Jenkins 29260 John Milton Bryant 29261 Russell Steven Thompson 29262 William Frank Prince 29263 Michael Robert Taylor 29264 Larry Allen Diekema 29265 Robert Lawrence Garman 29266 Marshall Oakley Larsen 29267 Thomas Anthony Shadis 29268 Edwin Charles Hirsch 29269 Robert Delony Ginn 29270 John Dee McDowell 29271 Bruce Bernard Nolte 29272 Peter Anthony Nell 29273 Wayne Robert Pembrook 29274 Albert Raymond Shiely 29275 Hunt Dorn Crawford 29276 William Stephen Johnson 29277 Claude Tatsuji Ishida 29278 Trevor Arthur Reid 29279 Richard Ward Coleman 29280 John Frank Epley 29281 Jay Wallace Kaine 29282 Eugene Howard Helmich 29283 William Youl Arcuri 29284 Daniel McGrath Lynch 29285 Joseph Wade McKinney 29286 Michael Vincent McCabe 29287 Michael Patrick Mullady 29288 Robert Ayres Walton 29289 John Robert Young 29290 William Paul Cater 29291 Louis Vance Hutchison 29292 Timothy Randall Carman 29293 Thomas Edward Oettinger 29294 Dan Darrell Shaw 29295 Nelson Perkins Johnson 29296 Mark Charles Gilbert 29297 Tommy Joe Boyce 29298 Cary Edmund Garner 29299 John Lee Carter 29300 Charles Bernard McGee 29301 William Robert Wessels 29302 Stephen H. Muse 29303 John Stephen Riley 29304 Mason James Young 29305 Walter Charles Conkin 29306 John Norton 29307 Joseph Francis Ferraro 29308 Daniel Leo Anderton 29309 John Howard Beasley 29310 Michael Henry Glawe 29311 John Michael Stetor 29312 Douglas Edward Stockton 29313 Larry Warren Krueger 29314 Michael John Pearce 29315 Larry Duane Walrod 29316 Calvin O'Neal Purdin 29317 Curtis Linn Newcomb 29318 Alfred Michael Lisi 29319 Quincy Anthony Deas 29320 Paul Vance Campbell 29321 John Henry Decker 29322 John Andrew Holm 29323 John J. Lazzeri 29324 David Michael Carr 29325 David Franklin Varnell 29326 John Stanley Howell 29327 Alan Duncan Fenty 29328 Roderick Henry Morgan 29329 Louis Anthony De Scioli 29330 Victor Elias Paris 29331 Stephen Ralph Baribeau 29332 Lawrence Bohemar Wilkins 29333 Nicholas Anthony Bonarrigo 29334 Donald Patrick De Cort 29335 Clark Donald Campbell 29336 Joseph Claude Neuman 29337 David Milo Herring 29338 Martin Robert Burns 29339 Carlos Romeo Velez 29340 Thomas William Anthony 29341 Gilbert Kwai Tung Tam 29342 Kenneth Paul Thompson 29343 Richard Edwin Murdoch 29344 James Eugene Oxley 29345 Jon Raymond Goodman 29346 Terry Lee Johnson 29347 Walter Franklin Huff 29348 James Kevin Murray 29349 William Stimson Trivette 29350 James Arland Osman 29351 Perry Clarkson Casto 29352 James N. Roland 29353 Ralph Byron Churchill 29354 John Laxton Kendrick 29355 James Lawrence Mowery 29356 Stephen Fletcher Garrett 29357 Charles Joseph Benardo 29358 Bartlett Jones Engram 29359 H. Michael Heffelfinger 29360 Edwin Griffin Clapp 29361 Daniel Drake Keiser 29362 Donald Gene Goff 29363 John Alan Norris 29364 Gerald Counts Minor 29365 Michael Lindbergh Jones 29366 Philip Robert Kensinger 29367 Carl Erwin Linke 29368 Robert William Wagner 29369 Gregory Newell Edwards 29370 John Alfred Fenili 29371 Francis Ancrum Clarkson 29372 William Martin Addy 29373 Frederick Carl Goeth 29374 Robert Lynn Archer 29375 John Robin Hostettler 29376 Jerryl Newman Ryan 29377 Stephen Kenneth Cook 29378 Bruce Edwin Robinson 29379 John William Carlson 29380 Thomas Sharp McChesney 29381 William Lester Terrill 29382 Gregory Raymond Webb 29383 Thomas Russell Auman 29384 Philip Stanley Bunch 29385 James Culligan Vernon 29386 Thomas Carson Dockery 29387 David Michael Peters 29388 Roger Frank Stahlak 29389 Bruce Clifford Raisor 29390 Terry Neil Hilderbrand 29391 Guy William Drab 29392 David John Young 29393 James Douglas Byrd 29394 James William Crawford 29395 Thomas Edward Martinez 29396 Kennard Ellsworth Gillihan 29397 Stephen Frederick Schwaderer 29398 Paul Frederick Franke 29399 Joseph Rodney Boswell 29400 William Benton Colson 29401 Jerome Bartholomew Sidio 29402 Timothy Edward Krebs 29403 Earl Stover Quirk 29404 Ross Stanley Kelly 29405 Charles Thomas Connatser 29406 Don Herman Meinhold 29407 James Orville Odermann 29408 John Kenneth Jaccard 29409 Francis Andrew Cannavo 29410 Ronald Hall Boggs 29411 Frank Pearce Whitlock 29412 Gerald Olivier Saari 29413 Michael Bradford Russ 29414 Henry Benjamin Bentley 29415 W. Dexter Brown 29416 Elmer William Schweninger 29417 Douglas Arnold LeFevre 29418 Matthew Henri Fleumer 29419 William Stevenson Waters 29420 Robert Edward Opatovsky 29421 Shelby Taylor Stevens 29422 William Alexander Coy 29423 Thomas Evans Fricks 29424 Glenn Joseph Broussard 29425 Charles Kirk Wagener 29426 Robert Werner 29427 Henry Joseph Andrzejczak 29428 Richard Lysle Williams 29429 Richard Neil Bradford 29430 Jeffrey Paul Woythal 29431 James Frederick Galloway 29432 William Albert Saunders 29433 Harold Halsey Dunwoody 29434 Tom Mercer Nicholson 29435 Fritz Joseph Hausmann 29436 John Asher Stidd 29437 Donald Joseph Greene 29438 Robert McFadden Stewart 29439 Roger Reid Fox 29440 Dale Raymond Fredrick 29441 Michael Winston Hobson 29442 Larry Leroy Gates 29443 George Wynn Alcorn 29444 Michael Thomas Murphy 29445 John Martin Vermillion 29446 Patrick Michael Dunphy 29447 Erick Wallace Sweet 29448 Donald Irvin Pratt 29449 Alan Lee Brace 29450 McDonald Plummer 29451 William Jonathan Ekman 29452 Larry Barrett Horacek 29453 Robert Allan Wallis 29454 John Charles Wells 29455 Lee Craig Carlson 29456 Gary Albert Gracyas 29457 John Philip DeLeo 29458 William Harvey Roedy 29459 James Patrick Sullivan 29460 Paul John Fardink 29461 Terence Joseph Tierney 29462 Kurtis Andrew Meyer 29463 Frank A. Terranova 29464 James R. Ward 29465 David Ric Gass 29466 Bruce Leigh Newby 29467 Edward Vincent Kelly 29468 Richard Allen Castleman 29469 Harry Wolfe Crumling 29470 Peter Byron Cramblet 29471 Thomas Gerard Bradley 29472 Peter B. Spivy 29473 Michael Alan Coulman 29474 Lewis Andrew Tully 29475 Frederick W. Conard 29476 Larry Keith Henderson 29477 Walter Joseph Ambrose 29478 Gary Richard Steele 29479 Francis Alfred Santangelo 29480 Michael Casmir Froncek 29481 C. John Roberts 29482 Richard A. Wennerberg 29483 Thomas Robert Rozman 29484 James Robert Haas 29485 Robert Edward Mason 29486 Willie Jefferson Price 29487 Edward J. Murphy 29488 Thomas Hardy Mylan 29489 James Allan Chandler 29490 Philip Sheridan Krieger 29491 Paul Richard McDowell 29492 Dominick Anthony Crea 29493 Frank Romano 29494 Victor J. Madeja 29495 Kurt Bernhardt Reineke 29496 Thomas Edward Miller 29497 Frank Michael Gyovai 29498 **1971** John William Murray Moore 29499 Robert Arnold Mohn 29500 Theodore W. Hoffman 29501 John Willard Pitts 29502 Frank Philip Bifulco 29503 John Francis Lilley 29504 John David Current 29505 John Sloan Brown 29506 Frank Kendall 29507 Christopher Cole Shoemaker 29508 Thomas Robert Watson 29509 Lawrence Cooper Merkl 29510 Charles Harvey Bayar 29511 Dennis Allen Wenker 29512 Charles Brimmer Wilson 29513 John Francis Reed 29514 Paul Taylor Dempsey 29515 Peter Andrew Andersen 29516 Dennis Carl Piper 29517 Michael Bismarck Hunter 29518 William Edward Benedict 29519 Glenn Michael Mason 29520 William Arnold Bearden 29521 Patrick Finnegan 29522 Robert Witherspoon Miller 29523 Thomas Lainis 29524 Robert Van Elliott 29525 Louis Michael Wenick 29526 William Ross Higley 29527 Thomas Charles Suermann 29528 Calvert Potter Benedict 29529 James W. Peterson 29530 J. Richard Capka 29531 Bruce L. Smith 29532 Timothy A. Wray 29533 Stephen Marshall Gooden 29534 Michael Albert Liberty 29535 Walter Jerome Wright 29536 Hans Alexander Van Winkle 29537 Patrick Reynolds Donald 29538 David Lee Kopp 29539 Wilbur A. Hitchcock 29540 Stephen Lindsay Baber 29541 Charles James Armogida 29542 Leslie Frank Steel 29543 Michael Lyle McNulty 29544 Stephen Daniel Bennett 29545 Steven Decker Harrison 29546 John Thomas Durgala 29547 David Bruce Hahn 29548 Robert Clinton Harvey 29549 Hugh Charles MacDonald 29550 Carl James Leininger 29551 Hubert Lane Morehead 29552 John Thomas Knowles 29553 Michael Eugene Richardson 29554 Roy Roger Hedtke 29555 Stephen A. Barneby 29556 William James Lennox 29557 E. Davisson Hardman 29558 Robert Burdette Ireland 29559 Timothy James Reischl 29560 Albert Love Patterson 29561 Gerald Paxson James 29562 Terrence Joseph McGuire 29563 William Thomas Sabata 29564 Harry Edgar Richards 29565 Neil Stuart Erwin 29566 Charles H. Swannack 29567 John Patrick Fogarty 29568 David Alan Duke 29569 Bartley C. Ackerman 29570 John Keith Wing 29571 John Murray McConaghy 29572 Sperry George Kaler 29573 John M. Kendall 29574 Thomas Edward Mannle 29575 Daniel Lawrence Turner 29576 Bernard B. Sapp 29577 Stephen Donald Vaughn 29578 James Cary Lovell 29579 Joe Stephen Chavara 29580 Joseph Edward Thomas 29581 Craig Vernon Gabbert 29582 Ronald Craig Gladney 29583 Donald T. Wynn 29584 David Daubney Brown 29585 James A. Walter 29586 William Henry Mattfeld 29587 Ll Soon Shin 29588 Samuel John Sutter 29589 Peter Bruce Root 29590 William George Doyne 29591 Clifford Phelan Kruthers 29592 George Robert McClelland 29593 Thomas Robert Frankenfield 29594 Herbert Charles Clifton 29595 Douglas Conrad Wagner 29596 Henry A. Schwartzstein 29597 Herbert John Gallagher 29598 David Christopher Arney 29599 Michael Cox Ryan 29600 Ronald Eugene Clary 29601 Charles Ray Hosack 29602 Eric John Jensen 29603 Charles Richard Taylor 29604 Ward D. King 29605 Thomas Joseph Teesdale 29606 David Lightner Kotzebue 29607 Thomas Alan Pyrz 29608 James Paul Albo 29609 Philip S. Kennedy-Grant 29610 Robert Kemp Holcombe 29611 David Scott Hutchison 29612 William D. Raymond 29613 John George Annis 29614 David Slayton Coughlin 29615 Narciso Lazo Abaya 29616 James Benton Edwards 29617 William George Parrot 29618 Thomas Frederic Metz 29619 E. Lawrence Sakas 29620 Richard Norman Seaman 29621 Steven Lee Moses 29622 William Ray Baldwin 29623 David Phillip Schlener 29624 Charles Hartley Bryce 29625 David Ray Humphrey 29626 John A. Spears 29627 Richard Morse Bridges 29628 John Richard Monastra 29629 David W. Rhyne 29630 John Weart Ogren 29631 John R. Robinson 29632 Thomas Edward Smith 29633 Michael Edward Hess 29634 John Casmir Szczepanski 29635 Guy Michael Church 29636 David R. Lewis 29637 Patrick Dennis McDonald 29638 Walter Ernest Heinz 29639 James Allen Conrad 29640 Robert M. Heffron 29641 Robert Arthur Fitton 29642 James Bradford Bond 29643 Scott Alan Crandall 29644 Terry Ray Moss 29645 William Joseph Ridder 29646 Roy Ernest Gogel 29647 Boonsrang Niumpradit 29648 Michael Lee Wamsted 29649 W. Ted Tornehl 29650 Stephen Frederick Wilcox 29651 William David Bernard 29652 David Armand Guerland 29653 Richard Anthony Kelly 29654 John Wendell Mitchell 29655 Thomas Randall Lujan 29656 Robert James Snyder 29657 Jeffrey B. Jones 29658 Stanley Charles Leja 29659 Gary Albert Wright 29660 Robert N. Anderson-Ludrick 29661 Lawrence P. Navin 29662 John Taylor Beard 29663 James R. Walters 29664 Terry Peter LaCasse 29665 Gary Wayne Nickel 29666 James Charles Kolding 29667 Joseph Stanley Kulik 29668 William Robert Brown 29669 Thomas V. Kruthers 29670 H. Eric Watkins 29671 John Patrick Doyle 29672 Stephen Girard Mirakian 29673 Luis Manuel Nido 29674 David Keith Sitler 29675 Michael Alan Heller 29676 William Joseph Barkovic 29677 William R. Hotze 29678 David V. DeParle 29679 Kenneth Matthew Matwiczak 29680 Joseph Leonard Yakovac 29681 Neal Robert Jensen 29682 Daniel Charles Scioletti 29683 Edward D. Postell 29684 Charles Harding Williams 29685 John Robert Neenan 29686 Glen Dale Worthington 29687 Michael Allen Bendas 29688 Kenneth Byron Karhuse 29689 Gary Douglas Kirchberger 29690 Robert Eric Armbruster 29691 Robert David Tyndall 29692 John P. Michael Hughes 29693 Michael Richard Cascini 29694 James Graceton Floyd 29695 Jeffrey Lee Hubsch 29696 Steven Joseph Wright 29697 James J. Grazioplene 29698 Peter David Weddle 29699 Michael Arthur Neyland 29700 Raymond Edward Pierce 29701 Glen Munro Macdonald 29702 David Thomas Smyth 29703 Odos Grant Young 29704 William Sumner Nichols 29705 William Edward Morrison 29706 Arthur Richard P. Wielkoszewski 29707 Alfred J. Estrella 29708 Lloyd Windle Sherfey 29709 Michael Anthony Masciello 29710 Ronald Allen Liss 29711 Max Elsworth Miller 29712 Edward Hill Matthews 29713 Charles E. Harrison 29714 John T. McLaughlin 29715 Kenneth Daryl Gitt 29716 Richard Coan Leclaire 29717 Gary Eugene Heuser 29718 James Anthony Sansone 29719 Wayland Merle Watts 29720 David Bruce Gorski 29721 Daniel Keith Patterson 29722 John Robert McHenry 29723 Daniel Stonert McMonagle 29724 John J. Koontz 29725 Joseph Council Rhyne 29726 William D. Carraway 29727 Thomas Wingfield Ogilvy 29728 Ronald Franklin Knight 29729 Vaughn Gerald Dille 29730 Gary Arthur Garrett 29731 James Stephen Schlesinger 29732 Christopher B. Benham 29733 Jerry Beard Edelen 29734 Richard Clarke Goodwin 29735 Geoffrey Lynn Finbar Keith 29736 Stephen K. Carroll 29737 James Carlin Eberle 29738 Joseph August Iacchei 29739 Charles Edward Libershal 29740 Steven A. Oaks 29741 O. Dennis Borcheller 29742 Gene Lawrence Baker 29743 Joseph Henry Beno 29744 James Patrick Schwei 29745 Michael Jon McRee 29746 Thomas Neal Theaux 29747 Dell Lee Dailey 29748 Timothy John Houseward 29749 William Randall Mann 29750 Ford Christopher Droegemueller 29751 David Anthony Ballantine Baker 29752 David Eugene Hardin 29753 James Richard Methered 29754 Dan Ross Howard 29755 Nelson Joseph Post 29756 Robert B. Cates 29757 Randolph Lyman Mase 29758 Douglas Hill Metcalf 29759 Douglas Robert Jorrey 29760 John Nicholas Bantsolas 29761 Michael Patrick Hopkins 29762 Donald James Hassin 29763 Robert Alan Lundy 29764 Don Albert Nelsen 29765

Leonidas Constantine Malleris 29766 Dale F. Pirkle 29767 Paul Martin Andrew 29768 Richard Victor Barbuto 29769 William Michael Penhallegon 29770 Michael Edward Tokarsky 29771 John David Pegg 29772 John Anthony Marsala 29773 Raymond Ernest Rasmussen 29774 Thomas Gary Martin 29775 Jeffrey Barnett Weinstock 29776 Paul Irving Finberg 29777 John Karl Anderson 29778 Hubert Burnette Wall 29779 Danton Gibbs Steele 29780 Frederick George Hitchcock 29781 Robert John Anderson 29782 Jerry Wayne Thompson 29783 Paul Barnett Watkins 29784 Earl Thomas Atchison 29785 Keith Vernon VonSeggern 29786 Stephen Douglas Rice 29787 Ronald Douglas Killpack 29788 Robert Edward Kempfe 29789 Robert Vance Lambert 29790 Eric McChesney Sundin 29791 Gregory Dixon Schrubbe 29792 James Russell Dawson 29793 Glenn Randolph Gaffney 29794 James L. Lindeman 29795 Richard Elliott Fate 29796 John Franz Nolde 29797 Edward A. Spohn 29798 James Harold Cox 29799 Joseph E. Mankowski 29800 Monty Lee Miller 29801 Phillip Leslie Wharton 29802 William Joseph Cullina 29803 William Joseph Tryon 29804 Donald Michael Rowland 29805 Richard E. Rentz 29806 Clifford Nelson Powell 29807 Ross Frederick Anderson 29808 Gerald Elden Cummins 29809 Gordon Scott Dietrich 29810 Warren Arthur Greer 29811 Guy A. Berry 29812 Edward Wayne Pogue 29813 Bard Knox Mansager 29814 John William Turk 29815 Joseph Richard Visinski 29816 Brian Wilson Roberts 29817 Peter L. Morash 29818 John Martin Dayman 29819 Clyde Baker Hoskins 29820 Donald Norman Elder 29821 James Leon West 29822 Michael D. Maples 29823 James Scott Hartley 29824 Richard Young Hartline 29825 William Clarence Roden 29826 Daniel William Pillasch 29827 George Thomas O'Brien 29828 Randall Glen Oliver 29829 Paul Drake 29830A David Harrison McIntyre 29830 Andrew Warren Smoak 29831 William Frederick Anderson 29832 James Neil Hickok 29833 Paul Patrick Jacobs 29834 Glenn Preston Barefoot 29835 Michael Paul Breithaup 29836 Robert Mason Satchell 29837 Frederick Anthon Forsyth 29838 Donald Edward Brodeur 29839 Robert Michael Tomasulo 29840 Gerald Charles Babayan 29841 William Walter Babic 29842 James B. Godwin 29843 Rodney Dean Miller 29844 John Michael Andreini 29845 Ronald Merl Musser 29846 Douglas James Eccleston 29847 James Michael O'Brien 29848 Stephen H. Rosenberg 29849 Ronald George Vlk 29850 Alexander Glass 29851 James Henry Gorczynski 29852 Raymond Richard Drummond 29853 Steve C. Rucker 29854 Terrill Kay Moffett 29855 Larry Stephen Socea 29856 Richard Frank Collins 29857 Joseph Anthony Halloran 29858 Robert Raymond Kulbick 29859 Joseph Richard Cerami 29860 Charles Thomas Hughes 29861 Ross Paul Witschonke 29862 Joseph Lloyd Bergantz 29863 William F. Field 29864 Steven James Rau 29865 Gary James Alexander 29866 Joseph Anthony Adelman 29867 Philip Rogers Beliveau 29868 Clifford Oscar Lindstrom 29869 Jerome Neal Carter 29870 Rodney Keith Erb 29871 David Richard Bell 29872 Brian Edgar McQuistion 29873 Byron Jake Stockstill 29874 Gene Wayne Boesch 29875 Michael Wayne Beard 29876 Comadora Millard Ferguson 29877 George Henry Gilmore 29878 Gregory Raymond Wenzloff 29879 Raymond H. McKinney 29880 Kevin Gerard Libby 29881 Claude M. Weldon 29882 Daniel Ralph Allemeier 29883 Franklin L. Hagenbeck 29884 James Darrell Morgeson 29885 Richard Graham deMoya 29886 Darrell William Harris 29887 Alan Jeffrey Rock 29888 Oscar A. Chappel 29889 Dean Lester Danielson 29890 Stanley G. Phernambucq 29891 Joseph John Waldhaus 29892 Kenneth Abbott MacAaron 29893 Randall K. Smith 29894 Richard Frederick Knight 29895 Lawrence John Varnas 29896 William Michael Currie 29897 George Peter Sivess 29898 W.E. Michael Renaud 29899 Walton Harris Walker 29900 Paul Allen Waddington 29901 David Michael Bond 29902 Michael Francis Ciferri 29903 Lawrence Abbott Kaden 29904 Roger L. Duckworth 29905 Terry Ray Lorenz 29906 Stephen Logan Cooch 29907 Jay Royer Schmieder 29908 Robert Bertrand Allaire 29909 Kevin James Cogan 29910 Anthony Raymond Lentini 29911 Jonathan Nantz Forest 29912 Robert P. St. Germain 29913 Donald Wilson Smith 29914 Timothy P. Mason 29915 Ronald William Carpenter 29916 Richard Outler Register 29917 Raymond Edward Halvatgis 29918 Russell Parlante Vaughan 29919 Michael John Roark 29920 Leonard P. Kloeber 29921 Robert Eugene Johnson 29922 Mark Mitchell Weiman 29923 Richard Paul Wiesler 29924 Patrick Francis Grant 29925 Hugh Michael Spivey 29926 Richard Thomas Keene 29927 Patrick J. O'Neill 29928 Michael Eric Erickson 29929 Michael Kevin Ryan 29930 Douglas Spohn Becker 29931 Charles H. Lautermilch 29932 Leon Duane Davis 29933 Robert C. Bishop 29934 James Michael Kesler 29935 Stuart C. Lindsay 29936 Raymond Craig Collins 29937 James Andrew Crowe 29938 Cordell Alan Pohl 29939 Raymond James Reitnour 29940 Maurice John Gustin 29941 William Theodore Shuff 29942 Kenneth Richard Hartlein 29943 Carl Kingsley Wake 29944 Richard L. Rowe 29945 Jeffrey Falder Ingram 29946 John Anthony Villecco 29947 Gregory William Doepke 29948 Donald R. Corn 29949 Carl Albert Dragstedt 29950 Timothy Thomas Kitt 29951 David Kenneth Curry 29952 William Courtney Trabue 29953 Douglas Lee Streeter 29954 Terry E. Thomason 29955 Stephen Richard Thomas 29956 August William Bremer 29957 Robert Thomas Payne 29958 Carl Beavan Marriott 29959 John Peter Buckner 29960 Gerald Sherman Petersen 29961 Richard Evans Ryder 29962 Donald Burt Johnson 29963 Archibald Vincent Arnold 29964 Jock Bartlett Hazeltine 29965 Kenneth Keith Landis 29966 Doyle Paul Perry 29967 Benjamin Bauer 29968 Christopher Van Dyke Cardine 29969 John H. Chiles 29970 Stephen J. Marshman 29971 John Joseph Spiezia 29972 Joseph Laurent Chabot 29973 Douglas Andrew Meier 29974 Danny Lynn Odom 29975 Thomas Joseph Rini 29976 Patrick D. Rivette 29977 Ronald C. Glatt 29978 Philip Edward Lower 29979 John Benjamin Howard 29980 William Charles Quinlan 29981 John W. Grigg 29982 Ronald Lee Munden 29983 Raymond Pawlicki 29984 Henry Hermann Bolz 29985 Richard Alan Dudley 29986 Steven O. Vandal 29987 Kirk J. Cottington 29988 William Andrew Jones 29989 Benjamin Clayton Hackman 29990 Robert Mark Jacobson 29991 Larry Eugene Kinder 29992 James Thomas Arietti 29993 Paul Frank Fasi 29994 Glenn Roger Weidner 29995 Charles Michael Williams 29996 Kevin Flanagan 29997 Michael Ken Nelson-Palmer 29998 Lee Howard Vagt 29999 William Harold Ewing 30000 Thomas Cobb Speight 30001 Ervin William Bazzle 30002 Richard Edward Graf 30003 Arden R. Jensen 30004 Russell Bennett Howell 30005 Frederick Alan Baldwin 30006 Russell Francis Procopio 30007 Wayne E. Grant 30008 Peter C. Cole 30009 Christopher Bradley Timmers 30010 Robert G. Shively 30011 Steven James Mura 30012 Allan Dorsey Payne 30013 Logan Rex Kelly 30014 John F. Flood 30015 Arthur Howland Baker 30016 Jeffrey Alan McNally 30017 Paul Quentin Laliberte 30018 William Ira Hancock 30019 Michael J. Kelly 30020 Christopher Scott Publow 30021 James J. Horton 30022 Gary Val Nichols 30023 Roy D. Carper 30024 Patrick Joseph O'Neil 30025 Kevin Francis Brennan 30026 Roy Walter F. Werthmuller 30027 Lyle Barber Nelson 30028 Robert Chier Kramer 30029 Michael H. Newell 30030 John D. Morrison 30031 Donald Edward Fowler 30032 Alan Anthony Fox 30033 Kent E. Petersen 30034 George Edwin Hale 30035 David Paul Gerlach 30036 Marcus Raymond Erlandson 30037 Stephen James White 30038 Ray Sidney Costner 30039 William Joseph Reiley 30040 William Joseph Tetu 30041 James George Buck 30042 William Floyd West 30043 Frank Andrew Baumann 30044 Alvin Dwayne Aaron 30045 Thomas Patrick Berry 30046 Arthur Dee Ives 30047 Thomas Frederick Dyne 30048 Bruce Edward Nead 30049 Richard Fleet McKenney 30050 John Ogden Shoemaker 30051 Stephen Watts Bracey 30052 Leo James FitzHarris 30053 Michael Richard Stith 30054 Larry Carl Schroeder 30055 Thomas Wayne Turner 30056 Dale Martin Abrahamson 30057 Michael Nastasi 30058 Ronald Henry Pfenning 30059 John Francis Scott 30060 Daniel Allen Miller 30061 Robert Ransom Gregorie Wade 30062 John Addis Dole 30063 Craig James McGrath 30064 William Thomas Stone 30065 Philip Kenneth Daniels 30066 Kenneth Edward Gordon 30067 Charles Dennis Moore 30068 Andrew Gordon Schnabel 30069 Patrick Wayne Plugge 30070 Stony Raine Lohr 30071 Ronald Andrew Barnabei 30072 Mark Allen Yrazabal 30073 Patrick Morris Cron 30074 Francis Louis Wyman 30075 Thomas Raymond Cafaro 30076 Robert Geza Breznovits 30077 Donald Ridgley MacLaren 30078 Michael James Shadell 30079 Bohdan Jurij Rudzinskyj 30080 Thomas Francis Burrell 30081 Bruce Douglas Litwin 30082 James W. Bapple 30083 Lawrence Michael Davis 30084 Joe H. Seitz 30085 Michael Gordon Carver 30086 Garry Andrew Mabry 30087 Keith Loren Fay 30088 John Travis Morrison 30089 Warren Patrick Fligg 30090 John Joseph Friel 30091 Richard D. Jones 30092 Michael George Ritchie 30093 James Christopher Clarke 30094 David Scott Albright 30095 William Bradford Hoelscher 30096 William Fredrick Diehl 30097 Charles Edward Enwright 30098 Thomas C. McKeon 30099 Arthur Ethridge Hays 30100 Lawrence Richard Boice 30101 Michael Allen Kelley 30102 Kim Lindsley Sellick 30103 Craig Barnell Hughes 30104 Kevin T. James 30105 Joseph Francis Passanante 30106 Hugh Mercer Bracey 30107 Norman Walter Bates 30108 Terrence David Fullerton 30109 David Alan Richardson 30110 Jerald Lee Thompson 30111 Palmer Frederick Smith 30112 James M. Hoover 30113 Richard Allen Williams 30114 Richard Earl Zimmerman 30115 Joseph Lanman Holcombe 30116 Edward Charles Fenske 30117 Bert Lowell Lennon 30118 Roy Richard Dodge 30119 Gerald Gene Stock 30120 Robert Joseph Werner 30121 Edward Mallory A. Fergusson 30122 Robert D. Weiss 30123 Charles Owen Smith 30124 Gary N. Phillips 30125 J. Murray Schrantz 30126 Robert Gary Worthington 30127 William Richard Lamborne 30128 Joseph Frank Albano 30129 William Harry Wier 30130 Randall Lee Fewel 30131 Ben Marley Smith 30132 John Michael Grissett 30133 Stephen Richard Lewis 30134 Daniel Joseph Ferris 30135 Thomas Nelson Harvey 30136 John Anthony Klevecz 30137 Thomas Lewis Montrone 30138 Steven Daniel Pjesky 30139 Donald John Coleman 30140 Thomas Elwin Crossman 30141 James Bruce Melesky 30142 Martin Paul Reese 30143 Joseph Preston Curry 30144 John Garrick Stevenson 30145 Gene A. Jones 30146 James Dale Ford 30147 Terry Michael Tighe 30148 Steven F. Wood 30149 William Beauford Carper 30150 Maurice Anthony Mussa 30151 Clyde James Hindes 30152 Louis Michael Kardonsky 30153 Milan James Fischer 30154 William John Carr 30155 Robert Earl Freeman 30156 Robert Latta Litchfield 30157 John Michael Cavalieri 30158 Alan Hilton Threatt 30159 Thomas Paul Pazak 30160 Thomas Kevin Ferguson 30161 John Joseph Pingel 30162 Jeffrey Alan Lincoln 30163 Joseph M. Fox 30164 David Peter Anderson 30165 George Francis Cullen 30166 Thomas Wayne Peterson 30167 Richard Walton Enners 30168 Jerry J. Edwards 30169 Robert Francis Fitzgerald 30170 Paul Douglas Oakley 30171 Richard Danny Kelley 30172 James M. Ebbesen 30173 Henry Carl Schrader 30174 William Wilberforce Plummer 30175 Mark Allan Dawson 30176 Jay Edward Levine 30177 David Edward Nelson 30178 Benjamin Joseph George 30179 Samuel Gregory Pride 30180 Stephen Joseph Marsh 30181 Robert Leaning Ashworth 30182 David Eldo Amos 30183 Paul Edwin Blaine 30184 Joe Ralph Nichols 30185 Jimmy Ray Grussmeyer 30186 David Ladlow Bearchell 30187 Kenneth John Kobes 30188 Johnny Wayne Brooks 30189 Harry Jacob Singer 30190 Louis Anthony Catti 30191 Bert Alison David 30192 Raymond Wesley Blaine 30193 Richard Stephen Scales 30194 Lewis Chesley Hester 30195 John Boursiquot Rose 30196 Joseph David Jenckes 30197 Jerome Arthur Keith 30198 Phillip Lee DenAdel 30199 John Michael Fogarty 30200 Raymond Michael Van Buskirk 30201 Michael Lawrence Raymo 30202 Douglas Eugene Clevenger 30203 Donald Keith Smith 30204 John Bernard Dierkes 30205 Robert B. Camp 30206 William Gerard Lord 30207 Thomas Aloysius Donahue 30208 Frank Dalton Durrum 30209 Leonard Anthony Chiacchia 30210 Michael Franzino 30211 Ronald Sergio Trowbridge 30212 Michael Marion Harmless 30213 David Michael Smith 30214 Jack Carlton Frink 30215 Myrl B. Jowell 30216 William C. Fothergill 30217 Kenneth Loy Wyrick 30218 Joseph Patrick Seletsky 30219 Paul Edward Reynolds 30220 James Andrew Landgraff 30221 Leonel Xavier Munoz 30222 Paul Henry Nelson 30223 John Robert Hamer 30224 John Michael Cristler 30225 Gary Vernon Fraaza 30226 **1972** Timothy Townley Lupfer 30227 Russell Bruce Hall 30228 Jefferson Johnson Irvin 30229 Stephen Bruce Tallman 30230 Sterling Gaylord West 30231 Robert Francis Holland 30232 Michael Glen Harper 30233 Thomas Robert Folk 30234 James Omar Kievit 30235 Michael Freeborn Stafford 30236 Michael Dee Jones 30237 John Edward LaSala 30238 Leo Joseph Troy 30239 John Paul Rainier 30240 James Malcolm Slone 30241 Douglas Martin Hoon 30242 John Anthony Vaccaro 30243 Richard Allan Redd 30244 Donald John Bergin 30245 Clifford Plummer Black 30246 Richard Allen Schrader 30247 James Emery Libhart 30248 John Stephen Sullivan 30249 Christopher Paul Tillman 30250 Scott Alan Moseley 30251 Jonathan A. Jacobsen 30252 William N. Alex 30253 Daniel Francis Grogan 30254 John Franklin Corbett 30255 Benroe W. Blount 30256 James L. Hickey 30257 Steven John Skoog 30258 Stanley Richard Gray 30259 Gerry Wayne Mitchell 30260 Grant Michael Smith 30261 Eric Thorne Olson 30262 Ronald Eugene Prier 30263 William Wardell Saylor 30264 David Wayne Talafuse 30265 Wayne Watson Boy 30266 Howard F. Kuenning 30267 Robert Weston Ash 30268 Joseph John Drach 30269 Christopher Luke Lawlor 30270 Gene Charles Barton 30271 Thomas Binn Nelson 30272 Bruce Edward van Dam 30273 Mark Benedict Bilodeau 30274 Robert Lewis Van Antwerp 30275 Floyd Gilbert Whitney 30276 Dan Whitney Hickox 30277 Donald Haryford Costello 30278 Raymond Louis Federici 30279 John Anthony Bonin 30280 Thomas Love Hendrix 30281 Robert Minutoli 30282 Gary Douglas Speer 30283 Walter William Shulits 30284 William Charles Guarino 30285 Eric Walter Bantz 30286 Earl Ike Patterson 30287 Kweon Il Stambaugh 30288 John M. Smith 30289 Steven Michael Dougan 30290 Paul George Gabelia 30291 Virgil Victor Becker 30292 James Lawrence Westphal 30293 Dean E. Wade 30294 F. Kenneth Davis 30295 Bruce Kenyon Scott 30296 James Richard Kerin 30297 Christopher Kane 30298 Jeffrey L. Schrepple 30299 Kevin John Fitzpatrick 30300 Brian Eric Dillon 30301 Timothy LeRoy Sanford 30302 Richard John Williams 30303 Thomas Kevin Ryan 30304 Michael J. Whitaker 30305 Michael Deegan 30306 John Irwin Boxberger 30307 Francis Patrick Hogan 30308 Lawrence Arthur Lansrud 30309 William Carl Smith 30310 Edward George Murdock 30311 Dennis Edward Leahy 30312 Do-Sun Chae 30313 Laurence John Best 30314 Daniel Mark Downs 30315 Bruce Cameron Clark 30316 Scott Edwin Peppler 30317 John Allen Geraci 30318 Gary James Holland 30319 Thom Scott Thomassen 30320 John Edward Baker 30321 Louis Canonico 30322 Bernie Ray Stein 30323 Steven Hornor Myer 30324 William Daniel James 30325 Joe Edward Wishcamper 30326 James Manly Lee 30327 Thomas Andrew Marks 30328 Mark William Ernst 30329 William Edwards Harlan 30330 Daniel Louis Breitenbach 30331 Kenneth J. Ratajczak 30332 Robert Estes Ludwig 30333 William Howard Shriver 30334 Philip Merkle Jones 30335 Holly Chester Howlett 30336 Troy M. Reyna 30337 Daniel Cover Doe 30338 Robert Frank Dees 30339 Anthony Charles DiRienzo 30340 John Paul Langlois 30341 John Anthony Cavalier 30342 Ronald Lee Hawthorne 30343 William Edward McConaghay 30344 Walter Richard Ennaco 30345 Harry Daniel Brown 30346 Gentry Stanton North 30347 John Paul McGuinness 30348 Robert Harold Wank 30349 Marvin King Foust 30350 Peter Alphonso Topp 30351 Edward James Mueller 30352 William George Bixby 30353 James F. Holcomb 30354 Andrew Francis Krepinevich 30355 Daniel Eugene Bappe 30356 Richard Townsend Martin 30357 Anthony R. Russo 30358 Kenneth David Hopper 30359 Dale Clark Packard 30360 Rodney Saku Azama 30361 Stephen John Gillon 30362 Frederick George Wilson 30363 James Robert Hougnon 30364 Richard Joseph McGrath 30365 Richard Alan Kinder 30366 Edwin Henry Bratton 30367 Mark P. Gay 30368 Robert Lee Bryant 30369 Douglas Kahele Apo 30370 George C. Wildrick 30371 Kenneth Edward Brockman 30372 Lee Keith Miller 30373 Thomas Steven Hrivnak 30374 Douglas Anthony Radz 30375 Greg Alan Bowman 30376 Frederick Van Vurst 30377 Paul Norman Dunn 30378 Thomas Joseph Pawlowski 30379 Edward Cleve Buntz 30380 William North Sterrett 30381 George James Murati 30382 Jonathan Morgan Cage 30383 James Alfred Frick 30384 David Campbell Kirk 30385 Christopher Francis Fornecker 30386 Richard Dean Amstutz 30387 George William McFetridge 30388 Peter Louis Odorico 30389 Steven Kent Mulliken 30390 Stephen Keehn 30391 Victor James Paci 30392 Paul Dale Eaton 30393 David Wayne Easton 30394 Edward Vance McCracken 30395 Robert John Bulger 30396 Joseph A. Scaniffe 30397 Joseph Dayle Horsfall 30398 Brian Lee Klemmer 30399 Stephen Coriell Fee 30400 Dean Robert Ertwine 30401 Paul Douglas Timmerberg 30402 Anthony Hall Colby 30403 Gene Craig Baumberger 30404 Charles Michael Coleman 30405 Michael Patrick Dugan 30406 James Roger Bowen 30407 Grant J. Moyer 30408 William N. Vinson 30409 William John Wilson 30410 Raymond S. Rollings 30411 Brian Lee Davie 30412 Robert Scott Beumer 30413 Gary Charles Micheau 30414 Bradford Gee Loo 30415 John Robert Wood 30416 Robert Dee Mattox 30417 Edward Joseph Collins 30418 Reginald Heber W. Sterns 30419 Lawrence Alan Aubrecht 30420 Randolph Allan Shelton 30421 Guy Harwood Richardson 30422 Daniel Anthony Perkowski 30423 Robert Paul Hieronymus 30424 Michael Warren Sawicki 30425 Ronald Crafton Murphree 30426 Wayne Alvin Kirkbride 30427 Michael Lee Crook 30428 Matthew Joseph Peterson 30429 Stephen Scott Smith 30430 Dennis Lynn Gray 30431 Howard Manley Voland 30432 Gordon Alan Israelson 30433 Richard James Lewis 30434 William Stephen Pavlick 30435 Michael Edward Fankell 30436 Francis X. Kaczynski 30437 Jay E. Lawson 30438 George Alan Higgins 30439 Marvin Alan Steinman 30440 Joseph Patrick Gallagher 30441 Paul Alexander Capofari 30442 Randy L. Jones 30443 Jim Dernar 30444 Jeffrey Dennis McCausland 30445 Michael Peter Murray 30446 Michael Kobbe 30447 Judson Randolph Belmont 30448 Felix Randal Bolding 30449 Shaun Sweeney Conlin 30450 Marion Thomas Davis 30451 Erik Kimber Polcrack 30452 Joseph Michael Hanratty 30453 Ted Dell Whitley 30454 Richard Lynn Wampler 30455 Jeffrey Thornton Tucker 30456 Bruce Malcolm Sandison 30457 Wayne Richard Godfrey 30458 Bruce Campbell 30459 John Charles Featherstone 30460 Patrick Francis Link 30461 Charles John Drobny 30462 John S. Lawrence 30463 Ronald Ira Karp 30464 Dennis R. Dowdy 30465 Randall Dee Bookout 30466 Daniel Keith Sullivan 30467 William Laird Henry 30468 David Edward Goins 30469 Jeffrey Leonard Spara 30470 Norman Dennis Greczyn 30471 John Robert Crouse 30472 David A. Grayson 30473 Richard Glynn Parsons 30474 Daniel George Rossbach 30475 David Bruce Levin 30476 Robert James Marr 30477 Garry Alan Williams 30478 Claude Richard Parmely 30479 Gary Jay Dennis 30480 Ward Lynn Bursley 30481 James Atticus Bowden 30482 Daniel Francis Lally 30483 Nicholas John Licht 30484 David Norman Nicholson 30485 Carl M. Kruger 30486 Allan Harold Magee 30487 Douglas Hartzler Wise 30488 Jan Randall Medusky 30489 John Alfred Roth 30490 Lawrence Kevin Turner 30491 Kurt Lee Kratz 30492 Paul Michael Vuksich 30493 Kenneth Thomas Walker 30494 Thomas Guffin Waller 30495 Arthur Ernest Batchelder 30496 Robert Wayne Hurst 30497 David Charles Lueneburg 30498 David Preston Inglee 30499 John Bradley Marvin 30500 Peter Bruce Slade 30501 George Kerr Devine 30502 Jeffery Lee Donald 30503 James Drew Walker 30504 John Franklin Johnson 30505 Mark Emil Eldridge 30506 Thurman Berg Tejan 30507 Donald David Newlin 30508 Ronald Andrew Bodre 30509 Harry Robert Irwin 30510 Philip W. Blair 30511 Myron Erich Pangman 30512 George Sidney Webb 30513 Franklin Homer Reiser 30514 James William Lewis 30515 A. Rhodes Wilson 30516 Frank Michael Juric 30517 John Edward King 30518 William Frank McLaughlin 30519 Thomas Kevin McNerney 30520 Raymond Patrick Canton 30521 Ralph Parker Fader 30522 Robert Michael McDannell

30523 Dennis John Miller 30524 Patrick Joseph Sinnott 30525 Richard Reynolds Rust 30526 Robert Dale Mercer 30527 Blake Patrick Gendron 30528 David Alan Shrewsbury 30529 James Eugene Lyon 30530 Charles Nicholas Ebel 30531 David Ballance Haseman 30532 William Dean James 30533 William Robert Phillips 30534 John Michael McWilliam 30535 Michael R. S. Donaghy 30536 James Merritt Spinks 30537 Edward Francis Augustyniak 30538 Ronald Dean Keenan 30539 Michael David Proctor 30540 Nathan Forrest Shoaf 30541 Paul Jacob Burton 30542 Steven Andrew Zurian 30543 Charles Steven Hughes 30544 James Francis Cordes 30545 Ernest Anthony Miller 30546 Paul John Cavise 30547 Jeffrey Bruce Staser 30548 Mark Alan Robershotte 30549 Douglas Fred Clark 30550 Paul Winston Albers 30551 John Moncure 30552 Antonio Socoro Lauglaug 30553 Paul Hardy Herbert 30554 Robert Wells Allbright 30555 Stephen James Curry 30556 Howard Charles Wilson 30557 Robert Davis Powers 30558 James Robertson McLean 30559 Robert McGregor Miller 30560 Jon Alan Burkley 30561 Louie Reyna 30562 Timothy John Norris 30563 Walter Rieckhoff Lincoln 30564 Kenny Alfred Searcy 30565 John Michael Gallagher 30566 John Charles Donovan 30567 Robert Alan Strong 30568 Lance Marquardt Giroux 30569 Walter Wojdakowski 30570 Merrill Anthony Miller 30571 Joseph Sorin Schneider 30572 Jeffrey Joseph Dufault 30573 Nicholas Clarence Salamone 30574 Rolland Archibald Dessert 30575 Charles William Hundley 30576 Daniel Cushing Kelso 30577 John Harold Northrop 30578 Alan Hamilton Brennan 30579 John Peter Kale 30580 James Leonard Griffin 30581 Richard Fleming Kane 30582 Lee Charles Stinson 30583 Leland Wayne Hall 30584 William Jlwy Siwy 30585 Bernard E. Pasierb 30586 Stephen Roy Dooley 30587 Michael Lee Lysfjord 30588 William D. Sanders 30589 James Andrew Hughes 30590 George Lester Sadler 30591 Peter Richard Scovill 30592 John G. Wheelock 30593 Jerome Sylvester Gabig 30594 Stephen Michael Sheppard 30595 Grant G. Hintze 30596 Frank Joseph Eich 30597 Ronald Ray Scott 30598 William Joseph Farmer 30599 Philip Anthony Crockett 30600 Robert Ridgway McLaughlin 30601 George Warren Heyworth 30602 Donald Carl MacMichael 30603 Jim Bob Plunkett 30604 Joris Michael Hogan 30605 Felipe Frocht 30606 Robert Mitchell Brown 30607 Charles Estes Frost 30608 Jerome A. Jacobs 30609 Milton Edward Koger 30610 Gereth Bruce Stillman 30611 David Gordon Wildes 30612 Glenn Aaron Gates 30613 Russell Clyde Wagnon 30614 Thomas William Pressler 30615 Scott Carleton Rowen 30616 Murro McCracken Martens 30617 William Earl Patrick Moyer 30618 Fernando Alfaro 30619 Charles Whitman Jones 30620 Robert Henry Crocker 30621 William Edward Wightman 30622 William Loyd Webb 30623 Burton William Tulkki 30624 Alexander G. McLaren 30625 Michael Dow Scisco 30626 Thomas Everett Cahill 30627 Sidney Edward Harvey 30628 Wilbur Ray Snyder 30629 Christopher Alan Bishop 30630 Robert Charles Wines 30631 H.R. Nick Lawrence 30632 David Ralph Gallay 30633 James Henry Le Febvre 30634 Charles Wesley Clements 30635 Benjamin Reyes Lazo 30636 Stephen Joseph Kiernan 30637 Arthur Starkey Vaeni 30638 David Tillson Bradford 30639 Robert Frank Effertz 30640 Henry Carlisle Johnson 30641 Brian Thomas Matthew Borders 30642 Albert J. Hamilton 30643 Richard Arthur Lien 30644 Ernest Philip Petersen 30645 Michael David Balderman 30646 Alan David McMurry 30647 Alan T. Ernst 30648 John Gayle Boynton 30649 David C. Grob 30650 William V. Tierney 30651 Craig Thomas Hatton 30652 Gregory Kam Moon Wong 30653 Charles Eugene Blakley 30654 Cornelius Joe Ergonis 30655 James Michael Tanner 30656 Gregory Michael Matiya 30657 Paul Joseph Johnson 30658 John Calvin Siemer 30659 Michael Neil Olson 30660 Richard John Joseph 30661 Craig William McKee 30662 James Stephen Park 30663 Glenn Steven Geary 30664 James Richard Wold 30665 Robert Hugh Dull 30666 Stephen Geoffrey Hannan 30667 Thomas Matthew Kriwanek 30668 Charles Allen Barlow 30669 B. Hudson Berrey 30670 Gary Franklin Moore 30671 James Henry Benner 30672 William Christopher North 30673 John Charles Eberly 30674 Robert Harlan Strong 30675 Kurt Leslie Musser 30676 Ulrich Richard Schmidt 30677 James H. Silcox 30678 Roger Masaaki Ueda 30679 Henry Lee Kinnison 30680 James Anthony Ryer Veeder 30681 Randall Reeves Parish 30682 Scott Howard Burner 30683 David Andrew Carlson 30684 Karl W. Johnson 30685 Benjamin Daigle Martin 30686 Scott Gregory Helgeson 30687 Edward Eugene Durham 30688 Gregory Ernest Lamb 30689 Gregory Richard True 30690 Jeffrey L. King 30691 William John Hatch 30692 Jonathan Mark Faith 30693 Joseph Benedict Wismann 30694 Keith R. Jones 30695 Gerry Russell Zmolek 30696 George Victor McIlvaine 30697 Joseph Arthur Edmyth Ivey 30698 Scott Frederick Miller 30699 Charles William Fletcher 30700 Brad Jackson 30701 Michael Morgan Toler 30702 Harvey Richard Jokinen 30703 Lawrence John Cook 30704 Michael Antoine Rodrigue 30705 Steven Michael Grantham 30706 Samuel William Koster 30707 Thomas Robert Rock 30708 Walter Roy Seifried 30709 Clifford Kenton Willis 30710 Roy L. Hiter 30711 Thomas Guy Carulli 30712 James Richard Wylie 30713 Alton Pozo Latimer 30714 David Andrew Mitchell 30715 Jeffrey M. Park 30716 John Francis Maggiolino 30717 Alan Bruce Clay 30718 William Edward Chalk 30719 Frank Paul Noto 30720 Tommy Willard Kirk 30721 Joe Ben Lamb 30722 Hayward Stanley Florer 30723 Steven Keith Hogan 30724 William Bradley Russell 30725 Charles William Minshew 30726 John A. Kidder 30727 Joseph Reginald Edwards 30728 John Leroy Hamlin 30729 Randall Louis Stein 30730 David Lloyd Hartman 30731 Aaron Oscar Stacchini 30732 Ernest Hinds 30733 Chris Joseph LeBlanc 30734 Paul Jefferson Harlow 30735 Alan Delbert Skillicorn 30736 Roger Dryden Cunningham 30737 Ronald Dee Golden 30738 Brian Stephen Keif 30739 Earl Paul Smith 30740 Donald Wayne Phillips 30741 James Edwin Birkhimer 30742 Michael Alan Godbout 30743 Kenneth David Dzombar 30744 Raymond R. Crawford 30745 Robert Lee Mahowald 30746 Robert Lowell Somers 30747 Henry Daniel Glaister 30748 Gary Peter Sarpen 30749 William Warren Gibson 30750 Gregory Thomas McGuckin 30751 Robert Baldwin Preston 30752 Richard Joseph O'Leary 30753 William Edward Walsh 30754 John Anthony A. Opiola 30755 George Robert Walter 30756 Robert J. Wittman 30757 John W. Klingelhoefer 30758 Ray Steven Idzior 30759 August Charles Manguso 30760 Charles Osborn Warner 30761 Michael Blaine Barker 30762 Steve Allen Hicks 30763 Harry Delbert Stumpf 30764 James Jackson Rackley 30765 Barry Edward Willey 30766 John Hodges Bentley 30767 Joseph Thomas Farrell 30768 Thomas John McGrann 30769 Ray Edward Ward 30770 Andrew Franklin Harvell 30771 Kenneth Lee Martin 30772 Thomas Clay McQuary 30773 Franklin Emerson Hoke 30774 Brian L. Travis 30775 Gary Donald Mirzoian 30776 Frank Ronald Turek 30777 Thomas Houston Boswell 30778 John C. Roggow 30779 Donald Lee Walter Kerr 30780 Daniel Burke Hennebry 30781 Michael M. Aldrich 30782 Thomas Allen Rooker 30783 Frederick William Sherman 30784 William John Staudenmeier 30785 Edwin W. Chamberlain 30786 Claude Monroe McQuarrie 30787 Robert Barlett Quimby 30788 Dale Ellick Morgan 30789 Scott Charles Adams 30790 Ken Richard Rash 30791 Howard Steve Etheridge 30792 Frederick Rogers Ferrin 30793 James Thomas Barnes 30794 Peter Brooks Palmer 30795 Craig A. Peterson 30796 James Dale Babington 30797 Laurence Lee Duncan 30798 Roger Duane Asper 30799 Thomas A. Ladd 30800 Dennis Anthony Wagner 30801 Philip Nelson Hurst 30802 James Raymond Benko 30803 Gary Wayne Potter 30804 Frank Rapier Hancock 30805 Gareth Edward Dobija 30806 Bradford John Holtz 30807 Craig Lewis Kaster 30808 Edward Albert Freund 30809 Charles Anthony Williams 30810 David Marshall Hayes 30811 Scott Eugene Nahrwold 30812 R. Mark McCauley 30813 Stephen Thomas Baranzyk 30814 Michael David Reeder 30815 Andrew Linas Eiva 30816 Michael O'Neal Collins 30817 Eric Hans Asker 30818 Thomas Joseph Abrahamsen 30819 Dales Morrison Kent 30820 Robert Price Bush 30821 Dennis L. Heath 30822 Chester James Phillips 30823 Barney E. Coale 30824 Michael Dominick Bellino 30825 Zoltan Ray Kollat 30826 William Richard Snader 30827 Stephen Clark Daly 30828 James Joseph Galioto 30829 Stan Woods Graff 30830 Robert M. Butt 30831 Thomas Kenneth Walton 30832 Joseph Stephen Dennehy 30833 Larry Vance Hill 30834 David Stephen Emery 30835 Peter Aloysius McDonald 30836 Donald Scott Bushnell 30837 Gordon Lamar Hart 30838 William Claude Jones 30839 Kenneth James Kiger 30840 Frank Joseph Cservak 30841 Roger Dean Magneson 30842 Roderick Charles Rice 30843 Brian Lee Buchanan 30844 Joel Clark Harris 30845 James Victor Walter 30846 Joseph Henry Kimmitt 30847 James Taggart Camp 30848 Charles Robert Hiatt 30849 Patrick Henry McGann 30850 Gerald Paul Hunt 30851 Steven James Powers 30852 James Dennis O'Brien 30853 John Cobbey Weekley 30854 Patrick Michael Flachs 30855 Hugh Christopher Ardleigh 30856 Elary Gromoff 30857 Clarence La Don Miller 30858 Jay Mark Augustenborg 30859 Douglas Howard Skeggs 30860 Edgar La Nolan Anderson 30861 Kenneth Lee Vogel 30862 Allen Jerry Williams 30863 John Michael Chaney 30864 William Guild Welch 30865 Joseph William Adamczyk 30866 Barry Harold Jenkins 30867 Robert L. A. Lossius 30868 John Andrew McCommons 30869 Charles Ward Shaklee 30870 William Curtiss Puddy 30871 Leland Bernard Stedge 30872 William Joseph Leszczynski 30873 Michael Henry Jackson 30874 Stephen Charles Main 30875 Michael Nelson McElhare 30876 David Lowell Pedersen 30877 Michael Patrick O'Dell 30878 Jerome Dillon Smalley 30879 John Arthur Goshorn 30880 William Joseph Herdrich 30881 John Francis Souza 30882 Robert James Curran 30883 Howard Charles Smith 30884 Alfred J. Weber 30885 Thomas Boone Giboney 30886 David Lee Brice 30887 James Howard Montgomery 30888 Lee R. Barnes 30889 Robert Elgin Woodside 30890 Daniel Edward Jenkins 30891 Christopher Vincent Feudo 30892 Henry Eric Peitz 30893 David Bryan Wohleen 30894 Paul Lee Doppel 30895 Roger Lee Miller 30896 Lawrence Allen Baltezore 30897 Robert Clair Edwards 30898 Thomas W. Waters 30899 Edward Carl Horton 30900 Harold George Thomas 30901 Don Dixon Tilton 30902 Gary Steen Walborn 30903 Robert Wayne Akers 30904 Robert Lewis Wyatt 30905 Ralph Joseph Cericola 30906 Tony Louis Dedmond 30907 Robert William MacArevey 30908 E. Duston Saunders 30909 Randolph Douglas Alastair Brown 30910 Daniel Lee Muchow 30911 Paul Edward La Bonte 30912 Gregory Lynn Hart 30913 John Gohmert Garner 30914 Steven Elmore Curtis 30915 Ronald Frank Nicholl 30916 Michael Lawrence Rudzis 30917 William Michael McDaniel 30918 Robert Peter Rhea 30919 John Clay Anderson 30920 Gordon Scott Scholler 30921 Theodore Franklin Leger 30922 Joseph Gerard Materia 30923 James Peter Kelliher 30924 Peter Anthony Rich 30925 Andrew Haa Num Kim 30926 Gary Charles McDonald 30927 Thomas Joseph Innamorato 30928 Joseph Pasquale Gatti 30929 James Ernest Seitz 30930 Richard Joseph Ducote 30931 John Paul Corcoran 30932 Robert Gregory Losey 30933 Danny Samuel Mension 30934 Lee Nace Perry 30935 James Samuel Ritter 30936 Kim Rolofson Putnam 30937 William Earl Simons 30938 Peter Joseph Bucha 30939 Howard John Carpenter 30940 Mark James Fischer 30941 William Douglas Waldbueser 30942 Michael Arnold Ceniceros 30943 Paul Anthony Oskvarek 30944 Robert W. Doyle 30945 Craig Borden Loucks 30946 Geoffrey Forrest Eaton 30947 Roger Donald Hershman 30948 Melbourne Kimsey 30949 Patrick Zane Ford 30950 Jay Edward Rossi 30951 Gregory Bruce Schneider 30952 Matthew W. Hussey 30953 William Fredrick Fennema 30954 David E. Schnabel 30955 Nestor Sanchez 30956 Thomas O'Hara Patrick Sweeney 30957 Richard Arthur Cody 30958 Donald Keene Strother 30959 William Wallace Britain 30960 William Johnson Ray 30961 William Kent Dermann 30962 Douglas Earle Merkl 30963 Stephen James Broussard 30964 Dennis Joseph Donahue 30965 Robert L. Miller 30966 James Moreau Gilly 30967 James Lee Mohney 30968 Daniel Allen Merritt 30969 Robert Gardner Kail 30970 Bruce Clayton LaVigne 30971 Robert Paul Coonan 30972 Guillermo Giandoni 30973 Richard Vincent Luczak 30974 Karl Eric Gorzelnik 30975 Benny Frank Harrell 30976 Philip Scott Stonecipher 30977 Richard Bruce Leibert 30978 James Louis Moran 30979 Tod John Wilson 30980 Bruce Rodney Ritter 30981 James David Morgan 30982 Eric Robert Mellinger 30983 John Matthew Buttine 30984 Edward Walter Vross 30985 Edgar Benjamin Williams 30986 Alexander Russell Bolling 30987 Thomas James Pollard 30988 Daniel Joseph Morgan 30989 Mark Gerald Cole 30990 Frederick Charles Heneman 30991 Frank Elsworth Galati 30992 Daniel Bernard Ostrowski 30993 Michael Walter Driscoll 30994 Richard Douglas Sinclair 30995 Joseph Raymond Taylor 30996 Randall Owen Chitwood 30997 David Anthony Leis 30998 Michael Eugene Jacob 30999 George Henry Linnemeier 31000 Richard Nathan Halvorson 31001 Clifford Wesley Stilgenbauer 31002 James Britton Clark 31003 Charles Michael Sela 31004 G. Thomas Greco 31005 Edward Lee Dyer 31006 Herbert David Barnhart 31007 Richard Ray Timboe 31008 Robert Campbell Lang 31009 Duane William Boswell 31010 William Joseph Miller 31011 Bruce Harris Barlow 31012 Charles Albert Zimmerman 31013 Albert Marcael Fleumer 31014 Jerry Lee Walker 31015 Bill Arthur Martin 31016 Richard Allen Ekman 31017 David Russell Ralph 31018 Peter Edward Galgay 31019 John David Ferguson 31020 A. David Lynch 31021 Thomas Wilson Dayvault 31022 John Charles Sturgeon 31023 Keith William Woznek 31024 Geoffrey Morgan Champion 31025 John Douglas Simar 31026 Clyde Paisley Gibson 31027 Dale Thomas McDonough 31028 Gary Nitta 31029 Roy Edward Maday 31030 Robert Stephen Jeska 31031 Thomas Howell Speairs 31032 Geoffrey John Wilhelmy 31033 Richard Joseph Lawson 31034 George Edward Summers 31035 Percy Squire 31036 Jack Owen Shafer 31037 David Everett Wicker 31038 Phillip Allan Drumheiser 31039 Raymond Donald Ritacco 31040 Gene W. Bailey 31041 Howard Kuschick 31042 Robert J. Rauk 31043 Bruce Martin Moore 31044 Stephen Dewitt Presley 31045 William John Hershenow 31046 John Larkin Lynch 31047 Cornelious Burns 31048 **1973** Jay Christopher Willis 31049 Richard Marvin Saunders 31050 Michael Joseph Mundt 31051 William Surles McArthur 31052 Donald Richard Ponikvar 31053 Thomas Lynn Mays 31054 James Frederick DeBroux 31055 Karl W. Eikenberry 31056 Jeffrey Charles Olson 31057 William Norman Lane 31058 Robert Lars Welo 31059 William John Quinn 31060 Thomas Edward Wiswell 31061 Scott B. Cottrell 31062 Mark Edward Vincent 31063 Richard Stephen Young 31064 Bruce Lamont Innis 31065 Lawrence Andrew Gaydos 31066 Danny Patrick Kaup 31067 Raymond Charles McCann 31068 Joseph Peter Mastrucci 31069 Joseph Dennis Palatka 31070 James Leroy Fuehrmeyer 31071 F. Thomas Lubozynski 31072 Eric George Daxon 31073 Gordon Graham Murdock 31074 William Michael James 31075 William John Pieper 31076 Richard Lloyd Cram 31077 William Stanley Bice 31078 Charles Thomas Hutzler 31079 Timothy Alan Jurek 31080 Charles Robert Kaylor 31081 Garrett L. Dietz 31082 Craig Douglas Wildrick 31083 Raymond David Zegley 31084 Joseph Phillips Tallman 31085 Douglas Charles Bender 31086 Donald Arthur Hollsten 31087 Paul Nathaniel Smith 31088 Donald Edward Brown 31089 John Philip Abizaid 31090 Murray Winn Williams 31091 Thomas John Leney 31092 Steven Paul Medaglia 31093 Henry D. Ramm 31094 Timothy Joseph Casey 31095 David Bruce Vaughan 31096 Patrick Allen Putignano 31097 Terry Dee Clark 31098 John Joseph Twomey 31099 William Henry Pearce 31100 Brent Allen Crabtree 31101 Bruce Edward Takala 31102 John Charles Linskey 31103 Phillip Leslie Smith 31104 Robert MacMullin 31105 Tommy E. Shook 31106 Richard John Maloney 31107 Hugh Darrow Bohlender 31108 Mark William Hemenway 31109 Robert Alfred Potter 31110 Uldric Lutgardt Fiore 31111 Timothy Jon Beatty 31112 Robert Douglas Knight 31113 Merlyn Dean Gibson 31114 Frederic John Pineau 31115 William Joseph Morris 31116 Kenneth Vaccaro 31117 Gerald Stephen Doyle 31118 Steven Robert Lindberg 31119 Paul Andrew Stipek 31120 George Leander Anderson 31121 Philip Ray Lindner 31122 Don Timothy Riley 31123 James Michael Gillcrist 31124 William Jack Armstrong 31125 John Lowell Storm 31126 Paul Frederick Benoit 31127 Alan Dana Worland 31128 John Robert Cotton 31129 Robert Myers Montgomery 31130 Scott Richard Eckelman 31131 Yaropolk Roland Hladkyj 31132 Byron Edward Luckett 31133 Stephen John Kirin 31134 Robert Murray Akscyn 31135 Scott Ross Feil 31136 Norman J. Hoerer 31137 Richard Leon Moskala 31138 John R. Hughes 31139 James Henry Hayes 31140 Michael J. DeBow 31141 John Richard Elliott 31142 Paul Anthony Meunier 31143 Bruce E. Boevers 31144 Michael Adair Berry 31145 Jeffrey Paul Cartwright 31146 Jer Donald Get 31147 Robert John Sweetman 31148 Hugh French T. Hoffman 31149 Charles H. Berlin 31150 Paul Wiles Trotti 31151 Joseph Bernard FitzHarris 31152 Gregory Mark Eckert 31153 Leslie Ray Alm 31154 John Francis Feeley 31155 Thomas Peter McKenzie 31156 Godfrey W. Brooks 31157 James Richard Burke 31158 Flynn Andrew 31159 Douglas Edward Warren 31160 Thomas Patrick Cusimano 31161 John Howard Bemis 31162 Jeffrey E. Jenkins 31163 Barry Thomas Hodge 31164 Edwin Charles Scharf 31165 Richard Paul Bauer 31166 Roy James Lyford-Pike 31167 Robert Francis Thomas 31168 Damian Patrick Kelly 31169 Andre Harding Sayles 31170 Bobby FLee Summers 31171 David Walter Tyner 31172 Richard Thomas Weeks 31173 Thomas Earl Shores 31174 Robert E. Morris 31175 Steven Geoffrey Carlson 31176 Gary Don Newsom 31177 John Hugh Fargason 31178 Elias Castro Bustamante 31179 John Stephen Klegka 31180 John D. Cook 31181 Robert Pentuk 31182 Stephen Francis Yunker 31183 Gary Michael Loberg 31184 Robert Lee Mace 31185 Ronnie E. Madera 31186 Kevin William Bond 31187 Thomas Lloyd Zieske 31188 Alex X. Z. Bendeck 31189 Martin William Moakler 31190 Wayne Gilbert Springer 31191 James Erwin Johnston 31192 D. Kirk Shaffer 31193 Albert Andrew Sciarretta 31194 Bruce Denison Chandler 31195 Thomas Joseph Fitzsimmons 31196 John William Holly 31197 James Vernon Elsey 31198 Mico John Miller 31199 Kerry Dean Figiel 31200 Richard Boyer Diver 31201 Glenn M. Rice 31202 Kelley Bean Mohrmann 31203 Paul Frederick Hamm 31204 Charles Frank Culclasure 31205 Stephen Barry Olsen 31206 Carter Francis Smith 31207 Ronald Bret Graef 31208 W. Clarke Edwards 31209 Gregory Mark Shaka 31210 Brendan Joseph Crowley 31211 George Wesley Crockatt 31212 Paul Dean Peterson 31213 William P. Goodwin 31214 John Joseph Zielinski 31215 David Edward Briggs 31216 Dee William Pettigrew 31217 John Robert Valant 31218 Jose Antonio Urgelles 31219 James Arthur Mayer 31220 Richard Allen Read 31221 Gary Leonard Gallo 31222 Michael Thomas Chychota 31223 Ben Ransom Cabell 31224 William Edward Jordan 31225 Roger Lee Bruley 31226 Terence Sean Meehan 31227 Manuel Aguila Briones 31228 Robert E. Gearheart 31229 Timothy John Georgelas 31230 Michael Lawrence Brown 31231 John Alan Anderson 31232 Thomas Alan Bauer 31233 Nage Lee Damas 31234 Christopher Lincoln Lingar 31235 David Ramon Marler 31236 Keith W. Rockwell 31237 Michael Patrick Stuhr 31238 William Read Gilmore 31239 Joseph Stanley Kuncel 31240 Howard Ross Frederick Condit 31241 Richard Murrell Carter 31242 James A. Herberg 31243 Peter Jean Kai 31244 Chaitram Singh 31245 David Wendell Schmitz 31246 Edward Bryant McGuire 31247 Michael Andrew Mutz 31248 George Charles Nobles 31249 William Redfield Brown 31250 Steven Thomas McKinney 31251 Gerald Harrison Reynolds 31252 Kevin Cameron Craig 31253 William Patrick Madigan 31254 Roth Stephen Schleck 31255 Lee Richard Pollock 31256 Alfred Guy Costantine 31257 Thomas Kermit Trettin 31258 Enrique Alberto Ortiz 31259 Thomas Frank Frein 31260 Gregory Mark Ellis 31261 Clyde Morris Leavelle 31262 David Duane Barber 31263 James Gerard O'Keefe 31264 Wayne Douglas Reynolds 31265 James Addison Baugh 31266 Robert Lawrence Schnabl 31267 John Morton Nolen 31268 George W. Weightman 31269 Charles Franklin Snow 31270 Thomas J. Hodgini 31271 Robert Hoole Sherwin 31272 Steven Paul Landry 31273 Dennis Michael Jackson 31274 Terry Edwin Smith 31275 Charles Lawrence Dokmo 31276 Michael Dillon Hockley 31277 George Ellsworth

Quillin 31278 David Jeffrey Wachter 31279 Michael R. Gibbs 31280 Robert Edward Cadow 31281 Walther Rowland Wroblewski 31282 Guy Michael Marsala 31283 David Bruce Kimball 31284 Thomas Owen McKernon 31285 James G. Victor 31286 Mark Douglas Venske 31287 George Stuart Perkins 31288 James Thomas Schroeder 31289 Jack Jay Oakley 31290 Francisco Ong Dominguez 31291 Michael A. Alden 31292 John Ross Docksey 31293 Ralph Barton Clare 31294 Dana Charles Mather 31295 Lavoy M. Thiessen 31296 Max Allen Skidmore 31297 Sanford Douglass Kreider 31298 Lynn Douglas Ferguson 31299 Michael Byrd Prewitt 31300 Michael Andrew Burton 31301 Daniel Jackson Baker 31302 Martin Robert Beck 31303 Grover Hugar Dailey 31304 Michael James Stewart 31305 Richard Gerhard Bjurstrom 31306 Mark Lloyd Hanna 31307 Steven Frederick Waters 31308 Stephen John Kuffner 31309 Bruce Edward Kasold 31310 James Delbert Wineland 31311 Eugene Joseph Iwanyk 31312 John Richard Olsen 31313 David L. Howard 31314 Dan Preston Krebill 31315 David Andrew Moody 31316 Thomas Michael Depkovich 31317 James Alan Hawkins 31318 William Paul Heilman 31319 Michael David Wilcomb 31320 Manuel Sosa 31321 Robert Edward Skiver 31322 Lawrence Andrew Watt 31323 Daniel Vincent Wright 31324 Richard Michael Dallaire 31325 John Anthony Snyder 31326 Bruce Edward Zukauskas 31327 Peter L. Smith 31328 Ronald Stanley Petricka 31329 Thomas J. Hanifen 31330 Joseph Key Bratton 31331 John W. Rutherford 31332 Walter Christoph Hunter 31333 Edwin Glenn Stikeleather 31334 Christopher Tonneson Westfall 31335 Bernard Walter Galing 31336 William Herbert Jockheck 31337 Steven Ray Gerhardt 31338 John Charles Gay 31339 Harold E. Yamashita 31340 Robert R. Simpson 31341 Ronald Earl McConnell 31342 Walter W. Olson 31343 Timothy P. Riggers 31344 Robert J. Hicks 31345 James Thomas Grenier 31346 Jan Lester Schultz 31347 Roy Davis Phillips 31348 Walter King Bendler 31349 Gregory Dale Lewis 31350 Robert Michael Garrant 31351 James William Leonard 31352 James Edward Bessler 31353 Kenneth J. Self 31354 Randolph Edward Noster 31355 Michael Karl Jelinsky 31356 Richard Jay Hoffman 31357 David Loren Marks 31358 Robert David Wilson 31359 Arthur Thomas Coumbe 31360 John Henry Farris 31361 James C. Cooke 31362 Robert B. Gregg 31363 Kevin Lee Murphy 31364 Merritt Maynard Smith 31365 Nicholas George A. Prospero 31366 Julian Bohdan Harwanko 31367 Daniel Alan Hahn 31368 Clifford Allen Reeser 31369 Henry Stephen Scharpenberg 31370 Peter Matthew Schoultis 31371 Gregory Fred Bergeret 31372 Dennis A. Hein 31373 George Larry Jent 31374 Dennis John Marine 31375 Richard Stanton Rokola 31376 Robert H. Johnson 31377 William James Haugh 31378 Robert G. Gillette 31379 Daniel Bradford Baker 31380 Dennis W. Rowe 31381 Charles Bernard Hendrick 31382 H. Lindsey Arison 31383 Frank Michael Maressa 31384 Richard Post Loiselle 31385 Michael William Ellis 31386 Michael Francis Basten 31387 Walter Tom Jervis 31388 Joseph Warren Miller 31389 Melvin Warren Brinkley 31390 James Anthony Milobowski 31391 Brian Edward Fredericks 31392 Leon B. Baker 31393 Thomas Patrick Gannon 31394 Richard Robert Babbitt 31395 Stephen Dwight Bull 31396 David Lee Bubb 31397 James Louis Janele 31398 Gregory Brent Hagen 31399 Stephen Edward Freeman 31400 Edward Baldwin McCaul 31401 William Edson Goodrich 31402 Thomas Owen Mason 31403 Douglas Herbert Hand 31404 Daniel J. Davis 31405 Thomas Lynn Reynolds 31406 John Bishop Gately 31407 Philip Hugh Lynch 31408 John Francis Whalen 31409 Frank Douglas Cozza 31410 Ricky Duane Wilkerson 31411 Frederick Anthony Zapka 31412 Richard Kent Arras 31413 Noel Dennis Habib 31414 Lee Terrell Waggener Bavaro 31415 Joseph Elliott Jaremko 31416 Nicholas Thomas Combs 31417 Paul K. Shaffer 31418 Henry Arnold Walters 31419 John Douglas Mills 31420 Edward John Spencer 31421 Davis Michael Richardson 31422 Dennis Alden Tone 31423 Grant Hurmiston Walker 31424 David Roy Jackson 31425 Robert Gordon Brown 31426 Henry Paul Hoffman 31427 Lester Francis McConville 31428 James Keith Kelling 31429 Robert Anthony Guardia 31430 Roldan Vea 31431 Wayne Dolor Roberts 31432 James Andrew Ripple 31433 Steven Edward Bothe 31434 Thomas Counter Shull 31435 Thomas Howard Brown 31436 Richard Charles Wilson 31437 William F. McManaway 31438 Dennis Patrick Geoghan 31439 Gary Louis Vogler 31440 Jon A. Marshall 31441 Galen Eugene Morris 31442 Benjamin Martin Adams 31443 Dennis Philip Pryor 31444 Emanuel M. Tornquist 31445 Richard Burton Cassidy 31446 Gilbert Soloman Jenkins 31447 Glenn Malcolm Green 31448 H. Roger Mills 31449 Michael Edward Denton 31450 Frank Joseph Ruvio 31451 Charles Joseph Venable 31452 Mark Durward Brigham 31453 Gregory Bruce Conover 31454 Bruce Craig Ressner 31455 Stanley C. Moore 31456 George William Everett 31457 Joseph Anthony Lucidi 31458 Gregory Charles Douglass 31459 Robert Alan Brown 31460 William Taylor White 31461 Charles Andrew Donnell 31462 Bruce Wayne Blevins 31463 Robert Thomas Hines 31464 Craig Douglas Vorselen 31465 Lloyd L. Sutton 31466 Lawrence P. MacPhee 31467 Paul Anthony Baldy 31468 Thomas Sopwith McLean 31469 Charles James Maxfield 31470 Jack Lee Kincart 31471 Dennis Patrick Finnigan 31472 Gordon Ray Jaehne 31473 David Bruce Mackay 31474 Gary Wayne Bowen 31475 John Lockrey Nicodemus 31476 William Arthur Snow 31477 Michael Earl Eichers 31478 Fred E. Weiderhold 31479 Douglas Henry Hartline 31480 Daniel George Braun 31481 Donald Paul Coover 31482 Donnie Kent Patterson 31483 Jesse Baker Adams 31484 James Robert Allen 31485 John Albert Hazel 31486 Greg Steven Johnson 31487 Arthur John Brown 31488 Conrad William Norville Taylor 31489 Bennie K. Wilson 31490 William Edward Griffin 31491 Gilbert Granger Spencer 31492 Raymond Teegardin Mercer 31493 Raymond Edward Paggi 31494 John Forrest Halstead 31495 Michael Robert VanZetta 31496 Richard Anthony Rodrigues 31497 Francis Scott Hinchion 31498 Thomas Duggan Slear 31499 James J. Pelosi 31500 Thomas Francis O'Connor 31501 Melvin Eugene Clark 31502 David Francis McDermott 31503 Michael Clark Spielberger 31504 Edward D. Crossett 31505 Allen Lloyd Nichley 31506 Alfred L. Samuel 31507 Paul C. Snipes 31508 Stephen Conro Pixley 31509 Timothy Eugene Killgrove 31510 Dale Leroy Kurtz 31511 Charles William Kranitzky 31512 Jeffrey Alan Sorenson 31513 Mark Morgan Tracy 31514 Robert Land Smith 31515 Michael Randolph Stanton 31516 Mark Camden Griffith 31517 James Richard MacSwain 31518 Ronald Peyton Turnicky 31519 Edward Joseph Durham 31520 Charles Flaveous Sargent 31521 Warren S. Jensen 31522 Charles Henry Hall 31523 Dan Arol Lynn 31524 Myron J. Griswold 31525 Alan William Sanborn 31526 Douglas L. Days 31527 James Michael Cersosimo 31528 William Willis Epley 31529 Glen R. Hawkins 31530 George Arthur Fulton 31531 William Henry Perry 31532 Christopher Paul Rajk 31533 Albert Frank Kaminsky 31534 John Anthony Cerny 31535 Thomas J. Daze 31536 Todd Byron Kersh 31537 Dana Bland Keeney 31538 Mark Wilson Sousa 31539 Ronald Mark Rowley 31540 Joseph Francis Gaziano 31541 Philip Paul Joseph O'Donnell 31542 James Miles Burd 31543 Stephen Francis Flynn 31544 David Paul Valcourt 31545 Patrick J. McInerney 31546 Robert Henry Meyer 31547 Jeremy King Miller 31548 Frederick Marshall Brooks 31549 Robert William Davis 31550 Scott Colson Marcy 31551 Andrew Julius Widlak 31552 Charles Eugene Rittenburg 31553 Stephen G. Kee 31554 James Hugh Varner 31555 Paul J. Tetlack 31556 Steven Douglas Church 31557 Carl L. Critchlow 31558 Charles Eugene Beresky 31559 Grady Richard Poole 31560 Dennis Michael Morgenstern 31561 Richard Hunt Dickinson 31562 William P. Drechsel 31563 Philip Wayne Hill 31564 James Elmer Young 31565 Clyde Joseph Christopher 31566 Donald Joseph Blane 31567 W. Kim Brady 31568 Richard E. Dakin 31569 George Christopher Thompson 31570 Harry Patrick Allen 31571 Stanley Jay Shipley 31572 Edward Michael Francis 31573 William Frederick Filter 31574 Peter William Fotheringham 31575 Todd R. Jones 31576 Timothy Jerome Sielski 31577 Norman Joseph White 31578 Richard M. Johnson 31579 Frederick Benjamin Poccia 31580 Dieter Hans Joachim Zerressen 31581 Courtland Clouis Bivens 31582 Hugh David Porter 31583 Stephen L. Maddox 31584 Michael Edward Farrell 31585 Brett William Bailey 31586 Michael Douglas Vidlak 31587 William David Karl Wilson 31588 Michael Thomas Anderson 31589 Robert Carrol Holcomb 31590 Louis James Bartok 31591 Patrick Edward Logan 31592 George William Hubbard 31593 Val Anthony Pakis 31594 Rudolph Thompson Schwab 31595 John William O'Maley 31596 Michael B. Schulte 31597 Charles Richard Rash 31598 Michael Wayne McKeeman 31599 Michael O'Hagan 31600 William C. Lee Phillips 31601 Garland Charles Bonner 31602 William Newton Deatherage 31603 Kent Merle Freise 31604 Henry Charles Keebler 31605 Arthur William Robinson 31606 Michael William Colbert 31607 Jeffrey Michael Leskowat 31608 Casey Rogers 31609 David Joseph Timmons 31610 Kenneth Norell Highland 31611 Theophlise L. Twitty 31612 Bruce Edward Simpson 31613 John Anthony Quartarone 31614 Henry Richard Canciglia 31615 Joseph Franklin Watson 31616 Kenneth Lynn Travis 31617 William L. Moore 31618 Donald James O'Donnell 31619 Alan Jerome Bacon 31620 Jack Fowler Fennel 31621 Keith Wesley Bakken 31622 Robert Eugene Johnson 31623 Carlton Ernest Young 31624 Robert Jeffrey Lee 31625 Lawrence Greg Bronstein 31626 William Donald Miller 31627 Robert James Looney 31628 Harley Eugene Venters 31629 Stephen Dennis Coats 31630 Cedric Carson Brown 31631 James Kevin Hughes 31632 Mark Steven Kopsky 31633 David P. Ford 31634 John Masich Vuksich 31635 Scott Erwin Stewart 31636 Nelson Eddy Torres 31637 Robert Scott Mair 31638 John Patrick Everett 31639 Rex Eugene Wamsley 31640 Douglas T. Cromack 31641 Paul T. H. Currie 31642 Joseph Paul Cyr 31643 Francis LaVerne Dougherty 31644 John R. Dunlap 31645 George Kelsey Saul 31646 Michael Patrick Schramp 31647 Michael Lynn Donaldson 31648 Timothy Lee Thomas 31649 Thomas Albert Popa 31650 Gary Eugene Topping 31651 Telford William Larew 31652 Mark E. Benoit 31653 Terry Allen Bossieux 31654 Alexander S. Rhodes 31655 James Milton Branham 31656 Douglas Paul Belnap 31657 Walter P. McMurtry 31658 Edward Christopher Johnson 31659 Bryan Scott Drouin 31660 William Edward Chancellor 31661 Ronald Alan Grosso 31662 Gregory Joseph Arceri 31663 Peter Christopher Correa 31664 Michael Joseph Ceurvels 31665 Louis Frank Putman 31666 Patrick Mark Hermanson 31667 Sidney K. Craig 31668 John Hall Frederick 31669 Harry Allan Horn 31670 Daniel Gallagher Dutro 31671 Mark Everett Caras 31672 Stephen Arvo Seppa 31673 Louis Joseph Sosler 31674 Gaylyn Ford Jones 31675 Patrick Oliver Richardson 31676 Mark J. Ivandick 31677 Dana Lynn Warehime 31678 Robert Erhardt Hoffmann 31679 Thomas Edward Michaels 31680 William Patrick Rooney 31681 James Schweithelm 31682 William Elton Barker 31683 Robert William Rankin 31684 Randall Jay Wartner 31685 Bradley James Erbes 31686 Dean Emerson Craig 31687 William R. Pearson 31688 Roger Lee Williamson 31689 Matthew Ward Raymond 31690 Edward Paul Hetrick 31691 Joseph Emby Porter 31692 William Roman Feltes 31693 Lee Bennett Ross 31694 Robert Joseph Fasulo 31695 Craig Vincent Landrith 31696 Paul Anthony Jones 31697 Thomas N. Thompson 31698 Stephen Paul Bogosian 31699 Gregory Ralston Pepin 31700 Joseph Edward Planchak 31701 Christopher Rogers Losey 31702 Charles G. Kershaw 31703 Robert Patrick Kane 31704 Ivar Martin Kaardal 31705 George C. Chobany 31706 William Ray Humphries 31707 Harold E. Hale 31708 Reginald Dean Olsen 31709 Michael Evan Jose 31710 Marc R. Grunseth 31711 Sal John William Federico 31712 Lyman Dale McCall 31713 Charles David Franklin 31714 Michael Clement Naum 31715 Mark Henry Gerner 31716 Philip Tumblin 31717 Matthew Jack Belford 31718 Denis Albert Sullivan 31719 Roger Leigh Rothwell 31720 James Kenneth O'Brien 31721 Roland Eustace Peixotto 31722 Charles Webster Pope 31723 J. Murray Ritter 31724 Ricardo Ernesto Castro 31725 Robert Edwin Miller 31726 Charles James Mitchell 31727 Alfredo Roberto Reynoso 31728 James Clyde Styron 31729 Terrence Joseph Eastman 31730 Jerry Alan Simonsen 31731 George Herman Ferris 31732 Thomas J. Gandolfo 31733 William Peyton Fox 31734 Gary Robert Hall 31735 Chris James Mortensen 31736 Thomas William Erndt 31737 Leonard Monroe Dixon 31738 Kihm Michael Schroeder 31739 John Richard Thomas 31740 Howard Deane Elliott 31741 Scott Alan Barry 31742 William Edwin Boerth 31743 John Joseph Scanlan 31744 Robert Thomas Machado 31745 Ronald Frank Danhof 31746 John Michael Rocco 31747 Richard Andrew Stibrik 31748 Robert Busill Tully 31749 Robert Michael Goett 31750 William Donsal Lewis 31751 Keith William Workman 31752 Daniel Michael Maguire 31753 Harold Glenn Waite 31754 R. Douglas MacIntyre 31755 Melvin Alan Orr 31756 James L. Bryan 31757 Robert B. McCullough 31758 Martin O'Shaughnessy 31759 Lawrence Baxter Hames 31760 Juan Manuel Verhelst 31761 Bernard Jerome Kerbawy 31762 Anthony Ross Strickler 31763 Kenn Allen Riordan 31764 Arthur John Peterson 31765 Kevin Kelly 31766 David A. Hicks 31767 Robert Allen Marsh 31768 William Vincent Martz 31769 George Steven Monteiro 31770 Charles Donald Atkins 31771 Jack Lee Masters 31772 Michael Anthony Pasquarella 31773 Raymund Victor Crandall 31774 Keith Otto Arlund 31775 James F. X. Daum 31776 Rex Gregory Beck 31777 David Winklbauer 31778 Glenn Dee Carriere 31779 Lawrence Allen Saksa 31780 Thomas John Mulyca 31781 Ronald Wayne Gerbers 31782 John A. Little 31783 Robert Jason Williamson 31784 Michael Roderick Thompson 31785 John W. Jones 31786 Robert Lee Maginnis 31787 Jon B. Crowell 31788 Barney Joe Oakes 31789 Jon Charles Housman 31790 Kevin Edward Keating 31791 David Henry Pickett 31792 Philip Allen Neil 31793 David Webster Rose 31794 Thomas John Wilson 31795 Joseph James Tamburelli 31796 Javier Octavio De La Rosa Perigault 31797 Joseph Michael Laura 31798 Thomas Atherton Godwin 31799 David Coleman Blackerby 31800 John Nicholas Robinson 31801 Walter Arnold Rolfs 31802 Thomas Brooke Lyndon Stanford 31803 Richard Kenneth Dembowski 31804 Brian Eugene Rasmussen 31805 James Calvin McGill 31806 Paul Scott Beaty 31807 Thomas Russell Wood 31808 Jerome Frederick Mossbarger 31809 Albert Carl Goit 31810 William Gary Chadick 31811 Michael Sylvester Altieri 31812 Dennis Paul Scott 31813 Robert David Boyd 31814 Dennis Laverne Johnson 31815 Regis John Carr 31816 Gordon MacDonald King 31817 Michael Harold Poore 31818 William Charles Dougherty 31819 Matthew Henry Eaton 31820 Stephen H. Frolich 31821 Charles Edward Dyke 31822 Michael S. Richburg 31823 John Joseph Purcell 31824 Sanford Robert Rubinstein 31825 David Francis Jamroz 31826 Jeffrey Alan Greene 31827 Ralph Edward Smith 31828 Creston Mark Cathcart 31829 Paul S. Gendrolis 31830 Michael Anthony Pearson 31831 Mark P. Timmers 31832 Pedro Marrero 31833 Lester Albert Jung 31834 Joe B. Davis 31835 James Allison Hunt 31836 Mark Jeffrey Dieterle 31837 Earl Alonzo Cooper 31838 William Paul Moline 31839 James William Burke 31840 John James Kreitner 31841 Kevin Michael Rice 31842 Ambrose Francis Cook 31843 Richard Dennis Lyons 31844 Jonathan L. Jacoby 31845 Joseph Anthony Murphy 31846 Peter Joseph Spring 31847 Robert T. Tapp 31848 Daniel Louis Edelstein 31849 Harry Franklin J. Campbell 31850 Richard Mark Weinstock 31851 Charles L. Carville 31852 David Nelson Dulong 31853 Michael John Masterson 31854 Steven Louis Daigle 31855 John O. Innes 31856 Mark Charles Collier 31857 Donald Thomas McMahon 31858 Ronald Scott Ross 31859 Steven Peter Palamar 31860 William John Pokorny 31861 Gregory L. Ervin 31862 Del W. Meincke 31863 Jeffry Stuart McDonald 31864 Richard Michael Maringer 31865 Matthew J. Wotell 31866 Stephen Scott McGill 31867 John Joseph Foster 31868 William Stephen Owens 31869 John Woodland Morris 31870 Donald Vaughn Neel 31871 Joseph Gerard Pallone 31872 Michael David Andrew Bollinger 31873 Daniel Peterjohn 31874 James Christopher Stroble 31875 David Holmes Huntoon 31876 Eric Vann Hinson 31877 William Raymond Sanborn 31878 Mark G. Clouse 31879 Kevin Eugene Finn 31880 Robert Alan Portante 31881 Edwin Leslie Martin 31882 Roy Lee Kelly 31883 David John Griffith 31884 James Mark Torpey 31885 Edward Joseph Grenchus 31886 Clyde Redding Hobby 31887 George Taylor Leatherman 31888 William Harley Held 31889 Lawrence Dennis Edwards 31890 Thomas C. Nunn 31891 Joachim Hagopian 31892 Donald Keith Takami 31893 James Michael Silva 31894 Gregory Allen Pierce 31895 John Edward Dowalgo 31896 John Craig Walsh 31897 Randel B. McIntyre 31898 Charles Smith Coats 31899 Michael Joseph Ruggiero 31900 Vincent Bennett Curasi 31901 James Allen Mitchell 31902 Gordon Russell Mayhew 31903 Glenen Vars Nance 31904 Paul Joseph Rana 31905 Charles Robert Sacrison 31906 Thomas Emery Williams 31907 John Harold Daly 31908 William Joseph Ciccotti 31909 Robert Richard Roe 31910 Daniel Leo Cullinan 31911 Joe F. Furloni 31912 James Robert Cooke 31913 John Robert Tapp 31914 Robert James Sansone 31915 Barry Wayne Woodruff 31916 William R. Orton 31917 Terry Eugene Wiese 31918 James Patrick McArdle 31919 Cletus A. Krater 31920 Kent Hughes Butts 31921 Peter William Kippie 31922 Buckner Lee Garrison 31923 Peter Michael Baldwin 31924 Michael James Shanahan 31925 Joseph Collins Marvil 31926 William Barnwell Gross 31927 Charles Joe Ostrand 31928 William Ira Crisp 31929 Michael D. Flannery 31930 Chris B. Petersen 31931 Harry Christian Ehlers 31932 Edward J. Roubian 31933 Terry Wayne Small 31934 Francis Edward Weiss 31935 Charles Dana Bickford 31936 Raymond Edward Morris 31937 Robert Cornell Aldrich 31938 Richard Lee Atha 31939 Apolonio Bernardino Garcia 31940 Mercer Emory Ferguson 31941 Clifford Christian Volz 31942 Richard Bell 31943 Alton C. McKennon 31944 Edward John Quinnan 31945 F. David Coleman 31946 Michael Lynn Mosier 31947 Michael John Rzeplinski 31948 John Henry Schultz 31949 Franklin Miciat Garabato 31950 William Benjamin Scott 31951 James Vincent Scott 31952 Matthew Augustine Tomasz 31953 Robert Vernon Kurrus 31954 Charles Duane Seaman 31955 William Joseph Handley 31956 Richard Cameron Diehl 31957 Charles Conan St. Mane 31958 James Phillip Schultz 31959 Richard Taliesen Reese 31960 Kim R. Wright 31961 Robert Bryant Jarrell 31962 Michael Joseph Spears 31963 Timothy J. Pfister 31964 Lee Frederick Hediger 31965 Lenwood Robinson 31966 Mark Page Lintz 31967 R. Clinton Miner 31968 Albin F. Irzyk 31969 Brett Hammond Lewis 31970 Foster Fillmore Fountain 31971 Michael Bruce Gaines 31972 John M. Cronin 31973 George Arthur Rollins 31974 Wesley Hughes Schermann 31975 Samuel Ernest Fleming 31976 Frederick Raymond Kenady 31977 Charles Eugene Woodrow 31978 Christopher Allan Torgerson 31979 Craig Alan Vanek 31980 Dallas Frank Britton 31981 Wayne Joseph Piechowiak 31982 Steven Peter Ankley 31983 Bradford Joseph Barker 31984 Ronald H. Milam 31985 Kerry Michael Karnan 31986 Robert Edward Souza 31987 William Thomas Hughes 31988 Charles Truett Crenshaw 31989 Paul Arnold Nelson 31990 Russell Alan Davis 31991 Harold Edward Weinberg 31992 **1974** Ralph Henry Graves 31993 Thomas Edward Rogers 31994 David Aaron Bosse 31995 Paul Konrad Fuhrmeister 31996 Harold Hayes Sullivan 31997 David Andrew Fastabend 31998 Kerry Kirwin Pierce 31999 Richard Douglas Plumley 32000 Thomas Vincent Daula 32001 Paul Michael Webber 32002 Andrew Joseph Green 32003 Robert John Nelson 32004 Larry Arthur Zieske 32005 Edward Andrew Cerutti 32006 James Alexander Mitchell 32007 Clifford Owen Clausen 32008 Jeffrey Wayne Anderson 32009 Thomas Joseph Downar 32010 Thomas James Anthony 32011 Cyrus William Davis 32012 Howard Everett Berner 32013 Robert Morton Metheny 32014 David J. Powell 32015 John Fred Troxell 32016 Dale Bruce Mowry 32017 Willis Freeman Marti 32018 Richard William Morton 32019 Christopher Bradford White 32020 Terry Robert Youngbluth 32021 Robert David Fierro 32022 John David Daigh 32023 Dominic John Izzo 32024 Albert Charles Malich 32025 Jerry T. Mohr 32026 Alan Thair Carver 32027 William Garland Higgs 32028 Merrill S. Blackman 32029 Mark L. Swinson 32030 Robert Steven Alexander 32031 David Howell Petraeus 32032 George Alfred Brown Peirce 32033 Donald Harry Dubia 32034 Thomas E. Hoefert 32035

Stephen Adam Sihelnik 32036 Jonathan P. Adams 32037 Perry Kevin Falk 32038 Eric Paul Fahrenthold 32039 Robert Sibbald Toomy 32040 Alan D. Landry 32041 Michael Richard Uram Clifford 32042 Conrad Charles Crane 32043 Daniel Lawrence French 32044 Stephen Richard Benton 32045 Richard Patrick Pate 32046 John Michael Sapanara 32047 Mark Peter Andreotta 32048 Barry Lee Scribner 32049 Steven Michael Di Silvio 32050 William R. Betson 32051 James Joseph O'Brien 32052 Richard J. Berish 32053 William John Hopkinson 32054 Stephen Alfred LaRocca 32055 Robert Emmet Roetzel 32056 Donald John Demetz 32057 Michael William Luce 32058 Roger L. Goodman 32059 Joseph W. Murphy 32060 James Lawrence Spinelli 32061 Michael Allen Kirby 32062 Timothy Thomas Tanner 32063 Stephan Gregory Smith 32064 Paul Bement Ingalls 32065 James Richard Brettell 32066 Stephen Charles Adams 32067 Eric Robert Wildemann 32068 Stephen Richard Trauth 32069 Bernard Lester Crosby 32070 Bradford Wallace Flora 32071 William Lawrence Conner 32072 John David Norwood 32073 William Watson Doe 32074 Van Eugene Wahlgren 32075 William Tyson Edwards 32076 Lawrence Michael Gehlhausen 32077 Raymond Michael Saunders 32078 Gary Stephen Coleman 32079 James Alan Wright 32080 Donald A. Galvanin 32081 John Weisz 32082 James Edward Thompson 32083 Clarence Auburn Harris 32084 Robert Herbert Thorsen 32085 Richard Lee Vincent 32086 Jeffrey Robert Sommerville 32087 Herbert William Male 32088 James Wallace Pickett 32089 John Richard Miller 32090 Stephen Wayne Houseworth 32091 Martin Henry Joyce 32092 James Stewart Davidson 32093 Peter Leigh Breton 32094 Richard Kirk de Jonckheere 32095 Joseph N. G. LeBoeuf 32096 Mark Wayne Austin 32097 Michael Richard Reopel 32098 Jon Russell Dutcher 32099 Charles Carroll Thebaud 32100 Mark Richard Kindl 32101 John Harmon Bruce Krueger 32102 James Edward Sweetnam 32103 Gene Allen Dickey 32104 Howard Douglas Patrick 32105 Ted Eugene Davis 32106 James Winthrop Fishback 32107 William G. Pierce 32108 Thomas Mellon Froneberger 32109 Richard Fulton Ballard 32110 Michel Lee Deeter 32111 Richard Franklin Norman 32112 Michael Quirante Cosio 32113 Charles T. Letcher 32114 William David Gabbard 32115 William Bernard Moore 32116 William George Mather 32117 John M. Fitzpatrick 32118 Norman Hill Andersson 32119 Michael Brian Kelly 32120 David Allen Bingham 32121 Richard Carl Oertel 32122 Gregory Guy Bean 32123 Robert Edward Bassler 32124 Russell Simmons Wolfe 32125 Robert Cook McFetridge 32126 Edward James Filiberti 32127 David Robert Stinson 32128 Dennis James Blasko 32129 Dwight Edward Morse 32130 Edward Francis Polom 32131 Thomas Patrick Reidy 32132 Samuel William France 32133 Paul Vance Lemley 32134 John Edward Majeroni 32135 John P. Gilmer 32136 Michael Rowen Brown 32137 John Anthony Corey 32138 Stephan Mark Vidmar 32139 John Henry McDonald 32140 Mark William Scott 32141 Reginald Joseph Fadden 32142 Clifford Gerald Barnes 32143 Richard Gary Rowe 32144 Anthony Joseph Stamilio 32145 Daniel Driscall O'Brien 32146 Myron Corbett Lynch 32147 Jeffrey Vance Rogers 32148 Bradley George Magness 32149 Lawrence John Frank 32150 William Thomas Johnsen 32151 Harold Stanton Hedberg 32152 Denis Gerald Rochette 32153 David Paul Rynd 32154 Charles Edward Cobb 32155 Ken Carlyle Hicks 32156 Daniel Joseph McCafferty 32157 Frederick William Stellar 32158 Marvin Scott Haswell 32159 Edwin Michael Perry 32160 David Wayne Buto 32161 Harvey D. Jones 32162 Robert Lynn Minor 32163 Milton Caldwell Spaulding 32164 Patrick Norman Johnson 32165 James Francis Byrne 32166 Thomas Michael McGinnis 32167 James Arthur Relyea 32168 Flayo O. Kirk 32169 Dionisio Aquino De Leon 32170 George Richard Gay 32171 James Reed Loy 32172 William Lee Allinder 32173 Homer James Bash 32174 Gregory Dean Lucas 32175 John Robert Martin 32176 Kim David Jones 32177 John Leopold Czarzasty 32178 Mark Jerome Redlinger 32179 Walter Edward Wentz 32180 Bruce Thomas Palmatier 32181 Gary Ronald Stinnett 32182 James Vincent Mudd 32183 Stephen M. Speakes 32184 Keith B. Alexander 32185 Charles Robert Herrick 32186 Joseph Malcolm Ward 32187 Gordon Wayne Lester 32188 Stephen Allan Shambach 32189 Dwight Antonio Helton 32190 Carl Ellsworth Case 32191 Brian Grosner 32192 Fred Blair Giacometti 32193 Donald Dale Cantwell 32194 Maceo Braxton 32195 Wendell Garcia 32196 Robert John Reese 32197 James Anthony Doyle 32198 Charles Mueller Westenhoff 32199 Glenn James Ruffenach 32200 Ronald Haskell Miller 32201 Stephan Vernon Ottesen 32202 Alan Keith Wright 32203 Thomas Arthur Lengnick 32204 Michael John Detore 32205 Arvidas Kazimieras Jarasius 32206 Martin Bartholomew Giandoni 32207 Morris J. Ingalls 32208 Jay F. Cook 32209 Michael G. Headly 32210 Kenneth Rudolph Buenzow 32211 Edward John Dlugolenski 32212 Joseph Paul Mackin 32213 Marvin Kim Decker 32214 Thomas A. Leahy 32215 Gregory Charles Gardner 32216 Courtnay Salisbury Whitman 32217 Steven Edward Wells 32218 Richard Glenn Binger 32219 James Robert Koenig 32220 Karl John Arunski 32221 Vayl Stanley Oxford 32222 Rex Nowers Osborne 32223 Michael James Bradley 32224 John Robert Herrin 32225 James Campbell Barclay 32226 Michael John Abdo 32227 Clinton D. Blunier 32228 Randall Lee Hughes 32229 Scott Vincent Myers 32230 Gregory Hugh Parlier 32231 David Randall Flyer 32232 Richard Halbert Schwamb 32233 John Alan Schaefer 32234 Donald Charles Seeber 32235 Stephen James Meibers 32236 Bradlee C. Lindsey 32237 James Douglas McMillan 32238 Joseph Stephen Rybczynski 32239 Victor Wallace Roeske 32240 Dale Eugene Hirst 32241 Albert Bryant 32242 Arthur Evan Exten 32243 Michael Eugene Rusho 32244 Christopher Booth Sinclair 32245 Charles Wilson Alexander 32246 Joseph Hunter 32247 Ambrose Robert Hock 32248 Gary Anthony Gorby 32249 George John Desiderio 32250 James Lawrence Laughlin 32251 Mark Edward Stengel 32252 Gregory Alan Schumacher 32253 Timothy Aleck Peterson 32254 Steven John Hashem 32255 Martin Edward Dempsey 32256 Daniel Lee Duncan 32257 Charles William Protasio 32258 James Robert Malcolm 32259 Terry Wade Freeze 32260 Robert Henry Buyson Dela-Cruz 32261 Charles Glen Poure 32262 Robert Bruce Muh 32263 Erik Sven Andren 32264 Thomas Schmidt 32265 John Emery Toth 32266 Jeffrey Noel LeBeau 32267 Kenneth D. Miner 32268 David E. Neely 32269 Jeffrey Joseph Knapp 32270 Robert Jay Kocher 32271 Clayton R. Wheeler 32272 Richard Alfred Kornacki 32273 James Elmer McDaniel 32274 Neil Patrick Krukar 32275 Harry William Rollins 32276 Stephen Michael Hughes 32277 Robert Gottfred Lundquist 32278 Paul Daniel Kure 32279 Phillip Leon Mallory 32280 Robert Milton Gates 32281 Morris Albert Pierce 32282 Richard T. Wallace 32283 Herbert Wilson Wells 32284 Dannie Ki Martz 32285 John Joseph Lacek 32286 Benjamin Guy Withers 32287 Gary Raymond Miller 32288 Thomas Alden Gandy 32289 Donald Morris Proeschel 32290 Allen E. Saum 32291 Vincent J. Connor 32292 William Alan Wolf 32293 Andrew George Ellis 32294 Richard Andrew Kurasiewicz 32295 Robert George Visnovsky 32296 Edward Joseph Lisecki 32297 Alan John Walker 32298 James A. Kelley 32299 John Charles Matousek 32300 Timothy Cyril Tyson 32301 Wayne Richard Kniskern 32302 Robert Eugene Duncan 32303 Mitchell Glenn Craigmile 32304 David Allen Dlugolenski 32305 Charles Peter Sauer 32306 William Ed Parker 32307 Dennis Leslie Phillips 32308 Atis Ojars Jurka 32309 John Grant Sweeney 32310 Alan Michael Przyworski 32311 Robert James Foss 32312 Duane Keith Bickings 32313 Arthur Maurice Herrmann 32314 Jeffrey Wayne Karhohs 32315 Edward Davis Jones 32316 Raymond Eric Peterson 32317 David Story Stevens 32318 Robert Daniel Meyer 32319 Rudy Theodore Veit 32320 Mark Peter Lennon 32321 Donald J. Borje 32322 Charles F. Markley 32323 William E. Myers 32324 William Alexander Burdumy 32325 Jeffrey Romont Ginther 32326 Randall Emil Bruch 32327 Brian Woodbridge Clowes 32328 James Albert O'Rourke 32329 John Anton Van Vleet 32330 James Randell Stratton 32331 Michael Boyden Bearce 32332 Richard Frank Goosen 32333 Mark Thomas Davis 32334 John Alan Minier 32335 Peter Hughes Zeigler 32336 Michael Peter Tulay 32337 Richard Anthony Hornburg 32338 Dennis Craig Brown 32339 Thomas John Weber 32340 Thomas P. Brennen 32341 John Franklin Blanco 32342 Randal William Studer 32343 Mark Alan Bokmeyer 32344 Jerry Wayne Dixon 32345 Kenneth Darrell Hoyle 32346 Timothy Joseph Kiggins 32347 John Wallace Denny 32348 Randal Gerald Tart 32349 Paul Joseph Tafone 32350 Donald A. Harris 32351 Gregory Howard DeVoe 32352 Daniel J. Kulich 32353 Edward Charles Clarke 32354 Dean Edgar Russell 32355 Roy Samuel Hubbard 32356 William Robert Nealson 32357 Gregory Alvin Moore 32358 Frank Albert Libby 32359 William Eugene Albrecht 32360 John P. DeWit 32361 Jeffrey Bretton Smith 32362 Richard Marino Gaudio 32363 James Allen Corman 32364 James Michael Grunseth 32365 David Eugene Rogers 32366 Robert Carl Jewart 32367 Joseph Cline Greer 32368 Randall Laverne Coffelt 32369 Emilio DiGiorgio 32370 Robert Joseph Forman 32371 Robert Chadwick Eagin 32372 Renard Ramon Rozzoni 32373 Robert Ford Hayden 32374 James Allen Blackwell 32375 Gordon Kent Moore 32376 Michael Lloyd Langley 32377 William Robert Sole 32378 Thomas Andrews Bradshaw 32379 Freddy Lee Polk 32380 Robert Mitchell Kimsey 32381 Arthur Howard Moore 32382 Timothy Alan Rippe 32383 George Daniel Hulsey 32384 David B. Cunningham 32385 Louis Vozzo 32386 Ronny Elliot Reid 32387 Dennis Carl Dimengo 32388 Roger Warren Astin 32389 Robert Carrel Anderson 32390 John Francis Shortal 32391 Ronald Anthony Morrell 32392 Robert Calvin Pinson 32393 Jack Edward McGehee 32394 Paul Tage Annis 32395 Maurice Emmett O'Brien 32396 Mark Steven Jensen 32397 William Neal McMillan 32398 Philip D. Coker 32399 Craig Thomas Robinson 32400 Robert Wilbur Mixon 32401 Thomas John Stavridis 32402 Mark Stephen Grazier 32403 Ralph Dennis Holweck 32404 Thomas Erwin Gleason 32405 Theodore Roosevelt Taylor 32406 Christopher Allen O'Reilly 32407 Jeffrey Douglas Cerny 32408 James D. Brown 32409 Steven Charles Sample 32410 James Herbert Bly 32411 James Gregory Gates 32412 Patrick Allen McBrayer 32413 Joe Edward Gonzalez 32414 David Ewing McCracken 32415 Timothy Joseph Tyler 32416 Eric Stephen Paternoster 32417 Thomas R. Turner 32418 Michael Angelo Pantaloni 32419 John Craig Koehler 32420 William Michael Davis 32421 John Emerson Kling 32422 Dennis Wayne Green 32423 Bruce D. Grant 32424 Christopher Lawrence Manos 32425 John Philip Geraci 32426 Craig Paul Wittman 32427 James Troy Chafin 32428 James H. W. Inskeep 32429 John Dennis Hoffman 32430 Timothy Vincent Mahar 32431 Duncan Calvert Turner 32432 Mark Warren Baker 32433 William Leo Reinhart 32434 John Lee Nations 32435 Todd Smith Bacastow 32436 Adrian Donald Robbe 32437 William Ames Fletcher 32438 Bruce Barton Bailey 32439 Michael Patrick McConnell 32440 William Robert Bell 32441 Kevin Marc Lewis 32442 Carles Michael Sitero 32443 Larry E. Milam 32444 Eugene Gerard Barbero 32445 Mark Steven Vincent 32446 Gary Bruce Rodvelt 32447 George P. Fenton 32448 John Michael Haetinger 32449 John Charles Mainwaring 32450 Kenneth David Duhm 32451 Stephen James Leggiero 32452 Gary Ellis Johnsen 32453 Olmedo Alfaro 32454 David William Lambert 32455 Nicholas Peter Jarem 32456 Denis Eugene McGuinness 32457 Gregory Frank Boron 32458 Joseph Jerome Deponai 32459 Stephen John Wiacek 32460 Thomas Edwin Mullen 32461 Merlin Lloyd Miller 32462 Philip Jeffrey Grimm 32463 George F. Oliver 32464 Lawrence Richard Adair 32465 Ralph Anthony Marks 32466 Stephen Alden Monks 32467 Colen K. Willis 32468 Michael L. Raney 32469 Peter James Stuart 32470 James William Wimberley 32471 Robert Lee Cleek 32472 Harry Lloyd Williams 32473 Robert Francis Joyce 32474 Daniel Patrick Mahoney 32475 Ejner Jens Fulsang 32476 Richard James Preece 32477 Roy Powers Crawford 32478 Albert Montgomery Lokey 32479 Jeffery Rand Vollmer 32480 Scott Lewis Shires 32481 Reggie N. Coats 32482 Michael Louis Helferd 32483 Lonnie Edwin Nesrsta 32484 William Morgan Bransford 32485 Bryan Lee Oliver 32486 Keith Bernarr Holmes 32487 Howard C. Renner 32488 Richard Bross 32489 Robert John Williams 32490 Gary Lee Hughes 32491 George Steven Trompak 32492 John Joseph Twohig 32493 James Thomas Barker 32494 Stephen Spencer Geraci 32495 Michael Lee Weidner 32496 Lloyd Mifflin Scott 32497 Dominick Angelo Lovallo 32498 Eric Ross Barnes 32499 William Robert Aldridge 32500 George Thomas Rooksby 32501 Thomas Joseph Palguta 32502 J. Richard Dillon 32503 David Lucas Fowler 32504 Gerald Wayne Topping 32505 David Randall Roemer 32506 Joseph James Fox 32507 Kenneth Lawrence St. Cyr 32508 Gary Nelson Rodriguez 32509 Karl Kuldrian Warner 32510 Kenneth Edward Cross 32511 Thomas K. Eads 32512 Gary Alan Maus 32513 Mark Phillip Joiner 32514 Thomas Robert Goedkoop 32515 Philip Newton Garito 32516 William Sudler Goodhand 32517 Michael Edward Milligan 32518 Joseph Oppus Flores 32519 Paul Kim Rappold 32520 Charles Eric Fardelmann 32521 John Robert Fabry 32522 Vincent Francis O'Connell 32523 Steven James Schenck 32524 Christopher John Wilcox 32525 Richard Charles Galli 32526 Charles Edward White 32527 Patrick Gale Potter 32528 Marvin Stuart Searle 32529 Douglas Alan Darling 32530 Paul Norman Sills 32531 Steve E. Featherstone 32532 Harold Edward Cooney 32533 Michael James Lombardi 32534 Patrick Eugene Pope 32535 Charles Philip Gates 32536 Gregory Dean Burkhart 32537 John Nicholas Aleshin 32538 Walter Lawrence Sharp 32539 William Issiac Chadwick 32540 Charles Bernard Rynearson 32541 Mark Henry Whitman 32542 Paul Pratt Millner 32543 Robert J. Beecher 32544 Dale Arthur Blinten 32545 Dennis R. Lewis 32546 Stephen Dominic Marino 32547 Steve Edward Stone 32548 John R. Hamilton 32549 Ralph Emerson Bower 32550 Brett Gerald Moonen 32551 Peter C. McLaughlin 32552 James A. Coggin 32553 Russell James Goehring 32554 William Aaron Hastie 32555 Donald William Fritz 32556 Steven Thomas Bollens 32557 Daniel Dwight Duesler 32558 Frederick Lowell Thielke 32559 Albert Farrant Turner 32560 Kenneth Michael Kalinich 32561 Matthew P. Reese 32562 Guy Martin Bourn 32563 John Robinson Batiste 32564 Brian William Anderson 32565 Richard John Dameron 32566 Carter Stott Thomas 32567 William Charles Muir 32568 Royce Gene Richardson 32569 Ernest Gilbert Chachere 32570 John Keith Dickerson 32571 Joseph Barker Dance 32572 John David Welt 32573 Charles William Barker 32574 David Fitzhugh Brown 32575 Ashby Minor Foote 32576 Steven Joseph Hargan 32577 Edward J. Toothman 32578 Mark Warren Russell 32579 Steven G. Hanna 32580 Benedict Jackson Beardsley 32581 Theodore Adam Taylor 32582 Robert Edward Dillon 32583 Christopher Lee Sargent 32584 John Francis Sladky 32585 Tam Minh Pham 32586 David Lee Wallinger 32587 Clark Andre Reynolds 32588 Dennis Michael Miller 32589 Frank Louis Prindle 32590 Harvey D. Jones 32591 Terry Bruce Callahan 32592 Carl Bruce McNutt 32593 Robert Joseph Weber 32594 French R. White 32595 Clifford Dane Krebs 32596 Blaine Warren Hyten 32597 Mark Hansley Jackson 32598 James Michael Rossi 32599 Vincent Joseph Mauro 32600 Martin John Svoboda 32601 David Rodarte 32602 John W. McCoy 32603 Martin Lee Robbins 32604 David Walter Thompsen 32605 Colin K. Dunn 32606 Ted Alan Martin 32607 Richard Denis Fetter 32608 George Alfred Runkle 32609 Daniel Anthony Zwack 32610 Siegfried W. Kirchner 32611 David Anthony Keller 32612 Paul Francis O'Sullivan 32613 Richard Alan Corson 32614 Edward Martin Sanders 32615 Roman Ciupak 32616 Timothy R. Rensema 32617 Michael William Rogers 32618 John Warren Ritchhart 32619 Bryan E. Smith 32620 John Scott Walker 32621 Gary Douglas Richmond 32622 Ned Alan Bumgarner 32623 Geary Owen Bauman 32624 Robert W. Richards 32625 Joseph Clarence Bonnet 32626 John Joseph Moore 32627 Terry Ervin Elmore 32628 Robert David Impellizzeri 32629 Mitchell Steven Dossett 32630 John Paul Mulroney 32631 Marlin Anthony Ressler 32632 Paul Richard Clark 32633 David Jeffrey Milidonis 32634 Stephen Michael Peer 32635 Patrick John Cooney 32636 Edward Francis Fagan 32637 Thomas Lansing Snyder 32638 Donald Vincent Harlin 32639 Darryl Rafael Carattini 32640 Byron Donald Canfield 32641 David Alan Mitchell 32642 Curtis W. Medill 32643 Jeffrey C. Richgels 32644 James Dale Martin 32645 Edgar Whitfield Duskin 32646 John Harrison Miller 32647 Cecil Garrenton Batchelor 32648 Richard Willard Madden 32649 Michael Lynn Combest 32650 William Thomas Marsh 32651 Marshall Larry Best 32652 John Walter Kussard 32653 Robert Todd Troxell 32654 William Cesar Fierro 32655 Robert Steven Williams 32656 Robert Carter Scharling 32657 Kerry Richard Parker 32658 Frank Bernard Janoski 32659 Thomas George Wills 32660 James Reagan Mitcham 32661 Clare Hibbs Armstrong 32662 Kurt D. Norman 32663 Charles Peyton Llewellyn 32664 Donald Howard Zacherl 32665 Herman Robert Yezak 32666 Barry Eugene Black 32667 Lucian Stanley Egrid 32668 Christian Paul Kaila 32669 Jeffrey Dean Sachau 32670 William Thurston Kenny 32671 James Michael Kinnaman 32672 Steven Raymond Robinson 32673 William Glenn Webster 32674 Tracy Lee Strickland 32675 Dana Robert Bondy 32676 Albert John Kuehn 32677 Eric Andreas Vonderscheer 32678 Richard Lee Furman 32679 Franklin Ray Taylor 32680 Michael John McCaffrey 32681 Donald Michael Johnson 32682 John William Ulrich 32683 James Alan Burden 32684 Michael Steven Crocker 32685 Russell Gene Quimby 32686 Thomas Jack Bennett 32687 Thomas James O'Leary 32688 Oscar Valentin Ortiz 32689 John Henry Porter 32690 Dale Alan Fletcher 32691 Kenton Howell Hendricks 32692 Timothy Shawn Shaver 32693 Samuel J. Hughes 32694 Rodney Dale Cooley 32695 David Ray Williamson 32696 Edward L. Fox 32697 Jerry Dwayne Johnson 32698 Dennis Joseph Mahoney 32699 Theodore John Lombard 32700 Alvah Lee Skaggs 32701 Stephen L. Brown 32702 David Andrew Shelden 32703 Matthew Stephen Klimow 32704 James Francis Cisek 32705 Michael Dale Dotson 32706 J. Kingsley Fink 32707 Julio Enrique Sanjines 32708 Louis Gelling 32709 Leonard Charles Peters 32710 James Lee Dixon 32711 Brian Irwin Geehan 32712 Dennis Lee Patrick 32713 Jeffrey Thomas Kallman 32714 James Brewton Millard 32715 James F. Ellington 32716 French L. MacLean 32717 Kim Allen Jacobs 32718 Steve Wayne Stevenson 32719 Anthony Bernard Petruzzi 32720 Douglas Williams Markel 32721 Sean Anthony Murray 32722 Nathan S. Mamura 32723 Charles Conrad Gleichenhaus 32724 Layton Robert Bull 32725 Francisco A. Sablan 32726 Jack Robert Kromer 32727 Lee Arnold Van Arsdale 32728 James Franklin Grim 32729 James Timothy Soncrant 32730 Richard Joseph Neske 32731 Joseph Frankie 32732 Jack Edward Pattison 32733 Michael David Wallace 32734 Glenn Allen Taylor 32735 Constantine George Mourtos 32736 Patrick Arthur Schado 32737 Winfield W. Scott 32738 Richard Lyle Phillips 32739 Douglas Farris Mow 32740 John Carroll Rivers 32741 Charles Kevin Tobin 32742 William Joseph Martinez 32743 David Lyle Hohnstine 32744 Douglas Christopher Cathcart 32745 Charles Gregory Kuklenski 32746 William J. Spencer 32747 Harold Dale Barnett 32748 Lawrence Charles Bethel 32749 Edward Rodney Ramey 32750 Frank Needham Roberts 32751 Leonard Irvin Huskey 32752 Robert Michael Humphreys 32753 Clark Bogh Sorensen 32754 David Edward Siegel 32755 Dwight Stuart Webster 32756 Andrew Marcus Knight 32757 Wilson Grooms 32758 James Thomas Sharp 32759 Thomas J. Loisel 32760 Warren Ballew 32761 Robert S. Silva 32762 David A. Molten 32763 Glenn F. Wilkinson 32764 Robert A. Hass 32765 Donald D. Jenkins 32766 Peter J. Martin 32767 Thomas N. Hinkel 32768 Antonio W. Messina 32769 Andrew Carl Nordby 32770 Terry L. Barton 32771 John C. Edgecomb 32772 Gary Michael Pestrak 32773 Champe W. Miller 32774 Craig M. Huffman 32775 Dennis L. Bilter 32776 Dennis L. Gum 32777 Kenneth C. Popielis 32778 John D. Walls 32779 Allan A. Banks 32780 James A. Vestermark 32781 David A. Deykes 32782 Gary W. Roberts 32783 George Paul Prate 32784 Robert J. Landseadel 32785 Thomas M. Harrison 32786 John L. Otte 32787 Paul B. Miller 32788 Michael J. Campo 32789 David J. Cronin 32790 Jimmie D. King 32791 Hy S. Rothstein 32792 Scott Larrabee 32793 Gary J. Anderson 32794 James MacMahan Hogan 32795 Victor A. Pasini 32796 Donald J. McGrath 32797

Keith P. Saddler 32798 Kenneth E. Webber 32799 Gerald W. Williams 32800 Robert R. Donoho 32801 John M. Draper 32802 Michael L. Tixier 32803 Joe R. Miller 32804 Edward M. Yeterian 32805 Edmund Ludger Chabot 32806 Allen L. Sample 32807 Gerard R. Markham 32808 Patrick Andrew Thomas 32809 Fred P. Borman 32810 Oliver H. Hunter 32811 Darryl C. Carroll 32812 Adrian C. Conley 32813 W. Douglas Shaw 32814 Stephen P. Arn 32815 David J. Herbison 32816 Douglas O. Crewse 32817 Gary T. Bishop 32818 Jesse A. McCorvey 32819 Danny R. Deaver 32820 David L. Burget 32821 James W. Ward 32822 Gregory A. Butson 32823 Larry Denis Moore 32824 Dennis J. Frisco 32825 **1975** John Moore McMurray 32826 Daniel W. Krueger 32827 Robert Elias Mockos 32828 Peter Lorentz Guth 32829 Robert John Bonometti 32830 Allen Gail Plumley 32831 Scott Louis Christensen 32832 Howe Preston Cochran 32833 Philip Julian Freeman 32834 Michael Wayne Wimmer 32835 John Henry Hug 32836 William Harley Venema 32837 Robert Alan McDonald 32838 Eric Jeffrey Zeidman 32839 Paul Steven Schaefer 32840 John Alexander Hook 32841 David Earle Johnston 32842 Timothy Horne Parker 32843 Robert William Enzenauer 32844 Robin Bradley Sellers 32845 William Patrick Cody 32846 Peter T. Madsen 32847 Richard Stanley Tokarz 32848 Stephen Paul Hetz 32849 Howard James Bush 32850 David John Rehbein 32851 Michael Luis Dominguez 32852 Gary Douglas Niederlander 32853 William Thomas Highfill 32854 Robert Albert Dunn 32855 James Jude Attaya 32856 Stephen Edward Lord 32857 William Marcus Morgan 32858 James Henry Algeo 32859 Brian Patrick Carr 32860 Alan Scott Rogers 32861 Harold David Pontious 32862 David Frank Pursell 32863 James Clyde Johns 32864 Michael Wayne Cannon 32865 Leonard A. Alt 32866 Lynn Merle Wahlgren 32867 James Michael Wark 32868 Walter Verle Lowe 32869 Edward Murray Bradford 32870 David J. Frenier 32871 Douglas Edward Lute 32872 Michael Rudolph Simone 32873 Michael A. Spasyk 32874 Dale Alan Dvorak 32875 David Owens Rittenhouse 32876 William Dale Ivey 32877 Robert Edward Johnson 32878 David Robert Ridenour 32879 Philip Leon Salmon 32880 Sheldon John Bruce 32881 Thomas Aloysius Holden 32882 Brian Douglas Fitzpatrick 32883 Joseph Schroedel 32884 Thomas Augustine Berens 32885 Thomas Henry Wallace 32886 Bruce Cameron Tyson 32887 Mike McBiles 32888 David Carl Ruck 32889 Patrick William Peter Lisowski 32890 Russell William Glenn 32891 Daniel George Heine 32892 Larry Eugene Hartman 32893 Gerald Wilson Cauley 32894 Harold A. Floyd 32895 Thomas Michael Howard 32896 Michael Steven McCall 32897 Charles Benjamin Skaggs 32898 Gregory N. Bender 32899 Edward Charles Shaffer 32900 Patrick Gerard Findlay 32901 John Martin Ruzicka 32902 John V. Rathbone Redington 32903 William John Barattino 32904 Raymond Kazmin Perkins 32905 Stephen Compton Moore 32906 Patrick Michael Owens 32907 Richard Edward Zak 32908 Steven Roy Grimes 32909 Robert Louis Smith 32910 Kerry Lynn Cailteux 32911 John Jeffrey Cimral 32912 Ricky Etcyel Boyd 32913 Michael Charles Strathearn 32914 Michael Francis Smith 32915 John Lawrence Lane 32916 Lynn Averil Westbrook 32917 Douglas Ashby Campbell 32918 Peter James Ferrara 32919 Thomas Richard Grubbs 32920 Matthew Dale Richardson 32921 Patrick John Dolan 32922 James William Yocum 32923 Timothy Shane Muchmore 32924 Howard Edwin Barton 32925 J. Scott Lewis 32926 James DeWitt Wisenbaker 32927 Michael Anthony Vane 32928 Stephen Matthew Remmert 32929 Ennis Clement Whitehead 32930 Robert James O'Neill 32931 Bill Thomas Whitesel 32932 Roger Kaplan 32933 Michael Douglas Fletcher 32934 Kevin Norris Wardlow 32935 Stephen Glenn Branscom 32936 Michael Sam Smith 32937 Joseph John Manzo 32938 Joseph Graham Dodd 32939 Gary Michael Koenig 32940 Edwin Albert Murdock 32941 Richard Allen Hoefert 32942 Michael Errol Haith 32943 Donald Harry Luzius 32944 James Kevin Abcouwer 32945 Ray Riddle 32946 Patrick John Gallagher 32947 Michael Thomas Ostrom 32948 Thomas Roger Noreen 32949 Steven Norwood Read 32950 John Patrick Leake 32951 Michael Lynn Lee 32952 Stephen Charles Ellis 32953 David Wesley Milton 32954 Thomas Raleigh Clark 32955 Michael A. Killham 32956 Danny Eugene Stroud 32957 Leonardo Victor Flor 32958 Gary Alan Mitchell 32959 Bradley Charles Hall 32960 David W. Washechek 32961 Stephen Bellene 32962 Thomas Reaves Douglas 32963 Gerard Thomas Hopkins 32964 David Ernest Geck 32965 Dennis Robert Kelley 32966 Gustave Hill Murby 32967 Paul Lawrence Peterson 32968 John Gregory Rice 32969 William Charles Weber 32970 Robert Wesley Hayes 32971 Emil Joseph Menk 32972 Charles Gary Rodriguez 32973 Daniel John Bonney 32974 James Michael Rigsby 32975 Glenn David McDermott 32976 Albert Stedman Wedemeyer 32977 Steven Fredrick Westfall 32978 Carl Kenji Aoki 32979 Anthony Thomas Rowan 32980 John David Brandt 32981 Ronald Anderson 32982 Malachy Patrick McGree 32983 Reinhard Albert Ratz 32984 William Charles Lloyd 32985 Peter King Fiorey 32986 Robert Edward Hoopes 32987 Donald Eugene Ramsey 32988 Joseph Francis Scalo 32989 Alan Jeffrey Renne 32990 Michael David Lorenz 32991 Joseph B. McCutcheon 32992 Mark Oliver Oetken 32993 William Curtis David 32994 Robert Vincent Walsh 32995 Mark Edward Heinen 32996 Timothy Lorn Bates 32997 Robert Michael Byers 32998 David John Schumann 32999 Douglas Colcock Lenz 33000 Steven George Fruscella 33001 Raymond Earl Garvey 33002 Donald Angelo Gagliano 33003 Charles Nethercott Cardinal 33004 Paul Robert Martin 33005 John Norman Davis 33006 Gordon Douglas Toney 33007 Michael Curtis Burnette 33008 John Herbert Carpenter 33009 John Mark Beeman 33010 Romeo De La Rosa Posadas 33011 Frederick D. G. Williams 33012 Cary Winthrop Mehlenbeck 33013 Richard Joseph Jardine 33014 Larry Lynn Ghormley 33015 Charles Albert Peddy 33016 Nicholas John Kolar 33017 Robert Michael Palatka 33018 Thomas Jones Huey 33019 Thomas K. Littlefield 33020 Daniel Robert Judy 33021 George Thomas Cherolis 33022 Tom Eugene Warren 33023 Jeffrey Hunter Boatright 33024 Stephen Charles Stacey 33025 Steven Gilbert Guthrie 33026 Gilberto Martell Lopez 33027 Richard Dale Cantwell 33028 Bruce Kevin Adams 33029 Francis Gabriel Caputo 33030 James L. Cain 33031 Griffith Scott Hughes 33032 Corydon Murray Loomis 33033 Joseph Henry Barget 33034 Jimmy Dean Swanson 33035 Larry Glen Baker 33036 Harry Ruel Byrd 33037 William Clair Britton 33038 Jerald Alpaugh Jones 33039 James Blake Myers 33040 Michael John Ulekowski 33041 Hilario Jose Ramirez 33042 Robert Alan Strom 33043 Donald Gerard Taylor 33044 Sidney R. Killebrew 33045 Royce Johnson Kincaid 33046 John Michael Uhorchak 33047 Mitchell Ray Lee 33048 Neil Warren Ahle 33049 Frank Di Domenico 33050 George Martin Scheets 33051 Raymond Mark Oscar 33052 John Frazer Brewer 33053 Richard Donald Lineburg 33054 William Joseph Troy 33055 John Baltzly Garver 33056 Richard Daniel Buckley 33057 Thomas M. Hogan 33058 Bernard Livingston Spence 33059 Alfred Perle 33060 William James Partridge 33061 James Eubank Armstrong 33062 William Ward Watkin 33063 Michael Anthony Collura 33064 Jeffrey Ray Gardner 33065 Mark Russell Girolamo 33066 William Joseph Reid 33067 Steven J. Benkufski 33068 Stephen L. Ward 33069 Leslie Norman Heddleston 33070 Richard John Doran 33071 Edward Olen Garland 33072 Thomas Claire Fiser 33073 Gary Francis Clark 33074 Kevin Charles Conlon 33075 James Keatley Given 33076 David Albert Bear 33077 Mark Owen Hehmeyer 33078 James Francis Trout 33079 Andrew Thomas Hamlin 33080 Michael Peter Weinstein 33081 Thomas Loren Oetjen 33082 Michael Edward Keller 33083 Willard Francis Quirk 33084 Charles William Rogers 33085 Gary Martin Bishop 33086 Harry Mohr Starn 33087 Jan Conrad Le Kander 33088 Charles Gregory Walls 33089 Robert Lynn Frank 33090 William Sidney Vogel 33091 Jared Glenn Menzie 33092 Charles Miloye Vuckovic 33093 David William Brooks 33094 Charles Edward Leal 33095 Karl J. Gunzelman 33096 Clark Lynn 33097 David Keith Bethea 33098 John Darwin Kilian 33099 Michael Dana Heredia 33100 Bart Douglas Cook 33101 Samuel Chew Powell 33102 William John Kay 33103 Robert Raymond Reynolds 33104 Charles Eric Diener 33105 Kenton Ray Canny 33106 Jose Arnaldo Picart 33107 James Brian Raney 33108 Gregory John List 33109 Scott Edward Mooney 33110 Leslie Haruo Nishida 33111 David Patrick Coughran 33112 Raymond Eugene Menard 33113 David Adrian Bentley 33114 Keith Alan Self 33115 John Mayland McFarland 33116 Gerald Norman Lebel 33117 Marvin Wayne Harrison 33118 Scott Biddle Huxel 33119 Joseph Earl Langan 33120 James Ira Pettit 33121 John Speer Peterson 33122 Cornelius Gabriel Begley 33123 Dean Lawrence Ashbaugh 33124 Steven Michael Strickland 33125 Carl Arthur Provencher 33126 Michael David Snyder 33127 John Stephen Backof 33128 Dean Eric Dickey 33129 Samuel John Hubbard 33130 Frederic Edward Abt 33131 William Scott Reed 33132 Randal R. Castro 33133 Robert James Harren 33134 Vernon Charles Bice 33135 Keith M. Huber 33136 John Allen Adams 33137 John Patrick Fiedler 33138 Robert Foster Webb 33139 Clifford Eric Nakayama 33140 Daniel Robert Alexander 33141 Michael David Tigner 33142 John William Talbot 33143 Frank Kolar 33144 Timothy Nick Bolyard 33145 Joseph Floyd Wilhelm 33146 Charles Wesley Ford 33147 John Clyde Schoonover 33148 Bruce James Yelverton 33149 Lee Edwin Quisenberry 33150 Robert Francis Acevedo 33151 Peter Craig Anderson 33152 James Gregory Tharp 33153 Norman Earl Stone 33154 Robert George Boyko 33155 Henry Spillman Evans 33156 Patrick Kevin Keating 33157 Steven Michael Harnois 33158 Alaric Gregory Fine 33159 James Daniel Klemashevich 33160 Carl Eugene Gerhiser 33161 Darryl James Egler 33162 Robert W. Dace 33163 Lawyn Clayton Edwards 33164 Fred Eric Dierksmeier 33165 George C. Harris 33166 Thomas Michael Pirog 33167 James Phyletus Williams 33168 James Courtney Morris 33169 Norman Gustaf Benson 33170 James Matlack Hughes 33171 Leonard Wood Pardue 33172 Duane Herbert Bjorlin 33173 Craig Bradley Hanford 33174 William Randolph Repass 33175 James Rupert Coffey 33176 Hugh Harnett Thomas 33177 Jeffrey Kent Ilseman 33178 Schaun H. Mobley 33179 James Lester Smith 33180 Patrick Edward Devens 33181 Robert Donald Merkl 33182 Harry William Jarnagan 33183 Timothy Peter Wasilition 33184 Jean-Luc Marcel Nash 33185 Jay Richard Bishop 33186 Trenton George Keeble 33187 Gary Merle Nicholas 33188 John Alt Crumplar 33189 Michael Anthony Colotti 33190 Bruce William Potter 33191 Michael R. Kershner 33192 Michael Hughes O'Brien 33193 Lee Douglas Lowrey 33194 Daniel Elliott Kinsey 33195 Louis Joseph Kovar 33196 David Nace Purcell 33197 Kenneth Stephen Kasprisin 33198 David Alan Thomas 33199 John Larkin Whisler 33200 Richard Bruce Anderson 33201 George Eugene Schrlau 33202 Kenneth Dale Beatty 33203 Raymond Eugene Johnson-Ohla 33204 Francis John O'Nell 33205 David James Whitney 33206 Joseph Weldon Parker 33207 George Henry Hazel 33208 John Richard Dornstadter 33209 David Gilbert Ford 33210 Robert Carl Nelson 33211 John William Pennington 33212 George Walter Koontz 33213 Ralph Dale Ghent 33214 James Parker Glasser 33215 Wayne Francis Chalupa 33216 Michael Robert Williams 33217 Theodore Garcia Osuniga 33218 Stephen Paul Beever 33219 James Matthew La Rivee 33220 Thomas Earl Richwine 33221 Keith William McNeely 33222 Salvatore John Colatarci 33223 Mark Siemer 33224 Sloan Duncan Gibson 33225 Daniel Dannecker Drummond 33226 John Robert Gilbert 33227 Leocadio Muniz 33228 Joseph Thomas Boylan 33229 John Scott Furman 33230 Charles Oliver Hammond 33231 Dan H. Hubbard 33232 Wayne Ford Hallgren 33233 Terrence Colin Campbell 33234 Dennis Michael Gassert 33235 Charles Barrett Haver 33236 Jay Steven Gruskowski 33237 Dale Alan Green 33238 John Joseph Tilley 33239 John Mark Sidoni 33240 Robert E. Durbin 33241 Dale Steven Cederle 33242 John Louis De Troye 33243 Gerald Danforth Hill 33244 Ralph Douglas Smith 33245 Daniel Anthony Fey 33246 Thomas Hunt St. Onge 33247 Gerald Patrick Kelley 33248 Gilbert Evans Mestler 33249 Russell Maynard Musser 33250 Eric Gordon Troup 33251 James Paul Jarvis 33252 James Russell Isaacs 33253 Donald Bruce Smith 33254 David Patrick Arthur Bentley 33255 Kevin Scott Wilson 33256 John Frederick Burnett 33257 John Francis Craven 33258 James Morris Grayson 33259 Bradley McLean Harris 33260 Bruce Anthony Casella 33261 Norman Frederick Reinhardt 33262 Frank Edward Holland 33263 Glenn Douglas Newell 33264 Michael Gregory Genetti 33265 John P. McMullen 33266 John E. Davis 33267 Randall Carl Robertson 33268 William J. A. O'Brien 33269 Douglas T. Wray 33270 Daniel O. Westover 33271 Jerry R. Bolzak 33272 Dennis J. Parrinello 33273 Robin W. Van Deusen 33274 David H. Meisell 33275 Douglas Rives Brown 33276 James E. Hicks 33277 George J. Mitchell 33278 E. Carl Barthelson 33279 Ephraim Martin 33280 Olaf Lee Elton 33281 James E. Erdly 33282 Ramon Nava 33283 Stephen P. Walsh 33284 Bruce R. Wells 33285 Dean Silverberg 33286 Barry K. Pepper 33287 James Michael Olsen 33288 Gerald Leland Buckner 33289 Leonard A. Grasso 33290 Loren Dumas Porr 33291 Denny Dumas Dresch 33292 John Stephen Chappell 33293 Ross William Weber 33294 James Ashmore Marks 33295 William Martin Campsey 33296 James Michael Missler 33297 Porcher L. Engle Taylor 33298 Peter Edward Haglin 33299 August J. Fucci 33300 Noel Thomas Jones 33301 David Butler McCrady 33302 David Jeffrey Thomas 33303 Lawrence Robert Haller 33304 Robert Louis Caslen 33305 Steven Randall Lollis 33306 Marshall Tupper Hillard 33307 William Henry Cleckner 33308 Gregory Auldredge Howard 33309 Ronald Richard Baynes 33310 Robert Ernest McNulty 33311 Charles Kimberly Hunt 33312 Keith Douglas Gordon 33313 Timothy Robert Kish 33314 Robert Alan Haviland 33315 Miguel Diaz Laffosse 33316 Steven R. Montgomery 33317 Richard Lee Swetman 33318 Michael John Fitzgerald 33319 Randy Charles Wright 33320 Ernest William Neilsen 33321 Glenn Scott Davis 33322 James H. Gerberman 33323 Edward John Grimm 33324 Patrick John O'Connor 33325 Harry Critz Hardy 33326 Luigi Richard Magnanti 33327 George Henry Andrews 33328 Peter Thomas Farrell 33329 Gerald James Hayes 33330 Stephen D. Townes 33331 Bradley Peter Coury 33332 Gregory John Moldovan 33333 Michael Charles Schulze 33334 William Michael Kociscak 33335 Robert Louis Johnson 33336 William Joseph Blankmeyer 33337 James Luke McIntyre 33338 Michael Larmas Smith 33339 Bart Davis Keiser 33340 Ralph Voss Showers 33341 William Wayne Wittman 33342 Gary Marvin Hale 33343 Jamie Devon Clark 33344 Howard Tayloe Styron 33345 William Dean Lewis 33346 William J. Wooley 33347 Mark James Novara 33348 Dell Harrison Nunaley 33349 Philip Jeffrey Edwards 33350 Charles Morgan Byrne 33351 David Charles White 33352 Jeffrey Scott Perry 33353 Ioane Keehu 33354 Richard Joseph Pevoski 33355 Rudolph Daguio Acojedo 33356 John William Mode 33357 David N. Blackledge 33358 Clyde Douglas Blankenship 33359 Bruce Alan Neese 33360 David Lawrence Macintire 33361 Malcolm Taylor Acree 33362 Lance Douglas Jordan 33363 Thomas Edward Eccleston 33364 Lynn Maynard McCrum 33365 Robert Flippin Burris 33366 James Frederick Benn 33367 Robert Samuel Berlin 33368 Gary Dennis Bauleke 33369 Thomas Patrick Connors 33370 Martin Amasisa Briggs-Hall 33371 Fred Richard Place 33372 Richard Howard Langhorst 33373 Gregory James Samson 33374 Edward Harrell Woodbery 33375 James Joseph Dunphy 33376 Michael John Hamilton 33377 Victor Macias 33378 James Patrick Pottorff 33379 William Franklin Hoffman 33380 Roger Henry Veenstra 33381 Dan Trimble 33382 Ben Flo Collins 33383 David Michael Annen 33384 Peter Francis Larson 33385 Joseph John Hennessy 33386 David Thomas Clark 33387 Benjamin Clark Freakley 33388 Dale Martin Petroff 33389 Malcolm Owen Everett 33390 William Forrest Crain 33391 Norman Grady Walker 33392 Terry Lee Shapiro 33393 Gregory William Ellison 33394 Alan August Tomson 33395 James John Maye 33396 Glen Steven Rowe 33397 Timothy Francis Sugrue 33398 Edward McCleave Dannemiller 33399 Mark Phillip Hertling 33400 Philip Joseph Baker 33401 James Scott Hoffman 33402 Henry A. Umanos 33403 Clarence Michael Hart 33404 Arthur Joseph Farrington 33405 John Joseph McNally 33406 Henry Frederick McCourt 33407 Bruce David Bachus 33408 Thomas Charles Wallace 33409 Van-George Raymond Belanger 33410 Joseph Andrew Kotch 33411 Michael John Scoba 33412 Dougald MacMillan 33413 Richard David Tellier 33414 Robert Walter Simons 33415 Neil Louis Putz 33416 Paul Michael Bonney 33417 Michael Louis Franklin Slavin 33418 Craig Douglas Jung 33419 Arthur Clinton Harrold 33420 Bruce Charles Haas 33421 Dennis John Manganiello 33422 Lawrence Donald Murphy 33423 Darryl Loyd Harris 33424 Marc Andrew Polzella 33425 George John Kaigh 33426 Thomas Alan Helms 33427 Paul Charles Parkins 33428 James Paul Pope 33429 Gregory Paul Holder 33430 David Bruce Edmonds 33431 John S. Sapienza 33432 James William Harris 33433 Kenneth William Hunzeker 33434 John Joseph Deacon 33435 John Lee Nance 33436 Dan Thomas Hitchcock 33437 Mark Evin Readinger 33438 Melvin F. Bennett 33439 Bernard Martin Farmer 33440 Robert Edward Johnson 33441 Jeffrey Robert Gillig 33442 Wade Owen Popovich 33443 Laurence Edward Thomas 33444 Frank Drummond Taylor 33445 Brent Lewis Clark 33446 Roderick Michael Pinkney 33447 Joseph Newton Jaggers 33448 Joseph E. Wasiak 33449 Jack G. Gulden 33450 Peter Ray Ramsberger 33451 Clarence Russell Hunley 33452 Patrick Andrew Pollard 33453 Stephan Joseph Tonello 33454 David Patrick Sykora 33455 Charles Larry Hamil 33456 Michael Wayne Means 33457 Charles Benjamin Lee 33458 John P. Mitcham 33459 Gerard Michael Johnson 33460 Bruce Wayne Hulsart 33461 Leonard Matthews Finley 33462 Earl Augustus Johnson 33463 Manuel Eduardo Gonzalez 33464 Chester Lee Smith 33465 Daniel D. Cappell 33466 James R. Taylor 33467 Bruce James Donlin 33468 Ralph Dean Antes 33469 David Gardner Loeschner 33470 Robert Pratt Ronne 33471 Vincent Joyce Scully 33472 Alan Kent Wagner 33473 John Dibble Vosilus 33474 Thomas Edward Lastoskie 33475 William Vernon Williams 33476 Edward Blake Anderson 33477 Henry William Suchting 33478 Mark Gordon Smith 33479 Albert B. Brown 33480 Joaquin Ricardo Ventura 33481 Kelly Daniel Monahan 33482 Andrew J. Stanley 33483 Mark Rogers Hatley 33484 Richard S. Gourley 33485 Ward Lance Jones 33486 Jeffrey Scott Hill 33487 Austin R. Omlie 33488 David Thomas DiGiacinto 33489 Bruce Arland Messinger 33490 Stephen MacRae Sanders 33491 John Peter Klepich 33492 Frederick Raymond Harvey 33493 Michael Alan Kirby 33494 William Thomas Downs 33495 Jack H. Cage 33496 Douglas Wayne Dupree 33497 Paul Wesley Leake 33498 Fred Dean Gianakouros 33499 Eugene Gordon Piasecki 33500 Thomas Glen Ayers 33501 Chris Stephen Ferguson 33502 Michael Richard Conners 33503 John Robert Lynes 33504 Richard W. Baldwin 33505 Martin Russell Conrad 33506 James Halim Burton 33507 Richard Wilson Groves 33508 Jeffrey Clyde Akamatsu 33509 Dennis Keith Lockard 33510 Larry Duane Gibbs 33511 Kevin Wayne Gaylor 33512 Forest Dean Williams 33513 Philip Robert Range 33514 Phillip Randolph Nelson 33515 Peter Bruce Marion 33516 Ricky Don McClure 33517 Philip Sloan Brewster 33518 Timothy David Williams 33519 Cody Steven Scace 33520 Robert Paul Busick 33521 Charles E. Motson 33522 William Henry McCowan 33523 Thomas Kevin Danaher 33524 Alfred Emanuel S. Burkhard 33525 Edwin Jeffrey Van Keuren 33526 Wells Kormann 33527 Barry Ames Rider 33528 James Jerome Davis 33529 Jimmy M. Rabon 33530 Robert August McNab 33531 Walter Philip Schaefer 33532 John A. Florio 33533 Kurt William Hansen 33534 Steven H. Garland 33535 Dennis James O'Rorke 33536 Lloyd James Austin 33537 Michael Robert Nichols 33538 Stephen Lee Pospisil 33539 Donald Lee Mooney 33540 Roy R. Allison 33541 David Willis Tate 33542 Steven Cary Ptacek 33543 Johnathan Earl Byrd 33544 David Anthony Morris 33545 Carl Harold South 33546 Vernon Michael Peters 33547 Gregory C. Fogg 33548 George Douglass Clark 33549 Donald William Browne 33550 Mark Thomas Dunaiski 33551 Thomas Paul Ryan 33552 Douglas Penn Stickley 33553 Rick Aslanian 33554 Peter Charles Kinney 33555 Nicholas Ronald Johnsen 33556 Edward Kevin Maney 33557 Victor J. Bero 33558 Craig Charles

Cunningham 33559 Robert Jeffrey Henning 33560 David Raymond Preast 33561 James Elwood Bonine 33562 Steven Harold Wallace 33563 John Frederick Cosgrove 33564 Gary Wayne Combs 33565 Allan George Dyer 33566 Robert James Coleman 33567 Christopher James Gaston 33568 Elmer Gary Glade 33569 Stephen Joseph Bittner 33570 John Arthur Hodges 33571 William Richard Thornton 33572 Charles J. Brady 33573 William Robert Aultman 33574 John Edward Boehmler 33575 Dorian Trent Anderson 33576 Douglas Michael Chesnulovitch 33577 Daniel Lawrence Monken 33578 Thomas Judson Hale 33579 Doyle Joseph Weishar 33580 Michael Ray Girrard 33581 John Cofer Dashiell 33582 David Francis Miles 33583 John Robert McConnell 33584 Robert Laughlin Dyke 33585 Melvin Lee DeVilbiss 33586 Richard Frederick Machamer 33587 Eric Ross Cunningham 33588 Francis Patrick McGarry 33589 Craig Lindsley Smith 33590 Vincent Francis Gwiazdowski 33591 Robert Judson Goodman 33592 Dean Edward Morningstar 33593 Johnie Ray McAlister 33594 William Richard Kline 33595 John Smith Lough 33596 James Kenneth Woolery 33597 David Birch Morris 33598 David Gregory Emswiler 33599 Ronald Anthony Cheese 33600 Roger Edward Cawthon 33601 Anthony John Cerri 33602 Gary Lee Williams 33603 Ronald Bryan Smith 33604 David Joseph Duncavage 33605 Brian Francis Haig 33606 Gary Pearce Melton 33607 David Lee Maas 33608 Patrick VanSchoyck 33609 Thomas Mowrey Fix 33610 Ossie B. Boddie 33611 David Joseph Buckley 33612 Bruce Joseph Ray 33613 Albert P. Lawson 33614 Ronald Lloyd Olney 33615 James Thomas Lockwood 33616 Mark Stephen Burington 33617 Keith Allen Sims 33618 Scott Kevin Johnson 33619 Michael John Cooley 33620 Myles Herbert Mierswa 33621 Terry Higdon Byce 33622 Jeffrey Lee Duncan 33623 Carl James Carrano 33624 Robert Steven Furst 33625 Barrington Montinez Armstrong 33626 Paul Edward Moran 33627 Marc L. Cates 33628 Lewis Townsend Wray 33629 Carl Robert Johnson 33630 Bruce Edward Jablonski 33631 Frank Andrew Mrak 33632 Rawskia Bradley 33633 Lorenzo J. Kelly 33634 Ralph Frederick D'Elosua 33635 John Robert Bailey 33636 Joseph D. Jones 33637 Robert Estes Grossman 33638 George Earl Sanford 33639 Barry Michoel Ward 33640 Patrick Dominic Hanly 33641 Robert Gary Schumpert 33642 Sidney Jerome Lewis 33643 Derwood Willhite 33644 Robert Russell Hadden 33645 Ronald P. Conley 33646 Mark H. Sweberg 33647 Charles Lane Beaudry 33648 Allan Dean Fehlings 33649 James Vincent Slavin 33650 Thomas Matthew Gross 33651 Enrico Alcide Mazzoli 33652 Norman Christopher Jordan 33653 Donald F. Hartung 33654 Thomas Adam Austin 33655 Dempsey Norbert Darrow 33656 Alan Barry Neidermeyer 33657 Edwin Sloan Borman 33658 Claude William Shipley 33659 Douglas Samuel Frazier 33660 Brian Mark Ludera 33661 Willie Lee Thigpen 33662 Richard Patrick Conniff 33663 Steven Paul Schook 33664 John D. Fischer 33665 Joseph Goldberg 33666 Alan Michael Batey 33667 Michael Donald Blom 33668 David Le Roi Williams 33669 Robert Steven Miske 33670 William Herbert Thrasher 33671 Harry Frank Weiskopf 33672 George Thomas Reynolds 33673 Eugene Emmett Shaw 33674 Randy Roland Rapp 33675 Robert Evans Patton 33676 Roger Mark Hamilton 33677 Ronald Ralph Richard 33678 Sam S. Walker 33679 Daniel Bruce Coles 33680 Darrell Wylie Edge 33681 Kenneth Lowell Decker 33682 Stanley Arthur Dickerson 33683 Francis Charles Baker 33684 Rickie L. Coston 33685 Joseph Thomas Corbett 33686 Kenneth Joseph George 33687 **1976** Danny Mac Davis 33688 Charles Manley Allen 33689 Justin Severance Huscher 33690 Thomas Rowland Thomas 33691 Bruce A. Berwick 33692 William Bartlett Newnam 33693 Michael John O'Donnell 33694 Clark Keith Ray 33695 John Byron McDaniel 33696 Ian Murchie Thompson 33697 Peter Hastings Greenman 33698 John Ember Sterling 33699 David Frederic Melcher 33700 Neil Francis Hasson 33701 John Manuel Cal 33702 James George Diehl 33703 Richard B. Jackson 33704 Stephen Allan Hanson 33705 David Wayne Hutchison 33706 Albert August Drewke 33707 John Christopher Brown 33708 Bruce V. Jackan 33709 Gregory Lester Schmitz 33710 David Lawrence Hayden 33711 Joseph Michael Schuessler 33712 William Edward Eichinger 33713 Richard Morales 33714 Dale Thomas Moeller 33715 Michael Ray Morris 33716 Douglas Raymond Koenig 33717 Scott Wahlgren MacKay 33718 William Clayton Harrington 33719 Dennis Michael Murphy 33720 Albert Shipman Freeman 33721 Carl Jens Stevens 33722 Foster Gianato Nickerson 33723 Karl Gustav Grunwald 33724 Mark Charles Coomer 33725 Michael Francis Kelley 33726 Glen Daniel Krc 33727 Jeffry Edward Dorney 33728 Robert Glenn Crosby 33729 Richard Gosaku Kaiura 33730 Jeffry Bruce Jones 33731 Richard Leroy Conte 33732 Joseph George Moyer 33733 Henry Joe Keirsey 33734 Henry Axel Krigsman 33735 Richard Eric Dean 33736 Lawrence Peter Abreu Burgess 33737 Dale R. Snyder 33738 Thomas Preston Swaim 33739 Edward Raymond Murdough 33740 Stephen Charles Nash 33741 Bradley Charles Houck 33742 Dale Stewart Vincent 33743 Kim Mergner Campbell 33744 John A. Henry 33745 Michael Roger Baker 33746 Stanley William Golis 33747 John Reynolds Bartley 33748 Thomas James Kelly 33749 James Augustus Coffey 33750 Charles Conrad Teising 33751 Vernon Bernard Crocker 33752 Edward James McCarthy 33753 Keith Christopher Walker 33754 Donald Winslow McCormick 33755 Michael Randall Pelkey 33756 Michael Francis Scully 33757 Harold Joseph Leeman 33758 Bruce Gene Harding 33759 Eric Arthur Brewner 33760 Brian Erich Osterndorf 33761 David Lawrence Diedrich 33762 Thomas F. Julich 33763 Richard David Heekin 33764 Scott Dale Gillogly 33765 Rand James Cuthbertson 33766 Lox Albert Logan 33767 Douglas M. Brown 33768 Michael George Mickalonis 33769 Russell Jon Hall 33770 Bob Eugene Spiegel 33771 Bruce Jackman Porter 33772 Thomas John Meyer 33773 Stover Singleton James 33774 Michael L. Findlay 33775 Stephen Jay Butler 33776 Gerald Ray Harrington 33777 Richard Cromie Rogers 33778 Richard John Wolff 33779 Keith Odin Nystrom 33780 John Edward Marshall Grech 33781 John Martin Williamson 33782 Richard Randolph Ryles 33783 Kip Cliffton Edwards 33784 Gregory Allan Stone 33785 John Donovan Gardner 33786 Jerry Lester Phillabaum 33787 Eric Brady Zimmerman 33788 James M. Ives 33789 David C. Morin 33790 Paul Thomas Migaki 33791 Bruce James Daniecki 33792 John Myron Geddes 33793 Timothy Jo Miller 33794 Ralph Eugene Gehrki 33795 John Roswell Cummings 33796 Lee Bennett Corney 33797 Robin Joseph Drescher 33798 Jorge Patrocinio Guzman 33799 Kevin Toshito Ryan 33800 John Andrew Johnson 33801 Robert T. Baratta 33802 Randy J. Kolton 33803 David William Barno 33804 Mark C. Nelson 33805 James S. Weller 33806 Jeffrey Albert Snyder 33807 Lonnie S. Keene 33808 Thomas Patrick Kelly 33809 Dennis Roy Kennedy 33810 Timothy R. Decker 33811 Joseph A. Speight 33812 Warren J. P. Brey 33813 John J. Midgley 33814 Jerry B. Warner 33815 Ronald D. Jantzen 33816 Paul D. Albertelli 33817 James M. Brege 33818 John Patrick Taylor 33819 Richard P. Bifulco 33820 F. Jefferson Hughes 33821 Robert L. McClure 33822 Robert A. Mazzoli 33823 David A. Kingston 33824 Gary L. Wingo 33825 Lance A. Locklear 33826 Paul F. Adams 33827 Francis H. Kearney 33828 Robert T. Taira 33829 Daniel Joseph Dowling 33830 Steven Fernand Finder 33831 Mark Richard Grotte 33832 Russell Bruce Lieurance 33833 Rolf Mowatt-Larssen 33834 Clyde A. Page 33835 John Arthur Chubb 33836 Guy Carleton Swan 33837 Stephen Todd Mauro 33838 Brin Arthur Tolliffe 33839 Mark Arnold Hedman 33840 Marc Charles Elgaway 33841 Martin R. Rollinson 33842 Milton Gregory Fields 33843 Randall Jackson Hall 33844 Bohdan Twerdowsky 33845 Volney James Warner 33846 William Joseph Seymour 33847 Michael David Maloney 33848 Robert Scott Myers 33849 Herbert Louis Shatzen 33850 William Thomas Grisoli 33851 Mark James Romaneski 33852 John Christian Hetzel 33853 Francisco Jose Pedrozo 33854 Wesley Arthur Reynolds 33855A John Hilmen Holler 33855 Randolph Chung 33856 Louis Kuhn 33857 John Parker Rodgers 33858 Myron Addison Spears 33859 Robert Dawson Glover 33860 Patrick Joseph Lusk 33861 Mark David Daniels 33862 Michael Kazumi Asada 33863 Donald Scott Stephenson 33864 Ronald Lee Johnson 33865 Paul Lawrence Hicks 33866 James Jerome Lullen 33867 Bruce Thomas Robinson 33868 Jeffrey Michael Welch 33869 Robert B. Shaw 33870 Edward Lowry Flinn 33871 James Leslie Travis 33872 James Louis Dumolt 33873 Kevin Thomas Kelley 33874 Edmund John Olsen 33875 Virgil Walter Cook 33876 James R. Meredith 33877 Peter Finley Tuebner 33878 Karl Edward Prinslow 33879 Timothy Conrad Felt 33880 Jon Charles Lewis 33881 Whitney James Robinson 33882 Howard Mordecia Williams 33883 Lawrence Adrian Klooster 33884 Alexander Pruitt 33885 Joseph Louis Schroeder 33886 Paul Douglas Harjung 33887 Harry Marrs Jarred 33888 Gordon Davis Cerow 33889 John Charles Ross 33890 William John Luk 33891 Daniel Adrian Nash 33892 Mark Edward Tillotson 33893 Edward Peter Negrelli 33894 Scott Thomas Collier 33895 Edward Charles Schults 33896 Richard C. Gonder 33897 Luther Jack Dunn 33898 William Ronald Medsger 33899 Paul Frederick Koch 33900 Stanley Drwal 33901 Michael Robert Rooney 33902 Michael F. Kerrigan 33903 Charles Richard Allison 33904 George Thomas Norris 33905 James A. Treadwell 33906 Walter Anthony Schrepel 33907 Michael R. Wood 33908 Robert Max Soeldner 33909 Shane Gil Stonesifer 33910 Martin Joseph Wisda 33911 Harvey Thomas Landwermeyer 33912 John Joseph Reidt 33913 Allan Burt Carroll 33914 Robert Masujima Gallo 33915 James Patrick Smith 33916 Kevin Philip Anastas 33917 Carl Robert Kikerpill 33918 Glenn Jeffrey Lesniak 33919 Mark James Carlson 33920 Gregory E. Bush 33921 Mark Miles Soeth 33922 Ransom Scott Brown 33923 Peter Richard Burke 33924 Stephen Goss Lewis 33925 Mark Richard DePue 33926 Dennis Richard McMahon 33927 Thomas Brockway House 33928 Walter John Sutterlin 33929 John S. Lidh 33930 Lowell Edward Sargeant 33931 John Bruce MacLeod 33932 James Richard Skelton 33933 David Fredrick Anderson 33934 Lee Anthony Bulman 33935 Raymond Bernando Quinones 33936 Stephen Donald Kidder 33937 Leonard Joseph Tylenda 33938 Benjamin Franklin Overbey 33939 Frank Alan Croshal 33940 John David Szoka 33941 Mark Wayne Harvey 33942 Michael Donald Beale 33943 Jeffrey Carlton Brooks 33944 Gary Lee Christensen 33945 Edward Chester Markiewicz 33946 James Leo Trayers 33947 John Marshall Kirby 33948 Francis Xavier Frugoli 33949 Steven Arthur Slade 33950 Michael Damian Kasun 33951 Paul John Pietryka 33952 Thomas Prokopchuk 33953 William Otto Wehrle 33954 Michael Steven Remias 33955 Joseph Alexander Lesini 33956 Michael Merie Kitts 33957 Mark Thomas Premont 33958 Jeffrey Shawn Wike 33959 Michael H. Davis 33960 Jonathan Paul Chase 33961 David Michael Finkelstein 33962 Lance Alan McAllister 33963 William Paul Rue 33964 Frank Edwin Williams 33965 Anthony Stephen McAnally 33966 Francis Dailey Collins 33967 Christopher Alan Headle 33968 Charles William Kilgore 33969 Sanders Monroe Holston 33970 Brad Alan Carlton 33971 Kenneth L. Pamperin 33972 Rodney Dale Cariker 33973 Michael John Wickham 33974 Robert Roy Beimler 33975 Harold H. Zaima 33976 Rick Blaine Manson 33977 Eric James Coulter 33978 Jeffrey William Meadows 33979 Philip Alan Gray 33980 Thomas Henry Jones 33981 Emmett Edward McDonough 33982 Daniel Joseph Ferrari 33983 David George Mabee 33984 Willie Henry Pruitt 33985 Stanley Allen McChrystal 33986 Gregory Robert Bornhoft 33987 Norman Lee Balliet 33988 Craig Edwin Kovach 33989 Brian Edmond Moretti 33990 Stuart Hadley Piermarini 33991 Donald Alan Knowles 33992 Peter Anthony Amico 33993 David Moore Shanahan 33994 Douglas Abbott MacGregor 33995 Hubert Phillips 33996 Robert Paul Farquhar 33997 Max Warren Thompson 33998 William Burns Caldwell 33999 Michael Peter DeMarco 34000 Leon Jon Begeman 34001 James Mark Dulong 34002 Gerald Peter Falkenstein 34003 Stephen Hollich 34004 James Robert Hibbard 34005 Michael Jerome Kazmierski 34006 William Joseph Hofmann 34007 James Andrew Mothorpe 34008 Paul John Perrone 34009 Bobby Dean Melvin 34010 Louis Herbert Brown 34011 Gary Lynn McKenzie 34012 Joseph Thomas Saffer 34013 Gregory Vince Stanley 34014 Orlando Ward Spalding 34015 Paul Richard Wilson 34016 Michael Casey McFarland 34017 Bruce Randolph Hoelscher 34018 Matthew Stuart Jun Hada 34019 Ralph P. Steen 34020 Steven Douglas Anderson 34021 George Edward Sherman 34022 Joseph Anthony Dubyel 34023 James Edward Covert 34024 Juan A. Jimenez 34025 Gary Franklin Easom 34026 Randolph Robin Rogel 34027 Dennis Louis Thompson 34028 Kenneth Allen Walker 34029 Daniel Morton Spangler 34030 Donald George Murdock 34031 Thomas Vernon Alexander 34032 Gregory Michael Saunders 34033 Matthew Lewis Smith 34034 Craig Alan Candelore 34035 David Paul Harris 34036 Allan Ray Osborn 34037 Richard B. Bowman 34038 James Vaughn Herndon 34039 Edmund Gerard Healy 34040 Demetrius Kevin Bivins 34041 Louis Eugene Held 34042 Gregory Donald Wallace 34043 Rimmer Fowler 34044 James E. Nickerson 34045 Michael Reuss Snipes 34046 Craig Stevens Murphy 34047 Malcolm Dayton Johnson 34048 Bradley Dean Gillund 34049 Joseph Patrick Pineau 34050 Rhett Anthony Hernandez 34051 Lewis George Aide 34052 James L. Jacobs 34053 Mark Edward Grimes 34054 James Albert Moerkerke 34055 Roger Leslie Maxwell 34056 Leonard Eugene Donahoo 34057 Michael Arnett Hamilton 34058 John Paul Lawrence 34059 David Eugene Titus 34060 Richard A. Carlin 34061 Thomas Casimir Kurasiewicz 34062 Bradford James Bryant 34063 Michael David Baca 34064 Gary K. Knapp 34065 John Henry Belser 34066 James Robert Reynolds 34067 James Cole Cartledge 34068 Gary Robert Kloepping 34069 Albert Lee Staerkel 34070 Charles Ravenscroft 34071 M. Dwayne Chambless 34072 Michael Cantrell 34073 Ernest Roland Morgan 34074 James Lee Williams 34075 Timothy Kevin Reddy 34076 Mark T. Kimmitt 34077 David Wallace McSween 34078 Robert C. Allgood 34079 Ronald Charles Russell 34080 Brian George Shellum 34081 George Baker Thomson 34082 Matthew P. Redmann 34083 James Robert Felty 34084 Robert Thomas Dalton 34085 August Joseph Raquipiso 34086 Kevin K. Olson 34087 Robert Ernest Finlay 34088 Francis David Swann 34089 Steven Allen Vernon 34090 Jack W. Myers 34091 William Roy Wolfe 34092 Thomas Joseph Steinbrunner 34093 Luciano Linsangan Gaboy 34094 Hector E. Topete 34095 Robert James Schuett 34096 Daniel J. Keefe 34097 Roger Anthony Reinhart 34098 John Walter Lemza 34099 Scott Douglas Gilbert 34100 David K. Eachus 34101 Stephen C. Horner 34102 Michael Gerald O'Donnell 34103 William Henry Patterson 34104 Kevin James O'Rourke 34105 Jonathan William Compton 34106 Steven John Rawlick 34107 Nicholas Francis Spinelli 34108 Steve George Capps 34109 Gary Duane Jerauld 34110 Keith R. McNally 34111 Robert Harold McEwin 34112 Bruce Donald Jette 34113 Keith Farrell Snider 34114 Douglas Jonathan Ward 34115 Daniel Lee Whiting 34116 Gary William Gerst 34117 Kevin David Koester 34118 Michael J. Driscoll 34119 Thomas Jay Rosener 34120 Louis Graham Burgess 34121 Charles Joseph O'Hara 34122 William Donald Clingempeel 34123 Douglas M. Taylor 34124 Robert Lawrence Taggart 34125 Richard Joseph Marchant 34126 Michael Zane Swisher 34127 Kerry Edmund Murphy 34128 Richard Duncan Myrand Downie 34129 Daniel Albert McManus 34130 Bruce Thomas Gridley 34131 Douglas Scott Rogers 34132 Richard N. Hawkins 34133 Frank David Cerny 34134 David Marvin Johnson 34135 Francis Paul Valentino 34136 Mark V. Montesclaros 34137 Jose Ramon Rodriguez Harrison 34138 Albert C. Johnson 34139 Douglas Mark McLean 34140 Robert William Kocher 34141 Samuel Joseph Butler 34142 Timothy D. Harrod 34143 Donald Myron Pierson 34144 Floyd Everett Bowles 34145 Carl Frank Menyhert 34146 Gary Annunziato 34147 Stephen David Bonneau 34148 Randall R. Braden 34149 Hugh Michael Denny 34150 Ronald Gerard Houle 34151 Larry Danelishen 34152 John Alfred Harkey 34153 Dale Allan Apple 34154 Richard Forrest Rachmeler 34155 Collyon Scott Koehler 34156 Kenneth Reuben Fugett 34157 Gerald Francis Lambert 34158 Robert Johnston Fritz 34159 Eduardo Cardenas 34160 Antonio Martin Cogliandro 34161 John Sebastian Labella 34162 Ellis Wayne Golson 34163 Timothy Richard Sweeney 34164 John Michael Carmichael 34165 Edwin L. Kennedy 34166 Lawrence George Shattuck 34167 Jerrold Timothy Sullivan 34168 Daniel Frank Korzym 34169 Troy Lynn Thames 34170 David Frederick Rees 34171 James Alexander Wiegel 34172 Earl L. Madison 34173 Carlos Joseph Negrete 34174 Michael William Byrne 34175 Todd Richard Decker 34176 James Edward McGinnis 34177 Laurence Cochia King 34178 George T. Greenlee 34179 Charles James Zaruba 34180 Joseph Stanley Drelling 34181 Kevin Richard Krebs 34182 Roger M. Clarizio 34183 Robert John Spiridigliozzi 34184 Richard Joseph Randolph 34185 Edward Allen Bent 34186 Ernest Robert Klawitter 34187 Douglas Alan Gendron 34188 Brad David Scott 34189 Herman Arthur Miles 34190 Jose David Riojas 34191 Carl William Horn 34192 Leo Arthur Leduc 34193 Ronald John Paul Ranalli 34194 Edward Joseph Sinclair 34195 Richard Earl Oelslager 34196 Ronnie Lee Squires 34197 Bernard Joseph Lachner 34198 Steven Allen Fondacaro 34199 James Ernest Lawson 34200 Robert Martin Topolewski 34201 Peter Edward Jurusik 34202 Scott Randall Peterson 34203 Duane Stephen Castro 34204 Stephen Paul Chubon 34205 Bradley Harold Matthews 34206 Robert Edward Twomey 34207 Alan Craig Dingfelder 34208 Roy Warren Bromfield 34209 John Harry McGhee 34210 Stephen David Nichols 34211 Mark Edward Berry 34212 Robert Russell Horback 34213 Robert Sterling Hawekotte 34214 Elliot Joseph Rosner 34215 Vincent DePaul Louis 34216 Russell Arnold Grimm 34217 Jeffrey Alan Moyer 34218 Nathan Daniel Workman 34219 Michael A. Pietrzyk 34220 William Frank Stefan 34221 Mark Thomas Hanna 34222 Frank G. Helmick 34223 Dennis Eugene Scaman 34224 Richard Louis Bogusky 34225 Gerald Claude Eversmeyer 34226 Kevin Michael Higgins 34227 George Kirk Strodtbeck 34228 John Robert Ruppert 34229 Thomas Kevin Fox 34230 Arthur Lawrence Voetsch 34231 Robert Lloyd Coxe 34232 Michael Walter Brady 34233 Richard T. Johnston 34234 Foid Kim Janes 34235 Charles Michael Cato 34236 Francis Hamilton Rocco Caponegro 34237 Michael James Perry 34238 Eric Larson Doane 34239 Jim Edward Mainwaring 34240 Robert Ermelindo Bernardi 34241 Saulius Jones Siemaska 34242 Ronald Charles Garrison 34243 Ky Wayne White 34244 Charles Rodney Layman 34245 Aaron Bernard Hayes 34246 John Louis Brenneman 34247 William Harold Walsh 34248 Gregg Alan Taylor 34249 Michael Anthony White 34250 Eric Richard Christensen 34251 David Richard Apt 34252 Andrew Francis Vail 34253 James Bruce Chudoba 34254 James Edward Hoffman 34255 Michael Patrick Tatu 34256 Mark Allen West 34257 Thomas Scott Kallman 34258 Michael John Delarede 34259 Arthur Ott Victor 34260 Richard Lee Weger 34261 Robert Emmett Smith 34262 Steven Gary Butler 34263 Edmundo Moises Colchado 34264 James Howard Wooley 34265 David Michael Lutz 34266 Phillippe Minez 34267 Gary Allen Reynolds 34268 William Frederick Wechsler 34269 Christopher Leland Baggott 34270 Eddie Don Mills 34271 Adam Samuel Lobert 34272 Douglas Theodore Slaybaugh 34273 Bruce William Fish-Gertz 34274 Robert Stephen Pikna 34275 Jeffrey Warren Davis 34276 John Jeffrey Martin 34277 James Ralph Critchlow 34278 Paul Francis Maier 34279 Michael William Metcalf 34280 Peter Edward Goodyear 34281 Edward D. Miller 34282 James H. Johnston 34283 William Patrick Vansant 34284 Jacob Marshall McFerren 34285 John Richard Warner 34286 Nathan Anderson Godwin 34287 Robert Joseph Lynch 34288 Earl J. Mazerolle 34289 Donald Calhoun Spiece 34290 Mark W. Hebrank 34291 Michael D. Barbero 34292 Steve Edward Dietrich 34293 William Ray Sipes 34294 Hal Reese Nyander 34295 James Edward Fletcher 34296 Stephen Bruce Pickering 34297 Timothy Michael Judge 34298 Raymond Thomas Odierno 34299 Steven Gilbert Brooks 34300 Robert William Surtees 34301 Daniel Thomas Murphy 34302 Daniel Kevin Croak 34303 Glenn Marshall Peach 34304 Richard John Chappo 34305 Paul Evan Goldich 34306 Stephen Paul Balint 34307 John Michael O'Toole 34308 David George Crouch 34309 Santiago Busa 34310 Joseph Leon Hardesty 34311 William George Foshay 34312

Steven Richard Babula 34313 Bruce Loring Weyrick 34314 Michael Robert Sloan 34315 John William Vanderschaaf 34316 Michael Allen Babb 34317 Kazimierz Stefan Rybak 34318 William Guy Minton 34319 Stanley Raymond Stajduhar 34320 Frederick Weaver 34321 David Lopez 34322 John Raymond Brower 34323 Jay S. Fordice 34324 Rhinnie Ruben Rohrback 34325 James Michael Donivan 34326 Donald Victor Booth 34327 Christopher Joseph Grates 34328 David Alan Hoopengardner 34329 Niel Arthur Youngberg 34330 Richard Harold Sumption 34331 B. Richard Blair 34332 Gregory Jenkin Dyson 34333 Cornell McKenzie 34334 Audie D. Zimmerman 34335 Brian Lee Kimsey 34336 Ronald Matthew Janowski 34337 Bruce Kevin Zophy 34338 Randy Lee Morgan 34339 Eric Stephen Gerencser 34340 Steven Joseph Naughton 34341 David Michael Kristick 34342 James Ronald Daron 34343 William David Staley 34344 Robert Thomas Wrightson 34345 Robert Anthony McEwan 34346 Steven Scott Daniel 34347 Francis Lynn Stoudenmire 34348 Steven Joseph Ricks 34349 Kevin Peter Christensen 34350 Woodrow Michael Ivandick 34351 Richard Allen Harris 34352 Steven Fane Banks 34353 Michael John Misyak 34354 David Allen Yatto 34355 Louis Ralph Liuzzo 34356 Willie Preston Whitlock 34357 Philip Francis Wright 34358 Charles Herbert Ockrassa 34359 John Lawrence Goetchius 34360 Roger Ronald Schleiden 34361 Herbert Dale Smiley 34362 Michael Francis McGuire 34363 William Monk 34364 Robert Phillip Chase 34365 James Van Scott 34366 Edward Thomas Carney 34367 Sigurd Anthony Jett 34368 Clifford Fitz Henry Cornell 34369 Curtis Randall Dangerfield 34370 Bruce Allen Hoover 34371 Steven Paul Best 34372 Michael John Thompson 34373 Matthew David Matey 34374 Jeffrey Hunter Stansberry 34375 Robert Craig Marshall 34376 John McLaughlin Gallagher 34377 Howard Patrick Murray 34378 James Ray Riffe 34379 James Kenneth Grammer 34380 Karl Lewis Kraus 34381 Edison Arceo Guillermo 34382 Charles Michael Robinson 34383 Matthew Grills Hyde 34384 Rno Philip Reinemer 34385 John Lewis Crown 34386 Michael Joseph Hall 34387 Joseph P. Riolo 34388 Richard Alan Koffinke 34389 Edward Albert Evans 34390 Stanley Carson Plummer 34391 David Walter Luken 34392 Richard Joseph Harrington 34393 Stephen Robert Canosa 34394 Jeffrey Lawrence Groh 34395 David Rupp 34396 James Henry Gordon 34397 Robert J. Tezza 34398 Arthur Kenneth Liepold 34399 Robert Michael Radin 34400 Marcus A. Alexander 34401 Gregory Gerald Fountain 34402 Jose Antonio Fernandez 34403 Gary Fields 34404 Jack Mills Harrill 34405 Stephen Philip Hayward 34406 Kenneth Gustavo Moncayo 34407 Joseph Ramsey Cook 34408 Stephen Harover Cass 34409 Daniel A. Nolan 34410 Terence Fong 34411 Steven W. Dickerson 34412 Lon Tomohisa Horiuchi 34413 Thomas Michael Valerio 34414 James Michael Rapkoch 34415 Cheng Yu Huang 34416 Alexander John Rouch 34417 Michael L. Dixon 34418 Robert Michael Urban 34419 Richard Louis Hinojosa 34420 Stephen Dale Milburn 34421 Thomas Burton Mitchell 34422 John Joseph Angell 34423 William Harold Roof 34424 Allan David Stuhlmiller 34425 Timothy Patrick Hill 34426 Wayne Joseph Trujillo 34427 Donald Davis Harvel 34428 Steven Richard Eisenhart 34429 Edward John Brennan 34430 Bruce Edward Black 34431 Geoffrey Lawrence Irons 34432 Curtis Andrew Barnhill 34433 David Sledge Noel 34434 Stuart Alan Carroll 34435 John Benson Stinson 34436 Joseph Robert Sanders 34437 Scott Francis Moss 34438 Kevin Charles Woody 34439 Joseph A. Cuellar 34440 Richard Lynn Elam 34441 Dennis Robert Trujillo 34442 Keith Eugene Sims 34443 William Eric Andersen 34444 John Arvids Spodris Birznieks 34445 Leonard Bernard Horning 34446 Richard A. Brisson 34447 David Lee Mossbarger 34448 Steven Edwards Barrett 34449 Don Victor Reginald Hicks 34450 Ray Lawrence Oden 34451 Ricky Allen Fontana 34452 Gary Lewis DellaRocco 34453 Ted Archer Crozier 34454 William Carlton Creighton 34455 Steven Eugene Miller 34456 Clinton Wendell Austin 34457 Gregory Joseph Mallon 34458 Darrell Evins Crawford 34459 John Jeffrey Scott 34460 John William Wallace 34461 Gary Alan May 34462 Scott Forrest Weidner 34463 Leonard Maxwell West 34464 Graham John Waugaman 34465 Lawrence Michael Pallotta 34466 Lawrence Kirk Slate 34467 Glen W. LaForce 34468 Kevin Francis Kiley 34469 Neil Bradley Dodrill 34470 Robert Alexander Zeige 34471 James Robert Webb 34472 Wayne Lee Converse 34473 Randy Perry Sager 34474 Bruce William Gamsby 34475 Patrick Tyrone Sullivan 34476 Chester Arvol Taylor 34477 David James Pyle 34478 Brian Ray Zahn 34479 Robert Gregory Klotzbach 34480 Warren G. H. A. Crecy 34481 John Thomas Matlach 34482 Jackie L. Merklein 34483 Thomas Arthur Gabel 34484 Calvin Blake Daley 34485 Geoffrey Michael Schmid 34486 James William Munday 34487 Vincent Steven Botto 34488 David P. Kapinos 34489 John Stefan Dearing 34490 Woitto Nestor Helenius 34491 Gerald Peter Araneo 34492 David Alexander Ball 34493 Paul David Ligman 34494 David Bontecou Deeter 34495 Richard Garland Holcombe 34496 John Robert Gordon 34497 David J. Williams 34498 Joseph Nathan Floyd 34499 David Mitchell Rodriguez 34500 Robert D. McClure 34501 James Willis Webb 34502 Reamer Welker Argo 34503 Maurice Edmund Hudson 34504 Stephen John Craig 34505 Wayne Terri Crafton 34506 Frederick William Tonsing 34507 David Louis Dickey 34508 Peter Edward Schunke 34509 James Joseph O'Connor 34510 Larry Kenneth Renfro 34511 Larry E. Shelton 34512 Carlos Adolfo Falcon 34513 Charlie Timothy Wall 34514 Andrew T. Gasparovic 34515 Mark Anthony Smith 34516 Hugh W. Perry 34517 Michael Louis Pinckert 34518 Robert William Colie 34519 Darrell Allen Baker 34520 Percy Reginald Simpson 34521 Jesse Frederick Owens 34522 Joseph Adams Higgs 34523 Kenneth R. Schnell 34524 Agustin Ortiz 34525 James Robert Rollins 34526 Charles E. Everett 34527 Glenn Martin Hulse 34528 Carl A. Cannon 34529 Lloyd Michael Lambeth 34530 Archie Elam 34531 Linwood Larmont Little 34532 Samuel Edward Fogarty 34533 Edward Francis Cawley 34534 Johnny Louis Brown 34535 John James Foy 34536 Donald Jay Moser 34537 Love Collins 34538 Robert Charles O'Leary 34539 Richard Gerard Meyer 34540 Jeffrey Milton Bruckner 34541 **1977** Greg Alden Bowers 34542 Mark Bradley Mengel 34543 Clyde Andrew Selleck 34544 David Alan Hruska 34545 Herbert L. Hess 34546 William David Stoutamire 34547 Alan Lawrence Beitler 34548 John Edward Shephard 34549 Keith M. Garrison 34550 Kevin George Scherrer 34551 John Scofield Prall 34552 Paul Christian Jensen 34553 Alan Grant Getts 34554 George Mortimer Tilley 34555 Stephen Arthur Spaulding 34556 Kelly Dean Ferrell 34557 Richard Alvin Wagner 34558 Michael Scott O'Bannon 34559 Robert Paul Lennox 34560 Kenneth Franklin Miller 34561 Terrence Joseph Daly 34562 Thomas George Hesse 34563 William Bruce Watkins 34564 Dean Clement Berry 34565 Jerome John Dittman 34566 Marion Wade Key 34567 Blake Van Leer Peck 34568 Robert Forrest Mull 34569 Richard Francis Davis 34570 John Louis Charvat 34571 Michael Francis Hullihan 34572 Robert M. Schmidt 34573 John Vernon Guenther 34574 George David Michael Mitroka 34575 Thomas Patrick Kuchar 34576 Robert Francis Zyck 34577 Patrick Bryan Achey 34578 Michael Roy Chritton 34579 Rex S. Takasugi 34580 Steven Clark Lefemine 34581 Stephen Kelly Barton 34582 Kenneth Lorne Wright 34583 Daniel Paul Doede 34584 Thomas Joseph Begines 34585 Alan Stanley Andon 34586 Robert Louis Ball 34587 Walter Vinson Horstman 34588 Stephen Kirk Morrow 34589 Jeffrey Paul Whitman 34590 Allen D. Lewis 34591 David Eugene Mechtly 34592 John Peter Robert 34593 Donald Paul Luke Fiorino 34594 George Bernard Fink 34595 David Nam Wah Young 34596 Robert James Huff 34597 John Charles Williams 34598 Michael Maurice Frost 34599 Robert W. Weller 34600 Donald C. Ecklin 34601 Paul Martin Gudeczauskas 34602 Ricky Lynch 34603 William Scott Anders 34604 Richard Kyle Douglas 34605 Richard Noel Kellett 34606 Andrew Stein Sandoy 34607 David Patrick Buchanan 34608 Mark Jeffrey Klaiber 34609 Frederick William Weber 34610 John Daniel Marks 34611 Robert Charles Larner 34612 Joseph Ralston Sullivan 34613 Timothy Charles Morris 34614 Frederick L. Clapp 34615 Andrew James Hill 34616 Hugh Douglas Sansom 34617 James Michael Bradbury 34618 Peter John Comodeca 34619 Alan Dale Chute 34620 Dennis Eric Scott 34621 Timothy Wayne Crain 34622 Ted Stephen Kanamine 34623 Frank Alan Appelfeller 34624 Robert Stanley Cymbalski 34625 Michael Kwan 34626 Karl Alan Fears 34627 Bruce Clifford Abbott 34628 Joseph Michael Erpelding 34629 Steven Charles Hadley 34630 David Ward Martin 34631 Craig Robert Pieringer 34632 Philip Dennis Dyer 34633 Kent Cuthbertson 34634 Stephen Harold Tupper 34635 Jerome Bartholomew Myers 34636 Alan Bret Becker 34637 George Richard Bruce 34638 Robert Alan Kehlet 34639 Robert Moeller Elliott 34640 John Charles Turowski 34641 Ralph Tibbs Garver 34642 Robert Harry Acker 34643 William Martin Mayes 34644 Niel Arlen Robbins 34645 Gary John Tocchet 34646 Thomas Hunter Garver 34647 John Cicerelle 34648 James Patrick Muldoon 34649 Kurt Steven Meckstroth 34650 Edward Michael Lawnick 34651 Gary Edward Simmons 34652 Lloyd Dayton Carmack 34653 Hugh Michael Hughes 34654 Lance Anthony Betros 34655 Donald D. Jacobovitz 34656 David Michael Patterson 34657 Joseph Herndon Rossetti 34658 Richard Steven Hunt 34659 Andrew Thomas Chmar 34660 Jeffrey Brian Wheeler 34661 Marc Kevin Collins 34662 Marc Jay Jacobson 34663 James Gregory Brecher 34664 Kevin H. Pilgrim 34665 Jeffrey Alan Elting 34666 Jesse Michael Pantalion 34667 Herman Nicholas Iorio 34668 Andrew Rosario Manuele 34669 Thomas McKay 34670 Cornelius Hendrik Goebertus 34671 Stephen Cary Hawkins 34672 James A. Fitch 34673 Patrick Daniel Linehan 34674 Harry Gray Looney 34675 James Phillip Nymark 34676 Max Ernest McDonald 34677 William Kenneth Orris 34678 James M. Modlin 34679 Randy Joe Hall 34680 Patrick Harry Zaiss 34681 James Robert Malcolm 34682 David Leland Morlock 34683 Thomas Darrel Molzahn 34684 Edwin D. Patterson 34685 Douglas Read Gault 34686 Patrick Joseph Vaughan 34687 Craig Allen Gaetzke 34688 Anthony John Gratson 34689 Michael Ray Campbell 34690 Steven Charles Gravlin 34691 F. Freeman Marvin 34692 Stewart Vincent Black 34693 David Lawrence Bolte 34694 James Michael Liedle 34695 Gordon Neil Peterson 34696 David Edgar Perry 34697 Ronald Bryan Vogt 34698 Richard Henry Naigle 34699 Harry Glenn Summers 34700 William Joseph Vanark 34701 Joseph Feliks Wartski 34702 James Brierley Wyman 34703 Riziero Fernando Montanari 34704 David Michael Owens 34705 Dustin Clyde Frazier 34706 Andrew McCoy Warner 34707 Brian Edward Michael Smith 34708 John D. Hightower 34709 James Gordon Connelly 34710 Stuart Bennion Alleman 34711 Stacey Katsuto Hirata 34712 Edward Nelson Rouse 34713 Mark James Lowery 34714 Francis Xavier Kinney 34715 Robert Martin Evans 34716 George Stanley Dowell 34717 John Mays Compton 34718 Gregory Stephen Kuhr 34719 John R. Kennedy 34720 Steve Norman Maring 34721 James Bernard McGuan 34722 Gary Marc McClelland 34723 Francis Andrew Imaikalani Bowers 34724 Michael E. Ivy 34725 Michael L. McGinnis 34726 John William Burdan 34727 Thomas Christian Odderstol 34728 William Earl Ryan 34729 James Lee Collins 34730 Robert Boyd Harnish 34731 Robert F. Mathis 34732 John Thomas Klauck 34733 Michael Clayton Bibby 34734 James Jay Carafano 34735 Murray Morgan Welch 34736 James Edward McShea 34737 Mario Andrew Carrillo 34738 William Douglas Malone 34739 James Logan Sowder 34740 Lewis Stuart Rowell 34741 Anthony James Manganiello 34742 Harry M. Knight 34743 David Eugene Anselmi 34744 Gray Lincoln Salada 34745 Philip Lee Campbell 34746 Freddie Jim Mills 34747 Ronald L. Bertha 34748 Douglas Benson Tesdahl 34749 Stephen Graham Findlay 34750 Jack Allen Keaton 34751 Terrance Thompson 34752 Mark William Creighton 34753 Dewey Leffler Blyth 34754 Thomas Frank Dougall 34755 Kurt Arthur Andrews 34756 Konrad Lee Cailteux 34757 Donald Wayne Washington 34758 Aivars Zigfrids Baumanis 34759 Frederick Kennedy 34760 John Bernard Wolters 34761 Carl Frederick Engelhardt 34762 Richard Stephen Grammier 34763 William Ray Tetro 34764 Darell Ladd Nepil 34765 Rand Alexander Ballard 34766 Bruce Le Bey Frasier 34767 Denis Paul Bilodeau 34768 Michael Daniel Nicholas 34769 Kerry Allan Mess 34770 Steven Peter Bucci 34771 Steven Herman Heinecke 34772 Andrew Stephen Lamb 34773 Michael T. Keith 34774 Gerald Edward Nelson 34775 Gary Alan Montgomery 34776 Odus Earl Harwood 34777 Blayne Alynn Hall 34778 Scott Thor Lofgren 34779 Alexander Francis Janisz 34780 Patrick Clyde Lafayette 34781 Timothy D. Lynch 34782 James Dennis Hodge 34783 Robert Allen Dow 34784 Donald Alan Carter 34785 James Graham Stevens 34786 Andrew C. Gjelsteen 34787 Bruce Elden Altizer 34788 William Harrison McDonald 34789 Robert William Sinclair 34790 Daniel Timothy Driscoll 34791 Charles Edward Harris 34792 Edward Joseph Merkler 34793 Mark Angelo Centra 34794 Paul Edward Melody 34795 William Casey Grier 34796 Alden Smith Bradstock 34797 James Kevin Greer 34798 Mark Robert Liebenow 34799 Kevin Charles Benson 34800 Robert Charles Lamb 34801 Steven L. Burkett 34802 Carl Axel Swanson 34803 Alberto Laureano Garcia 34804 Theodore S. Russell 34805 Bernard F. Gerasimas 34806 Eric Quinto Javier 34807 Mark Allen Henry 34808 Hoa Generazio 34809 Michael Montelongo 34810 Christopher Born 34811 Douglas Paul Scalard 34812 Steven Torres 34813 Robert J. Leonard 34814 John Joseph Curry 34815 Matthew J. Fair 34816 William James Butler 34817 Andrew Bernard Twomey 34818 John Francis Joseph Mangan 34819 Bruce Wayne Carlson 34820 Samuel Ruven Maizel 34821 Paul Arthur Petzrick 34822 Richard Wilson Shaw 34823 Ronny Ramos 34824 George Wellington Gotschall 34825 Warren Craig Chellman 34826 Wallace Allen Price 34827 Steve Franklin Pierce 34828 Michael Wayne Page 34829 Edward Page Lukert 34830 James Craig Naudain 34831 Ernest Richard Schelhaas 34832 Theodore Bryan Eilts 34833 Ivan Dominic Krestyn 34834 Ronald E. Loveland 34835 Kevin Gerard Kelly 34836 Paul Ervin Snapp 34837 Timothy Daniel Holden 34838 Leo Raymond Cullinan 34839 Clifford H. Harris 34840 Robert Gregory Curtis 34841 Timothy Alan Fong 34842 Paul Thomas Newell 34843 Derrill Melvin Goodson 34844 John Philip Mertens 34845 Dale Bruce Bodman 34846 Walter Gerard McCone 34847 Thomas Patrick O'Connell 34848 Jeffrey William Hetherington 34849 David W. Hoy 34850 Peter George Welsch 34851 Terry Gifford Stewart 34852 Martin Earl Long 34853 James Lee Ross 34854 Billy Eugene Conner 34855 John William Holbert 34856 Jeffrey Louis Kinard 34857 Mitchell Thomas Poodry 34858 Mark Allen McGuire 34859 Earl Thomas Hill 34860 David N. Calkins 34861 Robert S. Barnes 34862 Kenneth Mike Franklin 34863 William Emil Fitzgerald 34864 Thomas Andrew Hayden 34865 Jerry K. Hill 34866 John Francis Antal 34867 Michael D. Doubler 34868 Mark Frederick Gillespie 34869 Michael Andrew Sheehan 34870 William Joseph Hill 34871 Anthony Leo Paulo 34872 William Charles Dowd 34873 Charles Farrell Holloway 34874 Gerald James Belcher 34875 Daniel D. James 34876 John Stephen Brannis 34877 Robert E. Newman 34878 Richard Alan Wiggins 34879 Steven John Cox 34880 Vincent J. Viola 34881 Alonzo Stephen Kretzer 34882 John William Sprowl 34883 William Glenn LaPerch 34884 Thomas Milton Perrin 34885 Stephen M. Gouthro 34886 Thomas Durwood Greenhouse 34887 David Jeffrey Fletcher 34888 Timothy Lawrence Challans 34889 Mel Chito Bustamante Labrador 34890 Thomas James Kindel 34891 Earl Monroe Yerrick 34892 Donald Wayne Fuller 34893 Willes K. Lee 34894 Christopher Walter Lai 34895 Warren David Calkin 34896 Gary William Krahn 34897 William Arthur Carrington 34898 Robert Wesley Morris 34899 Christopher Scott Pritchett 34900 David Lyn Richardson 34901 Kenneth Steven Collier 34902 Steven Wade Rotkoff 34903 Randall George Banky 34904 Frank Delaplaine Turner 34905 Scott A. Leishman 34906 Randy L. J. Buckner 34907 Rodolfo Rolando Diaz-Pons 34908 Alan Edwin Ruegemer 34909 John Paul Weinzettle 34910 Eric William Stanhagen 34911 David A. Wood 34912 Alan David Phillips 34913 Mark Allen Ellis 34914 George John Samuelson 34915 Donald Lee Parmer 34916 Jerry Alan Aslinger 34917 Jeffrey Edward Tensfeldt 34918 Jack Bernard Tombrella 34919 Arthur Thomas Aylward 34920 Jack Donald Regan 34921 Trent Richard Frederickson 34922 Michael Joseph Donahue 34923 James Hayes Bickford 34924 George Christopher Tillery 34925 James Arthur Hubbard 34926 Walter James Lawrence 34927 David Timothy Cole 34928 William Lance Gatling 34929 Wesley F. Walters 34930 Daniel Decatur Wood 34931 John Robert Chapman 34932 Douglas Alan Waldrep 34933 Kenneth Roy Stevenson 34934 Donald Paul Walker 34935 Robert Floyd Jones 34936 Daniel Jeffrey Adelstein 34937 Paul Robert Smith 34938 Wayne Michael Chiusano 34939 Jay Tanner Kitzrow 34940 Patrick Olin McGranahan 34941 John Daniel Lafayette 34942 Bradford Keith Zuehlke 34943 David Richard Chepauskas 34944 John Leroy Nixon 34945 William Theodore Lasher 34946 Roland Spencer Lane 34947 John Joseph Powers 34948 Michael David Kanner 34949 James Michael Huskins 34950 Thomas Francis Kiggins 34951 Zachary Lee Smith 34952 Vincent Russell Collins 34953 David T. Wuensch 34954 William Edward Mosby 34955 Donnie Lee Henry 34956 John Walter Barchet 34957 Rex Garret Finley 34958 Robert Daniel Richardson 34959 James Clay 34960 John James Luther 34961 Richard Eugene Stinner 34962 William Rene Vermette 34963 Randal L. Gehler 34964 James Andrew Wilt 34965 Robert Stirling Goodman 34966 Alton Lee Woolley 34967 Kevin William Trehey 34968 Bernard Otha Greenwade 34969 Bernhard Georg Eugene 34970 Glenn Lew Morton 34971 James Kenneth Whiteman 34972 Kenneth Thomas Lamneck 34973 Patrick Thomas Healey 34974 Matthew Joseph Forbes 34975 Michael Bernard Wilson 34976 Richard Frank Sollner 34977 Mark Charles Wiley 34978 Michael James Malooley 34979 Mark William Palen 34980 Len Douglas Shartzer 34981 Calvin Eric Williams 34982 Clyde William Cocke 34983 David McCoach Dorman 34984 George David Harrington 34985 Jeffrey Patrick Kemp 34986 Kenneth Malone Hicks 34987 James Raymond Loba 34988 Leonard Keith Ewing 34989 Steven J. Hoogland 34990 David Ross Engstrom 34991 David Paul Miller 34992 Kurt James Sellers 34993 Frank Rainer Prautzsch 34994 Jesse C. Keeling 34995 Lee Andrew Phillips 34996 Paul T. Hengst 34997 Thomas P. Hanlon 34998 Michael Burnell Henry 34999 Stanley Lavon Warrick 35000 Jerry Lynn Minton 35001 Michael James Schweiger 35002 Daniel Walter Fuller 35003 Mark L. Van Drie 35004 Ronald Douglas Offut 35005 Gregory Alan Adams 35006 Richard Matthew Trotter 35007 David Louis Haueter 35008 Richard Henry Harris 35009 Jerome Frank Zazzera 35010 James Kermit Womack 35011 Larry H. Hysell 35012 Roy Michael Wnek 35013 George Tabor Heaton 35014 Thomas Paul Watson 35015 Charles C. Howard 35016 James Francis Karol 35017 Ralph Thomas Tierno 35018 Gregory Witham Copperthite 35019 Paul Anthony Ignacius Nardi 35020 Cory S. Manka 35021 Charles M. Martin 35022 Dale Edward Phelps 35023 William Bernard Keating 35024 Kenneth Lawrence Scott 35025 R. Mark Brown 35026 David Reed Brooks 35027 Carl Emery Sanders 35028 Robert Stephen Cowan 35029 Jamie Lee Jamieson 35030 Christopher Francis Kurek 35031 David Bryant King 35032 Dirk Nelson 35033 Peter Michael Zielinski 35034 Robert William Heun 35035 Richard Anthony McCollam 35036 David Powers Xavier Schneider 35037 Scott Maple 35038 Raymond Joseph Bosse 35039 James Leslie Holloway 35040 Denis Luke O'Keefe 35041 Mark Alan Kophamer 35042 Charles Loren Holzinger 35043 Clarence Raymond Kohs 35044 Gerhard B. Hartig 35045 David V. B. Price 35046 Kurt Laing Struder 35047 Larry Thomas Artman 35048 Chris Eric Tomsen 35049 Jean Peter Vreuls 35050 John Francis Short 35051 Paul W. Anderson 35052 William Gerard Mason 35053 Frederick King Alderson 35054 Robert John Skinner 35055 David Richard Plaza 35056 Eugene William Twilleager 35057 Michael Allen Shannon 35058 William Gene Johnson 35059 Kevin Brian Rue 35060 Philip Scott Thompson 35061 Arne Wesley Owens 35062 Leslie Francis Kayanan 35063 William Haller Woodson 35064 Tony Jesus Acosta 35065 Carl J. Witcher 35066 Brian D. Hughes 35067 Bernardo Alfonso Arce-Gutierrez 35068 Harry Daniel Scott 35069 Peter John Palmer 35070 Mark Edward Preston 35071

Richard Albert Rogers 35072 Donald Joseph McGhee 35073 Anthony Salvatore Lieto 35074 Mark Thomas Beck 35075 Angel David Velez 35076 Joseph Francis Santilli 35077 Michael Anthony Platz 35078 James H. Renfrow 35079 David Alan Youngker 35080 Lawrence John Zachmann 35081 James Mitchell Hogarth 35082 Terrell Lynn Carr 35083 Gregory Allen Harding 35084 Michael James Harwood 35085 Barry Don Bomier 35086 Jody Allan Fink 35087 Drew M. Willard 35088 Ralph John Masi 35089 John Albert Gagnon 35090 Lee Anthony Jackson 35091 Matthew Noell Pridgeon 35092 Patrick Charles Short 35093 Jeffrey Lewis Yeaw 35094 Michael Christian Phillips 35095 James Anthony Thiel 35096 John Kevin McKeown 35097 Robert Allan Stackhouse 35098 Daniel Kenneth Alberico 35099 Carlos Arturo Calderon 35100 Raymond Murphy Beverley 35101 Mark Brian Geisler 35102 Ronald James Kelley 35103 William Francis Chin 35104 Thomas Adolph Meyers 35105 Steven G. Maida 35106 John Keith Langhauser 35107 James Aaron Vaughn 35108 Greg Arthur Gorzelnik 35109 Robert Michael Bankey 35110 Gregory S. Tate 35111 Theodore James Goldsmith 35112 Ivory Douglas Carson 35113 Keith Daniel Bombaugh 35114 Stephen Joseph Wunder 35115 Thomas Walter Lagarenne 35116 Miguel Rafael Valladares 35117 Ralph Willcox Kingman 35118 John Arthur Kime 35119 William Palmer Woodcock 35120 Alfred Arthur Wilson 35121 John Nichols Pruett 35122 Thomas Edward Lederle 35123 David Park Olslund 35124 John Elmer Peeler 35125 Larry Lynn Wheeler 35126 Bruce Richard Cogossi 35127 Kevin John Hayes 35128 Edgar Edward Smith 35129 Robert Wade Sanders 35130 Ronald Gene McCandless 35131 Kevin Robert Gardner 35132 Dan Joseph McConnell 35133 Richard Wayne Anderson 35134 Ralph D. Harris 35135 James David Skopek 35136 Cranson Avila Butler 35137 Michael V.R. Johnson 35138 Howard J. Benkert 35139 Randall Jay Thady 35140 Timothy J. Regan 35141 Roger Lee Moyer 35142 Frank Paul Vellella 35143 James Russell Kline 35144 David Jesse Hall 35145 Mark Andrew Haselton 35146 Gene Louis Rodriguez 35147 William David Holtvoight 35148 Robert Lewis Mitchell 35149 Jeffrey Michael Jancek 35150 Edward Douglas Clark 35151 James Edward Ward 35152 Marc Brandon Gunnels 35153 Michael Richard Klein 35154 Reginald Bernard McFadden 35155 Gerald Douglas Pace 35156 Michael Leo Trubia 35157 John Howard Powell 35158 Donald F. Camden 35159 Ray Michael Dowe 35160 Andrew Edward Pehonsky 35161 Vance C. Riggs 35162 Vance Jackson Walden 35163 Jerry Dean Porter 35164 Denis Egan Zambetti 35165 Richard Albert Burns 35166 Michael Alan Hodges 35167 Simon John Taflan 35168 Thomas Douglas Vonkaenel 35169 Gilbert Richard Collins 35170 John D. Bechtold 35171 Thomas Edward Markiewicz 35172 Christopher Charles Batchelder 35173 Cecil Cicero Loyd 35174 John Alan Kappel 35175 Allen J. Light 35176 Michael Matthew O'Brien 35177 Joseph Patrick Lynem 35178 Matthew Manton Holm 35179 William Robert Terry 35180 Jerry Taliaferro 35181 Paul Boyd Neal 35182 Thomas W. Strehle 35183 James Paul McFadden 35184 Arne Ellermets 35185 Geoffrey Alan Clark 35186 Blair Maguire Turner 35187 Phillip Louis Pierson 35188 Armin Jose Cruz 35189 Steven Peter Lopez 35190 Anthony Allen Pyne 35191 James Burke Murphy 35192 Mark Allen Daniels 35193 Kenneth Roger Blanset 35194 William Vincent Paul 35195 Jesus Alberto Lugo 35196 Charles Norman Busick 35197 Duncan Stuart Cameron 35198 Arthur De Vandus Jackson 35199 Michael Weir Adamson 35200 Joseph Martin Lunsford 35201 Mitchell Anthony Howell 35202 Rory Quintin Miott 35203 Ronald Jay Bramlett 35204 John Stephen Dinnell 35205 John Lawrence Ortman 35206 Joseph Anthony Durso 35207 George Henry Grotheer 35208 Larry Brian O'Neill 35209 James Monroe Morris 35210 Westley Kwai Heen Chin 35211 Martin Philip Bricker 35212 Eliseo Bentivoglio Passacantando 35213 Bradley Robert Ardner 35214 Douglas Roy Arndt 35215 Curtis L. Jones 35216 Michael Lee Church 35217 Carlos Jesus Asencio 35218 Ronald Robert Porter 35219 David Clayton Rost 35220 John Raymond Geiger 35221 Gregory Leon Robinson 35222 Hazen Lawrence Baron 35223 Roger Vance McMaster 35224 Paul Thomas Richardson 35225 Darrell Peebles 35226 Mathias George Foster 35227 Nicholas Francis Altomare 35228 Eugene Frederick Nosco 35229 William Edward Francis Scully 35230 Jack Saylor Heacock 35231 Kevin Michael Clement 35232 David Mark Chadwick 35233 Donald Lee Hinton 35234 Brien McGaffigan 35235 William Paul Shine 35236 Joseph Michael Tedesco 35237 Fredrick Bishop Seeger 35238 Robert Gordon Simmons 35239 Broadus Earl Watson 35240 Francis Wingate Saul 35241 Herman Edwin Denzler 35242 Edward Scott Powers 35243 Brett Allen Lewis 35244 Carl Lee Sizemore 35245 Weldon Barry Willhite 35246 Frank William White 35247 Kevin Porter Thompson 35248 Victor Tise 35249 Douglas Alan Biggerstaff 35250 Jesus Leonardo Olivo 35251 Colonel Zane McFadden 35252 Walter Leslie Frankland 35253 Timothy James Flanagan 35254 Scott D. Callender 35255 Gary Edward Starkweather 35256 Michael McLaughlin Quinn 35257 Meredith Paul Stone 35258 Mark Anthony Milia 35259 Lawrence J. Joustra 35260 Ralph M. Garduno 35261 Steven G. McManus 35262 Michael Robert Deets 35263 Reginald Keith Chapman 35264 Craig Alfred Schwegman 35265 **1978** David Allen Adam 35266 Dexter Curtis Adams 35267 Terry Rantz Adams 35268 Paul James Aiello 35269 Stephen Randall Aldrich 35270 John William Alexander 35271 Hal Kevin Alguire 35272 Curtis J. Alitz 35273 Charles Dexter Allen 35274 Charles William Allen 35275 Lloyd McKinley Alston 35276 Anthony Ted Alt 35277 Robert Peter Anastos 35278 Alan Arthur Anderson 35279 Darcy Glenn Anderson 35280 John Robert Anderson 35281 Mark Dunn Anderson 35282 Steven Mark Anderson 35283 Walter Neal Anderson 35284 Brad Thomas Andrew 35285 Bill Ray Aquino 35286 Daniel Louis Arczynski 35287 Francis John Arduini 35288 Gerard Anthony Armstrong 35289 John Loveland Armstrong 35290 Steven Nicholson Aude 35291 Joseph Stanley Augustine 35292 Charles Edward Austin 35293 Allison Travis Aycock 35294 William Guy Bacon 35295 Biff Leland Baker 35296 Paul Nichols Baker 35297 Thomas Newton Baker 35298 Mark Henry Bangsboll 35299 Keith Allen Banks 35300 James Martin Bannantine 35301 James Michael Bannister 35302 James O. Barclay 35303 Rodney Vernon Barnum 35304 Willard Earl Bartlett 35305 Joseph Charles Barto 35306 John Thomas Bartocci 35307 Charles Joseph Bartolotta 35308 Thomas Glen Barton 35309 Joseph Anthony Basile 35310 John Peter Basilica 35311 Reginald Leon Bassa 35312 Bruce James Baugh 35313 Kevin Michael Beam 35314 Tony Edward Beam 35315 William Darryl Beatty 35316 Bennett Charles Beaudry 35317 John Philip Becker 35318 Martin Donald Beckman 35319 Richard Mark Bega 35320 Jessy Joseph Benavente 35321 Jeffery Charles Benchich 35322 Ricky Benito 35323 Stanley Paul Berceau 35324 Michael David Berendt 35325 Mark Thomas Berry 35326 David Lee Bhame 35327 Michael Wayne Biering 35328 David Masud Bilyeu 35329 Robert Paul Birmingham 35330 Alan Scott Black 35331 James Willard Blake 35332 William Albert Blanding 35333 Paul Wiley Blankenship 35334 Herbert Wayne Blomquist 35335 Robert Mark Blum 35336 Timothy Michael Blumer 35337 Ervin Clement Boger 35338 Robert Brougham Boggs 35339 Marc Howard Boin 35340 John Manning Bolchoz 35341 Johnnie Loyd Bone 35342 Keith Earle Bonn 35343 Kirk Alan Boothe 35344 Robert Correa Borja 35345 Michael Bosack 35346 Thomas Paul Bostick 35347 Douglas Roland Bowman 35348 Quinton Vonette Bowman 35349 Clifton E. Boyd 35350 Jeffrey A. Brandl 35351 Robert Eugene Brassell 35352 Charles Patrick Braungart 35353 Mark Nash Braunstein 35354 Charles Alan Breeding 35355 Barry William Breitenbach 35356 Kenneth Michael Bresnahan 35357 John William Bressler 35358 George Robert Bristow 35359 Roger Kenneth Brown 35360 Harry R. Bruderly 35361 Jon Howard Brundage 35362 Mark Edward Buck 35363 William M. Buckler 35364 John William Buckley 35365 Laurence Booth Buckley 35366 James Joseph Budney 35367 Herman Eugene Bulls 35368 Michael Anthony Bumbulsky 35369 Andrew Peter Burke 35370 Kevin John Burke 35371 Brian McMahon Burr 35372 Joshua B. Burress 35373 Michael Edward Burton 35374 Daniel James Busby 35375 Stephen Robert Bush 35376 Thomas Alan Bush 35377 Benjamin Hollis Butler 35378 Jerome Knox Butler 35379 Howard Eugene Cabiness 35380 Brian Douglas Cade 35381 Steven Daniel Cage 35382 James Walter Calder 35383 Louis Caldera 35384 Russell Lynn Prewittcampbell 35385 Russell Earl Canfield 35386 Christopher Anthony Cano 35387 Randy Virlin Cargill 35388 Salome Acosta Carrasco 35389 Thomas Christopher Carroll 35390 Thomas Michael Carroll 35391 Calvin George Carter 35392 Robert Lee Carter 35393 Michael James Casas 35394 James Francis Casey 35395 Richard James Cashman 35396 Michael Peter Castelli 35397 Mark Francis Cawley 35398 Ricardo Ceja 35399 Robert John Celski 35400 Joseph Henry Cerv 35401 Robert Lawrence Chadwick 35402 James Darwin Chandler 35403 Paul Steven Chang 35404 Douglas Earl Chapman 35405 Harold L. Chappell 35406 Steven Alan Chester 35407 Stephen B. Childers 35408 Darryl Kwock Hung Ching 35409 Paul Anthony Christiani 35410 William Kevin Citera 35411 Robert Philip Clair 35412 George Dennis Clark 35413 Michell Carnelious Clark 35414 Robert Clayton 35415 Terry L. Clemons 35416 Charles Thomas Cleveland 35417 Kevin Reuben Clowes 35418 James Henry Coffman 35419 Stewart Lynn Coker 35420 Craig Eugene College 35421 Michael H. Collins 35422 Terry Wayne Collins 35423 Michael Colpo 35424 Gary Gerard Conlon 35425 Thomas J. Conneran 35426 Enrique Contreras 35427 Patrick Boone Conway 35428 Jonathan S. Coomes 35429 John Emil Cornelius 35430 Charles D. Cornwell 35431 Randy Michael Cotton 35432 David S. Cottrell 35433 Michael Paul Coville 35434 Charles Thomas Coyle 35435 Paul Earl Crandall 35436 Randy Orison Crane 35437 Cameron Allen Crawford 35438 Kevin Kenneth Crawford 35439 Michael L. Creed 35440 Michael John Creen 35441 David Bruce Cripps 35442 Gordon Wendell Crom 35443 John Joseph Cronin 35444 Lawrence Martin Cuculic 35445 Winfred Scott Cummings 35446 Kenneth Raymond Curley 35447 Stephen Lee Curtis 35448 Leo Joseph Cyr 35449 Stephen Curtis Daffron 35450 John F. D'Agostino 35451 Milan Clarke Dahlquist 35452 Douglas Melvin Daily 35453 Paul Myron Daily 35454 Karl D. D'Amico 35455 William Ray Damsel 35456 Timothy Daniel 35457 Jay Franklin Daniels 35458 Glen Joseph D'Arcangelo 35459 Thomas James Darnell 35460 Donald Royce Davidson 35461 Richard Edward Davidson 35462 Addison Dimmitt Davis 35463 Alan LeRoy Davis 35464 Robert Francis Davis 35465 Donald Wight Dawson 35466 Richard Philip De Fatta 35467 Gregg Francis Degen 35468 Robert De Leon 35469 Maurice John Delorey 35470 Douglas Paul DeMoss 35471 John Richard DePiazza 35472 Terry Keith DeRouchey 35473 Glenn Marshall De Soto 35474 Charles Emil Dixon 35475 Nelson Craig Dodd 35476 Richard Craig Doerer 35477 George Thomas Dolan 35478 Keith R. Donnelly 35479 Dennis Patrick Donovan 35480 Jeffrey James Dorko 35481 Kevin C. Downey 35482 Curtis J. Downs 35483 James Evan Drake 35484 John Lawrence Drew 35485 Stuart Parker Drury 35486 Joseph John Duda 35487 Glen Paul Dudevoir 35488 George R. Dunaway 35489 Mark Edward Durant 35490 Stuart Morris Dyer 35491 Thomas Melroy Easton 35492 David Harley Eby 35493 Charles Raymond Eddy 35494 David Leo Edwards 35495 Earl Wayne Edwards 35496 Jens Curtis Egeland 35497 Richard W. Ehni 35498 Mark Andrew Eidem 35499 Albert A. Eisele 35500 Edward Clay Elias 35501 David C. Elliott 35502 Mark A. English 35503 Adolph Henry Ernst 35504 Peter Alan Eschbach 35505 Christopher G. Essig 35506 Allen C. Estes 35507 Gary Lynn Evans 35508 Wenzel Gayler Evans 35509 James William Ewing 35510 Jack E. Faires 35511 William Herbert Fairfield 35512 Edward Martin Fallon 35513 John William Faulconbridge 35514 Gary Michael Fechter 35515 Arnold Anthony Ferrando 35516 Robert Bruce Fess 35517 Charles James Fiala 35518 Glenn Robert Fisher 35519 Daniel Leroy Fitch 35520 Brian Fitzpatrick 35521 David John Fitzpatrick 35522 Manuel J.F. Hernandez 35523 Timothy Lee Flugum 35524 Jeffrey W. Foley 35525 Gordon James Folse 35526 Daniel Edward Ford 35527 Stanley Harrison Ford 35528 Henry Ray Fore 35529 William Howell Forrester 35530 William Martin Foster 35531 John Robert Fox 35532 William Lee Fox 35533 David Michael Frank 35534 Eric H. Franks 35535 Martin Calvert Frazier 35536 Brian Douglas Freund 35537 Donald Lau Fry 35538 Ronald David Frye 35539 Steven Leslie Fuller 35540 Raymond Victor Furstenau 35541 George Daniel Gagaris 35542 Ricardo Greg Galindo 35543 Jay Elgin John Gallagher 35544 John Robert Folino Gallo 35545 James Vance Galloway 35546 Gerald Paul Gallup 35547 Rudolph Nicasio Garcia 35548 John Alexander Garrido 35549 Robert R. Gaydos 35550 William Scott Gemma 35551 Richard Brian Georgi 35552 Ronald Jeffrey Geouque 35553 Craig Thompson Gilbert 35554 James Joseph Gildea 35555 Gray Moore Gildner 35556 Henry Dale Gill 35557 Henry S. Gillen 35558 Timothy Patrick Glenn 35559 Daniel Frank Goerke 35560 Randy George Goff 35561 Joe Robert Gonzalez 35562 Juan Gonzalez 35563 Thomas W. Grace 35564 Ramon R. Grado 35565 Reginald Antonio Grant 35566 Thomas Grant 35567 Kenneth Philip Graves 35568 William Gerald Graves 35569 Douglas Henry Gray 35570 Christopher Daniel Grech 35571 Robert Keefer Greenawalt 35572 Timothy James Greene 35573 Charles Steven Griffin 35574 John Gerald Griffith 35575 Todd David Griffith 35576 Andrew Mark Grimalda 35577 John David Gross 35578 Robert Kellam Grubbs 35579 Patrick Andrew Guinnane 35580 Gary John Gumm 35581 Michael John Guthrie 35582 Thomas Garland Guthrie 35583 Robert Gerald Gutjahr 35584 Thomas Jesse Guzman 35585 Terrance Paul Haack 35586 John Daniel Hackenberg 35587 William Joseph Haese 35588 David Campbell Hall 35589 Leamon Lamar Hall 35590 Max Noble Hall 35591 Millard Hall 35592 Ronald Mark Hall 35593 Donald Lee Halvorsen 35594 Dale Allen Hamby 35595 Robert William Hamilton 35596 William Wade Hamilton 35597 Daniel Robert Hammond 35598 Dawson Roger Hancock 35599 Daniel Quincy Hand 35600 Knute Edward Hankins 35601 Mark James Hansen 35602 Frank Austin Hardy 35603 Perry Hargrove 35604 Ronald Keith Haring 35605 Edward Gerard Harkin 35606 Randall Bradley Harkins 35607 William Eugene Harner 35608 Anthony William Harriman 35609 George Ray Harris 35610 Jonathan M. Harrison 35611 Robert L. Harrison 35612 Edward Arthur Hart 35613 William Edward Harter 35614 Jay Allan Hatch 35615 Thomas Wayne Hayes 35616 Steven Jordan Haynes 35617 James John Hays 35618 Stephen Varnell Heard 35619 Ted Earl Heath 35620 John William Hedberg 35621 Benny Coleman Hedden 35622 Thomas Patrick Hedge 35623 Thomas David Hedglin 35624 Charles Ford Heinlen 35625 Kurt Konrad Heinzerling 35626 Richard Nelson Helfer 35627 Daniel Lee Heller 35628 Karl David Heller 35629 Gustaf Alfred Hellzen 35630 Steven Evald Heltemes 35631 Robert Earl Hendrick 35632 Lonnie Dean Henley 35633 Peter A. Henry 35634 Randall Stephen Henson 35635 Thomas James Herbert 35636 Leo Sylvester Hergenroeder 35637 Robert Arthur Hernandez 35638 Herbert Elmo Herndon 35639 Keith Earl Herrington 35640 James Morgan Heverin 35641 Kirby Wayne Hicks 35642 Timothy Edward Higgens 35643 John Randall Higgins 35644 Ronald Paul Higham 35645 Randall William Hill 35646 Robert MacDonald Hill 35647 Cecil Thomas Hobbs 35648 James Luther Hodge 35649 Daniel Paul Hoeh 35650 James Allen Hoffman 35651 Terrence Keith Hoffman 35652 Robert Henry Hoisington 35653 Mark David Holdeman 35654 James Jujuan Hollingsworth 35655 Sanford Eugene Holman 35656 John Charles Holmberg 35657 Brent Leon Holmes 35658 Stephen G. Holt 35659 Thomas Duane Hook 35660 Charles Daimon Hooker 35661 Timothy William Hope 35662 Clinton Mack Horn 35663 Karl Raymond Horst 35664 David Wood Hough 35665 William Arthur Houtz 35666 Wayne Richard Hudry 35667 Eric Martin Hughes 35668 Joseph Ernest Hunt 35669 Paul Raymond Hunter 35670 Leroy Treft Hurt 35671 Stephen Scott Hutton 35672 Philip Cecil Hyland 35673 David Lawrence Innis 35674 Dewey Monroe Jackson 35675 Kevin Dale Jackson 35676 Kevin Michael Jackson 35677 Paul Joseph Jacobsmeyer 35678 Charles H. Jacoby 35679 Joseph Lee James 35680 Adam Jan Janczewski 35681 William John Janowski 35682 Terrance Edward Jedrziewski 35683 Scott Heyward Jeffers 35684 Peter Frank Jelen 35685 Howard Charles Jelinek 35686 David Alan Jellison 35687 James Streeter Jenkins 35688 Wallace David Jenkins 35689 David Canning Jennings 35690 Thomas William Jewell 35691 James David Jogerst 35692 Orley Harley Medford Johns 35693 Brent A. Johnson 35694 Harry Edwin Johnson 35695 Mark Bruton Johnson 35696 Michael James Johnson 35697 Paul Anthony Johnson 35698 Stephen Lee Johnson 35699 Keith Patrick Jones 35700 Kenneth Lee Jones 35701 Robert Daniel Jones 35702 Russell Leon Jones 35703 Daniel Scott Jorgenson 35704 Leland Thomas Jourdan 35705 Michael Edward Kaczmarek 35706 Kim Robert Kadesch 35707 Terrence Allen Kanka 35708 Robert Vincent Kazimer 35709 Scott Alden Kearby 35710 Leo Frank Keechi 35711 Brian Francis Keenan 35712 Gary Joseph Kelley 35713 Timothy Patrick Kelly 35714 Jon Warren Kerbs 35715 Robert Brian Keyser 35716 William G. Kimball 35717 John Patrick Francis Kimmel 35718 Earle Wadsworth Kirkland 35719 Craig Thomas Kirkpatrick 35720 Michael William Kiser 35721 Ronald Kearney Knapp 35722 James E. Knauff 35723 Robert James Knight 35724 William Frederick Knoll 35725 Robert Edward Knotts 35726 Abbott Clinton Koehler 35727 Royal Warren Koepsell 35728 Kenneth Dale Konigsmark 35729 Edward Joseph Kornish 35730 Alexander Dennis Korzyk 35731 Stephen Raymond Kostek 35732 Robert Kadgihn Koster 35733 Edward Robert Koucheravy 35734 Robert George Koval 35735 Michael Edward Krieger 35736 Kirk Matthew Krist 35737 Gary Allen Kussman 35738 Mark Phillip Kwasniewski 35739 Samuel John Lacombe 35740 William George Lake 35741 Michael J. Lally 35742 Robert Jones Lamb 35743 Ryan Williams LaMothe 35744 Raymond Paul Lamoureux 35745 Patrick George Landry 35746 Jackson Lee Lansford 35747 Thomas Calvin Lawing 35748 Stephen Richard Layfield 35749 Howard Scott Lazarus 35750 Geary Laverne Leathers 35751 David Marshall Lemcoe 35752 William Frederick Lemnitzer 35753 Henry Russell LePage 35754 Francis Arthur Lesieur 35755 Roberto Alfonso Levoit 35756 Donald Gene Lewis 35757 James Michael Lewis 35758 Danilo Delapuz Lim 35759 Robert Carl Lindquist 35760 Peter Charles Linskey 35761 Christopher John Littel 35762 Richard John Lohne 35763 John J. Londa 35764 Jeffrey Wayne Long 35765 William Dale Long 35766 James Ching Loo 35767 Scott Lyle Loomis 35768 Nicholas W. Lorber 35769 James Allen Loseke 35770 Jay C. Loufek 35771 John Michael Lovejoy 35772 James Hart Luckett 35773 Daniel S. Ludwig 35774 David Wayne Lutz 35775 Kurt O Neal Lynam 35776 John Peter Lynaugh 35777 Peter Leroy Lyon 35778 Richard Joseph Lyons 35779 Patrick John MacArevey 35780 Douglas Lance Machamer 35781 Tadeusz Stefan Maciuba 35782 John Francis Mack 35783 Robert W. Madden 35784 John David Mahony 35785 Christopher Benjamin Maitin 35786 Richard Anthony Makowski 35787 Anthony Louis Malagrino 35788 Robert Prentice Mallory 35789 Paul Bernard Malone 35790 Billy Mike Maloney 35791 Michael Eugene Mamer 35792 Edward J. Manion 35793 Robert Brooks Manion 35794 Gordon Harman Manley 35795 Jeff Alan Manley 35796 Jaime Marenco 35797 Dario Urbano Margve 35798 James Nicholas Marino 35799 John Eric Marlin 35800 John Maynard Marshall 35801 Stephen John Marshall 35802 Kevin Dean Martin 35803 Kevin M. Martin 35804 Quinton R. Martin 35805 Peter H. Martini 35806 John Francis Maskavich 35807 Robert Alan Maszarose 35808 George John Matis 35809 Julio Antonio Matos 35810 Gregory Blake Matthews 35811 R. Douglas Maurer 35812 Chris Clay Maxfield 35813 Jody Allen Maxwell 35814 Richard Eugene Maxwell 35815 David Scott Mayer 35816 Gerald Thomas Mayer 35817 Brian Keith Mays 35818 William Joseph McArdle 35819 Keith Charles McCaffrey 35820 Timothy Joseph McCarville 35821 Joseph Courtney McClendon 35822 Gary Lynn McCorkindale 35823 Mark McLean McCormick 35824 Curtis Lynn McCoy 35825 John Forrest McCue 35826 Floyd Ray McDaniel 35827 Patrick Oscar McGaugh 35828 Vol Forrest McGlothlin 35829 Kevin Peter McGrath 35830 Mark Lettelle McGruder 35831 Stephen John McHale

35832 Harry Lee McIntosh 35833 Michael Edwin McIntyre 35834 Tim Roberts McKaig 35835 Gary D. McKee 35836 Jackie Deane McKown 35837 Roy Edmon McLendon 35838 Keith R. McLoughlin 35839 Dennis Eugene McMichael 35840 Robert Lee McNamara 35841 James Neil McNeill 35842 Richard R. McPhee 35843 Joseph John McVeigh 35844 Thomas Andrew McWhorter 35845 Gary Russell Meden 35846 Stephen Roy Meek 35847 Gregory Lynn Melville 35848 Miguel Angel Mendoza 35849 Richard Allen Metro 35850 Larry Davie Meyer 35851 Robert Francis Xavier Meyer 35852 Floyd Mike Miles 35853 Paul Cutler Miles 35854 Jon Jeffrey Miller 35855 Richard Bruce Miller 35856 Richard Dean Miller 35857 Steven Joseph Miller 35858 Tod Weston Miller 35859 Wyatt Jay Mills 35860 Thomas Francis Milo 35861 Mark David Mingilton 35862 James Buford Misenheimer 35863 Joseph William Mislinski 35864 Charles Elijah Mitchell 35865 Darryl Levy Mobley 35866 William John Moeller 35867 Michael C. Monical 35868 Gary Allen Moody 35869 James Monte Moon 35870 Roger Michael Moore 35871 Daniel Fuller Moorer 35872 Jose Torres Morales 35873 Charles Joseph Moratz 35874 Craig Andrew Morehead 35875 Thomas John Moriarty 35876 Patrick Francis Morris 35877 Guy Arthur Morrison 35878 John Wilson Morrison 35879 Richard Edward Morrow 35880 Thomas Alan Mothorpe 35881 James Patrick Moye 35882 Myron Desverney Moye 35883 Michael Kent Moyer 35884 David Lee Mull 35885 Randall Paul Munch 35886 Lawrence Harvey Murphey 35887 Brian Francis Murphy 35888 Glenn Alan Murray 35889 Joseph Vincent Muscarella 35890 Cris P. Myers 35891 Jeffrey Ford Myers 35892 Joseph Dwan Myers 35893 Scott Dalton Myers 35894 Fred Haskell Naber 35895 James Joseph Nagy 35896 James Thomas Nalepa 35897 Bernard Joseph Nally 35898 William Fitzgerald Napier 35899 Joseph Victor Napoli 35900 Barrington Nelson Nash 35901 Michael James Neilson 35902 James Arthur Neumann 35903 Gary Francis Christopher Neuser 35904 James Warren Nichols 35905 David Simon Niekerk 35906 Wayne Joseph Nixon 35907 Dean Andrew Nowowiejski 35908 Timothy Joseph O'Brien 35909 William Vincent O'Brien 35910 Christopher Edward O'Connor 35911 Patrick Jay O'Connor 35912 David Orville Odegard 35913 Daniel Swain O'Dell 35914 John Bellis O'Dowd 35915 Rodger Alan Oetjen 35916 John Arthur Offerman 35917 Robert Francis Olds 35918 James Allen Olecki 35919 Jose Raul Olivero 35920 Arild Walter Olsen 35921 Edward Joseph O'Neill 35922 Mark Edward O'Neill 35923 Guy Poolanui Ontai 35924 Patrick J. O'Reilly 35925 Stephen Michael Orloff 35926 Frederick David Orr 35927 F. Raymond Ortega 35928 James M. Ortiz 35929 James Canty O'Shaughnessy 35930 Kelly David Osmer 35931 Gerard Matthew Ousley 35932 Carl D. Owens 35933 Eugene Joseph Palka 35934 Charles Russell Palm 35935 Douglas Charles Palmer 35936 Leonard Earl Palmer 35937 Roy Joseph Panzarella 35938 James Spero Pappafotis 35939 Joseph Mickler Parker 35940 Norman Sanford Parlier 35941 Donald Gilbert Patchell 35942 John Walter Paul 35943 Walter Esper Paulekas 35944 Jack Pearson 35945 Patrick Morgan Pedden 35946 Michael Eugene Perry 35947 Randy Marion Perry 35948 Daniel Ross Peterman 35949 James Dean Peterson 35950 Kendall Cox Peterson 35951 Joseph John Pfanzelter 35952 Michael Anthony Phillips 35953 David Steven Pickerell 35954 Thomas David Pijor 35955 Calvin Fitz Herbert Pilgrim 35956 Gerald William Pina 35957 Robert Lee Platt 35958 Terence Lyn Plautz 35959 Robert Michael Player 35960 Rex Anthony Ploederer 35961 Edward Tracy Poore 35962 William Lewis Post 35963 Charles Grady Powell 35964 Stephen Hibbert Powell 35965 Gerard Shanley Preece 35966 Michael William Price 35967 Wallace Walter Price 35968 Ronald Gene Prichard 35969 Mark Charles Prugh 35970 William Nathan Pulliam 35971 John Paul Quigley 35972 David Gregory Quimby 35973 Russell Edward Quirici 35974 Kenneth J. Rackers 35975 Joseph Bernard Raczkowski 35976 Burt George Ramos 35977 Calvin Tembrevilla Ramos 35978 Robert Mark Rapone 35979 Earl David Rasmussen 35980 James Edward Ray 35981 Terry Maxwell Reed 35982 Michael Patrick Regan 35983 Adam Joseph Reich 35984 Eric Francis Reichelt 35985 Gary Evan Reisenwitz 35986 Eugene K. Ressler 35987 Paul C. Reynolds 35988 Richard Allen Rhinehart 35989 Stephen Kelton Rice 35990 David Franklin Rich 35991 Larry Tim Rich 35992 David Lee Riese 35993 Michael Neal Riley 35994 Timothy Devall Ringgold 35995 Harry Niles Rising 35996 David Wayne Robbins 35997 David Matthew Roberson 35998 George Roberta 35999 Russell Lee Roberts 36000 James D. Rodgers 36001 Orlando Ramon Rodriguez 36002 Patrick Victor Rogers 36003 Robert Eugene Rogers 36004 John Edward Rogert 36005 Jeffrey Allen Romer 36006 Mark A. Roncoli 36007 Leland Dale Ronningen 36008 John Paul Rooney 36009 Joseph M. Rose 36010 Blair Arthur Ross 36011 Bradley Nolan Rounding 36012 Richard Leroy Routh 36013 David Michael Rudorfer 36014 Robert Joseph Rush 36015 Paul Steven Rusinko 36016 Robert Ryan 36017 Rory Alan Salimbene 36018 Douglas Warren Salzmann 36019 James Walter Sample 36020 Maynard Jackson Sanders 36021 Peter D. Sanders 36022 Steve Richard Sanders 36023 Robert Alvin Sarginger 36024 Stuart William Sarkela 36025 William Danny Sartin 36026 Gale Warren Satre 36027 Mark Christopher Savarese 36028 Carl Samuel Savino 36029 Curtis Michael Scaparrotti 36030 Michael Joseph Schaefer 36031 John Adam Schell 36032 Henry Louis Schnepf 36033 Gerard T. Scholz 36034 Wayne Evertt Schoonveld 36035 John F. Schorsch 36036 Daniel James Schultz 36037 Vincent James Schultz 36038 John Franklin Scott 36039 Randle Eric Scott 36040 Philip Harold Scriber 36041 Christopher Scroggins 36042 Marion Joseph Seaton 36043 Edward Christian Segaar 36044 Kenneth Robert Seitz 36045 Martin Earl Selleck 36046 Keith Lynn Sellen 36047 Ralph David Semmel 36048 Charles Frank Shaver 36049 Robert Grant Shaw 36050 Mortimer Charles Shea 36051 Franklin A. Shearer 36052 Kevin Patrick Sheehan 36053 Richard Earl T. Sheffield 36054 Robert Louis Sheffler 36055 Christopher L. Shepherd 36056 Milan William Shepherd 36057 Kevin Edmund Sherlock 36058 Mark Forrester Shields 36059 Scott Harmon Shorr 36060 Charles G. Short 36061 Stephen Gale Short 36062 Clarence Allan Shuford 36063 Michael John Sienicki 36064 Michael Joseph Silva 36065 Ward Ross Silvola 36066 Frank Paul Simpkins 36067 John H. Sinclair 36068 Michael John Six 36069 Michael Ray Skaggs 36070 Brian Edward Skutt 36071 Richard Clay Slack 36072 Michael David Slotnick 36073 Curtis Smith 36074 David John Smith 36075 John Edward Boker Smith 36076 Robert L. Smith 36077 Roland Charles Smith 36078 Thomas J. Snukis 36079 Robin Martin Snyder 36080 John Andrew Soldo 36081 Jose I. Solera 36082 Edward Jack Solomon 36083 Joseph Louis Spenneberg 36084 Oren D. Sprague 36085 Robert Elmer Sprague 36086 Ronnie Gordon Stauffenberg 36087 Matthew Daniel Stavish 36088 Gustave Ross Steenborg 36089 R. James Steiner 36090 Ralph Richard Steinke 36091 Gary L. Stenzel 36092 Andrew John Stevens 36093 John Francis Stewart 36094 George Warren Stone 36095 James Leighton Stover 36096 William Andrew Stranko 36097 Randolph Peter Strong 36098 Russell Charles Struble 36099 Thomas Edward Strutz 36100 Gregory Allan Stump 36101 Kevin Michael Stump 36102 Garrett James Sullivan 36103 James Francis Sullivan 36104 James Stephen Sullivan 36105 Paul Hugh Sullivan 36106 William Charles Sumner 36107 Thaddeus Lloyd Suter 36108 David Franklin Swafford 36109 David Arthur Swart 36110 Timothy Jay Sweeney 36111 Steven E. Sykes 36112 Leslie Szabolcsi 36113 Dennis J. Szydloski 36114 Robert Stephen Talianko 36115 Dale Clarence Tatarek 36116 Francis Phillip Taylor 36117 John Lawrence Taylor 36118 Timothy Taylor 36119 William Romayne Taylor 36120 Andrew MacDonald Tedesco 36121 Carl Maddams Tegen 36122 Mark Steven Tejan 36123 Peter Rudy Tellmann 36124 George M. Telthorst 36125 Nicholas Joseph Tessino 36126 John D. Thomas 36127 Ted Alan Thomas 36128 Richard Gregg Thompson 36129 Stuart Nelson Thompson 36130 William Richard Thompson 36131 John York Thornton 36132 Kenneth Robert Thronson 36133 Michael Timothy Tobin 36134 Lenobio S. Toledo 36135 John Michael Tomkovich 36136 Paul Lester Tomlinson 36137 Ryan Timothy Toole 36138 Peter Gregory Torok 36139 Arthur Thomas Mary Tracy 36140 Joseph John Tramposch 36141 Grant Edward Trobaugh 36142 Simeon George Trombitas 36143 George Marion Tronsrue 36144 Robert P. Ufford 36145 Carlos Antonio Usera 36146 Abraham George Valdez 36147 John Vance Vanderbleek 36148 Steven Leroy Van Drew 36149 Richard David Van Orsdale 36150 Vaughn Garner Akimeka Vasconcellos 36151 James Edward Veditz 36152 Doug A. Vermillion 36153 Arthur Veros 36154 Scott M. Vickers 36155 Mark Elliot Vinson 36156 Roderick Thomas Visser 36157 John Albert Vitagliano 36158 Martin Louis Vozzo 36159 Patrick D. Vye 36160 Leigh William Wacenske 36161 Robert Joseph Walcott 36162 John A. Walden 36163 John James Walker 36164 Stephen Leslie Walker 36165 Kevin Blaise Wall 36166 Jeffrey David Wallace 36167 Kevin Patrick Walsh 36168 Robert Gene Walters 36169 William John Wansley 36170 Monroe Payne Warner 36171 Thomas William Weafer 36172 James Edward Weger 36173 W. Bond Wells 36174 Alvis Archer Wheatley 36175 Jesse Allen White 36176 Monte Anthony White 36177 Wayne Lynn White 36178 Joseph Alexander Whitfield 36179 Cecil Duane Whittington 36180 Michael Vincent Wickham 36181 David Mark Wiener 36182 James Scott Wiggins 36183 Laurence Curt Wiggins 36184 Bruce A. Wilhelm 36185 David Yoe Williams 36186 Kenneth R. Williams 36187 Robert Gerard Williams 36188 Paul George Williamson 36189 William Gary Wilson 36190 Earl Roy Wingrove 36191 Gary Joseph Winton 36192 Dale William Wittig 36193 James Michael Wolfe 36194 William Joseph Wolfe 36195 Steven Stanley Wolszczak 36196 James Dankwerth Wookey 36197 Charles Floyd Wright 36198 William Earl Wrinkle 36199 Mark Benson Wroth 36200 Richard Habersham Wylly 36201 Joseph Stephen Yavorsky 36202 Bruce Phillip Yost 36203 Christopher J. Young 36204 James Lowen Young 36205 Victor James Young 36206 James Patrick Yuengert 36207 Paul Anthony Zacharzuk 36208 Phillip Joseph Zeller 36209 William John Zientek 36210 Douglas Kent Zimmerman 36211 Daniel Lee Zimmermann 36212 Robert William Zittleman 36213 George Louis Adamakos 36214 Michael Lowell Belter 36215 Jeffrey Mark Blower 36216 Philip Joseph Brandli 36217 George Michael Cuesta 36218 Anthony Brockton Dailey 36219 Thomas Gerard Day 36220 George Arthur Deitz 36221 Curtis Alexander Harris 36222 Gregory King 36223 Shawn Peter Lovett 36224 Kenneth Robert Lucas 36225 Steven Doyle MacLellan 36226 Benson Ocampo Malto 36227 Steven Eugene Marts 36228 Kevin Andrew McCaffrey 36229 Douglas Paul McIntosh 36230 Michael John Miller 36231 Marvis Moseley 36232 Mark Loyal Nancarrow 36233 James Gary Pentecost 36234 William Scott Potter 36235 Norman Dean Sams 36236 Keith Henry Wilson 36237 Edward Park Donnelly 36238 John Daniel Gallivan 36239 Jessie Milton Hartman 36240 James Michael Keating 36241 Matthew Peter Saitta 36242 Robert Aubrey Smentkowski 36243 Tony Glen Smith 36244 John Christopher Storbeck 36245 Mark William Jones 36246 **1979** Blaine Fidler Aaron 36247 Kent Wayne Abernathy 36248 Jesse Thomas Acosta 36249 William Dean Adams 36250 William Gregory Adams 36251 Thomas Paul Aeillo 36252 Marc I. Alderman 36253 Thomas Joseph Alfonso 36254 Thomas Allen Allmon 36255 Richard Frederick Ambruster 36256 Jeffrey Montgomery Ames 36257 Robert Koerner Amster 36258 Kurt William Andersen-Vie 36259 Joel Melvin Anderson 36260 Louis Brian Anderson 36261 Marvin Paul Anderson 36262 Neil Andres 36263 James A. Angelosante 36264 Dean William Anker 36265 Douglas Paul Anson 36266 Jeffrey Alan Appleget 36267 Stephen Anthony Arata 36268 Harry Martell Gwynn Argo 36269 Thomas Armstrong 36270 Kevin James Arnold 36271 Alan Dale Arthur 36272 Stuart Douglas Artman 36273 Charles James Atcitty 36274 Michael Duane Austin 36275 Stephen D. Austin 36276 Robert Edward Avey 36277 Mark S. Bahr 36278 Douglas Sharpe Baker 36279 George Ronald E. Baker 36280 Andrew Joseph Balafas 36281 Curtis Balom 36282 Gregory Thomas Banner 36283 Albert Florindo Barese 36284 Thomas William Barth 36285 J. Craig Bartsch 36286 Jeffrey Lynn Bassette 36287 Michael John Bates 36288 Bruce William Batten 36289 Kent Carleton Bauer 36290 Christopher Jennings Beam 36291 Michael D. Beasley 36292 Robert James Beatty 36293 Andrew Gregg Beeson 36294 David Robert Belcher 36295 John Carl Berger 36296 J. Kevin Berner 36297 Gregory Leroy Berry 36298 Larry Alan Besterman 36299 Charles N. Betack 36300 Stephen G. Bianco 36301 William Robertsmith Bishop 36302 Calvin Lawrence Black 36303 Marvin Carl Blackburn 36304 Bruce Eugene Blackmon 36305 John Melville Blaine 36306 David Mark Blakemore 36307 Albert Marshall Bleakley 36308 Dale Michael Bleckman 36309 Robert Elliot Bleimeister 36310 Gregory Paul Blenski 36311 Timothy Donald Bloechl 36312 Michael Edward Boatner 36313 Brian Francis Bocklage 36314 Bruce Alan Boldon 36315 Antonius Johannes Bom 36316 Marcus Bonds 36317 John Henry Bone 36318 Ronald Mark Bonesteel 36319 Douglas Alan Boone 36320 Bruce Keith Bornick 36321 James Joseph Bouchard 36322 Dennis Eugene Bowden 36323 William Earl Bowers 36324 Kevin Lee Bowles 36325 Jerry Logan Bowling 36326 Brent Murrey Boyles 36327 Gregory John Bozek 36328 Paul Richard Bozek 36329 Bruce William Brackett 36330 Gregory Keith Brannon 36331 Charles Bernard Breslin 36332 William Gerard Brinn 36333 Leo Austin Brooks 36334 Robert Regan Broome 36335 John David Brophy 36336 Matthew J. Brown 36337 William Michael Brown 36338 Clennie Lee Brundidge 36339 John William Bruno 36340 Bruce Edward Brydges 36341 Stephen Duane Buck 36342 Paul Acker Buckhout 36343 Paul Thomas Buhl 36344 Edward Jerome Bullard 36345 Hal Richard Burton 36346 Douglas Michael Busch 36347 Gary Stewart Butler 36348 Jerry Lee Butler 36349 Kevin Michael Butler 36350 Milton Thadd Buzan 36351 Michael John Cadle 36352 Robert Michael Caliva 36353 John Francis Campbell 36354 Roy Edward Campbell 36355 Todd Ross Campbell 36356 Peter Charles Campisi 36357 Mark Lee Cannady 36358 Pedro H. Cano 36359 David John Capp 36360 William Guillermo Cardenas 36361 Kelly John Carew 36362 Robert Lawrence Carney 36363 Thomas Joseph Carney 36364 Keith Allen Carpenter 36365 Robert William Case 36366 Alan Clifford Cate 36367 Florencio Tagle Cayco 36368 Carl Patrick Cecil 36369 Kevin Howard Chaples 36370 Arlen Dale Chapman 36371 James R. Charlton 36372 Michael Jay Cheng 36373 Donald Edward Chrans 36374 Gregory Peter Chura 36375 Stephen Gerard Chura 36376 Timothy Philip Clapp 36377 James P. Clarahan 36378 David Cecil Clark 36379 David Sheridan Clark 36380 John D. Clark 36381 Michael Gemmell Clark 36382 Jack Hines Cleland 36383 Edward F. Clemons 36384 Francis Drury Clepper 36385 Michael Francis Cochrane 36386 Louis Francis Cocker 36387 James Vance Cockerham 36388 Thomas M. Cole 36389 Samuel Jeffrey Colella 36390 Joe Thomas Coleman 36391 Thomas Edward Coleman 36392 Francis Anthony Colletti 36393 Matthew Samuel Collier 36394 Christopher Allan Collins 36395 Lynn Alan Collyar 36396 Michael Paul Comodeca 36397 Brian Paul Concannon 36398 Robert William Cone 36399 Michael John Conrad 36400 George Stephen Conwill 36401 Clair Edward Conzelman 36402 John Joseph Cook 36403 Eric C. Cooper 36404 Jeffrey Jay Cooper 36405 Mauro Antonio Cooper 36406 Mark A. Copperthite 36407 Liam Padraig Corballis 36408 Ernest Lee Cornell 36409 James Thomas Corrigan 36410 Steven Scott Cotariu 36411 Thomas Albert Couture 36412 David Oliveira Couvelha 36413 David Alan Cox 36414 Kendall Page Cox 36415 Michael Philip Coyle 36416 L. Steven Cramer 36417 Jerry A. Crane 36418 Timothy Lee Crane 36419 Francisco Antonio Crescioni 36420 Mark S. Crowson 36421 Steven Joel Crutchfield 36422 Anthony A. Cucolo 36423 Donald Reuben Curtis 36424 Richard Lane Dalzell 36425 Gary M. Danczyk 36426 Douglas Edward Danko 36427 Gregory James Dardis 36428 Lloyd Randolph Darlington 36429 Richard A. Davis 36430 Steven Scott Davis 36431 Mark Jeffrey Dawes 36432 James Sanders Day 36433 Timothy Kevin Deady 36434 Paul Edward DeBenedictis 36435 Christian E. de Graff 36436 Jack DeLeon 36437 Edward Nicholas DeLia 36438 Michael Francis DeMayo 36439 Lawrence Depriest DeRamus 36440 Peter Samuel DeRobertis 36441 James Stuart Dewitt 36442 Kevin Lee Dibb 36443 John Wesley Dietz 36444 Joseph F. DiGangi 36445 Mark Robert Dilandro 36446 Dominick Michael Dilauria 36447 Thomas Gregory Dillon 36448 Brian Albert Dionne 36449 Paul John Diorio 36450 Philip James DiSalvo 36451 Herbert Mahlon Dixon 36452 Kenneth Edmond Dixon 36453 John William Dluhos 36454 Douglas C. Doan 36455 John Breese Dollison 36456 Philip Lee Donihe 36457 Edwin Lafayette Dottery 36458 Edmund Alexander Dowling 36459 Gerald Fearn Drago 36460 Scott Richard Dratch 36461 Patrick Joseph Driscoll 36462 Robert Edwin Driscoll 36463 Ernest Allen Drott 36464 Robert Harry Drumm 36465 William Thomas Drummond 36466 Richard James Duckworth 36467 Scott Reynold Duffin 36468 Andrew James Duffy 36469 Michael Eugene Duffy 36470 William Ryan Duffy 36471 Jeffrey D. Duncan 36472 Richard Kent Duncan 36473 Merritt Thomson Durham 36474 Thomas Brian Durkin 36475 Drew Norman Early 36476 Scott Bailey Easton 36477 William Edward Ebel 36478 Richard Warren Ede 36479 Michael E. Edleson 36480 Rodney Scott Edmonds 36481 Roger Louis Engelau 36482 Marvin Anthony Englert 36483 John Joseph Enright 36484 Raymond Arthur Entringer 36485 Mark E. J. Estep 36486 Calvin Earl Evans 36487 David Norman Evans 36488 Joseph Charles Fahey 36489 John Robert Fain 36490 Steven Patrick Farmer 36491 Ross Faught 36492 George Michael Fedun 36493 Paul Michael Fenstermacher 36494 Brett Hadley Ferguson 36495 Timothy John Fiala 36496 Robert Gerard Fien 36497 Jose Maria Figueres 36498 Dennis Le Roy Filler 36499 Francis Alphonse Finelli 36500 Bruce Andrew Fink 36501 Scott Andrew Finlay 36502 Brendan Francis Flanagan 36503 Ralph Michael Flannery 36504 Gilbert Boughton Fletcher 36505 Robert George Fogg 36506 Timothy John Ford 36507 Ernest Thomas Forrest 36508 Patrick Graham Forrester 36509 Scott Thomas Forster 36510 David Robert Foster 36511 Essex Fowlks 36512 Kevin Jude Frantz 36513 Richard Kevin Freed 36514 Raymond Emmons Freeland 36515 Tracy Henry Freeman 36516 David Edward Freshwater 36517 Duane E. Fuller 36518 Matthew David Fuller 36519 John Robert Gaffney 36520 Kris Robert Gagnon 36521 Andrew Kelly Gale 36522 Timothy Paul Gannon 36523 David John Garcia 36524 Norman Emmanuel Garcia 36525 John Paul Gardner 36526 Thomas Gregory Gargiulo 36527 Patrick Steven Garrett 36528 Anthony J. Gasbarre 36529 Michael John Gearty 36530 Dan Lee Gehlbach 36531 Kurt David Gelke 36532 Charles Donald Gemar 36533 Thomas John Gibbons 36534 George William Gibbs 36535 Peter Rene Gibson 36536 Timothy J. Gibson 36537 Charles Browning Giesecke 36538 Philip K. Giles 36539 Ronald Darwin Gillette 36540 Jeffrey Thomas Gilling 36541 Norman George Girardin 36542 Michael David Goblirsch 36543 George Austin Godette 36544 Keith A. Godwin 36545 Timothy James Golden 36546 Albert Joe Gomez 36547 Francisco Javier Gonzalez 36548 Robert L. Gordon 36549 David John Gorenc 36550 Clifford Patrick Vance Graham 36551 Thomas Edward Graham 36552 Carl Ray Grantham 36553 Michael C. Gray 36554 Paul Greer 36555 Wesley Bernard Griffin 36556 Jeffrey John Grindrod 36557 Robert Louis Groller 36558 Elliott George Gruner 36559 Jeffrey David Gunzenhauser 36560 Mark Lind Haaland 36561 Thomas Mark Hagen 36562 Nelson A. Hager 36563 Robert Francis Hahn 36564 Kevin Louis Hall 36565 Donald Hallett 36566 David D. Halverson 36567 Mark David Hanson 36568 Harold Shaun Hardrick 36569 Bret Anthony Harlow 36570 James Edward Harris 36571 Patrick R. Harris 36572 James Mitchell Hartman 36573 Mark Alan Hartman 36574 George W. Hartnell 36575 David Joseph Hartsell 36576 Robert Paul Harwig 36577 Kenneth Alan Hawes 36578 Thomas William Hayden 36579 Timothy Loren Hayes 36580 Randy Mashar Hearn 36581 Jeffrey John Heckel 36582 Ralph Coleman Hedden 36583 James Andrew Helis 36584 Morris Joseph Herbert 36585 Tracy M. Herbert 36586 David Michael Hergenroeder 36587 Michael Louis Herman 36588 James Robert Hester 36589 James Robert Hickey 36590 Marc R. Hildenbrand 36591 Edward Loren

Hillenbrand 36592 Richard L. Hinchion 36593 Dennis August Hines 36594 Kevin Dale Hipple 36595 Rick Heber Hoff 36596 Lawrence William Hoffman 36597 Calvin Mark Holman 36598 Robert S. Holmes 36599 Frederick Lansing Hoon 36600 Charles Wayne Hooper 36601 William Gregory Hoover 36602 Michael Robert Horn 36603 Thomas David Horton 36604 Boyd Douglas Houck 36605 Maroc Leonard Howard 36606 Martin D. Howard 36607 Michael Francis Howe 36608 Tedd Jay Hoyt 36609 Jeffrey Matthew Hrutkay 36610 David Reed Huff 36611 Bernard Charles Hughes 36612 James E. Hughes 36613 Richard Paul Hughes 36614 Frank R. Hull 36615 Harvey Michael Humphrey 36616 Brian Harold Hunt 36617 Don Werner Lewis Huskey 36618 Steven Edward Hutek 36619 Robert Allison Hyatt 36620 Richard John Hyde 36621 Raul Armando Interiano 36622 Stanley Marion Jackson 36623 Jeffrey Alan Jacobs 36624 Barry Lee Jacobson 36625 Timothy Allen Jacobson 36626 John McGavock Jacocks 36627 Steven John Janis 36628 James Alexander Jankowski 36629 Lester C. Jauron 36630 Samuel Neff Jenkins 36631 Martin Arthur Jimenez 36632 John Richard Johnsen 36633 Dan Allen Johnson 36634 Gregory Lane Johnson 36635 James Scott Johnson 36636 Jeffrey Grant Johnson 36637 Charles Michael Johnston 36638 Keith James Johnston 36639 Donald E. Jones 36640 Jeffrey Samuel Jones 36641 Gregory Wayne Jordan 36642 Richard Alan Jordan 36643 Peter John Kale 36644 Michael E. Kallman 36645 James Joseph Kardas 36646 John Andrew Kardos 36647 Douglas Edward Karmel 36648 Patrick Joseph Kastner 36649 George Richard Kather 36650 Arthur George Kaub 36651 Francis Bret Kaufmann 36652 Michael Christopher Kavanaugh 36653 Charles Brian Keating 36654 Thomas John Kee 36655 John M. Keefe 36656 Robert Marshall Keith 36657 Brian Cassady Keller 36658 Byron Kelley 36659 Keith Douglas Kelley 36660 Donald Andrew Kelly 36661 Charles W. Kennedy 36662 Rein Edward Kiewel 36663 Richard Eldon Killblane 36664 Charles Herbert King 36665 Norman Douglas King 36666 Gary William Klaben 36667 Karl Kennedy Klett 36668 Charles Edward Knapp 36669 Richard Dale Knapp 36670 Daniel Thomas Knowles 36671 Gregory Michael Kogut 36672 Marin Hristos Kollef 36673 Roger Brent Kolts 36674 Joseph James Komperda 36675 Donald Francis Kopinski 36676 Michael Peter Kostoff 36677 Donald Paul Kotchman 36678 Steven Douglas Kraner 36679 Richard Daniel Krobock 36680 Robert Keith Kroening 36681 John Lawrence Krueger 36682 Kelly Dean Kruger 36683 Kevin Carl Kyzer 36684 Stephen John Labak 36685 J. Frank Lady 36686 Ronald James Lardie 36687 Charles D. Lawrence 36688 Raymond Joseph Lazzaro 36689 Miguel Noe Leal 36690 John Reuben Lee 36691 Mark E. Lee 36692 Robert Edward Lee 36693 Francis Michael LeGasse 36694 Joseph Louis LeGasse 36695 Donald Christopher Leins 36696 Michael Reynolds Lemmon 36697 John Thomas Lenahan 36698 Leslie Paul Leonard 36699 Charles Steven Lewis 36700 Jeffrey Linder Lewis 36701 Dean Allen Lindholm 36702 Robert C. Link 36703 Cary Thomas Linnerud 36704 Eric Boardman Lintz 36705 Mark Thomas Littel 36706 Stephen Gregory Loew 36707 Jeffrey Grady Lott 36708 William Robert Lough 36709 Douglas I. Luckett 36710 Peter Joseph Lunn 36711 Thomas Robert Lutman 36712 Charles McDonald Lyon 36713 Sanford David Lyons 36714 John Anthony Lytwynec 36715 Craig Mitchell Macallister 36716 John Alexander MacDonald 36717 Michael Allan MacDonald 36718 Michael Raymond Macedonia 36719 Kendall Scott MacGibbon 36720 William Robert MacHardy 36721 Russell Martin MacInnes 36722 Phillip Darnell Macklin 36723 Michael Drewry Macyauski 36724 John Phillip Madigan 36725 Daniel Michael Mahoney 36726 Steven Michael Mahoney 36727 Cornelius John Maney 36728 Mitchell Alan Mankosa 36729 Rolf Nikolaus Mann 36730 Thomas Leroy Mann 36731 John Anthony Marin 36732 James Joseph Marmora 36733 Gregg Forrest Martin 36734 Stephen Keith Martin 36735 William Raymond-Jesse Martin 36736 Joseph E. Martz 36737 Vincent Marucci 36738 Robert E. Mathis 36739 Timothy Aaron Mathis 36740 Jerry Frederick Matson 36741 John Patrick Maynard 36742 George Scott McAllister 36743 Michael Patrick McBride 36744 James T. McCall 36745 David Alexander McCann 36746 Thomas Wayne McCann 36747 Patrick McCarty 36748 Paul Thomas McDowell 36749 Mark Aaron McElrea 36750 Stuart A. McFarren 36751 Thomas Clarence McGiffin 36752 Sean Michael McGinn 36753 Scott Luther McGinnis 36754 Victor Grey McGlaughlin 36755 James Joseph McGorry 36756 Donald Charles McGraw 36757 Eugene Lee McIntyre 36758 Thomas Gary McIntyre 36759 Kevin Eugene McKedy 36760 Joseph Francis McKeon 36761 Isaac Vincent McKissick 36762 Patrick Joseph McManamon 36763 Joseph Bryant McMullin 36764 Patrick Brian McNiece 36765 Rickie Allen McPeak 36766 Michael Mark Medenis 36767 Ralph Frank Meoni 36768 James Ronald Merriken 36769 Samuel Judson Merrill 36770 Gary Lloyd Mesick 36771 Bryant Scott Messner 36772 Dean Frederick Mielke 36773 Douglas Charles Miller 36774 Gregory Earl Miller 36775 John Arthur Miller 36776 Kevin Leroy Miller 36777 James Harvey Minnon 36778 Jeffrey Lynn Misner 36779 Chris Terry Mitchell 36780 Bert Kameaaloha Mizusawa 36781 Michael Louis Modica 36782 Georges Molinari 36783 James Molnar 36784 William Francis Montgomery 36785 Joseph Allen Moore 36786 Robert Garvin Moore 36787 James Ross Moran 36788 Martin Michael Moratz 36789 Ricky A. Morlen 36790 Michael James Mos 36791 Lance Eugene Motley 36792 Steven Eric Mumm 36793 Martin Vincent Mundt 36794 Joseph Hoban Murnane 36795 Michael Richard Myers 36796 Walter Rudolph Myers 36797 Lennie M. Naeyaert 36798 William P. Nanry 36799 Stephen Robert Naru 36800 Gordon Scott Neal 36801 Brent Vincent Nelson 36802 Kevin Paul Nestor 36803 Joseph William Neubert 36804 Steven Ray Niblett 36805 David Alan Niedringhaus 36806 Joseph P. Nizolak 36807 Michael Keith Nobles 36808 Ben D. Nolan 36809 William Hillborn Nolan 36810 E. J. Nusbaum 36811 Clayton Anthony Tucker Nyberg 36812 Kurt Evan Nygaard 36813 Michael L. Oates 36814 Patrick William O'Brien 36815 Robert Joseph Ochman 36816 Timothy J. O'Connor 36817 Thomas James O'Donnell 36818 Jeffrey Gordon Ohstrom 36819 Francisco Manterola Ojeda 36820 Larry Moss Okuda 36821 Michael Francis O'Leary 36822 Joseph Pickett Oliver 36823 Jeffrey Lynn Olson 36824 Lee Frank Olson 36825 Michael Isamu Omura 36826 Thomas Jefferson O'Neal 36827 Timothy Peter O'Neill 36828 Carl Joseph Orler 36829 Richard Easterling Orr 36830 Charles C. Otterstedt 36831 James Robert Otto 36832 John Albert Owens 36833 Earl Pagan 36834 Gregory Scott Palmer 36835 Phillip Panzarella 36836 David Keith Parker 36837 Stephen Richard Parker 36838 Vincent John Pascal 36839 David Windell Patterson 36840 Philip Mark Patterson 36841 Gary Sheldon Patton 36842 Steve Pavlica 36843 Richard Norman Pedersen 36844 Paul Daniel Pelissero 36845 Patrick Ryan Penland 36846 Brian Neal Perkins 36847 Paul Fritz Perlwitz 36848 James Clifford Perry 36849 Alexander D. Perwich 36850 Robert Charles Peterson 36851 Charles Richard Petrie 36852 Carlous Tyrone Pettus 36853 Charles Edward Phillips 36854 Gregory Stephen Phillips 36855 Richard J. Phillips 36856 Robert Joseph Piechota 36857 Kenneth Lee Pieper 36858 James Richard Pierson 36859 Jeffrey Charles Pipik 36860 Howard Michael Place 36861 Peter Plassmann 36862 Bert Douglas Politoski 36863 David Wayne Polly 36864 Robin Merl Pope 36865 John Wally Powell 36866 Stephen Sugg Powell 36867 William Fuller Powers 36868 Bryon Eugene Powlus 36869 Gerald Louis Pretti 36870 Alan Lowell Price 36871 Christopher Stocker Prinslow 36872 Timothy Carl Pugh 36873 Robert Gerald Pyper 36874 Thomas Vincent Quinn 36875 Christopher W. Radlicz 36876 Kenneth C. Rathbun 36877 James Wallace Raycraft 36878 Michael Joseph Rayder 36879 Allen Dwight Raymond 36880 Donald Eugene Reed 36881 Robert Joseph Reed 36882 Richard Alan Rees 36883 David Lawrence Reeves 36884 Bruce Harold Reminger 36885 Stephen Ford Renfrow 36886 Stephen John Ressler 36887 Jerardo Reyes 36888 Paul Dilie Riddle 36889 Louis R. Riebe 36890 William R. Rieger 36891 Christopher M. Riley 36892 James Arlie Roberts 36893 James Stanley Roberts 36894 Victor M. Robertson 36895 Leslie Brian Roby 36896 Mark Daniel Rocke 36897 James Patrick Rodgers 36898 Rodney Bruce Roeber 36899 Paul Erik Roege 36900 Ernest Paul Rogers 36901 James Edward Rogers 36902 Robert Lee Root 36903 Gary L. Ross 36904 Thomas Jerome Roth 36905 John Ward Rotter 36906 Robert Henry Routier 36907 James Rudolph Rowan 36908 Peter James Rowan 36909 John Phillip Ruman 36910 Anthony Salvatore Ruocco 36911 William Joseph Sandbrook 36912 William John Sander 36913 David Craig Sanders 36914 Jay Michael Saredy 36915 Theodore Joe Sario 36916 Gary Glen Sauer 36917 Shepard Austin Sawyer 36918 Martin Leo Scanlan 36919 George Michael Schaertl 36920 Gary Robert Schamburg 36921 Arthur Andrew Scharein 36922 Steven Gerard Schauwecker 36923 Robert Mackie Schicktanz 36924 Wade Carter Schieber 36925 David Calvin Schlessman 36926 William Charles Schleyer 36927 Eric Jay Schlossberg 36928 Frederick Paul Schmalberger 36929 Brian G. Schmidtke 36930 Stephen Douglas Schneider 36931 Steven Roger Schooley 36932 Charles Louis Schott 36933 James Vernon Schultz 36934 John Frederick Schultz 36935 Frederick August Schulze 36936 Paul Lewis Schumack 36937 Fred Lee Schwien 36938 Brian Mark Scilzo 36939 Timothy John Scott 36940 John V. Scudder 36941 Einar Austin Seadler 36942 Walter Albert Sears 36943 Todd Thurston Semonite 36944 Steven Mitchell Seybert 36945 David William Shaffer 36946 Steven Ralph Shannon 36947 Charles Houston Shaw 36948 Josef Corwin Shaw 36949 Joseph Michael Sheairs 36950 Patrick Lee Sherman 36951 Russell Richard Sherrett 36952 Jeffrey Alan Shey 36953 Bradley W. Shike 36954 Douglas Allen Shipp 36955 Kenneth D. Shive 36956 Nelson Eugene Shive 36957 Martin W. Shubert 36958 Robert Sam Simis 36959 Steven Jay Curtis Simmons 36960 Daniel Mark Sims 36961 Mark C. Sims 36962 George Buster Singleton 36963 John Stephen Sink 36964 James Robert Sitlington 36965 Robert Paul Skertic 36966 Joseph Anthony Sladewski 36967 Douglas Frederick Slater 36968 William Mark Slayton 36969 Nathaniel Hawthorne Sledge 36970 Doak Kullman Smailer 36971 Carleton McNeill Smith 36972 David Jonathan Smith 36973 James Warren Smith 36974 Nicholas E. Smith 36975 Parker Kirwin Smith 36976 Stephen Michael Smith 36977 Charles Owen Smithers 36978 Deryl Paul Smoak 36979 William Archer Snead 36980 Charles T. Sniffin 36981 Daniel R. Snyder 36982 Steven Patrick Spaay 36983 Robert M. Speir 36984 Thomas F. Spellissy 36985 John Mott Spiller 36986 Robert Marcus Spillers 36987 Michael James Spoerl 36988 Mark Layton Spruill 36989 Lee Alan Staab 36990 Allan R. Starkie 36991 John Rud Staser 36992 Michael Ural Staten 36993 John Michael Andrew Stawasz 36994 John Stewart 36995 Jeffrey Alan Stonerock 36996 Robert Brian Stratton 36997 Michael John Streff 36998 Steven Robert Strong 36999 Paul Alan Struven 37000 Allen Hasty Stults 37001 Kevin J. Sturm 37002 Edward Joseph Sullivan 37003 Eric Arthur Sundt 37004 Mark Sutton 37005 Douglas Edward Swartz 37006 Victor A. Sweberg 37007 Patrick R. Sweeney 37008 David Kenneth Swindell 37009 Richard John Syslo 37010 Daniel Scott Szarenski 37011 Gerald Leonard Tabin 37012 Anthony Dean Tabler 37013 Thomas Lawrence Talty 37014 Albert Buck Tanner 37015 Michael Steven Tax 37016 Clarence E. Taylor 37017 David Harold Taylor 37018 Forest Archer Taylor 37019 Paul Henry Taylor 37020 William Laurence Taylor 37021 Todd S. Tetreault 37022 Michal A. Thalacker 37023 Frankie N. Thibodeau 37024 Donald Thomas Thiel 37025 Kirk Kevin Thomas 37026 Martin Spalding Thomas 37027 Michael Hutsen Thomas 37028 Steven P. Thomas 37029 Harry Hillard Thompson 37030 Jeffery James Thompson 37031 Terence Michael Tidler 37032 William James Tillo 37033 Michael Allan Toner 37034 John Bolling Towey 37035 James Thomas Treharne 37036 Brooks Frederick Troup 37037 Wm. Howard Trowbridge 37038 Robert Edward Troxel 37039 Franklin Scott Tuck 37040 Bruce Ray Tucker 37041 Tommy Glen Tucker 37042 John Marshall Turner 37043 John Nelson Turner 37044 Douglas Walter Turrell 37045 Kurt Frederick Ubbelohde 37046 Larry Lyn Uland 37047 Walter Francis Ulmer 37048 Robert Lewis Underberg 37049 Robert Boyden Underwood 37050 Thomas Foster Underwood 37051 Bruce W. Uphoff 37052 David Van Van Cleve 37053 Ross Leigh Vanderhye 37054 Thurston Van Horn 37055 Karl Michael Vanzant 37056 Robert Louis Vasta 37057 James Ellison Vaughn 37058 Mark McClain Vaughn 37059 David Wesley Veney 37060 Mitchell Vervoort 37061 Michael John Vetter 37062 David Jon Wabeke 37063 Mark Matthew Waclawski 37064 Edward Patrick Wade 37065 Roy Charles Waggoner 37066 Gordon Thompson Wales 37067 Hubert E. Waller 37068 Michael Bradford Smith Wallis 37069 James John Walton 37070 Byron Walter Ward 37071 Jay Warren Watai 37072 Gregory Lynn Watson 37073 Alan Wayne Watts 37074 John Alan Watz 37075 Kurt Elliott Webber 37076 Kevin John Weddle 37077 Christopher Julian Wegmann 37078 Peter Lawrence Weiland 37079 Davis Stuart Welch 37080 Donald Joseph Welch 37081 Mark Joseph Welker 37082 Gordon Marshall Wells 37083 James Patrick Wells 37084 Nicholas Craig Werling 37085 Mark Edward West 37086 Alan David Westfield 37087 Robert Michael White 37088 Wayne Edward Whiteman 37089 James Allen Whitt 37090 Stephen William Whittey 37091 S. Ward Whyte 37092 Warren Lee Wieland 37093 Andrew Townsend Wiener 37094 Francis John Wiercinski 37095 Anthony George Wiley 37096 Joseph Winfield Wilkerson 37097 Jeffery Gautier Wilkinson 37098 C. Kevin Williams 37099 Cleveland Williams 37100 James Irvin Williams 37101 Peter Griffith Williams 37102 Scott Douglas Williams 37103 Michael Brian Willis 37104 Daniel Marvin Wilson 37105 Douglas Lyle Wilson 37106 Keith K. Wilson 37107 Gregory Roy Wine 37108 John Wilson Wiseman 37109 George K. Withers 37110 James Phillip Witzerman 37111 William Thornton Wolf 37112 Terry A. Wolff 37113 Raymond Earl Womack 37114 Michael Jon Woodworth 37115 John Todd Worthington 37116 Mario F. Wozniak 37117 Jeffrey F. Wright 37118 David Thomas Yancey 37119 Alexander John Yarmie 37120 Anthony Lynn Yeldell 37121 Gary Michael Yerks 37122 Robert W. Zaccardi 37123 Curt S. Zargan 37124 Joseph A. Zator 37125 Kevin J. Zenner 37126 Kenneth Mark Zoeller 37127 Michael Anthony Zonfrelli 37128 Joseph Edmond Pecoraro 37129 Michael Dale Murray 37130 Michael Alimpich 37131 Toney L. Ash 37132 Thomas J. Chegosh 37133 James Floyd Dedmon 37134 Lawrence De Leon 37135 Erik Gilmore Eriksen 37136 Steven Otto Fischer 37137 Mark Chappelle Fuller 37138 Raymond Carl Gamble 37139 Michael John Karaman 37140 James Joseph Kelly 37141 Steven William Kerr 37142 William Joseph Krzan 37143 Keeyoung Lee 37144 John Nicholas Lesko 37145 Dale Grant Newman 37146 Eric William Oetjen 37147 Jules George Petit 37148 Francis Xavier Reidy 37149 Jose Amilcar Torres 37150 Dean Leroy Vaniter 37151 Damian Christopher Wackerman 37152 Peter Lewis Waldman 37153 Clifford Stephen Walter 37154 Robert Paul Wentzel 37155 Edward Peter Castle 37156 Walter Earl Wininger 37157 Matthew J. Duffy 37158 Tony Orville Jennings 37159 Mark R. Lees 37160 Richard Anthony Lochner 37161 Thaddeus Jude Noll 37162 John A. Harrison 37163 William Newsome Eichorn 37164 Michael W. Grant 37165 Curtis Bryan Hill 37166 Arthur Albert Sobers 37167 Jimmie Lee Traylor 37168 Thomas W. Williams 37169 **1980** Brian Jay Adams 37170 Charles Lucien Adams 37171 Douglass S. Adams 37172 Collin Alex Agee 37173 John Francis Agoglia 37174 Richard Allen Albrecht 37175 John Holland Albright 37176 Donna Alesch Newell 37177 James Michael Alexander 37178 Robert M. Algermissen 37179 Thomas William Allen 37180 Randal Andrew Almeter 37181 Russell Edward Altizer 37182 Daniel Taylor Ames 37183 Patrick Walter Amstein 37184 Eric Carl Andersen 37185 Charles Allan Anderson 37186 Kenneth Allan Anderson 37187 Thomas Michael Arielly 37188 Roger Allen Arnzen 37189 James Thomas Arriola 37190 James Edward Arsenault 37191 Peter John Ash 37192 Shelley Ann Richardson 37193 Thomas Robert Austin 37194 David Michael Autrey 37195 John Roderic Babb 37196 Stephen Walter Bachinski 37197 Mark Douglas Baehre 37198 Michael David Baehre 37199 John Paul Baker 37200 Joseph Thomas Baker 37201 Curtis James Balcer 37202 Elias Villegas Balderas 37203 Walter Ransford Barfield 37204 Carol Anne Barkalow 37205 Mark Adam Barowski 37206 Gerald Gordon Barrett 37207 Ronald Francis Barry 37208 Scott Thomas Bauman 37209 David Douglas Beach 37210 David Wayne Beals 37211 Michael Kerr Beans 37212 John Langworthy Beaudry 37213 Gregory Thomas Beck 37214 James Louis Becker 37215 Mark Alan Becker 37216 Ronald James Beebe 37217 David John Bender 37218 Glenn Joseph Benecke 37219 Elliott Marshall Benson 37220 Martin Allen Bentrott 37221 Brigid Benya Ockrassa 37222 Jon Kent Berlin 37223 Evan Edward Blanco 37224 Rebecca A. Hardy 37225 Daniel Norwood Bock 37226 Steven Joseph Bock 37227 Seth Peter Bokmeyer 37228 Christopher Jay Bolan 37229 Cliff Frederic Boltz 37230 Thomas L. Bosco 37231 Charles W. Boucher 37232 Christopher Ray Bowling 37233 David Michael Boyle 37234 Mark Anthony Boyle 37235 Diane Bracey 37236 William Custer Bradley 37237 William Charles Bradshaw 37238 Casey Leo Brady 37239 Kevin Michael Brady 37240 Jonathan Donald Bray 37241 Robert Ethan Brewster 37242 David John Bricker 37243 Donald W. Bridge 37244 James Thomas Brockway 37245 Robert Brooks 37246 Vincent Keith Brooks 37247 Bradley David Brown 37248 David Wayne Brown 37249 Michael Thomas Brunett 37250 Robert Louis Buckman 37251 Charles Alan Bull 37252 Richard Andrew Burke 37253 Michael Ray Burney 37254 Stephen Henry Button 37255 Peter John Cafaro 37256 Timothy John Cahill 37257 Charles Michael Caldwell 37258 James Anthony Caldwell 37259 Janis Marie Meyer 37260 James Philip Calve 37261 William Edward Camargo 37262 John Price Canby 37263 Michael Eric Cantor 37264 Joe Manuel Cantu 37265 John Alfred Capelli 37266 Paul Rupert Capstick 37267 Michael Cardarelli 37268 Peter Anthony Cardinal 37269 Douglas Charles Carpenter 37270 Larry A. Carpenter 37271 Robert Stephen Carrington 37272 Glen Alan Carroll 37273 Chris Cesare Casciato 37274 John Michael Castellano 37275 James Todd Caudle 37276 M. W. Dwight Cdebaca 37277 Gary Michael Cecchini 37278 Wayne Morrow Chancellor 37279 David Christopher Charest 37280 Joe Franklin Charsagua 37281 John Michael Cheatham 37282 Gary Harrison Cheek 37283 Curtis P. Cheeseman 37284 Owen William Cheney 37285 Ralph Kevin Chester 37286 Dana Kyle Chipman 37287 John Henry Chory 37288 Gregory Mark Chubon 37289 Michael Francis Chura 37290 Karen A. Cicchini 37291 David Paul Ciceri 37292 Charles Griffin Clark 37293 Daniel James Clark 37294 Perry Raymond Clawson 37295 James Peter Clifford 37296 Robert Clune 37297 Rick Lynn Coalwell 37298 James Arthur Coe 37299 Steven Allan Cohen 37300 Stephen Alan Cole 37301 Ruth Ann Colister 37302 Daniel Patrick Collins 37303 Peter Collins 37304 Ronald Stephen Collins 37305 Stephen Douglas Combs 37306 William Alec Comley 37307 Rick Dwight Compton 37308 William Francis Condron 37309 David Michael Conetsco 37310 Michael Kevin Connell 37311 Michael Gregory Conrad 37312 William Bryan Conrad 37313 Charles Joseph Conz 37314 David Anthony Cook 37315 David Christopher Cook 37316 James Philip Cooke 37317 Joseph William Cormack 37318 Don Spencer Cornett 37319 Moises Cortizo 37320 Andrew Paul Costa 37321 Albert McMullen Cox 37322 W. Scott Crawford 37323 William Travis Crawford 37324 Howard Bruce Crofoot 37325 Chet Huntley Cross 37326 Kent Michael Crossley 37327 James Patrick Cummings 37328 James Richard Curl 37329 Scott Anthony Cusimano 37330 Joy Suzanne Dallas 37331 Bret Glenn Dalton 37332 Darrell Randolf Davis 37333 Gregory Cady Davis 37334 John Allan Davis 37335 Mark Joseph Davis 37336 Paul Francis Davis 37337 Robert John Davis 37338 Denise Irene Dawson 37339 Daniel Mark Deeter 37340 Michael Scott Defferding 37341 David Dwight de Haan 37342 David Samuel DeHorse 37343 Daryl Craig Dennis 37344 David Lee DeVries 37345 Steven Leroy Dials 37346 David Martin DiDonato 37347 Michael Anthony DiGennaro 37348 Gary Francis Di Gesu 37349 Steven Robert DiGiulio 37350 Douglas John Dinon 37351 James Louis Di Simoni 37352 Robert Loren Doering 37353 William Russsell Doherty 37354 Stanley Edward

Domikaitis 37355 Patrick James Donahue 37356 John Edward Donlon 37357 Alex Dornstauder 37358 Bruce Philip Dow 37359 Joseph Craig Doyen 37360 Jeffrey Alan Doyle 37361 Timothy Loftin Doyle 37362 David Andrew Dryer 37363 William Alan Duelge 37364 Alan Douglas Duff 37365 William Francis Duffy 37366 Hinman Dunn 37367 Jeffrey Lawrence Durnford 37368 James Francis Dwyer 37369 Stephen Roy Dwyer 37370 Jeffrey A. Easley 37371 Marty Joe Eaton 37372 John Arthur Econom 37373 Andrew Anton Edmunds 37374 Dale Norman Egger 37375 Keith Douglas Emberton 37376 Henry William Embleton 37377 James Hubert Embrey 37378 Thomas Joseph Endres 37379 Timothy James Eno 37380 Mark James Eshelman 37381 Richard Michael Esposito 37382 William M. Ether 37383 Robert Charles Faille 37384 Edward C. Farnham 37385 Thomas John Farrell 37386 Donald Collins Feeney 37387 Mark Richard Feeney 37388 Sean Eugene Feeney 37389 Thomas Joseph Fencl 37390 Robin Fennessy Carrington 37391 Stephen Roy Ferguson 37392 William Roessler Ferrara 37393 Joseph Matthew Fetzer 37394 Bobbi Fiedler Prinslow 37395 Anne Fields Macdonald 37396 Randall Lee Fisher 37397 David Brennan Flanigan 37398 James Ralph Fleenor 37399 Charles Joseph Fogle 37400 Leo John Fontana 37401 Michael Anthony Ford 37402 Stephen Peter Ford 37403 James Anthony Foster 37404 Joseph Edward Foster 37405 Mark S. Foster 37406 Robert Edward Francis 37407 Thomas Alan Franke 37408 Rick Preston Friedman 37409 Robin Bretton Friedman 37410 William H. Friedman 37411 Robert Allen Fryling 37412 David Kazu Fukuda 37413 Brenda Sue Fulton 37414 Dale Alan Fye 37415 Bruce William Gafner 37416 Steven Eugene Galing 37417 Michael Allan Folino Gallo 37418 Samuel R. Garza 37419 William Gaul 37420 Michael Desha Gayle 37421 Randy Elmer Geiger 37422 Kathleen Gerard Snook 37423 William Henry Gerety 37424 Douglas Harvey Germann 37425 Daniel Martin Gerstein 37426 Michael William Gifford 37427 Reginald R. Gillis 37428 Tim Ronald Glaeser 37429 Charles Edward Glass 37430 Thomas Gerard Gleason 37431 Thomas O. Glenn 37432 John Joseph Gniadek 37433 Donald Grancis Gongaware 37434 John Allan Goodale 37435 Katharine Goodland 37436 Robert Allen Goodman 37437 Mike Davy Goodwin 37438 Karl Felton Grace 37439 Bruce Ihrig Graham 37440 Roy Jeffrey Graham 37441 William James Graham 37442 Mark Lawrence Graner 37443 Curtis Anthony Grayer 37444 Michael Thomas Greene 37445 Vernon Edward Greene 37446 Michael Andrew Greer 37447 Jeffrey Glenn Gregson 37448 Douglas Arthur Greig 37449 Daniel Gene Grey 37450 Mary Ellen Vaniter 37451 Eleanor Ruth Griffin 37452 Michael Patrick Griffin 37453 Paul Edwin Grim 37454 Michael Patrick Grogan 37455 Michael Angel Guardia 37456 Nancy L. Gucwa 37457 Gary Allan Gulyas 37458 Karl David Gustafson 37459 John Robert Gusz 37460 Carl Raul Gwin 37461 Ned Elton Hacker 37462 Joseph Edward Hafeman 37463 Thomas James Hagan 37464 Johnnie Alan Ham 37465 Alan Arthur Hamill 37466 Roy Scott Hamilton 37467 Ronald James Hansen 37468 Kurtis Harvey Hanson 37469 Donald Joseph Harrington 37470 Janet J. Smith 37471 Winburn Drew Harrington 37472 Stephen Daniel Harvey 37473 Thomas C. Hastings 37474 Christopher Nixon Hatley 37475 Richard Louis Haueter 37476 Chris Allen Hawkins 37477 Peter A. Hawkins 37478 Ronald James Hayne 37479 Scott Douglas Hazlett 37480 Michael Bruce Heacock 37481 Kenneth Charles Healy 37482 Bruce Jay Held 37483 Michael Reed Helmick 37484 Donald Curt Hendershot 37485 Mark Stephen Hendrix 37486 Richard Herbik 37487 Daniel James Hergenroeder 37488 Douglas Edward Herr 37489 Christopher Carl Herstrom 37490 George Albert Hervey 37491 Charles Ray Hillis 37492 Jeffrey William Hills 37493 Karen Jayne Hobson 37494 Mark Neal Hobart 37495 Robert Charles Hobbs 37496 Frederick Benjamin Hodges 37497 James Keith Hogue 37498 John Raymond Holland 37499 Andrea Lee Hollen 37500 Bayles Brett Holliday 37501 Benjamin Henry Holly 37502 Gerald John Hopkins 37503 William Charles Hopkinson 37504 Gary Bryan Hopper 37505 Charles Albert Horn 37506 William Dearl Horton 37507 Mark Wade House 37508 Kenneth Paul Howe 37509 Thomas Joseph Hrubovsky 37510 Mark Chwen Hu 37511 Earle Franklin Hudson 37512 Ann Marie Collier 37513 Thomas Gerard Hughes 37514 Elrin Lewis Hundley 37515 Anthony James Hunt 37516 David Presssley Hunter 37517 Mark Patrick Hurley 37518 Samuel Hutchins 37519 Steven John Ignat 37520 Gregory James Jackson 37521 William Charles Jahn 37522 Mark Stephen James 37523 Robert Eugene James 37524 Mark Robert Jaworski 37525 Alfred Theodore Jelinek 37526 Richard Bruce Jenkins 37527 David George Jesmer 37528 Rex Eugene Jessup 37529 David Randall Johnson 37530 Debra Ann Johnson 37531 George Edward Johnson 37532 Marcus Lynn Johnson 37533 Randy Dean Johnson 37534 Ernest W. Jones 37535 Jeffery Jones 37536 William Berrodin Jones 37537 John P. Joseph 37538 Jeffrey Robert Joyce 37539 Brent Leslie Kadesch 37540 Tamara Christine Watson 37541 Keith William Kaspersen 37542 Charles Scott Kellar 37543 Kevin Straith Kelleher 37544 Susan Puanani Kellett-Forsyth 37545 Karen Louise Stoner 37546 Kevin William Kelly 37547 Michael Paul Kelly 37548 Kevin Barry Kenny 37549 Thomas Edward Kick 37550 Charles Peter Kielkopf 37551 Jeffrey Mark Kildow 37552 Thomas Gerard Kilgore 37553 N. Wesley Kimata 37554 Gordon Thomas Kingma 37555 Karen M. Kinzler Strang 37556 Clare Kirby Jenkins 37557 John Thomas Kisiel 37558 Robert Edwin Klein 37559 Michael Stephen Knapp 37560 Robert K. Knight 37561 Thomas Warren Knottek 37562 Thomas Robert Knutilla 37563 Stephen Carter Knutson 37564 Thomas Lee Koning 37565 Kenneth Anthony Konstanzer 37566 Daniel E. Kostyshak 37567 Glenn Kenneth Kouhia 37568 Jacob P. Kovel 37569 Jan M. Kozlowski 37570 Stephen D. Kreider 37571 Mark Jay Kucera 37572 Mark Matthew Kulungowski 37573 Robert John Kuper 37574 Miroslav Paul Kurka 37575 John Robert Laird 37576 Steven Gorbandt Lamb 37577 Michael Cecil Lamberth 37578 Mark Nelson Laney 37579 Brian Douglas Langley 37580 Stephen Raymond Lanza 37581 Michael P. Larkin 37582 Paul William Lascelle 37583 James Henry Latham 37584 Michael J. Laurendi 37585 Geoffrey William Lea 37586 Glen Bryan Ledeboer 37587 Richard Yoshinobu Ledger 37588 John Lee 37589 William Fitzhugh Lee 37590 Craig Douglas Leiby 37591 David Michael Leigh 37592 Gregory David Leikvold 37593 Doug Leighton Lenhoff 37594 Richard Kent Lester 37595 Joel E. Levenduski 37596 Alan Thomas Levesque 37597 Darrell H. Lewis 37598 Debra M. Lewis 37599 Paul Stanley Lewza 37600 John Edward Ley 37601 Michael Merle Leyland 37602 David Alan Liebetreu 37603 Douglas Alan Liening 37604 Francisco Javier Linares 37605 James Francis Lindenmayer 37606 Michael Linnington 37607 Michael Gene Linthicum 37608 Douglas John Litavec 37609 Eric Charles Littleton 37610 James Gregory Liwski 37611 Douglas Irvin Lobdell 37612 Jody Christopher Locklear 37613 David Wayne Logan 37614 Ronald M. Loiselle 37615 Lonnie Gene Long 37616 Joseph Scott Lockadoo 37617 Nicholas Lordi 37618 Todd Owen Loudenslager 37619 Douglas Andrew Lowrey 37620 Nicolas George Lucariello 37621 John Ray Luce 37622 Jeffrey P. Lukens 37623 Michael Werner Luttmann 37624 Richard Scott MacDermott 37625 Kevin Vance MacGibbon 37626 James Ennis Macklin 37627 David Geoffrey MacLean 37628 Donald John Maggioli 37629 Eugene Paul Maggioncalda 37630 Marty E. Mahoney 37631 Robert Martin Maiberger 37632 Steven Jeffrey Mains 37633 Danna Rocque 37634 Thomas J. Mangan 37635 Edward Eugene Maran 37636 Scot Rondell Maring 37637 Von Kent Marler 37638 Michael Edmond Marmaro 37639 Bruce Michael Martin 37640 Paul Kindley Martin 37641 Vicki Louise Lundquist 37642 Michael Mario Martinez 37643 Vincent Charles Masi 37644 Daniel Victor Mason 37645 Karl Alan Masters 37646 Jacob Pope Matthews 37647 Richard W. Matthews 37648 John Anthony Mattingly 37649 John Matuscak 37650 Phillip Harvey May 37651 George Samuel Mayes 37652 Roger Wells Mayfield 37653 John Alan Mazzucca 37654 Peter Alexander McAnulty 37655 Kevin McCall 37656 Gilbert Carroll McCallum 37657 Debra McCarthy Schroeder 37658 Barry John McConnell 37659 Daniel Joseph McCormack 37660 Edward Daniel McCoy 37661 Jack Henry McCoy 37662 Jane M. Coumes 37663 Richard Paul McEvoy 37664 John Thomas McGrath 37665 Robert Francis McGurty 37666 Robert Dean McKercher 37667 Steven Mitchell McLemore 37668 Andrew Russell McMahon 37669 Scott Alan McManus 37670 Richard Douglas McMorris 37671 Scott Kevin McPheeters 37672 Gary Paul McVaney 37673 Russell Phillip Medina 37674 Dale Ray Meeks 37675 Robert William Meikle 37676 Keith Francis Melvin 37677 Michael Alexander Merritt 37678 John Donald Michel 37679 Brendan Thomas Miles 37680 Jeffrey Thomas Miles 37681 Lloyd Miles 37682 Christopher Gerard B. Miller 37683 Frank Lewis Miller 37684 Gregory Scott Miller 37685 John Edward Miller 37686 Thomas Michael Miller 37687 Laurence Coleman Milstead 37688 Gary A. Minadeo 37689 Robert Jerome Minkewicz 37690 Kenneth Michael Mishkel 37691 Michael Steven Mizusawa 37692 Paul Bruce Mobley 37693 David Edmund Moeller 37694 John Michael Moeller 37695 Michael Joseph Molohon 37696 Sylvia Thorpe Moran 37697 Michael Anthony Morgan 37698 Mark Francis Morgida 37699 Ed Mornston 37700 L. Paul Morris 37701 Robert Parker Morris 37702 Barron Thomas Motz 37703 James Christopher Moyers 37704 Albert Anthony Mrozek 37705 Michael Gerard Mudd 37706 Clarence Peter Mueller 37707 Daniel John Mueller 37708 Amy Jane Muir Murrell 37709 Gerard Patrick Mullane 37710 Earle Frank Mulrane 37711 Jeffrey W. Munn 37712 Barton Lawrence Munro 37713 Raymond Joseph Murchek 37714 David Brian Myers 37715 Joseph Francis Napoli 37716 Douglas Edward Nash 37717 James Daniel Neighbors 37718 Kevin Edward Nekula 37719 Douglas Harold Nelson 37720 Marlin Allen Ness 37721 Michael Edward Newell 37722 Robert Kirk Nicholson 37723 Frederick Harold Niedermeyer 37724 Douglas Edward Nielsen 37725 Sonya Elich Martin 37726 Koji Derwin Nishimura 37727 William Bryan Norman 37728 John David Norwood 37729 Rita Annette Kral 37730 Jon Kimbal Nussbaum 37731 Marene Nyberg Allison 37732 Thomas John O'Brien 37733 Erin O'Connor Misner 37734 David John O'Donnell 37735 James Gerard O'Donnell 37736 Paul Vincent Oettinger 37737 David Hanley Olwell 37738 Todd Edward Ostheller 37739 Eric Dean Ostrem 37740 Christopher Gerard Owens 37741 Raymond Edward Padro 37742 Peter Michael Palumbo 37743 Stephen Paul Parshley 37744 Daniel Albert Patton 37745 Francis Karl Pauc 37746 Edward William Payne 37747 John Whitcomb Peabody 37748 Steven Mark Peaslee 37749 Kevin Edward Pedersen 37750 Charles Andrew Peperak 37751 John Michael Peppers 37752 Rodney Perdue 37753 David Gerard Perkins 37754 Jane Perkins McKeon 37755 William Edward Perkins 37756 Tim Edward Perley 37757 Joseph Paul Perovich 37758 John Montgomery Perry 37759 David Lee Peters 37760 Steven Edward Peters 37761 Terry Dean Peters 37762 Jon Michael Peterson 37763 Robert Owen Petro 37764 Michael Francis Pfenning 37765 Lillian Ann Pfluke 37766 Michael Francis Kevin Phelan 37767 Ben Kirk Phillips 37768 Michael William Pick 37769 Donald Ray Pierce 37770 Alan Edward Pires 37771 William Mikell Platt 37772 Phillip Steven Plutt 37773 Richard J. Polo 37774 Michael Wayne Porch 37775 Mark Alan Porter 37776 David Deytheur Powell 37777 Michael Rodney Pracht 37778 David Walter Price 37779 George Prohoda 37780 Stanley Joseph Prusinski 37781 Anthony Jaye Puckett 37782 Daniel Pusty 37783 Michael Francis Pyrz 37784 John M. Qualls 37785 Wilson Albert Quinley 37786 Floyd Anthony Quintana 37787 Kenneth Allen Ragghanti 37788 David Anthony Rameden 37789 William Ramos 37790 Darrell Scott Ransom 37791 David L. Ransom 37792 Joseph Anthony Rapone 37793 John Steven Regan 37794 Susanne Reichelt Lamb 37795 Richard Scott Reid 37796 Joaquin F. Reis 37797 Kurt Charles Reitinger 37798 James Douglas Renbarger 37799 Michael Scott Repass 37800 Richard Henry Repetto 37801 James Michael Reynolds 37802 Stephen Carl Reynolds 37803 Robert Alden Rhein 37804 George Henry Rhynedance 37805 Marc Jean Richard 37806 Gregory Lee Ridderbusch 37807 Jay Clarke Rifenbary 37808 William Allen Rigby 37809 Eddie Lee Rivers 37810 Alan Dale Robertson 37811 Thomas William Robertson 37812 Hugh G. Robinson 37813 Timothy Andrew Rosemore 37814 Mary Grace Whitley 37815 Ronald David Ross 37816 Paul Charles Rossbach 37817 Thomas Paul Rost 37818 Robert L. Ruck 37819 Cristobal Jose Rugama 37820 Edward J. Ruggero 37821 Benigno Bern Punsalan Ruiz 37822 Laurence Dean Rund 37823 Charles Joseph Ruppert 37824 David Wayne Russell 37825 Rex Alan Russell 37826 Martin George Russo 37827 Stephen Layne Rust 37828 Randy Glenn Rutledge 37829 Robert Paul Ryan 37830 William Kenneth Rychener 37831 David Glenn Sadler 37832 Teodorico Valero Sanchez 37833 Alan Charles Sanger 37834 Mark Alan Sargent 37835 Frank Savin 37836 Gregg Alan Schamburg 37837 Bruce Bradley Schardt 37838 Michael Ross Schaub 37839 Madison Charles Schepps 37840 Ronald David Schiefer 37841 Mark Edward Schiller 37842 Kenneth Dale Schmidt 37843 John C. Schmit 37844 Michael W. Schneider 37845 Steven John Schowalter 37846 Robert Martin Schozer 37847 Mark Verne Schroeder 37848 Warren Roy Schultz 37849 Jeff Edward Schwartz 37850 James Clarence Scott 37851 Jeffrey Wallace Scott 37852 Michael Roll Scott 37853 Thomas Joseph Scruggs 37854 Bruce Edward Seeling 37855 Eric Duncan Seifarth 37856 William Anthony Serrao 37857 Max L. B. Shadle 37858 Edward Patrick Shanahan 37859 Jeffrey Daniel Sharp 37860 Daniel Paul Shaver 37861 Steven Lloyd Sheaffer 37862 Drew Lloyd Shearer 37863 Brynnen G. Hahn 37864 David Nelson Shelley 37865 Gilbert Wade Shepherd 37866 John Bolling Sheppard 37867 Andrew Nan Sherrill 37868 John Mondy Shimkus 37869 James Wade Shufelt 37870 John Fergerson Shults 37871 William Eric Siburg 37872 Mark Andrew Siem 37873 Kathleen Silvia 37874 Richard Lee Simis 37875 Jerry Tyler Simpson 37876 William Francis Skoda 37877 William Thornton Sledge 37878 George Robert Smith 37879 Jeffrey Craig Smith 37880 Joan Smith Grey 37881 William R. Sneddon 37882 Audy Ray Snodgrass 37883 Scott Andrew Snook 37884 Charles Reiner Snyder 37885 Thomas Reiji Sole 37886 Douglas Allan Sommer 37887 Anthony D. Songer 37888 Steven R. Sosland 37889 Michael Emerson Souder 37890 David John Speck 37891 William John Spencer 37892 Rex Alan Spitler 37893 Paul Franklin Springer 37894 Timothy Lee Staggs 37895 Brian Patrick Stapleton 37896 Douglas George Stearns 37897 Stephen Joseph Stefancin 37898 Barney Joseph Stenkamp 37899 Mark William Stephenson 37900 Michael Kent Stephenson 37901 Christi Lynn Stevens 37902 Mark Richard Stevens 37903 Michael James Stevens 37904 Michael Joseph Stevens 37905 Scott Lee Stich 37906 Dianne Louise Hamilton 37907 Chris Frederick Stoinoff 37908 Charles Lee Stone 37909 George Francis Stone 37910 James A. Stone 37911 John Keagy Stoner 37912 Patrick St. Pierre 37913 Kevin P. Stramara 37914 Timothy Paul Stranko 37915 John Christopher Stratis 37916 Keith Edward Strohschein 37917 Steven Maksym F. Stuban 37918 Joseph Nobuo Sugihara 37919 Eugene Francis Sullivan 37920 John Russell Sullivan 37921 Thomas Michael Sullivan 37922 Charles Lee Sutton 37923 Martin Swafford 37924 Wayne Lenn Swan 37925 Michael Charles Swezey 37926 Joel Vincent Swisher 37927 Paul Charles Szaro 37928 David Takacs 37929 Frederick Bill Takatori 37930 Michael Collin Talbott 37931 Paul Duane Tanner 37932 Lee Fulton Taylor 37933 Mark August Taylor 37934 Peter J. A. Tedford 37935 Scott Richard Teising 37936 Philip David Telander 37937 Terry Tepper Walters 37938 David Alan Tharp 37939 John Adam Thayer 37940 Paul Charles Thomas 37941 Raymond Anthony Thomas 37942 Walter William Thomas 37943 Michael Joseph Timlin 37944 John William Tindall 37945 Stephen Michael Tobin 37946 Regina Claire Todd 37947 Robert Masao Toguchi 37948 Mitchell Elich Toryanski 37949 Perry Alan Toscano 37950 Steven James Tourek 37951 Scott Winfield Tousley 37952 Donald Wesley Towers 37953 Barbara Lynn Treharne 37954 John Robert Trindle 37955 Clifton N. B. Triplett 37956 Larry Murray Trumbore 37957 Jeffrey Charles Tumm 37958 Doris Ann Turner 37959 Henry Clay Turner 37960 James Thomas Turner 37961 John Henry Hammond Turner 37962 Michael Jay Ungar 37963 Robert Chapman Upton 37964 Oscar Blanchard Valent 37965 John Ervin Valentine 37966 Anthony Gerald Vandermeys 37967 John A. Van Grouw 37968 Robert Hugh Vasse 37969 Robert Henry Vaughn 37970 Russell Owen Vernon 37971 Gilberto Villahermosa 37972 Robert William Jr. Viohl 37973 Anthony Michael Visk 37974 Randall Arthur Von Rosenberg 37975 Keith Robert Vore 37976 Joseph Leonard Votel 37977 Christopher Glenn Wagner 37978 Kenneth S. Wagner 37979 Christopher Wakim 37980 Michael John Waldier 37981 Joseph A. Waldron 37982 Harlan Murch Walker 37983 Priscilla Marie Locke 37984 Wally Zwolinski Walters 37985 William Randall Walton 37986 John Richard Ward 37987 Steven Ralph Ward 37988 William Franklin Ward 37989 Mark Gregory Wardlaw 37990 Eugene Casey Wardynski 37991 John Carson Warnke 37992 Vincent Edwin Warrick 37993 Jeffrey M. Weart 37994 Don Leeroy Webber 37995 James Michael Weeks 37996 William Ray Weeks 37997 Edward Joseph Wegel 37998 Edward Lee Weinberg 37999 Steven Nicholas Welks 38000 Paul Louis Wentz 38001 Thomas Joseph Werner 38002 Kurt Ogg Westerman 38003 Kathleen Wheless Gerstein 38004 James Benjamin White 38005 Stuart Allen Whitehead 38006 Stuart A. Whitfield 38007 Roger Francis Wieland 38008 Kathryn Annette Funk 38009 Edmund Anthony Wilhelm 38010 Thomas P. Wilhelm 38011 Fred Clayton Wilkins 38012 Charles Wesley Williams 38013 James B. Williams 38014 Jeffrey Nels Williams 38015 Frank Phillip Willingham 38016 Robert Stafford Wills 38017 James Scott Wilson 38018 Mark Edwin Wilson 38019 William Gregory Withers 38020 Keith Richard Wokowsky 38021 Guy Allen Wolf 38022 Paul Alan Wolfley 38023 Leonard Wong 38024 George Joseph Woods 38025 Willis Addison Woods 38026 Mark Leroy Work 38027 William Keeley Wray 38028 Charles Donald Wright 38029 Donna Marie Wright 38030 Paul Eugene Wright 38031 Mark Alan Yeshnik 38032 Carol Ann MacGibbon 38033 Kelly L. Zachgo-Lynch 38034 Gregory Joseph Zanetti 38035 Jerry David Zayas 38036 Joan Marie Gerth 38037 John Christopher Zizzi 38038 John Terry Zoccola 38039 Andrew Rufus Bland 38040 Stephen Lester Bragdon 38041 James Donald Campbell 38042 Raymond Martin Conner 38043 Ronald John DePaul 38044 Michael Duane Ellerbe 38045 Mark Adrian Flacy 38046 Mary E. Flynn O'Brien 38047 Richard Owen Funk 38048 John J. Kramer 38049 Winston Det Min Ling 38050 Richard Charles Martin 38051 Richard Irving McCaughey 38052 Albert Anton Nelwan 38053 Stephen Joseph Perez 38054 William Michael Pontius 38055 Donald K. Reeves 38056 Michael Rodemers 38057 Leopoldo Carrillo Scrivner 38058 Gregory Bernard Stephens 38059 Tollie Strode 38060 James Eric Thayer 38061 Kevin James Thomas 38062 David Wayne Vaden 38063 Timothy Joseph Walsh 38064 Russell Hans Wange 38065 John Lee Wolf 38066 George Robert Conrad 38067 Norman Hoover Hahn 38068 Joseph Huber Hall 38069 Steven Dale McKnight 38070 Jack Merlin Kerns 38071A Kirk William Schaumann 38071 Christopher Edwin Allen 38072 Jay Alan Harris 38073 John F. Hilliard 38074 Wayne Christopher Jackson 38075 Matthew Angelo Tavrides 38076 Charles J. Toomey 38077 Michael Ronald Trusty 38078 Mark Eugene Walden 38079 Donald Ewing Williams 38080 Miguel Antonio Gutierrez 38081 **1981** Douglas Adams Adams 38082 Randy Lee Adams 38083 William French Adams 38084 William Peter Adams 38085 Christopher Anthony Ager 38086 Gary Alfredo Agron 38087 Bruce Allen Ahlbrand 38088 James Kyongho Ahn 38089 Gregory Allen Aldrich 38090 David M. Alegre 38091 Blair Cartledge Alexander 38092 Curtis Duane Alexander 38093 Donald Allard 38094 Daniel Bartlett Allyn 38095 Jeffrey Joseph Altmire 38096 James Ernest Alty 38097 Bruce Cory Anderson 38098 Jeffry Lee Anderson 38099 Joseph Anderson 38100 Michael Robert Anderson 38101 Paul Allan Anderson 38102 William Fredrick Anderson 38103 John Antanies 38104 Michael Dean Anthony 38105 Edward James Apgar 38106 Edward Ritter Armstrong 38107 Mark Halsey Armstrong 38108 William Thomas Atkinson 38109 Robert John Avalle 38110 Adolfo Ayala 38111 Alan Joseph

Azzarita 38112 Michael John Bacevich 38113 James Donald Bagwell 38114 Steve J. Baham 38115 George Harold Baker 38116 Michael A. Baker 38117 William Balogh 38118 Kurt Charles Barthel 38119 Terrance James Bauer 38120 Franklin Roosevelt Baum 38121 Barry E. Bazemore 38122 Gary Allen Bechard 38123 Adele Marie Beck Kruegler 38124 Kevin John Becker 38125 Seth Walter Becker 38126 James Albert Bederka 38127 Michael Dargacz Beery 38128 Paul Jeffrey Begeman 38129 Gregory Robert Beliles 38130 Leslie Howard Belknap 38131 William J. Belknap 38132 Matthew John Benne 38133 Timothy Scott Bensley 38134 Thomas Charles Berger 38135 Raymond P. Bernhagen 38136 Fernando Berrios 38137 Paul Randall Bethea 38138 Fareed Michael Betros 38139 Michael David Bianchi 38140 George Martin Bilafer 38141 Eric Daniel Billig 38142 Victor Michael Bird 38143 John Elmer Birk 38144 Martin Bernard Bischoff 38145 Gregory Allen Bisig 38146 Thomas A. Blanchard 38147 Carl Stephen Bleyl 38148 John G. Blitch 38149 Jeffrey B. Blyth 38150 Brian Lee Boettner 38151 Kevin Michael Bolan 38152 Lewis Alexander Boore 38153 Liviu Emanuel Border 38154 Kenneth Paul Boretti 38155 Susan Bottorff Neumann 38156 John Michael Bowen 38157 Brian Joseph Bowers 38158 Barry G. Box 38159 Scott Edwin Boyd 38160 Christine Boyle Yuengert 38161 Matthew Steven Bradley 38162 Daniel Wesley Breckel 38163 Margaret Mary Bridgeman 38164 Peter Capwell Brigham 38165 Mark Anthony Brinkley 38166 Michael David Bristol 38167 John Michael Britten 38168 Randy A. Britton 38169 Gary Joseph Brockington 38170 Timothy John Brotherton 38171 Alvin Lyn Broussard 38172 David Richard Brown 38173 Heidi Virginia Brown 38174 Hubert William Brown 38175 James Ernest Brown 38176 Robert Brooks Brown 38177 Mark Scott Browne 38178 William Theodore Browne 38179 Robert Hall Bruce 38180 John Calvin Brudvig 38181 Richard Brudzynski 38182 Michael Lindsay Bruhn 38183 Michael Paul Bruyere 38184 Kevin Goeden Bryan 38185 Carlton Andrew Buchanan 38186 William Hamilton Buck 38187 John Brendan Buckley 38188 William Robert Buckley 38189 Eugene Russel Buckner 38190 Paul Edward Buechner 38191 William Frank Buechter 38192 Dea Bulen Hunt 38193 Stephen George Bullock 38194 Thomas William Buning 38195 Mark Wayne Burger 38196 Samuel Wayne Burkett 38197 Douglas Arthur Burrer 38198 Howard A. Burris 38199 C. Craig Buzan 38200 Ann L. Stroud 38201 Christopher Joseph G. Cachero 38202 Tymothy W. Caddell 38203 Robert J. Cadigan 38204 Steven Vincent Callan 38205 Ramiro David Canedo 38206 Franklin D. Canterbury 38207 John McWhirter Cape 38208 Magdaline C. Caradimitropoulo 38209 Kathryn Helen Carlson 38210 Robert Michael Carpenter 38211 John Con Carrano 38212 Patrick John Carroll 38213 Steven Whitney Carter 38214 Helias Casares 38215 Patrick Ernest Case 38216 Fabian Gustavo Castro 38217 Russell Keith Catron 38218 Robert Gene Caudle 38219 Dean Robert Cerny 38220 Michael H. Ceruti 38221 Mark Bret Cheben 38222 Dan W. Chesnut 38223 Clarence Kwan Kee Chinn 38224 Jeffrey John Chludzinski 38225 Kevin Daniel Clark 38226 Michael James Clidas 38227 Thomas Yardley Cobb 38228 Lewis Cole Cochran 38229 Todd T. Cochran 38230 Paul Douglas Coleman 38231 Nerius Alexis Collazo 38232 James Glenn Collins 38233 Carl James Colwell 38234 Thomas Joseph Comodeca 38235 Mark William Conforti 38236 Kevin Gerald Conlon 38237 Arthur William Connor 38238 Michael D. Connor 38239 Michael Scott Contratto 38240 Jeffery Scott Cook 38241 Keith Larue Cooper 38242 Dale N. Cope 38243 Richard Chase Coplen 38244 Alfred Anthony Coppola 38245 Mary Theresa Cotnoir Murtie 38246 Peter Normand Courtois 38247 Charles George Coutteau 38248 Martin John Coyne 38249 Stephen John Cozza 38250 Brian Matthew Craddock 38251 William Michael Crocoll 38252 Al Edward Crosby 38253 Ian Gillead Cunningham 38254 James Walter Czizik 38255 David James Daley 38256 Douglas Paul Dalpini 38257 Gregory Gerard Daly 38258 James Ralph Daly 38259 Patrick Joseph Daly 38260 Katherine Dammel Martins 38261 William Alfred Dauer 38262 James Edward David 38263 Peter Alan Davidson 38264 Robert Guinn Davidson 38265 Geoffrey Clark Davis 38266 Gordon Bryant Davis 38267 Kathleen M. Batton 38268 Stuart Daniel Davis 38269 Vernon Thomas Davis 38270 Philip Jon Davison 38271 T. D. Decker 38272 Peter DeFluri 38273 Matthew Jay DeHaven 38274 Perry Joseph Delahoussaye 38275 William Francis Delaney 38276 Robert Delisle 38277 Peter Charles DeMarco 38278 Stephen Craig DePew 38279 Donna Dermatis Jaye 38280 William Rudolph Derrick 38281 Michael Scott Desens 38282 Shane Macomber Deverill 38283 Donald Charles Devine 38284 Gregory L. Dewalt 38285 Richard Henry DiGiovanni 38286 Paul Richard Dillman 38287 Louis Amerigo DiMarco 38288 Stephen Carl Dinkel 38289 Charles J. Dionne 38290 Joseph Patrick DiSalvo 38291 Paul Joseph Divis 38292 Brian Augustine Doak 38293 Thomas Gregory Dodd 38294 Kevin Rumley Dodge 38295 Bryan Lee Dohrn 38296 Reinaldo Marques D'Oliveira 38297 Yvonne D. Doll 38298 Joseph William Dombi 38299 Paul Anthony Dombkowski 38300 Robert James Domitrovich 38301 Thomas Michael Donahue 38302 Robert Scott Donnelly 38303 Kevin Sean Donohue 38304 Michael Edward Donovan 38305 Floyd Terry Douthit 38306 Anthony Joseph Dowd 38307 Jon Nicholas Dowling 38308 Mary E. White 38309 Charles Henry Driessnack 38310 Patrick Joseph DuBois 38311 Stephen Campane Dumont 38312 Thomas Michael Dunn 38313 Donald Jeffrey Dunthorn 38314 John D. Dutchyshyn 38315 Kenneth P. Dzierzanowski 38316 Allen Cash East 38317 Nathan R. Eberle 38318 Antulio J. Echevarria 38319 A. Tommy Economy 38320 Timothy J. Edens 38321 Kent William Eisele 38322 Robert Steven Elias 38323 Joseph Robert Elledge 38324 Daniel Brian Elliott 38325 Charlotte Ann Johnston 38326 Stanley Jay Emelander 38327 Donald William Engen 38328 Bonney Sue Epstein 38329 Andrew Arthur Evans 38330 Leroy Michael Evans 38331 Matthew Brian Fagan 38332 Michael K. Fahnestock 38333 Glenn Arthur Falconi 38334 Joseph Edwin Fallon 38335 Michael Joseph Fallon 38336 David Joseph Farace 38337 Billy Robert Farrar 38338 Michael William Feil 38339 Robert Michael Felland 38340 Michael Fenn 38341 James Eric Ferrando 38342 John Joseph Ferraro 38343 Paul W. Ferriero 38344 John Garth Fiala 38345 Mark Alan Fichten 38346 Robert Grause Fix 38347 Kenneth Paul Fleischer 38348 Michael Angelo Florio 38349 Nathan Allen Fogt 38350 Robert Scott Forbes 38351 Todd H. Foreman 38352 Michael Wayne Fortanbary 38353 Daniel Arthur Fournie 38354 Christopher William Fowler 38355 Edward Joseph Fox 38356 Kathleen Freely Browning 38357 Ian Henry George Freeman 38358 Thomas Freeman 38359 Edward Dean Freesmeyer 38360 John Michael French 38361 Jeffrey R. Friedel 38362 Gregory John Fritz 38363 Keith John Fruge 38364 Christopher Charles Fry 38365 Joseph Lloyd Fulbright 38366 William Bewick Fullerton 38367 Christopher Todd Fulton 38368 Antoinette Gaidosik Smart 38369 Patrick William Gaines 38370 William Joseph Gallagher 38371 Robert Charles Galvan 38372 John Welch Garmany 38373 Daryl Roy Garner 38374 Guy Anthony Gasser 38375 Gaylin Wayne Gates 38376 J. A. Gates 38377 Karl Franklin Gebhart 38378 Edward Lee George 38379 Joseph Gerencser 38380 Christian Joseph Germain 38381 Gregory Michal Gerovac 38382 Paul Charles Gerton 38383 Byron J. Gibson 38384 William James Gillette 38385 Randal Louis Gitschlag 38386 Timothy Lee Gladura 38387 Arthur David Glikin 38388 Walter Michael Golden 38389 Keith V. Goodson 38390 Matthew Lee Gorevin 38391 Patrick Joseph Gormley 38392 Allen Keiichi Goshi 38393 Michael Gordon Gould 38394 Norman Mark Grady 38395 Catherine Graham Haight 38396 David G. Graham 38397 Douglas Eugene Graham 38398 Timothy Wayne Grant 38399 Gerald Lee Greb 38400 Emmett Fidel Green 38401 Joseph Gerard Green 38402 Matthew John Green 38403 Bryon E. Greenwald 38404 John Greiman 38405 Stuart Elton Grewatz 38406 David Leon Griffin 38407 Billie Eugene Grimm 38408 Brian Lee Groft 38409 Michael James Grove 38410 Randall Alan Grubb 38411 Daniel Joseph Guilmette 38412 Gasper Gulotta 38413 Gary Howard Guyll 38414 Bruce Leonard Gwilliam 38415 Henry David Hacker 38416 Margaret Haese Belknap 38417 John Barton Hager 38418 David Leon Hagg 38419 William Henry Haight 38420 Matthew Thomas Hale 38421 Thomas James Halinski 38422 Kimetha Hall Topping 38423 Brian D. Haller 38424 Jon Robert Hallingstad 38425 Rebecca Stevens Halstead 38426 Susan D. Halter 38427 David Bryant Hamilton 38428 Kevin James Hammond 38429 Thomas Gregory Hammoor 38430 Daniel Joseph Hanauer 38431 Joseph Michael Hanley 38432 Georgette Hansen Wilson 38433 Robert Patrick Hansen 38434 Jennifer Ann Alle 38435 Nancy Harman Stevens 38436 William Everett Harmon 38437 Jeffrey William Harris 38438 Thomas Gregory Harris 38439 James Warren Harrison 38440 William Terry Harrison 38441 David Lee Hartley 38442 Samuel Clinton Hartwell 38443 Paul Thomas Harvey 38444 Steven Paul Haustein 38445 Robert Field Hayes 38446 Edward William Hazel 38447 John David Healey 38448 Edward A. Healy 38449 Douglass Scott Heckman 38450 Joseph Patrick Heekin 38451 Howard Brian Heidenberg 38452 William Paul Hein 38453 Frederick Carl Hellwig 38454 James Edward Hembrey 38455 James Bruce Henderson 38456 Robert St. Clair Henderson 38457 Theodore Alan Hendy 38458 Mark Matthew Hennes 38459 John Bennett Hennessey 38460 Kermit P. Henninger 38461 Robert Joseph Henry 38462 Matthew John Herholtz 38463 Victor David Hernandez 38464 Ernest Joseph Herold 38465 Joe Elson Herr 38466 Gregory Keith Herring 38467 Dean William Hess 38468 Jorge Fidencio Hidalgo 38469 Gregory David Hiebert 38470 Terence Scott Higdon 38471 David Melvin Hildreth 38472 Jeffrey Alan Bond 38473 James Bernard Hill 38474 Kevin D. Hill 38475 Peter John Hillebrand 38476 William Jude Hine 38477 Curtis Timothy Hines 38478 William Clayton Hix 38479 R. Todd Hockenbury 38480 David Clayton Hoffman 38481 Michael Patrick Hoffman 38482 Mark Nelson Hogan 38483 Michael Edward Hogan 38484 Thomas Harold Hogan 38485 David Richard Hogg 38486 Leon William Hojnicki 38487 Richard David Hooker 38488 John Charles Hope 38489 Reinhold J. Horn 38490 James Allen Hornack 38491 Donald Howard Horner 38492 Pamela Odette Howard 38493 Richard Andrew Howley 38494 Russell James Hrdy 38495 Lawrence Ping Hu 38496 Billy Dean Hubbard 38497 Michael Gerard Hudachek 38498 James Kenneth Hudson 38499 Stephen E. Hughes 38500 David Lawrence Hull 38501 Kathleen Humphreys Ladig 38502 Ronald Leroy Humphreys 38503 John William Hustleby 38504 Christopher H. Jackson 38505 Michael Jack Jackson 38506 Robert Charles Jacobs 38507 Arlon Harm Jahnke 38508 Matthew Edward Janze 38509 Michael Joseph Jaye 38510 Roy Karl Jeffery 38511 Tim Alan Jensen 38512 Eric Malm Johnson 38513 Hiram N. Johnson 38514 Jace R. W. Johnson 38515 Steven Lowry Johnston 38516 William Francis Johnston 38517 David Theodore Jones 38518 Steven Michael Jones 38519 Frank Antim Jordano 38520 Steven Michael Karan 38521 James Karas 38522 James Mark Karditzas 38523 Robert Wade Karpiak 38524 David Jay Katz 38525 John Michael Katz 38526 Michael Vincent Kelly 38527 Patrick Eaton Kelly 38528 Alexander Dimitri Kendris 38529 Anthony Alan Kerhin 38530 Kenneth Anthony Kienle 38531 Christopher John Killoy 38532 Dean Stuart Kinghorn 38533 Andrew John Kinney 38534 D. Jill Kirby 38535 Richard Klatt 38536 Daniel John Klecker 38537 Stephen Douglas Klotz 38538 Dan Joe Knappenberger 38539 David Scot Knecht 38540 Earl Eugene Knight 38541 Kirk Barnes Knipp 38542 Michael Joseph Knippel 38543 Margaret Knox Kulungowski 38544 Gerald Stephen Koenig 38545 James Michael Kons 38546 Steven Haigaz Krikorian 38547 Michael Anthony Kriz 38548 Gary Thomas Kropkowski 38549 Robert Kruger 38550 James Michael Krushat 38551 Robert James Kuelzow 38552 Keith Charles Kurber 38553 Robert M. Kurtz 38554 Hon Cheun Kwan 38555 John Ray Labrucherie 38556 Sam Dewitt Lail 38557 Glen David Lambkin 38558 Michael Louis Lambright 38559 Lynn A. Lancaster 38560 Charles Edward Lane 38561 Edward George Lane 38562 Thomas Nathan Lanier 38563 Richard Christopher LaPerch 38564 Jon Alan LaPointe 38565 Peter Waller Lash 38566 Richard Brian Leap 38567 Randy Carroll LeCompte 38568 Brian Michael Lee 38569 David Matthew Lee 38570 J. Marc LeGare 38571 Gerard W. Lemanski 38572 David Brian Lemauk 38573 Theodore Gerhard Lemcke 38574 Michael Joseph Lessel 38575 Michael John Liesman 38576 Raymond Everett Lilley 38577 Michael Vincent Litwinowicz 38578 John Roulston Livingston 38579 John Thomas Lloyd 38580 Jeffrey Arthur Lochow 38581 Ernest Gordon Lockrow 38582 Guy Anthony Lofaro 38583 Kevin Paul Logan 38584 Jeffrey Kevin Longar 38585 Debra Lopez Fix 38586 Howard Wright Loso 38587 Randal Wayne Lovell 38588 Barrett Franquez Lowe 38589 Neil Marcus Lowe 38590 Stuart Henry Ludemann 38591 Robert Anthony Luster 38592 Drew Alan Lyle 38593 Eric Jon Lynam 38594 Dereck E. Lyons 38595 Geoffrey Allen MacDonald 38596 Sean Barry MacFarland 38597 Robert William Mackay 38598 Wayne Fraser MacKenzie 38599 Randall Lee Mackey 38600 Frederick M. Maddock 38601 David Raymond Madrid 38602 Anders Nelson Madsen 38603 Brian Ward Magerkurth 38604 William Thomas Maier 38605 David John Majdanski 38606 Marianne Patrice Malizia 38607 Robert Joseph Malley 38608 Paul David Mango 38609 William Fredrick Mann 38610 Kevin Ross Manos 38611 Charles Basil Manula 38612 David L. Maples 38613 Stanley Raymond March 38614 Mark Thomas Marino 38615 George Peter Marquardt 38616 Patrick Matthew Marr 38617 Andrew Hayden Marsh 38618 Jeffrey Eugene Marshall 38619 Scott William Marx 38620 Alan Brian Maskal 38621 Dean Allen Massman 38622 Theresa Matejov Freeze 38623 Heidi Mauk Gruner 38624 Robert John Mayer 38625 Robert Mazur 38626 Alphonso Franklin Mazyck 38627 Douglas Lawrence McAllaster 38628 Lawrence E. McAnneny 38629 Matthew Kevin McCarville 38630 Nathan Eugene McCauley 38631 Kevin James McClung 38632 James Charles McConville 38633 Douglas James McCord 38634 Thomas J. McCormick 38635 Cary S. McCoy 38636 Neil Earl McCray 38637 Frank Edward McDermott 38638 David R. McDonald 38639 John Joseph McDonald 38640 David Creaton McDowell 38641 Howard Ogle McGillin 38642 Michael Francis McGrath 38643 Stephen E. McGuire 38644 Mark John McKearn 38645 Michael James McMahon 38646 Shawn Sanders McMaster 38647 James D. McMullin 38648 James W. McNulty 38649 Warne David Mead 38650 Timothy K. Meade 38651 John Patrick Meehan 38652 Michael James Meese 38653 James Alridge Meredith 38654 Michael Anthony Mertz 38655 James Lloyd Messer 38656 Timothy John Metivier 38657 Daniel James Miklancic 38658 Melinda Miles 38659 Melissa Miles 38660 John Richard Minahan 38661 Michael Dewayne Miner 38662 Matthew Mirisola 38663 Charles William Mitchell 38664 James Eric Moentmann 38665 Robert Arthur Moore 38666 Christopher P. Moosmann 38667 Daniel Jerome Moravec 38668 David Alan Mosinski 38669 John Andrew Moskal 38670 John Thomas Mudlo 38671 Patrick John Mueller 38672 Gregory Allen Muilenburg 38673 Hugh Patrick Munson 38674 Neil Francis Murray 38675 Eric Scott Musser 38676 Barry William Muth 38677 Joseph Carney Myers 38678 Edward Paul Naessens 38679 Karl Burton Neblett 38680 Paul Matthew Nelson 38681 Duane Raynard Nesset 38682 Daniel Raymond Nevarre 38683 Michael Alan Newcomb 38684 Robert Board Newman 38685 Tracy Lane Newsome 38686 Robert Allen Newton 38687 James Marshall Nichol 38688 Brian Jay Nichols 38689 Camille Marie Nichols 38690 Mark Alan Nipper 38691 Duke Naoki Nishimura 38692 George Adelbert Nowak 38693 Robert Masaru Nozuka 38694 Robert Dale O'Brien 38695 David Christopher Ochs 38696 Christopher John O'Connell 38697 Edwin Sanderson O'Connor 38698 Francis Gerald O'Connor 38699 Mark O'Gara 38700 Gerald Brian O'Keefe 38701 Walter Joseph Olker 38702 Frederick J. Ondarza 38703 Cynthia O'Neil Hope 38704 Gary Gray Orton 38705 Thomas Sean O'Shaughnessy 38706 Alisande Osuch Gelineau 38707 Gail O'Sullivan Dwyer 38708 Scott Dean Owen 38709 Louis Joseph Pagentine 38710 Mark Alan Palmer 38711 Ralph Matthew Palmiero 38712 Raymond P. Palumbo 38713 William Scott Parker 38714 William Henry Parrish 38715 Mark Gregory Paslawsky 38716 Bonnie Patton Tidd 38717 Ross Douglas Pauley 38718 Eugene Pacelli Paulo 38719 John C. Paulson 38720 James Michael Pawlak 38721 Robert Andrew Payne 38722 Ronald Lee Pearson 38723 William Charles Peck 38724 Stephen Michael Pelicano 38725 David Robert Pelizzon 38726 Philip Walter Pellette 38727 Steven Patrick Perry 38728 Thomas Jay Perry 38729 Scott C. Peters 38730 Darryl W. Peterson 38731 Jeffrey N. Peterson 38732 Janet Petro Canavan 38733 James Echol Petty 38734 Dana James Hillian Pittard 38735 Debra Pittman Aaron 38736 Brian David Plaisted 38737 Mark Bennett Pliakos 38738 Andres Hinn Ploompuu 38739 Russell L. Poling 38740 Anita Polite Wabeke 38741 Randolph Wayne Ponder 38742 Edward Michael Poniatowski 38743 Ronald Anthony Porter 38744 Elizabeth Potter Burrer 38745 Kenneth Wayne Powell 38746 Robert Howard Pozsonyi 38747 William Joseph Prantl 38748 Richard Brent Pridgen 38749 John Joseph Prusiecki 38750 David Patrick Pursell 38751 Tommy E. Rader 38752 Daniel Joseph Ragsdale 38753 J. Kevin Rappold 38754 Gregory Scott Rassatt 38755 Roy Thornton Ray 38756 Charles Leonard Raymond 38757 Walter Russell Raymond 38758 William Curran Raynes 38759 Myles Reardon 38760 Keith Francis Reck 38761 Grady G. Reese 38762 Timothy Robert Reese 38763 Garon L. Reeves 38764 Thomas Arthur Rehm 38765 Carlton Barrow Reid 38766 Mark Alan Reisweber 38767 Michael Resty 38768 Manuel Joseph Reverie 38769 Frank Delbert Rhinesmith 38770 William Bradley Rice 38771 Charles Ross Rich 38772 Bryan Douglas Richardson 38773 Scott Richard Richardson 38774 Thomas Eric Richbourg 38775 Kyle M. Riddle 38776 Kevin Robert Riedler 38777 Ricardo Rogelio Riera 38778 Michael Andrew Rigg 38779 William E. Riker 38780 Lisa Riseling Bond 38781 Mark Lee Ritter 38782 Michael Rizzio 38783 Ricky J. Roberts 38784 Steven Wayne Robertson 38785 Daniel Keith Robie 38786 Timothy Von Robinson 38787 Humberto Rodriguez 38788 William Drew Rogers 38789 Jerry H. Roth 38790 Michael Edward Rounds 38791 Steven Eric Russell 38792 Douglas Edward Ryan 38793 Robert Joseph Sager 38794 James Robert Sajo 38795 Eugene Salazar 38796 Elizabeth Salvador Schowalter 38797 Ronald Frank Salyer 38798 David Wayne Samec 38799 Bryan Dirk Sampson 38800 Joe Benjamin Sanchez 38801 Donald Mark Sando 38802 John Paul Sankovitch 38803 David T. Santilli 38804 Wayne Allen Sauer 38805 David Michael Savage 38806 W. Michael Love 38807 Leonard J. Sbrocco 38808 Richard Andrew Schaefer 38809 Eric Paul Schellhorn 38810 Philip James Schlatter 38811 Gregory J. Schleyer 38812 Mark Robert Schmidt 38813 William Joseph Schneider 38814 Andrew Karl Schober 38815 David Dale Schoewe 38816 Mark Allen Schreder 38817 Mark James Schroeder 38818 Thomas Joseph Schwartz 38819 Tauno Bruun Schwelnus 38820 Braddock B. Scott 38821 Michael Patrick Scott 38822 Mark Ralph Seastrom 38823 David Mark Sheely 38824 Matthew Louis Sherman 38825 Peter K. Sherrill 38826 Timothy Mitchell Sherwood 38827 Robert Lee Shields 38828 Ronald Pier Shinego 38829 Kevin John Shuba 38830 John Sean Shultis 38831 Stephen Jon Simmerer 38832 Keith Douglas Simonson 38833 Jon Paul Smart 38834 Clark Lennon Smith 38835 Jack F. Smith 38836 Kevin Bruce Smith 38837 Stephen T. Smith 38838 David Wells Snyder 38839 Robert Donald Snyder 38840 Mark Carl Sofia 38841 Keith Donald Solveson 38842 Paul O. Somersall 38843 David Leon Sonnier 38844 William Wensten Spurgeon 38845 Patrick Thompson Stockpole 38846 Charles August Stafford 38847 Scott Robert Stahley 38848 Ronald Alfred Stanfield 38849 Amy Elizabeth Stearns 38850 Grant Douglas Steffan 38851 Dirk Edward Stevens 38852 Kevin Scott Stewart 38853 James K. Stiegler 38854 Bruce Michael Stiles 38855 John A. Stine 38856 Timothy Roger Stoy 38857 Kevin Anthony Streets 38858 Andrew B. Stroud 38859 James Merie Stuteville 38860 John Bartee Suddarth 38861 Steven Sukovich 38862 Christopher C. Sullivan 38863 Allen Michael Susie 38864 Everett James Sutherland 38865 Nancy Svoboda Rowe 38866 Sherrill L. Stramara 38867 Thomas Leslie Swaren 38868 Mark David Swope 38869 Paula Ann Sydenstricker 38870 Rand William Syslo

38871 Eric Frank Takatori 38872 William James Tarantino 38873 John A. Tartala 38874 Anthony Jean Tata 38875 Dean Curtis Taylor 38876 John James Taylor 38877 Patrick J. Teifer 38878 Bruce Alexander Thames 38879 Gary Eugene Thie 38880 John Steven Thiel 38881 Anthony Sterling Thomas 38882 Michael Curtis Thomas 38883 Vernon Thomas 38884 John P. Tidd 38885 Jeffrey Joseph Tierney 38886 Jeffrey Scott Todd 38887 M. Linwood Todd 38888 Christopher James Toomey 38889 Kenneth L. Topping 38890 David George Tosi 38891 David Michael Toth 38892 Bradford Clark Tousley 38893 James Vincent Towey 38894 James P. Trainor 38895 Michael E. Travis 38896 Raymond A. Trevino 38897 Chris Meredith Trotter 38898 G. Kent Troy 38899 Edward William Trudo 38900 Michael Joseph Tucci 38901 Rodney Duff Turner 38902 W. Bruce Turner 38903 Larry Charles Turrentine 38904 Lori Ann Utchel 38905 Francis Joseph Vahle 38906 Christopher Patrick Vanslager 38907 Robert John Vasta 38908 J. Mark Vaughn 38909 John Luther Vavrin 38910 Alfred Viana 38911 Robert Frank Vicci 38912 Malcolm Hugh Visser 38913 Roderick Karr Wade 38914 William Joseph Wadley 38915 Mark Richard Wagner 38916 Scott David Wagner 38917 Mark Ferguson Wait 38918 Chet George Walborn 38919 James Jolly Waldeck 38920 William Arthur Walk 38921 Anthony Keith Walker 38922 Kyle Edwin Walker 38923 Robert Scott Wall 38924 Robert C. Walter 38925 Rodney Wayne Walter 38926 Stephen Walters 38927 George Davisson Ward 38928 John F. Washuta 38929 James Louis Watson 38930 Michael Joseph Wawrzyniak 38931 Robert Edward Weafer 38932 John William Weatherford 38933 Anthony Vincent Webb 38934 James Richard Weber 38935 Kevin Allan Wedmark 38936 Mark Ralph Weitekamp 38937 Linda West Harmon 38938 Stephen Wayne Westbay 38939 Kenneth Richard Westlund 38940 Daisie Wheeler Boettner 38941 Stephen Lester White 38942 Leonard Kenneth Whitehead 38943 Malcolm A. Whitaker 38944 Steven Norman Wickstrom 38945 Deborah Widick Henderson 38946 Paul Albert Wiese 38947 John Douglas Wilhelm 38948 William Gerard Wilhelm 38949 Stephen Wilkins 38950 David Allen Will 38951 David Carson Williams 38952 Eddie Ermon Williams 38953 James Martin Williams 38954 Jeffrey Mooers Williams 38955 Michael Gordon Williams 38956 Duane Keven Wilson 38957 John P. Wilson 38958 Walter Merlin Wirth 38959 Daniel Victor Wise 38960 Peter Augustine Woloson 38961 John Keith Wood 38962 Kevin Bourne Wood 38963 Kent T. Woods 38964 E. Mark Woolen 38965 Edmund Winston Woolfolk 38966 Eugene Ray Woolridge 38967 Frederick Starr Wright 38968 James Edgar Wright 38969 Jerry Vernon Wright 38970 Victor Peter Wu 38971 Timothy Wayne Yahn 38972 Michael Stephen Yarmie 38973 Michael Lyman Yates 38974 Daniel Lee York 38975 James Frederick York 38976 Wayne Edward Young 38977 Gregory Frank Youst 38978 Louis Gerard Yuengert 38979 Brenda Zachary Linnington 38980 Daniel Louis Zajac 38981 Mark Albert Zamberlan 38982 Stephen Zapalla 38983 Holly Zarfoss Gumke 38984 Jess Victor Ziccarello 38985 Paul Joseph Zimmer 38986 Burkhardt Henry Zorn 38987 Paul Philip Barry 38988 Russ Howard Berkoff 38989 Melvin Haroyl Bland 38990 William Lindon Bowman 38991 Maitland Maines Browning 38992 Michael Philip Courts 38993 Richard James Everson 38994 Gregory Edward Ginter 38995 Peter Killan Goebel 38996 Neil Joseph Hamill 38997 Daryl Edward Harris 38998 Karla Spring Hayes 38999 Kathleen Henn Gambrell 39000 Mary Higgins Fletcher 39001 Paul Steven Hilton 39002 Frederick Morgan Isele 39003 David Jeffrey Key 39004 Robert Patton Kleinberger 39005 Robert Kirk Lawrence 39006 Timothy L. Libby 39007 Nicholas Liberatore 39008 David Harrison Ling 39009 Joseph Brown Lowder 39010 Morris Donald Minchew 39011 William Dale Osborne 39012 Charles E. Phillips 39013 John Thomas Phillips 39014 Patricia Savold McKinley 39015 Richard William Sellner 39016 Ralph Smith Siegrist 39017 Derek Anthony Soriano 39018 Scott Anthony Stangle 39019 William Scott Sullenberger 39020 Darrell George Vydra 39021 John Francis Wharton 39022 David Keith Wiggins 39023 William Henry York 39024 Henry Elbert Brown 39025 Jesse Robert Nutt 39026 Steven W. Berthot 39027A Harvey Leroy Pullen 39027 Paul Brian Dinardo 39028 Jeffry Paul Smith 39029 Patrick Joseph Carley 39030 Chet Cory Childers 39031 Archie Lee Davis 39032 Paul DeFluri 39033 John Anthony DiNome 39034 Timothy Charles Dolan 39035 Robin Emanuel-Smith 39036 Albert James Marcenkus 39037 Randall F. McElroy 39038 Charles William Swanson 39039 Kevin Scott Thompson 39040 Charles J. Young 39041 **1982** Paul Francis Abel 39042 Robert Bruce Abrams 39043 Crispiniano G. Acosta 39044 Christopher John Adams 39045 Peter Charles Adams 39046 Rashid Jan Afridi 39047 Mark Andrew Albe 39048 Richard Russel Allen 39049 Brian D. Allgood 39050 Ernest John Almanza 39051 Arthur G. Almore 39052 Oscar Nava Alvarez 39053 James Paul Amey 39054 Gregg Andres 39055 Mark J. Andrew 39056 David Arthur Anstey 39057 Steven Thomas Antrobus 39058 Manuel Aponte 39059 Francis Xavier Asencio 39060 David Edward Aucoin 39061 Stanley Fletcher Austin 39062 Michael Sidney Auzenne 39063 Mark Francis Averill 39064 Steven Michael Aviles 39065 James Brandon Bagby 39066 Joseph Percy Bailey 39067 Anita Lee Baker 39068 Ralph Otto Baker 39069 Charles J. Baldwin 39070 Monica Balkus Gorbandt-Smith 39071 Arthur Thomas Ball 39072 Dominic Rocco Baragona 39073 Michael Patrick Barbero 39074 Frans Carl Barends 39075 Robert Joel Barnhill 39076 Lee Alfred Bartholomew 39077 Scott Lamar Bass 39078 Richard Craig Bassett 39079 Maryann Cummings 39080 Edward Bator 39081 Robert Brian Bauder 39082 Roberta Baynes 39083 C. Richard Beard 39084 Daniel Thomas Beck 39085 Rene Donald Belanger 39086 Hugh Marshall Bell 39087 Oliver John Bell 39088 Helen B. Vislosky 39089 David Brian Bellows 39090 Monty Craig Benenhaley 39091 Jerryl Eugene Bennett 39092 Patricia Ann Vaninger 39093 Benjamin Roy Bergfelt 39094 Timothy James Bergin 39095 Steven Gosnell Berstler 39096 Thomas Murray Besch 39097 Mark Andrew Biehler 39098 Steven Thomas Bigari 39099 Karl M. Birkhimer 39100 Michael John Bittrick 39101 Kristi J. Blanchard 39102 Christopher Dale Bland 39103 Brett Alan Boerema 39104 Arie Douglas Bogaard 39105 Brian John Bogard 39106 John Spencer Boler 39107 Phillip Lewis Bond 39108 Joseph Alexander Bonometti 39109 Stephen Todd Boston 39110 Brian Matthew Boutte 39111 Dean Richard Bowden 39112 James Warren Bowen 39113 Thomas Scott Bowen 39114 Bradley Joseph Bower 39115 Craig Douglas Bowman 39116 James Vincent Boyle 39117 William Boyle 39118 David Martin Bradley 39119 Dennis Julian Bradley 39120 John R. Bray 39121 Hans-Christian Brechbuhl 39122 Barry Wade Brewer 39123 Gregory A. Brockman 39124 Boyd Bradley Brooks 39125 John Jackson Brooks 39126 Jon Brandon Broome 39127 Scott Lewis Brothers 39128 James Baggott Brown 39129 John Robert Brundige 39130 Thomas Arthur Bryant 39131 Robert Bryce 39132 Steven Michael Buc 39133 James Everette Buchwald 39134 Belinda Lee Buckman 39135 William Louis Buda 39136 Mark Robert Buechner 39137 Daniel C. Buning 39138 Gregory Glenn Burgamy 39139 Joseph Earl Burlas 39140 William Robinson Burlas 39141 Richard Joseph Burnett 39142 Torin Alan Bussey 39143 James Bryan Butler 39144 Louis Cline Byars 39145 Ponce Vina Cabinian 39146 Caren Elizabeth Cahill 39147 Paul Thomas Calbos 39148 Robert Bryan Call 39149 Dennis Franklin Callahan 39150 Joseph Andrew Camargo 39151 Stephen A. Campano 39152 Michael Francis Canavan 39153 Brian William Caputo 39154 Edward Charles Cardon 39155 Timothy Shawn Carlin 39156 Robert David Carlson 39157 Frederick Clyde Carr 39158 Lonnie Rudy Carroll 39159 Ronald Lee Carter 39160 Patrick James Cassidy 39161 Jack Holt Cassingham 39162 Rawlin Junior Castro 39163 Gene Arthur Catena 39164 John C. Caudle 39165 Michael Clyde Centers 39166 Robert Eugene Chadwick 39167 Chelsea Youngchele Chae 39168 Charles Amos Chase 39169 William Norris Cheesborough 39170 Peter Cheselka 39171 Robert Thomas Cheshire 39172 Anne Cianciolo Davis 39173 Ralph Magnus Ciccarelli 39174 Arthur Charles Cody 39175 Robin Darrell Cofer 39176 William A. Cofield 39177 Eugene Alexander Collett 39178 Bret Erryl Comolli 39179 Mark Edward Condry 39180 Thomas Kevin Connolly 39181 Russell Glenn Conrad 39182 William Jerome Cook 39183 Philip James Cooper 39184 John Willard Copp 39185 James Gregory Cordell 39186 Joseph William Corrigan 39187 David K. Cox 39188 Thomas Robert Crabtree 39189 David Lawrence Craig 39190 Donald Murray Craig 39191 Robert Stephen Craig 39192 Mark Farel Crawford 39193 James Larue Creighton 39194 Kenneth Paul Creighton 39195 David Alan Crenshaw 39196 Tommy S. Crenshaw 39197 William Roy Cronk 39198 Stephen Edward Croskrey 39199 Kevin B. Cruise 39200 Timothy John Cummings 39201 Rui Octavio Cunha 39202 Paul Frederick Cunningham 39203 Craig Jeffrey Currey 39204 Philip Joseph Curtin 39205 Steven Alan Cyr 39206 Harold James Dabney 39207 Kenneth Robert Dahl 39208 Thomas Edward Darby 39209 Douglas Wayne Daum 39210 Michael J. Davidson 39211 K. Mark Davis 39212 Norman Wayne Davis 39213 Paul Rodney Davis 39214 Thomas Gerard Davitt 39215 Kevin F. Dehart 39216 John Michael Delaney 39217 Deborah Delgiorno Reisweber 39218 Robert Francis Demange 39219 Brodford William Denham 39220 Ronald Nicholas DeSantis 39221 Roger Andrew Deveney 39222 Timothy John Devens 39223 Thomas Francis Devine 39224 Guy Napier DeYoung 39225 Dominic Theodore Diciro 39226 Michael Anthony Dietz 39227 Michael Jay Dixon 39228 Walter Kevin Dodson 39229 John Barry Domenick 39230 Robert Aloysius Donahue 39231 Kevin Wade Dotson 39232 Joseph Patrick Doty 39233 Norbert Silsbury Doyle 39234 Timothy Edwin Drake 39235 David Mark Drucker 39236 Matthew Eugene Duban 39237 Joseph P. Duffey 39238 Patrick Emmet Duffy 39239 Michael Alan Dukes 39240 James Fumiyo Dunn 39241 Danny Durrell Durham 39242 Robert Monroe Dyess 39243 Ronald Joseph Dykstra 39244 Mark Christopher Easton 39245 Todd James Ebel 39246 Charles Jude Eccher 39247 Bryan Scott Eckstein 39248 Steven J. Eden 39249 Steven Wayne Ellington 39250 Wesley Byron Elmore 39251 Lynnae Engdahl Boyd 39252 Daniel James Enright 39253 Craig Allen Ericks 39254 Eric David Erickson 39255 Jon Robert Eshelman 39256 Christopher Lee Estey 39257 Stephen Robert Fahy 39258 Wesley Errold Farmer 39259 Thomas Faupel 39260 Scott A. Fedorchak 39261 Ralph A. Fehlberg 39262 Andrew Donald Feickert 39263 James Cameron Ferguson 39264 Anthony Rudolph Ferrara 39265 Joe Eddie Fields 39266 David P. Fiely 39267 Keith Alan Fink 39268 Kelly Frank Fisk 39269 Robert Carl Fleming 39270 Charles E. Fletcher 39271 Shawn William Flora 39272 James Martin Flynn 39273 Rocco Foderaro 39274 Randall Len Fofi 39275 Robert Wayne Forrester 39276 Robert Alan Fortier 39277 Joan Fowler 39278 Craig Alan Fox 39279 Lynn Fox Lodwick 39280 Mark Dean Frakes 39281 Scott Andrew Francis 39282 William Raymond Francis 39283 Kent Peter Fredrickson 39284 Erik J. Fretheim 39285 Karl Michael Friedman 39286 Joe Anna F. Mastracchio 39287 Jed Dunn Fulk 39288 Amanda F. Perez 39289 Darel Robert Gallagher 39290 Timothy Jerome Gallagher 39291 Graham Wood Galloway 39292 Christopher Franklin Gandy 39293 Duane Paul Gapinski 39294 Rafael Jorge Garcia 39295 Keith Harold Gardner 39296 Terrence Francis Garland 39297 Patrick John Garman 39298 Donna Garrett Boltz 39299 John Leo Garrison 39300 Ralph H. Gay 39301 Kyle Alexander Gerlitz 39302 Stephen Joseph Gerras 39303 Holly G. Grange 39304 Robert Doyle Gibson 39305 Derek Christopher Gilbert 39306 Lee Jay Gilbert 39307 James C. Gillespie 39308 Deborah Gillette Nagle 39309 Thomas Wells Girouard 39310 Cindy Glazier Jebb 39311 Bryan Sam Goda 39312 William Peter Goetz 39313 Robert Michael Goldberg 39314 Michael Warren Goodwin 39315 Thomas Russell Goodwin 39316 Charles MacArthur Gorbandt 39317 Ozzie Hans Gorbitz 39318 Alex Gorsky 39319 Denise Ann Goudreau 39320 Keith Robert Gramke 39321 Nadja Y. West 39322 William Walter Graves 39323 David Lynn Green 39324 Priscilla B. Greene 39325 Vincent Evan Grewatz 39326 Carolyn Mary Grey 39327 Mark Christian Grieb 39328 Gerald Menzo Griffin 39329 Kevin Lynn Griffith 39330 Barbara L. Grofic 39331 Ellen Wood Houlihan 39332 Bryan Allen Groves 39333 Robert Daniel Grymes 39334 Alan Charles Guarino 39335 Robert S. Guarino 39336 Kellye Renae Guinn 39337 Dick Steven Habbinga 39338 John Kevin Hackney 39339 Dale R. Hajost 39340 Telemachus Christos Halkias 39341 Josef Roy Hallatschek 39342 Philip R. Hallenbeck 39343 James A. Hamaker 39344 Scott Eugene Hampton 39345 David John Hanauer 39346 Thomas Patrick Hand 39347 Eric Samuel Handler 39348 Gary Michael Hanko 39349 Lawrence Keizo Harada 39350 William Frederick Hargraves 39351 Holly Julaine Harlow 39352 Todd Andrew Harmanson 39353 Michael Patrick Harrington 39354 David Dean Harris 39355 Harry Noble Harris 39356 Keith Edward Hartlage 39357 Paula Gayle Hartman Hartman-Koehler 39358 Douglas Eric Harvey 39359 Casey Patrick Haskins 39360 Stephen M. Hasley 39361 Guy Thomas Hatch 39362 Joseph Jude Hawley 39363 Steve Carl Hawley 39364 Richard Allen Hayden 39365 Kerry Neal Haynes 39366 Lance Anthony Heard 39367 Robert Bruce Heather 39368 James Robert Heavner 39369 William Huntting Hedges 39370 Scott Anson Henry 39371 Thomas M. Henry 39372 Juan Jose Hernandez 39373 Eric Ferdinand Herzberg 39374 Mark Steven Hiatt 39375 Peter Anthony Hidalgo 39376 John Mitchell Hill 39377 Stephen Lawrence Hill 39378 Deborah Hinton Pawlowski 39379 Augustus Kwang Ho 39380 John Patrick Hoffman 39381 Mark Howard Hoffman 39382 Michael Wayne Hogan 39383 James Phillip Hogle 39384 Bruce Douglas Hogston 39385 Rodney DeLeon Hollifield 39386 Gregory Donald Holtkamp 39387 Timothy George Hopper 39388 John William Hornick 39389 Mark Abbott Horstman 39390 Steven Bradish Horton 39391 Richard Edwin Hoss 39392 Richard Anthony Howard 39393 Michael Rodney Hubbard 39394 John Mortimer Hudson 39395 Edward Lloyd Hughes 39396 Maxwell Ray Hughey 39397 April M. Vinson 39398 Laurel Hummel 39399 Jeffrey William Humphrey 39400 Thomas M. Hurley 39401 Steven James Hutchison 39402 Leslie H. Reis 39403 Jack Todd Hyder 39404 Jonathan Warren Hyman 39405 Kelly Gene Hyndman 39406 Francis Anthony Ignazzitto 39407 Lonnie Leroy Imlay 39408 Stephen A. Ingalls 39409 Raymond Christopher Iram 39410 Jeffrey Dallas Irwin 39411 Ernst Kangle Isensee 39412 Karl Brian Iverslie 39413 Roland Scott Jacobs 39414 Dennis Lee Jaeger 39415 Stephen Ward Jarrard 39416 John Curtis Jarrell 39417 Daryl DeFrance Jaschen 39418 Michael John Jasenak 39419 Joel Edward Jebb 39420 James F. Jennings 39421 Bradley Ray Johnson 39422 Chris Dey Johnson 39423 Michele Ann Johnson 39424 Samuel Holdman Johnson 39425 Terence Rhys Johnson 39426 Emmett Charles Jones 39427 Kermit Calvin Jones 39428 Michael Frederick Jones 39429 Phillip Nathaniel Jones 39430 Terence Arthur Jones 39431 Edward D. Jozwiak 39432 Kenneth Gregory Juergens 39433 Thomas A. Juric 39434 Kerry Charles Kachejian 39435 James John Kainec 39436 Stephen Paul Kalish 39437 Arthur Gilbert Kane 39438 John Howard Karaus 39439 Thomas Michael Kastner 39440 Russell Marvin Kautz 39441 Frank G. Keating 39442 Kevin Michel Keating 39443 John Chesley Keely 39444 Lyle Jay Kellman 39445 Paul Wilson Kelly 39446 Terrence Kane Kelly 39447 Kenneth Andrew Kennedy 39448 James T. Kenney 39449 Steven Leslie Kent 39450 Kevin James Keough 39451 Richard Jay Kimmey 39452 Curtis Steeble King 39453 David Thomas Kinsella 39454 Michael John Klingele 39455 David Michael Knapp 39456 Lester William Knotts 39457 James A. Knowlton 39458 Ole Albert Knudson 39459 Steven Karl Kocher 39460 Perry Lee Koehler 39461 Joseph Raymond Kolb 39462 Nencho Nikolay Kolev 39463 Matthew Casimer Kolodziejczyk 39464 Robert Steven Koratsky 39465 Jeffrey Korcan 39466 John W. Korsnick 39467 Bruce Alan Kowalski 39468 Scott David Kraner 39469 Tara Shelomith Krause 39470 Phillip Michael Kruk 39471 Richard S. Kubu 39472 Thomas Walter Kula 39473 Kevin Dean Kullander 39474 Sanjai Kumar 39475 David Shigeaki Kumura 39476 George Douglas Kunkel 39477 John Cormier Kuttruff 39478 Brian Patrick Lacey 39479 Denis Joseph Lambert 39480 William Wise Landefeld 39481 Craig Gerard Langhauser 39482 Patricia LaPlaca O'Keefe 39483 Norman Raymond Larson 39484 James Baltzell Lasche 39485 James Jonathan Lauer 39486 Brian W. Lauritzen 39487 Lars Eric LaVine 39488 Richard Lawrence Lavosky 39489 Brian R. Layer 39490 Edward Charles Leaver 39491 Walter John Leberski 39492 David Edward LeBlanc 39493 Thomas Guy LeBlanc 39494 Walter Robert Ledger 39495 James Dain Lee 39496 Kyu Ho Lee 39497 Knute Andrew Leidal 39498 John Anthony Lengenfelder 39499 Pamela Leonowich 39500 William Bradley Lewallen 39501 Kenneth Robert Lewis 39502 John Walter Lindberg 39503 Johnny Dwain Lock 39504 William Roy Lodwick 39505 Michael Richard Loew 39506 Mark David Lofgren 39507 Tom Charles Loomis 39508 Dale Lamar Love 39509 William Ivy Lowry 39510 John Steven Lukert 39511 James Patrick Lutz 39512 Thomas Francis Lynch 39513 Thomas Joseph Lynch 39514 Kyle Edward MacGibbon 39515 Michael Hugh MacNeil 39516 John Martin MacPherson 39517 John Charles Madrid 39518 John Joseph Mahoney 39519 Brian Freeman Malloy 39520 Kevin Wayne Mangum 39521 Charles Strader Mann 39522 Peter Raja Mansoor 39523 Jonathan A. Markol 39524 Prescott Lee Marshall 39525 Edward Thomas Martin 39526 Eileen Martin Volpe 39527 Rodrigo Grimmer Mateo 39528 William C. Mayville 39529 Michael Robert Mazzuki 39530 James Michael McAlister 39531 David Allen McBride 39532 Robert Mills McCaleb 39533 Thomas Lane McClellan 39534 James Michael McCormick 39535 Patricia Michelle McCormick 39536 Everett Koichi McDaniel 39537 Anthony Kirk McDonald 39538 John Alan McElree 39539 John Harold McGee 39540 David Lawrence McGlown 39541 Gregory Scott McGory 39542 Eric Fitzgerald McMillin 39543 Joseph Malcolm McNeill 39544 Kevin Michael McPoyle 39545 Sallye Jane Meek Allgood 39546 Kevin Girarde Merrigan 39547 Paul Alan Merritt 39548 Michael Lynn Mesick 39549 Robert William Metz 39550 Mark A. Milat 39551 Raymond Arthur Millen 39552 Cliff Miller 39553 Derek Alan Miller 39554 Linda J. Miller 39555 Michael Leslie Minear 39556 Michael Anthony Minney 39557 Joseph Bruce Moles 39558 Guy Robert Monagas 39559 John David Monger 39560 Paul Stanley Mooradian 39561 John Morgan Moore 39562 Robert Thomas Moore 39563 John Stephen Moorehead 39564 James Anthony Morales 39565 Joseph Frank Moravec 39566 Christopher Morey 39567 Glenn Edward Morgan 39568 Thomas Joseph Morgan 39569 Robert Philip Moritz 39570 Timothy John Morris 39571 Tom Curry Morris 39572 Douglas Jon Morrison 39573 Kevin Wayde Morse 39574 Stewart Junius Mosby 39575 Alan Michael Mosher 39576 Matthew Moten 39577 Thomas Michael Muir 39578 Daniel Francis Mulligan 39579 George Frederick Munro 39580 Thomas Eugene Murphy 39581 William Sargeant Murphy 39582 James Patrick Murtagh 39583 John Naccarelli 39584 David Charles Nadeau 39585 Robert Steven Nakamoto 39586 Roberto Natividad Nang 39587 Patrick Charles Neary 39588 Mark Daniel Needham 39589 Casey Alan Neff 39590 John Murray Negley 39591 John Michael Neilson 39592 Harlene A. Coutteau 39593 Walter Charles Nelson 39594 Emmerico Tan Nepomuceno 39595 Scott Franklin Netherland 39596 William Newman 39597 John William Nicholson 39598 Robert Jorgen Nielsen 39599 Charles Raymond Noll 39600 Robert Lloyd Norr 39601 James Hugh North 39602 David Allan Novak 39603 Gerald Raymond Nowotny 39604 Dennis Andrew O'Brien 39605 Liam Tomas O'Connell 39606 Robert Michael O'Connor 39607 Kevin Patrick O'Dwyer 39608 Patrick Daniel O'Farrell 39609 Elizabeth Ogden Rehwalt 39610 Brian Dennis O'Leary 39611 Edward Charles Olivares 39612 Charles Kenneth Oliver 39613 Pamela Kay Oliver 39614 Maritza Olmeda-Saenz Ryan 39615 John Gerard O'Lone 39616 Steven Olsen 39617 Bruce Bernard O'Neill 39618 Patrick Joseph O'Neill 39619 Timothy Sean O'Rourke 39620 Michael Lee Orr 39621 M. Rafael Ortiz 39622 Patrick Odoardi Ortland 39623 Andrew Alan Osborn 39624 Dennis Mark Ostrowski 39625 Noel Phillip Owen 39626 John Mann Page 39627 David Edward Palamar 39628 James Robert Palumbo 39629 Mark Warren Palzer 39630 Scott Charles Paoli 39631 Derek Joseph Paquette 39632

Christopher Joseph Paradies 39633 Don Seung Park 39634 Scott A. Pasolli 39635 Charles Abbot Pate 39636 William Damian Patterson 39637 Gregg Steven Pearson 39638 Anthony Fitzhugh Pecora 39639 William Maynard Pedersen 39640 Michael John Peffers 39641 Albert Paul Pehanick 39642 Ramon Thomas Perez 39643 Jay Ellis Perlberg 39644 Benjamin Perry 39645 Phillip Ward Person 39646 Richard Donald Peters 39647 Allen Leo Peterson 39648 Donna Kay Peterson 39649 Gunnar B. Peterson 39650 Roger William Peterson 39651 Steven William Peterson 39652 Glenda Petty O'Toole 39653 Mark Alan Philbrook 39654 Warren Edward Phipps 39655 John Ronald Piatak 39656 Mark R. Pires 39657 James Donald Pirkle 39658 Richard Lawrence Plasket 39659 James Alan Polo 39660 John Ripley Porter 39661 Maria Portera Pate 39662 Uwe Herbert Porth 39663 Jeffrey Scott Poulin 39664 Lesa Ann Powell 39665 Webster David Powell 39666 Gale Alicia Harrington 39667 Thomas I. Pratt 39668 Lawrence Allen Price 39669 Richard Frank Proietti 39670 John Philippe Proulx 39671 Michael Clovis Proulx 39672 Joseph Fallaw Puett 39673 John Edward Pulliam 39674 James Edward Quinn 39675 Mark Robert Quintana 39676 John David Radel 39677 Mario Orlando Ramirez 39678 William Robert Reagan 39679 Michael J. Reagor 39680 Donald Frederick Reich 39681 Richard Harry Reichelt 39682 Karl Edward Reinhard 39683 Edward Charles Reynolds 39684 Hughes Hamilton Rice 39685 Randall Baxter Richardson 39686 Anthony Morris Ridnell 39687 Mitchell James Riehle 39688 Brad H. Rinehart 39689 Ronald James Rintala 39690 Frank Alan Riott 39691 Jeffrey Leon Risher 39692 Bradley Craig Risser 39693 Scott Douglas Ritchey 39694 Kenneth Ray Robertson 39695 Russell Goodman Robertson 39696 Mark Allan Robinson 39697 Robert Kirkland Rockwood 39698 James Gregory Rodgers 39699 Michael Joseph Roemer 39700 William Dexter Rogers 39701 Eugene Joseph Rohrer 39702 William Christopher Roller 39703 Samuel Milton-Selby Rollinson 39704 Daniel S. Roper 39705 Michael Arnold Rossi 39706 Kevin Gerald Rousseau 39707 Robert Franklin Ruck 39708 Dawn S. Rucker 39709 Guy Paul Runkle 39710 Wade Drury Rush 39711 Jason Rushton 39712 Randall Robert Russo 39713 Richard Stanton Russo 39714 Janet Elizabeth Cortner 39715 John Morton Rutherford 39716 Robert Edward Ryan 39717 Sean Ryan 39718 Philip J. Rymiszewski 39719 Lori Sakauye Rousseau 39720 Steven Linsey Salazar 39721 Stephen Walter Sanders 39722 Jayson David Sawyer 39723 Gary Michael Saxton 39724 Michael Anthony Saylor 39725 Tarry Scaglione Hilliard 39726 Patricia Madeleine P. Schaeflern 39727 Eric Jon Schaertl 39728 John Arthur Schatzel 39729 Tad Frederick Schinke 39730 Thomas Frank Schneider 39731 John Stephen Schoen 39732 Christopher John Schopfer 39733 John Francis Schreiner 39734 Joseph Edward Schulz 39735 Michael Schwed 39736 Jeffrey Arnold Scott 39737 Benjamin Alberto Scrivner 39738 Paul Roger Scroggins 39739 Robert Edward Scurlock 39740 Wayne Tosh Seidler 39741 Lewis Frank Setliff 39742 Eric Clay Sexton 39743 Frederick Arthur Shambach 39744 Daniel Joseph Shanahan 39745 James Alfred Sharman 39746 David Alan Sherwin 39747 Manuel Cirino Silva 39748 Carl Frank Simmons 39749 Bruce Alan Simpson 39750 Gideon Ethan Sinasohn 39751 Eugene Windfield Skinner 39752 Todd W. Skulte 39753 Michael Eugene Slavin 39754 Anthony Scott Smith 39755 Michael Bernard Smith 39756 Michael Davis Smith 39757 Roger Douglas Smith 39758 Scott Ross Smith 39759 John Edward Snyder 39760 Dempsey Douglas Solomon 39761 Ralph Eric Dwayne Sorrell 39762 William Kenneth Sorrell 39763 Jonathan James Sosnowski 39764 Susan Risque Sowers 39765 Michael Anthony Spencer 39766 James Carter Spilman 39767 Warren Randolph Starr 39768 David Nathan Steer 39769 Robert Louis Steinrauf 39770 Joseph Cleveland Stevens 39771 Richard Lee Stevens 39772 Rosemary Ellen O'Hara 39773 Steven David Stewart 39774 Dean Chapman Stodter 39775 Thomas Joseph Stokowski 39776 Kevin Scott Stoleson 39777 James Arlon Straus 39778 Douglas John Strock 39779 Stuart Lawson Strong 39780 David Joel Styles 39781 Ricki Lynn Sullivan 39782 Mark Francis Supko 39783 Mark Edward Swanson 39784 John Joseph Swart 39785 Matthew Christopher Sweeney 39786 Patrick John Sweeney 39787 Andrew Charles Swick 39788 Kevin William Tate 39789 Howard Avery Taylor 39790 John Rae Taylor 39791 Peter Firey Taylor 39792 Jeffrey William Terhune 39793 Michael John Theriault 39794 David L. Thomas 39795 Stephen Arthur Thompson 39796 Eric Joel Thor 39797 Christian Charles Thudium 39798 Mark Edward Tillman 39799 David Patrick Todd 39800 Jack Christopher Todd 39801 Walter Emrich Tollefson 39802 John-Mary Tompkins 39803 Jeffrey Albert Tong 39804 Timothy Andrew Torchia 39805 Scott Robert Torgerson 39806 Lawrence George Tosi 39807 Richard Armond Totleben 39808 Stephen Miles Townsend 39809 John Howard Travers 39810 Janice Traxler Carr 39811 Robert Walter Turko 39812 Rocky James Tyler 39813 George Merrill Utley 39814 Ramiro Miguel Valderrama 39815 Christopher B. Valentine 39816 Clinton Daniel Valverde 39817 Thomas S. Vandal 39818 Paul Montgomery Vanderburgh 39819 Douglas Michael Vargas 39820 Brian Scott Veit 39821 Juan Manuel Vera 39822 Lawrence John Verbiest 39823 Anthony Joseph Vertin 39824 John Vislosky 39825 Gregory Alan Voigt 39826 William Albert Vollmer 39827 Thomas John Volpe 39828 Martin Carl Von Tersch 39829 Peter Michael Vozzo 39830 Ricky L. Waddell 39831 Michael Paul Wadsworth 39832 Marlin R. Wagner 39833 Ronald De Witt Waidlich 39834 Michael Lee Wakeman 39835 Stephen Kirby Walker 39836 Patricia M. Anderson 39837 William Wade Ward 39838 John Buckley Warden 39839 Frank Martin Warner 39840 John Henry Warren 39841 Patrick Theron Warren 39842 James Zygmunt Wartski 39843 Joseph Michael Warwick 39844 Mark George Washechek 39845 Richard J. Wassmuth 39846 John Dudley Wasson 39847 Dwane Edward Watsek 39848 Bryan Glenwood Watson 39849 Harold William Waugh 39850 David Charles Weeden 39851 David Anthony Wegrzyn 39852 Jeffrey Richard Weil 39853 Joseph Charles Weinhoffer 39854 Ronald Wayne Welch 39855 Marcus James Weldon 39856 Timothy Reece Welton 39857 Frank Stanley Weston 39858 Jordan Ray White 39859 Michael Patrick White 39860 Anthony Alan Wickham 39861 Darren Alan Wilcox 39862 Peter Robert Wilder 39863 Thomas Michael Wiley 39864 David Michael Wilkins 39865 Gregory Charles Willems 39866 L. Gene Willets 39867 Curtis Ray Williams 39868 Darrell Madison Williams 39869 David Thomas Williams 39870 Debbra Williams Head 39871 Gary Spencer Williams 39872 Margaret Burcham 39873 Patrick Michael Williams 39874 Robert Julius Williams 39875 Scott Charles Williams 39876 Stephen Charles Williams 39877 Yancey Roger Williams 39878 Donna Marie Williamson 39879 Brent David Willis 39880 Michael Clinton Wilmer 39881 David Charles Wilson 39882 Michael David Winstead 39883 Tey Carter Wiseman 39884 Francis Eugene Wolf 39885 Daniel G. Wolfe 39886 Renee S. Wolven 39887 Tezeon Yorkchoung Wong 39888 Paul Jeffrey Wood 39889 Michael Eugene Woodgerd 39890 Kurt Michael Woods 39891 Daniel Joseph Worth 39892 Robert Edward Wrenn 39893 Timothy Gerard Wright 39894 Thomas Anthony Wuchte 39895 Allen Gregory Wynder 39896 Kenneth Jon Yarberry 39897 Charles Michael Yomant 39898 Richard Gerard York 39899 Tracey Lee Zander 39900 James J. Zanoli 39901 James R. Zemet 39902 John C. Zemet 39903 David Bryan Ziegler 39904 Eugene Patrick Coddington 39905 Joseph Bradley Coleman 39906 Philip Gerard Connolly 39907 Richard Bryant Hook 39908 Steven Craig Jackan 39909 Thomas Williams Kaiser 39910 Mark Lawrence Kimmey 39911 James D. Meyer 39912 Richard Randolph Odom 39913 Bobby N. Rakes 39914 William John Sardella 39915 Martin Charles Smith 39916 Robert Bruce Smith 39917 Donald Richard Swygert 39918 Thomas Fleet Westfall 39919 Scott Morgan Wingate 39920 David Michael Yerks 39921 Edward Francis Boyle 39922 Michael Eugene Faessler 39923 Peter Sean Keller 39924 Clifford Scott Monroe 39925 Gregory Roman Perchatsch 39926 Robert Powledge Smith 39927 Reynaldo Daquil Antonio 39928 Medardo Tabios DelaCruz 39929 Christopher Mark DeToro 39930 Morrison Joseph Fenner 39931 Celia FlorCruz FlorCruz 39932 Paul David Guerra 39933 Joseph Bernard Hajost 39934 Cardell Hervey 39935 Dennis Wayne Sumner 39936 Alex George Sung 39937 Gary Lynn Terry 39938 Archie Wilmer 39939 **1983** Pamela Joan Slingsby 39940 Dencio Severo Acop 39941 Rex Mitchell Adams 39942 Robert Freeman Adams 39943 John Joseph Agostini 39944 Soong Bum Ahn 39945 Ronald Paul Alberto 39946 William Edward Alexander 39947 William T. Allen 39948 John Bart Alumbaugh 39949 David R. Amberger 39950 David Paul Anderson 39951 Harold G. Anderson 39952 Keith Allen Anderson 39953 Gerald Ronai Andrews 39954 John Elroy Anzalone 39955 Joseph Paul Aperfine 39956 Gregory John Argyros 39957 Todd William Arnold 39958 Edward David Arrington 39959 Ernest Carl Audino 39960 Alan Wayne Avery 39961 Mark Hartley Ayers 39962 Bruce Archer Babbitt 39963 Charles R. Babers 39964 Brian Neil Baker 39965 David John Baker 39966 David Paul Baker 39967 Brian Kerry Balfe 39968 Kurt Rayo Barker 39969 Jeter Scott Barnhill 39970 Laureen M. Barone 39971 James Edward Barringer 39972 Ercole Peter Barsotti 39973 Thomas Henry Barth 39974 Deborah Anne Nightingale 39975 Joseph Michael Bassil 39976 Philip F. Battaglia 39977 Kevin Michael Batule 39978 Brent Thomas Baty 39979 Chris William Bauer 39980 William Francis Bauer 39981 Bryan Lee Bear 39982 David Brian Bearden 39983 Philip Frederick Beaver 39984 Jeffrey Michael Bedard 39985 James Loyd Bedingfield 39986 Larry Dale Beisel 39987 Jonathon Anthony Bell 39988 Michael Stephen Bell 39989 Jeffrey Alan Belles 39990 Henry William Bennett 39991 John Joseph Benning 39992 Charles Roland Benway 39993 Daniel Wesley Berger 39994 Laurel J. McHargue 39995 Christian John Bezick 39996 David Lee Biacan 39997 Roger Bruce Bilas 39998 John Robert Black 39999 Carlos Blanchard 40000 Joseph Michael Blanco 40001 William Steven Bland 40002 Robert G. Blatz 40003 Martin Gerhardt Bobroske 40004 John Henry Bock 40005 Michael William Bohr 40006 Edward Hall Boland 40007 Neal Ernest Bonrud 40008 Kenneth John Bonville 40009 Thomas Harding Boone 40010 Barry Charles Bort 40011 David Boslego 40012 Michael George Boulegeris 40013 Thomas T. Bowe 40014 Michael Peter Bowman 40015 Brian T. Boyle 40016 Charles G. Boyle 40017 Matthew Lester Brand 40018 Curt Russell Brandt 40019 Jeffrey Ross Brantley 40020 Donna M. B. Brazil 40021 Brent B. Bredehoft 40022 William John Breitenbach 40023 Michael F. Brennan 40024 Robert Smiley Bridgford 40025 William John Bristow 40026 Franklin Porter Broadhurst 40027 Gerald Gerard Brolin 40028 Robert Alan Brooks 40029 Gregory Albert Brouillette 40030 Elizabeth Brouse Schweppe 40031 Clayton Edward Brown 40032 Gregory Robert Brown 40033 Mark Albert Brown 40034 Peter Keith Brual 40035 Mark Charles Bruegmann 40036 Michael Edward Bryson 40037 Otto Curtis Burnette 40038 John Charles Buss 40039 Brian James Butcher 40040 Mark Isham Byrd 40041 Joseph Albert Campano 40042 Jennifer Campbell Foster 40043 Gerard Olvera Canales 40044 John Frederick Cannizzaro 40045 Michael A. Capria 40046 Peter Thomas Carella 40047 Calvin Thomas Carlsen 40048 Christian Robert Carlson 40049 Robert Dwight Carman 40050 Courtney Palmer Carr 40051 Curtis Arthur Carver 40052 Anthony Wayne Castile 40053 Joanne F. Cavanaugh 40054 Christopher Mark Chambers 40055 Thomas William Charron 40056 Juan Carlos Chaves 40057 Rafael Checa 40058 Walter Roy Cheshire 40059 James Edward Chew 40060 Robert Joseph Ching 40061 Jeffrey Kwan J. Chinn 40062 Albert George Chlapowski 40063 Constance Ren-Tien Chu 40064 Paul Vincent Cino 40065 Anthony James Clarke 40066 Robert Theodore Clarke 40067 James Robert Clawson 40068 Phillip Anthony Clough 40069 William Baird Clowes 40070 John Shelby Coates 40071 John Daniel Cody 40072 John Franklin Coldren 40073 John Vernet Cole 40074 Robert George Cole 40075 Edward Charles Collazzo 40076 Frank Sylvester Collette 40077 Steven Nelson Collins 40078 James Arthur Combs 40079 Mark Connors 40080 James Wade Cook 40081 Judson Alexander Cook 40082 Richard Preston Cook 40083 Jennings Bryan Cooksey 40084 Peter Jeffrey Coote 40085 David Daniel Coover 40086 Kelly Dan Coppess 40087 Richard Alan Coppola 40088 Bruce Anthony Cordelli 40089 Maria Louisa Britt 40090 Ronald George Costella 40091 Mary Costello Forbes 40092 Michael Brian Cotter 40093 David Calhoun Couch 40094 Joseph Brian Cowan 40095 Thomas Houston Cowan 40096 Clifford Deal Crofford 40097 George Henry Crompton 40098 Nathan Roy Croskrey 40099 Shayne Patrick Crowley 40100 William James Crowley 40101 Michael Anthony Crumlin 40102 Charlie Wilson Crutcher 40103 Daniel Joseph Cummings 40104 Michael Patrick Cummings 40105 Terrence Cummings 40106 Jefferson Moore Curl 40107 Richard Curran-Kelley 40108 Paul Jerome Cutting 40109 John Richard Daluga 40110 Jeffrey Arnaz Daniel 40111 Sean Joseph Darragh 40112 Richard Frederick Dauch 40113 Jeffry Bennett Daun 40114 David Glyn Davies 40115 Albert Minh Davis 40116 Alfrazier Davis 40117 Eric Charles Davis 40118 Grant Martin Davis 40119 James Leroy Davis 40120 Jeffrey Harrison Davis 40121 Jimmy Dale Davis 40122 Mark A. Davis 40123 Kelly Day Wetzel 40124 Charles Edwin Dean 40125 Timothy James Dean 40126 Mark Francis Decoteau 40127 Charles Henry Dedekind 40128 Kim Michelle Barrier 40129 Michael Del Rosario 40130 Frank R. Demith 40131 Bruce Wayne Dempsey 40132 Charles Erwin Derrick 40133 Wayne L. Detwiler 40134 Michael Gerard Devereaux 40135 James Thomas Devine 40136 Glen Raymond Dewillie 40137 Merrell Dayne Dilks 40138 William Andrew Dispoto 40139 Monica Ann Divis 40140 Michael Kenneth Dodson 40141 Curt Walter Doescher 40142 Michael Joseph Dolan 40143 Robert Joseph Dombkowski 40144 Gary Robert Donaldson 40145 John Jackson Donnelly 40146 Gery William Donovan 40147 Kevin Joseph Dougherty 40148 Chris Roy Downey 40149 David Michael Doyle 40150 James Paul Drago 40151 Vincent M. Dreyer 40152 Douglas Arthur Dribben 40153 John William Driscoll 40154 James Everman Drummond 40155 Christopher J. Duell 40156 Brian T. Duemling 40157 John Egene Dumoulin 40158 Mark Laurence Dunlap 40159 Michael Kevin Dwyer 40160 Kally Lynn Eastman 40161 James Michael Ecklund 40162 William Declan Egan 40163 Randall Scott Eichelberger 40164 Jon Louis Elliott 40165 Bradley Sloan Elrod 40166 Mark Douglas Entner 40167 Frank Denina Espanto 40168 Tanner James Espey 40169 William Jones Estes 40170 James Ames Evans 40171 Douglas Alan Fabish 40172 Robert John Farrell 40173 Billy Don Farris 40174 Kenton George Fasana 40175 Philip Andrew Fauth 40176 Melvin Payne Fechner 40177 Eric Audette Feige 40178 Harold John Fennimore 40179 J. Brian Ferguson 40180 Jude Connor Fernan 40181 Scott Hauser Fewin 40182 James Robert Ficke 40183 Francis Fulton Figliola 40184 Mary Finch Finch 40185 Robert Griffith Finkenaur 40186 Hugo Jacob Fischer 40187 Robert Joseph Fischer 40188 Thomas Edward Fish 40189 Charles Hugh Fisher 40190 Gregory Scott Fitzgerald 40191 Joseph Patrick Fitzhenry 40192 John Leonard Fitzpatrick 40193 Vincent Thomas Flavia 40194 Raymond Travis Flewelling 40195 Ross Harmon Florey 40196 Louis Donald Flynn 40197 Scott Dale Follett 40198 John Louis Fontana 40199 Jeffrey Michael Forgach 40200 Steven Peter Foster 40201 Sara Fotsch Gaba 40202 Steven James Fraasch 40203 Louis Joseph Francis 40204 Andre Norman Fredette 40205 David Hugh Freedman 40206 Bo Hurbert Heinrich Friesen 40207 Michael Allen Fritsch 40208 Charles Ernest Fugarino 40209 Anthony Frank Fulco 40210 James Edwin Gaba 40211 James Joseph Galvin 40212 Dean Alan Gant 40213 Tracy Anne Mollet-St. Benoit 40214 Joseph R. Garrison 40215 Martin Michael Garrity 40216 Robert Eric Gates 40217 Willie E. Gates 40218 Clarence Lincoln Gayagas 40219 George Geczy 40220 Dean Frederick Gemberling 40221 Marc Cedric George 40222 Jeffrey Stephen Geraci 40223 Dianne Elizabeth Gerard 40224 Richard Gerard Gesing 40225 Joy Ann Gibbon 40226 Benjamin Neal Gilbert 40227 Daniel Alphonse Gilewitch 40228 Wayne L. Gillespie 40229 Mark W. Gillette 40230 Cheryl Gilligan 40231 Derek Gilman 40232 Francis Joseph Giordano 40233 Bruce Gnatowski 40234 Joseph Anthony Goetz 40235 Gregory James Gongaware 40236 Lori Good Loucks 40237 David Thomas Gorczynski 40238 Christopher Michael Gordon 40239 James Alan Gorske 40240 John Charles Gorske 40241 David Milton Graham 40242 Jo A. Dempsey 40243 James Combs Greenwell 40244 Charles Peter Grenchus 40245 Stephen Gricoski 40246 Fletcher Hugh Griffis 40247 Rease Littlefield Griffith 40248 William George Groeger 40249 Paul L. Grosskruger 40250 Joseph Richard Gruchacz 40251 Gregory Paul Gulia 40252 Edward Charles Gully 40253 Glenn Eugene Guyant 40254 David William Gwynn 40255 Mitchel E. Hadad 40256 Ralph William Haddock 40257 Kelley Haines Dolan 40258 John P. Hains 40259 Donald Lee Hall 40260 John David Hall 40261 Richard Alvin Hall 40262 William Russel Hall 40263 Paul James Hamill 40264 Marcus Keith Hamilton 40265 Joseph M. Hampton 40266 Ronald Barry Hancock 40267 Todd Allen Hann 40268 David Lee Harper 40269 John Charles Harre 40270 Denis Liam Harrington 40271 Richard Thomas Harrington 40272 Edwin Hawkins Harris 40273 Guy N. Harris 40274 Robert Mitchell Harris 40275 Stuart George Harrison 40276 Blake E. Hawkey 40277 Morris Grady Hayes 40278 Grant Wesley Hayne 40279 Carl Dewitt Haynes 40280 Mark W. Healy 40281 Mark Thomas Hefty 40282 Alex Jay Heidenberg 40283 Keith Douglas Heithcock 40284 Kevin Patrick Heller 40285 John Joseph Henry 40286 Bert C. Hensley 40287 Kenneth Clyde Henson 40288 David Martin Hernon 40289 Thomas Eugene Higgins 40290 Timothy Patrick Hill 40291 Bruce William Hilmes 40292 Joseph Edward Hoellerer 40293 Christopher Michael Holden 40294 Ross Easton Holley 40295 Roger Bruce Holt 40296 Simon Larz Holzman 40297 Joseph Raymond Homa 40298 Dallas William Homas 40299 Robin Scott Hood 40300 Reynold Nelson Hoover 40301 James Rogers Hopkins 40302 William Charles Hoppe 40303 Jerusalem Tadaishi Howard 40304 Lara Howard York 40305 Dale Eugene Hruby 40306 William Davis Huggins 40307 Allen Hull 40308 James David Hummer 40309 Kenneth Jay Humphries 40310 Diane Hunter Battaglia 40311 Shawn Hunter 40312 Paul Francis Husar 40313 Donald Ward Husted 40314 Nicholas Drew Hyslop 40315 Harry George Jackson 40316 Jerry Dewayne Jackson 40317 Julius Henry Jackson 40318 Libby Ann Bethea 40319 Matthew Warren Jackson 40320 Michele Jackson Caron 40321 Richard Lance Jackson 40322 Jeffrey Williams Jarabek 40323 Brice Howard Johnson 40324 Christine Monica Johnson 40325 David Henry Johnson 40326 James Michael Johnson 40327 Joel Munson Johnson 40328 Mark Angelo Johnstone 40329 Michael Allen Jolley 40330 Loran Steven Joly 40331 Brian David Jones 40332 Dallas Leigh Jones 40333 Raymond Dennis Jones 40334 Rebecca Winter Jones 40335 Robert Lee Jones 40336 Steven Wayne Jones 40337 William Gardiner Jones 40338 Tod Norman Jordan 40339 Byron Graham Jorns 40340 James Murray Judy 40341 Brad L. Julian 40342 Hal David Jungerheld 40343 William Joseph Kaiser 40344 Mark Edward Kamish 40345 Gregory Gerard Kapral 40346 James Michael Kearns 40347 Daniel James Keefe 40348 Daniel Bruce Kellas 40349 John Henry Kelleher 40350 Patrick Joseph Kelly 40351 Richard W. Kemp 40352 James Patrick Kenney 40353 Ronald Dean Kerr 40354 Christopher David Kerski 40355 Daniel A. Kessler 40356 Kurt Lawrence Keville 40357 Michael Dean Kiehnau 40358 Thomas Albert Kilmer 40359 Christopher Kisok Kim 40360 Hyo Chag Kim 40361 Lawrence John Kinde 40362 Chris Allan King 40363 Dion Joseph King 40364 Thomas Reed Kirkland 40365 Howard William Klei 40366 Steven Lee Klynsma 40367 Robert Daniel Knapp 40368 James Everly Knight 40369 Michael Robert Knott 40370 Carl Forrest Knowlton 40371 Robert John Kock 40372 Timothy Gerard Koenig 40373 Lee Gerald Kolbo 40374 David Andrew Kolvek 40375 John William Korevec 40376 Christopher Allen Kozak 40377 Jeffrey Allen Kralowetz 40378 Kenneth Donald Kramer 40379 Richard Gerard Kressin 40380 Cynthia Lee Kreuzmann Lotz 40381 Timothy Ray Kuklo 40382 Todd Allen Kulik 40383 George Kunzweiler 40384 Alexander F. Kwan 40385 Charlie Joel Lail 40386 Gary Andrew Laing 40387 Michael Christopher Lamarra 40388 Leonard Amos Landry 40389 Margaret C. Laneri 40390 William Leonard Lang 40391 Gary Drew Langford

40392 Christopher John Larsen 40393 Creighton Andrew Larson 40394 Larry Joseph Laseter 40395 Donald Junior Lash 40396 Jeffrey David Lau 40397 David Charles Lavery 40398 Nils David Lavine 40399 Michael Edward Lee 40400 Monte Wayne Bradford 40401 Thomas Legenza 40402 Michael Lawrence Lehto 40403 Roy Kieth Lembke 40404 David John Lemelin 40405 Michael Peter Lerario 40406 Lorraine Antoinette Lesieur 40407 John Glenn Levine 40408 Chipper McCoy Lewis 40409 Joel Vincent Liberto 40410 Donnell Lighthall 40411 David Walter Little 40412 Gregory Harrington Little 40413 Dennis Patrick Lochard 40414 Peter Michael Loebs 40415 Michael Everett Longo 40416 Edward Sanford Loomis 40417 Thomas Cameron Loper 40418 Juan Manuel Lopez 40419 Timothy Peder Loucks 40420 William Stewart Love 40421 Edward Bruce Lucci 40422 Paul T. Lukert 40423 Gregory James Lund 40424 William S. Lunde 40425 Michael Joseph Lyons 40426 Anthony Joseph Macchiavelli 40427 Brian James MacDonald 40428 Bruce R. MacDonald 40429 William A. Macon 40430 William Joseph Maddalena 40431 Amy Maier Okamoto 40432 Robert Earl Maier 40433 Jeffrey E. Malapit 40434 Randall John Malchow 40435 James Conrad Markley 40436 Bruce Alan Martin 40437 Christopher Wayne Martin 40438 Michael Dell Martin 40439 Michael Patrick Martin 40440 Peter Joseph Martin 40441 Mark Steven Martins 40442 Robert Edward Maruna 40443 Kenneth Joseph Massey 40444 Robert Lee Massie 40445 Michele Marie Putko 40446 Jill Ann Maurer 40447 Eric V. Mayer 40448 Gary Michael McAndrews 40449 Richard William McArdle 40450 James Francis McAree 40451 Mark Steffan McConkey 40452 G. Scott McConnell 40453 Richard Edward McDonald 40454 Roger Laney McDonald 40455 Timothy M. McDonald 40456 Willie James McFadden 40457 Harry Ian McGavisk 40458 Charles Hubbard McGould 40459 John John McGuiness 40460 Mike Kevin McHargue 40461 James Clayton McIntyre 40462 Joseph Ray McKenzie 40463 Richard Gordon McKiddie 40464 David Mark McNallan 40465 William Henry McQuail 40466 Leonard Scott McWherter 40467 Kathleen Medaris Widmer 40468 Marvin Lee Meek 40469 Hans Nicholas Meinhardt 40470 Will Garrison Merrill 40471 Jerry Christopher Meyer 40472 Austin Scott Miller 40473 James Franklin Miller 40474 Norman L. Miller 40475 Timothy James Miller 40476 Rudi Tsuneji Mizusawa 40477A Michael Mark Mills 40477 John Charles Moeller 40478 Manuel Edmund Molera 40479 William Thomas Monacci 40480 Paul Douglas Mongan 40481 John Wesley Monk 40482 Patrick Louis Moody 40483 Robert Jacob Moon 40484 Robert John Moore 40485 Mark Lee Moravits 40486 Mark Warren Morehouse 40487 Thomas Morgan 40488 James Kelly Morningstar 40489 Mark Richard Morrow 40490 Douglas J. Moulds 40491 Christopher William Mozina 40492 Brian Jeffrey Mueller 40493 Eileen T. Trainor 40494 Charles Ray Mulligan 40495 Gregory Murphy 40496 Kevin Paul Murphy 40497 Thomas Joseph Murphy 40498 Stephen Edward Murray 40499 John Bernard Myers 40500 Laura Krupka 40501 Lee Eric Myles 40502 William Dale Naessens 40503 David Allan d 40504 Raymond Carl Nelson 40505 Dale E. Neumann 40506 Bryan Terrence Newkirk 40507 Edward Carl Newman 40508 Peter Paul Nickolenko 40509 Dimitrije Nikolich 40510 Vincent Alan Nikonchuk 40511 Victoria L. Nilles 40512 Ruben Arturo Nogueira 40513 James A. North 40514 Curtis Henry Nutbrown 40515 Patrick Brian Oakes 40516 David Michael Oaks 40517 John Leo O'Brien 40518 Marianne O'Brien 40519 Brian Lynn Ochsner 40520 Daniel Patrick O'Connell 40521 Joseph Leonard O'Connell 40522 Jane Kathryn O'Connor Jollota 40523 Cristina O'Donnell Rhynedance 40524 Robert James Ogden 40525 Michael Jospeh Olsen 40526 Steven Eugene Olson 40527 Daniel Arthur O'Neil 40528 James Peter Orchard 40529 Ruben Ordonez 40530 Lionel Valentin Ortiz 40531 Brendan John O'Shea 40532 Michael James Ottens 40533 Darrell Ray Overcash 40534 Gerald Edgar Overstreet 40535 David E. Painter 40536 Yeong Pak 40537 Robert M. Panerio 40538 Charles Edward Parker 40539 Starr Parker 40540 Frank Ray Parris 40541 Jerome Joseph Pasierb 40542 Anthony Joseph Patricelli 40543 Kathryn Ann Gartland 40544 Daniel L. Paulo 40545 Daniel Wyatt Peck 40546 Charles Oscar Perez 40547 Joseph Francis Perez 40548 Steven Michael Perry 40549 Russell Arthur Peterson 40550 John Edmund Phelan 40551 Steven Charles Phelps 40552 Alan Burgess Phillips 40553 Gary John Pieringer 40554 John Anthony Pierson 40555 Norman Carlos Pimentel 40556 Sonja Pinoci Moyer 40557 Mark Thomas Pisko 40558 Robert Joseph Pittman 40559 Ray Arno Plagens 40560 Robert Joseph Plummer 40561 Christopher Daniel Pokorny 40562 Keith Alexander Polak 40563 Kevin George Polak 40564 Dennis Arthur Polaski 40565 Shawn Douglas Pompe 40566 N. Alec Portalupi 40567 Kevin Scott Porter 40568 John Lee Pothin 40569 Richard Anthony Powell 40570 Stacy Powell Cody 40571 William Henry Prentiss 40572 Donna Prep Alberto 40573 Lon Lewis Pribble 40574 Anthony Gerard Proulx 40575 Charles Walter Provine 40576 B. Alan Provins 40577 Larry Hardeman Pruitt 40578 Christopher Joseph Putko 40579 Robert Michael Pyne 40580 Bohdan Myron Pyskir 40581 Douglas James Quinlan 40582 Bruce Anthony Quint 40583 Rory Randall Radovich 40584 Joseph Francis Rangitsch 40585 Kenneth William Rathje 40586 Joseph William Rawlins 40587 William Montgomery Raymond 40588 Sharon Reardon Shiflet 40589 John O. Reas 40590 George Franklin Reasor 40591 Terence Jay Redmann 40592 Robert John Redzikowski 40593 William Brent Reece 40594 Brad Douglas Reid 40595 Patrick Anthony Reily 40596 David Michael Reinert 40597 Donald Arthur Renner 40598 Scott A. Reval 40599 Todd A. Rey 40600 Raul Alberto Reyes 40601 Wayne Gregory Richardson 40602 Duane H. Riddle 40603 Wesley Allen Riddle 40604 William Ira Riddle 40605 James Gordon Riley 40606 Jeffrey Holmes Ringer 40607 Brian John Roberts 40608 Michael Lee Roberts 40609 Patrick Wayne Robertson 40610 Dean Matthew Robinson 40611 Jose Manuel Robles-Maldonado 40612 Anthony Paulino Rodriguez 40613 Rand Alyn Rodriguez 40614 David Bruce Roeder 40615 Kyle John Rogers 40616 Robert George Rohlfing 40617 William B. Roka 40618 Steven Michael Root 40619 John G. Rossi 40620 Hugh Wade Rountree 40621 Michael H. Roy 40622 Arlen Ray Royalty 40623 Randy Jay Rubens 40624 Edgar K. Rugenstein 40625 Antonio Jorge Ruizcalderon 40626 Joseph Mark Rusbarsky 40627 Albert Edward Ryan 40628 David Shea Ryon 40629 Stephen Sabarese 40630 David Joseph Sacha 40631 Scott Michael Sajer 40632 Gregory Joseph Salata 40633 Harry Lee Salisbury 40634 Timothy Louis Salter 40635 Keith J. Samuels 40636 Kent Stuart Sanderson 40637 Michael Gene Santens 40638 Edward Karl Sauer 40639 John Lee Saufley 40640 Peter Ralph Scheffer 40641 Frederick Mich Schenkelberg 40642 Thomas R. Scheu 40643 Russell Roland Schleiden 40644 Kirk Rodney Schleifer 40645 James Michael Schless 40646 Karl Morris Schmidt 40647 Kathleen Schmidt Loper 40648 Thomas George Scholtes 40649 Kathleen K. Hildreth 40650 Steven Michael Schrader 40651 Robert Richard Schulz 40652 Henry Jerold Schumacher 40653 William M. Schumer 40654 Edwin William Selman 40655 Matthew Mark Seng 40656 Harold Clayton Shablom 40657 William E. Shannon 40658 Gerard James Shaw 40659 Robert George Shiflet 40660 Marc Damien Sierra 40661 Craig Lance Simoneau 40662 Eric Donald Sine 40663 Glenn Matthew Skawski 40664 Thomas P. Slafkosky 40665 Gordon George Roger Slifer 40666 John Eric Smidt 40667 Bruce Gordon Smith 40668 Jeffrey Dean Smith 40669 Richard William Smith 40670 Robert Paul Smith 40671 Steven Blaine Smith 40672 Wayne R. Smith 40673 David Bryan Snider 40674 Joseph Walter Snodgrass 40675 Jeffrey Joseph Snow 40676 William Mark Snyder 40677 Edward John Sobeck 40678 Steven Michael Soucek 40679 Linda Spenny Kalis 40680 John Frederick Spurrier 40681 Michael A. Stacey 40682 Bruce Walter Stachura 40683 Thomas Patrick Stall 40684 Martin James Stefanelli 40685 Michael James Stehlik 40686 James E. Stevens 40687 Kenneth Allen Stevens 40688 Brian Robert Stewart 40689 Eric George Stieber 40690 Eugene Francis Stockel 40691 Daniel Joseph Stoll 40692 Donald Joseph Stoll 40693 William Benn Stratton 40694 Mark Bryant Streeter 40695 Barry Todd Strope 40696 Kevin Michael Sullivan 40697 Michael Edmund Sullivan 40698 Shawn Joseph Sullivan 40699 Lori L. Sussman 40700 David Stewart Sutter 40701 Margaret Ann Olmstead 40702 Thomas P. Swanton 40703 Paul Swicord 40704 Dwight Paul Swift 40705 Bill Tanner 40706 John Andrew Tarpey 40707 Kenneth Scott Telk 40708 Joachim Jude Tenuta 40709 Curtis Larry Thalken 40710 William Dean Thames 40711 David Michael Thiede 40712 Peter H. Thimm 40713 Johnny F. Thomas 40714 Stanley Stanley Thomas 40715 James Arthur Thompson 40716 Michael Kalani Thompson 40717 William W. Thompson 40718 John Richard Tibbetts 40719 Jan T. Swicord 40720 James J. Timmer 40721 Gregory Ray Titus 40722 Neil Humphries Tolley 40723 Kerry John Tomasevich 40724 Michael John Tomaszewski 40725 Adorjan Sihamer Toth 40726 Kenneth Ernest Tovo 40727 Timothy Edgar Trainor 40728 Robert E. Traurig 40729 Mark David Troutman 40730 Brian Gregory Trueblood 40731 Stephen Paul Tryon 40732 David Richard Tucker 40733 Steven Alfred Tullia 40734 Allan Edgardo Tuquero 40735 Alan Ray Turbyfill 40736 Richard Anthony Turner 40737 Robert Michael Turner 40738 John Uberti 40739 Benjamin David Valenzuela 40740 Lorenzo Jose Valenzuela 40741 Gordon Wayne Van Dusen 40742 Steven Richard Van Kirk 40743 Thomas E. Van Meter 40744 John Kendrick Vaughn 40745 Joseph Mark Verser 40746 Patrick Alan Vess 40747 Alan James Villandre 40748 Eric John Von Tersch 40749 Mark Guenther Voss 40750 Linda Waeltz Morse 40751 Lewis George Wagner 40752 Warren Ralph Waldorff 40753 Gerald Jeffrey Walker 40754 James Woodrow Wallace 40755 James Edward Walsh 40756 Patrick Dean Walsh 40757 Jon Curtis Walter 40758 Kurt Philip Wangenheim 40759 Teresa Ward Gerton 40760 Joseph Allan Waverek 40761 Robert Charles Weddall 40762 Thomas Paul Weikert 40763 Jeffrey Scott Weissman 40764 Stephen Andrew Welcer 40765 Gordon E. Welch 40766 Todd Roger Wendt 40767 Paul David Werner 40768 Andrew Braune Wertin 40769 Theodore Scott Westhusing 40770 Douglas Harry Wheelock 40771 Michael Gerard White 40772 Rachel Robardey 40773 Stanley David White 40774 Shawn Eric Wiant 40775 Daniel John Wiley 40776 John Robert Wilkinson 40777 Cardell Williams 40778 Eric Scott Williams 40779 Michael Kelvin Williams 40780 William Frazer Willoughby 40781 Mark Edward Wiltse 40782 Gary Wayne Wittekind 40783 Glenn Paul Wittpenn 40784 Edward Robert Wohlwender 40785 Jefferson K. Won 40786 Robert Arthur Wood 40787 Michael Dewey Woodruff 40788 Michael Patrick Woods 40789 Charles M. Wright 40790 John S. Wright 40791 Kevin Wayne Wright 40792 Steven Gregory Wyman 40793 Andrew Claude Yee 40794 Scott Donald Zegler 40795 Joseph Fayad Zellmer 40796 Thomas George Ziek 40797 Paul Christian Zimmerman 40798 David Henry Zydanowicz 40799 Cheryl Zywicki Connors 40800 Randal Frederick Ames 40801 M.J.H. Armstrong 40802 Anthony E. Copeland 40803 Lisa Marie Engert 40804 Douglas Norman Fouser 40805 Mitchel Bruce Kugler 40806 Steven Edward Lavergne 40807 Stephen Joseph Low 40808 Theodore David Martin 40809 Mark Christopher Murtagh 40810 Stephen Dale Payne 40811 Gerald J. Schmitz 40812 Christopher William Short 40813 Nathan Thomas White 40814 Robert W. Widmer 40815 John Robert Lennon 40816 Sally Phoenik Greb 40817 Jeanette Marie McMahon 40818 Timothy John Rushatz 40819 Michael Lee Wojta 40820 Clinton Overton Allen 40821 Daniel Andrew Cox 40822 Mark Julius Hopson 40823 Richard Francis Klein 40824 Michael Scott McManigal 40825 Mary Brooke Myers 40826 Clarence Neason 40827 Gregory S. Pitts 40828 Michael Timothy Sullivan 40829 Darryl Anthony Williams 40830 Scott Damon Moschell 40831 William Salvatore Rabena 40832 **1984** Troy A. Aarthun 40833 Anycia Audrey Prukop 40834 Joseph Michael Accardi 40835 Patricia Aceves Carlson 40836 Glen Phillip Adams 40837 John Allison Adams 40838 Stephen Francis Ahrens 40839 Ronald James Aizer 40840 David A. Alberga 40841 Philip Lawrence Alibrandi 40842 Bryan Keith Allem 40843 Andrea Allen Baker 40844 Donald C. Allgrove 40845 Vincent Edward Alonso 40846 Brian Lee Alto 40847 Joseph Henry Alvarez 40848 Joseph Craig Ammon 40849 John Charles Andrews 40850 Paul Michael Angresano 40851 Christos Theodore Antoniou 40852 William Albert Arbaugh 40853 Thomas W. Ariail 40854 Andrew Brian Arnberg 40855 David Rice Arterburn 40856 Michael W. Asimos 40857 Herbert Andrew Aten 40858 David Dean Auge 40859 David Richard Auman 40860 Peter Yucho Au-Yeung 40861 Thomas Everett Ayres 40862 Jonathan Steven Baca 40863 James Sean Baird 40864 Keith Alan Baker 40865 James L. Baldi 40866 Cleophas Baldwin 40867 David J. Balland 40868 Vincent Andre Bandy 40869 David William Baragona 40870 Clayton L. Barker 40871 Gil Wayne Barnett 40872 Dana Patrick Barrette 40873 Gary Paul Bastin 40874 Nancy Ellen Bates 40875 Craig Steven Bayer 40876 Jeffrey Todd Bazemore 40877 Daniel A. Beach 40878 Dwight E. Beach 40879 Steven Russell Beach 40880 Paul Michael Beals 40881 Tommy Dan Beaty 40882 Christopher John Beben 40883 Frank Robert Beckwith 40884 Raymond Paul Bednar 40885 Eric Ray Belcher 40886 George P. Belsky 40887 Douglas Leo Bentley 40888 William Andrew Bentley 40889 Gary Frank Berenyi 40890 Jeffrey Jared Bergner 40891 James M. Bermudez 40892 Jeffrey David Bertocci 40893 Eric Cramer Besch 40894 Anthony Bibbo 40895 Jacob D. Biever 40896 Craig Daniel Billman 40897 Diane K. Klopsch 40898 Christy M. Samuels 40899 David Laurence Black 40900 Ben Anthony Blas 40901 Matthew Edwin Blyth 40902 Robert Stanley Bobinski 40903 James McCary Bogan 40904 Craig Edwin Bohn 40905 Kevin Gerard Bolyard 40906 Claud Robert Bond 40907 Donald Lee Boone 40908 Michael Clark Borsodi 40909 Andy Frank Bouckley 40910 Daniel Oliver Boyd 40911 Peter James Boylan 40912 Randy Jay Brach 40913 Allen Scott Bradley 40914 Kent Loring Bradley 40915 Sherry Bradley Holiday 40916 Jonathan Scott Brazier 40917 David R. Breuhan 40918 Douglas Lee Brimmer 40919 Brian Martin Brockson 40920 Michael Francis Broski 40921 Christopher Michael Brower 40922 Christopher Paul Brown 40923 James Gerard Brown 40924 Jay P. Brown 40925 Kenneth Brown 40926 Charles W. Browning 40927 Wallace Bradley Brucker 40928 Bruce Emile Bruno 40929 Todd Anthony Buchs 40930 John Leonard Buckheit 40931 Patricia Ann Buckingham 40932 Alexander Thomas Buehler 40933 Thomas Brandon Burke 40934 Larry Curtis Burner 40935 Mark William Burwell 40936 Aaron Gregory Butler 40937 John Marsh Buzzell 40938 Markus Stefan Bynum 40939 Guillermo Reyes Cabacungan 40940 Lawrence Panela Cabot 40941 George E. Cadena 40942 Dennis John Cahill 40943 Judith Baker Cain 40944 Philip Thomas Calbos 40945 Sean Michael Callahan 40946 Jeffrey Michael Callin 40947 Kelly Nicholas Campbell 40948 Cesar Julio Candanedo 40949 David Anthony Cannella 40950 Gregory Lawrence Cantwell 40951 Dominic J. Caraccilo 40952 Daniel Joseph Caraccio 40953 Robert K. Carl 40954 Christopher Carlin 40955 Robert E. Carney 40956 Lonny James Carpenter 40957 John Charles Carrington 40958 Barry Glen Carroll 40959 Michael Ross Carvelli 40960 William Henry Cattley 40961 Gregory Jerome Celestan 40962 Ronald Coleman Celeste 40963 Charlie Joseph Cepak 40964 George Jeffrey Ceremuga 40965 Marc Edward Cerniglia 40966 Donald Duane Cersovsky 40967 Stacey Chandler Fredenberg 40968 Dean I-Jen Chang 40969 E. Robert Chapman 40970 Thomas Clark Chapman 40971 Chester Anthony Yu Min Char 40972 William Alfred Childers 40973 John Ming Cho 40974 Louise Ann McKay 40975 Jon L. Christensen 40976 Matthew Mason Christensen 40977 Joey Lawrence Christmas 40978 Joseph Chu 40979 Tony Changyong Chung 40980 David Lyman Church 40981 Gary West Clark 40982 John Hays McCormick Clark 40983 Michael Joseph Clark 40984 Patrick James Clark 40985 Richard D. Clarke 40986 Jon Sharrock Cleaves 40987 Irina Clements Staats 40988 Thomas Eugene Clifford 40989 Leila Ryan Cluff 40990 Alma Jo Hulse 40991 Daniel Wilcox Coester 40992 Willard David Conklin 40993 David Alan Cook 40994 Edwin Charles Cook 40995 Gregory W. Cook 40996 Mark Charles Cook 40997 Troy Asao Kaleolani Cooper 40998 Charles Kevin Cornett 40999 William Nowlin Cosby 41000 Craig Scott Cotter 41001 Bernard Michael Coyle 41002 William Francis Coyle 41003 Curtis Wayne Cozart 41004 Paul Jeffrey Cozza 41005 Robert James Craig 41006 Mark Vincent Crane 41007 Michael Ray Criss 41008 Joshua Joseph Cronin 41009 James Arthur Crook 41010 Jerry Lawrence Crosby 41011 Andre Michael Cuerington 41012 Kenneth Paul Cullen 41013 Peter Joseph Curry 41014 Michael Patrick Cyr 41015 David Larsen Danielsen 41016 Keith Robison Darrow 41017 Randy Rebellon Dasalla 41018 Dag Peter Dascher 41019 Troy Eric Davidson 41020 Gerald Sheldon Davie 41021 Bruce H. Davison 41022 Charles Marcus Deal 41023 Joseph Paul DeAntona 41024 Susan De Benedictis Lee 41025 Diane L. Pitts 41026 Julie Delphin 41027 Ralph Christopher DeLuca 41028 John Anthony DeMaio 41029 Joseph Frank DeMarco 41030 William Richard DeMario 41031 Robert Lawrence DeMont 41032 Robert Carmine DeQuattro 41033 Steven Buffett Detwiler 41034 Thomas Edward Devens 41035 Steven C. Devney 41036 John Dudley DeWitt 41037 Bradley C. Dick 41038 Reuben Dabney Dickenson 41039 Douglas Lawrence Dickinson 41040 Robert A. Dobson 41041 Sean Kevin Dodgson 41042 David Lee Doerries 41043 Christopher Charles Dolt 41044 Joseph Michael Donahue 41045 Karen Elizabeth Jones 41046 Thomas Edmund Donovan 41047 John M. Dougherty 41048 Paul Dennis Dougherty 41049 Thurman Elliott Dow 41050 Dennis Joseph Dowd 41051 John F. Dowd 41052 Peter Thomas Doyle 41053 Martha Jean Drennan 41054 Stephen Joseph Driscoll 41055 Richard Donald Dubois 41056 Raymond Leroy Dudley 41057 Michael Duff 41058 Thomas Russell Duffy 41059 Robert Paul Duguay 41060 Robert L. Dunaway 41061 Maurice F. Dunne 41062 Darrell Daniel Durant 41063 Gregory Joe Dyekman 41064 Kenneth Wayne Dyson 41065 Arthur John Earl 41066 David Emerson Eckelbarger 41067 Alan D. Eckersley 41068 John Francis Edelen 41069 Brenda A. Edleson 41070 David Judd Edwards 41071 Scott Allan Edwards 41072 Brian Scott Eighmy 41073 Thomas Ivan Eisiminger 41074 Kent Marvel Elliott 41075 Stefan Elliott 41076 John Daniel Enloe 41077 Stephen Berrill Epling 41078 Jeffrey Michael Erickson 41079 Darrell Lee Eucker 41080 James Arthur Ewing 41081 Willard Gerard Fallon 41082 Daniel Malone Fancher 41083 Gerald Lavon Farber 41084 Ross James Faria 41085 Charles Martin Faris 41086 Joseph Thomas Farrell 41087 Joseph Richard Faucett 41088 Herbert Peter Fechter 41089 Emery Blane Fehl 41090 John Franklin Ferguson 41091 Robert Scott Ferro 41092 Michael James Ferry 41093 Alan David Fessenden 41094 Patrick L. Fetterman 41095 Richard Harlan Fields 41096 Herman H. Fierro 41097 Phillip Merrill Fine 41098 John D. Fink 41099 Craig Adam Finley 41100 John Christopher Finnessy 41101 Colby Dale Fisher 41102 Deborah Christine Fleming 41103 David Corson Flemings 41104 Timothy Scott Fliss 41105 Kenneth Allen Focht 41106 Jacqueline Foglia-Sandoval 41107 Troy Bayton Foote 41108 Paul William Forbes 41109 Gregory Scott Ford 41110 Charles Edwin Forshee 41111 Norbert Herve Fortier 41112 Cindy Ellen Foss 41113 Darrell Dean Fountain 41114 Mark D. Fox 41115 Walter Luther Fox 41116 Bruce C. Francis 41117 Steven Mark Franz 41118 Christopher Reed Frawley 41119 John E. Fredenberg 41120 Douglas Eugene Friedly 41121 David Aldrich Friedman 41122 Robert William Fry 41123 Lawrence Edward Fussner 41124 Paul W. Gaasbeck 41125 Christopher Wolfgang Gaertner 41126 Eddie L. Gamble 41127 Diana Gamboa Wiant 41128 Marcia Raleen Ganoe 41129 Matthew Gapinski 41130 Richard L. Garcia 41131 Kelvin Gerard Gardner 41132 Douglas Arthur Garmer 41133 Angela Marie Gaston 41134 Rafael M. Gavilan 41135 Christine Marie Gayagas 41136 Christopher Paul Gehler 41137 Richard Francis Gennaro 41138 William James Georgas 41139 Barbara Gethard Gerovac 41140 George Anthony Gialenios 41141 Brian Michael Gibbons 41142 Kevin Peter Gibbons 41143 Thomas Whitney Gibson 41144 James Burnham Gilbert 41145 Wesley Gerard Gillman 41146 Andrew Gordon Glen 41147 Richard Godfrey 41148 Glenn Harry Goldman 41149 Margaret Mary Gordon 41150 Joseph D. Goss 41151 Anthony M. Gowgiel 41152 Frederick Frederick Graboyes 41153 Gerren Spencer Groyer 41154

William Withington Greehey 41155 Jerry R. Green 41156 Tobin L. Green 41157 Bradley D. Greene 41158 Alison E. G. Estes 41159 Jeffrey Duren Grey 41160 Allen Leland Griffith 41161 Carl David Grunow 41162 Gerard Knauss Guiler 41163 William H. Guinn 41164 Luis Santiago Gutierrez 41165 Thomas Kyle Haase 41166 Michael Jon Hagen 41167 Thomas William Hagstrom 41168 Timothy Arthur Haight 41169 Paul Richard Haist 41170 David White Hall 41171 Byron Keith Hamilton 41172 Scott Reed Hamilton 41173 Steven William Hammond 41174 Robert Wayne Hand 41175 E. Shamus Hanlon 41176 Tracy Sue Hanlon 41177 John Thomas Hansen 41178 Monroe Bailey Harden 41179 Ellen Lois Haring 41180 Kelly Harriman Ziccarello 41181 Dennis John Harrington 41182 Gail Louise Harrison 41183 Arthur L. Hartman 41184 John Gregory Haugen 41185 Michael David Hauser 41186 Jeffrey Walter Hawley 41187 David Jonathan Hayes 41188 Richard Dwayne Hayes 41189 Stanley Neal Heath 41190 Wayne Edgar Heaton 41191 John Edward Heller 41192 John Joseph Heller 41193 R. Ross Hempstead 41194 Barbara S. Melendez 41195 Michelle Marie Fraley 41196 Paul Kevin Heun 41197 Richard Alan Hewitt 41198 Suzanne C. Hickey 41199 David Edward Hill 41200 Dwayne Thomas Hill 41201 Eddy James Hill 41202 Greg Francis Hill 41203 Jerry Peterson Hill 41204 John Stuart Hillestad 41205 George Steven Hluck 41206 Daniel Leo Hogan 41207 David Craig Hogan 41208 Melvin Scott Hogan 41209 Paul Richard Hogan 41210 Buddy Allan Holbert 41211 Karla Holden Donovan 41212 Hershel Louis Holiday 41213 Eric Thomas Holmes 41214 Susan Gail Moblo 41215 James Ernest Hooper 41216 Richard Nelson Horton 41217 Teresa Rose Hougnon 41218 Jeffrey Lee Hovey 41219 Rory James Howard 41220 Peter Tzuo Yuan Hsieh 41221 Kimball Mark Hubbert 41222 Scott Keith Huffman 41223 Johnny Mack Humphrey 41224 Paul Kevin Hurley 41225 Mather Burton Hutchens 41226 John Evans Hutton 41227 Michael S. Ingham 41228 Lawrence Edward Iram 41229 Bruce Henry Irwin 41230 Wesley James Jennings 41231 Thomas Ritchie Jezior 41232 Brent Philip Johnson 41233 David E. A. Johnson 41234 Derek V. Johnson 41235 Jay Kilcrest Johnson 41236 Jeffrey William Johnson 41237 Margaret Johnson Luke 41238 Matthew Arthur Johnson 41239 Paul Hanes Johnson 41240 Todd Milo Johnson 41241 William Carl Johnson 41242 Kevin Jones 41243 Timothy Alan Jones 41244 Gregory Donald Joyce 41245 Michael Alan Kahn 41246 Philip Edward Kaiser 41247 Gregory Louis Kammerer 41248 Christian Lyle Kammermann 41249 Gregory Charles Kane 41250 Hahn Sok Kang 41251 Edward Francis Kastner 41252 William D. Kavanaugh 41253 Robert Sean Keating 41254 John D. Keenan 41255 Thomas Michael Keene 41256 William Mark Kehrer 41257 James Joseph Kelly 41258 Steve Wilhelm Jefferson Kemp 41259 James Larry Kendrick 41260 James Joseph Kenney 41261 Paul Francis Kenny 41262 Timothy John Keppler 41263 Michael Meredith Kershaw 41264 James P. Kester 41265 Karie Leigh Barber 41266 William Tyler King 41267 Jeffrey M. Kingston 41268 John Kevin Kirby 41269 Edward Frederick Kleinschmidt 41270 James Jeffrey Klingaman 41271 Christopher Johanne Klinkmueller 41272 Norbert S. Klopsch 41273 David Hiscock Knapp 41274 James Willis Knickrehm 41275 Clifford T. Knight 41276 John Lance Knight 41277 Tracy David Knox 41278 Kenneth Ernest Koebberling 41279 Gregory Allan Kokoskie 41280 Hermann Kolev 41281 Kevin Michael Koziatek 41282 Stephen Gerard Kreipe 41283 William David Kuchinski 41284 Thomas Paul Kulich 41285 Joseph Lloyd Kulmayer 41286 Steven Ralph Kuring 41287 Michael J. Kwinn 41288 Frank Lacitignola 41289 Richard Arlynn Lacquement 41290 David Anthony Lagasse 41291 Peter G. Laky 41292 Alexander Leroy Lambert 41293 Garrett Randall Lambert 41294 John Douglas Lambert 41295 Roger William Lambert 41296 Wayne Winston Lambert 41297 Karl Dietrich Landsberg 41298 Jon Adrian Larsen 41299 Mark Michael Lauer 41300 Richard Wesley Laughlin 41301 Darryl Joseph Lavender 41302 Terry Gene Lawrence 41303 Andrew Paul Lawrisuk 41304 Jeffrey Alan Lawson 41305 Lance A. Lawson 41306 Jean Louise Gaslin 41307 Vincent John Leardi 41308 Bryant James Lee 41309 Randall Howard Lee 41310 Brian C. Lein 41311 Susan Lenio Sine 41312 Paul R. Lepine 41313 Maurice Albert Lescault 41314 Brett Geoffrey Lewis 41315 Michael David Lewis 41316 Thaddeus Thomas Lewis 41317 Kenneth Kopf Lindell 41318 Joseph Alan Lindhardt 41319 Maureen E. Linehan 41320 Gregory Scott Linville 41321 Donald Cubbison Little 41322 Richard Paul Livermore 41323 Timothy J. Livolsi 41324 Leslie Lochry Bryson 41325 Paul R. Logan 41326 Jay Robert Long 41327 John Charles Loomis 41328 Ruben Serna Lopez 41329 Stephen Richard Luhrs 41330 Timothy Allan Lukas 41331 Rod Lurie 41332 Walter Udo Lutes 41333 Royd Clifton Lutz 41334 Jason Carl Lynch 41335 Walter Joseph Lynch 41336 Dominic Macaluso 41337 Bruce Thomas MacDonald 41338 Mark David Madigan 41339 Paul James Mahoney 41340 Robert L. Mahoney 41341 Hector M. Maldonado 41342 Gerald Paul Malloy 41343 Efrain Atalig Manglona 41344 Michael John Maraccini 41345 Joseph V. Marigliano 41346 Christopher John Marshall 41347 Edward John Martin 41348 Jeffrey W. Martin 41349 James John Marziale 41350 Keith Edward Matthews 41351 Douglas Frank Matuszewski 41352 Donald Carl Matz 41353 Robert B. Maurio 41354 James Joseph Beda Maynez 41355 Peter Shealey McChrystal 41356 William Paul McCloud 41357 Joseph Jefferson McClung 41358 Michael Eugene McCormack 41359 J. Scott McCormick 41360 Richard R. McCracken 41361 Amy McDonald Mulligan 41362 Joel McDonald 41363 Timothy Patrick McFadden 41364 Douglas Wyman McGlothlin 41365 John Thomas McGrail 41366 Michael John McGuire 41367 Daniel Patrick McKenrick 41368 Stephen McKinney 41369 Herbert R. McMaster 41370 Kerry Vlondie McNair 41371 Robert William McNally 41372 John Thomas McNamara 41373 Arthur Craigg McRae 41374 Ellen M. McDonald 41375 Susan Elizabeth Meckfessel-Chavez 41376 Darrin Leigh Meek 41377 James Ryan Melanson 41378 Dean William Mengel 41379 Mark Thomas Menkhus 41380 Michael Francis Merrill 41381 Mark Stephen Messina 41382 Scott Gregory Messinger 41383 Karl Frederic Meyer 41384 John Christopher Meyers 41385 Stanley V. Mickens 41386 Susann Marie Miguel 41387 Michael Thaddeus Miklos 41388 Charles Bruce Millar 41389 Colin Kelly Miller 41390 Daniel Bryon Miller 41391 James E. Miller 41392 Kent Michael Miller 41393 Warren Richard Miller 41394 William Potter Miller 41395 Steven James Minear 41396 James Thomas Mitroka 41397 Timothy Eric Mock 41398 Robert W. Molinari 41399 Joseph Wray Molinaro 41400 Joseph M. Molloy 41401 Rodney Michael Monsees 41402 Monrad Lewis Monsen 41403 David M. Moore 41404 David R. Moore 41405 Leon Elwin Moores 41406 Gregory L. Morgan 41407 Robert Thomas Morgan 41408 Todd Andrew Moriarty 41409 Mark Anton Morin 41410 Roger Joseph Morin 41411 Edward Stanley Morris 41412 Peter Charles Morris 41413 David Reid Mothershed 41414 McCammon Reed Mottley 41415 Mark Richard Mueller 41416 Jeannie Mular Tibbetts 41417 Matthew Timothy Mullarkey 41418 Leonel Munoz 41419 Jerald D. Murphy 41420 Kenneth Franklin Murphy 41421 Randy Patrick Murphy 41422 James Andrew Muskopf 41423 Rickey Cee Myhand 41424 Carmine Joseph Naccarelli 41425 James R. Nagel 41426 Theodore James Nagel 41427 John Jacob Nagy 41428 Frank Robert Nappi 41429 Robert Glenn Nave 41430 Marty Tucker Neese 41431 Thomas A. Nelson 41432 James Everett Neumiller 41433 Earl Newsome 41434 Michael Anthony Newton 41435 David Paul Nichting 41436 Andrew Brent Nocks 41437 David Thomas Noesges 41438 Bradley Pawl Nordgren 41439 Michael Notto 41440 Paul Frederick Nus 41441 Keith Roland Nuzzo 41442 Demetrius Cevaughn Oatis 41443 Ralph Thomas Obermeier 41444 John J. O'Brien 41445 Juston Michael O'Brien 41446 Gregory P. Oelberg 41447 Jeffrey Marc Oettinger 41448 Robert John Oglesby 41449 Joel Oguete 41450 Glenn K. Okamoto 41451 Keith Allan Oldre 41452 Ernest M. Oliver 41453 Todd Jeffrey Olney 41454 Brian Keith Olson 41455 Warren Clement Olson 41456 Patrick Lee Olvey 41457 Crystal Orr Henderson 41458 Anthony Michael Orsini 41459 Kenneth Donald Osmonson 41460 Troy Bentley Overton 41461 Christopher Michael Pacheco 41462 Alfred Harlan Paddock 41463 Timothy John Pagano 41464 Deirdre Painter Dixon 41465 Patricia Marie Painton 41466 Francis Christopher Pais 41467 Stuart Michael Pandza 41468 Joseph A. Paniccia 41469 Mark Gerhard Pannenberg 41470 Luis Alberto Parada 41471 Michael Ignatius Parietti 41472 Thomas Otis Parker 41473 Brian Victor Patton 41474 Mark Richard Pauli 41475 Jeffrey John Paull 41476 Robert Dean Pearcy 41477 Phillip A. Pedersen 41478 Richard Edmund Parke 41479 William John Penny 41480 Randal Gene Penrice 41481 George Earl Peoples 41482 Roman Santiago Perez 41483 Roy E. Perkins 41484 Steven Wayne Perkins 41485 Thomas Andrew Perkins 41486 Stephen J. Perry 41487 Thomas Walter Pesch 41488 James Frederick Peterson 41489 Michael Blair Petring 41490 William Scott Phillips 41491 John Alphonse Picciuto 41492 Greg A. Pickell 41493 Brian Edward Pierson 41494 Dennis James Pinigis 41495 David Normand Plante 41496 Michael Peter Poel 41497 John Paul Poisson 41498 John William Polanowicz 41499 Peter Alexander Popovich 41500 Albert Victor Porambo 41501 Robert James Portigue 41502 Edward Benjamin Posey 41503 Jacob L. Potak 41504 David Scott Pound 41505 Harry Dean Prantl 41506 Pamela Prentiss Morrill 41507 Andrew Jay Preston 41508 Christopher Blair Preston 41509 Daniel Andrew Priatko 41510 Raymond Alan Prisk 41511 Robert Ralston Pritchard 41512 Brian D. Prosser 41513 Harold Kent Prukop 41514 Mark Joseph Prusiecki 41515 Edwin Gilchrist Pryor 41516 John Howard Quigg 41517 Heather Maria Scott 41518 Kenneth Paul Quintilian 41519 Wayne P. Rainford 41520 Ludlow Anthony Ramsay 41521 Gary Jerome Ramsdell 41522 William Edward Rapp 41523 Jonathan Lee Rariden 41524 Michael Stewart Rasmussen 41525 Scott Melvin Rathbun 41526 Frank David Read 41527 George Leslie Reed 41528 Joseph H. Reed 41529 Darryl Keith Reever 41530 John Michael Reich 41531 Michael Nunziato Reilly 41532 Susan Reinhard Robertson 41533 Glenn David Reisweber 41534 Robert E. Renner 41535 Roger James Rettke 41536 Ronald Lee Reusch 41537 Livingston Zeus Reynolds 41538 Reynaldo Reza 41539 Robert Earl Rhodes 41540 Michael Victor Riccardi 41541 Daniel Allen Rice 41542 Christopher James Richardson 41543 Ricky Wayne Richardson 41544 Randy Scot Richey 41545 Stephen Wesley Richey 41546 Jimmy Louis Ricks 41547 Mary L. Hoelscher 41548 Guillermo Rivera 41549 Christopher John Rizzo 41550 Dean Hollister Rizzo 41551 Sharon Roberts Aizer 41552 Bruce Eric Robinson 41553 Willard Luther Robinson 41554 David Lawrence Rocha 41555 Michael Francis Roche 41556 Luis Francisco Rodriguez 41557 Oscar Hugo Rodriguez 41558 Beverly Yvette Rogers Phillips 41559 S. Allen Roosa 41560 Mark L. Rosen 41561 David Andrew Rossi 41562 Barry Alan Roth 41563 Gregory Paul Rowe 41564 John R. Rowe 41565 Marjorie A. Rudinsky 41566 George A. Sabochick 41567 Richard Michael Sajkoski 41568 John Louis Salvetti 41569 Armando R. Sanchezcastellanos 41570 Steven Allan Sanford 41571 James Richard Santangelo 41572 Joseph Frank Sartiano 41573 Carol Saunders Pitts 41574 David Paul Savold 41575 Karl Eric Sayce 41576 Edward Anthony Sbrocco 41577 Darrell K. Scales 41578 Patrick Joseph Scanlan 41579 Michael Edward Schaller 41580 Jeff Stewart Schelde 41581 Jerry Lynn Schlabach 41582 John Carl Schleeter 41583 Jeffrey Carl Schmidt 41584 Laura Ann Moore 41585 Thomas A. Schmitt 41586 Thomas Roger Schmutz 41587 Thomas John Schneider 41588 Joyce M. Schossau 41589 Andrew Paxton Schubin 41590 Frank John Schumacher 41591 John Nicholas Schuster 41592 Glenn G. Schweitzer 41593 Michael William Schweppe 41594 Daniel David Schwitolla 41595 Robert Walter Scott 41596 Caroline Choppa 41597 Candace Yvette Sui-Sin Seto 41598 Jeffrey Thomas Sgro 41599 Jan Robert Shadwick 41600 Everett Matthew Shaw 41601 Richard Leonard Shaw 41602 Richard James Shea 41603 Gerald Dwayne Sheeks 41604 Raymond Virgil Shellman 41605 Michael Christopher Sheridan 41606 Todd Todd Sherrill 41607 David Paul Shimkus 41608 Kevin Eugene Shorter 41609 David John Showerman 41610 John H. Shuman 41611 Stephen Allen Shuster 41612 Steven Emerson Sibley 41613 John Alvan Simmons 41614 Dana Francis Simon 41615 David Thomas Simpson 41616 Alan Neal Sims 41617 Thomas Matthew Sistrunk 41618 George J. Slabowski 41619 William Brown Slade 41620 John Francis Sloan 41621 Derek Robert Smith 41622 Dorinda Smith Lambert 41623 Forrest E. Smith 41624 John E. Smith 41625 Lawrence James Smith 41626 Melody Smith Lutz 41627 Philip Alan Smith 41628 Randy Lee Smith 41629 Rodney Alfred Smith 41630 Steven James Smith 41631 Thomas Patrick Smith 41632 Troy Lee Smith 41633 Michael Stephen Snell 41634 John Tony Snider 41635 Richard Louis Sobrato 41636 Darrell John Sodergren 41637 Miracle David Solley 41638 Gary Scott Southard 41639 Joseph Arthur Southcott 41640 Robert Grant Southey 41641 Robert Craig Sparks 41642 Katherine Perkuchin 41643 Ronald W. Spence 41644 Timothy Charles Spence 41645 John Michael Spiszer 41646 Clark A. Spurrier 41647 Richard C. Staats 41648 James Robert Stanley 41649 Richard Louis St.Clair 41650 John Albert Steils 41651 Daniel Wellington Steiner 41652 Jeffrey Michael Stephany 41653 Adam Brandon Stephenson 41654 Lloyd A. Stephenson 41655 Ricky Gene Stephenson 41656 William John Sternhagen 41657 Robert Byron Stokes 41658 Robert James Stone 41659 Charles Michael Stover 41660 Stephen Mitchell Strickland 41661 Heidi Ann Stark 41662 Jay B. Stuart 41663 Lydia Stuban Antoniou 41664 Kevin J. Stubblebine 41665 Mark Allen Stump 41666 William Keith Suchan 41667 Edward James Suhr 41668 Jon David Sullenberger 41669 James Matthew Sullivan 41670 Chris T. Sultemeier 41671 Richard Lee Suter 41672 Michael Yutaka Suzuki 41673 John R. Szypko 41674 Napoleon Caballes Taas 41675 Neville Patrick Tai 41676 Thomas Patrick Taney 41677 James Cletus Tapp 41678 Rick William Taylor 41679 Steven Douglas Taylor 41680 Troy Lowry Taylor 41681 Charles Warren Teel 41682 Bryan Keith Thomas 41683 Fern Jeannine Thomas 41684 Jerome Edward Thomas 41685 Susan G. Lobsiger 41686 Lawrence Frederick Thoms 41687 Richard Alan Thornton 41688 Kenneth Franklin Thrasher 41689 Blair Andrew Tiger 41690 Theron W. Tindall 41691 Judson Martin Titchen 41692 Jeffrey Michael Tokar 41693 Mark A. Tolzmann 41694 Kurtiss Lee Tomasovich 41695 Wanda Teresa Toro 41696 Manuel Angel Torres 41697 Salvatore Luigi Tortora 41698 Jerry Lee Towe 41699 Michael Shawn Trainer 41700 Edward Lyle Trigg 41701 Mark William Triplett 41702 Joseph Louis Trujillo 41703 Harry Daniel Tunnell 41704 Drew Anthony Turinski 41705 Michael Wayne Turner 41706 Paul Anthony Turner 41707 Robb Eric Turner 41708 Thomas W. Van Alstyne 41709 Glen Gerard Veevaert 41710 Patrick Garrette Vessels 41711 Bernard Gilbert Vezeau 41712 David Kenneth Viggers 41713 Philip Anthony Vignola 41714 Francisco B. Villanueva 41715 Mark L. Visnovske 41716 Oskar Peter Vuskalns 41717 Brigitte W. Kwinn 41718 Scott Timothy Wakeland 41719 Charles Easterling Walker 41720 Thomas Daniel Walko 41721 Kevin J. Wallace 41722 Cathleen Mary Walsh Brown 41723 Timothy John Walsh 41724 Elizabeth Hale 41725 Terry T.T. Ward 41726 Chaim Ross Warshawsky 41727 Anthony J. Waters 41728 Roslyn Ann Houston 41729 Bettyann Watson Sheats 41730 Thomas Edward Weckel 41731 Peter James Weis 41732 William Nathaniel Weiss 41733 Robert J. Welch 41734 Thomas Patrick Welch 41735 Edward Henry Wentworth 41736 Brian Carl Wepking 41737 Cynthia Werner Sbrocco 41738 Robert William Werthman 41739 David C. Weston 41740 David Bruce Whaling 41741 Lawrence Gregory Whalley 41742 Richard Bradley White 41743 Ronald Olswyn White 41744 Rory Gene White 41745 Samuel Raymond White 41746 David Scott Wiggins 41747 Henry George Wilks 41748 Lawrence E. Williams 41749 Shaun Hayden Williams 41750 George Edward Willis 41751 Christopher Ernst Wilson 41752 Tee Gee Wilson 41753 Richard Charles Wink 41754 Gregory Ayers Wise 41755 James Howard Wise 41756 Thomas Dean Wock 41757 John K. Wohlever 41758 Philip Wayne Wojtalewicz 41759 Douglas William Wolfkill 41760 David Howard Wood 41761 Robert Alan Woodmansee 41762 Michael Warren Wooley 41763 William D. Woolf 41764 Patrick McClister Wray 41765 Donald C. Wright 41766 Millicent J. Wright 41767 Scott Gregory Wuestner 41768 Brian F. Wycoff 41769 John Soteros Xenos 41770 Michael Lee Yoder 41771 Lawrence Arthur Zaenker 41772 Arthur Joseph Zarone 41773 Aidis Lucius Zunde 41774 Matthew Herbert Adams 41775 Bryan Joseph Armstrong 41776 Monica M. Belisle 41777 Larry Lynn Carroll 41778 David James Faddis 41779 Wayne F. McGurk 41780 John J. Menard 41781 Robert Frederick Muska 41782 Harold W. Nelson 41783 Kyle W. Ray 41784 Daniel Michael Shea 41785 Daryl Graham Smith 41786 Milton William Sorensen 41787 Gregory David Thornton 41788 James Edward Amundsen 41789 Daniel Joseph Cottone 41790 Robert Charles Loomis 41791 David H. Mowry 41792 Dennis Mandel Alsberry 41793 Derric H. Anderson 41794 Bradley Bruce Becker 41795 Alexa Anne Bielefeld 41796 Anthony Junius Boling 41797 Alfred Llooyd Brooks 41798 Rene Gordon Burgess 41799 Nicholas Edward Coddington 41800 Oswald Enriquez 41801 Anthony Dale Garcia 41802 Edward Alfred Gomez 41803 Janice Higuera 41804 Robert Cary Hinton 41805 Jeffrey Kittredge Hoadley 41806 Matthew Murray Hull 41807 William Howard Jefferson 41808 Derek Johnson 41809 William Owen Kime 41810 Kevin Alan Meehan 41811 Gary Todd Morton 41812 James P. O'Grady 41813 Paul Malcolm Peterson 41814 John Thomas Smith 41815 Gary Neal Sparkman 41816 Marcus Edward Steele 41817 Robert Edward Thompson 41818 **1985** Derric Lynn Abrecht 41819 John Louis Abruscato 41820 Craig Hall Ackerman 41821 Joseph Franklin Adams 41822 Reginald O. Adams 41823 Michael Lee Adkins 41824 Stephen F. Agather 41825 Michael Corbitt Aid 41826 Elton Dominic Akins 41827 Robin Albertella Griffen 41828 Alec Eugene Alessandra 41829 Brian Joseph Alexander 41830 Brad D. Allen 41831 Michael Christopher Allen 41832 Oliver Blane Alt 41833 Brenda Leigh Amster-Parada 41834 Katherine Marie Carter 41835 Romney Christian Andersen 41836 Brad Lee Anderson 41837 Jon Todd Anderson 41838 K. Wendy Anderson 41839 Randall Charles Anderson 41840 Richard Garcia Anderson 41841 John Angelis 41842 John Glenn Angelo 41843 James Timothy Anibal 41844 Rodney Lee Apfelbeck 41845 Santiago Apodaca 41846 Juan L. Arcocha 41847 Mark Randall Arn 41848 Richard Spencer Arnold 41849 Michael Joseph Arrington 41850 John Anthony Aruzza 41851 Harvey Augustine 41852 John Martin Aveningo 41853 Alex Lewis Babers 41854 Michael Damien Bagg 41855 Brent Guenter Bahl 41856 Michael Kenneth Baisden 41857 Paul Alan Balek 41858 Daniel Lee Ball 41859 Macaire Balzano Benson 41860 W. Christopher Bandy 41861 Daniel Theodore Banks 41862 James Boyd Bankston 41863 Charles Richard Barbee 41864 Charles Eric Barnes 41865 Joseph Earl Barnes 41866 Terrence James Barno 41867 Pedro Barreda 41868 Troy A. Barring 41869 David Edward Bassett 41870 James Yale Bassuk 41871 Stuart David Bastin 41872 William Thomas Beck 41873 Jonathan Lee Beegle 41874 Steven Michael Behrend 41875 Mark Wesley Belcher 41876 Gordon Wayne Bell 41877 Ernest Charles Benner 41878 Eric E. Benson 41879 Randall Morris Bentz 41880 David Joseph Berczek 41881 Luis Antonio Berdecia 41882 Jacob Lanier Berlin 41883 Jonathan David Berry 41884 Kevin Keeley Berry 41885 Mark James Beyea 41886 Wesley Todd Bickford 41887 Steven Lynn Birch 41888 Garry Parrant Bishop 41889 Robert Lawrence Biskup 41890 Aurelia Lynn Black 41891 Rans Dow Black 41892 Jeffrey Robert Blackman 41893 Phillip E. Blalock 41894 James Constantine Blastos 41895 Anthony Latimer Blount 41896 Todd Mack Bluedorn 41897 Gerard Boden 41898 Michael Boeding 41899 Jeffrey John Bolebruch 41900 Robert Clarence Bollmer 41901 Louis George Boomsma 41902 Bradley William Booth 41903 William Harvey Both 41904 Jeanne Bouchard LaVake 41905 David Bowen 41906 Richard Frederick Bowyer 41907 Robert Winsor Boyes 41908 John Charles Bradford 41909 James Patrick Bradley 41910 Yong Chol Bradley 41911 Artem Paul Braginetz 41912 John Glenn Alexander 41913 Kevin Louis Brau 41914 Katherine Brenner Heiberger 41915 Gilbert Samuel Brindley 41916 Michael K. Brooks 41917 David J. Brost 41918

Robert Dale Brouwer 41919 James B. Brown 41920 James E. Brown 41921 Jeffrey Richard Brown 41922 Michael Thomas Brown 41923 Steven Glenn Brown 41924 Todd Alan Browne 41925 Stephen E. Bruch 41926 Deewitt Talmadge Bryant 41927 Vincent D. Bryant 41928 Paul Richard Buico 41929 Daniel Thomas Burger 41930 Patrick Michael Burns 41931 Dale Mark Busic 41932 Jeffery Dean Butcher 41933 Frederick Xavier Philip Cabulong 41934 Frank Thomas Cackowski 41935 Robert Edward Cahill 41936 Scott Loubet Cahoon 41937 Mary Kathleen Gilmartin 41938 Paul Louis Cal 41939 Jon David Call 41940 Maureen Cecilia Callan-Canwell 41941 Fred Lee Campbell 41942 William Patrick Campos 41943 Kathryn Cancelliere McKinney 41944 Mark Cannon 41945 Pamela L. Cardin Martis 41946 Thomas Joseph Carey 41947 Gina Smith 41948 Christopher Raymond Carlson 41949 Harold J. Carlson 41950 Patricia M. Buel 41951 Angela D. Ruddell 41952 Anthony Bryan Carr 41953 Jay D. Carr 41954 Francisco R. Carranza 41955 Bryan Edward Carroll 41956 Catherine Leigh Carroll 41957 Rodney Jay Carter 41958 Bernard Michael Casey 41959 Christopher William Casey 41960 Kevin Roger Casey 41961 Norbert Michael Castro 41962 Jose Angel Cecin 41963 Michael Richard Cero 41964 Joseph L. Chacon 41965 Dean Arthur Chamberlain 41966 Jon T. Chambless 41967 Jeffery T. Chandler 41968 Steven Mark Charbonneau 41969 Robert D. Charleston 41970 Arthur Braswell Chasen 41971 Davie Duane Chennault 41972 Anne Chiarella Marx 41973 Johnson Chin 41974 Colleen Elizabeth Ann Chorak 41975 Patrick Michael Chuinard 41976 Thomas Michael Cioppa 41977 Robert Alan Claflin 41978 Geoffrey Rene Clark 41979 James Howard Clark 41980 Kendall Robert Clark 41981 Martin Robert Clark 41982 Scott Robert Clark 41983 Brendan W. Clarke 41984 James P. Clarke 41985 Thomas Robert Clarke 41986 Timothy M. Clarke 41987 Timothy Joseph Clays 41988 Barry Keith Clements 41989 Valerie Coffey 41990 Harry Lawrence Cohen 41991 Robert Earl Collins 41992 John K. Collison 41993 Ray Arnold Combs 41994 Virginia A. Todd 41995 Kathleen E. Houston 41996 Barry James Conway 41997 James L. Cook 41998 Keith Kelton Cook 41999 Jeffrey C. Corbett 42000 Ralph Robert Corradi 42001 Frank Edward Cowden 42002 Craig William Cox 42003 Randall A. Cozzens 42004 Harold Wayne Craig 42005 James Douglas Craig 42006 Bobby Grant Crawford 42007 Michael Cingle Cresson 42008 John Woodson Crews 42009 Christopher Peter Crum 42010 Raymond Cruz 42011 Robert Gordon Culberg 42012 Michael L. Cumbee 42013 Gary Wood Cumbey 42014 John Francis Cummings 42015 Michael Paul Currivan 42016 Andrew Francis Curry 42017 Stephen Lee Curtis 42018 Patricia Cyr Reno 42019 Jeff Paul Czapiewski 42020 Jerry Robert Daily 42021 Jeff Burton Dallas 42022 Kurt Eugene Davidson 42023 Kenneth John Davies 42024 Amah Amelia Davis 42025 Deborah Trew Davis 42026 Steven Andrew Davis 42027 Brandon Alexander Steele 42028 Thomas Michael DeBerardino 42029 Kenneth Delbert DeFries 42030 Patrick James Delaney 42031 Denise Anne DeLawter 42032 Stephen Harold Delity 42033 John Edward Della-Giustina 42034 Kenneth Henry Demarest 42035 Douglas Richard Dennis 42036 William Michael Derrick 42037 Thomas J. Desrosier 42038 Rodger Jan Deuerlein 42039 Paul Turgeon Devereaux 42040 John S. Devlin 42041 Matthew Anthony DeVore 42042 Calvin Craig DeWitt 42043 Joseph Louis DiCamillo 42044 Floyd Sidney Dickson 42045 John Michael DiMarsico 42046 Paul Alfred Dinkel 42047 Robert C. Doerer 42048 Michael J. Doherty 42049 William Thomas Dolan 42050 Edward Joseph Dollar 42051 John Kevin Donahue 42052 Patricia Joan Donley 42053 Marc Calvin Donnelly 42054 Dean E. Dorko 42055 Brian Lawrence Dosa 42056 Roger William Dougherty 42057 Terry Lee Douglas 42058 Francis Xavier Doyle 42059 William Joseph Doyle 42060 Sandra Elise Draper 42061 Anne Elizabeth Drislane Quigley 42062 Thomas Arthur Dufresne 42063 Mark Thomas Dufton 42064 John Matthew Duguay 42065 John Richard Duke 42066 Manuel Duran 42067 Thomas Anthony Durso 42068 Kevin Lee Dyer 42069 Phillip Andrew Dyer 42070 David Micheal Dykes 42071 Jimmie Lee Eberhart 42072 Ramon Luis Echevarria 42073 Jeffrey R. Eckstein 42074 Robert Drew Edgerly 42075 Peter B. Edmonds 42076 Keith Robert Edwards 42077 Donald Joe Ehrie 42078 Scott Albert Eisenhauer 42079 Richard Berkeley Ellis 42080 Anthony Emmi 42081 Mark Rudolf Engelbaum 42082 Anthony Joseph English 42083 George John Ennis 42084 Steven Benedict Enos 42085 Joseph Thomas Erdie 42086 Samuel Scott Evans 42087 Peter Martin Everett 42088 Jeffrey Alan Fackler 42089 Jeffrey Arthur Farrar 42090 James Kevin Faulkner 42091 Kurt William Fedors 42092 Philip T. Feir 42093 Alan William Feistner 42094 Robert Placid Feliu 42095 Kevin Michael Felix 42096 Lucia Fernandez 42097 Kirk Ray Fields 42098 Daniel Craft Finch 42099 Noel Jean Guarino 42100 Stephane Henri Finkenbeiner 42101 Maureen L. Collins 42102 Anthony John Fiore 42103 Michael Joseph Fisher 42104 Bobby Fitzpatrick 42105 Michael T. Fleming 42106 Steven Douglas Fleming 42107 Keith Owen Flood 42108 Edgar Emil Flores 42109 Julius Stephen Q. Flores 42110 Timothy Joseph Flynn 42111 Michael Anthony Foley 42112 Michael Christopher Foley 42113 Anne Forrester Muska 42114 John Thomas Forrester 42115 Rose Forrester Burwell 42116 Mark Arthur Foster 42117 Raymond Todd Foster 42118 Andrew Hamilton Fowler 42119 John Christopher Franchek 42120 Douglas Robert Frank 42121 Charles Dudley Franks 42122 Christopher Carl Franks 42123 Michael Elliott Frantz 42124 William Court Frauen 42125 Francis Virgil Frazier 42126 Clark Dale Frederick 42127 Robert Edward Freehill 42128 Matt John Frerichs 42129 Michael Earl Frey 42130 Steven Paul Friedel 42131 John Allen Fritchman 42132 Vernon Charles Fuller 42133 Anthony Charles Funkhouser 42134 Michael Edward Furlong 42135 Curt Steven Gandy 42136 Gerhard Thomas Garcia 42137 Maria Victoria Garcia Coy 42138 Charles William Gardner 42139 Stanley Joseph Gardocki 42140 Michael David Garner 42141 Joseph Albert Garrity 42142 Robert Miller Garver 42143 Michael Wayne Gary 42144 Patrick Bernard Gaston 42145 Scott Daniel Gemberling 42146 Joseph Daniel Gentilucci 42147 David Thomas Gerard 42148 Sean David Ghidella 42149 Patrick Francis Giblin 42150 James Earl Gibson 42151 Steven A. Gibson 42152 Byron Joe Gilbreath 42153 Edward Earl Giles 42154 Mary Ann Gilgallon 42155 John Marshall Gill 42156 Robert Francis Gilmartin 42157 Jeffrey T. Girard 42158 Harry Clinton Glenn 42159 William Edward Glenn 42160 Brian Roger Gollsneider 42161 Raymond Anthony Gonzales 42162 David Lowell Goodling 42163 Timothy Wayne Goodly 42164 Robert Lawrence Goodman 42165 Alan Robert Goodrich 42166 Michael Lawrence Goodwin 42167 David Guinn Gordon 42168 Keith Paul Gordon 42169 William Bonham Gore 42170 Karen Rachelle DeLissio 42171 Daniel James Gorman 42172 Byron Jay Gorrell 42173 Timothy Grammel 42174 Daniel Charles Gray 42175 Deborah J. McDonald 42176 Kevin Lawrence Green 42177 Paul Stephen Greenhouse 42178 Patricia Jean Grey Johnson 42179 Donald Henry Grier 42180 Eric Samuel Griffin 42181 O. Charles Griffin 42182 Garrett C. Grimm 42183 Joseph Edward Gross 42184 Lisa Gross Sternhagen 42185 Richard Clayton Gross 42186 Michael William Grosz 42187 Patrick N. Grum 42188 Clorinda F. Guarino Nothstein 42189 Justin C. Gubler 42190 Jerry Guerra 42191 Robert Guevara 42192 John James Guidy 42193 Ginni Guiton 42194 Craig Sutter Guth 42195 Gregory Samuel Hadjis 42196 Michael Kelly Haider 42197 Michael Alan Hajost 42198 Corine Hall Fox 42199 Franklin Carlisle Hall 42200 Ren Stacey Hall 42201 Deborah Ann Seaman 42202 John Brendan Halligan 42203 Jon Matthew Halsey 42204 Karen Annette Carvelli 42205 James Noel Hamilton 42206 Marvin Karl Hamilton 42207 Joseph F. Hanna 42208 James John Hanson 42209 Peter Carl Harbers 42210 James Christopher Harren 42211 John William Harrington 42212 Cynthia Ann Harris 42213 Ronald Allen Harris 42214 Steven Lyn Harris 42215 Matthew Douglas Harrison 42216 Rex A. Harrison 42217 Edgar Davis Hartley 42218 Robert Paul Hattan 42219 Matthew C. Hayes 42220 Harold Paul Hazen 42221 Steven James Heaney 42222 Karl Jonathan Heineman 42223 John Benjamin Heiston 42224 Philip Eugene Helbling 42225 David Harmon Helms 42226 David Norman Hendrickson 42227 Joel Dean Henley 42228 Alejandro Samson Hernandez 42229 Rhonda Susan Hernandez Miller 42230 Glen William Herrick 42231 Douglas Alan Hersh 42232 Todd Andrew Hetherington 42233 Brethard Scott Hill 42234 Russ Andrew Hinds 42235 Elizabeth Hine Carey 42236 Brian Keith Hobson 42237 Kenneth William Hodgson 42238 Michael John Hoey 42239 Joseph Martin Hojnacki 42240 Henry Jameson Holcombe 42241 Thomas John Holguin 42242 Jarvis Vincent Hollingsworth 42243 Mark L. Holman 42244 Hans William Holmer 42245 Bennett Martin Holtzman 42246 Tom Gregory Hood 42247 Michael Phillip Horton 42248 Leesa Ruth House 42249 Donald William Houston 42250 Stephen T. Houston 42251 Richard Joseph Howard 42252 Robert Patrick Hoynes 42253 Dale Ernest Hudson 42254 Bryan David Hug 42255 Robert S. Hume 42256 Geoffrey Richard Hunnicutt 42257 Curtis James Hunter 42258 Gary Keith Hunter 42259 William Scott Husing 42260 Darrell James Irvin 42261 David A. Irvin 42262 Michael Dominick Isacco 42263 Susan I. Spieth 42264 Douglas Kurt Jackson 42265 Michael Lynn Jackson 42266 Ronald Jacobs 42267 Grant Arthur Jacoby 42268 John Alexander Jakub 42269 Bernard James Jansen 42270 James Robert Jennings 42271 Vanessa Jennings Weissman 42272 Jay R. Jensen 42273 James Ritchie Jezior 42274 Michel Jim William Jimerson 42275 Calvin Vernard Johnson 42276 David Wilson Johnson 42277 Eric Allan Johnson 42278 Eric T. Johnson 42279 John Peter Johnson 42280 Loren Alan Johnson 42281 Mark Allen Johnson 42282 Mark Andrew Johnson 42283 Mark D. Johnson 42284 Mark Stephen Johnson 42285 Timothy Ross Johnson 42286 David Alan Jones 42287 Leon Jones 42288 Michael Angelo Jones 42289 Peter Lincoln Jones 42290 Christopher Iwao Jose 42291 Robert Edward Kaelin 42292 Kendrick Nelson Kahler 42293 Ayron Scott Kamp 42294 Patrick F. Kane 42295 Marc Andrew Kapsalis 42296 Jeffrey John Karsonovich 42297 Francis Joseph Kaufman 42298 Mark Oliver Keeley 42299 Jacqueline Marie Keiser 42300 Edwin Clayton Keller 42301 Brian Gene Kelley 42302 Daniel Patrick Kelly 42303 Steven Everett Kelly 42304 John S. Kem 42305 William Stephen Kibler 42306 Rhonda Michelle King Harmon 42307 Robert Edward Kirkpatrick 42308 James Alfred Kitz 42309 Timothy Paul Klauck 42310 Robert Brian Kleesattel 42311 Michael Erik Klein 42312 Steven Shawn Klement 42313 Patrick F. Knapp 42314 Lisa Marie Knight 42315 John Russell Knotts 42316 David A. Knowlton 42317 Charles Joseph Koehler 42318 Robert Glen Koehler 42319 Brian Keith Kondrat 42320 Timothy Lennart Kopra 42321 William Stephen Koshansky 42322 Robert Joseph Koss 42323 Richard J. Koucheravy 42324 William Eugene Kowal 42325 Daniel Stewart Krack 42326 John Frederick Kragh 42327 Paul Christopher Krajeski 42328 David E. Krall 42329 Scott Thomas Krawczyk 42330 Dirk Van Kreunen 42331 Dennis Alan Krings 42332 Greg Thomas Kropkowski 42333 John Gerard Krupar 42334 Thomas Kelly Kruppstadt 42335 Martin Richard Kuhn 42336 Jeffry J. Kulp 42337 Gregory Walter Kuznecoff 42338 Hunchu Kwak 42339 James Graziano La-Giglia 42340 Kevin Anthony Labee 42341 Paul Joseph LaCamera 42342 James Bradford Lacey 42343 Russell Philip Lachance 42344 Morgan Mori Lamb 42345 Keith Alan Landry 42346 Charles Barnett Lane 42347 Deborah Louise Guerra 42348 Randall Charles Lane 42349 Anthony David Larson 42350 Nels-Olaf Larson 42351 John Brian Laschkewitsch 42352 Robert Paul Lasley 42353 Duane Joseph Laughlin 42354 Timothy Paul Lawrence 42355 John Henry Lawson 42356 David Allen Lee 42357 Eliot Sanghoon Lee 42358 Diane Leese Wilhelm 42359 Timothy Patrick Leonard 42360 Eugene Joseph Lesinski 42361 William Kurtis Levens 42362 Leslie Lewis Flewelling 42363 Thomas Matthew Lewis 42364 Robert Alan Ley 42365 Paul Lawrence Limpert 42366 Mary List Clermont 42367 T. Shelton Little 42368 Philip Whitney Lockett 42369 Jon Michael Lockey 42370 John Wesley Loffert 42371 Anthony Loglisci 42372 Nicholas Robert Loglisci 42373 John Joseph Lopes 42374 Carlos Manuel Lopez 42375 Andrew M. Lotwin 42376 Linda Ann Lougee 42377 Neal Todd Lovell 42378 Carl Wayne Lowe 42379 Brian Edward Lowell 42380 Eric Marc Lowy 42381 Bradley Elwyn Lucas 42382 Douglas Gerhard Lund 42383 Kathryn Louise Lunsford 42384 John Paul Lybrand 42385 Roderick James MacBride 42386 Richard Alan Machovina 42387 Anne Robbins Daugherty 42388 Scott Andrew MacPherson 42389 Vernard Clifford Madden 42390 Richard John Maffei 42391 Thomas Henry Magness 42392 Jerome J. Malczewski 42393 Charles Joseph Mallory 42394 John Joseph Malobicky 42395 Michael David Manley 42396 Penelope Manolis Johnson 42397 Tucker B. Mansager 42398 Tyrone Joseph Manzy 42399 John Robert Marafino 42400 Vincent Robert Marchionni 42401 Kim Alan Marcyes 42402 Bryan Keith Market 42403 Christopher Warner Markwood 42404 Thor Tristan Markwood 42405 Steven John Marquardt 42406 John Frederick Marriott 42407 Jacqueline Marshall Baptiste 42408 Andrew Newton Martin 42409 Brian Patrick Martin 42410 William Edwin Martin 42411 Luis Martinez 42412 Kim Joseph Martini 42413 Michael Edward Mason 42414 Pierre Edward Massar 42415 Nick Mastrovito 42416 Church Myall Matthews 42417 Phillip Nelson Maxwell 42418 Mark Elmer May 42419 Wylie Henry May 42420 Garrett John McAvoy 42421 Charles Arthur McCaffrey 42422 Michael Dennis McCain 42423 John Martin McCarthy 42424 Jamie McCloud Perez 42425 Kevin Arthur McCoy 42426 Vincent A. McDermott 42427 Sean Daniel McDevitt 42428 Kenneth William McDonald 42429 William Eric McDow 42430 John F. McFassel 42431 Mitchell Gerald McGee 42432 Patrick Michael McGerty 42433 Michael Sean McGurk 42434 William Kermit McKelvy 42435 Paul Joseph McKittrick 42436 Michael Jerome McMahon 42437 Christopher Paul McPadden 42438 Robert Francis Meier 42439 Curd Juergen Meine 42440 Sibylla Meine Albertson 42441 Angela M. Messer 42442 Dan M. Milanesa 42443 Kevin Frank Miles 42444 Fredrick Duane Miller 42445 Michael Eugene Miller 42446 Raymond Mark Porter Miller 42447 Scott Alan Milliren 42448 Kent Gale Milner 42449 Michael David Miscoe 42450 Daniel Garrett Mitchell 42451 Jennifer Joan Moehringer 42452 Keith Scott Moir 42453 Timothy Patrick Monahan 42454 John Willard Montgomery 42455 Michael Edward Montoya 42456 John Preston Moore 42457 Kevin Duval Moore 42458 Judith R. Shownkeen 42459 Maria Arcelia Moreno 42460 Michelle Morin Roth 42461 John S. Morris 42462 Peter Morrissey 42463 Andrew Joseph Morrow 42464 David John Motz 42465 Jeffrey Alan Mrochek 42466 John Joseph Muller 42467 Charles Hugh Murdock 42468 Darryl G. Murdock 42469 Marlin Dale Murphy 42470 David Owen Myers 42471 Carl Robert Nank 42472 Paul N. Nasi 42473 Blake Warren Nelson 42474 Michael Herbert Newsome 42475 Jean Q. Nguyen 42476 Timothy Alan Nielsen 42477 William Paul Nikonchuk 42478 Steven Peter Nixon 42479 James Michael Nolen 42480 Richard Daniel O'Brien 42481 Thomas Peter Ockenfels 42482 Richard Allen Oleksyk 42483 Vincent Henry O'Neil 42484 Douglas R. Orr 42485 Paul A. Ostrowski 42486 Patrick J. O'Sullivan 42487 Francoise Yoko Otey Gamble 42488 Charles Emmett Overbeck 42489 Charles J. Packard 42490 David Anders Paddock 42491 Chris Harold Palmer 42492 Daniel Malcolm Parietti 42493 Helene Mary Parker 42494 Richard Arthur Parker 42495 Jeffrey Gerard Parow 42496 Jeffrey Jay Parrish 42497 Michael D. Parrish 42498 William Arthur Parshall 42499 Michael H. Pasco 42500 Bruce Allen Patrick 42501 John Paul Patrick 42502 Ivan Noe Pawlowicz 42503 Gregory William Pearce 42504 George Christopher Penrod 42505 Matthew Frank Peretin 42506 Peter Joseph Perez 42507 Brett Thomas Perry 42508 Michael Nicholas Perry 42509 Thomas Perry 42510 David Michael Persselin 42511 Robert Dean Peterson 42512 Terence Eugene Peterson 42513 Timothy Mark Petit 42514 John David Phee 42515 Richard T. Phillips 42516 Ron Paul Pierce 42517 David Lee Pierson 42518 Michael Frank Pigozzo 42519 Jeffrey Allen Pike 42520 Damian James Pillatzke 42521 Samuel Thelmon Piper 42522 Kenneth Alan Pitts 42523 Vernon Chester Plack 42524 Jeffrey John Plank 42525 Kenneth Elijah Poinsette 42526 Robert Barrett Polk 42527 Christopher John Porras 42528 Thomas Cash Powell 42529 Thomas Lee Price 42530 Vincent Lee Price 42531 John Ethan Pritchard 42532 David Andrew Prugh 42533 Ivan Dale Puett 42534 Luis Enrique Puig 42535 Andrew John Pytel 42536 John E. Quackenbush 42537 William J. Quigley 42538 Charles Walter Quinn 42539 Robert C. Quinn 42540 Rollie Francis Quinn 42541 Romulo Quintos 42542 William Thomas Rabbitt 42543 Jose Michael Ramos 42544 James Edward Ramsey 42545 Brian Thomas Rapavy 42546 Shawn Allan Rasmussen 42547 Michael Anthony Rave 42548 John Marcus Ray 42549 Kristin L. Fuhr 42550 David Nicholas Reding 42551 Ronald Ray Reichart 42552 Paul Gregory Reiland 42553 Christopher Edmund Reimer 42554 Richard Darr Reimers 42555 Brad David Reuben 42556 David Alfred Reynolds 42557 Louis Clifford Rhodes 42558 Richard Thomas Ricci 42559 James Edward Rice 42560 William Anson Rice 42561 Timothy John Riehl 42562 David Alan Risler 42563 Daniel James Rizika 42564 David James Rizzo 42565 John Carter Robinson 42566 Keith Wayne Robinson 42567 Tasha Lyn Williams 42568 Christopher E. Rodney 42569 Paul James Rodney 42570 Leo V. Rodriguez 42571 Wilfred Rodriguez 42572 Patrick Findley Roemer 42573 Scott Gilbert Roesler 42574 Steven Michael Roesler 42575 Vanessa Ann Roesler 42576 Charles Buddy Rogers 42577 Dawne M. Davis 42578 Darlene Marie Wilson 42579 Douglas Harlan Rombough 42580 Eric Roland Romero 42581 John Patrick Roney 42582 Margaret Ada Roosma 42583 Beverly Ursula Durham 42584 Randolph Edmond Rosin 42585 John Y. Crawford Roth 42586 Randolph Richard Rotte 42587 Keith Michael Rowand 42588 Daniel Seth Roy 42589 Michael S.J. Rubitski 42590 Kevin David Ruddell 42591 William Matthew Rudnicki 42592 Jamie Ann Ruffing 42593 Katherine Ryan Derrick 42594 Ronald Albert Rynne 42595 Jeff McCleskey Ryscavage 42596 John Richard Ryther 42597 Tracy Sager Seymour 42598 Stephen John Sak 42599 John Mark Salazar 42600 Jay Michael Sams 42601 Rudolph St. Peter D. Samuel 42602 Thomas Bernard Sanborn 42603 Richard John Sands 42604 Juan Diego Sans 42605 Mickey Anthony Sanzotta 42606 Francis M. Saporito 42607 John Francis Sarkis 42608 Bradley Richard Sartor 42609 Nathan Mark Sassaman 42610 Frederick Satkowiak 42611 Dale Russel Savary 42612 James Edward Scarlett 42613 Louis Robert Schilling 42614 Bernd Friedrich Schliemann 42615 Mark Michael Schneider 42616 Michael Leonard Schodowski 42617 Christopher Porter Schoff 42618 Jeffrey Lyle Schroeder 42619 Harry J. Schute 42620 Randal A. Schwallie 42621 Michael Harris Sears 42622 Scott David Seeley 42623 Ernest C. Segundo 42624 Jon Alan Seitz 42625 Kent Ryan Selby 42626 Terry Lee Sellers 42627 Douglas David Sena 42628 Glenn Graham Seymour 42629 John Shakarjian 42630 Dennis John Shanahan 42631 William Jacob Sharbaugh 42632 John David Shaw 42633 Catherine Alison Shea 42634 Deane Anthony Shephard 42635 Joe Houser Shockcor 42636 Karen Elisabeth Short 42637 Peter George Short 42638 Susan K. Green 42639 Robert William Silver 42640 Robert John Sinnema 42641 Thomas Siomades 42642 Christopher John Skinner 42643 Sherry Alysine Slaughter Waters 42644 Christopher F. Smith 42645 Randy Smith 42646 Kevin Andre Smith 42647 Kevin Lee Smith 42648 Robert Edward Smith 42649 Rodney Damon Smith 42650 Brian Joseph Snarzyk 42651 R. Karson J. Snyder 42652 William M. Solms 42653 Timothy Joel Sommer 42654 Brett V. Sortor 42655 Jeffrey Paul Sottak 42656 Kevin Paul Spala 42657 David Lavern Spear 42658 Linda Jane Malczewski 42659 Martha Robinson Hogan 42660 Mary Elizabeth Spellman 42661 Douglas Arnold Sperandio 42662 Thomas Francis Stacey 42663 David Charles Stader 42664 Matthew Wilson Stanley 42665 William Joseph Stanton 42666 Wayne Thomas Starrs 42667 Michael John Staver 42668 Timothy J. Steinagle 42669 James Francis Stenson 42670 Victor Speight Stephenson 42671 Douglas Ross Stewart 42672 James Edward Stewart 42673 Lisa Stewart Glen 42674 William Russell Stewart 42675 Mark Steven Stich 42676 Michael Charles Stimson 42677 Lori Ann Wilson 42678 Michael F. Stollenwerk 42679 Michael Peter Stoneham 42680 Andrew Streznewski 42681 Cynthia Marie Strobel 42682 Todd Brian Strubbe 42683 Anthony J. Studebaker

42684 Melissa Ann Sturgeon 42685 Timothy Sean Sughrue 42686 Daniel Paul Sullivan 42687 Joseph Martin Sullivan 42688 Scott Patrick Sullivan 42689 Timothy Frank Sullivan 42690 Michael Sean Sundgaard 42691 John Robert Surdu 42692 Geoffrey Eric Sutton 42693 Jeff B. Swisher 42694 Kurt Thomas Switala 42695 Michael Thomas Symes 42696 Kenneth Robert Tarcza 42697 Alexander Fielding Taylor 42698 Davis Forrester Taylor 42699 John Taylor 42700 Jonathan Tyrone Taylor 42701 Lorraine Taylor Withers 42702 Michael Wesley Taylor 42703 Scott Roberts Taylor 42704 Timothy Gerard Taylor 42705 Thomas Joseph Terrian 42706 Kathleen Terry 42707 Alex John Tetreault 42708 James Edwin Thiele 42709 Clifton Richard Thomas 42710 Daniel Alan Thomas 42711 Michael J. Thomas 42712 Robert Brian Thomas 42713 Allene C. Martin 42714 James Gregory Tidd 42715 Danny A. Tidwell 42716 Edwin Ronald Tifre 42717 John Barry Todd 42718 Kurt Tolivaisa 42719 James I. Tolsma 42720 William David Tompkins 42721 Curt L. Torrence 42722 Joseph David Torrence 42723 Aniello Louis Tortora 42724 Vincent Peter Toscano 42725 Tommy James Tracy 42726 Douglas George Trapani 42727 Mark Trawinski 42728 Raymond Darren Trent 42729 Lelia B. True 42730 James G. Truesdell 42731 James Robert Tully 42732 Calvin Patrick Turns 42733 Ross William Turrini 42734 Francis James Twarog 42735 Robert James Ulses 42736 Philip Edwin VanWiltenburg 42737 Dennis Juan Vazquez 42738 Roberto Lewis Vazquez 42739 Louis Anthony Vellucci 42740 Frank William Vetter 42741 Vanessa M. Swisher 42742 Enrique Francis Villalba 42743 Paul Anthony Vitagliano 42744 Thomas Edward Vossman 42745 Hung Vu 42746 Keith Charles Wagner 42747 Russell James Wagner 42748 John Mark Waite 42749 Robert John Waldo 42750 Dwayne Anthony Walker 42751 James Gerard Walker 42752 Kevin Eric Walker 42753 Virginia Ann Kiernan 42754 Michelle Lynne Walla 42755 Lisa Kay Taylor 42756 Mark Thomas Walter 42757 Todd Eugene Walter 42758 Robert John Wardlow 42759 John Matthew Warmerdam 42760 Versalle Frederick Washington 42761 M. Scott Weaver 42762 Thomas Dale Webb 42763 Lee S. Webster 42764 Alan Brian Wedgeworth 42765 Dennis John Fitzgerald Weese 42766 Shawn Luttrell Weidmann 42767 Frederick Keith Weiss 42768 Thomas Anthony Weisz 42769 A. Bryan Welch 42770 Robert Gerald Welch 42771 William Kunold Weldon 42772 Scott C. Weliver 42773 Gregory Martin Wellman 42774 Mark Matthew Wescott 42775 Todd Hampton Wesson 42776 Scott James Weston 42777 Robert E. Weyand 42778 John Calvin Wheeler 42779 William Wade Wheeler 42780 Ed White 42781 Jeffrey Roberts White 42782 Douglass Lynn Whitehead 42783 Jay Foster Wigboldy 42784 Karen Victoria Wiggins-Fair 42785 Christian James Williams 42786 Daniel Edward Williams 42787 Ellis James Williams 42788 Karl Ethan Williams 42789 Marcus Jaudon Williams 42790 Phillip Carl Williams 42791 Morgan Pryse Williamson 42792 Albert Theodore Wilson 42793 Gregory Ray Wilson 42794 Henry L. Wilson 42795 Jon P. Wilson 42796 Kevin Bernard Wilson 42797 Lorelei Wilson Coplen 42798 Robert Benjamin Wilson 42799 Roderick Rod Wilson 42800 Karl Eduard Wingenbach 42801 Warren Richard Wintrode 42802 Nathalie Margaret Wisneski 42803 David Robert Withers 42804 Steven Ray Witkowski 42805 John M. Wolf 42806 Stephanie L. Sauter 42807 Yudi Wong 42808 David Charles Wood 42809 Jennifer Wood Barnes 42810 Darryl Keith Woolfolk 42811 W. David Woolfolk 42812 Degas Anglo Wright 42813 George G. Wright 42814 Robert Stephen Wright 42815 Todd Shawn Wright 42816 Keith James Wroblewski 42817 Peter Charles Yankowski 42818 Sunny Yi 42819 Lawrence Matthew Young 42820 Thomas Brian Young 42821 Thomas Gregory Young 42822 David Allen Youngberg 42823 Thomas Zarcone 42824 Douglas Paul Zingler 42825 John Lawrence Zornick 42826 Jamie Dawn Zucker 42827 David Lawrence Zylka 42828 Christopher James Burgin 42829 Michael L. Collins 42830 Carl Derrick Corbett 42831 Gregory Phillip Desrosier 42832 John Raymond Dundas 42833 Kent Micah Green 42834 Edwin L. Hightower 42835 Melvin Jones 42836 Jansen J. Jordan 42837 Michael John Keller 42838 Eric Joseph Larsen 42839 Veronica Ann Lowery Bush 42840 Bryford Glenn Metoyer 42841 Pamela Sue Miller 42842 William Bryant Miracle 42843 Steven Anthony O'Borsky 42844 Queen Esther Peterson 42845 Tracy Andrea Pohl 42846 Dennis Gerard Schlitt 42847 John David Schumaker 42848 George Ernest Shampy 42849 Bruce Mitchell Smith 42850 Theresa Southworth LaCamera 42851 Regina Marie Stoll Korecki 42852 Thomas Martin Wilson 42853 Mark Joseph Bergen 42854 Andrew William Kerber 42855 Douglas Paul Morris 42856 James Joseph Sheils 42857 Tyrone K. Stark 42858 Michael Anthony Steen 42859 John Patrick Appleton 42860 Herman Asberry 42861 Sharon Elizabeth Baisted Jezior 42862 Martin Nicholas Baptiste 42863 Charles James Faust 42864 James Anthony Gentile 42865 Jeffrey Douglas Hall 42866 Brian Michael Hood 42867 Paul P. Howell 42868 Elaine Kempisty Rainey 42869 Gary L. Ladson 42870 Maria Dimitra Rainford 42871 Brendan Boyd McAloon 42872 Robert Thomas Myers 42873 Drew Allen O'Donnell 42874 David Glenn Powell 42875 Charles Franklin Robinson 42876 Alfred Scott 42877 Richard Frederick Steiner 42878 Christopher Caswell Zupa 42879 Richard L. Barker 42880 Terrence J. McKenrick 42881 **1986** Eric Douglas Adams 42882 Rhys Kevin Adsit 42883 Robert Anthony Albino 42884 David Richardson Alexander 42885 Jeffrey Craig Allen 42886 Curtis W. Andersen 42887 David Earl Anderson 42888 Frank Hamilton Anderson 42889 Michael Edward Anderson 42890 Tom Davis Anderson 42891 Douglas Anthony Andrews 42892 Ronald Fred Anglin 42893 Steven Thomas Antoch 42894 Patrick Michael Antonietti 42895 Patrick Robert Appleman 42896 Kevin Anthony Arbanas 42897 Thomas Oliver Archinal 42898 Mary Bridget Reynolds 42899 Rocco Anthony Armonda 42900 Theresa E. Rudacille 42901 Alan Todd Arnholt 42902 Michael Wade Arthur 42903 Yolanda E. Arts 42904 Ricanthony Rene Ashley 42905 John Thomas Atkins 42906 Mark A. Aubrey 42907 Colyn K. Bacon 42908 Victor Badami 42909 John Michael Badovinac 42910 Joel B. Bagnal 42911 William Gregory Baier 42912 Eugene Abraham Baker 42913 Steve Mitchell Balentine 42914 William Russel Balkovetz 42915 Douglas Joseph Balsbough 42916 Aniceto Domingo Bantug 42917 Michael Jay Barbee 42918 Brett A. Barraclough 42919 John S. Barrington 42920 Rhonda L. Bright 42921 William W. Basnett 42922 Samuel Judson Bass 42923 Tommie William Bates 42924 David Scott Baum 42925 James Francis Baum 42926 Jeffrey Lee Baum 42927 James Brian Baumgardner 42928 Cleveland Derrick Bazemore 42929 William Terry Beane 42930 Arthur B. Beasley 42931 Peter Brooks Bechtel 42932 Bruce Alan Beck 42933 Douglas William Bedell 42934 James Richard Belanger 42935 Edward Wayne Belcher 42936 James Carroll Bell 42937 Nicholas Vincent Bellucci 42938 Kevin Scott Belmont 42939 Sandra E. Woodfint 42940 John William Bencivenga 42941 Albert F. Beninati 42942 Kemal Ian Benouis 42943 Kirk C. Benson 42944 Michael Bertha 42945 Anne Teresa Berton 42946 Andrew Philip Bessmer 42947 Burt Alexander Biebuyck 42948 Philip Michael Biggs 42949 John S. Billie 42950 William R. Birchfield 42951 Dale B. Bisek 42952 Russell Harry Bittle 42953 Douglas Coffey Black 42954 Kenneth Crawford Blakely 42955 Gregory Scott Bleszinski 42956 Howard Lee Blevins 42957 Jonathan David Blevins 42958 George Walter Bond 42959 Vincent Carl Bons 42960 David Anthony Bonsavage 42961 Darren Kerk Booth 42962 Christopher Nelson Borgerding 42963 John Knox Born 42964 Jeffery Wayne Bost 42965 John Richard Boule 42966 Oswald Stephen Boykin 42967 Therese Boylan Bell 42968 Richard Luther Bradford 42969 Mark Kealon Bradley 42970 Stephen Dale Bradley 42971 Mary M. Brady 42972 Matthew Brady 42973 John William Brau 42974 Thomas Ulrich Brechbuhl 42975 James Stephen Breen 42976 Nicholas Richard Brent 42977 Mark F. Brick 42978 Winston Jay Keezer Bridge 42979 Myra Jane Peterson 42980 Thomas Henry Brittain 42981 David M. Britten 42982 Stephen Edward Brooks 42983 Jeffery Allen Brown 42984 John Fitzgerald Brown 42985 Todd David Brown 42986 Scott F. Bruner 42987 Jeffrey Brian Bruno 42988 Edward Lee Brunot 42989 Mark Allen Bryant 42990 James Anthony Buck 42991 Aaron Alan Buckley 42992 Matthew David Buckner 42993 Brian Joseph Bulatao 42994 Robert Lee Bullard 42995 Christopher Todd Bump 42996 Andy Kyle Bunn 42997 Keith Norman Burnham 42998 Gregory Kenneth Butts 42999 Richard Michael Cabrey 43000 John Michael Callahan 43001 Terence Robert Callahan 43002 Charlotte Hallengren 43003 Dennis Lenore Calloway 43004 Tedson James Campagna 43005 John Lewis Cannon 43006 Stephen Craig Cannon 43007 Steven Randolph Cannon 43008 Gregory Lee Canter 43009 Duane Elliott Cantey 43010 Louis Joseph Capezzuto 43011 Steven G. J. Cardin 43012 Laura Carew Loftus 43013 Bruce Futoshi Carniglia 43014 Forrest Lee Carpenter 43015 Scott Anthony Carr 43016 Kenneth George Carrick 43017 Roger D. Carstens 43018 Richard Lewis Carter 43019 Thomas Edward Cartledge 43020 Robert James Carty 43021 James Robert Casey 43022 Matthew Damian Cashin 43023 Charles Edwin Cavin 43024 Scott Stephen Chaisson 43025 Benjamin Chambers 43026 Wendell M. Champion 43027 James Scott Chapel 43028 David William Chaplin 43029 Daniel Joseph Charron 43030 Christopher Paul Chiarello 43031 Willie James Childs 43032 Michael Kwan Lee Chinn 43033 Fredrick Seok Choi 43034 Michael Carl Chopp 43035 Matthew D. Christ 43036 James Tully Clancy 43037 Christopher Terrell Clark 43038 Curt James Clark 43039 Harley Walter Clark 43040 Linda Jo Clark 43041 Harris Grant Clarke 43042 Cary Grayson Clayborn 43043 Dale Douglas Cleland 43044 Ross Miner Clemons 43045 Charles Thomas Climer 43046 Mark Bigford Coats 43047 Christopher Cole 43048 Craig Arthur Collier 43049 Michell Loree Collins 43050 Edward M. Columbus 43051 Patrick Rowan Connelly 43052 Glenn Michael Connor 43053 Mark Perry Connor 43054 Eric Robert Paul Conrad 43055 Mark Frenn Conroe 43056 Maryellen Conway Picciuto 43057 William Wade Cook 43058 Byron Willie Cooper 43059 Richard Weber Cornman 43060 John Matthew Corsi 43061 Neil Francis Costello 43062 Wanda M. Costen 43063 Craig Donald Cotter 43064 Roger David Cotton 43065 David Paul Courtoglous 43066 James Henry Crawford 43067 William Patrick Creeden 43068 Joseph Powell Creekmore 43069 Cynthia Dianne Crenshaw 43070 Chad Edward Creveling 43071 Edward Hawksley Cummings 43072 Steven Francis Cummings 43073 Gerard Patrick Curran 43074 Michael Joseph Curran 43075 Michael Lance Curry 43076 Howard Zoll Curtis 43077 Kenneth Scott Curtis 43078 Charles Bancroft Cushman 43079 Patrick R. Cusick 43080 Patrick Daly 43081 Daniel Steven D'Amico 43082 Bruce Jay Davis 43083 Charles Edward Davis 43084 Sharri Janell Davis 43085 Steven Michael Davis 43086 Tanya Lynn Davis 43087 Thomas Earl Davis 43088 John Wesley Day 43089 Richard Alan Day 43090 Thomas Frank DeFilippo 43091 Ramon Caragnan DeLeon 43092 Jesus Humberto Delgado-Jenkins 43093 Julie Annette Del Giorno 43094 Terrence Patrick DeLong 43095 Andrew David Dempsey 43096 Joseph Michael DePinto 43097 David Brian Des Roches 43098 Lisa Diciro Baca 43099 Darcy Lynn Dierks Good 43100 David F. Dimeo 43101 James Fred Di Orio 43102 Barry Santi Di Ruzza 43103 Michael Durer Dishman 43104 Mark Christopher DiTrolio 43105 Craig Thomas Doescher 43106 Joseph Paul Dole 43107 Gary David Domke 43108 Randall Evan Donaldson 43109 Scott Eugene Donaldson 43110 Hope Blanche Donnelly 43111 George Thomas Donovan 43112 Sean Paul Donovan 43113 Dean Edward Dorman 43114 Edward William Dougherty 43115 Robert Lynn Douthit 43116 Shane Keefe Downey 43117 Robert M. Dowse 43118 Wayne Brendan Doyle 43119 Kevin Todd Drevik 43120 Brian M. Drinkwine 43121 Leighton Scott Drisdale 43122 Llewellyn Fogel Dryfoos 43123 William D. Duke 43124 Jeffrey Allan Duncan 43125 Todd Justin Dunlap 43126 Chester F. Dymek 43127 Patrick Thomas Echols 43128 Robert James Eckelbarger 43129 Michael Paul Eddy 43130 Keevin Bernard Edwards 43131 Brian John Egeling 43132 Andrew C. Eger 43133 Andrew Steven Eiseman 43134 Carolyn E. Elliot-Ingham 43135 Joseph Matthew Elliott 43136 Joshua Marvel Elliott 43137 Robert Eugene Elliott 43138 Steven Robert Elliott 43139 Michael Delane Ellis 43140 Douglas Stewart Elmore 43141 Michael Tracey Endres 43142 Gregory James Enochs 43143 Phyllis Erkins White 43144 Mark Thomas Esper 43145 Stephen Charles Ethen 43146 Tod Steven Etheredge 43147 Orel Michael Everett 43148 Dale Stuart Fakkema 43149 John Hall Farley 43150 Kevin W. Farrell 43151 James Fasone 43152 Timothy Allen Faulkner 43153 Bruce Wayne Fauth 43154 Peter James Feeney 43155 Benjamin Rudolph Felts 43156 Gregory Paul Fenton 43157 Michael Scott Ferrier 43158 Linda L. Fetko 43159 Robert C. Field 43160 Terrence Patrick Finley 43161 Mark Donald Fisher 43162 Gregory Paul Fitzharris 43163 Michael Patrick Flanagan 43164 Timothy Flanagan 43165 Lorie Fleming Blount 43166 David Charles Flint 43167 Franklin Snider Flowers 43168 Charles Nicholas Fluekiger 43169 Robert Kent Fogtman 43170 Brett Douglas Folse 43171 Joan Marie Close 43172 Robin Louise Fontes 43173 Timothy Ray Ford 43174 Matthew John Fortunato 43175 Kevin Lee Foster 43176 Thomas M. Fowler 43177 David Nelson Fralen 43178 Neal Owen Freeman 43179 Richard L. French 43180 Edward George Froelich 43181 Ronald Dewayne Frost 43182 Peter Richard Fuenfhausen 43183 Brian Paul Fues 43184 David V. Fulton 43185 David Edward Funk 43186 Richard Jose Gabaldon 43187 Bruce John Gagne 43188 Eric A. Gaines 43189 David Stanley Galloway 43190 Stephen Stanley Galloway 43191 Michael Dennis Garcia 43192 Paul Webb Garland 43193 Aubrey Lee Garner 43194 Leanne Marie Schiffer 43195 Loretta Garrigan Craig 43196 Patrick Michael Gavin 43197 James Dorsey George 43198 Scott Allen Gerig 43199 Mark Daniel Gibbons 43200 Marilyn M. Shazor 43201 James Salvador Gigrich 43202 Thomas Curtis Gilchrist 43203 Todd Alan Gile 43204 Kirk Lee Gill 43205 Alfred Lawrence Glaeser 43206 Randy Lee Glaeser 43207 Joseph Martin Gleeson 43208 Alyson Ann Goermar 43209 Jerome Charles Goodrich 43210 Michael Clair Goodridge 43211 David Michael Gordon 43212 Dana Edward Goulette 43213 Walter Lee Grandberry 43214 Thomas Christopher Graves 43215 Jonathan Blaine Green 43216 Mark Edward Green 43217 Dennis Gordon Greenwood 43218 Christopher Alan Greer 43219 Dixon Grant Greffey 43220 James Patrick Griffen 43221 Paul Jones Groce 43222 John Ford Groeschner 43223 Richard William Gronemeyer 43224 Donald Lee Groom 43225 Don Charles Guggemos 43226 Ronald P. Guiao 43227 Thomas Edward Guleff 43228 Douglas Brian Gurian 43229 Kurt Patrick Gutierrez 43230 Jonathan Connor Guy 43231 Daniel Allen Guzman 43232 Anthony John Guzzi 43233 Daniel Joseph Gwynn 43234 Michael Joseph Gwynn 43235 Molly Hagan Root 43236 Darwin L. Haines 43237 Thomas Samuel Haislop 43238 Jeffrey T. Hajduk 43239 Vivian Haley Glaeser 43240 Kathryn Ruth Hall 43241 Rex Edmund Hall 43242 John Brantley Halstead 43243 James Ethan Hamby 43244 Michael Kevin Hanifan 43245 Jeffrey Alan Hanko 43246 Theodore Ryan Hanley 43247 Christine Anne Hansen 43248 Craig Wilson Harlow 43249 David M. Harmon 43250 John Leonard Harnois 43251 Marc Damond Harris 43252 David Joseph Hartley 43253 Robert G. Hartley 43254 John M. Harwig 43255 Warren Everett Hauert 43256 Keith Bradley Hauk 43257 Michael Andrew Haydak 43258 William Scott Hays 43259 Robert Harry Hazen 43260 Robert Patrick Healy 43261 Lawrence Robert Heckel 43262 Timothy James Hein 43263 Joseph Lon Helmick 43264 Eve H. Tuset 43265 Michael Arthur Henderson 43266 Alan Aden Hendricks 43267 Edwin Steven Hendricks 43268 William Roger Hensley 43269 James Floyd Herron 43270 Graydon William Hicks 43271 Michael Simeon Higginbottom 43272 Richard Claude Higley 43273 Lloyd Jefferson Hill 43274 Matthew S. Hinkle 43275 Stephen Ernest Hitz 43276 John Andrew Hluck 43277 Ronald Kevin Hocker 43278 Joel E. Hodge 43279 Thomas A. Hoenstine 43280 Jud Hoff 43281 Daniel Robert Hokanson 43282 Thomas Gregory Hood 43283 Michael Francis Hoskinson 43284 Paul Jon Houge 43285 Christopher Edward Houseman 43286 David Ross Houston 43287 James Alex Howard 43288 Joe Garrett Howard 43289 Patrick Robert Hoyes 43290 James Edward Hoyt 43291 James Hradecky 43292 David Alan Hudock 43293 Kevin L. Huggins 43294 Lawrence Garfield Hughes 43295 Wendell Carol Hull 43296 Paul George Humphreys 43297 Kristopher Martin Hurst 43298 Anthony Charles Hylton 43299 Matthew William Igel 43300 Damon Leon Igou 43301 Lewis Gerald Irwin 43302 Cynthia M. Sauer 43303 Mark A. Iverson 43304 Darin Shawn Jackson 43305 Thurman Hinson Jackson 43306 David Charles Jacoppo 43307 Terry Mitchell James 43308 Jose Rene N. Jarque 43309 Howard Scott Jeffries 43310 James Herman Jenkins 43311 Donald Edward Johantges 43312 Beverly D. Johnson 43313 David Sanford Johnson 43314 James Houston Johnson 43315 Mark W. Johnson 43316 Royce Emanuel Johnson 43317 Howard Alan Johnston 43318 Ted E. Johnston 43319 Douglas Samuel Jones 43320 Jack R. Jones 43321 Jeffrey Glen Jones 43322 Wade Randall Jost 43323 Jaimy Susanna Just Rand 43324 Stephen John Kaczmarek 43325 Paul D. Kapsner 43326 William Stanley Kearney 43327 Barry Forde Kellar 43328 Richard Todd Kellar 43329 Caroline Ward Keller 43330 Philip Andrew Keller 43331 John Patrick Kelley 43332 Paul Timothy Kelley 43333 Thomas Aquinas Kelley 43334 Timothy Michael Kelley 43335 Kevin Joseph Kelly 43336 Sean Kenna 43337 Frank Melvin Kennedy 43338 Dennis Charles Kibby 43339 Richard Goodwin Kidd 43340 Verner Michael Kiernan 43341 Richard Killian 43342 David Faron Kilpatrick 43343 Patrick James Kilroy 43344 James Chan-Ho Kim 43345 Peter Yubin Inokoji-Kim 43346 Kevin Andrew Kimzey 43347 Mary Brandt Kinder 43348 Elaina King Hajduk 43349 William Parker King 43350 Walter John Kleinfelder 43351 Robert Charles Kleinhample 43352 Kristin Knapp French 43353 John Thomas Knier 43354 Timothy Alan Knight 43355 Roger Brian Knowles 43356 Reinhard Wolfram Koenig 43357 Richard Stephen Kolpasky 43358 Michael Fredrick Kommer 43359 Michael George Kosalko 43360 Theodore Michael Kostich 43361 David John Kozuch 43362 Robert Carl Krall 43363 David Timothy Kramer 43364 Wayne John Kropp 43365 Peter Andreas Kuring 43366 Christopher Douglas Kurkowski 43367 Landon Gilbert Lack 43368 Mark Edward LaDu 43369 Paul K. LaFontaine 43370 Tye Mallory Lageman 43371 Benjamin Shane Lambert 43372 John P. Landgraf 43373 Richard Edward Lange 43374 Kevin W. Lanham 43375 Kelly Gerard LaPorte 43376 Larry Robert Larimer 43377 James Eldon Larsen 43378 Wilma I. Larsen 43379 Mark Eugene Lassiter 43380 Kevin Scott Lauterjung 43381 John Matthew Lazar 43382 Jeffrey Arnold Leach 43383 Martin Gary Leal 43384 Kevin Lech 43385 Donna Lee Ariyoshi 43386 Mark Melvin Lee 43387 Michael Jason Lee 43388 James Peter Leise 43389 Michael J. Lemanski 43390 Mark Adrian Levesque 43391 David Alan Ley 43392 Elizabeth Anne Lind 43393 Greg Allen Lind 43394 Duane Allen Linenkugel 43395 Racheau Douglas Lipscomb 43396 Donald Gene Lobeda 43397 George Eugene Loche 43398 Ralph Charles Locke 43399 Robert F. Lockett 43400 Wayne Martin Locklin 43401 Andrew Philip Lombardo 43402 Lance David Lombardo 43403 Darold Joseph Londo 43404 Michael Emil Lonigro 43405 Victor Lee Losure 43406 Robert Thomas Lott 43407 David Stuart Lowe 43408 Douglas Arthur Luehe 43409 Charles Jake Luigs 43410 Mark William Lukens 43411 Eric Thomas Lund 43412 Rodney Leigh Lusher 43413 John Patrick Lynch 43414 Darryl Mark MacDonald 43415 Ann A. Brechbuhl 43416 Charles Allen MacMaster 43417 Joseph Robert Macrina 43418 Kurt Laurence Maggio 43419 John Michael Magness 43420 Michele Marie Barlean 43421 Raymond Joseph Maier 43422 Clifford Fulton Mainor 43423 Frederick Robert Maiocco 43424 Thomas C. Malloy 43425 John Edward Maloney 43426 Ranelle Agtarap Manaois 43427 Fred Vincent Manzo 43428 Raffi Paul Maranian 43429 Ernest Patrick Marcone 43430 John Joseph Markovich 43431 Paul Christopher Marks 43432 Price Hendricks Marr 43433 Ronald M. Marsh 43434 Todd Dennis Marsh 43435 James Paul Marshall 43436 Joseph M. Martin 43437 Steven James Martin 43438 Richard Edwin Martinez 43439 Victor Francis Maslak 43440 William Ross Mason 43441 Norman C. Massry 43442 James Vincent Matheson 43443 Peter Joseph Mattes 43444 Albert Thomas Maxwell 43445 Willis Richard

McAdams 43446 James Michael McAllister 43447 Todd Bullard McCaffrey 43448 Thomas Shane McCann 43449 William David McCarley 43450 Stephen George McCarty 43451 Timothy Francis McConvery 43452 Mark Allen McCoy 43453 P. McDermott Ryan 43454 Johanna Kathryn Elgin 43455 Douglas Mark McDowell 43456 Michael Boyd McDuffie 43457 Brian Stuart McFadden 43458 Michael Leo McGinn 43459 Brian E. McGowan 43460 John Michael McHugh 43461 John Randall McIlhaney 43462 Kevin Wayne McKelvy 43463 Michael Lewis McKinney 43464 Kaye McKinzie 43465 Alan Dennis McKirby 43466 Balvin Anthony McKnight 43467 Charles James McLaughlin 43468 Lynn McNames Johnson 43469 Patricia Medina Booth 43470 William Meehan 43471 Patricia Melcher Davies 43472 Garry Robert Melia 43473 Derrick Alan Mellberg 43474 Steven M. Merkel 43475 Mark Christian Merritt 43476 David Brian Mesick 43477 Brian F. Metcalf 43478 David Christopher R. Meyer 43479 Mark Andrew Michaelsen 43480 Jonathan Arthur Millen 43481 Dana David Milner 43482 Richard Michael Minicozzi 43483 John Mark Mitchell 43484 Laurence Martin Mixon 43485 Thomas Oliver Monahan 43486 Stephen P. Moniz 43487 Dexter Bernard Monroe 43488 Darren Michael Moore 43489 Kevin Alan Moore 43490 Edward H. Moran 43491 Patrick James Moran 43492 James Dean Morris 43493 Joseph Thomas Morris 43494 Charles Patrick Moses 43495 Edward Todd Motley 43496 Mark A. Moulton 43497 Marc Adrian Moyer 43498 John Julian Mulbury 43499 Michael Anthony Munoz 43500 William Francis Murphy 43501 Charles Shawn Murray 43502 Leslie James Murray 43503 Michael Francis Murray 43504 Robert Alton Nabb 43505 Dean Takema Nakadate 43506 Andre Antonio Napoli 43507 Bruce Lamar Nelson 43508 David Eugene Nelson 43509 Michael Richard Nelson 43510 Robert A. Ness 43511 Rodney C. Neudecker 43512 Miyako Newell Schanely 43513 Eric Newman 43514 Walter Keith Nichols 43515 James Dan Nickolas 43516 John William Noble 43517 William F. Noble 43518 Frederick John Nohmer 43519 Leonard Joseph Novak 43520 Erin R. Batt 43521 Kathryn Marie O'Brien Hall 43522 Maura A. Gillen 43523 Thomas Leighton O'Brien 43524 Raymond Ernest Obst 43525 Gerald Patrick O'Connor 43526 Patrick Michael O'Connor 43527 Michael Gerard O'Dea 43528 Von Graham Odenwald 43529 Thomas Bruce O'Driscoll 43530 Richard Allen O'Hare 43531 Scott J. Okesson 43532 Clay Olbon 43533 Michael Stephen O'Leary 43534 Van Charles Oler 43535 Lawrence Robert Oliver 43536 Bruce Warren Ollstein 43537 Stanley Bell Olson 43538 John Taylor Olvey 43539 Andrew John Ornatowski 43540 James Francis Orner 43541 Laurence Gregory Ortiz 43542 Gregory Allen Palka 43543 Kent Gregory Pankratz 43544 Steven Daniel Parker 43545 Bryan Scott Parlier 43546 Richard Wayne Pascoe 43547 Edward Francis Pasquina 43548 Douglas Joseph Pavek 43549 Matthew Peter Pawlikowski 43550 Gerald Michael Pearman 43551 Pamela D. Pearson 43552 Wendy Sue Coddington 43553 Mark Daniel Peasley 43554 David James Pekarek 43555 Robert John Peller 43556 Robert George Penna 43557 Donald Raymond Peperak 43558 Scott Leon Pepple 43559 Paul Gonzalo Pereira 43560 Felix Manuel Perez 43561 Broc Alan Perkuchin 43562 Gregory Stephen Perrotta 43563 Barry Norris Peterson 43564 Jody Lynn Petery 43565 Karen S. Phelps 43566 Elliott O. Phillips 43567 Dalton S. Pierce 43568 Scott Cory Pierce 43569 James Charles Piggott 43570 Edgar Herbert Pigott 43571 David Anthony Pinder 43572 Robert Walter Pitulej 43573 Bret Rexford Platt 43574 R. Scott Poirier 43575 Clark T. Poland 43576 Robert Lee Pollard 43577 Michael Richard Pompeo 43578 John Robert Poncy 43579 Joseph Robert Posusney 43580 Kristin Michelle Powell Thomas 43581 Glenn Robert Powers 43582 David Walden Pratt 43583 Michael John Preuss 43584 Douglas Patrick Prevost 43585 Jesus Alfonso Prieto 43586 Scott Kenric Prihoda 43587 Matthew Joseph Pruden 43588 Andrew Dela Rosa Pullenza 43589 La Von Rochelle Purnell 43590 William Lee Pursel 43591 James Walter Quaider 43592 Leopoldo Aquino Quintas 43593 Keith Alan Raines 43594 Keith W. Ramsey 43595 Edwin Bruce Randolph 43596 Patrick David Reardon 43597 John James Recke 43598 Christopher Douglas Reed 43599 Michael Thomas Reed 43600 David Michael Regan 43601 Daniel Jeffery Regna 43602 Sam Jeffery Reider 43603 Christopher D. Reilly 43604 Jonathan Thomas Reinebold 43605 Elaine Ruth Reinhard 43606 Hugh William Rhodes 43607 Ronald Jerry Rice 43608 Clifford Richardson 43609 Kenneth Elton Ring 43610 Daniel Francis Rizzo 43611 David Alan Roberts 43612 Ruben A. Robles 43613 Jonathan David Rodden 43614 Daniel J. Rodstrom 43615 James Paul Rogers 43616 Warren Dean Rogers 43617 Robert Richard Roggeman 43618 Craig Chadwick Rollins 43619 Michael Kevin Root 43620 John Wesley Roper 43621 Troy Wayne Roper 43622 Peter A. Rosen 43623 Matthew Romolo Rotella 43624 Bridget Marie Rourke 43625 Bryan L. Rudacille 43626 Paul Vincent Rush 43627 Robert M. Rush 43628 Matthew John Russo 43629 David Leonard Rutherford 43630 William Emmett Ryan 43631 Steven Sabia 43632 Robert William Sadowski 43633 James Andrew Saldivar 43634 Brian Andrew Samela 43635 Roger N. Sangvic 43636 Mark Todd Santarelli 43637 Gerald Sarnelli 43638 James Joseph Saso 43639 Scott Michael Sauer 43640 Daniel Patrick Sauter 43641 Thomas Edward Sawyer 43642 Michael Thomas Scanlin 43643 Eric O. Schacht 43644 Daniel Adair Schafer 43645 Joseph Hughes Schafer 43646 Mark Derryl Schake 43647 Jeffrey Brian Schamburg 43648 Eric Barclay Scheidemantel 43649 Robert Frederick Scheider 43650 Alfred Edwin Schellhorn 43651 Richard A. Schemel 43652 Mark Alan Schemine 43653 Chris Robert Schiavo 43654 Therese G. Schiffer Brehm 43655 William Michael Schiffer 43656 Joel Benjamin Schlachtenhaufen 43657 Beth Schleeter Ferrier 43658 V. Glenn Schoonover 43659 Daniel Robert Schultz 43660 Jill Ellen Schurtz 43661 Scott Schutzmeister 43662 Brent C. Schvaneveldt 43663 Gerard Louis Schwartz 43664 John R. Schwartz 43665 Gordon Anthony Scott 43666 Richard Ervin Scott 43667 Lawrence Paul Seaberg 43668 William Searcy 43669 Albert Nelson Sebright 43670 Daniel Christopher Selph 43671 James Frederick Seramba 43672 David Graham Seymour 43673 Terrence Anthony Shamblin 43674 Thomas Carter Sharp 43675 Richard Louis Shelton 43676 George Thatcher Shepard 43677 Monica M. McMillan 43678 Debra F. Shoemaker 43679 Brian P. Shoop 43680 Stephen J. Sicinski 43681 Alan Lawrence Simmons 43682 Robert Mark Simmons 43683 Emry Petering Sisson 43684 Joseph B. Skarupinski 43685 Anthony Joseph Skubi 43686 Steven A. Sliwa 43687 Donald Eugene Smith 43688 Eugene Daryl Smith 43689 Frederica S. Houston 43690 George Alfred Smith 43691 George Sidney Smith 43692 James Henry Smith 43693 Joel Keith Smith 43694 Lee Charles Smith 43695 Marielle E. Martin 43696 Michael Darren Smith 43697 Stephen Joseph Smith 43698 Thomas Joseph Smith 43699 Brian Anthony Snell 43700 Karl Edward Snyder 43701 Kelly J. Snyder 43702 James John Solano 43703 Kurt Lee Sonntag 43704 Anthony Francis Souza 43705 Jill Spangler Reilly 43706 Carolyn A. Spaulding-Wright 43707 Russell Bradford Spears 43708 Scott A. Spellmon 43709 Michael Sean Spingler 43710 Josef Wilkin Spudich 43711 Norman Ray Spurlock 43712 Michael Spurr 43713 Matthew Meacom Stanton 43714 Dustin Michael Starbuck 43715 Pernell Norman Staudt 43716 Troy Dewayne Stebbins 43717 Kevin Paul Steele 43718 Timothy Howard Steele 43719 Stephen J. Steffes 43720 Stephanie Lyn Stephens 43721 Katherine Anne Stewart 43722 Lori Stokan Stokan 43723 Steven Walter Stone 43724 Craig James Stopa 43725 Russell Louis Storms 43726 John Michael Stradinger 43727 Robert William Straub 43728 Frances Denise Strebeck-Pennington 43729 Daniel Charles Stredler 43730 Jon Erik Strickler 43731 Steven Wayne Strifler 43732 Bryan D. Strong 43733 Carrie Marlene Stroup 43734 Elizabeth Anne Wood 43735 Kent Matthew Stueve 43736 Rodney Xerxes Sturdivant 43737 Michael Sven Sturgeon 43738 Joseph Herbert Sullivan 43739 John Hayworth Sutton 43740 Brian P. Sweeney 43741 Michael Robert Switzer 43742 Thomas Gerard Szoka 43743 Curt A. Szuberla 43744 David Anthony Tafares 43745 Karl William Tappert 43746 Marc Andrew Taylor 43747 Thomas Randolph Telthorst 43748 David A. Thelen 43749 David Glenn Thomas 43750 Dawn Thomas Jeffries 43751 Jeffrey Eugene Thompson 43752 Mark William Thompson 43753 John Charles Thomson 43754 Harkley Runyan Thornton 43755 Jeffrey John Thramann 43756 Christopher Lawrence Tierney 43757 Christopher Brian Timmer 43758 Mark A. Tolmachoff 43759 Todd Fitzgerald Tolson 43760 Roy Carl Tomlinson 43761 Brien Windus Tonkinson 43762 Robert C. Townley 43763 Richard Travaglini 43764 Vincent Patrick Trollan 43765 Lawrence L. Tubbs 43766 Albert John Tumminello 43767 Karen Turner Lee 43768 William Allmond Turner 43769 Steven Earl Turpening 43770 Thomas Andrew Upp 43771 Bradley J. Upton 43772 David J. Urban 43773 Kristine Joanne Urbauer 43774 Mark Vakkur 43775 Matthew Franklin Van Kirk 43776 Steven James Van Straten 43777 Steven Vass 43778 John William Velliquette 43779 Patrick Joseph Venezia 43780 John Harold Vickers 43781 Mark Michael Visosky 43782 Marian E. Vlasak 43783 David Nord Volkman 43784 Mark Roland Von Heeringen 43785 Thomas E. Voris 43786 Thomas Michael Voytek 43787 William Edward Vredenburgh 43788 Robert Francis Vrindten 43789 Amanda Marie Hiatt 43790 John Hobart Wagner 43791 Mark Kenneth Waite 43792 Michael Wayne Wallace 43793 Nathan Emerae Wallace 43794 Kevin Scott Walrath 43795 William Charles Walter 43796 George William Ward 43797 William Edward Ward 43798 Stephen Henry Warnock 43799 Kimberly Kay Warren 43800 Vance Anderson Warren 43801 Valerie Lynn Washington 43802 Dennis Eugene Watson 43803 Roger A. Weilep 43804 Kevin D. Weiler 43805 Thomas William Weiss 43806 John Martin Wendel 43807 Thomas Harold Wenneson 43808 David Adams Werntz 43809 Eric J. Wesley 43810 Jeffrey J. Weston 43811 George Lee Whale 43812 Eric Newton Whipple 43813 Kevin Lawrence Whitaker 43814 Robert E. White 43815 Joseph Eugene Whitlock 43816 Steven James Whitmarsh 43817 Justin Edward Whitney 43818 Robert Gerald Wiggins 43819 Thomas John Wilk 43820 Antonio Williams 43821 Bryan Richard Williams 43822 Charles Edward Williams 43823 George S. Williams 43824 Jeffrey W. Williams 43825 Thearon Michael Williams 43826 Eric Bruce Wilson 43827 Jonathan Richard Wilson 43828 Troy S. Wilson 43829 Robert Kent Wineinger 43830 David Wisnosky 43831 Michael Howard Wayne Witherspoon 43832 Robert George Witzmann 43833 Mark David Wolf 43834 Randall Bernard Wolken 43835 Andreas Wolter 43836 Scott Ellis Womack 43837 Walter George Woodring 43838 William Otto Woodring 43839 Paul John Albert Wiliam Worsfold 43840 Gregory Don Wright 43841 Joseph A. Wucik 43842 Monica Wyras O'Connor 43843 James Gerard Yentz 43844 Kenston Kangson Yi 43845 Philip D. Yost 43846 Lissa Virginia Young 43847 Michael Neil Young 43848 Fouad Steve Zeidan 43849 Alfonso Eduardo Zelaya 43850 Allen Marshall Zick 43851 Robert Oliver Zinnen 43852 William Jay Ziomek 43853 Bernard Joseph Zoppa 43854 John Stanley Bachleda 43855 John Spratt Bacot 43856 John Alexander Collison 43857 Berkley Eugene Cooke 43858 Louis Gene Gibson 43859 John Dowling Holley 43860 Guy Dozier Holliday 43861 Eric T. Judkins 43862 Sherman Horton Lane 43863 Joseph McDonald Meadows 43864 Michael Anthony Mennelle 43865 Edward James Mount 43866 Danita Pope Stephens 43867 Ruben Rios 43868 Jeffrey Alan Stanclift 43869 Anne Michele Loeder 43870 Kendal K. Weidinger 43871 David Laverne Kemp 43872 Donald Ben Okura 43873 Earl Hughes Oxendine 43874 David Michael Shade 43875 Terrance Michael Greene 43876 Marybel H. Johnson 43877 Andrew Franklin Hutchinson 43878 Peter Joseph LaFleur 43879 William Joseph Logan 43880 Craig Michael McLeod 43881 Marko J. E. Nikituk 43882 Gary Edward Pearcy 43883 Dennis Woodrow Semmel 43884 Joseph Stevens Stanjones 43885 Jeanne Kincaid Tofferi 43886 James Starling White 43887 **1987** Derek Clarke Abbott 43888 Ellen A. Birch 43889 Thomas B. Adams 43890 Jeffrey Lyle Adkins 43891 Johan Kwanghee Ahn 43892 Thomas Charles Albanese 43893 Jeffrey Scott Allar 43894 Lawrence Charles Allen 43895 Robert Scott Allen 43896 Michael John Allibone 43897 Stephen F. Alvermann 43898 Matthew Henry Ambrose 43899 Anne-Marie Anderson 43900 David Farrell Anderson 43901 Wendy Kay Masson 43902 John Paul Andre 43903 Douglas A. Andrews 43904 Michael Scott Andrews 43905 Trent Malcolm Andrews 43906 James Arnold Andrus 43907 Jeffrey Paul Angers 43908 Gus Anton 43909 Kevin Vincent Arata 43910 Joseph Mori Argyros 43911 Mark Tsuyoshi Ariyoshi 43912 Michael A. Armstrong 43913 Peter James Armstrong 43914 Paul Lawrence Arthur 43915 Joseph Edwin Artiaga 43916 Jeffrey Alan Ashmore 43917 Richard Archibald Ast 43918 David James Atkinson 43919 Bobby Lee Aufdengarten 43920 Valarie Ruth Austin 43921 Randy J. Bachman 43922 Leonard John Badal 43923 Peter J. Badoian 43924 Troy Matthew Baer 43925 Joseph Carl Baldelli 43926 Bernard B. Banks 43927 Michael J. Bara 43928 Brace Eugene Barber 43929 William Edward Bardon 43930 Wensley Barker 43931 Donald J. Barlow 43932 Elizabeth Katherine Ford 43933 Samuel J. Barry 43934 Kerry Allen Barshinger 43935 Alfred Andrew Bartkiewicz 43936 Timothy John Barton 43937 Ljuban Lou Bartulovic 43938 Anthony Joseph Bartyczak 43939 Keith A. Basik 43940 Belinda Bauer Seidel 43941 Lisa Ann Bauer Hauschild 43942 Christopher John Beaudoin 43943 Gary S. Bedard 43944 Brian Patrick Bedell 43945 Anathea Beecher Wallace 43946 Jeannette J. Jones 43947 Mark Dennis Beitz 43948 Kevin Brian Bell 43949 Lisa Bembry Steptoe 43950 Robert Emanuel Benjamin 43951 Benjamin Michael Bennett 43952 Donald James Bennett 43953 Bradley Alan Berger 43954 Kenneth William Bergeron 43955 Lisa Bergers Titus 43956 Nathan Myer Berman 43957 Jonathan Wayne Bettner 43958 Larry Darrell Biggins 43959 Kenneth J. Biland 43960 Courtney Lance Billington 43961 Allan Leon Bilyeu 43962 Guy Edward Binegar 43963 Joseph Francis Birchmeier 43964 Darren Christopher Blackwell 43965 Michael Joseph Blatz 43966 Mark R. Bliese 43967 Mark Alan Blodgett 43968 Timothy Paul Bobroski 43969 Kurt Alan Bodiford 43970 Ralph Boeckmann 43971 Kenneth Louis Boehme 43972 Peter John Boehmer 43973 Stephen A. Bollinger 43974 Constance Boothe Bennett 43975 James E. Boston 43976 Rafael Antonio Botello 43977 Calvert Lee Bowen 43978 Martha Mary Bowman 43979 Robert L. Bowman 43980 Charles Darrin Boyd 43981 Jeffrey Allen Bradford 43982 Lawrence Bradley 43983 David John Brady 43984 Gilbert Patrick Brady 43985 Earl George Bragg 43986 Robert Allen Brenner 43987 Howard Keith Brewington 43988 Michael R. Bridges 43989 Paul C. Britton 43990 James David Brock 43991 Strom Lauren Brost 43992 Deanna Y. Cousino 43993 Kevin Peter Brown 43994 Ross Adam Brown 43995 Todd A. Brown 43996 Thomas L. Bruen 43997 Gerald Philip Bruening 43998 Shawn Paul Buck 43999 Jeffrey Paul Buczak 44000 Shawn Arthur Budke 44001 Robert David Burdette 44002 John Richard Burger 44003 Robert Earl Burks 44004 W. Todd Burns 44005 Robert Charles Buscher 44006 William Robert Bush 44007 James Taylor Byall 44008 Michael Stephen Cacic 44009 Robert Walker Cairns 44010 Michael Edmond Callahan 44011 Gregory Paul Calvin 44012 Eric Lee Campbell 44013 Ned Murphy Campbell 44014 Terrance Decosta Campbell 44015 Donald Wayne Canaday 44016 John Scott Canonico 44017 Anthony Carmine Cariello 44018 J. Daniel Carlo 44019 Mark Jonathan Carlson 44020 Douglas Alan Carr 44021 Thomas Joseph Cascino 44022 Stephen Thomas Cass 44023 Hugh C. Cate 44024 David Wayne Cauble 44025 Alexis Ceballos 44026 John W. Cephas 44027 William R. Chapin 44028 Marc D. Chareth 44029 Randall George Chavez 44030 Richard Mark Checkan 44031 T. Kent Cheeseman 44032 Shawn Thomas Chicoine 44033 Brenda Childs Jordan 44034 Gary William Chippendale 44035 Craig Allen Christensen 44036 Darius Payne Chronister 44037 John W. Ciarlo 44038 Carmine Cicalese 44039 Ronald Vincent Cieri 44040 Paul Joseph Cioni 44041 James Francis Clare 44042 Douglas Mark Clark 44043 Mary Katherine Clark 44044 Patrick Anthony Clark 44045 Timothy Richard Clarke 44046 James Julian Clausen 44047 Brad Alan Clay 44048 Janette Clor Skowron 44049 Edward P. Clukey 44050 Duncan Christopher Clyborne 44051 Kimberly Field 44052 David Michael Cole 44053 Edward Edwards Cole 44054 Malcolm C. Cole 44055 William Edward Cole 44056 John Joseph Combs 44057 Mica Mackenzie Comstock 44058 Natalie Ann Conroe 44059 Michael Anthony Cooper 44060 Paul James Cooper 44061 James Paul Cordell 44062 William Philip Corr 44063 Carlos V. Cortez 44064 Thomas Hans Costa 44065 Daniel Joseph Costigan 44066 Michael Joseph Cote 44067 Timothy Doane Covell 44068 Douglas Alvin Cox 44069 Alan Jeffrey Craft 44070 Donald Michael Crawford 44071 Michael John Creedon 44072 Robert Bryant Creveling 44073 John Richard Crino 44074 Joseph Perry Croskey 44075 John Leo Cullivan 44076 Daniel Jordan Cunningham 44077 Walter Lee Cunningham 44078 John Timothy Currier 44079 Catherine M. Whalen 44080 Todd Alexander Cyril 44081 Tamara Czekala Davies 44082 Louis Alan Dainty 44083 Walter Robert Daley 44084 Edward Michael Daly 44085 Joel Lamar Daniels 44086 Benton Allen Danner 44087 Cliff A. Daus 44088 Ronald Harold Davies 44089 Christopher Patrick Davis 44090 Fletcher Michael Davis 44091 Joseph Loren Davis 44092 Louis Joseph DeAngelo 44093 Stephen Joseph DeBerardino 44094 Bryan Donald DeCoster 44095 Paul Bruno DeGironimo 44096 Harold Russell DeGraff 44097 Daniel Paul DeLeo 44098 David Alan Della-Giustina 44099 John Patrick Delmar 44100 Dale Andrew Derischebourg 44101 Robert Philip Dickerson 44102 Joseph Patrick Diminick 44103 Paul John Dineen 44104 Robert Smith DiVincenzo 44105 Erin Andrew Doe 44106 Joseph Edward Doherty 44107 Michael James Donato 44108 Mark Wayne Donley 44109 John Ray Dorris 44110 David J. Doucette 44111 Eric Ramon Downey 44112 William Nicholas Doyle 44113 Lawrence P. Drinkwine 44114 Michael R. Duckworth 44115 David Andrew Duffy 44116 David Joel Duffy 44117 James Clark Dugan 44118 Kevin R. Dunlop 44119 Matthew James Dunlop 44120 Michael Charles Dunn 44121 Darik Dale Dvorshak 44122 Shelly R. Matautia 44123 Darwin Dean Ebeling 44124 Mark Aaron Ebersbach 44125 Brian William Ebert 44126 Reece Murdoch Eddy 44127 Rembert Alan Edwards 44128 Kimberly Ann Ehrlund 44129 Lori A. Eitreim-Harrington 44130 Peter Jon Ekberg 44131 Jeffrey G. Elliott 44132 Lisa Ann Funk 44133 Robert Cutler Elwell 44134 Harris Emmons 44135 Peter Thomas Ercoli 44136 Brenda Essenmacher Nelson 44137 Robert Dwayne Estes 44138 Rudy Aldo Esteves 44139 Robert George Estey 44140 Daniel Edward Evans 44141 Thomas Robert Evans 44142 Donna E. Rutten 44143 Erik Stephen Everton 44144 William John Ewing 44145 Jacqueline Elaine Fabrizzio 44146 Matthew Andrew Faiello 44147 Gerard Michel Falzon 44148 Robert Henry Fancher 44149 Brian Arthur Farlow 44150 Dennis Alan Farmer 44151 Geoffrey David Farrell 44152 John Fitzgerald Farrington 44153 Dennis Ray Farrow 44154 Timothy Wayne Fath 44155 Stewart Ross Fearon 44156 David Matthew Fee 44157 Kelly Naurine Fehrenbach 44158 Joseph George Felber 44159 Joseph Harold Felter 44160 David Christopher Fenton 44161 John George Ferrari 44162 Michael J. Ferrone 44163 Bertrand P. Finkenbeiner 44164 J. Worden Finnell 44165 Bonnie L. Smith 44166 Timothy Edward Fitzgerald 44167 Michael Joseph Fitzpatrick 44168 David Harlan Fleece 44169 Jon P. Fliss 44170 Dwight Timothy Flowers 44171 Thomas Patrick Joseph Flynn 44172 Aaron Bernard Fore 44173 Andrew C. Forgay 44174 Thomas Chapman Forrest 44175 Barry Dean Forston 44176 Gary Alan Foskuhl 44177 Carl Edward Fossa 44178 Michael Joseph Francesconi 44179 Ronald David Francis 44180 Sana M. Francis Mason 44181 Edwin Lawrence Frederick 44182 Richard Keith Fredricksen 44183 Todd Alvin Freesemann 44184 Michael L. French 44185 Norman Gunter Freund 44186 John Thomas Friedland 44187 Todd Aaron Friedman 44188 James Joseph Fritschi 44189 Shawn David Fritz 44190 Richard Thomas Fugate 44191 William Scott Fuller 44192 Reginald Fullwood 44193 Barry Allen Gaertner 44194 James Andrew Gagliano 44195 Thomas DeWitt Gaither 44196 Michael F. Gajewski 44197 John Perry Galassie 44198 Michael John Gallante 44199 Charles William Gameros 44200 Michael F. Garceau 44201 Marion Garcia 44202 James Robert Garrett 44203 Troy Wayne Garrett 44204

William Paul Garvey 44205 David Lionel Garza 44206 James Jay Gawryszewski 44207 Stephen James Gayton 44208 Robert Bruce Geddis 44209 Terry Michael Geliske 44210 Jesse Luke Germain 44211 John Lawrence Gifford 44212 Paula E. White 44213 Matthew Joseph Gilligan 44214 Angela Maria Lungu 44215 Howard Richard Givens 44216 James Anthony Glackin 44217 George Aaron Glaze 44218 Daniel James Gleason 44219 Laurie Ann Goetz 44220 Kent Jerome Goff 44221 Michael Anthony Gonzales 44222 Alissa Good Simon 44223 Bruce James Gorski 44224 Thomas Joseph Goss 44225 John Meigs Graham 44226 Jennifer A. Conwell 44227 Keith Dereck Greaux 44228 Mark Richard Green 44229 Paul Wendell Green 44230 Timothy Tyler Green 44231 Wayne Anthony Green 44232 Kurt B. Greene 44233 Alfred Joseph Grein 44234 Gene Edison Griffin 44235 Michael Walker Griffith 44236 Stephen P. Griggs 44237 John Joseph Grisillo 44238 Kenneth Richard Gross 44239 William L. Grove 44240 Christopher R. Guidry 44241 Matthew James Gulbranson 44242 Erik Ole Gunhus 44243 Steven Brett Guthrie 44244 Karen Haddock Fralen 44245 Ronald Raymond Haddock 44246 Holly Louise Hagan Olson 44247 James Patrick Hagan 44248 Gregg Louis Hagerty 44249 Katrina Darlene Hall 44250 Julia Ann Hamacher-Wagner 44251 Darcie Lynn Hammond 44252 William George Hamor 44253 Millard J. Hampton 44254 Deborah Lynn Hanagan 44255 D. Scott Hanson 44256 John Edward Hardt 44257 Jonathan Paul Harmon 44258 James C. Harris 44259 Karl Desmond Harrison 44260 John Jeffrey Hartley 44261 Jeffrey Thomas Hassman 44262 Lincoln Colin Haynes 44263 Jeffrey Kirk Hazelwood 44264 Charles Benjamin Hazzard 44265 Christina M. Manning 44266 Steven Paul Heidecker 44267 John Powell Heiskell 44268 David John Hemmert 44269 Joseph Patrick Henderson 44270 Andrew R. Heppelmann 44271 Javier Hernandez 44272 Robert Bradford Herndon 44273 Thomas K. Hickman 44274 Thomas Edward Hiebert 44275 John Randell Higgins 44276 David Bright Hilburn 44277 Steven Craig Hilliker 44278 James Knippenberg Hillman 44279 Kurt Louis Hoernlein 44280 Herbert L. Hoffman 44281 Damon Kirk Hofstrand 44282 Walter Matthew Hogan 44283 Martin J. Holland 44284 Charles Cleveland Holton 44285 Samuel Charles Homsy 44286 Amelia Hoogerwerf Underwood 44287 Nathaniel Demetric Hope 44288 William Todd Hopson 44289 Richard Dale Horsley 44290 William G. Horton 44291 Ricky Lee Hoskins 44292 Christopher Samuel Houston 44293 Kevin Houston 44294 William Bruce Howard 44295 Craig S. Howe 44296 Debra Alane Hower 44297 Daniel Harley Howett 44298 Clare Rose Walker 44299 Lisa Ann Wall 44300 Evan Andrew Huelfer 44301 Fernando M. Huerta 44302 Jeffrey Lee Huisingh 44303 Robert James Hulett 44304 Michael Patrick Hunt 44305 Yvette Nevert Hunter 44306 Karen K. Ward 44307 Ann M. McBee 44308 John Jeffrey Hurst 44309 Thomas Arthur Hutchison 44310 Matthew Raymond Hyre 44311 Michael Anthony Iacobucci 44312 Mica J. Imamura 44313 Gilbert Ben Inouye 44314 Paul Joseph Ives 44315 Charles J. Jackson 44316 Roderic Carl Jackson 44317 James Laurence Jacobson 44318 David Leray James 44319 Michael J. Janser 44320 Robert Adrain Jarvis 44321 Paul Rimas Jaselskis 44322 J. Brandon Jenkins 44323 Matthew Bradley Jennings 44324 Wayne Jerzak 44325 Frederick Haaken Jessen 44326 John Hampton Jessup 44327 Ramon Jimenez 44328 Michael Robert Johns 44329 Anthony James Johnson 44330 Brian Zane Johnson 44331 Christopher R. Johnson 44332 Darren Henry Johnson 44333 Donald Richard Johnson 44334 Kenneth Alan Johnson 44335 Michael James Johnson 44336 Nathan Johnson 44337 Steven Craig Johnson 44338 Robert Jon Johnston 44339 Clarence Contee Jones 44340 Craig William Jones 44341 Kim L. Jones 44342 Michael Jones 44343 Michael C. Jones 44344 Robert Stephen Jones 44345 Gary Allen Jordan 44346 Jeffrey Alan Jordan 44347 Fredric Earle Kaehler 44348 Kipling Van Kahler 44349 Eugene Thomas Kaiser 44350 Paul Anthony Kamnikar 44351 Clinton M. Kandle 44352 Scott Lee Kane 44353 Joseph Kurt Kaple 44354 Christopher Peter Kapsal 44355 Mark Alexius Karasz 44356 Daniel L. Karbler 44357 Brett Taketsugu Kawakami 44358 James Allan Kearse 44359 Todd Andrew Keck 44360 Kevin Paul Keenan 44361 Michael Alexander Kegler 44362 Matthew Kellerhals 44363 Laura L. FitzPatrick 44364 Thomas Meade Kelso 44365 Scott A. Kessel 44366 David Vanover Ketter 44367 Charles M. Kibler 44368 Timothy James Kielpinski 44369 Michael Edward Kiene 44370 Gregory Robert Kilby 44371 John Howard Kilroy 44372 Han J. Kim 44373 Jeffrey K. Sung Kim 44374 John Scott King 44375 Reginal Delandro King 44376 David Andrew Kingston 44377 Randall David Kirby 44378 Richard P. Klein 44379 James Cletus Klotz 44380 Everett Denton Knapp 44381 William Kyle Knauf 44382 Ronald Lewis Knipping 44383 Christopher Allen Knowlton 44384 Michael Edward Knutson 44385 Kevin Knuuti 44386 Christopher David Kolenda 44387 John Michael Kolessar 44388 Lawrence Anthony Kominiak 44389 John Louis Korfmacher 44390 James Thomas Korpela 44391 Leonard Adrian Kortekaas 44392 Elod A. Kovach 44393 Tina Sheri Kracke 44394 Paul A. Krause 44395 Fred Theodore Krawchuk 44396 Timothy John Kroll 44397 Gregory Edward Krystyniak 44398 Catherine Ann Conner 44399 Jeffrey Gerard Kuhl 44400 Matthew Philip Kuperstein 44401 George McClelland Kyle 44402 Kevin E. LaBorne 44403 Trese Anne LaCamera 44404 Michael Otis Lacey 44405 Keith D. Ladd 44406 Keith J. LaFrance 44407 Richard Andrew Lakis 44408 Russell Joseph Lamarre 44409 William Thomas Lampley 44410 Kenneth Mark Landes 44411 Robert Stanley Lane 44412 Brandy Langston Maranian 44413 Kevin Raymond Larochelle 44414 Gregory Paul Larson 44415 Stephen Richard Lasse 44416 Thomas Shingu Lavender 44417 Valerie Jeanne Adank 44418 Douglas Brent Layman 44419 Michael Louis Layrisson 44420 William Jay Leady 44421 Aimee Lenz Kominiak 44422 Veronica C. Fiore 44423 Mark Julian Leone 44424 Nicolas Gregory Leshock 44425 Glenn Michael Levanti 44426 Ronald Flynn Lewis 44427 Michael J. Liantonio 44428 Robert N. Lichtenberger 44429 Samuel M. Ligo 44430 Gary Walter Linhart 44431 Stephen Norman Lisle 44432 John Thomas Listermann 44433 Sean Terrence Long 44434 Cori Lowe Bergeron 44435 James Bernard Lowery 44436 Paul Anthony Lucey 44437 James Edward Lutz 44438 Michael Richard Lyman 44439 John Martin Lynch 44440 Kevin Scott MacWatters 44441 Eric A. Madoff 44442 Brian Maka 44443 Dale John Malzi 44444 Joseph Paul Manausa 44445 Karl Rippert Mance 44446 Bruce Joseph Marchetti 44447 Matthew W. Markel 44448 Daniel John Maroun 44449 Shawn Bernard Marshall 44450 Timothy James Marshall 44451 Andres Rafael Martin 44452 Vincent Gregory Martinelli 44453 Michael Ervin Mathes 44454 Patrick Eugene Mathes 44455 Michael James Mathias 44456 George Nelson Matthews 44457 Donna M. McAleer 44458 Michael Louis Maus 44459 Reynold M. Maus 44460 Robert Ray Mayfield 44461 Edward R. McAleer 44462 John Robert McCombs 44463 Calvin Russell McCommons 44464 William John McConomy 44465 Daniel Joseph McCormick 44466 David H. McCormick 44467 Michael Victor McCrea 44468 George Patrick McDonnell 44469 Lee Alan McFadden 44470 Gary Lee McFarlane 44471 Sean P. McGettigan 44472 Sammie Lee McGriff 44473 John Joseph McGuinness 44474 Timothy Patrick McGuire 44475 Pearline V. McKenzie 44476 Patrick Michael McMahon 44477 Phillip Andrew Mead 44478 James Robert Meisinger 44479 James Joseph Meskill 44480 Todd A. Messitt 44481 William P. Metheny 44482 Richard Karl Meyer 44483 Thomas H. Meyer 44484 Drew Robert Meyerowich 44485 Joseph J. Michaud 44486 Mark Francis Migaleddi 44487 David James Mikolaities 44488 Andrew Macklin Miller 44489 Christopher William Miller 44490 Darren Scott Miller 44491 Tara A. Feir 44492 Tracy Miller Richardson 44493 Scott Sivard Mills 44494 Angela Lisabet Minichiello 44495 Siegfred Bueno Mison 44496 Charles Sanford Mitchell 44497 Frank Eugene Mitchell 44498 John Alexander Mitchell 44499 Mark Hall Mitchell 44500 Michael Alexander Mitchell 44501 Phillip Eugene Mitchell 44502 Timothy D. Mitchell 44503 Bryan Peter Mix 44504 John Henry Moellering 44505 Thomas John Moffatt 44506 Edward McFadden Monk 44507 Donald Gabriel Monteyne 44508 Douglas Bruce Moody 44509 Eric Collins Moore 44510 Randall Mark Moore 44511 James Delgado Mora 44512 Ricardo M. Morillo 44513 Stephen Albert Raymond Morris 44514 Rickey Michael Morrison 44515 Frederick Paul Moser 44516 Christopher Moss 44517 Donald R. Mudford 44518 Fletcher M. Munter 44519 James Peter Murphy 44520 Paul Francis Murphy 44521 Hugh John Murtha 44522 Richard Charles Muschek 44523 Alfredo J. Mycue 44524 Stephen Charles Myers 44525 John Patrick Nalan 44526 James Harold Nelson 44527 John Joseph Nelson 44528 Mark Lewis Nelson 44529 Randall Wayne Nelson 44530 Teresa Nelson Givens 44531 Wendell Lewis Nelson 44532 Michael E. Nerstheimer 44533 Timothy Edward Newsome 44534 Co G. Nguyen 44535 Todd Stephen Nicholson 44536 Richard John Nieberding 44537 Thomas James Nigro 44538 Troy Owen Nix 44539 Howard Edward Norowitz 44540 John Eugene Novalis 44541 Steven John Nulty 44542 Timothy A. Oberschlake 44543 James Michael O'Brien 44544 James Robert O'Brien 44545 Jennifer Jennifer Sena 44546 Robert Francis O'Connor 44547 James Robert O'Dea 44548 Stephen Alexander O'Dell 44549 Thomas Martin O'Donoghue 44550 Garry Owen O'Grady 44551 Daniel J. Oh 44552 Carl John Ohlson 44553 Christopher Luke O'Keefe 44554 Stanley Joseph Olenginski 44555 Bryn C. Olexy 44556 Loretta Anne Dahnke 44557 C. Grace Fitton 44558 Gregory Allan Olson 44559 Robert Leslie Olson 44560 Elizabeth Ann O'Neal 44561 Jeffrey K. Opperman 44562 Terence McCabe Ormsby 44563 Edward Hector Orzetti 44564 Patricia M. Goodnite 44565 Robert Joseph Owens 44566 Paul G. N. Pacheco 44567 Ronald Eugene Pacheco 44568 Robert Ray Painter 44569 Daniel Pak 44570 Bradley Hoke Palmer 44571 Renard Randy Paras 44572 Todd Wayne Parish 44573 Hae-Sue Park 44574 Myung Jin Park 44575 James Louis Parker 44576 Mark Allen Parrish 44577 Paul F. Pasquina 44578 James Arthur Patton 44579 Marvin J. Pearce 44580 Steven Charles Friis Pedersen 44581 Douglas Edwin Pennebaker 44582 Edward F. Pero 44583 Richard James Perrelli 44584 Domenic Francis Perriello 44585 Axa Stella Perwich 44586 Larry E. Peters 44587 Scott Bowen Peters 44588 Jacqueline Peterson Campagna 44589 Jeffrey David Peterson 44590 Kris Allen Peterson 44591 James Michael Petro 44592 Matthew Edward Petrocelli 44593 Christopher James Petty 44594 Thomas William Piatak 44595 Katherine Louise Schlimm 44596 Andrew John Piffat 44597 Mark James Pincoski 44598 Jeffrey George Plante 44599 Miguel A. Polanco 44600 Patrick A. Pollard 44601 Stephanie Lorraine Foster 44602 Clinton Cooper Pollitt 44603 Stanley Darwin Pomichter 44604 William J. Poole 44605 Michael Steven Posovich 44606 Michael Joseph Pratt 44607 William Wayne Prior 44608 Samuel Houston Prugh 44609 Mark Thomas Puhalla 44610 Scott Alan Pulford 44611 Christopher John Pulskamp 44612 Wallace Putkowski 44613 Matthew Sullivan Quinn 44614 Nivaldo Ignacio Quintana 44615 John Frank Rabena 44616 Brian William Raftery 44617 Scott Arlington Rainey 44618 Kimberly Randall McDermott 44619 James Andrew Rankin 44620 C. Brian Ranne 44621 Patricia L. Krier 44622 David Frederick Ray 44623 Patrick James Reardon 44624 James Edward Rector 44625 John Gordon Reddy 44626 James Troy Redmon 44627 James David Redwine 44628 Stephen Scott Reed 44629 Michael Arthur Regalado 44630 Michael Christopher Regan 44631 Gary W. Reider 44632 Paul Kenneth Reist 44633 Mark Edward Relich 44634 Jeanne Marie Ives 44635 Alfred Eugene Renzi 44636 Michael John Repetski 44637 Brian Lee Rhonehouse 44638 Patrick Norwood Rhyne 44639 Jennifer Lynn Wineinger 44640 Mark Alan Rice 44641 Larry Nicolas Ridge 44642 David Wilburn Riggins 44643 Christopher J. Rigoni 44644 Nicola Irene Riley 44645 Theresa Wetzel 44646 Franklin Delano Rivera 44647 Laurence Clayton Roberts 44648 Daniel Scott Robertson 44649 Anthony Edward Robinette 44650 James Harvey Robinette 44651 Corey Claude Robinson 44652 Justin David Roby 44653 Clayce Cullin Rodamer 44654 Frederick Jay Rodenbach 44655 Darrin Henry Rodeschin 44656 Arthur George Rodriguez 44657 Daniel Rodriguez 44658 Edwin Rodriguez 44659 Rodney Lee Roederer 44660 Steven John Roemhildt 44661 Charles Courtney Rogers 44662 Christopher Joseph Rollins 44663 Paul Emery Rollins 44664 Kenneth Arden Romaine 44665 Mark Kollin Romeo 44666 Dwayne Leonard Romero 44667 Peter John Rosario 44668 Michael William Rose 44669 Scott P. Rosen 44670 Eric Jacob Roth 44671 Thomas James Roth 44672 Edward Verner Rowe 44673 Ronald Wayne Rowe 44674 Jonathan Ward Rue 44675 Todd Robert Ruggles 44676 Christian Edward Rush 44677 Christopher Richard Russell 44678 Joy Renee Russell 44679 James Robert Rutledge 44680 Michael Barrett Ryan 44681 Keith Joseph Sabol 44682 James Edward Saenz 44683 Samuel Jonathan Salada 44684 Joseph Vincent Samek 44685 Kenneth Clyde Sampson 44686 John Christopher Sanchez 44687 William Alton Sanders 44688 Earle Glenn Sanford 44689 Stephanie S. Armstrong 44690 Veronica D. Santopolo Zsido 44691 Michael Christopher Santos 44692 James Anthony Santucci 44693 Gregory Victor Sarka 44694 Roberto Jose Sartori 44695 Jeffrey Todd Sauer 44696 David Owen Scheyer 44697 Klaus Dieter Schmidt 44698 William Brian Scholl 44699 Dennis L. Schrecengast 44700 Christopher Warren Schroeder 44701 Jonathan Frederick Schupp 44702 Karl Otto Schwartz 44703 Scott Jerome Schwartz 44704 Virginia J. Moul 44705 Scott Alan Seebold 44706 Gunter Horst Seeger 44707 Brian R. Seidel 44708 Alan Seise 44709 Philip Alan Selton 44710 Michael James Serwacki 44711 Janez Andrej Sever 44712 Sandra Joann Kolb 44713 Joyce Midori Shannon Oakley 44714 Christopher Lee Sharp 44715 Douglas John Shaver 44716 Jennifer Louise Shaw 44717 Stephen Matthew Shea 44718 Michael Lewis Shearin 44719 Alan Todd Sheinwald 44720 David John Shepard 44721 Kathleen Sherman Fliss 44722 Tanja Karin Shipman 44723 Ronald Lee Shultis 44724 James Edward Siewertsen 44725 Thomas Joseph Simard 44726 Joseph Anthony Simonelli 44727 John Thomas Sipes 44728 Jaroslaw Peter Siwik 44729 Thaddeus Joseph Siwinski 44730 Gregg Andrew Skibicki 44731 W. Lee Skidmore 44732 John Hardin Skiles 44733 Ervin Wright Skinner 44734 John Jerome Skinner 44735 David John Skowron 44736 Peter Michael Sload 44737 Jeffrey Scott Smidt 44738 Brennan C. Smith 44739 David Roy Smith 44740 Irving Smith 44741 Jason August Smith 44742 Maria Yvette Smith 44743 Monica Lynne Baisden 44744 Paolo Francesco Smith 44745 Robert Eugene Smith 44746 Steven E. Smith 44747 Jeffrey Egan Smitherman 44748 Fernande Marie Smorra 44749 Daniel R. Smythe 44750 Ross W. Snare 44751 J. Lee Snow 44752 Bradford Layne Snowden 44753 Michael Francis Sobiesk 44754 John Steven Sogan 44755 Robert Julian Sollohub 44756 Cecil H. Solomon 44757 George Scott Solomon 44758 Norman E. Solomon 44759 Bryndol A. Sones 44760 William Thompson Sorrells 44761 Alexander Sousa 44762 Lynn K. Sprague Byers 44763 William Makoto Stacey 44764 Thomas Neville Stader 44765 Lucie Marie Stagg 44766 Kenneth Paul Staresinic 44767 Albert Joseph Starostanko 44768 Anneliese Margarita Steele 44769 Alan Karl Stempel 44770 Ronald Joseph Steptoe 44771 Michael Joseph Stewart 44772 Gregory Keith Stinson 44773 Alexander Stojadinovic 44774 Kevin Douglas Stringer 44775 Charles F. Stuart 44776 Michael L. Suggs 44777 Joseph Benedict Sweeney 44778 John Robert Swisher 44779 Kevin Larry Tally 44780 Jason Toshio Tanaka 44781 Gordon John Taras 44782 Michael J. Tarsa 44783 Vernon L. Tatum 44784 Janet T. Brdar 44785 Michael Lee Tease 44786 George Edwin Thompson 44787 Lisa Donley Angleson 44788 Ralph Culmer Thompson 44789 Kelly Fitzpatrick Thrasher 44790 John Kai Tien 44791 Pele Victoria Tierney 44792 Jerry Robert Tiller 44793 James Mark Tillotson 44794 Valen Scott Tisdale 44795 Timothy Joseph Todaro 44796 Michael A. Todd 44797 Michael Thad Tolbert 44798 William Edward Tomasi 44799 Mark Alan Torch 44800 Richard Mark Toy 44801 Peter Thomas Trebotte 44802 Rebecca A. T. Yacone 44803 Bryan Paul Truesdell 44804 Polyxeni Tsigounis Combs 44805 Eric Andre Tuggle 44806 John Nunzio Tumino 44807 Eric Christopher Turner 44808 James Lawrence Turner 44809 Keven Turner 44810 Michael Edward Turner 44811 Richard Randolph Turner 44812 Robert V. Tuscano 44813 John D'Aracy Tyree 44814 William Kennedy Uemura 44815 Robert Michael Underwood 44816 Christopher Charles Valentine 44817 Mark T. Valley 44818 John Franklin VanSant 44819 Gaetano Francis Vastano 44820 John Matthew Venhaus 44821 Jeffrey Michael Vezeau 44822 Anthony James Vicari 44823 Mark Richard Vilardi 44824 Kevin John Vink 44825 Albert John Visconti 44826 James Edward Vogel 44827 Victoria V. Flack 44828 Jennifer A. Vogt Vogt 44829 Jeffrey Ralph Voigt 44830 Christine Judith Voisinet Bender 44831 William Joseph Voss 44832 Ingrid Maria Jones 44833 Kevin Paul Waizenhofer 44834 Matthew Thomas Walsh 44835 Stephen P. Walsh 44836 John P. Waltner 44837 Donald Cameron Walton 44838 Marvin Richard Walworth 44839 Lawrence John Wark 44840 Paul Lawrence Washington 44841 William Payne Weathersby 44842 Brent Neil Weaver 44843 Regina Ann Weinpahl McCluskey 44844 Jonelle Amelia Welch 44845 Frederick Paul Wellman 44846 Robert L. Wells 44847 Jay Joseph Welu 44848 Frederick Carl Westerlund 44849 Ernst Henry Weyand 44850 John B. Whalen 44851 Timothy Joseph Whalen 44852 Gregory Adam Whann 44853 David Roscoe Whiddon 44854 Benjamin M. White 44855 Richard Glenn White 44856 Timothy M. White 44857 Paul Wayne Whitecar 44858 Douglas Arthur Whitehouse 44859 John David Whitenack 44860 Brett R. Wiggs 44861 Andrew Robert Wild 44862 Theodore William Wilkinson 44863 Charlene Corene Griffin 44864 Christopher Yoe Williams 44865 Dain E. Williams 44866 Daniel Edward Williams 44867 David Francis Williams 44868 Ila Nadine Tatum 44869 R. Eric Williams 44870 Terry Glenn Williamson 44871 Bernard Eugene Williford 44872 Brian E. Willis 44873 Dale Costello Willis 44874 Darrell T. Wilson 44875 Matthew Edward Wilson 44876 Stephen Wayne Wingard 44877 Ralph Edward Winkelman 44878 R. Kevin Winkle 44879 Natalie Winn Birchfield 44880 Craig Scott Winton 44881 Richard Darren Witte 44882 Elizabeth Anne Wixted Carpenter 44883 Casey Dennis Wood 44884 Zane Bivins Wood 44885 William Harrison Woods 44886 Benny Lee Wright 44887 Shaun Thomas Wurzbach 44888 James F. Yacone 44889 Thomas Jerome Yanoschik 44890 Michael James Yeager 44891 Glenn Arthur Yeaw 44892 Rush Spencer Yelverton 44893 Gregory Frederick York 44894 Cheryl Lynne Young 44895 Dennis Allen Young 44896 George R. Young 44897 Michael Steven Young 44898 Theodore Alan Young 44899 Irene M. Rosen 44900 Matthew James Zielinski 44901 Eric Vonn Zimmerman 44902 Robert Joseph Zoppa 44903 John Ronald Zsido 44904 John Gilbert Briegel 44905 Douglas J. Hildebrand 44906 Joseph Arthur Lynch 44907 Joseph Dwayne Pollhein 44908 David Peter Reyes 44909 Gregory Alan Schuliger 44910 Harry Lloyd Theus 44911 Jeffrey Charles Thor 44912 Rufus Booker Williams 44913 Preston Lee Forchion 44914 John Quentin Calhoun 44915 Matthew Clay Fly 44916 Carol A. Kler 44917 Glenn C. Baca 44918 Dean Ray Batchelder 44919 Richard Earl Baxter 44920 J. Mitchell Cobb 44921 Joseph K. Gillis 44922 Anne Denisse Hidalgo 44923 Terence G. McGuire 44924 George P. Mitschke 44925 Elbert George Ross 44926 Douglas Bowden Tumminello 44927 Spencer Clark Williams 44928 John C. Kalainov 44929 **1988** Jeffrey Alan Abramson 44930 Patricia Abt George 44931 Edward Francis Acevedo 44932 Joaquin Daguay Agsalud 44933 Antonio A. Aguto 44934 Maynard Charles Ahner 44935 Daniel Scott Albert 44936 Merritt Edward Alberti 44937 Carlise Euvonne Alberty 44938 Darren Wayne Alch 44939 Michael Stuart Aleman 44940 Gregory John Allen 44941 Joseph Kenton Allen 44942 John Martin Alvermann 44943 John William Amberg 44944 Craig James Amnott 44945 Gregory John Anderson 44946 James David Anderson 44947 Matthew Reid Anderson 44948 Steven Paul Anderson 44949 Gerald Howard Ankeny 44950 Christopher Lee Anstead 44951 Douglas Perry Appert 44952 Howard Edward Arey 44953 Brett Wade Avants 44954 Andrew Wayne Backus 44955 Douglas Arthur Baden 44956 Lance Taylor Bagley 44957 Joseph Michael Bagonis 44958 Curtiss Merkel Bailey 44959 James Edward Baker 44960 Steven Alexander Baker 44961 Christopher Lawrence

Ballard 44962 Jerald Christian Bangerter 44963 Paul Fredrick Barber 44964 Michael George Barger 44965 Russell Barnes 44966 William Clyde Barnes 44967 Thomas Alan Barnett 44968 Robert James Barrett 44969 Duncan Lawrence Barry 44970 Michael Keith Barsella 44971 Robert Gerard Bartholet 44972 Daniel Donato Barulli 44973 Michael Eric Bassel 44974 Richard Alan Bauer 44975 Patrick Michael Bearse 44976 Randall J. Bechtel 44977 Jay Fredrick Beckerman 44978 Michael J. Beckman 44979 David Charles Behrens 44980 William Joseph Beitzel 44981 John Nicholas Bender 44982 Joseph Anthony Benevento 44983 Lisa Marie Strine 44984 David Mark Bennett 44985 Paul Jorge Dos Santos Bento 44986 David Lee Berdan 44987 Walter W. Berg 44988 Deanna Benard O'Brien 44989 Robert Michael Betchley 44990 Peter Brock Bickford 44991 Susan A. Moynihan 44992 George Robert Bisker 44993 Russell Dieter Bissinger 44994 Michael A. Boden 44995 William Philip Bohnaker 44996 William Lawrence Boice 44997 Richard Kikuo Kuramitsu Bond 44998 Jeffrey Raymond Boone 44999 Craig Charles Borchelt 45000 Brent David Borden 45001 Stuart Kraneck Born 45002 James Grissom Bosworth 45003 Hugh French Boyd 45004 James Henry Bradley 45005 Gary Darnell Branch 45006 Mark Warren Brantley 45007 Lawrence Michael Brede 45008 James Francis Brennan 45009 Thomas M. Brennan 45010 Timothy Patrick Brereton 45011 Jeanne E. Hutchison 45012 Charles Edward Broadus 45013 Aaron William Brody 45014 Ilean Brook Keltz 45015 Howard Earl Brookshire 45016 James Earl Brown 45017 Kerk Baxtor Brown 45018 Timothy James Brown 45019 Kathleen M. Burns 45020 David P. Bruner 45021 Eric Bouvier Bruns 45022 Karen Burgin McLaughlin 45023 Stephen Alois Burk 45024 Willard McKenzie Burleson 45025 Norvin Deveril Burrus 45026 Troy Denward Busby 45027 Robert Dennis Butler 45028 Windsor Shane Buzza 45029 Leo Philip Buzzerio 45030 Jeffery Gaylord Byington 45031 Scott John Byrnes 45032 Lyle Jeffrey Caddell 45033 Jacqueline M. Cain 45034 Jeffrey S. Cain 45035 Albert Anthony Cala 45036 Robert D. Calderon 45037 Hugh S. Campbell 45038 Daniel Canales 45039 William Joseph Caprio 45040 Michael Angelo Carlino 45041 John Martin Carlisle 45042 Kenneth Richard Carlson 45043 Alvin Bernard Carroll 45044 Kevin M. Carroll 45045 Brian Alexander Carson 45046 Peter Murphy Carter 45047 Jeffry T. Chancey 45048 Kathleen Teresa Chandler 45049 David Patrick Chapman 45050 Mark A. Charette 45051 Joseph McClelland Chatfield 45052 Brian Edwin Chee 45053 Michael William Chenette 45054 Alan A. Cheney 45055 Paul James Chevlin 45056 Steve Sang Chi 45057 David P. Chrismer 45058 Benson Lucas Chu 45059 David Hyun Chung 45060 Paul Michael Cimino 45061 Christopher J. Clark 45062 Ronald P. Clark 45063 Scott Douglas Clarke 45064 David Ray Clonts 45065 Timothy John Clouser 45066 Melissa Rutkoske 45067 William John Coffin 45068 Daniel Patrick Colasanto 45069 Osborne McCormack Collins 45070 Scott Everett Collins 45071 Raymond Carl Colucciello 45072 Garth Conner 45073 William Chance Conner 45074 Timothy P. Connors 45075 Leah Conser Scherr 45076 W. Dale Conwell 45077 Chris Terrell Cook 45078 Rhonda K.R. Cook 45079 Anthony Charles Copeland 45080 Mark W. Coplen 45081 Robert M. Cornejo 45082 Lisa A. Letarte 45083 Sean Joseph Corrigan 45084 John William Coursey 45085 Glenn Ray Cover 45086 Tyler Lee Randolph 45087 Geoffrey Allen Craft 45088 Robert Alworth Craig 45089 Robert Raymond Craig 45090 Mark Steven Cravotta 45091 John Crawford 45092 John Jay Crawford 45093 Tory Jon Crawford 45094 Douglas C. Crissman 45095 Jonathan B. Crocker 45096 Charles Trent Crosby 45097 Robert Lucas Gregory Crouch 45098 Richard A. Crusan 45099 John Charles Cunniffe 45100 Albert Kelker Cushon 45101 Scott David Custer 45102 Erik C. Dahl 45103 William Edward Dahlberg 45104 John S. Dailey 45105 Theodore Joseph Daley 45106 Gail L. Sharpsten 45107 John Michael Davis 45108 William Charles Degutis 45109 Daniel V. Deleon 45110 Sean T. Deller 45111 James Raymond DeMoss 45112 Donna L. Vorpahl 45113 Lisa Marie Denny 45114 Barry Gerard Depot 45115 Thomas Joseph Desperito 45116 David Wayne DeTata 45117 Keith Andrew Detwiler 45118 Mary Devoe Sawyer 45119 Ellen Sue Dexter 45120 Ricardo Felix Diaz 45121 Amy Dickinson Stredler 45122 Anthony John DiNallo 45123 Douglas Allan Disinger 45124 Catherine Dix Caddell 45125 George Kenneth Dixon 45126 John Theodore Dluzak 45127 David J. Dluzyn 45128 Dean Morgan Dochterman 45129 James Edward Dodson 45130 Albert F. Dombrowski 45131 Steven Kent Donaldson 45132 Jennifer D. Taft 45133 Christopher Anthony Donovan 45134 Thomas Tracy Dorame 45135 Robert Lathrop Doran 45136 Timothy Thomas Doran 45137 John James Dorney 45138 Grant Russell Doty 45139 Scott Howard Douglas 45140 Michael Edward Doyle 45141 Patrick O'Rourke Doyle 45142 David Andrew Drotar 45143 Alan Hugh Drum 45144 Stephen Robert Duea 45145 Robert Lynn Duffy 45146 John M. Duhamel 45147 Gary V. Duncan 45148 Albert Harrison Dunfee 45149 Christopher Anthony Durand 45150 James Michael Durham 45151 James Franklin Dusenberry 45152 Colleen Ann Dwyer 45153 Patrick Ambrose Dwyer 45154 Thomas Aquinas Earls 45155 Matthew Patrick Easley 45156 Michael Odell East 45157 Christopher Ray Easter 45158 David Raymond Ebbrecht 45159 Andrew W. Eberhard 45160 Gregory Ralph Ebner 45161 Erin Paul Edgar 45162 John Bel Edwards 45163 John Francis Egan 45164 Stephen Matthew Egbert 45165 David George Ehlis 45166 Mark Edward Eichelman 45167 Paul Leonard Eisenmann 45168 Robert Eugene Eisiminger 45169 Raymond Kenneth Elderd 45170 Timothy J. Engling 45171 Theodore Matthew Epple 45172 Michael David Esch 45173 Steven Edward Eskridge 45174 Michael Croden Esquivel 45175 Pablo Estrada 45176 Arnold B. Evans 45177 Kelly Michael Evans 45178 Michael Douglas Evans 45179 Robert Philip Fabrizzio 45180 Samuel Paul Fagone 45181 Donald G. Fallin 45182 Michael Joseph Farley 45183 David Michael Farrick 45184 Barth Christopher Fassbender 45185 Thomas Clifford Feder 45186 Adrian John Fehl 45187 W. Scott Field 45188 Peter Alan Finken 45189 Karen Fish Hallett 45190 Robert Joseph Fitzsimmons 45191 Wade Andrew Foote 45192 David Douglas Forchielli 45193 Andrea F. Hodge 45194 Mary M. Foreman 45195 Joseph Eugene Foster 45196 Robert Fraire 45197 Brian David Fraley 45198 Douglas Edward Fraley 45199 George Henry Franco 45200 Steven Ronald Frank 45201 Antoine Freche 45202 Mark Allen Freitag 45203 Gregory Owen Friedland 45204 Vaughn Arthur Frigon 45205 Kenneth H. Fritzsche 45206 Malcolm Bradley Frost 45207 Walter D. E. Frye 45208 Jeff Bryan Fuchs 45209 Marc Duane Furey 45210 Dale K. Furrow 45211 Steven R. Fusinetti 45212 Norman Henry Fuss 45213 Michele Lori Futernick 45214 Thomas Bruce Gabriele 45215 Daniel Michael Gadbois 45216 Francine Ann Gagne 45217 Sandy Louis Galacio 45218 James Leonard Galante 45219 Christopher Earl Ganny 45220 Sean Gano 45221 Antonio Garcia 45222 William Anthony Garland 45223 Todd Garlick 45224 John Lopez Garnica 45225 George Todd Garrell 45226 Patrick Loren Gary 45227 Brian Keith Gates 45228 Gregory Andrew Gatti 45229 Joseph Martin Gaudette 45230 Marc Laurent Gauval 45231 John Anderson George 45232 Randy Alan George 45233 Bradley T. Gericke 45234 John Steven Gersch 45235 Anthony Craig Gilb 45236 Michael John Gillette 45237 Christina Marie Girard 45238 Kimberly Sue Glassford 45239 Peter Clarke Glover 45240 Simon Rupert Goerger 45241 John Cornelius Goetz 45242 Troy Michael Goldhammer 45243 Jose Maria Gomez 45244 Caren Anne Puckett 45245 Kenneth James Goodlow 45246 Jeri Lee Gordon 45247 Sanju Goswami 45248 Michael Joseph Gould 45249 Gregory Allen Graber 45250 Shawn Patrick Granger 45251 Sharon Lynn Grasley 45252 Gregory Howard Graves 45253 Delvakia Gray 45254 Kevin John Gray 45255 John Welch Green 45256 John E. Griffis 45257 Raymond Edwin Griffiths 45258 Christian Bernard Grinsell 45259 Karl G. Grizio 45260 William Arthur Grotz 45261 Michael John Gruber 45262 Athena C. Malloy 45263 Christopher K. Guyon 45264 Gregory James Haack 45265 Dylan Jedediah Haas 45266 Thomas James Hadel 45267 Joel Davis Hagy 45268 John Edward Haley 45269 Elizabeth Halford 45270 Dawn Patrice Hoopingarner 45271 James William Hall 45272 John Haller 45273 Thomas K. Hallett 45274 Linwood Q. Ham 45275 David Mark Hamilton 45276 Karlton Hamilton 45277 Paul Richard Hamilton 45278 David Allen Hamm 45279 Michael Wayne Hamm 45280 Morgan Patrick Hanlon 45281 Robert John Hannah 45282 Christopher Henry Hannon 45283 Lance D. Hansen 45284 Erik William Hanson 45285 Kirk W. Hansen 45286 Glenn David Harrington 45287 Benjamin M. Harris 45288 Kevin Scott Harris 45289 Robert David Harris 45290 Terrence Vaughn Harshfield 45291 Nicholas Joseph Hart 45292 Steven Derek Hart 45293 John Paul Hartke 45294 William F. J. Hasper 45295 Jacquelyn Haug Heer 45296 Michael Todd Hawn 45297 Peggy Anne Creveling 45298 Philip James Hayes 45299 Harold Martin Hays 45300 Charles Edward Haywood 45301 Michael Wayne Hazelwood 45302 Todd Jeffrey Hecker 45303 Jeffery James Heer 45304 Clark Hayden Heidelbaugh 45305 Christine Jo Held 45306 Carol A. Redfield 45307 George Eric Helms 45308 Todd Frederick Helt 45309 Jeremiah Shields Heneghan 45310 Michael Gary Henley 45311 Michael Wayne Henry 45312 Charles Thomas Hensley 45313 Jeffrey Hensley 45314 Curtis James Herrick 45315 Timothy Roy Hess 45316 Alan Wayne Hester 45317 Lisa Heveri Cariello 45318 John Patrick Hiatt 45319 Timothy Patrick Hiebert 45320 James Michael Hill 45321 Mark Christopher Hill 45322 Sidney Roye Deburgh Hinds 45323 Allan W. Hinkle 45324 Richard Carroll Hinman 45325 Clifford Alexander Hodge 45326 Gregory W. Hodge 45327 Jodi L. Horton 45328 Keith Dennis Hohman 45329 Michael Rodgers Holland 45330 Dean Harry Hommer 45331 Arthur Clifton Hood 45332 Paul Matthew Hoogenboom 45333 Robert Samuel Hookness 45334 Dennis Cecil Hopkins 45335 Kirk Edward Hotelling 45336 Colin Eugene Hotnit 45337 Eric John Howard 45338 Ronnie Wayne Howell 45339 Michael Christopher Hoynes 45340 Mark George Hreczuck 45341 Franz Jose Huber 45342 Leonard Scott Huff 45343 Robert Leland Huffaker 45344 Dean G. Hughes 45345 Edward Thomas Hughes 45346 Scott Allen Hunt 45347 Ian Percy Hunter 45348 Christopher Ralph Hupp 45349 Craig Alan Hurley 45350 Paul Joseph Hurley 45351 Wayne John Hutt 45352 Inku Hwang 45353 Patrick Joseph Hynds 45354 John Joseph Iannitello 45355 Jose Francisco Paterno Ibarra 45356 Warner A. Irizarry 45357 James Tim Isacco 45358 Walter Eugene Isler 45359 Colin Hiroki Itagaki 45360 Barry Gerard Ives 45361 Lawrence Matthew Iwanski 45362 Archie Jackson 45363 Gregory Alan Jackson 45364 John Stephen Jonowski 45365 Raymond Matthew Jefferson 45366 Mark E. Jeffris 45367 Gregory Michael Jenkins 45368 Sean Michael Jenkins 45369 Marilou Jilbert Shepard 45370 Charles Johnson 45371 Lewis Allen Johnson 45372 Michael William Johnson 45373 Mitchell Bradley Johnson 45374 Ronald Glen Johnson 45375 Scott Allen Johnson 45376 Darin Keith Jones 45377 Mark David Jones 45378 Mark David Jones 45379 Andrew J. Juknelis 45380 Michael Edward Kaffka 45381 Page Anthony Karsteter 45382 Ralph Lester Kauzlarich 45383 John Joseph Gerard Keating 45384 Brian Jeffrey Keen 45385 Michael J. Keith 45386 Eric Reed Keltner 45387 Eric C. Keltz 45388 James Todd Kennard 45389 Robert Hargreaves Kewley 45390 Carl J. Kielbasa 45391 R. Kent Kildow 45392 John Michael Kilgallon 45393 Christine Killoran Anderson 45394 David Yong Kim 45395 Won Sok Kim 45396 Jeffrey Alan Kimes 45397 Robert Leroy King 45398 Scott David King 45399 Steven Michael King 45400 Robert O'Connor Kirkland 45401 Matthew Brett Kirt 45402 Richard Michael Kivi 45403 John Edward Klatt 45404 Michael Kevin Klee 45405 Gina Klein Lavender 45406 Charles Henry Klinge 45407 Lori Jean Klinger 45408 Kevin Paul Kluetz 45409 Cecilia Anne Knecht 45410 J. Paul Knight 45411 Steven Duane Knight 45412 Mark Alan Knowlton 45413 Gerald Charles Kobylski 45414 Gordon Kohl 45415 Christopher John Kolly 45416 Stephen A. Koski 45417 Richard Harry Krafft 45418 David Mark Krall 45419 Judith Ruth Kress Marburger 45420 Philip S. Krichilsky 45421 Kevin John Kriesel 45422 Todd Joseph Kruse 45423 Frank Gregory Kubista 45424 Heidi H. Kuebler Kras 45425 Dale Clayton Kuehl 45426 Lisa Kuessner Jones 45427 Scott Duane Kunselman 45428 Michael E. Kurilla 45429 Aaron Matthias Kuzemka 45430 John Eric Lacksen 45431 David J. LaFontaine 45432 Devrie Ann Weliver 45433 Ramona Denise Plemmons 45434 Scott David Landry 45435 Coleman Richard Larlee 45436 Daniel Scott Larsen 45437 David Maitland Lauderdale 45438 Timothy Scott Laughrey 45439 Edward R. Lawson 45440 Bernard Won Lee 45441 Gregory Yoonwoo Lee 45442 Shane Evan Lee 45443 David Craig Leek 45444 Martin Thomas LeFevour 45445 Christopher Joseph Lehner 45446 Paul Edward Leistensnider 45447 Chad Gerard LeMay 45448 Robert Stephen Leonard 45449 Robin Marie Mims 45450 John W. Letarte 45451 Corey Russell Leverette 45452 John William Lewis 45453 J. Michael Lewis 45454 Lyle Edward Lewis 45455 Sean P. Lewis 45456 John J. Lindsay 45457 Paul Stephen Linkins 45458 Bruce George Lipp 45459 Thorsten Adolf Littau 45460 Jose-Ramon Geronca Lobaton 45461 Jan Kathryn Lockhart 45462 Steven Reno Loglisci 45463 Gregory Harold Louks 45464 Sharon K. Rogers 45465 Antonio Luciano 45466 Christopher W. Luhman 45467 James Patrick Mackin 45468 Paul William Maetzold 45469 Christopher Hendric Magee 45470 John Edward Maher 45471 Brian Bernard Mahoney 45472 Scott A. Maitland 45473 Anthony Michael Malba 45474 Michael Joseph Manion 45475 Rodney C. Manor 45476 John V. Maradits 45477 Francis Graziano Maresco 45478 Pablo Corpuz Mariano 45479 Joseph Raymond Markert 45480 David Scott Marks 45481 Ann T. Marshall Miller 45482 John Carl Marten 45483 David William Martin 45484 Eugene Joseph Martin 45485 Jorge L. Martin-Cintron 45486 Jeffrey Richard Martindale 45487 David Michael Martinez 45488 Edwin Martinez 45489 Monte Maurice Masters 45490 Thomas Paul Mathers 45491 Patrick Ernest Matlock 45492 Craig Matthew Matsuda 45493 Patrick L. Matthews 45494 Leonard Hubert Matz 45495 John Paul Maultsby 45496 John Patrick Maza 45497 Robert John McAleer 45498 Arthur Beard McAulay 45499 Douglas Carl McBroom 45500 Thomas Lee McCafferty 45501 Marc Gregory McClellan 45502 Marc Richard McCreery 45503 William Edward McDowell 45504 Craig S. McGinnis 45505 Paul Michael McGrath 45506 Patrick J. McHenry 45507 Gregory Wilson McIntyre 45508 Joseph Patrick McKay 45509 David Douglas McKee 45510 Bernadette Dorothy Hikins 45511 Mark Douglas McLaughlin 45512 Kelvin Dwight McLendon 45513 Joseph Larry John McMillen 45514 Timothy Russell McMinn 45515 Brian Stewart McNaughton 45516 George Bradley McNeely 45517 Dennis James McNulty 45518 James Randall Meade 45519 Edward James Melanson 45520 Michael A. Mellor 45521 John Walter Menges 45522 Brian Joseph Mennes 45523 Rodney Allen Mentzer 45524 Ronald Bryant Meredith 45525 Stephen Leopold Augustus Michael 45526 Walter Thomas Michel 45527 Brian Mark Michelson 45528 Donna M. Sweeney 45529 Gregory Jerome Miller 45530 Teresa Louise Miller Walker 45531 Todd D. Miller 45532 Douglas William Mills 45533 Rocco Matthew Minicucci 45534 Michael Sean Mitchiner 45535 Matthew Carl Moellering 45536 Eric Vern Mohney 45537 Richard Francis Molyneaux 45538 Cheryl Lynne Moman 45539 Victor F. Mondo 45540 David John Monk 45541 Joseph Arnold Montanaro 45542 Robert Mead Montgomery 45543 Caroline J. France 45544 Robert S. Moore 45545 Mark James Morasky 45546 Danny E. Morgan 45547 Jeffrey Scott Morgan 45548 Paul Freeman Morton 45549 John Byerly Mosher 45550 Jeffrey P. Muhlenkamp 45551 Dana Alan Munari 45552 James Patrick Murphy 45553 John James Murphy 45554 John Albert Nagl 45555 Alfred Najera 45556 Nancy Lynn Nakahara 45557 Phillip Joseph Napolitano 45558 William Wallace Nase 45559 Marcel Rainer Naujok 45560 Rafael Daniel Negron 45561 Jon Robert Nelson 45562 Suzanne R. Burk 45563 Darrel Bergeton Nerove 45564 Ernest Nichols 45565 Jason C. C. Nielsen 45566 Steven Bradley Nitsberg 45567 David Edward Noegel 45568 Sean M. Nolan 45569 John Blair Northrop 45570 John Firman Norton 45571 Daniel Scott Nunn 45572 Frederick Ira Nutter 45573 Patrick Michael O'Brien 45574 Leo James O'Donnell 45575 Eileen M. O'Grady 45576 Holly O. Rebelez 45577 John Joseph Oleinik 45578 Dan Stephen Olexio 45579 Eddie Oliver 45580 Keith Edward Olson 45581 Martin Joel Olson 45582 Anthony L. Olvey 45583 Frank Allen O'Neal 45584 Daniel Patrick O'Neill 45585 Jeffrey Thomas Oppenheim 45586 James R. Orbock 45587 Michael Vincent Ossanna 45588 Rosanne Frances Ott 45589 Mark Herbert Ottoson 45590 David Simpson Overton 45591 Mark F. Owens 45592 Curtis Bryan Paarmann 45593 John Valdo Painter 45594 John Edwin Palmer 45595 Michael Edward Panetta 45596 Jefferson Raymond Panton 45597 Michael John Pape 45598 Janice Paprocki Johnston 45599 Timothy Aloysius Parietti 45600 Keith J. Parker 45601 Benton John Partlow 45602 Justin Francis Patsey 45603 Andre Mauricio Pauka 45604 Richard Lee Paul 45605 Charles Aaron Pavlick 45606 Jack Ellison Peak 45607 Stannon Madson Pederson 45608 David Walter Penczar 45609 Shawn Patrick Penning 45610 Claude Clayton Perkins 45611 John Daryl Pero 45612 Jeff Dickson Petersen 45613 Andres Jaan Peterson 45614 Howard Kennedy Phelan 45615 Gordon William Phelps 45616 Daniel H. Picking 45617 Christopher Laurence Pietrzak 45618 Raul Antonio Pina 45619 Carmen Joseph Pino 45620 Bradley Wayne Pippin 45621 Gene Matthew Piskator 45622 Eric J. Pluckhorn 45623 Kenneth William Pollock 45624 Andrew Peter Poppas 45625 Michael Scott Porter 45626 Torrance James Porter 45627 William Anthony Porter 45628 Joel David Portuese 45629 Randy Eugene Powell 45630 John Graves Powers 45631 Gordon Troy Prairie 45632 Jeffrey C. Predmore 45633 Daniel Lorentz Pritchard 45634 Beth Ann Prost Manning 45635 James Daniel Pruneski 45636 Kenneth Scott Prygoski 45637 Alejandro M. Puig 45638 Brian Rodney Pulford 45639 Stephen Robert Purtell 45640 Robert James Rabb 45641 Curtis Todd Ramsey 45642 William L. Ratliff 45643 Craig Allen Raymond 45644 Peter John Rayna 45645 Larry Patrick Reback 45646 Darren M. Rebelez 45647 Robert Todd Redman 45648 Kevin Richard Reeves 45649 Randall Richard Reeves 45650 Robert Patrick Regan 45651 Lawrence Drew Reimers 45652 Myron John Reineke 45653 Erick Arthur Reinstedt 45654 Richard Martin Reyno 45655 Todd Roland Reynolds 45656 Kurt Thomas Ricci 45657 Daniel Edward Rice 45658 Frederick Lambrecht Rice 45659 Ryan Nelson Richardson 45660 Shawn Michael Richardson 45661 Laurel Ricketts Klinge 45662 Andrew Paul Rienstra 45663 Charles David Rigney 45664 Jerry Rodriguez 45665 Magda Rodriguez Bennett 45666 Edward Lee Roess 45667 Stuart Allen Roop 45668 Mark Howard Rose 45669 Patrick Martin Ross 45670 Michael John Rounds 45671 Kenneth Todd Royar 45672 Philip Peyton Rufe 45673 John Robert Ryan 45674 Michael Patrick Ryan 45675 Mark Harding Salas 45676 George James Salerno 45677 Scott Richard Sallah 45678 Benjamin James Sandford 45679 Warren Craig Sanks 45680 Celso Jerome Sandoval Santiago 45681 Jeffrey William Sauer 45682 Edward DeGrange Saulny 45683 Angelika Schaefer Morasky 45684 David Paul Schankin 45685 Karen M. Soscia 45686 James Raymond Schenck 45687 Clay S. Scherer 45688 Brenden Manuel Scherr 45689 Maribeth Ann Affeldt 45690 Linda Schimminger Lairson 45691 Sande Jon Schlesinger 45692 Rodney Jon Schlosser 45693 Matthew Clifford Limoges Schnaidt 45694 John Thomas Schoeppach 45695 Jeffery John Schorr 45696 John Edward Schotzko 45697 Eric Robert Schrenker 45698 Robert Schroder 45699 Eric Karl Schuster 45700 Francis John Schutte 45701 John Patrick Schwab 45702 Christopher Alan Schwartzbauer 45703 John Robert Schwetje 45704 Kelley Owen Scott 45705 Timothy Patrick Scott 45706 Jeffrey Scott Seay 45707 Matthew G. Sebenoler 45708 Michael John Seifert 45709 Marcie Seiner Johnson 45710 Monica R. Settles-White 45711 Kerry Keenen Shafer 45712 Jeffrey Mark Shapiro 45713 Christopher John Sharpsten 45714 John Bruce Shattuck 45715 Trevor W. Shaw 45716 Kirk Allen Shepherd 45717 Stacey Noel Johnson 45718 Jeffrey Brent Shiley 45719 Kevin John Shiller 45720 William David Shirley 45721 Wilson A. Shoffner 45722 Jay Scott Shonka 45723 Scott Alexander Shore 45724 Thomas Edward Shuler 45725 Shelly E. Muhlenkamp 45726 Jon Lee

Shupenus 45727 Christine Siegwarth Meyer 45728 Barry Jon Sievers 45729 Aaron Newell Silver 45730 Daniel Edward Simpson 45731 Sean Patrick Sinclair 45732 Michael Jay Sinnema 45733 Joseph Donald Skufca 45734 Laura Irene Slattery 45735 Allan G. Smith 45736 Patrick Ralph Smorra 45737 Scott Francis Snair 45738 David Broten Snodgrass 45739 Philip J. Sobiesk 45740 David Nelsen Sommerness 45741 Wayne Woo Young Song 45742 James Edward Sorensen 45743 William Louis Soscia 45744 Scott Richard Spaniol 45745 Brian Keith Spicer 45746 Joseph Michael Sroka 45747 William Sam Stallworth 45748 Darrell David Stanaford 45749 John Howard Stanley 45750 Jon Michael Staples 45751 Ronald Daryl Stappert 45752 Murray Paul Starkel 45753 Edwin Earl Starr 45754 Mark Daniel Steele 45755 Nicholas Todd Steele 45756 Mark Clinton Stevens 45757 Dale Bradley Stewart 45758 Steven Alexander Stoddard 45759 Peter R. Stoneham 45760 Veronica Annette Aldstadt 45761 Tim J. Strange 45762 Travis Cortez Strickland 45763 Scott Allan Strine 45764 Edward Anthony Struzik 45765 Scott Allen Suitts 45766 Dennis Sean Sullivan 45767 Gary Albert Sullivan 45768 Darren Jerod Sumter 45769 Edward Scott Surek 45770 Phon Dewey Sutton 45771 Barry Paul Sweeney 45772 Samuel Vansaun Swindell 45773 Stephanie Sykes Campbell 45774 Arunas Jonas Tamulaitis 45775 Frank W. Tate 45776 Gerald Lyn Taylor 45777 Jeffrey Alan Teach 45778 Michael Thomas Tetu 45779 John Allen Tewsbury 45780 Roy Therrien 45781 Andrew Edward Thompson 45782 John Lewis Thurman 45783 Donaldson Preston Tillar 45784 James Ivan Tilton 45785 Eric Kent Titus 45786 David Matthew Toczek 45787 Peter Michael Tofani 45788 Jeffery Keith Toomer 45789 Kerry James Trahan 45790 Douglas J. Trainor 45791 Matthew David Travers 45792 Luis Alfredo Trigo 45793 Jeffrey Ray Tronvold 45794 Sherise Brown 45795 Edward Mark Turner 45796 Morris A. Turner 45797 David Eric Tuttle 45798 Andreas Sebastian Ulrich 45799 David Juno Uyematsu 45800 Erik Valentzas 45801 Loyal Christopher Van Dyke 45802 Laura Lee Sauceda 45803 Timothy Richard Vara 45804 Anthony W. Vassalo 45805 David Dow Velloney 45806 Philip Michael Verges 45807 John Alfred Vigna 45808 Joseph James Volpe 45809 Larry H. Vorpahl 45810 Waymon Ray Votaw 45811 Nicholas James Vozzo 45812 Daniel Paul Wallace 45813 Daniel Raymond Walrath 45814 Michael Joseph Walsh 45815 Mark Lee Walters 45816 John Lanier Ward 45817 Kelly J. Ward 45818 David George Warner 45819 John Warner Washburn 45820 Jeffery Jay Watson 45821 Robert Lewis Watson 45822 Robert Michael Weaver 45823 Benjamin Earl Webb 45824 Robert Kentaro Webster 45825 William Vernon Wechsler 45826 Karen Anne Holmes 45827 David Matthew Weinerth 45828 Leonard E. Wells 45829 JoAnn Morrow 45830 Eric Wells Werner 45831 Michael Andrew Wernicke 45832 Christopher Kent West 45833 Gordon Warner Whatley 45834 Donald S. Whipp 45835 Shari Kay Garwick 45836 Paul Neal Wierschem 45837 David James Wilkie 45838 Charles Henry Williams 45839 Christopher Edward Williams 45840 Dennis Christopher Williams 45841 Kevin Wayne Williams 45842 Michael Jordan Williams 45843 Dennis M. Wince 45844 John Paul Winegarden 45845 Michael Joseph Wise 45846 Anthony Joseph Wisely 45847 Peter B. With 45848 Mark Raymond Wittlin 45849 Richard Eric Woehler 45850 Marvin Robert Wolgast 45851 Alan Roy Wood 45852 John Lebaron Woodbury 45853 Joseph Lee Woodbury 45854 Phillip Craig Woodham 45855 Carl Richard Woods 45856 Johnny D. Wright 45857 Scott Archer Wychgel 45858 Ledley Lewis Yaussy 45859 Carol Ray Young 45860 Kevin Patrick Young 45861 Robert Joseph Young 45862 Michael Yuschak 45863 Carlos A. Zamora 45864 Gwen Zemaitis Baker 45865 Rhonda S. Dunfee 45866 Scott John Zigmond 45867 Francisco Zuniga 45868 David Paul Hathaway 45869 Kevin Henry Adams 45870 James Stanley Baldree 45871 Vincent Anthony Bono 45872 Scott Allen Bradley 45873 George Norman Christensen 45874 James Conrad Gallup 45875 Adam Ray Grijalba 45876 Stuart Jefferson Gubler 45877 Jo Levern Hall 45878 Robert Edward Hamilton 45879 Darien P. Helmlinger 45880 Davis E. Jean-Louis 45881 Mary K. Crusan 45882 Anthony Stephen Ketron 45883 Richard Thomas Kidwell 45884 Bobby Jon Kirkpatrick 45885 Michael Roy Lover 45886 Michelle Ann Matthes 45887 Robert Dean Moran 45888 John Hamilton Nelson 45889 Michelle Patin Patin-Foote 45890 William Shannon Schleiden 45891 Kevin Leo Smith 45892 Paul Stephen Williams 45893 Kevin C. Fortier 45894 Patrick Earl Blair 45895 Andrew R. DeGuttadauro 45896 David Lynn Dellinger 45897 Garth Scott Estadt 45898 Richard Douglas Gillem 45899 Coll Stewart Haddon 45900 Ronald D. Herring 45901 William Do Kim 45902 Daniel Kane Kirk 45903 Thomas F. Lavallee 45904 Charles Edward Newbegin 45905 Michael Warren Noble 45906 Edward Dean Shultz 45907 Mark Edward Simmonds 45908 Michelle Williams Hannon 45909 Keith Robert Garwick 45910 **1989** Timothy F. Abbott 45911 Jenny W. Davis 45912 Robert Crawford Agans 45913 Mehmet Ali Agascioglu 45914 Jesus Aguirre 45915 Jeffrey Charles Ahrens 45916 Albert Llesis Alba 45917 Ronald Lee Albrecht 45918 Joel Patrick Alent 45919 Amber Delaine Allen 45920 Brian Christopher Allen 45921 Edwin Vernon Allen 45922 Hiroki Allen 45923 Scot Derek Allen 45924 John Chandler Allred 45925 Roy E. Alston 45926 Edward John Amato 45927 Mariano R. Amezcua 45928 Darrin Wayne Anderson 45929 Gregory Lee Anderson 45930 Jeffery Alan Anderson 45931 Jeffrey Norris Anderson 45932 John Charles Andonie 45933 Patricia Marie Anslow 45934 Vincente Javier Antolin 45935 Bruce Peter Antonia 45936 Quinton John Arnold 45937 Todd Alan Atwood 45938 Joseph Andrew Baalman 45939 David Edward Bailey 45940 Paul Derek Baisted 45941 Tina Marie Baker 45942 Robert Mark Balcavage 45943 Glenn Nazareth Balian 45944 Charles Earl Ball 45945 Michael A. Ball 45946 Thomas John Ballanco 45947 Kevin Edward Barber 45948 John Richard Barnett 45949 James Edward Barren 45950 Nathan D. Barrick 45951 John Matthew Barth 45952 Drew Charles Bartkiewicz 45953 Kimberly R. Sokol 45954 Brian Roger Bartos 45955 Robert M. Barush 45956 Roland Francis Batchelder 45957 Christopher Matthew Bates 45958 Randall E. Batson 45959 Christopher Randolph Beacham 45960 Michael Darren Bell 45961 Michael James Bell 45962 Shawn Patrick Bell 45963 Amy Elizabeth Bennett 45964 Arnold Anthony Bennett 45965 Nichelle Bennett Bruner 45966 Betsy Ann Jackson 45967 David Allen Biersach 45968 William P. Bijesse 45969 Jude Paul Bilafer 45970 Michael John Bindon 45971 R. Taft Blackburn 45972 Kimberly Blacker Tully 45973 David Laurence Blain 45974 Dennis W. Blaker 45975 Amy Blanchard Efaw 45976 Cary Lynn Blood 45977 Gary Edward Bloomberg 45978 Christopher Wayne Board 45979 George Scott Bobbitt 45980 Brett A. Boedeker 45981 James E. Boehl 45982 Shannon Lee Boehm 45983 John Zoltan Bohach 45984 Edward Thomas Bohnemann 45985 Joseph Edward Bolton 45986 Douglas Adam Boltuc 45987 Lawrence John Borkowski 45988 Joel Felix Bosco 45989 Brett Tedder Bowman 45990 George F. Bowman 45991 Earnest Eugene Boyd 45992 Robert Allen Boyer 45993 Robert G. Bozic 45994 Martin Joseph Brackett 45995 Christopher James Bradford 45996 Jane Brady Doucette 45997 Heather Brannon Fewell 45998 Michael D. Brantley 45999 Billy P. Braswell 46000 Michael Albert Braun 46001 Steven Lee Bray 46002 Jennifer L. Cowley 46003 Donald Charles Brewster 46004 Anthony Douglas Briggs 46005 Timothy Paul Brooks 46006 Scott Edward Brower 46007 Dean Alexander Brown 46008 Patrick Andrew Brown 46009 Michael I. Brownfield 46010 Lynette M.B. Arnhart 46011 Michael Alan Brumagin 46012 Frank Carl Brunner 46013 Jon G. Brunner 46014 David Joseph Brunnert 46015 Kerry Patrick Brunson 46016 Heather Lea Bryn 46017 Greg Stephen Buehler 46018 John Everett Burgess 46019 William Lewis Burruss 46020 Jeffrey A. Butler 46021 Matthew Paul Cadicamo 46022 Peter Louis Caldwell 46023 Steven Charles Calhoun 46024 James Joseph Callerame 46025 Eric M. Campany 46026 Ronald Lewis Campbell 46027 Wayne Anthony Cancro 46028 Michael Joseph Cannizzaro 46029 Bryan Eric Canter 46030 Stephan Alexander Capps 46031 John Christopher Carey 46032 Mark Bronson Carhart 46033 Michael Scott Carlson 46034 Stephen Harris Carlson 46035 Stephen T. Caro 46036 Brooke Thornton Carpenter 46037 Sean Michael Carroll 46038 Tyno Burnell Carter 46039 Martin Alan Case 46040 Stephen Hamilton Casey 46041 Roger Anthony Casillas 46042 Patrick David Cason 46043 Antony John Castagno 46044 Jeffrey Sean Castille 46045 Jonathan Neal Castle 46046 Roger Fainberg Cavazos 46047 Martin Hans Cesana 46048 James Leonard Chamlee 46049 William Eugene Champine 46050 Thomas Frederick Champion 46051 Gregory Paul Chandler 46052 Bumjin Chang 46053 J. Neil Chapman 46054 Emery John Chase 46055 Christella J. Chavez 46056 Christopher Matthew Chavez 46057 Gilbert Chavez 46058 Tonya Lashawn Carter 46059 Erik Chilian 46060 Richard Allen Chism 46061 Christine Moon Taran 46062 Song S. Choi 46063 Steven Bumjin Choi 46064 James Kuk Chan Choung 46065 Michael Scott Christians 46066 Wayne Bun Leung Chun 46067 Joe Woock Chung 46068 John E. Clady 46069 John Jeduthan Clark 46070 Jeffrey Craig Cleveland 46071 Valerie Marie Colangelo 46072 Daniel Matrin Cole 46073 John A. Cole 46074 Walter Preston Cole 46075 Charles C. Collins 46076 John Patrick Conboy 46077 Gregory John Conti 46078 David A. Converse 46079 Marc Cook Porterfield 46080 Terry Paul Cook 46081 Robert Stephen Cooley 46082 Mark Andrew Coons 46083 Brian Keith Coppersmith 46084 Alan Glenn C Suela Cordova 46085 Charles Christian Correll 46086 Brian Mark Cox 46087 Charles Clifford Crane 46088 Jeffrey Todd Crawford 46089 Michael John Crawford 46090 Richard Daniel Creed 46091 Neal L. Creighton 46092 Telita Crosland 46093 Donna A. Ward 46094 Daniel Lawrence Cruser 46095 Phillip Ray Cuccia 46096 Harry George Curley 46097 Matthew Leroy Curtis 46098 Nora P. Tellifson 46099 Francis Scott Cwiklinski 46100 Gregory Albert Daddis 46101 Chad Howard Dalton 46102 David A. Danikowski 46103 Lars Andreas Danner 46104 Douglas Dean Datka 46105 Jeffrey Allen Daws 46106 Joseph D'Costa 46107 John P. DeBlasio 46108 Timothy A. Decker 46109 Timothy James DeFoe 46110 Eric Joseph DeFrancisco 46111 Christopher Joseph Degutis 46112 Thomas Joseph Deierlein 46113 Douglas Jay DeLancey 46114 Kyle Paul Delaney 46115 Richard Alan Demaree 46116 Nicholas Roy DeMiro 46117 Ellen Anja Blackburn 46118 Randall Norman DeSoto 46119 Jeffrey Alan DeStefano 46120 Christopher Bean Destito 46121 Kevin E. Dice 46122 Michael Steven Dieroff 46123 Jeffrey David Dillemuth 46124 David William Dinger 46125 Janet Fern Seierstad 46126 Michael Joseph Ditullio 46127 Alan Michael Dodd 46128 Chae-Ung Um 46129 Francisco Jose Dominguez-Alvarez 46130 Juan Manuel Dominguez 46131 Christopher John Doniec 46132 Joseph Patrick Doran 46133 Jonathan Todd Drake 46134 John Francis Dunleavy 46135 David Paul Dunn 46136 Karen Dunn Braun 46137 Peter Claver Dunn 46138 Victor Valdimiro Duran 46139 Edward Joseph Dyke 46140 J. Arlen Ecker 46141 Paul Gerard Edwards 46142 Ronald Douglas Edwards 46143 Stephen Tyler Edwards 46144 Andrew Christopher Scott Efaw 46145 Michael George Ehard 46146 Mark Byron Elfendahl 46147 Jennifer A. Ellington 46148 Charles J. Emerson 46149 Nelson L. Emmons 46150 Charles Bryant England 46151 John Michael Epperly 46152 Todd William Erickson 46153 Treavor Keith Erney 46154 Bruce Andrew Estok 46155 Juan A. Estrella 46156 John Frederick Everhart 46157 Troy A. Faber 46158 Edward M. Falta 46159 John James Faria 46160 Shawn Montgomery Faunce 46161 Angelo Christi Fazio 46162 William Anthony Fecteau 46163 Andrew M. Fedorchek 46164 Dennis Charles Fehlinger 46165 Daniel Ferrara 46166 Michael Scott Ferris 46167 John Spencer Feutz 46168 Paul John Finken 46169 Matthew Patrick Finley 46170 Michael C. Fischer 46171 Todd Alexander Fisher 46172 Keith A. Flail 46173 Edward R. Fleming 46174 Antonio Manuel Fletcher 46175 Dean David Flint 46176 Robert Bruce Floersheim 46177 Jesse Clifton Folk 46178 James Gavin Ford 46179 John Arthur Ford 46180 John Scott Foresman 46181 Robert Anthony Forte 46182 John Clyde Fortson 46183 Christopher Daniel Fowler 46184 Peter Charles Fowler 46185 Roxanne Marie Fox 46186 Michael J. Francomb 46187 Cornell Parvin French 46188 James Edward Frezell 46189 Brian James Funfar 46190 Gregory Dmitri Gadson 46191 Bryan D. Galetano 46192 Jonathan Michael Gamm 46193 Edward R. Garcia 46194 John Angel Garcia 46195 Bret W. Garrett 46196 Michael Joseph Garvin 46197 Shawn Gregory Genal 46198 Jeffrey Willard Geoffroy 46199 John Michael George 46200 Oliver Clarence George 46201 Christian Stanley Gerig 46202 Thomas Troy Ghiglieri 46203 John K. Ghirardi 46204 Louis Craig Giammatteo 46205 Kenneth Clifton Gibson 46206 Robert Anthony Giczy 46207 Gary Thomas Giglio 46208 Brian Lee Gilbert 46209 Randall A. Glass 46210 Kirk William Gohlke 46211 Bradley Augustus Golden 46212 Stuart Paul Goldsmith 46213 Brian Kent Good 46214 Troy Murray Goodman 46215 William George Gould 46216 Troy Michael Gourrier 46217 George Steven Grabow 46218 Mark Vincent Grabski 46219 David William Grauel 46220 Scott Andrew Graves 46221 Michael Richard Greene 46222 Paul Edward Grey 46223 Kimberly Kathleen Griffin 46224 Kenneth Alan Griggs 46225 John G. Gromowsky 46226 Steven A. Gruenig 46227 M. Kevin Gullick 46228 Leif W. Gunhus 46229 Omar Francis Gutierrez 46230 Robert Arthur Gwinner 46231 Adolphus Rene Gwynn 46232 Teresa Ann Haering 46233 Frederick Hume Hager 46234 Larry Joseph Halida 46235 Arthur Lean Hall 46236 Thomas S. Hall 46237 David Shawn Halligan 46238 Michael J. Halpin 46239 Mark Dean Hamel 46240 Larry Wayne Hamm 46241 Robert Mac Hammond 46242 Richard Dwayne Hancock 46243 George Joseph Hanhauser 46244 Harold Mark Hannon 46245 Michael Christopher Hansen 46246 Cynthia Hargrow 46247 William Todd Harmon 46248 Dawn Marie Harold 46249 Jeffrey Paul Harrick 46250 James A. Harrington 46251 David Kevan Harris 46252 Charles W. Hartford 46253 Christopher Lee Hartle 46254 Kevin Dale Hartzell 46255 David Slade Harville 46256 George Pericles Hasapidis 46257 Sandra J. Hassett 46258 Wallace Howard Hastings 46259 Robert Stephen Hatala 46260 William Hal Hatchett 46261 David William Hauck 46262 Steven T. Haugenes 46263 Joseph Andre Hawes 46264 Frederick Barnes Hawkins 46265 Kathy Rohlena 46266 Timothy Patrick Healy 46267 Warren Eastman Hearnes 46268 Pamela T. Heckathorn Shaw 46269 Glenn Christopher Hedin 46270 Robert Richard Heininger 46271 John Maxie Hemmans 46272 Charles Scott Henderson 46273 Dale L. Henderson 46274 Darryl Gregory Henderson 46275 Kevin Dean Hendricks 46276 Richard Herbert Henkle 46277 Todd Michael Henry 46278 Matthew Scott Hergenroeder 46279 Guy Briggs Herman 46280 Donald Mathew Hermann 46281 Daryle J. Hernandez 46282 Arthur Paul Herold 46283 Lori K. Tompos 46284 Alexander C. Hicks 46285 James Michael Hill 46286 Ron J. Hill 46287 Stephen Francis Hillery 46288 Jamie Lorraine France 46289 Shirley Jayne Hitchcock Boyer 46290 Edward Jay Hlopak 46291 Michael John Hobbins 46292 Allan Eugene Hogue 46293 Marc Crosby Holden 46294 Robert Ivyl Holder 46295 Robert Wendell Holmes 46296 Brian P. Hopkins 46297 Charles Albert Hornak 46298 Jack Lionel Hornberger 46299 Garth Michael Horne 46300 Mark Dorian House 46301 Miguel Damian Howe 46302 Stephen Louis Hric 46303 Kevin F. Hub 46304 John Stephen Hurley 46305 Jeffrey Wade Hutchinson 46306 Melissa Jean Hyduchak Duhaime 46307 David Christopher Ice 46308 James Edward Illingworth 46309 Susan Christine Irons 46310 Corwin Fitzgerald Jackson 46311 Selwyn Rachon Jamison 46312 Frank Paul Janecek 46313 Peter Allen Janhunen 46314 Robert Richard Jankowski 46315 Mark Frank Janosy 46316 James Robert Janssen 46317 Thad Patrick Jarmon 46318 Alexander Jarotzky 46319 Thomas David Jarzen 46320 Brett Carlton Jenkinson 46321 Mark Mansfield Jennings 46322 Stewart Bruce Jesse 46323 Steven Tyler Joanis 46324 Donna Marie Johansen Dorminey 46325 Christopher Bruce Johnson 46326 Christopher Noel Johnson 46327 Eric Mitchell Johnson 46328 Frank R. Johnson 46329 Michael C. Johnson 46330 Timothy Jay Johnson 46331 Edward R. Jolley 46332 Bryan Neil Jones 46333 Gregory Scott Jones 46334 Jeffery Scott Jones 46335 Trudy J. Lewis 46336 William Edward Jones 46337 Daniel Gerard Jordan 46338 Robert Rothnick Jorgensen 46339 Cip C. Jungberg 46340 David James Kalb 46341 David James Kammen 46342 Kenneth Lee Kamper 46343 James Joseph Kardos 46344 Bruce Michael Karinshak 46345 Bryan Frederick Karinshak 46346 Deron Robert Kaseberg 46347 Roger R. Kashaninejad 46348 Kurt Joseph Kasun 46349 Timothy D. Keating 46350 Brendan Patrick Keegan 46351 John Arthur Kelly 46352 Stephen Denis Kennedy 46353 Amy Kerns Hawkins 46354 David Justin Kessler 46355 Richard Hamilton Kewley 46356 Jin S. Kim 46357 John Sok Kim 46358 Robert Shane Kimbrough 46359 Stuart Charles Kinder 46360 Julie Ann King Warner 46361 Stephen H. King 46362 Todd Joseph Kinser 46363 Dennis Patrick Kirby 46364 Jeffrey A. Klein 46365 Michael Patrick Klein 46366 Robert Louis Klucik 46367 Jeffrey Amos Knauer 46368 John Peter Knieriem 46369 Jay Evans Knox 46370 Kimberly Constance Knur 46371 Todd Mark Kobberdahl 46372 Mark Russell Koenig 46373 John Brian Kopchinski 46374 Victoria Ann Kost 46375 John Andrew Kotula 46376 Paul Andrew Kouri 46377 Cameron Alan Kramer 46378 Paul K. Kreis 46379 Mark S. Kremer 46380 Michael John Kristian 46381 Paul George Krueger 46382 Robert Arthur Kurzyna 46383 Jeffrey Joseph Kyburz 46384 Jonathan R. Lacey 46385 Patrick Michael Lacho 46386 Franklin Jerome Laden 46387 Cliff Michael Lairson 46388 Nathan Scott LaMar 46389 Theron Vincent Lambert 46390 Christopher James Landvogt 46391 Brian Buchanan Lane 46392 John Karl Lange 46393 Sherri Crystal Langston Whiteman 46394 Christian Adams LaPak 46395 Jill LaPlaunt Gould 46396 John Michael LaPorte 46397 Louis John Lartigue 46398 Todd Langston Lattimer 46399 Jonathan Dean Lau 46400 Timothy Merl Lauth 46401 Michael Anthony Lawter 46402 Lester Angelo Layman 46403 Kyle Eric Lear 46404 Emory Barger Leatherman 46405 Alec Sutton Lee 46406 Algustus Walton Lee 46407 Christopher Lee 46408 Dong W. Lee 46409 Ernest Changdae Lee 46410 Marc Alan Lee 46411 Preston Charles Lee 46412 Seung Joon Lee 46413 Kenneth Wayne Leisey 46414 Kevin Walters Lemke 46415 Marty Merle Leners 46416 Colleen Pana 46417 Joel James Levesque 46418 Brett David Lewis 46419 John W. Lewis 46420 Steven William Lewis 46421 Blaise Patrick Liess 46422 Reynolds James Lillibridge 46423 Joel Hongjy Lin 46424 Alvin B. Lindsay 46425 Troy Paul Lingley 46426 Kevin Robert Lingow 46427 Andrew John Lippert 46428 James Robert Lippincott 46429 Joan Hillary Landry 46430 Sarah De Los Angelas Llaguno 46431 Michael Scott Loccisano 46432 John Thomas Logsdon 46433 Andrew Davies Lohman 46434 Paul Anthony Lomtevas 46435 Joseph Flannery Lopes 46436 Ruben David Lopez 46437 Timothy M. Lorenz 46438 Christopher James Love 46439 Luke Robert Lozier 46440 James Henry IV Lynch 46441 Thomas Laurence Lynch 46442 William Henry Lynch 46443 Allyn David Lynd 46444 Philip Henry Macchi 46445 George Howell MacDonell 46446 Chelsea R. MacDougall 46447 Mark Gregor MacGregor 46448 Stacy Maciukenas Smith 46449 Jefferson Edgar Macklin 46450 Lisa Maria Maddox 46451 Billy Wade Mahaney 46452 William M. Mainor 46453 Thomas J. Maiwald 46454 Scott Thomas Mallory 46455 Christopher Michael Malloy 46456 Vincent F. Malone 46457 Melinda Anne Malskis Tarsa 46458 Dianne Maniuszko Falk 46459 Stephen C. Mannell 46460 Stephen J. Mapa 46461 Andrew Patrick Mapes 46462 Bert Delacruz Maqueda 46463 Charles Joseph Marcouiller 46464 Matthew Allen Marcy 46465 Virginia Therese Marion 46466 Robert Joseph Mark 46467 James Charles Markert 46468 Jay B. Marshall 46469 Craig James Martin 46470 Matthew Allen Martin 46471 Stanley Ronald Martin 46472 Lourdes Gisela Martinez 46473 Mary L. Martindale 46474 Steven Charles Mathews 46475 Douglas Dwayne Mathis 46476 John Wayne Matlock 46477 Dwayne Scott Matthews 46478 Peter Matthew Mavoides 46479 Jonathan Michael Mayer 46480 Paul Tillson Mayer 46481 Fernando Juan Maymi 46482 Louis Daniel Mayo 46483 Joseph P. Mazero 46484 Peter John McBreen 46485 Robert Allan McCann 46486 Bryan Stephen McClure 46487 Scott Russell McClure 46488 Douglas Scott McCoy 46489 Brian Robert McCullough 46490 James Alan

McDonald 46491 Jonathan Tobias McGlothian 46492 Chad Alan McGougan 46493 Michael James McGowan 46494 Scott Christopher McHenry 46495 Robert John McIlwaine 46496 Tad Michael McIntosh 46497 Scott Arnold McKechnie 46498 Joseph Stacey McLamb 46499 Edward Lingham McLarney 46500 Linda Marie McLaughlin 46501 Michael B. McManus 46502 Michael Joseph McManus 46503 Jeffrey Gordon McMillan 46504 William Edward McRae 46505 David E. McVay 46506 Timothy Allen McWain 46507 Kevin Patrick Meehan 46508 Paul Christopher Meggers 46509 Christopher Paul Melancon 46510 Gregory Scott Mellinger 46511 Gregg Eugene Merkel 46512 James Louis Merlo 46513 Mark Lyn Merrell 46514 Scott Allan Merriam 46515 Timothy Hiram Mersereau 46516 Alan Richard Metelko 46517 Glenn Jefferson Methvin 46518 Steven Elliott Metze 46519 Paul W. Metzloff 46520 William Michael Michaud 46521 Carla Miller Easter 46522 Eric Nathan Miller 46523 Joseph Wayne Miller 46524 Mark Allain Miller 46525 Stephen E. Miller 46526 William Darrin Miller 46527 David Bradley Millner 46528 Michael Roger Minogue 46529 Q. W. Cowart Misenheimer 46530 Douglas Michael Misenko 46531 Robert Charles Mitchell 46532 Randy Lee Moe 46533 William Gerard Montgomery 46534 James Marshall Moody 46535 Mark D. Mooney 46536 Patrick William Mooney 46537 Darren Wayne Moore 46538 Edmund W. Moore 46539 Guy Francis Moore 46540 Richard Scott Moore 46541 Samuel A. Moore 46542 William David Moore 46543 Ricardo Omar Morales 46544 Ian Robert Moran 46545 Christopher Philip Morris 46546 Robert Samuel Lewis Morris 46547 Scott Andrew Morrison 46548 Michael Edward Morrisroe 46549 Robert Charles Mueller 46550 Thom Michael Mukri 46551 Amy Lynn Anderson 46552 Richard Murg 46553 John Peter Murphy 46554 Scott Edward Murphy 46555 Patrick Brandon Muschamp 46556 John Paul Musone 46557 Ronald G. Myers 46558 James J. Nachazel 46559 Mary Nagrant Rigney 46560 Brian Kunio Nakamura 46561 Caroline Nalepa Phipps 46562 Mitchell Lewis Nance 46563 Michael Paul Napierala 46564 John C.M. Nelson 46565 Melinda Kay Nelson 46566 Scott Nelson 46567 David Michael Nero 46568 Jonathan Todd Neumann 46569 Christopher Michael Neville 46570 Craig Steven Newmaker 46571 Thomas Lee Niewald 46572 Marcellus Apostolos Niketas 46573 Vasilios Apostolos Niketas 46574 Kevin Scott Nikodym 46575 John P. Noback 46576 Frank Robert Nocerito 46577 Carolyn Nolan Morrison 46578 Eileen Patricia Nolan 46579 Robert M. Notch 46580 John Aubry Nowell 46581 Claude John Nusom 46582 William Crews Nyfeler 46583 Randall A. Nykanen 46584 W. Mark O'Brien 46585 John Joseph O'Connell 46586 Christopher J. O'Connor 46587 David Roy O'Connor 46588 Gerard Edmond O'Connor 46589 John Matthew O'Connor 46590 Robert Joseph Oehlers 46591 Patrick Sean O'Hanlon 46592 Dennis Michael O'Keefe 46593 David Aron Oksenberg 46594 William John Oliver 46595 Paul Martin Olsen 46596 Donald Lee Olson 46597 Michael James Opitz 46598 Frank Oprandy 46599 Robert Charles Orlando 46600 Lincoln Oro 46601 Kelly B. Butler 46602 Paul J. Ottariano 46603 Jack Albert Otteson 46604 Kelly Dean Ouderkirk 46605 William Glenn Padgett 46606 Keith Emery Page 46607 Hon Su Pak 46608 Robert Holden Paley 46609 Richard P. R. Pannell 46610 Melvin Frantrell Parker 46611 Robert Bryan Parker 46612 Steven Lloyd Parker 46613 Mark Steven Parrish 46614 Gregory Alton Parsons 46615 Peter K. Patacsil 46616 Anne Patterson Tuggle 46617 George E. Patterson 46618 Todd Bogan Paynter 46619 Wayne Cody Peck 46620 Ruth Pennington 46621 Kelly Crawford Perdew 46622 Joseph Thomas Perdue 46623 Carlos Perez 46624 Marcus Albert Marrero Perez 46625 Jeffrey Thomas Perkins 46626 Troy Douglas Perry 46627 Scott Alan Petersen 46628 Byron Douglas Peterson 46629 Randolph O. Petgrave 46630 Kevin Scanlon Petit 46631 Sandra Lee Petrin 46632 Salvatore Joseph Petrovia 46633 Ward Andrew Philips 46634 Donovan David Phillips 46635 Mark A. Phillips 46636 Matthew Joseph Phillips 46637 Steven Bradley Phillips 46638 Nicholas Alfred Piantanida 46639 Charles J. Pinigis 46640 Timothy Joseph Place 46641 Steven Charles Plank 46642 Gary Richard Polsinelli 46643 Michael Dushan Popovich 46644 Richard Lee Potterton 46645 Darius Anthony Powell 46646 Noel N. Pratap 46647 Richard Ray Preciado 46648 David Alexander Priatko 46649 Michael James Price 46650 Christopher Nixon Prigge 46651 Mark Stephen Provinsal 46652 Leo G. Pullar 46653 James Lloyd Pyatt 46654 David T. Quickstad 46655 John Patrick Quinn 46656 Robert Dean Radtke 46657 Charles Vaughn Raffay 46658 Mitchell Lawrence Rambin 46659 Harold William Rambusch 46660 Carl D. Ramsey 46661 Andrew William Randrup 46662 Scott Joseph Rauer 46663 Michael Winfred Rauhut 46664 John Charles Rayfield 46665 James Herbert Raymer 46666 David Richard Raymond 46667 Brian Joseph Reed 46668 Casey Allen Reed 46669 Joseph Oliver Reed 46670 Suzanne Reeder Miller 46671 Kathleen Regan Sullivan 46672 Stephanie Reich Kauzlarich 46673 David Dorsey Reichard 46674 Paul Gerard Reilly 46675 Nicholas Robert Reisdorff 46676 Matthew Martin Reyes 46677 John William Reynolds 46678 Christopher Aaron Richard 46679 Christina Richter Listermann 46680 Robert James Richtmyre 46681 Judith Rickenbacker Krause 46682 Andrew W. Riebe 46683 Ricky Dale Riley 46684 John Gerald Rippley 46685 Gary Brian Roberts 46686 Thomas Daniel Robertson 46687 Stephen John Robey 46688 Spencer William Robinson 46689 Javier Rodriguez 46690 Jonathan Michael Roitman 46691 Robert Ronald Rombough 46692 James S. Romero 46693 Nathan Eric Rosier 46694 Ian Cheney Ross 46695 Paul Hazen Ross 46696 David Edwin Rowell 46697 Melanie Lee Johnson 46698 Walter G. Roy 46699 Ross L. Ruchti 46700 Jeffrey Franklin Rufenacht 46701 Walter Thomas Rugen 46702 Adrienne Ruggles Eckstein 46703 Martin Anthony Ryan 46704 Lee A. Rysewyk 46705 John Joseph Sager 46706 Yurika Saito Karasz 46707 Michael James Saluto 46708 Ronald Louis Salvador 46709 Andrea Salvidio Brewster 46710 Theodore Andrew Samotis 46711 Frank Noll Sanders 46712 Thomas Lang Sands 46713 David John Santo 46714 George H. F. Sarabia 46715 Paul Victor Sariego 46716 Joseph Scott Sawyer 46717 Thomas James Scannell 46718 Darryl A. Scherb 46719 Christopher Andrew Schirner 46720 Robert R. Schmidt 46721 Charles Gerard Schretzman 46722 Adam John Schroeder 46723 Paul Franz Schubert 46724 Steven John Schulz 46725 Gillian S. Scice 46726 John Michael Scott 46727 Christopher Scuron 46728 John Edward Seamon 46729 Brian Edward Sebastian 46730 Anthony Sebo 46731 David Todd Seigel 46732 Timothy Raymond Seitz 46733 Kimberly J. Sebenoler 46734 Jaime Gerardo Serrano 46735 Janet A. Seufert 46736 Darren D. Shaffer 46737 Gregg Steven Sharp 46738 Lisa Anne Shay 46739 Michael Philip Shea 46740 John Lawrence Sheehan 46741 Thomas Gerald Sheehy 46742 Kathleen Marie Sherry 46743 Burton Kesler Shields 46744 J. Charles Shifferd 46745 Michael James Shinners 46746 Stephen Martin Shone 46747 H. David Silverman 46748 Benjamin M. Sim 46749 Robert Marshall Simmons 46750 Roger Allan Skavdahl 46751 Todd D. Smith 46752 Paul Steven Snyder 46753 Teresa Agnes Sobiesk 46754 Gregg Christopher Softy 46755 Mark Won Soh 46756 David Neil Sokol 46757 Mark William Solomon 46758 Lee Robert Sornson 46759 Pamela Jean Lohman 46760 Kelly L. Sowell 46761 James Alexander Sparkes 46762 Scott Andrew Sparks 46763 James William Spence 46764 Brian Keith Sperling 46765 Richard James Spinelli 46766 Eric N. Staat 46767 S. Peter Stark 46768 Curtis Lee Stedron 46769 Daniel Scott Stempniak 46770 Robert Lee Stephens 46771 Michael Allan Stevens 46772 Robert W. Stevens 46773 Todd Alan Stevens 46774 Eric W. Stewart 46775 Harold D. Stewart 46776 Ronald Scott Stewart 46777 Jason Lincoln Stine 46778 Mark Lincoln Stock 46779 Andrew Graham Stone 46780 Charles Shipman Stone 46781 David C. Stone 46782 Scott Allen Storkamp 46783 Andrew Joseph Strauser 46784 Diana Strickland Lyons 46785 Traci Lynette Strohl 46786 Eric M. Strong 46787 Mark Clifford Strong 46788 Lolita Stubblefield Davis 46789 Tracy Shawn Studer 46790 Brian Leroy Stumme 46791 Frank Douglas Sturek 46792 Douglas Vincent Stutz 46793 Adam Andrew Such 46794 Scott Richard Suhr 46795 Trent Matthew Suko 46796 Michael Matthew Sullivan 46797 Neil Joseph Sullivan 46798 Peter Traut Sullivan 46799 Douglas S. Sutter 46800 Robert Gerard Sutter 46801 Steven James Svoboda 46802 Erin Maureen Dulac 46803 Nathan Vose Sweetser 46804 James M. Swingle 46805 Stephannie Ann Tallent 46806 Christopher Paul Tapp 46807 Leafaina Olive Yahn 46808 Robert Joseph Taylor 46809 John Scott Telford 46810 Jon Emerson Tellier 46811 Beth Thomas Duffy 46812 Kimberly Jo Thomas 46813 Brian Lee Thompson 46814 P. Keith Thompson 46815 Timothy Trent Thompson 46816 Wiley Carl Thompson 46817 Bruce Kevin Thorn 46818 Eric David Tilley 46819 Linda Denise Timm Swann 46820 William Anthony Tohill 46821 Kenneth William Toney 46822 John Michael Tonra 46823 Robert F. Toole 46824 Onesimo Oscar Torres 46825 David Christopher Trybula 46826 Kevin Lee Tucker 46827 Philip Fortune Tull 46828 Charles Thomas Tully 46829 Norman Tallal Turfe 46830 Tracy Aaron Turner 46831 Jonathan Eric Ulsaker 46832 Edward J. Urbaniak 46833 Christopher James Vaka 46834 Bobbie Jo Vance Francis 46835 Richard John VanderWal 46836 Lee Matthew VanHouten 46837 Brent Alton Van Manen 46838 Sandra Vann Olejasz 46839 Paul Aaron Varner 46840 Michael Joseph Vassalotti 46841 Alex C. Vernon 46842 Joseph Hall Vest 46843 Scott Allen Vezeau 46844 John Vincent Viggiano 46845 Dennis Francis Villasenor 46846 Douglas Scott Vinson 46847 Kevin Michael Volk 46848 John Gary Voorhees 46849 Vincent Marcellus Wallace 46850 Charles Sebastian Walls 46851 Jason Louis Walrath 46852 William A. Walski 46853 James J. Walton 46854 Ann Wanner Holder 46855 Conan Michael Ward 46856 Michael James Ward 46857 Henry Benjamin Wardick 46858 Benjamin Fenton Warner 46859 David Paul Warshaw 46860 Glenn A. Waters 46861 Timothy Forbes Watson 46862 Michael Karl Wegler 46863 Thomas Edward Weisenfels 46864 Deborah A. W. Wellington 46865 William Brendan Welsh 46866 James Wenner 46867 Sally West Brownfield 46868 John Will Whatley 46869 John Whitley Wheeler 46870 Charles William White 46871 Kelly Ray Whiting 46872 Jon B. Wildermuth 46873 Amy Joellyn Franklin 46874 Maurice Lasalle Williams 46875 Robert Leroy Williams 46876 Thomas Roy Williams 46877 Russell Maurice Williamson 46878 James Richard Willis 46879 Isaiah Wilson 46880 John Nathan Wilson 46881 Margaret Rose Wilson 46882 Shawn Patrick Wilson 46883 William Todd Winklbauer 46884 Elizabeth Lyn Yarbrough 46885 Gregory Scott Winston 46886 Stephen William Witzmann 46887 Natee Wongissares 46888 Joyce Woo 46889 Bruce Michael Woolverton 46890 Michael John Worden 46891 Jeffrey Todd Workman 46892 Nicole A. Hagedorn 46893 Stephen Paul Workman 46894 Jon Arthur Wozniak 46895 Michael Andrew Wright 46896 Richard Andrew Wulff 46897 Michael David Wyant 46898 Ann Marie Bogshaw 46899 Amy Yaeger Paul 46900 Wade S. Yamada 46901 Roy Yan 46902 Scott David Yanagihara 46903 Eugene Arnold Yancey 46904 Dennis William Yates 46905 Kiyotaka Albert Yazawa 46906 Jose Christoble Ybarra 46907 Joseph Y. Yi 46908 Craig Alan Young 46909 Michael Anthony Young 46910 Susan M. Young 46911 Korta Yuasa 46912 Charles Kyoon Yun 46913 Daniel Yun 46914 Carl John Zaiser 46915 Bruce W. Zartman 46916 Craig Steven Zeitler 46917 James L. Ziegler 46918 Peter J. Ziomek 46919 Martin Adam Zybura 46920 Christopher Zigmund Barra 46921 Kevin Michael Barry 46922 Cid Fernando Carmona 46923 Leona C. Knight 46924 David Vincent D'Antonio 46925 Sigrun C. Denny 46926 Christopher Douglas Drinkard 46927 Randie Alexander Gardener 46928 George Chester Gatling 46929 William Eugene Gebhards 46930 Debarsher Nichol Gray Jackson 46931 Kenneth Dwight Hancock 46932 Eric De'Andre Handy 46933 Sherman William Henderson 46934 Mark Robert Hudak 46935 Michael C. Karsonovich 46936 James Christopher Kennedy 46937 Gerald E. Lilly 46938 Mark Lynwood Loggins 46939 Craig A. McCarthy 46940 Richard T. McCauley 46941 Andrew Arthur Merritt 46942 Damon Garnett Montgomery 46943 Lisa M. Fortin 46944 Amy M. Ritz 46945 Walter Randolph Robertson 46946 Brian Anthony Roeder 46947 K. Carlo Sampson 46948 Timothy Owen Sasser 46949 Tamara Singleton Broadnax 46950 Melody Denise Smith 46951 James Rodney Talley 46952 Mark Daniel Brewster 46953 Roberto Victor Hennessy 46954 Bryan Harold Babb 46955 Marco Julio Barrera 46956 Leslee Anne Wolf 46957 Diane L. Bodnar Nelson 46958 Marshall Benton Cain 46959 Tracey Clyde 46960 Everton Maurice Cranston 46961 Ron Davis 46962 Jack Donwyn Frey 46963 Douglas James Gels 46964 Russell Crofton Hayes 46965 Calvin Lewis Hines 46966 Victor Robert Horn 46967 Anthony Tyrone Jackson 46968 Jonathan Adam Lanciani 46969 Eric Christopher Niemann 46970 Ronald Wallace Smith 46971 James Michael Snow 46972 James Conrad Squire 46973 Timothy Paul Sullivan 46974 Sheryl Swofford Tullis 46975 Luis Fernando Zuna 46976 **1990** Albert Joseph Abbadessa 46977 Martin Lewis Abbott 46978 Allen G. Abell 46979 Joann Antonietta Acciarito 46980 William Eugene Acheson 46981 Clay Taylor Adams 46982 Darryl Keith Ahner 46983 Felisa Aldas Lewis 46984 Humberto J. Alexander 46985 Nathanael Lester Allen 46986 Michael C. Allison 46987 Jon Henry Amis 46988 Glenn Howard Amnott 46989 Lynn A. Delisle 46990 Albert Moulton Anderson 46991 David Charles Anderson 46992 Scott James Anderson 46993 Timothy Wayne Anderson 46994 Walter Boris Andonov 46995 Paul Patrick Andres 46996 Francis Lee Andrews 46997 Michael Logan Andrews 46998 Peter Burchard Andrysiak 46999 Richard D. Anthis 47000 Stephen Anthonavage 47001 Douglas William Apelt 47002 Albert Francis Armonda 47003 Michael Richard Armondo 47004 Sterritt Lee Armstrong 47005 Paul V. Ashcraft 47006 Jeffrey Jon Augeri 47007 Thomas David Augustin 47008 Christian Eric Aune 47009 John Hardin Austin 47010 Corey Roger Averill 47011 Scott Allan Baggett 47012 Brodrick Jerome Bailey 47013 Kristin Michelle Baker 47014 Paul Martin Baker 47015 William Blair Baldwin 47016 Troy Lee Bargmann 47017 David M. Barnes 47018 Benjamin Uriah Barnett 47019 Robert Leslie Barrie 47020 Myles Keough Bartley 47021 John Cornelius Baskerville 47022 John Alexander Basso 47023 Gregory Michael Bastien 47024 Daniel Garth Beatty 47025 Ivan Philip Beckman 47026 Jason Robert Begue 47027 Scott A. Belanger 47028 Robert Lee Bell 47029 Michael William Belzile 47030 Melissa Sloan House 47031 Edward Joseph Benz 47032 Elissa Marie Bergevin 47033 Michael Robert Berke 47034 Daniel Timothy Bernal 47035 Stephanie E. Paduchak 47036 Daniel Dupre Berry 47037 John Arthur Berry 47038 Joseph S. Bianchi 47039 Fred Lewis Bible 47040 Thomas Joseph Biel 47041 Benjamin James Bigelow 47042 Richard Hugh Bilello 47043 Brian Scott Birmingham 47044 Michael William Blaney 47045 Andrew David Blank 47046 William Tariel Bliss 47047 Betsy Block Gilland 47048 William Clarence Blume 47049 Patrice Mary Grace Sutherland 47050 Dawn M. Boland 47051 Expeditus B. Bolanos 47052 Scott Charles Bolick 47053 Douglas Michael Boone 47054 James Michael Booth 47055 James Frederick Borneman 47056 Mark Edward Borowski 47057 Morris Leonard Botkin 47058 David W. Bottcher 47059 Terrell Clinton Boyd 47060 Jonathan Thomas Boyer 47061 Leonard C. Boyer 47062 Patrick Michael Boyer 47063 Christopher Boyle 47064 Samuel Robert Boyles 47065 Cynthia L. Branch 47066 Bryan Andrew Brauer 47067 David N. Brechbuhl 47068 Ross Louis Brigger 47069 Hillery John Broadous 47070 Patrick Philip Brosseau 47071 Deborah Ann Brown 47072 John Mitchell Brown 47073 Michael Enloe Browne 47074 John Roger Bruellman 47075 John Francois Brumlik 47076 Joseph Paul Bruno 47077 Douglas Mattson Bryan 47078 Jonathan Douglas Buell 47079 James Christopher Bull 47080 Eric Francis Buller 47081 Ronald Boyd Bunch 47082 Eric Charles Burger 47083 Anthony Paul Burgess 47084 "William George, Jr. Burke 47085" Keith Wayne Burleson 47086 Brian Scott Burlingame 47087 David Ramon Bushee 47088 Steven Joseph Butler 47089 Catherine Mary Reyes 47090 Richard Van Cain 47091 Randall Keith Cales 47092 Mark Jude Camarena 47093 Bryan Edward Campbell 47094 Marjorie Mary Campbell 47095 Brian Wain Cannon 47096 Loren Glen Cannon 47097 Jeffery Allan Carlson 47098 Dawn M. Morris 47099 Joseph Arthur Carmody 47100 William Howard Carrier 47101 Eduardo Cartaya 47102 Kenneth Roland Casey 47103 Edward Allan Cashmere 47104 Timothy Mark Cauley 47105 Douglas Earl Chamberlin 47106 Dennis Patrick Chapman 47107 Kenneth Edward Chapman 47108 Tom S. Cheng 47109 Eric Michael Chibnik 47110 Raymond Inku Cho 47111 Benedict James Chu 47112 Randy Jae Chung 47113 Jon Joseph Chytka 47114 David A. Ciesinski 47115 Stephen David Cifrulak 47116 "Frank Stiles, III Clark 47117" Glenn Alan Clark 47118 Jeffrey J. Clark 47119 Kevin Earl Clark 47120 Richard M. Clark 47121 Andrew Todd Clements 47122 Mark Alan Clouse 47123 Samuel Cochrane 47124 Dennis Patrick Collins 47125 Timmy L. Collins 47126 Brian C. Cook 47127 James Clair Copenhaver 47128 Robert G. Cormier 47129 Eddie Joe Cottle 47130 David B. Cox 47131 Shannon Charlsi Cox 47132 Carl Anthony Curriera 47133 Scott Richard Curtis 47134 Paul Robert Cusack 47135 Travis L. Dalton 47136 Mark Richard Daniels 47137 Frederick James Danner 47138 Kimberly Lorraine Darby 47139 Marcus Ray Darnell 47140 Robert E. Davidson 47141 Patrick Burke Davie 47142 Ricardo Davila 47143 Brian Charles Davis 47144 Patrick Seely Davis 47145 Richard Allen Davis 47146 Rodney Allan Davis 47147 Joseph Luke Day 47148 Frank Joseph DeCarlo 47149 Gregory Allen Decker 47150 Rodney John Decker 47151 Bertrand Harold De Forest 47152 Christopher James DeGaray 47153 John Charles Dehn 47154 Joseph Nicholas DeJulius 47155 Dana Clement Delisle 47156 Todd Anthony Dellert 47157 James Todd Dell'Olio 47158 "Daniel Robert, Jr. Delp 47159" Steven Laurence Delvaux 47160 Kelly Marie Demers 47161 Sarah D. Parker 47162 Kelly D. Barnes 47163 Julie E. Morton 47164 Michael D. Detlefsen 47165 John Glenden DeVine 47166 Mario A. R. Diaz 47167 James Patrick Diggins 47168 George Alfred Dikeman 47169 Andrew Charles Dillon 47170 Debby Deanna Dines 47171 Barrett Shey Doane 47172 Kevin Butler Dodson 47173 Michael Gerard Dolan 47174 Jonathan Reidy Dols 47175 D. Glenn Donelin 47176 Moir P. Donelson 47177 Sean Lee Dorfman 47178 Sean D. Drake 47179 Ronald W. Draper 47180 Michael David Saunders Drisko 47181 Paul Stephen Dubbels 47182 Fitzhugh Lee Duggan 47183 Leannn Duhoski Berry 47184 Timothy L. Dukeman 47185 Michael Day Dullea 47186 Michelle Ann Dunne Beasley 47187 Steven Craig Durham 47188 Richard Scot Durost 47189 Eric Ashby Dutton 47190 Scott Alan Eader 47191 Kristin Marie Edwards Gagnon 47192 Eric Anderson Egan 47193 John Martin Eggert 47194 Michael Lee Eggleston 47195 Barry James Ehlers 47196 John Wesley Eisenhauer 47197 Charles B. Elliott 47198 Richard Lane Ellis 47199 Eric S. Enos 47200 Timothy John Ertmer 47201 David Anthony Esposito 47202 Andrew Roy Etnyre 47203 Jeffrey Scott Evans 47204 Michael Patrick Evans 47205 Jeffrey Nathaniel Evenson 47206 Daniel Neal Ewen 47207 Todd Darren Fath 47208 Daniel J. Fay 47209 Curtis Donald Feistner 47210 "Ronald Everett, Jr. Felder 47211" David Jarret Ferguson 47212 David Paul Ferguson 47213 Felipe Ferrer 47214 Thomas Joseph Fields 47215 Daniel Christopher Firlie 47216 Michael T. Fisher 47217 Tyler Falls Fitzgerald 47218 Brendan James Fitzpatrick 47219 Jennifer L. Fleming 47220 Jennifer Rae Flores 47221 Eric Paul Flowers 47222 Carolyn A. Ford 47223 Andrew John Forssell 47224 Collin J. Fortier 47225 Melynda M. Foye 47226 Michael Lee Foster 47227 "David Marsel, Jr. Foye 47228" Brian Patrick Freidhoff 47229 Kenneth S. Fu 47230 Michael Paul Gabel 47231 Mark Clement Gagnon 47232 Raoul Anthony Gaines 47233 Kimo Carter Gallahue 47234 Victor Gabriel Garcia 47235 James Thomas Garrett 47236 Brian Patrick Garrison 47237 Eric B. Gass 47238 Leo Thomas Gatewood 47239 Jonathan Douglas Gelman 47240 Michael David Gengler 47241 Brian R. Gephart 47242 Tad Loren Gerlinger 47243 William Edward Gibson 47244 Richard A. Gieseler 47245 Daniel J. Giesing 47246 Steven Wesley Gilland 47247 Gregory Alan Gilley 47248 Thomas W. Gilligan 47249 Andrew S. Girardi 47250 Bobby Earl Glaspie 47251 David Otto Gluth 47252 George Webster Godfrey 47253 Oleg Arkady Gostomelsky 47254 Jamie Gough 47255 Scott Allen

Graham 47256 Martha Giddings Granger 47257 Lance Matthew Granholm 47258 Taylor Lyn Gray 47259 William Morgan Gray 47260 Matthew K. Green 47261 Ronald James Green 47262 Kevin Patrick Gregoire 47263 Karl Allen Greiffendorf 47264 Darryl Carl Griffin 47265 Kimberly Lynn Sanborn 47266 Andrew Laurence Groeger 47267 Jennifer G. Buckner 47268 Robert Anthony Guerriero 47269 David James Gulick 47270 Thomas H. Guntrip 47271 Tritron R. Gurganus 47272 Jeffrey Carleton Hagler 47273 Scott George Hair 47274 Allison Hall Miller 47275 David Allen Hall 47276 Howard Pritchard Hall 47277 Edward Stephen Hallas 47278 Audrey Jeanette Hanagan 47279 Richard Lee Hansen 47280 David Wayne Hardy 47281 David McEachern Hart 47282 Russell Ray Harville 47283 Mark Alan Haseman 47284 Michael David Hassman 47285 Keith Arthur Hattes 47286 William Allan Hauschild 47287 Timothy Glen Havenhill 47288 Keith Austin Havenstrite 47289 Kenneth A. Hawley 47290 Lisa Haylett Pruett 47291 Garrett Durand Heath 47292 Ronald Everett Heatherly 47293 Christina Lee Herebert Mayer 47294 James Michael Heidenberger 47295 Jeffrey Paul Helbling 47296 Christopher Jon Helixon 47297 Brandon Keith Herl 47298 James Jay Hermacinski 47299 Heather Anne Yahn 47300 Keri Jean Robertson 47301 Matthew Wade Hester 47302 Paul Campbell Hester 47303 Donald A. Hicks 47304 Julianne Tracy Hodsden 47305 Daniel Lee Higgins 47306 Michael Scarth Higgins 47307 David C. Hill 47308 Kevin M. Hill 47309 Michael Scott Hill 47310 William Lewis Hinshaw 47311 Steven Brian Hocevar 47312 Scott Lawrence Hodsden 47313 Anthony John Hofmann 47314 Dallas Lowell Holverson 47315 John K. Hopf 47316 Kevin Lee Hoppens 47317 Kelso William Horst 47318 James Coulson Horton 47319 James Michael Houlahan 47320 Claude Edward House 47321 Edward Plater Hoyt 47322 Daniel F. Huantes 47323 Michael T. Hubbard 47324 Jeffrey Todd Hubert 47325 Ralph Marvin Hudnall 47326 Michail Sean Huerter 47327 Christopher Michael Hughes 47328 Beaver L. Huh 47329 Christina Lynn Schlosser 47330 David Evan Hurley 47331 Michael Joseph Hustead 47332 Robert Patrick Huston 47333 Paul Huszar 47334 Kevin Scott Hutchison 47335 Heyward Groverman Hutson 47336 Robert Waddington Hutson 47337 Todd Robert Hutton 47338 Derya Idemen 47339 Augusto A. Ingles 47340 Stephen Akira Inouye 47341 Stephen Donald Iram 47342 Robert Dean Irving 47343 Henry L. Jackson 47344 Louis Myles Jackson 47345 Mark Allen Jackson 47346 Michael S. Jackson 47347 James Frederic Jacobs 47348 Christopher Patrick Jenkins 47349 John Patrick Jenkins 47350 Bradford Linn Johnson 47351 Carol Ann Sumter 47352 Gordon Brett Johnson 47353 Joni Janine Johnson 47354 Todd Gregory Johnson 47355 Alan Richard Jones 47356 David Thomas Jones 47357 Derek Anderson Jones 47358 Fleming Holcombe Jones 47359 James E. Jones 47360 John Wilhelm Jones 47361 Quay Burton Jones 47362 Robert Scott Jones 47363 Thomas Keith Jones 47364 Thomas W. Jones 47365 Myer Joy 47366 Christina Stefanie Juhasz 47367 Joel Lee Kain 47368 Aaron Edward Kalloch 47369 Joseph Michael Kane 47370 Alan David Katz 47371 Mark Alan Keck 47372 Jason Ernest Kelley 47373 Robert Lawrence Kelley 47374 Susan Lynn Hardwick 47375 Andrew John Kelly 47376 Daniel Patrick Kennedy 47377 John Walter Kennedy 47378 Matthew John Kennedy 47379 Suzanne Marie Kennedy 47380 Matthew J. Kephart 47381 John Francis Kerish 47382 Richard Emerson Kern 47383 Stephen Kerwick 47384 Kumar Cortez Kibble 47385 Jeffrey S. Kieft 47386 Michael Andrew Kilbane 47387 Sean Michael Kilkenny 47388 Peter Gary Kilner 47389 Daniel Melvin King 47390 Joshua Allan King 47391 Kevin Christopher King 47392 Mark Creswell Kirby 47393 Lee Christian Kirschbaum 47394 Shawn Eric Klawunder 47395 Mark John Kneis 47396 Vann Patrick Knight 47397 John A. Knighten 47398 Sharlene J. Donovan 47399 Jean Elizabeth Henderson 47400 Jennie Margaret Koch 47401 Robert Allen Kokorda 47402 Jeffrey Scott Kopp 47403 Deborah Louise Kotulich 47404 James Nicholas Krakar 47405 Brian Eugene Kramer 47406 Michael L. Kramer 47407 Peter W. Kramer 47408 Richard Francis Kreuscher 47409 Joseph Wallace Krider 47410 Steven Allen Krnavek 47411 Steven Kurt Kroenlein 47412 Robert John Kroning 47413 Mark Richard Kuharich 47414 Aleksander Edgars Kupcis 47415 Paul Bryan Kuznik 47416 Paul Matthew Lackman 47417 Timothy Cann Ladouceur 47418 Walter Ayers Lamb 47419 Mark Hamilton Landes 47420 Scott David Lathrop 47421 Brian Michael Layton 47422 Diana Maureen Leach Holland 47423 David Jin Lee 47424 John Chung Lee 47425 Seung J. Lee 47426 Christopher Lehner 47427 Chad N. Lemond 47428 Michael Eugene Lenhart 47429 John J. Lenkart 47430 Penelope S. Glackin 47431 Daniel Keith Levenson 47432 David P. Lewis 47433 Michael Anthony Lewis 47434 Raymond Howard Lewis 47435 Theodore Marcus Liddell 47436 William Wayne Lidster 47437 James Buchanan Lincoln 47438 Christopher Elliot Lingle 47439 Patrick Sean Linnihan 47440 Garret Ronald Lipecky 47441 David Arthur Longhorn 47442 James Philip Lowe 47443 David Loren Lucas 47444 Jonathan Eric Lundstedt 47445 Peter Charles Lydon 47446 Darren Dodd Lynn 47447 Robert William Lyons 47448 Marcos A. Madrid 47449 Andrew Quijano Magracia 47450 Patrick G. L. Magras 47451 Michael James Mammay 47452 Patrick Edward Mangin 47453 Brian K. Mangus 47454 Albert Edward Mannes 47455 Tina R. Hartley 47456 Dale Russell Manry 47457 Scott Lee Mapstone 47458 Steven D. Marcontell 47459 Keith Arthur Markham 47460 Nikolai Fedge Markowitz 47461 Kristian Matthew Marks 47462 Andrew John Martin 47463 Matthew S. Martin 47464 Paul Jerome Mathews 47465 Ruben R. Matos 47466 Todd Michael Mattson 47467 Douglas Matthew Matty 47468 Frank Stefan Mayer 47469 John Eric Mayer 47470 Michael John Mazur 47471 Kevin Michael McAllister 47472 Troy Joseph McCann 47473 Daniel Joseph McCarthy 47474 Stewart Craig McCarver 47475 Thomas Daniel McCleskey 47476 David Matthew McCloskey 47477 Lloyd Milton McClure 47478 Shannon Michael McConnell 47479 Preston Franklin McCormick 47480 Gregory Wayne McCown 47481 Emily Jeanne McCracken 47482 Larry Frederick McElrath 47483 Joseph P. McGee 47484 John Gerard McGinn 47485 Brian Edward McGlumphy 47486 D. Scott McKean 47487 William Scott McKee 47488 Robert E. McKillop 47489 Terence Eugene McLinskey 47490 Markham Neil McMullen 47491 Michael Francis McNally 47492 James Francis McNulty 47493 William A. Medina 47494 Jeffrey Allan Meek 47495 Margaret Ann Meloch Manry 47496 Joel E. L. Meyer 47497 Stuart Lee Meyer 47498 Matthew Todd Michaelson 47499 Edward Otto Miiller 47500 Charles Russell Miller 47501 Fred Wallace Miller 47502 John Paul Miller 47503 Lawrence Charles Miller 47504 Mark Steven Miller 47505 O'Neal Miller 47506 Tyler Gabe Miller 47507 Steven Daniel Milstein 47508 Aleksandar Milutinovic 47509 Neil Joseph Minihane 47510 Don W. Minton 47511 Victoria Louise Miralda Miralda 47512 Steven Michael Miska 47513 Vickie Demetrios Stenfors 47514 Bradley Kent Mitchell 47515 Gregory Kent Mitchell 47516 Jonathan Scott Mitchell 47517 Michael Wade Mize 47518 Daniel Charles Moll 47519 Bryan Scott Monteith 47520 Sergio Mora 47521 Heriberto Moreno 47522 Raymond Richard Morin 47523 Charles David Morris 47524 Samuel Douglas Morris 47525 Kurt Arthur Mosher 47526 John Clarence Moyse 47527 Karl Eric Muehlheuser 47528 Garrett Emmett Mulrooney 47529 Robert Linton Reeves Munden 47530 Luis Antonio Muniz 47531 Scott Antonio Murock 47532 Kennard Michael Murphy 47533 Kevin Paul Murphy 47534 Mark Eugene Murray 47535 Michael Joseph Musiol 47536 Kenneth James Nadermann 47537 Richard Scott Nair 47538 George Phillips Nall 47539 Michael Christopher Nason 47540 Magatte Ndiaye 47541 Ramon A. Negron 47542 Lyndel Marie Nelson Stewart 47543 Eric Joseph Ness 47544 Mark C. Nester 47545 Frederick Alexander Nettles 47546 Edward J. Neveril 47547 Thomas Allison Neville 47548 Jon Michael Newhard 47549 Bryan Dewayne Newman 47550 Brian Terry Nichols 47551 Raymond Eugene Nichols 47552 Theresa Beryl Nichols 47553 Suzanne Christine Nielsen 47554 Jerry Wayne Nies 47555 James Lewis Noles 47556 James Eric Nygaard 47557 William John Nygaard 47558 John James O'Brien 47559 David Isaias O'Clander 47560 Jacob Wainwright O'Connell 47561 Patrick O'Dea 47562 Michael S. Odom 47563 Frederick Mark O'Donnell 47564 Rodney John Ofte 47565 Scott Douglas O'Hearen 47566 Clare P. O'Keeffe 47567 Shane Malcolm O'Kelly 47568 Suzanne Marie Oldenburg 47569 Stephen Nicholas Olejasz 47570 Joseph Olmeda 47571 Andrew Alan Olson 47572 Jeffrey Thomas O'Neal 47573 John P. O'Neil 47574 Catherine Claire Orpen Kilner 47575 James R. Orrange 47576 David Christopher Ortega 47577 Michael Aaron Ortelli 47578 Michael Joseph O'Toole 47579 David Frank Ottavianelli 47580 Joseph T. Owczarek 47581 Paul E. Owen 47582 Sean Patrick Owens 47583 Ronald Paduchak 47584 Jae Cherl Pak 47585 John Anthony Palazzolo 47586 Michael P. Panciera 47587 Michael John Papp 47588 Wendell Todd Pardue 47589 Jonathan Randall Parow 47590 Jonathan Mark Paschal 47591 Scott Allen Paul 47592 Brian Keath Paxton 47593 James P. Payne 47594 Gregory Thorman Pease 47595 Susan Peck Randrup 47596 Yale Sinclair Peebles 47597 Eric Lee Peltz 47598 Richard Wesley Pendell 47599 Larry Dodd Perino 47600 Theodore M. Perryman 47601 Richard Vance Petitt 47602 Christian Alfred Pfeil 47603 Robert Jay Phillips 47604 Wade Ernest Phillips 47605 Brian Thomas Pierce 47606 Scott Christopher Pierce 47607 William Todd Piett 47608 Anton Thor Ivan Morales Pineda 47609 Brian James Poe 47610 Stanley Paul Pokrywka 47611 Francis Patrick Polashek 47612 Kendal Vanpatrick Polk 47613 Paul A. Potter 47614 Michael J. Preisser 47615 Raymond Neal Pruett 47616 Donald Edward Pruitt 47617 Se Woo Pyo 47618 Richard John Rabago 47619 Anthony Paul Raia 47620 Cynthia Sienna Ramirez Lindenmeyer 47621 Nora Edna Ramirez 47622 Conrado Ramos 47623 Michael Edward Ransome 47624 Mark David Raschke 47625 Oscar Antonio Raudales 47626 Steven James Raymond 47627 Robert Wilby Redd 47628 Robert Nathaniel Reddix 47629 Paul Patrick Reese 47630 Philip Rey Regualos 47631 Theodore Herman Reich 47632 Christopher Brian Reid 47633 Glenn Joseph Reilly 47634 John Thomas Reim 47635 Michael David Reinert 47636 William Harvey Reinhart 47637 Celia Renteria Szelwach 47638 Edward Joseph Repetski 47639 Robert Stanley Reppa 47640 Marc Thomas Resch 47641 Joseph Allen Ricciardi 47642 Beth Ann Richards 47643 Scott Michael Richards 47644 George Walter Riggins 47645 Wesley Clarke Ritner 47646 David Christopher Roberts 47647 Joel Edward Roberts 47648 Joseph Jett Rodgers 47649 Thomas Charles Rodgers 47650 Douglas Taylor Rogers 47651 John C. Roou 47652 Tamara Tuschhoff 47653 Heath Christopher Roscoe 47654 James P. Ross 47655 Michael J. Ross 47656 Steven D. Rothert 47657 Pablo Esteban Ruiz 47658 James August Rupkalvis 47659 Kevin Joseph Ruth 47660 Marc James Ruyak 47661 Joseph J. Saccon 47662 James Vincent Saccone 47663 Lyn Betsy Sammons Eddy 47664 Jeffrey Michael Sanborn 47665 Rene Sanchez 47666 David Michael Sanders 47667 Gregory R. Sarafian 47668 Curtis Raymond Sawyer 47669 Malcolm George Schaefer 47670 Jill R. Whaley 47671 David Francis Scharf 47672 Paula Isolde Schasberger 47673 Thomas Carll Schermerhorn 47674 Eric Anderson Schimpf 47675 Paul John Schmitt 47676 Karl Michael Schreiber 47677 Robert John Schug 47678 James Anthony Schulz 47679 Jerome Scott Schulze 47680 Rafael Augusto Schulze 47681 Steven John Schweitzer 47682 Christopher Sclafani 47683 George H. Seaward 47684 Arnold Seay 47685 James E. Seckel 47686 Thor Andreas Sewell 47687 Robert Lawrence Shearer 47688 William Gordon Sheboy 47689 David Peter Shelstad 47690 Richard Vincent Sheridan 47691 Steve Sherlock 47692 Steven R. Shields 47693 John Keesoo Shin 47694 Timothy W. Shiveley 47695 Thomas Andrew Shoffner 47696 Michael Scot Shrout 47697 Gregory Francis Sierra 47698 John David Silvers 47699 Scott Edward Simpson 47700 Timothy Eugene Singley 47701 John David Sinsley 47702 Salvatore Thomas Sirna 47703 Alan Bruce Smith 47704 Benjamin Shannon Smith 47705 Charles Christopher Smith 47706 David Allen Smith 47707 Derick Clarke Smith 47708 Gerardus Johannes Smith 47709 Matthew McSperit Smith 47710 Pamela Stephanie Smith Pewitt 47711 Patrick Brennan Smith 47712 Warren Wilbur Smith 47713 David Paul Smole 47714 Joseph Christopher Sniezek 47715 Louis J. Snowden 47716 Sharon L. Cox 47717 Jon Erik Solem 47718 Kathleen A. O'Grady 47719 Martin C. Spake 47720 Donald L. Sparaco 47721 Clayton King Speed 47722 Mark Edward Stabile 47723 William Augustus Stack 47724 Jon C. Stanat 47725 Kristin Elizabeth Standing 47726 Charles D. Starbird 47727 Stacy Ross Starbuck 47728 Stephen J. Stark 47729 Brett Alan Steele 47730 Holly A. Stein 47731 Julie K. Abell 47732 Jacqueline Elizabeth Stennett 47733 Kenneth Allen Stevens 47734 Sandra S Muchow 47735 Catherine Anne Stewart Strobel 47736 James Christopher Stewart 47737 Richard B. Stikkers 47738 David C. Stockton 47739 Christopher Bernard Storey 47740 Frederick John Strampe 47741 Michael T. Strauss 47742 Frederick Daniel Streetman 47743 Paul Richard Stringfellow 47744 Daniel James Stringham 47745 Kevin Scott Strode 47746 Michael Allen Stuart 47747 Michael D. Sufnarski 47748 Ryung Suh 47749 Jammong Suksaeng 47750 Bridget Marie Sullivan 47751 Edward Sullivan 47752 Scott Richard Sutherland 47753 Michael Stanley Sutton 47754 Michael Thomas Swindell 47755 Peter Alexander Szelwach 47756 Darrel Shawn Tackett 47757 Neysa L. Bianchi 47758 Todd Andrew Taranto 47759 Karen Taylor Smith 47760 Michael Wayne Taylor 47761 Kevin S. Terrell 47762 John Dennis Thee 47763 George Konrad Thiebes 47764 David Edward Thomas 47765 Ryan O'Neal Thomas 47766 Blair F. Thompson 47767 Michael J. Thorson 47768 Andy Cheng-Chung Tiao 47769 Jonathan Wayne Tibbals 47770 Bradford Tieke 47771 Anthony Lawrence Tillman 47772 Geoffrey Long Tinelli 47773 Jay Michael Toland 47774 Mark Allen Tomkovicz 47775 Sharon Ann Tosi Moore 47776 Kristen L. Crino 47777 Todd J. Traczyk 47778 Dominic Herbert Trader 47779 Brian Keith Tramel 47780 Michael Fahey Traver 47781 Michael J. Tretola 47782 Mark David Tribus 47783 Michael Ray Trisler 47784 Joseph Eugene Tsagronis 47785 Scott Kenneth Tufts 47786 James Madison Tukpah 47787 Steven Charles Tullis 47788 Robert Tallal Turfe 47789 Juan Kruger Ulloa 47790 Robert Eugene Unger 47791 Kevin Dennis Universal 47792 Andrew D. Unwin 47793 Theodore Paul Valmassei 47794 Peter Reid Van Prooyen 47795 Joel Henri Van Timmeren 47796 Bruce Albert Vanderbush 47797 Robert Cash VanGorder 47798 Christopher Sean Vara 47799 Mark Steven Vara 47800 Michael Le Page Varuolo 47801 John Amandas Vermeesch 47802 Candace Marie Vernold 47803 Matthew D. Vertin 47804 Steven Andre Visosky 47805 Hiep Van Vo 47806 John A. Vogel 47807 Brian Russell Vowinkel 47808 Robert Anthony Wagner 47809 Philip Carl Wahlbom 47810 Paul C. Walheim 47811 Wright Northrop Wall 47812 Edward Thomas Wallace 47813 Patrick Michael Walsh 47814 Greggory Reed Walters 47815 Eric Tse Wang 47816 James Lee Warfield 47817 David Del Warns 47818 Bobby Wayne Watts 47819 Howard C. Webb 47820 David Joseph Weber 47821 James Allen Weber 47822 August Martin Wegner 47823 Veronica Joan Wendt Wendt 47824 Michael E. Wertz 47825 Jeffrey L. Westfield 47826 Vincent Paul Westover 47827 Fred Marshall Wetherington 47828 Christopher Kamerer Wetzel 47829 Kevin Tae Il Whang 47830 Brian E. Wheeler 47831 Jeffrey David Wheeler 47832 Roger Jewett Wheeler 47833 Timothy Wade White 47834 Robert Frederick Whittle 47835 Craig Jospeh Wiedl 47836 Dorne Leonard Wiese 47837 Bruce Howard Williams 47838 David Blair Williams 47839 David Eugene Williams 47840 Douglas Daniel Williams 47841 Hugh R. Williams 47842 James S. Williams 47843 John David Williams 47844 Walter Knight Williams 47845 Elexa D. Orrange 47846 Ronald Rea Wilson 47847 Robert G. Wilt 47848 Gary Wayne Winch 47849 Diane Elizabeth Wineinger 47850 John Joseph Wixted 47851 George Bryan Scott Wofford 47852 Hely Dave Wood 47853 Dana John Woodall 47854 Cameron Kyle Worsham 47855 Paul Leroy Wynn 47856 James D. Wyrwas 47857 Newman Yang 47858 Shannon Kole Yates 47859 David Joseph Yebra 47860 James Joseph Yee 47861 Daryl Ray Youngman 47862 Tae Hyun Yun 47863 Eric William Zeeman 47864 Kristofor Michael Zehm 47865 Stephen Joseph Ziegler 47866 John Graham Zierdt 47867 Eric Anthony Zilewicz 47868 Frank Harvey Zimmerman 47869 Kevin Karl Zurmuelen 47870 Marc D. Albanese 47871 William Allen Armelin 47872 Michael John Backus 47873 Stephen Michael Breagy 47874 Thomas Jerome Clancy 47875 Daniel Joseph Cooney 47876 Ira Ben Davis 47877 Albert F. Farrar 47878 Gregory Kent Fennewald 47879 Kay Linda Gelinas Emerson 47880 Jeffrey Todd Harrod 47881 Sean C. Jordan 47882 Jeffrey Allen McDougall 47883 Chauncy Conrad Nash 47884 John Anthony O'Grady 47885 Kevin Walter Parker 47886 George Ramirez 47887 Carlton Wayne Rice 47888 Larry John Schauer 47889 Tracy L. Roou 47890 Jose Martin Thompson 47891 John Thomas Wade 47892 Paul Kevin Tsatsos 47893 John Andre Scott 47894 Richard Patrick St. Rose 47895 Hugh David Bair 47896 Philip Reiner Boyd 47897 Kathryn Ann Donnelly 47898 Jeb Stuart Downing 47899 Joy Lynn Curriera 47900 Scott Allen Frank 47901 Jeffrey David Jack 47902 Robert Thomas Krumm 47903 Steven Marc Linn 47904 Joseph William Mack 47905 Timothy Todd Mulville 47906 Thomas Robert Raggio 47907 **1991** Anthony Parker Aaron 47908 John C. Abercrombie 47909 Darrin Alan Adams 47910 Martin Francis Adams 47911 Jorge Apollo Agcaoili 47912 Jose L. Aguilar 47913 Michael Alexander Aguilar 47914 Blace Chandler Albert 47915 Michael Victor Aldinger 47916 Ovidio Alfaro 47917 David Wayne Alley 47918 Mark Alan Amundson 47919 Gregory Kenneth Anderson 47920 Jeffrey Glen Anderson 47921 William J. Andre 47922 John F. Andrews 47923 John Robert Andrews 47924 Richard Earl Angle 47925 Rory Anthony Anglin 47926 Shawn David Arch 47927 Mark A. Arnott 47928 Mikael Ryan Ash 47929 Kimberly Ashton O'Keefe 47930 Lance Anthony Ashworth 47931 Dana Andrew Aubel 47932 Frank D. Auguston 47933 James Robert Auvil 47934 Donald H. Aven 47935 Joseph Gary Ayers 47936 John Harlow Babb 47937 Nicholas William Baer 47938 George Daniel Bailey 47939 Clinton Jay Baker 47940 Craig William Baker 47941 Harold D. Baker 47942 Lewis Demiles Baker 47943 Shane Aries Baker 47944 Thomas Edward Baker 47945 Bryan J. Balding 47946 Stephen Harold Bales 47947 Michael Andre Ball 47948 Vincent Lee Ball 47949 Kevin Patrick Banks 47950 Christopher Marsh Barden 47951 Vincent John Barnhart 47952 Michael John Barone 47953 Troy David Baronet 47954 Martin John Barr 47955 William Allen Barrow 47956 Robert James Barry 47957 Jeffrey S. Barson 47958 Flavio Bastiani 47959 Jonathan H. Bauman 47960 David Roger Baxter 47961 Derrick Emil Baxter 47962 Edward William Bayouth 47963 James M. Beamesderfer 47964 Douglas Riette Beaton 47965 Joseph Darien Beatty 47966 Jenifer Ida Beaudean 47967 Shannon Daves Beebe 47968 Mark Douglas Beech 47969 Paul Edward Begalka 47970 Perry Prine Beissel 47971 Brian D. Bell 47972 Philip James Belmont 47973 Eric Jay Benchoff 47974 Anthony Luis Benitez 47975 Robert John Bennett 47976 Alan T. Bernhard 47977 Kevin Lee Berry 47978 Shelley Ann Berry 47979 Mark Daniel Bieger 47980 Alfred Joseph Biland 47981 Geoffrey Scott Binney 47982 Thomas Brock Blake 47983 "Bonnie L Blanchard,#47984 Etnyre 47984" Carlos Adrian Blazquez 47985 Robert David Blomquist 47986 Frank L. Boersma 47987 Elizabeth Wensinger Boggs 47988 Michael Thomas Bogovich 47989 Shawn M. Boland 47990 Ronald Scott Bomkamp 47991 Ward P. Bond 47992 David Wade Boone 47993 Brent Dean Bourne 47994 James Clifford Bourque 47995 Brian Lee Bowen 47996 Timothy Vincent Bowler 47997 Steven Lamarr Bowman 47998 Thomas Lee Bowman 47999 Robert Francis Boyle 48000 Gregory Joseph Brady 48001 Jonathan P. Braga 48002 Robert Alan Brammer 48003 Vito Brancatella 48004 Bradley Scott Branderhorst 48005 James Carl Brau 48006 Dennis Richard Bray 48007 John Ronald Brence 48008 Scott A. Brender 48009 Frank Wayne Brewster 48010 My-Linh Brewster Shattan 48011 Jonalan Brickey 48012 Robert Wayne Brinson 48013 Jerome Philippe Brock 48014 Jason Matthew Brocke 48015 Desrae Dinah Broderick 48016 David Henry Brooks 48017 Paul Kevin Brooks 48018 Glenn Ronald Brown 48019 Keith Eric Brown 48020 Leonard G. Brown 48021 Lynne Dianne Destefano

48022 John George Buck 48023 James Arthur Buller 48024 Michael Lillis Burke 48025 Thomas Edward Burke 48026 Christina Lynn Mills 48027 Richard Owen Burney 48028 Timothy Horne Burnham 48029 Robert Eugene Burns 48030 Heather Lynn Peters 48031 Patrick Glenwood Burton 48032 Andrew Raymond Burzumato 48033 Robert Drue Bynum 48034 Robert Patrick Cahill 48035 Suzanne C. Aguilar 48036 Gary D. Calese 48037 Brian David Cameron 48038 Charles B. Campbell 48039 Richard M. Campbell 48040 Carlos J. Canino 48041 Sean Michael Caplice 48042 Frank T. Capone 48043 Ronnie Edward Cardwell 48044 Henry Brown Carlile 48045 Daniel J. Carlo 48046 Michael Howard Carr 48047 Robert James Carroll 48048 John Lee Carter 48049 Casino Frederick Casey 48050 Michael Sylvester Cashman 48051 Calvin Lee Cass 48052 Christiana Cassidy Runey 48053 Watson Gerrard Caudill 48054 David Phillip Chambers 48055 Christian Donald Chapman 48056 Kenneth Douglas Chase 48057 Christian Joseph Childs 48058 Michael J. Chmielecki 48059 Jesus Castro Chong 48060 Brooks Robert Chretien 48061 Bernhard Eric Christianson 48062 Thomas William Cipolla 48063 Traci Ruth Cisek Fisher 48064 Curt Jerome Cizek 48065 Brian Eugene Clark 48066 Daniel Leonard Clark 48067 Jan Lisa Malaikal 48068 Joseph Pomeroy Clark 48069 Christopher John Claytor 48070 Scott Allen Clemenson 48071 Andrew Franklin Clements 48072 Donald Eugene Clemons 48073 Daniel W. Clevenger 48074 Alexandre S. Clug 48075 Richard Edwin Colclough 48076 Christopher John Collins 48077 Richard Michael Collins 48078 Brian James Conjelko 48079 Kathleen M. Conmy Malone 48080 Ronald David Conwell 48081 Dreux Edward Coogan 48082 John W. Coogan 48083 Patrick Michael Cooley 48084 Ellis O'Neal Cooper 48085 Todd Christopher Cooper 48086 Matthew David Coose 48087 William L. Copenhaver 48088 Damion Herman Cordova 48089 Roger George Cordray 48090 Daniel Paul Correa 48091 Charles David Costanza 48092 Vonnette T. Monteith 48093 Phillip L. Coughran 48094 Dennis D. Cowher 48095 Shawn W. Cowley 48096 Brent Anthony Crabtree 48097 Robert Donald Craddock 48098 Holly Craig Pierce 48099 Douglas C. Cramer 48100 Erika Ingeborg Granville 48101 Mark Thompson Cramer 48102 Richard Kevin Crawford 48103 Reggie Levorn Crenshaw 48104 Colleen Ann Adams 48105 Jon Randal Crist 48106 Daniel Zene Crowe 48107 Sean Albert Crowley 48108 Martin F. Cudzilo 48109 Rodolfo Cuellar 48110 David Thomas Culkin 48111 Gail Anne Curley 48112 David Nelson Dadich 48113 Warren Todd Daniel 48114 Gregory Brent Davidson 48115 Russell Allen Davidson 48116 William Trent Davidson 48117 Lisa V. Davis 48118 Ralph W. Deatherage 48119 Brian Connell Deboda 48120 Anthony Richard DeBoom 48121 Fiore James Decosty 48122 Sharon Elizabeth DeCrane 48123 Lucie M. Deile 48124 Jason Andrew Dejarnett 48125 Eric J. DeJong 48126 Anthony Joseph Detoto 48127 Christopher D. DiCicco 48128 John Peter DiGiambattista 48129 Robert Pak Dill 48130 Jason Todd Dillman 48131 Jeffrey Jay DiLullo 48132 John Arthur Dinges 48133 David Paul Doane 48134 Rebecca D. McCorkendale 48135 Darrell D. Dodge 48136 Dana J. Duckro 48137 Patrick James Domingue 48138 Andrew Julian Doniec 48139 William Higgins Donohue 48140 Robert Wayne Dorta 48141 Robert Wilson Dotson 48142 Tim John Driscoll 48143 John Patrick Drohan 48144 John P. Dugan 48145 Joseph Michael Duncan 48146 Vince E . Duque 48147 Charles Wayne Durr 48148 Andrew James Duszynski 48149 Gregory Noble Duvall 48150 David Frederick Dwyer 48151 Dixon Dee Dykman 48152 Joseph Frederick Dziezynski 48153 Michael Richard Eastman 48154 John George Economou 48155 James Matthew Edelblute 48156 Beverly Denise Edwards 48157 John Kimball Edwards 48158 Janell Elizabeth Eickhoff 48159 Jon Michael Elkin 48160 David Paul Ellis 48161 Michael Wayne Ellis 48162 Christopher H. Engen 48163 Paul Adrian Eno 48164 William Luther Erwin 48165 Anthony Paul Etnyre 48166 Kenneth Allan Evans 48167 Robert Clayton Evans 48168 Carl T. Every 48169 Edward Stephen Falkowski 48170 Andre Fallot 48171 William Keeler Farmer 48172 James Andrew Farney 48173 Jerry L. Farnsworth 48174 Dane M. Farnworth 48175 Christopher M. Farrell 48176 Todd David Farrington 48177 John Scott D Feight 48178 Sean Emmett Fennelly 48179 Erik Warren Ferguson 48180 Robyn Elizabeth Ferguson 48181 Jarl Glenn Ferko 48182 Susan F. Boudet 48183 Michael Ferrari 48184 Jan F. Heffernan 48185 Troy Edward Filburn 48186 David Paul Filer 48187 Holly E. West 48188 Joseph Nathaniel Fisher 48189 Sean A. Fisher 48190 Michael Francis Fitzgerald 48191 Matthew Steven Fitzpatrick 48192 Peter Geoffrey Fontana 48193 Louis Peter Fortunato 48194 James Alfred Fowler 48195 Jonathan Michael Fox 48196 James Weldon Frazier 48197 H.E. Eugene Freeland 48198 Jeffrey Wellington French 48199 Charles B. Friden 48200 Nelson Daniel Fritz 48201 Gavin Andrew Frost 48202 Jeffrey D. Gabel 48203 Mark Allen Gahman 48204 Christopher Morin Galy 48205 Kenneth Richard Gamble 48206 Stuart Allan Gardner 48207 Grant G. Garrigan 48208 Peter William Gaudet 48209 Scott Charles Gensler 48210 Omuso Dabibi George 48211 Scott Robert Gerber 48212 Beth Ann German 48213 Jon Roger Gerold 48214 Manuel Federico Girbal 48215 Edward Wendell Givens 48216 Toni DeLancey 48217 Thomas Perrine Glover 48218 Winston Jerrome Glover 48219 Lawrence Arthur Gnewuch 48220 Robert H. Goldsmith 48221 Amy Lynn Peterson 48222 Filomeno Palacio Gonzalez 48223 Kenneth William Gonzalez 48224 Christopher Edward Good 48225 Andrew Carl Gorske 48226 Karl August Gossett 48227 Stephen J. Grabski 48228 Brian Matthew Grady 48229 Jonathan Kirk Graff 48230 Peter C. Graff 48231 Richard Allan Graham 48232 John Hallock Granville 48233 Janet Marie Greco Gibson 48234 Shaun Jeffrey Greene 48235 Benjamin Michael Greiner 48236 John Victor Griffin 48237 Jack Hammond Griswold 48238 Joseph Bernard Gudenburr 48239 Kevin Gilbert Guidry 48240 Martin Armando Guillen 48241 Peter James Habic 48242 William Christopher Haddad 48243 Robert Michael Haffey 48244 Daniel P. Hakala 48245 Andrew Oscar Hall 48246 Ronald Elmer Hall 48247 Timothy John Hall 48248 Brian Sean Halloran 48249 Scott William Halstead 48250 Burke Ryan Hamilton 48251 Melton Kristan Hamilton 48252 Erik Scott Hamilton-Jones 48253 Pearce Wheless Hammond 48254 Yee Chang Hang 48255 Jennifer Hankes Painter 48256 Brian Dale Hankinson 48257 Gregory Charles Hardewig 48258 Hugh Hiroshi Hardin 48259 Christopher George Harlan 48260 Lorenzo Harris 48261 Christopher S. Hart 48262 Christopher Michael Hartley 48263 Theodore Richard Harvala 48264 Stephen McCallum Havel 48265 William Fredrick Hecker 48266 Jeffrey Allen Helms 48267 Susan Hennessey Filburn 48268 Lewis E. Henry 48269 Dale Jerome Herr 48270 Salome Herrera 48271 Saul Herrera 48272 James Gregory Heslin 48273 Tracy A. O'Keefe 48274 Jerry Scott Hines 48275 Jon David Hirst 48276 Jason Whitney Hodell 48277 David Lee Hodge 48278 Kim Marie Evans 48279 Daniel Christopher Hodne 48280 David Matthew Hodne 48281 Fred Norbert Hoehne 48282 Michael W. Holder 48283 Eric Franklin Holt 48284 Scott Gordon Hooper 48285 Michael Brian Hoos 48286 John Martin Hoppmann 48287 Mohammad Mozammel Hoque 48288 David Jesse Horan 48289 Leonard John Horan 48290 Carl J. Horn 48291 Donna L. Moore 48292 Pamela Christa Harber 48293 Timothy Brian Hoskinson 48294 Michael Wayne Houmiel 48295 Scott D. Howarth 48296 Kirsten Anne Johnson 48297 Robert Stanley Hribar 48298 Martha Shiu-Tsong VanDriel 48299 Matthew Jason Hubbard 48300 William Matthew Huff 48301 Philip Charles Hughes 48302 Philip Dwight Hunt 48303 Kirk Stanley Hunter 48304 John Thomas Hyatt 48305 Lee Douglas Hyder 48306 Patrick J. Hynes 48307 Robert F. Hynes 48308 Kami M. Iannaco 48309 Catherine Marie Daly 48310 Andrew Thatcher Iliff 48311 Thomas P. Innis 48312 Thomas Lester Irby 48313 John M. Isakson 48314 Daniel James Izzo 48315 Jennifer Jenkins Ash 48316 Jeffrey Lee Jennette 48317 Carlos Alberto Jentimane 48318 David E. Jernigan 48319 William Garrison Jeter 48320 M. Hayden Johnson 48321 Rob Bradley Johnson 48322 William Braxton Johnson 48323 William Randy Johnson 48324 Jason Eldon Jones 48325 Jeffrey A. Jones 48326 Mark E. Jones 48327 Timothy Michael Jones 48328 Randolph Francis Judd 48329 James Brian Kane 48330 Rebecca Ann Kanis 48331 Adam C. Kapolka 48332 Clint Eastwood Karamath 48333 Patrick Joseph Keane 48334 Thomas Christopher Keane 48335 Kevin R. Kearns 48336 James Peter Keating 48337 John Michael Keenan 48338 Sean Keenan 48339 Kevin T. Keepfer 48340 Jenifer L. Kelley 48341 Troy Eric Kelley 48342 Eric Waid Kelly 48343 Jason Boyd Kennedy 48344 Pat Michael Kern 48345 Jeffrey Dean Kessler 48346 Brian Stuart Kewak 48347 Aaron Mark Kibbey 48348 Glenn Albert Kiesewetter 48349 Edward Kinyung Kim 48350 Kenneth Sang Kim 48351 Yu Shik Kim 48352 Christopher John Kindgren 48353 Eric Paul King 48354 Marilyn R.S. King 48355 Nadia Lorraine King 48356 Robert Andrew King 48357 John Frederick Klafin 48358 Brian T. Kleyensteuber 48359 Douglas William Kling 48360 Randall R. Klingaman 48361 David Leroy Knellinger 48362 Luke Augustus Knittig 48363 Scott A. Kobida 48364 Lance Worthington Kohler 48365 Bruce Alan Kososki 48366 Steven Michael Kozma 48367 Ralph E. Krall 48368 George Frederick Kratz 48369 Joseph Lee Kremer 48370 Michael Jason Krieg 48371 Mark Donald Krumin 48372 Charles David Krumwiede 48373 James Chien Ku 48374 Paul Donald Kucik 48375 Daniel Roger Kueter 48376 Karl Roland Kurz 48377 Sean Andrew Kushner 48378 Walter Hpueng Kwon 48379 David Paul Lambert 48380 Lennis Steven Lammers 48381 Craig Kenneth Larson 48382 Eric John Larson 48383 Andrew Daniel Lauman 48384 Earl David Lawson 48385 Sharon J. Helms 48386 James Rodney Leady 48387 Jeffry Lech 48388 Henry Hyun Kyu Lee 48389 Jon Yol Lee 48390 Long-Chain Lee 48391 Richard J. Lee 48392 John William Leffers 48393 Paul E. Lentini 48394 Hugo Franz Lentze 48395 Otto Paul Leone 48396 Jason Thomas LeRoy 48397 Jeffrey H. LeRoy 48398 Casey John Lessard 48399 Dana Letarte 48400 Steven Jerry Letzring 48401 Timothy Edward Lewicki 48402 Dean Edward Lewis 48403 Matthew Robert Lewis 48404 Jeffrey Alan Libby 48405 Todd Alan Liddell 48406 John Leonard Lieb 48407 Alexander John Lind 48408 Victor Charles Lindenmeyer 48409 Vincent Ray Lindenmeyer 48410 Jason Lee Linsey 48411 Charles I. Lipeles 48412 Lance Edward Lippencott 48413 Matthew Allen Lisowski 48414 Michael Edward Lisowski 48415 Norman Peter Litterini 48416 D. Mark Livesay 48417 Antonio Pierre Logan 48418 Matthew Joseph Louis 48419 William J. Love 48420 Christopher Robert Lovejoy 48421 Alan Lowson 48422 Clara Jane Meldrum 48423 Ronald Garth Lukow 48424 Bret Eric Luloff 48425 Christopher Lyga 48426 Matthew P. Lynch 48427 Patrick Dean Lynch 48428 Christopher P. Mackenzie 48429 Orlando Madrid 48430 Christopher Michael Magnuson 48431 Robert Charles Maindelle 48432 Mark A. Mais 48433 Mitchell A. Malone 48434 Stacy Lyn Manning-Richardson 48435 Nicolette Ann Mark 48436 Jeffrey John Marone 48437 Jason Edward Marquith 48438 Corby Wayne Marshall 48439 James Andrew Marshall 48440 William Patrick Marshall 48441 Robert R. Martinolli 48442 Albert Mategrano 48443 Mark Matheson 48444 Edward William Mathia 48445 David Warner Mathisen 48446 Edward Paul Mattison 48447 Nick Shaun Mauldin 48448 Timothy Lawrence Maybury 48449 Michael Mayweather 48450 Colleen Lightfoot 48451 Kevin Delong McComas 48452 Douglas Paul McCormick 48453 Bradley Joseph McIlwee 48454 Michael J. McIntee 48455 Dennis John McKernan 48456 James Charles McKinnon 48457 Andrew Hayes McLaughlin 48458 Stephen Mark McMillion 48459 Thomas Anthony McTigue 48460 Bryan Leon McWilliams 48461 Richard James Meehan 48462 Robert Brian Meldrum 48463 Keith Thomas Melinson 48464 Brian Douglas Melton 48465 Miguel Mendoza 48466 Luciano Mercado 48467 John Frederick Meyer 48468 Paul R. Miles 48469 Karen L. Flaherty 48470 Andrew James Miller 48471 Matthew McCabe Miller 48472 Charlene Gwynn 48473 Michael James Mingee 48474 Robert Richard Minner 48475 Kenneth Jules Mintz 48476 Charles Scott Mitchell 48477 Todd Erik Mitchell 48478 Gregory Raymond Mogavero 48479 Francis Cesare Monestere 48480 James W. Montgomery 48481 Eric Thomas Moore 48482 Kenneth C. Moore 48483 Reginald L. Moore 48484 Stephen Douglas Moore 48485 David John Morgan 48486 Scott Hudson Morgan 48487 Dan John Morley 48488 Dennis Louis Morris 48489 Harris Lee Morris 48490 Craig David Morrow 48491 David Paul Morrow 48492 Matthew D. Morton 48493 Ronald J. Mouw 48494 Kenneth Jerome Mrozek 48495 Adam Wright Muller 48496 Patrick John Mullin 48497 Jeffrey Bryan Mullins 48498 Mark Benjamin Mydland 48499 Chester John Nadolski 48500 Victor Masano Nakano 48501 David Gregory Neary 48502 Patrick Lee Neuschwanger 48503 Corey Andrew New 48504 Hung Viet Nguyen 48505 Rhett James Nichol 48506 Curtis William Nichols 48507 Bret Tatsuo Ninomiya 48508 Anthony Joseph Noto 48509 George M. Novak 48510 James Alexander Nowell 48511 James Nugent 48512 Patrick Charles O'Brien 48513 Patrick E. O'Brien 48514 William G. O'Brien 48515 Michael Paul O'Day 48516 Thomas Joseph O'Donnell 48517 Richard Olejniczak 48518 Jennifer E. Olinger 48519 Eric Robert Olsen 48520 Darren Arnold Olson 48521 Michelle Lea Olson 48522 John R. O'Neil 48523 Michael Joseph Onufrow 48524 Johnson F. Ododa Opiyo 48525 Mark Edwin Orwat 48526 Chris Errol Ostrander 48527 Robert William Otto 48528 Erik Richard Overby 48529 Michael William Pace 48530 Michael Victor Palaza 48531 John David Palcisko 48532 Marc Stephen Pana 48533 Tom P. Pappas 48534 Johannes Magbanua Paraan 48535 Rafael Antonio Paredes 48536 Michael Edmund Parker 48537 Guy Brynt Parmeter 48538 Michael Jared Parsons 48539 Theodore Michael Parsons 48540 Ernest L. Pasteur 48541 Matthew Fred Pasvogel 48542 Steven Jude Patin 48543 Eric Alan Patterson 48544 William Paul Patterson 48545 Christopher Allan Patton 48546 Carence Emmise Agans 48547 Vu Le Pearson 48548 David Eugene Peek 48549 Todd Andrew Pendelton 48550 Theodore Mark Permuth 48551 Sean Allen Peters 48552 Shane Michael Peters 48553 Craig M. Peterson 48554 John M. Petracca 48555 Thomas Fulton Pettit 48556 Scott Lee Pfeifer 48557 Curtis Eugene Phelps 48558 Clinton L. Phillips 48559 Kendell Jay Phillips 48560 William Sato Pierce 48561 Gravelle Linnion Pierre 48562 Edward Jonas Pintar 48563 Charles Curtis Poche 48564 Jerome Anthony Pofi 48565 Aaron Robert Pogue 48566 John Carl Pomory 48567 Drew Corbett Popson 48568 Alexander Raphael Porcelli 48569 Yolanda Renita Porter 48570 Brian Wade Post 48571 Mark Blaine Potter 48572 William Michael Potter 48573 Robert Alfred Powalski 48574 Joanne C. Moore 48575 Thomas Lloyd Prescott 48576 William Troy Prestenberg 48577 Joseph David Preuth 48578 Trent Mitchell Price 48579 Eric Kenneth Prichard 48580 Shawn Thomas Prickett 48581 Michael A. Princi 48582 Frederick Earle Prins 48583 Robert Eppes Proctor 48584 Ronald Earl Pruitt 48585 Blake Kendall Puckett 48586 Sanjay Vijay Purandare 48587 Michael Marty Purpura 48588 Craig Eugene Quadrato 48589 Joel Rod Quinn 48590 Patrick D. Quinn 48591 Brian E. Rae 48592 Nathanial Wayne Rainey 48593 Robert Anthony Ramirez 48594 Diego Isidro Ramos 48595 John Phoenix Rann 48596 Roy Michael Raugh 48597 James R. Ray 48598 David Christopher Reardon 48599 Gregory Steven Recker 48600 Edward Charles Reddington 48601 Kevin Rone Reed 48602 Bryan William Reese 48603 John Nuno Rei 48604 Laurie D. Reider 48605 Terence Martin Rice 48606 John Buchanan Richardson 48607 David Michael Richey 48608 Paul Ritkouski 48609 Craig T. Rivet 48610 Kathleen M. Rivet Quinn 48611 William Michael Robare 48612 John Morgan Robb 48613 Kurt D. Roberts 48614 Richard Alfred Rockweiler 48615 James D. Rockwell 48616 Frederick A. Rodgers 48617 Jerry L. Rodgers 48618 Carter Lance Rogers 48619 Lumen Dillard Roley 48620 Richard C. Rooney 48621 Mark Edward Rose 48622 Thomas Burke Rossman 48623 Raymond Boyd Rowles 48624 James Crawford Royse 48625 Ronald B. Rueppel 48626 Todd W. Rumbles 48627 "Michael, Dennis Runey 48628" Edward Fuller Russ 48629 Andrew Grinnell Russell 48630 Anthony R. Russillo 48631 Randy Dean Rustman 48632 Joseph Andrew Ryan 48633 Richard Joseph Ryan 48634 Beach Nicole Sachse 48635 Fernando Salazar 48636 Matthew Robert Sampson 48637 Anthony Casmer Santora 48638 Jed Jeffrey Schaertl 48639 John Christian Scharrett 48640 James Walter Schirmer 48641 James Gerard Schleck 48642 Eric Rand Schmacker 48643 Mark Edward Schmitt 48644 Todd David Schmitt 48645 Edward Joseph Schober 48646 Russell Joseph Schott 48647 Clinton William Schreckhise 48648 Robin Marie Schuck 48649 Michael Anton Schultz 48650 Silke Edwards 48651 Bernard Renaud Seeger 48652 John Stephen Seehorn 48653 Stephen Frank Segundo 48654 Matthew Lawrence Seldin 48655 Jeffrey Steven Settle 48656 Robert Alan Seymour 48657 Robert A. Seymour 48658 Scott Taylor Seymour 48659 Terri Lee Grow 48660 Brian David Sharpe 48661 Mark D. Shattan 48662 Thomas J. Sheehan 48663 Daniel L. Shekleton 48664 J. Andrew Sherrard 48665 Hyonwoo Shin 48666 James M. Shinn 48667 Brian Douglas Shoemaker 48668 Jeffrey Mark Shoemaker 48669 Jason Khoa Shrader 48670 David Eidson Sibert 48671 Dean Larry Sievers 48672 Mark Linwood Simmons 48673 Michael Shawn Simon 48674 Jeffrey Scott Simpson 48675 Douglas Arthur Sims 48676 Cheryl Lynn Sirna 48677 John I. Slater 48678 Howard M. Slee 48679 John Franklin Sloboda 48680 Christopher Andrew Smith 48681 Darren Robert Smith 48682 Debra Lynn Smith 48683 John Scott Smith 48684 Michael Leviel Smith 48685 Todd Wesley Smith 48686 Wade Richard Smith 48687 Paul Louis Smolchek 48688 Deborah Anne Chovancek 48689 Brian J. Sonka 48690 Robert R. Soto 48691 Daniel Frederick C. Soucek 48692 Kara Lynne Soules 48693 John Cranmer Soupene 48694 Elizabeth Amelia Southard 48695 Stephanie J. Dullea 48696 Kris A. Spadavecchia Belanger 48697 William Anthony Speier 48698 William Joseph Spencer 48699 Robert Gerald Spignesi 48700 L. Kyle Spinks 48701 John Robert Stark 48702 Gary Eugene Starzmann 48703 Andrew Conrad Steitz 48704 Allen H. Stephan 48705 William D. Stewart 48706 William L. Stone 48707 Alan Charles Streeter 48708 Richard Edward Stroiney 48709 Mark Page Struss 48710 Edward Charles Sudzina 48711 Michael Patrick Sullivan 48712 Catherine A. Hansen 48713 James P. Sutton 48714 Kirk Leighton Swanson 48715 Steven Matthew Swierkowski 48716 Gabriel Boris Sylvia 48717 Samuel Orock Tabot 48718 David Leroy Talley 48719 Todd Arginio Tamburino 48720 Joseph John Tanona 48721 Peter John Tate 48722 Owen Jay Tatsuta 48723 Joseph Patrick Taylor 48724 Brian H.E. Tebrock 48725 Elisa M. Westfield 48726 Timothy Allen Thatcher 48727 Todd V. Thiel 48728 Thanh Tieu 48729 Eric Russell Timmerman 48730 John Joel Tiner 48731 Alvin Yuhico Tiu 48732 James Phillip Tobey 48733 Kevin Michael Tohill 48734 David Charles Tomasi 48735 Damion O. Topping 48736 Vincent Hugo Torza 48737 Kristopher Antony Towers 48738 Thomas Vincent Traczyk 48739 Michael J. Tripp 48740 Vernon James Tryon 48741 Brian Charles Turner 48742 Martin Edward Tursky 48743 Stephanie Jean Tutton 48744 Douglas Michael Vallejo 48745 Nathan H. VanDuzer 48746 William F. Van Mullen 48747 David Richard Velasquez 48748 Stephen F. Vensor 48749 Mark Andrew Viney 48750 Craig Thomas Vosper 48751 Mark Patrick Wade 48752 Kevin Eugene Wainwright 48753 Patrick L. Walden 48754 David Joseph Walker 48755 James Alexander Walsh 48756 Karen J. Walsh 48757 Robert John Walthouse 48758 Paul B. Walton 48759 Bradley Scott Wanek 48760 Charles Brook Ward 48761 Robert Joseph Wardrop 48762 Monique Yvette Washington 48763 John A. Wasko 48764 Todd R. Wasmund 48765 Christopher J. Watrud 48766 Jeffrey Carl Weber 48767 Martin Joseph Weber 48768 Randall Scott Weisner 48769 Robert Russell Welch 48770 Christopher D. Wells 48771 Mark D. Wells 48772 Bernita Elizabeth Russo 48773 Mark Robertson West 48774 Walter Lee Wheatfall 48775 Donald H. White 48776 Douglas Eric White 48777 Kevin Christopher White 48778 Michael Renard White 48779 Craig A. Whiteside 48780 Jason Scott Wieman 48781 Gregory S. Wilcox 48782 Mark Anthony Wildermuth 48783 Brian Earl Wilkerson 48784 Don Lars Willadsen 48785 Guy Edwin Willebrand 48786 David H. Williams 48787 Kevin David Williams 48788 Scott Thomas Williams 48789 Christopher Ray Willis 48790 Douglas Everett Willis 48791 David Raymond Wills 48792 Eugene Wiley Wilson

48793 George Brian Wilson 48794 Douglas Walter Winton 48795 Anthony Mario Wizner 48796 Julie Ann Wood Goldsmith 48797 Lisa M. Woodman-Rumbles 48798 Bradley Keith Woods 48799 Joseph Paul Wortmann 48800 Courtney Agnew Wright 48801 Neiland Lee Wright 48802 Teresa Ann Wyatt 48803 Peter Kyung Yi 48804 Ugur Z. Yildirim 48805 Samuel Louis Yingst 48806 Richard Berry Yoder 48807 Naftali Elad Yoran 48808 Shaw Yoshitani 48809 Steven Edward Yost 48810 Robert Thomas Yow 48811 William Francis Ystueta 48812 Terry Ji-Won Yun 48813 Richard Ronald Zareck 48814 Shane William Zehnder 48815 Dennis Duane Ziegler 48816 Francesca Ziemba 48817 Matthew Christopher Zimmerman 48818 Michael J. Zuerlein 48819 Michael Warren Brogan 48820 Laurel Jean Coesens 48821 John R. Cook 48822 Geraldine Renee Daniels 48823 Darrell Edwin Eikner 48824 Brian Patrick Fitzgerald 48825 Anthony L. Garcia 48826 Richard Henry Gordon 48827 Paul Joseph Haggerty 48828 Bradley J. Hamacher 48829 Matthew Christian Hayes 48830 Stephen Tyler Jasper 48831 Christopher Bryan Johnson 48832 Richard John Little 48833 Philip Lee Mayberry 48834 Todd Charles McCoskey 48835 Charles David Michaelsen 48836 Richard Ronald Navarro 48837 Richard Douglas Orman 48838 Malcolm Xavier Perry 48839 Laura Marie Pritz Elliott 48840 Natalie Mandry 48841 Craig Ronald Romanowski 48842 Clement Van Beuren Sawin 48843 George Johnnie Stroumpos 48844 R. Mark Teixeira 48845 Daniel Thomas Warner 48846 Todd Lamart Woodson 48847 Derrick Clinton Wright 48848 Bryne Corey Zuege 48849 Joseph M. Harris 48850 Herb Booth Petry 48851 Andrew T. Rendon 48852 Allen R. Brenner 48853 Patrick D. Brundidge 48854 Norine C. D'Arcy Friden 48855 Bradley H. Doebel 48856 Grant Edwin Goldsmith 48857 Robert A. Gutierrez 48858 Clemens S. Kruse 48859 Kelly Dean Laughlin 48860 Brian Thomas Mackey 48861 Glenn Mark McRill 48862 Edward D. Nieto 48863 Bret Steven Petkus 48864 Paul Warren Poole 48865 Ingrid Powell-Dawkins 48866 David E. Romano 48867 James R. Romanski 48868 Rodd E. Thrower 48869 Andrew C. Ulrich 48870 Kimberly L. Whittington 48871 Jonathan K. Williams 48872 **1992** David Allan Abke 48873 Earl Eric Khalid Abonadi 48874 R. Christian Ackerman 48875 Alex Jeffrey Adelman 48876 Jeffrey Allen Agee 48877 Frederick Ahn 48878 John Scot Aita 48879 Terry Francis Alger 48880 Craig Joseph Alia 48881 Peter Michael Allen 48882 Daniel Peter Aloisi 48883 Mark Robert Amato 48884 Mark McClellan Ambrose 48885 Victor Andrew Ames 48886 Neal Albert Amodio 48887 James Fuller Anderson 48888 John Gregory Anderson 48889 Thomas Larry Anderson 48890 Stacy Ruth Anselmi Zotter 48891 Joel K. Aoki 48892 Glenn Edwin Arnold 48893 Michael Jon Arntson 48894 Paul Michael Arrambide 48895 William Michael Artigliere 48896 Harold W. Askins 48897 Andrew Gene Aull 48898 Steven Erickson Bach 48899 Corbin Kai Backman 48900 Brett Edward Bagwell 48901 Lance Michael Bailey 48902 Craig Richard Baker 48903 David A. Balan 48904 James Scott Ball 48905 Bethany L. Lee 48906 Y. Ho Andrew Bang 48907 James J. Bankey 48908 Nathan Hezekiah Banks 48909 Kenneth Charles Baran 48910 Guy Richard Barattieri 48911 Daniel David Barber 48912 Ballard C. Barker 48913 Leroy Ronald Barker 48914 Kelly Suzanne Barnes 48915 Mary Jude Barnes 48916 Troy Donnell Barnes 48917 Skip Daniel Barnett 48918 Shannon S. Rigby 48919 Nathan Edward Barto 48920 Alexander Joshua Basse 48921 Kevin Lee Bates 48922 Ryan Derric Bates 48923 Daniel H. Bath 48924 Michael Joseph Battles 48925 Michael Anthony Baumeister 48926 Jennifer R. Ryan 48927 John Christopher Beatty 48928 William E. S. Beaty 48929 Deannalee Marie Beauvais 48930 William Vernon Beck 48931 Gregory Scott Beckman 48932 Alec Carl Beekley 48933 Jeffrey Frank Bellinger 48934 Scott Patrick Belveal 48935 Jeffrey William Bencik 48936 Sharon S. Laahs 48937 James Justin Bents 48938 Joseph Bertrand Berger 48939 Jeffery John Berkmeyer 48940 Sean Cardona Bernabe 48941 Paul Thomas Berquist 48942 David Lee Beshears 48943 Eric Stephen Betts 48944 Jason Neil Beyer 48945 Don Michael Bice 48946 David Patrick Biron 48947 Andrew David Blake 48948 Matthew Buchanan Blitch 48949 Marc Earl Boberg 48950 Jennifer Catherine Boggs 48951 John A. Bojescul 48952 Thomas Robert Bolen 48953 Stephen Anthony Boltja 48954 Gregory Scott Bonds 48955 Robert Gayle Booze 48956 David William Borgognoni 48957 David Todd Borowicz 48958 Paula Kay Rickleff 48959 Kimberly Ann Bowers 48960 John Michael Boyer 48961 Jose R. Bracero 48962 Jennifer Ann Bradac 48963 Tracey LaDawn Brame 48964 Matthew Francois Brantley 48965 Amy L. Tribus 48966 Jeffrey Paul Bray 48967 Trevor Jon Bredenkamp 48968 David Scott Brewster 48969 William Luther Brice 48970 David Aaron Briles 48971 Lance Edward Broeking 48972 David Anthony Brown 48973 Douglas Charles Brown 48974 Ivan Ellery Brown 48975 Jeffrey Vaughn Brown 48976 Kile Daniel Brown 48977 Kimberly Jean Brown 48978 Kyle Matthew Bruner 48979 Marc Albert Brunner 48980 Sean P. Buchholtz 48981 Emily C. Burgess Felvus 48982 Heidi K. Burghart 48983 F. John Burpo 48984 William Michael Burris 48985 Guy Matthew Burrow 48986 Curtis Alan Buzzard 48987 Benjamin Barton Cable 48988 Enrico J. Cacciatore 48989 Jennifer L. Hawkins 48990 Giorgio Ferdinando Caldarone 48991 Gerald Van Cammack 48992 Scott Alan Campbell 48993 William John Campbell 48994 Jerome Merle Cap 48995 David Reginald Capps 48996 Peter Grant Carey 48997 Brian David Carlock 48998 Charles A. Carlton 48999 Joseph Richard Carmen 49000 Christopher Franklin Carr 49001 Richard Quinn Carroll 49002 Kedran Juanrez Carter 49003 Jason Franklin Cartwright 49004 Stephen John Cavoli 49005 Steven J. Chaloult 49006 Lance Floyd Chambers 49007 Michael David Chandler 49008 Edward Yusam Ching 49009 Ennocent Chivhima 49010 Hang Jin Cho 49011 Joo Cho 49012 Yong U. Choi 49013 Dana Jo Carran 49014 Erik Loren Christiansen 49015 Daniel Yong Pom Chun 49016 Gregg T. Clark 49017 Jason Ray Clark 49018 Kevin Burns Clark 49019 Matthew Paul Clark 49020 Andrew Davenport Clarke 49021 Gregory Jay Cleveland 49022 Sean Douglas Cleveland 49023 Sean Tracy Code 49024 Christopher Michael Coglianese 49025 Barak Cohen 49026 Gail C. Seymour 49027 Mark Albert Colbrook 49028 Larry Leon Coleman 49029 Craig Wyatt Collar 49030 Liam Collins 49031 Andrew Austin Collum 49032 Richard Michael Colucciello 49033 Sean Mannon Condron 49034 Christopher Lyn Connolly 49035 Patrick Russell Cook 49036 Mark L. Coomes 49037 Daniel Wayne Kennedy Cooper 49038 Jimmy L. Cooper 49039 Adrian Ariel Maaray Cordovi 49040 Daniel Philip Core 49041 Clark M. Cornelius 49042 James Thomas Corrigan 49043 Cory Nathan Costello 49044 Marc Elliott Cottle 49045 Matthew Heath Coulter 49046 James Warby Crichton 49047 Gerald Franklin Crook 49048 Christopher Jon Crosby 49049 Michael Joseph Crossett 49050 David Dean Crossley 49051 Tobin M. Crowder 49052 Ann G. Finley 49053 Matthew Wayne Currie 49054 David Matthew Curry 49055 Craig Andrew Cutlip 49056 Douglas Wendell Cutright 49057 Christopher William Dailey 49058 John Christian Damm 49059 Benjamin Clark Danielson 49060 Laurin J. Darnell 49061 Michael Leo Dauer 49062 Paul Gerard Davidson 49063 Antonio C. Davis 49064 Edward Dale Davis 49065 Jason Daniel Davis 49066 Jeffrey Scot Davis 49067 Toya Jeneen Davis 49068 Mark Alexander Dawkins 49069 Guillermo De Los Santos 49070 Curtis Laray Decker 49071 Rollan Jay Degeare 49072 Harold C. Demby 49073 J. Michael Denning 49074 Mark Junior Derber 49075 Michael Craig Derosier 49076 Rose Nguyen Sulley 49077 David Richard Dickison 49078 Rebecca Lynne Dieck 49079 Joseph Francis Dillon 49080 Matthew Anthony Dimmick 49081 Brian Keith Diven 49082 Michael Scott Doheny 49083 Christopher Todd Donahue 49084 Michael Christopher Donahue 49085 Brian C. Donovan 49086 Daniel Lee Dorchinsky 49087 Erik Herbert Dowgos 49088 Christopher Thomas Drew 49089 Gerald Raymond Dull 49090 Percy Elford Dunagin 49091 Peter Michael Dunaway 49092 John Lee Duncan 49093 Scott Michael Dunderdale 49094 Charles Thomas Duray 49095 Robert Lee Eason 49096 Tony James Ebert 49097 Randall Dale Eccleston 49098 Ezra Abram Eckhardt 49099 Marshall Vincent Ecklund 49100 Raymond Gerald Edgar 49101 Robert Thomas Edmondson 49102 William Burl Eger 49103 Stephen K. Ehrenberg 49104 Karl Phillip Eimers 49105 Matthew Lee Elam 49106 Daniel Prentice Elliott 49107 Deborah Marie Ellis 49108 Marc Christopher Emery 49109 Melissa J. E. McCarthy 49110 Michael Anthony Emons 49111 John Brunner Ende 49112 Chad E. Enders 49113 Arthur Bryan Endres 49114 Michael Taylor Engle 49115 Joseph Francis English 49116 Anthony Eugene Enrietto 49117 Ross Alan Erzar 49118 Christopher Brian Ewing 49119 Andrew Forrest Farnsler 49120 Matthew Harold Fath 49121 Nathan Robert Fawkes 49122 Grant Douglas Fay 49123 Kyle Eric Feger 49124 Melissa Dawn Feit 49125 Daniela Clara Ferchmin 49126 Boris Jorge Fernandez 49127 Thomas A. Feuerborn 49128 Darren Earl Fey 49129 Troy C. Figgins 49130 Kurt Anthony Filosa 49131 Rodney James Fischer 49132 Darren Phillips Fitz Gerald 49133 Sean Stanley Fitzgerald 49134 James Regis Fitzgibbon 49135 James Daniel Flandreau 49136 David E. Flieg 49137 Brian Keenan Flood 49138 Craig Roy Fluharty 49139 Robert Jerry Foltynowicz 49140 James Spenzer Forbes 49141 Kenneth A. Foret 49142 Stuart Franklin Fowler 49143 Kevin M. Frank 49144 Timothy Mark Frederick 49145 Joseph J. Frescura 49146 Joseph Lewis Frey 49147 James Aubrey Frick 49148 Lakeisha R. Davis 49149 Eric Carl Frutchey 49150 James L. Fry 49151 Mathew James Fry 49152 Peter Lyndon Gabriel 49153 Keith Andrew Gallew 49154 Jacob Lawrence Garcia 49155 Paul Nathan Garcia 49156 Stace Wayne Garrett 49157 James E. Gaylord 49158 Marcia J. Geiger Isakson 49159 James Christopher Geiser 49160 Charles Andrew Gibbs 49161 Brendon Shoichi Gibson 49162 Jason Carlton Giles 49163 Norman William Gill 49164 Jaime L. Gilliam-Swartz 49165 Exter Garfield Gilmore 49166 Jeffrey Scott Gloede 49167 John Kevin Goertemiller 49168 Romeo Gonzales 49169 James Tristan Gorman 49170 William David Goss 49171 Gregory Peter Gosselin 49172 Angela Elaine Mysliwiec 49173 Katherine Elsie Brooks 49174 Joel Walker Gray 49175 Sharette Kirsten Gray 49176 Peter Nikolay Greany 49177 Alex Norman Green 49178 Herbert Leonard Green 49179 Quincy Justin Greene 49180 Stephen Christopher Greene 49181 Scot William Greig 49182 Iris M. Cowher 49183 Rhett Bolden Griner 49184 Cindy M. Doane 49185 Fred John Grospin 49186 James David Guenter 49187 Bartholomew A. Gutierrez 49188 Douglas Berwin Guttormsen 49189 Jennifer J. Gwinn 49190 Gregory Wayne Haas 49191 Cem Hacioglu 49192 Andrew Scott Hager 49193 Gerald William Hahn 49194 Young Peter Hahn 49195 Allen Dudgeon Haight 49196 Michael P. Graham 49197 Jeffrey Thomas Hajek 49198 Eric Reed Hall 49199 John David Hall 49200 Lee Forest Hall 49201 Maria L. Hall 49202 Charles Albert Hallman 49203 Christopher Dean Hamel 49204 Robert Glen Hamill 49205 Roderick James Hammond 49206 Philip Lain Hancock 49207 David Christopher Haney 49208 Earl Carlos Hanson 49209 Michael Patrick Hanson 49210 Thomas Jacob Hardin 49211 Garrick M. Harmon 49212 Scott Anthony Harmon 49213 David Lee Harris 49214 Richard Earl Harris 49215 Ky Brent Harrod 49216 Anita Beth Harvey 49217 Stuart Anthony Hatfield 49218 John Roy Haubert 49219 Shauna Marie Hauser 49220 Corina Hausherr 49221 William F. Hausman 49222 Albert Lee Hawkins 49223 Bradley Brian Hawkins 49224 Shawn Lee Hawkins 49225 Kwasi Lumumba Hawks 49226 Brandon Coleman Hayes 49227 James Emmett Hayes 49228 Jason R. Hayes 49229 John Thomas Head 49230 Robert R. Hebert 49231 Galen Wade Hedlund 49232 Neil Robert Hedtke 49233 Thomas David Heinold 49234 David James Hejl 49235 Ronald Barry Hildner 49236 Teresa L. Rae 49237 Terrence Edward Hill 49238 William Martin Hilton 49239 Timothy Paul Himes 49240 Burl Shannon Hinkle 49241 Mark John Hoepner 49242 Jason T. Hoffman 49243 Marc Frederick Hoffmeister 49244 Dierk Christopher Hohman 49245 Thomas Pope Holliday 49246 Carl Jerome Hollister 49247 Glenn Capicotto Hollister 49248 Stacey R. Hollyer-Dunagin 49249 Lance Gerard Homan 49250 Edward E. Horne 49251 Michael Patrick Hosie 49252 Derk S. Hoskin 49253 Nelson Scott Howard 49254 William Relle Howard 49255 Patrick Vincent Howell 49256 Christopher P. Hsu 49257 Helmut Wilhelm Huber 49258 Dana L. Huckbody-Ball 49259 Harry Brian Hudick 49260 Carolyn M. Copenhaver 49261 Jay Scott Hulett 49262 Wayne Andrew Hunt 49263 Patrick Langdon Hurley 49264 Harlan Lafe Hutcheson 49265 Patrick Forrest Hymel 49266 Joong B. Im 49267 James Philo Isenhower 49268 Brian Taylor Jackson 49269 Latonya Cherise Jackson 49270 Thomas Joseph Jacobs 49271 Gregory Knox Jacobsen 49272 Jeffrey P. Jagielski 49273 Jack Alan James 49274 Michael Edward James 49275 Frank Edward Jenio 49276 Jason Miller Jenkins 49277 Melvin Christopher Jenks 49278 James Jennings 49279 Michael S. Jensen 49280 Michele Lisa Jensen 49281 Scott R. Jerald 49282 Geoffrey James Jeram 49283 Jeffrey H. Johnson 49284 Karin Alice Johnson 49285 Linda M.J. Lamm 49286 Paul L. Johnson 49287 Todd Christopher Johnston 49288 David Edward Morgan Jones 49289 Omar James Jones 49290 James Jeffrey Jordano 49291 Jeffrey Howat Julkowski 49292 William H. Kaczynski 49293 Darrell J. Kain 49294 Scott Christopher Kaine 49295 Peter Kalamaras 49296 John William Karagosian 49297 Thomas Allen Karinshak 49298 Kim Thu Thi Kawamoto 49299 Jeffrey Anthony Kazaglis 49300 Edward C. Kelly 49301 Nelson Glenn Kerley 49302 David Richard Kershaw 49303 Donald Sean Kettering 49304 Amali Bin Ahmad Khairol 49305 Josiah Leslie Kibe 49306 Christopher John Kidd 49307 Joel Eric Kiefer 49308 Charlie Henry Kim 49309 Jin Woo Kim 49310 Sally Joanne Taverni 49311 Sanford Jong Kim 49312 Sang H. Park 49313 Jeffrey Suk Kyu Kim 49314 Todd G. King 49315 Howard Clinton Kirk 49316 James M. Kisiel 49317 Stephen Roman Kiziuk 49318 Jeremy Stefan Klages 49319 Kevin M. Klopcic 49320 Stephen Gerald Kneeland 49321 Richard Warren Knight 49322 Aaron Keith Knudsen 49323 Gretchen Manus 49324 Andrew Warren Koloski 49325 Brian John Kouba 49326 John Christopher Kowalewski 49327 David Richard Kramer 49328 Edith Elizabeth Krause 49329 Jeanine Elizabeth Kruger 49330 Robert M. Kulis 49331 Michelle Lee Kurbiel 49332 Steven Edward LaCasse 49333 Stephen William Ladd 49334 Christopher Stephen LaGullo 49335 Duncan Lamb 49336 Susan M. Williamson 49337 John C. Lamphere 49338 Paul A. Landt 49339 Joseph Edward Langenderfer 49340 Mary K. King 49341 Michael Winston Lanier 49342 Eric David Larkin 49343 Thomas Lane Larson 49344 Melanie A. Lauben Little 49345 Dawne Elizabeth Laughlin 49346 Gregory Matthew Law 49347 Joseph Paul Lazzari 49348 Barton Corbett Leatherwood 49349 Carleton A. Lee 49350 Heok Chye Lee 49351 Kang Min Lee 49352 Yong Jik Lee 49353 Kerry A. LeFrancis 49354 Christopher David Lepp 49355 Jason Lerner 49356 Bobby Valton Lewallen 49357 Nicholas Gene Lewis 49358 William Irvin Lewis 49359 Correna Ann Leiding Panagiotou 49360 Douglas C. Ligor 49361 David George Limberg 49362 Christopher Joseph Limerick 49363 William Penn Peter Linder 49364 William Clark Lindner 49365 Carl Thomas Linnington 49366 Richard T. Little 49367 David Tshombe London 49368 Deborah Lynn Long 49369 Michael Junker Loos 49370 Clayton Lamont Lowe 49371 Brian Joseph Lunday 49372 John Shannon Lyerly 49373 Thomas James Lynch 49374 John Idris Lyons 49375 Brian John Lyttle 49376 Mary Frances Mace Baumeister 49377 Matthew J. Machon 49378 Andrew Walter Mack 49379 Kenneth Leon Mack 49380 David Eldred Mackey 49381 Robert Matheson Macleod 49382 Charles W. Macune 49383 Craig Merlin Magerkurth 49384 George Edward Malcom 49385 Saleem Ahmad Malik 49386 Marshall John Malinowski 49387 David Shepherd Mallory 49388 Joseph Patrick Maloney 49389 Shon J. Manasco 49390 Peter Charles Manza 49391 Monica L. Cater 49392 Patrick Scott Marcoux 49393 Kyle Joseph Marsh 49394 James P. Marshall 49395 Curtis Lewis Martin 49396 Robert Anthony Martinez 49397 Roberto Loya Martinez 49398 Silas Martinez 49399 Ronald Florian Massey 49400 Jeffrey A. Mathis 49401 Caroline Mauro Jagielski 49402 Paul Edward Maxwell 49403 Matthew Joseph May 49404 Timothy J. Maynard 49405 Thomas G. McCann 49406 Paul James McCarthy 49407 Richard E. McCarthy 49408 Brian Douglas McCarver 49409 R. Keith McClung 49410 Matthew Alexander McConnell 49411 Daryl Scott McCormick 49412 William Lance McCoskey 49413 Stephen J. McCullough 49414 Michael Thomas McDonnell 49415 Michael Eugene McDuffie 49416 Kimberly D. McGavern 49417 Darrick Lamar McGill 49418 Kenny Wayne McGuffee 49419 James Carroll McGuire 49420 Marshall Arthur McKay 49421 Michael Delbert McKay 49422 Kevin Andrew McKenna 49423 Benjamin Darrell McKenzie 49424 Michael Andrew McLarney 49425 Heather Ann Davidson 49426 Edward Joseph McManus 49427 Vance Clayton McMurry 49428 Christopher William Mead 49429 Aaron Paul Mebust 49430 Robert K. Meek 49431 Mitchell Leonard Meier 49432 Edward Gerard Melton 49433 John J. Melton 49434 Mark Anthony Membrino 49435 Christopher M. Mendes 49436 Christopher Allan Mendez 49437 Daniel Ramon Menendez 49438 Gerardo V. Meneses 49439 Karl Theodore Messmer 49440 Garret K. Messner 49441 John L. Miles 49442 Bernard Paul Miller 49443 Charles N. Miller 49444 Jason John Miller 49445 John Mark Miller 49446 Jeffrey M. Mills 49447 Kevin Ray Mills 49448 Daniel Dickinson Miner 49449 Ronald Jon Minty 49450 Bill Mills Miranda 49451 Mark Steven Osorio Mistal 49452 Darren S. Mitchell 49453 Korey Otis Mitchell 49454 Russel T. Mizelle 49455 John Adrian Moberly 49456 Bradley F. Mock 49457 Robert J. Molinari 49458 Mark Edward Maloney 49459 Christopher Anthony Monaco 49460 John B. Monroe 49461 Jon Lee Monroe 49462 Alex Sean Montoya 49463 King Starr Moon 49464 Lance D. Moore 49465 Matthew Randolph Moore 49466 Vincent P. Moore 49467 Mark John Moran 49468 Sean MacKenzie Morgan 49469 Jason R. Morris 49470 Robert Bailey Moseley 49471 Dewey Alexander Mosley 49472 David Burkette Moulder 49473 John W. Mullens 49474 Joseph Timothy Munko 49475 Jennifer Murtagh Hagwood 49476 John Howard Myers 49477 Vincent Mysliwiec 49478 John Eun-Jun Myung 49479 Christopher P. Navoa 49480 Bronson Neal 49481 David Robert Nehring 49482 Landy Thomas Nelson 49483 Michael Jot Neri 49484 Melissa C. Hamel 49485 David Michael Newman 49486 John Patrick Newman 49487 Nicholas Han Nguyen 49488 Jennifer Anne Spencer 49489 Demetrios J. Nicholson 49490 Heath Joshua Niemi 49491 T. Bradley Ninness 49492 Scott Edward Noble 49493 Michael Eugene Noel 49494 Gerald John O'Donnell 49495 Alvaro Velasquez Obregon 49496 Robert A. O'Brien 49497 Charles Francis O'Donnell 49498 Charles Howard Ogden 49499 Thomas Ogden 49500 Steven J. Oh 49501 Gregory Stephen Olinger 49502 Edrian Oliver 49503 Thomas William Olsen 49504 Craig T. Olson 49505 Joel Carter Olson 49506 Patrick Knute Olson 49507 George Alan O'Neal 49508 William Peter O'Neill 49509 Perry Perry Orr 49510 Jennifer O. Smestad 49511 Gary Lee Ostendorf 49512 Michael Todd Ozeranic 49513 Wesley P. Padilla 49514 John Michael Paganini 49515 Stephen Edward Paganucci 49516 Sang-Woo Pak 49517 James Robert Papenberg 49518 Mark Frederick Parcells 49519 John Parente 49520 Daniel Daehyun Park 49521 Steven Kyehong Park 49522 Allanna Michele Cook 49523 David Allen Parsons 49524 Cheryl A. Lamphere 49525 Andrew James Pasterchick 49526 Matthew Paul Henry Pasulka 49527 Jacqueline Latanya Patten 49528 John Scott Payne 49529 Thomas Wray Payne 49530 Amanda Martha Greig 49531 William Edward Pearson 49532 Isaac Bernard Peay 49533 Lawrence Edward Penn 49534 Celestino Perez 49535 Marc Alexander Perez-Venero 49536 Thomas Wayne Perkins 49537 Andrew Joseph Pero 49538 J.Stephen Stephen Peterson 49539 Michael Charles Peterson 49540 Dennis Lee Phillips 49541 Jo David Phillips 49542 Robert Terry Phillips 49543 Kenneth Dale Pickett 49544 Justin Earle Pierce 49545 Daniel Vincent Pillitiere 49546 Clinton J. Pincock 49547 John Rattaporn Pippy 49548 Aaron Christopher Pitney 49549 William R. Pittman 49550 Christiane Lynn Ploch 49551 John Andrew Polhamus 49552 Frank Anthony Pometti 49553 Angela P. Shinn 49554 James Scott Powell 49555 Christopher Scott Prentice 49556 Arthur Fredrick Pressel 49557 Bernard A. Radcliffe 49558 Eric C. Rannow 49559 John E. Ransford 49560 Scott

Mitchell Ransom 49561 Stephen Patrick Rawles 49562 Joel Dawson Rayburn 49563 Mark R. Read 49564 Alton Todd Real 49565 John Henry Reese 49566 Jason Marc Reherman 49567 Chad Allan Reiman 49568 Richard Frank Richkowski 49569 Darin Thomas Richter 49570 William S. Rielly 49571 Mark Randall Rigby 49572 Michael Edward Worthen Ritter 49573 Aaron David Roberson 49574 Julie Ann Robert Hall 49575 Daniel M. Roberts 49576 Michael Andrew Roberts 49577 Dale Allen Robison 49578 Paul William Robyn 49579 Armando Rodriguez 49580 Carolina Coll 49581 Jasper Latney Rogers 49582 Stephen Christopher Rogers 49583 John Louis Roper 49584 Craig Patrick Rose 49585 Craig Steven Roseberry 49586 Douglas Gerald Ross 49587 L. Daniel Rotenberry 49588 Blaine Edmond Roth 49589 James Donald Rouse 49590 William Leslie Ruddock 49591 Averill Ruiz 49592 Eric Gordon Ruselink 49593 Amy Madeline Zimmerman 49594 Noel Lendol Russell 49595 Christopher Anthony Russo 49596 Philip J. Ryan 49597 Bruce Alan Ryba 49598 John Anthony Sabatini 49599 John Randolph Sadler 49600 Juan Manuel Saldivar 49601 Gene Anthony Salkovsky 49602 Gail E. Yoshitani 49603 Thomas William Sanders 49604 Christopher Neves Santos 49605 Gregory Pandley Sarakatsannis 49606 Kerry Lee Sarver 49607 William Gordon Savage 49608 Reid Leslie Sawyer 49609 Michelle Ann Schmidt 49610 Christopher F. Schmitt 49611 David Lee Schmitt 49612 Kurt Albert Schosek 49613 Eric Dan Schourek 49614 Lee W. Schreiter 49615 Brian David Schuler 49616 Morgan Malcolm Xavier Schulz 49617 Bruce Edward Schuman 49618 Christina M. Guthrie 49619 Jason Daniel Schwers 49620 Aaron D. Scott 49621 Linda Susanne Scott 49622 Richard Anthony Seaman 49623 James Stuart Seamon 49624 Amy C. Brinson 49625 Lara Ann Seligman 49626 Daniel Louie Sevall 49627 Jennifer Jill Shafer-Odom 49628 Deborah Marie Shahid 49629 Christopher Scott Shannon 49630 Michael Dean Shapiro 49631 Dewayne Dean Sharp 49632 Thomas Everett William Shea 49633 Phillip Jon Shearer 49634 Robert Edward Sheets 49635 Brett Harry Shelley 49636 Timothy O'Harra Sheridan 49637 Scott Marshall Sherman 49638 Edward W. Shim 49639 Yong Myung Shin 49640 Andrew Van Shipe 49641 Alan Bradley Shorey 49642 Robert Lee Shults 49643 Jeremy Todd Siegrist 49644 Robert A. Sierens 49645 Jeffery B. Siler 49646 James Arthur Sinkus 49647 Deidre M. Sisson 49648 Rosalynn Gloria Johnson 49649 Stephen Eugene Small 49650 Jason Lane Smallfield 49651 Andrew Fitzgerald Smith 49652 Arlen Lavon Smith 49653 Catherine Ann Smith 49654 Coniculus Bonifay Smith 49655 Edward Scott Smith 49656 Frank Henry Smith 49657 Jason Mark Smith 49658 John Anthony Smith 49659 Kevin Joseph Smith 49660 Michael Anthony Smith 49661 Raymond Patrick Smith 49662 Rodney Brent Smith 49663 Sean M. Smith 49664 Steven Christopher Smith 49665 Torrence Jae Smith 49666 Todd Matthew Snell 49667 Frank Kenneth Sobchak 49668 Robert Sobeski 49669 Theodore Edward Sokolowski 49670 Omar Soto-Jimerez 49671 Christopher P. Soucie 49672 Matthew Victor Sousa 49673 Everett Stuart Palmer Spain 49674 Michael Rea Spears 49675 William Terence Speegle 49676 Jamelle C. Feuerborn 49677 Scott D. Stanley 49678 Jackson Archibald Jackson Steele 49679 Joel Russell Stephenson 49680 Margaret Dunlop Stewart 49681 Timothy Richard Stiansen 49682 Geoffrey Melvin Stoker 49683 Michael E. Stokes 49684 John Herbert Stone 49685 John J. Strange 49686 Christopher Michael Struve 49687 Marc Daniel Suarez 49688 Craig Edward Suydan 49689 Philip Adam Swabsin 49690 Christopher W. Swiecki 49691 Bradley J. Swim 49692 Joel Travis Tanaka 49693 Ramon A. Tancinco 49694 Hubert Pierce Tankersley 49695 Joseph James Taranto 49696 Scott Brian Tardif 49697 Eric Paul Tauch 49698 Darryl Lynwood Taylor 49699 David Jerome Taylor 49700 Grady Scott Taylor 49701 Jason James Thacker 49702 Dean Darrel Thimjon 49703 Walter Gene Thomas 49704 Henrik Howard Thomsen 49705 John Lathrop Throckmorton 49706 Melinda Kathryn Tilton 49707 Aaron P. Tipton 49708 Matthew A. Tolle 49709 Monte A. Tomasino 49710 Julius Ancheta Tomines 49711 William M. Torpey 49712 Laura Leticia Torres 49713 Cory Henry Touard 49714 Peter William Travis 49715 Brian Tribus 49716 Thomas Todd Trinter 49717 Ryan Matthew Tritschler 49718 Michael Neil Trotter 49719 Douglas Lee Truax 49720 John Carlton Tucker 49721 Robert Scott Tucker 49722 Michael Todd Tunnell 49723 Yolanda Rochelle Turner 49724 Brian Francis Tuson 49725 Jon Michael Tussing 49726 Charles Henry Uchill 49727 Jeffrey Matthew Vajda 49728 John Timothy Vallely 49729 Reid Evan Vander Schaaf 49730 Donald Lee Van Fossen 49731 Deborah Macrae Vann 49732 Bret Patrick Van Poppel 49733 Jack Edwin Vantress 49734 Michael Scott Velasco 49735 Kenneth J. Verhulst 49736 Jonathan William Vernau 49737 Niave F. Knell 49738 Eric D. Verzola 49739 Steven Dallas Vestal 49740 Peter Jerome Vlakancic 49741 Son Phi Vo 49742 Glenn James Voelz 49743 Donald A. Vollmar 49744 Ronald Anthony Voves 49745 Edward J. Vozzo 49746 Damon Matthew Vrabel 49747 Chaka Luthuli Wade 49748 M. David Wagner 49749 Kevin Andre Walker 49750 Nathaniel Franklin Wallace 49751 Steven M. Walter 49752 Christian J. Walters 49753 Edward W. Walters 49754 James Edward Ward 49755 Kermit Demetrius Ward 49756 Samuel J. Warf 49757 Paul Allan Warmuskerken 49758 Christopher Wells Waters 49759 Timothy Thomas Waters 49760 Michael J. Weatherwax 49761 Jeffery Alan Weaver 49762 Kristina E. Weber 49763 John Berdette Weisner 49764 James David Wells 49765 Theresa R. Drushal 49766 Brian James West 49767 Mark Andrew White 49768 Richard Lyle White 49769 Wilbert Eugene Whitten 49770 John K. Wickiser 49771 Thomas Alan Wiers 49772 Stephen M. Wilbur 49773 David A. Wilkins 49774 Patrick Brian Wilkison 49775 James Robert Willcox 49776 Elizabeth L. Tolle 49777 Michael Patrick Williams 49778 Myreon Williams 49779 Scott Michael Williams 49780 Jack William Williamson 49781 Neil James Willis 49782 Kevin Michael Wilson 49783 Michael John Wilson 49784 Ingrid W. Lynch 49785 Larry Nicholas Wittwer 49786 Eric James Wolf 49787 Desi Levon Wyatt 49788 Donald Steven Yamagami 49789 William Michael Yanek 49790 Garth G. Yarnall 49791 Robert A. Yeager 49792 Peter C. Yoon 49793 Brian E. Young 49794 Ericka Anne Young 49795 Peter James Young 49796 Arron B. Yount 49797 Richard L. Zellmann 49798 Roy Frederick Zinser 49799 Neal Jeffrey Zuckerman 49800 Joseph John Zwirecki 49801 Peter Cole Adamoyurka 49802 Michael David Blomquist 49803 Matthew Michael Bowman 49804 Kevin Wesley Carruth 49805 Frank Anthony DeGeorge 49806 Kristen Melissa Duncan 49807 Randall Glen Lee 49808 Sidney Jerome Loyd 49809 Philip Randall Matthewson 49810 Fritzgerald Francis McNair 49811 Timothy John Rausch 49812 Robert McKie Salley 49813 Fombah Teh Sirleaf 49814 Callian Maurice Thomas 49815 John T. Bair 49816 Thomas David Hansbarger 49817 Matthew Ho Nuhse 49818 Jay J. Petty 49819 Matthew Phillip Bartlett 49820 Chris Anthony Castillon 49821 Todd Randall Feemster 49822 John Stevens Frost 49823 John Dunn Hayes 49824 David Michael Lacy 49825 Dennis Michael Malone 49826 Edward John McGuire 49827 William H. McMillian 49828 Bradley W. Rockow 49829 Karen Jane Roe 49830 Gregory Karl Smith 49831 Rodney Allan Teasley 49832 Leslie Lee Wiese Narel 49833 Kevin Patrick Driscoll 49834 **1993** Erik J. Aasterud 49835 David S. Abrahams 49836 David B. Abshire 49837 Eric Achenbach 49838 James R. Acosta 49839 Lamar D. Adams 49840 Sherri R. Ehrenberg 49841 Calvin L. Addison 49842 Thomas L. Aiello 49843 Thomas L. Ailinger 49844 Steven T. Alch 49845 Virginia A. Wells 49846 Brent Alexander 49847 Dennis G. Alff 49848 Chad E. Allen 49849 Derrick Allen 49850 Kenneth S. Allen 49851 Robert K. Allison 49852 Joel N. Allmandinger 49853 Jonathan K. Alt 49854 David T. Ambrose 49855 Jason Luke Amerine 49856 Paul M. Amrhein 49857 Kirk J. Anderegg 49858 Erik N. Anderson 49859 James E. Anderson 49860 Jeffrey F. Anderson 49861 Cort W. Andrews 49862 Jimmy Andrews 49863 Brian N. Andrusin 49864 Steve Ansley 49865 Andrew S. Apgar 49866 Brian P. Apgar 49867 Austin T. Appleton 49868 Lynda R. Royse 49869 Charles S. Armstrong 49870 Ryan Arne 49871 Reynold R. Arredondo 49872 Randall J. Arvay 49873 Thomas J. Atkins 49874 Paul Ernest Aus 49875 Jose S. Azcona 49876 Kevin M. Backus 49877 Berkley Baker 49878 Bobby J. Baker 49879 John M. Baker 49880 Paul G.V. Baker 49881 Allana J. Balkam 49882 Jeremy A. Ball 49883 Richard P. Banez 49884 Bobby H. Bang 49885 Young Joon Bang 49886 Mandy L. Banther 49887 Darren M. Barker 49888 Gilberto J. Barrera 49889 Clark Christian Barrett 49890 James T. Bartelme 49891 Lee J. Barton 49892 Darrin J. Batchelor 49893 William A. Bates 49894 Steven Dennis Battleson 49895 Chadwick T. Bauld 49896 Craig S. Baumgartner 49897 Scott T. Beall 49898 James M. Beals 49899 Jason D. Beam 49900 Kristine Beardsley 49901 Jennifer Beason 49902 Brian Christian Beck 49903 Christopher G. Beck 49904 Gregg H. Bell 49905 Richard C. Bell 49906 Treavor J. Bellandi 49907 Peter N. Benchoff 49908 James E. Bennett 49909 Jennifer M. Bennett 49910 Charles K. Bergman 49911 Mark Berneti 49912 Richard K. Berube 49913 John Allen Best 49914 Michael Best 49915 William H. Bestermann 49916 Kurt L. Beurmann 49917 Kevin A. Bigelman 49918 John R. Bird 49919 Alan Dale Bisenieks 49920 John W. Bittner 49921 Tricia E. Achenbach 49922 Michael F. Blandino 49923 Jeffrey D. Blaney 49924 Benjamin C. Block 49925 Wendy A. Stringer 49926 Bradley T. Bodi 49927 Dennis E. Bogdan 49928 Douglas J. Bohrer 49929 John Joseph Bonin 49930 Robert A. Borcherding 49931 Christopher C. Bowen 49932 Darrion L. Bowers 49933 Paul Lewis Bowers 49934 David A. Bowlus 49935 Lance P. Boyce 49936 James J. Boyle 49937 Scott Boyle 49938 Steven Braddom 49939 William K. Bradford 49940 Joseph F. Bradley 49941 Schawn L. Branch 49942 Jeffrey A. Brandsma 49943 Gregory C. Braunton 49944 Kevin W. Breedlove 49945 Gregory Allen Breitenfeld 49946 Andrew P. Brickson 49947 William R. Brigmon 49948 Michael D. Brinegar 49949 Stephen M. Brooks 49950 Michael W. Brough 49951 Donald M. Brown 49952 John C. Brown 49953 Kevin S. Brown 49954 Lori Lee Brown 49955 William N. Brown 49956 Bradley K. Brumbach 49957 Patrick D. Buckley 49958 Chad A. Buffington 49959 Charles W. Buffington 49960 Stephen P. Burke 49961 Kenneth W. Burkman 49962 Doug R. Bush 49963 James H. Bush 49964 Todd Butler 49965 Kevin J. Byrne 49966 Brian E. Bzdawka 49967 Samuel L. Calkins 49968 Lance Calvert 49969 Paul F. Campagna 49970 Cameron M. Cantlon 49971 Brook W. Capps 49972 Anthony T. Carango 49973 Daniel Miller Carey 49974 Christopher P. Carlton 49975 Lincoln R. Carroll 49976 Nicole J. Carroll 49977 Peter Carroll 49978 James R. Carson 49979 Brandon Robert Carteen 49980 Wilbert B. Carter 49981 David M. Cascio 49982 John J. Casisa 49983 Donald R. Cathcart 49984 Jonathan D. Caudill 49985 Kerry S. Cecil 49986 Christopher C. Cerniauskas 49987 Paul A. Cerniauskas 49988 Daniel L. Chandler 49989 William H. Chapman 49990 Jason A. Charland 49991 William C. Chess 49992 Mary Rebekah Cheyne 49993 Darren J. Chiappinelli 49994 David Brant Chiesa 49995 Shane J. Chin 49996 Timothy H. Cho 49997 Michael H. Choi 49998 Michael Chong 49999 Jeffrey D. Chuck 50000 Allyson M. Ross 50001 Michael N. Clancy 50002 Jeremy S. Clark 50003 Philip R. Clark 50004 Eddie Clay 50005 Michael B. Coachys 50006 Robert R. Cochran 50007 Charles R. Coe 50008 David Colebank 50009 Chad A. Collier 50010 Lara E. Colton 50011 Thomas J. Combs 50012 Kurt P. Connell 50013 Christopher J. Conrad 50014 Charles A. Cook 50015 Edwin Allan Cook 50016 Nathan E. Cook 50017 Jimmy B. Cooper 50018 Krista L. Bonino 50019 Thomas M. Corbitt 50020 David Coslin 50021 David E. Covolesky 50022 William H. Cox 50023 Paul G. Craft 50024 James R. Craig 50025 Steven P. Cram 50026 Jacob E. Crawford 50027 Jeremy A. Crist 50028 John J. Critelli 50029 Jay F. Crook 50030 John Denver Cross 50031 James William Crossley 50032 Mason William Crow 50033 Stephen J. Crumblish 50034 Gretchen Cudaback 50035 Emma A. Cuevas 50036 Cecil W. Culbreth 50037 Craig P. Cummings 50038 Thomas Cupit 50039 David Curl 50040 William R. Currence 50041 Karen A. Fay 50042 John Michael Cushing 50043 John W. Daberkow 50044 Shawn L. Daniel 50045 Peter A. Dannenberg 50046 Peter E. Dargle 50047 Paul T. Darling 50048 Richard W. Darouse 50049 Michael L. Davidson 50050 Daniel M. Davis 50051 James Robeson Davis 50052 Robert W. Davis 50053 Russell Davis 50054 Soo L. Davis 50055 J. Kirk Day 50056 Jeffrey A. Dean 50057 Judith A. Musgrove 50058 Shad H. Deering 50059 Steven M. Delgado 50060 Gregg Michael Dellert 50061 Christopher Delossantos 50062 C. Russell DeMartino 50063 Anthony Demasi 50064 Jason Kyle Dempsey 50065 James A. Densmore 50066 Selina K. Deviney 50067 Phillip J. DeVries 50068 Torrey A. DiCiro 50069 Ronald J. Diehl 50070 Charles S. Dietrich 50071 Larry Dillard 50072 James Dillon 50073 Richard P. DiMeglio 50074 John P. Dina 50075 Luke Stan Dodds 50076 Ross Dolgoff 50077 Roy L. Donelson 50078 Christopher P. Donnelly 50079 Mark Lee Dotson 50080 Thomas W. Doughty 50081 Tracy Dowling 50082 Patrick M. Downes 50083 David S. Doyle 50084 Dan J. Driscoll 50085 Brian C. Dudley 50086 William H. Dunbar 50087 Landy Dunham 50088 James K. Dunivan 50089 David Dunphy 50090 Jon R. Durant 50091 Frank Michael Duriancik 50092 James Duthu 50093 Frank E. Dwyer 50094 James P. Dyke 50095 Arthur Dymond 50096 James D. Dzwonchyk 50097 Mark Eberle 50098 Dennis V. Eclarin 50099 Adam T. Edwards 50100 James M. Efaw 50101 Matthew L. Eichburg 50102 Josef K. Eichinger 50103 Robert M. Einfalt 50104 Robert W. Eldred 50105 Elliott S. Elliott 50106 R Shawn Elliott 50107 Jon E. Ellis 50108 Michael David Ellis 50109 Henry P. Ellison 50110 Robert J. Ells 50111 Ronald L. Ells 50112 Daniel J. Engel 50113 Charles B. Engle 50114 James C. English 50115 Teresa Marie Erb 50116 Jeffrey M. Erickson 50117 Reed G. Erickson 50118 Pedro R. Espinoza 50119 Brad Michael Evangelist 50120 Scott Ewald 50121 Christopher T. Faber 50122 Phillip E. Fant 50123 Scott G. Farester 50124 Timothy W. Farmer 50125 Kenneth E. Farris 50126 Kristina D. Feemster 50127 Carl R. Fehrenbacher 50128 Christian Henrik Fellows 50129 Douglas Norman Ferrel 50130 Bruce Ferrell 50131 Victor W. Ferson 50132 Michael L. Figliuolo 50133 Toney E. Filsotrat 50134 Scot A. Fischer 50135 Scott M. Fitzgerald 50136 David G. Fivecoat 50137 Stephen Paul Fleming 50138 Paul R. Flood 50139 Louis A. Florence 50140 Benjamin C. Ford 50141 Brian A. Forn 50142 Vincent J. Fortunato 50143 Jamison L. Fox 50144 Marc G. Franklin 50145 Dwight E. Fraser 50146 John P. Frederick 50147 Charles W. Fritz 50148 Preston L. Funkhouser 50149 Stuart Douglas Furner 50150 Marcus Gaccione 50151 Edward A. Gaffney 50152 Daniel E. Gallagher 50153 Michael P. Gallagher 50154 Erin Patacsil 50155 Samuel Gannelli 50156 Ralph Richard Garcia 50157 Scott T. Gardiner 50158 Jason T. Garkey 50159 Elizabeth G. Kubala 50160 Stephen Gauthier 50161 Kara Michele Geisler 50162 Stephen Georgian 50163 Darren S. Gerblick 50164 Darryl Lee Gerow 50165 Dennis J. Geyer 50166 Grant S. Geyer 50167 Bryan R. Gibby 50168 Thomas M. Gilleran 50169 Sean M. Gladieux 50170 William Glaser 50171 James P. Goddard 50172 Ari Goetz 50173 Mark R. Goldschmidt 50174 Homer Gonzalez 50175 Rodney Shawn Gonzalez 50176 John J. Gordan 50177 Aaron P. Gordon 50178 Robert E. Gordon 50179 Nimrod M. Goredema 50180 John M. Gorkos 50181 Nicholas G. Gouzoulis 50182 Alexander S. Graham 50183 Daniel Graham 50184 Norman D. Grant 50185 David R. Grayson 50186 Thomas A. Greason 50187 Michael V. Greco 50188 Jean-Pierre Green 50189 Richard Adam Green 50190 Gaylord Greene 50191 William W. Griswold 50192 Jeffery M. Grosso 50193 Mathew D. Guerrie 50194 Christopher C. Guerriero 50195 William C. Deile 50196 Kent G. Guffy 50197 Eugenia K. Guilmartin 50198 Yi Se Gwon 50199 Anna Maria Haberzettl 50200 Eric R. Hadlock 50201 Michael Haggard 50202 James T. Hagy 50203 Remi Hajjar 50204 Anthony Shane Hale 50205 Matt Thomas Halferty 50206 Justin R. Hall 50207 Richard H. Halliburton 50208 Charles S. Haltiwanger 50209 Akemi L. Haman 50210 Warren Hamilton 50211 Thad S. Hand 50212 Charles E. Hansell 50213 Dane L. Hanson 50214 Douglas D. Hanson 50215 Travis D. Hanson 50216 Charles T. Hardman 50217 Gregory S. Harkins 50218 Matthew Jason Harleman 50219 Matthew Harless 50220 Stephen R. Harold 50221 Jerad I. Harper 50222 John Keith Harris 50223 Gerald Hart 50224 Raphael Hart 50225 James W. Hartman 50226 Steven Charles Hartman 50227 Michael D. Harvey 50228 Lorna J. Hastings 50229 Kenneth R. Hathaway 50230 Harry A. Hatzis 50231 Justin Hawke Hawke 50232 Johnny D. Hawkins 50233 Scott E. Hayford 50234 Donald J. Hazelwood 50235 John Heaton 50236 Keith R. Hedgspeth 50237 Steven B. Hedrick 50238 George S. Hegedus 50239 Trevor L. Heilman 50240 Steve Heller 50241 Roger G. Henderson 50242 Jason Henneke 50243 Gary G. Hennigan 50244 Matthew O. Hennigan 50245 Simon J. Hernaez 50246 Mark E. Hewitt 50247 John M. Hicks 50248 Joshua J. Higgins 50249 Kraig M. Hill 50250 Richard C. Hill 50251 Brodie R. Hodges 50252 Greg Hodnett 50253 Timothy W. Hoffner 50254 Christopher Hogan 50255 William B. Holden 50256 Scott Holstine 50257 Deanna M. Holt Cascio 50258 Abraham Y. Hong 50259 Sonki Hong 50260 Katey H. Mobley 50261 Christopher Hopkins 50262 James R. Hoskin 50263 Martha A. House 50264 Erik K. Hovda 50265 Jason Alan Howe 50266 Jeffery D. Hudson 50267 Peter P. Hudson 50268 Timothy Patrick Hughes 50269 Kristen C. Hull 50270 D'Hania J. Hunt 50271 Michael H. Hunter 50272 Thomas R. Hustead 50273 Mark C. Hustis 50274 Andrew J. Hyatt 50275 Joseph P. Iacono 50276 Luke A. Ihde 50277 David C. Im 50278 Kevin C. Inglin 50279 Tyrone Benjamin Ingo 50280 Culpepper F. Ingram 50281 Sean Innes 50282 Frank P. Intini 50283 Steven L. Isenhour 50284 Edward Jackman 50285 James W. Jackson 50286 John C. Jackson 50287 Jennifer A. Jacobs 50288 Carl Rodger Jacquet 50289 Joseph E. Janczyk 50290 Ryan M. Janovic 50291 Abel Jaramillo 50292 Christopher G. Jarvis 50293 Michael A. Jaskowiec 50294 Harold A. Jenkins 50295 Shawn T. Jenkins 50296 Matthew Jennings 50297 Jason A. Joerg 50298 Tina L.M. Taylor 50299 Ann Marie Johnson 50300 Christopher D. Johnson 50301 Donald S. Johnson 50302 J. Duncan Johnson 50303 Jeffrey Clinton Johnson 50304 Lauri Johnson 50305 Shannon Roxanne Abercrombie 50306 Steven K. Johnson 50307 Dana M. Probert 50308 James A. Jones 50309 Raymond T. Jones 50310 Sean Jones 50311 Jason Michael Jowers 50312 Amy D.J. Spangler 50313 Anthony Gustave Judge 50314 Edgar R. Jugueta 50315 Dano M. Jukanovich 50316 Matt A. Jury 50317 Shawn C. Jury 50318 Todd A. Justman 50319 Michael A. Kachure 50320 Michael S. Kaczmarek 50321 Robert Kaderavek 50322 James W. Kaine 50323 Jacqueline M. Kalata-Whiteside 50324 Douglas M. Katz 50325 Brent A. Kauffman 50326 Robert R. Keeter 50327 Danny Mack Kelley 50328 Mark P. Kempf 50329 Michael T. Kenny 50330 Michael P. Keown 50331 David J. Keppel 50332 Matthew B. Kezar 50333 Robert G. Kilborn 50334 Kevin W. Kilkelly 50335 Dean Kim 50336 Ike W. Kim 50337 Richard H. Kim 50338 Terence A. Kimball 50339 George B. Kimes 50340 Eric J. Kindgren 50341 Patrick V. Kinsman 50342 Jason A. Kirk 50343 Michael E. Kisner 50344 Shara McGowan 50345 Douglas L. Kitani 50346 Dean T. Klopotoski 50347 Robert J. Klopp 50348 J. Christopher Knox 50349 Adam C. Kocheran 50350 Stephen S. Koh 50351 Michael A. Konczey 50352 Laura Anne Lee 50353 G. Joseph Kopser 50354 Douglas M. Korneski 50355 Donald J. Kosatka 50356 Christian R. Koshinski 50357 Patrick G. Koster 50358 Edward A. Kovaleski 50359 Derek A. Kreager 50360 March L. Krotee 50361 Eric C. Krumin 50362 Maryann Min Yen Hawke 50363 Mark E. Kuleck 50364 Masami Marie Knox 50365 Keoki P. Kusano 50366 Paul H. Kwon 50367 Willie J. Lacy 50368 Troy L. Lambeth 50369 Brian B. Lane 50370 Grover Jake LaPorte 50371 Andrew Lathrop 50372 James R. Laughlin 50373 Leonard Andre Leassear 50374 Brent L. Lechner 50375 Derrick S. Lee 50376 James Kenneth Lee 50377 Sang K. Lee 50378 Ronald A. Lehman 50379 John F. Leide 50380 G. Christopher Leighow 50381 Shawn J. Leight 50382 Kenneth R. Lemire 50383 Robert J. Lenz 50384 Rene Lerma 50385 Yale F. Levin 50386 Charles W. Lewis 50387 Brian M. Lincoln 50388 Scott T. Lindberg 50389 Robin

Jane Robertson 50390 Stephen Michael Livezey 50391 John E. Livingstone 50392 George M. Lopez 50393 Thomas D. Lopez 50394 Joseph R. Loren 50395 Dario N. Lorenzetti 50396 Frank Paul Loria 50397 Peter A. Luhowy 50398 Michael S. Lynch 50399 Patricia Zoch 50400 Kevin Charles Mackenzie 50401 Alex N. MacMaster 50402 Oscar L. Magee 50403 James M. Malakoff 50404 Patmon A. Malcom 50405 Stanley A. Malloy 50406 Philip M. Mandry 50407 Thomas J. Mangine 50408 Joseph V. Mangolini 50409 Marshall W. Manley 50410 Tracy L. Mann 50411 Todd A. Manninen 50412 William Olee Manning 50413 Robert R. Mansell 50414 Brian Scott Manus 50415 Eve Marie Manzke 50416 Sava C. Marinkovich 50417 Joseph A. Marino 50418 Mark P. Markowski 50419 Sean Marshall 50420 William M. Martin 50421 Kofo A. Martins 50422 James M. Marucci 50423 Scott D. Mason 50424 Thomas Mathis 50425 William B. Matier 50426 Miki Carstens 50427 Scott D. Maxwell 50428 Christopher T. Mayer 50429 Jeffrey W. Mayo 50430 Jeffrey W. Mazikowski 50431 Michael J. Mazzocco 50432 John A. McAfee 50433 Thomas M. McCardell 50434 David B. McCarson 50435 Jeffrey J. McConihay 50436 John D. McDonald 50437 Raymond M. McDonald 50438 Michael P. McElrath 50439 Suzette M. McGee 50440 Theodore J. McGovern 50441 Christopher McGowan 50442 Richard K. McGowan 50443 James A. McInerney 50444 Charles E. McIntyre 50445 Howard Douglas McInvale 50446 Alex B. McKindra 50447 Evan H. McNamara 50448 Kenneth T. Meno 50449 David C. Menser 50450 Chance J. Mercure 50451 Aaron Merrill 50452 Charles M. Merrimon 50453 John R. Meyer 50454 Dale Michalk 50455 Fernando D. Miguel 50456 Sean Richard Mikula 50457 Marshall C. Miles 50458 Bradley J. Miller 50459 Wendy F. Milling 50460 Michael B. Mills 50461 Lorraine M. Rojas 50462 Joseph Michael Minasola 50463 Jennifer L. Mischler Silva 50464 Trevor Anthony Mishler 50465 Patrick M. Mitchell 50466 Thomas Blake Mitchell 50467 Webb Mitchell 50468 Timothy T. Mobley 50469 David M. Moga 50470 Charles I. Montana 50471 Mark G. Montgomery 50472 Todd C. Mooney 50473 Daniel W. Moore 50474 Mark A. Morex 50475 John R. Moritz 50476 Darrin A. Morris 50477 Andrew J. Muench 50478 David Mulligan 50479 Kathryn M. Mulligan 50480 Brent T. Mumford 50481 Thomas M. Murphy 50482 Mark C. Nace 50483 Joseph T. Napier 50484 Michelle Dannenberg 50485 Micah J. Narel 50486 Jeremy Peter Nathan 50487 David Navratil 50488 John Douglas Nawoichyk 50489 Dean S. Newman 50490 Julie A. Lepp 50491 Thu Nguyen 50492 James W. Niemiec 50493 Matthew T. Nilson 50494 Glenn W. Nocerito 50495 John Noh 50496 Charles W. Nolan 50497 Lisa A. Ansley 50498 Eric A. Nord 50499 Kenneth Scott Noyes 50500 Ralph C. Obert 50501 Michael C. O'Brien 50502 William T. O'Brien 50503 Carloyn Faye Belveal 50504 John E. O'Donnell 50505 John S. Oh 50506 Patrick O'Hara 50507 Metin A. Oktay 50508 Donovan Dwight Jurgens Ollar 50509 Kim H. Olmstead 50510 Michael Gregory Olmstead 50511 Jason A. Olson 50512 Lance R. Olson 50513 William T. Olson 50514 Jerome W. O'Neal 50515 Dennis W. O'Neill 50516 Charina Navratil 50517 James M. Orosz 50518 Jeffrey Ortoli 50519 Carl Raymond Ott 50520 Jason J. Ottman 50521 Steven R. Overby 50522 Damon E. Owens 50523 Michael P. Owens 50524 David L. Painter 50525 Lisa Johnson 50526 John W. Panhorst 50527 Mark S. Parker 50528 Ronald A. Parungao 50529 Gary F. Parvin 50530 Neal E. Pason 50531 John S. Passyn 50532 Tarak Patel 50533 Jason Andrew Pates 50534 Andrew M. Patterson 50535 Thomas C. Paudler 50536 Michael J. Peck 50537 David S. Pelkey 50538 Michel V. Peloquin 50539 Eric Peltzer 50540 James Pennella 50541 William S. Penzel 50542 Doug Peplowski 50543 Allen J. Pepper 50544 Jeremy G. Perkins 50545 Donald J. Perry 50546 Paul S. Perry 50547 Antony E. Peters 50548 Dwight J. Peters 50549 Andrew M. Phalan 50550 Derek R. Phillips 50551 John E. Pirog 50552 John Nicholas Pistone 50553 Mischa A. Plesha 50554 Todd Plotner 50555 Douglas E. Portrey 50556 William Gibbons Portwood 50557 Joshua J. Potter 50558 Adrian Roberto Pratt 50559 Michael G. Pratt 50560 J. Douglas Preston 50561 Christopher S. Prevo 50562 Robert D. Prins 50563 Matthew G. Pryor 50564 Michael K. Quillinan 50565 Milton S. Quiros 50566 Jennifer M. Lyle 50567 James C. Ragan 50568 Gerardo Ramirez 50569 Richard A. Randazzo 50570 Ashleigh D. Raney Wehmeyer 50571 John P. Rapisarda 50572 David Lee Raugh 50573 Anthony M. Ray 50574 Christopher A. Recker 50575 Matthew James Reed 50576 Simon R. Reese 50577 Stephen C. Reich 50578 Kevin H. Reilly 50579 Marcus R. Reinhart 50580 Kristin Marie Smith 50581 Joshua Ian Reitz 50582 Christopher C. Riccardi 50583 Lucas B. Rice 50584 J. Shelby Richardson 50585 Ronald W. Richardson 50586 Adam Alexander Riddle 50587 Thomas A. Rider 50588 Frank M. Rieser 50589 Thomas Rippert 50590 Jeffrey A. Ritsick 50591 Aldolphus Shirrell Roberts 50592 Gregory L. Roberts 50593 Kristyn Jones 50594 Michael Robertson 50595 Veronica Robertson 50596 Jay Howard Robinson 50597 Irving S. Rogers 50598 Kristian A. Rogers 50599 Jose A. Rojas 50600 Rob Roland 50601 Jason E. Roncoroni 50602 J M. Rose 50603 Marco V. Rosito 50604 John S. Ross 50605 Kenneth E. Rotkoff 50606 Scott A. Rousseau 50607 Stephanie Erickson 50608 Robert S. Rowe 50609 Stephen B. Royall 50610 James D. Ruchti 50611 Dana Rucinski 50612 Melissa L. Rucker 50613 Billy B. Ruhling 50614 Kathleen M. Rumely 50615 Darryl A. Rupp 50616 Edgar Allison Russell 50617 Richard M. Russo 50618 Wilson R. Rutherford 50619 Scott G. Ryan 50620 Jeffrey Alyn Rynbrandt 50621 Lexa Saboe Saboe 50622 Eliza M. Sacco 50623 David A. Sadler 50624 Scott A. Salmon 50625 David Wayne Sandoval 50626 John D. Sarabia 50627 Gina Louise Scarsella 50628 Sean Steven Scharnikow 50629 Joanne E. Schell 50630 Bruce T. Schempp 50631 Michael E. Scheuing 50632 Mary E. Schmelzer 50633 Eric M. Schoenhauer 50634 Kurt A.J. Schumacher 50635 Eric R. Secl 50636 Douglas A. Seaworth 50637 Jeffrey A. Seggi 50638 Jackson J. Seims 50639 Michael E. Senn 50640 Dennis S. Sentell 50641 Jon Dorian Shafer 50642 Bryan R. Shaw 50643 Chris D. Shaw 50644 Desmond Jamal Shaw 50645 Jason K. Shepard 50646 James Mchugh Sheridan 50647 Paul D. Sherman 50648 Bradley P. Sherrill 50649 Raymond Y. Shetzline 50650 Chadwick W. Shields 50651 James M. Shifferd 50652 Timothy J. Shin 50653 James F. Shuman 50654 Brian W. Siefering 50655 Christopher J. Sierakowski 50656 Adam Leigh Silva 50657 Eric C. Silver 50658 Michael J. Simmering 50659 Julie A. Simoni 50660 Samuel K. Simpson 50661 Sean D. Simpson 50662 Kenneth J. Simurdiak 50663 Alan M. Skaggs 50664 Jeremy M. Slagley 50665 David J. Slivka 50666 James R. Slowinski 50667 Michael A. Smit 50668 Andy Smith 50669 Daniel R. Smith 50670 Drew P. Smith 50671 Elizabeth R. Smith 50672 Joel A. Smith 50673 Kevin M. Smith 50674 Leumas J. Smith 50675 Stephen B. Smith 50676 William D. Smith 50677 Richard H. Sneed 50678 Jennifer Snider 50679 Mark S. Snyder 50680 Brian T. Soldon 50681 Benjamin R. Sommerness 50682 Dale S. Song 50683 Darren D. Sorgenfrei 50684 James R. Sosnicky 50685 Todd C. Soucy 50686 David A. Spangler 50687 Kurt H. Sparkman 50688 Philip B. Spencer 50689 Philip P. Speth 50690 George J. Stalter 50691 Timothy M. Steckel 50692 Mitchell P. Steidl 50693 Jon Steinke 50694 Gregory K. Stephens 50695 Mark A. Stephens 50696 Dan T. Stephenson 50697 Bart D. Stewart 50698 George A. Stewart 50699 Marek Rafal Stobbe 50700 Frederick M. Storey 50701 David B. Stouffer 50702 David B. Stringer 50703 Jack T. Strother 50704 Heidi R. Dillard 50705 Richard A. Stuhrke 50706 Walter B. Sturek 50707 Gregory Suchanek 50708 Charles H. Suh 50709 Gerard J. Sullivan 50710 Chad Raymond Sundem 50711 Paul F. Sutter 50712 Scott R. Swartzwelter 50713 Christopher J. Sweeney 50714 Christopher D. Swenson 50715 Robert M. Swisher 50716 Brian C. Symonds 50717 Drew Merrill Syphus 50718 Thane J. Syverson 50719 Stacy D. Takats 50720 Mark E. Talbot 50721 David P. Tamburri 50722 Todd M. Tarantelli 50723 Scott A. Tardanico 50724 Douglas J. Taylor 50725 James W. Taylor 50726 Paul J. Taylor 50727 Patrick A. Terhune 50728 Albert B. Terrell 50729 Anthony John Testa 50730 G. Troy Thames 50731 Allen T. Thiessen 50732 James J. Thome 50733 Theodore M. Thome 50734 Benjamin Thompson 50735 James Earl Thompson 50736 Jeffrey B. Thompson 50737 Matthew G. Thompson 50738 Brent A. Thomsen 50739 John Thong 50740 Jill Troutner 50741 Randall J. Thorn 50742 Donald W. Tidwell 50743 Robert J. Tisch 50744 Jeffrey J. Tlapa 50745 Charlotte Tobin 50746 Patrick R. Tomlinson 50747 Scott C. Tompkins 50748 Michael J. Torreano 50749 Darryl J. Torres 50750 Chandra M. Roberts 50751 Felix J. Trinidad 50752 Stephen F. Troutner 50753 Cary J. Tucker 50754 Renee M. Underwood 50755 Brian Alexander Urkiel 50756 Elias Ursitti 50757 Benjamin S. Valentine 50758 Stephen Joseph Vanaskie 50759 Tong Fu Vang 50760 Thomas F. Veale 50761 James L. Veler 50762 Kirk J. Venable 50763 Zachary L. Venegas 50764 James D. Vickrey 50765 Michael Viera 50766 Corina Villegas 50767 Kevin W. Vina 50768 Saranyu Viriyavejakul 50769 Bruce A. Vitor 50770 Jennifer S. Minus 50771 Russell Vowinkel 50772 Jill Wagner 50773 Eric L. Walker 50774 Robert W. Walker 50775 Anthony B. Wall 50776 Brian F. Waltman 50777 Frank J. Walton 50778 Eric G. Waltz 50779 Shane R. Ward 50780 Jared L. Ware 50781 David A. Warnick 50782 Michael J. Washington 50783 William R. Watson 50784 Jonathan K. Weaver 50785 Paul V. Webb 50786 Stephen A. Webb 50787 David Webber 50788 Timmy Weber 50789 Dean D. Wegner 50790 Marc A. Wehmeyer 50791 Todd M. Weidow 50792 Devin A. Weil 50793 Melissa Werner 50794 Joe D. West 50795 Patricia Larsen 50796 Edward A. Whatley 50797 Harold H. Whiffen 50798 Randy E. White 50799 Thomas E. White 50800 Todd D. Wielinski 50801 Ann Elizabeth Koh 50802 Craig A. Wilhelm 50803 David G. Williams 50804 Josh Williams 50805 Philip Williams 50806 Robert S. Williams 50807 Jason Brian Wills 50808 William J. Wilshire 50809 Brant A. Wilson 50810 Eric Michael Wilson 50811 Robert Winters 50812 Terri A. Wise 50813 Brent V. Witherington 50814 Sarah E. Woehrman 50815 Eric H. Wojtkun 50816 James E. Wolfe 50817 William L. Wong 50818 Berkeley Wood 50819 Christopher L. Woods 50820 Jason L. Wos 50821 Timothy D. Wright 50822 Todd J. Wright 50823 Joseph Leo Wyszynski 50824 Mark Yankopoulos 50825 Mike Yerkic 50826 Katherine A. Yerovi-Ribaudo 50827 Amit Yoran 50828 Adam M. Young 50829 Jason J. Young 50830 Martin S. Young 50831 Matthew T. Zacher 50832 Christine D. Pennella 50833 John A. Zimmerman 50834 Daniel E. Zink 50835 Patrick D. Zoch 50836 Jesse William Zuck 50837 Joseph P. McNally 50838 Jason J. Sidel 50839 Jason E. Cook 50840 Laura L. Kesler 50841 John D. McNeill 50842 Kenneth B. Wojcik 50843 Chad William Bixby 50844 James Crawford Durant 50845 Brian Charles Hale 50846 Eric Charles Kotouc 50847 Jeffrey Peirce McGuckin 50848 John Pedroza 50849 Johann Anthony Perera 50850 Samuel James Saine 50851 Nicole M. Lucas 50852 **1994** Derek Gene Abrams 50853 Craig Alan Achtzehn 50854 Marcus Paul Acosta 50855 Harry Ben Adams 50856 Shawn A. Adams 50857 Steven James Adams 50858 Enrique Aguilar 50859 Soner Akgul 50860 Daniel Adam Alexander 50861 Evagelia Nicholas Alexapoulos Alexopoulos 50862 Coren Jonathan Allen 50863 James Christopher Allen 50864 Jason Emory Allen 50865 Jason S. Allen 50866 Mark C. Allen 50867 Dana Catrice Allmond 50868 Samuel Holland Amber 50869 Matthew J. Andersen 50870 Erik Gunnar Anderson 50871 Delyn A. Schuler 50872 Douglas Wayne Andresen 50873 Paul Bryan Andrzejewski 50874 Kerrie Esther Arata 50875 Lorenzo Isabel Arciniaga 50876 David O. Ardayfio 50877 Loren Gordon Armstrong 50878 Chad G. Arnold 50879 Edward Preston Ash 50880 John T. Auxter 50881 Georgina A. Biehl 50882 William Russell Bailey 50883 Christopher Masten Baker 50884 David G.R. Balch 50885 Eric Barbosa 50886 Bradley Donalthon Barker 50887 Jason Wade Barrie 50888 Jonathan Michael Barrow 50889 Craig Hamilton Barstow 50890 Phillip Allen Bartlett 50891 Mark Robert Battistoni 50892 Jeffrey John Beamon 50893 Christopher Anthony Bean 50894 Beth Anne Behn 50895 Jason Michael Bell 50896 Mark Wyatt Bellomy 50897 Brian Michael Benko 50898 Steve Scott Benko 50899 Michael John Benson 50900 Erik Michael Berdy 50901 Cary Lynne Berta 50902 Jennifer Therese Bhalla 50903 Mark R. Biehl 50904 Jason Michael Bingo 50905 Rex Allen Binns 50906 Christopher Jon Birchard 50907 Michael John Birmingham 50908 Frederick Harold Black 50909 Scott D. Blackwell 50910 Noelle Marie Grosso 50911 John Frances Blankenhorn 50912 Darin Jed Blatt 50913 Wayne Austin Blevins 50914 Bradley W. Bloodworth 50915 Brian Dennis Bobo 50916 Andrea Elizabeth Hartman 50917 Christopher A. Bogue 50918 Leslie Kern Bond 50919 Todd Michael Bookless 50920 Bret Rayburn Bowser 50921 Adam James Boyd 50922 Gregory Louis Boylan 50923 Alison J. Jette 50924 Elisabeth C. Kusano 50925 Robert Charles Braggs 50926 Hannibal Rock Bray 50927 Leslie Christine Bresko 50928 David Michael Bresser 50929 Blake Forsyth Brewer 50930 Nathaniel North Brewster 50931 Eric Thomas Briggle 50932 Brian J. Briggman 50933 Jason Michael Brizek 50934 Geoffrey Craig Brown 50935 Brandi Caprice Bryan 50936 Douglas Paul Bryant 50937 Heather Bryant Mattson 50938 John Karl Buehler 50939 Joel Mark Buenaflor 50940 Jonathan David Bulseco 50941 James L. Bunch 50942 Michael Kent Burba 50943 Gary Matthew Burden 50944 Jeffrey Clement Burg 50945 Stuart Justin Burke 50946 Barrett Adams Burns 50947 Christopher Arthur Burns 50948 James Scott Burrow 50949 Curtis Anthony Bush 50950 Gerald Reyes Cabacungan 50951 Rita Callahan Flaherty 50952 Vanderick James Camacho 50953 Decker Ardean Cammack 50954 Marion Patino Candava 50955 Charles Wilson Canfield 50956 Argot Carberry 50957 Brian S. Carey 50958 Dominique Nicole Braggs 50959 Shannon Christopher Carney 50960 Charles Burton Carpenter 50961 Shawn Everett Carpenter 50962 Daniel Eugene Carr 50963 Chad Gabriel Carroll 50964 Michael Collier Carter 50965 Annah Mara McDowell 50966 Roderick Manuel Castillo 50967 Jeffrey M. Casucci 50968 Randolph John Cestone 50969 Charles B. Chalfont 50970 Elizabeth J. Chao 50971 David Samuel Choe 50972 Min Wook Chong 50973 Steve Chie-Woo Chong 50974 Cynthia Y.W. Childress 50975 Mark David Cieplinski 50976 Jonathan Paul Clancy 50977 Thomas Dale Clark 50978 David Murrill Clolinger 50979 Andrew Charles Clough 50980 Mark Stephen Clough 50981 Ross Max Coffey 50982 John Patrick Cogbill 50983 Faren R. Cole 50984 Kenneth Christopher Cole 50985 Samuel Ross Coleman 50986 Lisa A. Willadsen 50987 Todd E. Combs 50988 John Ambrose Compton 50989 Robert Paul Conlin 50990 James Leondaious Connally 50991 Dawn E. Conniff 50992 Kristina A. Connors 50993 Matthew Thomas Conway 50994 Jason Gene Coon 50995 Renee LaVone Paulus 50996 Arthur Thomas Cornelson 50997 Jeffrey John Corton 50998 Christopher Levzat Cosie 50999 Albert Maurice Costello 51000 Kevin Lee Cotman 51001 Beth Lisa Coughlin 51002 Hunter Justin Crandall 51003 Christopher Edward Crane 51004 Joseph Carlisle-Eric Crawford 51005 Joaquin Maurice Croslin 51006 Nance Kate Csoka 51007 Samuel Johnson Cubberley 51008 Peter John Cuenca 51009 John A. Culley 51010 Erin Marie Cunningham 51011 Paul Edward Cunningham 51012 Tyrone David Curtin 51013 David Barton Cushen 51014 David Robert Cwik 51015 Michael Paul Cyr 51016 Kevin Louis Czarnecki 51017 Lawrence Joseph Daley 51018 Harry Scott Dalton 51019 Monte Allen Davenport 51020 James Alexander Davidson 51021 Chadwick Gerrell Davis 51022 Michael James Davis 51023 Neil Anthony Davis 51024 Wayne Albert Davis 51025 Daniel Archer DeBroux 51026 Anthony Thomas Deguia 51027 Derek Dela Dela-Cruz 51028 Carlos Delagarza 51029 David George Delaney 51030 Vaughn Duane DeLong 51031 John David Delsignore 51032 Thomas Patrick Demitrovic 51033 David J.P. Dennison 51034 Toshikazu Dezaki 51035 James Albert Dickerson 51036 Mary Catherine Dillon 51037 James Edward Dimon 51038 Jeffrey Jay Dirkse 51039 Minhluan Nguyen Doan 51040 William James Dobosh 51041 Spencer David Dodge 51042 Nathan Patrick Donahoe 51043 Alfred Walden Donaldson 51044 Matthew Aaron Dooley 51045 William Davis Douglass 51046 William Spencer Downing 51047 Seamus Kinnear Doyle 51048 John Robert Dube 51049 Roger H. Duda 51050 Ronald Leopold Dufresne 51051 Chad Michael Duhe 51052 Glenn Dale Duhon 51053 David Guy Dumas 51054 Richard Eugene Dunaway 51055 Daniel Jerome Durbin 51056 Jason Marion Du Terroil 51057 Michael Robert Dyer 51058 Marvin Jeffrey Joseph Dyke 51059 Jack Eames 51060 Raymond Larry Eason 51061 Jesse Lee Easter 51062 Christopher Jonathan Eddy 51063 Sebastian Alexander Edwards 51064 Sean D. Egan 51065 Steven Francis Egan 51066 Anthony Richard Elias 51067 Patrick James Ellis 51068 Anthony Joseph Encarnacao 51069 Mark Anthony Escobedo 51070 Todd Anthony Esh 51071 Donald Robert Esser 51072 James Alan Etchechury 51073 Michael Eugene Etley 51074 Ryan Ray Fairman 51075 Kristoffer Brady Fale 51076 Luke David Falk 51077 Bryan Richard Fangman 51078 Timothy Lance Farmer 51079 Sean Edward Farrar 51080 Darren Joseph Feher 51081 Jon Gary Ferko 51082 Daniel Andres Fickel 51083 Jeremy Van Fine 51084 John David Fio Rito 51085 Elliott Guthrie Fishburne 51086 John Charles Flanagan 51087 Jeffrey William Fleece 51088 Anthony Jo Flores 51089 Sean Thomas Flynn 51090 David Clifford Foley 51091 Lukas Peter Forbes 51092 Ethan W. Ford 51093 Brian D. Forrest 51094 Corbett Allan Foster 51095 Todd Michael Fox 51096 Melissa Janet Fozman 51097 Jeffrey John Friesen 51098 Edie J. Fuchs 51099 Brett Thompson Funck 51100 Patton James Gade 51101 Ryan Joseph Gagliano 51102 John Patrick Gallagher 51103 Jeffrey Robert Galloway 51104 Vinaya Anand Garde 51105 David Wayne Gardner 51106 James Robert Garrett 51107 Stephen M. Garrett 51108 Robert D. Gatliff 51109 Patrick Lewis Gaydon 51110 Tyrone Gabriel Gayeski 51111 Dean T. Gels 51112 Jason Everett George 51113 Matthew J. Geraci 51114 Byron Keith German 51115 Jason Timothy Ghetian 51116 Kirk Ellis Gibbs 51117 Clair Austin Gill 51118 Leslie Lee Gillespie 51119 Kennon Shane Gilliam 51120 Carl Nicholas Giordano 51121 Nicholas H. Gist 51122 Joel David Glockler 51123 Jeremy Stephen Gocke 51124 Darlene Marie Godfrey 51125 Kent Matthew Gonser 51126 Eric Michael Gooley 51127 William Chapman Gottmeier 51128 Matthew Edward Grady 51129 Thomas William Graepel 51130 Frank Earl Graham 51131 Philip Edward Graham 51132 Sean Michael Graham 51133 Anthony David Grant 51134 Gary Robert Graves 51135 Phillip John Raymond Graves 51136 Christopher Lynn Gray 51137 Brian Russell Greata 51138 Jennifer Helen Greenberg 51139 Channing M. Greene 51140 Timothy David Grein 51141 Gregory Carlton Griffin 51142 Gregory Glen Griffin 51143 Marvin Lee Griffin 51144 Scott Randolph Griffith 51145 Randall Darrell Grigg 51146 David Bachlotte Grizzle 51147 Christopher James Grose 51148 Adam Philip Gryglas 51149 Richard Brian Gussenhoven 51150 Danny Toku Gusukuma 51151 Mark William Guy 51152 Joseph Edward Guzman 51153 Karin Ann Gventer 51154 Karsten Jeffery Haake 51155 Kyle Herman Hadlock 51156 Samuel John Hagadorn 51157 David Daniell Haight 51158 Decker Bradley Hains 51159 Darrell Early Hale 51160 Derek Edwin Hall 51161 James Anthony Hall 51162 John William Hall 51163 Erik Scott Hallas 51164 David Theodore Hamann 51165 Ralph C. Hamm 51166 Jimmy Warren Hamner 51167 Glen Reed Hampton 51168 Darren Defoe Hanna 51169 Andrew Scott Hanson 51170 Mohamad Imad Haque 51171 Sean G. Hardin 51172 Nathan Sean Harrigan 51173 Robert McNamara Harris 51174 Bradley Chase Harrison 51175 Jeffrey Todd Harry 51176 Devin Wayne Hartfield 51177 Brian Joel Harthorn 51178 Jason William Hartman 51179 Christopher Michael Hasty 51180 Kenneth Christopher Hatcher 51181 Eric Robertson Hatchett 51182 Suzanne Michelle Hauf 51183 Keith Wayne Haufler 51184 Mark R. Hauser 51185 Todd Curtis Hawkins 51186 Tracel Hawkins Runyan 51187 Andrew Clark Hayes 51188 Edward Bryan Hayes 51189 Paul Rosser Hayes 51190 Kerri Kristen Casino 51191 James Edward Healy 51192 Troy Louis Hedgpeth 51193 John Michael Hefner 51194 Richard Lynn Heine 51195 Alice Heldt Quesenberry 51196 Matthew Patrick Helm 51197 Bryan Scott Helsel 51198 Bradley Dean Helton 51199 Jennifer Ann Henderson 51200

Steven James Henderson 51201 Kendall Lyon Henry 51202 Peter Dean Hesford 51203 Charles Gideon Heupel 51204 Kenneth Curtis Heyman 51205 Tony S. Park Hicks 51206 Kevin Sean Hicks 51207 Christopher James Higgins 51208 Michael Harold Hill 51209 Andrew Jon Hittner 51210 Brian Edward Hittner 51211 John D. Hixson 51212 Tanesha Lachele Hartfield 51213 Vanessa Adele Hodge 51214 John Gregory Hodgson 51215 Laura M. Offstein 51216 Howard Henry Hoege 51217 Christopher Jason Holm 51218 Kenneth Eric Holt 51219 Aaron Frederick Hood 51220 Jason Craig Hook 51221 Michael Lowell Hoover 51222 Walter John Horin 51223 John Paul Horning 51224 Brian Joseph Hornung 51225 Charles Oliver Howald 51226 David William Howard 51227 Preston Taylor Howard 51228 Heidi Jo McClung 51229 Joseph Robert Hsu 51230 Ryan Andrew Hudak 51231 Christian Hermann Huettemeyer 51232 Derek Alan Huffer 51233 Richard Seungkwon Huh 51234 Jack C. Hunnicutt 51235 James Uksu Hwang 51236 Eugene Seok Hwangbo 51237 Aaron Paul Ingebritson 51238 Reizal Arif Ismail 51239 Todd Eugene Jackins 51240 Chad Theodore Jagmin 51241 Philip W. Jalufka 51242 Khadija T. Jenkins 51243 Anthony John Jamora 51244 Jamal Kamau Jenkins 51245 Loren B. Jerlow 51246 Kyle F. Jette 51247 Anthony Eugene Johnson 51248 Cheri Lynn Johnson 51249 Harry Marshall Johnson 51250 Jeremiah John Johnson 51251 Michael Henry Johnson 51252 Randy Tyrie Johnson 51253 Thomas Michael Johnson 51254 Tory James Johnson 51255 Clayton Mason Jones 51256 Margaret Jones Thomas 51257 Steven Kyle Jones 51258 Thomas B. Jones 51259 Todd Bradley Jones 51260 Russell L. Jordan 51261 Samuel Eugene Joyner 51262 Chad Vernon Jubela 51263 Anthony A Kajencki 51264 Jason Robert Kalainoff 51265 Theresa A. Benchoff 51266 Samuel W. Kan 51267 John F. Kane 51268 Kurt Andrew Kane 51269 King York Kao 51270 Michael J. Kays 51271 Gregory Blake Kehler 51272 Andrew Donald Kelly 51273 Jason Erik Kelly 51274 Michael T. Kelly 51275 Kurt Peter Kempkes 51276 Timothy P. Keneally 51277 Joshua Stuart Kennedy 51278 Michael Lee Kennedy 51279 Kaylan Eugene Kennel 51280 Keven Jay Kercher 51281 Dennis W. Kerwood 51282 Neil Kumman Khatod 51283 Suthep Khiewpakdee 51284 Muawiya Tahsin Khreis 51285 Siobhain Ita Cushen 51286 Robert Louis Kilroy 51287 Ha Jung Kim 51288 Janel Kim 51289 Jenny Ann Kim 51290 Michael Minho Kim 51291 Sophia Kim 51292 Patricia Lynn Kinerson 51293 Charles B. King 51294 Nickolas T. Kioutas 51295 Robert Christopher Kissane 51296 Bryan Peter Klatt 51297 Brian Francis Knapp 51298 Laura Louise Knapp 51299 Lara Susan Knight 51300 Peter Gerald Knight 51301 Kent Allen Korunka 51302 Andrew Stephen Kos 51303 Robert Anthony Kovach 51304 Brian G. Koyn 51305 Alan Hubert Kral 51306 Brendan Gerard Krasinski 51307 Michael Gabriel Krause 51308 Christopher Michael Krebs 51309 Chance Kriesel 51310 Ronald W. Krisak 51311 Jay W. Krueger 51312 Joseph Richard Krupa 51313 Daniel J. Kudrna 51314 Kevin R. Kugel 51315 Geoffrey Dale Kuhlmann 51316 Clifford Edward Kump 51317 Manu Joseph Kusano 51318 Mark Gregory Kustelski 51319 Marc Dietrich Kutter 51320 William Carl Kuttler 51321 Roger Dean Kuykendall 51322 Dirk Michael Kvale 51323 Spencer Talbot Kympton 51324 Duc Dinh Lai 51325 Michael Edward Lamke 51326 Kevin Matthew Lamphere 51327 Michael Harrington Landers 51328 Theodore J. Landgraf 51329 John Dennis Lane 51330 Stephen John Lapekas 51331 Duncan John Larkin 51332 Tod Jerrett Larson 51333 Kar P. Lau 51334 Duane Schindler Lauchengco 51335 Zachary Creighton Lauer 51336 Sarah Lynn Zinser 51337 Laura Alberta Law 51338 Mark Abel LeBlanc 51339 George Whan Lee 51340 Tyson Jerrod Lee 51341 Young Chan Lee 51342 Tacildayus Legrand Andrews 51343 Jeffrey S. Leischner 51344 Patrick C. Lemoine 51345 Philip Jacob Lenz 51346 Karen K. Leonard 51347 Kent Michael Lersch 51348 Jason Lee Lewallen 51349 Eric James Lewis 51350 Green Pryor Lewis 51351 James Monroe Lewis 51352 Paul Libretta 51353 Aaron Benjamin Lilley 51354 Paul Anthony Lipps 51355 Erik M. Littlejohn 51356 Ernest Litynski 51357 Rafael Romualdo Lizardi 51358 David Joseph Long 51359 Jason Douglas Long 51360 Loren McKinley Long 51361 Michael Alvin Long 51362 Thomas Claude Longfellow 51363 Thomas Callan Lopresti 51364 Arol Joseph Lora 51365 Aaron J. Loudon 51366 Nicholas Leonard Louis 51367 David Christopher Love 51368 Zachary Truman Lowe 51369 Langdon John Lucas 51370 David S. Lyle 51371 John Bradley MacDougall 51372 Donald Maciag 51373 Cy Michael Macko 51374 Jennifer Lynn Cantello 51375 Cecil Rolf Dietter MacPherson 51376 Gabrielle Marie Maddaloni 51377 Brian David Maddox 51378 Michael Bernard Madkins 51379 Peter Grant Madrinan 51380 Michael Francis Magajne 51381 Robert Edward Lee Magee 51382 Eric Daniel Magnell 51383 Carol Marie Pilarski 51384 William Jewel Major 51385 Jeffrey F. Maliska 51386 Michael William Mangino 51387 Scott Robert Marcoux 51388 Scott Stanley Marhold 51389 John Michael Markatos 51390 Amy Lynn Markutsa 51391 Adrian Andrew Marsh 51392 Heather M. Throne 51393 Todd Herron Marshburn 51394 Douglas William Martin 51395 Hollie Jean Martin 51396 Jay Clinton Martin 51397 Maria Young 51398 Phillip Grant Martin 51399 Michael James Masters 51400 Melinda Sue Masterson 51401 Gregory S. Mathews 51402 Michael J. Matison 51403 John Christian Matthews 51404 Jeffrey A. Mattson 51405 Odessa Yumi Maxwell 51406 Sean Patrick McAllister 51407 Kevin Alan McAninch 51408 Patrick William McCabe 51409 Robert M. McCarthy 51410 Robert Edward McClintock 51411 Shon Arthur McCormick 51412 Christopher David McCune 51413 Craig Campbell McFarland 51414 Dexter Lane McFarlin 51415 Joseph J. McGraw 51416 David George McGurk 51417 Stephen Richard McHale 51418 Stephen H. McIntyre 51419 Sean Kameeiamoku McKeague 51420 Thailand Addrell McMillan 51421 Jennifer Jo Loutzenheiser 51422 Matthew John Andrew McNiel 51423 James Wilson McPherson 51424 Michael Timothy McTigue 51425 Rodney Shane McWhorter 51426 William Michael Medof 51427 Amy M. Meeks 51428 Stephen Todd Mefford 51429 Anthony Marks Mello 51430 Jim Melton 51431 William Henry Mengel 51432 Thomas Richard Mervine 51433 Thomas Brian Messervey 51434 Christopher Lee Metzger 51435 Russell Allen Metzler 51436 Paul Martin Meyer 51437 Eric Alexander Meyerson 51438 Jon Adam Michael 51439 Martin Michael Michna 51440 Kurt Alan Miesner 51441 Allison Elizabeth Miller 51442 Heather Anne Bouton 51443 Ian Matthew Miller 51444 Jason Lee Miller 51445 Jeffery Donald Miller 51446 Joel Matthew Miller 51447 Ryan Stephen Miller 51448 Kyung IL Min 51449 Christian John Miner 51450 Aaron Wade Mitchell 51451 Chad Thomas Mitchell 51452 Samuel Thomas Mitchell 51453 Paul Francis Mlakar 51454 Michael R. Molino 51455 Rachel Molnar Shetzline 51456 Tara L. Mondt Lenz 51457 Joshua Lee Moon 51458 Crystal L. Jennings 51459 David Arthur Samuel Moore 51460 Louis Wesley Morales 51461 Gary Joseph Morea 51462 Thomas Joseph Morelli 51463 Todd R. Morgenfeld 51464 Michael Randal Morrell 51465 Robert Bruce Morris 51466 Joseph Michael Morrison 51467 Brent David Morrow 51468 Jason Macrae Morwick 51469 Douglas James Moschkau 51470 Roy A. Moss 51471 Nathaniel E. Mostajo 51472 Scott William Mueller 51473 David Edwin Mugg 51474 Kevin Patrick Muir 51475 Christopher W. Muller 51476 Michael Joseph Muller 51477 Melanie Munk 51478 Jeffrey Burton Murphy 51479 Richard Michael Murphy 51480 Torrey Matthew Murphy 51481 Kendall Dale Musgrove 51482 Ernest Dewitt Napier 51483 Travis Jordan Narum 51484 Stephanie Marie Rice 51485 Christopher Brian Nead 51486 Emily C. Schiffer 51487 Mark Eugene Neubauer 51488 Chadd Timothy Newman 51489 Louie Hoang Ngoc Nguyen 51490 Nhiem Thanh Nguyen 51491 Scott M. Nieman 51492 Toomas Arthur Niemann 51493 John Andrew Noesser 51494 Mark Edward Nogalski 51495 Brodrick Leonard Norman 51496 Geoffrey A. Norman 51497 Joseph Allen Notch 51498 Seth David O'Brien 51499 Thomas Walter O'Connor 51500 Evan Hayden Offstein 51501 Colleen T. Rogers 51502 Walter Robert Ohl 51503 Curtis William Ohland 51504 John Nevel Oldham 51505 Shawn Nathan Olds 51506 Mark Patrick Olin 51507 Michael Romine Olive 51508 John Alfred Oliver 51509 Jay Randal Olsen 51510 Dennis Patrick O'Neil 51511 Humberto A. Orantes 51512 Frank Orellana 51513 John Anthony Orlando 51514 Stephen John Orloski 51515 Kevin Edward O'Rourke 51516 Carlos E Ortiz 51517 David Duane Orton 51518 Brian Keith Orwig 51519 Gary Allan Ostby 51520 Larry Joseph Ostendorf 51521 Colin John O'Sullivan 51522 Christopher Lee Ott 51523 Jeffrey David Owen 51524 Ray Owen 51525 Bartt Derek Owens 51526 Brett Douglas Owens 51527 Jincy Rebecca Pace 51528 Jason Corey Padilla 51529 Jin Hyong Pak 51530 Raul Guadalupe Palacios 51531 Jeffrey David Palmer 51532 Douglas John Paluti 51533 Bill Aristidis Papanastasiou 51534 Donna Lynn Parent 51535 Grace Park 51536 John H. Park 51537 Steve Junsik Park 51538 Graeme R. Parnell 51539 Robbie Joe Passinault 51540 Keith K. Patterson 51541 Curtis Wayne Patteson 51542 Edward Lee Pearce 51543 John A. Pearson 51544 Richard Gene Pearson 51545 Robert Ernest Pearson 51546 Samuel Claude Pearson 51547 Joseph Gregory Penkala 51548 Adrian Emil Perica 51549 Edward J. Perkins 51550 Keye E. Perry 51551 Justin Carl Perusek 51552 Michael Anthony Peters 51553 Jonathan Joseph Petrucelli 51554 Kevin Ray Pettet 51555 John Rife Petty 51556 Christopher Joseph Pflanz 51557 Charles Ray Phariss 51558 Layne Phillips 51559 Kevin B. Phipps 51560 Joseph Irwin Pierce 51561 David Edward Pilarski 51562 Hugh Scott Pittman 51563 Theresa Fay Placette 51564 Michael Anthony Plaia 51565 Gretchen B. Platt 51566 James M. Plumlee 51567 Jose Luis Polanco 51568 Scott Michael Polk 51569 James Erickson Pool 51570 Robert Earle Poole 51571 Matthew Adam Posner 51572 William Tecumseh Potter 51573 Elita S. Perusek 51574 Marcus Tanz Powell 51575 Steven Matthew Powell 51576 Troy Nicholas Prehar 51577 Edward A. Presley 51578 Brian Douglas Prettyman 51579 Sean Michael Pritchard 51580 James Richard Pugh 51581 Eric Pulwicz 51582 Mark T. Purdy 51583 Justin Thomas Putnam 51584 Stephanie Q. Howard 51585 Ross Wayne Raburn 51586 Bill Rafael Rainusso 51587 Roberto Ramirez 51588 Thomas Jason Ratcliff 51589 Leon Hiawatha Cress Rawlings 51590 Matthew John Redmond 51591 Heather Louise Reed 51592 Kristin Austra Reed 51593 Ryland Michael Reed 51594 Tristan Chellew Reeve 51595 Christopher Norbert Reichart 51596 Aaron William Reisinger 51597 Kyle Norman Remick 51598 Laurent Louis Renard 51599 Matthew Edward Resnick 51600 Eric Scott Rhind 51601 Kevin Paul Rhoads 51602 Brett Laurence Rice 51603 Christopher F. Riemer 51604 Wendy D. Martin 51605 John David Ring 51606 George Scott Ringler 51607 Jason Raymond Rios 51608 Robert M. Ripperger 51609 John Lawrence Ritter 51610 Timothy James Roach 51611 Kendric H. Robbins 51612 Ryan Neil Roberson 51613 Daniel Frederick Robinson 51614 Kirsten E. Kennedy 51615 Darryl William Rodgers 51616 Jace L. Rodgers 51617 Adrian Lenin Rodriguez 51618 Bryant V. S. Rogers 51619 Michael Laurence Rolli 51620 Francisco Romero-Acosta 51621 William Ellis Rooker 51622 Eric John Rosenfelder 51623 Ashley Hope Rosenthal 51624 Donald Roy 51625 Paul Underwood Royle 51626 Daniel L. Rucker 51627 Daniel Michael Ruiz 51628 Chad Alan Rupe 51629 William Aloysius Ryan 51630 Troy F. Ryder 51631 Jeffrey Scott Salerno 51632 Paul John Salmon 51633 James Robert Salome 51634 Aaron David Sane 51635 Mark Ryan Sanford 51636 Curt Gary Sansoucie 51637 Robert Charles Santamaria 51638 Eric Egydio Sassi 51639 Michael E. Saxon 51640 Tracy John Saxon 51641 Jason Christian Schaaf 51642 Dominic John Schaffer 51643 Matthew Charles Schell 51644 Lisa A. Cline 51645 Thomas Edward Schiffer 51646 Bryan Scott Schiller 51647 Joseph Thomas Schmidt 51648 Phillip Raymond Schmitz 51649 Christopher D. Schneider 51650 Ryan David Schneider 51651 George Watts Schrader 51652 Jason Edward Schroeder 51653 Jeremy Jing-Wun Schroeder 51654 Scott Jay Schroeder 51655 James Christopher Schug 51656 Sheri Lyn Schweiker 51657 Michael John Scimeca 51658 Brett Anthony Sciotto 51659 Dominic M. Scola 51660 Beverly Sue Casiano 51661 Erik Bert Scott 51662 Alexander Jorg Seifert 51663 Gerald D. Sentell 51664 Lawrence Mark Seward 51665 John Randall James Shagena 51666 Stuart Frederick Shapiro 51667 Stephen Ralph Sharpe 51668 Robert Daniels Shear 51669 Michael Edward Sheehy 51670 Michelle L. Sherwood 51671 Brian Christopher Shields 51672 John Kesler Shields 51673 Jay Joseph Shininger 51674 Roy Jonathan Shipley 51675 Mark John Shogren 51676 Stephen Timothy Shore 51677 Trenton Little Shuping 51678 Jeffrey Alan Shusta 51679 Zachary Andrew Sikes 51680 David Michael Simmons 51681 Major Jell Simmons 51682 David Ronald Siry 51683 Geoffrey Shane Skipworth 51684 Maria M. Slaughter 51685 Christopher Curtis Sleight 51686 Deborah Sue Karagosian 51687 Julie S. Gallagher 51688 James Edward Slomka 51689 Bradley Clayton Smith 51690 Brett George Smith 51691 Brian Lawrence Smith 51692 Camille D. Griffin 51693 Chad Mitchell Smith 51694 Eric Brian Smith 51695 Henry Louis Smith 51696 Linwood E. Smith 51697 Matthew Paul Smith 51698 Michael William Smith 51699 Milton S. Smith 51700 Nathaniel Starbuck Smith 51701 Teresa Anne Condron 51702 Travis Allen Smith 51703 William Charles Snider 51704 Mike Solis 51705 Tom Min Son 51706 Grover R. Southerland 51707 Marissa Victoria Souza 51708 Stephen Scott Sowell 51709 Christopher Andrew Spence 51710 Donald Masao Spire 51711 Eric James St. Amand 51712 Jason Charles Stacy 51713 Matthew Nicholas Stader 51714 Richard Elliott Stanfield 51715 Jennifer L. Stanley 51716 Dwayne Thomas Stanton 51717 Elisabeth Adele Stark 51718 Scott Russell Steele 51719 Adam Corey Steelhammer 51720 Peter Eric Stelling 51721 James Matthew Stepien 51722 Jason P. Stewart 51723 Shane Patton Stogner 51724 Scott Taylor Stratton 51725 Adam Christopher Straub 51726 Matthew Alexander Strickler 51727 Mark David Strong 51728 William A. Strout 51729 Slade Alan Suchecki 51730 John Francis Sullivan 51731 Michael Donald Sullivan 51732 Shane Michael Sullivan 51733 Christie Marie Summers 51734 Jennifer Marie Summers 51735 Brad David Sutek 51736 Jason W. Sutton 51737 Adam Carl Swiecki 51738 Richard Joseph Swift 51739 Brett Gareth Sylvia 51740 James William Sytsma 51741 John Christopher Szczepanski 51742 Gregory Leonard Szczesny 51743 Lance Adam Tacquard 51744 Keith Allen Tahtinen 51745 Ting Jennifer Tai 51746 Curtis Don Tait 51747 Stephen Paul Talbott 51748 Wel-Shi Tan 51749 Michael Stephen Tarquinto 51750 Curtis David Taylor 51751 Daniel Eric Taylor 51752 Modupe Taylor-Pearce 51753 Daniel L. Teeter 51754 Rigdon T. Terrell 51755 Anthony James Testa 51756 Allan R. Thomas 51757 David Alan Thomas 51758 Devon Trent Thomas 51759 Mark David Thomas 51760 Christopher A. Thompson 51761 John Brian Thompson 51762 Kurt Travis Thompson 51763 Michael Gary Thornberry 51764 Brian J. Thorne 51765 Eric Jon Thorne 51766 Robert John Thornfelt 51767 Steven Michael Thornton 51768 Kermit Grady Threatte 51769 George Miguel Tiaffay 51770 Scott Allen Tikalsky 51771 Matthew J. Timbario 51772 Juan Bernardino Tirona 51773 Eric S. Tollefson 51774 Stephen Richard Trimborn 51775 Steven Wayne Trisler 51776 Grant Alan Troxell 51777 Carlos Antonio Trujillo 51778 Vu Truong 51779 Creighton Collins Tubb 51780 Geoffrey R. Tumlin 51781 David L. Tummonds 51782 Brian Mark Tung 51783 Lori L. Turbak 51784 Christopher Edward Turco 51785 Scott Garo Turkington 51786 Bess Kathleen Turner 51787 Frank Lee Turner 51788 Joel Todd Turner 51789 Sean James Turner 51790 William J. Turturro 51791 Douglas Christopher Uken 51792 Christopher M. Upton 51793 Lydia Yvette Uribarri 51794 Ricardo Berton Valdez 51795 Jeremy B. Vance 51796 Todd Bryce Vandawater 51797 Jonathan Jackson Vannatta 51798 Michael Ray Vastag 51799 John Chancellor Veasey 51800 Daniel Luis Velazquez 51801 John Allen Vest 51802 Brian Douglas Vile 51803 Thomas P. Vogel 51804 Timothy James Volkmann 51805 Peter James von Alt 51806 Jason Rudy Vranes 51807 Aaron Alan Wagner 51808 Wendi Michelle Waits 51809 Gary Alan Walenda 51810 Ross Shively Walker 51811 John Michael Wallace 51812 Kimberly Anne Walter 51813 Danyelle Juel Wambach Robinson 51814 Dustin Jon Wambeke 51815 Jason Christopher Ward 51816 Richard Ian Ward 51817 Wendy Cole Ward 51818 Kevin James Warner 51819 Kaye Dunham 51820 Monica Patrice Washington 51821 Jamey Douglas Webb 51822 John Lewis Wedges 51823 James Stuart Wells 51824 Christopher William Wendland 51825 Michael William Werner 51826 Jason A. Wesbrock 51827 Martin J. Whalen 51828 Michael James Whalen 51829 Alexander Peter Whitaker 51830 Christopher Michael White 51831 Matthew Bradford White 51832 Lisa Devonne Whittaker 51833 Michael Stewart Whitten 51834 John Patrick Whyte 51835 James Gilbert Wideman 51836 John Spencer Wieman 51837 Lawrence Albert Wilkinson 51838 Dorsey Franklin Williams 51839 Julie Justine Williams 51840 Shon Patrick Williams 51841 Steven James Williams 51842 Tara Ann Ann Patricia Green 51843 Theodore Duffy Williams 51844 Tracey J. Koyn 51845 Samuel James Willmon 51846 Ramey Luther Wilson 51847 Byron Clifford Wimmer 51848 David G. Winget 51849 David Wise 51850 Thomas Lloyd Witt 51851 David Eugene Wojczynski 51852 Jonathan Edward Wolfe 51853 Jason Aric Wolter 51854 Ernest Yat-Kwan Wong 51855 John Douglas Wood 51856 Marc D. Wood 51857 John Draper Woodall 51858 Alan Clark Woodmansey 51859 Catherine Ann Kohn 51860 Timothy Glen Workman 51861 Anthony Matthew Wright 51862 Jason Michael Wright 51863 Michael F. Yankovich 51864 Todd Carter Yant 51865 Jason Anthony Yee 51866 Robert W. York 51867 Terrence Youmans 51868 Daniel Shaw Young 51869 James W. Young 51870 Robert Eugene Young 51871 Victor Young Yu 51872 Richard Henry Zampelli 51873 Michael J. Zatlukal 51874 John Joseph Zavage 51875 Patrick Smith Zelley 51876 Lars Niclas Zetterstrom 51877 Gregory Thomas Ziegler 51878 Yima Zikria 51879 Travis C. Zimmer 51880 Jeffrey Wade Zimmerman 51881 Christopher Michael Ziniti 51882 Anthony D. Zuress 51883 Megan Anne Uken 51884 Dirk Patrick Barber 51885 Isaac Alexander Barnes 51886 Reginald Maurice Dobson 51887 Jennifer Rebecca Perkins 51888 Jennifer Sue Hodges 51889 Ronald Patrick Morrison 51890 E. Jonathan Mundorf 51891 Gregory D. Perry 51892 Mickey Jang-Won Suh 51893 Robert Mark Summers 51894 Marvin Glen Haynes 51895 Robert Alan Krieg 51896 Jason Christopher Patrick 51897 Jawara Riley 51898 **1995** Thomas Harold Aarsen 51899 James Francis Adamouski 51900 Brett Nathan Adams 51901 Geoffrey Randall Adams 51902 Nurudeen Balogun Adeyemi 51903 Ronald Richard Adimey 51904 Mark Christopher Adinolfi 51905 Eric Louis Adler 51906 Robert Joseph Ahern 51907 Dorothea L. C. Abraham 51908 Syed Omar Ali 51909 Shaffir Alikhan 51910 Kimberly Danielle Allen 51911 Bridget Drury Altenburg 51912 Patrick Sedler Altenburg 51913 James Rolf Anderson 51914 Jason Lynn Anderson 51915 Robyn J. Anderson 51916 Wayne Michael Anderson 51917 Richard Karl Anselmi 51918 Adam David Appleby 51919 Kristen Leigh Argus 51920 Michael Sean Armstrong 51921 Paul Mathew Armstrong 51922 Stephanie Rochelle Ahern 51923 Patrick Charles Aspland 51924 Christopher Stephen Auclair 51925 Christopher Michael Austin 51926 Rodrick Lavelle Austin 51927 Jean-Pierre Bado 51928 Chad Allen Bagley 51929 David Brannon Bailey 51930 Marshanna Marie Bain 51931 Jeffrey Edwin Baker 51932 John Tofft Baker 51933 Koo Baker 51934 Scott Reginald Baker 51935 Troy Robinson Baker 51936 Brian Christopher Baldrate 51937 Chad B. Balfanz 51938 Amber B. Dossey 51939 Aryn Alyssa Ballard 51940 Adam Vincent Balukonis 51941 Joe Dave Banner 51942 Kevin Scott Bardonner 51943 Thomas H. Barnard 51944 Brandon Eric Barr 51945 Sunny Diane Barse 51946 Aaron Charles Barta 51947 James Boone Bartholomees 51948 Heather June Grodin 51949 Michael A Baseluos 51950 Chad Thomas Bates 51951 John William Bauer 51952 Richardo Abnel Bautista 51953 David Mandel Beaird 51954 Slade Henry Beaudoin 51955 Kimberly Ann Beck 51956 Damon Andrew Becknel 51957 Shawn Daryl Beebe 51958 Jeff Ronald Beierlein 51959 David Graham Bell 51960 Michelle M. Olmstead 51961 Jack W. Benecke 51962 Andrew Marcus Benjamin 51963 Paul Temple Berghaus 51964 Robbie William Berglund 51965 Michael L. Bernstein 51966 Christopher Edward Berry 51967 Peter John Bertanzetti 51968 Joseph Douglas Bertrand

51969 Thomas Beverley 51970 Chad Mitchell Bilbrey 51971 Michael Eugene Bindas 51972 Philip Erwin Bindon 51973 Matthew Shannon Bird 51974 Daniel J. Birnbaum 51975 Todd Allen Blackwell 51976 John Hawkins Blaha 51977 Tyrone Marcellus Bland 51978 Brian John Bledsoe 51979 Mark Alan Bliss 51980 Thomas George Blount 51981 Paul C. Boatman 51982 Brian C Bolio 51983 Patricia Dee Borcher 51984 Michael C. Borchers 51985 Theodore Sinclair Bosley 51986 Christopher Edward Bove 51987 Tanya M. Bovetsky 51988 Melanie Dawn Bowers 51989 Matthew Robert Bowler 51990 Bradley Loren Bowman 51991 Brandon Neil Box 51992 David N. Box 51993 Edward Affsa Brady 51994 Peter Arthur Brandt 51995 Terry Daniel Brannan 51996 Jonathan Paul Breazeale 51997 Erich David Brelje 51998 John Edward Brennan 51999 Shannon Lee Warder 52000 Jennifer Ann Brewer 52001 Reid Sinclair Brewer 52002 Jason A. Brizic 52003 Herbert J. Brock 52004 Jarett Daniel Broemmel 52005 Ann M. Stinnett 52006 Brent E. Brown 52007 Dante Orlando Brown 52008 Kelly Coppin Brown 52009 Bradley N. Bruce 52010 James Eric Bryan 52011 Charles Edwin Bryant 52012 Stanley Michael Buchesky 52013 Shelby Lee Buchly 52014 Mehmet Ilker Budak 52015 John Fenwick Buergler 52016 Joel Nicholas Buffardi 52017 Todd E. Buhr 52018 An Hong Bui 52019 Robert Scott Buiniskis 52020 Dale Wendall Burbank 52021 Joel Christian Burbank 52022 Kenneth John Burkeen 52023 Erin Burns Lunday 52024 Scott Andrew Burns 52025 Frank Byrne 52026 Jonathan Curt Byrom 52027 Brian Richard Cahak 52028 Matthew A. Calarco 52029 Christy Jo Dirks 52030 Dianna Kaye Caldwell 52031 Jason Christopher Caldwell 52032 Anthony Mario Callandrillo 52033 James Joseph Cameron 52034 Martin David Camp 52035 Chad Eugene Campfield 52036 Christian Thomas Cannon 52037 James Samuel Capps 52038 Kevin S. Capra 52039 Thomas Joseph Carey 52040 Peter Philip Carnegie 52041 Thomas Michael Carnevale 52042 John Mimoso Carreiro 52043 Andrew Thomas Carter 52044 Stephen Patrick Case 52045 Kent Douglas Cavallini 52046 Michael E. Cerniauskas 52047 Chad Christopher Chalfont 52048 Kevin Scott Chaney 52049 Hannah A. Birnbaum 52050 Shaun Patrick Chelf 52051 Christa Marie Chewar 52052 Mickey Seong Koo Cho 52053 Steven Nicholas Cho 52054 Richard Jong-Youl Chong 52055 Clayton S. Christman 52056 John Soojin Chu 52057 James Hoon Chun 52058 Kevin Kee-yup Chung 52059 Blake Forrester Church 52060 Luis Arturo Cifuentes 52061 John Dee Clark 52062 Megan Brooke Peguero 52063 Robert Walter Clark 52064 Jennifer Ruth Clegg 52065 Spencer James Clouatre 52066 Noah Christian Cloud 52067 Marco Michael Coen 52068 Kyler Scott Cole 52069 Steven R. Cole 52070 Bryan Arthur Coleman 52071 Shannon Lee Horne 52072 Clyde Edward Collins 52073 Michael Joseph Colon 52074 John David Colwell 52075 Peter Grover Conboy 52076 William Merrill Conde 52077 Trisha Leigh Wright 52078 Jose Alejandro Cora 52079 Andrew S. Cornelius 52080 Jason Douglas Cornett 52081 Ernesto Allen Cortez 52082 Stuart Randall Coston 52083 Jose Alfonso Cotto Rivas 52084 Philip Alcuin Cowley 52085 Brian Arthur Cox 52086 Nathan Adam Cox 52087 Richard Ryan Coyle 52088 James Gordon Craig 52089 Douglas B. Crandall 52090 Neavolia Nguyen Speirs 52091 Franklin Eugene Crawford 52092 Jeremy William Crawford 52093 Troy Dale Creason 52094 Michael Crenshaw 52095 Jesse Andrew Crispino 52096 Garry Franklin Crossland 52097 Richard Anthony Crosson 52098 James Cornelius Crowley 52099 Cord Wayne Cunningham 52100 Jason Alexander Curl 52101 Philip Joseph Dacunto 52102 Larry Sherrod Daffin 52103 Frances Stephanie Danaher 52104 Anthony James Daniel 52105 Todd J. David 52106 Neil Brian Davids 52107 Warren Earl Davidson 52108 Scott Frederick Davis 52109 Vendeck M. Davis 52110 William Earl Davis 52111 Paul Woolsey Davison 52112 Dale G. Degen 52113 Clayton Hale Degiacinto 52114 Joseph Stefano Degliuomini 52115 Gilbert Franklin Deimel 52116 James Julio De La Pena 52117 Travis Clay Delk 52118 Keith Roy DeLoach 52119 Anthony Michael Deluca 52120 Brady Alan Demarest 52121 Sean Edward Demeule 52122 Ronald T. Demott 52123 Richard Andrew Dennis 52124 Matthew Scott Denny 52125 Gerald Allen Derrick 52126 Douglas Michael Descamps 52127 Michael Gregory Dhunjishah 52128 Bret Michael Diaz 52129 Michael Wayne Dickson 52130 Jonathan Lee Dietrich 52131 Mark Christopher Dille 52132 Abrahm Charles Dimarco 52133 Brian J Dimeo 52134 Marc Jason Distefano 52135 Christopher L. Dodd 52136 Scot Alan Doepker 52137 James Joseph Doheny 52138 Carol Mary Doleski 52139 Calondra Lavet Fortson 52140 Jennifer Marie Dormire 52141 Matthew Daniel Dossey 52142 James Levon Doty 52143 Edward Joseph Doyle 52144 Jonathan Howard Doyle 52145 Kelly Sean Doyle 52146 Edward W. Dresch 52147 Christopher Charles Drexel 52148 Charles Edward Driscoll 52149 Eric Jason Duckworth 52150 James Paul Duncan 52151 Joseph A Dunlop 52152 John Rand Dyke 52153 Eric Christopher Eaves 52154 Cristina M. Moore 52155 Matthew Ryan Edmond 52156 Brent Thomas Edwards 52157 Dominick L. Edwards 52158 Larry D. Edwards 52159 Sarah Veronica Eichinger 52160 Troy James Eigner 52161 Janet M. Elbert 52162 Daniel Gregory Elliott 52163 Kyle Thomas Elliott 52164 Brad Walton Endres 52165 Ethan Michael Herman Epstein 52166 Hans Gary Erickson 52167 Ross Tyler Erickson 52168 Matthew David Erlacher 52169 Michael Todd Etter 52170 Christopher J. Ewolski 52171 Eric A. Farkas 52172 Mark Wesley Faulkner 52173 Mark Vincent Favetti 52174 Scott William Felde 52175 Craig William Fellman 52176 Thomas Bryan Fenoseff 52177 Troy C. Ferguson 52178 Ronald Albert Ferlazzo 52179 Robert Allen Ferris 52180 Jonathan David Field 52181 Jason Edward Figueiredo 52182 Taras T. Filenko 52183 Kevin Eugene Finch 52184 Sean Patrick Finnegan 52185 Douglas Alan Fischer 52186 Jordan Jason Fisher 52187 Robert John Fisher 52188 Kerry Shamuson Fletcher 52189 Kathelina C. Flury 52190 Sean Christopher Flynn 52191 Timothy Hoyt Flynn 52192 Brian T. Fogarty 52193 Brian James Foldenauer 52194 Michael Dennis Forbis 52195 Joseph Paul Fragnito 52196 David Alan Francomb 52197 Johnathan B Frasier 52198 Steven Jon Frederiksen 52199 James Davis Freeman 52200 Joshua Michael Freeman 52201 Zebedee Freeman 52202 Luis Angel Fregoso 52203 Andrea J. French Viera 52204 Michael Patrick Friters 52205 Joseph Alexander Funderburke 52206 John Anthony Gabbert 52207 Armand Leon Gadoury 52208 Catherine Noelle Gaffigan 52209 Dennis Charles Gansen 52210 Robert Jude Garbarino 52211 Nicole K. Thomsen 52212 Carrie Lou Blair 52213 Greg Patrick Garrison 52214 Patrick Nicholas Gasparro 52215 Matthew Adam Gehrmann 52216 Randell Edwin Gelzer 52217 Corey Scott Gerving 52218 Anthony William Giannetti 52219 Peter Nicholas Giavara 52220 Thomas Pepe Giglio 52221 Timothy Stephen Gillette 52222 Scott David Gilman 52223 John Clark Giordano 52224 Justin Jonathan Gittler 52225 William Clayton Glidewell 52226 Karine Ann Sutler 52227 Brandon Scott Glover 52228 David Michael Gloystein 52229 Gary Maurice Godbee 52230 Steven Florian Gratzer 52231 Thomas Matthew Greco 52232 Christopher Lee Green 52233 Michael Harold Greenberg 52234 Brett Samuel Greene 52235 Timothy Paul Greene 52236 Jon Michael Greeson 52237 Eugene John Gregory 52238 Jeffrey Scott Gribschaw 52239 Brandon Robert Grogan 52240 Gregory A. Gualtieri 52241 Rey Dominique Lucero Gumboc 52242 Paul Burton Gunnison 52243 Eric Alan Guttormsen 52244 Matthew Howard Haas 52245 Leon Raymond Hachat 52246 Justen Drue Hackenberg 52247 Kyle Oku Hair 52248 David Lloyd Hall 52249 John Francis Hall 52250 John Noble Hall 52251 Robert-Teofilo Alcausin Hall 52252 Charles Kirby Hammond 52253 Thomas Morgan Hammond 52254 Jason Michael Hance 52255 Jeffrey T. Hanson 52256 Ryan Warren Hanson 52257 Eric Brian Hardy 52258 Kevin Patrick Hare 52259 Patrick Koll Harkins 52260 Grover Claude Harms 52261 Mikell Calloway Harper 52262 Todd Douglas Harrington 52263 Peter Garrison Hart 52264 Ezekiel Harvey 52265 Frowene Selestine Harvey 52266 Robert John Haskin 52267 Derek T. Hasty 52268 Ronald Conrad Hasz 52269 Joshua Anthony Hatfield 52270 Tiffany Suzanne Orcesi 52271 Jeffrey William Haverty 52272 Brandon Heath Havron 52273 John Michael Hawkins 52274 Joseph Scott Haynes 52275 Nathan John Hays 52276 Daniel Thomas Head 52277 Mark Steven Hebert 52278 Robert Ray Heckathorne 52279 John Knute Hedstrom 52280 Brian Scott Hefner 52281 Kurt Frederick Heiss 52282 Robert Brandon Hendry 52283 Brian Thomas Hennaman 52284 Sean Patrick Hennessy 52285 Edward Carter Henrichson 52286 Garth Stephen Herbert 52287 Manuel Hernandez 52288 William Lamar Hickman 52289 Christopher Shane Hicks 52290 Joshua Patrick Higgins 52291 Justin Leroy Highley 52292 John Thomas Hildebrant 52293 Andrew Christopher Hilmes 52294 Gregory Ellis Hinson 52295 Troy Eugene Hively 52296 Francis Quang Hoang 52297 Eric Michael Hobson 52298 Benjamin Heath Hockenberry 52299 Christopher Dale Hockenberry 52300 Frederick Allen Hockett 52301 Timothy Harold Hocking 52302 Shaughnessy Dion Hodge 52303 Daniel A. Hoffman 52304 Joseph Patrick Hogan 52305 Nancy Lynn Hogan 52306 Jeremy David Hoit 52307 Emily Brenna Holcomb 52308 Margaret Elizabeth Pratt 52309 Ronald James Hollmann 52310 Johnell Rochelle Holly 52311 Matthew Jeremy Holly 52312 John Clinton Hopkins 52313 Andrew William Hospodar 52314 Daniel Harry Houseworth 52315 Mark C Houston 52316 Andrew Todd Howard 52317 Nathan Paul Huber 52318 Samuel Fate Hudson 52319 Jason Todd Hull 52320 Jason Craig Hutton 52321 Benjamin Eugene Hwang 52322 John Hwang 52323 Anthony Severino Iasso 52324 Kyu-bin Im 52325 Brian Alan Ivie 52326 Demaris Bernice Johanek 52327 Bruce Aaron Jaggard 52328 Gene Young Jahng 52329 Jeffrey P. Jajack 52330 Michael Alexander James 52331 Nathan Patrick Janysek 52332 Michael David Jason 52333 Sharon A. Jefferies 52334 Joel Matthew Jensen 52335 Jon Michael Jepko 52336 Matthew Alan Jesop 52337 John Anthonie Jettinghoff 52338 James W. Johng 52339 Kevin Michael Clarke Johnson 52340 Mark Christian Johnson 52341 Mark D. Johnson 52342 Jennifer A. McAfee 52343 Paul David Johnston 52344 Tige A. Johnston 52345 Dondra Trevor Jolly 52346 Eusi Mumina Jordan 52347 Marco Antonio Juarez 52348 Thomas Gregory Juetten 52349 Eduardo Allan Degala Jugueta 52350 Jong Ho Jun 52351 Edward Arthur Just 52352 Aaron John Justice 52353 Lucas Daniel Kagel 52354 Cynthia Marie Kanis 52355 Mark Glenn Kappelmann 52356 Nicholas Theodore Karabatsos 52357 Katherine Shirley Karwan 52358 Michael J. Karwatka 52359 Nakizito Namazzi Kazigo 52360 Jeannine Marie Koehler 52361 Stephen Lee Keefe 52362 LaMarcus Chevas Keels 52363 John Joseph Keleher 52364 Scott Wilson Kelly 52365 Joseph Thomas Kemmer 52366 John Patrick Kennedy 52367 John Scot Kennedy 52368 Stephen Jack Kent 52369 Thomas George Kent 52370 Justin Robert Keppy 52371 Kevin Harrison Kerby 52372 Jon Dennis Kerr 52373 Stephen Wayne Kersh 52374 Matthew Frederick Ketchum 52375 Jason Thomas Kidder 52376 Thomas Patrick Kilkenney 52377 David Suk Hoon Kim 52378 Douglas Duk Sung Kim 52379 Glenn T Kim 52380 William Lee Kim 52381 Raymond Andrew Kimball 52382 James Mobley Kimbrough 52383 Milton Lewis Kinslow 52384 Daryl Scott Kirkland 52385 Paul Alan Kirschbaum 52386 Heather Michele Kitson 52387 Eric Carol Klingeman 52388 Jonathan Page Klug 52389 Zachary Tait Knepper 52390 Matthew H Knorr 52391 John A. Koehler 52392 Ronald L. Koelsch 52393 Marcus Anthony Koepplinger 52394 Natasha Graham 52395 James Stanley Kotwis 52396 Paula Dean Kranz 52397 Alyssa Joanne Edwards 52398 Robert Latshaw Krotee 52399 Kurt Jerard Krummenacker 52400 Joseph P. Kuchan 52401 Cornelius William Kugler 52402 Christopher Thomas Kuhn 52403 John F Kurth 52404 Yong Duk Kwon 52405 Tarra Laguens Bopp 52406 Aaron Gillen Lambert 52407 Justin Lee Lambert 52408 Michael Terry Laney 52409 Lee Shin Langford 52410 Gwendolyn Sue Langton 52411 Cindy T. Atkins 52412 Paul Walker Laroque 52413 Robert Kyle Lashbrook 52414 Lance Joseph Lauchengco 52415 Fredric Ryan Laughlin 52416 Wayne C. Lawler 52417 Gavin A. Lawrence 52418 Gregory Alan Leavell 52419 Arte R. Ledyard 52420 Corey Eugene Lee 52421 Joseph Chong Jin Lee 52422 Robert Hyung-ku Lee 52423 Eric William Leetch 52424 Damien Jude Leigh 52425 Paul Eduardo Leon Lima 52426 Sandra L. Sizemore 52427 Charlotte Ann Lincoln 52428 Arturo Zambrano Lincon 52429 Travis Jason Lindberg 52430 Kent Randall Lindner 52431 Rachael Ann Deeds 52432 William D. Linn 52433 Jennifer Lisi 52434 Matthew Ryan Little 52435 Reed Allan Little 52436 Richard Cheng-An Liu 52437 Christopher Lo Weng Wah 52438 Timothy Ryan Loveland 52439 Raymond A. Lund 52440 Gregory Tyson Lundahl 52441 Cass Donlin Lundgren 52442 Andrew Joseph Lyman 52443 Diane E. Kinney 52444 Daniel George Lynn 52445 Kory Thomas Lyons 52446 Peter Joseph Macakanja 52447 Romeo Reyes Macalintal 52448 Alexander Duncan MacCalman 52449 Kelly Glen Macdonald 52450 Tara Elizabeth Cook 52451 Robie Cornelius Maclaughlin 52452 Andrew Fullerton Maclean 52453 Thomas Justin Madalo 52454 Jon-Paul N. Maddaloni 52455 Paul Joseph Maggiano 52456 John P. Maguire 52457 Dennis Barry Maier 52458 Michael John Makovec 52459 Mark Samuel Manfredonia 52460 Jeremy Todd Manning 52461 Christopher Robert Manske 52462 Stephen Todd Marchant 52463 Stephen Vincent Marchesani 52464 Matthew Robert Marciniak 52465 Allan Mari 52466 Rebecca Elizabeth Marier 52467 Lawrence Clyde Marion 52468 Grant Charles Marks 52469 Damian Cole Marquith 52470 Stephen Clifford Marr 52471 John Todd Marro 52472 Ryan Matthew Marro 52473 Ryan Thomas Marsh 52474 Bartholomew Phillip Martin 52475 Edgar Earl Martin 52476 Samuel Luke Martin 52477 John Robert Mathers 52478 Kurt Matheson 52479 Diedra Verlaine Turner 52480 Theresa Marie Matuszak 52481 David Matthew Mauer 52482 Eric Lee Maxwell 52483 Lisa Michelle Maxwell 52484 Matthew Ross Maybouer 52485 Matthew Morrison Mayfield 52486 Emily M. Rowe 52487 Daniel James McAuliffe 52488 Katie Jane Judge 52489 Scott Daniel McCarty 52490 Ryan William McCausland 52491 John James Mcdermott 52492 Brian D. Mcdonald 52493 John David Mcdonald 52494 William Patrick McDonough 52495 Paul Gerard Mcglyn 52496 Michael Charles McGovern 52497 Thomas Joseph Mcgrath 52498 Colin Patrick McGraw 52499 Troy Edward McHenry 52500 Sean Patrick Mchugh 52501 Andrew Scott McIntyre 52502 Michael Fredrick McLaughlin 52503 Thomas Andrew Mcnally 52504 Kris Medeiros Colwell 52505 Yuttana Meecharoen 52506 Joseph Lester Mehrten 52507 Gretchen Marie Meier 52508 Aaron M. Meilleur 52509 Brian Andrew Meinshausen 52510 Joseph Scott Meisinger 52511 Brian Anthony Mello 52512 Eugene M. Mello 52513 Richard Vincent Melnyk 52514 Otmaro Antonio Menjivar 52515 Oagile Mompa Merafhe 52516 Jason John Merchant 52517 Marvin Thomas Mercier 52518 Eric Peter Meyer 52519 John Carroll Michaud 52520 Mark David Miles 52521 Eric Bradley Miller 52522 Casey Russell Minott 52523 Jason Augustus Miseli 52524 John Charles Moffitt 52525 Aaron Thomas Morgan 52526 Devon M. Blake 52527 John Bennett Mountford 52528 Daniel Edward Mouton 52529 Richard Allen Moyers 52530 Mandi Jo Moynihan 52531 Neil Edward Mulac 52532 Patrick Daniel Munson 52533 John Patrick Murphy 52534 Stephen O. Murphy 52535 Matthew Charles Myllykangas 52536 Kevin Yoshida Nabb 52537 Ralph Dogra Nacey 52538 Regina Nanez 52539 Gregory John Nardi 52540 Walter Edward Narramore 52541 Benjamin Light Nash 52542 Cornelius B. Nash 52543 Scott Charles Nauman 52544 James Theodore Naylor 52545 Michael Joseph Neilitz 52546 Eric Jason Nelson 52547 John Edward Nelson 52548 Leon John Nesti 52549 Daniel D. Nettesheim 52550 Ethan Spencer Neuenschwander 52551 Landinh Ngo 52552 Thomas Hong-Phuc Nguyen 52553 Clayton Joseph Nicholas 52554 Christopher James Nicolini 52555 James Darby Nielson 52556 Quentin Carlyle Noreiga 52557 Taw D. North 52558 Andrew Joseph Norton 52559 Marcus David Novacheck 52560 John Rudolph Novak 52561 Ronald Joseph Novotny 52562 Roderick John O'Connor 52563 Shawn Patrick O'Connor 52564 Romy Dion O'Daniel 52565 Joseph Robert Odell 52566 Andrew Bobb Off 52567 Eric R. Oliver 52568 Paul Eldon Olson 52569 Steven James Olson 52570 Luke Andrew Omey 52571 Arthur Lee O'Neal 52572 P. Peter Orabona 52573 Aaron Dwight Osburn 52574 Carlos Eduardo Palacios 52575 Jason Nigel Palmer 52576 Noel Frederick Palmer 52577 Chad Michael Palodichuk 52578 Jennifer Param Finch 52579 Jason Knox Parker 52580 William M. Parker 52581 Matthew Jason Passante 52582 Joel Lawrence Pates 52583 James Richard Patton 52584 Eric William Pavlick 52585 Abdiel Enrique Peart 52586 Angela P. Weston 52587 Michael Bruce Peffley 52588 Gabriel Angelo Pennone 52589 Phoebe Lashay Penny 52590 Jason G. Pepsnik 52591 Brian Thomas Perez 52592 Jeffrey Dennis Perry 52593 Lee I. Peters 52594 Rebecca Anne Peters 52595 Glen Aulin Peterson 52596 Patrick Daniel Pflaum 52597 David Charles Phillips 52598 David John Phillips 52599 James Patrick Phillips 52600 Stacey Lee Pittman 52601 Warren Lee Pittman 52602 Derek William Placke 52603 Thomas Patrick Poepping 52604 Patrick James Pollock 52605 Marcus C. Ponce de Leon 52606 Joshua Walter Porten 52607 Quentin Jameson Portis 52608 Jeffrey Henry Powell 52609 Lewis Jerroldton Powers 52610 Kerry Shurron Prowell 52611 Darrin Christopher Puckett 52612 Hans Joseph Pung 52613 Ajit Vijay Purandare 52614 Rossel James Purcell 52615 Mark Christopher Quander 52616 Jeffrey Allen Quinn 52617 Matthew Tyrone Quinn 52618 Colleen Marie Compton 52619 William Neil Radicic 52620 Jeffrey Scott Rains 52621 Gerard Rapisarda 52622 Ayman Mohamed Naguid Rateb 52623 Scott William Rath 52624 Steven Michael Ray 52625 Douglas Allen Raymond 52626 Mark Gerald Reardanz 52627 Shad Alexander Reed 52628 Mark David Reel 52629 Nathan R. Reel 52630 Dale Richard Rehkopf 52631 John Anthony Reiss 52632 Kevin Dewayne Releford 52633 Clayton Mark Rempe 52634 Craig Donald Rennard 52635 Michael Allen Reyburn 52636 Erick Lee Rheam 52637 Rose Ellen Rice 52638 William Martin Ricks 52639 Andrew Douglas Rieger 52640 Ana Luisa Turner 52641 Christopher J. Roach 52642 Robin Lee Robbins Lloyd 52643 Walter Grady Roberson 52644 Kurt William Roberts 52645 David Joseph Roehn 52646 August Jameson Rolling 52647 Eduardo Romero 52648 Richard Keith Roper 52649 Katherine Victoria Rose 52650 Maria V. Burger 52651 Donald Joseph Ross 52652 Jennifer Elizabeth Waterman 52653 Sarah Gibson Ross 52654 Michael Matthew Rossi 52655 Marc Alain Rousseau 52656 Jason T. Rowe 52657 John Patrick Rowe 52658 Jonathan Allen Rufenacht 52659 Anthony Wayne Rush 52660 Lisa Marie Russell 52661 Scott William Rutler 52662 Paul Mccafferty Ryan 52663 Heather B. Sheldon 52664 Daniel Lee Salisbury 52665 Bryan Wesley Salyers 52666 Leona Marie Sanders 52667 Alexander Sime Saric 52668 Dennis M Sarmiento 52669 Ryan John Saulsbury 52670 William Christian Saunders 52671 David Thomas Sawyer 52672 Matthew Scalia 52673 Paul W Schaefer 52674 Robert Joseph Schexnayder 52675 Joseph B. Schino 52676 Robert F. Schlicht 52677 Timothy O'Neal Schmitt 52678 Brian Michael Schoenbaechler 52679 Timothy James Scholma 52680 Conrad Alan Schupay 52681 Heather Lynn Schwalber 52682 Craig William Schwartz 52683 Michael Robert Seawood 52684 Charles Morgan Seeger 52685 Jon Matthew Selle 52686 Arthur W. Sellers 52687 Christine Margaret Senin 52688 Craig Neil Senzon 52689 Mark Andrew Seris 52690 Encer Ray Shaffer 52691 Baqar A. Shah 52692 William J. Shavce 52693 Robert George Shaw 52694 Anthony Edwin Shepard 52695 Ryan Jiun-huei Shih 52696 Andrea Arlene Kagel 52697 Alexander Vidal Simmons 52698 Heather Kirsten Simmons 52699 Kristina Sinacori 52700 Nicole Ann Lashbrook 52701 John Mitchell Sizelove 52702 William Walter Sjolinder 52703 Ryan Frost Skinner 52704 Edward Simmons Sledge 52705 Andrew Reid Smith 52706 Bradford William Smith 52707 Brian Joseph Smith 52708 Craig Scott Smith 52709 Dana Lynn Smith 52710 Douglas Mark Smith 52711 Kimberly Ann O'Neal 52712 Sean Matthew Smith 52713 Lenard Dean Sollami 52714 Michael Chinsuk Song 52715 David Roy Sonne 52716 William Joseph Sorg 52717 Tracey Ann Ryser 52718 Phillip Dean Sounia 52719 Joseph Randolph Sowers 52720 Michael David Spake 52721 Robert Hunter Spash 52722 Steven Scott Spaulding 52723 Jeffrey Stuart Spear 52724 Kenneth A. Spearman 52725 Deidre Nicola Spence

52726 Stephen Charles Sprengnether 52727 Christopher Leir Squier 52728 Ryan Richard Squires 52729 Scott Jay St. Germain 52730 Mark Edward Stachelski 52731 Michael Craig Stajura 52732 Luke Edward Stall 52733 Alison Blythe Stanley 52734 Paul Terence Stanton 52735 Jonathan Phillip Starkenburg 52736 Matthew Francis Starry 52737 Stephen James Stasevich 52738 Jenness Farnham Steele 52739 Christopher Michael Steiner 52740 Kyle Blazej Stelma 52741 James Edward Stephens 52742 William Ronald Stewart 52743 Michael Alan Stinnett 52744 Matthew Michael Straub 52745 Donald B. Streater 52746 John Clinton Stull 52747 Diana Elizabeth Stumpf 52748 Brian Patrick Sullivan 52749 Richard Charles Sullivan 52750 Victor Herbert Sundquist 52751 Brian Eugene Surratt 52752 Ronald Dean Sutek 52753 Shawn M. Svob 52754 Mark William Swanson 52755 Trevor Robinson Swartz 52756 Graham Robert Swenson 52757 John Colquhoun Swift 52758 Stephen P. Szymanski 52759 David Brian Tabor 52760 Aaron Elliott Talbert 52761 Jacob Danny Talbot 52762 Ian James Tarasevitsch 52763 Michael John Tauber 52764 T. G. Taylor 52765 William Cooper Taylor 52766 Edward Bernard Teague 52767 Cristiano Duarte Teixeira 52768 Ryan Dain Teksten 52769 Thomas Anthony Terese 52770 Erich Robert Then 52771 Michael Austin Thoman 52772 Abigail Hope Linnington 52773 Gregory Irvin Thompson 52774 Malcolm Fredrick Thompson 52775 Mark William Thompson 52776 Erik W. Thomsen 52777 Darin John Thomson 52778 Derek Keith Thomson 52779 Jeanne Marie Neumeyer 52780 Michael A. Tobey 52781 Allyson M.T. Houston 52782 Derrick Wade Toddy 52783 Tanya Thais Tolles 52784 Joshua Mathew Toman 52785 Wayne Clinton Townsend 52786 Thomas Anthony Traficano 52787 Gerardo Antonio Trevino 52788 Mark Stephen Trott 52789 Michael Jeffrey Trotter 52790 Heidi Anne Trush 52791 James Joseph Tuite 52792 Yvette R. Turner 52793 Matthew J. Turpin 52794 David Benjamin Udall 52795 Paul Matthew Urban 52796 Geoffrey Ryan Van Epps 52797 Christina L. Perera 52798 Kevin Gerard Vaughn 52799 Robert Anthony Vedra 52800 Richard James Velloff 52801 Paul Austin Vencill 52802 Jason Charles Verkay 52803 Todd J. Verrill 52804 Ethan T. Vessels 52805 Timothy Charles Viles 52806 Todd Christopher Villines 52807 Christopher Charles Vine 52808 Kevin Ray Virgil 52809 Whitney Coleman Vogt 52810 Tasha Michelle Vohs 52811 Samuel Louis Volkman 52812 Michael Morgan Volpe 52813 William David Voorhies 52814 Constantine Yaroslav Voyevidka 52815 Jacob Thomas Wade 52816 Karen Ann Wakefield 52817 David A. Waldron 52818 Jacob A. Walker 52819 Adam D. Wallen 52820 Douglas Ronald Walter 52821 Mark Douglas Walters 52822 Richard Lynn Wampler 52823 Albert Y. Wang 52824 Kenneth Michael Wanless 52825 James Eric Warder 52826 Brian Ray Warner 52827 Ronald Aubrey Warner 52828 Todd Eric Warren 52829 Michael Stephen Waterman 52830 Edward James Watto 52831 Clinton Wayne Watts 52832 Gregory Boylan Waugh 52833 Geoffrey Alan Webb 52834 Charles Lee Weber 52835 Eric George Weber 52836 Robert M. Weber 52837 Noah Franklin Webster 52838 Alex Lane Wehmeyer 52839 Daniel Carl Weiss 52840 James Robert West 52841 David Bond Westlake 52842 Garth Andrew Whitacre 52843 Jackie Lynn White 52844 Justin Michael White 52845 Stephanie Troylynn White 52846 Jean Suzin Whitten 52847 Rocco Timothy Wicks 52848 Luther Roswell Wiest 52849 Justin Patrick Daniel Wilcox 52850 Dennis Gregory Wille 52851 Danny Jude Williams 52852 Michael Todd Williams 52853 Sean Christopher Williams 52854 Younga Williams 52855 Wesley James Williamson 52856 Gail Elizabeth Atkins 52857 Matthew Wesley Wineriter 52858 Meredith Catherine Winkle 52859 James Arthur Witham 52860 Jamison Richard Wolocko 52861 Sung Hun Won 52862 Brian Valdez Wood 52863 James Patrick Work 52864 Brian Keith Wortinger 52865 Brian Matthew Wray 52866 Jason Conrad Wright 52867 Joshua Matthew Wyatt 52868 Melissa Marie Wyka 52869 James Robert Wynkoop 52870 Leo Joseph Wyszynski 52871 Chong Hyon Yim 52872 Dunn Yoshitani 52873 Christopher J. Young 52874 Kenneth L. Young 52875 Jonathan Inkoo Yun 52876 Mark Andrew Yurko 52877 Brigitte J. Nettesheim 52878 Michael R. Zahuranic 52879 Thad D. Zak 52880 Claudia Zavala 52881 Robert Jeffrey Zeunik 52882 Andrew Stephen Zieseniss 52883 David Joseph Zinn 52884 Michael Zelker Zizza 52885 Jeb Stuart Zoller 52886 Mark Andrew Boeke 52887 Linwood Buford 52888 Steven A. Cline 52889 Carolyn M. Davis 52890 Mark Clayton Dean 52891 Eric A. Duvall 52892 Randy Joel Erickson 52893 Marc A. Folsom 52894 John Carl Mostellar 52895 Matthew P. Neumeyer 52896 Terry Dennis Phillips 52897 Michael Otto Williams 52898 Aaron Matthew Zelhart 52899 Anna M. K. Candler 52900 Andrew Henry Christiansen 52901 Robert P. Damare 52902 Gennie Leon Gantt 52903 Krista Martina Hoffman 52904 Juan Sheldon Jones 52905 Lyle E. Larkworthy 52906 Stephen L Lessar 52907 Kyle Richard McIntyre 52908 Michelle Ann Meier 52909 Roger Daniel Plaster 52910 Michael Paul Rossi 52911 Kevin Christopher Saatkamp 52912 Corey Tremayne Settles 52913 **1996** Andre B. Abadie 52914 Kevin John Ach 52915 David William Acker 52916 James Melvin Adams 52917 Michael Lee Adams 52918 Timothy Duane Adams 52919 Nirzarni J. Adhvaryu 52920 Jason Pfab Affolder 52921 Phillip Raymond Ahn 52922 John Bernard Ahrens 52923 Alexis Marie Albano 52924 Adam Aaron Albrich 52925 Timothy Taylor Alden 52926 Philip Jacob Aldrich 52927 Mary Olufunmilayo Belemo Alfred-Ockiya 52928 Mark Wesley Anders 52929 Devry Calvin Anderson 52930 Eric David Anderson 52931 Michael Andrew Anderson 52932 Trever Shaw Anderson 52933 Stephanie Gayle Andrasek 52934 Christine Dianne Andrews 52935 Sureyya Ardic 52936 Robert Collin Armstrong 52937 John Edwin Arnold 52938 Michael Arriaga 52939 Robert Mills Arthur 52940 Mary Katherine Ashworth 52941 David William Averett 52942 Matthew Joseph Avery 52943 Jacques Alain Ba'Ana Tsogo 52944 Kevin Scott Badger 52945 Michael David Bagully 52946 Brent A. Baker 52947 Cullen Griffin Barbato 52948 Daniel T. Bard 52949 Keith Craig Bardo 52950 Robert Elliott Barnsby 52951 Brian Keith Barry 52952 Steven Thomas Barry 52953 Jason Patrick Batchelor 52954 Archie Lee Bates 52955 Heath Thomas Bates 52956 David Gerard Bauer 52957 Doel Dwayne Baughman 52958 Joseph Aaron Beard 52959 Ryan Brandon Beaver 52960 Brian Jeffrey Bechard 52961 Michael Murray Beckwith 52962 Julia Bell 52963 Michael Jonathan Bellack 52964 Edward Todd Bennett 52965 Lance Byron Bennett 52966 Morgan Alan Berglund 52967 Jeffrey Scott Bergmann 52968 Jeanne K. Kenady 52969 Ryan Christopher Berry 52970 Drew Peter Berwanger 52971 Brett William Bielawski 52972 Jeffrey Scott Biggans 52973 Leanne Michelle Seguin 52974 Lynyetta Catrean Blackshear 52975 William Joseph Blair 52976 Timothy Andrew Block 52977 Kevin Dean Boates 52978 David Jay Boettcher 52979 Kenneth M. Bolin 52980 Peter Christopher Bonin 52981 Gary Lee Boone 52982 Robert Grason Born 52983 Christian Nielsen Bottcher 52984 Richard Thurmond Bowen 52985 Alan Jeffrey Boyer 52986 Kory Earl Boyer 52987 Corey Allen Braddock 52988 Matthew Wayne Bradshaw 52989 Thomas Jerome Brady 52990 Jason Raymond Brandt 52991 Matthew K. Brandt 52992 Richard Michael Bratt 52993 Donald Ray Braught 52994 Casey Lynn Bredewater Cox 52995 Thomas Paul Brennan 52996 Brett Martin Brewer 52997 Chad David Broski 52998 Daniel Francis Brostek 52999 Jason Paul Brown 53000 Justin Wayne Brown 53001 Leland Blair Brown 53002 Peter Allen Brown 53003 Robert S. Brown 53004 Theodore Robert Brown 53005 Jeremy Paul Browne 53006 Michael Daniel Buchheit 53007 Geoffrey Robert Bull 53008 Brandi Lynn Bult 53009 Jessica Lynn Bunin 53010 John Franklyn Burger 53011 James Torrance Burgess 53012 Thomas F. Burrell 53013 Derek F. Burt 53014 Jose Miguel Bustamante 53015 Anthony Lynn Butler 53016 Michael Kahlil Byard 53017 Joshua Todd Byers 53018 James Maximillien Cadet 53019 Molly C. Capra 53020 Adrian Paul Calame 53021 Erik Russell Caldwell 53022 Gordon Andrew Callender 53023 John Joseph Camiolo 53024 Christopher Ryan Campbell 53025 Jonathan Alan Campbell 53026 Whitney Alfred Campbell 53027 Michael Vincent Cangolosi 53028 James Frank Cantelupe 53029 Eric Christopher Capers 53030 Aaron Scott Carlisle 53031 Karin Marie Carolan 53032 Steven Paul Carpenter 53033 Bradley Matthew Carr 53034 Christopher Daniel Carrano 53035 Elizabeth Ann Casely 53036 Robert Peter Cassery 53037 Kristen Elise Lewis 53038 Andrew Douglas Cecil 53039 Shane Douglas Celeen 53040 Vincenzo Santino Centamore 53041 Matthew Preston Champion 53042 Scott Asber Chance 53043 Brandyn Potter Chapman 53044 Young Dong Chase 53045 Chad Nathan Chegwidden 53046 Daniel Moo-Yuan Chen 53047 Brian Victor Chernauskas 53048 Gabriel Andres Chinchilla 53049 Brian H. P. Cho 53050 Michael Nam Jae Cho 53051 Brian Choi 53052 Sung Hwan Chon 53053 Sook Ping Chong 53054 Paul Anthony Christianson 53055 William Wu Chang Chung 53056 David Michael Church 53057 Michael Vito Ciaramella 53058 Aaron Matthew Cichocki 53059 Max Wesley Clegg 53060 Bo Shaler Cockrell 53061 Bryan M. Cofer 53062 Dwayne Leon Coffey 53063 William Gregory Colbert 53064 Robert Carrol Cole 53065 John James Coleman 53066 Tausha Eudora Coleman 53067 Richard Louis Comitz 53068 Jason F. Conrad 53069 John Thomas Conroy 53070 Marc Edward Conselman 53071 Carlos Alberto Contreras 53072 Paul Andrew Cook 53073 Sean M. Cooney 53074 Lenton Douglas Cooper 53075 Michael Nicholas Coppa 53076 Thomas P. Cornelius 53077 Stephen J. Courreges 53078 Richard Jay Covert 53079 Michael Thomas Cowperthwait 53080 James Edward Cox 53081 Richard Thomas Cranford 53082 Chad Austin Crank 53083 William G. Crans 53084 Brian Andrew Crawley 53085 Justin Lee Cremer 53086 Scott Charles Crissey 53087 Robert Ellison Croft 53088 John Raymond Crombie 53089 Matthew Arthur Crouch 53090 John Downing Crow 53091 Patrick Connley Cruser 53092 Mathew Aaron Cunningham 53093 Ian Scott Currier 53094 Lewis Martin Curry 53095 Kevin Robert Cutright 53096 Patrick James Dagon 53097 Matthew David Dall 53098 Rebecca Leigh Damm 53099 Glen Oh Dare 53100 Jonathan Peter Darr 53101 Joel E. Davis 53102 Brian James Dawson 53103 Michael R. DeBock 53104 V. James DeBoer 53105 Mark Alexander Delaar 53106 Douglas Logan Delp 53107 Robert G. Deluca 53108 Richard Kenneth Dembowski 53109 Michael Ross Dempsey 53110 Andrew Thomas Deponai 53111 Dale Coleman Destefano 53112 Daniel Justin DeVries 53113 Coninyah Ben Dan Ben Dew 53114 Jeffrey Wheeler Hurt Dickey 53115 Jason Stuart Dickie 53116 Richard Dean Dickson 53117 Alan Harris Dinerman 53118 Shawn C. Dinsmore 53119 Aaron Zimmerman Dirks 53120 Robert William Doering 53121 Amy Lynn Donaldson 53122 Glen Garrett Donnelly 53123 Edward Allen Donovan 53124 William Daniel Doran 53125 Marc Christopher Dorrer 53126 William Delos Doutt 53127 Floyd Donald Drake 53128 Steven Edmund Droste 53129 Michael Joseph Drulis 53130 Jason Patrick Duane 53131 Daniel Davis Duchai 53132 Christopher Sean Dudley 53133 Paul Vincent D'Ulisse 53134 Jonathan Stewart Dunn 53135 Ryan Michael Duran 53136 J. Keller Durkin 53137 Peter Carl Earle 53138 Andrew Blake Eckel 53139 Dion Miguel Edge 53140 Dale Rodney Edmiston 53141 Emily Jean Edson 53142 Nathaniel Manuel Edwards 53143 Ryan Arnold Edwards 53144 Kara Kristen Bates 53145 Jefferson York Emblen 53146 Raymond Jacob Emerson 53147 Michel Allen Enos 53148 Stein Bernard Ericsson 53149 Paul Francis Evangelista 53150 Robert Vincent Ewers 53151 James Anderson Ewing 53152 Jude Ogbonna Ezeagu 53153 Bret Cooper Faler 53154 Michael James Feeley 53155 Joel Scott Ferguson 53156 Paul John Ferrigno 53157 Thomas James Fezza 53158 Bradley Martin Fisher 53159 Matthew Robert Fix 53160 Jon Charles Fleck 53161 Amanda Hope Flint 53162 Richard John Fonyi 53163 Gregory Steven Fortier 53164 David Maurice Fortson 53165 Damien Edward Fosmoe 53166 Lawrence Douglas Foss 53167 Chad Stephen Foster 53168 Aaron J. Francis 53169 John Richard Frederick 53170 Christopher G. Freeman 53171 Yelankan Zachary Freeman 53172 Jason Ryan Freidt 53173 John Aaron Frick 53174 Everett Tomio Fuller 53175 Robert L. Fuqua 53176 Douglas M. Gafney 53177 Thomas Loren Galli 53178 Jonathan Allan Gano 53179 Rogelio Javier Garcia 53180 Benjamin A. Gardner 53181 Whitney Benjamin Gardner 53182 Joseph Walker Garrard 53183 Richard James Gash 53184 Brian Peter Gavula 53185 Liane Theresa Geary 53186 Vincent Paul Generoso 53187 Edward John Gengaro 53188 Chad Alan Giacomozzi 53189 Everett Nobel Gibbens 53190 Daniel D. Gick 53191 Carl Adam Giorgi 53192 Burton Cook Glover 53193 Matthew Pardee Gnau 53194 Willie Joe Godchaux 53195 Joseph Lockett Goddu 53196 Adelaido Godinez 53197 Kevin Richard Golinghorst 53198 Trinidad Gonzalez 53199 Amy Leigh Gouge 53200 John David Graves 53201 Patrick Michael Gray 53202 Seth W. Green 53203 Janelle Ann Cole 53204 Darin Lee Griffin 53205 Benjamin Kelly Grimes 53206 Michael Todd Grissom 53207 Alan Richard Gronewold 53208 Michael Joseph Gunning 53209 Charles Michael Gutowski 53210 Robert Claiburn Hagedorn 53211 Jerry Edward Haley 53212 Charles Wellborn Hall 53213 John Stephen Hall 53214 Jason Douglas Hallock 53215 James Martin Halloran 53216 Dimitri P. Haloulos 53217 John Henry Hampton 53218 Kimberly Marie Hanson 53219 Frank Stanton Hardee 53220 Kenneth Dale Hardesty 53221 Kevin Michael Hare 53222 Anna Lisa Harmon Spear 53223 Tyson Wood Harmon 53224 Richard Jeffrey Harris 53225 Waymond Eli Harris 53226 Sarah Rachel Hart 53227 David Paul Harvie 53228 Gar Allen Haugo 53229 Clinton Wayne Hawkins 53230 Charles Edward Hawthorne 53231 Stewart Marshall Hayes 53232 Bradley Eugene Haynie 53233 Ralph David Heaton 53234 Glenn David Hemminger 53235 Oliver Thomas Henderson 53236 Matthew P. Hennigan 53237 Armando Hernandez 53238 David Matthew Hernke 53239 Jason Lambert Hester 53240 Jesse Stuart Hester 53241 Jason Cody Hick 53242 James Neil Hickok 53243 David Timothy Hills 53244 David Maxwell Hilsman 53245 Gerald Eugene Himes 53246 Frederick Milton Hinshaw 53247 James Allen Hiser 53248 Christopher Charles Hoag 53249 Cynthia Lenore Hobbs 53250 Tobin Lee Hobbs 53251 Randall Wade Hoberecht 53252 Joshua Alan Hobson 53253 Timothy Douglas Hoch 53254 Wilton Norman Hockaday 53255 Matthew Berrigan Holloway 53256 Ryan A. Honl 53257 Mark Howard Hoovestol 53258 Thomas Robert Horrobin 53259 Benjamin John Howard 53260 Christopher William Howard 53261 Thomas Hand Howarth 53262 Christopher L. Howsden 53263 Matthew Timothy Hueman 53264 Holly Flores 53265 John R. Hughes 53266 Fred Lee Huh 53267 David Marshall Hull 53268 Victoria Joan Hulse 53269 Michael Lawrence Hummel 53270 Timothy Dale Hummel 53271 Peter John Huybers 53272 Mindy Ann Kimball 53273 James Udosen Imoh 53274 Gerald Duane Ingalls 53275 Kirk Alyn Ingold 53276 Matthew Damian Iram 53277 Jaime Alexander Irick 53278 Avram Jacob Isaacson 53279 Matthew Lars Isaacson 53280 Thomas Andrew Jackson 53281 Harry Anthony Janiski 53282 Nicholas Phillip Jaskolski 53283 Carrie Ann Jeanneret 53284 Jaroslaw Adam Jedrzejowski 53285 Jason Keith Jefferis 53286 Kevin Lee Jefferson 53287 Jeremiah Joseph Jette 53288 Eduardo Javier Jimenez 53289 Barton Leroy Johnke 53290 Benjamin Franklin Johnson 53291 Brad Alan Johnson 53292 David Timothy Johnson 53293 Derek Gawain Johnson 53294 Eric M. Johnson 53295 Jeffrey James Johnson 53296 Jennifer Renee Johnson 53297 Jeremy Daniel Johnson 53298 Ryan Wade Johnson 53299 Timothy Werner Johnson 53300 Christena Anne Johnston 53301 Carolanne Marie Bard 53302 Elliot Richard Jones 53303 Garrett Preston Jones 53304 Michael Lindbergh Jones 53305 Ryan Macray Jones 53306 Brian Louis Juhasz 53307 Steven Michael Kapcoe 53308 Andrew Michael Karczewski 53309 Damien Curtis Katzenmeyer 53310 Kevin Francis Kaveney 53311 Ryan William Kay 53312 John Baptist Kazigo 53313 Kimberly Ann Kazinski 53314 Christopher Anthony Kearns 53315 Carlos Lamar Keith 53316 James Shane Kelly 53317 Brian F. Kenady 53318 Matthew Ernest Kenneway 53319 Jason Eugene Kerr 53320 John Eric Kettula 53321 So Yon Ki 53322 John D. Kiernan 53323 Katharyn Suzanne Hiebert 53324 Sean Patrick Kilcawley 53325 David Brian Killion 53326 Peter Sungjun Kim 53327 Curtis Wade King 53328 Joshua Lane Kinley 53329 Christopher S. Kinney 53330 Ioannis Eustathiou Kiriazis 53331 Scott Walker Kirkpatrick 53332 David Lee Kirman 53333 Kamthorn Kirtthamai 53334 Todd Richard Kishpaugh 53335 Jeffrey T. Kittell 53336 Derek Timothy Klein 53337 Steven John Klubertanz 53338 Andrew Ferrieres Knaggs 53339 Matisse Maxson Knight 53340 Scott Phillip Knight 53341 Devon Eric Knox 53342 Aaron Theodore Kohler 53343 Ivan Matthew Konermann 53344 Christopher Michael Korpela 53345 Charlene C. Kow 53346 Gary Ralph Kramlich 53347 Michael Lee Kreh 53348 Bridget Amanda Kroger 53349 Timothy Harold Krueger 53350 Andrew M. Krug 53351 Todd Jesse Kuehnlein 53352 Paul Lawrence Kuettner 53353 Brandon Geremiah Kulik 53354 Jereld Craig Kunard 53355 Bryan Akira Kunitake 53356 Daniel J. Kustelski 53357 Michael Joseph Kuzara 53358 Erik R. Laaken 53359 Cameron Gregory LaBrache 53360 Alexander Charles Ladage 53361 Gregory Aloysius Lafata 53362 Baron Hayden Lambert 53363 Conrad Anthony Langenegger 53364 Robert W. Lanz 53365 Marc Vincent La Roche 53366 Kirk David Larson 53367 Rebecca Ann Lash 53368 Jonathan C. Lauer 53369 Edward Joseph Lavelle 53370 J. David Leamon 53371 Frederick D. Ledfors 53372 Justin Adam Ledzinski 53373 James Joo Lee 53374 James W. Lee 53375 Larry Scott Lee 53376 Russell S. Lee 53377 Joseph William Lehman 53378 Craig Thomas Lennon 53379 Paul Bryant Lester 53380 Michelle Renee Lewis 53381 Charles Sumner Lientz 53382 Kevin Dion Lilly 53383 Padraic Richard Lilly 53384 Bryce Inwood Lindsay 53385 Aaron David Lindstrom 53386 Natalie Rose Linendoll 53387 Eric Thomas Ling 53388 Ian Justin Llewellyn 53389 Eric Paul Lopez 53390 Bryan Maxwell Love 53391 Stephen Anthony Love 53392 Travis Joel Loving 53393 Patrick Sean Lowry 53394 Joshua Mathew Lubarsky 53395 Thomas Wayne Lucario 53396 Aaron Blaine Luck 53397 Michael Edward Lucy 53398 Mark D. Lueking 53399 Amy Jo Luyster Nelson 53400 Darcy Lynn Schnack 53401 Mark Andrew Lynskey 53402 Stephan Edward Lynskey 53403 Bryon Joseph Mace 53404 Craig Michael Maceri 53405 Deann Rana Machlan 53406 Amy E. Knight 53407 Fredric Ryan Maddox 53408 Landis Courtney Maddox 53409 Tobin Andrew Magsig 53410 Ferdinand Espiritu Malasmas 53411 James Ernest Malphurs 53412 Michael William Mandarino 53413 Robert R. Manning 53414 Michael Ray Mansell 53415 George Andrew Marcontell 53416 Chad Thomas Marley 53417 Benjamin J. Marlin 53418 Hunter Marc Marshall 53419 Steven Goudreau Marshall 53420 Lawrence D. Martin 53421 Damien E. Mason 53422 Scott Richard Masson 53423 Christopher Paul Masters 53424 Glenn Ray Matlock 53425 Curtis Lee Mattson 53426 Ryan David Matulka 53427 Carmen May 53428 Eric Lynn Mayer 53429 Melissa Anne Mazur 53430 Eric Paul McAllister 53431 Sim Joelken McArthur 53432 Kevin E. McAuliffe 53433 Joseph Andrew McCabe 53434 Thomas J. McCarron 53435 Matthew Paul McCarthy 53436 Kellie Jane Barry 53437 Christopher Lowell McCrea 53438 Joshua Lee McCullough 53439 Michael Aaron McCullough 53440 Michael Alexander McDonald 53441 Thomas I.M. McDonough 53442 David Howard McDowell 53443 Patrick Wayne McGee 53444 Gregory Russell McIntyre 53445 Kelli Ann McKechnie 53446 Geoffrey Jonathan McKeel 53447 Brian Francis McMahon 53448 John Joseph McNally 53449 Brad Alan McNeilly 53450 Nicole Anne McPherson 53451 Justin Clifford McQuary 53452 Andrew David Mees 53453 Christian Butler Meisel 53454 Gustavo Rene Mendiola 53455 Matthew Scott Merrill 53456 Terry David Meyer 53457 Edward Meyers 53458 Nathaniel Christian Midberry 53459 Jason Langdon Millam 53460 Mark Daniel Miller 53461 Darin Wyatt Mills 53462 Steven Brian Mills 53463 William Donald Mills 53464 Oliver Friedrich Mintz 53465 Stephen Andrew Mohme 53466 David John Molinari 53467 Francis Joseph Monaco 53468 Jeffrey Raymond Montanari 53469 Aaron Lane Montgomery 53470 Michael Robert Moon 53471 Ann Marie Moore 53472 Kevin Lee Moore 53473 Ryan Eugene Moore 53474 Bryan Augustus Morgan 53475 Eileen Moritz 53476 Scott Bryan Morris 53477 Theodore Scott Morris 53478 Dale Michael Mouch 53479 Jason D. Moura 53480 Abdullah Muhammad 53481 William Edward Mullee 53482

Daniel Patrick Murphy 53483 Kevin Michael Myers 53484 Ronald Francis Myers 53485 Scott Andrew Myers 53486 Karen Gnau 53487 Thomas James Nagle 53488 John Durand Nail 53489 T. Gregory Naples 53490 Kimberly Dawn Nash 53491 Scott Mariner Naumann 53492 Michael Thomas Neary 53493 Michael Joseph Nebesky 53494 James Harold Nelson 53495 Kenneth Joseph Nelson 53496 Ross F. Nelson 53497 Dustin Phillip Neuberger 53498 Anthony Eugene New 53499 Matthew Angelo Newgent 53500 Joel Daniel Newsom 53501 Evin Shay Nieradka 53502 Henry Gerard Nixon 53503 Eric Michael Noe 53504 Kevin Michael Norman 53505 Samuel Griffin Norquist 53506 Matthew Edward Novak 53507 Thomas Edward Novak 53508 Brian John Novoselich 53509 John J. Nowogrocki 53510 Andrew David Nygaard 53511 Christopher Michael O'Brien 53512 Suzanne Michelle O'Barr 53513 James Michael O'Brien 53514 John William Ocana 53515 Michael Bryant Ochs 53516 Shawn Morris O'Connor 53517 Buckley Earl O'Day 53518 Kevin Dean Offel 53519 Jody Bennett Offstein 53520 Eric Andrew Ogborn 53521 Benjamin Ray Ogden 53522 Jennifer Danella Oliva 53523 Tyler Kent Olson 53524 Patrick Scott O'Neal 53525 Matthew James O'Neil 53526 Joseph Robert Oppold 53527 James Baisden Osborne 53528 Heather Lynn Perry 53529 Christopher Edward Oxendine 53530 Robert John Ozanich 53531 Alisha P. Barnsby 53532 Jeffrey Owen Paine 53533 David John Palazzo 53534 Benjamin Newby Palmer 53535 James Gatbonton Pangelinan 53536 Hanna Maaria Parikka 53537 Andrew Young Park 53538 Angela Marie Wyatt 53539 John E. Patterson 53540 Paul Edward Patterson 53541 Brian William Pavlick 53542 David Baird Peeples 53543 Justin Michael Pelkey 53544 Theodore Joseph Pelzel 53545 Katherine Lynn Pendry 53546 James Lee Perrine 53547 Charles C. Perry 53548 Henry Christopher Perry 53549 Nathaniel Wayne Peters 53550 Thomas Jon Petersen 53551 Jacob Arthur Peterson 53552 Joseph A. Petty 53553 Mark Andrew Pflanz 53554 Brian Matthew Phelan 53555 Matthew Aaron Phelps 53556 Erin A. Phillips 53557 Jeremy David Phillips 53558 Casey John Phoenix 53559 David Wayne Picard 53560 Timothy J. Piccirilli 53561 Stephen Patrick Pirner 53562 Patrick Joseph Pittenger 53563 Stephen Justin Platt 53564 Tito Gerome Pope 53565 Carl Andrew Poppe 53566 Michael Alan Pressel 53567 Cameron Stalker Price 53568 Howard Milton Price 53569 Donald Christopher Prograis 53570 Peter Prozik Jr. 53571 Toby Warren Prudhomme 53572 Bryan Taylor Purdom 53573 Matthew Cassius Purdy 53574 Joseph Albert Puskas 53575 Jeremy James Putman 53576 Peter Townsend Quimby 53577 Franz Louis Rademacher 53578 Theodore William Radtke 53579 Eugene Joseph Ragasa 53580 Timothy Paul Raker 53581 Andrew Lawrence Ramos 53582 Anthony Pasquale Randall 53583 Courtland Adam Rankin 53584 Robert William Ratcliffe 53585 Joel David Raup 53586 James Albert Ray 53587 Mark Davis Ray 53588 Brendan Collin Raymond 53589 Shelley Ann Raymond 53590 Cynthia L. Reams 53591 Joseph Daniel Reap 53592 Mikael Bomani Reckley 53593 Jonathan B. Redmond 53594 Lenore Marie Hobbs 53595 John Stephen Reed 53596 Leslie Byron Reese 53597 Shane Richardson Reeves 53598 Philip Glenn Reuss 53599 David Mark Richkowski 53600 Devin Lawrence Rickey 53601 James Garrett Riely 53602 Benjamin Albert Ring 53603 Kirk Michael Ringbloom 53604 Nicole Rene Riva 53605 Librado Kim Rivas 53606 Jose David Rivera 53607 Glenn Barry Robbins 53608 Alistair Jay Roberts 53609 Dean Byron Roberts 53610 Matthew Aaron Roberts 53611 Glenn S. Robertson 53612 Benjamin Cooke Rodgers 53613 Timothy James Rodgers 53614 Ismael Roberto Rodriguez 53615 Jonathan Walter Roginski 53616 Philip John Root 53617 Jason Wallace Ross 53618 Donald C. Rucker 53619 Hernan Eduardo Ruiz 53620 Vincent Kenneth Russell 53621 Amy Hunter Ruth 53622 Kevin Rogers Ryan 53623 Laura Rebecca Sabatini 53624 Anthony John Sabino 53625 Brian Johnathan Salie 53626 Eric Michael Sass 53627 Charles Edward Saunders 53628 Paul Andrew Savel 53629 Todd Alfred Scattini 53630 Curtis Edward Schaefer 53631 Andrew George Schanno 53632 John Frederic Schepflin 53633 David Paul Schleiff 53634 Troy Allan Schnack 53635 Michael P. Schock 53636 Todd Schultz 53637 Gregory Eugene Schwarz 53638 Andrea L.A. Scott 53639 Jamar Darrion Scott 53640 Nathaniel Scott 53641 Alexander Dale Seguin 53642 Daniel Adrian Segura 53643 John J. Senneff 53644 Michael Jilly Sessa 53645 Marc Norman Shafer 53646 Andrew Douglas Shaller 53647 Gregory Kenneth Sharpe 53648 Daniel Pierce Shaw 53649 Timothy Ryan Shaw 53650 Christopher Martin Shearer 53651 David Valentine Shebalin 53652 Brendan John Sheehan 53653 Michael Anthony Shekleton 53654 Jeffry Wayne Shetterly 53655 Stanley Jiyong Shin 53656 David Anthony Shirley 53657 Devin Micah Shirley 53658 Matthew Aaron Shirley 53659 Adekunle Olaolu Sholeye 53660 Barry Lee Simmons 53661 Christopher Todd Simpson 53662 Steven Daniel Sims 53663 Eren Paul Sitki 53664 Michael Scott Sivulka 53665 Bryan K. Sizemore 53666 Samuel Aaron Skiles 53667 Scott Christopher Slater 53668 John Clark Slawter 53669 Staci Marie Gash 53670 Jared Andrew Sloan 53671 Brian Jeffrey Smith 53672 Christopher William Smith 53673 Erik Van Smith 53674 James Nelson Smith 53675 Jarrad Nathan Smith 53676 Kenneth Dale Smith 53677 Meosha K. Smith 53678 Michael Tucker Smith 53679 Richard Francis Smith 53680 Richard W. Smith 53681 Travis Marion Smith 53682 Tyler Bradford Smith 53683 Sara Ann Berner 53684 Gregory J. Sovich 53685 Brian Andrew Speas 53686 Alexander Quenton Spencer 53687 Tamara Lyn Spicer 53688 Spencer Harold Spiker 53689 Warren Elsey Sponsler 53690 Christine Elaine St. John 53691 Nancy Elizabeth Starbuck 53692 Peter Bryan Steed 53693 Nathaniel Joseph Steinwachs 53694 Thomas Mcallister Stevenson 53695 Robert McKinley Steward 53696 Nicole S. Lee 53697 Daxton Thomas Stilwell 53698 Neil Richard Stockmaster 53699 Eric James Stoner 53700 Mark William Stouffer 53701 Maria Lisa Streba 53702 Frances Ann Sugrue 53703 Wardell Owens Sullivan 53704 Ryan Lee Sumstad 53705 Brian Andrew Sumutka 53706 Jeffrey Kenneth Sutton 53707 Levi Jesse Sutton 53708 David Lawrence Swenson 53709 Joseph Timothy Swiecki 53710 Christina Ann Swindlehurst 53711 Brian Ernest Swinehart 53712 Scott Allen Tackett 53713 Jason Clifford Taliaferro 53714 Catherine Taylor Wilkinson 53715 Gregory James Taylor 53716 William Bradford Taylor 53717 William Todd Tebbe 53718 Brandon Russell Tegtmeier 53719 Cory D. Tereick 53720 William Scott Tharp 53721 Roxanne Marie Theobald 53722 Carla Thomas Joyner 53723 Ronald Purnell Thomas 53724 Ryan Michael Thomas 53725 Travis Michael Thomas 53726 Kenneth Dwight Thompson 53727 Stephen Joseph Thorley 53728 Charles Galloway Thrash 53729 Raymond John Tomasits 53730 Frederick Joseph Toti 53731 Marc Edward Toulouse 53732 Kyle William Towns 53733 Joseph Anthony Triano 53734 Christopher Andrew Tubbs 53735 John Christopher Tucker 53736 John Timothy Turner 53737 Michael Ryan Turner 53738 Duncan Edwin Tye 53739 Jeffery David Ugino 53740 Thaddeus Lydell Underwood 53741 Abraham Tyler Usher 53742 James A. Van Atta 53743 Michael S. Van Buskirk 53744 Todd Michael Van Sickle 53745 Peter Herman Vangeertruyden 53746 Lance Kevin Vanzandt 53747 Michael Wayne Vargo 53748 Marcus Robert Vartan 53749 Mark Curtis Vetter 53750 James Shannon Vinall 53751 Jay Andrew Virgil 53752 Christopher Terennce Viscovich 53753 Joseph W. Vongsvarnrungruang 53754 Todd R. Vydareny 53755 Baxter Francis Wade 53756 Krista Leigh Wagner 53757 Thomas James Waldron 53758 Michael Wayne Wall 53759 Benjamin Michael Wallen 53760 James N.R. Walser 53761 James Andrew Walsh 53762 Matthew Thomas Walsh 53763 George Henry Walter 53764 John Patrick Walton 53765 Lawrence Richard Walton 53766 Mathew Aaron Wanchick 53767 Katherine Patricia Ward 53768 Daniel Edward Warn 53769 Christopher Hugh Warner 53770 Laura Christina Watson 53771 Scott Thomas Watson 53772 James Allen Wayne 53773 Trent Robby Webb 53774 Jason B. Weekes 53775 Robert Samuel Weller 53776 Michael William Wells 53777 Kyle Justin Werking 53778 Ryan Michael Werling 53779 Emett Austin White 53780 Christopher William Whitmark 53781 Glen Porcher Whitner 53782 Matthew Timothy Wiger 53783 Baasil Toussaint Wilder 53784 Kenneth James Wilkinson 53785 Barry Wixx Williams 53786 Blair Shaffer Williams 53787 Colin Lee Williams 53788 Tacuma Sekou Williams 53789 Kathy Marina Brown 53790 Kip Alan Wilson 53791 Mark Allen Wilson 53792 Jonathan Caleb Winchester 53793 Ian Scott Winer 53794 Thaddeus Andrew Wojtusik 53795 Stefan Robert Wolfe 53796 Daman Richard Wood 53797 Timothy Scott Wren 53798 Benjamin Dean Wright 53799 Stuart Busse Wright 53800 Gary Herbert Wynn 53801 William Arthur Wyrovsky 53802 Gerald Tan Yap 53803 Christopher J. Yeaton 53804 John Lee Yi 53805 Abel Estes Young 53806 Dillard Wesley Young 53807 Kyung Min Yu 53808 Andrew Eugene Yuliano 53809 Eric Zampedri 53810 Richard Louis Zanardi 53811 Jeffrey Scott Zanelotti 53812 Laurel Colleen Sitki 53813 James Edward Zopelis 53814 Brian William Zuck 53815 Gregory C. Alfred 53816 Jay Robert Bucci 53817 David Leroy Buffaloe 53818 Paul Andrew Forgey 53819 Baris Murat Guner 53820 Darren Michael Harbst 53821 Benjamin David Herring 53822 Aaron William Rumfelt 53823 Brad Edward Smith 53824 Richard E. Stiek 53825 Edward Lee Stover 53826 Charles Anthony Sulewski 53827 Brian Lee Tucker 53828 Jason Robert Villas 53829 Nathaniel Glen Wissmar 53830 J. B. Worley 53831 Tony L. Dedmond 53832 Amy Dee West 53833 Robert Dale Griffin 53834 Scott L. Hamilton 53835 Irvin Randolph Hawkins 53836 Nathan Edward Johnson 53837 Justin Brooks Lane 53838 **1997** Robert J Aaron 53839 Christine Elizabeth Campion 53840 Jeffrey W Adams 53841 Kevin J Adams 53842 Christopher Brando Agbayani 53843 Adam K Ake 53844 Thomas C Akerlund 53845 Babatunde I Alaya 53846 James G Alden 53847 Joseph F Alderete 53848 Alicia Michelle Chivers 53849 Christopher T Altavilla 53850 Angela M Altieri 53851 Luis M Alvarez 53852 Michael R Amrine 53853 Larry C Anderson 53854 Mitchell E Anderson 53855 Brandy M Andrews 53856 Michael P Andrzejewski 53857 Aaron Angell 53858 Jeffrey C Angerman 53859 David A Anthony 53860 Edgar Anzaldua 53861 Matthew T Archambault 53862 Aaron M Armstrong 53863 Steven N Arne 53864 David M Arnold 53865 Michael C Arnold 53866 Don G. Artman 53867 James M Ashburn 53868 Andrew W Ashley 53869 David M. Ashley 53870 Charles L Assadourian 53871 Beth A. Assenmacher 53872 Matthew J August 53873 Donald E Augustus 53874 Thomas E Austin 53875 Christian C Ayers 53876 Nicholas E Ayers 53877 Christopher A Bachl 53878 Thomas J Backenson 53879 Kevin Bae 53880 Houston E Baker 53881 Michael A Baker 53882 Rodney S Baker 53883 Travis L Bales 53884 Richard R Balestri 53885 Julie Anne Balten 53886 Jennifer R Barcomb 53887 Matthew S Barrow 53888 Gary C Battista 53889 Michael B Baumann 53890 Scott J Baumgartner 53891 Jeremy D Bell 53892 Stephen A Bell 53893 Andrew T Bellocchio 53894 Jonathan M Bentley 53895 Matthew J Berberian 53896 Michael A Berdy 53897 Steve D Berlin 53898 Sherri L Bernal 53899 Anthony J Bianchi 53900 Shannon B Bican 53901 Mekola Bidanec 53902 William F Billeter 53903 Derek A Bird 53904 Boyd E Bishop 53905 Eric R Bjorklund 53906 Daniel D Blackmon 53907 Shawn Blackwell 53908 Rex L Blair 53909 James A. Bland 53910 Daniel J Blank 53911 Matthew L Blome 53912 Stephen R Boeckels 53913 Michael A Bonura 53914 Timothy J Booth 53915 David J Borden 53916 Kevin D. Bouren 53917 Zachary L Boyd 53918 Richard M Bradley 53919 James A Brady 53920 Scott E Brady 53921 Kenneth J Braeger 53922 Alexander Braszko 53923 Jeffrey T Breloski 53924 Tara S Brewer 53925 Thomas J Brewer 53926 Matthew P Brewster 53927 Bryan R Brickell 53928 Jeffrey A Brizic 53929 Kase H Brock 53930 Colin N Brooks 53931 George L Brooks 53932 Jason S Brown 53933 Matthew W Brown 53934 Wade D Brown 53935 Daniel J Browne 53936 Jimmie A Browning 53937 Harris J Brumer 53938 Corey A Brunkow 53939 Terrence H Buckeye 53940 Alexander J Buehler 53941 Brian W Buehler 53942 Alexander L Bullock 53943 Jonathon T. Bunch 53944 William D Bundy 53945 Kristopher M Bunting 53946 James J Burdsall 53947 Steven J Burkart 53948 Lisa M Burns 53949 Tiffany Q Burns 53950 Myndret C Busack 53951 Jeffrey S. Button 53952 Peter C Bylone 53953 Christopher J Byrd 53954 Todd W Cabell 53955 Charles E Calvert 53956 Darren A Campion 53957 Caren L Carbone 53958 Salomon A Carias 53959 Kristen Elizabeth Sloan 53960 Melanie I Carlson 53961 Scott D Carow 53962 Andrew C Carr 53963 Jeffrey J Carroll 53964 Michael B Carson 53965 Robert A Castillo 53966 Sedat Cevikparmak 53967 Douglas R Chadwick 53968 Adam M Chalmers 53969 Richard C Chandler 53970 Douglas L Chapman 53971 Andres F. Chaves 53972 Yvonne Chavez Miller 53973 Katina M Chesser 53974 Matthew T Chilbert 53975 James H Chipman 53976 Bryan J Chivers 53977 Damien W Choi 53978 James C Chung 53979 John G Chung 53980 Kwang U Chung 53981 Samuel A Clare 53982 Jason P Clark 53983 Rachel J Bellamy 53984 Rebecca A Clark 53985 Elisabeth A Claus 53986 Tommy J Clement 53987 David T Cloft 53988 Leo R Coddington 53989 Cactus B Coker 53990 Kaci H Cole 53991 Paul B. Cole 53992 Johnathan J Collier 53993 Michael Collorafi 53994 Jason W Condrey 53995 Christopher L Connelly 53996 Brian T Conroy 53997 David M Cook 53998 Aaron K Coombs 53999 Leah Copeland 54000 Robert C Cordray 54001 Susanne E Corlett 54002 Carla J Cornish 54003 Justin A Coussoule 54004 Daniel D Cox 54005 Justin D Cox 54006 Robyn Lynn Munson 54007 David F Coy 54008 Thomas M Coyle 54009 James R Crane 54010 Michael E Crane 54011 Timothy A Crane 54012 Kevin A Crawford 54013 Frank A Cristaudo 54014 Matthew N Cromly 54015 David A. Crossett 54016 Kobie Crowder 54017 Jeffrey L Csoka 54018 MaryHelene Cudd 54019 Craig R Cudzilo 54020 Tonya R Cultice 54021 Brian H Cunningham 54022 Joel J Cunningham 54023 Hoby F Cupp 54024 Patrick C Curran 54025 Matthew F Dabkowski 54026 Sorrel B Daggett 54027 Ian D Dancel 54028 Zachary D D'Angelo 54029 William R Daniel 54030 Brad W Davey 54031 Mark A Davino 54032 Brian M Davis 54033 Bryan J Davis 54034 Jeffry B Davis 54035 Philip D. Davis 54036 Arleigh W Dean 54037 Judson D Dean 54038 Rebecca K Dean 54039 Bryan P Decker 54040 Joel C Dees 54041 Robert L Degand 54042 Keith W DeGregory 54043 Matthew A Deloia 54044 Mark C DeLorenzo 54045 Karen Elizabeth Hernandez 54046 Thomas M Deveans 54047 Sara D Dewitz 54048 Ronald P Dibisceglie 54049 Anthony M DiCarlo 54050 Hannon A Didier 54051 Joel L Dillon 54052 John A Dimuzio 54053 Daniel F Dittenber 54054 Kelly L Dobert 54055 Richard L Dodson 54056 Linda M Donahue 54057 Samuel T Donnelly 54058 Daniel K Dorado 54059 John P Doyle 54060 Marcus J Doyle 54061 Matthews Drewery 54062 Richard J Ducote 54063 Brian E Dugan 54064 Steven J Dullack 54065 Quinntine A Dunford 54066 Che P Dungan 54067 Jeremy M Dunn 54068 Robert M Dutton 54069 Ryan W Dutton 54070 Pamela L Dziedzic 54071 Roger W Eades 54072 Jason W Easley 54073 Eric J Eberline 54074 Brendan G Ederle 54075 Scott A Ederr 54076 Kevin M Edler 54077 Gary P Edwards 54078 Jeremy V Edwards 54079 Michael S Edwards 54080 Scott A Eichelberger 54081 Aaron D Eide 54082 Aaron A Eklund 54083 Kristina M. Encarnacao 54084 James P Engelbrecht 54085 Erin P English 54086 Eric M Engquist 54087 Jeffrey R Enquist 54088 Jan R Enriquez 54089 Christopher R Erikson 54090 Phillip T Esposito 54091 Charles W Estes 54092 Joshua A Etzel 54093 Robert D Evans 54094 Daniel J Everett 54095 Joseph M Ewers 54096 Stephen A Fabiano 54097 Stephen A Fairless 54098 Michael J Falhamer 54099 Matthew N Fandre 54100 James M. Faust 54101 Frank P Fede 54102 Brad D Fenske 54103 Matthew M Ferguson 54104 Marcus M Ferrara 54105 Paul M Ferro 54106 Guy L. Filippelli 54107 Jeramie D Fitzgerald 54108 Michael O Fleener 54109 Douglas M Fletcher 54110 Andrew D Flor 54111 Michael A Florczyk 54112 Nathan A Folkert 54113 William E Fork 54114 Peter D Fraccaroli 54115 Marc J Franciszkowicz 54116 Adam B Frederick 54117 Richard P Fredricks 54118 Will B Freds 54119 Kevin M Frosch 54120 Alexis M Frum 54121 Timothy J Fuemmeler 54122 Edsel R Gacasan 54123 Daniel M Gade 54124 Matthew E Gaffigan 54125 Jeneen K Galvin 54126 Christopher P Garbarino 54127 Israel Garcic 54128 Jamie Garcia 54129 Damien T Garner 54130 Leticia Shirley Fay Boatman 54131 Garland R Gay 54132 Rebecca A. Geist 54133 Mark T Germano 54134 Hise O Gibson 54135 Lee F Gibson 54136 Christopher S Gilbert 54137 Jeremy A Gilkes 54138 Daniel J Gilmore 54139 Stephen J Gilmore 54140 Terence P Gilroy 54141 Christopher C Giunta 54142 Peter J Gizzi 54143 John P Glass 54144 Jonathan W Gleason 54145 Christian S Glowe 54146 Chet C Gnagey 54147 Joseph C Goetz 54148 Michael J Gorman 54149 Kimiko E Sullins 54150 Andrew R Graham 54151 Eric J. Grandeo 54152 Newton E Grant 54153 Richard J Grasfeder 54154 David R Graves 54155 Charles B Gray 54156 Michael E Greenbaum 54157 Jason P. Gresh 54158 Steven J Gribschaw 54159 Phillip B Griffith 54160 Marcus W Grimes 54161 Andrew C Gross 54162 David J Grossman 54163 Casey S Groves 54164 Gregory W Guimont 54165 Xiao P Guo 54166 Jonathan A Hadley 54167 Jarid L Halverson 54168 Daniel W Hampton 54169 Shepherd N Han 54170 Nathan H Hancock 54171 Eric R Hanes 54172 Taylor W Hanes 54173 Carl J Hanks 54174 Leif A Hansen 54175 Adam R Harben 54176 Michael A Harding 54177 Eric H Harmon 54178 Michael G Harris 54179 Daniel C Hart 54180 Ian W Hartley 54181 Michael J Harvey 54182 Thomas J Haslemann 54183 Nicholas P Haugen 54184 Jason M Havey 54185 Heath A Hawk 54186 Robert M Heffington 54187 Josh W. Helms 54188 Heather A Hennessy 54189 Bart G Hensler 54190 Ryan O Herath 54191 Marc L Herdegen 54192 Ernesto J Hernandez 54193 Anthony Justin Hewitt 54194 William L Heyward 54195 Randal E. Hickman 54196 Michael D Hicks 54197 Aaron T Hill 54198 Trevor W Hill 54199 Darrin M Hinman 54200 Martin C Hodell 54201 Rashad T. Hodge 54202 Russell V Hoff 54203 Christopher M Hoffman 54204 Gregory D Holt 54205 Jerry L Hood 54206 Matthew M. Hope 54207 Gavin K Hoppie 54208 Shawn E Horton 54209 John E Houk 54210 Scott L Howell 54211 Sean E Hubbard 54212 Ann Marie Perkins 54213 Ian Woodington Humphrey 54214 Mark R Hunsicker 54215 Wesley M Hunt 54216 Martin N Hunter 54217 Guy C Huntsinger 54218 Scott G Hurdis 54219 Daniel M Hurley 54220 Greg Iannuccilli 54221 Sean P Imbs 54222 Joseph F. Ingemi 54223 Brent J Ishizaki 54224 Kirk S Jackson 54225 Marcus J Jackson 54226 Matthew D Jackson 54227 Eric M Jamison 54228 Karl D Jansen 54229 James M Jardinella 54230 Piotr A Jaskolski 54231 Charles P Johnson 54232 Eric J Johnson 54233 John T. Johnson 54234 Jonathan P Johnson 54235 Matthew K Johnson 54236 William J Johnson 54237 Melissa A Jones 54238 Alan A Jordan 54239 Joe D Junguzza 54240 Matthew R Junko 54241 Theodore J Kaiser 54242 Adam P Kamann 54243 Louis J Karnes 54244 Aleksander Toom Kask 54245 Sung K Kato 54246 John M Kays 54247 Charles W Kean 54248 Colin P Kearns 54249 William R Keating 54250 Jeffrey M Kelley 54251 Peter T Kellogg 54252 George J Kelly 54253 Matthew J Kemkes 54254 James D Kemter 54255 John H. Kendall 54256 Christopher S Kennedy 54257 Joshua C Kennedy 54258 Gregory D Kent 54259 Walter E Kent 54260 Eero R Keravuori 54261 Sean P Kernan 54262 Brian A Kessens 54263 Christopher P Keup 54264 Bryan J Kewley 54265 Adib R Khoury 54266 Gregory C Kies 54267 John P Kilbride 54268 George J Kim 54269 Jin Kim 54270 John J Kim 54271 Marvin L King 54272 Stephen D King 54273 Brian P Klawikowski 54274 Theodore W Kleisner 54275 Joseph A Kling 54276 Michael F Kloepper 54277 Joshua A Knittel 54278 Timothy G Knoth 54279 Erik K Kober 54280 Timothy J Koester 54281 Pamela K Kolongowski 54282 Bernard J Kotwica 54283 Michael J Kovacevic 54284 Jacob M Kramer 54285 Jeffrey M Krassin 54286 Paul T Krattiger 54287 Daren A Krause 54288 Colleen K Kremin 54289 Kevin L Kretzschmar 54290 Jason A Kreulen 54291 Justin S Krider 54292 Kirsten A. Krucker 54293 Diana Kuykendall 54294 Ryan J Kuypers 54295 Chandra L Lagrone 54296 Michael J Lally 54297 Christopher I Lammie 54298 Edward E Lanham 54299 Erik A Larson 54300 Jonathan D Larson 54301 Kevin D Lasater 54302 Krzysztof

Laski 54303 Ayodele O Lawson 54304 David F Leavell 54305 Eun U Lee 54306 Llewellyn V Lee 54307 Mark Y Lee 54308 Rance A Lee 54309 William F Lefever 54310 Douglas M Legan 54311 Dianna H Lehn 54312 John C Lemay 54313 Richard D Lencz 54314 Jaimie E Leonard 54315 Ryan G Leonard 54316 Leo C Lesch 54317 Ronald F Leshinski 54318 Allen D. Leth 54319 Michael Lewczak 54320 Jonathan C Lewis 54321 Wei L Lim 54322 Ralph R Lindsey 54323 Robyn D Lindstrom 54324 Christopher A Linz 54325 Sean M Lock 54326 Joseph E Long 54327 Marc A Lopez 54328 Rose H Lopez 54329 Joseph R Losievsky 54330 Downing Lu 54331 Joshua J Lucas 54332 Joshua B Ludwig 54333 Ryan P Lueders 54334 Holand P Lujan 54335 Matthew W Luzzatto 54336 Robert G Lynch 54337 Jason P Maassel 54338 Brian J MacKenzie 54339 Michael J MacKinnon 54340 Thomas J Mahoney 54341 David N Main 54342 Richard A Malaga 54343 Zaheer A. Malik 54344 Sloan C Mann 54345 Katina L Manning 54346 Daniel K Mark 54347 Jonathan W Mark 54348 John N Martin 54349 Michael W Martin 54350 Mitchell Z Martin 54351 Christopher J Martindale 54352 Jon B Martinez 54353 Shane A Matarelli 54354 Amanda L May 54355 Ronnie E McAda 54356 Michael R McBride 54357 John P McCollum 54358 Ryan E McCormack 54359 Joseph R McCoy 54360 Michael D McCoy 54361 James A McDonald 54362 Richard M McDonald 54363 James K McDonough 54364 Andrew G McGlyn 54365 John K McGuire 54366 Andrew M McKee 54367 Joseph P McLaine 54368 Brian K McLaughlin 54369 Jason B McMurrough 54370 Patrick J McNamara 54371 Scott C McQuery 54372 Daniel C McTigue 54373 Jeremy G McVey 54374 James W Mechling 54375 Hector M Melendez 54376 Alexander S Mentis 54377 David S Merrill 54378 Wade D Merritt 54379 Lino Miani 54380 Richard J Michalski 54381 Benjamin D Miller 54382 Daniel R Miller 54383 Gregory W Miller 54384 Jabari M Miller 54385 Jeffrey S Miller 54386 Mickey A Miller 54387 Shay S Miller 54388 Stephen M Miller 54389 Thomas J Miller 54390 Zachary L Miller 54391 Nathan A Minami 54392 Kenneth D. Mitchell 54393 Michael J Mitchell 54394 Victoria L Mitchell 54395 Daisy C Mo 54396 Michael A Molnar 54397 Maria L Monforte 54398 Brandon J Moore 54399 Peter J Mooren 54400 Jarrod P Moreland 54401 Clay A Morgan 54402 Ryan J Morgan 54403 Alexander O Morris 54404 William J Morrison 54405 Jason D Mrochek 54406 Victor A Mroczkowski 54407 Sean C Mullin 54408 Thomas O Mullins 54409 Richard D Munson 54410 Craig M Murphy 54411 Joshua R Nagtzaam 54412 Adam J Nelson 54413 David V Nelson 54414 Shawn L Nelson 54415 William C Nelson 54416 Yu S Ng 54417 Darnell M Nicholas 54418 Keith T Nichols 54419 Joshua P Norbury 54420 Jeffrey P Nors 54421 Danielle M Kays 54422 Michael T Nuckowski 54423 Dennis E Nutt 54424 Penny M O'Kelley 54425 Jason C Oates 54426 John F Oconnor 54427 Paul S Oh 54428 Eric J Okimoto 54429 Thomas J Oliver 54430 Victor S Olshansky 54431 Erik H Olson 54432 Michael A Opdenaker 54433 Dana R Orvis 54434 Scott M Osterling 54435 Timothy R O'Sullivan 54436 Amy Ebba Edwards 54437 Eric T Paliwoda 54438 Ali W Palmer 54439 James S Palmer 54440 Jeremy C Pamplin 54441 Everett B Pannkuk 54442 Luis A Parilli 54443 Ronnie Park 54444 Joseph H Parker 54445 Rhinard D. Parry 54446 Jeremy M Patrick 54447 Ezekiel W Paxton 54448 Kelly A Rose 54449 Gregory R Pearly 54450 Jonathan J Peppard 54451 Kevin P Perakslis 54452 Stanislav R Perchev 54453 Scott M Percival 54454 Jason D. Perez 54455 David J Perkins 54456 Christopher J. Perron 54457 Ronald L Perry 54458 Stephen T Peterson 54459 Douglas S Philippone 54460 Dwight E Phillips 54461 Melissa Sue Sims 54462 Rachael Elyse Johnson 54463 Nathan J. Pickup 54464 Sandra J Willis 54465 Randy S Plotnitzky 54466 Jonathan J Pontius 54467 Jason C Porter 54468 Benjamin K Potter 54469 David C Preece 54470 Eric G Preister 54471 Kevin G Price 54472 Lawrence R Price 54473 Douglas M Pulley 54474 Jorn A Pung 54475 Jayson H Putnam 54476 Charles J Querriera 54477 Edwin J Quimby 54478 David J Radford 54479 Ralph W Radka 54480 Michael J Radke 54481 Michael S Rainey 54482 Chrispin N Rainford 54483 Cassandra Ralls 54484 Jeremy M Ramage 54485 Benjamin G Ramos 54486 Paul J Reader 54487 Jeffrey D Reamer 54488 Adam T Reese 54489 Christopher G Reid 54490 Brian M Reidy 54491 Gregory D Reim 54492 Brad A Reisinger 54493 Christopher L Reitsma 54494 Ross N Revenaugh 54495 Joanna L Reynolds 54496 William V Rice 54497 Giselle M Richards 54498 Timothy S Rickey 54499 Mary Jayne Riley 54500 Leonardo V Rinaldi 54501 Carlos E Rios 54502 Marcus M Ritter 54503 Ian R Robbins 54504 Andrew S Roberts 54505 Anne E Robertson 54506 Daniel W Robinson 54507 Robert A Robinson 54508 Christopher J Rocheleau 54509 Robert Jo Rodenmayer 54510 Elliott D Rodgers 54511 Chad M Roehrman 54512 Raul Romero 54513 Aaron K Roof 54514 Charles C Rose 54515 Michael D Rose 54516 Evangeline Grace Perry 54517 Robert K Ross 54518 Robert L Rossi 54519 Ryan J Rothmeyer 54520 Anthony C Rovano 54521 Melinda D Rowan 54522 Stephen B. Rubright 54523 Daniel W Ruecking 54524 James E Runkel 54525 Michael S Ruppert 54526 Brandon L Russell 54527 Jason L Russell 54528 John D Rutledge 54529 Jason M Sabat 54530 Matthew J Sabatino 54531 Jose D. Salinas 54532 Ike L Sallee 54533 Karen L Fluck 54534 Joseph M Savage 54535 Patrick S Saxman 54536 Megan A Scanlon 54537 Thomas D Scarberry 54538 Christopher S Schaefer 54539 Scott R Schaller 54540 Julie S Schellhase 54541 Bryce A Schlosser 54542 John H Schmonsees 54543 Kirk M Schneider 54544 Robert R Schramm 54545 Elliot D Schroeder 54546 Jonathan A Schudmak 54547 Kyle H Schultz 54548 Matthew E Schulz 54549 Bradley E Schwan 54550 David E Scott 54551 Erik J Scott 54552 Jerrod L Scott 54553 Kevin A Scott 54554 Kyle T Scott 54555 Marlon O Scott 54556 Michael C Scott 54557 Sean A Scott 54558 Thomas A Scott 54559 Scott F Scroggins 54560 Scott B Seidel 54561 Adam L Seldow 54562 Lance I Sells 54563 Aubrey D Semien 54564 David S Sentell 54565 Bryan T Shadduck 54566 Benefsheh D Shamley 54567 Joseph B Sharrock 54568 Corey N Shea 54569 Jeffrey A Sheehan 54570 Douglas J Shelton 54571 Brian D. Sherrick 54572 John W Shields 54573 Leslie A Shiozawa 54574 Andrew J Short 54575 Richard Bryan Simon 54576 William L Skimmyhorn 54577 Brent O Skinner 54578 Randie Lee Herdegen 54579 Jonathan P. Sloan 54580 Brian S Smith 54581 Christopher M. Smith 54582 Shawn D Smith 54583 William T Smith 54584 Michael C Sohn 54585 Christopher M. Soldi 54586 Joseph S Somers 54587 Peter J Song 54588 David W Spangler 54589 Michael P Speiser 54590 Richard J Spencer 54591 Tevina M Sprang 54592 Christopher J Springer 54593 Mark D Spungin 54594 Christopher T Stanford 54595 Joseph E Staromana 54596 Brian P Steele 54597 Joel I Stein 54598 Leslie A Stein 54599 Jonathan M Steinhauer 54600 Patrick B Steinhoff 54601 David T Sterling 54602 Joshua W Stewart 54603 Brady L Stout 54604 Chad A Stover 54605 Ryan L Strom 54606 Carra J Stuart 54607 Joshua M Stubbs 54608 Kurt D Stuckwisch 54609 Stephen A Suhr 54610 Brian T Sullivan 54611 Robert I Sundy 54612 Anthony A Suzzi 54613 Danny L Swancey 54614 Chihung Szeto 54615 Roger J Taneus 54616 James H Taumoepeau 54617 Momoevi S Tawake 54618 Jonathan C Taylor 54619 Mark R Taylor 54620 Matthew K Teague 54621 Matthew A Templeman 54622 Nathan V Tennant 54623 Christian G Teutsch 54624 Casey Z. Thomas 54625 Ronald F Thomas 54626 Mikkel L Thompson 54627 Todd G Thornburg 54628 Michael B Tice 54629 Robert B Tier 54630 Anthony L Tingle 54631 Aaron J Titus 54632 Laurel A Toffey 54633 Kevin R Toner 54634 Ethan E Topping 54635 George M. Torres 54636 Brandon K Trevino 54637 Rebecca Anna Clement 54638 Patricia A Byrd 54639 Keven G Truesdell 54640 Michael S Tudor 54641 Duane A Turner 54642 John F Turner 54643 Timothy Scott Turner 54644 Edward S Twaddell 54645 Peter J Twedell 54646 Jerrold J Tyquiengco 54647 Jackie J Ulrich 54648 Brad A Underwood 54649 Daniel J Underwood 54650 Robert M Urban 54651 Kyle A Vahle 54652 Eric A Vanek 54653 Travis M Van Hecke 54654 Johannas C Vanlierop 54655 Zachary A Vann 54656 Tony K Verenna 54657 James T Vibbert 54658 Juan P. Villasenor 54659 Matthew C Vinton 54660 David P Vodila 54661 Petr Vohralik 54662 Jared H Voigts 54663 Josh L Waddy 54664 Michael P Wagner 54665 Randolph J Wagner 54666 Robert M Wagner 54667 Joseph C Walchko 54668 Leland W Waldrup 54669 Gregory Harold Wall 54670 Timothy Scott Wallace 54671 Wayne M Wallace 54672 Eric R Wallet 54673 Kathleen J Walls 54674 John R. Walters 54675 Keith R Walters 54676 Jason A Wands 54677 Brian K Ward 54678 Jason T Warren 54679 David D Watkins 54680 William J Watson 54681 Leo J Waugh 54682 Christopher M Weathers 54683 Michael V Weaver 54684 Robert E Webb 54685 Ian P Weikel 54686 Aaron S Welch 54687 Holly A Wells 54688 Edwin B Werkheiser 54689 Brandon A West 54690 Michael R West 54691 Joseph E Whaley 54692 Jeffrey D Wheaton 54693 John C White 54694 Anthony M. Wilcox 54695 Edwin A Williams 54696 Steven M Williams 54697 Demitra LaTon Williamson 54698 Joseph M Willis 54699 Elizabeth A Wilson 54700 John M Wilson 54701 Keith W Wilson 54702 Susan L Alden 54703 David M Wimberley 54704 James E Winland 54705 Heather A Winters 54706 Matthew H Winters 54707 Christopher B Witt 54708 Diane W. Ashley 54709 Michael J Woitalla 54710 Erik E Wolbach 54711 Jacob G Wolf 54712 Thomas T Wong 54713 Kevin M Woods 54714 Daniel A Woolverton 54715 Patrick E. Workman 54716 Ryan L Worthan 54717 Dena M Braeger 54718 Jason P Wright 54719 Pamela Shonette Blackwell 54720 James R Yastrzemsky 54721 Samuel C Yim 54722 Christopher S. Young 54723 David G Young 54724 James L Young 54725 John B Young 54726 Virgil J Yumo 54727 Walter D Zacherl 54728 Mark M Zais 54729 Matthew M Zais 54730 Michael A Zeppieri 54731 Kenneth R Ziniti 54732 Vasiliki Droste 54733 Anthony E Zupancic 54734 Carlos K Fernandez 54735 Patricia M Gabriel 54736 Paul O Hartman 54737 Mark C Paine 54738 Salamasinaleilani Tamara Strokin 54739 Fernando D. Vaughn 54740 Christopher J Farmer 54741 Joseph Lane Bader 54742 Sargent M. Binkley 54743 Eugene Henry Cabusao 54744 Michael F. Coerper 54745 Nelson J. David 54746 Sean P. Falconi 54747 Christopher L. T. Harris 54748 James R. Henry 54749 Timothy J. Michalek 54750 Wayne D. Pare 54751 Tony E. Reed 54752 Sean M. Sebastian 54753 Nathan W. Smith 54754 Michael E. Tews 54755 **1998** Brian Edward Abell 54756 Scott Alan Abram 54757 Barclay Ray Adams 54758 Freddy Lee Adams 54759 David Nelson Addams 54760 James Patrick Adkins 54761 Travis Dean Adkins 54762 Kyle Dean Aemisegger 54763 Jarvis Toa Afualo 54764 Richard Caesar Aguirre 54765 Joseph Curtis Alexander 54766 Christopher Gregg Alff 54767 Michael Peter Allman 54768 Benjamin Thomas Ambrose 54769 Anon Allen Ames 54770 Russell Jacob Ames 54771 Robert Renn Amstead 54772 Kenneth Joseph Anderle 54773 James Jeffrey Anderson 54774 Ryan James Anderson 54775 Jonathan David Angelo 54776 Robert Paul Appledorn 54777 Zachary Marshall Arthurs 54778 Jamie Janine Arundell 54779 Jeffrey William Au 54780 Andrew Vilis Auns 54781 Michael Steven Avey 54782 Caroline Jacora Ayres 54783 Scott Anthony Bacco 54784 Christopher Henry Bachmann 54785 Stephanie Anne Bagley 54786 Peter Erik Bailey 54787 Kevin Michael Baird 54788 Michael Brian Baka 54789 Gregory Wayne Baker 54790 Larry V Baker 54791 Darren Ryan Baldwin 54792 Antoinette Marie Bonenberger 54793 Dennis Kevin Banks 54794 David Arquiza Barber 54795 Martin James Barnes 54796 William Andrew Barresi 54797 Manuel Joseph Bartolini 54798 Louray Cheryl Barton 54799 David Thomas Beard 54800 Thomas Arland Beckstrand 54801 Stephen Reed Beckwith 54802 Adolf Jerry Beil 54803 Jerry Jr Bell 54804 Nathan Thomas Bellinger 54805 David Matthew Benedict 54806 Lawrence William Bengal 54807 Matthew Curran Benigni 54808 Mark Earl Bennett 54809 Erik Wayne Benton 54810 Joseph William Berendzen 54811 Joshua Franklin Berry 54812 Sean Michael Bick 54813 Wade Chandler Birdwell 54814 Richard Alan Blackburn 54815 Banaise Patrick Blake 54816 William Carl Blake 54817 David Lee Blank 54818 Veronika Martina Blasko 54819 James Frederick Block 54820 Eric Arthur Blomstedt 54821 Brian Richard Bodenman 54822 Charles Dewayne Bonner 54823 Ann Elizabeth Bonney 54824 Joshua Randall Bookout 54825 Jackson Robert Booth 54826 Albert George Bossar 54827 Ryan Walter Boulais 54828 Shannon Marie Boyce 54829 Robert Douglas Boyd 54830 John Patrick Boyle 54831 Kenneth Paul Bradley 54832 Scott Alexander Bradley 54833 Anthony Lee Bradway 54834 Christopher Nathan Breard 54835 Brian William Brennan 54836 Christian Thomas Bright 54837 Kirk Evans Brinker 54838 Joseph John Brocht 54839 Barbara Marie Brodzinski 54840 Timothy Mark Brower 54841 Andrew Robert Brown 54842 Matthew Philip Brown 54843 Phillip Byron Brown 54844 Robert Gerome Brown 54845 Jason Edward Brumbelow 54846 Joshua William Bryan 54847 Robert Kevin Bryant 54848 Jerry Robert Buchanan 54849 Kevin Thomas Buehler 54850 Michael Timothy Bukowski 54851 Rebecca Louise Bunch 54852 David Russell Bunker 54853 Rhett Erin Burbank 54854 Matthew Anthony Burkholder 54855 Anthony J Burns 54856 Keith James Burns 54857 Louis Joseph Burts 54858 Andrew Robert Bury 54859 Matthew Dwight Butt 54860 Jack Wallace Butters 54861 Raymond Joseph Butts 54862 Melvin Leon Byrd 54863 Jonathan E Cacy 54864 Bryce Lee Callahan 54865 Brendan Callanan 54866 Matthew Thomas Camire 54867 Jason Lee Campbell 54868 Keith Mitchell Campbell 54869 Richard Terrance Capka 54870 Edward Scott Carden 54871 Christopher Alan Carey 54872 Joshua Andrew Carlisle 54873 Neal David Carlson 54874 Kathleen Elizabeth Carr 54875 Daniel Martin Cartaya 54876 Daniel Patrick Castellaneta 54877 Charles Dylan Cathey 54878 Rachel Dawn Cazier 54879 Joseph Ross Cenni 54880 Daryl Allen Chamberlain 54881 Brian Allen Chapin 54882 Jeremy Jiggs Chapman 54883 Peter Henry Chapman 54884 Peter Kerr Chase 54885 David Allen Cheek 54886 Peter Peihung Chen 54887 James Clifton Cheney 54888 Gary Robert Chisholm 54889 Kwok Fai Chiu 54890 Ryan Thomas Choate 54891 Eugene Stewart Choi 54892 Chaval Chompucot 54893 Jonathan Matthew Chung 54894 John Joseph Ciccarello 54895 Andrew David Claar 54896 Darren Michael Clapprood 54897 Robert Michael Clement 54898 Alan Theodore Clinard 54899 Thomas Richard Coccaro 54900 Robert James Coker 54901 Justin Kendig Colbert 54902 Njeri Sana Colbert 54903 Matthew William Coldsnow 54904 Matthew Hersh Cole 54905 David Joseph Conk 54906 Christopher Francis Conley 54907 William Patrick Connelly 54908 Alan Ardist Conner 54909 John Philip Cooney 54910 Nathan Lane Cooper 54911 Carolyn Jane Copcutt 54912 Ben Coronado 54913 Anthony Lee Costello 54914 Tiwana Lynn Coutee 54915 Edward Lee Cox 54916 Donald Eugene Crawford 54917 Eric Daniel Crispino 54918 Robert Allen Croke 54919 Wade Allen Cross 54920 Jason Howard Cuneo 54921 Cuyler Gavin Cunningham 54922 Steven Boyd Cunningham 54923 Ryan William Currie 54924 Daphne Denise Curtin 54925 Quinn Colin Cusson 54926 Wyatt Edwin Cutler 54927 Matthew Paul Cuviello 54928 Nathan Stephen Dalley 54929 Marc Thomas Dalziel 54930 Martin James Damato 54931 Matthew Wayne Damborsky 54932 Daniel Andrew Danczyk 54933 Rebecca Jean Dangelo 54934 Dustin Michael Davis 54935 Eric Robert Davis 54936 John Robert Davison 54937 Paul Marino Dececchis 54938 Richard De Nava 54939 William Francis Deakyne 54940 Robert Andrew Dees 54941 Damon Andrew Delarosa 54942 Krista Nicole Delaura 54943 Joseph-Manue Rober Delemos 54944 Christopher Scott Denham 54945 Sharla Jean Denlinger 54946 Mark Joseph Derocchi 54947 Anthony John Desimone 54948 Joshua John Detillio 54949 Allan William Deware 54950 Ludwig Diaz 54951 Danielle Marie Dibacco 54952 Jeffrey Stephen Dietz 54953 Michael Lee Dinkins 54954 David Andrew Djuric 54955 Darren Shane Doherty 54956 Kenneth Henry Dojaquez 54957 Mark Allen Donaphon 54958 Aram Mourad Donigian 54959 John Colin Donlin 54960 Riley Drew Donoho 54961 Robert Frank Douglas 54962 Stephen Edward Douglas 54963 James William Downing 54964 Lyman Cummings Doyle 54965 Brian Michael Dudzik 54966 Andrew Dudzikowski 54967 Jonathan Lee Due 54968 Patrick Gavin Duffy 54969 Brian Mitschele Duncan 54970 Bryan Gustave Dunn 54971 Christian Dean Dunning 54972 Andrew John Duus 54973 Kenneth Edward Dworczyk 54974 Holly Anne Dzwilefsky 54975 Joseph Christopher Demike 54976 Katrina Eaker Walters 54977 Jeffrey Alexander Edmonds 54978 Jeffrey Edward Edwards 54979 Stein William Edwards 54980 William David Edwards 54981 James Michael Egan 54982 Christian Elliott Ehret 54983 Nathan Israel Eldredge 54984 James Thomas Eldridge 54985 Gabriel Enrique Elvir 54986 Steven K Emanuel 54987 Scott Joseph Emmel 54988 Jeffrey John Enck 54989 William Curtis Enger 54990 Cynthia Mae Ensell 54991 Sherilyn Ann Epperson 54992 Jolie Ann Erickson 54993 Peter Anthony Escalle 54994 Jamison Anne Fadely 54995 Scott Brian Fagan 54996 Karen F. Radka 54997 Adeyinka Akanbi Faleti 54998 Matthew Sean Farmer 54999 Anthony Philip Felice 55000 Reubin Benjamin Felkey 55001 Timothy Joseph Ferber 55002 Raymond Joseph Fields 55003 James Patrick Finan 55004 Lawrence Howard Fink 55005 Jeremy Jon Finn 55006 Elizabeth Ann Fiston 55007 Joseph Edward Fitts 55008 Michael Sherida Fitzharris 55009 Brian Edward Flores 55010 Jason Alexander Foerter 55011 John Patrick Fogarty 55012 Alonzo Quentin Ford 55013 Jeffrey Edward Forgach 55014 Chad Robert Foster 55015 Stephen William Frank 55016 Aaron Lee Freeman 55017 Bo Bradley French 55018 Taneha Niche Friend 55019 Candice Elaine Frost 55020 Christopher Fuhriman 55021 James Glen Fussell 55022 William Nathan Gaddis 55023 Marc Paul Gaguzis 55024 Matthew Joseph Gallant 55025 Scott Robert Galloway 55026 Mark Allen Gardner 55027 Gregory Paul Gass 55028 Joseph Rich Geary 55029 John Joseph Geis 55030 Edward Frank Gelsone 55031 Christian Dennis Gemar 55032 Joseph Carl Geraci 55033 Kevin Joseph Gersch 55034 Jeffrey Tyler Gibbons 55035 William Ray Gibbs 55036 Jill Nadine Giddings 55037 Nathan Douglas Ginos 55038 Corey Aaron Givens 55039 Peter Glantzis 55040 Kelby Tyson Glass 55041 Joshua Logan Glendening 55042 Philip Woodrow Goddard 55043 William Howard Goin 55044 Michael Thomas Golden 55045 Patsky Oridel Gomez 55046 Matthew Jacob Gomlak 55047 Jason Luz Gonzalez 55048 Jason Dale Good 55049 Brian Thomas Gordon 55050 Neal Harry Gouck 55051 Richard Scott Goyette 55052 David Lee Graves 55053 David C. Gray 55054 Jason Gabriel Green 55055 Sakima A.G. Brown 55056 Matthew Evan Greer 55057 Jordan Christopher Gros 55058 Gretchen Sue Grotrian 55059 Bryan Nelson Groves 55060 George Kostanty Guszcza 55061 Chandler Lewis Hadlock 55062 Jennifer Lynn Hafey 55063 Michael James Hahn 55064 Steven Martin Haley 55065 Shawn David Hall 55066 Stephen Mark Hall 55067 Joseph Cread Halsey 55068 Stephen Samuel Hamilton 55069 Todd Richard Hamilton 55070 Lorraine Leslie Hampton 55071 Martin Radell Handy 55072 Robert James Hannah 55073 Brian Russell Hannon 55074 Brian Michael Hansen 55075 Brian Patrick Hare 55076 Burke Alexander Hare 55077 Sally Dolan Harrington 55078 Scott Michael Harrington 55079 Bryan Mark Harris 55080 Ralph John Harting 55081 Jonathan Michael Hartley 55082 Douglas Randolph Haskin 55083 Matthew Douglas Hasting 55084 John Jeremy Hawbaker 55085 Marcus Christian Hay 55086 Malcolm Gibran Haynes 55087 Clinton Sean Hays 55088 Kevin Matthew Heffernan 55089 Kevin Patrick Hegarty 55090 Eric Craig Heinle 55091 Michael Don Helton 55092 Thomas Edwin Hemphill 55093 Harold Paulk Henderson 55094 Shawn Christian Henley 55095 Luke Martin Herbert 55096 Wade Druery Herman 55097 Nicholas Morgan Hermes 55098 Joel Martin Hermsdorfer 55099 Randall Manuel Herrera 55100 Aaron Fisher Hetherington 55101 Eric Alex Hettinga 55102 Michael Brandon Hiatt 55103 Jaime Elizabeth Hicks 55104 George Adam Hodges 55105 Charles Peter Hoenig 55106 Luke Jamin Hofmann 55107 Zachary Benjamin Hohn 55108 Robert Carrol Holcomb 55109 Robert Joseph Holcombe 55110 Vanessa Lindley Holden 55111 Jason Brett Holeman 55112 Paul William Hollenack 55113 James Kevin Hopping 55114 Christopher Michael Hosmer 55115 Katherine Anne Howard 55116 James David Hoyman 55117

Joseph James Hudak 55118 Samuel Harris Huddleston 55119 Jay Todd Huffman 55120 Anthony Emanuel Hughley 55121 Michael Raymond Hunt 55122 Beth Anne Hurlburt 55123 Micaela R Hurley 55124 John Daniel Hurst 55125 Nathan Coleman Hurt 55126 John Damon Huse 55127 John Milton Huzinec 55128 Daniel S Hwang 55129 Kristina Ann Hymore 55130 Thomas John Iak 55131 Michael Christopher Igoe 55132 Richard Ken Inae 55133 Maureen Elizabeth August 55134 Jeffrey Eugene Ivey 55135 Kevin Darrell Jackson 55136 Charles Hillman Jacobs 55137 Jeremy Wayne James 55138 Randy Paul James 55139 Ho Jang 55140 Shannon Estelle Janosky 55141 Erica Lynn Jeffries 55142 Joshua Richard Jent 55143 William Steven Joachim 55144 Christopher Branden Johnson 55145 Eric Andrew Johnson 55146 Jeffrey Titus Johnson 55147 Jennifer Toby Johnson 55148 Justin Robert Johnson 55149 Matthew Carl Johnson 55150 Harry Howard Jones 55151 Paul Anthony Jones 55152 Therese Elena Jones 55153 Nathaniel Glover Jordan 55154 Corey Robert Joyal 55155 Brett Michael Judkins 55156 Andrew Gabriel Jugan 55157 Erin Elizabeth Julien 55158 Oliver William Kabry 55159 Jeffrey Casimer Kacala 55160 Sean Douglas Kaine 55161 Robert Lawrence Kay 55162 Joshua Monroe Keena 55163 Leonard Cornelius Kennedy 55164 Matthew Roman Kestian 55165 Ryan Daniel Keys 55166 Erin Easter Kilgore 55167 Stephen Lloyd Killion 55168 Eugene Hong Kim 55169 Joseph Kim 55170 Byron Wayne King 55171 Jason Mendel King 55172 Matthew Keith King 55173 Judson Andrew Kingman 55174 Aaron David Kirkpatrick 55175 John Christian Klag 55176 Jennifer Jeane Knight 55177 Kyle Andrew Knotts 55178 Jeffrey Russell Knudson 55179 Matthew Damien Koehler 55180 Jason Thomas Kostal 55181 Mark Alan Kotasek 55182 Tiffany Marie Chapman 55183 Louis John Kousouris 55184 George Evangel Koutsopetras 55185 Gregorz Krol 55186 Jeffrey Christopher Kunard 55187 Eric Chikara Kunitake 55188 Erik Michael Lacom 55189 Sara Michelle Lacy 55190 Donald Judd Lagrange 55191 Brian Joseph Lamarca 55192 Kashta Amad Lambert 55193 Kevin Wayne Landtroop 55194 Jason Robert Lantrip 55195 Thomas Stuart Lark 55196 Jacob Jeremy Larkowich 55197 Lynden Latiak 55198 Matthew Joseph Lawton 55199 Thomas Edward Laybourn 55200 Randy John Laylo 55201 Thomas Earle Layton 55202 Viet Quoc Le 55203 Christopher Edwa Leadbetter 55204 Eddy June Lee 55205 Carlo David Legge 55206 Emily Elizabeth Regennitter 55207 Sally Catherine Levotch 55208 Adam James Lewis 55209 Anthony Michael Leyva 55210 Theodore Terence Liebreich 55211 Ted Tae Lim 55212 Michael Lee Lindley 55213 Edward Charles Linneweber 55214 Jesse John Lipscomb 55215 Michael Andrew Lipsner 55216 Kelley D'Arcy Litzner 55217 Daryl Dean Looney 55218 Bavy Uriah Lopez 55219 Scot Alan Lord 55220 John Frederick Lory 55221 Steven Robert Lott 55222 Catherine Anne Loughman 55223 Daniel Wayne Lowry 55224 David Victor Lozano 55225 Fernando Martinez Lujan 55226 Jeffrey Raymond Luke 55227 Andrew Saul Lunoff 55228 Michael Frank Luraschi 55229 Phillip Leslie Lust 55230 Brent Herman Lyew 55231 Katarzyna Maria Maas 55232 Steven Copeland Madray 55233 Shadwell Alan Madsen 55234 Patrick James Maginn 55235 Timothy Michael Mahoney 55236 John Anthony Mailman 55237 Franklin Duane Maizner 55238 David Ian Malkin 55239 Anthony Charles Mancari 55240 David Thomas Manley 55241 Peter Joseph Manternach 55242 Christopher Edward Marks 55243 Peter James Marques 55244 Lawrence Morales Martin 55245 Matthew Benjamin Martin 55246 Scott Evan Martin 55247 William Joseph Martin 55248 Alex Tomas Martinez 55249 Kimberly Titilayo Martins 55250 John Spencer Mask 55251 Franklin Craig Massey 55252 Jarret Daniel Mathews 55253 Daniel Patrick Mauro 55254 David Neal Mayo 55255 Phillip Walker Mazingo 55256 James Louis Mazurek 55257 Corbett Finley McCallum 55258 Shannon Marie McCarthy 55259 Andrew Spencer McCleery 55260 Travis Ryan McCollum 55261 Kevin Patrick McCoy 55262 Yolanda Dee McCray 55263 Shamgar Elijah McDowell 55264 Douglas Alan McElravy 55265 Kyle Alan McFarland 55266 Joshua David McGary 55267 Travis Lyn McIntosh 55268 Brian David McKell 55269 Kristian Roy McKenney 55270 Geoffrey Michael McKenzie 55271 Jeremy Joseph McKnight 55272 James Butler McLean 55273 Keith David McManus 55274 Geoffrey Leroy McMurray 55275 Evan Raymond McNamara 55276 Christopher Willi McQuillan 55277 Timothy Tyler Measner 55278 Margarita Georgieva Vencill 55279 Patrick Mcmahon Mellon 55280 Vanessa Lawson 55281 Todd Andrew Messinger 55282 Elizabeth Lacourse Mahoney 55283 Jason Paul Meyer 55284 John Jeremy Meyers 55285 Ryan Mark Miedema 55286 Jonathan Michael Mihalka 55287 Craig Alan Mikolajchak 55288 Brian Paul Miles 55289 Bradley Stephen Miller 55290 Christopher Mclennan Miller 55291 Conor Hayes Miller 55292 Edward Daniel Miller 55293 Erin Catherine Miller 55294 Katharine King Corliss 55295 Patrick Joseph Miller 55296 Zachary Forrest Miller 55297 Charles Dion Milliner 55298 Mardi Loreane Mills 55299 Robert Granville Mitchell 55300 Sonya Lynn Mitchell 55301 Andrew William Moehring 55302 Samuel Edward Mokhiber 55303 Michael Paul Monaco 55304 Daniel George Monahan 55305 Jason Charles Monteiro 55306 Peter Jeong Moon 55307 Alexander Quintin Moore 55308 Nathan John Moore 55309 Adam Warren Morgan 55310 Andrew Richard Morgan 55311 Christopher Scott Morris 55312 Steven Wayne Morris 55313 Jerome Loren Moss 55314 Kristi Jo Mouw 55315 Pedro Gilberto Moya 55316 Peter Daniel Muench 55317 Michael Francis Mulherin 55318 James Edward Mullin 55319 Anthony Wallace Mullinax 55320 Joseph Dean Mullins 55321 Daniel Steele Murray 55322 Ian Harold Murray 55323 Wayne Bactad Nankil 55324 Philip James Nazzaro 55325 Hauke Guenter Nehrenheim 55326 Scott Jay Nelson 55327 Douglas Chamberlain Nesmith 55328 Jason William Newby 55329 Ryan Dean Newman 55330 Jonathan Aaron Newsom 55331 David James Nightengale 55332 Michael David Nordeen 55333 Rudy Gregorio Noriega 55334 Ian Alexander Northrop 55335 Inez Margaret Nowicki 55336 Neil Clement Nunberg 55337 John Henry O'Brien 55338 Timothy Joseph O'Connor 55339 Joseph Eugene O'Hanlon 55340 Jefferson Oakes 55341 Therese Lela Obidinski 55342 John Joseph O'Connell 55343 Laura Lynn Olen 55344 Joshua Grover Olf 55345 Stephen William Oliver 55346 Jeremy Lynn Olson 55347 Roger Bernal Ordonez 55348 Frederick Harada Orndorff 55349 Daniel Russell Ostrowski 55350 Stanley Kipper Overstreet 55351 Jennifer Vreeland Owens 55352 Michael Shane Owings 55353 Gasper Victor Pace 55354 Christopher Sutton Page 55355 Ramit Palmer 55356 Nicola Jason Palmisciano 55357 Gregory Glimis Pappas 55358 Randolph Jihoon Park 55359 Geoffrey Adam Parker 55360 Brad Aaron Pasho 55361 Mark Anthony Patanella 55362 Bradley Scott Paulsen 55363 Andrew Lindsay Pearce 55364 Robert David Peatman 55365 Timothy Edward Peck 55366 Holly Anne Pedley 55367 Manuel Antonio Perotin 55368 Brian David Perry 55369 Christopher Theodore Perry 55370 Demetrius Rashun Perry 55371 Benjamin Jacob Peterson 55372 Christopher Allan Pickett 55373 Dennis Lloyd Pintor 55374 Gregory Dale Pipes 55375 Bryan Christopher Pohlman 55376 Sara Elizabeth Pollak 55377 Michael Jason Ponchak 55378 Matthew Shane Pounders 55379 James Joseph Powell 55380 Christopher Andrew Powers 55381 Joel Craig Prather 55382 Bryan Christopher Price 55383 Bradley Michael Prugh 55384 Anderson Harwell Puckett 55385 Gregory Edward Punch 55386 Justin Craig Purdy 55387 Ryan Scott Purdy 55388 Adrienne Christine Quimby 55389 Adam Eugene Radicic 55390 Chad Michael Ramskugler 55391 Jay Perry Rangaram 55392 Melissa Elisabeth Rau 55393 Eric Wilhelm Rawie 55394 Christopher B Regennitter 55395 Thomas Matthew Register 55396 Kristoff Rewi Reid 55397 Malcolm Brian Reid 55398 Mitchell Lawrence Reid 55399 Jason Stephen Reiss 55400 Andrew Warren Reiter 55401 Kevin Edward Remus 55402 Nathan Paul Rettig 55403 John Benjamin Richey 55404 William Bryan Riddle 55405 Chad Frederick Rising 55406 Michelle Madeleine Robbins 55407 John Thomas Roberson 55408 David Michael Roberts 55409 Phylisha Artena Robinson 55410 Rafael Angel Rodriguez 55411 Matthew Byrne Rogers 55412 Craig Bruce Rohrbough 55413 Scott James Roney 55414 Daniel Alan Rowell 55415 Francisco Carlos Rubio 55416 Kurt Warren Ruch 55417 Juan-Carlos Federico Ruck 55418 Robert Thomas Ruckman 55419 Ryan Thomas Ruhl 55420 Page Anndi Emmel 55421 Bradley Joseph Ruther 55422 Andrew Tyrell Sabata 55423 Steven Alex Sabo 55424 Joseph Henry Sachitano 55425 Lee Edward Sagerson 55426 Darcy Rozel Saint-Amant 55427 Amy Ann Sanchez 55428 Heather Lee Dawson 55429 Nathan Allen Sandvig 55430 Gregory Vincent Santillo 55431 Allison Durga Saunders 55432 John Charles Scalia 55433 Thomas Michael Scanzillo 55434 Justin Charles Schaeffer 55435 Paul Andrew Schaffer 55436 Michael Edward Schauss 55437 Johnathan Christoph Scheele 55438 Joel Wesley Schell 55439 Franklin Bernard Scherra 55440 Rodney Paul Schmucker 55441 Dustin James Schrock 55442 Gerald Patrick Schuck 55443 Michael Scott Scioletti 55444 Douglas Cameron Scott 55445 Ryan Daniel Seagreaves 55446 Jason Raymond Sedlak 55447 Nathan Erick Self 55448 Robert Paul Semmens 55449 Andre W Senenko 55450 Amanda Marie Sentelle 55451 John Sheldon Serafini 55452 Jeremy Scott Sereno 55453 Michael Chad Setliff 55454 Jonathan Kirby Shaffner 55455 Daniel Frank Shaheen 55456 Jacob Wesley Shaver 55457 James Anthony Shaw 55458 Steven Bryant Shaw 55459 Timothy George Shelhamer 55460 Justin Rennie Shell 55461 Courtney Craig Shepherd 55462 Jeffrey Anderson Showalter 55463 Bryan Padraic Shrank 55464 Alan Dale Sicat 55465 Benjamin Fons Siebold 55466 Michael Joseph Silvestro 55467 Benjamin Raymond Simms 55468 Shane Derek Sims 55469 Stephen Andrew Skinner 55470 Timothy Jay Slicker 55471 Domenico Smeraglia 55472 Justin Jon Smeya 55473 Lyncoln Daniel Smith 55474 Matthew Lee Smith 55475 Ryan Mitchell Smith 55476 Troy Steven Smith 55477 Coler Don Snelleman 55478 Sang-Min Sok 55479 Michael Thomas Sokoll 55480 Bill Chang Song 55481 Darin Michael Souza 55482 John Charles Speece 55483 Sean Alistair Spence 55484 Scott Christopher Spieth 55485 Michael John Spinello 55486 Ryan Sol Spoon 55487 Scott Ryan Sprawls 55488 Scott Robert Spurrier 55489 Michael Thomas Squires 55490 Nicholas Stankovich 55491 William Joseph Starr 55492 Bonnie Blue Stefan 55493 Paul Daniel Stefens 55494 Sarah Grace Watts 55495 Anthony Jacob Stokely 55496 Bradley Howard Stoltz 55497 Marc Thomas Stotz 55498 Shannondoah Dairl Strange 55499 David Christian Strohm 55500 Gregory Michael Stroud 55501 Toihunta Stubbs 55502 Jason Paul Suber 55503 Jang Hyuk Suh 55504 Matthew Yulkwon Sung 55505 Nathan Scott Surrey 55506 Matthew Alan Sutton 55507 Aaron Coleman Swain 55508 Wendy Theresa Weikel 55509 John Paul Sweeny 55510 Eric Raymond Swenson 55511 Robert John Tackett 55512 Michael Morgan Talbot 55513 Jenny Kai-Yee Tam 55514 Elizabeth Frances Angerman 55515 Melinda Beth Thein 55516 Michael Glenn Taylor 55517 Robert Wesley Taylor 55518 Stephen Cadigan Taylor 55519 Thomas Howard Taylor 55520 William Jeremy Taylor 55521 Abelardo Damian Terpin 55522 John Kristen Terrill 55523 Krist George Thodoropoulos 55524 Amy Elizabeth Thomas 55525 Jerry James Thomas 55526 Adam Courtney Thompson 55527 Sonny Angelo Thompson 55528 John David Thresher 55529 Timothy John Tiger 55530 Gregory Scott Tily 55531 Jason Matthew Todd 55532 William Scott Todd 55533 Michael John Todryk 55534 Stacy Marie Tomic 55535 Jason Louis Torczynski 55536 Mario Andres Tovar 55537 Gabriel Robert Trexler 55538 Matthew Perry Tucker 55539 Richard Patrick Tucker 55540 James Edward Tully 55541 Bunyamin Tuner 55542 James Nathan Turner 55543 Jeremy Richmond Turner 55544 Scott Christopher Turner 55545 Theodore O'bryan Unbehagen 55546 Raymond George Val 55547 Andrew Joseph Valles 55548 Jeffrey Alan VanAntwerp 55549 Stephen Anthony Vanduzee 55550 Peter Davis Van Epps 55551 Robert Anthony Vecchiarelli 55552 Pattie Maria Showalter 55553 Adrian Velazquez 55554 Joseph Scott Viles 55555 Scott Matthew Virgil 55556 Andrew Kyle Visser 55557 Johny Michael Vlachakis 55558 Paul Clarke Voelke 55559 Victor Albert Vogel 55560 Matthew Aaron Wade 55561 Kandace Michelle Walker 55562 Craig Forest Walsh 55563 James Andrew Walton 55564 Scott Robert Wangen 55565 Mark John Wanish 55566 Matthew John Wanzeck 55567 Victor Bryant Ward 55568 Margaret Elizabeth Warner 55569 Charles Burtis Warren 55570 Erik Michael Watson 55571 Rufus Dwayne Watson 55572 James Anthony Watts 55573 Jason Watts 55574 Mark Christian Weaver 55575 John Christopher Webb 55576 Scott Edward Weiss 55577 Thad Daniel Weist 55578 Jacob Michael Wenz 55579 Timothy Sean Werner 55580 William Schyler West 55581 Jason Robert Whipple 55582 Eric William Widmar 55583 Bryan Joseph Wiley 55584 James Bradley Wilke 55585 Christopher Todd Williams 55586 Colin Jay Williams 55587 Edward O. Williams 55588 Sai Gabriel Williams 55589 Jason Alvin Wilson 55590 Robert Brian Wilson 55591 Samuel David Wilson 55592 David Charles Wimberly 55593 Benjamin Michael Witt 55594 Nathon Allen Woelke 55595 Courtlandt Dixon Wolbe 55596 Ryan John Wolfe 55597 Marie Elizabeth Wolff 55598 Burris Douglas Wollseiffer 55599 John Steven Woo 55600 Michael Christian Woodall 55601 George Lee Woods 55602 Cally Lynne Worman 55603 Patrick Elonious Wright 55604 Jim Shun Wu 55605 Ryan Brendan Wylie 55606 Gerald Todd Wyngaard 55607 Daniel Misha Yaciuk 55608 Anthony Weston Yeatts 55609 Jessica Beth Yerdon 55610 Hyeong-Jin Yoon 55611 Matthew Johns Yost 55612 Daniel Robert Young 55613 David James Young 55614 Karen Elizabeth Hofmann 55615 Bradley Richard Zagol 55616 Lisa Z. Geis 55617 Troy Edward Zeidman 55618 Michael Carl Zievers 55619 Dan Emilian Zugrav 55620 Young Seung-Moo Kam 55621 James David Maxwell 55622 John Nathan Maynard 55623 Wesley Gene McDonald 55624 Jason Anderson Reese 55625 Amanda Kathleen Zimon 55626 Paul Bates Bednar 55627 Richard Eugene Bratton 55628 Robert Hyun Chung 55629 June Shamine Copeland 55630 James Charles Hundt 55631 Christopher John Kirk 55632 Jeffrey Blanton Martinez 55633 Mark Peter Oskar 55634 Joseph John Shimerdla 55635 Chad Alan Suitonu 55636 Douglas Spencer Williams 55637 Steven Phillip Wright 55638 **1999** Michael Paul Abar 55639 Matthew Darrell Abel 55640 Abigail Lynn Adams 55641 Cary Lee Adams 55642 James Joseph Adams 55643 Roger Edwin Adamson 55644 Frederick Nicholas Albrecht 55645 Jason Pierre Albright 55646 Edith Elizabeth Alcorn 55647 Joshua Andrew Alcorn 55648 Nathan Gerard Allard 55649 Robert Frederick Allee 55650 David Mark Allen 55651 Mark Richard Allen 55652 Hugh Randolph Allyn 55653 Norine Mali Miller 55654 Charlotte Leigh Anders 55655 David Tansu Anders 55656 Derek Jason Anderson 55657 Heath Ernest Anderson 55658 Joseph Edward Anderson 55659 Kelley Lynn Anderson 55660 Robert Brian Anderson 55661 Spencer Myles Anderson 55662 Jakub Hubert Andrews 55663 Marc Richard Angle 55664 Donald Paul Appleman 55665 William Charles Arnett 55666 Dion Eric Atchison 55667 Lance Damon Awbrey 55668 Thomas Adam Babbitt 55669 Trent Nathan Baer 55670 Bradley Ryan Baggett 55671 Brian Wade Bagley 55672 Aaron Samuel Bailey 55673 Marc Rolland Bailey 55674 Andrew John Baker 55675 Ian Wesley Baldwin 55676 Myra Lynn Baldwin 55677 Samara Rene Ballard 55678 Todd Patrick Balog 55679 Andrew William Balthazor 55680 Anthony Paul Barbina 55681 Robert Leonard Barnes 55682 Aaron Daniel Barreda 55683 Eric David Barrett 55684 Robert James Barrett 55685 Francois Andre Bates 55686 Shawn Michael Bault 55687 Ryan David Baum 55688 Daniel George Beatty 55689 James Lawrence Bechard 55690 Richard Vernon Beevers 55691 Emory Dilworth Bellard 55692 Jonathan Thomas Belmont 55693 Shane Gannon Belvin 55694 Rebecca Day Benedict 55695 Aaron Arthur Bennett 55696 Christopher James Benshoof 55697 Daniel Kent Benson 55698 Joseph Edward Benson 55699 Eric Tyson Benting 55700 Joseph Emerson Berg 55701 Timothy Jude Bertocci 55702 Dale Edwin Betz 55703 Bradford David Bigler 55704 Matthew David Birck 55705 Elliott Journal Bird 55706 Ryan Lucas Bird 55707 John Douglas Bishop 55708 Richard Andrew Blenz 55709 Richard Jason Block 55710 Brandon White Bloodworth 55711 Edward Allan Bloom 55712 Carl Michael Bloomfield 55713 Craig Alan Blow 55714 Christy Leigh Blum 55715 James Edward Bluman 55716 Robert David Bohr 55717 Anthony Michael Bonarti 55718 Lance Bergin Borden 55719 Joshua Michael Borge 55720 Erik Bradley Borggren 55721 David Albin Boris 55722 Joseph Michael Borovicka 55723 Scott Jon Boston 55724 Elizabeth Audrey Bottcher 55725 Michael Jeremy Bovan 55726 Brian Daniel Bowden 55727 Brian Michael Boyer 55728 Christopher John Boyer 55729 Joshua Jannings Bradley 55730 Kevin David Bradley 55731 Matthew Fraser Brady 55732 Jennifer Jean Brand 55733 William Edward Braniff 55734 Jeffrey Thomas Braun 55735 Matthew Allan Breitbach 55736 Gerald Donald Brennan 55737 Kyle John Brennan 55738 James Bert Brindle 55739 Christopher Alan Britt 55740 Scott Alan Bronikowski 55741 Donald Kent Brooks 55742 Stephen Cooper Brown 55743 Herbert Fredrick Brychta 55744 Stephen Joseph Buchanan 55745 Gregory Alvin Buckmeier 55746 Bryce Kiffin Bucknell 55747 Antonio Francis Buehler 55748 Kevin Paul Buettner 55749 Troy Allen Bupp 55750 Brian Keith Burchfield 55751 Geoffrey Steven Burgess 55752 Reed Adam Burggrabe 55753 Justin Adam Burns 55754 Tessa Leah Burns 55755 Jake Spencer Bursack 55756 William Gentry Bushman 55757 Michael Joseph Bustos 55758 Craig William Butera 55759 James Aaron Byrd 55760 Sean David Byrnes 55761 Murphy Andrew Caine 55762 Aaron Lee Caldwell 55763 Chad Warner Caldwell 55764 Karen Maureen Callahan 55765 Alex Kenneth Cammenga 55766 Brian Joseph Campbell 55767 Bryan William Campbell 55768 Regan Nathan Campbell 55769 Gregory Vaughn Campion 55770 Jennifer Lee Cannan 55771 Joel James Canon 55772 Kevin Kenneth Carlile 55773 Paul Douglas Carron 55774 Joseph Nicholas Casabonne 55775 Lorna Barbara Case 55776 Andrew William Casey 55777 Susan Ann Castorina 55778 Larry Dale Caswell 55779 Philip Thomas Cattanach 55780 Colin Fordyce Cave 55781 Mehmet M Celebioglu 55782 Edward Mathias Cerer 55783 Michael In Cha 55784 Ricardo Jose Chamorro 55785 Brandon Carlyle Chance 55786 Kaci Lyn Vogel 55787 Mark Addison Chandler 55788 Mark Anthony Chaney 55789 Antionette Nicole Pulley 55790 Jubert John Chavez 55791 Varman Sok Chhoeung 55792 Alicia Amy Chin 55793 Jason Inhoon Choi 55794 Christopher Adam Cisneros 55795 Heather Joy Clancy 55796 Timothy Michael Clauss 55797 Ian Robert Claxton 55798 Steven Dennis Clay 55799 Russell David Clayton 55800 Christopher Leong Cline 55801 Aaron Paul Close 55802 Ryan Philip Close 55803 Frankie Corpuz Cochiaosue 55804 Matthew Kevin Coffey 55805 Christopher Paul Colbert 55806 Geoffrey Jason Cole 55807 Jack McRae Collins 55808 Nayda E Concina 55809 Brian Michael Connolly 55810 Joseph Francis Connolly 55811 Gary Michael Conway 55812 Forrest Viehweg Cook 55813 James Peter Cook 55814 Justin David Cook 55815 Heather Lyn Cooper 55816 Jessica Nicole Cooper 55817 Walter Raymond Cooper 55818 Sean Richard Copeland 55819 Daniel Vincent Cordaro 55820 Christopher David Corliss 55821 Scott Thomas Corwin 55822 Eric Walter Cosper 55823 James Armour Craig 55824 Jared Alexander Crain 55825 Roger Lavaughn Cravens 55826 Christopher Scott Crawford 55827 Michael Scott Crowell 55828 Jonathan March Culp 55829 Michael Seth Cunneen 55830 Clint Hollie Cunningham 55831 Colin Grant Cunningham 55832 Christopher Jordan Curry 55833 Joe Derrick Curtis 55834 Daniel William Czirjak 55835 Jacob Penn Dalton 55836 Gregory Wright Dameron 55837 Eric Martin Damman 55838 Andre Major Davis 55839 Heyward Hardy Davis 55840 Jeremy Michael Davis 55841 Joseph Patrick Day 55842 Jowanna Sue Day 55843 Jennifer Rae Debruin 55844 Matthew Raymond Debiec 55845 Nathan Wilfred DeForest 55846 Valencia Ann DeLaVega 55847 William Joseph Delbagno 55848 Jason Robert Delmar 55849 John Stacy DeLong 55850 Philip Wayne Denton 55851 Daniel Paul Devries 55852 Ethan Patrick Dial 55853 Douglas Andrew DiCenzo 55854 Julius Jeremiah Dickens 55855 Khanh Tuyet Diep 55856 Jeffrey Paul DiMarzio 55857 Gretchen Ann Dobert 55858 Thomas Paul Donatelle 55859 Brendan John Donnelly 55860 Michael Benjamin Dorschner 55861 John Casey Doss 55862 Jonathan Todd

Drake 55863 Claude Leon Drevet 55864 Kenneth William Driscoll 55865 Brian Michael Ducote 55866 Matthew Brian Duffy 55867 Michael Erik Dugan 55868 Christine Danielle Thornberg 55869 David Allen Dulaney 55870 Joseph Anthony Dunn 55871 Joseph Michael Duracinsky 55872 Jose David Durbin 55873 Matthew Lee Dyer 55874 Brian Ray Easley 55875 Christopher Ian Eastburg 55876 Kingsley Kenyatta Edwards 55877 Shay Edwards 55878 Joshua David Ekis 55879 Aaron Charles Elliott 55880 James Clay Elliott 55881 Keola Jordan Elobt 55882 Benjie Batatan Esguerra 55883 Thomas Michael Eskola 55884 Paul Andre Espinoza 55885 Charles Richard Evans 55886 Craig Laurence Evans 55887 Elizabeth Harlan Ewing 55888 Kellie Lynn Fabin 55889 Charles Gregory Fagerquist 55890 Frank Junior Fair 55891 Jeffrey Alan Farmer 55892 Christopher Lynn Farnsworth 55893 Jennifer Catherine Farrell 55894 Edward Patrick Farren 55895 Brian Matthew Fecteau 55896 Gregory Arthur Fend 55897 Jack Wayne Ferguson 55898 Kimberly Ann Ferguson 55899 Benjamin James Fernandes 55900 Richard Francis Ferrance 55901 Evan Ross Fertel 55902 Anthony Maurice Fields 55903 Joshua David Fields 55904 J Kingsley Fink 55905 James Conzetti Finocchiaro 55906 Nicole Elyse Fischer 55907 Jeremy Craig Fisk 55908 Joshua Michael Fleming 55909 Juddson Clayton Floris 55910 Adam James Florkowski 55911 Stanley Florkowski 55912 Jarat Lee Ford 55913 Scott Richard Ford 55914 Jonathan Ashley Fornes 55915 Karyn Susanne Forsyth 55916 Andrew Michael Foss 55917 Robert Lawrence Foster 55918 Michael Luther Fransen 55919 Sara Maria Frazier 55920 Brian Scott Freeman 55921 Jamey Edward Friel 55922 Matthew Frank Frombach 55923 Michael Vincent Fuchs 55924 James Keith Gadoury 55925 Susan Marie Galich 55926 Kevin Francis Galligan 55927 James Leland Galloway 55928 Nathan Richard Garaas 55929 John David Garcia 55930 Omar Garcia 55931 Kirsten Lindsay Garrett 55932 Bradford Isaac Garrison 55933 April Lynn Gasparri 55934 Timothy Dewayne Gatlin 55935 Benjamin Thomas Gatzke 55936 Christopher Alan Gay 55937 Kenneth Riley Gaylor 55938 James Jinlong Geishaker 55939 Dominick Salvatore Gerace 55940 Stephen Andrew Gerber 55941 Thomas Richard Germano 55942 Theodore Lawrence Gerstle 55943 Alexander Barrett Giambone 55944 Adisa Mosi Gibson 55945 Jennifer Margaret Gibson 55946 Keith Michael Gieseke 55947 Brian Paul Gilbert 55948 Philip Matthew Giusto 55949 Johnny Louis Goff 55950 Scott Richard Goff 55951 Augustine Christop Gonzales 55952 Stephen Grant Good 55953 John Thomas Goodrich 55954 Justin Charles Gordon 55955 Justin Matthew Gordon 55956 Richard Eugene Gorini 55957 Robert Pilny Gosling 55958 Elizabeth Asheley Gowdy 55959 John Joseph Gowel 55960 Jonathan Bradley Goza 55961 Andrew James Graham 55962 William Henry Grannis 55963 Paul Michael Grant 55964 Jason Alexander Grassbaugh 55965 David Shannon Gray 55966 Zachary Neal Gray 55967 Scott Wherry Greco 55968 Micah Shane Green 55969 Scott Allan Greenwood 55970 Melissa Anne Ringhisen 55971 Robert Paul Grimming 55972 Patrick Baldwin Grow 55973 Nathan Paul Gruver 55974 David Patrick Guerriero 55975 Joseph Charles Guido 55976 Daniel Stanley Gulick 55977 Michael Raymond Guzman 55978 Margaret Haenn Vineyard 55979 Nicholas Paul Hallam 55980 Brian Philip Hallberg 55981 Lindsey Elizabeth Halter 55982 James Edward Halton 55983 Christopher John Hammer 55984 Alan Mathew Hammons 55985 Joshua Daniel Hampton 55986 Jason Paul Hamre 55987 Richard Kent Harding 55988 Matthew Townley Hargrove 55989 Emily Ann Harrington 55990 Kevin Michael Harrington 55991 Scott Mark Harrington 55992 Ronald Wade Havniear 55993 Jerrod Eugene Hawk 55994 James Patrick Hayes 55995 Joseph Maddison Hays 55996 Benjamin Hunter Hayward 55997 Stacy Raquel Hazel 55998 David Charles Hazelton 55999 Sarah Elisabeth Knudson 56000 Stephen Comegys Hedger 56001 David Scott Heigle 56002 Glen Thomas Helberg 56003 Diane Shahin Held 56004 Robert Brandon Helm 56005 Patrick Thomas Hemmer 56006 Erica Pearle Brewer 56007 Stephen Wayne Henderson 56008 Cory Edmond Henry 56009 Christopher Jeremy Herndon 56010 Marc William Herr 56011 Donald Arthur Herzog 56012 Douglas Cooper Hess 56013 Dustin Garey Heumphreus 56014 Eric Andrew Hildebrandt 56015 Michael Lee Hill 56016 Rashidi Tabasuri Hodari 56017 Andrew Carl Hodges 56018 Daniel Aaron Holbrook 56019 Mathew Newton Holladay 56020 Heather Linnea Holm 56021 Joel Clynton Holmes 56022 Matthew Byron Holmes 56023 Brandon Terrell Hoskins 56024 Nathaniel Christof Howard 56025 Brody Justin Howatt 56026 Thomas Donald Howell 56027 Wilbur W Hsu 56028 Nathan MacFarlane Hubbard 56029 David Michael Hudson 56030 Kevin Geoffrey Hueman 56031 Ronald Jack Hughes 56032 Edward Anthony Hulten 56033 Manet Hun 56034 Alex Benjamin Hunt 56035 Nicole Rae Hunt 56036 Hillix Scott Huyette 56037 Daniel Phan Huynh 56038 Antonio Gallardi Ignacio 56039 Brandon Joel Iker 56040 Joshua Paul Illian 56041 Donna Louise Ingram 56042 William Howard Ingram 56043 David Ricardo Inniss 56044 Dreama Leah Sicat 56045 Elena Ivanova Ivanova 56046 Brian Joseph Jackiw 56047 Brian Anthony Jacobs 56048 Travis Robert Jadlot 56049 Corey Matthew James 56050 Kevin Lee James 56051 Joel Robert Jamison 56052 Christopher Noah Jarman 56053 Andrew John Jaskolski 56054 Paul Michael Jellison 56055 Colby Cecil Jenkins 56056 Shoshannah Brienz Jenni 56057 Jorge Duland Jensen 56058 Michael Lee Johns 56059 Cayton Loren Johnson 56060 Matthew Joseph Johnson 56061 Noah Orlando Johnson 56062 Richard Baard Johnson 56063 Richard Lee Johnson 56064 Steven Murrah Johnson 56065 Todd Levi Johnson 56066 Jonathan Jeffrey Johnston 56067 Steven Mark Johnston 56068 Marcus Jahaeziel Jolley 56069 Alison Michele Jones 56070 Cullen Albert Jones 56071 Hugh William Jones 56072 Jeremy Christopher Jones 56073 Matthew Steven Jones 56074 Paula Andrea Jones 56075 Shannon Kelleen Jones 56076 Michael Turner Jordan 56077 Christopher Andrew Joseph 56078 Barbara Jozwik 56079 Bryan Gerald Juntunen 56080 Melissa Anne Kaiser 56081 Brant Edward Kananen 56082 Kristian Cosmo Karafa 56083 David Anthony Kasza 56084 Joseph Arthur Katz 56085 Janette Lynn Kautzman 56086 Steven Michael Kedrowski 56087 David Allen Kegerreis 56088 Kevin Michael Kelly 56089 John Walter Kemp 56090 Ryan Calvin Kendall 56091 Samuel Carl Kicker 56092 Timothy Arthur Kiesow 56093 Sean Charles Kilbride 56094 Shawn Patrick Kilcoyne 56095 Christopher Michael Kim 56096 Jimmy H Kim 56097 Timothy James Klapec 56098 Christopher Donald Klein 56099 Andrew James Knight 56100 Matthew Arnold Knudson 56101 Todd Andrew Koch 56102 J. William Kohowski 56103 Kenneth Sakichi Kondo 56104 Andrew Matthew Kovanen 56105 Tomasz Krzysztof Kowalik 56106 Steven Lee Kreh 56107 Christina Joyce Kretchman 56108 James Lawrence Krueger 56109 Kwenton Kambridge Kuhlman 56110 Matthew John Kuntz 56111 Kristofer Hardy Kvam 56112 Babejohn Dominic Kwasniak 56113 Michael Frederick LaBrecque 56114 James Joseph Lacaria 56115 Michael Patrick LaChance 56116 Jeffrey Thomas Laczek 56117 Bernadette Kristen-A Gorini 56118 Robert Louis Lalumondier 56119 Graham Collin Landry 56120 Jarred Matthew Lang 56121 Jeffrey Anthony LaPlante 56122 Paul Joseph Lavigna 56123 Elizabeth Susan Lawney 56124 Shawn Michael Lawrence 56125 Heather Dawne Lawson 56126 Lindsay Jill Leatherman 56127 Andrew Chong Lee 56128 Genoa Nichole Lee 56129 Jae Min Lee 56130 Jimmy Jusuk Lee 56131 Jong Ung Lee 56132 Eric Lee Leiby 56133 Lucas Randall Leonard 56134 Melanie Lynn Koehler 56135 Joseph Mackenzie Letko 56136 Matthew James Levantovich 56137 Jason Todd Lewis 56138 Robert P Lewis 56139 Andrew Michael Lhamon 56140 Travis James Lieb 56141 John Theodore Liesen 56142 Christian Marc Liflander 56143 John Francis Lighting 56144 Barry Chris Lingelbach 56145 Dennis O'neal Lockhart 56146 Romarius Lamar Longmire 56147 Todd Lee Looney 56148 Cesar Lopez 56149 Nicole Dell Losonsky 56150 Harvey Richard Lowell 56151 Quan Hai Lu 56152 Jason Edward Luby 56153 Andrew Alan Lundbohm 56154 Angela Renee Lundholm 56155 Jonathan Henry Luttwak 56156 Ian Jeremy Lynch 56157 Kelly Marie Lynch 56158 Jeffrey Grant Lynes 56159 Sean Todd Macrae 56160 Margo Myra Mahan 56161 Francis Xavier Mahoney 56162 Robert William Mahowald 56163 Stephen Paul Maire 56164 Michael Edward Major 56165 Cheri Marie Benedict 56166 Jason Howard Mallory 56167 Isaac David Malson 56168 Nicole Andrea Manara 56169 Nathan Mark Mann 56170 Jonathan Andrew Markum 56171 William James Marm 56172 Gabriel Mackay Marriott 56173 Andrew Jeremy Marshall 56174 Andrew David Martin 56175 Bryan Michael Martin 56176 Wynn David Martin 56177 Timothy John Marvich 56178 Charles Ashley Matlach 56179 Jeffrey Travis Matson 56180 Edwin David Matthaidess 56181 Jason Michael Mattila 56182 Sean Mathew Mattingly 56183 Casey Lynn Maxfield 56184 Christine Angel Mayo 56185 Michael Christian McCafferty 56186 John Owen McClusky 56187 David Edward McCourtney 56188 Vanessa Ann McDermott 56189 Sharon Lynn McDonald 56190 Stefan Reid McFarland 56191 Sean Patrick McGee 56192 Michael Todd McGowan 56193 Steven Berle McGunegle 56194 Michael Edward McInerney 56195 George Critz McIngvale 56196 Ryan Wayne McKee 56197 Thurman Chester McKenzie 56198 David Lynn McLaughlin 56199 Richard Warren McPhillips 56200 Ryan Whitson McQueen 56201 Michael Patrick McWilliams 56202 Jeffrey Douglass Means 56203 Christian Daniel Meighan 56204 Jerrod Eugene Melander 56205 Faith Mellott 56206 Tia Nichole Melvin 56207 Catherine Mae Baka 56208 Jude T Metoyer 56209 Christopher James Midberry 56210 Robert Yoshio Mihara 56211 Janis Christopher Mikits 56212 Robert John Milan 56213 Aaron Christopher Miller 56214 Christopher John Miller 56215 Jacob Winston Miller 56216 Samuel Robert Miller 56217 Scott David Miller 56218 Scott Matthew Miller 56219 John David Mini 56220 Stephen Marcus Mintz 56221 Daniel David Mitchell 56222 Forrest Todd Mitchell 56223 William David Mitchell 56224 Jeffrey David Mix 56225 Casey Michelle Moes 56226 David McBurney Moffat 56227 Bryan Michael Moffatt 56228 Patrick Charles Moffett 56229 Kevin Roger Mogavero 56230 Aydin Mohtashamian 56231 Nathan Alan Molica 56232 Choyce Joseph Moon 56233 Brian Eric Moore 56234 Cynthia Louise Moore 56235 Scott Anthony Moretz 56236 Matthew James Morgan 56237 John David Moris 56238 John Alvin Morris 56239 Louis Alfonso Morris 56240 Michael Edward Morrison 56241 Jessie Richard Moser 56242 David Michael Muhlenkamp 56243 Terry Paul Muhlenkamp 56244 Michael Joseph Mulcahy 56245 Jamar Edmund Mullen 56246 Zachary Jared Mundell 56247 Derek Brandon Nagel 56248 Steven Costas Naum 56249 Randall Jason Neel 56250 Andrew John Nelson 56251 Peter Christopher Nelson 56252 Ryan Bruce Nelson 56253 David Lee Newell 56254 Jeffrey Woodrow Ng 56255 Hac Duc Nguyen 56256 Quan Thanh Nguyen 56257 Cecil C Nix 56258 Joseph Barre Novak 56259 Robert Allan Nowicki 56260 Eric Samuel Nye 56261 James Michael O'Boyle 56262 Brian Mccue O'Malley 56263 Terrence John O'Connor 56264 Derek Kristopher Odom 56265 Christopher William O'Gwin 56266 Eric Alan Olsen 56267 Eric Michael Olsen 56268 Jennifer Serwa Opoku 56269 Justin Dennis Orr 56270 Marc Joseph Ortiz 56271 Kalian Edward Osborn 56272 Shaun H S Owen 56273 Sterling James Packer 56274 Jeffrey Steven Palazzini 56275 Jonathan Michael Palin 56276 John Michael Pandich 56277 Kent Wesley Park 56278 Gregory Benedict Parranto 56279 Michael Parrella 56280 Clark Kaemper Patterson 56281 Peter Andrew Patterson 56282 Sarah Catherine Pattinson 56283 Cyril Scott Paulo 56284 Susan Kay Paulson 56285 Casey Vaughan Payne 56286 Alan Lee Pearson 56287 Matthew Gregory Peck 56288 Robert Michael Perchard 56289 Summer Ann Perkins 56290 Edward Wayne Petrik 56291 Jeremy Michael Phillips 56292 Jason Wayne Piechowiak 56293 Joanna Elyce Pierantonio 56294 Rebecca Elizabeth Platt 56295 Christopher Lee Plekenpol 56296 William Todd Pohlmann 56297 Aaron Scott Polsgrove 56298 Brian Lee Pond 56299 Mark Albert Ponikvar 56300 Emil Theodore Popov 56301 Thomas Dwayne Postlewait 56302 Brian William Potter 56303 David Anthony Pounds 56304 Matthew Reid Powell 56305 Stuart Monro Prins 56306 Christopher Joseph Puglisi 56307 Keith Scott Pund 56308 Gregory John Quimby 56309 Robert August Radtke 56310 Suresh Chinniah Ramgopal 56311 John Matthew Raso 56312 Neil Ravitz 56313 Travis Jay Rayfield 56314 Peter Michael Rayls 56315 Michael Patrick Raymo 56316 Cheryl Lynn Redline 56317 Jennifer Diana Reed 56318 Jeremy Theodore Reed 56319 Morgan Beth Reese 56320 Corey Vincent Reeves 56321 Ty Steven Remington 56322 Stephen Andrew Resch 56323 Jason Lee Reynolds 56324 Kristina Lynn Richardson 56325 Roderick Jamal Richardson 56326 Thomas Andrew Richardson 56327 William Stephen Riddle 56328 Dena Marie Ridenour 56329 Jeremy Scott Riegel 56330 John Justin Ringhisen 56331 David Preston Ritter 56332 Jason Scott Ritter 56333 Nathan Paul Ritter 56334 Aristotle Castro Rivera 56335 Cesar Augusto Rivera 56336 Andre Gerald Rivier 56337 Ryan Matthew Roberts 56338 Angela Shante Robinson 56339 Kevin Allen Robinson 56340 Shawnette Michaela Rochelle 56341 Michael Peter Rogowski 56342 Eric Anthony Rolfs 56343 Carrie Rose Rollins 56344 Christopher Thomas Romig 56345 Michael John Roposh 56346 David Joseph Roseland 56347 Michael Craig Ross 56348 Ulf Roland Rota 56349 Richard Mathew Roth 56350 Mark Andrew Rothemich 56351 Shannon Jean Rowe 56352 David Brian Rowland 56353 Kenneth Dale Rowland 56354 Ranee Rubio 56355 Pamela Sue Ruscio 56356 Shawn Patrick Russell 56357 Timothy David Rustad 56358 Philip Anthony Rutkowski 56359 Aaron Joseph Sadusky 56360 Benjamin Richard Saine 56361 Gillian Barbara Sakai 56362 Jason Victor Sama 56363 Michael Allan Sapp 56364 Charles Anthony Sawicky 56365 Brian David Sawser 56366 Matthew Thomas Sawyer 56367 Richard Anthony Schega 56368 Nicholas Charles Schenck 56369 Elizabeth Drew Scherer 56370 Ryan Joseph Schley 56371 Raymond James Schmotzer 56372 Michael Anthony Schneider 56373 James Charles Schreiner 56374 Kearson Louise Schuck 56375 Eric Stephen Schwartz 56376 Agostino Salvat Scicchitano 56377 Katherine Martha Gowel 56378 Michael Anthony Scott 56379 Sean Michael Scott 56380 Travene Althea Crawford 56381 Michael Steven Searcy 56382 Stephanie Diane Secosky 56383 Rachel Arlene Seguin 56384 Keith Terry Sellers 56385 Brittain Lynn Shafer 56386 Matthew Michael Shanahan 56387 Michael Dwayne Shaner 56388 Devan Joseph Shannon 56389 Saleem Akbar Sharif 56390 Michael Bernard Shattan 56391 Robert Michael Shaw 56392 Ryan Lee Shaw 56393 Kevin Allan Shea 56394 Andrew Lee Sherrill 56395 Michael Ray Shifferd 56396 Daniel Christian Shin 56397 Light Kwangwon Shin 56398 Andrew Timothy Short 56399 James William Shupe 56400 Amy Prentiss Siegenthaler 56401 Scott Floyd Siegfried 56402 Edwin Wade Sikking 56403 Daniel David Silva 56404 Donald John Simko 56405 Peter Folk Simms 56406 Raymond Min-young Simms 56407 Larry Wayne Simon 56408 Daniel Stephen Sinclair 56409 Terence Andwele Sinkfield 56410 Donald Christopher Sisson 56411 Andrew Morse Slack 56412 Terry Wayne Slaybaugh 56413 Adam Keith Smith 56414 Benedict Joseph Smith 56415 David Burton Smith 56416 David Ronald Smith 56417 Gabriel Keith Smith 56418 Jeremy David Smith 56419 Robert Lebrun Smith 56420 Scott Christopher Smith 56421 Travis Barrett Smith 56422 Lynn Marie Smolinski 56423 Mario Augusto Soto 56424 Andrew Joseph Sparkman 56425 Parke Pius Speth 56426 Robert Joseph Spivey 56427 Aaron Christopher Stachel 56428 Joseph Bradley Stanyer 56429 Scott Russell Stechschulte 56430 Robert Dirk Steinfort 56431 Colleen Marie Stevens 56432 Joshua Bryan Stewart 56433 Richard Allen Stewart 56434 Brian Jeffrey Stickney 56435 John Colon Stillwell 56436 Heather Lynn Stone 56437 Michael Andrew Stone 56438 Robert Keith Stone 56439 Jason Leslie Stoneman 56440 Gregory Stopyra 56441 David Brian Storch 56442 Brian Joseph Storm 56443 Brian James Stramaglia 56444 Michelle Susan Stratton 56445 John Carlton Stroh 56446 Margaret Anne Strom 56447 Craig Andrew Stucker 56448 Dennis Patrick Sugrue 56449 Philip Min-Suk Suh 56450 Brian Elliott Supko 56451 Holland McKissick Sutton 56452 Jordon Edwin Swain 56453 Jerem Gregory Swenddal 56454 Michael Paul Szczepanski 56455 Gabriel Aaron Szody 56456 Gregory Britten Szulis 56457 Kimberly Anne Bursack 56458 Brian Jason Talley 56459 Anthony Joseph Tanner 56460 Matthew Paul Tarjick 56461 George Tereik Tatum 56462 Charles Onehunga Taumoepeau 56463 Benjamin Austin Taylor 56464 Kevin Ryan Taylor 56465 Katherine Ann Teliska 56466 Peter Wesley Tepper 56467 Nathan Daniel Terra 56468 Kevin James Terrazas 56469 Jesus Ubaldo Terrones 56470 Michael James Tess 56471 Joshua Wyatt Thibeault 56472 William Karl Thiele 56473 Benjamin A Thomas 56474 Richard David Thomas 56475 Zachary Lee Thomas 56476 Andrea Cecilia Thompson 56477 Daniel James Thompson 56478 Paul Cameron Tijerina 56479 Eric Lee Tisland 56480 Marc Aaron Titler 56481 Michael David Todd 56482 Aaron Christopher Tolson 56483 Andrew Brown Tompkins 56484 Frank Joel Toney 56485 William Raymond Torrey 56486 Jeffery Michael Townsend 56487 Jennifer Nicole Trainor 56488 John Eric Travland 56489 Kenneth Aaron Tumelson 56490 Corry Paul Tyler 56491 Hayley Catherine Ulrich 56492 Robert Edward Underwood 56493 James Uptgraft 56494 Michael Scott Vaccaro 56495 Jennifer Michelle Vaden 56496 Elizabeth Lee Vallette 56497 Lucas Scott VanAntwerp 56498 Neil David Vance 56499 Alexander Vela 56500 Stephen L Vergamini 56501 Eric James Vihinen 56502 Matthew Joseph Villa 56503 Michael Alan Vineyard 56504 Ryan Kenneth Wainwright 56505 Stephen Larue Waldrop 56506 Roger Paul Waleski 56507 Brendan James Walker 56508 Jason Lee Walker 56509 Robert Willis Walker 56510 Stephen Clayton Walker 56511 Brennan Victor Wallace 56512 Mark Edward Warder 56513 Ralph Leon Ware 56514 Alan Ronald Warmbier 56515 Jason William Warren 56516 Steven Charles Watkins 56517 John Douglas Watson 56518 Jay Joseph Weatherwax 56519 Remus Tererus Webb 56520 Paul Jason Weber 56521 Jeffrey David Weeks 56522 Robert Jose Weeks 56523 Ryan Norman Wehner 56524 Rebecca Ann Weingart 56525 Keith Allen Weinstein 56526 Matthew Edward Wells 56527 Melinda Jane Wengert 56528 David William West 56529 Julie Laura Mundell 56530 Justus Eugene White 56531 Jason Wayne Whiteley 56532 Robert Mitchel Whitten 56533 Richard Terrance Whittington 56534 Jason Wright Wicks 56535 Marek Adam Wiernusz 56536 Christopher Micha Wilkinson 56537 Bart D Wilkison 56538 Benjamin Reid Williams 56539 Bobby Ray Williams 56540 Charles Malcom Williams 56541 Clinton Sheridan Williams 56542 Daniel Mark Williams 56543 Matthew Thomas Williams 56544 Scott Patrick Williams 56545 Norman Lee Wilson 56546 Ryan Jeffrey Wilson 56547 Jason Duane Windau 56548 John David Wingeart 56549 Carl Herbert Wohlfeil 56550 Carl Jonathan Wojtaszek 56551 Raymond Charles Wong 56552 Dan J Woods 56553 Nathan Ty Woods 56554 Gavin Ward Woody 56555 Laura Annette Worthing 56556 Hannibal Sebastian Wright 56557 William Charles Wright 56558 Kriston Robert Yagel 56559 Colin William Yankee 56560 Raffie Ruben Yeremian 56561 Patrick Mulligan Yonnone 56562 Christopher Terry Young 56563 Justin Robert Zadnichek 56564 Christine Marie Zalucki 56565 James Andrew Zanella 56566 Benjamin Brian Zelno 56567 Shannon Leigh Zerbey 56568 David Wayne Zickafoose 56569 Elliot Stephen Zimmer 56570 Jonathan Stanley Zimmer 56571 Janet Aileen Zimmerman 56572 Tyriene Vaughn Amey 56573 Dorian Anne Brown 56574 LeShon Keith King 56575 Timothy Duane Cook 56576 Jason David Barnes 56577 John Smith Berry 56578 Roberto Nicolas Bran 56579 Raina Jo Chesser 56580 Leroy Harris 56581 Brian Antoine King 56582 Luann Rose Hoyseth 56583 Stephen Thorton Melton 56584 Robert Lane Sammon 56585 Kerwin Lendon Smith 56586 Glenda Louise Wrenn 56587 **2000** Jason Michael Abelli 56588 Andrew Patrick Adams 56589 Charles Henry Adams 56590 Dennis Edward Adams 56591 Eric Ronald Adams 56592 David Curtis Ahl 56593 John Stephen Albright 56594 Danial Calab Alexander 56595 Matthew David Alexander 56596 Nicholas Ryan Alioto 56597 Andrew Sidney Allen 56598 Anita Felice Allen 56599 Dean MacDonald Allison 56600 Brett Sheridan Allmond 56601 Christine Ann Almy 56602 Jesus Janeo Altuna 56603 Richard Manuel Alvarez 56604 Dennis Chong An 56605 Reginald Jerome Anderson 56606 Daniel Yasuo Arai

56607 Nicholas John Armstrong 56608 Tyler Lawrence Arnold 56609 Andrew Ross Atkins 56610 Darby Lee Aviles 56611 Scott Adrian Bailey 56612 Steven Eric Baker 56613 Beneka Bali 56614 Sean Alan Barbaras 56615 Justin Christopher Barclay 56616 Charles Ernest Barker 56617 Jamie Michelle Barker 56618 Christopher Quay Barnett 56619 Barnes Kemp Barton 56620 Kenneth Charles Bateman 56621 Sean Wesley Baxter 56622 David Moreau Beach 56623 James Christopher Bean 56624 Brian Christopher Beatty 56625 Jarrett Franklin Beck 56626 Ralph Lee Becki 56627 Cornelius Gabriel Begley 56628 Jayna Teresa Bell 56629 Kimberly H Belmont 56630 Christina Ann Gaguzis 56631 Ann Elizabeth Benford 56632 Derek Howard Bennett 56633 Andrew William Benson 56634 Waitman Wade Beorn 56635 Sarah Anne Bercaw 56636 Heather Anne Berg 56637 Jeffrey Bryant Berg 56638 Jake Allen Bergman 56639 Chad Edward Bettac 56640 Brian David Betts 56641 Achim Miguel Biller 56642 Jason Daniel Billington 56643 Scott Rene Blanchard 56644 Jennifer Tuero Blatty 56645 John Thomas Bleigh 56646 Penny Melissa Bloedel 56647 Brian Blum 56648 Jeremy Shane Boardman 56649 Nicholas Paul Bobrowski 56650 Kyle Nelson Bockey 56651 Jonathan Andrew Bodenhamer 56652 Bryan Myles Bogardus 56653 Jonathan Matthew Boggiano 56654 John Mathias Bohnen 56655 John Donald Boland 56656 Michael Peter Bolcek 56657 Bryson Sheridan Bort 56658 Robert Alan Bowers 56659 Timothy Lee Bowers 56660 Robyn Marlene Bowland 56661 Bryce Hatfield Bowman 56662 David Joshua Boytim 56663 Jonathan Mark Bradford 56664 Jeffrey John Bradley 56665 Kari Liona-Lynn Hadley 56666 Tiffani Annette Braswell 56667 Cedric Devlin Bray 56668 Jessie James Brewster 56669 Christine Rita Farrell 56670 Brian Michael Brinson 56671 Kari Jean Brizius 56672 James Matthew Brocato 56673 David Clayson Brockbank 56674 David Joseph Brodsky 56675 Charles Plummer Brooks 56676 Eric Anton Brooks 56677 Ericka Marie Brooks 56678 Jason Layne Brothers 56679 Jason Brown 56680 John Eric Brown 56681 William Robert Brown 56682 Michael John Browning 56683 Alisha Ann Bryan 56684 Jason Wayne Bryant 56685 Tiffany Kristin Bryant 56686 David James Buehler 56687 Greg Bennett Buehler 56688 Leo Victor Buehler 56689 Nicholas Thomas Bugajski 56690 Joshua Michael Bundt 56691 Ryan Thomas Burkert 56692 Adrian Alan Burleigh 56693 Michael Meredith Burns 56694 Travis Carter Burns 56695 Benjamin Joseph Burris 56696 Josh Alston Burton 56697 Kerry Anne Burzynski 56698 Philip Alexander Buswell 56699 Emile George Buzaid 56700 Adam Clark Byrd 56701 Michael Sebastian Cahill 56702 Maria Callo 56703 Brian Michael Calvasina 56704 Victor Emmanuel Camaya 56705 Braden Kawailani Camp 56706 William Roderick Canda 56707 Matthew Patrick Capobianco 56708 Briah Leigh Carey 56709 Sally Miranda Carlson 56710 Patrick Boyd Carneal 56711 Vaughn Hai Carpenter 56712 Christopher Edwin Carter 56713 Richard Lee Cartwright 56714 Kirk Edward Cassel 56716 Luis Andres Castellanos 56717 Shaun Corbin Castillo 56718 Jennifer Reeves Cave 56719 Benjamin Celver 56720 Kurt Chapman 56721 Justin Andre Charise 56722 Jennifer Louise Charron 56723 Stephanie Anastasia Chase 56724 David Henry Chen 56725 Matthew Wayne Childers 56726 David Matthew Childress 56727 Rae Cho 56728 Christopher Michael Chung 56729 Matthew Norman Cini 56730 Carl John Ciovacco 56731 Bronston Allen Clough 56732 Jason Allen Coats 56733 Anthony Terron Coaxum 56734 Adria Maite Cobeaga 56735 Mark Anthony Cobos 56736 Jason Robert Cody 56737 Sara Lynn Coffland 56738 Charles Lee Coggins 56739 George Howard Coleman 56740 Marcus Henry Colyer 56741 Christina Lynn Congo 56742 Nathaniel Fairbank Conkey 56743 David Matthew Conner 56744 Meghan Anne Conroy 56745 Nathaniel Riley Cook 56746 Samuel Patrick Cook 56747 Gordon Campbell Cooke 56748 Charles James Coombe 56749 Timothy John Cooper 56750 Max Alberto Cortes 56751 Christian Cloud Cosner 56752 Andrew Bartholow Costello 56753 Keegan Bryson Cotton 56754 Michael Issac Couture 56755 Gordon-Michael Angelo Cox 56756 Yanson Tupper Cox 56758 John Christopher Craft 56759 Nathaniel Thomas Crain 56760 Thomas Ulysses Crary 56761 Kevin James Craw 56762 Malaika Iyana Crowe 56763 Patrick John Culpepper 56764 Kevin Francis Cummiskey 56765 Patrick Ryan Cunanan 56766 Anthony Alphonse D'Aguillo 56767 Shawn David Dalton 56768 Molly Kathleen Dammyer 56769 Steven Mathew Danelson 56770 Clayton Collins Daniels 56771 Kyle Andrew Davis 56772 Justin Lester DeArmond 56773 Jennifer Leigh Delaney 56774 Jason Matthew Delmarty 56775 Brian Andrew Demcher 56776 Christopher Martin Dempsey 56777 Christopher James DeMure 56778 Kirby Robert Dennis 56779 Christopher Glenn Deppoliti 56780 Robb Ryan Dettmer 56781 Travis Patrick Dettmer 56782 Rachel Erin Dickes 56783 Derek Lyle Diener 56784 Geoffrey Christian Dietrich 56785 Joseph Albert DiFilippo 56786 Peter DiGiorgio 56787 Robert Jefferson Dillard 56788 Stephen Frederick Dinetz 56789 Lee Allen Dingman 56790 Jiordan Jude Diorio 56791 Michael Steven Dirks 56792 Jonathan Patrick Dishaw 56793 Matthew Edward Doherty 56794 Christopher James Doran 56795 Anthony Earl Douglas 56796 Ashley Marie Dozier 56797 Jasen Drnasin 56798 Christina Lynn Dugan 56799 Thomas Patrick Duggan 56800 James Derrick Dunn 56801 John Neumann Dvorak 56802 Jason Ruy Dye 56803 David John Dyrenforth 56804 James Lee Ealy 56805 David Christian Eckley 56806 Brandon Lee Edlefsen 56807 Cameron Ray Edlefsen 56808 Daniel Alexander Edwards 56809 James Tyrone Edwards 56810 Samuel James Ehmer 56811 Jennifer Sue Eilen 56812 Ralph Edward Elder 56813 Heather Leanne Ellinger 56814 Jack Francis Emmons 56815 Duane Stanley Enger 56816 Rachel Lynette Enicks 56817 James Robert Enos 56818 Nicholas Mark Eremita 56819 Eli Espericueta 56820 Elizabeth Ann Evans 56821 Kenneth Clay Evans 56822 Lee Alan Evans 56823 James Bruce Evarts 56824 Peter Dale Everson 56825 Katherine Elizabeth Evey 56826 David Fagergren 56827 Margaret Mary Fahy 56828 Joseph Victor Faiella 56829 Rafael Valentin Fajardo 56830 Jesse Leon Falk 56831 Justin Adam Falk 56832 Kevin Ashley Farmer 56833 Patrick David Farrell 56834 Thomas John Fauvell 56835 George Wallace Feese 56836 Dustin Landon Felix 56837 Daryl Adewale Ferguson 56838 Vincent Joseph Ferreri 56839 Reno Ferri 56840 James Michael Few 56841 William Joseph Fick 56842 Aaron Michael Flecker 56843 Esteban Flores 56844 Michael Christopher Flynn 56845 Scott Daniel Folger 56846 Samuel Formunyam Fomundam 56847 Kevin Matthew Forader 56848 Kelly Alleen Fork 56849 Edward Anthony Fornataro 56850 Sean David Foster 56851 Jordan Makana Francis 56852 Douglas Timothy Frank 56853 Lucas Nathaniel Frank 56854 Mark Daniel Frank 56855 John Thomas Franz 56856 Justin Andrew Fregia 56857 Michael Conrad Freidl 56858 Michael John Frick 56859 Sarah Otelia Fritts 56860 Steven Craig Fritz 56861 Matthew Frederick Frosch 56862 Reid Epler Furman 56863 Alexander Watson Fyfe 56864 Ian Matthew Gallagher 56865 Jeffery Christopher Gallart 56866 Andrew Gallo 56867 Jason John Galui 56868 Daniel Allen Galvan 56869 Daniel Michael Ganci 56870 Lucais Levi Garden 56871 Nathan Edward Gargus 56872 Randall Edward Garver 56873 Markus Jason Garza 56874 Michael Edward Gates 56875 Shellie Marie Gato 56876 Jennifer Caryn Gauthier 56877 Eric George Gautier 56878 Plinio Geolingo Gayares 56879 Eric Douglas Geary 56880 Brian John Gebhardt 56881 Jonathan Derrick Gensler 56882 James John Geric 56883 Prescott Miller Gerling 56884 Marc Andrew Giammatteo 56885 Arne Paul Gibbs 56886 Chad Michael Gibson 56887 John Galloway Gibson 56888 Katrina Christine Gier 56889 Robert Bruce Gillespie 56890 John Bolling Gilliam 56891 Joshua John Gilliam 56892 Brian Michael Gillo 56893 Khalilah Latori Gilmore 56894 George Sotirios Giouzelis 56895 Andrew Paul Glaze 56896 Stephen Courtland Gleason 56897 Thomas Allen Goettke 56898 David Mark Gohlich 56899 Albert Thomas Goins 56900 Lowell Alexander Goldman 56901 Carlos Gaspar Gonzales 56902 Jason Michael Gonzalez 56903 Paul Denison Gonzalez 56904 Michael Scott Gordon 56905 Robert Douglas Gordon 56906 Stephen Michael Gordon 56907 Ryan Todd Gould 56908 Robert Benjamin Graetz 56909 Thomas Jerrold Graham 56910 Jamaine Andre Granger 56911 Kevin Gregory Grant 56912 Marius Antoninus Greene 56913 Christopher David Gries 56914 Daniel Dale Grieve 56915 William John Griffith 56916 Adam McCullough Grim 56917 Sean Matthew Grobosky 56918 Sean Michael Groves 56919 Charles Christopher Gunst 56920 Toni Susanne Gyssels 56921 Leah Joy Haberer 56922 David Mandus Hageman 56923 Mehis Hakkaja 56924 Johnny Ilman Ham 56925 Freya Lee Hamre 56926 Jennifer Kum Han 56927 Jeremy Raymond Hancock 56928 Scott Paul Handler 56929 Jason Paul Hanson 56930 Karl Rekvold Hanson 56931 Eric Matthew Harbaugh 56932 David Michael Harkness 56933 Jacob Raynor Harmeson 56934 Mark Brewster Harper 56935 Matthew Evan Harper 56936 Fredrick Harrell 56937 Carolyn Swift Harris 56938 Charla Nicole Harris 56939 Andrew Delaney Hartland 56940 Richard Edgar Hartney 56941 Lynn Taylor Haseman 56942 Aaron James Hatok 56943 Sarah Ann Hatton 56944 Jason Solomon Hawksworth 56945 Francis Michael Hayes 56946 Michael Lynn Haywood 56947 Trevor Jeremy Head 56948 Joseph Dean Heaton 56949 Melvin Dennis Helgeson 56950 Eric Mikal Helland 56951 William Henry Henderson 56952 Thomas Love Hendrix 56953 Michael Scott Hequembourg 56954 Brian Anthony Herman 56955 Thomas Joseph Hernandez 56956 Joseph David Hess 56957 James Jonathan Hickman 56958 Sean Victor Hicks 56959 Elizabeth Jeanne Higgins 56960 Hunter Bradley Hill 56961 Jason Earl Hill 56962 Roger Truman Hill 56963 James David Hochstetler 56964 Luther Robert Hoffmann 56965 Leah Tess Hofmann 56966 Michael Ward Holcomb 56967 Brandon Dale Holden 56968 Michael John Holifield 56969 Walter William Hollis 56970 Hurl Dean Holloway 56971 Clinton Allen Holmes 56972 Joshua Lee Holst 56973 Elise Margit Holtan 56974 Jeremy James Holz 56975 Stanton Michael Hom 56976 Michael Eric Hooper 56977 Joseph Flores Howard 56978 Colin Dale Hoyseth 56979 Jackson Yu-Hao Huang 56980 Amy Leah Huggler 56981 Scott Douglas Hughes 56982 Jeanne Frances Hull 56983 Jacob Isaac Hunter 56984 Nathanael Sargent Hunterton 56985 Michael John Hurst 56986 David Joon Hwangbo 56987 David X Iannuccilli 56988 Thomas Fitzgerald Ingram 56989 Sharif Malcolm Irick 56990 Roman Dominic Izzo 56991 Alana Rae Jackman 56992 Marcus Alden Jackson 56993 Michael Thomas Jackson 56994 Jeffrey Scott Jager 56995 Conrad Joseph Jakubow 56996 Robert Alexander James 56997 Rebecca Ann Jarabek 56998 Aimee Jeanette Jaskot 56999 Grady Dewayne Jett 57000 Kenrick Wayne Johnson 57001 Stephen Mark Johnson 57002 Mark Liston Johnston 57003 Angela Marie Jones 57004 Jessica Anne Jones 57005 Joseph Scott Jones 57006 Craig Martin Julien 57007 Steven Yoon Jung 57008 Nicholas Ryan Kahler 57009 Jeffrey Matthew Kaldahl 57010 Jennifer Alice Kamrowski 57011 Louis Michael Kangas 57012 Thomas Alexander Kapla 57013 Vince Mcadam Kaster 57014 Aaron James Kaufman 57015 Brian Fitzgerald Kavanagh 57016 Daniel Joseph Keenaghan 57017 Jessica Ann Kehren 57018 Michael Thomas Keilty 57019 David Samuel Keller 57020 Brandon Lee Kelley 57021 Bratcha Jermaine Kellum 57022 Keith Jones Kelly 57023 Richard Arthur Kelo 57024 Michael Leo Kendra 57025 Jeffrey David Kenewell 57026 Edward Elliott Kennedy 57027 John Robert Kennedy 57028 Michael Edward Kennedy 57029 Thomas Elliott Kennedy 57030 Andrew Kerigan Kernan 57031 William Alois Kesselring 57032 Charles Albert Ketterman 57033 Samantha Lay Khoo 57034 Twila Ann Khouri 57035 Mary Catherine Kidd 57036 Sara Agnes Kierpiec 57037 Laura Michelle Kiger 57038 Michael Joseph Kilbourne 57039 Brian Stuart Kilgore 57040 William Patrick Kilrain 57041 Austin Kwangjun Kim 57042 Esther Kim 57043 Simon Kim 57044 Sung Min Kim 57045 Thomas Chul Kim 57046 Gabriel Randall Kimble 57047 Christopher Jam Kirkpatrick 57048 Ryan Mason Kirkpatrick 57049 Jonathan Ernest Klink 57050 Jonathan Scott Kluck 57051 Jason Matthew Kneisc 57052 Parker Thomas Knight 57053 Charles Milburn Knoll 57054 Shane Austin Knopp 57055 Kevin James Koger 57056 Brian Koh 57057 Temidayo Latonia Koledoye 57058 Rachel Ann Balog 57059 Scott A Kozak 57060 Adam Taichi Kraft 57061 Ryan Kwang-Huie Kuo 57062 Stephen Shih-Pai Kuo 57063 Ryan Behrendsen Kurrus 57064 Anthony Francis Kurz 57065 Michael Coyle LaBroad 57066 Phillip Matthew LaCasse 57067 Gregory Ernest Ladeveze 57068 Erica Lynn Lamb 57069 Michael Lawrence Lamey 57070 Lisa Reyn Landreth 57071 Travis Allen Landrith 57072 Christopher Charles Lane 57073 Michael Patrick Lang 57074 Nicholas James Lange 57075 Michael Patrick Langelotti 57076 Beth Anne Larrabee 57077 Melissa Lawton 57078 Cedric Ghunwook Lee 57079 In Ah Lee 57080 Sung Woo Lee 57081 Lance Sebastian Leonard 57082 Jeffrey Hunter Lester 57083 Roberto Alfredo Letona 57084 Danielle May Levesque 57085 Michael Lamar Levy 57086 Tyler Smith Lewison 57087 Lillian Lien 57088 Duane Harold Limpert 57089 Conway Lin 57090 H Steve Lin 57091 Eric Robert Lindberg 57092 Harry Laverne Lindenmuth 57093 Christopher Ryan Lloyd 57094 Olivia Shea Locker 57095 Arlyn Edward Logan 57096 Brett Ronald Long 57097 Kevin Neal Long 57098 Michael Adam Long 57099 Ryan Daniel Long 57100 John R Longley 57101 Jose Karl Lopez-Galle 57102 Charles Melvin Lott 57103 Karen Elizabeth Loughman 57104 Timothy Ryan Love 57105 Michael Bryan Loveall 57106 Christopher Lee Lovell 57107 Ryan Joseph Lowry 57108 Eliasib Lozano 57109 Eric Francis Lucas 57110 Sean Patrick Lucas 57111 Gavin Oldenburg Luher 57112 Randall Arron Lummer 57113 Ryan Lamont Lundberg 57114 Philip Xuan Luu 57115 Andrew Joe Lynch 57116 Jason Ryan Lynn 57117 Nathan Michael MacCarter 57118 Lorna Nicolette Magnus 57119 Michael Robert Mai 57120 Timothy William Maneval 57121 John Patrick Manfra 57122 Tyson Pete Mangum 57123 Yun Kyong Mann 57124 Anthony John Margiotta 57125 Anthony John Marinos 57126 Casey David Markovitz 57127 William Paul Marseglia 57128 Robert John Martin 57129 Thomas Sutton Martin 57130 Casey Ann Martinez 57131 Manuel Martinez 57132 John Bradley Marvin 57133 Jeffrey Lamont Matsen 57134 Christopher Paul Matthew 57135 Joseph Michael Matthews 57136 David Anthony Mattox 57137 Thomas Craig Mattox 57138 Boyd Maughan 57139 Neil Richard Maunu 57140 Raymond Kevin McBride 57141 Sean Patrick McCafferty 57142 Michael Brian McCarthy 57143 Christopher Shawn McClure 57144 Calvin Walter McConnell 57145 Jess McConnell 57146 Jason Ryan McCoy 57147 Sean Michael McCoy 57148 Scott Eugene McCraney 57149 George Edward McCullough 57150 Jason Victor McCullough 57151 Ryan Patrick McDermott 57152 Matthew John McDonough 57153 John Paul McDougall 57154 Brian Charles McDowell 57155 Jeffrey Scott McFarland 57156 Michael Patrick McGaffigan 57157 Sara Elsbeth McGhie 57158 Christopher Ian McGrail 57159 Tyler James McIntyre 57160 Alex McKinlay 57161 Brian Christopher McLean 57162 Thomas Joseph McMeniman 57163 Jennifer Marie McMinn 57164 John Jude McNally 57165 Meighan Kathleen McNulty 57166 Willie Curtis McRae 57167 Jack Raymond Mead 57168 Devin Michael Medeiros 57169 Robert Eric Medina 57170 Jedediah Jamin Medlin 57171 Christopher Jinchul Melary 57172 Jason Robert Melchior 57173 Nicholas Obrien Melin 57174 Heath Aleka Melton 57175 Thomas Howard Melton 57176 Christopher Lloyd Meng 57177 Michael Richard Messner 57178 Michael Andre Michaud 57179 Seth David Middleton 57180 Kathleen Marie Miles 57181 Thomas Bailey Miller 57182 James Patrick Milligan 57183 Benjamin Doughman Minchhoff 57184 Roman Mirczak 57185 John Gorman Misenheimer 57186 Cheryl Lynn Mitchell 57187 James Mitchell 57188 Jennifer Maddin Mitchell 57189 George Andrew Mitroka 57190 Clifton Craig Mo 57191 Austin P Moffitt 57192 Darren Reed Moniot 57193 John Gordon Mooney 57194 Arthur Stanley Moore 57195 Brian James Moore 57196 James Michael Moore 57197 Trent Michael Moore 57198 Benjamin Louis Morales 57199 David Wynne Morehan 57200 Louis Todd Morelli 57201 Zachariah George Morford 57202 Brad Alan Morgan 57203 Kenneth Scott Morley 57204 Christopher Frank Morrell 57205 Christopher John Morris 57206 John Edson Morrison 57207 Matthew James Morrison 57208 Thomas Keith Morrow 57209 Christopher Toby Morton 57210 James Leon Moseley 57211 Craig M Mullaney 57212 Clayton Thomas Multer 57213 Nicholas Carl Mumm 57214 Matthew James Munger 57215 Robert Paul Murphy 57216 Aimee Marie Muscato 57217 Sven John Myrberg 57218 Jason Michael Nadon-Rzasa 57219 Reid Thomas Nahm 57220 Brian Whalen Nash 57221 Mikhael Daniel Nassif 57222 James Thomas Nati 57223 William Navarro 57224 Craig Ashley Nazareth 57225 Christopher James Nelson 57226 Ryan Lee Nenaber 57227 Heath Alan Nero 57228 Robert Julian Newbauer 57229 Kevin Patrick Newell 57230 Henry Arthur Newton 57231 Thomas Alan Nicot 57232 Patrick Allen Nielsen 57233 Jacob Paul Ninas 57234 Douglas Andrew Noble 57235 Ryan Paul Noble 57236 Steven Warren Noess 57237 Jeffrey David Noll 57238 Micah Zachary Nordquist 57239 Jason Shawn Northrop 57240 Leif E Nott 57241 Emmanuel Nouga 57242 Russell Gladieux Nowels 57243 Peter O'Dea 57244 Michael Joseph O'Hare 57245 Kristin Marie O'Keefe 57246 Kerry Ann O'Loughlin 57247 Thomas James O'Loughlin 57248 Thomas William Oakley 57249 Joseph Michael Odorizzi 57250 William Peter Oehlrich 57251 Aaron James Oelrich 57252 Erik Chinmu Oksenvaag 57253 Mary Faith Oliastro 57254 Andrew James Olson 57255 Matthew Peter Orlousky 57256 Philip Andrew Orotelli 57257 Elias David Otoshi 57258 Justin Robert Pabis 57259 Nicholas Keith Padgalskas 57260 Kurt Michael Page 57261 Michael Angelo Panaro 57262 Douglas Oscar Pardo 57263 James Chunin Park 57264 Matthew Lucion Parker 57265 Thomas Charles Parks 57266 Brandon Wayne Parrish 57267 Huber Raymond Parsons 57268 William Wesley Parsons 57269 Eric Andrew Parthemore 57270 Rodric Gabriel Pauletto 57271 Brian Matthew Pearson 57272 Paul Pellegrino 57273 Lisa Anne Peplinski 57274 Michael Paul Perkins 57275 Timothy Neville Peterman 57276 Gavin Lynn Peterson 57277 Jasmine Tyne Peterson 57278 Patrick Joseph Petrino 57279 Clindon Joseph Phillips 57280 Jessica Irene Phillips 57281 Bradford Wallace Pieper 57282 Brent Marshall Pipkin 57283 Michael Joseph Pisarik 57284 Alison Frances Pliske 57285 George Gregory Plitt 57286 Robert R. Plotts 57287 Theodis J Pope 57288 Jeffrey Alan Poquette 57289 Jason Richard Posey 57290 Katie Elizabeth Powell 57291 Trenton Welton Powell 57292 John Scofield Prall 57293 Mark F Prehar 57294 Phoebe Evelyn Price 57295 William Aric Prost 57296 Michele Lynette Pryor 57297 Bryant Gerard Puerto 57298 Melissa Lynn Pulliam 57299 Kathleen Elizabeth Quinlan 57300 Elsa Marn Racen 57301 Isaac Joseph Rademacher 57302 Daniel Omar Ramos 57303 Matthew Byron Rapp 57304 Amelia Corine Rappin 57305 Jesse Ray Reed 57306 Walter A Reed 57307 Jonathan Scott Reggio 57308 Nicholas James Rengel 57309 Hartleigh Ann Richard 57310 Robert Benjamin Richards 57311 Joshua Royce Richardson 57312 Christopher Bryan Riley 57313 Maijaliisa Ann Rimstad 57314 Omar Tashanka-Ali Ritter 57315 Walter Otto Rittger 57316 Garner Lowell Rivard 57317 Alberto Rivera 57318 Jeffrey Nathan Roberts 57319 Racine Weade Robertson 57320 Guyton Lee Robinson 57321 Juan Carlos Rodriguez 57322 Michelle Devonne Rogers 57323 James Riordan Rogowski 57324 Myron Anthony Rone 57325 Curtis Wells Roney 57326 Brandan Timothy Rooney 57327 Scott Edward Ross 57328 Zachary Evans Rossley 57329 Marie Lou Hatch 57330 Chad Donald Ruby 57331 Bronwyn Leah Ruddy 57332 Erin Alice Runci 57333 Lloyd Austin Runser 57334 Daniel Broderick Russo 57335 Sean Whiting Ruthe 57336 Kenneth Joseph Rutka 57337 Joshua Whitman Rutledge 57338 Seung Han Ryu 57339 David Anthony Saftner 57340 Patrick Henry Sagebiel 57341 Shaun Michael Salmon 57342 Stephen Patrick Salomone 57343 Matthew Joseph Salvo 57344 David Allen Sarrette 57345 Nathan Christian Saul 57346 Adam Mark Sawyer 57347 Nelson Roger Schaffner 57348 Mark Kramer Schenck 57349 Erin Michelle Scheu 57350 Stephen Mark Schlesinger 57351 Alexander Richard Schneider 57352 Joshua Andrew Schneider 57353 Nicholas John Schommer 57354 Amber Elise Schrank 57355 Mark Andrew Schulz 57356 Clarence Christopher Scott 57357 James Henry Scullion 57358 Joseph Francis Semien 57359 Aleksandr Michael

Sergek 57360 Alcario Serros 57361 Dustin Garner Shannon 57362 Kimberley Louise Shea 57363 Eric Russell Sigmon 57364 James Edward Silliman 57365 Briana Elaine Simpson 57366 Richard Brett Simpson 57367 Terron Daniel Sims 57368 Sarah Ann Sinclair 57369 Eldridge Rajanoji Singleton 57370 Jeremy Paul Singleton 57371 James Allen Sink 57372 Sandra Kay Smalley 57373 Neal Christopher Smiley 57374 Adam Michael Smith 57375 Alwyn Vincent Smith 57376 Christopher Kostas Smith 57377 Christopher Vaughan Smith 57378 David Joseph Smith 57379 Duncan Alfred Smith 57380 Kerry Ann Smith 57381 Lorenzo Ray Smith 57382 Ryan C Smith 57383 Brett Charles Smithley 57384 Curtis Mitchell Snider 57385 Eunice Jiyun Sohn 57386 Vance Young Sohn 57387 Tatiana Ivanova Sohrakoff 57388 Joshua Boyd Soper 57389 Andrew Christian Sorum 57390 Matthew Ryan Spears 57391 Matthew Paul Stafford 57392 David James Stalker 57393 Matthew Cavanaugh Stanley 57394 Robert Cook Stanton 57395 Charles Raymond Starr 57396 Michael Henderson Starz 57397 Thomas Augustus Stauber 57398 Rosemarie Staun 57399 Kevin Lee Steele 57400 Jason Jon Steger 57401 Shannon Elizabeth Stein 57402 Earl Macaine Stevenson 57403 Thomas Charles Stewart 57404 Orrin Gregory Stitt 57405 Samuel Gene Storrer 57406 Thomas Andrew Stott 57407 William Edward Stovall 57408 Povilas Jonas Strazdas 57409 Bradley K Streich 57410 Justin Edward Strevig 57411 Richard Michael Strong 57412 Vaughn Douglas Strong 57413 Matthew Shunk Stuckey 57414 Joshua James Stuhrmann 57415 Melissa Irene Sturm 57416 Michael James Suckow 57417 Michael John Sullivan 57418 Ryan Patrick Sullivan 57419 Christopher Jay Sutton 57420 Jason Thomas Svoboda 57421 Julie Kaye Swartzlande 57422 Andrew Davis Swedberg 57423 Wade Louis Sweeny 57424 Brian MacArthur Sweigart 57425 James Symanski 57426 Nathanael Simon Tagg 57427 Christopher Patrick Taylor 57428 Joshua Scott Taylor 57429 Ryan Christopher Taylor 57430 William Christopher Taylor 57431 John Malone Teal 57432 Timothy Sean Tehan 57433 Audrey Suzanne Terry 57434 Dylan Joseph Tete 57435 Joshua Paul Thiel 57436 Benjamin James Thogersen 57437 Patrick Andrew Thomas 57438 Allen Maurice Thompson 57439 Anthony Maurice Thompson 57440 Daniel Royce Thompson 57441 James Bradford Thompson 57442 Lee Carey Thompson 57443 John R Thurman 57444 Benjamin David Tiffner 57445 Jonathan Hunter Tilley 57446 Lucius Eli Tillman 57447 Travis Shane Tilman 57448 Michael William Tilton 57449 Natalie Kae Tinianow-Pe 57450 Jason Daniel Torpy 57451 Jason Allen Toth 57452 Jade Christopher Totman 57453 Mark Julius Tricano 57454 Craig Alan Tripp 57455 Lance Mcarther Trotter 57456 Paul Erny Troy 57457 Victor Esteban Trujillo 57458 Nha-trang Thi Truong 57459 Joseph Leslie Tryon 57460 Christopher John Tucker 57461 Coley Daniel Tyler 57462 Kyle Lee Upshaw 57463 Kristofer Kevin Upson 57464 Jose Antonio Valera 57465 Dirk van Langenb 57466 Tresa Marie VanHeusen 57467 Erik Scott VanLaningha 57468 Jeffery Brett VanSickle 57469 David Prescott Varnes 57470 Christopher Richard Vegas 57471 Matthew John Vetter 57472 Albert Anthony Vigilante 57473 Andrew James Vincent 57474 Christopher David Visosky 57475 Timothy Adam Waddell 57476 Christian P Wade 57477 Christopher Klieber Wagar 57478 Russell O'Neill Wagner 57479 Shawn Michael Wagoner 57480 Jennifer Terry Ahl 57481 Jacob Matthew Wallace 57482 Daniel Jon Wallestad 57483 Steven Burnell Wargny 57484 Joseph Lamont Warner 57485 John Bernard Wauhop 57486 Wade Michael Weaver 57487 Cecilio Webb 57488 Whitney Webster Weeks 57489 Brian Hale Weightman 57490 Albert Joseph Weinnig 57491 Jason Craig Wells 57492 Frank Walker Wendt 57493 Edward Thurston Wenner 57494 Christopher Francis West 57495 Jonathan Gideon Westfield 57496 Walter Edwin Whatley 57497 Graham Richard White 57498 Wesley Thomas White 57499 Steven Robert Whiteside 57500 Nathan Seymore Whitfield 57501 Andrew John Whitford 57502 Carrie Lyn Wibben 57503 Gary Lee Williams 57504 Jamal Tarmin Williams 57505 John Thomas Williams 57506 Lindy Kay Williams 57507 Mark Justin Williams 57508 Aaron Lee Willis 57509 Eric Michael Willis 57510 Jared Paul Wilson 57511 Andrew Glynn Wilson-Ruta 57512 Corey Derek Winer 57513 Adam Christopher Wojcik 57514 James Robert Wojcik 57515 Christopher Paul Wolfe 57516 Andrew Robert Wolfrum 57517 Brandon Scott Woll 57518 Kerlan P Wolsey 57519 Michael Patrick Woods 57520 Matthew Tyler Work 57521 Ryan Keith Workman 57522 Timothy Flynn Wright 57523 Yang Xia 57524 Young-Bai M Yea 57525 Troy Alan Yegge 57526 Chee Leung Yew 57527 Elizabeth Olivia Young 57528 Robert Andrew Zimmerle 57529 Kathryn Mary Ziniti 57530 Melanie Rae Baltero 57531 John Warren Brengle 57532 Elijah Virgil Ham 57533 Grayson Matthew Hassmann 57534 Fred Furat Odisho 57535 James Matthew Prestenberg 57536 Charles Francis Thompson 57537 Kobbe Daniel Shaw 57538 George Augustus Aubert 57539 Matthew Scott Brooks 57540 Curtis Lee Edwards 57541 John Edward Johnson 57542 Craig Edward Johnston 57543 Adisa Theophilus King 57544 Michael Aaron Lefler 57545 Henry E Opolot 57546 Randy Thomas Overstreet 57547 Renee Christine Pomroy 57548 Jonathan Robert Ritz 57549 Meghann Elizabeth Sullivan 57550 Brian Douglas Truitt 57551 Michael H Winder 57552 **2001** Anthony Vincent Abbruscato 57553 Geoffrey Paul Abraham 57554 Matthew Taft Adamczyk 57555 Tracy Lynn Adamovich 57556 Angelo Anthony Adams 57557 Buck Adams 57558 Gregory Alan Adams 57559 Max Samuel Adams 57560 Thomas Christopher Adkins 57561 Scott Joseph Akerley 57562 Michael Andrew Akeroyd 57563 Jamie Lynn Alexander 57564 Jerrid Kyle Allen 57565 Aaron Adam Allison 57566 Angela Nicole Kreh 57567 Rodney Kevin Alston 57568 David Joel Alvarey 57569 David Allen Amamoo 57570 Rachel Amilcar 57571 Clayton Wayne Amsler 57572 Jonathan J Anastasia 57573 Ivan Alberto Anaya 57574 Ian Christopher Anderson 57575 Merlin Floyd Anderson 57576 Elizabeth Agnes Andreichuk 57577 Daniel John Andrews 57578 Brian Matthew Anthony 57579 Leandre Raj Anthony 57580 Ivan Josef Antosh 57581 James Eubank Armstrong 57582 Kevin Patrick Arnett 57583 Russel James Arnold 57584 Todd William Arnold 57585 Randall Lee Ashby 57586 Aaron David Ashley 57587 Jason William Atkinson 57588 Jerrad Ryan Avery 57589 Catherine Marie Babbitt 57590 Joseph Eugene Bagaglio 57591 Jonathan David Baker 57592 Carl Frederick Bakke 57593 Ravi Alexander Balaram 57594 David Paul Balcom 57595 Daniel P Baldi 57596 Casey Marie Baldwin 57597 Robert Francis Ball 57598 Andrae Tremayne Ballard 57599 Marc Stephen Balog 57600 Jeremy Kyle Barden 57601 Ryan Antes Bardo 57602 Richard Justin Bardsley 57603 John Benoit Barker 57604 Lawrence Charlie Barnard 57605 John Parnell Barnwell 57606 Jason Paul Barr 57607 Melissa Nell Barrett 57608 Seth Elias Barrett 57609 Timothy Scott Batig 57610 Linda Ellen Batkin 57611 Joseph Charles Becherer 57612 William Robert Beerbower 57613 Richard Bell 57614 Melissa Victoria Bembenek 57615 Ryan Matthew Berdiner 57616 Dwayne Gerard Bernal 57617 Jason Michael Berndt 57618 David Richard Bernstein 57619 David Michael Beskow 57620 Thomas Michael Bigger 57621 Sarah Beth Biggerstaff 57622 Patrick Michael Biggs 57623 Adam Lowell Bird 57624 David Russell Birie 57625 Benjamin Alan Biroschak 57626 Bryan Ward Blair 57627 Kurt Michael Blankenship 57628 Jason Michael Blaylock 57629 Jason Copeland Blonstein 57630 Gregory Paul Bock 57631 Seth Andrew Bodnar 57632 Paul Ray Boethel 57633 Mario Bogunovic 57634 Dennis Davin Bonavilla 57635 Laura Kathleen Bong 57636 Jason Patrick Boone 57637 Heidi Marie Borden 57638 Michael Robert Bordes 57639 Benjamin David Boring 57640 Bryan Aaron Bowdish 57641 Kristen Michelle Bowles 57642 Angela Christine Boyle 57643 Trevor William Bradna 57644 Marcus Williams Brakewood 57645 Christopher R Brautigam 57646 Ramon Brigantti 57647 Heidi Ann Brockmann 57648 Jeffrey Jordan Brooks 57649 Matthew Garrett Brougham 57650 Deborah Jean Brown 57651 Michael Jay Brownstein 57652 Audrey Eileen Bruun 57653 Rachael Anne Smith 57654 Mark Aaron Brzozowski 57655 Diosabelle Tabita Buack 57656 Boyce Ryan Buckner 57657 Edward Thomas Buffa 57658 Jeremy Bukowczyk 57659 William Anderson Burdette 57660 Daniel Scott Burges 57661 Michael Allen Burgwald 57662 Andrew Burke 57663 Jason Kenneth Burris 57664 Kyle John Button 57665 David Y Byrne 57666 Curtis Lee Byron 57667 Kevin Wayne Caflin 57668 Brandon M Calhoun 57669 Laura E Callahan 57670 Shawn Christopher Callahan 57671 Jared Daniel Cameron 57672 James Holmes Campbell 57673 Charles Henry Cannon 57674 Richard Matthew Caponi 57675 Anthony Daniel Caracio 57676 Brian Thomas Carlidge 57677 Brendan J Carroll 57678 Michelle Marie Casabonne 57679 Francisco Casanova 57680 Thomas William Casey 57681 Nile Lamar Cassett 57682 Robert Pinkney Cathey 57683 Christian Catron 57684 Brandon Croy Cave 57685 Joseph Jerome Ceasar 57686 George Nicolae Cernat 57687 Ryan Louis Chalupsky 57688 Matthew Aaron Chaney 57689 Dallas Quincy Cheatham 57690 Richard Teh Chen 57691 James Michael Cheng 57692 David Scott Chiappinelli 57693 John Daniel Childress 57694 Bryan Philip Childs 57695 George Wesley Childs 57696 Yoon Young Choi 57697 Lucas J Cioffi 57698 Joseph Michael Clark 57699 Henry Marshall Clay 57700 Bo William Clift 57701 Trevor John Cobb 57702 Scott Robert Cochran 57703 Sean Robert Cohen 57704 Matthew Jacob Cole 57705 Richard Thomas Colonna 57706 Christopher Dillon Connor 57707 Elinor M Connors 57708 Matthew Ryan Considine 57709 Nicholas Michael Cook 57710 Jason Andrew Cooper 57711 James Carlton Corbett 57712 Shawn Patrick Corcoran 57713 Michael John Costanzo 57714 Kevin Michael Coughlin 57715 Christina Kay Coward 57716 Andrew Alderman Cox 57717 Matthew David Cox 57718 John Kyle Crain 57719 Douglas Steven Crate 57720 Jesse Crawford-Mancin 57721 Christopher Bundick Creaghe 57722 Benjamin Ross Crombe 57723 Sean Glendon Cronin 57724 Kathleen Anne Crossett 57725 Richard Peter Crowley 57726 Jeffrey Donald Cullen 57727 Marcus Eddy Cunningham 57728 Lane Peterson Cutler 57729 Eric Peter Dalbom 57730 Heather Lee Dandrilli 57731 Larry Terrell Daniel 57732 Jon Eric Danielson 57733 Jason Nathaniel Daugherty 57734 Nicholas Joseph Davalla 57735 James Nathaniel Davis 57736 Jerrell Davis 57737 Alan Phillip Davison 57738 Joseph Mark Davison 57739 Christian Andrew Dawson 57740 Ashok Kumar Deb 57741 Jason Rex Defoor 57742 Deana Marie Delporto 57743 Bryan William Demare 57744 Megan Kylene Dempsey 57745 Andrew Carl Dermanoski 57746 Mohamed Ahmed Desoky 57747 Meghan M Devine 57748 Andrew Joseph Dial 57749 Victor Michael Diaz 57750 Robert William Dickerson 57751 Nicole Leigh Dieso 57752 Christian Nickey Dietz 57753 Robert Scott Dillard 57754 Robert Edward Dion 57755 Giao Trang Do 57756 Charles Owen Dodson 57757 Jessica Elisabeth Donckers 57758 Thomas Charles Dowd 57759 Dawn M Drango 57760 Gary Thomas Ducote 57761 Thomas Joseph Dunaway 57762 Bryan Russell Duncan 57763 Scott Wade Dunkle 57764 James Imani Dupree 57765 Justin Adrian Duvall 57766 Wesley John Dykema 57767 James Clifford Dywan 57768 Emily Elizabeth Eagan 57769 Jeremy Wayne Easley 57770 Merrell Greenwood Edney 57771 Steven Lee Elgan 57772 Robert Richard Elliott 57773 Nicole Ann Elwell 57774 Jeremy Adam England 57775 Angela Yvonne Ervine 57776 David Ernesto Escobar 57777 Sam Escobar 57778 John Evangelista 57779 Jerel Dion Evans 57780 Neal Eugene Everson 57781 Peter Riley Exline 57782 Michael Alexander Fairman 57783 Kathryn Mary Falato 57784 Robert Todd Falzone 57785 Andrew G Farina 57786 Brett Andrew Farmer 57787 Kory Jonathan Farmer 57788 John Irwin Faunce 57789 Ashden Fein 57790 Lorelei Marie Felix 57791 Christina Kimberly Feliz 57792 Vincent Charles Fellone 57793 Michael Albert Ferlazzo 57794 John Anthony Fernandez 57795 Robert William Fields 57796 Kevin Colin Finnegan 57797 Ian Fishback 57798 Anne Elizabeth Havniear 57799 Matthew Peter Fix 57800 Michael Patrick Flanigan 57801 Nancy Flores 57802 Daniel Eric Forsman 57803 Bradley Scott Foster 57804 Daniel Richard Fox 57805 Richard Raymond Fox 57806 Adria Olson Fraser 57807 Douglas George Fraser 57808 Kristin Charlotte Freberg 57809 Jeremiah Casey Fritz 57810 Michele Kathleen Frymier 57811 Jeffrey Robert Fuller 57812 Douglas Kerwin Fullerton 57813 David Andrew Fulton 57814 William Wickliffe Fulton 57815 Lindsey Yvonne Fultz 57816 Evan Joseph Gagnepain 57817 Kalina K Galabova 57818 Matthew Gregory Galan 57819 Alexander Michael Gallo 57820 Sara Sinead Galvin 57821 Ashling Therese Ganes 57822 Nicholas Clifton Gantt 57823 Alex Robert Garn 57824 Benjamin Chad Garner 57825 Matthew Thomas Garrett 57826 Andrew Michael Gash 57827 Paul Douglas Gates 57828 Ivan Iordanov Gaydarov 57829 William Thomas Gehrum 57830 Brett Cortland Gendron 57831 Jonathon Michael Genge 57832 Gabriel J Gengler 57833 Lamarl Sawyer Gerald 57834 Joseph Louis Gerena 57835 Craig Thomas Germano 57836 Marlow Ghorstygrbrakoxfdeis 57837 Jonathan Sutton Gibbs 57838 Meghan Mary Giddings 57839 Natalie Nicole Gielata 57840 James Hart Gifford 57841 Alfred Giles 57842 Michael Tiernan Gilmartin 57843 John Patrick Gilmour 57844 Jamie Jo Glassford 57845 James Thomas Golby 57846 Chris Manuel Gonzalez 57847 Joshua Aaron Gonzalez 57848 Daniel David Goode 57849 Derrick Lewis Goodwin 57850 Ryan Randall Goyings 57851 Matthew Frederick Graessle 57852 Douglas MacArthur Graham 57853 Nathan Alan Grant 57854 Brandon Herbert Graves 57855 Ashley Brooke Greaves 57856 Kelly Lynn Green 57857 Jessica Anne Grembi 57858 Timothy Jon Gries 57859 Matthew E Griffin 57860 Michael John Gruber 57861 Roger Dennis Gruneisen 57862 Thomas Anthony Grywalski 57863 Michael Ray Gudith 57864 Jonathan David Guinn 57865 Shawn Harlan Gundrum 57866 Jennifer Lynn Gurski 57867 Justin Alan Haas 57868 Scott Hady 57869 Dawn Frances Halfaker 57870 Charles Dewitt Hall 57871 John Louis Hallett 57872 Cheryl Lynn Hamilton 57873 Matthew Ryan Hamilton 57874 Jeffrey James Han 57875 Ryan Patrick Hanrahan 57876 Benjamin Karl Hansen 57877 Jason Conway Hansen 57878 Jason L Hansford 57879 Nathan James Harber 57880 Cristin Colleen Hargadon 57881 David Owen Harlan 57882 Jeffrey Christopher Harmon 57883 Scott David Harris 57884 William David Harris 57885 Harlan Ariel Harrison 57886 Joseph Merrill Harrison 57887 Richard Warren Hartfelder 57888 Allan Harvey 57889 Andrew James Haskell 57890 Keith Allen Haskin 57891 Andrew Ryan Hattman 57892 David Lucian Hawk 57893 Jeffrey Douglas Hay 57894 Scott Bradley Heal 57895 Jeffrey Thomas Helle 57896 Kristin Katherine Henningsen-Brengle 57897 Adam James Hensel 57898 David Walter Hensel 57899 William Mikell Herrington 57900 Andrew Lucas Herzberg 57901 Christopher Matthew Hetz 57902 Jason Scott Hetzel 57903 Micala Christie Hicks 57904 Terry Neil Hilderbrand 57905 Aaron Lee Hill 57906 Keith Robert Hille 57907 Eric William Hillerson 57908 Bryan Saint John Hilton 57909 Robert Edward Hilton 57910 Linda Christin Hird 57911 Joshua Ryan Hodge 57912 Matthew Thomas Hofmann 57913 Daniel Lee Hofstra 57914 Clara Jean Hoisington 57915 Ryan Craig Holtz 57916 Jonathan James Hopkins 57917 Matthew Don Hopper 57918 Randy Ray Hopper 57919 Aaron Dell Horn 57920 James Aron Horn 57921 John Joseph Horton 57922 Jewell Marie Hoscila 57923 Stacy Kathryn Mumm 57924 Andrew Ryan Houghton 57925 Terrance Ramon Houston 57926 Betsy Anne Hove 57927 Jacob Daniel Huber 57928 Timothy Philip Hudson 57929 David William Hughes 57930 Jennifer Marie Hughes 57931 Kristiaan Curtis Hughes 57932 Benjamin Wei Hung 57933 Fred Bradley Hunstable 57934 Hollis Christopher Hurst 57935 Zachary Michael Hurst 57936 Donnie Joe Hurt 57937 Barry Farrell Huston 57938 Star Adeline Hy 57939 Peter Joseph Inskeep 57940 Joshua Tetsuo Ishibashi 57941 Benjamin Fredricks Iverson 57942 Carl Michael Jackson 57943 Mark Eric Jacobson 57944 Adrian Francis Jasso 57945 Keith Weetman Jennings 57946 Thomas Lee Jensen 57947 Steven Donald Jette 57948 Arthur Eugene Jimenez 57949 Jose M Jimenez Padilla 57950 Ricardo Juan Jimenez 57951 Arthur Johnson 57952 Christopher Miles Johnson 57953 Daniel Isaac Johnson 57954 Jeffrey Wayne Johnson 57955 Kevin McBroom Johnson 57956 Perry Lee Johnson 57957 Jacob Matthew Johnston 57958 Ariel Anne Jones 57959 Bryan Donovan Jones 57960 Elisa Dulcinea Jones 57961 Justin Keith Jones 57962 Micheal Christopher Jones 57963 Michael Edward Jones 57964 Jeffrey J Jordan 57965 Alexis Charles Jung 57966 Christopher Edward Kane 57967 Matthew Austin Kapinos 57968 Jonathan Talbot Karpuk 57969 Mark Stephen Kaschenbach 57970 John Corey Kashner 57971 Jeremy Ray Kasper 57972 Justin J Kato 57973 Bryce Kiichi Kawaguchi 57974 Clifford Allen Kazmarek 57975 Daniel Arden Keener 57976 Jim Dan Keirsey 57977 David Robert Keiser 57978 Scott M Keller 57979 Jeffery M Kelley 57980 Terence Martin Kelley 57981 Therese Marjorie Kelley 57982 Kristen Ann Lewis 57983 Jeffrey Stuart Ker 57984 Eric Edwin Kessler 57985 Joshua Shehadeh Khoury 57986 Jennifer Sue Kicker 57987 Matthew Yun Kim 57988 Robert Alexander Kim 57989 Tae Hoon Kim 57990 Yung Jin Kim 57991 Jeremy John Kindseth 57992 Caleb Joshua King 57993 Ryan Donald Kistner 57994 Chad Allen Klascius 57995 Robyn Joy Klein 57996 Thomas Howard Klump 57997 Ryan Melink Knight 57998 Joshua David Knobel 57999 Jennifer Nicole Knowlden 58000 Allison Lynette Koenig 58001 Kacie Mackenzie Kolb 58002 Michael Lee Kolodzie 58003 Ryan David Kracht 58004 Carolyn Michelle Krahn 58005 Philip Roland Kreck 58006 Seth Adam Kretser 58007 Calvin Allen Kroeger 58008 Travis Barnes Krug 58009 Joshua Allen Kuehl 58010 Joshua Andrew Kurtzman 58011 Matthew Warren Kuskie 58012 Nathan J Kutsko 58013 Cory John Kwarta 58014 Clifton Carl Kyle 58015 Christian Anthony Labra 58016 Joseph Michael Lacanlale 58017 Kirsten Rita Lafond 58018 Steven John Lagan 58019 Bryan Kenneth Lake 58020 David Michael Lamborn 58021 Jeremy Edwin Lane 58022 Robert Brett Lanier 58023 Ford Michael Lannan 58024 Neal Jeffrey Lape 58025 Michael Patrick Larkin 58026 Ryan Thomas Larson 58027 Jozef Laski 58028 Adam Flemings Latham 58029 Michael Patrick Lavalle 58030 Andrew Joseph Layman 58031 Ryan William Leary 58032 Ricardo Antonio Ledesma 58033 Gregory George Lee 58034 Matt Dennis Lee 58035 Steven Sang Lee 58036 Vincent Warren Lee 58037 Jennifer Ann Leidel 58038 Wesley Allen Leisinger 58039 Andrew Elton Lembke 58040 Russell Paul Lemler 58041 Robert James Lentz 58042 Joshua Lewis 58043 Kristopher Brady Lewis 58044 Ryan Frederick Liebhaber 58045 Ryan Andrew Linares 58046 Clay Livingston 58047 Michael Alexander Lockhart 58048 Peter Charles Lohman 58049 Chris Robert Luke 58050 Eric Lee Lundy 58051 Joe Fenton Lusk 58052 Aaron Lee Lykling 58053 Clayton Edwin Lynch 58054 Sean Patrick Lynch 58055 Glen Anthony MacIsaac 58056 Dylan Alexander Mack 58057 Joel Stephen Maganza 58058 Peter Francis Magnetto 58059 Melissa Barbara Malone 58060 Dion Francis Mancenido 58061 Charles Jeffrey Maranich 58062 Joseph Thomas Marcee 58063 Elizabeth Siobhan Marken 58064 Joseph Robert Martel 58065 Aaron Lee Martin 58066 Adam Patrick Martin 58067 Carolyn Mclain Martin 58068 John Christopher Martinko 58069 John Paul Marzec 58070 Brendan David Masini 58071 Matthew Thomas Mason 58072 Michael Hayes Mason 58073 Patrick Earl Mather 58074 Oswaldo Alonso Maxwell 58075 David Drew May 58076 Mark Allen McBride 58077 Paul Matthew McBride 58078 Mark Roger McClellan 58079 Liam Charles McConville 58080 Brad Christopher McCoy 58081 Gerrod Adam McDaniel 58082 Ryan Joseph McDonough 58083 Sean Coleman McElhenny 58084 Robert William McFarren 58085 Erin Kathleen McGill 58086 Matthew Brian McGuire 58087 Laura Kathleen McKenna 58088 Simon Antonio McKenzie 58089 Benjamin Emmett McLaughlin 58090 Douglas Arthur McLeod 58091 Thomas Hugh McMurtrie 58092 Derick Paul McNally 58093 Mark Edwin McNamara 58094 Megan Laura McNicol 58095 Thomas Patrick McQuary 58096 Brendan Thomas McShea 58097 Timothy Paul Meadors 58098 Dwight Steven Mears 58099 Luis R. Mejia-Roman 58100 Nancy Elisabeth Mellette 58101 Brendan James Melly 58102 Garrett John Meyers 58103 Chad Christopher Mihalek 58104 Brian James Miller 58105 Brooks Bryant Miller 58106 James Michael Miller 58107 Matthew Gerar Miller 58108 Robert Douglas Miller 58109 Craig William Milliron 58110 Joseph Scott Minor 58111 Dominic Anthony Mirabella 58112 Gary Randall Mitchell 58113 Anthony Vincent Mitek 58114 Kathleen

Mary Mitroka 58115 Kristine Marie Mitroka 58116 Michelle Renee Molinaro 58117 Thomas Paul Molton 58118 John Henry Moltz 58119 Joy Ellen Monson 58120 Jacqueline Marie Cochiaosue 58121 Timothy Eric Morgan 58122 James Andrew Morin 58123 Thomas Edward Morley 58124 Aaron Franklin Morris 58125 Dean William Morrison 58126 Brian Michael Morrissey 58127 Sean Michael Morrow 58128 Michael Anthony Mosby 58129 Nicholas Stephen Mudd 58130 Brendan Burkart Mullen 58131 Stephen Peter Muller 58132 Eric Matthew Musgrave 58133 Matthew Robert Myer 58134 Amanda Leigh Nagy 58135 John Koji Nakata 58136 Justin Conroy Nash 58137 Christian Nelson 58138 Peter Andrew Nesbitt 58139 Charles Abram Neveau 58140 Mary Shannon Newell 58141 Frank Woodrow Newman 58142 James Alan Nicholson 58143 William Mcneal Nicholson 58144 Dennis Kazuki Nishikawa 58145 John William Njock 58146 Megan Jane Noble 58147 Alejandro Mauricio Nunez 58148 Lawrence Randall Nunn 58149 Thomas Nosakhare Obaseki 58150 Anthony Karl Odierno 58151 Gregory Michael Ogborn 58152 Marc Christopher Ogborn 58153 Daniel J Oh 58154 Brendan Bernard Ohern 58155 Darryl Tyrone Olden 58156 Matthew John Oldenburg 58157 Ryan Casey O'Neill 58158 Angelica Ontiveros 58159 Katherine R Opie 58160 Matthew Ryan Oren 58161 Marisa Pace 58162 Ryan John Pagels 58163 Joseph Curtis Palen 58164 Eric Ian Palicia 58165 Rebecca Marie Palitka 58166 Ann Liang Papanos 58167 Chong Woo Park 58168 David Jinchul Park 58169 Sang Yong Park 58170 Seo Woo Park 58171 Sarah Jennifer Parker 58172 Nathan Harold Parrish 58173 Benjamin Ryan Parry 58174 Andrew Reuben Pearson 58175 Gregory Arthur Pearson 58176 Ryan Peter Peckyno 58177 Irena Peharda 58178 John David Pelikan 58179 Francis Balaye Pera 58180 William Thomas Perkins 58181 Jonathan Goodwin Perry 58182 Charles David Peters 58183 Paul James Peters 58184 Paul Andrew Peterson 58185 Kyle David Petroskey 58186 Andrew Ross Pfluger 58187 David Anthony Phelps 58188 Michael Joseph Phillips 58189 Thomas Enrique Piazze 58190 Geoffrey Alexander Pickett 58191 Jeffrey Wayne Pickler 58192 Chad Michael Piechocki 58193 Brian John Piekielko 58194 Richard Carl Pifer 58195 Re Olivier Pinkcombe 58196 John M Pinter 58197 Anastasia Marie Piotrowski 58198 Ryan Matthew Piotrowski 58199 Michael Carl Piro 58200 Jonathan Michael Poe 58201 James Lyle Pope 58202 Riley John Post 58203 Emily Jane Potter 58204 Richard Allen Powers 58205 Seth David Pullen 58206 Sukhdev Singh Purewal 58207 Matthew Glenn Purtle 58208 Donald Michael Pytash 58209 Edwin Gerard Quan 58210 David C Rachal 58211 Pierre Antoine Rachal 58212 Matthew Jon Radik 58213 Donald Les Raines 58214 Juliza Jordan Ramirez 58215 Timothy Kyle Randall 58216 Adam Daniel Rankin 58217 Matthew Stephen Rasmussen 58218 Colin Kile Raymond 58219 Damon Paul Reed 58220 Joshua Genaro Reeves 58221 Richard Thomas Reggero 58222 Bernard J Reilly 58223 Barret J Rhoden 58224 Jessica Ann Rice 58225 Jessica Veronica Rice 58226 James E Richards 58227 Ingebrigt Andreas Riise 58228 Michael James Rimstad 58229 Daniel Patrick Rivette 58230 Christopher Adam Robbins 58231 Matthew Urey Robertson 58232 Andrew P Robin 58233 John Joe Rocha 58234 Joseph M Rodibaugh 58235 Robert Reade Rodock 58236 Chad Aaron Roe 58237 Timothy Daniel Roepke 58238 Spencer Lamb Rogers 58239 Beau Gabriel Rollie 58240 Carlys Louann Romano 58241 Robert Carmen Romano 58242 Michael Steven Rosol 58243 Matthew Steven Ross 58244 Nadine Idelia Ross 58245 Timothy Hemphill Ross 58246 Allison Andrea Rowe 58247 Grant Douglas Rowland 58248 John Warren Ruch 58249 Travis William Rudge 58250 Reuben Claude Rudisill 58251 Krista Marie Ruschak 58252 Diana Marie Russell 58253 Theodore Charles Ruzicka 58254 Eugene Edward Sacco 58255 Jared Daniel Sainato 58256 Jackson Tracy Salter 58257 Marc J Sanborn 58258 Andrew Philip Sanders 58259 Dale Shaune Sanders 58260 Erik Nathan Sanders 58261 Robert Armando Santamaria 58262 Luke J Santillo 58263 Jason Elliott Sapp 58264 Charles Flaveous Sargent 58265 David Morgan Sattelmeyer 58266 Dana Louise Savage 58267 Tereh Amelia Sayles 58268 Mark Edward Scabavea 58269 Thomas Dale Scaife 58270 Charcillea Ann Schaefer 58271 Travis Michael Schega 58272 William Harman Schmid 58273 Shane Robert Schmutz 58274 Sheri Lynn Schneider 58275 Jeremy Scott Scholtes 58276 Adam Justin Schrader 58277 Kurt Thomas Schraml 58278 Ryan Lee Schrock 58279 Jason Paul Schuerger 58280 Steven Joel Schuldt 58281 Fred Willis Schwark 58282 Shane Paul Scott 58283 Brent Ryan Scurci 58284 Torrey Verrayle Searles 58285 Sindie Denise Secosky 58286 Alison Lorraine Semanoff 58287 Jordan Jon Sembower 58288 James Bryan Sharp 58289 Thomas J Shaughnessy 58290 Brandon Smith Shell 58291 Benjamin Layman Shepherd 58292 Yosup Shim 58293 Shane Mark Shipman 58294 David James Shoemaker 58295 Jason Scott Sigler 58296 Jason Alan Simmons 58297 Jerry Alan Simonsen 58298 Michael Lee Sixsmith 58299 Kelly Lynn Skrdlant 58300 Patrick George Sleem 58301 Gary Steven Sliver 58302 Blayne Paul Smith 58303 Brian Joseph Smith 58304 Diane April Smith 58305 Jana Kehau Smith 58306 Jeffrey Adam Smith 58307 Joseph Brinton Smith 58308 Kelly Keith Smith 58309 Kevin D Smith 58310 Ryan Clay Smith 58311 Andrew Joseph Snelgrove 58312 Jason Owen Snellings 58313 Elizabeth Ann Snyder 58314 Jessica Anne Snyder 58315 Adrienne Elizabeth Sommers 58316 Young Il Song 58317 Kristin Elizabeth Sonne 58318 Vojko Sotlar 58319 Scott C Spahr 58320 Nathan Ward Speanburg 58321 Adam Spencer 58322 Clayton Brian Spicer 58323 Ronald George Sporer 58324 Kevin Herbert Stacy 58325 Erin K Stair 58326 David Paul Stairs 58327 Tyler James Standish 58328 Sebastian Staszeczka 58329 Melissa Marie Stavola 58330 Erick John Stenborg 58331 Tod Daniel Stephens 58332 Charles Robert Stewart 58333 Eric Dale Stoutenburg 58334 David Martin Sturgis 58335 Matthew Thomas Sullivan 58336 Joshua Mac Summerlin 58337 Michael John Superior 58338 Robert Lewis Swartwood 58339 Seth Owen Swartz 58340 Adrian Sykes 58341 Brian Douglas Szydlik 58342 Tyler Jameson Tafelski 58343 James Russell Taft 58344 Adrian Talapan 58345 Kevin Michael Taylor 58346 Michael Merchant Taylor 58347 Scott Carl Taylor 58348 Christopher Dale Terrill 58349 Aaron Matthew Thomas 58350 John William Thomas 58351 Laura Jean Thomas 58352 Matthew Jonathan Thomas 58353 Brandon Scott Thompson 58354 Melissa Ann Thompson 58355 Eric John Thornburg 58356 Sarah Dolores Thornton 58357 Michelle Alano Timajo 58358 Howard Charles Titzel 58359 Michael Terry Tobias 58360 Matthew David Tobin 58361 Thomas Earl Tolman 58362 Jonathan Todd Tolson 58363 Frank Casper Tortella 58364 Crosby Hideo Toyama 58365 Michael David Traugutt 58366 Scott Franklin Travis 58367 Thomas Patrick Traylor 58368 Roger Larocque Trimble 58369 Garrett William Trott 58370 Keith Douglas Tully 58371 Michael Patrick Tumlin 58372 Julie Blaine Turner 58373 David Albert Uthlaut 58374 Jennifer L Uyeshiro 58375 Michael Kenneth Vahle 58376 Steven Reeves Valentine 58377 Jason Bernard Alle Van Camp 58378 Matthew Thomas Van de Vender 58379 Blaine Van Gansbeke 58380 Tyler Gregory VanHorn 58381 Kyle Matthew VanSchoyck 58382 Jeremy Dale Vaughan 58383 Matthew Wade Vea 58384 Nicholas Paul Verska 58385 Nathanael James Vodila 58386 Melissa Lynn Vones 58387 Christopher Wayne Waddell 58388 William McFall Waddell 58389 Brian Michael Wade 58390 Neilson Winters Wahab 58391 Christian Anthony Walker 58392 William Christopher Walker 58393 Chad Curtis Wallet 58394 Kyle M Walton 58395 Ryan Joseph Wampler 58396 James Robert Warren 58397 Jesse Martin Waters 58398 Keith Phillip Watrob 58399 Christopher Richard Watroba 58400 Patrick James Watson 58401 Jason Robert Wayne 58402 Carilynne Janene Weatherwax 58403 Ann Marie Weber 58404 Renee Anne Vigilante 58405 Andrew John Wentzler 58406 John Andrew Wenzel 58407 Erik Paul Westerberg 58408 Laura Marie Westley 58409 Chad Christopher Wetherill 58410 Jaron Seth Wharton 58411 Andrew Allen White 58412 Michael John White 58413 Robert James White 58414 Joseph Lee Whitener 58415 Gary Edward Wiesner 58416 Kyle Evan Wiginton 58417 Nathan Andrew Wilbourn 58418 Andrew Brian Wild 58419 Clarence Wesley Wilhite 58420 Christopher George Wilkens 58421 Christopher John Williams 58422 Matthew Charles Williams 58423 Ryan Thomas Williams 58424 James John Williamson 58425 Douglas M Willig 58426 Meghan Barker Wilmore 58427 Matthew Lee Wilson 58428 Joseph Edward Wise 58429 Michael Donald Wise 58430 Susan Jane Woo 58431 Edward Ryan Wood 58432 Mckinley Charles Wood 58433 Matthew William Woodcock 58434 Amy Lynn Woodell 58435 Roscoe Eugene Woods 58436 Emily Rose Woolsey 58437 Shawn David Wray 58438 Vashaun Antonio Wrice 58439 Benjamin John Wunderlich 58440 Daniel Yang 58441 Lisa Renee Yates 58442 David A Yeoman 58443 Charlotte Eileen Yerdon 58444 Ahmet Yildiz 58445 Duke Gotthard Yim 58446 Tamara Deann Yolo 58447 Gene Yu 58448 Peter Domminic Zaffina 58449 Brett Zeleznik 58450 Matthew Conlin Zimmerman 58451 Darren Zychek 58452 Eddi Zyber Zyko 58453 Brian Gregory Bergen 58454 Jacob Ryan Cavins 58455 Ryan Hamilton Forshee 58456 Celso David Galvez 58457 Jayson Alexander Hwang 58458 Michael Allen Irvine 58459 George Thomas Jones 58460 Harry Kirias 58461 Ernesto Lopez 58462 Robert Austin Mahoney 58463 Erica Michelle Pitts 58464 Christopher Lennox Rapp 58465 Corrie Small 58466 Lyle Elton Weaver 58467